For Students

MEANINGFUL HELP AND FEEDBACK

- Personalized interactive learning aids are available for point-of-use help and immediate feedback.
  These learning aids include:

  - Help Me Solve This walks students through solving an algorithmic version of the questions they are working,
    with additional detailed tutorial reminders. These informational cues assist the students and help them
    understand concepts and mechanics.

  - Demo Docs are entire problems worked through step by step from start to finish, replicating the in-class experience
    for students anytime, anywhere.

  - Accounting Simplified videos give students a 3- to 5-minute lesson on concepts. Our new videos are engaging
    whiteboard animations that help illustrate concepts for students.

  - NEW! Accounting Cycle Tutorial provides students with an interactive and simulated exercise to reinforce the
    concepts critical to success in Accounting.

  - eText links students directly to the concept covered in the problem they are completing.

  - Homework and practice exercises with additional algorithmically generated problems are available for further
    practice and mastery.

  - NEW! Worked Out Solutions—now available to students when they are reviewing their submitted and graded
    homework. The Worked Out Solutions provide step-by-step explanations on how to solve select problems using
    the exact numbers and data that were presented to the student in the problem.

- NEW! Dynamic Study Modules—Using a highly personalized, algorithmically driven process, Dynamic Study
  Modules continuously assess students' performance and provide additional practice in the areas where they
  struggle the most.

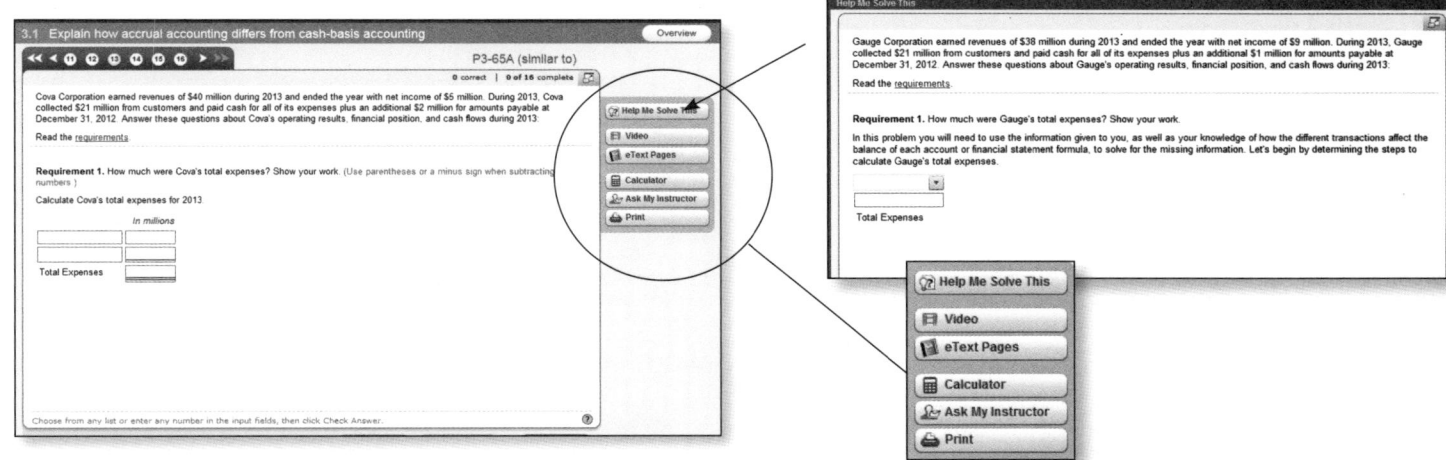

PERSONALIZED AND ADAPTIVE STUDY PATH

- Assist students in monitoring their own progress by offering them a
  customized study plan powered by Knewton, based on Homework,
  Quiz, and Test results.

- Regenerated exercises offer unlimited practice and the opportunity to
  prove mastery through Quizzes on recommended learning objectives.

Financial Accounting

Tenth Edition

Walter T. Harrison Jr.
Baylor University

Charles T. Horngren
Stanford University

C. William (Bill) Thomas
Baylor University

PEARSON

Boston   Columbus   Indianapolis   New York   San Francisco   Upper Saddle River
Amsterdam   Cape Town   Dubai   London   Madrid   Milan   Munich   Paris   Montréal   Toronto
Delhi   Mexico City   São Paulo   Sydney   Hong Kong   Seoul   Singapore   Taipei   Tokyo

Editor in Chief: Donna Battista
Acquisitions Editor: Lacey Vitetta
Development Editor: Mignon Worman Tucker
Editorial Assistant: Christine Donovan
Director of Marketing: Maggie Moylan Leen
Marketing Manager: Alison Haskins
Team Lead, Project Management: Jeff Holcomb
Senior Production Project Manager: Elizabeth Gale
  Napolitano
Manager, Rights & Permissions: Michael Joyce
Rights & Permissions Coordinator: Samantha Graham
Photo Researcher: Rachel Youdelman
Senior Manufacturing Buyer: Carol Melville

Interior Designer: Liz Harasymcuk
Cover Design: PreMediaGlobal
Cover Art: Sergign/Shutterstock
Media Producer: James Bateman
Supplements Project Manager: Jill Kolongowski
Full-Service Project Management: Lynn Steines,
  S4Carlisle Publishing Services
Composition: S4Carlisle Publishing Services
Printer/Binder: Courier/Kendallville
Cover Printer: Lehigh-Phoenix Color/
  Hagerstown
Typeface: 10/12 Caslon

Credits and acknowledgments borrowed from other sources and reproduced, with permission, in this textbook appear on the appropriate page within text.

Microsoft and/or its respective suppliers make no representations about the suitability of the information contained in the documents and related graphics published as part of the services for any purpose. All such documents and related graphics are provided "as is" without warranty of any kind. Microsoft and/or its respective suppliers hereby disclaim all warranties and conditions with regard to this information, including all warranties and conditions of merchantability, whether express, implied or statutory, fitness for a particular purpose, title and non-infringement. In no event shall Microsoft and/or its respective suppliers be liable for any special, indirect or consequential damages or any damages whatsoever resulting from loss of use, data or profits, whether in an action of contract, negligence or other tortious action, arising out of or in connection with the use or performance of information available from the services.

The documents and related graphics contained herein could include technical inaccuracies or typographical errors. Changes are periodically added to the information herein. Microsoft and/or its respective suppliers may make improvements and/or changes in the product(s) and/or the program(s) described herein at any time. Partial screen shots may be viewed in full within the software version specified.

Microsoft® and Windows® are registered trademarks of the Microsoft Corporation in the U.S.A. and other countries. This book is not sponsored or endorsed by or affiliated with the Microsoft Corporation.

Many of the designations by manufacturers and sellers to distinguish their products are claimed as trademarks. Where those designations appear in this book, and the publisher was aware of a trademark claim, the designations have been printed in initial caps or all caps.

Library of Congress Cataloging-in-Publication Data
Harrison, Walter T.
  Financial accounting / Walter T. Harrison Jr., Baylor University, Charles T. Horngren, Stanford University, C. William (Bill) Thomas, Baylor University. — Tenth edition.
      pages cm
  Includes index.
  ISBN-13: 978-0-13-342753-0
  ISBN-10: 0-13-342753-6
  1. Accounting. I. Horngren, Charles T., 1926- II. Thomas, C. William. III. Title.
  HF5636.H37 2015
  657—dc23

                                          2013042426

10 9 8 7 6 5 4 3 2

ISBN 10:   0-13-342753-6
ISBN 13: 978-0-13-342753-0

ABOUT THE AUTHORS

Walter T. Harrison Jr. is professor emeritus of accounting at the Hankamer School of Business, Baylor University. He received his BBA from Baylor University, his MS from Oklahoma State University, and his PhD from Michigan State University.

Professor Harrison, recipient of numerous teaching awards from student groups as well as from university administrators, has also taught at Cleveland State Community College, Michigan State University, the University of Texas, and Stanford University.

A member of the American Accounting Association and the American Institute of Certified Public Accountants, Professor Harrison has served as chairman of the Financial Accounting Standards Committee of the American Accounting Association, on the Teaching/Curriculum Development Award Committee, on the Program Advisory Committee for Accounting Education and Teaching, and on the Notable Contributions to Accounting Literature Committee.

Professor Harrison has lectured in several foreign countries and published articles in numerous journals, including *Journal of Accounting Research*, *Journal of Accountancy*, *Journal of Accounting and Public Policy*, *Economic Consequences of Financial Accounting Standards*, *Accounting Horizons*, *Issues in Accounting Education*, and *Journal of Law and Commerce*.

He is co-author of *Financial & Managerial Accounting*, second edition, 2009 and *Accounting*, eighth edition, 2009 (with Charles T. Horngren and M. Suzanne Oliver), published by Pearson Prentice Hall. Professor Harrison has received scholarships, fellowships, and research grants or awards from PricewaterhouseCoopers, Deloitte & Touche, the Ernst & Young Foundation, and the KPMG Foundation.

Charles T. Horngren (1926–2011) was the Edmund W. Littlefield professor of accounting, emeritus, at Stanford University. A graduate of Marquette University, he received his MBA from Harvard University and his PhD from the University of Chicago. He was also the recipient of honorary doctorates from Marquette University and DePaul University.

A certified public accountant, Horngren served on the Accounting Principles Board for six years, the Financial Accounting Standards Board Advisory Council for five years, and the Council of the American Institute of Certified Public Accountants for three years. For six years he served as a trustee of the Financial Accounting Foundation, which oversees the Financial Accounting Standards Board and the Government Accounting Standards Board.

Horngren is a member of the Accounting Hall of Fame.

A member of the American Accounting Association, Horngren was its president and its director of research. He received its first annual Outstanding Accounting Educator Award.

The California Certified Public Accountants Foundation gave Horngren its Faculty Excellence Award and its Distinguished Professor Award. He was the first person to have received both awards.

The American Institute of Certified Public Accountants presented its first Outstanding Educator Award to Horngren.

Horngren was named Accountant of the Year, in Education, by the national professional accounting fraternity, Beta Alpha Psi.

Professor Horngren was also a member of the Institute of Management Accountants, from whom he received its Distinguished Service Award. He was a member of the institute's Board of Regents, which administers the Certified Management Accountant examinations.

Horngren is the author of these other accounting books published by Pearson: *Cost Accounting: A Managerial Emphasis*, Fifteenth Edition, 2015 (with Srikant Datar and George Foster); *Introduction to Financial Accounting*, Eleventh Edition, 2014 (with Gary L. Sundem, John A. Elliott, and Donna Philbrick); *Introduction to Management Accounting*, Sixteenth Edition, 2014 (with Gary L. Sundem, Jeff Schatzberg, and Dave Burgstahler); *Financial & Managerial Accounting*, Sixteenth Edition, 2014 and Horngren's *Accounting*, Tenth Edition, 2014 (revised by Tracie Nobles, Brenda Mattison, and Ella Mae Matsumura).

Horngren was the consulting editor for Pearson's Charles T. Horngren Series in Accounting.

C. William (Bill) Thomas is the J. E. Bush Professor of Accounting and a Master Teacher at Baylor University. A Baylor University alumnus, he received both his BBA and MBA there and went on to earn his PhD from The University of Texas at Austin.

With primary interests in the areas of financial accounting and auditing, Bill Thomas has served as the J. E. Bush Professor of Accounting since 1995. He has been a member of the faculty of the Accounting and Business Law Department of the Hankamer School of Business since 1971, and served as chair of the department from 1983 until 1995. He was recognized as an Outstanding Faculty Member of Baylor University in 1984 and Distinguished Professor for the Hankamer School of Business in 2002. Dr. Thomas has received several awards for outstanding teaching, including the Outstanding Professor in the Executive MBA Programs in 2001, 2002, and 2006. In 2004, he received the designation as Master Teacher.

Thomas is the author of textbooks in auditing and financial accounting, as well as many articles in auditing, financial accounting and reporting, taxation, ethics and accounting education. His scholarly work focuses on the subject of fraud prevention and detection, as well as ethical issues among accountants in public practice. His most recent publication of national prominence is "The Rise and Fall of the Enron Empire" which appeared in the April 2002 *Journal of Accountancy*, and which was selected by Encyclopedia Britannica for inclusion in its *Annals of American History*. He presently serves as both technical and accounting and auditing editor of *Today's CPA*, the journal of the Texas Society of Certified Public Accountants, with a circulation of approximately 28,000.

Thomas is a certified public accountant in Texas. Prior to becoming a professor, Thomas was a practicing accountant with the firms of KPMG, LLP, and BDO Seidman, LLP. He is a member of the American Accounting Association, the American Institute of Certified Public Accountants, and the Texas Society of Certified Public Accountants.

In memory of *Charles T. Horngren* 1926–2011

Whose vast contributions to the teaching and learning of accounting impacted and will continue to impact generations of accounting students and professionals.

For our wives,

Nancy and Mary Ann

BRIEF CONTENTS

CONTENTS

Chapter 8

Long-Term Investments & the Time Value of Money 428

Spotlight: Intel Holds Several Different Types of Investments 428

Chapter 9

Liabilities 482

Spotlight: Southwest Airlines: Still Flying High! 482

Account for Current and Contingent Liabilities 484

Current Liabilities of Known Amount 484

Current Liabilities That Must Be Estimated 490

Contingent Liabilities 491

Are All Liabilities Reported on the Balance Sheet? 492

Summary of Current Liabilities 493

Mid-Chapter Summary Problem 493

Account for Bonds Payable, Notes Payable, and Interest Expense 494

Bonds: An Introduction 494

Issuing Bonds Payable at Par (Face Value) 497

Issuing Bonds Payable at a Discount 499

What Is the Interest Expense on These Bonds Payable? 499

Interest Expense on Bonds Issued at a Discount 501

Partial-Period Interest Amounts 504

Issuing Bonds Payable at a Premium 504

The Straight-Line Amortization Method: A Quick and Dirty Way to Measure Interest Expense 508

Should We Retire Bonds Payable Before Their Maturity? 509

Convertible Bonds and Notes 509

Analyze and Differentiate Financing with Debt Versus Equity 510

The Leverage Ratio 512

The Times-Interest-Earned Ratio 513

Understand Other Long-Term Liabilities 513

Leases 513

Types of Leases 513

Do Lessees Prefer Operating Leases or Capital Leases? 514

Pensions and Postretirement Liabilities 515

Report Liabilities 516

Reporting on the Balance Sheet 516

Disclosing the Fair Value of Long-Term Debt 517

Reporting Financing Activities on the Statement of Cash Flows 517

End-of-Chapter Summary Problems 518

Chapter 10

Stockholders' Equity 550

Spotlight: The Home Depot: Building Toward Success 550

Explain the Features of a Corporation 552

Organizing a Corporation 553

Stockholders' Rights 554

Stockholders' Equity 555

Classes of Stock 555

Account for the Issuance of Stock 557

Common Stock 557

A Stock Issuance for Other Than Cash Can Create an Ethical Challenge 560

Preferred Stock 561

Mid-Chapter Summary Problem 562

Authorized, Issued, and Outstanding Stock 564

Show how Treasury Stock Affects a Company 564

How Is Treasury Stock Recorded? 564

Retirement of Treasury Stock 566

Resale of Treasury Stock 566

Issuing Stock for Employee Compensation 566

Summary of Treasury-Stock Transactions 567

Account for Retained Earnings, Dividends, and Splits 567

Should the Company Declare and Pay Cash Dividends? 568

Cash Dividends 568

Analyzing the Stockholder's Equity Accounts 569

Dividends on Preferred Stock 570

Stock Dividends 571

Stock Splits 572

Summary of the Effects on Assets, Liabilities, and Stockholders' Equity 573

CHANGES FOR THE TENTH EDITION

In general, the Tenth Edition content has been substantially redesigned and enhanced:

- The text font has been enlarged from the Ninth Edition to Tenth Edition to make the text easier to read.
- Chapter openers now only take up one or two pages, with a small silhouetted image of the spotlight company.
- Most financial statements, general ledger, and journal entries have been converted to Excel.
- Special sections called Try It in Excel have been added to every chapter, giving students explicit instructions as to how to access the chapter focus company's most recent financial statements in Excel from the website of the U.S. Securities and Exchange Commission (www.sec.gov).
- Other sections of most chapters give explicit instructions on how to build Excel templates that streamline and simplify various accounting tasks. These tasks include preparation of the adjusted trial balance worksheet, preparation of financial statements, computation of depreciation by various methods, and computation of effective-interest bond discount and premium amortization.
- In all chapters, a new "focus on analysis" company, Yum! Brands, Inc., was selected to replace Radio Shack. Selections of the financial statement appear in Appendix B.
- Demo Docs are removed from the text and are now relocated to MyAccountingLab.

Within Chapters 1 through 3:

- Chapter discussions were revised to be more integrative, using a continuing example of one company that carries through all three chapters.
- Excel is used as a facilitating tool to both prepare and analyze financial statements. Excel data files are available for problems in the end of chapter material for these chapters, also incorporating them into MyAccountingLab.
- Summary problems for each of these three chapters are reworked using the Excel format.

Below are the content changes to the Tenth Edition, listed chapter-by-chapter:

Chapter 1

- Chapter Opener: Spotlight company changed to The Gap, Inc.
- Provides detailed instructions as to how to access current financial statements of The Gap, Inc. in Excel on the website of the U. S. Securities and Exchange Commission (SEC).
- Real World Financial Statement changed to The Gap, Inc. and used to illustrate the interrelationships of the financial statements.
- Added coverage of the new financial reporting framework for small and midsize entities that are not public and that have no intention of going public.
- Updated information on international financial reporting standards (IFRS) in light of the more recent trend toward convergence rather than adoption of IFRS on the part of U.S. public companies.
- Chapter contains eight simulated Excel exercises and problems, gradable Excel exercises and problems in MyAccountingLab.

Chapter 2

- Chapter Opener: Spotlight company changed to Whole Foods Market, Inc.
- Real World company, Freddy's Auto Service, Inc., is used to illustrate recording of hypothetical transactions and posting entries.
- Provides instructions on how to access current financial statements of Whole Foods Market, Inc. in Excel on the website of the U. S. Securities and Exchange Commission (SEC).

- Provides detailed instructions as to how to prepare a financial statement in worksheet format using Excel.
- Detailed instructions provided as to how to prepare a trial balance using Excel.
- End of Chapter Summary Problem: Transactional analysis company name changed from Genie Car Wash, Inc. to Magee Service Center, Inc.
- Simulated Excel exercises and problems increased from two to six.

Chapter 3

- Provides instructions on how to access current financial statements of Starbucks Corporation in Excel on the website of the U. S. Securities and Exchange Commission (SEC).
- Provides detailed instructions as to how to prepare an adjusted trial balance worksheet using Excel.
- End of Chapter Summary Problem: Transactional analysis company name changed from Genie Car Wash, Inc. to Badger Ranch, Inc.
- Simulated Excel exercises and problems increased from 9 to 11.

Chapter 4

- Chapter Opener: Changed name of Spotlighted Cooking the Books company to Mid-Atlantic Manufacturing Company.
- Updated internal control discussion.
- Emphasized use of electronic bank reconciliations.
- Detailed instructions provided on how to prepare a cash budget using Excel.
- Two simulated Excel problems have been added.

Chapter 5

- Chapter Opener: Spotlight company changed to Apple, Inc.
- Provides detailed instructions on how to access current financial statements of Apple, Inc. in Excel on the website of the U. S. Securities and Exchange Commission (SEC).
- Updated and clarified discussion of accounting for short-term investments, illustrating distinction between accounting for trading securities and accounting for available-for-sale securities.
- Updated discussion on revenue recognition to correspond with new GAAP/IFRS standard.
- Simulated Excel exercises and problems increased from seven to eight.

Chapter 6

- Chapter Opener: Changed Spotlight company to Family Dollar Stores, Inc.
- Provides detailed instructions as to how to access current financial statements of Family Dollar Stores, Inc. in Excel on the website of the U. S. Securities and Exchange Commission (SEC).
- Expanded coverage (including journal entries) of how to account for purchase returns and discounts.
- Simulated Excel exercises and problems increased from 9 to 10.

Chapter 7

- Chapter Opener: Retained Spotlight company, FedEx Corporation, and updated information used in chapter using the FedEx Corporation 2012 Annual Report.
- Provides detailed instructions as to how to access current financial statements of FedEx Corporation in Excel on the website of the U. S. Securities and Exchange Commission (SEC).
- Changed exhibits on three depreciation methods to Excel format, with detailed instructions as to how to use Excel to compute depreciation expense, accumulated depreciation, and asset book value.
- Simulated Excel exercises and problems increased from 9 to 11.

Chapter 8

- Chapter Opener: Retained spotlight company, Intel Corporation and updated information in chapter using the 2012 Intel Corporation Annual Report.

- Provides detailed instructions as to how to access current financial statements of Intel Corporation in Excel on the website of the U. S. Securities and Exchange Commission (SEC).
- Simulated Excel exercises and problems increased from 9 to 10.

Chapter 9

- Chapter Opener: Retained Spotlight company, Southwest Airlines, and updated information in chapter using the Southwest Airlines 2012 Annual Report.
- Provides detailed instructions as to how to access current financial statements of Southwest Airlines Company in Excel on the website of the U. S. Securities and Exchange Commission (SEC).
- Modified chapter exhibits for bond discount and premium amortization to Excel format, and provided detailed instructions as to how to prepare effective-interest amortization tables in Excel format.
- Simulated Excel exercises and problems increased from eight to nine.

Chapter 10

- Chapter Opener: Changed Spotlight company to The Home Depot, Inc., and updated information in chapter using the Home Depot, Inc. 2012 Annual Report.
- Provides detailed instructions as to how to access current financial statements of The Home Depot, Inc. in Excel on the website of the U. S. Securities and Exchange Commission (SEC).
- Relocated coverage of Statement of Stockholders' Equity from Chapter 11 to Chapter 10 and changed end of chapter material to reflect this modified coverage.
- Simulated Excel exercises and problems increased from five to six.

Chapter 11

- Chapter Opener: Retained Spotlight company, The Gap, Inc. and updated information in chapter using the The Gap, Inc. 2012 Annual Report.
- Provides detailed instructions as to how to access current financial statements of The Gap, Inc. in Excel on the website of the U. S. Securities and Exchange Commission (SEC).
- Moved coverage of Statement of Stockholders' Equity to Chapter 10 and deleted related end of chapter material in Chapter 11.
- Added a section on non-financial measures of performance, such as corporate social responsibility.
- Added a section on use of footnote disclosures in financial analysis, including segment information. Added end-of-chapter materials to reflect this expanded coverage.
- Simulated Excel exercises and problems increased from five to seven.

Chapter 12

- Chapter Opener: Retained Spotlight company, Google, Inc. and updated information in chapter using the Google 2012 Annual Report.
- Provides detailed instructions as to how to access current financial statements of Google, Inc. in Excel on the website of the U. S. Securities and Exchange Commission (SEC).
- Simulated Excel exercises and problems increased from four to seven.

Chapter 13

- Chapter Opener: Retained Spotlight company, Amazon.com, Inc. and updated information in chapter using the Amazon.com 2012 Annual Report.
- Provides detailed instructions as to how to access current financial statements of Amazon.com, Inc. in Excel on the website of the U. S. Securities and Exchange Commission (SEC).
- Provided detailed instructions as to how to use Excel to perform both horizontal and vertical analyses of comparative financial statements.
- Expanded analysis of Amazon.com, Inc., providing comprehensive tables of key financial ratios in Excel format.
- Simulated Excel exercises and problems increased from six to nine.

VISUAL WALK-THROUGH

NEW!

Try It in Excel

Describes line-by-line how to retrieve and prepare accounting information (such as adjusted trial balance worksheets, ratio computations, depreciation schedules, bond discount and premium amortization schedules, and financial statement analysis) in Excel.

If you built the straight-line depreciation schedule in Exhibit 7-5 with Excel, changing the spreadsheet for units-of-production depreciation is a snap. Steps 1–3 and 6–8 are identical. Only steps 4 and 5, dealing with columns C and D, change. You might want to start by opening the straight-line schedule you prepared and saving it under another name: "units-of-production depreciation." Next, change the column headings for column C and column D. Column C should be labeled "Rate per unit." Column D should be labeled "Number Units." Assuming you do this, here are the modified steps 4 and 5 of the process we used before:

4. In column C, calculate a per-unit (rather than per-year as we did with straight-line) depreciation rate by dividing the depreciable cost ($41,000 − $1,000 in Exhibit 7-4) by the number of units (100,000 miles) to get a fixed depreciation rate per mile ($0.40). Enter .4 in cell C3 and copy down through cell C7.

5. In cells D3 through D7, respectively, enter the number of miles driven in years 1 through 5 of the asset's useful life. These are 20,000, 30,000, 25,000, 15,000, and 10,000, respectively.

All of the other amounts in the table will automatically recalculate to reflect units-of-production depreciation, exactly as shown in Exhibit 7-6. ■

Excel! Integrated Throughout Text!

Excel-based financial statements are used so that students will familiarize themselves with the accounting information format actually used in the business world.

A1		
A	**B**	**C**
FedEx Corporation		
Consolidated Balance Sheets (Partial, Adapted)		
(In millions of $)	**May 31, 2012**	**May 31, 2011**
CURRENT ASSETS		
Cash and cash equivalents	$ 2,843	$ 2,328
Receivables, less allowances of $178 and $182	4,704	4,581
Spare parts, supplies and fuel, less allowances	440	437
Deferred income taxes	533	610
Prepaid expenses and other	536	329
Total current assets	9,056	8,285
PROPERTY AND EQUIPMENT, AT COST		
Aircraft and related equipment	14,360	13,146
Package handling and ground support equipment	5,912	5,591
Computer and electronic equipment	4,646	4,408
Vehicles	3,654	3,294
Facilities and other	7,592	7,247
Gross property and equipment	36,164	33,686
Less accumulated depreciation and amortization	(18,916)	(18,143)
Net property and equipment	17,248	15,543
OTHER LONG-TERM ASSETS		
Goodwill	2,387	2,326
Other assets	1,212	1,231
Total other long-term assets	3,599	3,557
TOTAL ASSETS	$ 29,903	$ 27,385

A1	
A	**B**
FedEx Corporation	
Statement of Cash Flows (Partial, Adapted)	
Year Ended May 31, 2012	
	(In millions)
Cash Flows from Operating Activities:	
Net income	$ 2,032
Adjustments to reconcile net income	
to net cash provided by operating activities:	
Depreciation and amortization	2,113
Other items (summarized)	690
Net cash provided by operating activities	4,835
Cash Flows from Investing Activities:	
Capital expenditures	(4,007)
Other asset acquisitions and dispositions, net	(42)
Net cash (used in) investing activities	(4,049)
Cash Flows from Financing Activities:	
Net cash (used in) financing activities	(244)
Effect of exchange rate changes on cash	(27)
Net (increase) in cash and cash equivalents	515
Cash and cash equivalents, beginning of period	2,328
Cash and cash equivalents, end of period	$ 2,843

NEW! Accounting Cycle Examples Simplified

Accounting Cycle Tutorial (ACT)

For more practice and review of accounting cycle concepts in chapters 1 through 3, use ACT, the Accounting Cycle Tutorial, online at www.myaccountinglab.com. The Tutorial portion of ACT reviews major concepts, the Application provides practice exercises, and the Glossary reviews important terms.

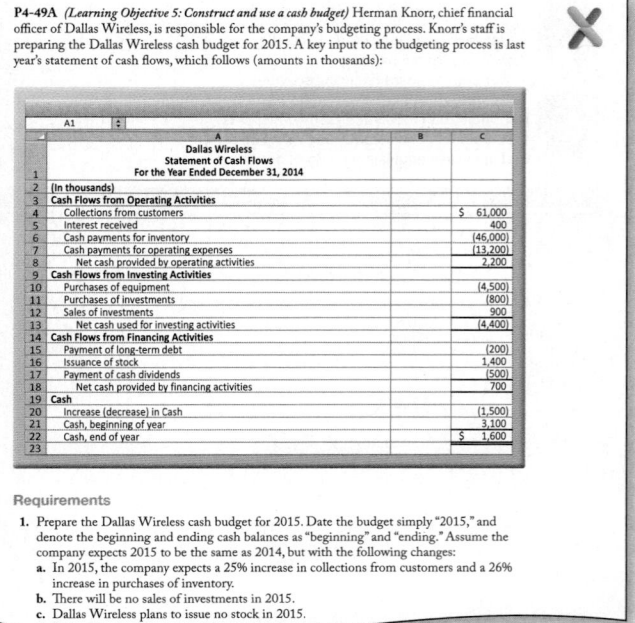

NEW! Excel Opportunities in MyAccountingLab Increased

Now students can get even more real-world Excel practice in their classes in every chapter:

- Instructors have the option to assign students end-of-chapter questions that can be completed in an Excel-simulated environment. These selected questions are indicated with a green Excel marginal icon.

- Questions will be auto-graded, reported to, and visible in the grade book.

- Excel remediation will be available to students.

E8-29B. *(Learning Objective 4: Prepare a consolidated balance sheet)* Zeta, Inc., owns Theta Corp. These two companies' individual balance sheets follow:

	Zeta, Inc.	Theta Corp.	Elimination Debit	Elimination Credit
Zeta, Inc. Consolidation Work Sheet				
Cash	$ 48,000	$ 18,000		
Accounts receivable, net	82,000	58,000		
Note receivable from Zeta	—	33,000		
Inventory	54,000	83,000		
Investment in Theta	119,000	—		
Plant assets, net	288,000	98,000		
Other assets	29,000	11,000		
Total	$ 620,000	$ 301,000		
Accounts payable	$ 49,000	$ 35,000		
Notes payable	152,000	23,000		
Other liabilities	78,000	124,000		
Common stock	107,000	82,000		
Retained earnings	234,000	37,000		
Total	$ 620,000	$ 301,000		

Requirements

1. Prepare a consolidated balance sheet of Zeta, Inc. It is sufficient to complete the consolidation work sheet. Use Exhibit 8-7 as a model.
2. What is the amount of stockholders' equity for the consolidated entity?

E8-30B. *(Learning Objective 1: Analyze and report held-to-maturity security transactions)* Assume that on September 30, 2014, Rentex, Inc., paid 96 for 7% bonds of Oleander Corporation as a long-term held-to-maturity investment. The maturity value of the bonds will be $80,000 on September 30, 2019. The bonds pay interest on March 31 and S⋯

P4-49A *(Learning Objective 5: Construct and use a cash budget)* Herman Knorr, chief financial officer of Dallas Wireless, is responsible for the company's budgeting process. Knorr's staff is preparing the Dallas Wireless cash budget for 2015. A key input to the budgeting process is last year's statement of cash flows, which follows (amounts in thousands):

Dallas Wireless Statement of Cash Flows For the Year Ended December 31, 2014	
(In thousands)	
Cash Flows from Operating Activities	
Collections from customers	$ 61,000
Interest received	400
Cash payments for inventory	(46,000)
Cash payments for operating expenses	(13,200)
Net cash provided by operating activities	2,200
Cash Flows from Investing Activities	
Purchases of equipment	(4,500)
Purchases of investments	(800)
Sales of investments	900
Net cash used for investing activities	(4,400)
Cash Flows from Financing Activities	
Payment of long-term debt	(200)
Issuance of stock	1,400
Payment of cash dividends	(500)
Net cash provided by financing activities	700
Cash	
Increase (decrease) in Cash	(1,500)
Cash, beginning of year	3,100
Cash, end of year	$ 1,600

Requirements

1. Prepare the Dallas Wireless cash budget for 2015. Date the budget simply "2015," and denote the beginning and ending cash balances as "beginning" and "ending." Assume the company expects 2015 to be the same as 2014, but with the following changes:
   a. In 2015, the company expects a 25% increase in collections from customers and a 26% increase in purchases of inventory.
   b. There will be no sales of investments in 2015.
   c. Dallas Wireless plans to issue no stock in 2015.
   d. Dallas Wireless plans to end the year with a cash b⋯

How would FedEx divide a $120,000 lump-sum purchase price for land, building, and equipment with estimated market values of $40,000, $95,000, and $15,000, respectively?

Answer:

	Estimated Market Value	Percentage of Total Market Value	×	Total Cost	=	Cost of Each Asset
Land................	$ 40,000	26.7%*	×	$120,000	=	$ 32,040
Building............	95,000	63.3%	×	$120,000	=	75,960
Equipment.........	15,000	10.0%	×	$120,000	=	12,000
Total	$150,000	100.0%				$120,000

*$40,000/$150,000 = 0.267, and so on

Stop & Think. . .

Found within various points of a chapter, this tool includes a question-and-answer snapshot asking students to apply what they just learned.

Challenge Problem

P11-62. *(Learning Objectives 1, 2, 4, 5: Analyze how various transactions affect the income statement and EPS)* Aerostar, Inc., operates as a retailer of casual apparel. A recent, condensed income statement for Aerostar follows:

	A	B	C
	Income Statement		
1	**For the Year Ended January 31, 2012**		
2	Sales revenue		$ 2,400,000
3	Operating expenses:		
4	Cost of goods sold	$ 1,500,000	
5	Selling and administrative expenses	500,000	2,000,000
6	Operating income		400,000
7	Other revenue (expenses)		50,000
8	Income before tax		450,000
9	Income tax expense (40% tax rate)		180,000
10	Net income		$ 270,000
11	Earnings per share (50,000 shares)		$ 5.40
12			

A1

Requirements

1. Assume that the following transactions were inadvertently omitted at the end of the year. Using the categories in the table, indicate the effect of each of the transactions on each category; use + for increase, − for decrease, and NE for no effect. Provide dollar amounts for each column except Earnings per Share.

Transaction	Operating Income	Income Before Tax	Net Income	Earnings per Share
Unadjusted balances	400,000	450,000	270,000	
a.				
b.				
c.				
d.				
e.				
f.				
g.				
h.				
i.				
Totals				

a. Purchased inventory on account from a German company. The price was 100,000 euros. The exchange rate of the euro was $1.47.

b. Sold inventory on account, $120,000 (cost of inventory, $75,000).

Critical Thinking Challenge Problems Increased!

Additional problems developed to provide students with the opportunity for applied critical thinking.

Dear Valued Colleagues,

Welcome to the Tenth Edition of *Financial Accounting*. We are grateful for your support as an adopter of our text as we celebrate over 20 years of success in the market. The Tenth Edition of *Financial Accounting* has been improved in many respects, as explained below.

Several editions ago, we shifted the focus of *Financial Accounting* more toward meeting the needs of users of accounting information for a more balanced presentation. Despite this shift, we still cover the "basic nuts-and-bolts of financial accounting"—the accounting cycle and financial statement preparation. In this edition, we added more discussion of key financial ratios, detailing what those ratios measure and how they are used.

Try It in Excel. As educators, we often have conversations with those who recruit our students. Based on these conversations, we found that students often complete their study of financial accounting without sufficient knowledge of how to use Excel to perform accounting tasks. To respond to this concern, we have adapted most of the illustrations of key accounting tasks in the book to Excel format and have added new sections in key chapters entitled "Try It in Excel," which describe line-by-line how to retrieve and prepare accounting information (such as adjusted trial balance worksheets, ratio computations, depreciation schedules, bond discount and premium amortization schedules, and financial statement analysis) in Excel format. In addition, we have designated many applications to homework exercises and problems that can be completed in Excel and that are automatically graded in MyAccountingLab.

Student success. We feel we have the most advanced student learning materials in the market with MyAccountingLab. These include automatically graded homework, DemoDocs, learning aid videos, and audio PowerPoints. We believe that the use of MyAccountingLab homework will greatly enhance student understanding of accounting with its instantaneous feedback. MyAccountingLab makes the study of financial accounting a more interactive and fun experience for students.

Professor expectations. As professors, we know that you want a book that contains the most relevant and technically correct content available. We also know that you want excellent end-of-chapter material that is as up-to-date and error-free as possible. We reviewed and created the end-of-chapter questions, exercises, problems, and cases taking into account the types of assignments we ourselves use in class and assign as homework. Based on comments from adopters, we have thoroughly reviewed every end-of-chapter exercise and problem, with the goal of eliminating redundancy and adding relevance. The textbook and solutions manual have been put through a rigorous accuracy check to ensure that they are as complete and error-free as possible.

We welcome your comments and suggestions. Please don't hesitate to send feedback about this book to: HorngrensAccounting@pearson.com

Walter Harrison
Bill Thomas

STUDENT AND INSTRUCTOR RESOURCES

For Students

MyAccountingLab

MyAccountingLab online Homework and Assessment Manager includes:

- Pearson eText
- Simulated Excel exercises and problems
- Audio and Student PowerPoint® Presentations
- Data Files
- Accounting Cycle Tutorial
- Videos
- MP3 Files with Chapter Objectives and Summaries
- Demo Docs
- Flash Cards
- Working Papers

Student resource website: pearsonhighered.com/harrison

This website contains the following:

- Data Files: Select end-of-chapter problems have been set up in different software applications, including Excel, QuickBooks 2012, and general ledger software.
- Working Papers

For Instructors

MyAccountingLab

Instructor Resource Center: pearsonhighered.com/accounting

For the instructor's convenience, the instructor resources are available on CD or can be downloaded from the textbook's catalog page (pearsonhighered.com/harrison) and MyAccountingLab.

Available resources include the following:

- Online Instructor's Manual: Includes chapter summaries, teaching tips provided by reviewers, pitfalls for new students, and "best of" practices from instructors across the country.

  Additional resources offered in this online manual include the following:

  - Introduction to the Instructor's Manual with a list of resources and a roadmap to help navigate what's available in MyAccountingLab.
  - Instructor tips for teaching courses in multiple formats—traditional, hybrid, or online.
  - "First Day of Class" student handout that includes tips for success in the course, as well as an additional document that shows students how to register and log on to MyAccountingLab.
  - Sample syllabi for 10- and 16-week courses.
  - Chapter overview and teaching outline that includes a brief synopsis and overview of each chapter.
  - Key topics that walk instructors through what material to cover and what examples to use when addressing certain items within the chapter.
  - Student chapter summary handout.
  - Assignment grid that outlines all end-of-chapter exercises and problems, the topic being covered in that particular exercise or problem, estimated completion time, level of difficulty, and availability in Excel templates.
  - Ten-minute quizzes that quickly assess students' understanding of the chapter material.
  - Demonstration Problems for use in class.

- Instructor's Solutions Manual: Contains solutions to all end-of-chapter questions, including short exercises, exercises, and problems.
- TestBank: Includes more than 3,000 questions. Both objective-based questions and computational problems are available.
- PowerPoint Presentations: These presentations help facilitate classroom discussion by demonstrating where the numbers come from and what they mean to the concept at hand. Includes NEW Demonstration Problem slides:
  - Instructor PowerPoint Presentations—complete with lecture notes
  - Student PowerPoint Presentations
  - Audio Narrated PowerPoint Presentations
  - Clicker Response System (CRS) PowerPoint Presentations
- Working Papers and Solutions in Excel and PDF Format
- Image Library
- Data and Solution Files: Select end-of-chapter problems have been set up in different software applications, including QuickBooks 2012 and General Ledger. Corresponding solution files are also provided.

ACKNOWLEDGMENTS

A special thank you to Betsy Willis and Mignon Worman Tucker for their dedication throughout the project. Thank you to Carolyn Streuly for her help with accuracy checking and to Jill Kolongowski for managing the supplements.

Thanks also to Carolyn Streuly for preparing the Test Bank, to Betsy Willis for preparing the Instructor's Resource Manual, and to Coby Harmon for preparing the PowerPoint presentation.

We would like to thank the following reviewers for the Tenth Edition for their valuable input: Mary Ewanechko, MBA, Monroe Community College; Dr. Geoffrey J. Gurka, PhD, Colorado Mesa University; Maria U. Ku, CPA, Accounting Instructor, Ohlone College & Diablo Valley College; Molly McFadden-May, MT (Master of Taxation), Tulsa Community College; and Sue Van Boven, Paradise Valley Community College.

In revising previous editions of *Financial Accounting*, we had the help of instructors from across the country who have participated in online surveys, chapter reviews, and focus groups. Their comments and suggestions for both the text and the supplements have been a great help in planning and carrying out revisions, and we thank them for their contributions.

Past Reviewer Participants

Shawn Abbott, College of the Siskiyous, CA
Linda Abernathy, Kirkwood Community College
Sol Ahiarah, SUNY College at Buffalo (Buffalo State)
M. J. Albin, University of Southern Mississippi
Gary Ames, Brigham Young University, Idaho
Elizabeth Ammann, Lindenwood University
Brenda Anderson, Brandeis University
Kim Anderson, Indiana University of Pennsylvania
Florence Atiase, University of Texas at Austin
Walter Austin, Mercer University, Macon GA
Brad Badertscher, University of Iowa
Sandra Bailey, Oregon Institute of Technology
Patrick Bauer, DeVry University, Kansas City
Barbara A. Beltrand, Metropolitan State University, MN
Jerry Bennett, University of South Carolina–Spartanburg
Peg Beresewski, Robert Morris College, IL
Lucille Berry, Webster University, MO
John Bildersee, New York University, Stern School
Brenda Bindschatel, Green River Community College
Candace Blankenship, Belmont University, TN
Charlie Bokemeier, Michigan State University
Patrick Bouker, North Seattle Community College
Amy Bourne, Oregon State University
Scott Boylan, Washington and Lee University, VA
Robert Braun, Southeastern Louisiana University
Linda Bressler, University of Houston Downtown
Michael Broihahn, Barry University, FL
Rada Brooks, University of California, Berkeley
Elizabeth Brown, Keene State College
Carol Brown, Oregon State University
Helen Brubeck, San Jose State University, CA
Scott Bryant, Baylor University
Marcus Butler, University of Rochester, NY
Marci Butterfield, University of Utah
Mark Camma, Atlantic Cape Community College, NJ
Kay Carnes, Gonzaga University, WA
Brian Carpenter, University of Scranton, PA
Sandra Cereola, James Madison University, VA
Kam Chan, Pace University
Hong Chen, Northeastern Illinois University
C. Catherine Chiang, Elon University
Freddy Choo, San Francisco State University, CA
Charles Christy, Delaware Tech and Community College, Stanton Campus
Lawrence Chui, Ph.D., CPA, Opus College of Business, University of St. Thomas
Shifei Chung, Rowan University, NJ
Bryan Church, Georgia Tech at Atlanta
Carolyn Clark, Saint Joseph's University, PA
Dr. Paul Clikeman, University of Richmond
Charles Coate, St. Bonaventure University, NY
Dianne Conry, University of California State College Extension–Cupertino
Ellen D. Cook, University of Louisiana at Lafayette

John Coulter, Western New England College
Sue Counte, Saint Louis Community College–Meramec
Julia Creighton, American University
Sue Cullers, Buena Vista University
Donald Curfman, McHenry County College, IL
Alan Czyzewski, Indiana State University
Laurie Dahlin, Worcester State College, MA
Bonita Daly, University of Southern Maine
Kreag Danvers, Clarion University
Betty David, Francis Marion University
Patricia Derrick, George Washington University
Peter DiCarlo, Boston College
Charles Dick, Miami University
Barbara Doughty, New Hampshire Community Technical College
Allan Drebin, Northwestern University
Carolyn Dreher, Southern Methodist University
Emily Drogt, Grand Valley State University
Carol Dutton, South Florida Community College
James Emig, Villanova University, PA
Ellen Engel, University of Chicago
Alan Falcon, Loyola Marymount University, CA
Janet Farler, Pima Community College, AZ
Dr. Andrew Felo, Penn State Great Valley
Ken Ferris, Thunderbird College, AZ
Dr. Mary Fischer, Professor of Accounting, The University of Texas at Tyler
Dr. Caroline Ford, Baylor University
Clayton Forester, University of Minnesota
Lou Fowler, Missouri Western State College
Timothy Gagnon, Northeastern University
Terrie Gehman, Elizabethtown College, PA
Lucille Genduso, Nova Southeastern University, FL
Alvin Gerald Smith, University of Northern Iowa
Frank Gersich, Monmouth College, IL
Bradley Gillespie, Saddleback College, CA
Lisa Gillespie, Loyola University, Chicago
Marvin Gordon, University of Illinois at Chicago
Brian Green, University of Michigan at Dearborn
Anthony Greig, Purdue University
Ronald Guidry, University of Louisiana at Monroe
Konrad Gunderson, Missouri Western State College
William Hahn, Southeastern College, FL
Jack Hall, Western Kentucky University
Gloria Halpern, Montgomery College, MD
Penny Hanes, Associate Professor, Mercyhurst College
Dr. Heidi Hansel, Kirkwood Community College
Kenneth Hart, Brigham Young University, Idaho
Al Hartgraves, Emory University
Michael Haselkorn, Bentley University
Thomas Hayes, University of North Texas
Larry Hegstad, Pacific Lutheran University, WA
Candy Heino, Anoka-Ramsey Community College, MN
Mary Hollars, Vincennes University

Anit Hope, Tarrant County College, TX
Thomas Huse, Boston College
Fred R. Jex, Macomb Community College, MI
Grace Johnson, Marietta College
Celina Jozsi, University of South Florida
John Karayan, Woodbury University
Beth Kern, Indiana University, South Bend
Irene Kim, The George Washington University
Hans E. Klein, Babson College, MA
Robert Kollar, Duquesne University
Willem Koole, North Carolina State University
Emil Koren, Hillsborough Community College, FL
Dennis Kovach, Community College of Allegheny
    County–North Campus
Ellen Landgraf, Loyola University Chicago
Howard Lawrence, Christian Brothers University, TN
Barry Leffkov, Regis College, MA
Elliott Levy, Bentley University
Chao-Shin Liu, Notre Dame
Barbara Lougee, University of California, Irvine
Heidemarie Lundblad, California State University,
    Northridge
Joseph Lupino, Saint Mary's College of California
Anna Lusher, West Liberty State College, WV
Harriet Maccracken, Arizona State University
Constance Malone Hylton, George Mason University
Carol Mannino, Milwaukee School of Engineering
Herb Martin, Hope College, MI
Aziz Martinez, Harvard University, Harvard
    Business School
Anthony Masino, Queens University / NC Central
Lizbeth Matz, University of Pittsburgh, Bradford
Bruce Maule, College of San Mateo
Michelle McEacharn, University of Louisiana at Monroe
Nick McGaughey, San Jose State University, CA
Allison McLeod, University of North Texas
Scott Miller, Gannon University
Cynthia J. Miller, Gatton College of Business &
    Economics, University of Kentucky
Cathleen Miller, University of Michigan–Flint
Mary Miller, University of New Haven
Mark Miller, University of San Francisco, CA
Frank Mioni, Madonna University, MI
Dr. Birendra (Barry) K. Mishra, University of California,
    Riverside
Theodore D. Morrison III, Wingate University, NC
Lisa Nash, Vincennes University
Rosemary Nurre, College of San Mateo
Bruce L. Oliver, Rochester Institute of Technology
Stephen Owen, Hamilton College
Charles Pedersen, Quinsigamond Community College, MA
Richard J. Pettit, Mountain View College

George Plesko, Massachusetts Institute of Technology
David Plumlee, University of Utah
Gregory Prescott, University of South Alabama
Rama Ramamurthy, College of William and Mary
Craig Reeder, Florida A&M University
Barb Reeves, Cleary University
Bettye Rogers-Desselle, Prairie View A&M University, TX
Darren Roulstone, University of Chicago
Norlin Rueschhoff , Notre Dame
Anwar Salimi, California State Polytechnic
    University, Pomona
Philippe Sammour, Eastern Michigan University
Angela Sandberg, Jacksonville State University, AL
George Sanders, Western Washington University, WA
Betty Saunders, University of North Florida
Albert A Schepanski, University of Iowa
William Schmul, Notre Dame
Arnie Schnieder, Georgia Tech at Atlanta
Allmen School of Accountancy, University of Kentucky
Gim Seow, University of Connecticut
Itzhak Sharav, CUNY–Lehman Graduate School
    of Business
Allan Sheets, International Business College
Lily Sieux, California State University, East Bay
James Smith, Community College of Philadelphia
Virginia Smith, Saint Mary's College of California
Beverly Soriano, Framingham State College, MA
Vic Stanton, Stanford University
Carolyn R. Stokes, Frances Marion University, SC
J. B. Stroud, Nicholls State University, LA
Gloria J. Stuart, Georgia Southern University
Al Taccone, Cuyamaca College, CA
Diane Tanner, University of North Florida
Martin Taylor, University of Texas at Arlington
Howard Toole, San Diego State University
Vincent Turner, California State Polytechnic University,
    Pomona
Marcia Veit, University of Central Florida
Bruce Wampler, Louisiana State University, Shreveport
Suzanne Ward, University of Louisiana at Lafayette
Craig Weaver, University of California, Riverside
Frederick Weis, Claremont McKenna College, CA
Frederick Weiss, Virginia Wesleyan College
Betsy Willis, Baylor University, Waco, TX
Ronald Woan, Indiana University of Pennsylvania
Allen Wright, Hillsborough Community College, FL
Dr. Jia Wu, University of Massachusetts, Dartmouth
Yanfeng Xue, George Washington University
Barbara Yahvah, University of Montana-Helena
Myung Yoon, Northeastern Illinois University
Lin Zeng, Northeastern Illinois University
Tony Zordan, University of St. Francis, IL

The Financial Statements

➤ SPOTLIGHT: The Gap, Inc.

Where do you go when you need to shop for casual clothes and accessories? Perhaps you've recently needed to replace or replenish your supply of jeans, casual shirts, tees, or sweaters in order to return to campus this fall. How about a new jacket or a pair of khakis and a belt to complete your look for the first campus party? Your parents have probably been buying clothing for you at some Gap-affiliated store (GapKids, Gap, Banana Republic, or Old Navy) since you were a baby! Based in San Francisco, California, The Gap, Inc. has been offering quality clothing and accessories to its customers since 1969. Its global portfolio of distinct brands crosses multiple demographic and geographic boundaries, with products designed for customers from a wide range of lifestyles and incomes. The company has a network of almost 3,500 company-operated and franchise store locations in the United States, Canada, the United Kingdom, France, Ireland, Japan, China, and Italy. The Gap, Inc.'s products are also available to customers in over 90 countries through company-owned websites. It operates under the brand names of Gap, babyGap, GapKids, Banana Republic, Old Navy, Piperlime, and Althea. Something you may not know is that The Gap, Inc., has been a top-rated corporate citizen several times since 2000 in a yearly report produced by *Corporate Responsibility Magazine*. In 2012, the company ranked #13 overall and #4 in employee relations on the magazine's list of 100 Best Corporate Citizens, measuring such areas as the environment, climate change, human rights, and philanthropy.

As you can see, The Gap, Inc., sells lots of clothing and accessories—its net sales were about $14.5 billion for the year ended January 28, 2012 (see line 4 of The Gap, Inc.'s Consolidated Statements of Income on page 2). On these net sales, The Gap, Inc., earned net income of $833 million for the year ended January 28, 2012 (line 10).

Q-Images/Alamy

	A	B	C	D	E
1	The Gap, Inc. Consolidated Statements of Income				
2	Adapted, in millions of $	12 Months Ended			
3		Jan. 28, 2012	Jan. 29, 2011		
4	Net sales	$ 14,549	$ 14,664		
5	Cost of goods sold and occupancy expenses	9,275	8,775		
6	Operating expenses	3,836	3,921		
7	Interest (income)/expense, net	69	(14)		
8	Income taxes	536	778		
9	Total expenses	13,716	13,460		
10	Net income	$ 833	$ 1,204		
11					

These terms—net sales and net income—may be unfamiliar to you now. But after you read this chapter, you'll be able to use these and other business terms. Welcome to the world of accounting! ●

Each chapter of this book begins with an actual financial statement. In this chapter, it's the Consolidated Statements of Income of The Gap, Inc., for the two years ended January 28, 2012 and January 29, 2011. The core of financial accounting revolves around the basic financial statements:

- Income statement (sometimes known as the statement of operations)
- Statement of retained earnings (usually included in the statement of stock-holders' equity)
- Balance sheet (sometimes known as the statement of financial position)
- Statement of cash flows

Financial statements are the business documents that companies use to report the results of their activities to various user groups, which can include managers, investors, creditors, and regulatory agencies. In turn, these parties use the reported information to make a variety of decisions, such as whether to invest in or loan money to the company. To learn accounting, you must learn to focus on decisions.

In this chapter, we explain generally accepted accounting principles, their underlying assumptions and concepts, and the bodies responsible for issuing accounting standards. We discuss the judgment process that is necessary to making good accounting decisions. We also discuss the contents of the four basic financial statements that report the results of those decisions. In later chapters, we will explain in more detail how to construct the financial statements, as well as how user groups typically use the information contained in them to make business decisions.

Learning Objectives

1. **Explain** why accounting is the language of business

2. **Explain and apply** underlying accounting concepts, assumptions, and principles

3. **Apply** the accounting equation to business organizations

4. **Evaluate** business operations through the financial statements

5. **Construct** financial statements and **analyze** the relationships among them

6. **Evaluate** business decisions ethically

You can access the most current annual report of The Gap, Inc., in Excel® format at **www.sec.gov**. Using the "filings" link on the toolbar at the top of the page, select "company filings search." This will take you to the "EDGAR Company Filings" page. Type "Gap" in the company name box, and select "search." This will produce the "EDGAR Search Results" page showing the company name. Click on the "CIK" link beside the company name. This will pull up all of the reports the company has filed with the SEC. Under the "filing type" box, type "10-K," and click the "search" box. Form 10-K is the SEC form for the company's latest annual report. Find the year that you wish to view. Click on the "Interactive Data" box, which takes you to the "View Filing Data" page. Find and click on the "View Excel Document" link at the top of this page. You may choose to either open or download the Excel files containing the company's most recent financial statements. ■

MyAccountingLab

The Gap, Inc.'s managers make lots of decisions. Which product is selling fastest—khakis, jeans, or casual slacks? Are tees more profitable than collared shirts? Should the company expand operations into Eastern Europe or the Middle East? Accounting information helps companies make these decisions.

Take a look at The Gap, Inc.'s Consolidated Statements of Income on page 2. Focus on net income (line 10). Net income (profit) is the excess of revenues (net sales) over expenses. You can see that The Gap, Inc., earned $833 million of net income in the year ended January 28, 2012. That's good news because it means that The Gap, Inc., had $833 million more revenue (net sales) than expenses for the year.

The Gap, Inc.'s Consolidated Statements of Income present more interesting news. Net sales (line 4) declined by about 0.8% during the period compared with the previous year (from $14,664 million to $14,549 million). Furthermore, net income declined by 31% (from $1,204 million to $833 million).

Suppose you have $10,000 to invest. What information would you need before deciding to invest that money in stock of The Gap, Inc.? Let's see how accounting works.

EXPLAIN WHY ACCOUNTING IS THE LANGUAGE OF BUSINESS

Accounting is an information system. It measures business activities, processes data into reports, and communicates results to decision makers. Accounting is "the language of business." The better you understand the language, the better you can manage your finances, as well as those of your business.

Accounting produces financial statements, which report information about a business. The financial statements measure performance and communicate where a business stands in financial terms. In this chapter we focus on The Gap, Inc. After completing this chapter, you'll begin to understand financial statements.

Don't confuse bookkeeping and accounting. Bookkeeping is a mechanical part of accounting, just as arithmetic is a part of mathematics. Exhibit 1-1 on page 4 illustrates the flow of accounting

1 **Explain** why accounting is the language of business

Exhibit 1-1 | The Flow of Accounting Information

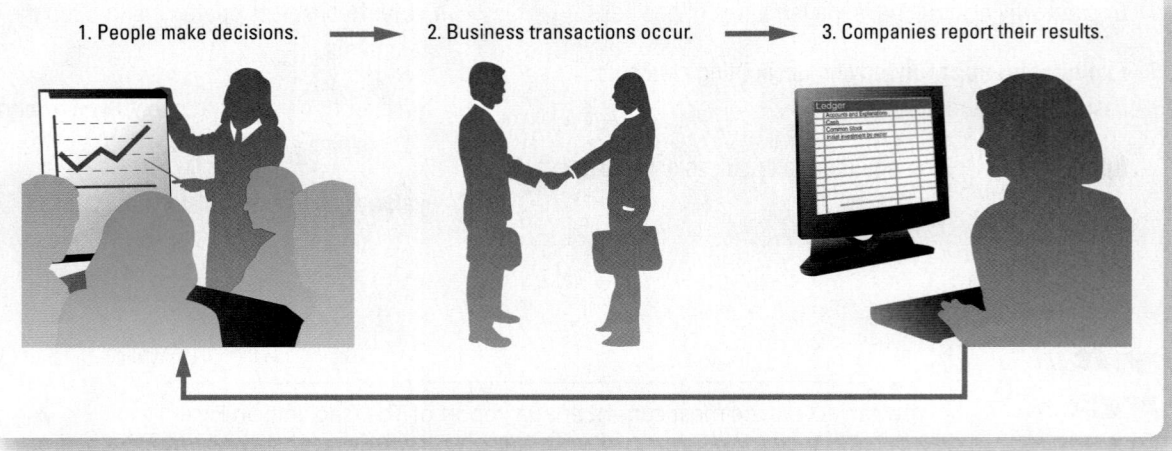

1. People make decisions. → 2. Business transactions occur. → 3. Companies report their results.

information and helps illustrate accounting's role in business. The accounting process begins and ends with people making decisions.

Who Uses Accounting Information?

Decision makers use many types of information; a banker needs information to decide who gets a loan or The Gap, Inc., uses accounting to decide where to locate a new store. Let's see how decision makers use accounting information.

- *Individuals.* People like you manage their personal bank accounts, decide whether to rent an apartment or buy a house, and budget the monthly income and expenditures of their businesses. Accounting provides the necessary information to allow individuals to make these decisions.

- *Investors and creditors.* Investors and creditors provide the money to finance The Gap, Inc. Investors want to know how much income they can expect to earn on an investment. Creditors want to know when and how The Gap, Inc., is going to pay them back. These decisions also require accounting information.

- *Regulatory bodies.* All kinds of regulatory bodies use accounting information. For example, the Internal Revenue Service (IRS) and various state and local governments require businesses, individuals, and other types of organizations to pay income, property, excise, and other taxes. The U.S. Securities and Exchange Commission (SEC) requires companies whose stock is traded publicly to provide it with many kinds of periodic financial reports. All of these reports contain accounting information.

- *Nonprofit organizations.* Nonprofit organizations—churches, hospitals, and charities such as Habitat for Humanity and the Red Cross—base many of their operating decisions on accounting data. In addition, these organizations have to file periodic reports of their activities with the IRS and state governments, even though they may owe no taxes.

Two Kinds of Accounting: Financial Accounting and Management Accounting

Both *external* and *internal users* of accounting information exist. We can therefore classify accounting into two branches.

Financial accounting provides information for decision makers outside the entity, such as investors, creditors, government agencies, and the public. This information must be relevant for the needs of decision makers and must faithfully give an accurate picture of the entity's economic activities. This textbook focuses on financial accounting.

Management accounting provides information for managers of The Gap, Inc. Examples of management accounting information include budgets, forecasts, and projections that are used in making the strategic decisions of the entity. Internal information must still be accurate and relevant for the decision needs of managers. Management accounting is covered in a separate course that usually follows this one.

Organizing a Business

Accounting is used in every type of business. A business generally takes one of the following forms:

- Proprietorship
- Partnership
- Limited-liability company (LLC)
- Corporation

Exhibit 1-2 compares ways to organize a business.

Exhibit 1-2 | The Various Forms of Business Organization

	Proprietorship	Partnership	LLC	Corporation
1. *Owner(s)*	Proprietor—one owner	Partners—two or more owners	Members	Stockholders—generally many owners
2. *Personal liability of owner(s) for business debts*	Proprietor is personally liable	General partners are personally liable; limited partners are not	Members are *not* personally liable	Stockholders are *not* personally liable

Proprietorship. A **proprietorship** has a single owner, called the proprietor. Dell Computer started out in the college dorm room of Michael Dell, the owner. Proprietorships tend to be small retail stores or solo providers of professional services—physicians, attorneys, or accountants. Legally, the business *is* the proprietor, and the proprietor is personally liable for all the business's debts. But for accounting purposes, a proprietorship is a distinct entity, separate from its proprietor. Thus, the business records should not include the proprietor's personal finances.

Partnership. A **partnership** has two or more parties as co-owners, and each owner is a partner. Individuals, corporations, partnerships, or other types of entities can be partners. Income and losses of the partnership "flow through" to the partners, and they recognize them based on their agreed-upon percentage interest in the business. The partnership is not a tax-paying entity. Instead, each partner takes a proportionate share of the entity's taxable income and pays tax according to that partner's individual or corporate rate. Many retail establishments, professional service firms (law, accounting, etc.), real estate, and oil and gas exploration companies operate as partnerships. Many partnerships are small or medium-sized but some are gigantic, with thousands of partners. Partnerships are governed by agreement, usually spelled out in writing in the form of a contract between the partners. General partnerships have mutual agency and unlimited liability, meaning that each partner may conduct business in the name of the entity and can make agreements that legally bind all partners without limit for the partnership's debts. Partnerships are therefore quite risky, because an irresponsible partner can create large debts for the other general partners without their knowledge or permission. This feature of general partnerships has spawned the creation of limited-liability partnerships (LLPs).

A *limited-liability partnership* is one in which a wayward partner cannot create a large liability for the other partners. In LLPs, each partner is liable for partnership debts only up to the extent of his or her investment in the partnership, plus his or her proportionate share of the liabilities. Each LLP, however, must have one general partner with unlimited liability for all partnership debts.

Limited-Liability Company (LLC). A **limited-liability company** is one in which the business (and not the owner) is liable for the company's debts. An LLC may have one owner or many owners, called *members*. Unlike a proprietorship or a general partnership, the members of an LLC do *not* have unlimited liability for the LLC's debts. An LLC pays no business income tax. Instead, the LLC's income "flows through" to the members, and they pay income tax at their own tax rates, just as they would if they were partners. Today, many multiple-owner businesses are organized as LLCs, because members of an LLC effectively enjoy limited liability while still being taxed like members of a partnership.

Corporation. A **corporation** is a business owned by the **stockholders**, or **shareholders**, who own **stock** representing shares of ownership in the corporation. One of the major advantages of doing business in the corporate form is the ability to raise large sums of capital from issuance of stock to the public. All types of entities (individuals, partnerships, corporations, or other types) may be shareholders in a corporation. Even though proprietorships and partnerships are more numerous, corporations transact much more business and are larger in terms of assets, income, and number of employees. Most well-known companies, such as The Gap, Inc., Amazon.com, Inc., Google, General Motors, Toyota, and Apple, Inc., are corporations. Their full names include *Corporation* or *Incorporated* (abbreviated as *Corp.* and *Inc.*) to indicate that they are corporations—for example, Starbucks Corporation. A few bear the name *Company*, such as Ford Motor Company.

A corporation is formed under state law. Unlike proprietorships and partnerships, a corporation is legally distinct from its owners. The corporation is like an artificial person and possesses many of the same rights that a person has. The stockholders have no personal obligation for the corporation's debts. So, stockholders of a corporation have limited liability, as do limited partners and members of an LLC. However, unlike partnerships or LLCs, a corporation pays a business income tax as well as many other types of taxes. Furthermore, the shareholders of a corporation are effectively taxed twice on distributions received from the corporation (called dividends). Thus, one of the major disadvantages of the corporate form of business is *double taxation of distributed profits.*

Ultimate control of a corporation rests with the stockholders, who generally get one vote for each share of stock they own. Stockholders elect the **board of directors**, which sets policy and appoints officers. The board elects a chairperson, who holds the most power in the corporation and often carries the title chief executive officer (CEO); it also appoints the president as chief operating officer (COO). Corporations have vice presidents in charge of sales, accounting, finance (the chief financial officer or CFO), and other key areas.

EXPLAIN AND APPLY UNDERLYING ACCOUNTING CONCEPTS, ASSUMPTIONS, AND PRINCIPLES

2 **Explain and apply** underlying accounting concepts, assumptions, and principles

Accountants follow professional frameworks for measurement and disclosure of financial information. The most common of these frameworks is called **generally accepted accounting principles (GAAP)**. In the United States, the **Financial Accounting Standards Board (FASB)** formulates GAAP. The **International Accounting Standards Board (IASB)** sets global—or international financial reporting standards (IFRS), as discussed in a later section.

Exhibit 1-3 gives an overview of the joint conceptual framework of accounting developed by the FASB and the IASB. Financial reporting standards (whether U.S. or international), at the bottom, follow this conceptual framework. The overall *objective* of accounting is to provide financial information about the reporting entity that is useful to existing and potential investors, lenders, and other creditors in making decisions about providing resources to the entity.

To be useful, information must have the fundamental qualitative characteristics, which include

- relevance, and
- faithful representation.

To be relevant, information must be capable of making a difference to the decision maker, in helping them to predict or confirm value. In addition, the information must be *material*, which means it must be important enough to the informed user so that, if it were omitted or incorrect, it would make a difference in the user's decision. Only information that is material needs to be separately *disclosed* (listed or discussed) in the financial statements. If not, it does not need separate disclosure but may be combined with other information. To make a faithful representation, the information must be complete, neutral (free from bias), and free from error (accurate). Accounting information must focus on the *economic substance* of a transaction, event, or circumstance, which may or may not always be the same as its legal form. Faithful representation makes the information *reliable* to users.

Exhibit 1-3 | Conceptual Foundations of Accounting

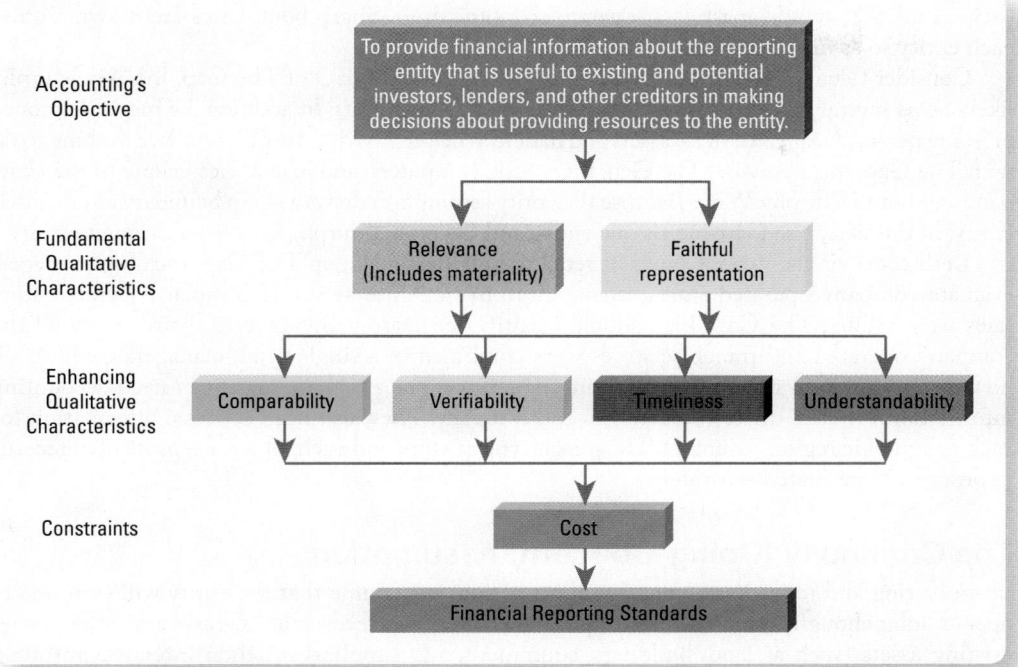

Based on Financial Accounting Standards Board (FASB) and International Accounting Standards Board (IASB), *Joint Conceptual Framework for Reporting* (2010).

Accounting information must also have a number of *enhancing or supplementary qualitative characteristics.* These include

- comparability,
- verifiability,
- timeliness, and
- understandability.

Comparability means that the accounting information for a company must be prepared in such a way as to be capable of being compared with information from other companies in the same period; it should also be *consistent* with similar information for that company in previous periods. *Verifiability* means that the information must be capable of being checked for accuracy, completeness, and reliability. The process of verifying information is often done by *internal* as well as *external auditors.* Verifiability enhances the reliability of information and thus makes the information more representative of economic reality. *Timeliness* means that the information must be made available to users early enough to help them make decisions, thus making the information more relevant to their needs. *Understandability* means the information must be sufficiently transparent so that it makes sense to reasonably informed users of the information (investors, creditors, regulatory agencies, and managers).

Accounting information is costly to produce. A primary constraint in the decision to disclose accounting information is that the *cost of disclosure should not exceed the expected benefits* to users. The management of an entity is primarily responsible for preparing accounting information. Managers must exercise judgment in determining whether the information is necessary for a complete understanding of economic facts and is not excessively costly to provide.

This course will expose you to GAAP as well as to relevant international financial reporting standards (IFRS). We summarize GAAP in Appendix D and IFRS in Appendix E. In the following section, we briefly summarize some of the basic assumptions and principles that underlie the application of these standards.

The Entity Assumption

The most basic accounting assumption (underlying idea) is the **entity**, which is any organization (or person) that stands apart as a separate economic unit. Sharp boundaries are drawn around each entity so as not to confuse its affairs with those of others.

Consider Glenn K. Murphy, chairman of the board and CEO of The Gap, Inc. Mr. Murphy likely owns several homes, automobiles, and other personal assets. In addition, he may owe money on some personal loans. All these assets and liabilities belong to Mr. Murphy and have nothing to do with The Gap, Inc. Likewise, The Gap, Inc.'s cash, computers, and inventories belong to the company and not to Murphy. Why? Because the entity assumption draws a sharp boundary around each entity; in this case, The Gap, Inc., is one entity, and Glenn K. Murphy is a second, separate entity.

Let's consider the various types of retail outlets that make up The Gap, Inc. Top managers evaluate company-operated stores separately from franchise stores. If company-operated store sales were falling, The Gap, Inc., should identify the reason. But if sales figures from all the company-operated and franchise stores were combined in a single total, managers couldn't tell how differently each unit was performing. To correct the problem, managers need accounting information for each division (entity) in the company. They also need separate information for each geographic region (country). Thus, each type of store and each region keeps its own records in order to be evaluated separately.

The Continuity (Going-Concern) Assumption

In measuring and reporting accounting information, we assume that the entity will continue to operate long enough to sell its inventories and convert any receivables to cash, and to use other existing assets (such as land, buildings, equipment, and supplies) for their intended purposes, and settle its obligations in the normal course of business. This is called the **continuity (going-concern) assumption**.

Consider the alternative to the **going-concern assumption**: the quitting concern, or going out of business assumption. An entity that is not continuing would have to sell all of its assets in the process. In that case, the most *relevant* measure of the value of the assets would be their liquidating values (or the amount the company can receive for the assets when sold in order to go out of business). But going out of business is the exception rather than the rule. Therefore, the continuity assumption says that a business should stay in business long enough to convert its inventories and receivables to cash and pay off its obligations in the ordinary course of business, and to continue this process of operating into the future.

The Historical Cost Principle

The **historical cost principle** states that assets should be recorded at their *actual cost,* measured on the date of purchase as the amount of cash paid plus the dollar value of all noncash consideration (other assets, privileges, or rights) also given in exchange. For example, suppose The Gap, Inc., purchases a building for a new store. The building's current owner is asking $600,000 for the building. The management of The Gap, Inc., believes the building is worth $585,000 and offers the present owner that amount. Two real estate professionals appraise the building at $610,000. The buyer and seller compromise and agree on a price of $590,000 for the building. The historical cost principle requires The Gap, Inc., to initially record the building at its actual cost of $590,000—not at $585,000, $600,000, or $610,000, even though those amounts were what some people believed the building was worth. At the point of purchase, $590,000 is both the *relevant* amount for the building's worth and the amount that *faithfully represents* a reliable figure for the price the company paid for it.

The *historical cost principle* and the *continuity assumption* (discussed previously), also maintain that The Gap, Inc.'s accounting records should continue to use historical cost to value the asset for as long as the business holds it. Why? Because cost is a *verifiable* measure that is relatively *free from bias.* Suppose that The Gap, Inc., owns the building for six years. Real estate prices increase during this period. As a result, at the end of the period, the building can be sold for $650,000. Should The Gap, Inc., increase the carrying value of the building on the company's books to $650,000? No. According to the historical cost principle, the building remains on The Gap, Inc.'s books at its historical cost of $590,000. According to the continuity assumption, The Gap, Inc., intends to stay in business and use the building, not to sell it, so its historical cost is the most relevant and the most faithful representation of its carrying value. It is also the most easily verifiable (auditable) amount. Should the company decide to sell the building later at a price above or below its carrying value, it will record the cash received, remove the carrying value of the building from the books, and record a gain or a loss for the difference at that time.

The historical cost principle is not used as widely in the United States as it once was. Accounting is moving in the direction of reporting more and more assets and liabilities at their fair values. **Fair value** is the amount that the business could sell the asset for, or the amount that the business could pay to settle the liability. The FASB has issued guidance for companies to report many assets and liabilities at fair values.[1] Moreover, in recent years, the FASB has agreed to "harmonize" GAAP with International Financial Reporting Standards (IFRS). These standards generally allow for broader measurement of different types of assets with fair values than GAAP, which may cause more assets to be revalued periodically to fair market values. We will discuss the trend toward globalization of accounting standards on the next page, and we will illustrate it in later chapters throughout the book.

The Stable-Monetary-Unit Assumption

In the United States, we record transactions in dollars because that is our medium of exchange. British accountants record transactions in pounds sterling, Japanese in yen, and some continental Europeans in euros.

Unlike a liter or a mile, the value of a dollar changes over time. A rise in the general price level is called *inflation*. During inflation, a dollar will purchase less food, less toothpaste, and less of other goods and services. When prices are stable—there is little inflation—a dollar's purchasing power is also stable.

Under the **stable-monetary-unit assumption**, accountants assume that the dollar's purchasing power is stable over time. We ignore inflation, and this allows us to add and subtract dollar amounts as though the dollar over successive years has a consistent amount of purchasing power. This is important because businesses that report their financial information publicly usually report comparative financial information (that is, the current year along with one or more prior years). If we could not assume a stable monetary unit, assets and liabilities denominated in prior years' dollars would have to be adjusted to current year price levels. Inflation has been at very low levels in developed countries for several decades and is expected to remain so for the foreseeable future. Thus, inflation adjustments to accounting information to make it comparable over time are not considered necessary.

Global View **International Financial Reporting Standards (IFRS)** We live in a global economy! The global credit crisis of 2008 originated in the United States but rapidly spread throughout the world. Investors in the United States can easily trade stocks on the Hong Kong, London, and Brussels stock exchanges over the Internet. Each year, American companies such as Starbucks Corporation, The Gap Inc., McDonalds Corp., Microsoft Corp., and The Walt Disney Company conduct billions of dollars of business around the globe. Conversely, foreign companies such as Nokia, Samsung, Toyota, and Nestlé conduct billions of dollars of business in the United States. American companies have merged with foreign companies to create international conglomerates such as Pearson (the publisher of this textbook) and Anheuser-Busch InBev (producers of alcoholic beverages). No matter where your career starts, it is very likely that it will eventually take you into global markets.

---

[1] In 2013, the American Institute of Certified Public Accountants (AICPA) adopted a separate "financial reporting framework for small and medium-sized entities" (FRF-SME) that avoids some of the complexities of full-blown GAAP. Many SMEs are owner-managed, and prepare financial statements mostly for the use of their bankers, who do not require all of the complex disclosures of GAAP. FRF-SME is less complicated than GAAP, and, while it requires accrual accounting, it emphasizes use of historical cost more than fair values for assets. Most of the principles we employ in this text are applicable to both FRF-SMEs and GAAP. Accrual accounting is discussed in Chapter 3.

Until recently, one of the major challenges of conducting global business has been the fact that different countries have adopted different accounting standards for business transactions. Historically, the major developed countries in the world (United States, United Kingdom, Japan, Germany, etc.) have all had their own versions of GAAP. As investors seek to compare financial results across entities from different countries, they have had to restate and convert accounting data from one country to the next in order to make them comparable. This takes time and can be expensive.

The solution to this problem lies with the IASB, which has developed International Financial Reporting Standards (IFRS). These standards are now being used by most countries around the world. For years, accountants in the United States did not pay much attention to IFRS because our GAAP was considered to be the strongest single set of accounting standards in the world. In addition, the application of GAAP for public companies in the United States is overseen carefully by the U.S. Securities and Exchange Commission (SEC), a body that at present has no global counterpart.

Nevertheless, in order to promote consistency in global financial reporting, the SEC is studying whether and how to require all U.S. public companies to adopt some version of IFRS within the next decade. The advantage to adopting a uniform set of high-quality global accounting standards is that financial statements from a U.S. company (say, Hershey Corporation in Pennsylvania) will be comparable to those of a foreign company (say, Nestlé in Switzerland). Using these standards, it will be easier for investors and businesspeople to evaluate information of various companies in the same industries from across the globe, and companies will have to prepare only one set of financial statements instead of multiple versions. Thus, in the long run, a uniform set of high-quality global accounting standards should significantly reduce costs of doing business globally.

Does this mean that the accounting information you are studying in this textbook will soon become outdated? Fortunately, no. For one thing, the vast majority of the introductory material you learn from this textbook, including the underlying conceptual framework outlined in the previous section, is *already* part of IFRS as well. The most commonly used accounting practices are essentially the same under both U.S. GAAP and IFRS. Additionally, the FASB is working hand-in-hand with the IASB toward *convergence* of standards, that is, gradually adjusting both sets of standards to more closely align them over time so that, if transition to IFRS in the United States ever occurs, it will occur smoothly. At the time of the publication of this text, there are still some areas of disagreement between GAAP and IFRS. For example, certain widely accepted U.S. practices, such as the use of the last-in, first-out (LIFO) inventory costing method (discussed in Chapter 6), are disallowed under IFRS. Other differences exist as well, which must be resolved before IFRS can be fully adopted in the United States.

In general, the main difference between U.S. GAAP and IFRS is that U.S. GAAP has become rather "rules-based" over its long history, while IFRS (not in existence as long) allows more professional judgment on the part of companies. One other major difference between IFRS and U.S. GAAP lies in the valuation of long-term assets (plant assets and intangibles) and liabilities. In U.S. GAAP, the historical cost principle tells us to value assets at historical cost. In contrast, IFRS prefers more of a fair-value approach, which reports assets and liabilities on the balance sheet at their up-to-date values rather than at historical cost. This may seem like a big difference, but U.S. GAAP already allows for a partial fair-value approach with rules such as lower-of-cost-or-market, accounting for the impairment of long-term assets, and adjusting certain investments to fair values. We cover these concepts in more depth in later chapters.

Throughout the remainder of this textbook, in chapters that cover concepts where major differences between GAAP and IFRS exist, we will discuss those differences. Because this is an introductory textbook in financial accounting, our discussion will be brief in order to focus on the changes that are relevant for this course. Appendix E includes a table, cross-referenced by chapter, that summarizes all of these differences, as well as their impacts on financial statements once IFRS is fully adopted.

You can expect to hear more about the global harmonization of accounting standards in the future. When you do, the most important things to remember will be that these changes will be beneficial for financial statement users in the long run and that most of what you learned in this accounting course will still apply. Remember that there are far more areas of common ground than of disagreement. Whatever may come, your knowledge of international accounting principles will benefit you in the future. The globalization of the world economy provides a wonderful opportunity for you to succeed in the business world.

APPLY THE ACCOUNTING EQUATION TO BUSINESS ORGANIZATIONS

The Gap, Inc.'s financial statements tell us how the business is performing and where it stands. But how do we arrive at the financial statements? Let's examine the *elements of financial statements*, which are the building blocks from which statements are made.

3 **Apply** the accounting equation to business organizations

Assets and Liabilities

The financial statements are based on the **accounting equation**. This equation presents the resources of a company and the claims to those resources.

- **Assets** are economic resources that are expected to produce a benefit in the future. The Gap, Inc.'s cash, merchandise inventory, and equipment are examples of assets.

Claims on assets come from two sources:

- **Liabilities** are "outsider claims." They are debts that are payable to outsiders, called *creditors*. For example, a creditor who has loaned money to The Gap, Inc., has a claim—a legal right—to a part of The Gap, Inc.'s assets until the company repays the debt.
- **Owners' equity** (also called **capital**, or **stockholders' equity** for a corporation) represents the "insider claims" of a business. Equity means ownership, so The Gap, Inc.'s stockholders' equity is the stockholders' interest in the assets of the corporation.

The accounting equation shows the relationship among assets, liabilities, and owners' equity. Assets appear on the left side and liabilities and owners' equity on the right. As Exhibit 1-4 shows, the two sides must be equal:

Exhibit 1-4 | The Accounting Equation

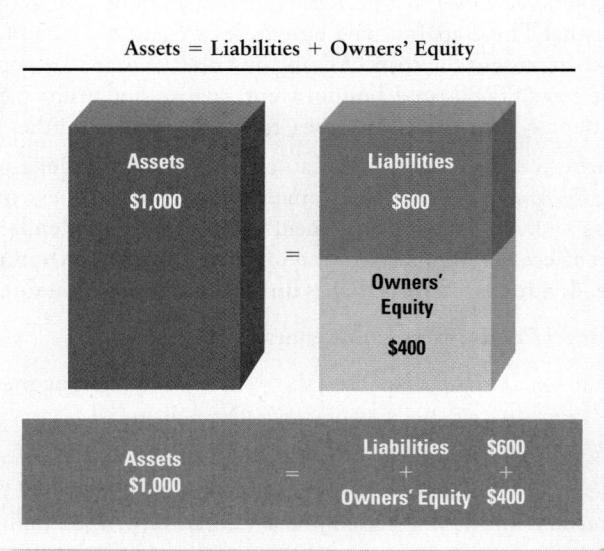

Assets = Liabilities + Owners' Equity

Assets	Liabilities
$1,000	$600
	Owners' Equity
	$400

Assets		Liabilities	$600
$1,000	=	Owners' Equity	+ $400

What are some of The Gap, Inc.'s assets? The first asset is *cash and cash equivalents*, the liquid assets that are the medium of exchange. Another important asset is merchandise inventory (often called inventories)—the clothing items—that The Gap, Inc.'s stores sell. The Gap, Inc., also has assets in the form of *property, plant, and equipment*, or *fixed assets*. These are the long-lived assets the company uses to do business—store equipment, buildings, computers, and so on.

The Gap, Inc.'s liabilities include a number of payables, such as accounts payable and federal and state income taxes payable. The word *payable* always signifies a liability. An account payable is a liability for goods or services purchased on credit and supported by the credit standing of the purchaser. Accounts payable typically have to be paid within 30 to 60 days. *Long-term debt* is a liability that's payable beyond one year from the date of the financial statements. The *current portion of long-term debt* is the amount due within the next year, and it has to be disclosed separately in current liabilities.

Owners' Equity

The owners' equity of any business is its assets minus its liabilities. We can write the accounting equation to show that owners' equity is what's left over when we subtract liabilities from assets.

$$\text{Assets} - \text{Liabilities} = \text{Owners' Equity}$$

A corporation's equity—called stockholders' equity—has two main subparts:

■ Paid-in capital

■ Retained earnings

The accounting equation can be written as

$$\text{Assets} = \text{Liabilities} + \text{Stockholders' Equity}$$
$$\text{Assets} = \text{Liabilities} + \text{Paid-in Capital} + \text{Retained Earnings}$$

■ **Paid-in capital** is the amount the stockholders have invested in the corporation. The basic component of paid-in capital is **common stock**, which the corporation issues to the stockholders as evidence of their ownership. All corporations have common stock.

■ **Retained earnings** is the amount earned by income-producing activities and kept for use in the business. Three major types of transactions affect retained earnings: revenues, expenses, and dividends.

■ **Revenues** are inflows of resources that increase retained earnings by delivering goods or services to customers. For example, a Gap store's sale of a pair of jeans brings in revenue and increases The Gap, Inc.'s retained earnings.

■ **Expenses** are resource outflows that decrease retained earnings due to operations. For example, the wages that The Gap, Inc. pays employees are an expense and decrease retained earnings. Expenses represent the costs of doing business; they are the opposite of revenues. Expenses include cost of goods sold, building rent, salaries, and utility payments. Expenses also include the depreciation of display cases, racks, shelving, and other equipment.

■ **Dividends** decrease retained earnings, because they are distributions to stockholders of assets (usually cash) generated by net income. A successful business may pay dividends to shareholders as a return on their investments. Remember: **dividends are not expenses. Dividends never affect net income. Instead of being subtracted from revenues to compute net income, dividends are recorded as direct reductions of retained earnings.**

Businesses strive for *profits*, the excess of revenues over expenses.

■ When total revenues exceed total expenses, the result is called **net income, net earnings,** or **net profit**.

■ When expenses exceed revenues, the result is a **net loss**.

■ Net income or net loss is the "bottom line" on an income statement. The Gap, Inc.'s bottom line reports net income for the year ended January 28, 2012, of $833 million (line 10 on the Consolidated Statements of Income on page 2).

Exhibit 1-5 shows the relationships among the following:

- Retained earnings
- Revenues − Expenses = Net income (or net loss)
- Dividends

Exhibit 1-5 | The Components of Retained Earnings

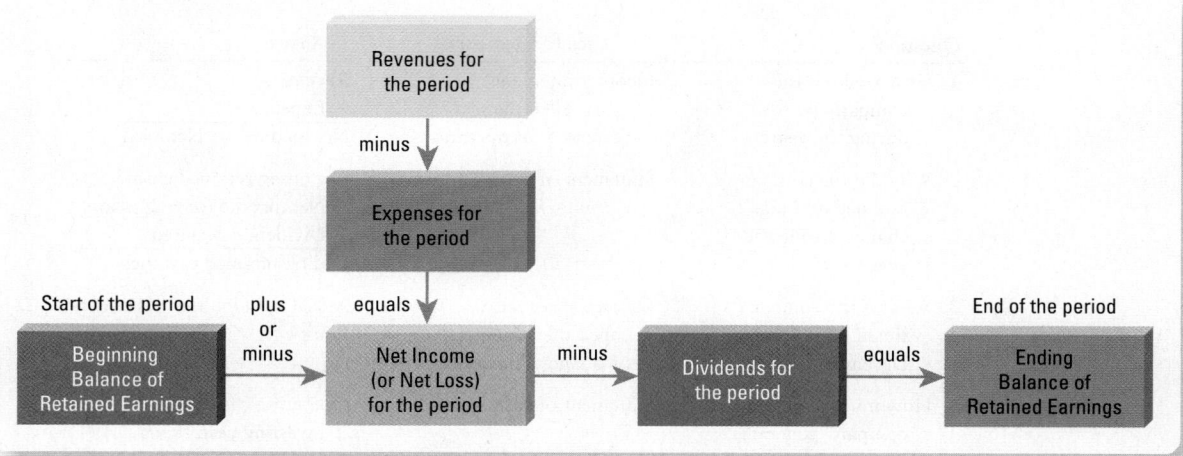

The owners' equity of proprietorships and partnerships is different from that of corporations. Proprietorships and partnerships don't identify paid-in capital and retained earnings separately. Instead, they use a single heading: Capital. Examples include "Randall Waller, Capital"— for a proprietorship; and "Powers, Capital" and "Salazar, Capital"—for a partnership.

▷Stop & Think...

(1) If the assets of a business are $360,000 and the liabilities are $120,000, how much is the owners' equity?

(2) If the owners' equity in a business is $180,000 and the liabilities are $100,000, how much are the assets?

(3) A company reported monthly revenues of $325,000 and expenses of $85,000. What is the result of operations for the month?

(4) If the beginning balance of retained earnings is $150,000, revenue is $75,000, expenses total $35,000, and the company declares and pays a $10,000 dividend, what is the ending balance of retained earnings?

Answers:

(1) $240,000 ($360,000 − $120,000)

(2) $280,000 ($180,000 + $100,000)

(3) Net income of $240,000 ($325,000 − $85,000); revenues minus expenses

(4) $180,000 [$150,000 beginning balance + net income $40,000 ($75,000 − $35,000) − dividends $10,000]

EVALUATE BUSINESS OPERATIONS THROUGH THE FINANCIAL STATEMENTS

4 Evaluate business operations through the financial statements

The financial statements present a company to the public in financial terms. Each financial statement relates to a specific date or time period. What would investors want to know about The Gap, Inc., at the end of its fiscal year? Exhibit 1-6 lists four questions that decision makers may ask. Each answer comes from one of the financial statements.

Exhibit 1-6 | Information Reported in the Financial Statements

Question	Financial Statement	Answer
1. How well did the company perform during the year?	Income statement (also called the Statement of operations)	Revenues − Expenses Net income (or Net loss)
2. Why did the company's retained earnings change during the year?	Statement of retained earnings	Beginning retained earnings + Net income (or − Net loss) − Dividends declared Ending retained earnings
3. What is the company's financial position at December 31?	Balance sheet (also called the Statement of financial position)	Assets = Liabilities + Owners' Equity
4. How much cash did the company generate and spend during the year?	Statement of cash flows	Operating cash flows ± Investing cash flows ± Financing cash flows Increase (decrease) in cash

To learn how to use financial statements, let's work through The Gap, Inc.'s financial statements for the year ended January 28, 2012. The following diagram shows how the data flow from one financial statement to the next. The order is important.

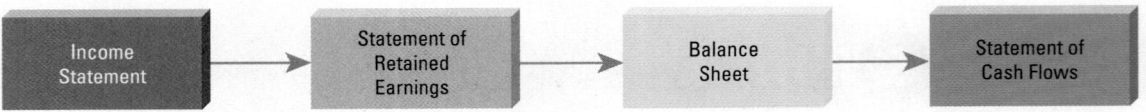

We begin with the income statement in Exhibit 1-7.

The Income Statement Measures Operating Performance

The **income statement**, or **statement of operations**, reports revenues and expenses for the period. The bottom line is net income or net loss *for the period*. At the top of Exhibit 1-7 is the company's name: The Gap, Inc. On the second line is the term "Consolidated Statements of Income."

The Gap, Inc., is actually made up of several corporations that are owned by a common group of shareholders. Commonly controlled corporations like this are required to combine, or consolidate, all of their revenues, expenses, assets, liabilities, and stockholders' equity and to report them all as one.

The dates of The Gap, Inc.'s Consolidated Statements of Income are "12 months Ended January 28, 2012 and 12 months Ended January 29, 2011." The Gap, Inc., like many retailers, uses a *fiscal year* consisting of the 52 weeks ending closest to January 31 as the accounting year. This is because the holiday season is the busiest time of the year and includes Christmas, while January is typically the slowest month of the year for retailers, allowing the company time to get its books in order. Companies often adopt a fiscal year that ends at the low point of their operations. Whole

Exhibit 1-7 | The Gap, Inc., Consolidated Statements of Income

	A	B	C	D	E
	The Gap, Inc.				
1	**Consolidated Statements of Income**	**Fiscal 2011**	**Fiscal 2010**		
2	Adapted, in millions of $	12 Months Ended			
3		Jan. 28, 2012	Jan. 29, 2011		
4	Net sales	$ 14,549	$ 14,664		
5	Cost of goods sold and occupancy expenses	9,275	8,775		
6	Operating expenses	3,836	3,921		
7	Interest (income)/expense, net	69	(14)		
8	Income taxes	536	778		
9	Total expenses	13,716	13,460		
10	Net income	$ 833	$ 1,204		
11					

Foods Market, Inc., uses a fiscal year consisting of the 52 weeks ending closest to September 30. FedEx Corp.'s fiscal year-end falls on May 31. Alternatively, about 60% of the largest companies, such as RadioShack Corporation, use a fiscal year corresponding to the calendar year.

The Gap, Inc.'s Consolidated Statements of Income in Exhibit 1-7 report operating results for two fiscal years in order to show trends for revenues, expenses, and net income. To avoid clutter, The Gap, Inc., reports its results in millions of dollars.

During the fiscal year ended January 28, 2012, The Gap, Inc.'s net sales (line 4) declined from $14,664 million to $14,549 million, less than 1 percentage point. However, net income declined from $1,204 million to $833 million (line 10), about 31 percent. The Gap, Inc., sold only slightly less merchandise during the current year than the previous year, but its costs of doing business actually increased over the same period, resulting in greatly reduced income. Focus on the 12 months ended January 28, 2012 (we show the 12 months ended January 29, 2011 for comparative purposes). An income statement reports two main categories:

- Revenues and gains
- Expenses and losses

We measure net income as follows:

Net Income = Total Revenues and Gains − Total Expenses and Losses

In accounting, the word *net* refers to an amount after a subtraction. *Net* income is the profit left over after subtracting expenses and losses from revenues and gains. **Net income is the single most important item in the financial statements.**

Revenues. The Gap, Inc.'s major source of revenue is net sales, which means sales revenue after subtracting all the goods customers have returned to the company. All retailers must accept some returned goods from customers due to product defects or items that customers do not want for other reasons. The Gap, Inc. also reports revenue from interest (line 7) which is offset against interest expense, or combined with various smaller amounts and reported as "interest expense, net." Interest and other smaller amounts of income and expense are sometimes combined into a category labeled "other income and expense." The term "other" generally notes that the amount is not sufficiently material to label separately on an ongoing basis. We explain this item in greater detail below.

Expenses. Not all expenses have the word *expense* in their title. For example, The Gap, Inc.'s largest expense is for cost of goods sold and occupancy expenses (line 5). In this line, The Gap, Inc., includes the direct cost of the items sold, as well as the cost of occupying store space, including some depreciation costs, as well as rent expense. As an example of cost of goods sold, suppose a component jacket costs The Gap, Inc., $30. Assume the company sells the jacket for $75. Sales revenue is $75, and cost of goods sold is $30. Cost of goods sold is the major expense of merchandising entities such as The Gap, Inc., Target Corp., Walmart Stores, Inc., and Whole Foods Market, Inc.

The Gap, Inc., has some other categories of expenses:

- **Operating expenses** (line 6) are the costs of everyday operations that are not directly related to merchandise purchases and occupancy. Many expenses may be included in this category, including sales commissions paid to employees, catalog production, mailing costs, warehousing expenses, depreciation, executive salaries, and other home-office expenses. These expenses amounted to $3,836 million during the 12 months ended January 28, 2012.

- **Interest expense, net** (line 7) was $69 million for the 12 months ended January 28, 2012. Interest expense, net represents The Gap, Inc.'s net cost of borrowing money. It actually includes interest expense of $74 million offset by interest income of $5 million, which is the amount of interest a company earns on amounts they have loaned to other companies. Companies are allowed to offset items like interest income and interest expense against each other and show only the difference (in this case the larger item is interest expense, and so the net amount appears as an expense).

- **Income taxes** (line 8) are expenses levied on The Gap, Inc.'s taxable income by the federal government. This is often one of a corporation's largest expenses. The Gap, Inc.'s income tax expense for the 12 months ended January 28, 2012, was a whopping $536 million (39.2% of its net income before taxes)!

Now let's examine the statement of retained earnings in Exhibit 1-8.

The Statement of Retained Earnings Shows What a Company Did with Its Net Income

MyAccountingLab

Retained earnings means exactly what the term implies, which is that portion of net income the company has kept over a period of years. If, historically, revenues exceed expenses, the result will be a positive balance in retained earnings. On the other hand, if, historically, expenses have exceeded sales revenues, the accumulation of these losses will result in an accumulated **deficit** in retained earnings (usually shown in parentheses). Net income (lines 4 and 7 in Exhibit 1-8) flows from the income statement (line 10 of Exhibit 1-7) to the **statement of retained earnings**.

Exhibit 1-8 | The Gap, Inc., Consolidated Statements of Retained Earnings

	A	B	C	D
	A1			
1	**The Gap, Inc.** **Consolidated Statements of Retained Earnings** **For the Two Years Ending January 28, 2012**			
2	**Adapted, in millions of $**			
3	Retained earnings, January 30, 2010	$ 10,815		
4	Net income, year ended January 29, 2011	1,204		
5	Cash dividends declared, year ended January 29, 2011	(252)		
6	Retained earnings, January 29, 2011	11,767		
7	Net income, year ended January 28, 2012	833		
8	Cash dividends declared, year ended January 28, 2012	(236)		
9	Retained earnings, January 28, 2012	$ 12,364		
10				

Net income increases retained earnings, and net losses and dividends decrease retained earnings. A positive balance in retained earnings indicates that a corporation has been able to accumulate earnings over its lifetime in order to expand, as well as to return a portion of its assets in the form of dividends to shareholders, if the corporation distributes dividends.

Let's review The Gap, Inc.'s Consolidated Statements of Retained Earnings for the two-year period ending January 28, 2012. At the beginning of fiscal 2010 (January 30, 2010), The Gap, Inc., had $10,815 million in retained earnings (line 3). During fiscal 2010, the company earned net income of $1,204 million (line 4) and declared dividends of $252 million to shareholders (line 5).

It ended the 2010 fiscal year with a retained earnings balance of $11,767 million, which carried over and became the beginning balance of retained earnings in fiscal 2011 (line 6).

During fiscal 2011, the company earned net income of $833 million (line 7). As shown on line 8, it then declared dividends to shareholders in the amount of $236 million (line 8), to end the 2011 fiscal year with a retained earnings balance of $12,364 million (line 9).

Which item on the statement of retained earnings comes directly from the income statement? It is net income. Lines 4 and 7 of the retained earnings statement come directly from line 10 of the income statement (see Exhibit 1-7) for fiscal 2010 and 2011, respectively. Take a moment to trace this amount from one statement to the other. Then give yourself a pat on the back—you're already learning how to analyze financial statements!

After a company earns net income, the board of directors decides whether to pay a dividend to the stockholders. Corporations are not obligated to pay dividends unless their boards decide to pay (i.e., declare) them. Usually, companies that are in a development stage or growth mode elect not to pay dividends, opting instead to plow resources back into the company to expand operations or purchase property, plant, and equipment. However, established companies like The Gap, Inc., usually have enough accumulated retained earnings (and cash) to pay dividends. Dividends decrease retained earnings because they represent a distribution of a company's assets (usually cash) to its stockholders.

The Balance Sheet Measures Financial Position

A company's **balance sheet**, also called the **statement of financial position**, reports three items: assets (line 12), liabilities (line 24), and stockholders' equity (line 31). The Gap, Inc.'s Consolidated Balance Sheets, shown in Exhibit 1-9, are dated at the *moment in time* when the accounting periods end (January 28, 2012, and January 29, 2011).

Exhibit 1-9 | The Gap, Inc., Consolidated Balance Sheets

	A	B	C	D
	A1			
1	The Gap, Inc. Consolidated Balance Sheets			
2	Adapted, In millions of $	Jan. 28, 2012	Jan. 29, 2011	
3	Current assets:			
4	Cash and cash equivalents	$ 1,885	$ 1,561	
5	Short-term investments	0	100	
6	Merchandise inventory	1,615	1,620	
7	Other current assets	809	645	
8	Total current assets	4,309	3,926	
9	Long-term assets:			
10	Property and equipment, net	2,523	2,563	
11	Other long-term assets	590	576	
12	Total assets	$ 7,422	$ 7,065	
13	Current liabilities:			
14	Current maturities of long-term debt	$ 59	$ 3	
15	Accounts payable	1,066	1,049	
16	Accrued expenses and other current liabilities	998	993	
17	Income taxes payable	5	50	
18	Total current liabilities	2,128	2,095	
19	Long-term liabilities:			
20	Long-term debt	1,606	0	
21	Other long-term liabilities	933	890	
22	Total long-term liabilities	2,539	890	
23	Commitments (see Notes 10 and 14)			
24	Total liabilities	4,667	2,985	
25	Stockholders' equity:			
26	Common stock	55	55	
27	Additional paid-in capital	2,867	2,939	
28	Retained earnings	12,364	11,767	
29	Accumulated other comprehensive income	229	185	
30	Treasury stock at cost	(12,760)	(10,866)	
31	Total stockholders' equity	2,755	4,080	
32	Total liabilities and stockholders' equity	$ 7,422	$ 7,065	
33				

Assets. There are two main categories of assets: current and long-term. **Current assets** are assets that are expected to be converted to cash, sold, or consumed during the next 12 months or within the business's operating cycle if longer than a year. Current assets include Cash and cash equivalents, Short-term investments, Accounts and notes receivable, Merchandise inventory, and Other current assets like prepaid expenses. The Gap, Inc.'s current assets at January 28, 2012 total $4,309 million (line 8). Let's examine each current asset that The Gap, Inc., holds.

- All companies have cash. Cash is the liquid asset that's the medium of exchange, and *cash equivalents* include money-market accounts or other financial instruments that are easily convertible to cash. The Gap, Inc., owns $1,885 million in cash and cash equivalents at January 28, 2012 (line 4). This is up from $1,561 million at January 29, 2011. We will explain this further when we discuss the statement of cash flows later.

- *Short-term investments* (line 5) include stocks and bonds of other companies that The Gap, Inc., intends to sell within the next year. The Gap, Inc., held $100 million of these types of investments at January 29, 2011, but converted all of them to cash equivalents during the year ended January 28, 2012, leaving none of these as of the year-end.

- *Merchandise inventories* (line 6) are a merchandising company's most important, and often its largest, current asset. The Gap, Inc.'s merchandise inventories at January 28, 2012, total $1,615 million (about 37% of total current assets and 22% of total assets). *Inventory* is a common abbreviation for *merchandise inventory*, and the two terms are used interchangeably.

- *Other current assets* (line 7) may include *prepaid expenses*, which represent amounts paid in advance for advertising, rent, insurance, and supplies. These are current assets because the company will benefit from these expenditures within the next year. The Gap, Inc., owns $809 million in other current assets as of January 28, 2012.

- An asset always represents a future benefit.

Long-term (non-current) assets include *Property and equipment* (also called *plant assets*, line 10). Other long-term assets (line 11) may include *other investments* that are expected to benefit the company for long periods of time or certain types of *intangible assets*.

- *Property and equipment* includes The Gap, Inc.'s land, buildings, computers, store fixtures, and equipment. The Gap, Inc., reports property and equipment on one line, *net,* meaning that the historical acquisition cost of the assets has been reduced by *accumulated depreciation*. Accumulated depreciation represents the amount of the historical cost of plant assets that has been allocated to expense in the income statement over time as the asset has been used in producing revenue. Thus, accumulated depreciation represents the used-up portion of the plant asset. We subtract accumulated depreciation from the cost of property and equipment to determine its net book value ($2,523 million on line 10). We will discuss the concept of depreciation further in later chapters.

- *Other long-term assets* (line 11) is a catchall category for assets that are difficult to classify. The Gap, Inc., owns about $590 million of these assets as of January 28, 2012. These primarily represent long-term tax benefits, due to the company's different reporting purposes—for financial versus tax purposes. The category also includes *intangible assets* with no physical form, such as patents, trademarks, and goodwill. We discuss goodwill and other intangible assets in Chapter 7.

- Overall, The Gap, Inc., reports total assets of $7,422 million at January 28, 2012 (line 12).

Liabilities. Liabilities are also divided into current and long-term categories. **Current liabilities** (lines 14–18) are debts generally payable within one year. Chief among the current liabilities are Current maturities of long-term debt, Accounts payable, Accrued expenses, and Income taxes payable. *Long-term liabilities* are payable after one year.

- *Current maturities of long-term debt* represent the portion of long-term liabilities (usually notes payable) that the company will have to pay off within the next year. Notice on line 20 that, at January 28, 2012, the company had about $1,606 million in long-term debt. Within the category of long-term debt, another $59 million was due and payable within 12 months (line 14), making a total of $1,665 million in long-term debt. GAAP requires companies to segregate and report the portion of long-term debt due and payable within 12 months as a current liability, rather than long-term. We'll talk about this more in Chapter 9.

- *Accounts payable* (line 15) of $1,066 million represents amounts owed to The Gap, Inc.'s vendors and suppliers for purchases of inventory.

- *Accrued expenses and other current liabilities* (line 16). Included in this $998 million are interest payable on borrowed money, accrued liabilities for salaries, utilities, and other expenses that The Gap, Inc., owes but has not yet paid as of January 28, 2012.

- *Income taxes payable* are tax debts owed to the government. The Gap, Inc., owes $5 million of federal and state income taxes as of January 28, 2012 (line 17).

- At January 28, 2012, The Gap, Inc.'s current liabilities total $2,128 million (line 18). The company also owes $2,539 million in long-term liabilities (line 22). These liabilities include long-term debt and other payables due after one year.

- At January 28, 2012, total liabilities are $4,667 million (line 24). This represents about 63% of total assets and indicates a moderately strong financial position.

Stockholders' Equity. The accounting equation states that

$$\text{Assets} - \text{Liabilities} = \text{Owners' Equity}$$

The assets (resources) and the liabilities (debts) of The Gap, Inc., are fairly easy to understand. Owners' equity is harder to pin down. Owners' equity is simple to calculate, but what does it *mean*?

The Gap, Inc., calls its owners' equity *Stockholders' equity* (line 31), and this title is descriptive. Remember that a corporation's owners' equity represents the stockholders' ownership of the business's assets. The Gap, Inc.'s stockholders' equity consists of the following:

- *Common stock* (line 26), represented by shares issued to stockholders for about $55 million at January 28, 2012. This amount represents the face amount (par value) of the stock. Par value is an artificial amount set by the company for the stock. Par value is explained in Chapter 10.

- *Additional paid-in capital* (line 27) represents amounts of cash received on initial sale of the company's stock in excess of the par value. This amounts to about $2,867 million at January 28, 2012.

- *Retained earnings* (line 28) are $12,364 million and $11,767 million at January 28, 2012, and January 29, 2011, respectively. We saw these figures on the statement of retained earnings in Exhibit 1-8 (lines 6 and 9). Retained earnings' final resting place is the balance sheet.

- The Gap, Inc.'s stockholders' equity holds two other items. *Treasury stock* (line 30) represents amounts paid by the company to repurchase its own stock. *Accumulated other comprehensive income (loss)* (line 29) represents items of gain or loss that are allowed by the FASB to bypass the income statement and be recorded directly into stockholders' equity. We will discuss the reasons for this in Chapters 8 and 11. For now, focus on the two main components of stockholders' equity: paid-in capital (consisting of common stock and additional paid-in capital) and retained earnings.

- At January 28, 2012, The Gap, Inc., has total stockholders' equity of $2,755 million (line 31). We can now prove that The Gap, Inc.'s total assets equal total liabilities and stockholders' equity at January 28, 2012 (amounts in millions):

MyAccountingLab

Total assets (line 12)	$7,422
Total liabilities (line 24)	$4,667
+ Total stockholders' equity (line 31)	$2,755
Total liabilities and stockholders' equity (line 32)	$7,422

Must equal

The statement of cash flows is the fourth required financial statement.

The Statement of Cash Flows Measures Cash Receipts and Payments

Companies engage in three basic types of activities:

Cash
Flow

- **Operating activities**
- **Investing activities**
- **Financing activities**

The **statement of cash flows** reports cash receipts and cash payments in each of these categories:

- *Companies operate by selling goods and services to customers.* **Operating activities** result in net income or net loss, and they either increase or decrease cash. The income statement of The Gap, Inc., reveals whether the company is profitable. The statement of cash flows reports whether operations increased the company's cash balance. Operating activities are most important, and they should be the company's main source of cash. Continuing negative cash flow from operations can lead to bankruptcy.

- *Companies invest in long-term assets.* The Gap, Inc., buys store fixtures and equipment, for which it must often spend cash. When these assets wear out, the company might sell them, which often increases cash. Both purchases and sales of long-term assets are investing cash flows. Investing cash flows are the next most important after operations.

- *Companies need money for financing.* Financing activities include issuing stock, paying dividends, borrowing, and repayments of borrowed funds. The Gap, Inc., issues stock to its shareholders and borrows from banks. These are cash receipts. The company may also pay loans, pay dividends, and repurchase its own stock. These payments are examples of financing cash flows.

Overview. Each category of cash flows—operating, investing, and financing—either increases or decreases cash. On a statement of cash flows, cash receipts appear as positive amounts. Cash payments are negative amounts and are enclosed by parentheses.

In Exhibit 1-10, which shows The Gap, Inc.'s Consolidated Statements of Cash Flows, operating activities provided net cash of $1,363 million in the 12 months ended January 28, 2012 (line 7). Notice that this is $530 million more than net income ($833 million in line 5), caused primarily by depreciation and amortization expenses, which were deducted from net sales in order to compute net income, but which did not use cash. Investing activities for the fiscal year (purchase of property, plant, and equipment and changes in other assets) used cash of about $454 million (line 11). That signals expansion.

Financing activities used another $602 million (line 17). Examining the details, we find that The Gap, Inc., used a whopping $2,092 million in cash to repurchase common stock from existing shareholders during the year (line 15). This represents the largest single transaction reflected on the cash flow statement, exceeding the total amount of cash provided from operating activities by $729 million! In addition, the company paid another $236 million in dividends to shareholders (line 16). We will discuss the reasons why companies purchase treasury stock and pay dividends in Chapter 10.

Overall, The Gap, Inc.'s cash and cash equivalents increased by $324 million during the 12 months ended January 28, 2012 (line 19) and ended the year at $1,885 million (line 21). Trace ending cash and cash equivalents back to the balance sheet in Exhibit 1-9 (line 4). Cash and cash equivalents links the statement of cash flows to the balance sheet. You've just performed more financial-statement analysis!

Exhibit 1-10 | The Gap, Inc., Consolidated Statements of Cash Flows

	A	B	C	D	E
		A1			
1	The Gap, Inc. Consolidated Statements of Cash Flows				
2	Adapted, In millions of $	12 Months Ended			
3		Jan. 28, 2012	Jan. 29, 2011		
4	**Cash flows from operating activities:**				
5	Net income	$ 833	$ 1,204		
6	Adjustments to reconcile net income to net cash provided by operating activities	530	540		
7	Net cash provided by operating activities	1,363	1,744		
8	**Cash flows from investing activities:**				
9	Purchases of property and equipment	(548)	(557)		
10	Change in other assets, net	94	128		
11	Net cash used for investing activities	(454)	(429)		
12	**Cash flows from financing activities:**				
13	Proceeds from issuance of debt	1,651	3		
14	Issuance of stock related to share-based payments	75	81		
15	Repurchases of common stock	(2,092)	(1,959)		
16	Cash dividends paid	(236)	(252)		
17	Net cash used for financing activities	(602)	(2,127)		
18	Effect of foreign exchange rate fluctuations on cash	17	25		
19	Net increase (decrease) in cash and cash equivalents	324	(787)		
20	Cash and cash equivalents at beginning of period	1,561	2,348		
21	Cash and cash equivalents at end of period	$ 1,885	$ 1,561		
22					

CONSTRUCT FINANCIAL STATEMENTS AND ANALYZE THE RELATIONSHIPS AMONG THEM

Exhibit 1-11 summarizes the relationships among the financial statements of The Gap, Inc., for the fiscal year ending January 28, 2012. These statements are condensed, so the details of Exhibits 1-7 through 1-10 are omitted. Study the exhibit carefully because these relationships apply to all organizations. Specifically, note the following:

5 **Construct** financial statements and **analyze** the relationships among them

1. The income statement for the 12 months ended January 28, 2012
   a. Reports revenues (net sales) and expenses of the year. Revenues and expenses are reported *only* on the income statement.
   b. Reports net income if total revenues exceed total expenses. If expenses exceed revenues, there is a net loss.

2. The statement of retained earnings for the 12 months ended January 28, 2012
   a. Opens with the beginning retained earnings balance.
   b. Adds net income (or subtracts net loss). Net income comes directly from the income statement (arrow 1 in Exhibit 1-11).
   c. Subtracts dividends declared.
   d. Reports the retained earnings balance at the end of the year.

3. The balance sheet at January 28, 2012, end of the accounting year
   a. Reports assets, liabilities, and stockholders' equity at the end of the year. Only the balance sheet reports assets and liabilities.
   b. Reports that assets equal the sum of liabilities plus stockholders' equity. This balancing feature follows the accounting equation and gives the balance sheet its name.
   c. Reports retained earnings, which comes from the statement of retained earnings (arrow 2 in Exhibit 1-11).

MyAccountingLab

4. The statement of cash flows for the 12 months ended January 28, 2012
    a. Reports cash flows from operating, investing, and financing activities. Each category results in net cash provided (an increase) or used (a decrease).
    b. Reports whether cash and cash equivalents increased (or decreased) during the year. The statement shows the ending cash and cash equivalents balance, as reported on the balance sheet (arrow 3 in Exhibit 1-11).

Exhibit 1-11 │ Relationships among the Financial Statements (in millions of $)

	A	B	C	D	E
	The Gap, Inc. **Consolidated Statement of Income (Adapted)** **12 Months Ended January 28, 2012**				
1					
2	Net sales	$ 14,549			
3	Expenses	13,716			
4	Net income	$ 833			
5					

	A	B	C	D	E
1	**Consolidated Statement of Retained Earnings (Adapted)**				
2	Beginning retained earnings	$ 11,767			
3	Net income	833			
4	Cash dividends declared	(236)			
5	Ending retained earnings balance	$ 12,364			
6					

	A	B	C	D	E
1	**Consolidated Balance Sheet (Adapted)**				
2	Assets				
3	Cash and cash equivalents	$ 1,885			
4	All other assets	5,537			
5	Total assets	$ 7,422			
6	Liabilities				
7	Total liabilities	$ 4,667			
8	Stockholders' Equity				
9	Common stock and additional paid-in capital	2,922			
10	Retained earnings	12,364			
11	Other equity	(12,531)			
12	Total stockholders' equity	2,755			
13	Total liabilities and stockholders' equity	$ 7,422			
14					

	A	B	C	D	E
1	**Consolidated Statement of Cash Flows (Adapted)**				
2	Net cash provided by operating activities	$ 1,363			
3	Net cash used in investing activities	(454)			
4	Net cash used in financing activities	(602)			
5	Effect of foreign exchange rate fluctuations on cash	17			
6	Net increase (decrease) in cash and cash equivalents	324			
7	Cash and cash equivalents, beginning of year	1,561			
8	Cash and cash equivalents, end of year	$ 1,885			
9					

● Decision Guidelines

IN EVALUATING A COMPANY, WHAT DO DECISION MAKERS LOOK FOR?

These Decision Guidelines illustrate how people use financial statements. Decision Guidelines appear throughout the book to show how accounting information aids decision making.

Suppose you are considering an investment in The Gap, Inc., stock. How do you proceed? Where do you get the information you need? What do you look for?

Decision	Guidelines
1. Can the company sell its products?	1. Net sales revenue on the income statement. Are sales growing or falling?
2. What are the main income measures to watch for trends?	2. a. Gross profit (Sales – Cost of goods sold) b. Operating income (Gross profit – Operating expenses) c. Net income (bottom line of the income statement) All three income measures should be increasing over time.
3. What percentage of sales revenue ends up as profit?	3. Divide net income by sales revenue. Examine the trend of the net income percentage from year to year.
4. Can the company collect its receivables?	4. From the balance sheet, compare the percentage increase in accounts receivable to the percentage increase in sales. If receivables are growing much faster than sales, collections may be too slow, and a cash shortage may result.
5. Can the company pay its a. current liabilities? b. current and long-term liabilities?	5. From the balance sheet, compare a. current assets to current liabilities. Current assets should be somewhat greater than current liabilities. b. total assets to total liabilities. Total assets must be somewhat greater than total liabilities.
6. Where is the company's cash coming from? How is cash being used?	6. On the cash flows statement, operating activities should provide the bulk of the company's cash during most years. Otherwise, the business will fail. Examine investing cash flows to see if the company is purchasing long-term assets—property, plant, and equipment and intangibles (this signals growth).

EVALUATE BUSINESS DECISIONS ETHICALLY

Good business requires decision making, which in turn requires the exercise of good judgment, both at the individual and corporate levels. For example, you may work for or eventually run a company like **Starbucks Corporation** that has decided to plow back a portion of its profits to support social development projects in the communities that produce its coffee, tea, and cocoa. Can that be profitable in the long run?

Perhaps as an accountant, you may have to decide whether to record a $50,000 expenditure for a piece of equipment as an asset on the balance sheet or an expense on the income statement. Alternatively, as a sales manager for a company like IBM, you may have to decide whether $25 million of goods and services delivered to customers in 2014 would be more appropriately

6 **Evaluate** business decisions ethically

recorded as revenue in 2014 or 2015. As mentioned earlier, the transition from U.S. GAAP to IFRS *will require an increased emphasis on judgment*, because IFRS contains fewer rules than U.S. GAAP. Depending on the type of business, the facts and circumstances surrounding accounting decisions may not always make them clear-cut, and yet the decision may determine whether the company shows a profit or a loss in a particular period! What are the factors that influence business and accounting decisions, and how should these factors be weighed? Generally, three types of factors influence business and accounting decisions: *economic, legal, and ethical.*

The *economic* factor states that the decision being made should *maximize the economic benefits* to the decision maker. Based on economic theory, every rational person faced with a decision will choose the course of action that maximizes his or her own welfare, without regard to how that decision impacts others. In summary, the combined outcome of each person acting in his or her own self-interest will maximize the benefits to society as a whole.

The *legal* factor is based on the proposition that free societies are governed by laws. Laws are written to provide clarity and to prevent abuse of the rights of individuals or society. Democratically enacted laws both contain and express society's moral standards. Legal analysis involves applying the relevant laws to each decision and then choosing the action that complies with those laws. A complicating factor for a global business may be that what is legal in one country might not be legal in another. In that case, it is usually best to abide by the laws of the most restrictive country.

The *ethical* factor recognizes that while certain actions might be both economically profitable and legal, they may still not be right. Therefore, most companies, and many individuals, have established standards for themselves to enforce a higher level of conduct than that imposed by law. These standards govern how we treat others and the way we restrain our selfish desires. This behavior and its underlying beliefs are the essence of ethics. **Ethics** are shaped by our cultural, socioeconomic, and religious backgrounds. An *ethical analysis* is needed to guide judgments when making decisions.

The decision rule in an ethical analysis is to choose the action that fulfills ethical duties— responsibilities of the members of society to each other. The challenge in an ethical analysis is to identify specific ethical duties and stakeholders to whom you owe these duties. As with legal issues, a complicating factor in making global ethical decisions may be that what is considered ethical in one country is not considered ethical in another.

Among the questions you may ask in making an ethical analysis are the following:

- *Which options are most honest, open, and truthful?*
- *Which options are most kind and compassionate and will build a sense of community?*
- *Which options create the greatest good for the greatest number of stakeholders?*
- *Which options result in treating others as I would want to be treated?*

Ethical training starts at home and continues throughout our lives. It is reinforced by the teaching that we receive in our church, synagogue, or mosque; the schools we attend; and by the persons and companies we associate with.

A thorough understanding of ethics requires more study than we can accomplish in this book. However, remember that when you are making accounting decisions, you should not check your ethics at the door!

In the business setting, ethics work best when modeled "from the top." Ethisphere Institute (www.ethisphere.com) has recently established the Business Ethics Leadership Alliance (BELA), aimed at "reestablishing ethics as the foundation of everyday business practices." BELA members agree to embrace and uphold four core values that incorporate ethics and integrity into all their practices: (1) legal compliance, (2) transparency, (3) conflict identification, and (4) accountability. Each year, Ethisphere Institute publishes a list of the World's Most Ethical Companies. The 2012 list includes corporations like United Parcel Service, Inc., Starbucks Corp., Pepsico, Inc., The Gap, Inc., and Target Corp. Excerpts from many of these companies' financial statements will be featured in later chapters of this text. As you begin to make your decisions about future employers, put these companies on your list! It's easier to act ethically when you work for companies that recognize the importance of ethics in business practices. These companies have learned from experience that, in the long run, ethical conduct pays big rewards—not only socially, morally, and spiritually, but economically as well!

❯ Decision Guidelines

DECISION FRAMEWORK FOR MAKING ETHICAL JUDGMENTS

Weighing tough ethical judgments in business and accounting requires a decision framework. Answering the following four questions will guide you through tough decisions:

Decision	Guidelines
1. What is the issue?	1. The issue will usually deal with making a judgment about an accounting measurement or disclosure that results in economic consequences, often to numerous parties.
2. Who are the stakeholders, and what are the consequences of the decision to each?	2. Stakeholders are anyone who might be impacted by the decision—you, your company, and potential users of the information (investors, creditors, regulatory agencies). Consequences can be economic, legal, or ethical in nature.
3. Weigh the alternatives.	3. Analyze the impact of the decision on all stakeholders, using economic, legal, and ethical criteria. Ask "Who will be helped or hurt, whose rights will be exercised or denied, and in what way?"
4. Make the decision and be prepared to deal with the consequences.	4. Exercise the courage to either defend the decision or to change it, depending on its positive or negative impact. How does your decision make you feel afterward?

To simplify, we might ask three questions:

1. Is the action legal? If not, steer clear, unless you want to go to jail or pay monetary damages to injured parties. If the action is legal, go on to questions 2 and 3.
2. Who will be affected by the decision and how? Be as thorough about this analysis as possible, and analyze it from all three standpoints (economic, legal, and ethical).
3. How will this decision make me feel afterward? How would it make me feel if my family reads about it in the newspaper?

   In later chapters throughout the book, we will apply this model to different accounting decisions.

Freddy's Auto Service, Inc., began operations on April 1, 2014. During April, the business provided services for customers. It is now April 30 and investors wonder how well Freddy's performed during its first month. The investors also want to know the company's financial position at the end of April and its cash flows during the month.

The following data are listed in alphabetical order.

Accounts payable	$ 1,800	Land	$18,000
Accounts receivable	2,000	Payments of cash:	
Adjustments to reconcile net		Acquisition of land	40,000
income to net cash provided		Dividends	2,100
by operating activities	(3,900)	Rent expense	1,100
Cash balance at beginning of April	0	Retained earnings at beginning	
Cash balance at end of April	?	of April	0
Cash receipts:		Retained earnings at end of April	?
Issuance (sale) of stock to owners	50,000	Salary expense	1,200
Sale of land	22,000	Service revenue	10,000
Common stock	50,000	Supplies	3,700
		Utilities expense	400

Requirements

1. Prepare the income statement, the statement of retained earnings, and the statement of cash flows for the month ended April 30, 2014, and the balance sheet at April 30, 2014. Draw arrows linking the statements.

2. Answer the following questions:

   a. How well did Freddy's Auto Service, Inc., perform during its first month of operations?

   b. Where does Freddy's Auto Service, Inc., stand financially at the end of April?

Answers

Requirement 1

Financial Statements of Freddy's Auto Service, Inc.

	A	B	C	D
	A1 ⬍			
1	Freddy's Auto Service, Inc. Income Statement Month Ended April 30, 2014			
2	Revenue:			
3	Service revenue		$ 10,000	
4	Expenses:			
5	Salary expense	$ 1,200		
6	Rent expense	1,100		
7	Utilities expense	400		
8	Total expenses		2,700	
9	Net Income		$ 7,300	
10				

①

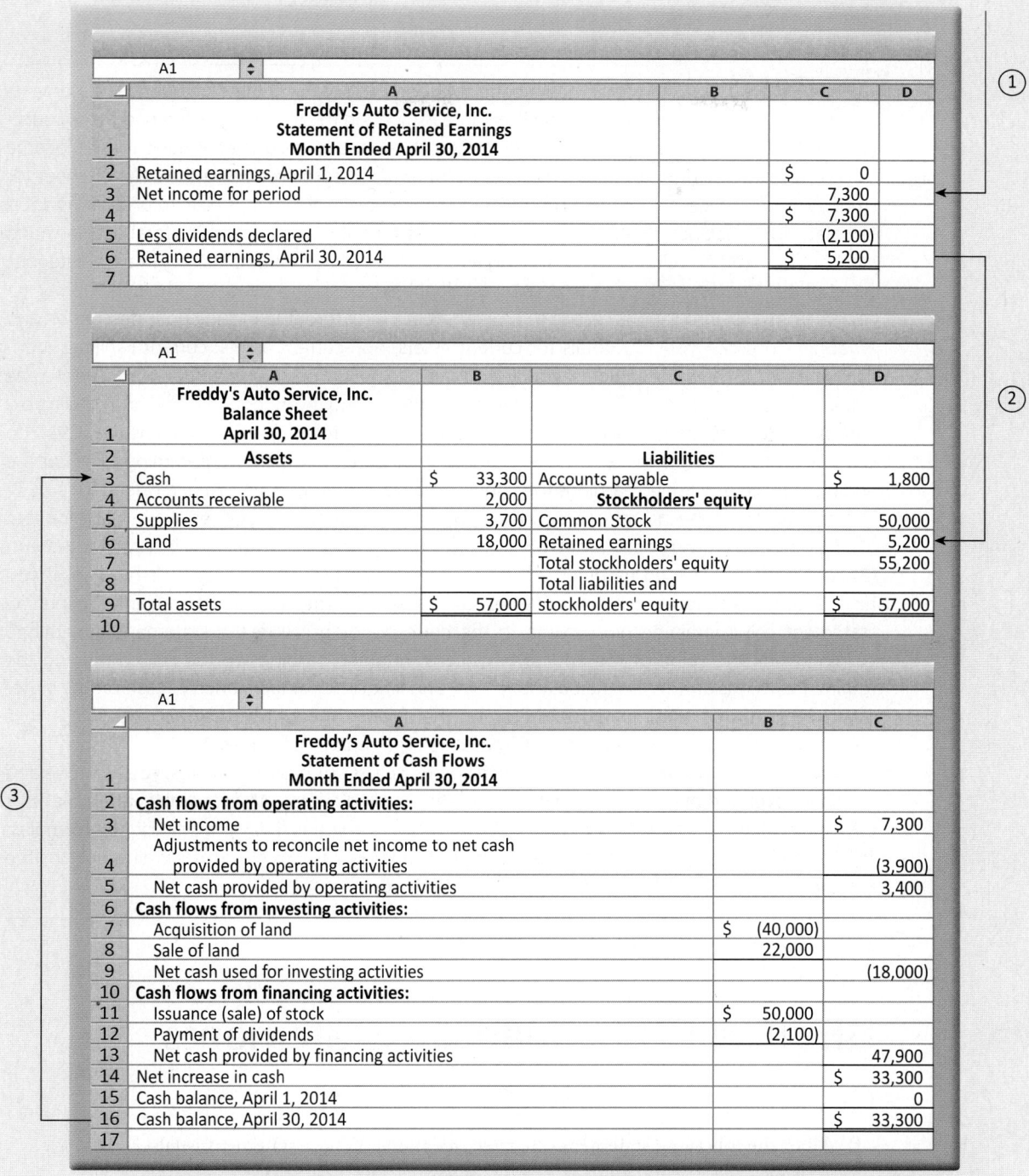

Freddy's Auto Service, Inc.
Statement of Retained Earnings
Month Ended April 30, 2014

	A	B	C	D
1				
2	Retained earnings, April 1, 2014		$ 0	
3	Net income for period		7,300	
4			$ 7,300	
5	Less dividends declared		(2,100)	
6	Retained earnings, April 30, 2014		$ 5,200	
7				

Freddy's Auto Service, Inc.
Balance Sheet
April 30, 2014

	A	B	C	D
2	Assets		Liabilities	
3	Cash	$ 33,300	Accounts payable	$ 1,800
4	Accounts receivable	2,000	Stockholders' equity	
5	Supplies	3,700	Common Stock	50,000
6	Land	18,000	Retained earnings	5,200
7			Total stockholders' equity	55,200
8			Total liabilities and	
9	Total assets	$ 57,000	stockholders' equity	$ 57,000
10				

Freddy's Auto Service, Inc.
Statement of Cash Flows
Month Ended April 30, 2014

	A	B	C
2	Cash flows from operating activities:		
3	Net income		$ 7,300
4	Adjustments to reconcile net income to net cash provided by operating activities		(3,900)
5	Net cash provided by operating activities		3,400
6	Cash flows from investing activities:		
7	Acquisition of land	$ (40,000)	
8	Sale of land	22,000	
9	Net cash used for investing activities		(18,000)
10	Cash flows from financing activities:		
11	Issuance (sale) of stock	$ 50,000	
12	Payment of dividends	(2,100)	
13	Net cash provided by financing activities		47,900
14	Net increase in cash		$ 33,300
15	Cash balance, April 1, 2014		0
16	Cash balance, April 30, 2014		$ 33,300
17			

Requirement 2

a. Freddy's Auto Service, Inc., performed rather well in April. Net income was $7,300—very good in relation to service revenue of $10,000. The company was able to pay cash dividends of $2,100.

b. Freddy's Auto Service, Inc., ended April with cash of $33,300. Total assets of $57,000 far exceed total liabilities of $1,800. Stockholders' equity of $55,200 provides a good cushion for borrowing. The business's financial position at April 30, 2014, is strong.

If you've had a basic course in Excel, you can prepare financial statements easily using an Excel spreadsheet! In this chapter, you learned the accounting equation (see Exhibit 1-4 on page 11). In Exhibit 1-5 you learned the formulas for net income as well as how to compute the ending balance of retained earnings. Using the balance sheet for Freddy's Auto Service, Inc., in the End-of-Chapter Summary Problem, it is easy to prepare an Excel template for a balance sheet by programming cells for total assets (cell B9), total liabilities and stockholders' equity (cell D9). Then, as long as you know what accounts belong in each category, you can use the insert function to insert individual assets, liabilities, and stockholders' equity accounts from a list into various cells of the spreadsheet (don't forget to include both description and amounts). You can insert subtotals for current assets, non-current assets, current liabilities, non-current liabilities, and stockholders' equity. You can also build a basic Excel template for the income statement for Freddy's Auto Service, Inc. by listing and totaling revenues and listing and totaling expenses, then subtracting total expenses from total revenues to compute net income (cell C9). You can build an Excel template for the statement of retained earnings by programming a cell for the ending balance of retained earnings (beginning balance + net income (loss) − dividends) (cell C6). Then merely insert the individual amounts, and bingo, your spreadsheet does all the math for you.

Don't forget the proper order of financial statement preparation: (1) income statement, (2) statement of retained earnings, (3) balance sheet, and (4) statement of cash flows. If you have to prepare all four statements, it's best to follow that order so that you can link the income statement cell containing net income to the corresponding cell in the statement of retained earnings; link the value of the ending balance of retained earnings to the cell containing the retained earnings amount in the balance sheet; and link the ending balance of cash on the statement of cash flows to the balance of cash on the balance sheet as of the year end. These links correspond to the amounts connected by arrows (1, 2, and 3) on pages 26–27.

The beauty of this approach is that once you build a set of basic templates, you can save and use them over and over again as you progress through the course. **MyAccountingLab** makes it easy for you by providing the templates, but in most cases you will have to provide the formulas. Try it! You'll not only be learning accounting but refining your Excel skills as well! Look for the Excel icon in both the text and **MyAccountingLab**. ■

REVIEW | The Financial Statements

Quick Check (Answers are given on page 52.)

1. All of the following statements are true except one. Which statement is false?
   a. A proprietorship is a business with several owners.
   b. Bookkeeping is only a part of accounting.
   c. Professional accountants are held to a high standard of ethical conduct.
   d. The organization that formulates generally accepted accounting principles in the United States is the Financial Accounting Standards Board.

2. The valuation of assets on the balance sheet is generally based on
   a. selling price.
   b. what it would cost to replace the asset.
   c. current fair market value as established by independent appraisers.
   d. historical cost.

3. The accounting equation can be expressed as
   a. Assets + Liabilities = Owners' equity
   b. Owners' equity − Assets = Liabilities
   c. Assets − Liabilities = Owners' equity
   d. Assets = Liabilities − Owners' equity

4. The nature of an asset is best described as
   a. something owned by a business that has a ready market value.
   b. an economic resource that's expected to benefit future operations.
   c. something with physical form that's valued at cost in the accounting records.
   d. an economic resource representing cash or the right to receive cash in the future.

5. Which financial statement covers a period of time?
   a. Income statement
   b. Balance sheet
   c. Statement of cash flows
   d. Both a and c

6. How would net income be most likely to affect the accounting equation?
   a. Increase assets and increase stockholders' equity
   b. Increase assets and increase liabilities
   c. Decrease assets and decrease liabilities
   d. Increase liabilities and decrease stockholders' equity

7. During the year, Aynsley, Inc., has $280,000 in revenues, $145,000 in expenses, and $6,000 in dividend declarations and payments. Stockholders' equity changed by
   a. +$135,000.
   b. +$129,000.
   c. −$129,000.
   d. +$141,000.

8. Aynsley, Inc., in question 7 had
   a. net income of $129,000.
   b. net income of $135,000.
   c. net income of $141,000.
   d. net loss of $135,000.

9. Mighty Corporation holds cash of $8,000 and owes $31,000 on accounts payable. Mighty has accounts receivable of $47,000, inventory of $28,000, and land that cost $40,000. How much are Mighty's total assets and liabilities?

	Total assets	Liabilities
a.	$123,000	$31,000
b.	$123,000	$59,000
c.	$95,000	$59,000
d.	$83,000	$71,000

10. Which item(s) is (are) reported on the balance sheet?
    a. Retained earnings
    b. Inventory
    c. Accounts payable
    d. All of the above

11. During the year, Romero Company's stockholders' equity increased from $98,000 to $116,000. Romero earned net income of $25,000. Assume no changes in the capital stock accounts. How much in dividends did Romero declare during the year?
    a. $18,000
    b. $7,000
    c. $25,000
    d. $0

12. Parret Company had total assets of $175,000 and total stockholders' equity of $78,000 at the beginning of the year. During the year, assets increased by $42,000 and liabilities increased by $12,000. Stockholders' equity at the end of the year is
    a. $108,000.
    b. $120,000.
    c. $132,000.
    d. $139,000.

13. Which of the following is a true statement about International Financial Reporting Standards?
    a. They are not needed for U.S. businesses since the United States already has the strongest accounting standards in the world.
    b. They are not being applied anywhere in the world yet, but soon they will be.
    c. They are converging gradually with U.S. standards.
    d. They are more exact (contain more rules) than U.S. generally accepted accounting principles.

14. Which of the following is the most accurate statement regarding ethics as applied to decision making in accounting?
    a. Ethics involves making difficult choices under pressure and should be kept in mind in making every decision, including those involving accounting.
    b. It is impossible to learn ethical decision making, since it is just something you decide to do or not to do.
    c. Ethics has no place in accounting, since accounting deals purely with numbers.
    d. Ethics is becoming less and less important as a field of study in business.

Accounting Vocabulary

accounting (p. 3) The information system that measures business activities, processes that information into reports and financial statements, and communicates the results to decision makers.

accounting equation (p. 11) The most basic tool of accounting: Assets = Liabilities + Owners' equity.

asset (p. 11) An economic resource that is expected to be of benefit in the future.

balance sheet (p. 17) List of an entity's assets, liabilities, and owners' equity as of a specific date. Also called the *statement of financial position.*

board of directors (p. 6) Group elected by the stockholders to set policy for a corporation and to appoint its officers.

capital (p. 11) Another name for the *owners' equity* of a business.

common stock (p. 12) The most basic form of capital stock.

continuity assumption (p. 8) See going-concern assumption.

corporation (p. 6) A business owned by stockholders. A corporation is a legal entity, an "artificial person" in the eyes of the law.

current asset (p. 18) An asset that is expected to be converted to cash, sold, or consumed during the next 12 months, or within the business's normal operating cycle if longer than a year.

current liability (p. 18) A debt due to be paid within one year or within the entity's operating cycle if the cycle is longer than a year.

deficit (p. 16) Negative balance in retained earnings caused by net losses over a period of years.

dividends (p. 12) Distributions (usually cash) by a corporation to its stockholders.

entity (p. 8) An organization or a section of an organization that, for accounting purposes, stands apart from other organizations and individuals as a separate economic unit.

ethics (p. 24) Standards of right and wrong that transcend economic and legal boundaries. Ethical standards deal with the way we treat others and restrain our own actions because of the desires, expectations, or rights of others, or because of our obligations to them.

expenses (p. 12) Decrease in retained earnings that results from operations; the cost of doing business; opposite of revenues.

fair value (p. 9) The amount that a business could sell an asset for, or the amount that a business could pay to settle a liability.

financial accounting (p. 4) The branch of accounting that provides information to people outside the firm.

Financial Accounting Standards Board (FASB) (p. 6) The regulatory body in the United States that formulates generally accepted accounting principles (GAAP).

financial statements (p. 2) Business documents that report financial information about a business entity to decision makers.

financing activities (p. 20) Activities that obtain from investors and creditors the cash needed to launch and sustain the business; a section of the statement of cash flows.

generally accepted accounting principles (GAAP) (p. 6) Accounting guidelines, formulated by the Financial Accounting Standards Board, that govern how accounting is practiced.

going-concern assumption (p. 8) Holds that the entity will remain in operation for the foreseeable future.

historical cost principle (p. 8) Principle that states that assets should be recorded at their actual cost.

income statement (p. 14) A financial statement listing an entity's revenues, expenses, and net income or net loss for a specific period. Also called the *statement of operations.*

International Financial Reporting Standards (IFRS) (p. 9) Accounting guidelines, formulated by the **International Accounting Standards Board (IASB)**. U.S. GAAP is being harmonized with IFRS. At that time, U.S. companies are expected to adopt these principles for their financial statements so that they can be compared with those of companies from other countries.

investing activities (p. 20) Activities that increase or decrease the long-term assets available to the business; a section of the statement of cash flows.

liability (p. 11) An economic obligation (a debt) payable to an individual or an organization outside the business.

limited-liability company (p. 5) A business organization in which the business (not the owner) is liable for the company's debts.

long-term debt (p. 12) A liability that falls due beyond one year from the date of the financial statements.

management accounting (p. 4) The branch of accounting that generates information for the internal decision makers of a business, such as top executives.

net earnings (p. 12) Another name for *net income.*

net income (p. 12) Excess of total revenues over total expenses. Also called *net earnings* or *net profit.*

net loss (p. 12) Excess of total expenses over total revenues.

net profit (p. 12) Another name for *net income.*

operating activities (p. 20) Activities that create revenue or expense in the statement of cash flows. Operating activities affect the income statement.

owners' equity (p. 11) The claim of the owners of a business to the assets of the business. Also called *capital, stockholders' equity,* or *net assets.*

paid-in capital (p. 12) The amount of stockholders' equity that stockholders have contributed to the corporation. Also called *contributed capital.*

partnership (p. 5) An association of two or more persons who co-own a business for profit.

proprietorship (p. 5) A business with a single owner.

retained earnings (p. 12) The amount of stockholders' equity that the corporation has earned through profitable operations and has not given back to stockholders.

revenues (p. 12) Increase in retained earnings from delivering goods or services to customers or clients.

shareholder (p. 6) Another name for *stockholder.*

stable-monetary-unit assumption (p. 9) The reason for ignoring the effect of inflation in the accounting records, based on the assumption that the dollar's purchasing power is relatively stable.

statement of cash flows (p. 20) Reports cash receipts and cash payments classified according to the entity's major activities: operating, investing, and financing.

statement of financial position (p. 17) Another name for the *balance sheet.*

statement of operations (p. 14) Another name for the *income statement.*

statement of retained earnings (p. 16) Summary of the changes in the retained earnings of a corporation during a specific period.

stock (p. 6) Shares into which the owners' equity of a corporation is divided.

stockholder (p. 6) A person who owns stock in a corporation. Also called a *shareholder.*

stockholders' equity (p. 11) The stockholders' ownership interest in the assets of a corporation.

ASSESS YOUR PROGRESS

Short Exercises

S1-1. *(Learning Objective 3: Apply the accounting equation)* Suppose you manage a Coffee Plus! restaurant. Identify the missing amount for each situation:

	Total Assets	=	Total Liabilities	+	Stockholders' Equity
a.	$?		$320,000		$340,000
b.	135,000		57,000		?
c.	401,000		?		356,000

S1-2. *(Learning Objective 6: Evaluate business decisions ethically)* Good business and accounting practices require the exercise of good judgment. How should ethics be incorporated into making accounting judgments? Why is ethics important?

S1-3. *(Learning Objective 1: Explain and differentiate between business organizations)* Taylor Signs, Inc., needs funds, and Taylor Stamp, the president, has asked you to consider investing in the business. Answer the following questions about the different ways that Stamp might organize the business. Explain each answer.

    a. What forms of organization will enable the owners of Taylor Signs to limit their risk of loss to the amounts they have invested in the business?

    b. What form of business organization will give Stamp the most freedom to manage the business as she wishes?

    c. What form of organization will give creditors the maximum protection in the event that Taylor Signs, Inc., fails and cannot pay its debts?

S1-4. *(Learning Objective 2: Explain underlying accounting concepts, assumptions, and principles of accounting)* Meagan Wallace is chairman of the board of New Age Foods, Inc. Suppose Ms. Wallace has just founded New Age Foods, and assume that she treats her home and other personal assets as part of New Age Foods. Answer these questions about the evaluation of New Age Foods, Inc.

  1. Which accounting assumption governs this situation?

  2. How can the proper application of this accounting assumption give Wallace and others a realistic view of New Age Foods, Inc.? Explain in detail.

S1-5. *(Learning Objective 2: Apply underlying accounting concepts, assumptions, and principles)* Identify the accounting concept, assumption, or principle that best applies to each of the following situations:

    a. Inflation has been around 5.5% for some time. Woodlake Realtors is considering measuring its land values in inflation-adjusted amounts.

    b. You get an especially good buy on a fax machine, paying only $300 when it normally costs $800. What is your accounting value for this fax machine?

    c. Burger King, the restaurant chain, sold a store location to McDonald's. How can Burger King determine the sale price of the store—by a professional appraisal, Burger King cost, or the amount actually received from the sale?

    d. General Motors wants to determine which division of the company—Chevrolet or GMC—is more profitable.

S1-6. *(Learning Objective 3: Apply the accounting equation)*

  1. If you know the assets and the owners' equity of a business, how can you measure its liabilities? Give the equation.

  2. Use the accounting equation to show how to determine the amount of a company's owners' equity. How would your answer change if you were analyzing your own household or a single IHOP restaurant?

S1-7. *(Learning Objectives 1, 4: Explain accounting language; evaluate business operations)* Accounting definitions are precise, and you must understand the vocabulary to properly use accounting. Sharpen your understanding of key terms by answering the following questions:

  1. How do the assets and owners' equity of Apple, Inc., differ from each other? Which one (assets or owners' equity) must be at least as large as the other? Which one can be smaller than the other?

  2. How are Apple, Inc.'s liabilities and owners' equity similar? Different?

S1-8. *(Learning Objective 1: Explain accounting language)* Consider Walmart, a large retailer. Classify the following items as an Asset (A), a Liability (L), or Stockholders' Equity (S) for Walmart:

a. ____ Accounts receivable		**g.** ____ Notes payable	
b. ____ Long-term debt		**h.** ____ Retained earnings	
c. ____ Merchandise inventory		**i.** ____ Land	
d. ____ Prepaid expenses		**j.** ____ Accounts payable	
e. ____ Accrued expenses payable		**k.** ____ Common stock	
f. ____ Equipment		**l.** ____ Supplies	

S1-9. *(Learning Objective 1: Explain accounting language)*
1. Identify the two basic categories of items on an income statement.
2. What do we call the bottom line of the income statement?

S1-10. *(Learning Objective 5: Construct an income statement)* O'Malley Services, Inc., began 2014 with total assets of $216 million and ended 2014 with assets of $358 million. During 2014, O'Malley Services earned revenues of $398 million and had expenses of $167 million. O'Malley Services paid dividends of $25 million in 2014. Prepare the company's income statement for the year ended December 31, 2014, complete with an appropriate heading.

S1-11. *(Learning Objective 5: Construct a statement of retained earnings)* Canada Corp. began 2014 with retained earnings of $286 million. Revenues during the year were $482 million, and expenses totaled $337 million. Canada declared dividends of $59 million. What was the company's ending balance of retained earnings? To answer this question, prepare Canada's statement of retained earnings for the year ended December 31, 2014, complete with its proper heading.

S1-12. *(Learning Objective 5: Construct a balance sheet)* At December 31, 2014, Washington Products has cash of $21,000, receivables of $17,600, and inventory of $79,000. The company's equipment totals $185,000. Washington owes accounts payable of $25,000 and long-term notes payable of $169,000. Common stock is $30,500. Prepare Washington's balance sheet at December 31, 2014, complete with its proper heading. Use the accounting equation to compute retained earnings.

S1-13. *(Learning Objective 5: Construct a statement of cash flows)* Guling Legal Services, Inc., ended 2013 with cash of $15,000. During 2014, Guling earned net income of $75,000 and had adjustments to reconcile net income to net cash provided by operations totaling $8,000 (this is a negative amount). Guling paid $29,000 to purchase equipment during 2014. During 2014, the company paid dividends of $31,000. Prepare Guling's statement of cash flows for the year ended December 31, 2014, complete with its proper heading.

S1-14. *(Learning Objectives 1, 5: Explain accounting language; construct financial statements)* Suppose you are analyzing the financial statements of Adams Medical, Inc. Identify each item with its appropriate financial statement, using the following abbreviations: Income statement (IS), Statement of retained earnings (SRE), Balance sheet (BS), and Statement of cash flows (SCF). Three items appear on two financial statements, and one item shows up on three statements.

a. _____ Accounts payable	**h.** _____ Dividends
b. _____ Inventory	**i.** _____ Increase or decrease in cash
c. _____ Interest revenue	**j.** _____ Net income
d. _____ Long-term debt	**k.** _____ Net cash provided by operating activities
e. _____ Net cash used for financing activities	**l.** _____ Retained earnings
f. _____ Salary expense	**m.** _____ Sales revenue
g. _____ Cash	**n.** _____ Common stock

S1-15. *(Learning Objectives 2, 4: Apply accounting concepts; evaluate business activity)* Apply your understanding of the relationships among the financial statements to answer these questions.
  a. How can a business earn large profits but have a small balance of retained earnings?
  b. Give two reasons why a business can have a steady stream of net income over a five-year period and still experience a cash shortage.
  c. If you could pick a single source of cash for your business, what would it be? Why?
  d. How can a business be unprofitable several years in a row and still have plenty of cash?

Exercises

Group A

E1-16A. *(Learning Objectives 3, 4: Apply the accounting equation; evaluate business operations)* Compute the missing amount in the accounting equation for each company (amounts in billions):

	Assets	Liabilities	Stockholders' Equity
Beautiful Florals	$?	$47	$36
Corner Groceries	26	?	19
State Bank	33	11	?

Which company appears to have the strongest financial position? Explain your reasoning.

E1-17A. *(Learning Objectives 3, 4: Apply the accounting equation; evaluate business operations)* City Car Wash, Inc., has current assets of $180 million; property, plant, and equipment of $300 million; and other assets totaling $110 million. Current liabilities are $105 million and long-term liabilities total $280 million.

Requirements

1. Use these data to write City Car Wash's accounting equation.
2. How much in resources does City Car Wash have to work with?
3. How much does City Car Wash owe creditors?
4. How much of the company's assets do the City Car Wash stockholders actually own?

E1-18A. *(Learning Objectives 3, 4: Apply the accounting equation; evaluate business operations)* Norton, Inc.'s comparative balance sheet at January 31, 2015, and 2014, reports the following (in millions):

	2015	2014
Total assets	$76	$52
Total liabilities	23	14

Requirements

Three situations about Norton's issuance of stock and declaration and payment of dividends during the year ended January 31, 2015, follow. For each situation, use the accounting equation and the statement of retained earnings to compute the amount of Norton's net income or net loss during the year ended January 31, 2015.
1. Norton issued $7 million of stock and declared no dividends.
2. Norton issued no stock but declared dividends of $5 million.
3. Norton issued $29 million of stock and declared dividends of $8 million.

E1-19A. *(Learning Objective 5: Identify financial statement by type of information)* Assume Hi Tech, Inc., is expanding into Australia. The company must decide where to locate and how to finance the expansion. Identify the financial statement where these decision makers can find the following information about Hi Tech, Inc. In some cases, more than one statement will report the needed data.

- **a.** Revenue
- **b.** Dividends
- **c.** Ending cash balance
- **d.** Total assets
- **e.** Selling, general, and administrative expense
- **f.** Adjustments to reconcile net income to net cash provided by operations
- **g.** Cash spent to acquire the building
- **h.** Current liabilities
- **i.** Income tax expense
- **j.** Net income
- **k.** Common stock
- **l.** Ending balance of retained earnings
- **m.** Income tax payable
- **n.** Long-term debt

E1-20A. *(Learning Objectives 3, 5: Apply the accounting equation; construct a balance sheet)* Amounts of the assets and liabilities of Alan Sanders Realty Company, as of July 31, 2014, are given as follows. Also included are revenue, expense, and selected stockholders' equity figures for the year ended on that date (amounts in millions):

Total revenue	$ 37.8	Investment assets (long-term)	$135.6
Receivables	0.6	Property and equipment, net	1.9
Current liabilities	2.1	Other expenses	5.3
Common stock	21.8	Retained earnings, beginning	16.9
Interest expense	0.6	Retained earnings, ending	?
Salary and other employee expenses	13.8	Cash	1.8
Long-term liabilities	102.2	Other assets (long-term)	10.7

Requirement

1. Construct the balance sheet of Alan Sanders Realty Company at July 31, 2014. Use the accounting equation to compute ending retained earnings.

E1-21A. *(Learning Objective 5: Construct an income statement and a statement of retained earnings)* This exercise should be used with Exercise 1-20A. Refer to the data of Alan Sanders Realty Company in Exercise 1-20A.

Requirements

1. Prepare the income statement of Alan Sanders Realty Company for the year ended July 31, 2014.
2. What amount of dividends did Alan Sanders declare during the year ended July 31, 2014? (*Hint*: Prepare a statement of retained earnings.)

E1-22A. *(Learning Objective 5: Construct an income statement and a statement of retained earnings)* Assume the Island Coffee Roasters Corp. ended the month of August 2015 with these data:

Payments of cash:			
Acquisition of equipment	$205,000	Cash balance, August 1, 2015	$ 0
Dividends	2,400	Cash balance, August 31, 2015	5,500
Retained earnings		Cash receipts:	
August 1, 2015	0	Issuance (sale) of stock	
Retained earnings		to owners	24,400
August 31, 2015	?	Rent expense	1,800
Utilities expense	5,200	Common stock	24,400
Adjustments to reconcile		Equipment	205,000
net income to net cash		Office supplies	7,400
provided by operations	1,400	Accounts payable	8,800
Salary expense	78,500	Service revenue	272,600

Requirement

1. Prepare the income statement and the statement of retained earnings of Island Coffee Roasters Corp., for the month ended August 31, 2015.

E1-23A. *(Learning Objective 5: Construct a balance sheet)* Refer to the data in Exercise 1-22A.

Requirement

1. Prepare the balance sheet of Island Coffee Roasters Corp., for August 31, 2015.

E1-24A. *(Learning Objective 5: Construct a statement of cash flows)* Refer to the data in Exercises 1-22A and 1-23A.

Requirement

1. Prepare the statement of cash flows of Island Coffee Roasters Corp., for the month ended August 31, 2015. Using Exhibit 1-11 as a model, show with arrows the relationships among the income statement, statement of retained earnings, balance sheet, and statement of cash flows.

E1-25A. *(Learning Objective 4: Evaluate business operations through the financial statements)* This exercise should be used in conjunction with Exercises 1-22A through 1-24A.

The owner of Island Coffee Roasters Corp. seeks your advice as to whether he should cease operations or continue the business. Complete the report giving him your opinion of net income, dividends, financial position, and cash flows during his first month of operations. Cite specifics from the financial statements to support your opinion. Conclude your memo with advice on whether to stay in business or cease operations.

Group B

E1-26B. *(Learning Objectives 3, 4: Apply the accounting equation; evaluate business operations)* Compute the missing amount in the accounting equation for each company (amounts in billions):

	Assets	Liabilities	Stockholders' Equity
Clayton Homes	$?	$17	$21
Howard Automotive	70	?	46
Bella Boutique	51	15	?

Which company appears to have the strongest financial position? Explain your reasoning.

E1-27B. *(Learning Objectives 3, 4: Apply the accounting equation; evaluate business operations)* Jaska Services, Inc., has current assets of $208 million; property, plant, and equipment of $338 million; and other assets totaling $107 million. Current liabilities are $156 million and long-term liabilities total $100 million.

Requirements

1. Use these data to write Jaska Services Inc.'s accounting equation.
2. How much in resources does Jaska Services have to work with?
3. How much does Jaska Services owe creditors?
4. How much of the company's assets do the Jaska Services, Inc.'s stockholders actually own?

E1-28B. *(Learning Objectives 3, 4: Apply the accounting equation; evaluate business operations)* Burchette, Inc.'s comparative balance sheet at January 31, 2015, and 2014, reports the following (in millions):

	2015	2014
Total assets	$48	$29
Total liabilities	13	11

Requirements

Three situations about Burchette's issuance of stock and declaration and payment of dividends during the year ended January 31, 2015, follow. For each situation, use the accounting equation and the statement of retained earnings to compute the amount of Burchette's net income or net loss during the year ended January 31, 2015.

1. Burchette issued $6 million of stock and declared no dividends.
2. Burchette issued no stock but declared dividends of $5 million.
3. Burchette issued $31 million of stock and declared dividends of $3 million.

E1-29B. *(Learning Objective 5: Identify financial statement by type of information)* Assume Chen, Inc., is expanding into France. The company must decide where to locate and how to finance the expansion. Identify the financial statement where these decision makers can find the following information about Chen, Inc. In some cases, more than one statement will report the needed data.

  a. Net income
  b. Current liabilities
  c. Cash spent to acquire the building
  d. Adjustments to reconcile net income to net cash provided by operations
  e. Selling, general, and administrative expenses
  f. Ending cash balance
  g. Ending balance of retained earnings
  h. Income tax expense
  i. Long-term debt
  j. Revenue
  k. Total assets
  l. Dividends
  m. Income tax payable
  n. Common stock

E1-30B. *(Learning Objectives 3, 5: Apply the accounting equation; construct a balance sheet)* Amounts of the assets and liabilities of Diaz Design Company, as of July 31, 2014, are as follows. Also included are revenue, expense and selected stockholders' equity figures for the year ended on that date (amounts in millions):

Total revenue	$ 41.4	Investment assets (long-term)	$108.9
Receivables	1.6	Property and equipment, net	57.6
Cash	4.7	Other expenses	2.9
Other assets (long-term)	31.7	Retained earnings, beginning	55.1
Interest expense	0.3	Retained earnings, ending	?
Salary and other employee expenses	13.6	Current liabilities	5.3
Long-term liabilities	99.5	Common stock	21.5

Requirement

1. Construct the balance sheet of Diaz Design Company at July 31, 2014. Use the accounting equation to compute ending retained earnings.

E1-31B. *(Learning Objective 5: Construct an income statement and a statement of retained earnings)* This exercise should be used with Exercise 1-30B.

Requirements

1. Prepare the income statement of Diaz Design Company for the year ended July 31, 2014.
2. What amount of dividends did Diaz Design declare during the year ended July 31, 2014? (*Hint*: Prepare a statement of retained earnings.)

E1-32B. *(Learning Objective 5: Construct an income statement and a statement of retained earnings)* Assume Office Plus Copy Center, Inc. ended the month of May 2014 with these data:

Payments of cash:			Cash balance, May 1, 2014........	$ 0
Acquisition of equipment.......	$402,700		Cash balance, May 31, 2014......	20,300
Dividends..............................	12,500		Cash receipts:	
Retained earnings			Issuance (sale) of stock	
May 1, 2014	0		to owners	200,000
Retained earnings			Rent expense.............................	3,700
May 31, 2014	?		Common stock..........................	200,000
Utilities expense	10,500		Equipment.................................	402,700
Adjustments to reconcile			Office supplies...........................	4,400
net income to net cash			Accounts payable	33,800
provided by operations...........	29,400		Service revenue..........................	450,300
Salary expense...........................	230,000			

Requirement

1. Prepare the income statement and the statement of retained earnings of Office Plus Copy Center, Inc., for the month ended May 31, 2014.

E1-33B. *(Learning Objective 5: Construct a balance sheet)* Refer to the data in Exercise 1-32B.

Requirement

1. Prepare the balance sheet of Office Plus Copy Center, Inc., at May 31, 2014.

E1-34B. *(Learning Objective 5: Construct a statement of cash flows)* Refer to the data in Exercises 1-32B and 1-33B.

Requirement

1. Prepare the statement of cash flows of Office Plus Copy Center, Inc., for the month ended May 31, 2014. Using Exhibit 1-11 as a model, show with arrows the relationships among the income statement, statement of retained earnings, balance sheet, and statement of cash flows.

E1-35B. *(Learning Objective 4: Evaluate business operations through the financial statements)* This exercise should be used in conjunction with Exercises 1-32B through 1-34B.

The owner of Office Plus Copy Center now seeks your advice as to whether he should cease operations or continue the business. Complete the report giving him your opinion of net income, dividends, financial position, and cash flows during his first month of operations. Cite specifics from the financial statements to support your opinion. Conclude your memo with advice on whether to stay in business or cease operations.

Quiz

Test your understanding of the financial statements by answering the following questions. Select the best choice from among the possible answers given.

Q1-36. The *primary* objective of financial reporting is to provide information
   a. useful for making investment and credit decisions.
   b. to the federal government.
   c. on the cash flows of the company.
   d. about the profitability of the enterprise.

Q1-37. Which type of business organization provides the least amount of protection for bankers and other creditors of the company?
    a. Proprietorship   **c.** Partnership
    b. Corporation   **d.** Both a and c

Q1-38. Assets are usually reported at their
    a. historical cost.
    b. current market value.
    c. appraised value.
    d. none of the above (fill in the blank) _____.

Q1-39. During February, assets increased by $84,000 and liabilities increased by $26,000. Stockholders' equity must have
    a. decreased by $110,000.   **c.** decreased by $58,000.
    b. increased by $110,000.   **d.** increased by $58,000.

Q1-40. The amount a company expects to collect from customers appears on the
    a. income statement in the expenses section.
    b. balance sheet in the stockholders' equity section.
    c. balance sheet in the current assets section.
    d. statement of cash flows.

Q1-41. All of the following are current assets except
    a. Cash.   **c.** Sales Revenue.
    b. Inventory.   **d.** Accounts Receivable.

Q1-42. Revenues are
    a. decreases in liabilities resulting from paying off loans.
    b. increases in retained earnings resulting from selling products or performing services.
    c. increases in paid-in capital resulting from the owners investing in the business.
    d. all of the above.

Q1-43. The financial statement that reports revenues and expenses is called the
    a. statement of retained earnings.   **c.** statement of cash flows.
    b. balance sheet.   **d.** income statement.

Q1-44. Another name for the balance sheet is the
    a. statement of operations.   **c.** statement of profit and loss.
    b. statement of financial position.   **d.** statement of earnings.

Q1-45. Morton Corporation began the year with cash of $140,000 and land that cost $24,800. During the year Morton earned service revenue of $285,000 and had the following expenses: salaries, $209,000; rent, $86,000; and utilities, $27,000. At year-end, Morton's cash balance was down to $79,000. How much net income (or net loss) did Morton experience for the year?
    a. ($10,000)   **c.** ($37,000)
    b. $76,000   **d.** ($98,000)

Q1-46. Williams Instruments had retained earnings of $350,000 at December 31, 2013. Net income for 2014 totaled $183,750, and dividends declared for 2014 were $78,750. How much retained earnings should Williams report at December 31, 2014?
    a. $455,000   **c.** $10,000
    b. $533,750   **d.** $35,000

Q1-47. Net income appears on which financial statement(s)?
    a. Balance sheet   **c.** Income statement
    b. Statement of retained earnings   **d.** Both b and c

Q1-48. Cash paid to purchase a building appears on the statement of cash flows among the
    a. operating activities.   **c.** investing activities.
    b. stockholders' equity.   **d.** financing activities.

Q1-49. The stockholders' equity of Kozlozsky Company at the beginning and end of 2014 totaled $126,000 and $138,000, respectively. Assets at the beginning of 2014 were $150,000. If the liabilities of Kozlozsky Company increased by $70,000 in 2014, how much were total assets at the end of 2014? Use the accounting equation.

a. $232,000

b. $220,000

c. $68,000

d. $218,000

Q1-50. Stockman Company had the following on the dates indicated:

	12/31/14	12/31/13
Total assets	$ 570,000	$ 350,000
Total liabilities	229,000	126,000

Stockman had no stock transactions in 2014; thus, the change in stockholders' equity for 2014 was due to net income and dividends. If dividends were $56,000, how much was Stockman's net income for 2014? Use the accounting equation and the statement of retained earnings.

a. $61,000

b. $173,000

c. $117,000

d. $237,000

Problems

All of the following problems can be found within MyAccountingLab, an online homework and practice environment. Your instructor may ask you to complete these problems using **MyAccountingLab**.

MyAccountingLab

Group A

P1-51A. *(Learning Objectives 3, 4: Apply the accounting equation; evaluate business operations)* Compute the missing amount (?) for each company—amounts in millions.

	Diamond Co.	Hagar, Inc.	Lowell Corp.
Beginning			
Assets	$101	$ 54	$?
Liabilities	63	22	4
Common stock	6	5	3
Retained earnings	?	27	6
Ending			
Assets	$?	$ 85	$16
Liabilities	65	32	?
Common stock	6	?	4
Retained earnings	37	?	?
Income statement			
Revenues	$340	?	$21
Expenses	331	156	?
Net income	?	?	?
Statement of retained earnings			
Beginning RE	$ 32	$ 27	$ 6
+ Net income	?	14	3
− Dividends declared	(4)	(6)	(0)
= Ending RE	$ 37	$ 35	$ 9

At the end of the year, which company has the
- highest net income?
- highest percent of net income to revenues?

P1-52A. *(Learning Objectives 1, 3, 4, 5: Explain accounting language; apply the accounting equation; evaluate business operations; construct a balance sheet)* The manager of Philly Automotive, Inc., prepared the company's balance sheet as of June 30, 2014, while the accountant was ill. The balance sheet contains numerous errors. In particular, the manager knew that the balance sheet should balance, so he plugged in the stockholders' equity amount needed to achieve this balance. The stockholders' equity amount is *not* correct. All other amounts are accurate.

	A	B	C	D
1	Philly Automotive, Inc. Balance Sheet June 30, 2014			
2	Assets		Liabilities	
3	Cash	$ 44,100	Notes receivable	$ 33,400
4	Equipment	78,300	Interest expense	5,300
5	Accounts payable	18,800	Office supplies	1,700
6	Utilities expense	3,600	Accounts receivable	5,800
7	Advertising expense	2,500	Note payable	122,400
8	Land	184,700	Total	168,600
9	Salary expense	35,900	**Stockholders' Equity**	
10			Stockholders' equity	199,300
11	Total assets	$ 367,900	Total liabilities	$ 367,900
12				

Requirements

1. Prepare the correct balance sheet and date it properly. Compute total assets, total liabilities, and stockholders' equity.
2. Is Philly Automotive actually in better (or worse) financial position than the erroneous balance sheet reports? Give the reason for your answer.
3. Identify the accounts listed on the incorrect balance sheet that should not be reported on the balance sheet. State why you excluded them from the correct balance sheet you prepared for Requirement 1. On which financial statement should these accounts appear?

P1-53A. *(Learning Objectives 2, 4, 5: Apply underlying accounting concepts; evaluate business operations; construct a balance sheet)* Jose Alvarado is a realtor. He organized the business as a corporation on April 16, 2015. The business received $60,000 cash from Alvarado and issued common stock. Consider the following facts as of April 30, 2015:

    a. Alvarado has $18,000 in his personal bank account and $43,000 in the business bank account.

    b. Alvarado owes $7,500 on a personal charge account with Sears.

    c. Alvarado acquired business furniture for $19,800 on April 24. Of this amount, the business owes $15,000 on accounts payable at April 30.

    d. Office supplies on hand at the real estate office total $2,000.

    e. Alvarado's business owes $128,000 on a note payable for some land acquired for a total price of $150,000.

    f. Alvarado's business spent $16,000 for a USA Realty franchise, which entitles him to represent himself as an agent. USA Realty is a national affiliation of independent real estate agents. This franchise is a business asset.

    g. Alvarado owes $197,000 on a personal mortgage on his personal residence, which he acquired in 2009 for a total price of $361,000.

Requirements

1. Prepare the balance sheet of the real estate business of Jose Alvarado Realtor, Inc., at April 30, 2015.
2. Does it appear that the realty business can pay its debts? How can you tell?
3. Identify the personal items given in the preceding facts that should not be reported on the balance sheet of the business.

P1-54A. *(Learning Objectives 4, 5: Construct and analyze an income statement, a statement of retained earnings, and a balance sheet; evaluate business operations)* The assets and liabilities of Cameron Services, Inc., as of December 31, 2014, and revenues and expenses for the year ended on that date follow:

Equipment............................	$112,000	Land.....................................	$ 26,200
Interest expense....................	10,800	Note payable......................	99,300
Interest payable...................	3,100	Property tax expense..........	7,700
Accounts payable................	28,900	Rent expense......................	41,600
Salary expense.....................	108,700	Accounts receivable............	84,800
Building...............................	401,000	Service revenue..................	457,600
Cash....................................	46,800	Supplies..............................	6,100
Common stock....................	5,500	Utilities expense	8,500

Beginning retained earnings was $364,800, and dividends declared totaled $105,000 for the year.

Requirements

1. Prepare the income statement of Cameron Services, Inc., for the year ended December 31, 2014.
2. Prepare the company's statement of retained earnings for the year.
3. Prepare the company's balance sheet at December 31, 2014.
4. Analyze Cameron Services, Inc., by answering these questions:
   a. Was Cameron Services profitable during 2014? By how much?
   b. Did retained earnings increase or decrease? By how much?
   c. Which is greater, total liabilities or total stockholders' equity? Who owns more of Cameron Services' assets, creditors of the company or the Cameron Services' stockholders?

P1-55A. *(Learning Objectives 4, 5: Construct a statement of cash flows; evaluate business opera-tions)* The following data come from the financial statements of Mitchell Company for the year ended March 31, 2015 (in millions):

Purchases of property,		Other investing cash	
plant, and equipment for cash....	$ 2,640	payments..	$ 120
Net income......................................	2,287	Accounts receivable..........................	600
Adjustments to reconcile net		Payment of dividends	199
income to net cash provided		Common stock.................................	3,630
by operating activities	1,778	Issuance of common stock...............	154
Revenues..	44,400	Cash proceeds on sale of	
Cash, beginning of year.................	203	property, plant, and equipment.....	26
end of year	1,489	Retained earnings.............................	9,675
Cost of goods sold.........................	28,162		

Requirements

1. Prepare a cash flow statement for the year ended March 31, 2015. Not all items given appear on the cash flow statement.
2. What activities provided the largest source of cash? Is this a sign of financial strength or weakness?

P1-56A. *(Learning Objective 5: Construct financial statements)* Summarized versions of Heartstring Corporation's financial statements are given for two recent years.

	A	B	C	D
		A	B	C	D
1				
2		2015	2014	
3	**Income Statement**	**(in Thousands)**		
4	Revenues	$ k	$ 28,300	
5	Cost of goods sold	18,090	a	
6	Other expenses	1,210	3,590	
7	Income before income taxes	4,580	4,760	
8	Income taxes (35%)	l	1,666	
9	Net income	$ m	$ b	
10	**Statement of Retained Earnings**			
11	Beginning balance	$ n	$ 6,907	
12	Net income	o	c	
13	Dividends declared	(94)	(140)	
14	Ending balance	$ p	$ d	
15	**Balance Sheet**			
16	**Assets**			
17	Cash	$ q	$ e	
18	Property, plant, and equipment	14,870	13,760	
19	Other assets	r	9,541	
20	Total assets	$ s	$ 27,806	
21	**Liabilities**			
22	Current liabilities	$ t	$ 10,590	
23	Long-term debt	7,100	6,420	
24	Other liabilities	110	255	
25	Total liabilities	$ 16,905	$ f	
26	**Stockholders' equity:**			
27	Common stock	$ 500	$ 500	
28	Retained earnings	u	g	
29	Other stockholders' equity	90	180	
30	Total stockholders' equity	v	10,541	
31	Total liabilities and stockholders' equity	$ w	$ h	
32	**Cash Flow Statement**			
33	Net cash provided by operating activities	$ x	$ 3,050	
34	Net cash used in investing activities	(200)	(325)	
35	Net cash used in financing activities	(560)	(500)	
36	Increase (decrease) in cash	(15)	i	
37	Cash at beginning of year	y	2,280	
38	Cash at end of year	$ z	$ j	
39				

Requirement

1. Complete Heartstring Corporation's financial statements by determining the missing amounts denoted by the letters.

Group B

P1-57B. *(Learning Objectives 3, 4: Apply the accounting equation; evaluate business operations)*
Compute the missing amount (?) for each company—amounts in millions.

	Kenley Corp.	Verde Co.	Thompson, Inc.
Beginning			
Assets.............................	$ 87	$52	$?
Liabilities	59	24	2
Common stock...................	4	3	12
Retained earnings..............	?	25	14
Ending			
Assets.............................	$?	$60	$ 44
Liabilities	50	17	?
Common stock...................	4	?	12
Retained earnings..............	36	?	?
Income statement			
Revenues..........................	$228	$?	$ 29
Expenses	214	156	?
Net income........................	?	?	?
Statement of retained earnings			
Beginning RE	$ 24	$25	$ 14
+ Net income......................	?	18	13
− Dividends declared............	(2)	(3)	(5)
= Ending RE........................	$ 36	$40	$ 22

Which company has the
- highest net income?
- highest percent of net income to revenues?

P1-58B. *(Learning Objectives 1, 3, 4, 5: Explain accounting language; apply the accounting equation; evaluate business operations; construct a balance sheet)* The manager of Fast Break Sports, Inc., prepared the company's balance sheet as of March 31, 2014, while the accountant was ill. The balance sheet contains numerous errors. In particular, the manager knew that the balance sheet should balance, so he plugged in the stockholders' equity amount needed to achieve this balance. The stockholders' equity amount is *not* correct. All other amounts are accurate.

	A1			
	A	**B**	**C**	**D**
1	Fast Break Sports, Inc. Balance Sheet March 31, 2014			
2	**Assets**		**Liabilities**	
3	Cash	$ 20,500	Notes receivable	$ 16,000
4	Equipment	47,000	Interest expense	3,100
5	Accounts payable	14,500	Office supplies	1,600
6	Utilities expense	2,000	Accounts receivable	2,700
7	Advertising expense	900	Note payable	49,000
8	Land	33,000	Total	72,400
9	Salary expense	3,800	**Stockholders' Equity**	
10			Stockholders' equity	99,300
11	Total assets	$ 171,700	Total liabilities	$ 171,700
12				

Requirements

1. Prepare the correct balance sheet and date it properly. Compute total assets, total liabilities, and stockholders' equity.
2. Is Fast Break Sports, Inc. in better (or worse) financial position than the erroneous balance sheet reports? Give the reason for your answer.
3. Identify the accounts that should *not* be reported on the balance sheet. State why you excluded them from the correct balance sheet you prepared for Requirement 1. On which financial statement should these accounts appear?

P1-59B. *(Learning Objectives 2, 4, 5: Apply underlying accounting concepts; evaluate business operations; construct a balance sheet)* Nancy Boyd is a realtor. She organized her business as a corporation on September 16, 2015. The business received $80,000 from Boyd and issued common stock. Consider these facts as of September 30, 2015.

    a. Boyd has $22,000 in her personal bank account and $56,000 in the business bank account.
    b. Boyd owes $2,000 on a personal charge account with Ann Taylor Clothing Stores.
    c. Boyd acquired business furniture for $50,000 on September 25. Of this amount, the business owes $41,000 on accounts payable at September 30.
    d. Office supplies on hand at the real estate office total $3,000.
    e. Boyd's business owes $86,000 on a note payable for some land acquired for a total price of $117,000.
    f. Boyd's business spent $25,000 for a Nationwide Realty franchise, which entitles her to represent herself as an agent. Nationwide Realty is a national affiliation of independent real estate agents. This franchise is a business asset.
    g. Boyd owes $124,000 on a personal mortgage on her personal residence, which she acquired in 2009 for a total price of $375,000.

Requirements

1. Prepare the balance sheet of the real estate business of Nancy Boyd Realtor, Inc., at September 30, 2015.
2. Does it appear that the realty business can pay its debts? How can you tell?
3. Identify the personal items given in the preceding facts that should not be reported on the balance sheet of the business.

P1-60B. *(Learning Objectives 4, 5: Construct and analyze an income statement, a statement of retained earnings, and a balance sheet; evaluate business operations)* The assets and liabilities of Weston, Inc., as of December 31, 2014, and revenues and expenses for the year ended on that date follow:

Equipment........................	$ 37,100	Land.................................	$ 68,000	
Interest expense..................	2,900	Note payable.....................	54,000	
Interest payable..................	1,200	Property tax expense..........	2,100	
Accounts payable	9,000	Rent expense	17,000	
Salary expense...................	30,800	Accounts receivable............	25,000	
Building............................	123,000	Service revenue..................	161,000	
Cash.................................	17,000	Supplies............................	2,300	
Common stock...................	27,100	Utilities expense	8,700	

Beginning retained earnings was $109,600, and dividends declared totaled $28,000 for the year.

Requirements

1. Prepare the income statement of Weston, Inc., for the year ended December 31, 2014.
2. Prepare the company's statement of retained earnings for the year.
3. Prepare the company's balance sheet at December 31, 2014.
4. Analyze Weston, Inc., by answering these questions:
   a. Was Weston profitable during 2014? By how much?
   b. Did retained earnings increase or decrease? By how much?
   c. Which is greater, total liabilities or total stockholders' equity? Who owns more of Weston's assets, creditors of the company or Weston's stockholders?

P1-61B. *(Learning Objectives 4,5: Construct a statement of cash flows; evaluate business operations)* The following data come from the financial statements of Fun Gun Sales Company for the year ended May 31, 2015 (in millions):

Purchases of property, plant, and equipment for cash....	$ 5,305	Other investing cash payments...........................	$ 155
Net income...........................	4,050	Accounts receivable...............	900
Adjustments to reconcile net income to net cash provided by operating activities	2,860	Payment of dividends	145
		Common stock......................	4,810
		Issuance of common stock......	1,180
Revenues..............................	59,000	Cash proceeds on sale of property, plant, and	
Cash, beginning of year........	230		
end of year	2,880	equipment	165
Cost of goods sold...............	37,600	Retained earnings..................	12,980

Requirements

1. Prepare a cash flow statement for the year ended May 31, 2015. Not all the items given appear on the cash flow statement.
2. Which activities provided the largest source of cash? Is this a sign of financial strength or weakness?

P1-62B. *(Learning Objective 5: Construct financial statements)* Summarized versions of Kelley Corporation's financial statements follow for two recent years:

	A1	⬍			
	A		**B**	**C**	**D**
1					
2			2015	2014	
3	**Income Statement**		(in Thousands)		
4	Revenues		$ k	$ 14,600	
5	Cost of goods sold		8,050	a	
6	Other expenses		1,230	1,180	
7	Income before income taxes		2,590	2,870	
8	Income taxes (35%)		l	1,005	
9	Net income		$ m	$ b	
10	**Statement of Retained Earnings**				
11	Beginning balance		$ n	$ 2,690	
12	Net income		o	c	
13	Dividends declared		(96)	(70)	
14	Ending balance		$ p	$ d	
15	**Balance Sheet**				
16	**Assets**				
17	Cash		$ q	$ e	
18	Property, plant, and equipment		10,500	9,750	
19	Other assets		r	5,381	
20	Total assets		$ s	$ 16,261	
21	**Liabilities**				
22	Current liabilities		$ t	$ 4,640	
23	Long-term debt		5,400	6,691	
24	Other liabilities		90	110	
25	Total liabilities		$ 10,761	$ f	
26	**Stockholders' equity:**				
27	Common stock		$ 325	$ 225	
28	Retained earnings		u	g	
29	Other stockholders' equity		190	110	
30	Total stockholders' equity		v	4,820	
31	Total liabilities and stockholders' equity		$ w	$ h	
32	**Cash Flow Statement**				
33	Net cash provided by operating activities		$ x	$ 1,050	
34	Net cash used in investing activities		(230)	(350)	
35	Net cash used in financing activities		(570)	(550)	
36	Increase (decrease) in cash		(60)	i	
37	Cash at beginning of year		y	980	
38	Cash at end of year		$ z	$ j	
39					

Requirement

1. Complete Kelley Corporation's financial statements by determining the missing amounts denoted by the letters.

APPLY YOUR KNOWLEDGE

Decision Cases

Case 1. (*Learning Objectives 1, 4: Explain accounting language; evaluate business operations through financial statements*) Two businesses, Brown Bag Corp. and April Sales Co., have sought business loans from you. To decide whether to make the loans, you have requested their balance sheets.

	A	B	C	D
	A1			
	A	B	C	D
1	**Brown Bag Corp.** **Balance Sheet** **August 31, 2015**			
2	**Assets**		**Liabilities**	
3	Cash	$ 5,000	Accounts payable	$ 50,000
4	Accounts receivable	10,000	Note payable	80,000
5	Land	75,000	Total liabilities	130,000
6	Furniture	15,000	**Stockholders' Equity**	
7	Equipment	45,000	Stockholders' equity	20,000
8			Total liabilities and	
9	Total assets	$ 150,000	stockholders' equity	$ 150,000
10				

	A	B	C	D
	A1			
	A	B	C	D
1	**April Sales Co.** **Balance Sheet** **August 31, 2015**			
2	**Assets**		**Liabilities**	
3	Cash	$ 5,000	Accounts payable	$ 6,000
4	Accounts receivable	10,000	Note payable	9,000
5	Merchandise inventory	15,000	Total liabilities	15,000
6	Building	35,000	**Stockholders' Equity**	
7			Stockholders' equity	50,000
8			Total liabilities and	
9	Total assets	$ 65,000	stockholders' equity	$ 65,000
10				

Requirement

1. Using only these balance sheets, to which entity would you be more comfortable lending money? Explain fully, citing specific items and amounts from the respective balance sheets. (Challenge)

Case 2. *(Learning Objectives 4, 5: Correct errors; construct financial statements; evaluate business operations through financial statements)* A year out of college, you have $10,000 to invest. A friend has started Hunters Unlimited, Inc., and he asks you to invest in his company. You obtain the company's financial statements, which are summarized at the end of the first year as follows:

A1	⬍		
	A	**B**	**C**
1	Hunters Unlimited, Inc. Income Statement Year Ended December 31, 2014		
2	Revenues		$ 100,000
3	Expenses		80,000
4	Net Income		$ 20,000
5			

A1	⬍			
	A	**B**	**C**	**D**
1	Hunters Unlimited, Inc. Balance Sheet December 31, 2014			
2	Cash	$ 6,000	Liabilities	$ 60,000
3	Other assets	100,000	Stockholders' equity	46,000
4	Total assets	$ 106,000	Total liabilities and stockholders' equity	$ 106,000
5				

Visits with your friend turn up the following facts:

    a. Hunters Unlimited delivered $140,000 of services to customers during 2014 and collected $100,000 from customers for those services.

    b. Hunters recorded a $50,000 cash payment for software as an asset. This cost should have been an expense.

    c. To get the business started, your friend borrowed $10,000 from his parents at the end of 2013. The proceeds of the loan were used to pay salaries for the first month of 2014. Since the loan was from his parents, your friend did not reflect the loan or the salaries in the accounting records.

Requirements

    1. Prepare corrected financial statements.

    2. Use your corrected statements to evaluate Hunters Unlimited's results of operations and financial position. (Challenge)

    3. Will you invest in Hunters Unlimited? Give your reason. (Challenge)

Ethical Issue

(Learning Objective 6: Evaluate ethical decisions) You are studying frantically for an accounting exam tomorrow. You are having difficulty in this course, and the grade you make on this exam can make the difference between receiving a final grade of B or C. If you receive a C, it will lower your grade point average to the point that you could lose your academic scholarship. An hour ago, a friend, also enrolled in the course but in a different section under the same professor, called you with some unexpected news. In her sorority test files, she has just found a copy of an old exam from the previous year. In looking at the exam, it appears to contain questions that come right from the class notes you have taken, even the very same numbers. She offers to make a copy for you and bring it over.

You glance at your course syllabus and find the following: "You are expected to do your own work in this class. Although you may study with others, giving, receiving, or obtaining information pertaining to an examination is considered an act of academic dishonesty, unless such action is authorized by the instructor giving the examination. Also, divulging the contents of an essay or objective examination designated by the instructor as an examination is considered an act of academic dishonesty. Academic dishonesty is considered a violation of the student honor code and will subject the student to disciplinary procedures, which can include suspension from the university." Although you have heard a rumor that fraternities and sororities have cleared their exam files with professors, you are not sure.

Requirements

1. What is the ethical issue in this situation?
2. Who are the stakeholders? What are the possible consequences to each?
3. Analyze the alternatives from the following standpoints: (a) economic, (b) legal, and (c) ethical.
4. What would you do? How would you justify your decision? How would your decision make you feel afterward?
5. How is this similar to a business situation?

Focus on Financials | Amazon.com, Inc.

(Learning Objectives 3, 4: Apply the accounting equation; evaluate business operations) This and similar cases in succeeding chapters are based on the consolidated financial statements of **Amazon.com, Inc.** As you work with Amazon.com, Inc., throughout this course, you will develop the ability to use the financial statements of actual companies.

Requirements

Refer to the Amazon.com, Inc., consolidated financial statements in Appendix A at the end of the book.

1. Go on the Internet and do some research on Amazon.com, Inc., and its industry. Use one or more popular websites like http://finance.yahoo.com or http://www.google.com/finance. Write a paragraph (about 100 words) that describes the industry, some current developments, and a projection for future growth.
2. Read Part I, Item 1 (Business) of Amazon.com, Inc.'s annual report. What do you learn here and why is it important?
3. Name at least one of Amazon.com, Inc.'s competitors. Why is this information important in evaluating Amazon.com, Inc.'s financial performance?
4. Suppose you own stock in Amazon.com, Inc. If you could pick one item on the company's Consolidated Statements of Operations to increase year after year, what would it be? Why is this item so important? Did this item increase or decrease during fiscal 2012? Is this good news or bad news for the company?
5. What was Amazon.com, Inc.'s largest expense each year? In your own words, explain the meaning of this item. Give specific examples of items that make up this expense. The chapter gives another title for this expense. What is it?
6. Use the Consolidated Balance Sheets of Amazon.com, Inc., in Appendix A to answer these questions: At the end of fiscal 2012, how much in total resources did Amazon.com, Inc.,

have to work with? How much did the company owe? How much of its assets did the company's stockholders actually own? Use these amounts to write Amazon.com, Inc.'s accounting equation at December 31, 2012.

7. How much cash and cash equivalents did Amazon.com, Inc., have at the beginning of the most recent year? How much cash and cash equivalents did Amazon.com have at the end of the year?

Focus on Analysis | Yum! Brands, Inc.

(Learning Objectives 3, 4: Apply the accounting equation; evaluate business operations) This and similar cases in each chapter are based on the consolidated financial statements of **Yum! Brands, Inc.**, given in Appendix B at the end of this book. As you work with Yum! Brands, Inc., you will develop the ability to analyze the financial statements of actual companies.

Requirements

1. Go on the Internet and do some research on Yum! Brands, Inc., and its industry. Use one or more popular websites like http://finance.yahoo.com or http://www.google.com/finance. Write a paragraph (about 100 words) that describes the industry, some current developments, and a projection for where the industry is headed.
2. Read Note 1—(Description of Business) of Yum! Brands, Inc.'s annual report. What do you learn here and why is it important?
3. Name two of Yum! Brands, Inc.'s competitors. Why is this information important in evaluating Yum! Brands, Inc.'s financial performance?
4. Write Yum! Brands, Inc.'s accounting equation at December 31, 2012 (express all items in millions and round to the nearest $1 million). Does Yum! Brands, Inc.'s financial condition look strong or weak? How can you tell?
5. What was the result of Yum! Brands, Inc.'s operations during 2012? Identify both the name and the dollar amount of the result of operations for 2012. Does an increase (or decrease) signal good news or bad news for the company and its stockholders?
6. Examine retained earnings in the Consolidated Statements of Shareholders' Equity. What caused retained earnings to increase during 2012?
7. Which statement reports cash and cash equivalents as part of Yum! Brands, Inc.'s financial position? Which statement tells *why* cash and cash equivalents increased (or decreased) during the year? Which activities caused Yum! Brands, Inc.'s cash and cash equivalents to change during 2012, and how much did each activity provide or use?

Group Projects

Project 1. As instructed by your professor, obtain the annual report of a well-known company.

Requirements

1. Take the role of a loan committee of Bank of America, a large banking company headquartered in Charlotte, North Carolina. Assume a company has requested a loan from Bank of America. Analyze the company's financial statements and any other information you need to reach a decision regarding the largest amount of money you would be willing to lend. Go as deeply into the analysis and the related decision as you can. Specify the following:
   a. The length of the loan period—that is, over what period will you allow the company to pay you back?
   b. The interest rate you will charge on the loan. Will you charge the prevailing interest rate, a lower rate, or a higher rate? Why?
   c. Any restrictions you will impose on the borrower as a condition for making the loan.

Note: The long-term debt note to the financial statements gives details of the company's existing liabilities.

2. Write your group decision in a report addressed to the bank's board of directors. Limit your report to two double-spaced word-processed pages.
3. If your professor directs, present your decision and your analysis to the class. Limit your presentation to 10 to 15 minutes.

Project 2. You are the owner of a company that is about to "go public"—that is, issue its stock to outside investors. You wish to make your company look as attractive as possible to raise $1 million of cash to expand the business. At the same time, you want to give potential investors a realistic picture of your company.

Requirements

1. Design a booklet to portray your company in a way that will enable outsiders to reach an informed decision as to whether to buy some of your stock. The booklet should include the following:
   a. Name and location of your company.
   b. Nature of the company's business (be as detailed as possible).
   c. How you plan to spend the money you raise.
   d. The company's comparative income statement, statement of retained earnings, balance sheet, and statement of cash flows for two years: the current year and the preceding year. Make the data as realistic as possible with the intent of receiving $1 million.
2. Word-process your booklet, not to exceed five pages.
3. If directed by your professor, make a copy for each member of your class. Distribute copies to the class and present your case with the intent of interesting your classmates in investing in the company. Limit your presentation to 10 to 15 minutes.

MyAccountingLab

> **For online homework, exercises, and problems that provide you with immediate feedback, please visit www.myaccountinglab.com.**

Quick Check Answers

1. *a*

2. *d*

3. *c* [This is not the typical way the accounting equation is expressed (Assets = Liabilities + Owners' equity), but it may be rearranged this way].

4. *b*

5. *d*

6. *a*

7. *b* ($280,000 − $145,000 − $6,000 = $129,000)

8. *b* ($280,000 − $145,000 = $135,000)

9. *a* [Total assets = $123,000 ($8,000 + $47,000 + $28,000 + $40,000). Liabilities = $31,000]

10. *d*

11. *b* ($98,000 + Net income $25,000 − Dividends $7,000 = $116,000)

12. *a*

	Assets	=	Liabilities	+	Equity
Beginning	$175,000	=	$97,000	+	$78,000
Increase	$42,000	=	$12,000	+	$30,000
Ending	$217,000*	=	$109,000*	+	$108,000*

Must solve for these amounts

13. *c*

14. *a*

2 Transaction Analysis

> **SPOTLIGHT: Whole Foods Market, Inc.**

Do you ever get a craving for a big juicy apple, orange or banana? Do you enjoy a great steak, grilled chicken breast, or fresh salmon fillet every now and then, accompanied by a baked potato and fresh garden salad? How about the smell of fresh bread baking? Getting hungry? Then you might head for your friendly neighborhood Whole Foods Market, where you'll find a wonderland of organically grown delights! Besides being good to eat, Whole Foods products are designed to be good for you, promoting a healthy lifestyle.

Whole Foods Market, Inc., is the world's leading retailer of natural and organic foods and America's first national "Certified Organic Grocer." Based in Austin, Texas, the company launched over 30 years ago, before "organic" was a household word, and it has led the charge to nation-wide acceptance of organically grown foods. It completed its initial public offering (IPO) in 1992. The mission of the company is to promote the vitality and well-being of all individuals by sup-plying the highest quality, most wholesome foods available. The company's mission is devoted to the promotion of organically grown foods, healthy eating, and sustainability of the world's ecosystem. You'll see Whole Foods Market stores in all of the larger cities, usually in affluent neighborhoods. How does Whole Foods Market, Inc., determine its revenues, expenses, and net income? Like all other companies, Whole Foods Market, Inc., has a comprehensive account-ing system. Whole Foods Market, Inc.'s consolidated statement of operations (income state-ment) is given at the start of this chapter. The statement of operations shows that during fiscal year 2012, Whole Foods Market, Inc., made almost $11.7 billion of sales and earned net income of $465.6 million. Where did those figures come from? ●

Jeff Greenberg/Alamy

A1				
	A		B	C
1	**Whole Foods Market, Inc.** **Consolidated Statements of Operations (Adapted)**			
2	(In Thousands)		**12 Months Ended**	
3			Sep. 30, 2012	Sep. 25, 2011
4				
5	Sales		$ 11,698,828	$ 10,107,787
6	Cost of goods sold and occupancy costs		7,543,054	6,571,238
7	Gross profit		4,155,774	3,536,549
8	Direct store expenses		2,983,419	2,628,811
9	General and administrative expenses		372,065	310,920
10	Pre-opening expenses		46,899	40,852
11	Relocation, store closure, and lease termination costs		9,885	8,346
12	Operating income		743,506	547,620
13	Interest expense		(354)	(3,882)
14	Investment and other income		8,892	7,974
15	Income before income taxes		752,044	551,712
16	Provision for income taxes		286,471	209,100
17	Net income		$ 465,573	$ 342,612
18				

Chapter 1 introduced the financial statements. Chapter 2 will show you how companies record the transactions that eventually become part of the financial statements.

Learning Objectives

1. Explain what a transaction is

2. Define "account," and **list** and **differentiate** between different types of accounts

3. Show the impact of business transactions on the accounting equation

4. Analyze the impact of business transactions on accounts

5. Record (journalize and post) transactions in the books

6. Construct and use a trial balance

MyAccountingLab

>> Try It in Excel

You can access the most current annual report of Whole Foods Market, Inc., in Excel format at **www.sec.gov**. Using the "filings" link on the toolbar at the top of the home page, select "company filings search." This will take you to the "EDGAR Company filings" page. Type "Whole Foods" in the company name box, and select "Search." This will produce the "EDGAR Search Results" page showing the company name. Click on the "CIK" link beside the company name. This will pull up all of the reports the company has filed with the SEC. Under the "filing type" box, type "10-K," and click the search box. Form 10-K is the SEC form for the company's latest annual report. Find the year that you wish to view. Click on the "Interactive Data" box, which takes you to the "View Filing Data" page. Find and click on the "View Excel Document" link at the top of the page. You may choose to either open or download the Excel files containing the company's most recent financial statements. ■

EXPLAIN WHAT A TRANSACTION IS

Business activity is all about transactions. A **transaction** is any event that has a financial impact on the business and can be measured reliably. For example, Whole Foods Market, Inc., purchases fresh produce, meat, and natural nutritional supplements. Whole Foods Market, Inc., sells products, borrows money, and repays the loan—three separate transactions.

But not all events qualify as transactions. Whole Foods Market, Inc., may be featured in *Progressive Grocer* or a prospective customer may read an ad in the local newspaper or other media. These events may create awareness and, ultimately, new business for Whole Foods Market, Inc. But no transaction occurs until someone actually buys Whole Foods Market products or otherwise engages in an exchange with them. Transactions provide objective information about the financial impact of an exchange on an entity:

- It gives something.
- It receives something in return.

In accounting we always record both sides of a transaction. We must be able to measure the financial impact of the event on the business before recording it as a transaction.

1 **Explain** what a transaction is

DEFINE "ACCOUNT," AND LIST AND DIFFERENTIATE BETWEEN DIFFERENT TYPES OF ACCOUNTS

As we saw in Chapter 1, the accounting equation expresses the basic relationship of accounting:

2 **Define** "account," and **list** and **differentiate** between different types of accounts

$$\text{Assets} = \text{Liabilities} + \text{Stockholders' (Owners') Equity}$$

For each asset, each liability, and each element of stockholders' equity, we use a record called the account. An **account** is the record of all the changes in a particular asset, liability, or stockholders' equity during a period. The account is the basic summary device of accounting. Before launching into transaction analysis, let's review the accounts used by a company such as Whole Foods Market, Inc.

Assets

Assets are economic resources that provide a future benefit for a business. Most firms use the following asset accounts:

Cash. Money and any medium of exchange including bank account balances, paper currency, coins, certificates of deposit, and checks.

Accounts Receivable. Whole Foods Market, Inc., like most other companies, sells its goods and services and receives a promise for future collection of cash. The Accounts Receivable account holds these amounts.

Notes Receivable. Whole Foods Market, Inc., may receive a note receivable from a customer, who signed the note promising to pay Whole Foods Market, Inc. A note receivable is similar to an account receivable, but a note receivable is more binding because the customer signed the note. Notes receivable usually specify an interest rate.

Inventory. Whole Foods Market, Inc.'s most important asset is its inventory—the organically grown foods that Whole Foods Market, Inc., sells to customers. Other titles for this account include *Merchandise* and *Merchandise Inventory*.

Prepaid Expenses. Whole Foods Market, Inc., pays certain expenses in advance, such as insurance and rent. A prepaid expense is an asset because the payment provides a *future* benefit for the business. Prepaid Rent, Prepaid Insurance, and Supplies are prepaid expenses.

Land. This account shows the cost of the land Whole Foods Market, Inc., uses in its operations.

Buildings. The costs of Whole Foods Market, Inc.'s office buildings, warehouses, and the like appear in the Buildings account.

Equipment, Furniture, and Fixtures. Whole Foods Market, Inc., has a separate asset account for each type of furniture, fixture, and equipment, for example, food display cases, heating and air conditioning, computers, and office furniture. These types of assets are depreciated over their estimated useful lives, and those with similar estimated lifespans are usually grouped together.

Liabilities

Recall that a *liability* is a debt. A payable is always a liability. The most common types of liabilities include:

Accounts Payable. The Accounts Payable account is the direct opposite of Accounts Receivable. Whole Foods Market, Inc.'s promise to pay a debt (perhaps arising from a credit purchase of inventory or from a utility bill) appears in the Accounts Payable account.

Notes Payable. A note payable is the opposite of a note receivable. The Notes Payable account includes the amounts Whole Foods Market, Inc., must *pay* because it signed notes promising to pay a future amount. Notes payable, like notes receivable, also bear interest.

Accrued Liabilities. An **accrued liability** is a liability for an expense you have not yet paid. Interest Payable and Salary Payable are accrued liability accounts for most companies. Income Tax Payable is another accrued liability.

Stockholders' (Owners') Equity

The owners' claims to the assets of a corporation are called *stockholders' equity, shareholders' equity,* or simply *owners' equity.* A corporation such as Whole Foods Market, Inc., uses Common Stock, Retained Earnings, and Dividends accounts to record the company's stockholders' equity. In a proprietorship, there is a single capital account. For a partnership, each partner has a separate owner's equity account.

Common Stock. The Common Stock account shows the owners' investment in the corporation. Whole Foods Market, Inc., receives cash and issues common stock to its stockholders. A company's common stock is its most basic element of equity. All corporations have common stock.

Retained Earnings. The Retained Earnings account shows the cumulative net income earned by Whole Foods Market, Inc., over the company's lifetime, minus its cumulative net losses and dividends.

Dividends. Dividends are optional; they are decided (declared) by the board of directors. After profitable operations, the board of directors of Whole Foods Market, Inc., may declare and pay a cash dividend. The corporation may keep a separate account titled *Dividends*, which indicates a decrease in Retained Earnings.

Revenues. The increase in stockholders' equity from delivering goods or services to customers is called *revenue.* The company uses as many revenue accounts as needed. Whole Foods Market, Inc., uses a Sales Revenue account for revenue earned by selling its products. A service-oriented business has a Service Revenue account for the revenue it earns by providing services to customers. A lawyer provides legal services for clients and also uses a Service Revenue account. A business that loans money to an outsider needs an Interest Revenue account. If the business rents a building to a tenant, the business needs a Rent Revenue account.

Expenses. The cost of operating a business is called an *expense.* Expenses *decrease* stockholders' equity, the opposite effect of revenues. A business needs a separate account for each type of expense, such as Cost of Goods Sold, Salary Expense, Rent Expense, Advertising Expense, Insurance Expense, Utilities Expense, and Income Tax Expense. Businesses strive to minimize expenses and thereby maximize net income.

> Stop & Think...

Name two things that **(1)** increase Whole Foods Market, Inc.'s stockholders' equity and **(2)** decrease Whole Foods Market, Inc.'s stockholders' equity.

Answer:

(1) Increases in stockholders' equity: Sale of stock and net income (revenue greater than expenses).

(2) Decreases in stockholders' equity: Dividends and net loss (expenses greater than revenue).

SHOW THE IMPACT OF BUSINESS TRANSACTIONS ON THE ACCOUNTING EQUATION

Example: Freddy's Auto Service, Inc.

To illustrate the accounting for transactions, let's return to Freddy's Auto Service, Inc. In Chapter 1's End-of-Chapter Problem, Freddy Kish opened Freddy's Auto Service, Inc., in April 2014.

We will consider 11 transactions and analyze each in terms of its effect on Freddy's Auto Service. We will begin by using the accounting equation to build the financial statements in spreadsheet format. In the second half of the chapter, we will record transactions using the journal and ledger of the business.

3 **Show** the impact of business transactions on the accounting equation

Try It in Excel

As you review the 11 transactions, build an Excel template. Use the accounting equation on page 55 as a model. Remember that each transaction has either an equal effect on both the left- and right-hand sides of the accounting equation, or an offsetting effect (both positive and negative) on the same side of the equation. Recreate the spreadsheet in Exhibit 2-1, Panel B (page 63), step by step, as you go along. In Excel, open a new blank spreadsheet.

Step 1 Format the worksheet. Label cell A2 "Trans." You will put transaction numbers corresponding to the transactions below in the cells in column A. Row 1 will contain the elements of the accounting equation. Enter "Assets" in cell D1. Enter an "=" sign in cell F1. Enter "Liabilities + Stockholders' equity" in cell G1. Enter "Type of SE (abbreviation for stockholders' equity) Transaction" in cell J1. Highlight cells B1 through E1 and click "merge and center" on the top toolbar. Highlight cells G1 through I1 and click "merge and center." Now you will have a spreadsheet organized around the elements of the accounting equation: "Assets = Liabilities + Stockholders' equity" and, for all transactions impacting stockholders' equity, you will be able to enter the type (capital stock, revenue, expense, or dividends). This will be important for later when you construct the financial statements (Exhibit 2-2, page 65).

Step 2 Continue formatting. In cells B2 through E2, enter the asset account titles that transactions 1–11 deal with. B2: Cash; C2: AR (an abbreviation for accounts receivable); D2: Supplies; E2: Land. In cells G2 through I2, enter the liability and stockholders' equity account titles that Freddy's Auto Service, Inc.'s transactions deal with. G2: AP (an abbreviation for accounts payable); H2: CStock (an abbreviation for common stock); and I2: RE (abbreviation for retained earnings; this is where all transactions impacting revenue, expenses, and dividends will go for now).

Step 3 In row 15, sum each column from B through E and G through I. For example, the formula in cell B15 should be "=sum(B3:B14)." In cell A15, enter "Bal." This will allow you to keep a running sum of the accounts in the balance sheet as you enter each transaction.

Step 4 In cell A16, enter "Totals." In cell C16, enter "=sum(B15:E15)." In cell H16, enter "=sum(G15:I15). You can use the short cut symbol "Σ" followed by highlighting the respective cells. Excel allows you to keep a running sum of the column totals on each side of the equation. You should find that the running sum of the column totals on the left-hand side of the equation always equals the running sum of the column totals on the right-hand side, so the accounting equation always stays in balance. As a final formatting step, highlight cells B3 through I16. Using the "number" tab on the toolbar at the top of the spreadsheet, select "Accounting" as for format with no $ sign, and select "decrease decimal" to zero places. Now you're ready to process the transactions. ■

Transaction 1. On April 1, Freddy Kish and a few friends invest $50,000 to open Freddy's Auto Service, Inc., and the business issues common stock to the stockholders. The effect of this transaction on the accounting equation of Freddy's Auto Service, Inc., is a receipt of cash and issuance of common stock:

Assets		Liabilities	+	Stockholders' Equity	Type of Stockholders' Equity Transaction
Cash	=			Common Stock	
(1) + 50,000				+ 50,000	Issued common stock

Every transaction's net amount on the left side of the equation must equal the net amount on the right side. The first transaction increases both the cash and the common stock of the business. If you're following along in Excel, enter 1 in cell A3 of the spreadsheet you are creating. Enter 50000 in cell B3 (under Cash) and 50000 in cell H3 (under CStock). To the right of the transaction in cell J3 write "Issued common stock" to show the reason for the increase in stockholders' equity. You don't have to enter commas; Excel will do that for you. Notice that the sum of Cash (cell B15) is now 50,000 and the sum of Common Stock (cell H15) is also 50,000. The total of accounts on the left side of the accounting equation is 50,000 (cell C16) and it equals the total of accounts on the right side of the accounting equation (cell H16).

Every transaction affects the financial statements of the business, and we can prepare financial statements after one, two, or any number of transactions. For example, Freddy's Auto Service, Inc., could create the company's balance sheet from our spreadsheet after its first transaction, shown here.

	A	B	C	D	E	F
1	**Freddy's Auto Service, Inc.** **Balance Sheet** **April 1, 2014**					
2	**Assets**			**Liabilities**		
3	Cash		$ 50,000	None		
4				**Stockholders' Equity**		
5				Common stock	$ 50,000	
6				Total stockholders' equity	50,000	
7				Total liabilities and		
8	Total assets		$ 50,000	stockholders' equity	$ 50,000	
9						

This balance sheet shows that the business holds cash of $50,000 and owes no liabilities. The company's equity (ownership) is denoted as *Common Stock* on the balance sheet. A bank would look favorably on this balance sheet because the business has $50,000 cash and no debt—a strong financial position.

As a practical matter, most entities report their financial statements at the end of the accounting period, and not after each transaction. But an accounting system based on a structure similar to our Excel spreadsheet can produce statements whenever managers need to know where the business stands.

Transaction 2. Freddy's purchases land for a new location and pays cash of $40,000. The effect of this transaction on the accounting equation is as follows:

	Assets			=	Liabilities + Stockholders' Equity	Type of Stockholders' Equity Transaction
	Cash	+	Land		Common Stock	
(1)	50,000				50,000	Issued common stock
(2)	− 40,000		+ 40,000		―――	
Bal	10,000		40,000		50,000	
		50,000			50,000	

The purchase increases one asset (Land) and decreases another asset (Cash) by the same amount. If you're following along in Excel, enter a 2 in cell A4. Enter −40000 in cell B4 and 40000 in cell E4. The spreadsheet automatically updates, showing that after the transaction is completed, Freddy's has cash of $10,000, land of $40,000, total assets of $50,000 and no liabilities. Stockholders' equity is unchanged at $50,000. Note that, as shown in cells C16 and H16, total assets must always equal total liabilities plus stockholders' equity.

Transaction 3. The business buys supplies on account, agreeing to pay $3,700 within 30 days. This transaction increases both the assets and the liabilities of the business. Its effect on the accounting equation follows:

	Assets					=	Liabilities	+	Stockholders' Equity
	Cash	+	Supplies	+	Land		Accounts Payable	+	Common Stock
Bal	10,000				40,000				50,000
(3)	―――		+ 3,700		―――		+ 3,700		―――
Bal	10,000		3,700		40,000		3,700		50,000
			53,700					53,700	

The new asset is Supplies, and the liability is an Account Payable. Freddy's signs no formal promissory note, so the liability is an account payable, not a note payable. If you're following along in Excel, enter 3 in cell A5, 3700 in cell D5 under the account "Supplies" and 3700 in cell G5 under "AP" (accounts payable). Notice that the spreadsheet now reflects 3 assets in row 15: cash with a balance of $10,000 (cell B15), supplies with a balance of $3,700 (cell D15), and land with a balance of $40,000 (cell E15), for total assets of $53,700 (cell C16). On the right-hand side of the accounting equation, Freddy's now has accounts payable (a liability) of $3,700 (cell G15) and common stock (cell H15) of $50,000, for a total of $53,700 (cell H16).

Transaction 4. Freddy's earns $7,000 of service revenue by providing services for customers. The business collects the cash. The effect on the accounting equation is an increase in the asset Cash and an increase in Retained Earnings, as follows:

	Assets					=	Liabilities	+	Stockholders' Equity			Type of Stockholders' Equity Transaction
	Cash	+	Supplies	+	Land		Accounts Payable	+	Common Stock	+	Retained Earnings	
Bal	10,000		3,700		40,000		3,700		50,000			
(4)	+ 7,000		―――		―――		―――		―――		+ 7,000	Service revenue
Bal	17,000		3,700		40,000		3,700		50,000		7,000	
			60,700						60,700			

In the Excel spreadsheet on line 6, we enter 7000 under Cash (cell B6) and 7000 under Retained Earnings (cell I6). In cell J6, we enter "Service revenue" to show where the $7,000 of increase in Retained Earnings came from. Our grand totals on the bottom of the spreadsheet now show $60,700 for total assets as well as $60,700 for total liabilities and stockholders' equity.

Transaction 5. Freddy's performs service on account, which means that Freddy's lets some customers pay later. Freddy's earns revenue but doesn't receive the cash immediately. In transaction 5, Freddy's repairs a fleet of UPS delivery trucks, and UPS promises to pay Freddy's $3,000 within one month. This promise is an account receivable—an asset—of Freddy's Auto Service. The transaction record is:

			Assets				Liabilities	+	Stockholders' Equity		Type of Stockholders' Equity Transaction
	Cash	+	Accounts Receivable	+ Supplies	+ Land		Accounts Payable	+	Common Stock +	Retained Earnings	
Bal	17,000			3,700	40,000	=	3,700		50,000	7,000	
(5)			+ 3,000							+ 3,000	Service revenue
Bal	17,000		3,000	3,700	40,000		3,700		50,000	10,000	
			63,700						63,700		

It's performing the service that earns the revenue—not collecting the cash. Therefore, Freddy's records revenue when it performs the service—regardless of whether Freddy's receives cash now or later. In your Excel spreadsheet, enter 3000 under Accounts Receivable on the left-hand side (cell C7) and 3000 under Retained Earnings on the right-hand side (cell I7). Also enter "Service revenue" in cell J7 to keep a record of the type of transaction (revenue) that affects stockholders' equity (SE).

Transaction 6. During the month, Freddy's Auto Service, Inc., pays $2,700 for the following expenses: rent, $1,100; employee salaries, $1,200; and utilities, $400. The effect on the accounting equation is:

			Assets				Liabilities	+	Stockholders' Equity		Type of Stockholders' Equity Transaction
	Cash	+	Accounts Receivable	+ Supplies	+ Land		Accounts Payable	+	Common Stock +	Retained Earnings	
Bal	17,000		3,000	3,700	40,000		3,700		50,000	10,000	
(6)	− 2,700					=				− 1,100	Rent expense
										− 1,200	Salary expense
										− 400	Utilities expense
Bal	14,300		3,000	3,700	40,000		3,700		50,000	7,300	
			61,000						61,000		

This transaction will take up lines 8, 9, and 10 of the Excel spreadsheet. Enter −2700 under Cash (cell B8); −1100 under Retained Earnings (cell I8); −1200 under Retained Earnings (cell I9); and −400 under Retained Earnings (cell I10). Enter the type of transaction (rent expense, salary expense, utilities expense) to account for the type of transaction impacting stockholders' equity (SE). These expenses decrease Freddy's Auto Service, Inc.'s Cash and Retained Earnings. List each expense separately to keep track of its amount and to facilitate the preparation of the income statement later.

Transaction 7. Freddy's pays $1,900 on account, which means to make a payment toward an account payable. In this transaction Freddy's pays the store from which it purchased supplies in transaction 3. The transaction decreases Cash (cell B11 on the Excel spreadsheet) and also decreases Accounts Payable (cell G11):

	Assets						Liabilities	+	Stockholders' Equity		
	Cash	+	Accounts Receivable	+	Supplies	+	Land		Accounts Payable	+	Common Stock	+	Retained Earnings
Bal	14,300		3,000		3,700		40,000	=	3,700		50,000		7,300
(7)	− 1,900								− 1,900				
Bal	12,400		3,000		3,700		40,000		1,800		50,000		7,300
			59,100								59,100		

Transaction 8. Freddy Kish, the major stockholder of Freddy's Auto Service, paid $30,000 out of his personal (not business) bank account to remodel his home. This event is a personal transaction of the Kish family. It is not recorded by the Freddy's Auto Service business. We focus solely on the business entity, not on its owners. This transaction illustrates the entity assumption from Chapter 1.

Transaction 9. In transaction 5, Freddy's performed services for UPS on account. The business now collects $1,000 from UPS. We say that Freddy's *collects the cash on account*, which means that Freddy's will record an increase in Cash and a decrease in Accounts Receivable. This is not service revenue because Freddy's already recorded the revenue in transaction 5. The effect of collecting cash on account is:

	Assets						Liabilities	+	Stockholders' Equity		
	Cash	+	Accounts Receivable	+	Supplies	+	Land		Accounts Payable	+	Common Stock	+	Retained Earnings
Bal	12,400		3,000		3,700		40,000	=	1,800		50,000		7,300
(9)	+ 1,000		− 1,000										
Bal	13,400		2,000		3,700		40,000		1,800		50,000		7,300
			59,100								59,100		

This transaction is entered on line 12 of the Excel spreadsheet as an increase in Cash (cell B12) and a decrease in AR (cell C12).

Transaction 10. Freddy's sells some land for $22,000, which is the same amount that Freddy's paid for the land. Freddy's receives $22,000 cash, and the effect on the accounting equation is:

	Assets							Liabilities	+	Stockholders' Equity		
	Cash	+	Accounts Receivable	+	Supplies	+	Land	Accounts Payable	+	Common Stock	+	Retained Earnings
Bal	13,400		2,000		3,700		40,000	1,800		50,000		7,300
(10)	+ 22,000						− 22,000					
Bal	35,400		2,000		3,700		18,000	1,800		50,000		7,300
			59,100							59,100		

Note that the company did not sell all its land; Freddy's still owns $18,000 worth of land. This transaction is entered in the Excel spreadsheet as an increase in Cash (cell B13) and a decrease in Land (cell E13).

Transaction 11. Freddy's Auto Service, Inc., declares a dividend and pays the stockholders $2,100 cash. The effect on the accounting equation is:

	Assets				Liabilities	+	Stockholders' Equity			Type of Stockholders' Equity Transaction
	Cash +	Receivable +	Supplies +	Land	Accounts Payable	+	Common Stock	+	Retained Earnings	
Bal	35,400	2,000	3,700	18,000	1,800		50,000		7,300	
(11)	− 2,100								− 2,100	Dividend
Bal	33,300	2,000	3,700	18,000	1,800		50,000		5,200	
		57,000					57,000			

The dividend decreases both Cash (cell B14) and the Retained Earnings (cell I14) of the business. *However, dividends are not an expense.* They are a separate type of reduction of stockholders' equity. Therefore, enter "Dividend" in cell J14. We should now have all of the transactions impacting stockholders' equity labeled properly, which will facilitate the preparation of the financial statements later.

Transactions and Financial Statements

Exhibit 2-1 summarizes the 11 preceding transactions. Panel A gives the details of the transactions, and Panel B shows the transaction analysis. If you prepared an Excel spreadsheet as you followed the discussion of the 11 transactions, it should look very similar to Panel B. As you study the exhibit, note that every transaction maintains the equality:

$$Assets = Liabilities + Stockholders' \ Equity$$

Exhibit 2-1 | Transaction Analysis: Freddy's Auto Service, Inc.

PANEL A—Transaction Details

(1) Received $50,000 cash and issued stock to the owners
(2) Paid $40,000 cash for land
(3) Bought $3,700 of supplies on account
(4) Received $7,000 cash from customers for service revenue earned
(5) Performed services for a customer on account, $3,000
(6) Paid cash expenses: rent, $1,100; employee salary, $1,200; utilities, $400

(7) Paid $1,900 on the account payable created in transaction 3
(8) Major stockholder paid personal funds to remodel home, *not* a transaction of the business
(9) Received $1,000 on account
(10) Sold land for cash at the land's cost of $22,000
(11) Declared and paid a dividend of $2,100 to the stockholders

PANEL B—Transaction Analysis

	A	B	C	D	E	F	G	H	I	J
				A1						
	A	B	C	D	E	F	G	H	I	J
1			Assets			=	Liabilities +	Stockholders' Equity		Type of SE transaction
2	Trans	Cash	AR	Supplies	Land		AP	C Stock	RE	
3	1	50,000						50,000		Issued common stock
4	2	(40,000)			40,000					
5	3			3,700			3,700			
6	4	7,000							7,000	Service revenue
7	5		3,000						3,000	Service revenue
8	6	(2,700)							(1,100)	Rent expense
9									(1,200)	Salary expense
10									(400)	Utilities expense
11	7	(1,900)					(1,900)			
12	9	1,000	(1,000)							
13	10	22,000			(22,000)					
14	11	(2,100)							(2,100)	Dividend
15	Bal	33,300	2,000	3,700	18,000		1,800	50,000	5,200	
16	Totals		57,000					57,000		
17										

Statement of Cash Flows Data (bracket spanning rows 3–15, columns A–B)

Income Statement Data (bracket spanning rows 6–10, column J)

Statement of Retained Earnings Data (bracket spanning rows 14, column J)

Balance Sheet Data (bracket below table)

Panel B of Exhibit 2-1 provides the data for Freddy's Auto Service, Inc.'s financial statements:

■ *Income statement* data appear as revenues and expenses under Retained Earnings. The revenues increase retained earnings; the expenses decrease retained earnings.

■ The *balance sheet* data are composed of the ending balances of the assets, liabilities, and stockholders' equities shown at the bottom of the exhibit. The accounting equation shows that total assets ($57,000) equal total liabilities plus stockholders' equity ($57,000).

■ The *statement of retained earnings* repeats net income (or net loss) from the income statement. Dividends are subtracted. Ending retained earnings is the final result.

■ Data for the *statement of cash flows* are aligned under the Cash account. Cash receipts increase cash, and cash payments decrease cash. *Note: We did not reproduce the statement of cash flows in Exhibit 2-2.*

Exhibit 2-2 shows the Freddy's Auto Service, Inc.'s income statement, statement of retained earnings, and balance sheet at the end of April, the company's first month of operations. Follow the flow of data to observe the following:

1. The income statement reports revenues, expenses, and either a net income or a net loss for the period. During April, Freddy's Auto Service, Inc., earned net income of $7,300. From the transaction analysis spreadsheet in Exhibit 2-1, Panel B, service revenue consists of the sum of cells I6 and I7 ($7,000 for cash and $3,000 on account). Expenses (salary $1,200 from cell I9, rent $1,100 from cell I8, and utilities $400 from cell I10) are listed separately in the income statement. The sum of these expenses is $2,700. Net income consists of the difference between service revenue and total expenses ($10,000 − $2,700 = $7,300). This is known as a "single-step" income statement. Compare Freddy's income statement with that of Whole Foods Market, Inc., at the beginning of the chapter. Freddy's income statement includes only two types of accounts: revenues and expenses. In contrast, Whole Foods Market, Inc.'s consolidated statement of income illustrated in the chapter opening includes multiple types of revenue (sales, investment and other income) and several types of expenses (cost of goods sold, operating expenses, other expenses), segregated by type. It has important subheadings that segregate different types of income (gross profit, operating income, income before income taxes, net income). This is known as a "multiple-step" income statement. You will learn more about it in Chapters 3 and 11.

2. The statement of retained earnings starts with the beginning balance of retained earnings (zero for a new business). Add net income for the period from the income statement (arrow ①), subtract dividends ($2,100 from cell I14 of the transaction analysis spreadsheet in Exhibit 2-1, Panel B), and compute the ending balance of retained earnings ($5,200).

3. The balance sheet lists the assets, liabilities, and stockholders' equity of the business at the end of the period. The assets consist of the totals of cash, accounts receivable, supplies, and land (see cells B15 through E15 in Exhibit 2-1 Panel B). Liabilities consist of only accounts payable (cell G15). Common stock carries over from cell H15. Also included in stockholders' equity is retained earnings, which comes from the statement of retained earnings (arrow ②). It has also been accumulated in cell I15 of Exhibit 2-1, Panel B.

Exhibit 2-2 | Financial Statements of Freddy's Auto Service, Inc.

A1					
	A		**B**	**C**	**D**
1	Freddy's Auto Service, Inc. Income Statement Month Ended April 30, 2014				
2	Revenues				
3	Service revenue ($7,000 + $3,000)			$ 10,000	
4	Expenses				
5	Salary expense		$ 1,200		
6	Rent expense		1,100		
7	Utilities expense		400		
8	Total expenses			2,700	
9	Net income			$ 7,300	
10					

①

A1					
	A		**B**	**C**	**D**
1	Freddy's Auto Service, Inc. Statement of Retained Earnings Month Ended April 30, 2014				
2	Retained earnings, April 1, 2014			$ 0	
3	Add: Net income for the month			7,300	
4	Subtotal			7,300	
5	Less: Dividends declared			(2,100)	
6	Retained earnings, April 30, 2014			$ 5,200	
7					

②

A1						
	A	**B**	**C**	**D**	**E**	**F**
1	Freddy's Auto Service, Inc. Balance Sheet April 30, 2014					
2	**Assets**			**Liabilities**		
3	Cash		$ 33,300	Accounts payable	$ 1,800	
4	Accounts receivable		2,000	**Stockholders' Equity**		
5	Supplies		3,700	Common stock	50,000	
6	Land		18,000	Retained earnings	5,200	
7				Total stockholders' equity	55,200	
8				Total liabilities and		
9	Total assets		$ 57,000	stockholders' equity	$ 57,000	
10						

>> **Try It** in **Excel**

If you are familiar with Excel, a quick look at Exhibit 2-2 should convince you of how easy it is to prepare the income statement, statement of retained earnings, and balance sheet in Excel. Prepare three simple templates for each of these financial statements for Freddy's Auto Service, Inc. You may use these templates again, and add to them, in Chapter 3 as you learn the adjusting entry process. Selected problems in MyAccountingLab have already prepared these templates for you. The midchapter summary problem will illustrate with another small company. ■

Let's put into practice what you have learned so far.

Mid-Chapter Summary Problem

Shelly Herzog opens a research service near a college campus. She names the corporation Herzog Researchers, Inc. During the first month of operations, July 2014, the business engages in these transactions:

a. Herzog Researchers, Inc., issues its common stock to Shelly Herzog, who invests $25,000 to open the business.

b. The company purchases on account office supplies costing $350.

c. Herzog Researchers pays cash of $20,000 to acquire a lot next to the campus. The company intends to use the land as a building site for a business office.

d. Herzog Researchers performs research for clients and receives cash of $1,900.

e. Herzog Researchers pays $100 on the account payable that it created in transaction b.

f. Herzog pays $2,000 of personal funds for a vacation.

g. Herzog Researchers pays cash expenses for office rent ($400) and utilities ($100).

h. The business sells a small parcel of the land for its cost of $5,000.

i. The business declares and pays a cash dividend of $1,200.

Requirements

1. Using Excel, build a spreadsheet to analyze the preceding transactions in terms of their effects on the accounting equation of Herzog Researchers, Inc. Use Exhibit 2-1, Panel B, as a guide.

2. Using Excel, prepare the income statement, statement of retained earnings, and balance sheet of Herzog Researchers, Inc., after recording the transactions. Draw arrows linking the statements. Use Exhibit 2-2 as a guide.

Answers

Requirement 1

PANEL B—Transaction Analysis: Herzog Researchers, Inc.

	A	B	C	D	E	F	G	H	I
			Assets		=	Liabilities +	Stockholders' Equity		Type of SE transaction
1									
2	Trans	Cash	Office Supplies	Land		AP	C Stock	RE	
3	a	25,000					25,000		Issued common stock
4	b		350			350			
5	c	(20,000)		20,000					
6	d	1,900						1,900	Service revenue
7	e	(100)				(100)			
8	f (n/a)								
9	g	(400)						(400)	Rent expense
10		(100)						(100)	Utilities expense
11	h	5,000		(5,000)					
12	i	(1,200)						(1,200)	Dividend
13	Bal	10,100	350	15,000		250	25,000	200	
14	Totals		25,450				25,450		
15									

Requirement 2

A1		A	B	C	D
1		**Herzog Researchers, Inc.** **Income Statement** **Month Ended July 31, 2014**			
2	**Revenues**				
3	Service revenue			$ 1,900	
4	**Expenses**				
5	Rent expense		$ 400		
6	Utilities expense		100		
7	Total expenses			500	
8	Net income			$ 1,400	
9					

A1		A	B	C	D
1		**Herzog Researchers, Inc.** **Statement of Retained Earnings** **Month Ended July 31, 2014**			
2	Retained earnings, July 1, 2014			$ 0	
3	Add: Net income for the month			1,400	
4	Subtotal			1,400	
5	Less: Dividends declared			(1,200)	
6	Retained earnings, July 31, 2014			$ 200	
7					

	A	B	C	D	E	F
1	**Herzog Researchers, Inc.** **Balance Sheet** **July 31, 2014**					
2	**Assets**			**Liabilities**		
3	Cash		$ 10,100	Accounts payable	$ 250	
4	Office supplies		350	**Stockholders' Equity**		
5	Land		15,000	Common stock	25,000	
6				Retained earnings	200	
7				Total stockholders' equity	25,200	
8				Total liabilities and		
9	Total assets		$ 25,450	stockholders' equity	$ 25,450	
10						

The analysis in the first half of this chapter can be used, but even in Excel, it can be cumbersome. Whole Foods Market, Inc., has hundreds of accounts and millions of transactions. The spreadsheet to account for Whole Foods Market, Inc.'s transactions would be huge! In the second half of this chapter we discuss double-entry accounting as it is actually used in business.

ANALYZE THE IMPACT OF BUSINESS TRANSACTIONS ON ACCOUNTS

4 **Analyze** the impact of business transactions on accounts

Every business transaction involves an exchange of at least two things:

- You give something.
- You receive something in return.

Accounting is, therefore, based on a double-entry system, which records the *dual effects* on the entity. *Each transaction affects at least two accounts.* For example, Freddy's Auto Service, Inc., received $50,000 cash in exchange for the issuance of stock. This transaction increased both Cash and Common Stock by $50,000. It would be incomplete to record only the increase in Cash or only the increase in Common Stock.

The T-Account

An account can be represented by the letter T. We call this a *T-account*. The vertical line in the letter T represent the division of the account into its two sides: left and right. The account title appears at the top of the T. For example, the Cash account can appear as follows:

	Cash
(Left side)	(Right side)
Debit	*Credit*

The left side of each account is called the **debit** side, and the right side is called the **credit** side. Often, students are confused by the words *debit* and *credit*. To become comfortable using these terms, remember that *every business transaction involves both a debit and a credit.* You should remember that *debit* means "left-hand side" and *credit* means "right-hand side."

Debit = Left side	Credit = Right side

Increases and Decreases in the Accounts:
The Rules of Debit and Credit

The type of account determines how we record increases and decreases. *The rules of debit and credit* are illustrated in Exhibit 2-3.

- Increases in *assets* are recorded on the left (debit) side of the account. Decreases in *assets* are recorded on the right (credit) side. You receive cash and debit the Cash account. You pay cash and credit the Cash account.
- Conversely, increases in *liabilities* and *stockholders' equity* are recorded by credits. Decreases in *liabilities* and *stockholders' equity* are recorded by debits.

Exhibit 2-3 | Accounting Equation and the Rules of Debit and Credit

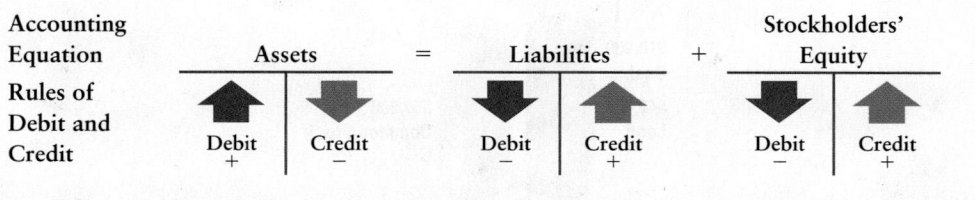

To illustrate the ideas diagrammed in Exhibit 2-3, let's review the first transaction. Freddy's Auto Service, Inc., received $50,000 and issued (gave) stock. Which accounts are affected? The Cash account and the Common Stock account will hold these amounts:

Exhibit 2-4 | The Accounting Equation after Freddy's Auto Service's First Transaction

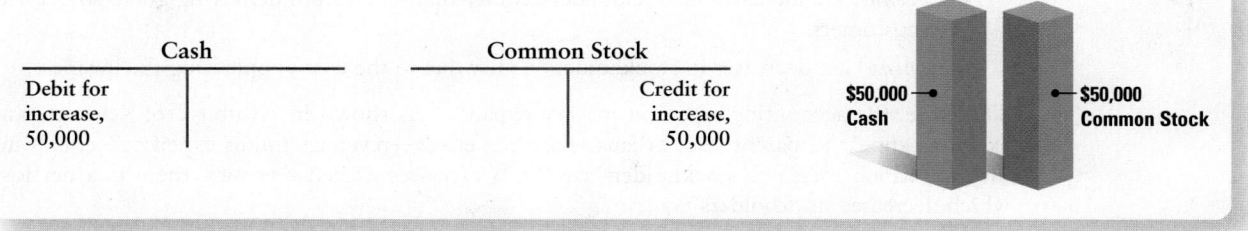

The amount remaining in an account is called its *balance*. This first transaction gives Cash a $50,000 debit balance and Common Stock a $50,000 credit balance. Exhibit 2-4 shows this relationship.

Freddy's' second transaction is a $40,000 cash purchase of land. This transaction decreases Cash with a credit and increases Land with a debit, as shown in the following T-accounts (focus on Cash and Land):

Cash				Common Stock	
Bal	50,000	Credit for decrease, 40,000		Bal	50,000
Bal	10,000				

Land	
Debit for increase, 40,000	
Bal	40,000

After this transaction, Cash has a $10,000 debit balance, Land has a debit balance of $40,000, and Common Stock has a $50,000 credit balance, as shown in Exhibit 2-5.

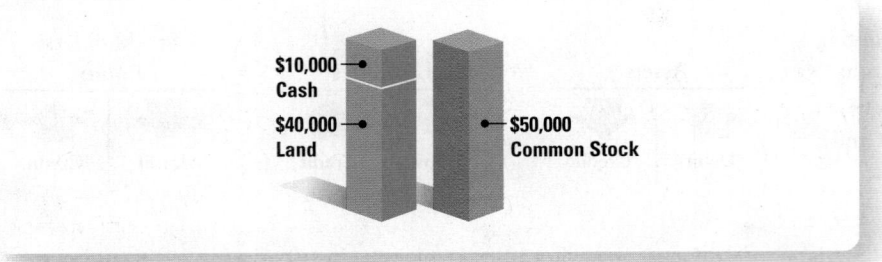

Additional Stockholders' Equity Accounts:
Revenues and Expenses

Stockholders' equity also includes the two categories of income statement accounts, Revenues and Expenses:

- *Revenues* are increases in stockholders' equity that result from delivering goods or services to customers.
- *Expenses* are decreases in stockholders' equity due to the cost of operating the business.

Therefore, the accounting equation may be expanded as shown in Exhibit 2-6. Revenues and expenses appear in parentheses because their net effect—revenues minus expenses—equals net income, which increases stockholders' equity. If expenses exceed revenues, there is a net loss, which decreases stockholders' equity.

We can now express the final form of the rules of debit and credit, as shown in Exhibit 2-7. *You should not proceed until you have learned these rules.* For example, you must remember that

- a debit increases an asset account;
- a credit decreases an asset account.

Exhibit 2-6 | Expansion of the Accounting Equation

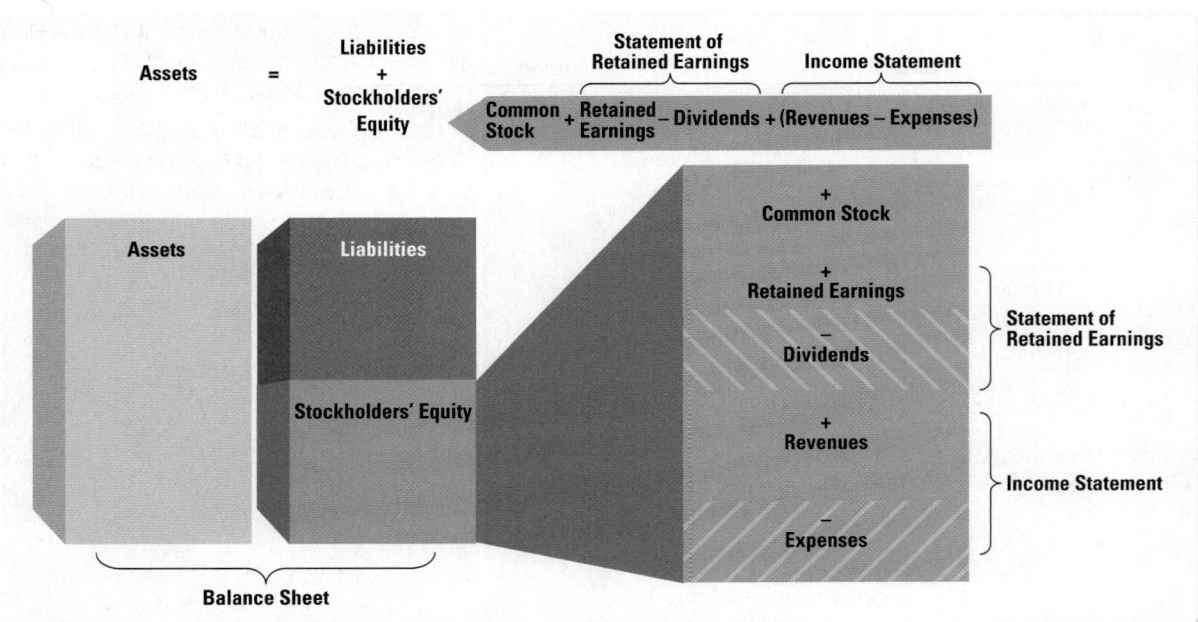

Exhibit 2-7 | Final Form of the Rules of Debit and Credit

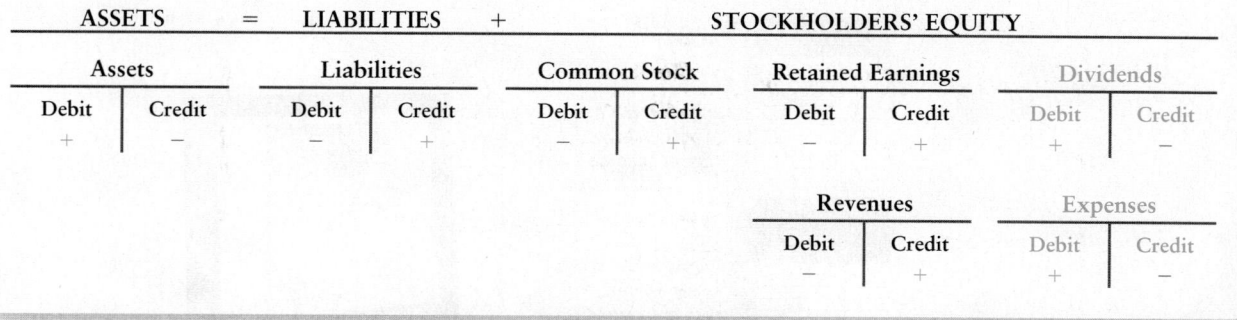

Liabilities and stockholders' equity are the opposite.

- A credit increases a liability or stockholders' equity account.
- A debit decreases a liability or stockholders' equity account.

Dividends and Expense accounts are exceptions to the rule. Dividends and Expenses are equity accounts that are increased by a debit. Dividends and Expense accounts are negative (or *contra*) equity accounts.

Revenues and expenses are treated as separate account categories because users of financial statements need to keep track of each separately. Exhibit 2-7 shows revenues and expenses below the other equity accounts.

RECORD (JOURNALIZE AND POST) TRANSACTIONS IN THE BOOKS

Accountants use a chronological record of transactions called a **journal**, also known as the *book of original entry*. The journalizing process follows three steps:

1. Specify each account affected by the transaction and classify each account by type (asset, liability, stockholders' equity, revenue, or expense).

2. Determine whether each account is increased or decreased by the transaction. Use the rules of debit and credit to increase or decrease each account.

3. Record the transaction in the journal, including a brief explanation. The debit side is entered on the left margin, and the credit side is indented to the right.

5 Record (journalize and post) transactions in the books

Step 3 is also called "booking the journal entry" or "journalizing the transaction." Let's apply the steps to journalize the first transaction of Freddy's Auto Service, Inc.

Step 1 The business receives cash and issues stock. Cash and Common Stock are affected. Cash is an asset, and Common Stock is stockholders' equity.

Step 2 Both Cash and Common Stock increase. Debit Cash to record an increase in this asset. Credit Common Stock to record an increase in this equity account.

Step 3 Journalize the transaction:

	A1	▲▼				
	A	**B**	**C**	**D**	**E**	**F**
		JOURNAL				
1	**Date**	**Accounts and Explanation**	**Debit**	**Credit**		
2	Apr 1	Cash	50,000			
3		Common Stock		50,000		
4		Issued common stock.				
5						

When analyzing a transaction, first pinpoint the effects (if any) on Cash. Did Cash increase or decrease? Typically, it is easiest to identify Cash effects. Then identify the effects on the other accounts.

Exhibit 2-8 | The Ledger (Asset, Liability, and Stockholders' Equity Accounts)

Copying Information (Posting) from the Journal to the Ledger

The journal is a chronological record of all company transactions listed by date. But the journal does not indicate how much cash or accounts receivable the business has.

The **ledger** is a grouping of all the T-accounts, with their balances. For example, the balance of the Cash T-account shows how much cash the business has. The balance of Accounts Receivable shows the amount due from customers. Accounts Payable shows how much the business owes suppliers on open account, and so on.

In the phrase "keeping the books," *books* refers to the journals as well as the accounts in the ledger. In most accounting systems, the ledger is computerized. Exhibit 2-8 shows how asset, liability, and stockholders' equity accounts are grouped in the ledger. Revenue and expense accounts also appear in the general ledger, which may contain hundreds or even thousands of accounts.

Entering a transaction in the journal does not get the data into the ledger. Data must be copied to the ledger—a process called **posting**. Debits in the journal are always posted as debits in the accounts, and likewise for credits. Exhibit 2-9 shows how Freddy's Auto Service, Inc.'s stock issuance transaction is posted to the accounts.

Exhibit 2-9 | Journal Entry and Posting to the Accounts

PANEL A—Journal Entry

	A	B	C
	A1		
	Accounts and Explanation	**Debit**	**Credit**
1			
2	Cash	50,000	
3	Common Stock		50,000
4	*Issued common stock.*		
5			

PANEL B—Posting to the Accounts

Cash	Common Stock
50,000	50,000

Exhibit 2-10 | Flow of Accounting Data

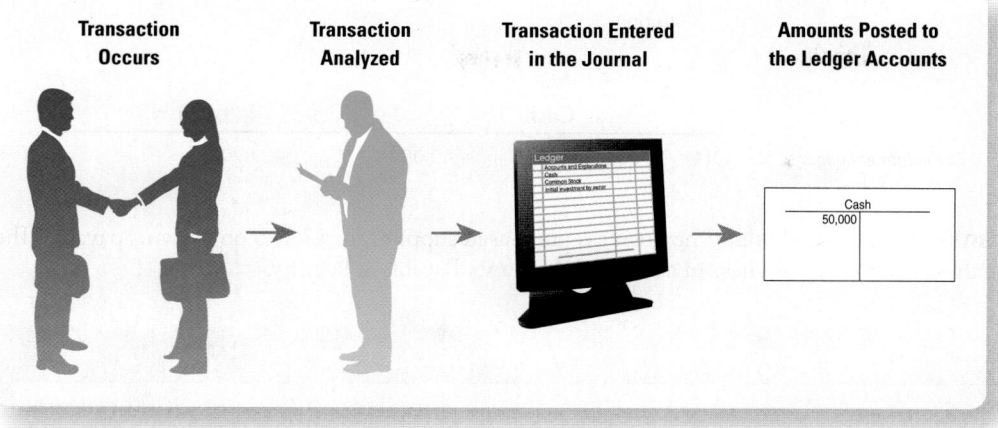

| Transaction Occurs | Transaction Analyzed | Transaction Entered in the Journal | Amounts Posted to the Ledger Accounts |

The Flow of Accounting Data

Exhibit 2-10 summarizes the flow of accounting data from the business transaction to the ledger. Let's continue the example of Freddy's Auto Service, Inc., and account for the same 11 transactions we illustrated earlier. Here we use the journal and the accounts. Each journal entry posted to the accounts is keyed by date or by transaction number. This linking allows you to locate any information you may need.

Transaction 1 Analysis. Freddy's Auto Service, Inc., received $50,000 cash from the stockholders and in turn issued common stock to them. The journal entry, accounting equation, and ledger accounts follow:

	A1					
		A	**B**	**C**	**D**	**E**
1	Cash		50,000			
2	Common Stock			50,000		
3	*Issued common stock.*					
4						

	Assets	**=**	**Liabilities**	**+**	**Stockholders' Equity**
Accounting equation	+50,000	=	0	+	50,000

	Cash		Common Stock	
The ledger accounts	(1) 50,000			(1) 50,000

Transaction 2 Analysis. The business paid $40,000 cash for land. The purchase decreased cash; therefore, credit Cash. The purchase increased the asset land; to record this increase, debit Land.

	A1					
		A	**B**	**C**	**D**	**E**
1	Land		40,000			
2	Cash			40,000		
3	*Paid cash for land.*					
4						

	Assets	=	Liabilities	+	Stockholders' Equity
Accounting equation	+ 40,000	=	0	+	0
	− 40,000				

	Cash					Land	
The ledger accounts	(1)	50,000	(2)	40,000	(2)	40,000	

Transaction 3 Analysis. The business purchased supplies for $3,700 on account payable. The purchase increased Supplies, an asset, and Accounts Payable, a liability.

	A	B	C	D	E
1	Supplies	3,700			
2	Accounts Payable		3,700		
3	Purchased office supplies on account.				
4					

	Assets	=	Liabilities	+	Stockholders' Equity
Accounting equation	+ 3,700	=	+ 3,700	+	0

	Supplies			Accounts Payable	
The ledger accounts	(3)	3,700		(3)	3,700

Transaction 4 Analysis. The business performed services for clients and received cash of $7,000. The transaction increased cash and service revenue. To record the revenue, credit Service Revenue.

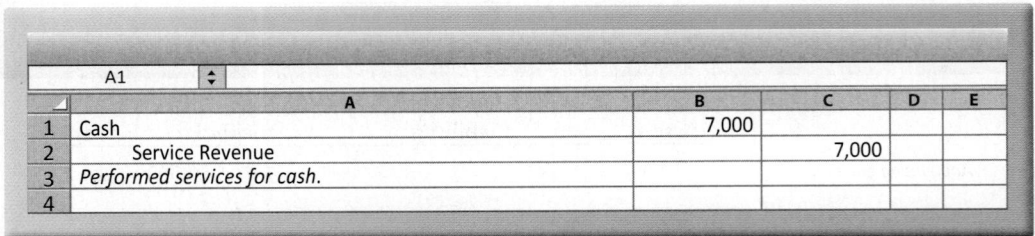

	A	B	C	D	E
1	Cash	7,000			
2	Service Revenue		7,000		
3	Performed services for cash.				
4					

	Assets	=	Liabilities	+	Stockholders' Equity	+	Revenues
Accounting equation	+ 7,000	=	0			+	7,000

	Cash				Service Revenue	
The ledger accounts	(1)	50,000	(2)	40,000	(4)	7,000
	(4)	7,000				

Transaction 5 Analysis. Freddy's performed services for UPS on account. UPS did not pay immediately, so Freddy's billed UPS for $3,000. The transaction increased accounts receivable; therefore, debit Accounts Receivable. Service revenue also increased, so credit the Service Revenue account.

A1			A	B	C	D	E
1		Accounts Receivable		3,000			
2			Service Revenue		3,000		
3		*Performed services on account.*					
4							

	Assets	=	Liabilities	+	Stockholders' Equity	+	Revenues
Accounting equation	+ 3,000	=	0			+	3,000

	Accounts Receivable			Service Revenue	
The ledger accounts	(5) 3,000			(4)	7,000
				(5)	3,000

Transaction 6 Analysis. The business paid $2,700 for the following expenses: rent, $1,100; employee salary, $1,200; and utilities, $400. Credit Cash for the sum of the expense amounts. The expenses increased, so debit each expense account separately.

A1			A	B	C	D	E
1		Rent Expense		1,100			
2		Salary Expense		1,200			
3		Utilities Expense		400			
4		Cash			2,700		
5		*Paid expenses.*					
6							

	Assets	=	Liabilities	+	Stockholders' Equity	−	Expenses
Accounting equation	− 2,700	=	0			−	2,700

	Cash				Rent Expense	
The ledger accounts	(1)	50,000	(2)	40,000	(6) 1,100	
	(4)	7,000	(6)	2,700		

	Salary Expense			Utilities Expense	
	(6) 1,200			(6) 400	

Transaction 7 Analysis. The business paid $1,900 on the account payable created in transaction 3. Credit Cash for the payment. The payment decreased a liability, so debit Accounts Payable.

	A	B	C	D	E
1	Accounts Payable	1,900			
2	Cash		1,900		
3	*Paid cash on account.*				
4					

	Assets	=	Liabilities	+	Stockholders' Equity
Accounting equation	− 1,900	=	− 1,900	+	0

	Cash			Accounts Payable	
The ledger accounts	(1) 50,000 | (2) 40,000 (7)			1,900 | (3)	3,700
	(4) 7,000 | (6) 2,700				
	(7) 1,900				

Transaction 8 Analysis. Freddy Kish, the major stockholder of Freddy's Auto Service, Inc., remodeled his personal residence. This is not a transaction of the business, so the business does not record the transaction.

Transaction 9 Analysis. The business collected $1,000 cash on account from the client in transaction 5. Cash increased, so debit Cash. The asset accounts receivable decreased; therefore, credit Accounts Receivable.

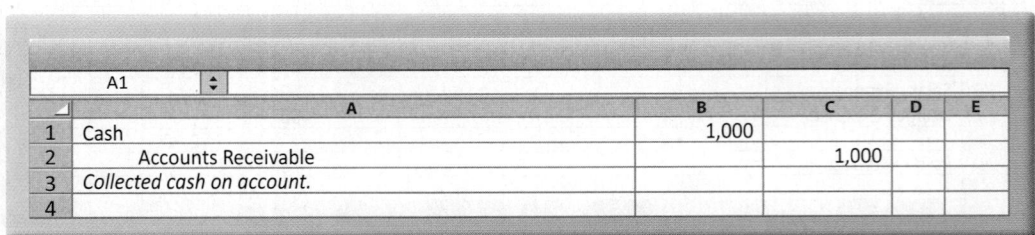

	A	B	C	D	E
1	Cash	1,000			
2	Accounts Receivable		1,000		
3	*Collected cash on account.*				
4					

	Assets	=	Liabilities	+	Stockholders' Equity
Accounting equation	+ 1,000	=	0	+	0
	− 1,000				

	Cash			Accounts Receivable	
The ledger accounts	(1) 50,000 | (2) 40,000	(5)		3,000 | (9)	1,000
	(4) 7,000 | (6) 2,700				
	(9) 1,000 | (7) 1,900				

Transaction 10 Analysis. The business sold land for its cost of $22,000, receiving cash. The asset cash increased; debit Cash. The asset land decreased; credit Land.

	A	B	C	D	E
	A1				
1	Cash	22,000			
2	Land		22,000		
3	Sold land.				
4					

	Assets	=	Liabilities	+	Stockholders' Equity
Accounting equation	+ 22,000	=	0	+	0
	− 22,000				

	Cash				Land		
The ledger accounts	(1)	50,000	(2)	40,000	(2)	40,000	(10) 22,000
	(4)	7,000	(6)	2,700			
	(9)	1,000	(7)	1,900			
	(10)	22,000					

Transaction 11 Analysis. Freddy's Auto Service, Inc., declared and paid its stockholders cash dividends of $2,100. Credit Cash for the payment. The transaction also decreased stockholders' equity and requires a debit to an equity account. Therefore, debit Dividends.

	A	B	C	D	E
	A1				
1	Dividends	2,100			
2	Cash		2,100		
3	Declared and paid dividends.				
4					

MyAccountingLab

	Assets	=	Liabilities	+	Stockholders' Equity	−	Dividends
Accounting equation	− 2,100	=	0			−	2,100

	Cash				Dividends	
The ledger accounts	(1)	50,000	(2)	40,000	(11)	2,100
	(4)	7,000	(6)	2,700		
	(9)	1,000	(7)	1,900		
	(10)	22,000	(11)	2,100		

MyAccountingLab

Accounts after Posting to the Ledger

Exhibit 2-11 shows the accounts after all transactions have been posted to the ledger. Group the accounts under assets, liabilities, and stockholders' equity.

Each account has a balance, denoted as Bal, which is the difference between the account's total debits and its total credits. For example, the Accounts Payable's balance of $1,800 is the difference between the credit ($3,700) and the debit ($1,900). Cash has a debit balance of $33,300.

Exhibit 2-11 | Freddy's Auto Service, Inc.'s Ledger Accounts after Posting

| Assets | = | Liabilities | + | Stockholders' Equity |

Cash

(1)	50,000	(2)	40,000
(4)	7,000	(6)	2,700
(9)	1,000	(7)	1,900
(10)	22,000	(11)	2,100
Bal	33,300		

Accounts Receivable

| (5) | 3,000 | (9) | 1,000 |
| Bal | 2,000 | | |

Supplies

| (3) | 3,700 | |
| Bal | 3,700 | |

Land

| (2) | 40,000 | (10) | 22,000 |
| Bal | 18,000 | | |

Accounts Payable

| (7) | 1,900 | (3) | 3,700 |
| | | Bal | 1,800 |

Common Stock

| | | (1) | 50,000 |
| | | Bal | 50,000 |

Revenue

Service Revenue

		(4)	7,000
		(5)	3,000
		Bal	10,000

Dividends

| (11) | 2,100 | |
| Bal | 2,100 | |

Expenses

Rent Expense

| (6) | 1,100 | |
| Bal | 1,100 | |

Salary Expense

| (6) | 1,200 | |
| Bal | 1,200 | |

Utilities Expense

| (6) | 400 | |
| Bal | 400 | |

A horizontal line separates the transaction amounts from the account balance. If an account's debits exceed its total credits, that account has a debit balance, as for Cash. If the sum of the credits is greater than the debits, the account has a credit balance, as for Accounts Payable.

CONSTRUCT AND USE A TRIAL BALANCE

6 Construct and use a trial balance

A **trial balance** lists all accounts with their balances—assets first, then liabilities and stockholders' equity (including revenue and expense accounts). The trial balance summarizes all the account balances for the financial statements and *shows whether total debits equal total credits*. A trial balance may be taken at any time, but the most common time is at the end of the period. Exhibit 2-12 is the trial balance of Freddy's Auto Service, Inc., after all transactions have been journalized and posted at the end of April.

Exhibit 2-12 | Trial Balance

MyAccountingLab

MyAccountingLab

	A	B	C	D	E
1	Freddy's Auto Service, Inc. Trial Balance April 30, 2014				
2		Balance			
3	Account Title	Debit	Credit		
4	Cash	$33,300			
5	Accounts receivable	2,000			
6	Supplies	3,700			
7	Land	18,000			
8	Accounts payable		$ 1,800		
9	Common stock		50,000		
10	Dividends	2,100			
11	Service revenue		10,000		
12	Rent expense	1,100			
13	Salary expense	1,200			
14	Utilities expense	400			
15	Total	$61,800	$61,800		
16					

The trial balance *facilitates the preparation of the financial statements.* It is possible to prepare an income statement, statement of retained earnings, and balance sheet from the data shown in a trial balance such as the one in Exhibit 2-12. For Freddy's Auto Service, Inc., the financial statements would appear exactly as shown in Exhibit 2-2 on page 65. However, the financial statements are normally not constructed at this point, because they do not yet contain end-of-period adjustments, which are covered in Chapter 3.

Try It in Excel

A trial balance can be one of the most simple and useful applications of Excel. Try building Exhibit 2-12 in Excel. Open a new blank worksheet. Format the title (company name, trial balance, and date), and provide column headings (account title, debit, and credit) exactly as shown in Exhibit 2-12. Then on successive lines, enter account titles and amounts from the general ledger accounts, being careful to enter amounts in the proper debit or credit columns. Finally, sum both debit and credit columns. The total amounts of debits and credits should agree. ■

Analyzing Accounts

You can often tell what a company did by analyzing its accounts. This is a powerful tool for a manager who knows accounting. For example, if you know the beginning and ending balances of Cash, and if you know total cash receipts, you can compute your total cash payments during the period.

In our chapter example, suppose Freddy's Auto Service began May with cash of $1,000. During May, Freddy's received cash of $8,000 and ended the month with a cash balance of $3,000. You can compute total cash payments by analyzing Freddy's Cash account:

Cash

			x = beginning balance + cash receipts − ending balance
			= 1,000 + 8,000 − 3,000
Beginning balance	1,000		
Cash receipts	8,000	Cash payments	x = 6,000
Ending balance	3,000		

Or, if you know Cash's beginning and ending balances and total payments, you can compute cash receipts during the period—for any company!

You can compute either sales on account or cash collections on account by analyzing the Accounts Receivable account (using assumed amounts):

Accounts Receivable

			x = beginning balance + sales on account − ending balance
			= 6,000 + 10,000 − 5,000
Beginning balance	6,000		
Sales on account	10,000	Collections on account	x = 11,000
Ending balance	5,000		

Also, you can determine how much you paid on account by analyzing Accounts Payable (using assumed amounts):

Accounts Payable

x = beginning balance + purchases on account − ending balance			
= 9,000 + 6,000 − 11,000			
		Beginning balance	9,000
Payments on account	x = 4,000	Purchases on account	6,000
		Ending balance	11,000

Please master this powerful technique. It works for any company and for your personal finances! You will find this tool very helpful when you become a manager.

Correcting Accounting Errors

Accounting errors can occur even in computerized systems. Input data may be wrong, or they may be entered twice or not at all. A debit may be entered as a credit, and vice versa. You can detect the reason or reasons behind many out-of-balance conditions by computing the difference between total debits and total credits in the trial balance. Then perform one or more of the following actions:

1. Search the records for a missing account. Trace each account back and forth from the journal to the ledger. A $200 transaction may have been recorded incorrectly in the journal or posted incorrectly to the ledger. Search the journal for a $200 transaction.

2. Divide the out-of-balance amount by 2. A debit treated as a credit, or vice versa, doubles the amount of error. Suppose Freddy's Auto Service, Inc., added $300 to Cash instead of subtracting $300. The out-of-balance amount is $600, and dividing by 2 identifies $300 as the amount of the transaction. Search the journal for the $300 transaction and trace to the account affected.

3. Divide the out-of-balance amount by 9. If the result is an integer (no decimals), the error may be a

   - *slide* (e.g., writing $400 as $40). The accounts would be out of balance by $360 ($400 − $40 = $360). Dividing $360 by 9 yields $40. Scan the trial balance in Exhibit 2-12 for an amount similar to $40. Utilities Expense (balance of $400) is the misstated account.
   - *transposition* (e.g., writing $2,100 as $1,200). The accounts would be out of balance by $900 ($2,100 − $1,200 = $900). Dividing $900 by 9 yields $100. Trace all amounts on the trial balance back to the T-accounts. Dividends (balance of $2,100) is the misstated account.

Chart of Accounts

As you know, the ledger contains the accounts grouped under these headings:

1. **Balance sheet accounts: Assets, Liabilities, and Stockholders' Equity**
2. **Income statement accounts: Revenues and Expenses**

Organizations use a **chart of accounts** to list all their accounts and account numbers. Account numbers usually have two or more digits. Asset account numbers may begin with 1, liabilities with 2, stockholders' equity with 3, revenues with 4, and expenses with 5. The second, third, and higher digits in an account number indicate the position of the individual account within the category. For example, Cash may be account number 101, which is the first asset account. Accounts Payable may be number 201, the first liability. All accounts are numbered by using this system.

Organizations with many accounts use lengthy account numbers. For example, the chart of accounts of Whole Foods Market, Inc., may use five-digit account numbers. The chart of accounts for Freddy's Auto Service, Inc., appears in Exhibit 2-13. The gap between account numbers 111 and 141 leaves room to add another category of receivables, for example, Notes Receivable, which may be numbered 121.

Appendix C to this book gives two expanded charts of accounts that you will find helpful as you work through this course. The first chart lists the typical accounts that a *service* corporation, such as Freddy's Auto Service, Inc., would have after a period of growth. The second chart is for a *merchandising* corporation, one that sells a product instead of a service.

Exhibit 2-13 | Chart of Accounts—Freddy's Auto Service, Inc.

Balance Sheet Accounts		
Assets	**Liabilities**	**Stockholders' Equity**
101 Cash	201 Accounts Payable	301 Common Stock
111 Accounts Receivable	231 Notes Payable	311 Retained Earnings
141 Supplies		312 Dividends
151 Land		
191 Office Furniture		

Income Statement Accounts (Part of Stockholders' Equity)	
Revenues	**Expenses**
401 Service Revenue	501 Rent Expense
	502 Salary Expense
	503 Utilities Expense

The Normal Balance of an Account

An account's *normal balance* falls on the side of the account—debit or credit—where increases are recorded. The normal balance of assets is on the debit side, so assets are *debit-balance accounts*. Conversely, liabilities and stockholders' equity usually have a credit balance, so these are *credit-balance accounts*. Exhibit 2-14 illustrates the normal balances of all the assets, liabilities, and stockholders' equities, including revenues and expenses.

As explained earlier, stockholders' equity usually contains several accounts. Dividends and expenses carry debit balances because they represent decreases in stockholders' equity. In total, the equity accounts show a normal credit balance.

Exhibit 2-14 | Normal Balances of the Accounts

Assets	Debit	
Liabilities		Credit
Stockholders' Equity—overall		Credit
Common stock		Credit
Retained earnings		Credit
Dividends	Debit	
Revenues		Credit
Expenses	Debit	

Account Formats

So far we have illustrated accounts in a two-column T-account format, with the debit column on the left and the credit column on the right. Another format has four *amount* columns, as illustrated for the Cash account in Exhibit 2-15. The first pair of amount columns on the left are for the debit and credit amounts of individual transactions. The last two columns are for the account balance. This four-column format keeps a running balance in the two right columns. The format of the accounts is determined by the type of computer software that the company uses.

MyAccountingLab

Exhibit 2-15 | Account in Four-Column Format

Account: Cash					Account No. 101

				Balance	
Date	Item	Debit	Credit	Debit	Credit
2014					
Apr 2		50,000		50,000	
3			40,000	10,000	

Analyzing Transactions Using Only T-Accounts

Businesspeople must often make decisions without the benefit of a complete accounting system. For example, the managers of Whole Foods Market, Inc., may consider borrowing $100,000 to buy equipment. To see how the two transactions [(a) borrowing cash and (b) buying equipment] affect Whole Foods Market, Inc., the manager can go directly to T-accounts:

T-accounts:

Cash		Note Payable	
(a) 100,000			(a) 100,000

T-accounts:

Cash		Equipment		Note Payable	
(a) 100,000	(b) 100,000	(b) 100,000			(a) 100,000

This informal analysis shows immediately that Whole Foods Market, Inc., will add $100,000 of equipment and a $100,000 note payable. Assuming that Whole Foods Market, Inc., began with zero balances, the equipment and note payable transactions would result in the following balance sheet (date assumed for illustration only):

A1				
	A	B	C	D
1	Whole Foods Market, Inc. Balance Sheet September 30, 2014			
2	Assets		Liabilities	
3	Cash	$ 0	Note payable	$100,000
4	Equipment	100,000		
5			Stockholders' Equity	0
6			Total liabilities and	
7	Total assets	$100,000	stockholders' equity	$100,000
8				

MyAccountingLab

Companies don't actually keep records in this shortcut fashion. But a decision maker who needs information quickly may not have time to journalize, post to the accounts, take a trial balance, and prepare the financial statements. A manager who knows accounting can analyze the transaction and make the decision quickly.

Now apply what you've learned. Study the Decision Guidelines, which summarize the chapter.

◉ Decision Guidelines

HOW TO MEASURE RESULTS OF OPERATIONS AND FINANCIAL POSITION

Any entrepreneur must determine whether the venture is profitable. To do this, he or she needs to know its results of operations and financial position. If a shareholder of Whole Foods Market, Inc., wants to know whether the business is making money, the Guidelines that follow will help:

Decision	Guidelines
Has a transaction occurred?	If the event affects the entity's financial position and can be reliably recorded—Yes If either condition is absent—No
Where to record the transaction?	In the *journal*, the chronological record of transactions
How to record an increase or decrease in the following accounts?	Rules of *debit* and *credit*:

	Increase	Decrease
Assets	Debit	Credit
Liabilities	Credit	Debit
Stockholders' equity...............	Credit	Debit
Revenues...............................	Credit	Debit
Expenses	Debit	Credit

Decision	Guidelines
Where to store all the information for each account?	In the *ledger*, the book of accounts
Where to list all the accounts and their balances?	In the *trial* balance
Where to report the following:	
results of operations?	In the income statement (Revenues − Expenses = Net income or net loss)
financial position?	In the balance sheet (Assets = Liabilities + Stockholders' equity)

End-of-Chapter Summary Problem

The trial balance of Magee Service Center, Inc., on March 1, 2014, lists the entity's assets, liabilities, and stockholders' equity on that date.

| | Balance | |
Account Title	Debit	Credit
Cash	$26,000	
Accounts receivable	4,500	
Accounts payable		$ 2,000
Common stock		10,000
Retained earnings		18,500
Total	$30,500	$30,500

During March, the business completed the following transactions:

a. Borrowed $45,000 from the bank, with Magee signing a note payable in the name of the business.

b. Paid cash of $40,000 to a real estate company to acquire land.

c. Performed service for a customer and received cash of $5,000.

d. Purchased supplies on credit, $300.

e. Performed customer service and earned revenue on account, $2,600.

f. Paid $1,200 on account.

g. Paid the following cash expenses: salaries, $3,000; rent, $1,500; and interest, $400.

h. Received $3,100 on account.

i. Received a $200 utility bill that will be paid next week.

j. Declared and paid a dividend of $1,800.

Requirements

1. Make the following accounts, with the balances indicated, in the ledger of Magee Service Center, Inc. Use the T-account format.

   ▪ Assets—Cash, $26,000; Accounts Receivable, $4,500; Supplies, no balance; Land, no balance

   ▪ Liabilities—Accounts Payable, $2,000; Note Payable, no balance

   ▪ Stockholders' Equity—Common Stock, $10,000; Retained Earnings, $18,500; Dividends, no balance

   ▪ Revenues—Service Revenue, no balance

   ▪ Expenses—(none have balances) Salary Expense, Rent Expense, Interest Expense, Utilities Expense

2. Journalize the preceding transactions. Key journal entries by transaction letter.

3. Post the transactions from the journal to the ledger and compute the balance in each account after all the transactions have been posted.

4. Prepare the trial balance of Magee Service Center, Inc., at March 31, 2014.

5. To determine the net income or net loss of the entity during the month of March, prepare the single step income statement for the month ended March 31, 2014. List expenses in order from the largest to the smallest.

Answers

Requirement 1

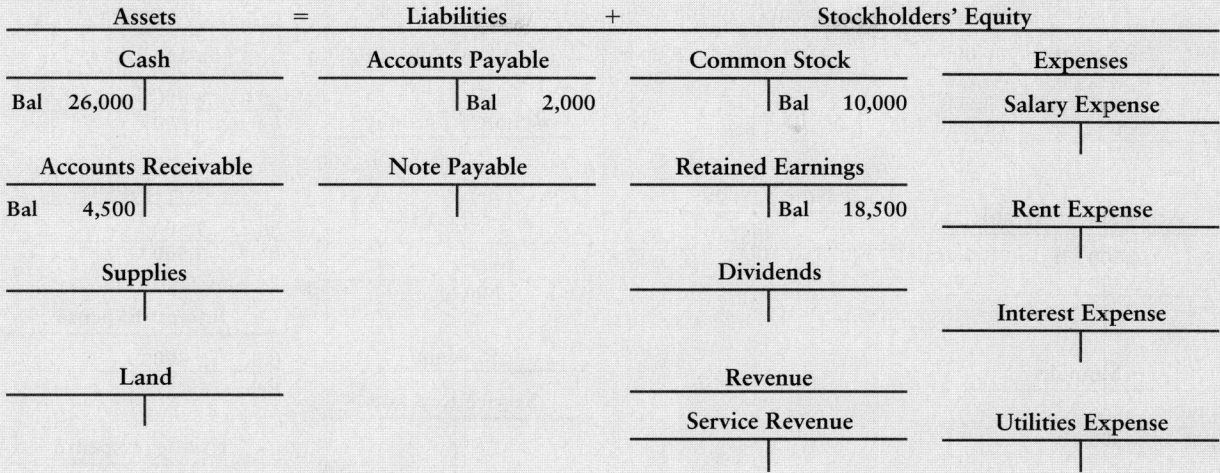

	Assets	=	Liabilities	+	Stockholders' Equity	

Assets = Liabilities + Stockholders' Equity

Cash
Bal 26,000 |

Accounts Payable
| Bal 2,000

Common Stock
| Bal 10,000

Expenses
Salary Expense
|

Accounts Receivable
Bal 4,500 |

Note Payable
|

Retained Earnings
| Bal 18,500

Rent Expense
|

Supplies
|

Dividends
|

Interest Expense
|

Land
|

Revenue

Service Revenue
|

Utilities Expense
|

Requirement 2

Accounts and Explanation	Debit	Credit	Accounts and Explanation	Debit	Credit
a. Cash	45,000		**g.** Salary Expense	3,000	
Note Payable		45,000	Rent Expense	1,500	
Borrowed cash on note payable.			Interest Expense	400	
b. Land	40,000		Cash		4,900
Cash		40,000	Paid cash expenses.		
Purchased land for cash.			**h.** Cash	3,100	
c. Cash	5,000		Accounts Receivable		3,100
Service Revenue		5,000	Received on account.		
Performed service and received cash.			**i.** Utilities Expense	200	
d. Supplies	300		Accounts Payable		200
Accounts Payable		300	Received utility bill.		
Purchased supplies on account.			**j.** Dividends	1,800	
e. Accounts Receivable	2,600		Cash		1,800
Service Revenue		2,600	Declared and paid dividends.		
Performed service on account.					
f. Accounts Payable	1,200				
Cash		1,200			
Paid on account.					

Requirement 3

Assets	=	Liabilities	+	Stockholders' Equity

Cash

Bal	26,000	(b)	40,000
(a)	45,000	(f)	1,200
(c)	5,000	(g)	4,900
(h)	3,100	(j)	1,800
Bal	31,200		

Accounts Receivable

Bal	4,500	(h)	3,100
(e)	2,600		
Bal	4,000		

Supplies

(d)	300	
Bal	300	

Land

(b)	40,000	
Bal	40,000	

Accounts Payable

(f)	1,200	Bal	2,000
		(d)	300
		(i)	200
		Bal	1,300

Note Payable

		(a)	45,000
		Bal	45,000

Common Stock

	Bal	10,000

Retained Earnings

	Bal	18,500

Dividends

(j)	1,800	
Bal	1,800	

Revenue

Service Revenue

	(c)	5,000
	(e)	2,600
	Bal	7,600

Expenses

Salary Expense

(g)	3,000	
Bal	3,000	

Rent Expense

(g)	1,500	
Bal	1,500	

Interest Expense

(g)	400	
Bal	400	

Utilities Expense

(i)	200	
Bal	200	

Requirement 4

	A1					

	A	B	C	D	E
1	Magee Service Center, Inc. Trial Balance March 31, 2014				
2		Balance			
3	**Account Title**	**Debit**	**Credit**		
4	Cash	$ 31,200			
5	Accounts receivable	4,000			
6	Supplies	300			
7	Land	40,000			
8	Accounts payable		$ 1,300		
9	Notes payable		45,000		
10	Common stock		10,000		
11	Retained earnings		18,500		
12	Dividends	1,800			
13	Service revenue		7,600		
14	Salary expense	3,000			
15	Rent expense	1,500			
16	Interest expense	400			
17	Utilities expense	200			
18	Total	$ 82,400	$ 82,400		
19					

Requirement 5

	A	B	C	D	E
1	**Magee Service Center, Inc.** **Income Statement** **Month Ended March 31, 2014**				
2	**Revenues**				
3	Service revenue		$ 7,600		
4					
5	**Expenses**				
6	Salary expense	$ 3,000			
7	Rent expense	1,500			
8	Interest expense	400			
9	Utilities expense	200			
10	Total expenses		5,100		
11	Net income		$ 2,500		
12					

REVIEW | Transaction Analysis

Quick Check (Answers are given on page 112.)

1. A debit entry to an account

   a. increases assets.

   b. increases liabilities.

   c. increases stockholders' equity.

   d. both b and c.

2. Which account types normally have a credit balance?

   a. Expenses

   b. Revenues

   c. Liabilities

   d. Both b and c

3. An attorney performs services of $1,100 for a client and receives $400 cash with the remainder on account. The journal entry for this transaction would

   a. debit Cash, credit Accounts Receivable, credit Service Revenue.

   b. debit Cash, debit Accounts Receivable, credit Service Revenue.

   c. debit Cash, debit Service Revenue, credit Accounts Receivable.

   d. debit Cash, credit Service Revenue.

4. Accounts Payable had a normal beginning balance of $1,000. During the period, there were debit postings of $500 and credit postings of $600. What was the ending balance?

   a. $900 debit

   b. $1,100 credit

   c. $900 credit

   d. $1,100 debit

5. The list of all accounts with their balances is the

   a. balance sheet.

   b. chart of accounts.

   c. trial balance.

   d. journal.

6. The basic summary device of accounting is the

   a. journal.

   b. trial balance.

   c. account.

   d. ledger.

7. The beginning Cash balance was $3,000. At the end of the period, the balance was $4,000. If total cash paid out during the period was $27,000, the amount of cash receipts was
   a. $28,000.   **c.** $30,000.
   b. $26,000.   **d.** $31,000.

8. In a double-entry accounting system,
   a. liabilities, owners' equity, and revenue accounts all have normal debit balances.
   b. half of all the accounts have a normal credit balance.
   c. a debit entry is recorded on the left side of a T-account.
   d. both a and b are correct.

9. Which accounts appear on which financial statement?

Balance sheet	*Income statement*
a. Cash, receivables, payables	Revenues, expenses
b. Cash, revenues, land	Expenses, payables
c. Expenses, payables, cash	Revenues, receivables, land
d. Receivables, land, payables	Revenues, supplies

10. A doctor purchases medical supplies of $640 and pays $290 cash with the remainder on account. The journal entry for this transaction would be which of the following?
    a. Supplies
       Accounts Payable
          Cash
    b. Supplies
       Accounts Payable
       Cash
    c. Supplies
       Accounts Receivable
          Cash
    d. Supplies
       Cash
          Accounts Payable

11. Which is the correct sequence for recording transactions and preparing financial statements?
    a. Financial statements, trial balance, ledger, journal
    b. Ledger, trial balance, journal, financial statements
    c. Ledger, journal, trial balance, financial statements
    d. Journal, ledger, trial balance, financial statements

12. The error of posting $50 as $500 can be detected by
    a. totaling each account's balance in the ledger.
    b. dividing the out-of-balance amount by 2.
    c. examining the chart of accounts.
    d. dividing the out-of-balance amount by 9.

Accounting Vocabulary

account (p. 55) The record of the changes that have occurred in a particular asset, liability, or stockholders' equity during a period. The basic summary device of accounting.

accrued liability (p. 56) A liability for an expense that has not yet been paid by the company.

cash (p. 55) Money and any medium of exchange that a bank accepts at face value.

chart of accounts (p. 80) List of a company's accounts and their account numbers.

credit (p. 68) The right side of an account.

debit (p. 68) The left side of an account.

journal (p. 71) The chronological accounting record of an entity's transactions.

ledger (p. 72) The book of accounts and their balances.

posting (p. 72) Copying amounts from the journal to the ledger.

transaction (p. 55) Any event that has a financial impact on the business and can be measured reliably.

trial balance (p. 78) A list of all the ledger accounts with their balances.

ASSESS YOUR PROGRESS

Short Exercises

S2-1. *(Learning Objective 2: Differentiate between different types of accounts)* Bill Alexander opened a software consulting firm that immediately paid $17,000 for a computer. Was Alexander's computer an expense of the business? If not, explain.

S2-2. *(Learning Objective 4: Analyze the impact of business transactions on accounts)* Cathey's Catering began with cash of $15,000. Cathey then bought supplies for $4,400 on account. Separately, Cathey paid $7,500 for equipment. Answer these questions.
   a. How much in total assets does Cathey have?
   b. How much in liabilities does Cathey owe?

S2-3. *(Learning Objectives 1, 4: Explain what a transaction is; analyze the impact of business transactions on accounts)* Dora Patel, MD, opened a medical practice. The business completed the following transactions:

July 1	Patel invested $60,000 cash to start her medical practice. The business issued common stock to Patel.
1	Purchased medical supplies on account totaling $12,000.
2	Paid monthly office rent of $4,700.
3	Recorded $10,300 revenue for service rendered to patients, received cash of $4,200, and sent bills to patients for the remainder.

After these transactions, how much cash does the business have to work with? Use a T-account to show your answer.

S2-4. *(Learning Objectives 3, 4: Show the impact of business transactions on the accounting equation; analyze the impact of business transactions on accounts)* Refer to Short Exercise 2-3. Which of the transactions of Dora Patel, MD, increased the total assets of the business? For each transaction, identify the asset that was increased.

S2-5. *(Learning Objectives 1, 3: Explain what a transaction is; show the impact of transactions on the accounting equation)* King Design specializes in imported clothing. During March, King completed a series of transactions. For each of the following items, give an example of a transaction that has the described effect on the accounting equation of King Design.
   a. Increase an asset and increase a liability.
   b. Decrease an asset and decrease owners' equity.
   c. Decrease an asset and decrease a liability.
   d. Increase an asset and increase owners' equity.
   e. Increase one asset and decrease another asset.

S2-6. *(Learning Objective 5: Record (journalize) transactions)* After operating for several months, architect Zach Talbot completed the following transactions during the latter part of October:

Oct 15	Borrowed $64,000 from the bank, signing a note payable.
22	Performed service for clients on account totaling $17,100.
28	Received $10,300 cash on account from clients.
29	Received a utility bill of $1,450, an amount that will be paid during November.
31	Paid monthly salaries of $10,100 to employees.

Journalize the transactions of Zach Talbot, Architect. Include an explanation with each journal entry.

S2-7. *(Learning Objectives 3, 5: Show the impact of transactions on the accounting equation; record (journalize and post) transactions in the books)* Architect Wendy Watson purchased supplies on account for $4,800. Later Watson paid $1,350 on account.

1. Journalize the two transactions on the books of Wendy Watson, architect. Include an explanation for each transaction.
2. Open a T-account for Accounts Payable and post to Accounts Payable. Compute the balance and denote it as Bal.
3. How much does the business owe after both transactions? In which account does this amount appear?

S2-8. *(Learning Objective 5: Record (journalize and post) transactions in the books)* Bush Consulting performed service for a client who could not pay immediately. Bush expected to collect the $3,900 the following month. A month later, Bush received $2,000 cash from the client.

1. Record the two transactions on the books of Bush Consulting. Include an explanation for each transaction.
2. Post to these T-accounts: Cash, Accounts Receivable, and Service Revenue. Compute each account balance and denote it as Bal.

S2-9. *(Learning Objective 6: Construct and use a trial balance)* Assume that First Mortgage Company reported the following summarized data at December 31, 2014. Accounts appear in no particular order; dollar amounts are in millions.

Other liabilities	$ 2	Revenues	$38
Other assets	20	Cash	5
Expenses	27	Accounts payable	6
Stockholders' equity	6		

Prepare the trial balance of First Mortgage at December 31, 2014. List the accounts in their proper order. How much was First Mortgage Company's net income or net loss?

S2-10. *(Learning Objective 6: Use a trial balance)* McAllen, Inc.'s trial balance follows:

	A1		

	A	B	C	D	E
1	McAllen, Inc. Trial Balance December 31, 2014				
2		Balance			
3	**Account Title**	**Debit**	**Credit**		
4	Cash	$ 5,400			
5	Accounts receivable	18,300			
6	Supplies	2,500			
7	Land	40,600			
8	Equipment	21,700			
9	Accounts payable		$ 26,000		
10	Note payable		22,900		
11	Common stock		14,500		
12	Retained earnings		5,200		
13	Service revenue		63,600		
14	Salary expense	33,000			
15	Rent expense	8,000			
16	Utilities expense	2,700			
17	Total	$ 132,200	$ 132,200		
18					

Compute these amounts for the business:
1. Total assets
2. Total liabilities
3. Net income or net loss during December

S2-11. *(Learning Objective 6: Use a trial balance)* Refer to McAllen, Inc.'s trial balance in Short Exercise 2-10. The purpose of this exercise is to help you learn how to correct three common accounting errors.

> *Error 1.* Slide. Suppose the trial balance lists Land as $4,060 instead of $40,600. Recompute column totals, take the difference, and divide by 9. The result is an integer (no decimals), which suggests that the error is either a transposition or a slide.
>
> *Error 2.* Transposition. Assume the trial balance lists Accounts Receivable as $13,800 instead of $18,300. Recompute column totals, take the difference, and divide by 9. The result is an integer (no decimals), which suggests that the error is either a transposition or a slide.
>
> *Error 3.* Mislabeling an item. Assume that McAllen, Inc., accidentally listed Accounts Receivable as a credit balance instead of a debit. Recompute the trial balance totals for debits and credits. Then take the difference between total debits and total credits, and divide the difference by 2. You get back to the original amount of Accounts Receivable.

S2-12. *(Learning Objective 2: Define accounting terms)* Accounting has its own vocabulary and basic relationships. Match the accounting terms at the left with the corresponding definition or meaning at the right.

_____ 1. Debit	**A.**	The cost of operating a business; a decrease in stockholders' equity
_____ 2. Expense		
_____ 3. Net income	**B.**	Assets – Liabilities
_____ 4. Ledger	**C.**	Grouping of accounts
_____ 5. Posting	**D.**	Copying data from the journal to the ledger
_____ 6. Normal balance	**E.**	Record of transactions
_____ 7. Payable	**F.**	Revenues – Expenses
_____ 8. Journal	**G.**	Left side of an account
_____ 9. Receivable	**H.**	Always an asset
_____ 10. Owners' equity	**I.**	Side of an account where increases are recorded
	J.	Always a liability

S2-13. *(Learning Objective 4: Analyze the impact of business transactions on accounts)* Robinson Investments, Inc., began by issuing common stock for cash of $200,000. The company immediately purchased computer equipment on account for $56,000.
1. Set up the following T-accounts of Robinson Investments, Inc.: Cash, Computer Equipment, Accounts Payable, and Common Stock.
2. Record the first two transactions of the business directly in the T-accounts without using a journal.
3. Show that total debits equal total credits.

Exercises

All of the A and B exercises can be found within MyAccountingLab, an online homework and practice environment. Your instructor may ask you to complete these exercises using **MyAccountingLab**.

MyAccountingLab

Group A

E2-14A. *(Learning Objectives 1, 4: Explain what a transaction is; analyze the impact of transactions on accounts)* Assume Dresses Unlimited opened a store in San Antonio, starting with cash and common stock of $150,000. Patti Brown, the store manager, then signed a note payable to purchase land for $75,000 and a building for $204,000. Brown also paid $39,000 for equipment and $6,100 for supplies to use in the business.

Suppose the home office of Dresses Unlimited requires a weekly report from store managers. Write Brown's memo to the home office to report on her purchases. Include the store's balance sheet as the final part of your memo. Prepare a T-account to compute the balance for Cash.

E2-15A. *(Learning Objective 4: Analyze the impact of business transactions on accounts)* The following selected events were experienced by either Quick Medical Services, Inc., a corporation, or George Quick, the major stockholder. State whether each event (1) increased, (2) decreased, or (3) had no effect on the total assets of the business. Identify any specific asset affected.

    a. Borrowed $65,000 from the bank for use in the business.
    b. Quick used personal funds to purchase a flat-screen TV for his home.
    c. Sold land and received cash of $71,000 (the land was carried on the company's books at $71,000).
    d. Received $16,300 cash from customers on account.
    e. Made cash purchase of land for a building site for the business, $84,000.
    f. Received $11,000 cash and issued stock to a stockholder.
    g. Paid $8,900 cash on accounts payable.
    h. Purchased medical equipment and signed a $100,000 promissory note in payment.
    i. Purchased office supplies on account for $1,700.
    j. The business paid Quick a cash dividend of $7,000.

E2-16A. *(Learning Objective 3: Show the impact of business transactions on the accounting equation)* Dr. Rebecca Gray opened a medical practice specializing in physical therapy. During the first month of operation (January), the business, titled Dr. Rebecca Gray, Professional Corporation (P.C.), experienced the following events:

Jan	6	Gray invested $150,000 in the business, which in turn issued its common stock to her.
	9	The business paid cash for land costing $63,000. Gray plans to build an office building on the land.
	12	The business purchased medical supplies for $1,900 on account.
	15	Dr. Rebecca Gray, P.C., officially opened for business.
	15–31	During the rest of the month, Gray treated patients and earned service revenue of $9,600, receiving cash for half the revenue earned.
	15–31	The business paid cash expenses: employee salaries, $3,300; office rent, $1,200; utilities, $900.
	31	The business sold supplies to another physician for cost of $700.
	31	The business borrowed $35,000, signing a note payable to the bank.
	31	The business paid $500 on account.

Requirements

1. Analyze the effects of these events on the accounting equation of the medical practice of Dr. Rebecca Gray, P.C.
2. After completing the analysis, answer these questions about the business.
    a. How much are total assets?
    b. How much does the business expect to collect from patients?
    c. How much does the business owe in total?
    d. How much of the business's assets does Gray really own?
    e. How much net income or net loss did the business experience during its first month of operations?

E2-17A. *(Learning Objective 5: Record (journalize) transactions in the books)* Refer to Exercise 2-16A.

Requirement

1. Record the transactions in the journal of Dr. Rebecca Gray, P.C. List the transactions by date and give an explanation for each transaction.

E2-18A. *(Learning Objectives 4, 5, 6: Analyze the impact of business transactions on accounts; record (post) transactions in the books; construct and use a trial balance)* Refer to Exercises 2-16A and 2-17A.

Requirements

1. After journalizing the transactions of Exercise 2-17A, post the entries to the ledger, using T-accounts. Key transactions by date.
2. Prepare the trial balance of Dr. Rebecca Gray, P.C., at January 31, 2014.
3. From the trial balance, determine total assets, total liabilities, and total stockholders' equity on January 31.

E2-19A. *(Learning Objectives 1, 4, 5: Explain what a transaction is; analyze the impact of business transactions on the accounts; record (journalize) transactions)* The first seven transactions of Follett Advertising, Inc., have been posted to the company's accounts:

Cash						Supplies				Land			Equipment	
(1)	8,700	(4)	3,000		(3)	500	(5)	65	(4)	33,000		(7)	3,500	
(2)	9,000	(6)	270											
(5)	65	(7)	3,500											

Accounts Payable				Note Payable			Common Stock		
(6)	270	(3)	500		(2)	9,000		(1)	8,700
					(4)	30,000			

Requirement

1. Prepare the journal entries that served as the sources for the seven transactions. Include an explanation for each entry. As Follett moves into the next period, how much cash does the business have? How much does Follett owe in total liabilities?

E2-20A. *(Learning Objective 6: Construct and use a trial balance)* The accounts of Lake Oaks Pool Service, Inc., follow with their normal balances at April 30, 2014. The accounts are listed in no particular order.

Account	Balance	Account	Balance
Dividends..........................	$ 3,500	Common stock..................	$ 16,800
Utilities expense	1,800	Accounts payable	4,800
Accounts receivable..........	5,300	Service revenue.................	20,910
Delivery expense	450	Equipment........................	29,200
Retained earnings..............	4,700	Note payable....................	21,500
Salary expense..................	8,700	Cash.................................	19,760

Requirements

1. Prepare the company's trial balance at April 30, 2014, listing accounts in proper sequence, as illustrated in the chapter. For example, Accounts Receivable comes before Equipment. List the expense with the largest balance first, the expense with the next largest balance second, and so on.

2. Prepare the financial statement for the month ended April 30, 2014, that will tell the company the results of operations for the month.

E2-21A. *(Learning Objective 6: Construct and use a trial balance)* The trial balance of Amanda's Candies, Inc., at September 30, 2014, does not balance:

Cash..................................	$ 14,200	
Accounts receivable..............	12,800	
Inventory.............................	17,300	
Supplies...............................	400	
Land....................................	41,000	
Accounts payable		$11,600
Common stock......................		47,100
Sales revenue.......................		33,800
Salary expense......................	2,200	
Rent expense.......................	1,000	
Utilities expense	1,000	
Total	$89,900	$92,500

The accounting records hold the following errors:
   a. Recorded a $200 cash revenue transaction by debiting Accounts Receivable. The credit entry was correct.
   b. Posted a $1,000 credit to Accounts Payable as $100.
   c. Did not record utilities expense or the related account payable in the amount of $640.
   d. Understated Common Stock by $200.
   e. Omitted Insurance Expense of $3,700 from the trial balance.

Requirement

   1. Prepare the correct trial balance at September 30, 2014, complete with a heading. Journal entries are not required.

E2-22A. *(Learning Objective 4: Analyze the impact of business transactions on accounts)* Set up the following T-accounts: Cash, Accounts Receivable, Office Supplies, Office Furniture, Accounts Payable, Common Stock, Dividends, Service Revenue, Salary Expense, and Rent Expense. Record the following transactions directly in the T-accounts without using a journal. Use the letters to identify the transactions.
   a. Stephen Garner opened a law firm by investing $25,000 cash and office furniture with a fair value of $10,400. Organized as a professional corporation, the business issued common stock to Garner.
   b. Paid monthly rent of $1,800.
   c. Purchased office supplies on account, $1,050.
   d. Paid employees' salaries of $3,600.
   e. Paid $500 of the account payable created in transaction c.
   f. Performed legal service on account, $10,000.
   g. Declared and paid dividends of $3,200.

E2-23A. *(Learning Objective 6: Construct and use a trial balance)* Refer to Exercise 2-22A.
   1. After recording the transactions in Exercise 2-22A, and assuming they all occurred in the month of November 2014, prepare the trial balance of Stephen Garner, Attorney, at November 30, 2014. Use the T-accounts that have been prepared for the business.
   2. How well did the business perform during its first month? Compute net income (or net loss) for the month.

Group B

E2-24B. *(Learning Objectives 1, 4: Explain what a transaction is; analyze the impact of transactions on accounts)* Assume L. Deveta Fashions opened a store in New Orleans, starting with cash and common stock of $100,000. Lori Lyons, the store manager, then signed a note payable to purchase land for $86,000 and a building for $125,000. Lyons also paid $43,000 for equipment and $7,500 for supplies to use in the business.

Suppose the home office of L. Deveta Fashions requires a weekly report from store managers. Write Lyon's memo to the head office to report on her purchases. Include the store's balance sheet as the final part of your memo. Prepare a T-account to compute the balance for Cash.

E2-25B. *(Learning Objective 4: Analyze the impact of business transactions on accounts)* The following selected events were experienced by either Landscapes Deluxe, Inc., a corporation, or Bill Tinsley, the major stockholder. State whether each event (1) increased, (2) decreased, or (3) had no effect on the total assets of the business. Identify any specific asset affected.

- **a.** Received $150,000 cash and issued stock to a stockholder.
- **b.** Purchased land for a building site for the business and signed a $100,000 promissory note to the bank.
- **c.** Purchased supplies on account for $3,000.
- **d.** Tinsley used personal funds to purchase a pool table for his home.
- **e.** Purchased equipment for the business for $87,000 cash.
- **f.** Received $38,000 cash from customers for services performed.
- **g.** Sold land and received a note receivable of $46,000 (the land was carried on the company's books at $46,000).
- **h.** Earned $12,000 in revenue for services performed. The customer promises to pay Landscapes Deluxe in one month.
- **i.** Paid $19,000 cash on accounts payable.
- **j.** The business paid Tinsley a cash dividend of $5,000.

E2-26B. *(Learning Objective 3: Show the impact of business transactions on the accounting equation)* Fred Grimes opened a medical practice specializing in surgery. During the first month of operation (March), the business, titled Dr. Fred Grimes, Professional Corporation (P.C.), experienced the following events:

Mar	6	Grimes invested $40,000 in the business, which in turn issued its common stock to him.
	9	The business paid cash for land costing $21,000. Grimes plans to build an office building on the land.
	12	The business purchased medical supplies for $3,500 on account.
	15	Dr. Fred Grimes, P.C., officially opened for business.
	15–31	During the rest of the month, Grimes treated patients and earned service revenue of $20,100, receiving cash for half the revenue earned.
	15–31	The business paid cash expenses: employee salaries, $7,500; office rent, $2,400; utilities, $3,600.
	31	The business sold supplies to another physician for cost of $920.
	31	The business borrowed $32,000, signing a note payable to the bank.
	31	The business paid $500 on account.

Requirements

1. Analyze the effects of these events on the accounting equation of the medical practice of Dr. Fred Grimes, P.C.
2. After completing the analysis, answer these questions about the business.
   - **a.** How much are total assets?
   - **b.** How much does the business expect to collect from patients?
   - **c.** How much does the business owe in total?
   - **d.** How much of the business's assets does Grimes really own?
   - **e.** How much net income or net loss did the business experience during its first month of operations?

E2-27B. *(Learning Objective 5: Record (journalize) transactions in the books)* Refer to Exercise 2-26B.

Requirement

1. Record the transactions in the journal of Dr. Fred Grimes, P.C. List the transactions by date and give an explanation for each transaction.

E2-28B. *(Learning Objectives 4, 5, 6: Analyze the impact of business transactions on accounts; record (post) transactions in the books; construct and use a trial balance)* Refer to Exercises 2-26B and 2-27B.

Requirements

1. Post the entries to the ledger, using T-accounts. Key transactions by date.
2. Prepare the trial balance of Dr. Fred Grimes, P.C., at March 31, 2014.
3. From the trial balance, determine total assets, total liabilities, and total shareholders' equity on March 31.

E2-29B. *(Learning Objectives 1, 4, 5: Explain what a transaction is; analyze the impact of business transactions on accounts; record (journalize) transactions in the books)* The first seven transactions of Big Horn Advertising, Inc., have been posted to the company's accounts:

	Cash				Supplies			Land			Equipment	
(1)	7,000	(3)	5,900	(4)	820	(5)	130	(6)	36,000	(3)	5,900	
(2)	8,300	(6)	7,000									
(5)	130	(7)	140									

	Accounts Payable				Note Payable			Common Stock	
(7)	140	(4)	820		(2)	8,300		(1)	7,000
					(3)	29,000			

Requirement

1. Prepare the journal entries that served as the sources for the seven transactions. Include an explanation for each entry. As Big Horn moves into the next period, how much cash does the business have? How much does Big Horn owe in total liabilities?

E2-30B. *(Learning Objective 6: Construct and use a trial balance)* The accounts of Castlerock Tree Service, Inc., follow with their normal balances at September 30, 2014. The accounts are listed in no particular order.

Account	Balance	Account	Balance
Dividends..........................	$ 5,100	Common stock.................	$ 12,000
Utilities expense	2,700	Accounts payable	5,100
Accounts receivable...........	8,200	Service revenue.................	32,300
Delivery expense	800	Land.................................	29,600
Retained earnings..............	13,100	Note payable.....................	21,700
Salary expense...................	18,500	Cash.................................	19,300

Requirements

1. Prepare the company's trial balance at September 30, 2014, listing accounts in proper sequence, as illustrated in the chapter. For example, Accounts Receivable comes before Land. List the expense with the largest balance first, the expense with the next largest balance second, and so on.
2. Prepare the financial statement for the month ended September 30, 2014, that will tell the company the results of operations for the month.

E2-31B. *(Learning Objective 6: Construct and use a trial balance)* The trial balance of Yellow Car Sales, Inc., at June 30, 2014, does not balance.

Cash	$ 9,600	
Accounts receivable	13,200	
Inventory	17,100	
Supplies	800	
Land	53,000	
Accounts payable		$12,200
Common stock		47,400
Sales revenue		37,100
Salary expense	1,900	
Rent expense	1,100	
Utilities expense	1,100	
Total	$97,800	$96,700

The accounting records hold the following errors:
  a. Recorded a $600 cash revenue transaction by debiting Accounts Receivable. The credit entry was correct.
  b. Posted a $3,000 credit to Accounts Payable as $300.
  c. Did not record utilities expense or the related account payable in the amount of $650.
  d. Understated Common Stock by $200.
  e. Omitted Insurance Expense of $1,800 from the trial balance.

Requirement

  1. Prepare the correct trial balance at June 30, 2014, complete with a heading. Journal entries are not required.

E2-32B. *(Learning Objective 4: Analyze the impact of business transactions on accounts)* Set up the following T-accounts: Cash, Accounts Receivable, Office Supplies, Office Furniture, Accounts Payable, Common Stock, Dividends, Service Revenue, Salary Expense, and Rent Expense. Record the following transactions directly in the T-accounts without using a journal. Use the letters to identify the transactions.
  a. Laura Hull opened a law firm by investing $26,000 cash and office furniture with a fair value of $8,100. Organized as a professional corporation, the business issued common stock to Hull.
  b. Paid monthly rent of $2,600.
  c. Purchased office supplies on account, $1,900.
  d. Paid employee salaries of $3,700.
  e. Paid $1,000 of the accounts payable created in transaction c.
  f. Performed legal service on account, $9,100.
  g. Declared and paid dividends of $2,800.

E2-33B. *(Learning Objective 6: Construct and use a trial balance)* Refer to Exercise 2-32B.

Requirements

  1. After recording the transactions in Exercise 2-32B, and assuming they all occurred in the month of July 2014, prepare the trial balance of Laura Hull, Attorney, at July 31, 2014. Use the T-accounts that have been prepared for the business.
  2. How well did the business perform during its first month? Compute net income (or net loss) for the month.

Serial Exercise

Exercise 2-34 begins an accounting cycle that will be completed in Chapter 3.

E2-34. *(Learning Objectives 1, 4, 5, 6: Explain what a transaction is; analyze the impact of business transactions on accounts; record (journalize and post) transactions in the books; construct and use a trial balance)* Sean Huffman, Certified Public Accountant, operates as a professional corporation (P.C.). The business completed these transactions during the first part of January 2014:

Jan	2	Received $11,000 cash from Huffman, and issued common stock to him.
	2	Paid monthly office rent, $700.
	3	Paid cash for a Dell computer, $3,900, with the computer expected to remain in service for five years.
	4	Purchased office furniture on account, $4,700, with the furniture projected to last for five years.
	5	Purchased supplies on account, $400.
	9	Performed tax services for a client and received cash for the full amount of $1,000.
	12	Paid utility expenses, $200.
	18	Performed consulting services for a client on account, $1,500.

Requirements

1. Journalize the transactions. Explanations are not required.
2. Post to the T-accounts. Key all items by date and determine the ending balance in each account. Denote an account balance on January 18, 2014, as Bal.
3. Using **Excel**, prepare a trial balance at January 18, 2014. In the Serial Exercise of Chapter 3, we add transactions for the remainder of January and will require a trial balance at January 31.

Quiz

Test your understanding of transaction analysis by answering the following questions. Select the best choice from among the possible answers.

Q2-35. An investment of cash by stockholders into the business will
  a. decrease total liabilities.
  b. increase stockholders' equity.
  c. have no effect on total assets.
  d. decrease total assets.

Q2-36. Purchasing a laptop computer on account will
  a. increase total assets.
  b. have no effect on stockholders' equity.
  c. increase total liabilities.
  d. all of the above.

Q2-37. Performing a service on account will
  a. increase stockholders' equity.
  b. increase total assets.
  c. increase total liabilities.
  d. both a and b.

Q2-38. Receiving cash from a customer on account will
  a. have no effect on total assets.
  b. decrease liabilities.
  c. increase total assets.
  d. increase stockholders' equity.

Q2-39. Purchasing computer equipment for cash will
  a. increase both total assets and total liabilities.
  b. decrease both total assets and stockholders' equity.
  c. have no effect on total assets, total liabilities, or stockholders' equity.
  d. decrease both total liabilities and stockholders' equity.

Q2-40. Purchasing a building for $95,000 by paying cash of $25,000 and signing a note payable for $70,000 will
  a. decrease total assets and increase total liabilities by $25,000.
  b. increase both total assets and total liabilities by $70,000.
  c. decrease both total assets and total liabilities by $25,000.
  d. increase both total assets and total liabilities by $95,000.

Q2-41. What is the effect on total assets and stockholders' equity of paying the telephone bill as soon as it is received each month?

Total assets	Stockholders' equity
a. No effect	No effect
b. Decrease	No effect
c. Decrease	Decrease
d. No effect	Decrease

Q2-42. Which of the following transactions will increase an asset and increase a liability?
  a. Purchasing office equipment for cash   **c.** Payment of an account payable
  b. Issuing stock   **d.** Buying equipment on account

Q2-43. Which of the following transactions will increase an asset and increase stockholders' equity?
  a. Performing a service on account for a customer
  b. Borrowing money from a bank
  c. Collecting cash from a customer on an account receivable
  d. Purchasing supplies on account

Q2-44. Where do we first record a transaction?
  a. Ledger   **c.** Journal
  b. Trial balance   **d.** Account

Q2-45. Which of the following is not an asset account?
  a. Salary Expense   **c.** Common Stock
  b. Service Revenue   **d.** None of the above accounts is an asset.

Q2-46. Which statement is false?
  a. Dividends are increased by credits.   **c.** Liabilities are decreased by debits.
  b. Assets are increased by debits.   **d.** Revenues are increased by credits.

Q2-47. The journal entry to record the receipt of land and a building and issuance of common stock
  a. debits Land and credits Common Stock.
  b. debits Land and Building and credits Common Stock.
  c. debits Land, Building, and Common Stock.
  d. debits Common Stock and credits Land and Building.

Q2-48. The journal entry to record the purchase of supplies on account
  a. credits Supplies and debits Accounts Payable.
  b. debits Supplies Expense and credits Supplies.
  c. debits Supplies and credits Accounts Payable.
  d. credits Supplies and debits Cash.

Q2-49. If the credit to record the purchase of supplies on account is not posted,
  a. stockholders' equity will be understated.
  b. liabilities will be understated.
  c. assets will be understated.
  d. expenses will be overstated.

Q2-50. The journal entry to record a payment on account will
  a. debit Accounts Payable and credit Retained Earnings.
  b. debit Cash and credit Expenses.
  c. debit Expenses and credit Cash.
  d. debit Accounts Payable and credit Cash.

Q2-51. If the credit to record the payment of an account payable is not posted,
  a. expenses will be understated.
  b. cash will be overstated.
  c. cash will be understated.
  d. liabilities will be understated.

Q2-52. Which statement is false?
  a. A trial balance lists all the accounts with their current balances.
  b. A trial balance can be taken at any time.
  c. A trial balance is the same as a balance sheet.
  d. A trial balance can verify the equality of debits and credits.

Q2-53. A business's receipt of a $105,000 building, with a $90,000 mortgage payable, and issuance of $15,000 of common stock will
  a. increase assets by $15,000.
  b. increase stockholders' equity by $15,000.
  c. increase stockholders' equity by $105,000.
  d. decrease assets by $90,000.

Q2-54. FourStar, a new company, completed these transactions. What will FourStar's total assets equal?
  1. Stockholders invested $54,000 cash and inventory with a fair value of $30,000.
  2. Sales on account, $22,000.

  a. $106,000
  b. $54,000
  c. $84,000
  d. $76,000

Problems

All of the A and B problems can be found within MyAccountingLab, an online homework and practice environment. Your instructor may ask you to complete these problems using **MyAccountingLab**.

MyAccountingLab

Group A

P2-55A. *(Learning Objective 6: Construct and use a trial balance)* The trial balance of Dallas Design Specialties, Inc., follows:

	A	B	C	D	E
A1					
1	Dallas Design Specialties, Inc. Trial Balance December 31, 2014				
2	Cash	$ 31,600			
3	Accounts receivable	65,000			
4	Prepaid expenses	3,000			
5	Building	104,000			
6	Equipment	235,000			
7	Accounts payable		$ 52,200		
8	Note payable		132,000		
9	Common stock		66,000		
10	Retained earnings		182,000		
11	Dividends	18,000			
12	Service revenue		180,600		
13	Rent expense	59,000			
14	Advertising expense	12,000			
15	Wage expense	76,200			
16	Supplies expense	9,000			
17	Total	$ 612,800	$ 612,800		
18					

Annie May, your best friend, is considering investing in Dallas Design Specialties, Inc. Annie seeks your advice in interpreting this information. Specifically, she asks how to use this trial balance to compute the company's total assets, total liabilities, and net income or net loss for the year.

Requirement

1. Write a short note to answer Annie's questions. In your note, state the amounts of Dallas Design Specialties' total assets, total liabilities, and net income or net loss for the year. Also show how you computed each amount.

P2-56A. *(Learning Objectives 3, 4: Show the impact of business transactions on the accounting equation; analyze the impact of business transactions on accounts)* The following amounts summarize the financial position of Taylor Computing, Inc., on October 31, 2014:

	Assets				=	Liabilities	+	Stockholders' Equity		
	Cash	+ Accounts Receivable	+ Supplies	+ Equipment	=	Accounts Payable	+	Common Stock	+	Retained Earnings
Bal	2,600	3,300		11,700		8,100		6,500		3,000

During November 2014, Taylor Computing completed these transactions:
   a. The business received cash of $4,000 and issued common stock.
   b. Performed services for a customer and received cash of $6,300.
   c. Paid $4,100 on accounts payable.
   d. Purchased supplies on account, $1,200.
   e. Collected cash from a customer on account, $1,700.
   f. Consulted on the design of a computer system and billed the customer for services rendered, $4,200.
   g. Recorded the following business expenses for the month: (1) paid office rent—$1,600; (2) paid advertising—$1,200.
   h. Declared and paid a cash dividend of $2,700.

Requirements

1. Analyze the effects of the preceding transactions on the accounting equation of Taylor Computing, Inc.
2. Prepare the income statement of Taylor Computing, Inc., for the month ended November 30, 2014. List expenses in decreasing order by amount.
3. Prepare the entity's statement of retained earnings for the month ended November 30, 2014.
4. Prepare the balance sheet of Taylor Computing, Inc., at November 30, 2014.

P2-57A. *(Learning Objectives 4, 5: Analyze the impact of business transactions on accounts; record (journalize and post) transactions in the books)* This problem can be used in conjunction with Problem 2-56A. Refer to Problem 2-56A.

Requirements

1. Journalize the November transactions of Taylor Computing, Inc. Explanations are not required.
2. Prepare T-Accounts for each account. Insert in each T-account its October 31 balance as given (example: Cash $2,600). Then, post the November transactions to the T-accounts.
3. Compute the balance in each account.

P2-58A. *(Learning Objectives 4, 5, 6: Analyze the impact of business transactions on accounts; record (journalize and post) transactions in the books; construct and use a trial balance)* During the first month of operations, Wortham Services, Inc., completed the following transactions:

Jan	2	Wortham Services received $65,000 cash and issued common stock to the stockholders.
	3	Purchased supplies, $1,000, and equipment, $12,000, on account.
	4	Performed services for a customer and received cash, $5,500.
	7	Paid cash to acquire land, $39,000.
	11	Performed services for a customer and billed the customer, $4,100. Wortham expects to collect within one month.
	16	Paid for the equipment purchased January 3 on account.
	17	Paid for newspaper advertising, $600.
	18	Received partial payment from customer on account, $2,000.
	22	Paid the water and electricity bills, $430.
	29	Received $2,600 cash for servicing the heating unit of a customer.
	31	Paid employee salary, $2,900.
	31	Declared and paid dividends of $1,800.

Requirements

1. Record each transaction in the journal. Key each transaction by date. Explanations are not required.
2. Post the transactions to the T-accounts, using transaction dates as posting references. Label the ending balance of each account Bal, as shown in the chapter.
3. Prepare the trial balance of Wortham Services, Inc., at January 31 of the current year.
4. Mark Wortham, the manager, asks you how much in total resources the business has to work with, how much it owes, and whether January was profitable (and by how much).

P2-59A. *(Learning Objectives 4, 6: Analyze the impact of business transactions on accounts; construct and use a trial balance)* During the first month of operations (September 2014), Holt Music Services Corporation completed the following selected transactions:

   a. The business received cash of $50,000 and a building with a fair value of $107,000. The corporation issued common stock to the stockholders.
   b. Borrowed $60,000 from the bank; signed a note payable.
   c. Paid $47,000 for music equipment.
   d. Purchased supplies on account, $450.
   e. Paid employees' salaries, $6,100.
   f. Received $3,790 for music services performed for customers.
   g. Performed services for customers on account, $12,800.
   h. Paid $100 of the account payable created in transaction d.
   i. Received a $700 bill for utility expense that will be paid in the near future.
   j. Received cash on account, $1,600.
   k. Paid the following cash expenses: (1) rent, $1,400; (2) advertising, $400.

Requirements

1. Record each transaction directly in the T-accounts without using a journal. Use the letters to identify the transactions.
2. Prepare the trial balance of Holt Music Services Corporation at September 30, 2014.

Group B

P2-60B. *(Learning Objective 6: Construct and use a trial balance)* The trial balance of Tampa Outdoor Design, Inc., follows:

	A	B	C	D	E
A1					
	Tampa Outdoor Design, Inc.				
	Trial Balance				
1	**December 31, 2014**				
2	Cash	$ 27,300			
3	Accounts receivable	38,100			
4	Prepaid expenses	6,000			
5	Building	197,000			
6	Equipment	140,900			
7	Accounts payable		$ 54,000		
8	Note payable		135,300		
9	Common stock		75,000		
10	Retained earnings		112,200		
11	Dividends	16,000			
12	Service revenue		164,700		
13	Rent expense	24,700			
14	Advertising expense	10,000			
15	Wage expense	77,000			
16	Supplies expense	4,200			
17	Total	$ 541,200	$ 541,200		
18					

Ramona Robinson, your best friend, is considering making an investment in Tampa Outdoor Design, Inc. Ramona seeks your advice in interpreting the company's information. Specifically, she asks how to use this trial balance to compute the company's total assets, total liabilities, and net income or net loss for the year.

Requirement

1. Write a short note to answer Ramona's questions. In your note, state the amounts of Tampa Outdoor Design's total assets, total liabilities, and net income or net loss for the year. Also show how you computed each amount.

P2-61B. *(Learning Objectives 3, 4: Show the impact of business transactions on the accounting equation; analyze the impact of business transactions on accounts)* The following amounts summarize the financial position of Computer Works on May 31, 2014:

	Assets				=	Liabilities	+	Stockholders' Equity	
	Cash +	Accounts Receivable +	Supplies +	Equipment =		Accounts Payable +		Common Stock +	Retained Earnings
Bal	2,050	3,350		21,700		8,900		13,600	4,600

During June 2014, the business completed these transactions:
  a. The business received cash of $9,800 and issued common stock.
  b. Performed services for a customer and received cash of $5,800.
  c. Paid $4,900 on accounts payable.
  d. Purchased supplies on account, $700.
  e. Collected cash from a customer on account, $600.
  f. Consulted on the design of a computer system and billed the customer for services rendered, $3,400.
  g. Recorded the following expenses for the month: (1) paid office rent—$1,500; (2) paid advertising—$2,000.
  h. Declared and paid a cash dividend of $2,400.

Requirements

1. Analyze the effects of the preceding transactions on the accounting equation of Computer Works, Inc.
2. Prepare the income statement of Computer Works, Inc., for the month ended June 30, 2014. List expenses in decreasing order by amount.
3. Prepare the statement of retained earnings of Computer Works, Inc., for the month ended June 30, 2014.
4. Prepare the balance sheet of Computer Works, Inc., at June 30, 2014.

P2-62B. *(Learning Objectives 4, 5: Analyze the impact of business transactions on accounts; record (journalize and post) transactions in the books)* This problem can be used in conjunction with Problem 2-61B. Refer to Problem 2-61B.

Requirements

1. Journalize the transactions of Computer Works, Inc. Explanations are not required.
2. Prepare T-accounts for each account. Insert in each T-account its May 31 balance as given (example: Cash $2,050). Then, post the June transactions to the T-accounts.
3. Compute the balance in each account.

P2-63B. *(Learning Objectives 4, 5, 6: Analyze the impact of business transactions on accounts; record (journalize and post) transactions in the books; construct and use a trial balance)* During the first month of operations, Arguetta Brickworks, Inc., completed the following transactions:

Apr	2	Arguetta received $70,000 cash and issued common stock to the stockholders.
	3	Purchased supplies, $2,000, and equipment, $9,200, on account.
	4	Performed services for a client and received cash, $1,400.
	7	Paid cash to acquire land, $42,500.
	11	Performed services for a customer and billed the customer, $2,800. Arguetta expects to collect within one month.
	16	Paid for the equipment purchased April 3 on account.
	17	Paid the telephone bill, $150.
	18	Received partial payment from customer on account, $300.
	22	Paid the water and electricity bills, $170.
	29	Received $2,500 cash for repairing a customer's brick walkway.
	30	Paid employee salaries, $4,900.
	30	Declared and paid dividends of $2,600.

Requirements

1. Record each transaction in the journal. Key each transaction by date. Explanations are not required.
2. Post the transactions to the T-accounts, using transaction dates as posting references.
3. Prepare the trial balance of Arguetta Brickworks, Inc., at April 30 of the current year.
4. Dave Arguetta, the manager, asks you how much in total resources the business has to work with, how much it owes, and whether April was profitable (and by how much).

P2-64B. *(Learning Objectives 4, 6: Analyze the impact of business transactions on accounts; construct and use a trial balance)* During the first month of operations (March 2014), Lone Star Entertainment Corporation completed the following selected transactions:

  a. The business received cash of $38,000 and a building with a fair value of $110,000. The corporation issued common stock to the stockholders.
  b. Borrowed $50,000 from the bank; signed a note payable.
  c. Paid $45,500 for music equipment.
  d. Purchased supplies on account, $1,900.
  e. Paid employees' salaries, $4,200.
  f. Received $4,600 for music service performed for customers.
  g. Performed service for customers on account, $3,600.
  h. Paid $400 of the account payable created in transaction d.
  i. Received a $900 bill for utilities expense that will be paid in the near future.
  j. Received cash on account, $1,200.
  k. Paid the following cash expenses: (1) rent—$1,800; (2) advertising—$950.

Requirements

1. Record each transaction directly in the T-accounts without using a journal. Use the letters to identify the transactions.
2. Prepare the trial balance of Lone Star Entertainment Corporation at March 31, 2014.

Challenge Exercises and Problem

E2-65. *(Learning Objective 4: Analyze the impact of business transactions on accounts)* The manager of Southwest Furniture needs to compute the following amounts:

a. Total cash paid during December.

b. Cash collections from customers during December. Analyze Accounts Receivable.

c. Cash paid on a note payable during December. Analyze Notes Payable.

Here's the additional data you need to analyze the accounts:

| | Balance | | Additional Information |
Account	Nov 30	Dec 31	for the Month of December
1. Cash.............................	$10,000	$ 5,000	Cash receipts, $96,000
2. Accounts Receivable.......	27,000	25,000	Sales on account, $47,000
3. Notes Payable	11,000	19,000	New borrowing, $28,000

Requirement

1. Prepare a T-account to compute each amount, *a* through *c*.

E2-66. *(Learning Objectives 4, 6: Analyze the impact of business transactions on accounts; construct and use a trial balance)* The trial balance of 3PT, Inc., at October 31, 2014, does not balance.

Cash....................................	$ 3,900	Common stock....................	$20,100
Accounts receivable.............	7,400	Retained earnings................	7,500
Land....................................	34,400	Service revenue...................	9,500
Accounts payable	6,000	Salary expense.....................	3,300
Note payable......................	5,500	Advertising expense.............	1,100

Requirements

1. Prepare a trial balance for the ledger accounts of 3PT, Inc., as of October 31, 2014.

2. Determine the out-of-balance amount. The error lies in the Accounts Receivable account. Add the out-of-balance amount to, or subtract it from, Accounts Receivable to determine the correct balance of Accounts Receivable. After correcting Accounts Receivable, advise the top management of 3PT, Inc., on the company's

   a. total assets.

   b. total liabilities.

   c. net income or net loss for October.

E2-67. *(Learning Objective 4: Analyze the impact of business transactions on accounts)* This question concerns the items and the amounts that two entities, Burlington Co. and Gardner Hospital, should report in their financial statements.

During November, Gardner provided Burlington with medical exams for Burlington employees and sent a bill for $44,000. On December 7, Burlington sent a check to Gardner for $30,000. Burlington began November with a cash balance of $53,000; Gardner began with cash of $0.

Requirements

1. For this situation, show everything that both Burlington and Gardner will report on their November and December income statements and on their balance sheets at November 30 and December 31.

2. After showing what each company should report, briefly explain how the Burlington and Gardner data relate to each other.

P2-68. *(Learning Objectives 3, 4, 5: Analyze the impact of errors and compute correct amounts)*
Richards Advertising creates, plans, and handles advertising needs in the Tri-State area. Recently, Richards had to replace an inexperienced office worker in charge of bookkeeping because of some serious mistakes that had been uncovered in the accounting records. You have been hired to review these transactions to determine any corrections that might be necessary. In all cases, the bookkeeper made an accurate description of the transaction.

	A		B	C	D
			A1		
1	May	1	Accounts receivable	300	
2			Service revenue		300
3			Collected an account receivable.		
4					
5		2	Rent expense	5,000	
6			Cash		5,000
7			Paid monthly rent, $500.		
8					
9		5	Cash	1,000	
10			Accounts receivable		1,000
11			Collected cash for services provided.		
12					
13		10	Supplies	2,500	
14			Accounts payable		2,500
15			Purchased office equipment on account.		
16					
17		16	Dividends	2,000	
18			Cash		2,000
19			Paid salaries.		
20					
21		25	Accounts receivable	1,500	
22			Cash		1,500
23			Paid for supplies purchased earlier on account.		
24					

Requirements

1. For each of the preceding entries, indicate the effect of the error on cash, total assets, and net income. The answer for the first transaction has been provided as an example.

Date	Effect on Cash	Effect on Total Assets	Effect on Net Income
May 1	Understated $300	Overstated $300	Overstated $300

2. What is the correct balance of cash if the balance of cash on the books before correcting the preceding transactions was $5,500?
3. What is the correct amount of total assets if the total assets on the books before correcting the preceding transactions was $25,000?
4. What is the correct net income for May if the reported income before correcting the preceding transactions was $10,000?

APPLY YOUR KNOWLEDGE

Decision Cases

Case 1. *(Learning Objectives 4, 6: Analyze the impact of transactions on business accounts; construct and use a trial balance; measure net income or loss; decide whether to continue a business)* A friend named Jay Barlow has asked what effect certain transactions will have on his company. Time is short, so you cannot apply the detailed procedures of journalizing and posting. Instead, you must analyze the transactions without the use of a journal. Barlow will continue the business only if he can expect to earn monthly net income of at least $5,000. The following transactions occurred this month:

- **a.** Barlow deposited $5,000 cash in a business bank account, and the corporation issued common stock to him.
- **b.** Borrowed $5,000 cash from the bank and signed a note payable due within 1 year.
- **c.** Paid $1,300 cash for supplies.
- **d.** Purchased advertising in the local newspaper for cash, $1,800.
- **e.** Purchased office furniture on account, $4,400.
- **f.** Paid the following cash expenses for one month: employee salary—$2,000; office rent— $1,200.
- **g.** Earned revenue on account, $7,000.
- **h.** Earned revenue and received $2,500 cash.
- **i.** Collected cash from customers on account, $1,200.
- **j.** Paid on account, $1,000.

Requirements

1. Set up the following T-accounts: Cash, Accounts Receivable, Supplies, Furniture, Accounts Payable, Notes Payable, Common Stock, Service Revenue, Salary Expense, Advertising Expense, and Rent Expense.
2. Record the transactions directly in the accounts without using a journal. Key each transaction by letter.
3. Construct a trial balance for Barlow Networks, Inc., at the current date. List expenses with the largest amount first, the next largest amount second, and so on.
4. Compute the amount of net income or net loss for this first month of operations. Why or why not would you recommend that Barlow continue in business?

Case 2. *(Learning Objective 4: Analyze the impact of transactions on business accounts; correct erroneous financial statements; decide whether to expand a business)* Sophia Loren opened an Italian restaurant. Business has been good, and Loren is considering expanding the restaurant. Loren, who knows little accounting, produced the following financial statements for Little Italy, Inc., at December 31, 2014, the end of the first month of operations:

	A1			
	A		**B**	**C**
1	Little Italy, Inc. Income Statement Month Ended December 31, 2014			
2	Sales revenue			$ 42,000
3	Common stock			10,000
4	Total revenue			52,000
5				
6	Accounts payable			8,000
7	Advertising expense			5,000
8	Rent expense			6,000
9	Total expenses			19,000
10	Net income			$ 33,000
11				

	A	B	C
	Little Italy, Inc.		
	Balance Sheet		
1	**December 31, 2014**		
2	Assets		
3	Cash		$ 12,000
4	Cost of goods sold (expense)		22,000
5	Food inventory		5,000
6	Furniture		10,000
7	Total Assets		$ 49,000
8	Liabilities		
9	None		
10	Owners' Equity		$ 49,000
11			

In these financial statements all *amounts* are correct, except for Owners' Equity. Loren heard that total assets should equal total liabilities plus owners' equity, so she plugged in the amount of owners' equity at $49,000 to make the balance sheet come out even.

Requirement

1. Sophia Loren has asked whether she should expand the restaurant. Her banker says Loren may be wise to expand if (a) net income for the first month reached $10,000 and (b) total assets are at least $35,000. It appears that the business has reached these milestones, but Loren doubts whether her financial statements tell the true story. She needs your help in making this decision. Prepare a corrected income statement and balance sheet. (Remember that Retained Earnings, which was omitted from the balance sheet, should equal net income for the first month; there were no dividends.) After preparing the statements, give Sophia Loren your recommendation as to whether she should expand the restaurant.

Ethical Issues

Issue 1. Scruffy Murphy is the president and principal stockholder of Scruffy's Bar & Grill, Inc. To expand, the business is applying for a $250,000 bank loan. To get the loan, Murphy is considering two options for beefing up the owners' equity of the business:

> *Option 1.* Issue $100,000 of common stock for cash. A friend has wanted to invest in the company. This may be the right time to extend the offer.
>
> *Option 2.* Transfer $100,000 of Murphy's personal land to the business, and issue common stock to Murphy. Then, after obtaining the loan, Murphy can transfer the land back to himself and zero out the common stock.

Requirements

Use the ethical decision model in Chapter 1 to answer the following questions:
1. What is the ethical issue?
2. Who are the stakeholders? What are the possible consequences to each?
3. Analyze the alternatives from the following standpoints: (a) economic, (b) legal, and (c) ethical.
4. What would you do? How would you justify your decision? How would your decision make you feel afterward?

Issue 2. Part a. You have received your grade in your first accounting course, and to your amazement, it is an A. You feel the instructor must have made a big mistake. Your grade was a B going into the final, but you are sure that you really "bombed" the exam, which is worth 30% of the final grade. In fact, you walked out after finishing only 50% of the exam, and the grade report says you made 99% on the exam!

Requirements

1. What is the ethical issue?
2. Who are the stakeholders? What are the possible consequences to each?
3. Analyze the alternatives from the following standpoints: (a) economic, (b) legal, and (c) ethical.
4. What would you do? How would you justify your decision? How would it make you feel afterward?

Part b. Now assume the same facts that were just provided, except that you have received your final grade for the course and the grade is a B. You are confident that you "aced" the final. In fact, you stayed to the very end of the period and checked every figure twice! You are confident that the instructor must have made a mistake grading the final.

Requirements

1. What is the ethical issue?
2. Who are the stakeholders and what are the consequences to each?
3. Analyze the alternatives from the following standpoints: (a) economic, (b) legal, and (c) ethical.
4. What would you do? How would you justify your decision? How would it make you feel?

Part c. How is this situation like a financial accounting misstatement? How is it different?

Focus on Financials | Amazon.com, Inc.

(Learning Objectives 3, 4: Record transactions; compute net income) Refer to **Amazon.com, Inc.**'s financial statements in Appendix A at the end of the book. Assume that Amazon.com completed the following selected transactions during 2012.

   a. Made company sales (revenue) of $61,093 million, all on account (debit Accounts Receivable, net and other).
   b. Collected cash on accounts receivable $60,300 million.
   c. Purchased inventories on account, $47,010 million (credit Accounts Payable).
   d. Incurred cost of sales in the amount of $45,971 million. Debit the Cost of Sales (expense) account. Credit the Inventories account.
   e. Paid accounts payable in cash, $44,837 million.
   f. Paid operating expenses of $14,446 million in cash.
   g. Paid non-operating expenses (net) in cash, $132 million.
   h. Paid income taxes, $428 million in cash (debit Provision for Income Taxes).
   i. Accounted for income from other investment activity net of taxes in the amount of $155 million. Credit Other Assets. Debit the account entitled Equity Method Investment Activity, net of tax.
   j. Paid cash for Property and Equipment, $2,643 million; paid cash for Other Assets, $291 million.

Requirements

1. Set up T-accounts for beginning balances of Cash ($5,269 million); Accounts Receivable, net and other (debit balance of $2,571 million); Inventories (debit balance $4,992 million); Other Assets (debit balance of $ 1,388 million); Property and Equipment, net (debit balance of $4,417 million); Accounts Payable (credit balance of $11,145 million); Net Sales ($0 balance); Cost of Sales ($0 balance); Operating Expenses ($0 balance); Non-operating Income (expense), net ($0 balance); Provision for Income Taxes ($0 balance); Equity Method Investment Activity, net of tax ($0 balance).
2. Journalize Amazon.com's transactions a–j. Explanations are not required.
3. Post to the T-accounts, and compute the balance for each account. Key postings by transaction letters a–j.

4. For each of the following accounts, compare your computed balance to Amazon.com, Inc.'s actual balance as shown on its 2012 Consolidated Statement of Operations or Consolidated Balance Sheet in Appendix A at the end of the book. Your amounts should agree with the actual figures.
   a. Accounts Receivable, net and other
   b. Inventories
   c. Property and Equipment, net (assume no other activity in fixed assets than given in the problem)
   d. Other Assets
   e. Accounts Payable
   f. Net Sales
   g. Cost of Sales
   h. Operating Expenses
   i. Non-operating Income (expenses), net
   j. Provision for Income Taxes
   k. Equity Method Investment Activity, net of tax

5. Use the relevant accounts from requirement 4 to prepare a summary income statement for Amazon.com, Inc., for 2012. Compare the net income (loss) you computed to Amazon.com, Inc.'s actual net income (loss). The two amounts should be equal.

Focus on Analysis | Yum! Brands, Inc.

(Learning Objective 4: Analyze financial statements) Refer to the **Yum! Brands, Inc.'s** financial statements in Appendix B at the end of the book. Suppose you are an investor considering buying Yum! Brands, Inc.'s common stock. The following questions are important. Show amounts in millions.

1. Which was larger for Yum! Brands, Inc. during 2012: (1) sales revenue, or (2) cash collected from customers? Why? Show computation. (Challenge)
2. Investors are vitally interested in a company's sales and profits and its trends of sales and profits over time. Consider Yum! Brands, Inc.'s sales and net income (net loss) during the period from 2010 through 2012. Compute the percentage increase or decrease in net sales and also in net income (net loss) from 2010 to 2012. Which item grew faster during this two-year period—net sales or net income (net loss)? Can you offer a possible explanation for these changes? (Challenge)

Group Projects

Project 1. You are promoting a rock concert in your area. Your purpose is to earn a profit, so you need to establish the formal structure of a business entity. Assume you organize as a corporation.

Requirements

1. Make a detailed list of 10 factors you must consider as you establish the business.
2. Describe 10 of the items your business must arrange to promote and stage the rock concert.
3. Identify the transactions that your business can undertake to organize, promote, and stage the concert. Journalize the transactions, and post to the relevant T-accounts. Set up the accounts you need for your business ledger. Refer to the chart of accounts in Appendix C at the end of the book if needed.
4. Prepare the income statement, statement of retained earnings, and balance sheet immediately after the rock concert—that is, before you have had time to pay all the business bills and to collect all receivables.
5. Assume that you will continue to promote rock concerts if the venture is successful. If it is unsuccessful, you will terminate the business within three months after the concert. Discuss how to evaluate the success of your venture and how to decide whether to continue in business.

Project 2. Contact a local business and arrange with the owner to learn what accounts the business uses.

Requirements

1. Obtain a copy of the business's chart of accounts.
2. Prepare the company's financial statements for the most recent month, quarter, or year. You may use either made-up account balances or balances supplied by the owner.

If the business has a large number of accounts within a category, combine related accounts and report a single amount on the financial statements. For example, the company may have several cash accounts. Combine all cash amounts and report a single Cash amount on the balance sheet.

You will probably encounter numerous accounts that you have not yet learned. Deal with these as best you can. The charts of accounts given in Appendix C at the end of the book could be helpful.

MyAccountingLab	**For online homework, exercises, and problems that provide you with immediate feedback, please visit www.myaccountinglab.com.**

Quick Check Answers

1. *a*
2. *d*
3. *b*
4. *b* ($1,000 + $600 − $500)
5. *c*
6. *c*
7. *a* ($3,000 + *x* − $27,000 = $4,000; *x* = $28,000)
8. *c*
9. *a*
10. *b*
11. *d*
12. *d*

Accrual Accounting & Income

3

> **SPOTLIGHT:** Starbucks Corporation

Starbucks has changed coffee from a breakfast drink to an experience. It opened its first store in 1971 in Seattle, Washington. After studying the popularity of espresso bars in Italy, the company introduced the coffee house concept in Seattle in 1984. They incorporated as a public company in 1985 and, as of the end of 2012, had grown to over 17,500 stores in 60 countries around the world.

As you can see from Starbucks' Consolidated Statements of Earnings on the next page, the company had operating revenues, representing sales of coffee and related products, of about

Imagebroker/Alamy

$13.3 billion during the year ended September 30, 2012. That represented 13.7% growth over the previous year and translated into $1.38 billion in profits. That's a lot of coffee!

But at Starbucks, it's about more than coffee. The company's mission is "to inspire and nurture the human spirit—one person, one cup, and one neighborhood at a time." From the aromas and music to the wifi connection, having a latte, frappucino, Tazo chai tea, or caramel macchiato at Starbucks is designed to be a friendly, "socially connected" experience. It's also about a Shared Planet™. An integral part of the company's mission and values is to do business in a way that demonstrates a strong commitment to people and to the environment. The company has developed standards for environmentally, socially, and economically responsible coffee-buying to help assure better prices for farmers who do business with Starbucks. Starbucks works with Conservation International to encourage coffee growers to use sustainable farming practices that help protect the environment. The company has developed reusable and recyclable cups. It also sponsors employee programs that contribute hundreds of thousands of service hours to the communities where Starbucks stores operate. Starbucks is even committed to constructing "green" buildings that reduce its environmental footprint. All of these socially responsible practices

A1					
	A	B	C	D	E

	A	B	C	D	E
1	**Starbucks Corporation** **Consolidated Statements of Earnings (Adapted)**				
2	(in millions of USD)	12 months ended			
3		Sep. 30, 2012	Oct. 02, 2011		
4	**Net revenues:**				
5	Net operating revenues	$ 13,299	$ 11,701		
6	Other income and gains (net)	273	286		
7	Total net revenue	13,572	11,987		
8	Cost of sales including occupancy costs	5,813	4,916		
9	Store operating expenses	3,918	3,595		
10	Other operating expenses	430	393		
11	Depreciation and amortization expenses	550	523		
12	General and administrative expenses	802	749		
13	Other expenses	1	2		
14	Total operating expenses	11,514	10,178		
15	**Income before income taxes**	2,058	1,809		
16	Income tax expense	674	563		
17	**Net income**	$ 1,384	$ 1,246		
18					

cost money, which can be hard to justify during difficult economic times. But Starbucks is committed to using its resources for good as well as for gain. Think about that when you buy your next latte. ●

This chapter completes our coverage of the accounting cycle. It gives the basics of what you need before tackling topics such as receivables, inventory, and cash flows.

Learning Objectives

1. Explain how accrual accounting differs from cash-basis accounting

2. Apply the revenue and expense recognition principles

3. Adjust the accounts

4. Construct the financial statements

5. Close the books

6. Analyze and evaluate a company's debt-paying ability

» *Try It in* **Excel**

You may access the most current annual report of Starbucks Corporation in Excel format at **www.sec.gov**. Using the "filings" link on the toolbar at the top of the home page, select "company filings search." This will take you to the "Edgar Company Filings" page. Type "Starbucks" in the company name box, and select "search." This will produce the "EDGAR Search Results" page showing the company name. Click on the "CIK" link beside the company name. This will pull up all of the reports the company has filed with the SEC. In the "filing type" box, type "10-K" and click the search box. Form 10-K is the SEC form for the company's latest annual report. Find the year that you wish to view. Click on the "Interactive Data" box, which takes you to the "View Filing Data" page. Find and click on the "View Excel Document" link at the top of this page. You may choose to either open or download the Excel files containing the company's most recent financial statements in Excel format. ■

EXPLAIN HOW ACCRUAL ACCOUNTING DIFFERS FROM CASH-BASIS ACCOUNTING

Managers want to earn a profit. Investors search for companies whose stock prices will increase. Banks seek borrowers who will pay their debts. Accounting provides the information these people use for decision making. Accounting can be based on either the

1 Explain how accrual accounting differs from cash-basis accounting

- accrual basis, or the
- cash basis.

Accrual accounting records the impact of a business transaction as it occurs. When the business performs a service, makes a sale, or incurs an expense, the accountant records the transaction, even if the business receives or pays no cash.

Cash-basis accounting records only cash transactions—cash receipts and cash payments. Cash receipts are treated as revenues, and cash payments are handled as expenses.

Generally Accepted Accounting Principles (GAAP) Require Accrual Accounting.

Under accrual accounting, a business records revenues as the revenues are earned and expenses as the expenses are incurred—not necessarily when cash changes hands. Suppose you sell inventory that cost you $500, for $800 on account, and that you collect the $800 from the customer 30 days later. The sale and the subsequent cash collection are actually two separate transactions. Which transaction increases your wealth—making an $800 sale on account, or collecting the $800 cash 30 days later? Making the sale increases your wealth by $300 because you gave up inventory that cost you $500 and you got a receivable worth $800. Collecting cash later merely swaps your $800 receivable for $800 cash—no wealth is created by this transaction. Making the sale—not collecting the cash—increases your wealth.

The basic defect of cash-basis accounting is that the cash basis ignores important information. That makes the financial statements incomplete. The result? People using the statements make decisions based on incomplete information, which can lead to mistakes.

Suppose your business makes a sale on account. The cash basis does not record the sale because you received no cash. You may be thinking, "Let's wait until we collect cash and then record the sale. After all, we pay the bills with cash, so let's ignore transactions that don't affect cash."

What's wrong with this argument? There are two defects—one on the balance sheet and the other on the income statement.

Balance-Sheet Defect.
If we fail to record a sale on account, the balance sheet reports no account receivable. Why is this so bad? The receivable represents a claim to receive cash in the future which is a real asset, and it should appear on the balance sheet. Without this information, assets are understated on the balance sheet.

Income-Statement Defect.
A sale on account provides revenue that increases the company's wealth. Ignoring the sale understates revenue and net income on the income statement.

The take-away lessons from this discussion are as follows:

- Companies that use the cash basis of accounting do not follow GAAP. Their financial statements omit important information.
- All but the smallest businesses use the accrual basis of accounting.

Accrual Accounting and Cash Flows

Accrual accounting is more complex—and, in terms of the Conceptual Foundations of Accounting (Exhibit 1-3), is a more faithful representation of economic reality—than cash-basis accounting. To be sure, accrual accounting records cash transactions, such as the following:

- Collecting cash from customers
- Receiving cash from interest earned
- Paying salaries, rent, and other expenses
- Borrowing money
- Paying off loans
- Issuing stock

But accrual accounting also records *noncash* transactions, such as the following:

- Sales on account
- Purchases of inventory on account
- Accrual of expenses incurred but not yet paid
- Depreciation expense
- Usage of prepaid rent, insurance, and supplies
- Earning of revenue when cash was collected in advance

Accrual accounting is based on a framework of concepts and principles additional to those we discussed in Chapter 1. We turn now to the time-period concept, the revenue principle, and the expense recognition principle.

The Time-Period Concept

The only way for a business to know for certain how well it performed is to shut down, sell the assets, pay the liabilities, and return any leftover cash to the owners. This process, called liquidation, means going out of business. Ongoing companies can't wait until they go out of business to measure income! Instead, they need regular progress reports. Accountants, therefore, prepare financial statements for specific periods. The **time-period concept** ensures that accounting information is reported at regular intervals.

The basic accounting period is one year, and virtually all businesses prepare annual financial statements. Around 60% of large companies—including Amazon.com, eBay, and YUM! Brands—use the calendar year from January 1 through December 31.

A *fiscal* year may end on a date other than December 31. Most retailers, including Walmart, The Gap Inc., and J.C. Penney, use a fiscal year that ends on or near January 31 because the low point in their business activity falls in January, after Christmas. Starbucks Corporation uses a fiscal year that ends on or near September 30.

Companies also prepare financial statements for interim periods of less than a year, such as a month, a quarter (three months), or a semiannual period (six months). Most of the discussions in this text are based on an annual accounting period.

APPLY THE REVENUE AND EXPENSE RECOGNITION PRINCIPLES

The Revenue Principle

2 **Apply** the revenue and expense recognition principles

The **revenue principle** deals with two issues:

1. When to record (recognize) revenue
2. What amount of revenue to record

When should you record (recognize) revenue? After it has been earned—and not before. In most cases, revenue is earned when the business has delivered a good to, or has performed a service for, a customer. Revenue is recognized when the business transfers promised goods or services to a customer in an amount that reflects the cash (or fair market value of other consideration) that the entity expects to receive in exchange for those goods or services.

Global View

The FASB and IASB have recently issued a joint new standard that provides a globally consistent, converged, and simplified way to recognize revenue. The standard is based on the idea that all business transactions involve contracts that exchange goods or services for cash or claims to receive cash. The selling entity must: (1) identify the contract with the customer; (2) identify the separate performance obligations in the contract; (3) determine the transaction price; (4) allocate the transaction price to the separate performance obligations in the contract; and (5) recognize revenue when (or as) the entity satisfies the performance obligation. This text deals mostly with the retail industry, where businesses enter into relatively simple and straightforward contracts to purchase and sell largely finished goods and render services. In other industries, such as computer software, long-term construction, motion pictures, natural resources, or real estate, contracts can be more complex, making the issue of how and when to recognize revenue more complicated. Fortunately, in the retail industry, U.S. GAAP and IFRS have historically been consistent with respect to general principles of revenue recognition, so the issuance of the new standard has not substantially changed the rules by which revenue is recognized in the retail industry.

Exhibit 3-1 shows two situations that provide guidance on when to record revenue for Starbucks Corporation. In Situation 1, no transaction has occurred, so no contract exists. Starbucks Corporation records nothing. In Situation 2, a customer places an order for a latte. A transaction has occurred, producing a contract that both parties are obligated to fulfill. Starbucks recognizes revenue when it delivers the product, satisfying its contractual obligation and entitling it to collect cash. The customer receives the product and pays, satisfying the customer's contractual obligation.

By contrast, suppose that a plumbing company (a service-type business) signs a contract to perform plumbing services for a customer who is remodeling a home. The value of the services is $50,000. In signing the contract, the plumbing company becomes obligated to complete the plumbing services by a certain date. Revenue may not be recognized until the plumbing company has substantially completed its obligation and has finished performing the services for the customer.

The *amount* of revenue to record is the cash value of the goods or services transferred to the customer. For example, suppose that in order to promote business, Starbucks runs a promotion and sells lattes for the discount price of $2 per cup. Let's suppose Starbucks would ordinarily

Exhibit 3-1 | When to Record Revenue

charge $4 for this drink. How much revenue should Starbucks record? The answer is $2—the cash value of the transaction. The amount of the sale, $2, is the amount of revenue earned—not the regular price of $4.

The Expense Recognition Principle

The **expense recognition principle** is the basis for recording expenses. Expenses are the costs of assets used up, and of liabilities created, in earning revenue. Expenses have no future benefit to the company. The expense recognition principle includes two steps:

1. Identify all the expenses incurred during the accounting period.
2. Measure the expenses and recognize them in the same period in which any related revenues are earned.

To *recognize* expenses along with related revenues means to subtract expenses from related revenues to compute net income or net loss. Exhibit 3-2 illustrates the expense recognition (sometimes referred to as matching) principle.

Exhibit 3-2 | The Expense Recognition Principle

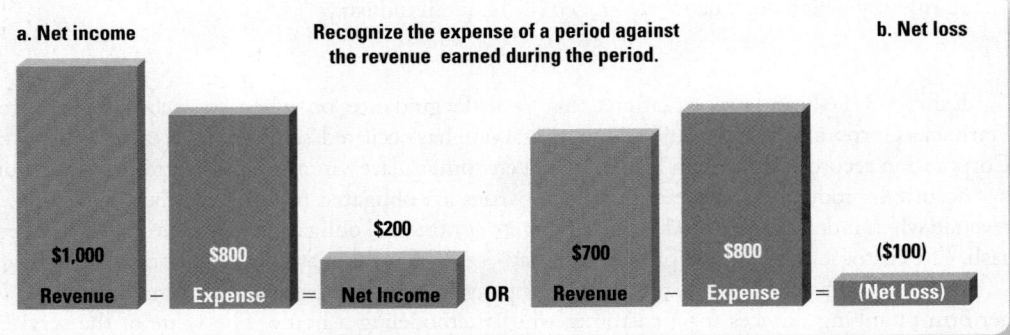

Some expenses are paid in cash. Other expenses arise from using up an asset such as supplies. Still other expenses occur when a company creates a liability. For example, Starbucks' salary expense occurs when employees work for the company. Starbucks may pay the salary expense immediately, or Starbucks may record a liability for the salary to be paid later. In either case, Starbucks has salary expense. The critical event for recording an expense is the employees' working for the company, not the payment of cash.

> Stop & Think...

(1) A customer pays Starbucks $250 on March 15 for coffee to be served at a party in April. Has Starbucks earned revenue on March 15? When will Starbucks earn the revenue?

(2) Starbucks pays $6,000 on July 1 for store rent for the next three months. Has Starbucks incurred an expense on July 1?

Answers:

(1) No. Starbucks has received the cash but will not deliver the coffee until later. Starbucks earns the revenue when it delivers the product to the customer and the customer assumes control over it.

(2) No. Starbucks has paid cash for rent in advance. No expense has yet been incurred because the company has not yet occupied the space. This prepaid rent is an asset because Starbucks has acquired the use of a store location in the future.

Ethical Issues in Accrual Accounting

Accrual accounting provides some ethical challenges that cash accounting avoids. For example, suppose that in 2014, Starbucks Corporation prepays a $4.5 million advertising campaign to be conducted by a large advertising agency. The advertisements are scheduled to run during September, October, and November. In this case, Starbucks is buying an asset, a prepaid expense.

Suppose Starbucks pays for the advertisements on September 1 and the ads start running immediately. Under accrual accounting, Starbucks should record one-third of the expense ($1.5 million) during the year ended September 30, 2014, and two-thirds ($3 million) during October and November, which are part of fiscal 2015.

Suppose fiscal 2014 is a great year for Starbucks—net income is better than expected. However, Starbucks' top managers believe that fiscal 2015 will not be as profitable as 2014. In this case, the company has a strong incentive to expense the full $4.5 million during fiscal 2014 in order to report all the advertising expense in the fiscal 2014 income statement. This unethical action would keep $3 million of advertising expense off the fiscal 2015 income statement and make 2015's net income look $3 million better than it actually is.

ADJUST THE ACCOUNTS

3 Adjust the accounts

At the end of the period, the business reports its financial statements. This process begins with the trial balance introduced in Chapter 2. We refer to this trial balance as unadjusted because the accounts are not yet ready for the financial statements. In most cases, the simple label "Trial Balance" means "unadjusted."

Which Accounts Need to Be Updated (Adjusted)?

The stockholders and management need to know how well Freddy's Auto Service, Inc. is performing. The financial statements report this information, and all accounts must be up-to-date. That means some accounts must be adjusted. Exhibit 3-3 gives the unadjusted trial balance of Freddy's Auto Service, Inc., at June 30, 2014.

This trial balance reflects the same accounts as those in Chapter 2 (see Exhibit 2-12) except for two additional months of transaction activity—May and June 2014. Still, the trial balance is unadjusted. That means it's not completely up-to-date. It's not quite ready for preparing the financial statements for presentation to the public.

Exhibit 3-3 | Unadjusted Trial Balance

A1					
	A	B	C	D	E
1	Freddy's Auto Service, Inc. Unadjusted Trial Balance June 30, 2014	Debit	Credit		
2	Cash	$36,800			
3	Accounts receivable	2,200			
4	Supplies	700			
5	Prepaid rent	3,000			
6	Land	18,000			
7	Equipment	24,000			
8	Accounts payable		$13,100		
9	Unearned service revenue		400		
10	Common stock		50,000		
11	Retained earnings		18,800		
12	Dividends	3,200			
13	Service revenue		7,000		
14	Salary expense	900			
15	Utilities expense	500			
16	Total	$89,300	$89,300		
17					

Cash, Land, Equipment, Accounts Payable, Common Stock, and Dividends are up-to-date and need no adjustment at the end of the period. Why? Because the day-to-day transactions provide all the data for these accounts.

Accounts Receivable, Supplies, Prepaid Rent, and the other accounts are another story. These accounts are not yet up-to-date on June 30. Why? Because certain transactions have not yet been recorded. Consider Supplies. During June, Freddy's Auto Service, Inc. used cleaning supplies to service autos. But Freddy's didn't make a journal entry for supplies used every time it serviced a car. That would waste time and money. Instead, Freddy's waits until the end of the period and then records the supplies used up during the entire month.

The cost of supplies used up is an expense. An adjusting entry at the end of June updates both Supplies (an asset) and Supplies Expense. We must adjust all accounts whose balances are not yet up-to-date.

Categories of Adjusting Entries

Accounting adjustments fall into three basic categories: deferrals, depreciation, and accruals.

Deferrals. A **deferral** is an adjustment for payment of an item or receipt of cash in advance. Starbucks purchases supplies for use in its operations. During the period, some supplies (assets) are used up and become expenses. At the end of the period, an adjustment is needed to decrease the Supplies account for the supplies used up. This is Supplies Expense. Prepaid Rent, Prepaid Insurance, and all other prepaid expenses require deferral adjustments.

There are also deferral adjustments for liabilities. Companies such as Starbucks may collect cash from a grocery-store chain in advance of earning the revenue. When Starbucks receives cash up front, Starbucks has a liability to provide coffee for the customer. This liability is called Unearned Sales Revenue. Then, when Starbucks delivers the goods to the customer, it earns Sales Revenue. This earning process requires an adjustment at the end of the period. The adjustment decreases the liability and increases the revenue for the revenue earned. Publishers such as Time, Inc., and your cell-phone company collect cash in advance. They too must make adjusting entries for revenues earned later.

Depreciation. **Depreciation** allocates the cost of a plant asset to expense over the asset's useful life. Depreciation is the most common long-term deferral. Starbucks buys buildings and equipment. As Starbucks uses the assets, it records depreciation for wear-and-tear and obsolescence. The accounting adjustment records Depreciation Expense and decreases the asset's book value over its life. The process is identical to a deferral-type adjustment; the only difference is the type of asset involved.

Accruals. An **accrual** is the opposite of a deferral. For an accrued *expense*, Starbucks records the expense before paying cash. For an accrued *revenue*, Starbucks records the revenue before collecting cash.

Salary Expense can create an accrual adjustment. As employees work for Starbucks Corporation, the company's salary expense accrues with the passage of time. At September 30, 2014, Starbucks owed employees some salaries to be paid after year-end. At September 30, Starbucks recorded Salary Expense and Salary Payable for the amount owed. Other examples of expense accruals include interest expense and income tax expense.

An accrued revenue is a revenue that the business has earned and will collect next year. At year-end, Starbucks must accrue the revenue. The adjustment debits a receivable and credits a revenue. For example, accrual of interest revenue debits Interest Receivable and credits Interest Revenue.

Let's see how the adjusting process actually works for Freddy's Auto Service, Inc. at June 30. We start with prepaid expenses.

Prepaid Expenses

A **prepaid expense** is an expense paid in advance. Therefore, prepaid expenses are assets because they provide a future benefit for the owner. Let's make the adjustments for prepaid rent and supplies.

Prepaid Rent. Companies pay rent in advance. This prepayment creates an asset for the renter, who can then use the rented item in the future. Suppose Freddy's Auto Service, Inc. prepays three months' store rent ($3,000) on June 1. The entry for the prepayment of three months' rent debits Prepaid Rent as follows:

	A	B	C	D	E	F
1	Jun 1	Prepaid Rent ($1,000 × 3)	3,000			
2		Cash		3,000		
3		Paid three months' rent in advance.				
4						

The accounting equation shows that one asset increases and another decreases. Total assets are unchanged.

Assets	=	Liabilities	+	Stockholders' Equity
3,000	=	0	+	0
− 3,000				

After posting, the Prepaid Rent account appears as follows:

Prepaid Rent

Jun 1	3,000

Throughout June, the Prepaid Rent account carries this beginning balance, as shown in Exhibit 3-3 (p. 119). The adjustment transfers $1,000 from Prepaid Rent to Rent Expense as follows:*

Adjusting entry a

	A	B	C	D	E	F
1	Jun 30	Rent Expense ($3,000 × 1/3)	1,000			
2		Prepaid Rent		1,000		
3		To record rent expense.				
4						

Both assets and stockholders' equity decrease.

Assets	=	Liabilities	+	Stockholders' Equity	−	Expenses
− 1,000	=	0				− 1,000

After posting, Prepaid Rent and Rent Expense appear as follows (with the adjustment highlighted):

Prepaid Rent   **Rent Expense**

Jun 1	3,000	Jun 30	1,000	→	Jun 30	1,000	
Bal	2,000				Bal	1,000	

---

*See Exhibit 3-8 (p. 130), for a summary of adjustments a–g.

This adjusting entry illustrates application of the expense recognition principle. We record an expense when incurred in order to measure net income.

Supplies. Supplies are another type of prepaid expense. On June 2, Freddy's Auto Service paid cash of $700 for cleaning supplies:

	A	B	C	D	E	F
1	Jun 2	Supplies	700			
2		Cash		700		
3		*Paid cash for supplies.*				
4						

Assets	=	Liabilities	+	Stockholders' Equity
700	=	0	+	0
− 700				

The cost of the supplies Freddy's used is Supplies Expense. To measure June's supplies expense, the business counts the supplies on hand at the end of the month. The count shows that $400 of supplies remain. Subtracting the $400 of supplies on hand from the supplies available ($700) measures supplies expense for the month ($300):

Asset Available During the Period	−	Asset on Hand at the End of the Period	=	Asset Used (Expense) During the Period
$700	−	$400	=	$300

The June 30 adjusting entry debits the expense and credits the asset:

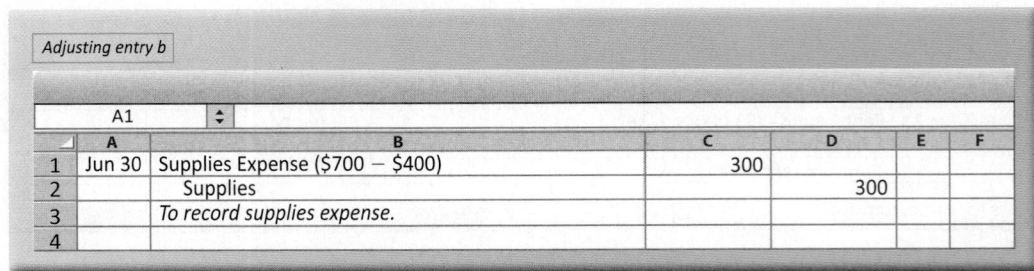

Adjusting entry b

	A	B	C	D	E	F
1	Jun 30	Supplies Expense ($700 − $400)	300			
2		Supplies		300		
3		*To record supplies expense.*				
4						

Assets	=	Liabilities	+	Stockholders' Equity	−	Expenses
− 300	=	0				− 300

After posting, the Supplies and Supplies Expense accounts appear as follows. The adjustment is highlighted for emphasis.

	Supplies				Supplies Expense	
Jun 2	700	Jun 30	300 →	Jun 30	300	
Bal	400			Bal	300	

At the start of July, Supplies has a $400 balance, and the adjustment process is repeated each month.

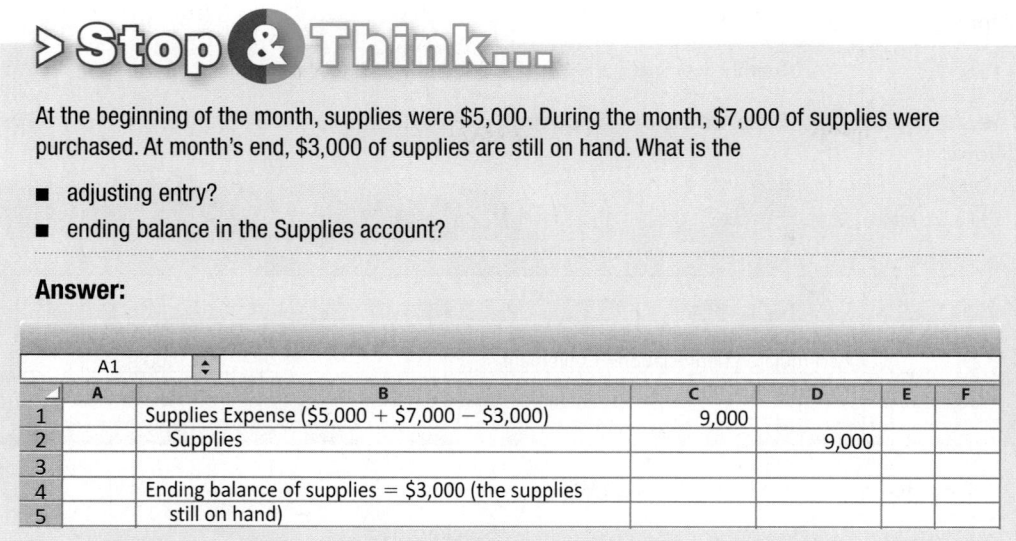

> **Stop & Think...**
>
> At the beginning of the month, supplies were $5,000. During the month, $7,000 of supplies were purchased. At month's end, $3,000 of supplies are still on hand. What is the
>
> - adjusting entry?
> - ending balance in the Supplies account?
>
> **Answer:**

	A	B	C	D	E	F
1		Supplies Expense ($5,000 + $7,000 − $3,000)	9,000			
2		Supplies		9,000		
3						
4		Ending balance of supplies = $3,000 (the supplies				
5		still on hand)				

Depreciation of Plant Assets

Plant assets are long-lived tangible assets, such as land, buildings, furniture, and equipment. All plant assets except land decline in usefulness, and this decline is an expense. Accountants spread the cost of each plant asset, except land, over its useful life. Depreciation is the process of allocating cost to expense for a long-term plant asset.

To illustrate depreciation, consider Freddy's Auto Service. Suppose that on June 3 Freddy's purchased equipment on account for $24,000:

	A	B	C	D	E	F
1	Jun 3	Equipment	24,000			
2		Accounts Payable		24,000		
3		Purchased equipment on account.				
4						

	Assets	=	Liabilities	+	Stockholders' Equity
	24,000	=	24,000	+	0

After posting, the Equipment account appears as follows:

Equipment

Jun 3   24,000

Freddy's records an asset when it purchases machinery and equipment. Then, as the asset is used, a portion of the asset's cost is transferred to Depreciation Expense. The machinery and equipment are being used to produce revenue. The cost of the machinery and equipment should be allocated (matched) against that revenue. This is another illustration of the expense recognition principle. Computerized systems program the depreciation for automatic entry each period.

Freddy's equipment will remain useful for five years and then be worthless. One way to compute the amount of depreciation for each year is to divide the cost of the asset ($24,000 in our example) by its expected useful life (five years). This procedure—called the straight-line depreciation method—gives annual depreciation of $4,800. The depreciation amount is an estimate. (Chapter 7 covers plant assets and depreciation in more detail.)

$$\text{Annual depreciation} = \$24,000/5 \text{ years} = \$4,800 \text{ per year}$$

Depreciation for June is $400.

$$\text{Monthly depreciation} = \$4{,}800/12 \text{ months} = \$400 \text{ per month}$$

The Accumulated Depreciation Account. Depreciation expense for June is recorded as follows:

		A	B	C	D	E	F
			Adjusting entry c				
A1	↕						
1		Jun 30	Depreciation Expense—Equipment	400			
2			Accumulated Depreciation—Equipment		400		
3			To record depreciation.				
4							

Total assets decrease by the amount of the expense:

Assets	=	Liabilities	+	Stockholders' Equity	−	Expenses
− 400	=	0				− 400

The Accumulated Depreciation—Equipment account (not Equipment) is credited to preserve the original cost of the asset in the Equipment account. Managers can then refer to the Equipment account if they ever need to know how much the asset cost.

The **Accumulated Depreciation** account shows the sum of all depreciation expense from using the asset. Therefore, the balance in the Accumulated Depreciation account increases over the asset's life.

Accumulated Depreciation is a contra asset account—an asset account with a normal credit balance. A **contra account** has two distinguishing characteristics:

1. It always has a companion account.

2. Its normal balance is opposite that of the companion account.

In this case, Accumulated Depreciation—Equipment is the contra account to Equipment, so it appears directly after Equipment on the balance sheet. A business carries an accumulated depreciation account for each depreciable asset, for example, Accumulated Depreciation—Building and Accumulated Depreciation—Equipment.

After posting, the plant asset accounts of Freddy's Auto Service, Inc. are as follows—with the adjustment highlighted:

Equipment			Accumulated Depreciation—Equipment			Depreciation Expense—Equipment		
Jun 3	24,000			Jun 30	400	Jun 30	400	
Bal	24,000			Bal	400	Bal	400	

Book Value. The net amount of a plant asset (cost minus accumulated depreciation) is called that asset's **book value (of a plant asset)**, or carrying amount. Exhibit 3-4 shows how Freddy's would report the book value of its land and equipment at June 30.

Exhibit 3-4 | Plant Assets on the Balance Sheet of Freddy's Auto Service

		A	B	C	D	E
A1	↕					
1		Freddy's Auto Service, Inc. Plant Assets at June 30				
2		Land		$18,000		
3		Equipment	$24,000			
4		Less: Accumulated Depreciation	(400)	23,600		
5						
6		Book value of plant assets		$41,600		
7						

At June 30, the book value of equipment is $23,600.

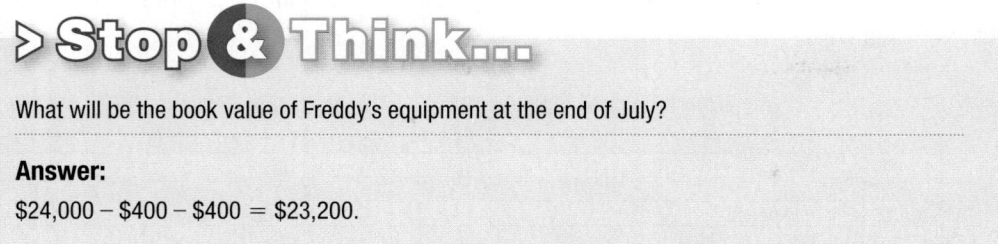

What will be the book value of Freddy's equipment at the end of July?

Answer:

$24,000 − $400 − $400 = $23,200.

Exhibit 3-5 shows how Starbucks Corporation reports property, plant, and equipment in its September 30, 2012 annual report. Lines 3 to 9 list specific assets and their cost. Line 10 shows the gross cost of all Starbucks' plant assets. Line 11 gives the amount of accumulated depreciation, and line 12 shows the assets' book value ($2,659 million and $2,356 million in the current and prior periods, respectively).

Exhibit 3-5 | Starbucks Corporation's Reporting of Property, Plant, and Equipment (Adapted, in millions)

	A	B	C	D	E
	A1				
1	Starbucks Corporation's Reporting of Property, Plant, and Equipment				
2	(Adapted) in millions of USD	September 30, 2012	October 2, 2011		
3	Land	$ 46	$ 45		
4	Buildings	225	219		
5	Leasehold improvements	3,958	3,618		
6	Store equipment	1,251	1,102		
7	Roasting equipment	323	295		
8	Furniture, fixtures, and other	836	758		
9	Work in progress	264	127		
10	Property, plant, and equipment, gross	6,903	6,164		
11	Less accumulated depreciation	(4,244)	(3,808)		
12	Property, plant, and equipment, net	$ 2,659	$ 2,356		
13					

Accrued Expenses

Businesses may incur expenses before they pay cash. Consider an employee's salary. Starbucks' expense and payable grow as the employee works, so the liability is said to accrue. Another example is interest expense on a note payable. Interest accrues as the clock ticks. The term **accrued expense** refers to a liability that arises from an expense that has not yet been paid.

Companies don't record accrued expenses daily or weekly. Instead, they wait until the end of the period and use an adjusting entry to update each expense (and related liability) for the financial statements. Let's look at salary expense.

Most companies pay their employees at set times. Suppose Freddy's Auto Service, Inc. pays its employee a monthly salary of $1,800, half on the 15th and half on the last day of the month. The following calendar for June has the paydays circled:

			June			
Sun.	Mon.	Tue.	Wed.	Thur.	Fri.	Sat.
						1
2	3	4	5	6	7	8
9	10	11	12	13	14	⑮
16	17	18	19	20	21	22
23	24	25	26	27	28	29
㉚						

Assume that if a payday falls on a Sunday, Freddy's pays the employee on the following Monday. During June, Freddy's paid its employee the first half-month salary of $900 and made the following entry:

	A	B	C	D	E	F
		A1				
1	Jun 15	Salary Expense	900			
2		Cash		900		
3		To pay salary.				
4						

Assets	=	Liabilities	+	Stockholders' Equity	−	Expenses
− 900	=	0				− 900

After posting, the Salary Expense account appears as follows:

Salary Expense	
Jun 15	900

The trial balance at June 30 (Exhibit 3-3, p. 119) includes Salary Expense with its debit balance of $900. Because June 30, the second payday of the month, falls on a Sunday, the second half-month amount of $900 will be paid on Monday, July 1. At June 30, therefore, Freddy's adjusts for additional salary expense and salary payable of $900:

Adjusting entry d

	A	B	C	D	E	F
		A1				
1	Jun 30	Salary Expense	900			
2		Salary Payable		900		
3		To accrue salary expense.				
4						

An accrued expense increases liabilities and decreases stockholders' equity:

Assets	=	Liabilities	+	Stockholders' Equity	−	Expenses
0	=	900				− 900

After posting, the Salary Payable and Salary Expense accounts appear as follows (adjustment highlighted):

Salary Payable				Salary Expense	
	Jun 30	900		Jun 15	900
	Bal	900		Jun 30	900
				Bal	1,800

The accounts now hold all of June's salary information. Salary Expense has a full month's salary, and Salary Payable shows the amount owed at June 30. All accrued expenses are recorded this way—debit the expense and credit the liability.

Computerized systems contain a payroll module. Accrued salaries can be automatically journalized and posted at the end of each period.

Accrued Revenues

Businesses often earn revenue before they receive the cash. A revenue that has been earned but not yet collected is called an **accrued revenue**.

Assume that FedEx hires Freddy's on June 15 to service FedEx delivery trucks each month. Suppose FedEx will pay Freddy's $600 monthly, with the first payment on July 15. During June, Freddy's will earn half a month's fee, $300, for work done June 15 through June 30. On June 30, Freddy's makes the following adjusting entry:

Adjusting entry e

A1	

	A	B	C	D	E	F
1	Jun 30	Accounts Receivable ($600 × 1/2)	300			
2		Service Revenue		300		
3		To accrue service revenue.				
4						

Revenue increases both total assets and stockholders' equity:

Assets	=	Liabilities	+	Stockholders' Equity	+	Revenues
300	=	0				+ 300

Recall that Accounts Receivable has an unadjusted balance of $2,200, and Service Revenue's unadjusted balance is $7,000 (Exhibit 3-3, p. 119). This June 30 adjusting entry has the following effects (adjustment highlighted):

	Accounts Receivable			Service Revenue	
	2,200				7,000
Jun 30	300		Jun 30		300
Bal	2,500		Bal		7,300

All accrued revenues are accounted for similarly—debit a receivable and credit a revenue.

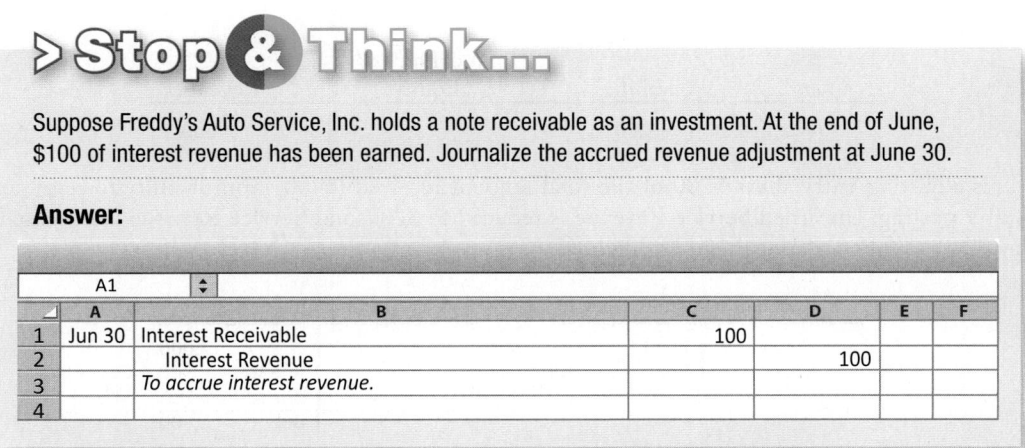

> **Stop & Think...**

Suppose Freddy's Auto Service, Inc. holds a note receivable as an investment. At the end of June, $100 of interest revenue has been earned. Journalize the accrued revenue adjustment at June 30.

Answer:

A1	

	A	B	C	D	E	F
1	Jun 30	Interest Receivable	100			
2		Interest Revenue		100		
3		To accrue interest revenue.				
4						

Unearned Revenues

Some businesses collect cash from customers before earning the revenue. This creates a liability called **unearned revenue**. Only when the job is completed does the business earn the revenue. Suppose **Home Depot** engages Freddy's Auto Service, Inc. to perform routine oil changes on Home Depot trucks, agreeing to pay Freddy's $400 monthly, beginning immediately. If Freddy's collects the first amount on June 15, then Freddy's records this transaction as follows:

	A	B	C	D	E	F
1	Jun 15	Cash	400			
2		Unearned Service Revenue		400		
3		*Received cash for revenue in advance.*				
4						

Assets	=	Liabilities	+	Stockholders' Equity
400	=	400	+	0

After posting, the liability account appears as follows:

Unearned Service Revenue

	Jun 15	400

Unearned Service Revenue is a liability because Freddy's is obligated to perform services for Home Depot. The June 30 unadjusted trial balance (Exhibit 3-3, p. 119) lists Unearned Service Revenue with a $400 credit balance. During the last 15 days of the month, Freddy's will earn one-half of the $400, or $200. On June 30, Freddy's makes the following adjustment:

Adjusting entry f

	A	B	C	D	E	F
1	Jun 30	Unearned Service Revenue ($400 × 1/2)	200			
2		Service Revenue		200		
3		*To record unearned service revenue that has been earned.*				
4						
5						

Assets	=	Liabilities	+	Stockholders' Equity	+	Revenues
0	=	− 200				+ 200

This adjusting entry shifts $200 of the total amount received ($400) from liability to revenue. After posting, Unearned Service Revenue is reduced to $200, and Service Revenue is increased by $200, as follows (adjustment highlighted):

Unearned Service Revenue					**Service Revenue**	
Jun 30	200	Jun 15	400			7,000
		Bal	200		Jun 30	300
					Jun 30	200
					Bal	7,500

All revenues collected in advance are accounted for this way. An unearned revenue is a liability, not a revenue.

One company's prepaid expense is the other company's unearned revenue. For example, Home Depot's prepaid expense is Freddy's Auto Service, Inc.'s liability for unearned revenue.

Exhibit 3-6 diagrams the distinctive timing of prepaids and accruals. Study prepaid expenses all the way across. Then study unearned revenues across, and so on.

Exhibit 3-6 | Prepaid and Accrual Adjustments

PREPAIDS—Cash First

	First		Later	
Prepaid expenses	Pay cash and record an asset: Prepaid Expense...... XXX Cash..............	XXX	Record an expense and decrease the asset: Expense............................. XXX Prepaid Expense.........	XXX
Unearned revenues	Receive cash and record unearned revenue: Cash........................ XXX Unearned Revenue	XXX	Record revenue and decrease unearned revenue: Unearned Revenue .... XXX Revenue	XXX

ACCRUALS—Cash Later

	First		Later	
Accrued expenses	Accrue expense and a payable: Expense.................. XXX Payable...........	XXX	Pay cash and decrease the payable: Payable............................. XXX Cash............................	XXX
Accrued revenues	Accrue revenue and a receivable: Receivable............... XXX Revenue	XXX	Receive cash and decrease the receivable: Cash................................... XXX Receivable.................	XXX

The authors thank Professors Darrel Davis and Alfonso Oddo for suggesting this exhibit.

Summary of the Adjusting Process

Two purposes of the adjusting process are to

- measure income, and
- update the balance sheet.

Therefore, every adjusting entry affects both of the following:

- Revenue or expense—to measure income
- Asset or liability—to update the balance sheet

Exhibit 3-7 summarizes the standard adjustments.

Exhibit 3-7 | Summary of Adjusting Entries

Category of Adjusting Entry	Type of Account	
	Debit	Credit
Prepaid expense...................	Expense	Asset
Depreciation.......................	Expense	Contra asset
Accrued expense.................	Expense	Liability
Accrued revenue.................	Asset	Revenue
Unearned revenue...............	Liability	Revenue

Exhibit 3-8 summarizes the adjustments of Freddy's Auto Service, Inc., at June 30—the adjusting entries we've examined over the past few pages.

- Panel A repeats the data for each adjustment.
- Panel B gives the adjusting entries.
- Panel C on the following page shows the accounts after posting the adjusting entries. The adjustments are keyed by letter.

Exhibit 3-8 | The Adjusting Process of Freddy's Auto Service, Inc.

PANEL A—Information for Adjustments at June 30, 2014	PANEL B—Adjusting Entries		
(a) Prepaid rent expired, $1,000.	(a) Rent Expense	1,000	
	Prepaid Rent		1,000
	To record rent expense.		
(b) Supplies used, $300.	(b) Supplies Expense	300	
	Supplies...		300
	To record supplies used.		
(c) Depreciation on equipment, $400.	(c) Depreciation Expense—Equipment	400	
	Accumulated Depreciation—Equipment		400
	To record depreciation.		
(d) Accrued salary expense, $900.	(d) Salary Expense	900	
	Salary Payable......................................		900
	To accrue salary expense.		
(e) Accrued service revenue, $300.	(e) Accounts Receivable..................................	300	
	Service Revenue....................................		300
	To accrue service revenue.		
(f) Amount of unearned service revenue that has been earned, $200.	(f) Unearned Service Revenue.........................	200	
	Service Revenue....................................		200
	To record unearned revenue that has been earned.		
(g) Accrued income tax expense, $600.	(g) Income Tax Expense	600	
	Income Tax Payable.............................		600
	To accrue income tax expense.		

PANEL C—Ledger Accounts

Assets	Liabilities	Stockholders' Equity

Assets

Cash

Bal 36,800 |

Accounts Receivable

	2,200	
(e)	300	
Bal	2,500	

Supplies

	700	(b)	300
Bal	400		

Prepaid Rent

	3,000	(a)	1,000
Bal	2,000		

Land

Bal 18,000 |

Equipment

Bal 24,000 |

Accumulated Depreciation—Equipment

		(c)	400
		Bal	400

Liabilities

Accounts Payable

	Bal 13,100

Salary Payable

		(d)	900
		Bal	900

Unearned Service Revenue

(f)	200		400
		Bal	200

Income Tax Payable

		(g)	600
		Bal	600

Stockholders' Equity

Common Stock

	Bal 50,000

Retained Earnings

	Bal 18,800

Dividends

Bal 3,200 |

Revenue

Service Revenue

			7,000
		(e)	300
		(f)	200
		Bal	7,500

Expenses

Rent Expense

(a)	1,000	
Bal	1,000	

Salary Expense

	900	
(d)	900	
Bal	1,800	

Supplies Expense

(b)	300	
Bal	300	

Depreciation Expense—Equipment

(c)	400	
Bal	400	

Utilities Expense

Bal	500	

Income Tax Expense

(g)	600	
Bal	600	

Exhibit 3-8 includes an additional adjusting entry that we have not yet discussed—the accrual of income tax expense. Like individual taxpayers, corporations are subject to income tax. They typically accrue income tax expense and the related income tax payable as the final adjusting entry of the period. Freddy's Auto Service, Inc. accrues income tax expense with adjusting entry g:

Adjusting entry g

A1

	A	B	C	D	E	F
1	Jun 30	Income Tax Expense	600			
2		Income Tax Payable		600		
3		To accrue income tax expense.				
4						

The income tax accrual follows the pattern for accrued expenses.

The Adjusted Trial Balance

This chapter began with the unadjusted trial balance (see Exhibit 3-3, p. 119). After the adjustments are journalized and posted, the accounts appear as shown in Exhibit 3-8, Panel C. A useful step in preparing the financial statements is to list the accounts, along with their adjusted balances, on an **adjusted trial balance**. This document lists all the accounts and their final balances in a single place. Exhibit 3-9 shows the worksheet for preparing the adjusted trial balance of Freddy's Auto Service, Inc.

Exhibit 3-9 | Trial Balance Worksheet

	A1								
		A	**B**	**C**	**D**	**E**	**F**	**G**	**H**
1	Freddy's Auto Service, Inc. Trial Balance Worksheet June 30, 2014								
2			**Trial Balance**		**Adjustments**		**Adjusted Trial Balance**		
3	Account title		Debit	Credit	Debit	Credit	Debit	Credit	
4	Cash		36,800				36,800		
5	Accounts receivable		2,200		(e) 300		2,500		
6	Supplies		700			(b) 300	400		
7	Prepaid rent		3,000			(a) 1,000	2,000		
8	Land		18,000				18,000		
9	Equipment		24,000				24,000		Balance sheet
10	Accumulated depreciation, equipment					(c) 400		400	(Exhibit 3-12)
11	Accounts payable			13,100				13,100	
12	Salary payable					(d) 900		900	
13	Unearned service revenue			400	(f) 200			200	
14	Income tax payable					(g) 600		600	
15	Common stock			50,000				50,000	
16	Retained earnings			18,800				18,800	Statement of retained
17	Dividends		3,200				3,200		earnings (Exhibit 3-11)
18	Service revenue			7,000		(e) 300		7,500	
19						(f) 200			
20	Rent expense				(a) 1,000		1,000		Income statement
21	Salary expense		900		(d) 900		1,800		(Exhibit 3-10)
22	Supplies expense				(b) 300		300		
23	Depreciation expense, equipment				(c) 400		400		
24	Utilities expense		500				500		
25	Income tax expense				(g) 600		600		
26	Totals		89,300	89,300	3,700	3,700	91,500	91,500	
27									

Note how clearly this worksheet presents the data. The Account Title and the Trial Balance data come from the unadjusted trial balance. The two Adjustments columns summarize the adjusting entries. The Adjusted Trial Balance columns then give the final account balances. Each adjusted amount in Exhibit 3-9 is the unadjusted balance plus or minus the adjustments. For example, Accounts Receivable starts with a balance of $2,200. Add the $300 debit adjustment to get Accounts Receivable's ending balance of $2,500. Spreadsheets are designed for this type of analysis.

MyAccountingLab

》 **Try It** in **Excel**

Envision Exhibit 3-9 as an Excel spreadsheet. By preparing one, you can use it as a template to solve future problems just by changing the initial trial balance data. To prepare the template, follow these steps:

1. Open a blank Excel spreadsheet. Format the spreadsheet header and column headings exactly as you see in Exhibit 3-9.
2. Enter the account titles and account balances from the unadjusted trial balance (Exhibit 3-3).
3. Calculate a sum for both the debit and credit columns labeled "trial balance."

4. Enter adjusting journal entries (a) through (g) one at a time in the "adjustments" columns. For example, for adjusting journal entry (a) enter 1,000 in the debit column on the "rent expense" line, and 1,000 in the credit column of the "prepaid rent" line. Do not enter the letters (a) through (g); use only the amounts.

5. In the adjusted trial balance debit and credit columns, enter formulas as follows:
   - For asset, dividend, and expense accounts: = + (debit amounts from "trial balance" and "adjustments" columns) – (credit amounts from "adjustments" columns).
   - For contra asset, liability, common stock, retained earnings, and service revenue accounts: = + (credit amounts from "trial balance" and "adjustments" columns) – (debit amounts from "adjustments" columns)

6. Sum the adjustments debit and credit columns.

7. Sum the adjusted trial balance debit and credit columns.

Formatted spreadsheets for adjusting journal entries are provided for you in selected problems in MyAccountingLab. ■

CONSTRUCT THE FINANCIAL STATEMENTS

The June financial statements of Freddy's Auto Service, Inc. can be prepared from the adjusted trial balance. At the far right, Exhibit 3-9 shows how the accounts are distributed to the financial statements.

4 Construct the financial statements

- The income statement (Exhibit 3-10) lists the revenue and expense accounts.
- The statement of retained earnings (Exhibit 3-11) shows the changes in retained earnings.
- The balance sheet (Exhibit 3-12) reports assets, liabilities, and stockholders' equity.

The arrows in Exhibits 3-10, 3-11, and 3-12 (all on the following page) show the flow of data from one statement to the next.

Try It in **Excel**

If you have already prepared Excel templates for the income statement, statement of retained earnings, and balance sheet for Freddy's Auto Service, Inc. in Chapter 2 (see Exhibit 2-2), you may update these, inserting additional amounts, and copying and pasting values from cells in the worksheet in Exhibit 3-9 to the appropriate cells in the financial statements. The value of Excel is that once you have prepared the templates for the worksheet and financial statements, you can reuse them multiple times for different sets of facts. ■

Why is the income statement prepared first and the balance sheet last?

1. The income statement reports net income or net loss, the result of revenues minus expenses. Revenues and expenses affect stockholders' equity, so net income is then transferred to retained earnings. The first arrow (1) tracks net income.

2. Retained Earnings is the final balancing element of the balance sheet. To solidify your understanding, trace the $18,500 retained earnings figure from Exhibit 3-11 to Exhibit 3-12. Arrow 2 tracks retained earnings.

Exhibit 3-10 | Income Statement

	A	B	C	D	E
	A1				
1	**Freddy's Auto Service, Inc.** **Income Statement** **Month ended June 30, 2014**				
2	Revenue:				
3	Service revenue		$7,500		
4	Expenses:				
5	Salary expense	$1,800			
6	Rent expense	1,000			
7	Utilities expense	500			
8	Depreciation expense	400			
9	Supplies expenses	300	4,000		
10	Income before tax		3,500		
11	Income tax expense		600		
12	Net income		$2,900		
13					

Exhibit 3-11 | Statement of Retained Earnings

	A	B	C	D	E
	A1				
1	**Freddy's Auto Service, Inc.** **Statement of Retained Earnings** **Month ended June 30, 2014**				
2	Retained earnings, May 31, 2014	$18,800			
3	Add: Net income	2,900			
4		21,700			
5	Less: Dividends	(3,200)			
6	Retained earnings, June 30, 2014	$18,500			
7					

① ②

Exhibit 3-12 | Balance Sheet

	A	B	C	D	E	F
	A1					
1	**Freddy's Auto Service, Inc.** **Balance Sheet** **June 30, 2014**					
2	**Assets**			**Liabilities**		
3	Cash		$36,800	Accounts payable	$13,100	
4	Accounts receivable		2,500	Salary payable	900	
5	Supplies		400	Unearned service revenue	200	
6	Prepaid rent		2,000	Income tax payable	600	
7	Land	$18,000		Total liabilities	14,800	
8	Equipment	24,000				
9	Less: Accumulated			**Stockholders' Equity**		
10	depreciation	(400)	41,600	Common stock	50,000	
11				Retained earnings	18,500	
12				Total stockholders' equity	68,500	
13				Total liabilities and		
14	Total assets		$83,300	stockholders' equity	$83,300	
15						

The given trial balance of Badger Ranch Company pertains to December 31, 2014, which is the end of its year-long accounting period. Data needed for the adjusting entries include:

a. Supplies on hand at year end, $2,000.

b. Depreciation on furniture and fixtures, $20,000.

c. Depreciation on building, $10,000.

d. Salaries owed but not yet paid, $5,000.

e. Accrued service revenue, $12,000.

f. Of the $45,000 balance of unearned service revenue, $32,000 was earned during the year.

g. Accrued income tax expense, $35,000.

	A1					
	A	**B**	**C**	**D**	**E**	
1	**Badger Ranch Company** **Trial Balance** **December 31, 2014**					
2	Cash	$ 198,000				
3	Accounts receivable	370,000				
4	Supplies	6,000				
5	Building	250,000				
6	Accumulated depreciation—building		$ 130,000			
7	Furniture and fixtures	100,000				
8	Accumulated depreciation—furniture and fixtures		40,000			
9	Accounts payable		380,000			
10	Salary payable					
11	Unearned service revenue		45,000			
12	Income tax payable					
13	Common stock		100,000			
14	Retained earnings		193,000			
15	Dividends	65,000				
16	Service revenue		286,000			
17	Salary expense	172,000				
18	Supplies expense					
19	Depreciation expense—building					
20	Depreciation expense—furniture and fixtures					
21	Income tax expense					
22	Miscellaneous expense	13,000				
23	Total	$1,174,000	$1,174,000			
24						

Requirements

1. Open the ledger accounts with their unadjusted balances. We show the accounts receivable account as an example:

Accounts Receivable
370,000

2. Journalize the Badger Ranch Company adjusting entries at December 31, 2014. Key entries by letter, as in Exhibit 3-8 (p. 130).

3. Post the adjusting entries to the accounts.

4. Using an Excel spreadsheet, prepare a worksheet for the adjusted trial balance, as shown in Exhibit 3-9 (p. 132).

5. Prepare the income statement, the statement of retained earnings, and the balance sheet. (At this stage, it is not necessary to classify assets or liabilities as current or long term.) Draw arrows linking these three financial statements.

Answers

Requirements 1 and 3

Assets

Cash

Bal 198,000	

Accounts Receivable

370,000	
(e) 12,000	
Bal 382,000	

Supplies

	6,000	(a)	4,000
Bal 2,000			

Building

Bal 250,000	

Accumulated Depreciation—Building

	130,000
	(c) 10,000
	Bal 140,000

Furniture and Fixtures

Bal 100,000	

Accumulated Depreciation— Furniture and Fixtures

	40,000
	(b) 20,000
	Bal 60,000

Liabilities

Accounts Payable

	Bal 380,000

Salary Payable

	(d) 5,000
	Bal 5,000

Unearned Service Revenue

(f)	32,000		45,000
		Bal	13,000

Income Tax Payable

	(g) 35,000
	Bal 35,000

Stockholders' Equity

Common Stock

	Bal 100,000

Retained Earnings

	Bal 193,000

Dividends

Bal 65,000	

Revenues

Service Revenue

	286,000
	(e) 12,000
	(f) 32,000
	Bal 330,000

Expenses

Salary Expense

172,000	
(d) 5,000	
Bal 177,000	

Supplies Expense

(a) 4,000	
Bal 4,000	

Depreciation Expense— Building

(c) 10,000	
Bal 10,000	

Depreciation Expense— Furniture and Fixtures

(b) 20,000	
Bal 20,000	

Income Tax Expense

(g) 35,000	
Bal 35,000	

Miscellaneous Expense

Bal 13,000	

Requirement 2

	A	B	C	D	E	F	G
1	(a)	Dec 31	Supplies Expense ($6,000 − $2,000)	4,000			
2			Supplies		4,000		
3			*To record supplies used.*				
4							
5	(b)	31	Depreciation Expense—Furniture and Fixtures	20,000			
6			Accumulated Depreciation—Furniture and Fixtures		20,000		
7			*To record depreciation expense on furniture and fixtures.*				
8							
9	(c)	31	Depreciation Expense—Building	10,000			
10			Accumulated Depreciation—Building		10,000		
11			*To record depreciation expense on building.*				
12							
13	(d)	31	Salary Expense	5,000			
14			Salary Payable		5,000		
15			*To accrue salary expense.*				
16							
17	(e)	31	Accounts Receivable	12,000			
18			Service Revenue		12,000		
19			*To accrue service revenue.*				
20							
21	(f)	31	Unearned Service Revenue	32,000			
22			Service Revenue		32,000		
23			*To record unearned service revenue that has been earned.*				
24							
25	(g)	31	Income Tax Expense	35,000			
26			Income Tax Payable		35,000		
27			*To accrue income tax expense.*				
28							

Requirement 4

	A1	⬍					
	A	**B**	**C**	**D**	**E**	**F**	**G**
1	**Badger Ranch Company Trial Balance Worksheet December 31, 2014**						
2		**Trial Balance**		**Adjustments**		**Adjusted Trial Balance**	
3	**Account title**	**Debit**	**Credit**	**Debit**	**Credit**	**Debit**	**Credit**
4	Cash	198,000				198,000	
5	Accounts receivable	370,000		(e) 12,000		382,000	
6	Supplies	6,000			(a) 4,000	2,000	
7	Building	250,000				250,000	
8	Accumulated depreciation—building		130,000		(c) 10,000		140,000
9	Furniture and fixtures	100,000				100,000	
10	Accumulated depreciation—furniture and fixtures		40,000		(b) 20,000		60,000
11	Accounts payable		380,000				380,000
12	Salary payable				(d) 5,000		5,000
13	Unearned service revenue		45,000	(f) 32,000			13,000
14	Income tax payable				(g) 35,000		35,000
15	Common stock		100,000				100,000
16	Retained earnings		193,000				193,000
17	Dividends	65,000				65,000	
18	Service revenue		286,000		(e) 12,000		330,000
19					(f) 32,000		
20	Salary expense	172,000		(d) 5,000		177,000	
21	Supplies expense			(a) 4,000		4,000	
22	Depreciation expense—building			(c) 10,000		10,000	
23	Depreciation expense—furniture and fixtures			(b) 20,000		20,000	
24	Income tax expense			(g) 35,000		35,000	
25	Miscellaneous expense	13,000				13,000	
26		1,174,000	1,174,000	118,000	118,000	1,256,000	1,256,000
27							

Requirement 5

	A	B	C	D	E
1	**Badger Ranch Company** **Income Statement** **Year ended December 31, 2014**				
2	Revenue:				
3	Service revenue		$330,000		
4	Expenses:				
5	Salary expense	$177,000			
6	Depreciation expense—furniture and fixtures	20,000			
7	Depreciation expense—building	10,000			
8	Supplies expense	4,000			
9	Miscellaneous expenses	13,000	224,000		
10	Income before tax		106,000		
11	Income tax expense		35,000		
12	Net income		$ 71,000		
13					

①

	A	B	C	D	E
1	**Badger Ranch Company** **Statement of Retained Earnings** **Year ended December 31, 2014**				
2	Retained earnings, December 31, 2013	$193,000			
3	Add: Net income	71,000			
4		264,000			
5	Less: Dividends	(65,000)			
6	Retained earnings, December 31, 2014	$199,000			
7					

②

	A	B	C	D	E	F
1	**Badger Ranch Company** **Balance Sheet** **December 31, 2014**					
2	**Assets**			**Liabilities**		
3	Cash		$198,000	Accounts payable	$380,000	
4	Accounts receivable		382,000	Salary payable	5,000	
5	Supplies		2,000	Unearned service revenue	13,000	
6	Building	$250,000		Income tax payable	35,000	
7	Less: Accumulated			Total liabilities	433,000	
8	depreciation	(140,000)	110,000			
9				**Stockholders' Equity**		
10	Furniture and fixtures	$100,000		Common stock	100,000	
11	Less: Accumulated			Retained earnings	199,000	
12	depreciation	(60,000)	40,000	Total stockholders' equity	299,000	
13				Total liabilities and		
14	Total assets		$732,000	stockholders' equity	$732,000	
15						

CLOSE THE BOOKS

It is now June 30, the end of the month. Freddy Kish, the manager, will continue Freddy's Auto Service, Inc. into July, August, and beyond. But wait—the revenue and the expense accounts still hold amounts for June. At the end of each accounting period, it is necessary to close the books.

5 **Close** the books

Closing the books means to prepare the accounts for the next period's transactions. The **closing entries** set the revenue, expense, and dividends balances back to zero at the end of the period. The idea is the same as setting the scoreboard back to zero after a game.

Closing is easily handled by computers. Recall that the income statement for a particular year reports only one year's income. For example, net income for Starbucks Corporation in fiscal 2012 relates exclusively to the year ended September 30, 2012. At each year-end, Starbucks accountants close the company's revenues and expenses for that year.

Temporary Accounts. Because revenues and expenses relate to a limited period, they are called **temporary accounts**. The Dividends account is also temporary. The closing process applies only to temporary accounts (revenues, expenses, and dividends).

Permanent Accounts. Let's contrast the temporary accounts with the **permanent accounts**: assets, liabilities, and stockholders' equity. The permanent accounts are not closed at the end of the period because they carry over to the next period. Consider Cash, Receivables, Equipment, Accounts Payable, Common Stock, and Retained Earnings. Their ending balances at the end of one period become the beginning balances of the next period.

Closing entries transfer the revenue, expense, and dividends balances to Retained Earnings, where they will reside on a permanent basis. Here are the steps to close the books of a company such as Starbucks Corporation or Freddy's Auto Service, Inc.:

1. Debit each revenue account for the amount of its credit balance. Credit Retained Earnings for the sum of the revenues. This process transfers the sum of all revenues into Retained Earnings, thereby increasing Retained Earnings.

2. Credit each expense account for the amount of its debit balance. Debit Retained Earnings for the sum of the expenses. This process transfers the sum of the expenses into Retained Earnings, thereby decreasing Retained Earnings.

3. Credit the Dividends account for the amount of its debit balance. Debit Retained Earnings. This entry places the dividends amount in the debit side of Retained Earnings. Remember that dividends are not expenses, but represent a permanent reduction of retained earnings.

Assume that Freddy's Auto Service, Inc. closes the books at the end of June. Exhibit 3-13 presents the complete closing process for the business. Panel A gives the closing journal entries, and Panel B shows the accounts after closing.

After closing the books, the Retained Earnings account of Freddy's Auto Service, Inc. appears as follows (data from Exhibits 3-10 and 3-11 on p. 134):

	Retained Earnings		
		Beginning balance	18,800
Expenses	4,600	Revenues	7,500
Dividends	3,200		
		Ending balance	18,500

Exhibit 3-13 | Journalizing and Posting the Closing Entries

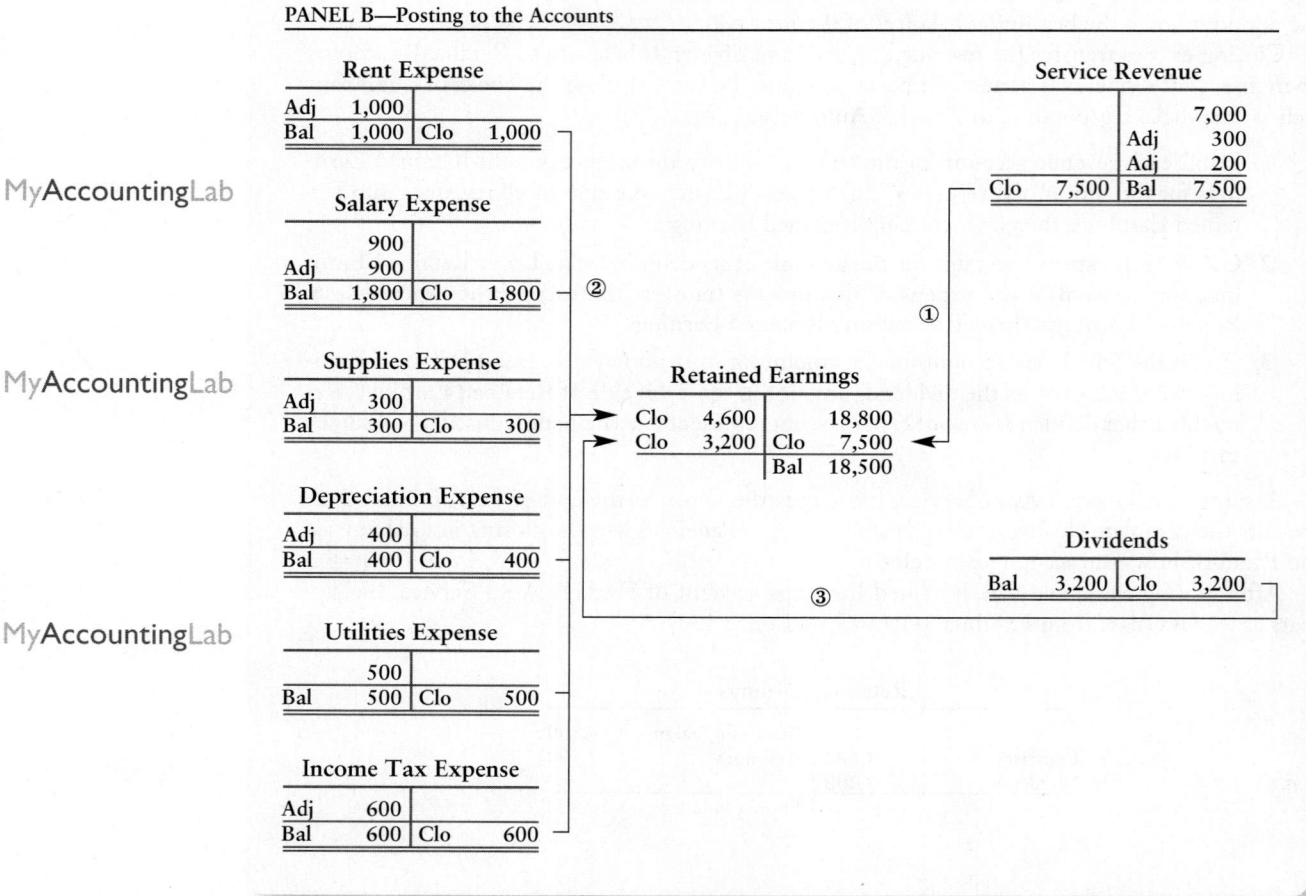

PANEL A—Journalizing the Closing Entries   Page 5

		Closing Entries		
①	Jun 30	Service Revenue...............................	7,500	
		Retained Earnings....................		7,500
②	30	Retained Earnings............................	4,600	
		Rent Expense...........................		1,000
		Salary Expense.........................		1,800
		Supplies Expense......................		300
		Depreciation Expense..............		400
		Utilities Expense......................		500
		Income Tax Expense...............		600
③	30	Retained Earnings...........................	3,200	
		Dividends.................................		3,200

PANEL B—Posting to the Accounts

Rent Expense

Adj	1,000		
Bal	1,000	Clo	1,000

Salary Expense

	900		
Adj	900		
Bal	1,800	Clo	1,800

Supplies Expense

Adj	300		
Bal	300	Clo	300

Depreciation Expense

Adj	400		
Bal	400	Clo	400

Utilities Expense

	500		
Bal	500	Clo	500

Income Tax Expense

Adj	600		
Bal	600	Clo	600

Service Revenue

			7,000
		Adj	300
		Adj	200
Clo	7,500	Bal	7,500

Retained Earnings

Clo	4,600		18,800
Clo	3,200	Clo	7,500
		Bal	18,500

Dividends

Bal	3,200	Clo	3,200

②   ①   ③

MyAccountingLab

Adj = Amount posted from an adjusting entry
Clo = Amount posted from a closing entry
Bal = Balance
As arrow   in Panel B shows, we can make a compound closing entry for all the expenses.

Classifying Assets and Liabilities Based on Their Liquidity

On the balance sheet, assets and liabilities are classified as current or long term to indicate their relative liquidity. **Liquidity** measures how quickly an item can be converted to cash. Cash is the most liquid asset. Accounts receivable are relatively liquid because cash collections usually follow quickly. Inventory is less liquid than accounts receivable because the company must first sell the goods. Equipment and buildings are even less liquid because these assets are held for use and not for sale. A balance sheet lists assets and liabilities in the order of relative liquidity.

Current Assets. As we saw in Chapter 1, **current assets** are the most liquid assets. They will be converted to cash, sold, or consumed during the next 12 months or within the business's normal operating cycle if longer than a year. The **operating cycle** is the time span during which cash is paid for goods and services, and these goods and services are sold to bring in cash.

For most businesses, the operating cycle is a few months. Cash, Short-Term Investments, Accounts Receivable, Merchandise Inventory, and Prepaid Expenses are the typical current assets.

Long-Term Assets. **Long-term assets** are all assets not classified as current assets. One category of long-term assets is plant assets, often labeled Property, Plant, and Equipment. Land, Buildings, Furniture and Fixtures, and Equipment are plant assets. Of these, Freddy's Auto Service, Inc. has only Land and Equipment. Long-Term Investments, Intangible Assets, and Other Assets (a catch-all category for assets that are not classified more precisely) are also long-term.

Current Liabilities. As we saw in Chapter 1, **current liabilities** are debts that must be paid within one year or within the entity's operating cycle if longer than a year. Accounts Payable, Notes Payable due within one year, Salary Payable, Unearned Revenue, Interest Payable, and Income Tax Payable are current liabilities.

Bankers and other lenders are interested in the due dates of an entity's liabilities. The sooner a liability must be paid, the more pressure it creates. Therefore, the balance sheet lists liabilities in the order in which they must be paid. Balance sheets usually report two liability classifications: current liabilities and long-term liabilities.

Long-Term Liabilities. All liabilities that are not current are classified as **long-term liabilities**. Many notes payable are long term. Some notes payable are paid in installments, with the first installment due within one year, the second installment due the second year, and so on. The first installment is a current liability and the remainder is long term.

Let's see how Starbucks Corporation reports these asset and liability categories on its balance sheet.

Reporting Assets and Liabilities: Starbucks Corporation

Exhibit 3-14 on the following page shows a classified balance sheet: The Consolidated Balance Sheets of Starbucks Corporation as of September 30, 2012 and October 2, 2011. A **classified balance sheet** separates current assets from long-term assets and current liabilities from long-term liabilities. You should be familiar with most of Starbucks' accounts. Study the Starbucks balance sheet all the way through—line by line.

Formats for the Financial Statements

Companies can format their financial statements in different ways. Both the balance sheet and the income statement can be formatted in two basic ways.

Balance Sheet Formats. The **report format** lists the assets at the top, followed by the liabilities and stockholders' equity below. The comparative Consolidated Balance Sheets of Starbucks Corporation in Exhibit 3-14 illustrate the report format. The report format is more popular, with approximately 60% of large companies using it.

The **account format** lists the assets on the left and the liabilities and stockholders' equity on the right in the same way that a T-account appears, with assets (debits) on the left and liabilities and equity (credits) on the right. Exhibit 3-12 (p. 134) shows an account-format balance sheet for Freddy's Auto Service, Inc. Either format is acceptable.

Income Statement Formats. A **single-step income statement** (statement of earnings) lists all the revenues together under a heading such as Revenues, or Revenues and Gains. The expenses are listed together in a single category titled Expenses, or Expenses and Losses. There is only one step, the subtraction of the sum of Expenses and Losses from the sum of Revenues and Gains, in arriving at income before income tax expense. Starbucks' single-step statement of earnings in the opening section of this chapter (p. 114) appears in single-step format.

A **multi-step income statement** reports a number of subtotals to highlight important relationships between revenues and expenses. Exhibit 3-15 shows Starbucks Corporation's

Exhibit 3-14 | Classified Balance Sheet of Starbucks Corporation

	A	B	C	D	E
	A1				
1	**Starbucks Corporation** **Consolidated Balance Sheets (Classified) (Adapted)**				
2	In millions of USD	Sep. 30, 2012	Oct. 02, 2011		
3	ASSETS				
4	Current assets:				
5	Cash and cash equivalents	$ 1,189	$ 1,148		
6	Short-term investments	848	903		
7	Accounts receivable, net	486	387		
8	Inventories	1,242	966		
9	Prepaid expenses and other	435	391		
10	Total current assets	4,200	3,795		
11	Long-term investments–available-for-sale securities	116	107		
12	Equity and cost investments	460	372		
13	Property, plant, and equipment, net	2,659	2,355		
14	Goodwill	399	322		
15	Other assets	385	409		
16	Total assets	$ 8,219	$ 7,360		
17	LIABILITIES AND SHAREHOLDERS' EQUITY				
18	Current liabilities:				
19	Accounts payable	$ 398	$ 540		
20	Accrued liabilities	1,134	941		
21	Insurance reserves	168	146		
22	Deferred revenue	510	449		
23	Total current liabilities	2,210	2,076		
24	Long-term debt	550	550		
25	Other long-term liabilities	345	347		
26	Total liabilities	3,105	2,973		
27	Shareholders' equity:				
28	Common stock	1	1		
29	Additional paid-in capital	39	41		
30	Retained earnings	5,046	4,297		
31	Accumulated other comprehensive income	23	46		
32	Total shareholders' equity	5,109	4,385		
33	Noncontrolling interests	5	2		
34	Total equity	5,114	4,387		
35	Total liabilities and shareholders' equity	$ 8,219	$ 7,360		
36					

Exhibit 3-15 | Starbucks Corporation Income Statement in Multi-Step Format

	A	B	C	D	E
	A1				
1	**Starbucks Corporation** **Consolidated Statements of Earnings (Adapted)**				
2	(in millions of USD)	12 months ended			
3		Sep. 30, 2012	Oct. 02, 2011		
4	Net revenues:				
5	Net operating revenues	$ 13,299	$ 11,701		
6	Cost of sales including occupancy costs	5,813	4,916		
7	**Gross profit**	7,486	6,785		
8	Store operating expenses	3,918	3,595		
9	Other operating expenses	430	393		
10	Depreciation and amortization expenses	550	523		
11	General and administrative expenses	802	749		
12	Total operating expenses	5,700	5,260		
13	**Operating income attributable to Starbucks**	1,786	1,525		
14	Gain on sale of properties	-	30		
15	Income from equity investees	211	174		
16	**Operating income**	1,997	1,729		
17	Interest income and other, net	94	114		
18	Interest expense	(33)	(34)		
19	**Income before income taxes**	2,058	1,809		
20	Income taxes	674	563		
21	**Net income**	$ 1,384	$ 1,246		
22					

comparative Consolidated Statements of Earnings in multi-step format. Gross profit, various levels of operating income, income before taxes, and net income are highlighted for emphasis.

In particular, operating income ($1,997 million) is separated from other types of income (i.e., interest income) that Starbucks did not earn by selling coffee. Operating income reflects the earnings from the company's core business activities. The other income consists mainly of interest income and other investment income. Most investors consider it important for the companies they own to report operating income separately from non-operating income such as interest and dividends so that they can evaluate the profitability of the company's core business activities.

Most companies' income statements do not conform to either a pure single-step format or a pure multi-step format. Business operations are too complex for all companies to conform to rigid reporting formats. We will discuss the components of the income statement in more detail in Chapter 11.

ANALYZE AND EVALUATE A COMPANY'S DEBT-PAYING ABILITY

6 **Analyze** and evaluate a company's debt-paying ability

As we've seen, accounting provides information for decision making. A bank considering lending money must predict whether the borrower can repay the loan. If the borrower already has a lot of debt, the probability of repayment may be low. If the borrower owes little, the loan may go through. To analyze a company's financial position, decision makers use data and ratios computed from various items in the financial statements. Let's see how this process works.

Net Working Capital

Net working capital is computational data that represents operating liquidity. Its computation is simple:

$$\text{Net working capital} = \text{Total current assets} - \text{Total current liabilities}$$

For Starbucks Corporation, at September 30, 2012 (amounts in millions in Exhibit 3-14),

$$\text{Net working capital} = \$4,200 - \$2,210 = \$1,990$$

Generally, to be considered sufficiently liquid, entities should have a sufficient excess of current assets over current liabilities. The amount of that excess is usually expressed in terms of the current ratio discussed below, and the amount considered "sufficient" varies with the industry. Starbucks Corporation's current assets exceed its current liabilities by $1,990 million, meaning that after the company pays all of its current liabilities, it will still have almost $2 billion in cash and other assets that can be converted into cash. Thus, Starbucks Corporation is considered highly "liquid."

Current Ratio

Another means of expressing operating liquidity through the relationship between current assets and current liabilities is the **current ratio**, which divides total current assets by total current liabilities.

$$\text{Current ratio} = \frac{\text{Total current assets}}{\text{Total current liabilities}}$$

For Starbucks Corporation, at September 20, 2012 (amounts in millions from Exhibit 3-14),

$$\text{Current ratio} = \frac{\text{Total current assets}}{\text{Total current liabilities}} = \frac{\$4,200}{\$2,210} = 1.90$$

Like net working capital, the current ratio measures the company's ability to pay current liabilities with current assets. A company prefers a high current ratio, which means that the business has plenty of current assets to pay current liabilities. An increasing current ratio from period to period indicates improvement in financial position.

As a rule of thumb, a strong current ratio is 1.50, which indicates that the company has $1.50 in current assets for every $1.00 in current liabilities. A company with a current ratio of 1.50

would probably have little trouble paying its current liabilities. Most successful businesses operate with current ratios between 1.20 and 1.50. A current ratio of less than 1.00 is considered low. That would mean that current liabilities exceed current assets.

Starbucks' current ratio of 1.90 indicates a strong current ratio position. The company makes most sales for cash. It has 90% more cash and other current assets that can be converted into cash than the amount needed to pay off accounts payable and other liabilities that must be met with cash immediately.

Debt Ratio

Still another measure of debt-paying ability is the **debt ratio**, which is the ratio of total liabilities to total assets.

$$\text{Debt ratio} = \frac{\text{Total liabilities}}{\text{Total assets}}$$

For Starbucks, at September 30, 2012 (amounts in millions from Exhibit 3-14),

$$\text{Debt ratio} = \frac{\text{Total liabilities}}{\text{Total assets}} = \frac{\$3,105}{\$8,219} = 0.38$$

The debt ratio indicates the proportion of a company's assets that is financed with debt. This ratio measures a business's ability to pay both current and long-term debts (total liabilities).

A low debt ratio is safer than a high debt ratio. Why? Because a company with few liabilities has low required debt payments. This company is unlikely to get into financial difficulty. By contrast, a business with a high debt ratio may have trouble paying its liabilities, especially when sales are low and cash is scarce.

Starbucks' debt ratio of 38% (0.38) is low compared to most companies in the United States. The norm for the debt ratio ranges from 60% to 70%. Starbucks' debt ratio indicates low risk for the company.

When a company fails to pay its debts, some of its creditors might be in a position to take the company away from its owners. Most bankruptcies result from high debt ratios. Companies that continue in this pattern are often forced out of business.

How Do Transactions Affect the Ratios?

Companies such as Starbucks are keenly aware of how transactions affect their ratios. Lending agreements often require that a company's current ratio not fall below a certain level. Another loan requirement is that the company's debt ratio may not rise above a threshold, such as 0.70. When a company fails to meet one of these conditions, it is said to default on its lending agreements. The penalty can be severe: The lender can require immediate payment of the loan. Starbucks has a sufficiently small amount of debt that the company is not in danger of default. But many companies are. To help keep debt ratios within normal limits, companies might adopt one or more of the following strategies:

- Increase revenue and decrease costs, thus increasing current assets, net income, and retained earnings without increasing liabilities
- Sell stock, thus increasing cash and stockholders' equity
- Choose to borrow less money

Let's use Starbucks Corporation to examine the effects of some transactions on the company's current ratio and debt ratio. As shown in the preceding section, Starbucks' ratios are as follows (dollar amounts in millions):[1]

---

[1]Because of the relatively small amounts of these particular illustrative transactions compared to the original components, we have chosen to carry current ratio and debt ratio computations to three decimal places in order to illustrate the impact of individual transactions on the current ratio and debt ratio. The larger the individual transaction in comparison with the original components (for example, see the End-of-Chapter Summary Problem), the less necessary this will be.

$$\text{Current ratio} = \frac{\$4,200}{\$2,210} = 1.900$$

$$\text{Debt ratio} = \frac{\$3,105}{\$8,219} = 0.378$$

The managers of any company would be concerned about how inventory purchases, payments on account, expense accruals, and depreciation would affect its ratios. Let's see how Starbucks would be affected by some typical transactions. For each transaction, the journal entry helps identify the effects on the company.

a. Issued stock and received cash of $50 million.

	A	B	C	D	E	F
1	Journal entry:	Cash	50			
2		Common Stock		50		
3						

Cash, a current asset, affects both the current ratio and the debt ratio as follows:

$$\text{Current ratio} = \frac{\$4,200 + \$50}{\$2,210} = 1.923 \qquad \text{Debt ratio} = \frac{\$3,105}{\$8,219 + \$50} = 0.375$$

The issuance of stock improves both ratios slightly.

b. Paid cash to purchase buildings for $20 million.

	A	B	C	D	E	F
1	Journal entry:	Buildings	20			
2		Cash		20		
3						

Cash, a current asset, decreases, but total assets stay the same. Liabilities are unchanged.

$$\text{Current ratio} = \frac{\$4,200 - \$20}{\$2,210} = 1.891 \qquad \text{Debt ratio} = \frac{\$3,105}{\$8,219 + \$20 - \$20} = 0.378; \text{ no change}$$

A cash purchase of a building hurts the current ratio but doesn't affect the debt ratio.

c. Made a $30 million sale on account to a grocery chain.

	A	B	C	D	E	F
1	Journal entry:	Accounts Receivable	30			
2		Sales Revenue		30		
3						

The increase in Accounts Receivable increases current assets and total assets, as follows:

$$\text{Current ratio} = \frac{\$4,200 + \$30}{\$2,210} = 1.914 \qquad \text{Debt ratio} = \frac{\$3,105}{\$8,219 + \$30} = 0.376$$

A sale on account improves both ratios slightly.

    d. Collected the account receivable, $30 million.

	A	B	C	D	E	F
		A1 ⬍				
1	*Journal entry:*	Cash	30			
2		Accounts Receivable		30		
3						

This transaction has no effect on total current assets, total assets, or total liabilities. Both ratios are unaffected.

    e. Accrued expenses at year end, $40 million.

	A	B	C	D	E	F
		A1 ⬍				
1	*Journal entry:*	Expenses	40			
2		Expenses Payable		40		
3						

$$\text{Current ratio} = \frac{\$4,200}{\$2,210 + \$40} = 1.867 \qquad \text{Debt ratio} = \frac{\$3,105 + \$40}{\$8,219} = 0.383$$

Most expenses hurt both ratios.

    f. Recorded depreciation, $80 million.

	A	B	C	D	E	F
		A1 ⬍				
1	*Journal entry:*	Depreciation Expense	80			
2		Accumulated Depreciation		80		
3						

No current accounts are affected, so only the debt ratio is affected.

$$\text{Current ratio} = \frac{\$4,200}{\$2,210} = 1.900 \qquad \text{Debt ratio} = \frac{\$3,105}{\$8,219 - \$80} = 0.381$$

Depreciation decreases total assets and therefore hurts the debt ratio.

    g. Earned interest revenue and collected cash, $40 million.

Cash, a current asset, affects both the current ratio and the debt ratio as follows:

	A	B	C	D	E	F
		A1 ⬍				
1	*Journal entry:*	Cash	40			
2		Interest Revenue		40		
3						

$$\text{Current ratio} = \frac{\$4,200 + \$40}{\$2,210} = 1.919 \qquad \text{Debt ratio} = \frac{\$3,105}{\$8,219 + \$40} = 0.376$$

A revenue improves both ratios.

    Now, let's wrap up the chapter by seeing how to use net working capital, the current ratio, and the debt ratio for decision making. The Decision Guidelines feature offers some clues.

● Decision Guidelines

EVALUATE DEBT-PAYING ABILITY USING NET WORKING CAPITAL, THE CURRENT RATIO, AND THE DEBT RATIO

In general, a larger amount of net working capital is preferable to a smaller amount. Similarly, a *high* current ratio is preferable to a low current ratio. *Increases* in net working capital and increases in the current ratio improve financial position. By contrast, a *low* debt ratio is preferable to a high debt ratio. Improvement is indicated by a *decrease* in the debt ratio.

No single ratio gives the whole picture about a company. Therefore, lenders and investors use many ratios to evaluate a company. Let's apply what we have learned. Suppose you are a loan officer at Bank of America and Starbucks Corporation has asked you for a $20 million loan to launch a new blend of coffee. How will you make this loan decision? The Decision Guidelines show how bankers and investors use two key ratios.

➤ USING NET WORKING CAPITAL AND THE CURRENT RATIO

Decision	Guidelines
How can you measure a company's ability to pay current liabilities with current assets?	Net working capital = Total current assets − Total current liabilities $$\text{Current ratio} = \frac{\text{Total current assets}}{\text{Total current liabilities}}$$
Who uses net working capital and the current ratio for decision making?	*Lenders and other creditors*, who must predict whether a borrower can pay its current liabilities. *Stockholders*, who know that a company that cannot pay its debts is not a good investment because it may go bankrupt. *Managers*, who must have enough cash to pay the company's current liabilities.
What is a good value of net working capital and the current ratio?	There is no correct answer for this. It depends on the industry as well as the individual entity's ability to generate cash quickly and primarily from operations. An entity with strong operating cash flow can operate successfully with a low amount of net working capital as long as cash comes in through operations at least as fast as accounts payable become due. A current ratio of, say, 1.10–1.20 is sometimes sufficient. An entity with relatively slow cash flow from operations needs a higher current ratio of, say, 1.30–1.50. Traditionally, a current ratio of 2.00 was considered ideal. Recently, acceptable values have decreased as companies have been able to operate more efficiently; today, a current ratio of 1.50 is considered strong. Although not ideal, cash-rich companies like Starbucks can operate with a current ratio below 1.0.

▶ USING THE DEBT RATIO

Decision	Guidelines
How can you measure a company's ability to pay total liabilities?	$$\text{Debt ratio} = \frac{\text{Total liabilities}}{\text{Total assets}}$$
Who uses the debt ratio for decision making?	*Lenders and other creditors*, who must predict whether a borrower can pay its debts. *Stockholders*, who know that a company that cannot pay its debts is not a good investment because it may go bankrupt. *Managers*, who must have enough assets to pay the company's debts.
What is a good value of the debt ratio?	It depends on the industry: A company with strong cash flow can operate successfully with a high debt ratio of, say, 0.70–0.80. A company with weak cash flow needs a lower debt ratio of, say, 0.50–0.60. Traditionally, a debt ratio of 0.50 was considered ideal. Recently, values have increased as companies have been able to operate more efficiently; today, a normal value of the debt ratio is around 0.60–0.70.

End-of-Chapter Summary Problem

Refer to the Mid-Chapter Summary Problem that begins on page 135. The adjusted trial balance appears on page 139.

Requirements

1. Make Badger Ranch Company's closing entries at December 31, 2014. Explain what the closing entries accomplish and why they are necessary.
2. Post the closing entries to Retained Earnings and compare Retained Earnings' ending balance with the amount reported on the balance sheet on page 140. The two amounts should be the same.
3. Prepare Badger Ranch Company's classified balance sheet to identify the company's current assets and current liabilities. (Badger Ranch Company has no long-term liabilities.) Use the

account format. Then compute the company's net working capital, current ratio, and debt ratio at December 31, 2014.

4. The top management of Badger Ranch Company has asked you for a $500,000 loan to expand the business. Badger Ranch proposes to pay off the loan over a 10-year period. Recompute Badger Ranch Company's debt ratio assuming you make the loan. Use the company financial statements plus the ratio values to decide whether to grant the loan at an interest rate of 8%, 10%, or 12%. Badger Ranch Company's cash flow is strong. Give the reasoning underlying your decision.

Answers

Requirement 1

2014			
Dec 31	Service Revenue..	330,000	
	Retained Earnings		330,000
31	Retained Earnings	259,000	
	Salary Expense		177,000
	Depreciation Expense—		
	Furniture and Fixtures............................		20,000
	Depreciation Expense—Building		10,000
	Supplies Expense		4,000
	Income Tax Expense		35,000
	Miscellaneous Expense...............................		13,000
31	Retained Earnings	65,000	
	Dividends..		65,000

Explanation of Closing Entries

The closing entries set the balance of each revenue, expense, and dividend account back to zero for the start of the next accounting period. We must close these accounts because their balances relate only to one accounting period.

Requirement 2

Retained Earnings

			193,000
Clo	259,000	Clo	330,000
Clo	65,000		
		Bal	199,000

The balance in the Retained Earnings account agrees with the amount reported on the balance sheet, as it should.

Requirement 3

	A	B	C	D	E
1	**Badger Ranch Company** **Balance Sheet** **December 31, 2014**				
2	**Assets**			**Liabilities**	
3	Current assets:			Current liabilities:	
4	Cash		$198,000	Accounts payable	$380,000
5	Accounts receivable		382,000	Salary payable	5,000
6	Supplies		2,000	Unearned service revenue	13,000
7	Total current assets		582,000	Income tax payable	35,000
8	Building	$250,000		Total current liabilities	433,000
9	Less: Accumulated			**Stockholders' Equity**	
10	depreciation	(140,000)	110,000	Common stock	100,000
11	Furniture and fixtures	$100,000		Retained earnings	199,000
12	Less: Accumulated			Total stockholders' equity	299,000
13	depreciation	(60,000)	40,000	Total liabilities and	
14	Total assets		$732,000	stockholders' equity	$732,000
15					

$$\text{Net working capital} = \$582,000 - \$433,000 = \$149,000$$

$$\text{Current ratio} = \frac{\$582,000}{\$433,000} = 1.34$$

$$\text{Debt ratio} = \frac{\$433,000}{\$732,000} = 0.59$$

Requirement 4

$$\begin{array}{c}\text{Debt ratio assuming}\\ \text{the loan is made}\end{array} = \frac{\$433,000 + \$500,000}{\$732,000 + \$500,000} = \frac{\$933,000}{\$1,232,000} = .76$$

Decision: Make the loan at 10%.

Reasoning: Prior to the loan, the company's financial position and cash flow are strong. The current ratio is in a middle range, and the debt ratio is not too high. Net income (from the income statement) is high in relation to total revenue. Therefore, the company should be able to repay the loan.

The loan will increase the company's debt ratio from 59% to 76%, which is more risky than the company's financial position at present. On this basis, a midrange interest rate appears reasonable—at least as the starting point for the negotiation between Badger Ranch Company and the bank.

REVIEW | Accrual Accounting & Income

Quick Check (Answers are given on page 191.)

1. On November 1, Brownstone Apartments received $3,600 from a tenant for four months' rent. The receipt was credited to Unearned Rent Revenue. What adjusting entry is needed on December 31?

   a. Cash   900
       Rent Revenue   900
   b. Unearned Rent Revenue   1,800
       Rent Revenue   1,800
   c. Unearned Rent Revenue   900
       Rent Revenue   900
   d. Rent Revenue   900
       Unearned Rent Revenue   900

2. The following normal balances appear on the *adjusted* trial balance of Adams Company:

Equipment..	$90,000
Accumulated depreciation, equipment................	12,000
Depreciation expense, equipment.......................	3,000

   The book value of the equipment is
   a. $78,000.   **c.** $66,000.
   b. $87,000.   **d.** $75,000.

3. Sullivan, Inc., purchased supplies for $1,500 during 2014. At year-end, Sullivan had $400 of supplies left. The adjusting entry should
   a. debit Supplies $1,100.   **c.** debit Supplies $400.
   b. credit Supplies $400.   **d.** debit Supplies Expense $1,100.

4. The accountant for Max Corp. failed to make the adjusting entry to record depreciation for the current year. The effect of this error is which of the following?
   a. Assets, net income, and stockholders' equity are all overstated.
   b. Assets and expenses are understated; net income is understated.
   c. Net income is overstated and liabilities are understated.
   d. Assets are overstated; stockholders' equity and net income are understated.

5. Interest earned on a note receivable at December 31 equals $225. What adjusting entry is required to accrue this interest?

   a. Interest Expense   225
       Cash   225
   b. Interest Payable   225
       Interest Expense   225
   c. Interest Receivable   225
       Interest Revenue   225
   d. Interest Expense   225
       Interest Payable   225

6. If a real estate company fails to accrue commission revenue,
   a. liabilities are overstated, and owners' equity is understated.
   b. revenues are understated, and net income is overstated.
   c. net income is understated, and stockholders' equity is overstated.
   d. assets are understated, and net income is understated.

7. All of the following statements are true except one. Which statement is false?

    a. Accrual accounting produces better information than cash-basis accounting.

    b. Adjusting entries are required for a business that uses the cash basis.

    c. The expense recognition principle directs accountants to identify and measure all expenses incurred and deduct them from revenues earned during the same period.

    d. A fiscal year may end on some date other than December 31.

8. The account Unearned Revenue is a(n)

    a. revenue.   c. expense.

    b. asset.   d. liability.

9. Adjusting entries

    a. are needed to measure the period's net income or net loss.

    b. do not debit or credit Cash.

    c. update the accounts.

    d. all of the above.

10. An adjusting entry that debits an expense and credits a liability is which type?

    a. Depreciation expense   c. Accrued expense

    b. Prepaid expense   d. Cash expense

    Use the following data for questions 11 and 12.

    Here are key figures from the balance sheet of Stamper, Inc., at the end of 2014 (amounts in thousands):

	December 31, 2014
Total assets (of which 30% are current)	$7,000
Current liabilities	700
Bonds payable (long-term)	1,300
Common stock	1,200
Retained earnings	3,800
Total liabilities and stockholders' equity	7,000

11. Stamper's current ratio at the end of 2014 is

    a. 3.00.   c. 1.05.

    b. 0.55.   d. 10.00.

12. Stamper's debt ratio at the end of 2014 is (all amounts are rounded)

    a. 10%.   c. 1.05%.

    b. 29%.   d. 14%.

13. On a trial balance, which of the following would indicate that an error has been made?

    a. Salary Expense has a debit balance.

    b. Accumulated Depreciation has a credit balance.

    c. Service Revenue has a debit balance.

    d. All of the above indicate errors.

14. The entry to close Management Fee Revenue would be which of the following?

    a. Management Fee Revenue
           Service Revenue

    b. Management Fee Revenue
           Retained Earnings

    c. Retained Earnings
           Management Fee Revenue

    d. Management Fee Revenue does not need to be closed.

15. Which of the following accounts is not closed?
  a. Accumulated Depreciation   **c.** Depreciation Expense
  b. Dividends   **d.** Interest Revenue

16. FedEx earns service revenue of $750,000. How does this transaction affect FedEx's current and debt ratios?
  a. Hurts the current ratio and improves the debt ratio
  b. Improves the current ratio and doesn't affect the debt ratio
  c. Improves both ratios
  d. Hurts both ratios

17. Suppose Rose Corporation borrows $10 million on a 10-year note payable. How does this transaction affect Rose's current ratio and debt ratio?
  a. Hurts both ratios
  b. Hurts the current ratio and improves the debt ratio
  c. Improves both ratios
  d. Improves the current ratio and hurts the debt ratio

Accounting Vocabulary

account format (p. 143) A balance-sheet format that lists assets on the left and liabilities and stockholders' equity on the right.

accrual (p. 120) An expense or a revenue that occurs before the business pays or receives cash. An accrual is the opposite of a deferral.

accrual accounting (p. 115) Accounting that records the impact of a business event as it occurs, regardless of whether the transaction affected cash.

accrued expense (p. 125) An expense incurred but not yet paid in cash.

accrued revenue (p. 127) A revenue that has been earned but not yet received in cash.

accumulated depreciation (p. 124) The cumulative sum of all depreciation expense from the date of acquiring a plant asset.

adjusted trial balance (p. 131) A list of all the ledger accounts with their adjusted balances.

book value (of a plant asset) (p. 124) The asset's cost minus accumulated depreciation.

cash-basis accounting (p. 115) Accounting that records only transactions in which cash is received or paid.

classified balance sheet (p. 143) A balance sheet that shows current assets separate from long-term assets and current liabilities separate from long-term liabilities.

closing the books (p. 141) The process of preparing the accounts to begin recording the next period's transactions. Closing the accounts consists of journalizing and posting the closing entries to set the balances of the revenue, expense, and dividends accounts to zero. Also called closing the accounts.

closing entries (p. 141) Entries that transfer the revenue, expense, and dividends balances from these respective accounts to the Retained Earnings account.

contra account (p. 124) An account that always has a companion account and whose normal balance is opposite that of the companion account.

current asset (p. 142) An asset that is expected to be converted to cash, sold, or consumed during the next 12 months or within the business's normal operating cycle if longer than a year.

current liability (p. 143) A debt due to be paid within one year or within the entity's operating cycle if the cycle is longer than a year.

current ratio (p. 145) Current assets divided by current liabilities. Measures a company's ability to pay current liabilities with current assets.

debt ratio (p. 146) Ratio of total liabilities to total assets. States the proportion of a company's assets that is financed with debt.

deferral (p. 120) An adjustment for which the business paid or received cash in advance. Examples include prepaid rent, prepaid insurance, and supplies.

depreciation (p. 120) Allocation of the cost of a plant asset to expense over its useful life.

expense recognition principle (p. 118) The basis for recording expenses. Directs accountants to identify all expenses incurred during the period, to measure the expenses, and to match them against the revenues earned during that same period.

liquidity (p. 141) Measure of how quickly an item can be converted to cash.

long-term asset (p. 143) An asset that is not a current asset.

long-term liability (p. 143) A liability that is not a current liability.

multi-step income statement (p. 143) An income statement that contains subtotals to highlight important relationships between revenues and expenses.

net working capital (p. 145) A measure of liquidity; current assets − current liabilities.

operating cycle (p. 142) Time span during which cash is paid for goods and services that are sold to customers who pay the business in cash.

permanent accounts (p. 141) Asset, liability, and stockholders' equity accounts that are not closed at the end of the period.

plant assets (p. 123) Long-lived assets, such as land, buildings, and equipment, used in the operation of the business. Also called fixed assets.

prepaid expense (p. 120) A category of miscellaneous assets that typically expire or get used up in the near future. Examples include prepaid rent, prepaid insurance, and supplies.

report format (p. 143) A balance-sheet format that lists assets at the top, followed by liabilities and stockholders' equity below.

revenue principle (p. 116) The basis for recording revenues; tells accountants when to record revenue and the amount of revenue to record.

single-step income statement (p. 143) An income statement that lists all the revenues together under a heading such as Revenues or Revenues and Gains. Expenses appear in a separate category called Expenses or perhaps Expenses and Losses.

temporary accounts (p. 141) The revenue and expense accounts that relate to a limited period and are closed at the end of the period are temporary accounts. For a corporation, the Dividends account is also temporary.

time-period concept (p. 116) Ensures that accounting information is reported at regular intervals.

unearned revenue (p. 128) A liability created when a business collects cash from customers in advance of earning the revenue. The obligation is to provide a product or a service in the future.

ASSESS YOUR PROGRESS

Short Exercises

S3-1. *(Learning Objective 1: Explain how accrual accounting differs from cash-basis accounting)* Southeast Corporation made sales of $825 million during 2014. Of this amount, Southeast collected cash for all but $27 million. The company's cost of goods sold was $255 million, and all other expenses for the year totaled $325 million. Also during 2014, Southeast paid $350 million for its inventory and $255 million for everything else. Beginning cash was $75 million. Southeast's top management is interviewing you for a job and they ask two questions:

    a. How much was Southeast's net income for 2014?
    b. How much was Southeast's cash balance at the end of 2014?

You will get the job only if you answer both questions correctly.

S3-2. *(Learning Objective 1: Explain how accrual accounting differs from cash-basis accounting)* Westwood Corporation began 2014 owing notes payable of $4.7 million. During 2014 Westwood borrowed $1.7 million on notes payable and paid off $1.6 million of notes payable from prior years. Interest expense for the year was $0.6 million, including $0.2 million of interest payable accrued at December 31, 2014.

Show what Westwood should report for these facts on the following financial statements:

    1. Income statement for 2014
        a. Interest expense
    2. Balance sheet as of December 31, 2014
        a. Notes payable
        b. Interest payable

S3-3. *(Learning Objectives 1, 2: Explain how accrual accounting differs from cash-basis accounting; apply the revenue and expense recognition principles)* As the controller of Brumley Consulting, you have hired a new employee, whom you must train. She objects to making an adjusting entry for accrued salaries at the end of the period. She reasons, "We will pay the salaries soon. Why not wait until payment to record the expense? In the end, the result will be the same." Write a reply to explain to the employee why the adjusting entry is needed for accrued salary expense.

S3-4. *(Learning Objective 2: Apply the revenue and expense recognition principles)* A large auto manufacturer sells large fleets of vehicles to auto rental companies, such as Budget and Hertz. Suppose Budget is negotiating with the auto manufacturer to purchase 827 vehicles. Write a short paragraph to explain to the auto manufacturer when the company should, and should not, record this sales revenue and the related expense for cost of goods sold. Mention the accounting principles that provide the basis for your explanation.

S3-5. *(Learning Objective 2: Apply the expense recognition principle)* Write a short paragraph to explain in your own words the concept of depreciation as used in accounting.

S3-6. *(Learning Objective 2: Apply the revenue and expense recognition principles)* Identify the accounting concept or principle that gives the most direction on how to account for each of the following situations:

  a. Salary expense of $48,000 is accrued at the end of the period to measure income properly.
  b. March has been a particularly slow month, and the business will have a net loss for the second quarter of the year. Management is considering not following its customary practice of reporting quarterly earnings to the public.
  c. A physician performs a surgical operation and bills the patient's insurance company. It may take three months to collect from the insurance company. Should the physician record revenue now or wait until cash is collected?
  d. A construction company is building a highway system, and construction will take four years. When should the company record the revenue it earns?
  e. A utility bill is received on December 27 and will be paid next year. When should the company record utility expense?

S3-7. *(Learning Objective 3: Adjust the accounts)* Answer the following questions about prepaid expenses:

  a. On October 1, Paradise Travel prepaid $6,000 for six months' rent. Give the adjusting entry to record rent expense at October 31. Include the date of the entry and an explanation. Then post all amounts to the two accounts involved, and show their balances at October 31. Paradise Travel adjusts the accounts only at October 31, the end of its fiscal year.
  b. On October 1, Paradise Travel paid $950 for supplies. At October 31, Paradise Travel has $270 of supplies on hand. Make the required journal entry at October 31. Then post all amounts to the accounts and show their balances at October 31.

S3-8. *(Learning Objectives 1, 3: Explain how accrual accounting differs from cash–basis accounting; adjust the accounts for depreciation)* Suppose that on January 1 Brothers Golf Company paid cash of $35,000 for equipment that is expected to remain useful for five years. At the end of five years, the equipment's value is expected to be zero.

  1. Make journal entries to record (a) purchase of the equipment on January 1 and (b) annual depreciation on December 31. Include dates and explanations, and use the following accounts: Equipment; Accumulated Depreciation—Equipment; and Depreciation Expense—Equipment.
  2. Post to the accounts and show their balances at December 31.
  3. What is the equipment's book value at December 31?

S3-9. *(Learning Objective 2: Apply the revenue and expense recognition principles)* During 2014, U-Commute Airlines paid salary expense of $44.1 million. At December 31, 2014, U-Commute accrued salary expense of $2.2 million. U-Commute then paid $3.8 million to its employees on January 3, 2015, the company's next payday after the end of the 2014 year. For this sequence of transactions, show what U-Commute would report on its 2014 income statement and on its balance sheet at the end of 2014.

S3-10. *(Learning Objective 3: Adjust the accounts for interest expense)* Perfect Travel Services borrowed $75,000 on October 1 by signing a note payable to Community Bank. The interest expense for each month is $312. The loan agreement requires Perfect Travel to pay interest on December 31.

1. Make Perfect Travel's adjusting entry to accrue monthly interest expense at October 31, at November 30, and at December 31. Date each entry and include its explanation.
2. Post all three entries to the Interest Payable account. You need not take the balance of the account at the end of each month.
3. Record the payment of three months' interest at December 31.

S3-11. *(Learning Objective 3: Adjust the accounts for interest revenue)* Return to the situation in Short Exercise 3-10. Here you are accounting for the same transactions on the books of Community Bank, which lent the money to Perfect Travel Services.

1. Make Community Bank's adjusting entry to accrue monthly interest revenue at October 31, at November 30, and at December 31. Date each entry and include its explanation.
2. Post all three entries to the Interest Receivable account. You need not take the balance of the account at the end of each month.
3. Record the receipt of three months' interest at December 31.

S3-12. *(Learning Objectives 1, 3: Explain how accrual accounting differs from cash-basis accounting; adjust the accounts for unearned revenue)* Write a paragraph to explain why unearned revenues are liabilities instead of revenues. In your explanation, use the following actual example: *The World Star*, a national newspaper, collects cash from subscribers in advance and later delivers newspapers to subscribers over a one-year period. Explain what happens to the unearned revenue over the course of a year as *The World Star* delivers papers to subscribers. Into what account does the earned subscription revenue go as *The World Star* delivers papers? Give the journal entries that *The World Star* would make to (a) collect $60,000 of subscription revenue in advance and (b) record earning $40,000 of subscription revenue. Include an explanation for each entry, as illustrated in the chapter.

S3-13. *(Learning Objectives 3, 4: Adjust the accounts for prepaid expenses; construct the financial statements)* Bowden Golf Co. prepaid three years' rent ($36,000) on January 1, 2014. At December 31, 2014, Bowden prepared a trial balance and then made the necessary adjusting entry at the end of the year. Bowden adjusts its accounts once each year—on December 31.

What amount appears for Prepaid Rent on
  a. Bowden's *unadjusted* trial balance at December 31, 2014?
  b. Bowden's *adjusted* trial balance at December 31, 2014?

What amount appears for Rent Expense on
  c. Bowden's *unadjusted* trial balance at December 31, 2014?
  d. Bowden's *adjusted* trial balance at December 31, 2014?

S3-14. *(Learning Objective 3: Adjust the accounts for accrued and unearned revenue)* Selenna, Inc., collects cash from customers two ways:

  a. **Accrued revenue.** Some customers pay Selenna after Selenna has performed service for the customer. During 2014, Selenna made sales of $19,000 on account and later received cash of $8,000 on account from these customers.
  b. **Unearned revenue.** A few customers pay Selenna in advance, and Selenna later performs the service for the customer. During 2014, Selenna collected $3,000 cash in advance and later earned $2,000 of this amount.

Journalize the following for Selenna:
  a. Earning service revenue of $19,000 on account and then collecting $8,000 on account
  b. Receiving $3,000 in advance and then earning $2,000 as service revenue

S3-15. *(Learning Objective 4: Construct the financial statements)* Suppose Uptown Sporting Goods Company reported the following data at July 31, 2014, with amounts in thousands:

Retained earnings, July 31, 2013	$ 36,500	Cost of goods sold.................	$136,000
Accounts receivable.......	28,000	Cash.......................................	26,700
Net revenues	180,500	Property and equipment, net ...	19,800
Total current liabilities..	55,100	Common stock.......................	22,500
All other expenses	29,600	Inventories	35,000
Other current assets	5,000	Long-term liabilities	7,500
Other assets...................	22,000	Dividends.............................	0

Use these data to prepare Uptown Sporting Goods Company's single step income statement for the year ended July 31, 2014; statement of retained earnings for the year ended July 31, 2014; and classified balance sheet at July 31, 2014. Use the report format for the balance sheet. Draw arrows linking the three statements.

S3-16. *(Learning Objective 5: Close the books)* Use the Uptown Sporting Goods Company data in Short Exercise 3-15 to make the company's closing entries at July 31, 2014. Then set up a T-account for Retained Earnings and post to that account. Compare Retained Earnings' ending balance to the amount reported on Uptown's statement of retained earnings and balance sheet. What do you find?

S3-17. *(Learning Objective 6: Analyze and evaluate liquidity and debt–paying ability)* Uptown Sporting Goods reported the following data at July 31, 2014, with amounts adapted in thousands:

	A1						
		A		B	C	D	E
1		Uptown Sporting Goods Company Income Statement Year ended July 31, 2014					
2	(Amounts in thousands)						
3	Net revenues			$180,500			
4	Cost of goods sold			136,000			
5	All other expenses			29,600			
6	Net income			$ 14,900			
7							

	A1						
		A		B	C	D	E
1		Uptown Sporting Goods Company Statement of Retained Earnings Year ended July 31, 2014					
2	(Amounts in thousands)						
3	Retained earnings, July 31, 2013				$36,500		
4	Add: Net income				14,900		
5	Retained earnings, July 31, 2014				$51,400		
6							

A1	▲▼					
	A	B	C	D	E

	A	B	C	D	E
1	**Uptown Sporting Goods Company** **Balance Sheet** **July 31, 2014**				
2	*(Amounts in thousands)*				
3	**Assets**				
4	Current:				
5	Cash	$ 26,700			
6	Accounts receivable	28,000			
7	Inventories	35,000			
8	Other current assets	5,000			
9	Total current assets	94,700			
10	Property and equipment, net	19,800			
11	Other assets	22,000			
12	Total assets	$136,500			
13	**Liabilities**				
14	Total current liabilities	$ 55,100			
15	Long-term liabilities	7,500			
16	Total liabilities	62,600			
17	**Stockholders' Equity**				
18	Common stock	22,500			
19	Retained earnings	51,400			
20	Total stockholders' equity	73,900			
21	Total liabilities and stockholders' equity	$136,500			
22					

1. Compute Uptown's net working capital.
2. Compute Uptown's current ratio. Round to two decimal places.
3. Compute Uptown's debt ratio. Round to two decimal places.

Do these values and ratios look strong, weak, or middle-of-the-road?

S3-18. *(Learning Objective 6: Analyze and evaluate liquidity and debt-paying ability)* Refer to the Uptown Sporting Goods Company data in Short Exercise 3-17.

At July 31, 2014, Uptown Sporting Goods Company's current ratio was 1.72 and its debt ratio was 0.46. Compute Uptown's (a) net working capital, (b) current ratio, and (c) debt ratio after each of the following transactions (all amounts in thousands, as in the Uptown financial statements):

1. Uptown earned revenue of $10,000 on account.
2. Uptown paid off accounts payable of $10,000.

When calculating the revised ratios, treat each of the above scenarios independently. Round ratios to two decimal places.

Exercises

All of the A and B exercises can be found within MyAccountingLab, an online homework and practice environment. Your instructor may ask you to complete these exercises
using **MyAccountingLab**.

MyAccountingLab

Group A

E3-19A. *(Learning Objectives 1, 2: Explain how accrual accounting differs from cash-basis
accounting; apply the revenue and expense recognition principles)* During 2014, Boyd Network, Inc.,
which designs network servers, earned revenues of $730 million. Expenses totaled $410 million.
Boyd collected all but $26 million of the revenues and paid $425 million on its expenses. Boyd's
top managers are evaluating 2014, and they ask you the following questions:

    a. Under accrual accounting, what amount of revenue should Boyd Network report for
        2014? How does the revenue principle help to answer these questions?

    b. Under accrual accounting, what amount of total expense should Boyd Network report
        for 2014? Which accounting principle helps to answer this question?

    c. Re-do parts a and b using the cash basis. Explain how the accrual basis differs from the
        cash basis.

    d. Which financial statement reports revenues and expenses? Which statement reports
        cash receipts and cash payments?

E3-20A. *(Learning Objectives 1, 3: Explain how accrual accounting differs from cash-basis
accounting; adjust the accounts)* An accountant made the following adjustments at December 31,
the end of the accounting period:

    a. Prepaid insurance, beginning, $600. Payments for insurance during the period, $2,400.
        Prepaid insurance, ending, $700.

    b. Interest revenue accrued, $2,600.

    c. Unearned service revenue, beginning, $1,700. Unearned service revenue, ending, $500.

    d. Depreciation, $5,800.

    e. Employees' salaries owed for two days of a five-day work week; weekly payroll, $20,000.

    f. Income before income tax, $21,000. Income tax rate is 35%.

Requirements

1. Journalize the adjusting entries.
2. Suppose the adjustments were not made. Compute the overall overstatement or understatement of net income as a result of the omission of these adjustments.

E3-21A. *(Learning Objectives 2, 3: Apply the revenue and expense recognition principles; adjust
the accounts)* Wolfe Nurseries, Inc., experienced four situations for its supplies. Compute the
amounts that have been left blank for each situation. For situations 1 and 2, journalize the
needed transaction. Consider each situation separately.

	Situation			
	1	**2**	**3**	**4**
Beginning supplies......................................	$ 2,000	$ 300	$1,000	$1,000
Purchases of supplies during the year........	?	800	?	400
Total amount to account for	2,800	?	?	1,400
Ending supplies	(1,050)	(600)	(700)	?
Supplies Expense.......................................	$1,750	$?	$1,300	$ 900

E3-22A. *(Learning Objective 3: Adjust the accounts)* Red Truck Rentals Company faced the following situations. Journalize the adjusting entry needed at December 31, 2014, for each situation. Consider each fact separately.

a. The business has interest expense of $3,600 that it must pay early in January 2015.

b. Interest revenue of $4,100 has been earned but not yet received.

c. On July 1, 2014, when the business collected $16,000 rent in advance, it debited Cash and credited Unearned Rent Revenue. The tenant was paying for two years' rent.

d. Salary expense is $6,000 per day—Monday through Friday—and the business pays employees each Friday. This year, December 31 falls on a Thursday.

e. The unadjusted balance of the Supplies account is $3,200. The total cost of supplies on hand is $1,650.

f. Equipment was purchased at the beginning of this year at a cost of $60,000. The equipment's useful life is five years. There is no residual value. Record depreciation for this year and then determine the equipment's book value.

E3-23A. *(Learning Objective 4: Construct the financial statements)* The adjusted trial balance of California Bulbs, Inc., follows.

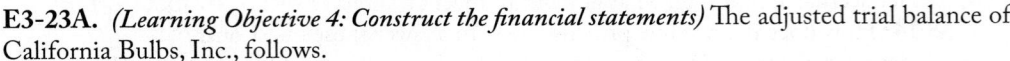
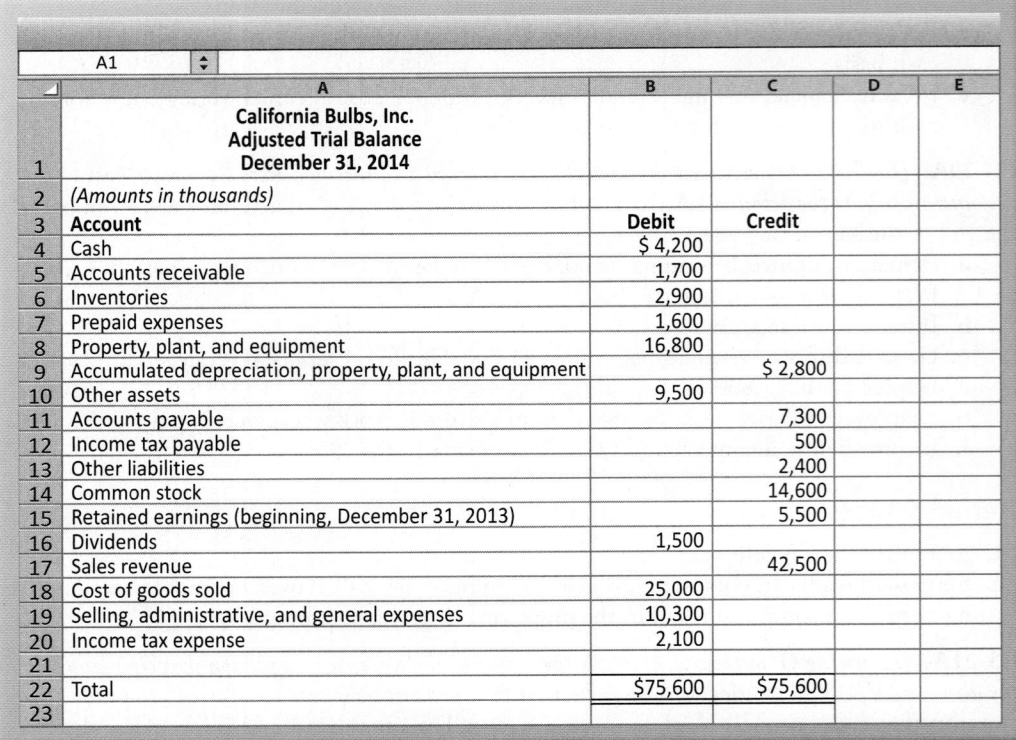

A1						
	A	**B**	**C**	**D**	**E**
1	California Bulbs, Inc. Adjusted Trial Balance December 31, 2014				
2	*(Amounts in thousands)*				
3	**Account**	**Debit**	**Credit**		
4	Cash	$ 4,200			
5	Accounts receivable	1,700			
6	Inventories	2,900			
7	Prepaid expenses	1,600			
8	Property, plant, and equipment	16,800			
9	Accumulated depreciation, property, plant, and equipment		$ 2,800		
10	Other assets	9,500			
11	Accounts payable		7,300		
12	Income tax payable		500		
13	Other liabilities		2,400		
14	Common stock		14,600		
15	Retained earnings (beginning, December 31, 2013)		5,500		
16	Dividends	1,500			
17	Sales revenue		42,500		
18	Cost of goods sold	25,000			
19	Selling, administrative, and general expenses	10,300			
20	Income tax expense	2,100			
21					
22	Total	$75,600	$75,600		
23					

Requirement

1. Prepare California Bulbs, Inc.'s single step income statement and statement of retained earnings for the year ended December 31, 2014, and its balance sheet on that date.

E3-24A. *(Learning Objectives 3, 4: Adjust the accounts; construct the financial statements)* The adjusted trial balances of Rosa Corporation at August 31, 2014, and August 31, 2013, include these amounts (in millions):

	2014	2013
Receivables..	$460	$290
Prepaid insurance..	370	450
Accrued liabilities payable (for other operating expenses).....	780	670

Rosa completed these transactions (in millions) during the year ended August 31, 2014.

Collections from customers..	$20,400
Payment of prepaid insurance	440
Cash payments for other operating expenses...............	4,300

Compute the amount of sales revenue, insurance expense, and other operating expenses to report on the income statement for the year ended August 31, 2014.

E3-25A. *(Learning Objective 5: Close the books)* Prepare the closing entries from the following selected accounts from the records of K. Perez Services Corporation at December 31, 2014:

Cost of services sold............	$14,300	Service revenue.......................	$31,900
Accumulated depreciation...	41,100	Depreciation expense	4,100
Selling, general, and		Other revenue	400
administrative expenses....	6,400	Dividends declared................	300
Retained earnings,		Income tax expense...............	600
December 31, 2013.........	2,600	Income tax payable	1,200

How much net income did K. Perez Services earn during 2014? Prepare a T-account for Retained Earnings to show the December 31, 2014, balance of Retained Earnings.

E3-26A. *(Learning Objectives 3, 5: Adjust the accounts; close the books)* The unadjusted trial balance and income statement amounts from the December 31 adjusted trial balance of Warfield Production Company follow.

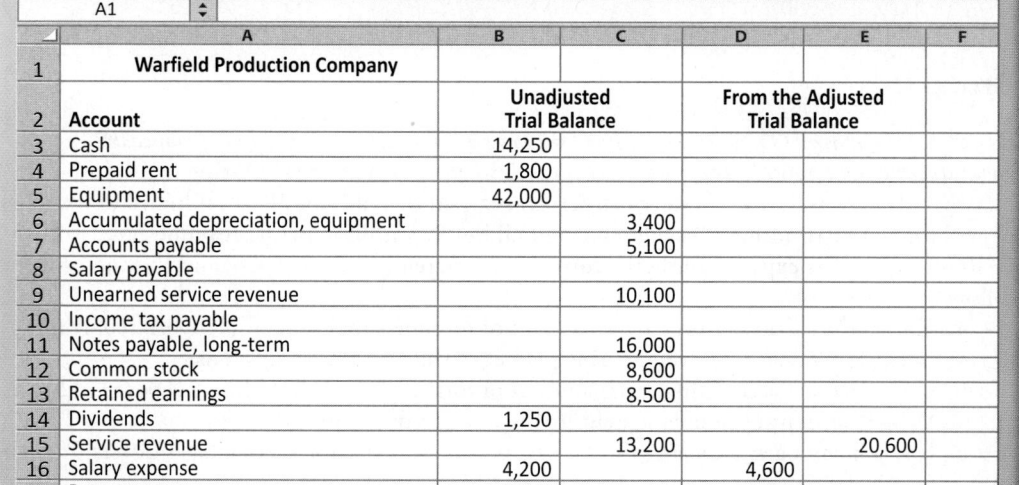

	A	B	C	D	E	F
	A1					
1	Warfield Production Company					
2	Account	Unadjusted Trial Balance		From the Adjusted Trial Balance		
3	Cash	14,250				
4	Prepaid rent	1,800				
5	Equipment	42,000				
6	Accumulated depreciation, equipment		3,400			
7	Accounts payable		5,100			
8	Salary payable					
9	Unearned service revenue		10,100			
10	Income tax payable					
11	Notes payable, long-term		16,000			
12	Common stock		8,600			
13	Retained earnings		8,500			
14	Dividends	1,250				
15	Service revenue		13,200		20,600	
16	Salary expense	4,200		4,600		
17	Rent expense	1,400		1,600		
18	Depreciation expense			850		
19	Income tax expense			1,450		
20	Total	64,900	64,900	8,500	20,600	
21						

Requirement

1. Journalize the adjusting and closing entries of Warfield Production Company at December 31. There was only one adjustment to Service Revenue.

E3-27A. *(Learning Objectives 4, 6: Construct the financial statements; analyze and evaluate liquidity and debt-paying ability)* Refer to Exercise 3-26A.

Requirements

1. Use the data in the partial worksheet to prepare Warfield Production Company's classified balance sheet at December 31 of the current year. Use the report format. First you must compute the adjusted balance for several of the balance-sheet accounts.
2. Compute Warfield Production Company's net working capital, current ratio, and debt ratio at December 31. A year ago, net working capital was $6,400, the current ratio was 1.67, and the debt ratio was 0.40. Indicate whether the company's ability to pay its debts—both current and total—improved or deteriorated during the current year.

E3-28A. *(Learning Objective 6: Analyze and evaluate liquidity and debt-paying ability)* Hermann Company reported these ratios at December 31, 2014 (dollar amounts in millions):

$$\text{Current ratio} = \frac{\$50}{\$40} = 1.25$$

$$\text{Debt ratio} = \frac{\$40}{\$70} = 0.57$$

Hermann Company completed these transactions during 2015:
- **a.** Purchased equipment on account, $8
- **b.** Paid long-term debt, $5
- **c.** Collected cash from customers in advance, $7
- **d.** Accrued interest expense, $2
- **e.** Made cash sales, $6

Determine whether each transaction improved or hurt Hermann's current ratio and debt ratio.

Group B

E3-29B. *(Learning Objectives 1, 2: Explain how accrual accounting differs from cash-basis accounting; apply the revenue and expense recognition principles)* During 2014, Jolleff Network, Inc., which designs network servers, earned revenues of $860 million. Expenses totaled $610 million. Jolleff collected all but $25 million of the revenues and paid $630 million on its expenses. Jolleff's top managers are evaluating 2014, and they ask you the following questions:
- **a.** Under accrual accounting, what amount of revenue should Jolleff Network report for 2014? How does the revenue principle help to answer these questions?
- **b.** Under accrual accounting, what amount of total expense should Jolleff report for 2014? Which accounting principle helps to answer this question?
- **c.** Rework parts a and b using the cash basis. Explain how the accrual basis differs from the cash basis.
- **d.** Which financial statement reports revenues and expenses? Which statement reports cash receipts and cash payments?

E3-30B. *(Learning Objectives 1, 3: Explain how accrual accounting differs from cash-basis accounting; adjust the accounts)* An accountant made the following adjustments at December 31, the end of the accounting period:

a. Prepaid insurance, beginning, $450. Payments for insurance during the period, $1,600. Prepaid insurance, ending, $500.

b. Interest revenue accrued, $2,700.

c. Unearned service revenue, beginning, $1,400. Unearned service revenue, ending, $300.

d. Depreciation, $5,400.

e. Employees' salaries owed for two days of a five-day work week; weekly payroll, $25,000.

f. Income before income tax, $26,000. Income tax rate is 35%.

Requirements

1. Journalize the adjusting entries.
2. Suppose the adjustments were not made. Compute the overall overstatement or understatement of net income as a result of the omission of these adjustments.

E3-31B. *(Learning Objectives 2, 3: Apply the revenue and expense recognition principles; adjust the accounts)* New York Sales, Inc., experienced four situations for its supplies. Compute the amounts that have been left blank for each situation. For situations 1 and 2, journalize the needed transaction. Consider each situation separately.

	Situation			
	1	2	3	4
Beginning supplies...................................	$ 560	$ 1,400	$ 1,100	$ 900
Purchases of supplies during the year........	?	1,100	?	600
Total amount to account for	2,040	?	?	1,500
Ending supplies	(200)	(400)	(1,000)	?
Supplies Expense.......................................	$1,840	$?	$ 1,600	$1,200

E3-32B. *(Learning Objective 3: Adjust the accounts)* Valley Company faced the following situations. Journalize the adjusting entry needed at December 31, 2014, for each situation. Consider each fact separately.

a. The business has interest expense of $2,100 that it must pay early in January 2015.

b. Interest revenue of $3,900 has been earned but not yet received.

c. On July 1, 2014, when the business collected $14,000 rent in advance, it debited Cash and credited Unearned Rent Revenue. The tenant was paying for two years' rent.

d. Salary expense is $2,300 per day—Monday through Friday—and the business pays employees each Friday. This year, December 31 falls on a Wednesday.

e. The unadjusted balance of the Supplies account is $3,110. The total cost of supplies on hand is $1,600.

f. Equipment was purchased at the beginning of this year at a cost of $120,000. The equipment's useful life is five years. There is no residual value. Record depreciation for this year and then determine the equipment's book value.

E3-33B. *(Learning Objective 4: Construct the financial statements)* The adjusted trial balance of Oregon Flowers, Inc., follows:

	A	B	C
	A1		
	Oregon Flowers, Inc. Adjusted Trial Balance December 31, 2014		
1			
2	(Amounts in thousands)		
3	Account	Debit	Credit
4	Cash	$ 2,510	
5	Accounts receivable	1,900	
6	Inventories	3,800	
7	Prepaid expenses	1,700	
8	Property, plant, and equipment	16,700	
9	Accumulated depreciation, property, plant, and equipment		$ 2,500
10	Other assets	9,700	
11	Accounts payable		7,500
12	Income tax payable		600
13	Other liabilities		2,400
14	Common stock		14,500
15	Retained earnings (beginning, December 31, 2013)		4,610
16	Dividend	1,400	
17	Sales revenue		43,600
18	Cost of goods sold	25,500	
19	Selling, administrative, and general expenses	10,000	
20	Income tax expense	2,500	
21			
22	Total	$ 75,710	$ 75,710
23			

Requirement

1. Prepare Oregon Flowers, Inc.'s single step income statement and statement of retained earnings for the year ended December 31, 2014, and its balance sheet on that date. Draw the arrows linking the three statements.

E3-34B. *(Learning Objectives 3, 4: Adjust the accounts; construct the financial statements)* The adjusted trial balances of Falcon Corporation at March 31, 2014, and March 31, 2013, include these amounts (in millions):

	2014	2013
Receivables..	$350	$210
Prepaid insurance	200	140
Accrued liabilities payable (for other operating expenses)	720	640

Falcon completed these transactions (in millions) during the year ended March 31, 2014.

Collections from customers	$20,900
Payment of prepaid insurance	470
Cash payments for other operating expenses	4,200

Compute the amount of sales revenue, insurance expense, and other operating expenses to report on the income statement for the year ended March 31, 2014.

E3-35B. *(Learning Objective 5: Close the books)* Prepare the closing entries from the following selected accounts from the records of Amanda's Jewels, Inc. at December 31, 2014:

Cost of services sold............	$14,600	Service revenue........................	$32,300
Accumulated depreciation...	41,200	Depreciation expense	4,500
Selling, general, and		Other revenue	200
administrative expenses....	6,000	Dividends declared................	400
Retained earnings,		Income tax expense...............	510
December 31, 2013	2,200	Income tax payable	500

How much net income did Amanda's Jewels earn during 2014? Prepare a T-account for Retained Earnings to show the December 31, 2014, balance of Retained Earnings.

E3-36B. *(Learning Objectives 3, 5: Adjust the accounts; close the books)* The unadjusted trial balance and income statement amounts from the December 31 adjusted trial balance of Terrell Production Company follow:

	A	B	C	D	E
	A1 ⬍				
1	**Terrell Production Company**				
2	**Account**	**Unadjusted Trial Balance**		**From the Adjusted Trial Balance**	
3	Cash	14,450			
4	Prepaid rent	2,500			
5	Equipment	44,000			
6	Accumulated depreciation, equipment		3,500		
7	Accounts payable		4,700		
8	Salary payable				
9	Unearned service revenue		9,100		
10	Income tax payable				
11	Notes payable, long-term		17,000		
12	Common stock		8,700		
13	Retained earnings		11,160		
14	Dividends	1,110			
15	Service revenue		14,100		20,600
16	Salary expense	4,600		5,600	
17	Rent expense	1,600		2,300	
18	Depreciation expense			750	
19	Income tax expense			1,360	
20	Total	68,260	68,260	10,010	20,600
21					

Requirement

1. Journalize the adjusting and closing entries of Terrell Production Company at December 31. There was only one adjustment to Service Revenue.

E3-37B. *(Learning Objectives 4, 6: Construct the financial statements; analyze and evaluate liquidity and debt-paying ability)* Refer to Exercise 3-36B.

Requirements

1. Use the data in the partial worksheet to prepare Terrell Production Company's classified balance sheet at December 31 of the current year. Use the report format. First you must compute the adjusted balance for several of the balance-sheet accounts.
2. Compute Terrell Production Company's net working capital, current ratio, and debt ratio at December 31. A year ago, the net working capital was $7,000, the current ratio was 1.72,

and the debt ratio was 0.40. Indicate whether the company's ability to pay its debts—both current and total—improved or deteriorated during the current year.

E3-38B. *(Learning Objective 6: Analyze and evaluate liquidity and debt-paying ability)* Cecilia Crawford Consulting Company reported these ratios at December 31, 2014 (dollar amounts in millions):

$$\text{Current ratio} = \frac{\$60}{\$50} = 1.20$$

$$\text{Debt ratio} = \frac{\$70}{\$90} = 0.78$$

Cecilia Crawford Consulting completed these transactions during 2015:
  a. Purchased equipment on account, $10
  b. Paid long-term debt, $6
  c. Collected cash from customers in advance, $7
  d. Accrued interest expense, $4
  e. Made cash sales, $8

Determine whether each transaction improved or hurt the business's current ratio and debt ratio.

Serial Exercise

Exercise 3-39 continues the Sean Huffman, Certified Public Accountant, P.C., situation begun in Exercise 2-34 of Chapter 2.

E3-39. *(Learning Objectives 3, 4, 5, 6: Adjust the accounts; close the books; construct the financial statements; analyze and evaluate liquidity and debt-paying ability)* Refer to Exercise 2-34 of Chapter 2. Start from the trial balance and the posted T-accounts that Sean Huffman, Certified Public Accountant, Professional Corporation (P.C.), prepared for his accounting practice at January 18. A professional corporation is not subject to income tax. Later in January, the business completed these transactions:

Jan 21	Received $2,400 in advance for tax work to be performed over the next 30 days.
21	Hired a secretary to be paid on the 15th day of each month.
26	Paid $400 for the supplies purchased on January 5.
28	Collected $1,500 from the client on January 18.
31	Declared and paid dividends of $1,200.

Requirements

1. Journalize the transactions of January 21 through 31.
2. Post the January 21 to 31 transactions to the T-accounts, keying all items by date.
3. Prepare an Excel spreadsheet showing the unadjusted trial balance at January 31.
4. At January 31, Huffman gathers the following information for the adjusting entries:
   a. Accrued service revenue, $2,000
   b. Earned $800 of the service revenue collected in advance on January 21
   c. Supplies on hand, $200
   d. Depreciation expense equipment, $65; furniture, $78
   e. Accrued expense for secretary's salary, $500

Refer to the Excel spreadsheet you prepared in requirement 3. Make these adjustments in the adjustments columns and complete the adjusted trial balance at January 31.

5. Journalize and post the adjusting entries. Denote each adjusting amount as Adj and an account balance as Bal.
6. Prepare the single step income statement and statement of retained earnings of Sean Huffman, Certified Public Accountant, P.C., for the month ended January 31 and the classified balance sheet at that date.
7. Journalize and post the closing entries at January 31. Denote each closing amount as Clo and an account balance as Bal.
8. Compute the net working capital, current ratio, and the debt ratio of Sean Huffman, Certified Public Accountant, P.C., and evaluate these values as indicative of a strong or weak financial position.

Quiz

Test your understanding of accrual accounting by answering the following questions. Select the best choice from among the possible answers given.

Questions 40–42 are based on the following facts: Beryl Strauss began a music business in July 2014. Strauss prepares monthly financial statements and uses the accrual basis of accounting. The following transactions are Strauss Company's only activities during July through October:

Jul 14	Bought music on account for $25, with payment to the supplier due in 90 days.
Aug 3	Performed a job on account for Jimmy Jones for $40, collectible from Jones in 30 days. Used up all the music purchased on July 14.
Sep 16	Collected the $40 receivable from Jones.
Oct 22	Paid the $25 owed to the supplier from the July 14 transaction.

Q3-40. In which month should Strauss record the cost of the music as an expense?
    a. August   **c.** September
    b. July   **d.** October

Q3-41. In which month should Strauss report the $40 revenue on its income statement?
    a. July   **c.** October
    b. September   **d.** August

Q3-42. If Strauss Company uses the *cash* basis of accounting instead of the accrual basis, in what month will Strauss report revenue and in what month will it report expense?

	Revenue	**Expense**
a.	August	August
b.	September	October
c.	September	July
d.	August	October

Q3-43. In which month should revenue be recorded?
    a. In the month that the invoice is mailed to the customer
    b. In the month that goods are ordered by the customer
    c. In the month that goods are shipped to the customer
    d. In the month that cash is collected from the customer

Q3-44. On January 1 of the current year, Chuy Company paid $2,400 rent to cover six months (January–June). Chuy recorded this transaction as follows:

	A	B	C	D	E	F
	A1					
1		Journal Entry				
2	Date	Accounts	Debit	Credit		
3	Jan 1	Prepaid Rent	2,400			
4		Cash		2,400		
5						

Chuy adjusts the accounts at the end of each month. Based on these facts, the adjusting entry at the end of January should include
  a. a credit to Prepaid Rent for $2,000.
  b. a debit to Prepaid Rent for $400.
  c. a credit to Prepaid Rent for $400.
  d. a debit to Prepaid Rent for $2,000.

Q3-45. Assume the same facts as in question 3-44. Chuy's adjusting entry at the end of February should include a debit to Rent Expense in the amount of
  a. $0.   c. $800.
  b. $1,600.   d. $400.

Q3-46. What effect does the adjusting entry in question 3-45 have on Chuy's net income for February?
  a. Decrease by $400   c. Decrease by $800
  b. Increase by $400   d. Increase by $800

Q3-47. An adjusting entry recorded June salary expense that will be paid in July. Which statement best describes the effect of this adjusting entry on the company's accounting equation?
  a. Assets are decreased, liabilities are increased, and stockholders' equity is decreased.
  b. Assets are not affected, liabilities are increased, and stockholders' equity is decreased.
  c. Assets are decreased, liabilities are not affected, and stockholders' equity is decreased.
  d. Assets are not affected, liabilities are increased, and stockholders' equity is increased.

Q3-48. On April 1, 2014, Arizona Insurance Company sold a one-year insurance policy covering the year ended March 31, 2015. Arizona collected the full $6,000 on April 1, 2014. Arizona made the following journal entry to record the receipt of cash in advance:

	A	B	C	D	E	F
	A1					
1		Journal Entry				
2	Date	Accounts	Debit	Credit		
3	Apr 1	Cash	6,000			
4		Unearned Revenue		6,000		
5						

Nine months have passed, and Arizona has made no adjusting entries. Based on these facts, the adjusting entry needed by Arizona at December 31, 2014, is

	A	B	C	D	E	F
1	a.	Insurance Revenue	1,500			
2		Unearned Revenue		1,500		
3	b.	Unearned Revenue	1,500			
4		Insurance Revenue		1,500		
5	c.	Unearned Revenue	4,500			
6		Insurance Revenue		4,500		
7	d.	Insurance Revenue	4,500			
8		Unearned Revenue		4,500		
9						

Q3-49. The Unearned Revenue account of Muffett Incorporated began 2014 with a normal balance of $5,000 and ended 2014 with a normal balance of $15,000. During 2014, the Unearned Revenue account was credited for $26,100 that Muffett will earn later. Based on these facts, how much revenue did Muffett earn in 2014?

    a. $26,100   **c.** $6,100

    b. $16,100   **d.** $36,100

Q3-50. What is the effect on the financial statements of recording depreciation on equipment?

    a. Net income, assets, and stockholders' equity are all decreased.

    b. Net income and assets are decreased, but stockholders' equity is not affected.

    c. Assets are decreased, but net income and stockholders' equity are not affected.

    d. Net income is not affected, but assets and stockholders' equity are decreased.

Q3-51. For 2014, Wyndham Company had revenues in excess of expenses. Which statement describes Wyndham's closing entries at the end of 2014 (assume there is only one closing entry for both revenue and expenses)?

    a. Revenues will be debited, expenses will be credited, and retained earnings will be debited.

    b. Revenues will be credited, expenses will be debited, and retained earnings will be debited.

    c. Revenues will be credited, expenses will be debited, and retained earnings will be credited.

    d. Revenues will be debited, expenses will be credited, and retained earnings will be credited.

Q3-52. Which of the following accounts would *not* be included in the closing entries?

    a. Accumulated Depreciation   **c.** Service Revenue

    b. Depreciation Expense   **d.** Retained Earnings

Q3-53. A major purpose of preparing closing entries is to

    a. zero out the liability accounts.

    b. close out the Supplies account.

    c. update the Retained Earnings account.

    d. adjust the asset accounts to their correct current balances.

Q3-54. Selected data for the Rubio Company follow:

Current assets..............	$ 29,700	Current liabilities	$ 25,100
Long-term assets	188,500	Long-term liabilities	113,000
Total revenues..............	195,000	Total expenses.................	176,000

Based on these facts, what are Rubio's current ratio and debt ratio?

	Current ratio	Debt ratio
a.	1.108	0.222
b.	1.183	0.633
c.	1.580	0.633
d.	8.693	0.845

Q3-55. Unadjusted net income equals $10,500. Calculate what net income will be after the following adjustments:
  1. Salaries payable to employees, $610
  2. Interest due on note payable at the bank, $125
  3. Unearned revenue that has been earned, $920
  4. Supplies used, $200

Q3-56. Salary Payable at the beginning of the month totals $20,000. During the month salaries of $136,000 were accrued as expense. If ending Salary Payable is $6,000, what amount of cash did the company pay for salaries during the month?
  a. $162,000   c. $150,000
  b. $110,000   d. $143,000

Problems

MyAccountingLab	All of the A and B problems can be found within MyAccountingLab, an online homework and practice environment. Your instructor may ask you to complete these problems using **MyAccountingLab**.

Group A

P3-57A. *(Learning Objective 1: Explain how accrual accounting differs from cash–basis accounting)* Ruiz Consulting had the following selected transactions in October:

October	1	Prepaid insurance for October through December, $2,000.
	4	Purchased office furniture for cash, $8,000.
	5	Performed services and received cash, $1,700.
	8	Paid advertising expense, $700.
	11	Performed service on account, $6,400.
	19	Purchased computer on account, $2,000.
	24	Collected for October 11 service.
	26	Paid account payable from October 19.
	29	Paid salary expense, $1,500.
	31	Adjusted for October insurance expense (see October 1).
	31	Earned revenue of $1,000 that was collected in advance back in September.
	31	Recorded October depreciation expense on all fixed assets, $208.

Requirements

  1. Show how each transaction would be handled (in terms of recognizing revenues and expenses) using the cash basis and the accrual basis.
  2. Compute October income (loss) before tax under each accounting method.
  3. Indicate which measure of net income or net loss is preferable. Use the transactions on October 11 and October 24 to explain.

P3-58A. *(Learning Objective 3: Adjust the accounts)* Journalize the adjusting entry needed on December 31, end of the current accounting period, for each of the following independent cases affecting Hall Corp. Include an explanation for each entry.

    a. Details of Prepaid Insurance are shown in the account:

	Prepaid Insurance		
Jan 1 Bal	2,100		
Mar 31	4,800		

    Hall prepays insurance on March 31 each year. At December 31, $1,800 is still prepaid.

    b. Hall pays employees each Friday. The amount of the weekly payroll is $5,800 for a five-day work week. The current accounting period ends on Wednesday.

    c. Hall has a note receivable. During the current year, Hall has earned accrued interest revenue of $600 that it will collect next year.

    d. The beginning balance of supplies was $3,200. During the year, Hall purchased supplies costing $6,100, and at December 31 supplies on hand total $2,100.

    e. Hall is providing services for Milam Investments, and the owner of Milam paid Hall $10,200 as the annual service fee. Hall recorded this amount as Unearned Service Revenue. Hall estimates that it has earned 80% of the total fee during the current year.

    f. Depreciation for the current year includes Office Furniture, $3,200, and Equipment, $5,300. Make a compound entry.

P3-59A. *(Learning Objectives 3, 4: Adjust the accounts; construct the financial statements)* Consider the unadjusted trial balance of WOW, Inc., at July 31, 2014, and the related month-end adjustment data.

	A1						
	A	**B**	**C**	**D**	**E**	**F**	**G**
1	WOW, Inc. Trial Balance Worksheet July 31, 2014						
2		Trial Balance		Adjustments		Adjusted Trial Balance	
3	Account	Debit	Credit	Debit	Credit	Debit	Credit
4	Cash	9,500					
5	Accounts receivable	1,600					
6	Prepaid rent	3,000					
7	Supplies	2,100					
8	Furniture	90,000					
9	Accumulated depreciation, furniture		3,000				
10	Accounts payable		3,200				
11	Salary payable						
12	Common stock		14,000				
13	Retained earnings		76,060				
14	Dividends	3,900					
15	Service revenue		17,700				
16	Salary expense	3,400					
17	Rent expense						
18	Utilities expense	460					
19	Depreciation expense						
20	Supplies expense						
21	Total	113,960	113,960				
22							

Adjustment data at July 31, 2014:

    a. Accrued service revenue at July 31, $3,950.

    b. Prepaid rent expired during the month. The unadjusted prepaid balance of $3,000 relates to the period July 1, 2014, through September 30, 2014.

    c. Supplies used during July, $1,630.

    d. Depreciation on furniture for the month. The estimated useful life of the furniture is five years.

    e. Accrued salary expense at July 31 for Monday, Tuesday, and Wednesday. The five-day weekly payroll of $15,000 will be paid on Friday.

Requirements

1. Using Exhibit 3-9 as an example, prepare the adjusted trial balance of WOW, Inc., at July 31, 2014. Key each adjusting entry by letter.
2. Prepare the single step monthly income statement, the statement of retained earnings, and the classified balance sheet. Draw arrows linking the three statements.

P3-60A. *(Learning Objective 3: Adjust the accounts)* MGS Rentals, Inc.'s unadjusted and adjusted trial balances at June 30, 2014, follow.

	A1						
	A		**B**	**C**	**D**	**E**	
1	**MGS Rentals, Inc.** **Trial Balance Worksheet** **June 30, 2014**						
2			**Trial Balance**		**Adjusted Trial Balance**		
3	**Account**		**Debit**	**Credit**	**Debit**	**Credit**	
4	Cash		$ 7,500		$ 7,500		
5	Accounts receivable		6,200		6,830		
6	Interest receivable				500		
7	Note receivable		3,800		3,800		
8	Supplies		1,200		900		
9	Prepaid insurance		2,400		1,000		
10	Building		70,100		70,100		
11	Accumulated depreciation, building			$ 9,100		$ 11,000	
12	Accounts payable			6,800		6,800	
13	Wages payable					850	
14	Unearned rental revenue			1,700		1,280	
15	Common stock			19,000		19,000	
16	Retained earnings			40,200		40,200	
17	Dividends		3,800		3,800		
18	Rental revenue			19,700		20,750	
19	Interest revenue			800		1,300	
20	Depreciation expense				1,900		
21	Supplies expense				300		
22	Utilities expense		100		100		
23	Wage expense		1,600		2,450		
24	Property tax expense		600		600		
25	Insurance expense				1,400		
26	Total		$97,300	$97,300	$101,180	$101,180	
27							

Requirements

1. Make the adjusting entries that account for the differences between the two trial balances.
2. Compute MGS Rental's total assets, total liabilities, net income, and total equity.

P3-61A. *(Learning Objectives 4, 6: Construct the financial statements; analyze and evaluate debt-paying ability)* The adjusted trial balance of Griffith Corporation at March 31, 2014, follows.

	A1	

	A	B	C
1	Griffith Corporation Adjusted Trial Balance March 31, 2014		
2	**Account**	**Debit**	**Credit**
3	Cash	$ 12,400	
4	Accounts receivable	18,800	
5	Supplies	2,600	
6	Prepaid rent	1,700	
7	Equipment	36,000	
8	Accumulated depreciation, equipment		$ 5,600
9	Accounts payable		9,100
10	Interest payable		700
11	Unearned service revenue		800
12	Income tax payable		2,400
13	Note payable		18,400
14	Common stock		13,000
15	Retained earnings		2,900
16	Dividends	9,000	
17	Service revenue		105,500
18	Depreciation expense	1,300	
19	Salary expense	49,800	
20	Rent expense	10,700	
21	Interest expense	2,700	
22	Insurance expense	4,000	
23	Supplies expense	2,400	
24	Income tax expense	7,000	
25	Total	$ 158,400	$ 158,400
26			

Requirements

1. Prepare Griffith Corporation's 2014 single step income statement, statement of retained earnings, and balance sheet. List expenses (except for income tax) in decreasing order on the income statement, and show total liabilities on the balance sheet. Draw arrows linking the three financial statements.

2. Griffith's lenders require that the company maintain a debt ratio no higher than 0.50. Compute Griffith's debt ratio at March 31, 2014, to determine whether the company is in compliance with this debt restriction. If not, suggest a way that Griffith could have avoided this difficult situation.

P3-62A. *(Learning Objective 5: Close the books, and evaluate retained earnings)* The accounts of Red River Services, Inc., at January 31, 2014, are listed in alphabetical order.

Accounts payable	$12,600	Interest expense	$ 300
Accounts receivable	16,600	Note payable, long term	15,700
Accumulated depreciation,		Other assets	10,100
equipment	6,700	Prepaid expenses	5,000
Advertising expense	11,300	Retained earnings,	
Cash	17,200	January 31, 2013	13,800
Common stock	10,800	Salary expense	26,900
Current portion of long-term		Salary payable	2,500
note payable	2,000	Service revenue	95,300
Depreciation expense	1,000	Supplies	4,700
Dividends declared	12,500	Supplies expense	5,000
Equipment	52,500	Unearned service revenue	3,700

Requirements

1. All adjustments have been journalized and posted, but the closing entries have not yet been made. Journalize Red River's closing entries at January 31, 2014.
2. Set up a T-account for Retained Earnings and post to that account. Then compute Red River Services' net income for the year ended January 31, 2014. What is the ending balance of Retained Earnings?
3. Did Retained Earnings increase or decrease during the year? What caused the increase or the decrease?

P3-63A. *(Learning Objectives 4, 6: Construct the financial statements; analyze and evaluate liquidity and debt-paying ability)* Refer back to Problem 3-62A.

Requirements

1. Use the Red River Services data in Problem 3-62A to prepare the company's classified balance sheet at January 31, 2014. Show captions for total assets, total liabilities, and total liabilities and stockholders' equity.
2. Compute Red River's net working capital, current ratio, and debt ratio at January 31, 2014, rounding to two decimal places. At January 31, 2013, net working capital was $21,800, the current ratio was 1.90, and the debt ratio was 0.32. Did Red River Services' ability to pay both current and total debts improve or deteriorate during fiscal 2014? Evaluate Red River Services' debt position as strong or weak and give your reason.

P3-64A. *(Learning Objective 6: Analyze and evaluate liquidity and debt-paying ability)* This problem demonstrates the effects of transactions on the current ratio and the debt ratio of McClain Company. McClain's condensed and adapted balance sheet at December 31, 2014, follows:

	(In millions)
Total current assets	$15.8
Properties, plant, equipment, and other assets	16.3
	$32.1
Total current liabilities	$ 8.6
Total long-term liabilities	5.3
Total stockholders' equity	18.2
	$32.1

Assume that during the first quarter of the following year, 2015, McClain completed the following transactions:

 a. Earned revenue, $2.4 million, on account.
 b. Borrowed $2.0 million on long-term debt.
 c. Paid half the current liabilities.
 d. Paid selling expense of $0.7 million.
 e. Accrued general expense of $0.5 million. Credit General Expense Payable, a current liability.
 f. Purchased equipment for $4.0 million, paying cash of $1.5 million and signing a long-term note payable for $2.5 million.
 g. Recorded depreciation expense of $0.4 million.

Requirements

1. Compute McClain's current ratio and debt ratio at December 31, 2014. Round to two decimal places.
2. Consider each transaction separately. Compute McClain's current ratio and debt ratio after each transaction during 2015—that is, seven times. Round ratios to two decimal places.
3. Based on your analysis, you should be able to readily identify the effects of certain transactions on the current ratio and the debt ratio. Test your understanding by completing these statements with either "increase" or "decrease":
 a. Revenues usually _____ the current ratio.
 b. Revenues usually _____ the debt ratio.
 c. Expenses usually _____ the current ratio. (*Note:* Depreciation is an exception to this rule.)
 d. Expenses usually _____ the debt ratio.
 e. If a company's current ratio is greater than 1.0, as it is for McClain, paying off a current liability will always _____ the current ratio.
 f. Borrowing money on long-term debt will always _____ the current ratio and the debt ratio.

Group B

P3-65B. (*Learning Objective 1: Explain how accrual accounting differs from cash-basis accounting*) Hudson Tax Consulting had the following selected transactions in December:

Dec	1	Prepaid insurance for December through April, $3,500.
	4	Purchased office furniture for cash, $900.
	5	Performed services and received cash, $1,500.
	8	Paid advertising expense, $140.
	11	Performed service on account, $3,100.
	19	Purchased computer on account, $2,800.
	24	Collected for December 11 service.
	26	Paid account payable from December 19.
	29	Paid salary expense, $800.
	31	Adjusted for December insurance expense (see December 1).
	31	Earned revenue of $400 that was collected in advance back in November.
	31	Recorded December depreciation expense on all fixed assets, $210.

Requirements

1. Show how each transaction would be handled (in terms of revenue and expense recognition) using the cash basis and the accrual basis.
2. Compute December income (loss) before tax under each accounting method.
3. Indicate which measure of net income or net loss is preferable. Use the transactions on December 11 and December 24 to explain.

P3-66B. *(Learning Objective 3: Adjust the accounts)* Journalize the adjusting entry needed on December 31, the end of the current accounting period, for each of the following independent cases affecting Bennett Corp. Include an explanation for each entry.

  a. Details of Prepaid Insurance are shown in the account:

Prepaid Insurance	
Jan 1 Bal 800	
Mar 31 3,600	

Bennett prepays insurance on March 31 each year. At December 31, $1,200 is still prepaid.

  b. Bennett pays employees each Friday. The amount of the weekly payroll is $5,500 for a five-day work week. The current accounting period ends on Monday.

  c. Bennett has a note receivable. During the current year, Bennett has earned accrued interest revenue of $500 that it will collect next year.

  d. The beginning balance of supplies was $2,700. During the year, Bennett purchased supplies costing $6,400, and at December 31 supplies on hand total $2,420.

  e. Bennett is providing services for Tesha Investments, and the owner of Tesha paid Bennett $11,900 as the annual service fee. Bennett recorded this amount as Unearned Service Revenue. Bennett estimates that it has earned 60% of the total fee during the current year.

  f. Depreciation for the current year includes Office Furniture, $3,500, and Equipment, $5,800. Make a compound entry.

P3-67B. *(Learning Objectives 3, 4: Adjust the accounts; construct the financial statements)* Consider the unadjusted trial balance of Kingston, Inc., at March 31, 2015, and the related month-end adjustment data.

	A	B	C	D	E	F	G
1	Kingston, Inc. Trial Balance Worksheet March 31, 2015						
2		Trial Balance		Adjustments		Adjusted Trial Balance	
3	Account	Debit	Credit	Debit	Credit	Debit	Credit
4	Cash	11,200					
5	Accounts receivable	2,900					
6	Prepaid rent	2,100					
7	Supplies	2,400					
8	Furniture	63,000					
9	Accumulated depreciation, furniture		3,700				
10	Accounts payable		4,000				
11	Salary payable						
12	Common stock		13,000				
13	Retained earnings		52,300				
14	Dividends	2,300					
15	Service revenue		14,030				
16	Salary expense	2,600					
17	Rent expense						
18	Utilities expense	530					
19	Depreciation expense						
20	Supplies expense						
21	Total	87,030	87,030				
22							

Adjustment data at March 31, 2015, include the following:

    a. Accrued advertising revenue at March 31, $3,650.

    b. Prepaid rent expired during the month. The unadjusted prepaid balance of $2,100 relates to the period March 2015 through June 2015.

    c. Supplies used during March, $2,090.

    d. Depreciation on furniture for the month. The furniture's expected useful life is three years.

    e. Accrued salary expense at March 31 for Monday, Tuesday, and Wednesday. The five-day weekly payroll is $10,500 and will be paid on Friday.

Requirements

1. Using Exhibit 3-9 as an example, prepare the adjusted trial balance of Kingston, Inc., at March 31, 2015. Key each adjusting entry by letter.
2. Prepare the monthly single step income statement, the statement of retained earnings, and the classified balance sheet. Draw arrows linking the three statements.

P3-68B. (*Learning Objective 3: Adjust the accounts*) Driftwood Apartments, Inc.'s unadjusted and adjusted trial balances at April 30, 2014, follow:

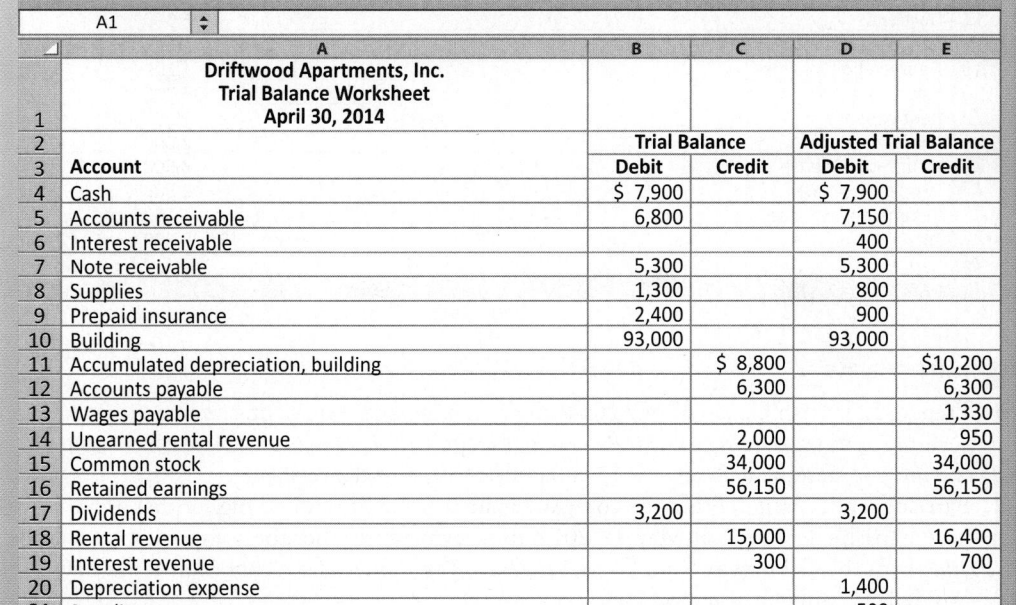

	A1						
	A		**B**	**C**	**D**	**E**	
1	Driftwood Apartments, Inc. Trial Balance Worksheet April 30, 2014						
2			**Trial Balance**		**Adjusted Trial Balance**		
3	**Account**		**Debit**	**Credit**	**Debit**	**Credit**	
4	Cash		$ 7,900		$ 7,900		
5	Accounts receivable		6,800		7,150		
6	Interest receivable				400		
7	Note receivable		5,300		5,300		
8	Supplies		1,300		800		
9	Prepaid insurance		2,400		900		
10	Building		93,000		93,000		
11	Accumulated depreciation, building			$ 8,800		$10,200	
12	Accounts payable			6,300		6,300	
13	Wages payable					1,330	
14	Unearned rental revenue			2,000		950	
15	Common stock			34,000		34,000	
16	Retained earnings			56,150		56,150	
17	Dividends		3,200		3,200		
18	Rental revenue			15,000		16,400	
19	Interest revenue			300		700	
20	Depreciation expense				1,400		
21	Supplies expense				500		
22	Utilities expense		700		700		
23	Wage expense		1,300		2,630		
24	Property tax expense		650		650		
25	Insurance expense				1,500		
26	Total		$ 122,550	$122,550	$126,030	$126,030	
27							

Requirements

1. Make the adjusting entries that account for the differences between the two trial balances.
2. Compute Driftwood Apartment's total assets, total liabilities, net income, and total equity.

P3-69B. *(Learning Objectives 4, 6: Construct the financial statements; analyze and evaluate debt-paying ability)* The adjusted trial balance of L. Farrish Corporation at May 31, 2014, follows:

	A	B	C
		A1 ⇕		
	A	**B**	**C**
1	**L. Farrish Corporation** **Adjusted Trial Balance** **May 31, 2014**		
2	**Account**	**Debit**	**Credit**
3	Cash	$ 21,500	
4	Accounts receivable	10,600	
5	Supplies	2,100	
6	Prepaid rent	1,800	
7	Equipment	37,300	
8	Accumulated depreciation, equipment		$ 3,600
9	Accounts payable		8,700
10	Interest payable		500
11	Unearned service revenue		900
12	Income tax payable		2,100
13	Note payable		17,700
14	Common stock		15,000
15	Retained earnings		3,500
16	Dividends	6,000	
17	Service revenue		90,600
18	Depreciation expense	1,200	
19	Salary expense	36,200	
20	Rent expense	10,100	
21	Interest expense	2,600	
22	Insurance expense	3,600	
23	Supplies expense	2,500	
24	Income tax expense	7,100	
25	Total	$ 142,600	$ 142,600
26			

Requirements

1. Prepare L. Farrish Corporation's 2014 single step income statement, statement of retained earnings, and balance sheet. List expenses (except for income tax) in decreasing order on the income statement, and show total liabilities on the balance sheet.
2. Farrish's lenders require that the company maintain a debt ratio no higher than 0.50. Compute Farrish's debt ratio at May 31, 2014, to determine whether the company is in compliance with this debt restriction. If not, suggest a way L. Farrish Corporation could have avoided this difficult situation.

P3-70B. *(Learning Objective 5: Close the books, evaluate retained earnings)* The accounts of Lazy River Service, Inc., at January 31, 2014, are listed in alphabetical order.

Accounts payable	$ 13,900	Interest expense................	$ 400
Accounts receivable...............	17,200	Note payable, long-term...	15,600
Accumulated depreciation,		Other assets......................	12,200
equipment	6,900	Prepaid expenses	5,500
Advertising expense...............	11,500	Retained earnings,	
Cash......................................	17,400	January 31, 2013	10,600
Common stock......................	13,200	Salary expense.................	21,700
Current portion of long term		Salary payable.................	2,600
note payable......................	2,700	Service revenue................	92,700
Depreciation expense	2,000	Supplies...........................	4,000
Dividends declared................	22,300	Supplies expense..............	4,800
Equipment............................	42,800	Unearned service revenue ...	3,600

Requirements

1. All adjustments have been journalized and posted, but the closing entries have not yet been made. Journalize Lazy River's closing entries at January 31, 2014.
2. Set up a T-account for Retained Earnings and post to that account. Then compute Lazy River's net income for the year ended January 31, 2014. What is the ending balance of Retained Earnings?
3. Did Retained Earnings increase or decrease during the 2014 fiscal year? What caused the increase or decrease?

P3-71B. *(Learning Objectives 4, 6: Construct the financial statements; analyze and evaluate liquidity and debt-paying ability)* Refer back to Problem 3-70B.

Requirements

1. Prepare the company's classified balance sheet in report form at January 31, 2014. Show captions for total assets, total liabilities, and total liabilities and stockholders' equity.
2. Compute Lazy River's net working capital, current ratio, and debt ratio at January 31, 2014, rounding to two decimal places. At January 31, 2013, the net working capital was $21,000, the current ratio was 1.81, and the debt ratio was 0.45. Did Lazy River's ability to pay both current and total liabilities improve or deteriorate during fiscal 2014? Evaluate Lazy River's debt position as strong or weak and give your reason.

P3-72B. *(Learning Objective 6: Analyze and evaluate liquidity and debt-paying ability)* This problem demonstrates the effects of transactions on the current ratio and the debt ratio of Cole Company. Cole's condensed and adapted balance sheet at December 31, 2013, follows:

	(In millions)
Total current assets	$15.4
Properties, plant, equipment, and other assets..............	15.8
	$31.2
Total current liabilities...	$ 9.4
Total long-term liabilities...	5.5
Total shareholders' equity...	16.3
	$31.2

Assume that during the first quarter of the following year, 2014, Cole completed the following transactions:

a. Earned revenue of $2.4 million, on account.
b. Borrowed $3.0 million on long-term debt.
c. Paid half of the current liabilities.
d. Paid selling expense of $0.6 million.
e. Accrued general expense of $0.3 million. Credit General Expense Payable, a current liability.
f. Purchased equipment for $4.9 million, paying cash of $2.0 million and signing a long-term note payable for $2.9 million.
g. Recorded depreciation expense of $0.9 million.

Requirements

1. Compute Cole's current ratio and debt ratio at December 31, 2013. Round to two decimal places.
2. Consider each transaction separately. Compute Cole's current ratio and debt ratio after each transaction during 2014—that is, seven times. Round ratios to two decimal places.
3. Based on your analysis, you should be able to readily identify the effects of certain transactions on the current ratio and the debt ratio. Test your understanding by completing these statements with either "increase" or "decrease."
    a. Revenues usually _____ the current ratio.
    b. Revenues usually _____ the debt ratio.
    c. Expenses usually _____ the current ratio. (*Note:* Depreciation is an exception to this rule.)
    d. Expenses usually _____ the debt ratio.
    e. If a company's current ratio is greater than 1.0, as for Cole, paying off a current liability will always _____ the current ratio.
    f. Borrowing money on long-term debt will always _____ the current ratio and _____ the debt ratio.

Challenge Exercises and Problems

E3-73. (*Learning Objective 6: Analyze and evaluate liquidity and debt-paying ability*) Baltimore Corporation reported the following current accounts at December 31, 2014 (amounts in thousands):

Cash	$1,500
Receivables	5,900
Inventory	2,700
Prepaid expenses	1,000
Accounts payable	2,600
Unearned revenue	1,600
Accrued expenses payable	1,900

During January 2015, Baltimore completed these selected transactions:

- Sold services on account, $9,000
- Depreciation expense, $400
- Paid for expenses, $7,300
- Collected from customers on account, $8,100
- Accrued expenses, $500
- Paid on account, $1,400
- Used up prepaid expenses, $700

Compute Baltimore's net working capital and current ratio at December 31, 2014, and again at January 31, 2015. Did the net working capital and current ratio improve or deteriorate during January 2015? Comment on the level of the company's net working capital and current ratio.

E3-74. *(Learning Objectives 3, 4: Adjust the accounts; compute financial statement amounts)* The accounts of Bracken Ltd. Services Company prior to the year-end adjustments follow:

Cash	$ 7,300	Common stock	$ 14,000
Accounts receivable	7,500	Retained earnings	46,000
Supplies	4,600	Dividends declared	16,000
Prepaid insurance	3,500	Service revenue	161,000
Building	110,000	Salary expense	37,000
Accumulated depreciation—		Depreciation expense—	
building	15,600	building	
Land	53,000	Supplies expense	
Accounts payable	6,100	Insurance expense	
Salary payable		Advertising expense	7,300
Unearned service revenue	5,500	Utilities expense	2,000

Adjusting data at the end of the year include the following:
   a. Unearned service revenue that has been earned, $1,650
   b. Accrued service revenue, $32,200
   c. Supplies used in operations, $3,100
   d. Accrued salary expense, $3,500
   e. Prepaid insurance expired, $1,500
   f. Depreciation expense—building, $2,600

Carter Bracken, the principal stockholder, has received an offer to sell Bracken Ltd. Services Company. He needs to know the following information within one hour:
   a. Net income for the year covered by these data
   b. Total assets
   c. Total liabilities
   d. Total stockholders' equity
   e. Proof that Total assets = Total liabilities + Total stockholders' equity after all items are updated

Requirement

Without opening any accounts, making any journal entries, or using a work sheet, provide Mr. Bracken with the requested information. The business is not subject to income tax.

P3-75. *(Learning Objective 4: Construct a balance sheet from given financial data)* Mobile Detail, Inc. provides mobile detailing to its customers. The Income Statement for the month ended January 31, 2014, the Balance Sheet for December 31, 2013, and details of postings to the Cash account in the general ledger for the month of January 2014 follow:

	A	B	C	D	E
1	**Mobile Detail, Inc.** **Income Statement** **Month ended January 31, 2014**				
2	Revenue:				
3	Detailing revenue	$29,400			
4	Gift certificates redeemed	600	$30,000		
5	Expenses:				
6	Salary expense	$12,000			
7	Depreciation expense—equipment	6,000			
8	Supplies expense	4,000			
9	Advertising	2,000	24,000		
10	Net income		$ 6,000		
11					

	A	B	C	D	E	F
1			**Mobile Detail, Inc.** **Balance Sheet** **December 31, 2013**			
2	**Assets**			**Liabilities**		
3	Cash		$ 1,300	Accounts payable	$ 5,000	
4	Accounts receivable		2,000	Salary payable	1,000	
5	Supplies		1,500	Unearned service revenue	800	
6	Equipment	$30,000		Total liabilities	6,800	
7	Less: Accumulated			**Stockholders' Equity**		
8	depreciation	(6,000)	24,000	Common stock	10,000	
9				Retained earnings	12,000	
10				Total stockholders' equity	22,000	
11				Total liabilities and		
12	Total assets		$28,800	stockholders' equity	$28,800	
13						

Cash

Bal 12/31/2013	1,300		
Cash collections from customers	31,000	Salaries paid	12,500
Issuance of common stock	8,000	Dividends paid	500
		Purchase of equipment	5,000
		Payments of accounts payable	5,500
		Advertising paid	1,500
Bal 1/31/2014	?		

The following additional information is also available:

1. $1,000 of the cash collected from customers in January 2014 was for gift certificates for detailing services to be performed in the future. As of January 31, 2014, $1,200 of gift certificates were still outstanding.
2. $3,500 of supplies were purchased on account.
3. Employees are paid monthly during the first week after the end of the pay period.

Requirement

Based on these statements, prepare the Balance Sheet for January 31, 2014.

APPLY YOUR KNOWLEDGE

Decision Cases

Case 1. *(Learning Objectives 3, 6: Adjust the accounts; analyze and evaluate liquidity)* The unadjusted trial balance of Grant Computer Services, Inc., at January 31, 2015, does not balance. The list of accounts and their balances is given below. The trial balance needs to be prepared and adjusted before the financial statements at January 31, 2015, can be prepared. The manager of Grant Computer Services also needs to know the business's current ratio.

Cash..	$ 8,000
Accounts receivable............................	4,200
Supplies..	800
Prepaid rent..	1,200
Land..	43,000
Accounts payable	12,000
Salary payable.....................................	0
Unearned service revenue	700
Note payable, due in three years	23,400
Common stock.....................................	5,000
Retained earnings...............................	9,300
Service revenue...................................	9,100
Salary expense.....................................	3,400
Rent expense.......................................	0
Advertising expense............................	900
Supplies expense..................................	0

Requirements

1. How much *out of balance* is the trial balance? Notes Payable (the only error) is understated.
2. Grant Computer Services needs to make the following adjustments at January 31:
   a. Supplies of $400 were used during January.
   b. The balance of Prepaid Rent was paid on January 1 and covers the whole year 2015. No adjustment was made on January 31.
   c. At January 31, Grant Computer Services owed employees $1,000.
   d. Unearned service revenue of $500 was earned during January.

   Prepare a corrected, adjusted trial balance. Give Notes Payable its correct balance.

3. After the error is corrected and after these adjustments are made, compute the current ratio of Grant Computer Services, Inc. If your business had this current ratio, could you sleep at night?

Case 2. *(Learning Objectives 4, 6: Construct the financial statements; analyze and evaluate liquidity and debt-paying ability)* On October 1, 2014, Mark Brandford opened Mark's Coffee Shop, Inc. Brandford is now at a crossroads. The October financial statements paint a glowing picture of the business, and Brandford has asked you whether he should expand the business. To expand the business, Brandford wants to be earning net income of $10,000 per month and have total assets of $50,000. Brandford believes he is meeting both goals.

To start the business, Brandford invested $25,000, not the $15,000 amount reported as "Common stock" on the balance sheet. The business issued $25,000 of common stock to Brandford. The bookkeeper "plugged" the $15,000 "Common stock" amount into the balance sheet (entered the amount necessary without any support) to make it balance. The bookkeeper made some other errors too. Brandford shows you the following financial statements that the bookkeeper prepared:

A1				
A	**B**	**C**	**D**	**E**
Mark's Coffee Shop **Income Statement** **Month ended October 31, 2014**				
Revenue:				
Investments by owner	$25,000			
Unearned banquet sales revenue	3,000			
		$28,000		
Expenses:				
Wages expense	$ 5,000			
Rent expense	4,000			
Dividends	3,000			
Depreciation expense—fixtures	1,000			
		13,000		
Net income		$ 15,000		

A1				
A	**B**	**C**	**D**	**E**
Mark's Coffee Shop **Balance Sheet** **October 31, 2014**				
Assets		**Liabilities**		
Cash	$ 8,000	Accounts payable	$ 7,000	
Prepaid insurance	1,000	Sales revenue	32,000	
Insurance expense	1,000	Accumulated depreciation—		
Food inventory	5,000	fixtures	1,000	
Cost of goods sold (expense)	12,000		40,000	
Fixtures (tables, chairs, etc.)	24,000	**Stockholders' Equity**		
Dishes and silverware	4,000	Common stock	15,000	
	$55,000		$55,000	

Requirement

1. Prepare corrected financial statements for Mark's Coffee Shop, Inc.: single step Income Statement, Statement of Retained Earnings, and Balance Sheet. Then, based on Brandford's goals and your corrected statements, recommend to Brandford whether he should expand the restaurant.

Case 3. *(Learning Objectives 3, 4: Adjust the accounts; construct the financial statements; evaluate a business based on financial statements)* Stanley Williams has owned and operated SW Advertising, Inc., since it began 10 years ago. Recently, Williams mentioned that he would consider selling the company for the right price.

Assume that you are interested in buying this business. You obtain its most recent monthly trial balance, which follows. Revenues and expenses vary little from month to month, and June is a typical month. Your investigation reveals that the trial balance does not include the effects of monthly revenues of $4,000 and expenses totaling $1,100. If you were to buy SW Advertising, you would hire a manager so you could devote your time to other duties. Assume that your manager would require a monthly salary of $5,000.

	A	B	C
	SW Advertising, Inc.		
	Trial Balance		
1	**June 30, 2014**		
2	Cash	$ 12,000	
3	Accounts receivable	6,900	
4	Prepaid expenses	3,200	
5	Land	158,000	
6	Plant assets	125,000	
7	Accumulated depreciation, plant assets		$ 81,500
8	Accounts payable		13,800
9	Salary payable		
10	Unearned advertising revenue		58,700
11	Common stock		50,000
12	Retained earnings		93,000
13	Dividends	9,000	
14	Advertising revenue		22,000
15	Rent expense		
16	Salary expense	4,000	
17	Utilities expense	900	
18	Depreciation expense		
19	Supplies expense		
20	Total	$319,000	$319,000
21			

Requirements

1. Assume that the most you would pay for the business is 16 times the amount of monthly net income *you could expect to earn* from it. Compute this possible price.
2. Williams states that the least he will take for the business is two times its stockholders' equity on June 30. Compute this amount.
3. Under these conditions, how much should you offer Williams? Give your reason. (Challenge)

Ethical Issues

Issue 1. Cross Timbers Energy Co. is in its third year of operations, and the company has grown. To expand the business, Cross Timbers borrowed $15 million from Bank of Fort Worth. As a condition for making this loan, the bank required that Cross Timbers maintain a current ratio of at least 1.50 and a debt ratio of no more than 0.50.

Business recently has been worse than expected. Expenses have brought the current ratio down to 1.47 and the debt ratio up to 0.51 at December 15. Lane Collins, the general manager, is considering the result of reporting this current ratio to the bank. Collins is considering recording this year some revenue on account that Cross Timbers will earn next year. The contract for this job has been signed, and Cross Timbers will deliver the natural gas during January of next year.

Requirements

1. Journalize the revenue transaction (without dollar amounts), and indicate how recording this revenue in December would affect the current ratio and the debt ratio.
2. Analyze this transaction according to the Decision Framework for Making Ethical Judgments in Chapter 1:
   a. What is the issue?
   b. Who are the stakeholders and what are the alternatives? Weigh them from the standpoint of economic, legal, and ethical implications.
   c. What decision would you make?
3. Propose for Cross Timbers a course of action that is ethical.

Issue 2. The net income of Solas Photography Company decreased sharply during 2014. Lisa Almond, owner of the company, anticipates the need for a bank loan in 2015. Late in 2014, Almond instructed Brad Lail, the accountant and a personal friend of yours, to record a $10,000 sale of portraits to the Almond family, even though the photos will not be shot until January 2015. Almond also told Lail *not* to make the following December 31, 2014, adjusting entries:

Salaries owed to employees $10,000
Prepaid insurance that has expired $1,000

Requirements

1. Compute the overall effect of these transactions on the company's reported income for 2014. Is reported net income overstated or understated?
2. Why did Almond take these actions? Are they ethical? Give your reason, identifying the parties helped and the parties harmed by Almond's action. Consult the Decision Framework for Making Ethical Judgments in Chapter 1. Which factor (economic, legal, or ethical) seems to be taking precedence? Identify the stakeholders and the potential consequences to each.
3. As a personal friend of Brad's, what advice would you give him?

Focus on Financials | Amazon.com, Inc.

(Learning Objectives 3, 4, 6: Adjust the accounts; construct financial statements; evaluate debt-paying ability) **Amazon.com, Inc.**—like all other businesses—adjusts accounts prior to year-end to get correct amounts for the financial statements. Examine Amazon.com, Inc.'s Consolidated Balance Sheets in Appendix A, and pay particular attention to "accrued expenses and other."

Requirements

1. Why does a company have accrued expenses payable at year-end?
2. Open a T-account for "Accrued Expenses and Other." Insert Amazon.com, Inc.'s balance (in millions) at December 31, 2011.
3. Journalize the following transactions for the year ended December 31, 2012. Key entries by letter, and show amounts in millions. Explanations are not required.
   a. Paid off the beginning balance of "Accrued Expenses and Other"
   b. Recorded operating expenses, other than cost of sales, of $14,446 million, paying $8,762 million in cash and accruing the remainder
4. Post these entries to "Accrued Expenses and Other" and show that the ending balance of the account agrees with the corresponding amount reported in Amazon.com, Inc.'s December 31, 2012, Consolidated Balance Sheets.
5. Compute net working capital, the current ratio, and the debt ratio for Amazon.com, Inc., at December 31, 2011, and December 31, 2012. Did the amount of working capital and ratio values improve, deteriorate, or hold steady during 2012? Do Amazon.com, Inc.'s ratio values indicate relative financial strength or weakness?

Focus on Analysis | Yum! Brands, Inc.

(Learning Objective 1: Explain accruals and deferrals) Refer to the consolidated financial statements of **Yum! Brands, Inc.** in Appendix B. During 2012, the company reported total revenues of $13,633 in its consolidated statement of income. In addition, the company had numerous accruals and deferrals. As a new member of Yum! Brands, Inc.'s accounting staff, it is your job to explain the company's revenue recognition policy, as well as the effects of accruals and deferrals on net income for 2012.

1. Examine the Summary of Significant Accounting Policies. Explain the company's policy for recognizing each type of revenue that is included in the Consolidated Statements of Income.

2. Examine Yum! Brands, Inc.'s comparative balance sheets at December 29, 2012, and December 31, 2011 as well as its Summary of Significant Accounting Policies. Ending net accounts and notes receivable for 2011 (beginning balance for 2012) were $286 million. Ending net receivables for 2012 were $301 million. Explain the source of these receivables. Which of these amounts did Yum! Brands, Inc. earn in 2011? Which amount is included in Yum! Brands, Inc. 2012 net income? Explain the makeup of the parties who owed Yum! Brands, Inc. and the amounts as of December 29, 2012. Were all of these amounts considered collectible? Why or why not?

3. Refer to Note 8, Supplemental Balance Sheet Information, and examine the details of the account entitled "prepaid expenses and other current assets". Why are these recorded as current assets? The beginning balance is $338 million and the ending balance is $272 million. Construct a journal entry or entries that might account for the change.

4. In Note 8, Supplemental Balance Sheet Information, focus on Property, Plant, and Equipment. Notice that accumulated depreciation and amortization stood at $3,225 million at the end of 2011 and at $3,139 million at year end 2012. Assume that depreciation and amortization expense for 2012 was $645 million. Explain what must have happened to account for the remainder of the change in the accumulated depreciation account during 2012. (Challenge)

5. In Note 8, Supplemental Balance Sheet Information, Accounts Payable and Other Current Liabilities, focus on accrued compensation and benefits. This account carried a credit balance of $440 million at the end of 2011 and $487 million at the end of 2012. What type of account is accrued compensation and benefits? What year's income statement did the $487 million accrued compensation and benefits affect? What year's income statement did the $440 million accrued compensation and benefits affect? Did the company's compensation and benefits expense increase, decrease, or stay the same from 2011 to 2012?

Group Project

Upon graduation from Texas State Technical College in Waco, Texas, your neighbor John Abel immediately accepted a position as an electrician's assistant for a large electrical repair company in Austin, Texas. After three years of hard work, John received a master electrician's license and decided to open his own business. John had saved $10,000, which he invested in the business, transferring the money from his personal savings account. His attorney advised him to set up the business as a corporation. He received 10,000 shares of capital stock in exchange for this transfer.

John purchased a used panel truck for $6,000 cash and some used tools for $1,200 cash. He signed a lease on a small shop building at 4240 East Oltorf in Austin and paid $3,000 in advance for the first six months' rent. He obtained an iPhone on a two-year contract, paying a $100 deposit, which he will get back at the end of the contract term. He also placed a small advertisement on Craigslist. John opened the doors of Abel Electronics, Inc., on October 1, 2014.

John's telephone immediately began ringing, with potential customers requesting small repairs and construction projects. After the first month, John was so busy that he had to employ an assistant.

Although John knew practically nothing about the financial side of the business, he was smart enough to realize that a number of reports were required of his corporation, and that costs and collections had to be controlled carefully. At the end of the year, prompted in part by concern about his income tax situation (corporations have to pay taxes as well as their employees) and partly by a $15,000 loan application at South Congress Bank for some new tools and shop expansion, John realizes that he needs to prepare financial statements. Knowing that you, his neighbor, are attending the University of Texas at Austin's business program, he comes to you for some help. After all, anyone trained in business should be able to prepare a set of financial statements to help a buddy out, right? He has brought all of his records (kept in a shoe box) to you, from which you gather the following information for the three months ended December 31, 2014:

- Bank account deposits for collections from customers for services totaled $33,000.
- Services billed to customers but not yet collected totaled $3,000.
- Checks written included: John's salary $5,000; his assistant's salary $3,500 (he still owes the assistant $500); payroll taxes $575; supplies purchased $9,500 (count of supplies still on hand on December 31 is $1,000); fuel and maintenance on truck $1,200; insurance $700; utilities including telephone $825; advertising $600 (he still owes $100).
- According to the Internal Revenue Service, the estimated life of the truck is five years and the estimated life of the tools is three years. These assets have no estimated salvage value and you recommend that John use the straight-line method of depreciation.
- You plug Abel Electronics, Inc.'s revenue and expenses for the quarter into Excel and it computes an estimated quarterly income tax payable of $1,680.

Requirements

1. Analyze the paragraphs above for evidence of business transactions. As you do so, prepare an Excel spreadsheet that includes every financial statement account involved (e.g., cash, accounts receivable, supplies, property & equipment, etc.). Use the spreadsheet format from Exhibit 2-1 as a model. (*Hint:* To make sure you enter the transactions correctly and completely, number the transactions consecutively as you recognize them.)
2. From the spreadsheet you created in requirement 1, prepare the single step income statement of Abel Electronics, Inc., using generally accepted accounting principles, for the three months ended December 31, 2014.
3. From the spreadsheet you created in requirement 1, prepare the statement of retained earnings of Abel Electronics, Inc. for the three months ended December 31, 2014.
4. From the spreadsheet you created in requirement 1, prepare the balance sheet for Abel Electronics, Inc., as of December 31, 2014.
5. Analyze the account "cash" that you created in requirement 1, and prepare a statement of cash flows for Abel Electronics, Inc., for the three months ended December 31, 2014. Divide the various increases and decreases to the account into three categories: operating, investing, and financing. Discuss among your team members what these categories mean. (Challenge)
6. Thoroughly analyze Abel Electronics, Inc.'s creditworthiness for the loan at South Congress Bank. For this purpose, assume that the term of the loan is 5 years, and that the principal balance is not due and payable until the end of the term of the loan. Only interest is payable yearly. Use all of the ratios you have learned so far. Consider not only Abel's present position but its position should the loan be granted. If you were a loan officer for the bank, would you approve Abel's request for the loan? Why or why not?

Quick Check Answers

1. *b*	7. *b*	13. *c*
2. *a*	8. *d*	14. *b*
3. *d*	9. *d*	15. *a*
4. *a*	10. *c*	16. *c*
5. *c*	11. *a*	17. *d*
6. *d*	12. *b*	

Internal Control & Cash

> **SPOTLIGHT:** Cooking the Books: Mid-Atlantic Manufacturing Company Takes a Hit

This account is adapted from a true story:

"I've never been so shocked in my life!" exclaimed Cal Collins, manager of the Mid-Atlantic Manufacturing Company office in Dover, Delaware. "I never thought this could happen to us. We are such a close-knit organization where everyone trusts everyone else. Why, people at Mid-Atlantic feel like family! I feel betrayed, violated."

Collins had just returned from the trial of Mandy Mintz, who had been convicted of embezzling over $600,000 from Mid-Atlantic Manufacturing over a six-year period. Mintz had been one of Mid-Atlantic's most trusted employees for 10 years. A single mom with two teenage daughters, Mintz had pulled herself up by her own bootstraps, putting herself through community college, where she had obtained an associate's degree in accounting. Collins had hired

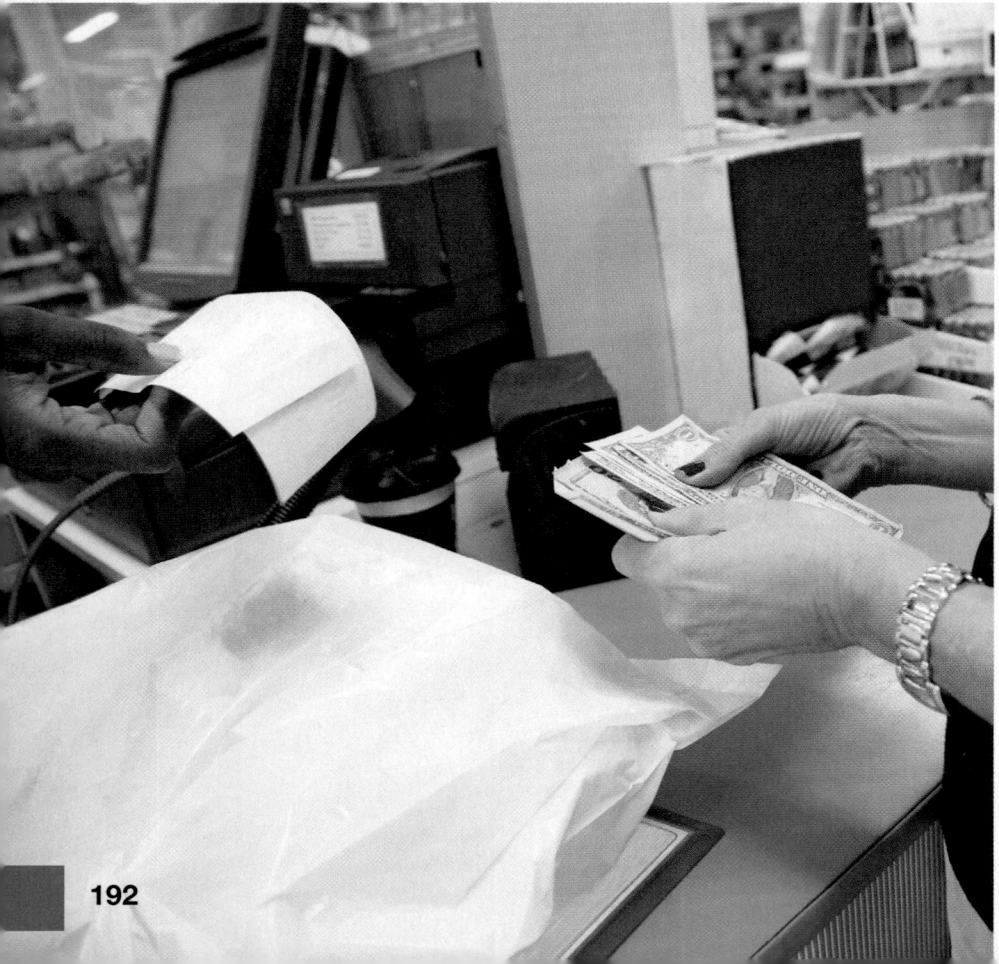

Fotofrog/iStockphoto

her as a part-time bookkeeper at Mid-Atlantic while Mintz was in college to help her out. She had done such a good job that, when she completed her degree, Collins asked her to stay on and assigned her the additional role of cashier, in charge of accumulating the daily cash receipts from customers and taking them to the night depository at the bank each day after work. Through the years, he also awarded her with what he considered good raises, compensating her at a rate that was generally higher than that of other employees with her education and experience levels.

Mintz rapidly became the company's "go-to" financial employee. She was eager to learn, dependable, and responsible. In 10 years she never took a day of vacation, choosing instead to take advantage of the company's policy that allowed employees to draw additional compensation for vacation accrued but not taken at the end of each year. Collins grew to depend on Mintz more and more each month, as the business grew to serve over 1,000 customers. Mintz's increased involvement on the financial side of the business freed Collins to spend his time working on new business, spending less and less time on financial matters. Collins had noticed that, in the past few years, Mintz had begun to wear better clothes and drive a shiny late-model convertible around town. Both of her teenagers also drove late-model automobiles, and the family had recently moved into a new home in an upscale subdivision of the city. Collins had been pleased that he had contributed to Mintz's success. But in recent months, Collins was becoming worried because, in spite of increasing revenues, the cash balances and cash flows from operations at Mid-Atlantic had been steadily deteriorating, sometimes causing the company difficulty in paying its bills on time.

Mintz, on the other hand, had felt underappreciated and underpaid for all of her hard work. Having learned the system well, and observing that no one was monitoring her, Mintz fell into a simple but deadly trap. As cashier, she was in charge of receiving customer payments that came in by mail. Unknown to Collins, Mintz had been **lapping** accounts receivable, an embezzlement scheme nicknamed "robbing Peter to pay Paul." Mintz began by misappropriating (stealing) some of the customers' checks, endorsing them, and depositing them into her own bank account. To cover up the shortage in a particular customer's account, Mintz would apply the collections received later from another customer's account. She would do this just before the monthly statements were mailed to the first customer, so that the customer wouldn't notice when he or she received the statement that someone else's payment was being applied to the amount owed Mid-Atlantic. Of course, this left the second customer's account short, so Mintz had to misapply the collection from a third customer to straighten out the discrepancy in the second customer's account. She did this for many customers, over a period of many months, boldly stealing more and more each month. With unlimited access to both cash and customer accounts, and with careful planning and constant diligence, Mintz became very proficient at juggling entries in the books to keep anyone from discovering her scheme. This embezzlement went on for six years, allowing Mintz to misappropriate $622,000 from the company. The customer accounts that were misstated due to the fraud eventually had to be written off.

What tipped off Collins to the embezzlement? Mintz was involved in an automobile accident and couldn't work for two weeks. The employee covering for Mintz was swamped with telephone calls from customers wanting to discuss unexplained differences in their billing statements for amounts they could prove had been paid. The ensuing investigation pointed straight to Mintz, and Collins turned the case over to the authorities.●

The excerpt from the Mid-Atlantic Manufacturing balance sheet on the following page reports the company's assets. Focus on the top line, Cash and cash equivalents. At December 31, 2014, Mid-Atlantic reported cash and cash equivalents of $6,260. Due to Mintz's scheme, the company had been cheated of $622,000 over several years that it could have used to buy new equipment, expand operations, or pay off debts.

Mid-Atlantic Manufacturing has now reviewed its internal controls. The company has hired a separate person, with no access to cash, to keep customer accounts receivable records. The company now uses a **lock-box system** for all checks received by mail. They are sent to Mid-Atlantic's bank lock box, where they are gathered by a bank employee and immediately deposited. The remittance advices accompanying the checks are electronically scanned and forwarded to Mid-Atlantic's accounts receivable bookkeeper where they are used as the source documents for posting amounts collected from customers. A summary of cash received goes to Collins, who reviews it for reasonableness and compares it with the daily bank deposit total. Another employee, who has neither cash handling nor customer bookkeeping responsibilities, reconciles Mid-Atlantic's monthly bank statement and reconciles the total cash deposited per the daily listings with the total credits to customer accounts receivable. Now Collins requires every employee to take time off for earned vacation and rotates other employees through those positions while those employees are away.

	A	B	C
	A1		
1	**Mid-Atlantic Manufacturing Company** **Balance Sheet (Partial, Adapted)** **December 31, 2014**		
2	**Assets**		
3	Cash and cash equivalents		$ 6,260
4	Cash pledged as collateral		2,000
5	Accounts receivable		8,290
6	Inventories		36,200
7	Prepaid expenses		1,400
8	Investments (long-term)		10,000
9	Equipment and facilities (net of accumulated depreciation of $2,400)		13,170
10	Other assets		3,930
11	Total assets		$81,250
12			

Lapping is a type of fraud known as "misappropriation of assets." Although it doesn't take a genius to accomplish it, lapping requires some *motivation* and is usually *rationalized* by distorted and unethical thinking. The *opportunity* to commit this type and other types of frauds arises through a weak internal control system. In this case, Mintz's access to cash and the customer accounts receivable, along with Collins's failure to monitor Mintz's activities, proved to be the deadly combination that provided the opportunity for this fraud.

This chapter begins with a discussion of fraud, its types, and common characteristics. We then discuss internal controls, which are the primary means by which fraud, as well as unintentional financial statement errors, are prevented. We also discuss how to account for cash. These three topics—fraud, internal control, and cash—go together. Internal controls help prevent fraud. Cash is the asset that is most often misappropriated through fraud.

1. Describe fraud and its impact

2. Explain the objectives and components of internal control

3. Design and **use** a bank reconciliation

4. Evaluate internal controls over cash receipts and cash payments

5. Construct and **use** a cash budget

6. Report cash on the balance sheet

DESCRIBE FRAUD AND ITS IMPACT

Fraud is an intentional misrepresentation of facts, made for the purpose of persuading another party to act in a way that causes injury or damage to that party. For example, in the chapter-opening story, Mandy Mintz intentionally misappropriated money from Mid-Atlantic and covered it up by making customer accounts look different from how they actually were. In the end, her actions caused $622,000 in damages to Mid-Atlantic.

Fraud is a huge problem and is getting bigger, not only in the United States but across the globe. In its 2012 survey titled *Report to the Nations on Occupational Fraud and Abuse,*[1] the Association for Certified Fraud Examiners (ACFE) revealed:

- A typical organization loses 5% of its revenue each year to fraud. Applied to the 2011 Gross World Product, this translates to a projected annual fraud loss of over $3.5 trillion. In the United States alone, this amounts to about $4,500 per employee.

- The median loss in occupational fraud cases is $140,000; these tended to be cases involving employee theft.

- More than one-fifth of reported fraud cases caused losses of at least $1 million; these larger cases tended to involve misleading financial statements.

- Occupational fraud is a significant risk for small business.

- Industries most commonly victimized by fraudsters include banking and financial services, government and public administration, and manufacturing.

- The longer a perpetrator has worked for an organization, the higher the fraud losses tend to be.

- The majority (77%) of reported frauds are perpetrated by employees in one of six departments: accounting, operations, sales, executive/upper management, customer service, and purchasing.

- Most occupational fraudsters are one-time offenders with clean employment histories.

- In 81% of reported cases, fraudsters exhibit one or more behavioral red flags, including: (a) living beyond one's means; (b) financial difficulties; and (c) unusually close associations with vendors or customers.

Fraud has exploded with the expansion of e-commerce via the Internet. In addition, studies have shown that the percentage of losses related to fraud from transactions originating in "third world" or developing countries via the Internet is even higher than in economically developed countries.

What are the most common types of fraud? What causes fraud? What can be done to prevent it?

There are many types of fraud. Some of the most common types are insurance fraud, check forgery, Medicare fraud, credit card fraud, and identity theft. The two most common types of fraud that impact financial statements are:

- **Misappropriation of assets** *This type of fraud is committed by employees of an entity who steal money from the company and cover it up* through erroneous entries in the books. The

1 **Describe** fraud and its impact

---

[1]Association for Certified Fraud Examiners, 2012.

Mid-Atlantic case is an example. Other examples of asset misappropriation include employee theft of inventory, bribery or kickback schemes in the purchasing function, or employee overstatement of expense reimbursement requests.

- **Fraudulent financial reporting** *This type of fraud is committed by company managers who make false and misleading entries in the books,* making financial results of the company appear to be better than they actually are. The purpose of this type of fraud is to deceive investors and creditors into investing or loaning money to the company that they might not otherwise have invested or loaned.

Both of these types of fraud involve making false or misleading entries in the books of the company. We call this *cooking the books.* Of these two types, asset misappropriation is the most common, but fraudulent financial reporting is by far the most expensive. Perhaps the two most notorious recent cases involving fraudulent financial reporting in the United States involved **Enron Corporation** in 2001 and **WorldCom Corporation** in 2002. These two scandals alone rocked the U.S. economy and impacted financial markets across the world. Enron (discussed in Chapter 8) committed fraudulent financial reporting by overstating profits through bogus sales of nonexistent assets with inflated values. When Enron's banks found out, they stopped loaning the company money to operate, causing it to go out of business almost overnight. WorldCom (discussed in Chapter 7) reported expenses as plant assets and overstated both profits and assets. The company's internal auditor blew the whistle on WorldCom, resulting in the company's eventual collapse. Sadly, the same international accounting firm, Arthur Andersen, LLP, had audited both companies' financial statements. Because of these and other failed audits, the once mighty firm of Arthur Andersen was forced to close its doors in 2002.

Each of these frauds, and many others revealed about the same time, involved losses in billions of dollars and thousands of jobs when the companies went out of business. Widespread media coverage sparked adverse market reaction, loss of confidence in the financial reporting system, and losses through declines in stock values that ran in the trillions of dollars! We will discuss some of these cases throughout the remaining chapters of the text as examples of how accounting principles were deliberately misapplied, through cooking the books, in environments characterized by *weak internal controls.*

Exhibit 4-1 explains in graphic form the elements that make up virtually every fraud. We call it the **fraud triangle**.

Exhibit 4-1 | The Fraud Triangle

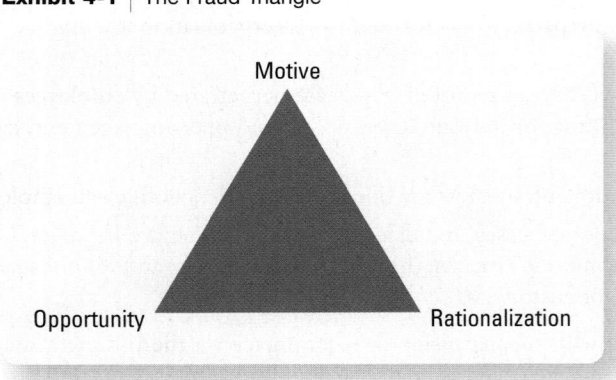

The first element in the fraud triangle is *motive*. This usually results from either critical need or greed on the part of the person who commits the fraud (the perpetrator). Sometimes it is a matter of just never having enough (because some persons who commit fraud are already rich by most people's standards). Other times the perpetrator of the fraud might have a legitimate financial need, such as a medical emergency, but he or she uses illegitimate means to meet that need. A recent article in *The Wall Street Journal* indicated that employee theft was on the rise due to economic hard times. In any case, the prevailing attitude on the part of the perpetrator is, "I want it, and someone else has it, so I'm going to do whatever I have to do to get it."

The second element in the fraud triangle is *opportunity*. As in the case of Mid-Atlantic Manufacturing, the opportunity to commit fraud usually arises through weak internal controls. It might be a breakdown in a key element of controls, such as improper *segregation of duties* and/or *improper access to assets*. Or it might result from a weak *control environment*, such as a domineering CEO, a weak or conflicted board of directors, or lax ethical practices, allowing top management to override whatever controls the company has placed in operation for other transactions.

The third element in the triangle is *rationalization*. The perpetrator engages in distorted thinking, such as "I deserve this;" "Nobody treats me fairly;" "No one will ever know;" "Just this once, I won't let it happen again;" or "Everyone else is doing it."

Fraud and Ethics

As we pointed out in our decision model for making ethical accounting and business judgments introduced in Chapter 1, the decision to engage in fraud is an act with economic, legal, and ethical implications. The perpetrators of fraud usually do so for their own short-term *economic gain*, while others incur *economic losses* that may far outstrip the gains of the fraudsters. Moreover, fraud is defined by state, federal, and international law as *illegal*. Those who are caught and found guilty of fraud ultimately face penalties which include imprisonment, fines, and monetary damages. Finally, from an *ethical* standpoint, fraud violates the rights of many for the temporary betterment of a few and for the ultimate betterment of no one. At the end of the day, everyone loses! **Fraud is the ultimate unethical act in business!**

EXPLAIN THE OBJECTIVES AND COMPONENTS OF INTERNAL CONTROL

The primary way that fraud, as well as unintentional error, is prevented, detected, or corrected in an organization is through a proper system of internal control. **Internal control** is a plan of organization and a system of procedures implemented by company management and the board of directors designed to accomplish the following five objectives:

2 **Explain** the objectives and components of internal control

1. *Safeguard assets.* A company must safeguard its assets against waste, inefficiency, and fraud. As in the case of Mid-Atlantic Manufacturing, if management fails to safeguard assets such as cash or inventory, those assets will slip away.

2. *Encourage employees to follow company policies.* Everyone in an organization—managers and employees—needs to work toward the same goals. A proper system of controls provides clear policies that result in fair treatment of both customers and employees.

3. *Promote operational efficiency.* Companies cannot afford to waste resources. They work hard to make a sale, and they don't want to waste any of the benefits. If the company can buy something for $30, why pay $35? Effective controls minimize waste, which lowers costs and increases profits.

4. *Ensure accurate, reliable accounting records.* Accurate records are essential. Without proper controls, records may be unreliable, making it impossible to tell which part of the business is profitable and which part needs improvement. A business could be losing money on every product it sells—unless it keeps accurate records for the cost of its products.

5. *Comply with legal requirements.* Companies, like people, are subject to laws, such as those of regulatory agencies like the SEC, the IRS, and state, local, and international governing bodies. When companies disobey the law, they are subject to fines, or in extreme cases, their top executives may even go to prison. Effective internal controls help ensure compliance with the law and avoidance of legal difficulties.

How critical are internal controls? They're so important that the U.S. Congress has passed a law to require public companies—those that sell their stock to the public—to maintain a system of internal controls and to require that their auditors examine those controls and issue audit reports as to their reliability. Exhibit 4-2 is Mid-Atlantic Manufacturing Management's Discussion of Financial Responsibility.

Exhibit 4-2 | Mid-Atlantic Manufacturing Management's Responsibility

> **Management's Discussion of Financial Responsibility**
>
> Mid-Atlantic Manufacturing Company regularly reviews its framework of internal controls, which includes the company's policies, procedures, and organizational structure. Corrective actions are taken to address any control deficiencies, and improvements are implemented as appropriate.

The Sarbanes-Oxley Act (SOX)

As the Enron and WorldCom scandals unfolded, many people asked, "How can these things happen? If such large companies that we have trusted commit such acts, how can we trust any company to be telling the truth in its financial statements? Where were the auditors?" To address public concerns, Congress passed the Sarbanes-Oxley Act of 2002 (SOX). SOX revamped corporate governance in the United States and profoundly affected the way that accounting and auditing is done in public companies. Here are some of the SOX provisions:

1. Public companies must issue an internal control report, and the outside auditor must evaluate and report on the soundness of the company's internal controls.
2. A special body, the Public Company Accounting Oversight Board, has been created to oversee the audits of public companies.
3. An accounting firm may not both audit a public client and also provide certain consulting services for the same client.
4. Stiff penalties await violators—25 years in prison for securities fraud; 20 years for an executive making false sworn statements.

The former CEO of WorldCom was convicted of securities fraud and sentenced to 25 years in prison. The top executives of Enron were also sent to prison. You can see that a lack of internal controls and related matters can have serious consequences.

Exhibit 4-3 diagrams the shield that internal controls provide for an organization. Protected by this shield, which provides protection from fraud, waste, and inefficiency, companies can do business in a trustworthy manner that ensures public confidence—an extremely important element in maintaining the stability of financial markets around the world.

Exhibit 4-3 | The Shield of Internal Control

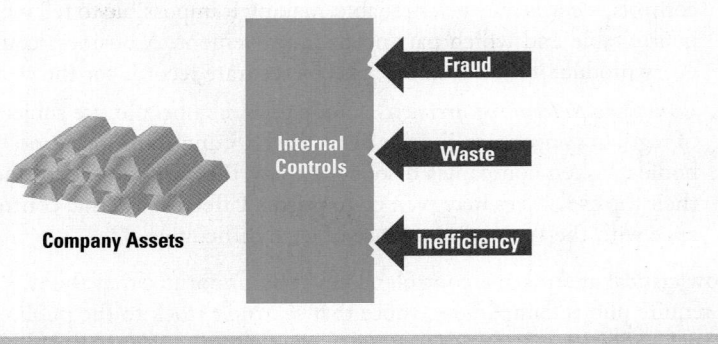

How does a business achieve good internal controls? The next section identifies the components of internal control.

The Components of Internal Control

Internal control can be broken down into five components:

- Control environment
- Risk assessment
- Information system
- Control procedures
- Monitoring of controls

Exhibit 4-4 diagrams the components of internal control.

Exhibit 4-4 | The Components of Internal Control

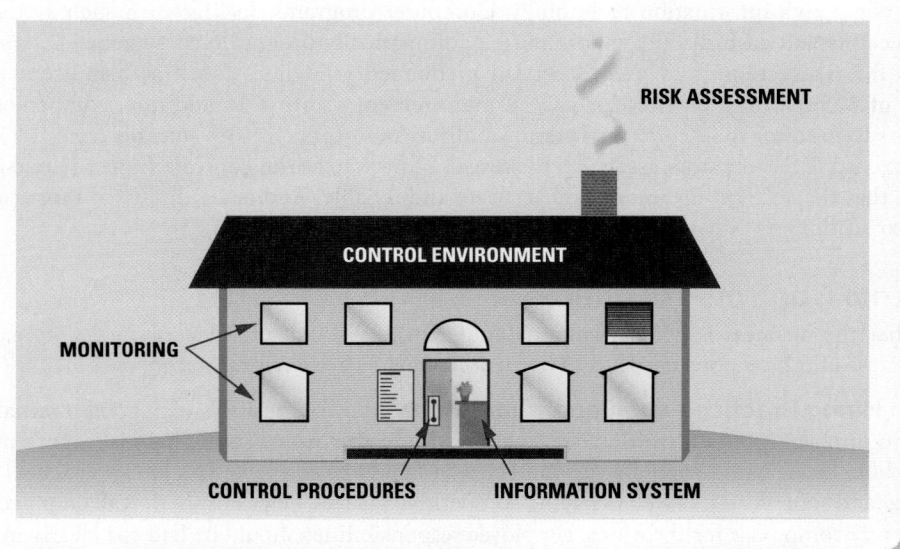

Control Environment. The control environment, symbolized by the roof over the building in Exhibit 4-4, is the "tone at the top" of the business. It starts with the owner and the top managers. They must behave honorably to set a good example for company employees. The owner must demonstrate the importance of internal controls if he or she expects employees to take the controls seriously. A key ingredient in the control environment of many companies is a corporate code of ethics, modeled by top management, which includes such provisions as prohibition against giving or taking bribes or kickbacks from customers or suppliers, prohibition of transactions that involve conflicts of interest, and provisions that encourage good citizenship and corporate social responsibility.

Risk Assessment. Symbolized by the smoke rising from the chimney, assessment of risks that a company faces offers hints of where mistakes or fraud might arise. A company must be able to identify its business risks, as well as to establish procedures for dealing with those risks to minimize their impacts on the company. For example, Kraft Foods faces the risk that its food products may harm people. Southwest Airlines' planes may crash. And all companies face the risk of bankruptcy. The managements of companies, supported by their boards, have to identify these risks and do what they can to prevent those risks from causing financial or other harm to the company, its employees, its owners, and its creditors.

Information System. Symbolized by the door of the building, the information system is the means by which accounting information enters and exits. The owner of a business needs accurate information to keep track of assets and measure profits and losses. Every system within the business that processes accounting data should have the ability to capture transactions as they occur, record (journalize) those transactions in an accurate and timely manner, summarize (post) those transactions in the books (ledgers), and report those transactions in the form of account balances or footnotes in the financial statements.

Control Procedures. Also symbolized by the door, control procedures built into the control environment and information system are the means by which companies gain access to the five objectives of internal controls discussed previously. Examples include proper separation of duties, comparison and other checks, adequate records, proper approvals, and physical safeguards to protect assets from theft. The next section discusses internal control procedures.

Monitoring of Controls. Symbolized by the windows of the building, monitoring provides "eyes and ears" so that no one person or group of persons can process a transaction completely without being seen and checked by another person or group. With modern computerized systems, much of the monitoring of day-to-day activity is done through controls programmed into a company's information technology. Computer programs dealing with such systems as cash receipts and cash disbursements can be automatically programmed to generate *exception reports* for transactions that exceed certain predefined guidelines (such as disbursements in excess of $15,000 in a payroll) for special management scrutiny. In addition, companies hire auditors to monitor their controls. Internal auditors monitor company controls from the inside to safeguard the company's assets, and external auditors test the controls from the outside to ensure that the accounting records are accurate and reliable. Audits are discussed more fully in the next section.

Internal Control Procedures

Whether the business is Mid-Atlantic Manufacturing, Microsoft, or a Starbucks store, every major class of transactions needs to have the following *internal control procedures*.

Smart Hiring Practices and Separation of Duties. In a business with good internal controls, no important duty is overlooked. Each person in the information chain is important. The chain should start with hiring. Background checks should be conducted on job applicants. Proper training and supervision, as well as paying competitive salaries, helps ensure that all employees are sufficiently competent for their jobs. Employee responsibilities should be laid out clearly in position descriptions. For example, the **treasurer**'s department should be in charge of cash handling, as well as signing and approving checks. Warehouse personnel should be in charge of storing and keeping track of inventory. With clearly assigned responsibilities, all important jobs get done.

In processing transactions, smart management *separates three key duties: asset handling, record keeping, and transaction approval.* For example, in the case of Mid-Atlantic Manufacturing, separation of the duties of cash handling from record keeping for customer accounts receivable would have removed Mandy Mintz's incentive to engage in fraud, because it would have made it impossible for her to have lapped accounts receivable if another employee had been keeping the books. Ideally, someone else should also review customer accounts for collectability and be in charge of writing them off if they become completely uncollectible.

The accounting department should be completely separate from the operating departments, such as production and sales. What would happen if sales personnel who are compensated based on a percentage of the amount of sales they make approved the company's sales transactions to customers? Sales figures could be inflated and might not reflect the eventual amount collected from customers.

At all costs, accountants must not handle cash, and cash handlers must not have access to the accounting records. If one employee has both cash-handling and accounting duties, that person can steal cash and conceal the theft. This is what happened at Mid-Atlantic Manufacturing.

For companies that are *too small* to hire separate persons to do all of these functions, the key to good internal control is *getting the owner involved*, usually by approving all large transactions, making bank deposits, or reconciling the monthly bank account.

Comparisons and Compliance Monitoring. No person or department should be able to completely process a transaction from beginning to end without being cross-checked by another person or department. For example, some division of the treasurer's department should be responsible for depositing daily cash receipts in the bank. The **controller**'s department should be responsible for recording customer collections to individual customer accounts receivable. A third employee (perhaps the person in the controller's department who reconciles the bank statement) should compare the treasurer department's daily records of cash deposited with totals of collections posted to individual customer accounts by the controller's department.

One of the most effective tools for monitoring compliance with management's policies is the use of **operating budgets** and **cash budgets**. A **budget** is a quantitative financial plan that helps control day-to-day management activities. Management may prepare these budgets on a yearly, quarterly, monthly, or more frequent basis. Operating budgets are budgets of future periods' net income. They are prepared by line item of the income statement. Cash budgets, discussed in depth later in this chapter, are budgets of future periods' cash receipts and cash disbursements. Often these budgets are "rolling," being constantly updated by adding a time period a year away while dropping the time period that has just passed. Computer systems are programmed to prepare exception reports for data that are out of line with expectations. This data can include variances for each account from budgeted amounts. Department managers are required to explain the variances and to take corrective actions in their operating plans to keep the budgets in line with expectations. This is an example of the use of **exception reporting**.

To validate the accounting records and monitor compliance with company policies, most companies have an audit. An **audit** is an examination of the company's financial statements and its accounting system, including its controls.

Audits can be internal or external. *Internal auditors* are employees of the business. They ensure that employees are following company policies and that operations are running efficiently. Internal auditors also determine whether the company is following legal requirements.

External auditors are completely independent of the business. They are hired to determine whether or not the company's financial statements agree with generally accepted accounting principles. Auditors examine the client's financial statements and the underlying transactions in order to form a professional opinion on the accuracy and reliability of the company's financial statements.

Adequate Records. *Accounting records* provide the details of business transactions. The general rule is that all major groups of transactions should be supported by either hard copy documents or electronic records. Examples of documents include sales invoices, shipping records, customer remittance advices, purchase orders, vendor invoices, receiving reports, and canceled (paid) checks. Documents should be prenumbered to ensure completeness of processing and proper transaction cutoff and to prevent theft and inefficiency. A gap in the numbered document sequence draws attention to the possibility that transactions might have been omitted from processing.

Limited Access. To complement segregation of duties, company policy should limit access to assets only to those persons or departments that have custodial responsibilities. For example, access to cash should be limited to persons in the treasurer's department. Cash receipts might be processed through a lock-box system. Access to inventory should be limited to persons in the company warehouse where inventories are stored or to persons in the shipping and receiving functions. Likewise, the company should limit access to records to those persons who have record-keeping responsibilities. All manual records of the business should be protected by lock and key, and electronic records should be protected by passwords. Only authorized persons should have access to certain records. Individual computers in the business should be protected by user identification and password. Electronic data files should be encrypted (processed through a special code) to prevent their recognition if accessed by a "hacker" or other unauthorized person.

Proper Approvals. No transaction should be processed without management's general or specific approval. The bigger the transaction, the more specific approval it should have. For individual small transactions, management might delegate approval to a specific department, such as in the following examples:

- Sales to customers on account should all be approved by a separate *credit department* that reviews all customers for creditworthiness before goods are shipped to customers on credit.

This helps ensure that the company doesn't make sales to customers who cannot afford to pay their bills.

- Purchases of all items on credit should be approved by a separate *purchasing department* that specializes in that function. Among other things, a purchasing department should only buy from approved vendors, on the basis of competitive bids, to ensure that the company gets the highest quality products for the most competitive prices.

- All personnel decisions, including hiring, firing, and pay adjustments, should be handled by a separate *human resources (HR) department* that specializes in personnel-related matters.

Very large (material) transactions should generally be approved by top management and may even go to the board of directors.

What's an easy way to remember the basic control procedures for any class of transactions? Look at the first letters of each of the headings in this section:

Smart hiring practices and **S**eparation of duties

Comparisons and compliance monitoring

Adequate records

Limited access to both assets and records

Proper approvals (either general or specific) for each class of transaction

So, if you can remember SCALP and how to apply each of these attributes, you can have great controls in your business!

Information Technology

Accounting systems are relying less on manual procedures and more on information technology (IT) than ever before for record keeping, asset handling, approval, and monitoring, as well as for physically safeguarding the assets. For example, retailers such as Target Stores and Macy's control inventory by attaching an *electronic sensor* to merchandise. The cashier must remove the sensor before the customer can walk out of the store. If a customer tries to leave the store with the sensor attached, an alarm sounds. According to Checkpoint Systems, these devices reduce theft by as much as 50%. *Bar codes* speed checkout at retail stores, performing multiple operations in a single step. When the sales associate scans the merchandise at the register, the computer records the sale, removes the item from inventory, and computes the amount of cash to be tendered.

David R. Frazier/Photolibrary, Inc./Photo Researchers, Inc.

When a company employs sophisticated IT, the basic attributes of internal control (SCALP) do not change, but the procedures by which these attributes are implemented change substantially. For example, segregation of duties is often accomplished by separating mainframe computer departments from other user departments (i.e., controller, sales, purchasing, receiving, credit, HR, and treasurer) and restricting access to the IT department only to authorized personnel. Within the computer department, programmers should be separated from computer operators and data librarians. Access to sensitive data files is protected by **password** and data encryption. Electronic records must be saved routinely, or they might be written over or erased. Comparisons of data (such as cash receipts with total credits to customer accounts) that might otherwise be done by hand are performed by the computer. Computers can monitor inventory levels by item, generating a purchase order for inventory when it reaches a certain level.

The use of computers has the advantage of speed and accuracy (when programmed correctly). However, a computer that is *not* programmed correctly can corrupt *all* the data, making it unusable. It is therefore important to hire experienced and competent people to run the IT department, to restrict access to sensitive data (and the IT department) only to authorized personnel, to check data entered into and retrieved from the computer for accuracy and completeness, and to test and retest programs on a regular basis to ensure data integrity and accuracy.

Safeguard Controls

Businesses keep important documents in *fireproof vaults*. *Burglar alarms* safeguard buildings, and *security cameras* safeguard other property. *Loss-prevention specialists* train employees to spot suspicious activity.

Employees who handle cash are in a tempting position. Many businesses purchase **fidelity bonds** on cashiers. The bond is an insurance policy that reimburses the company for any losses due to employee theft. Before issuing a fidelity bond, the insurance company investigates the employee's background.

Mandatory vacations and *job rotation* improve internal control. Companies move employees from job to job. This improves morale by giving employees a broad view of the business. Also, knowing someone else will do your job next month keeps you honest. Mid-Atlantic Manufacturing didn't rotate employees to different jobs, and it cost the company $622,000.

Internal Controls for E-Commerce

E-commerce creates its own risks. Hackers may gain access to confidential information such as account numbers and passwords. E-commerce pitfalls include:

- Stolen credit card numbers
- Computer viruses and Trojan Horses
- Phishing expeditions

Stolen Credit Card Numbers. Suppose you buy CDs from EMusic.com. To make the purchase, your credit card number must travel through cyberspace. Wireless networks (Wi-Fi) are creating new security hazards.

Amateur hacker Carlos Salgado, Jr., used his home computer to steal 100,000 credit card numbers with a combined limit exceeding $1 billion. Salgado was caught when he tried to sell the numbers to an undercover FBI agent.

Computer Viruses and Trojan Horses. A **computer virus** is a malicious program that enters program code without consent and performs destructive actions in the victim's computer files or programs. A **Trojan Horse** is a malicious computer program that hides inside a legitimate program and works like a virus. Viruses can destroy or alter data, make bogus calculations, and infect files. Most firms have found a virus in their system at some point.

Suppose the U.S. Department of Defense takes bids for a missile system. Raytheon and Lockheed-Martin are competing for the contract. A hacker infects Raytheon's system and alters Raytheon's design. The government would label the Raytheon design as flawed and award the contract to Lockheed. The success of a business can be seriously affected by technological fraud.

Phishing Expeditions. Thieves **phish** by creating bogus websites, such as AOL4Free.com and BankAmerica.com. The almost-authentic-sounding website attracts lots of visitors, and the thieves obtain account numbers and passwords from unsuspecting people. The thieves then use the data for illicit purposes.

Security Measures

To address the risks posed by e-commerce, companies have devised a number of security measures, including

- encryption and
- firewalls.

Encryption. The server holding confidential information may not be secure. One technique for protecting customer data is encryption. **Encryption** rearranges messages by a mathematical process. The encrypted message can't be read by those who don't know the code. An accounting example uses check-sum digits for account numbers. Each account number has its last digit equal to the sum of the previous digits. For example, consider Customer Number 2237, where $2 + 2 + 3 = 7$. Any account number that fails this test triggers an error message.

Firewalls. **Firewalls** limit access into a local network. Members can access the network but nonmembers can't. Usually, several firewalls are built into the system. Think of a fortress with multiple walls protecting the company's computerized records in the center. At the point of entry, passwords, personal identification numbers (PINs), and signatures are used. More sophisticated firewalls are placed deeper in the network. Start with Firewall 1 and work toward the center.

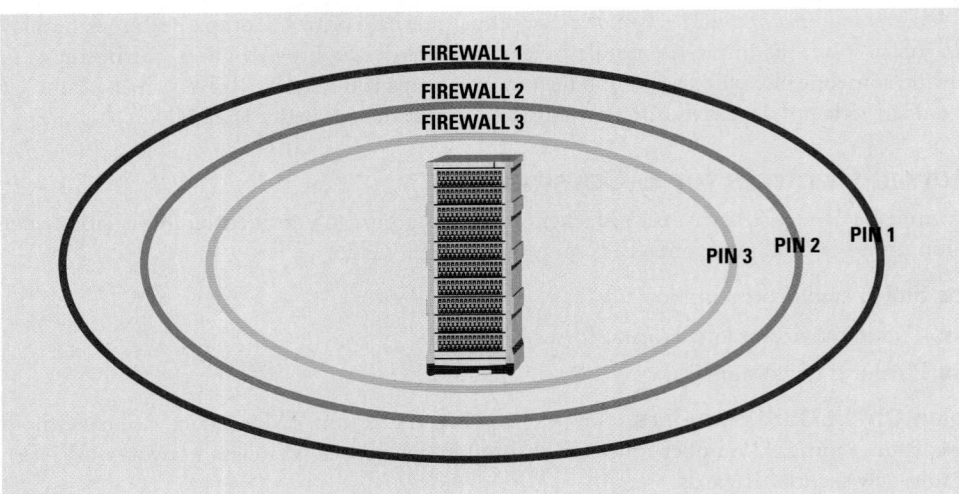

The Limitations of Internal Control—Costs and Benefits

Unfortunately, most internal controls can be overcome. Collusion—two or more people working together—can beat internal controls. Consider Mid-Atlantic Manufacturing, discussed in the chapter opening. Even if Collins were to hire a new person to keep the books, if that person had a relationship with Mintz and they conspired with each other, they could design a scheme to lap accounts receivable, the same as Mintz did, and split the takings. Other ways to circumvent a good system of internal controls include management override, human limitations such as fatigue and negligence, and gradual deterioration over time due to neglect. Because of the cost/benefit principle, discussed in the next paragraph, internal controls are not generally designed to detect these types of breakdowns. The best a company can do in this regard is to exercise care in hiring honest persons who have no conflicts of interest with existing employees and to exercise constant diligence in monitoring the system to ensure it continues to work properly.

The stricter the internal control system, the more it costs. An overly complex system of internal control can strangle the business with red tape. How tight should the controls be? Internal controls must be judged in light of their costs and benefits. Here is an example of a good cost/benefit relationship: A part-time security guard at a **Walmart** store costs about $28,000 a year. On average, each part-time guard prevents about $50,000 of theft. The net savings to Walmart is $22,000. Most people would say the extra guard is well worth the cost!

DESIGN AND USE A BANK RECONCILIATION

3 **Design** and **use** a bank reconciliation

Cash is the most liquid asset because it's the medium of exchange. Cash is easy to conceal and relatively easy to steal. As a result, most businesses create specific controls for cash.

Keeping cash in a bank account helps control cash because banks have established practices for safeguarding customers' money. The documents used to control a bank account include

- signature card,
- deposit ticket,
- check,
- bank statement, and
- bank reconciliation.

Signature Card

Banks require each person authorized to sign on an account to provide a *signature card*. This protects against forgery.

Deposit Ticket

Banks supply standard forms such as *deposit tickets*. The customer fills in the amount of each deposit. As proof of the transaction, the customer keeps a deposit receipt.

Check

To pay cash, the depositor can write a **check**, which tells the bank to pay the designated party a specified amount. There are three parties to a check:

- The maker, who signs the check
- The payee, to whom the check is paid
- The bank on which the check is drawn

Exhibit 4-5 shows a check drawn by Mid-Atlantic Manufacturing, the maker. The check has two parts, the check itself and the **remittance advice** below. This optional attachment, which may often be scanned electronically, tells the payee the reason for the payment and is used as the source document for posting to proper accounts.

Exhibit 4-5 | Check with Remittance Advice

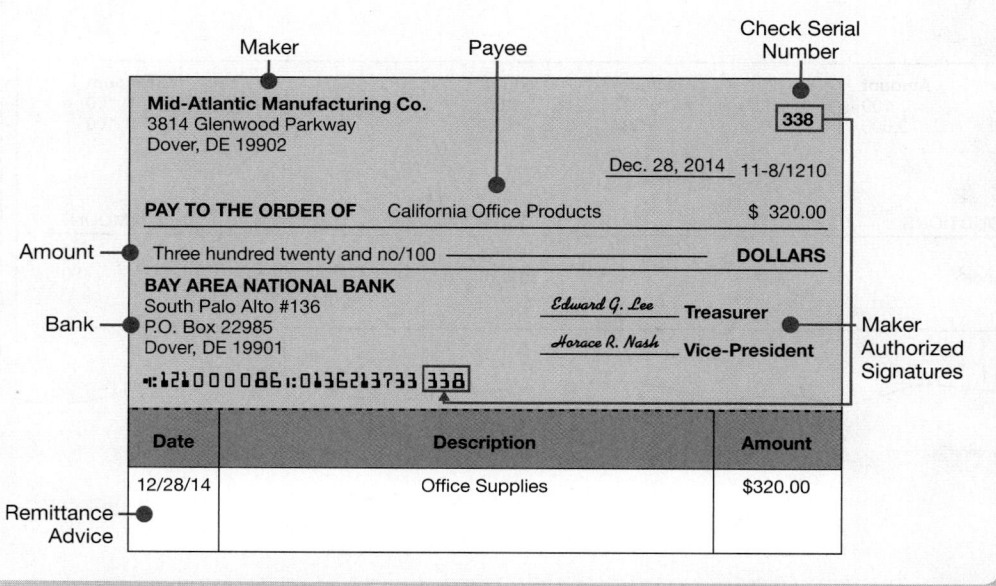

Bank Statement

Banks send monthly statements to customers. A **bank statement** reports what the bank did with the customer's cash. The statement shows the account's beginning and ending balances, cash receipts, and payments. Included with the statement is a list, and often visual images, of the maker's *canceled checks* (or the actual paid checks). Exhibit 4-6 is the December bank statement of the Dover, Delaware office of Mid-Atlantic Manufacturing.

Electronic funds transfer (EFT) moves cash by electronic communication. It is cheaper to pay without having to mail a check, so many businesses and individuals pay their mortgages, rent, utilities, and insurance by EFT.

Exhibit 4-6 | Bank Statement

BANK STATEMENT

BAY AREA NATIONAL BANK
SOUTH PALO ALTO #136 P.O. BOX 22985 Dover, DE 19901

Mid-Atlantic Manufacturing Co.
3814 Glenwood Parkway
Dover, DE 19902

CHECKING ACCOUNT 136–213733

December 31, 2014

BEGINNING BALANCE	TOTAL DEPOSITS	TOTAL WITHDRAWALS	SERVICE CHARGES	ENDING BALANCE
6,550	4,370	5,000	20	5,900

—— TRANSACTIONS ——

DEPOSITS	DATE	AMOUNT
Deposit	12/04	1,150
Deposit	12/08	190
EFT—Receipt of cash dividend	12/17	900
Bank Collection	12/26	2,100
Interest	12/31	30

CHARGES	DATE	AMOUNT
Service Charge	12/31	20

CHECKS

Number	Amount	Number	Amount	Number	Amount
307	100	333	150	335	100
332	3,000	334	100	336	1,100

OTHER DEDUCTIONS	DATE	AMOUNT
NSF	12/04	50
EFT—Insurance	12/20	400

Bank Reconciliation

There are two records of a business's cash:

1. The Cash account in the company's general ledger. Exhibit 4-7 shows that Mid-Atlantic Manufacturing's ending cash balance is $3,340.

2. The bank statement, which shows the cash receipts and payments transacted through the bank. In Exhibit 4-6, the bank shows an ending balance of $5,900 for Mid-Atlantic Manufacturing.

Exhibit 4-7 | Cash Records of Mid-Atlantic Manufacturing

General Ledger:

ACCOUNT Cash

Date	Item	Debit	Credit	Balance
2014				
Dec 1	Balance			6,550
2	Cash receipt	1,150		7,700
7	Cash receipt	190		7,890
31	Cash payments		6,150	1,740
31	Cash receipt	1,600		3,340

Cash Payments:

	A	B	C	D
	A1			
1	Check No.	Amount	Check No.	Amount
2	332	$3,000	337	$ 280
3	333	510	338	320
4	334	100	339	250
5	335	100	340	490
6	336	1,100	Total	$6,150
7				

The books and the bank statement usually show different cash balances. Differences arise because of a time lag in recording transactions. Here are some examples:

- When you write a check or use your bank debit card, you immediately deduct it in your checkbook. But the bank does not subtract the check or EFT from your account until the bank pays the item a few days later. And you immediately add the cash receipt for all your deposits or EFT credits. But it may take a day or two for the bank to add deposits or EFT credits to your balance.

- Your EFT payments and cash receipts are recorded by the bank before you learn of them.

To ensure accurate cash records, you need to update your cash record—either online or after you receive your bank statement. The result of this updating process creates a **bank reconciliation**, which you must prepare. The bank reconciliation explains all the differences between your cash records and your bank balance. The person who prepares the bank reconciliation should have no other cash duties. Otherwise, he or she can steal cash and manipulate the reconciliation to conceal the theft.

Preparing the Bank Reconciliation

Panel B of Exhibit 4-8 illustrates a typical bank reconciliation. It lists items that account for differences between the bank balance and the book balance. We call the cash record (also known as a "checkbook") the "Books."

Bank Side of the Reconciliation

1. Items to show on the *Bank* side of the bank reconciliation include the following:

   a. **Deposits in transit** (outstanding deposits). You have recorded these deposits, but the bank has not. Add deposits in transit on the bank reconciliation.

   b. **Outstanding checks.** You have recorded these checks, but the bank has not yet paid them. Subtract outstanding checks.

   c. **Bank errors.** Correct all bank errors on the Bank side of the reconciliation. For example, the bank may erroneously subtract from your account a check written by someone else.

Book Side of the Reconciliation

1. Items to show on the *Book* side of the bank reconciliation include the following:

   a. **Bank collections.** Bank collections are cash receipts that the bank has recorded for your account, but you haven't recorded the cash receipt yet. Many businesses have their customers pay directly to their bank. This is called a *lock-box system* and reduces theft. An example is a bank collecting an account receivable for you. Add bank collections on the bank reconciliation.

   b. **Electronic funds transfers.** The bank may receive or pay cash on your behalf. An EFT may be a cash receipt or a cash payment. Add EFT receipts and subtract EFT payments.

   c. **Service charge.** This cash payment is the bank's fee for processing your transactions. Subtract service charges.

   d. **Interest revenue on your checking account.** On certain types of bank accounts, you earn interest if you keep enough cash in your account. The bank statement tells you of this cash receipt. Add interest revenue.

   e. **Nonsufficient funds (NSF) checks.** These are cash receipts from customers for which there are not sufficient funds in the bank to cover the amount. NSF checks (sometimes called hot checks) are treated as cash payments on your bank reconciliation. Subtract NSF checks.

   f. **The cost of printed checks.** This cash payment is handled like a service charge. Subtract this cost.

   g. **Book errors.** Correct all book errors on the Book side of the reconciliation. For example, you may have recorded a $150 check that you wrote as $510.

Bank Reconciliation Illustrated. The bank statement in Exhibit 4-6 shows that the December 31 bank balance of Mid-Atlantic Manufacturing is $5,900 (upper right corner). However, the company's Cash account has a balance of $3,340, as shown in Exhibit 4-7. This situation calls for a bank reconciliation. Exhibit 4-8, Panel A, lists the reconciling items for easy reference, and Panel B shows the completed reconciliation.

Exhibit 4-8 | Bank Reconciliation

PANEL A—Reconciling Items

Bank side:

1. Deposit in transit, $1,600.
2. Bank error: The bank deducted $100 for a check written by another company. Add $100 to the bank balance.
3. Outstanding checks—total of $1,340.

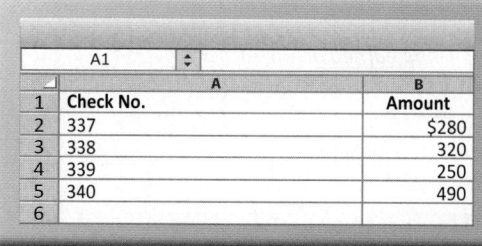

	A	B
1	Check No.	Amount
2	337	$280
3	338	320
4	339	250
5	340	490
6		

Book side:

4. EFT receipt of your dividend revenue earned on an investment, $900.
5. Bank collection of your account receivable, $2,100.
6. Interest revenue earned on your bank balance, $30.
7. Book error: You recorded check no. 333 for $510. The amount you actually paid on account was $150. Add $360 to your book balance.
8. Bank service charge, $20.
9. NSF check from a customer, $50. Subtract $50 from your book balance.
10. EFT payment of insurance expense, $400.

PANEL B—Bank Reconciliation

	A	B	C	D	E	F
1	Mid-Atlantic Manufacturing Co. Bank Reconciliation December 31, 2014					
2	Bank			Books		
3	Balance, December 31		$ 5,900	Balance, December 31		$ 3,340
4	Add:			Add:		
5	1. Deposit in transit		1,600	4. EFT receipt of dividend revenue		900
6	2. Correction of bank error		100	5. Bank collection of account		
7			7,600	receivable		2,100
8				6. Interest revenue earned on		
9				bank balance		30
10				7. Correction of book error—		
11				overstated our check no. 333		360
12	Less:					6,730
13	3. Outstanding checks					
14	No. 337	$280		Less:		
15	No. 338	320		8. Service charge	$ 20	
17	No. 339	250		9. NSF check	50	
18	No. 340	490	(1,340)	10. EFT payment of insurance expense	400	(470)
19	Adjusted bank balance		$ 6,260	Adjusted book balance		$ 6,260
20						

These amounts should agree.

SUMMARY OF THE VARIOUS RECONCILING ITEMS:

BANK BALANCE—ALWAYS

- *Add* deposits in transit.
- *Subtract* outstanding checks.
- *Add* or *subtract* corrections of bank errors.

BOOK BALANCE—ALWAYS

- *Add* bank collections, interest revenue, and EFT receipts.
- *Subtract* service charges, NSF checks, and EFT payments.
- *Add* or *subtract* corrections of book errors.

Journalizing Transactions from the Bank Reconciliation. The bank reconciliation is an accountant's tool separate from the journals and ledgers. It does *not* account for transactions in the journal. To get the transactions into the accounts, we must make journal entries and post to the ledger. All items on the *Book* side of the bank reconciliation require journal entries.

The bank reconciliation in Exhibit 4-8 requires Mid-Atlantic Manufacturing to make journal entries to bring the Cash account up-to-date. The numbers in red correspond to the reconciling items listed in Exhibit 4-8, Panel A.

	A	B	C	D	E
1	4.	Dec 31	Cash	900	
2			Dividend Revenue		900
3			*Receipt of dividend revenue earned on investment.*		
4					
5	5.	31	Cash	2,100	
6			Accounts Receivable		2,100
7			*Account receivable collected by bank.*		
8					
9	6.	31	Cash	30	
10			Interest Revenue		30
11			*Interest earned on bank balance.*		
12					
13	7.	31	Cash	360	
14			Accounts Payable		360
15			*Correction of check no. 333.*		
16					
17	8.	31	Miscellaneous Expense[1]	20	
18			Cash		20
19			*Bank service charge.*		
20					
21	9.	31	Accounts Receivable	50	
22			Cash		50
23			*NSF check returned by bank.*		
24					
25	10.	31	Insurance Expense	400	
26			Cash		400
27			*Payment of monthly insurance.*		
28					

[1]Miscellaneous Expense is debited for the bank service charge because the service charge pertains to no particular expense category.

The entry for the NSF check (entry 9) requires explanation. Upon learning that a customer's $50 check was not good, Cash must be credited to update the Cash account. Unfortunately, there is still a receivable from the customer, so Accounts Receivable must be debited to reinstate the receivable.

Online Banking

Online banking allows you to pay bills and view your account electronically. You don't have to wait until the end of the month to get a bank statement. With online banking, you can reconcile transactions at any time and keep your account current whenever you wish. Exhibit 4-9 shows a page from the account history of Toni Anderson's bank account.

Exhibit 4-9 | Online Banking—Account History

Account History for Toni Anderson Checking # 5401-632-9
as of Close of Business 07/27/2014

Account Details

Current Balance $4,136.08

Date ↓	Description	Withdrawals	Deposits	Balance
	Current Balance			**$4,136.08**
07/27/14	DEPOSIT		1,170.35	
07/26/14	28 DAYS INTEREST		2.26	
07/25/14	Check #6131 View Image	443.83		
07/24/14	Check #6130 View Image	401.52		
07/23/14	EFT PYMT CINGULAR	61.15		
07/22/14	EFT PYMT CITICARD PAYMENT	3,172.85		
07/20/14	Check #6127 View Image	550.00		
07/19/14	Check #6122 View Image	50.00		
07/16/14	Check #6116 View Image	2,056.75		
07/15/14	Check #6123 View Image	830.00		
07/13/14	Check #6124 View Image	150.00		
07/11/14	ATM 4900 SANGER AVE	200.00		
07/09/14	Check #6119 View Image	30.00		
07/05/14	Check #6125 View Image	2,500.00		
07/04/14	ATM 4900 SANGER AVE	100.00		
07/01/14	DEPOSIT		9,026.37	

FDIC EQUAL HOUSING LENDER   E-Mail

The account history—like a bank statement—lists deposits, checks, EFT payments, ATM withdrawals, and interest earned on your bank balance. It also often lists the running balance in the account (the updated balance after each addition and subtraction).

> ### Stop & Think...

The bank statement balance is $4,500 and shows a service charge of $15, interest earned of $5, and an NSF check for $300. Deposits in transit total $1,200; outstanding checks are $575. The bookkeeper recorded as $152 a check of $125 in payment of an account payable. This created a book error of $27 (positive amount to correct the error).

(1) What is the adjusted bank balance?

(2) What was the book balance of cash before the reconciliation?

Answers:

(1) $5,125 ($4,500 + $1,200 − $575).

(2) $5,408 ($5,125 + $15 − $5 + $300 − $27). The adjusted book and bank balances are the same. The answer can be determined by working backward from the adjusted balance.

Using the Bank Reconciliation to Control Cash. The bank reconciliation can be a powerful control device. Tim Bosworth is a CPA in New Orleans, Louisiana. He owns several apartment complexes that are managed by his aunt. His aunt signs up tenants, collects the monthly rents, arranges maintenance work, hires and fires employees, writes the checks, and performs the bank reconciliation. In short, she does it all. This concentration of duties in one person is evidence of weak internal control. Bosworth's aunt could be stealing from him and, as a CPA, he is aware of this possibility.

Bosworth trusts his aunt because she is a member of the family. Nevertheless, Bosworth exercises some controls over his aunt's management of his apartments. Bosworth periodically drops by the apartments to see whether the maintenance staff is keeping the property in good condition. To control cash, Bosworth occasionally examines the bank reconciliation that his aunt has performed. Bosworth would know immediately if his aunt were writing checks to herself. By examining the copy of each check, Bosworth establishes control over cash payments.

Bosworth has a simple method for controlling cash receipts. He knows the occupancy level of his apartments. He also knows the monthly rent he charges. Bosworth multiplies the number of apartments—say 20—by the monthly rent (which averages $500 per unit) to arrive at expected monthly rent revenue of $10,000. By tracing the $10,000 revenue to the bank statement, Bosworth can tell if all his rent money went into his bank account. To keep his aunt on her toes, Bosworth lets her know that he periodically audits her work.

Control activities such as these are critical. If there are only a few employees, separation of duties may not be feasible. The manager must control operations, or the assets will slip away.

Mid-Chapter Summary Problem

The cash account of Ayers Associates at February 28, 2014, follows:

	Cash		
Feb 1	Bal 3,995	Feb 3	400
6	800	12	3,100
15	1,800	19	1,100
23	1,100	25	500
28	2,400	27	900
Feb 28	Bal 4,095		

Ayers Associates received the bank statement on February 28, 2014 (negative amounts are in parentheses):

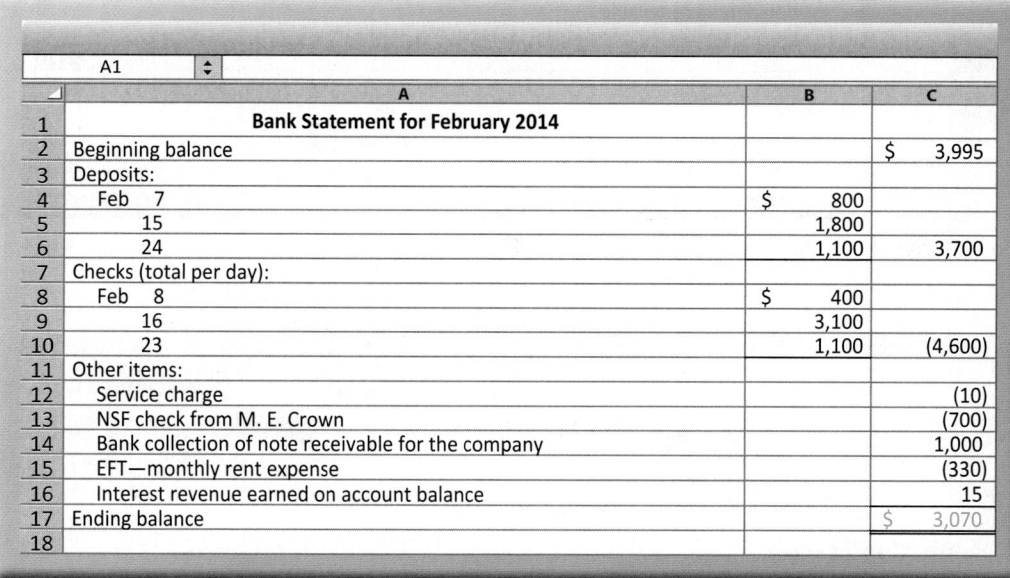

	A	B	C
1	**Bank Statement for February 2014**		
2	Beginning balance		$ 3,995
3	Deposits:		
4	Feb 7	$ 800	
5	15	1,800	
6	24	1,100	3,700
7	Checks (total per day):		
8	Feb 8	$ 400	
9	16	3,100	
10	23	1,100	(4,600)
11	Other items:		
12	Service charge		(10)
13	NSF check from M. E. Crown		(700)
14	Bank collection of note receivable for the company		1,000
15	EFT—monthly rent expense		(330)
16	Interest revenue earned on account balance		15
17	Ending balance		$ 3,070
18			

Additional data: Ayers deposits all cash receipts in the bank and makes all payments by check.

Requirements

1. Prepare the bank reconciliation of Ayers Associates at February 28, 2014.
2. Journalize the entries based on the bank reconciliation.

Answers

Requirement 1

	A	B	C
1	**Ayers Associates** **Bank Reconciliation** **February 28, 2014**		
2	**Bank:**		
3	Balance, February 28, 2014		$ 3,070
4	Add: Deposit of February 28 in transit		2,400
5			5,470
6			
7	Less: Outstanding checks issued on Feb 25 ($500)		
8	and Feb 27 ($900)		(1,400)
9	Adjusted bank balance, February 28, 2014		$ 4,070
10			
11	**Books:**		
12	Balance, February 28, 2014		$ 4,095
13	Add: Bank collection of note receivable		1,000
14	Interest revenue earned on bank balance		15
15			5,110
16	Less: Service charge	$ 10	
17	NSF check	700	
18	EFT—Rent expense	330	(1,040)
19	Adjusted book balance, February 28, 2014		$ 4,070
20			

equal

Requirement 2

	A	C	D	G
1	Feb 28	Cash	1,000	
2		Note Receivable		1,000
3		*Note receivable collected by bank.*		
4				
5	28	Cash	15	
6		Interest Revenue		15
7		*Interest earned on bank balance.*		
8				
9	28	Miscellaneous Expense	10	
10		Cash		10
11		*Bank service charge.*		
12				
13	28	Accounts Receivable	700	
14		Cash		700
15		*NSF check returned by bank.*		
16				
17	28	Rent Expense	330	
18		Cash		330
19		*Monthly rent expense.*		
20				

EVALUATE INTERNAL CONTROLS OVER CASH RECEIPTS AND CASH PAYMENTS

Cash requires some specific internal controls because it is relatively easy to steal and it's easy to convert to other forms of wealth. Moreover, all transactions ultimately affect cash. That's why cash is called the "eye of the needle." Let's see how to control cash receipts.

All cash receipts should be deposited for safekeeping in the bank—quickly. Companies receive cash over the counter and through the mail. Each source of cash has its own security measures.

4 Evaluate internal controls over cash receipts and cash payments

Cash Receipts Over the Counter

Exhibit 4-10 illustrates the purchase of products in a grocery store. The point-of-sale terminal provides control over the cash receipts, while also recording the sale and reducing inventory for the appropriate cost of the goods sold. Consider a **Whole Foods Market** store. For each transaction, the Whole Foods sales associate issues a receipt to the customer as proof of purchase. The cash drawer opens when the sales associate enters a transaction, and the machine electronically transmits a record of the sale to the store's main computer. At the end of each shift, the sales associate delivers the cash drawer to the office, where it is combined with cash from all other terminals and delivered by armored car to the bank for deposit. Later, a separate employee in the accounting department reconciles the electronic record of the sales per terminal to the record of the cash turned in. These measures, coupled with oversight by a manager, discourage theft.

Point-of-sale terminals also provide effective control over inventory. For example, in a restaurant, these devices track sales by menu item and total sales by cash, type of credit card, gift card redeemed, etc. They create the daily sales journal for that store, which, in turn, interfaces with the general ledger. Managers can use records produced by point-of-sale terminals to check inventory levels and compare them against sales records for accuracy. For example, in a restaurant, an effective way to monitor sales of expensive wine is for a manager to perform a quick count of the bottles on hand at the end of the day and compare it with the count at the end of the previous day, plus the record of any purchased. The count at the end of the previous day, plus the record of bottles purchased, minus the count at the end of the current day should equal the amount sold as recorded by the point-of-sale terminals in the restaurant.

An effective control for many chain retail businesses, such as restaurants, grocery stores, or clothing stores, to prevent unauthorized access to cash as well as to allow for more efficient management of cash, is the use of "depository bank accounts." Cash receipts for an individual store are deposited into a local bank account (preferably delivered by armored car for security reasons) on a daily basis. The corporate headquarters arranges for its centralized bank to draft the local depository accounts on a frequent (perhaps daily) basis to get the money concentrated into the company's centralized account, where it can be used to pay the corporation's bills. Depository accounts are "one-way" accounts where the local management may only make deposits; it has no authority to write checks on the account or take money out of the store's account.

Exhibit 4-10 | Cash Receipts over the Counter

Catherine Yeulet/iStockphoto/Getty Images

Cash Receipts by Mail

Many companies receive cash by mail. Exhibit 4-11 shows how companies control cash received by mail. All incoming mail is opened by a mailroom employee. The mailroom then sends all customer checks to the treasurer, who has the cashier deposit the money in the bank. The remittance advices go to the accounting department for journal entries to Cash and customer Accounts Receivable. As a final step, the controller compares the records for the day:

- Bank deposit amount from the treasurer
- Debit to Cash from the accounting department

The debit to Cash should equal the amount deposited in the bank. All cash receipts are safe in the bank, and the company books are up-to-date.

Exhibit 4-11 | Cash Receipts by Mail

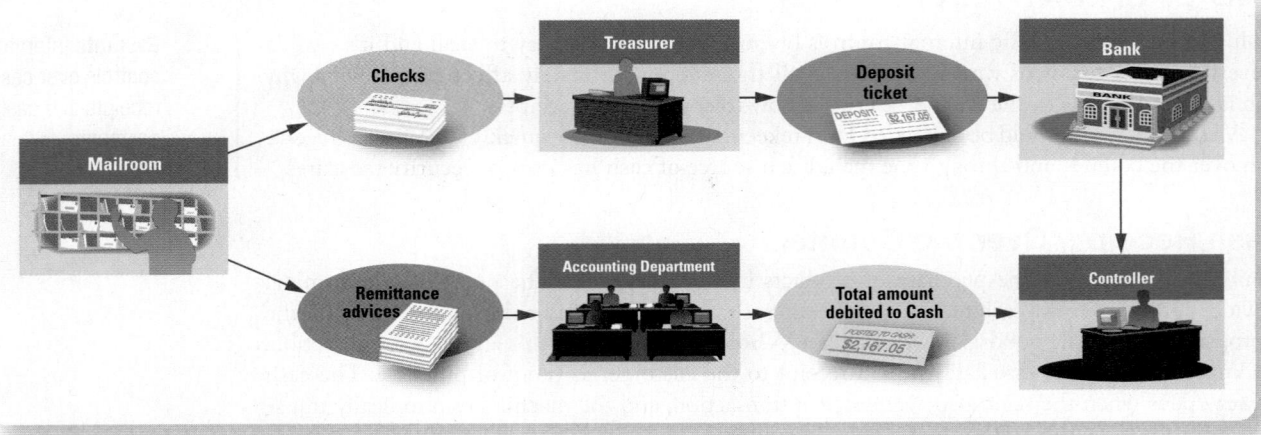

To prevent unauthorized access to cash, many companies use a bank lock-box system rather than risk processing checks through the mailroom. Customers send their checks by return mail directly to a post office box controlled by the company's bank. The bank sends a detailed record of cash received, by customer, to the company for use in posting collections to Accounts Receivable. Internal control is tight because company personnel never touch incoming cash. The lock-box system also gets the cash to the bank in a more timely manner, allowing the company to put the cash to work faster than would be possible if it were processed by the company's mailroom.

Controls over Payment by Check

Companies make most payments by check or electronic funds transfer (EFT). As we have seen, a company needs good separation of duties between (a) operations and (b) writing checks or authorizing EFTs for cash payments. Payment by check or EFT is an important internal control, as follows:

- The check or EFT provides a record of the payment.
- The check must be signed by an authorized official. The EFT must be approved by an authorized official.
- Before signing the check or authorizing the EFT, the official should study the evidence supporting the payment.

Controls over Purchase and Payment. To illustrate the internal control over cash payments by check, suppose Mid-Atlantic Manufacturing buys some of its inventory from Hanes Textiles. The purchasing and payment process follows these steps, as shown in Exhibit 4-12. Start with the box for Mid-Atlantic Manufacturing on the left side.

1. Mid-Atlantic faxes or e-mails an electronic *purchase order* to Hanes Textiles. Mid-Atlantic says, "Please send us 100 T-shirts."
2. Hanes Textiles ships the goods and sends an electronic or paper *invoice* back to Mid-Atlantic. Hanes sent the goods.
3. Mid-Atlantic receives the *inventory* and prepares a *receiving report* to list the goods received. Mid-Atlantic got its T-shirts.
4. After approving and agreeing all documents, Mid-Atlantic sends a *check* to Hanes or authorizes an electronic funds transfer (EFT) directly from its bank to Hanes' bank. By this action, Mid-Atlantic says, "Okay, we'll pay you."

For good internal control, the purchasing agent should neither receive the goods nor approve the payment. If these duties aren't separated, a purchasing agent can buy goods and have them shipped to his or her home. Or a purchasing agent can spend too much on purchases, approve

Exhibit 4-12 | Cash Payments by Check or EFT

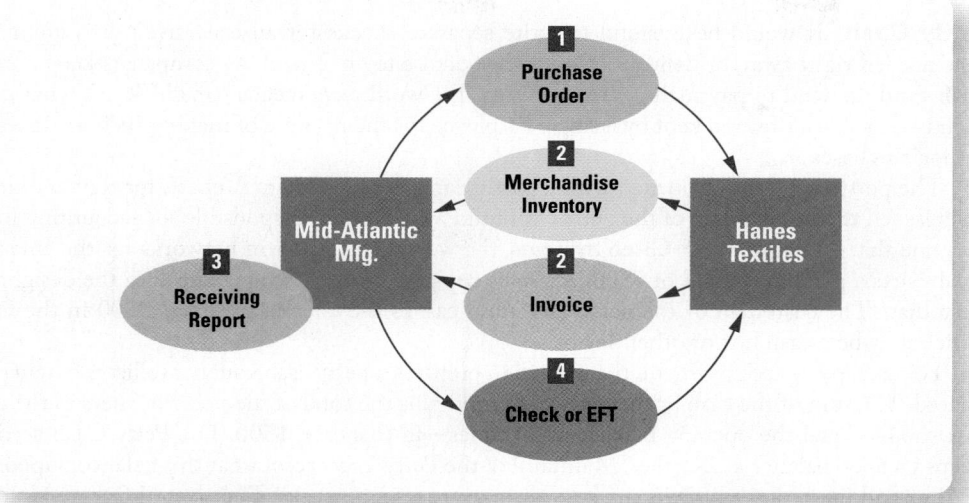

the payment, and split the excess with the supplier. To avoid these problems, companies split the following duties among different employees:

- Purchasing goods
- Receiving goods
- Approving and paying for goods

Exhibit 4-13 shows Mid-Atlantic's payment packet of documents. Before signing the check or approving the EFT, the treasurer's department should examine the packet to prove that all the documents agree. Only then does the company know that

1. it received the goods ordered, and
2. it is paying only for the goods received.

Exhibit 4-13 | Payment Packet

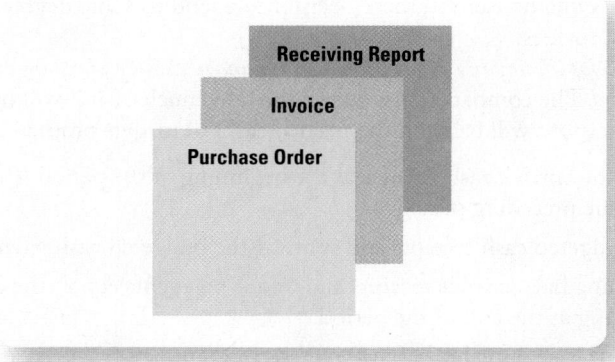

After payment, the person in the treasurer's department who has authorized the disbursement stamps the payment packet "paid" or punches a hole through it to prevent it from being submitted a second time. Dishonest people have tried to run a bill through twice for payment. The stamp or hole shows that the bill has been paid. If checks are used, they should then be mailed directly to the payee without being allowed to return to the department that prepared them.

To do so would violate separation of the duties of cash handling and record keeping, as well as allowing unauthorized access to cash.

Petty Cash. It would be wasteful to write separate checks for an executive's taxi fare, name tags needed right away, or delivery of a package across town. Therefore, companies keep a **petty cash** fund on hand to pay such minor amounts. The word *petty* means "small." That's what petty cash is—a small cash fund kept by a single employee for the purpose of making such on-the-spot minor purchases.

The petty cash fund is opened with a particular amount of cash. A check for that amount is then issued to the custodian of the petty cash fund, who is solely responsible for accounting for it. Assume that on February 28 **Cisco Systems**, the worldwide leader in networks for the Internet, establishes a petty cash fund of $500 in a sales department by writing a check to the designated custodian. The custodian of the petty cash fund cashes the check and places $500 in the fund, which may be a cash box or other device.

For each petty cash payment, the custodian prepares a petty cash voucher to list the item purchased. The sum of the cash in the petty cash fund plus the total of the paid vouchers in the cash box should equal the opening balance at all times—in this case, $500. The Petty Cash account keeps its $500 balance at all times. Maintaining the Petty Cash account at this balance, supported by the fund (cash plus vouchers), is how an **imprest system** works. The control feature is that it clearly identifies the amount for which the custodian is responsible.

In recent years, banks have instituted the practice of *debit cards*, which are used to make cash purchases of relatively small amounts. A company employee who needs to make a small purchase may obtain permission from a supervisor to use a company debit card. Supervisors require receipts for all such purchases and compare them with EFT amounts on the bank statement. Debit cards are taking the place of petty cash systems in many companies.

CONSTRUCT AND USE A CASH BUDGET

5 Construct and **use** a cash budget

As mentioned earlier in the chapter, a budget is a financial plan that helps coordinate business activities. Managers control operations with an operating budget. They also control cash receipts and cash payments, as well as ending cash balances, through use of a cash budget.

How, for example, does Mid-Atlantic Manufacturing decide when to invest in new inventory-tracking technology? How will Mid-Atlantic decide how much to spend? Will borrowing be needed, or can Mid-Atlantic finance the purchase with internally generated cash? What do ending cash balances need to be in order to provide a "safety margin" so the company won't unexpectedly run out of cash? A cash budget for a business works on roughly the same concept as a personal budget. By what process do you decide how much to spend on your education? On an automobile? On a house? All these decisions depend to some degree on the information that a cash budget provides.

A *cash budget helps a company or an individual manage cash by planning receipts and payments during a future period.* The company must determine how much cash it will need and then decide whether or not operations will bring in the needed cash. Managers proceed as follows:

1. Start with the entity's cash balance at the beginning of the period. This is the amount left over from the preceding period.

2. Add the budgeted cash receipts and subtract the budgeted cash payments.

3. The beginning balance plus receipts and minus payments equals the cash available before new financing at the end of the period.

4. Compare the cash available before new financing to the budgeted cash balance at the end of the period. Managers know the minimum amount of cash they need (the budgeted balance). If the budget shows excess cash, managers can invest the excess. But if the cash available falls below the budgeted balance, the company will need additional financing. The company may need to borrow the shortfall amount. The budget is a valuable tool for helping the company plan for the future.

Exhibit 4-14 | Cash Budget

	A	B	C
	A1 ⬍		
1	**Mid-Atlantic Manufacturing Company** **Cash Budget** **For the Year Ended December 31, 2014**		
2	Cash balance, December 31, 2013		$ 6,260
3	Budgeted cash receipts:		
4	Collections from customers		55,990
5	Dividends on investments		1,200
6	Sale of store fixtures		5,700
7			69,150
8	Budgeted cash payments:		
9	Purchases of inventory	$ 33,720	
10	Operating expenses	11,530	
11	Expansion of store	12,000	
12	Payment of long-term debt	5,000	
13	Payment of dividends	3,000	65,250
14	Cash available (needed) before new financing		$ 3,900
15	Budgeted cash balance, December 31, 2014		(5,000)
16	Cash available for additional investments, or		
17	(New financing needed)		$ (1,100)
18			

The budget period can span any length of time—a day, a week, a month, or a year. Exhibit 4-14 shows a cash budget for Mid-Atlantic Manufacturing, Inc., for the year ended December 31, 2014. Study it carefully because, at some point, you will use a cash budget.

Mid-Atlantic Manufacturing's cash budget in Exhibit 4-14 begins with $6,260 of cash at the end of the previous year (line 2). Then add budgeted cash receipts and subtract budgeted payments for the current year. In this case, Mid-Atlantic expects to have $3,900 of cash available at year-end (line 14). Mid-Atlantic managers need to maintain a cash balance of at least $5,000 (line 15). Line 17 shows that Mid-Atlantic must arrange $1,100 of financing in order to achieve its goals for 2014.

» *Try It in* **Excel**

The cash budget represents a perfect opportunity to use your Excel skills. Usually, budgeted cash receipts and budgeted cash payments (item 2 in the list on page 218) are derived by starting with cash receipts and cash payments of the current period and multiplying them by estimated percentage changes for next period. For example, assume that the current year's actual collections from customers are $1,000,000 and that, because of improved policies, management estimates a 10% increase in collections next year. Budgeted collections for next year will be $1,100,000 ($1,000,000 × 1.10). Similarly, assume that current-year expenditures for employee salaries are $500,000 and that the company grants all employees a 2% cost-of living raise. Assuming no change in personnel next year, budgeted cash payments for employee salaries will be $510,000 ($500,000 × 1.02). Following the format of Exhibit 4-14, prepare an Excel spreadsheet using formulas based on accurate estimates for next year. This can make preparation of the cash budget a breeze for next year as well as every year thereafter! ■

REPORT CASH ON THE BALANCE SHEET

6 Report cash on the balance sheet

Most companies have numerous bank accounts, but they usually combine all cash amounts into a single total called "Cash and Cash Equivalents." **Cash equivalents** include liquid assets such as time deposits, certificates of deposit, and high-grade U.S. or foreign government securities that are very close to maturity (3 months or less at the time of purchase). Time deposits are interest-bearing accounts that can be withdrawn for immediate use. Slightly less liquid than cash, cash equivalents are sufficiently similar to be reported along with cash. The balance sheet of Mid-Atlantic Manufacturing reported the following:

	A	B	C
	A1		
1	Mid-Atlantic Manufacturing Company Balance Sheet (Excerpts, adapted) December 31, 2014		
2	Assets		
3	Cash and cash equivalents		$ 6,260
4	Cash pledged as collateral		2,000
5			

Most public companies include additional information about cash and cash equivalents in the footnotes to their financial statements. For example, Note 1 (Description of Business and Accounting Policies) of Amazon.com, Inc.'s 2012 financial statements contains the following brief comment about cash and cash equivalents:

> ### Cash and Cash Equivalents
>
> We classify all highly liquid instruments with an original maturity of three months or less at the time of purchase as cash equivalents.

Note 2 (Cash, Cash Equivalents, and Marketable Securities) contains a more detailed description of the types of securities included in this category, as well as the method used to value those securities. We discuss these methods further in Chapter 5.

Compensating Balance Agreements

The Cash account on the balance sheet reports the liquid assets available for day-to-day use. None of the Cash balance is restricted in any way.

Any restricted amount of cash should *not* be reported as Cash on the balance sheet. For example, on the Mid-Atlantic Manufacturing balance sheet, *cash pledged as collateral* is reported separately because that cash is not available for day-to-day use. Instead, Mid-Atlantic has pledged the cash as security (collateral) for a loan. If Mid-Atlantic fails to pay the loan, the lender can take the pledged cash. For this reason, the pledged cash is less liquid.

Also, banks often lend money under a compensating balance agreement. The borrower agrees to maintain a minimum balance in a checking account at all times. This minimum balance becomes a long-term asset and is therefore not cash in the normal sense. Suppose Mid-Atlantic Manufacturing borrowed $10,000 at 8% from First Interstate Bank and agreed to keep 20%

($2,000) on deposit at all times. The net result of the compensating balance agreement is that Mid-Atlantic actually borrowed only $8,000. And by paying 8% interest on the full $10,000, Mid-Atlantic's actual interest rate is really 10%, as shown here:

$$\$10,000 \times .08 = \$800 \text{ interest}$$
$$\$800/\$8,000 = .10 \text{ interest rate}$$

» End-of-Chapter Summary Problem

Assume the following financial data for PepsiCo, Inc.: PepsiCo ended 2014 with cash of $200 million. At December 31, 2014, Bob Detmer, the CFO of PepsiCo, is preparing the cash budget for 2015.

During 2015, Detmer expects PepsiCo to collect $26,400 million from customers and $80 million from interest earned on investments. PepsiCo expects to pay $12,500 million for its inventories and $5,400 million for operating expenses. To remain competitive, PepsiCo plans to spend $2,200 million to upgrade production facilities and an additional $350 million to acquire other companies. PepsiCo also plans to sell older assets for approximately $300 million and to collect $220 million of this amount in cash. PepsiCo is budgeting dividend payments of $550 million during the year. Finally, the company is scheduled to pay off $1,200 million of long-term debt plus the $6,600 million of current liabilities left over from 2014.

Because of the growth planned for 2015, Detmer budgets the need for a minimum cash balance of $300 million.

Requirement

1. How much must PepsiCo borrow during 2015 to keep its cash balance from falling below $300 million? Prepare the 2015 cash budget to answer this important question. You may want to use Excel to streamline this task.

Answer

	A	B	C
1	**PepsiCo, Inc.** **Cash Budget** **For the Year Ended December 31, 2015**		
2	(In millions)		
3	Cash balance, December 31, 2014		$ 200
4	Estimated cash receipts:		
5	Collections from customers		26,400
6	Receipt of interest		80
7	Sales of assets		220
8			26,900
9	Estimated cash payments:		
10	Purchases of inventory	$ 12,500	
11	Payment of operating expenses	5,400	
12	Upgrading of production facilities	2,200	
13	Acquisition of other companies	350	
14	Payment of dividends	550	
15	Payment of long-term debt and other liabilities ($1,200 + $6,600)	7,800	(28,800)
16	Cash available (needed) before new financing		$ (1,900)
17	Budgeted cash balance, December 31, 2015		(300)
18	Cash available for additional investments, or		
19	(New financing needed)		$ (2,200)
20			

PepsiCo must borrow $2.2 billion.

REVIEW | Internal Control & Cash

Quick Check (Answers are given on page 244.)

1. Internal control has its own terminology. On the left are some key internal control concepts. On the right are some key terms. Match each internal control concept with its term by writing the appropriate letter in the space provided. Not all letters are used.

   _____ Internal control cannot always safeguard against this problem.

   _____ This is often mentioned as the cornerstone of a good system of internal control.

   _____ Pay employees enough to require them to do a good job.

   _____ This procedure limits access to sensitive data.

   _____ This type of insurance policy covers losses due to employee theft.

   _____ Trusting your employees can lead you to overlook this procedure.

   _____ This is the most basic purpose of internal control.

   a. Fidelity bond

   b. Supervision

   c. Separation of duties

   d. Encryption

   e. Competent personnel

   f. Firewalls

   g. Collusion

   h. Safeguarding assets

   i. External audits

2. Each of the following is an example of a control procedure, *except*

   a. a sound marketing plan.   **c.** sound personnel procedures.

   b. limited access to assets.   **d.** separation of duties.

3. Which of the following is an example of poor internal control?

   a. Rotate employees through various jobs.

   b. The mailroom clerk records daily cash receipts in the journal.

   c. Employees must take vacations.

   d. The accounting department compares goods received with the related purchase order.

Trisha Corporation has asked you to prepare its bank reconciliation at the end of the current month. Answer questions 4–8 using the following code letters to indicate how the item described would be reported on the bank reconciliation.

   a. deduct from the bank balance

   b. add to the book balance

   c. does not belong on the bank reconciliation

   d. deduct from the book balance

   e. add to the bank balance

4. The bank statement showed interest earned of $50.

5. The bank statement showed that the bank had credited Trisha's account for a $500 deposit made by Tryon Company.

6. A check for $753 written by Trisha during the current month was erroneously recorded as a $375 payment.

7. The bank statement included a check from a customer that was marked NSF.

8. A $600 deposit made on the last day of the current month did not appear on this month's bank statement.

9. Which of the following reconciling items does not require a journal entry?

   a. Bank service charge   **c.** Deposit in transit

   b. Bank collection of note receivable   **d.** NSF check

10. A check was written for $462 to purchase supplies. The check was recorded in the journal as $426. The entry to correct this error would

   a. increase Supplies, $36.   **c.** decrease Supplies, $36.

   b. decrease Cash, $36.   **d.** both a and b.

11. A cash budget helps control cash by

   a. developing a plan for increasing sales.

   b. ensuring accurate cash records.

   c. helping to determine whether additional cash is available for investments or new financing is needed.

   d. all of the above.

Accounting Vocabulary

audit (p. 201) A periodic examination of a company's financial statements and the accounting systems, controls, and records that produce them. Audits may be either external or internal. External audits are usually performed by certified public accountants (CPAs).

bank collections (p. 208) Collection of money by the bank on behalf of a depositor.

bank reconciliation (p. 207) A document explaining the reasons for the difference between a depositor's records and the bank's records about the depositor's cash.

bank statement (p. 206) Document showing the beginning and ending balances of a particular bank account listing the month's transactions that affected the account.

budget (p. 201) A quantitative expression of a plan that helps managers coordinate the entity's activities.

cash budget (p. 201) A budget that projects the entity's future cash receipts and cash disbursements.

cash equivalent (p. 220) Investments such as time deposits, certificates of deposit, or high-grade government securities that are considered so similar to cash that they are combined with cash for financial disclosure purposes on the balance sheet.

check (p. 205) Document instructing a bank to pay the designated person or business the specified amount of money.

computer virus (p. 203) A malicious program that enters a company's computer system by e-mail or other means and destroys program and data files.

controller (p. 201) The chief accounting officer of a business.

deposits in transit (p. 208) A deposit recorded by the company but not yet by its bank.

electronic funds transfer (EFT) (p. 206) System that transfers cash by electronic communication rather than by paper documents.

encryption (p. 203) Mathematical rearranging of data within an electronic file to prevent unauthorized access to information.

exception reporting (p. 201) Identifying data that is not within "normal limits" so that managers can follow up and take corrective action. Exception reporting is used in operating and cash budgets to keep company profits and cash flow in line with management's plans.

fidelity bond (p. 203) An insurance policy taken out on employees who handle cash.

firewall (p. 204) An electronic barrier, usually provided by passwords, around computerized data files to protect local area networks of computers from unauthorized access.

fraud (p. 195) An intentional misrepresentation of facts, made for the purpose of persuading another party to act in a way that causes injury or damage to that party.

fraud triangle (p. 196) The three elements that are present in almost all cases of fraud. These elements are motive, opportunity, and rationalization on the part of the perpetrator.

fraudulent financial reporting (p. 196) Fraud perpetrated by management by preparing misleading financial statements.

imprest system (p. 218) A way to account for petty cash by maintaining a constant balance in the petty cash account, supported by the fund (cash plus payment tickets) totaling the same amount.

internal control (p. 197) Organizational plan and related measures adopted by an entity to safeguard assets, encourage adherence to company policies, promote operational efficiency, and ensure accurate and reliable accounting records.

lapping (p. 193) A fraudulent scheme to steal cash through misappropriating certain customer payments and posting payments from other customers to the affected accounts to cover it up. Lapping is caused by weak internal controls (i.e., not segregating the duties of cash handling and accounts receivable bookkeeping, allowing the bookkeeper improper access to cash, and not appropriately monitoring the activities of those who handle cash).

lock-box system (p. 194) A system of handling cash receipts by mail whereby customers remit payment directly to the bank, rather than through the entity's mail system.

misappropriation of assets (p. 195) Fraud committed by employees by stealing assets from the company.

nonsufficient funds (NSF) check (p. 208) A "hot" check, one for which the payer's bank account has insufficient money to pay the check. NSF checks are cash receipts that turn out to be worthless.

operating budget (p. 201) A budget of future net income. The operating budget projects a company's future revenue and expenses. It is usually prepared by line item of the company's income statement.

outstanding check (p. 208) A check issued by the company and recorded on its books but not yet paid by its bank.

password (p. 202) A special set of characters that must be provided by the user of a computerized program or data files to prevent unauthorized access to those files.

petty cash (p. 218) Fund containing a small amount of cash that is used to pay minor amounts.

phish (p. 203) Creating bogus websites for the purpose of stealing unauthorized data, such as names, addresses, Social Security numbers, and bank account and credit card numbers.

remittance advice (p. 205) An optional attachment to a check (sometimes a perforated tear-off document and sometimes capable of being electronically scanned) that indicates the payer, date, and purpose of the cash payment. The remittance advice is often used as the source documents for posting cash receipts or payments.

treasurer (p. 200) In a large company, the individual in charge of the department that has final responsibility for cash handling and cash management. Duties of the treasurer's department include cash budgeting, cash collections, writing checks, investing excess funds, and making proposals for raising additional cash when needed.

Trojan Horse (p. 203) A malicious program that hides within legitimate programs and acts like a computer virus.

ASSESS YOUR PROGRESS

Short Exercises

S4-1 *(Learning Objective 1: Define fraud)* Define "fraud." List and briefly discuss the three major components of the "fraud triangle."

S4-2 *(Learning Objective 1: Describe fraud and its impact)* Charlene Clyde, an accountant for Otto Brothers Limited, discovers that her supervisor, Bob Lusk, made several errors last year. Overall, the errors overstated the company's net income by 20%. It is not clear whether the errors were deliberate or accidental. What should Clyde do?

S4-3 *(Learning Objective 1: Describe fraud involving e-commerce)* How do computer viruses, Trojan Horses, and phishing expeditions work? How can these e-commerce pitfalls hurt you? Be specific.

S4-4 *(Learning Objective 2: Describe components of internal control)* List the components of internal control. Briefly describe each component.

S4-5 *(Learning Objective 2: Explain the objectives of internal control)* Explain why separation of duties is often described as the cornerstone of internal control for safeguarding assets. Describe what can happen if the same person has custody of an asset and also accounts for the asset.

S4-6 *(Learning Objective 2: Explain the components of internal control)* Identify the other control procedures usually found in a company's system of internal control besides separation of duties, and tell why each is important.

S4-7 *(Learning Objective 2: Explain the objectives of internal control)* Cash may be a small item on the financial statements. Nevertheless, internal control over cash is very important. Why is this true?

S4-8 *(Learning Objectives 2, 4: Explain the objectives of internal control; evaluate controls over cash payments)* Cardinal Company requires that all documents supporting a check be canceled by punching a hole through the packet. Why is this practice required? What might happen if it were not?

S4-9 *(Learning Objective 3: Design and use a bank reconciliation)* The Cash account of Vincente Corp. reported a balance of $3,640 at August 31. Included were outstanding checks totaling $800 and an August 31 deposit of $300 that did not appear on the bank statement. The bank statement, which came from Tri State Bank, listed an August 31 balance of $4,775. Included in the bank balance was an August 30 collection of $685 on account from a customer who pays the bank directly. The bank statement also shows a $15 service charge, $20 of interest revenue that Vincente earned on its bank balance, and an NSF check for $55.

Prepare a bank reconciliation to determine how much cash Vincente actually has at August 31.

S4-10 *(Learning Objective 3: Design and use a bank reconciliation)* After preparing Vincente Corp.'s bank reconciliation in Short Exercise 4-9, make the company's journal entries for transactions that arise from the bank reconciliation. Date each transaction August 31, 2014, and include an explanation with each entry.

S4-11 *(Learning Objective 3: Design and use a bank reconciliation)* Suzie Hargis manages T. Oliver Manufacturing. Hargis fears that a trusted employee has been stealing from the company. This employee receives cash from clients and also prepares the monthly bank reconciliation. To check up on the employee, Hargis prepares her own bank reconciliation, as follows:

	A	B	C	D	E
1	**T. Oliver Manufacturing** **Bank Reconciliation** **July 31, 2014**				
2	**Bank**		**Books**		
3	Balance, July 31	$ 3,050	Balance, July 31		$ 2,880
4	Add:		Add:		
5	Deposits in transit	300	Bank collections		450
6			Interest revenue		35
7	Less:		Less:		
8	Outstanding checks	(760)	Service charge		(65)
9	Adjusted bank balance	$ 2,590	Adjusted book balance		$ 3,300
10					

Does it appear that the employee has stolen from the company? If so, how much? Explain your answer. Which side of the bank reconciliation shows the company's true cash balance?

S4-12 *(Learning Objective 4: Evaluate internal control over cash receipts)* Gordon Young sells memberships to the Denver Symphony Association in Denver, Colorado. The symphony's procedure requires Young to write a patron receipt for all memberships sold. The receipt forms are prenumbered. Young is having personal financial problems, and he stole $600 received from a customer. To hide his theft, Young destroyed the company copy of the receipt that he gave the patron. What will alert manager Sabrina Sims that something is wrong?

S4-13 *(Learning Objective 4: Evaluate internal control over cash payments)* Answer the following questions about internal control over cash payments:
1. Payment by check carries three controls over cash. What are they?
2. Suppose a purchasing agent receives the goods that he purchases and also approves payment for the goods. How could a dishonest purchasing agent cheat the company? How do companies avoid this internal control weakness?

S4-14 *(Learning Objective 5: Construct a cash budget)* Farm-to-Market (FM) is a major food cooperative. Suppose FM begins 2015 with cash of $7 million. FM estimates cash receipts during 2015 will total $103 million. Planned payments will total $97 million. To meet daily cash needs next year, FM must maintain a cash balance of at least $11 million. Prepare the organization's cash budget for 2015.

S4-15 *(Learning Objective 6: Report cash on the balance sheet)* Describe the types of assets that are typically included under the heading "cash and cash equivalents" on the balance sheet. What is a "cash equivalent"?

Exercises

MyAccountingLab

All of the Group A and Group B exercises can be found within MyAccountingLab, an online homework and practice environment. Your instructor may ask you to complete these exercises using **MyAccountingLab**.

Group A

E4-16A *(Learning Objectives 1, 2: Describe fraud and its impact; identify internal controls)* Identify the internal control weakness in the following situations. State how the person can hurt the company.

  a. Juan Higaredo works as a security guard at VALID parking in Denver. Higaredo has a master key to the cash box where customers pay for parking. Each night Higaredo prepares the cash report that shows (a) the number of cars that parked on the lot and (b) the day's cash receipts. Becca Chen, the VALID treasurer, checks Higaredo's figures by multiplying the number of cars by the parking fee per car. Chen then deposits the cash in the bank.

b. Isabella Valdez is the purchasing agent for McGehee Sports Equipment. Valdez prepares purchase orders based on requests from division managers of the company. Valdez faxes the purchase order to suppliers, who then ship the goods to McGehee. Valdez receives each incoming shipment and checks it for agreement with the purchase order and the related invoice. She then routes the goods to the respective division managers and sends the receiving report and the invoice to the accounting department for payment.

E4-17A *(Learning Objective 4: Evaluate internal control)* The following situations describe two cash payment situations and two cash receipt situations. In each pair, one set of internal controls is better than the other. Evaluate the internal controls in each situation as strong or weak, and give the reason for your answer.

Cash payments:

a. Gerald Munn Construction policy calls for construction supervisors to request the equipment needed for their jobs. The home office then purchases the equipment and has it shipped to the construction site.

b. Redstone, Inc., policy calls for project supervisors to purchase the equipment needed for jobs. The supervisors then submit the paid receipts to the home office for reimbursement. This policy enables supervisors to get the equipment quickly and keep construction jobs moving.

Cash receipts:

a. At Clifton Auto Parts, cash received by mail goes straight to the accountant, who debits Cash and credits Accounts Receivable to record the collections from customers. The Clifton accountant then deposits the cash in the bank.

b. Cash received by mail at Eagle Dermatology Clinic goes to the mailroom, where a mail clerk opens envelopes and totals the cash receipts for the day. The mail clerk forwards customer checks to the cashier for deposit in the bank and forwards the remittance advices to the accounting department for posting credits to customer accounts.

E4-18A *(Learning Objectives 1, 2, 4: Describe fraud and its impact; explain the objectives and components of internal control; evaluate internal controls)* Marcia Munson served as executive director of Downtown Columbia, an organization created to revitalize Columbia, South Carolina. Over the course of 11 years, Munson embezzled $444,000. How did Munson do it? By depositing subscriber cash receipts in her own bank account, writing Downtown Columbia checks to herself, and creating phony entities that Downtown Columbia wrote checks to.

Downtown Columbia was led by a board of directors comprised of civic leaders. Munson's embezzlement went undetected until Downtown Columbia couldn't pay its bills.

Give four ways Munson's embezzlement could have been prevented.

E4-19A *(Learning Objective 3: Prepare a bank reconciliation)* F. L. Callan's checkbook lists the following:

Date	Check No.	Item	Check	Deposit	Balance
3/1					$ 640
4	622	Landry's Cafe	$ 15		625
9		Dividends received		$ 115	740
13	623	City Tire Co.	155		585
14	624	Jiffy Lube	18		567
18	625	Cash	60		507
26	626	Shalom Baptist Church	90		417
28	627	Greenside Apartments	270		147
31		Paycheck		1,325	1,472

The March bank statement shows

Balance		$640	
Add: Deposits		115	
Debit checks:	No.	Amount	
	622	$15	
	623	155	
	624	81*	
	625	60	(311)
Other charges:			
NSF check......................................		$28	
Service charge		7	(35)
Balance			$409

*This is the correct amount for check number 624.

Requirement

1. Prepare Callan's bank reconciliation at March 31, 2015.

E4-20A *(Learning Objective 3: Use a bank reconciliation)* Ryan Patrick operates a roller skating center. He has just received the monthly bank statement at June 30 from Citizens National Bank, and the statement shows an ending balance of $750. Listed on the statement are an EFT rent collection of $409, a service charge of $7, two NSF checks totaling $120, and a $10 charge for printed checks. In reviewing his cash records, Patrick identifies outstanding checks totaling $610 and a June 30 deposit in transit of $1,765. During June, he recorded a $270 check for the salary of a part-time employee as $27. Patrick's Cash account shows a June 30 cash balance of $1,876. How much cash does Patrick actually have at June 30, 2014?

E4-21A *(Learning Objective 3: Design and use a bank reconciliation)* Use the data from Exercise 4-20A to make the journal entries that Patrick should record on June 30 to update his Cash account. Include an explanation for each entry.

E4-22A *(Learning Objective 4: Evaluate internal control over cash receipts)* McIntosh Stores use point-of-sale terminals as cash registers. The register shows the amount of each sale, the cash received from the customer, and any change returned to the customer. The machine also produces a customer receipt but keeps no record of transactions. At the end of the day, the clerk counts the cash in the register and gives it to the cashier for deposit in the company bank account.

Write a memo to convince the store manager that there is an internal control weakness over cash receipts. Identify the weakness that gives an employee the best opportunity to steal cash, and state how to prevent such a theft.

E4-23A *(Learning Objective 4: Evaluate internal control over cash payments)* Blue Manufacturing Company manufactures a popular line of work clothes. Blue Manufacturing employs 125 workers and keeps their employment records on time sheets that show how many hours the employee works each week. On Friday the shop foreman collects the time sheets, checks them for accuracy, and delivers them to the payroll department for preparation of paychecks. The treasurer signs the paychecks and returns the checks to the payroll department for distribution to the employees.

Identify the main internal control weakness in this situation, state how the weakness can hurt Blue Manufacturing, and propose a way to correct the weakness.

E4-24A *(Learning Objective 5: Construct and use a cash budget)* Dexter Communications, Inc., is preparing its cash budget for 2015. Dexter ended 2014 with cash of $68 million and managers need to keep a cash balance of at least $70 million for operations.

Collections from customers are expected to total $11,325 million during 2015, and payments for the cost of services and products should reach $6,196 million. Operating expense payments are budgeted at $2,553 million.

During 2015, Dexter expects to invest $1,822 million in new equipment and sell older assets for $157 million. Debt payments scheduled for 2015 will total $538 million. The company forecasts net income of $893 million for 2015 and plans to pay dividends of $348 million.

Prepare Dexter Communications' cash budget for 2015. Will the budgeted level of cash receipts leave Dexter with the desired ending cash balance of $70 million, or will the company need additional financing? If so, how much?

Group B

E4-25B *(Learning Objectives 1, 2: Describe fraud and its impact; evaluate internal controls)* Identify the internal control weakness in the following situations. State how the person can hurt the company.

a. Kirk Kennedy works as a security guard at TOWN parking in Des Moines. Kennedy has a master key to the cash box where customers pay for parking. Each night Kennedy prepares the cash report that shows (a) the number of cars that parked on the lot and (b) the day's cash receipts. Linda Alton, the TOWN treasurer, checks Kennedy's figures by multiplying the number of cars by the parking fee per car. Alton then deposits the cash in the bank.

b. Meagan Morales is the purchasing agent for RG Sports Equipment. Morales prepares purchase orders based on requests from division managers of the company. Morales faxes the purchase order to suppliers, who then ship the goods to RG Sports Equipment. Morales receives each incoming shipment and checks it for agreement with the purchase order and the related invoice. She then routes the goods to the respective division managers and sends the receiving report and the invoice to the accounting department for payment.

E4-26B *(Learning Objective 4: Evaluate internal control)* The following situations describe two cash payment situations and two cash receipt situations. In each pair, one set of internal controls is better than the other. Evaluate the internal controls in each situation as strong or weak, and give the reason for your answer.

Cash payments:

a. Gary Chapman Construction policy calls for construction supervisors to request the equipment needed for their jobs. The home office then purchases the equipment and has it shipped to the construction site.

b. Outdoor Buildings, Inc., policy calls for project supervisors to purchase the equipment needed for jobs. The supervisors then submit the paid receipts to the home office for reimbursement. This policy enables supervisors to get the equipment quickly and keep construction jobs moving.

Cash receipts:

a. At Westfield Auto Parts, cash received by mail goes straight to the accountant, who debits Cash and credits Accounts Receivable to record the collections from customers. The Westfield accountant then deposits the cash in the bank.

b. Cash received by mail at Hillcrest Heart Clinic goes to the mailroom, where a mail clerk opens envelopes and totals the cash receipts for the day. The mail clerk forwards customer checks to the cashier for deposit in the bank and forwards the remittance slips to the accounting department for posting credits to customer accounts.

E4-27B *(Learning Objectives 1, 2, 4: Describe fraud and its impact; explain the objectives and components of internal control; evaluate internal controls)* James Henry served as executive director of Downtown Huntsville, an organization created to revitalize Huntsville, Alabama. Over the course of 14 years, Henry embezzled $236,000. How did Henry do it? He did it by depositing subscriber cash receipts in his own bank account, writing Downtown Huntsville checks to himself, and creating phony entities to which Downtown Huntsville wrote checks.

Downtown Huntsville was led by a board of directors comprised of civic leaders. Henry's embezzlement went undetected until Downtown Huntsville couldn't pay its bills.

Give four ways Henry's embezzlement could have been prevented.

E4-28B *(Learning Objective 3: Prepare a bank reconciliation)* A. C. Mazanek's checkbook and May bank statement show the following:

Date	Check No.	Item	Check	Deposit	Balance
5/1					$ 645
4	622	Sun Cafe	$ 20		625
9		Dividends received		$ 110	735
13	623	Hartford Co.	145		590
14	624	FastMobil	58		532
18	625	Cash	60		472
26	626	First Baptist Church	75		397
28	627	Willow Tree Apartments	265		132
31		Paycheck		1,320	1,452

Balance				$645
Add: Deposits				110
Debit checks:	No.	Amount		
	622	$20		
	623	145		
	624	85*		
	625	60		(310)
Other charges:				
NSF check			$37	
Service charge			3	(40)
Balance				$405

*This is the correct amount for check number 624.

Requirement

1. Prepare Mazanek's bank reconciliation at May 31, 2014.

E4-29B *(Learning Objective 3: Use a bank reconciliation)* Joe Donney operates a roller skating center. He has just received the monthly bank statement at August 31 from Citizens National Bank, and the statement shows an ending balance of $638. Listed on the statement are an EFT rent collection of $375, a service charge of $9, two NSF checks totaling $137, and a $20 charge for printed checks. In reviewing his cash records, Donney identifies outstanding checks totaling $756 and an August 31 deposit in transit of $1,695. During August, he recorded a $280 check for the salary of a part-time employee as $28. Donney's Cash account shows an August 31 cash balance of $1,620. How much cash does Donney actually have at August 31, 2014?

E4-30B *(Learning Objective 3: Design and use a bank reconciliation)* Use the data from Exercise 4-29B to make the journal entries that Donney should record on August 31 to update his Cash account. Include an explanation for each entry.

E4-31B *(Learning Objective 4: Evaluate internal control over cash receipts)* Roper Stores use point-of-sale terminals as cash registers. The register shows the amount of each sale, the cash received from the customer, and any change returned to the customer. The machine also produces a customer receipt but keeps no record of transactions. At the end of the day, the clerk counts the cash in the register and gives it to the cashier for deposit in the company bank account.

Write a memo to convince the store manager that there is an internal control weakness over cash receipts. Identify the weakness that gives an employee the best opportunity to steal cash, and state how to prevent such a theft.

E4-32B *(Learning Objective 4: Evaluate internal control over cash payments)* Quick Kick Company manufactures a popular brand of footballs. Quick Kick employs 142 workers and keeps its employment records on time sheets that show how many hours the employee works each week. On Friday the shop foreman collects the time sheets, checks them for accuracy, and delivers them to the payroll department for preparation of paychecks. The treasurer signs the paychecks and returns the checks to the payroll department for distribution to the employees.

Identify the main internal control weakness in this situation, state how the weakness can hurt Quick Kick, and propose a way to correct the weakness.

E4-33B *(Learning Objective 5: Construct and use a cash budget)* Carron Communications, Inc., is preparing its cash budget for 2015. Carron ended 2014 with cash of $72 million, and managers need to keep a cash balance of at least $65 million for operations.

Collections from customers are expected to total $11,233 million during 2015, and payments for the cost of services and products should reach $6,129 million. Operating expense payments are budgeted at $2,756 million.

During 2015, Carron expects to invest $1,543 million in new equipment and sell older assets for $108 million. Debt payments scheduled for 2015 will total $611 million. The company forecasts net income of $884 million for 2015 and plans to pay dividends of $316 million.

Prepare Carron Communications' cash budget for 2015. Will the budgeted level of cash receipts leave Carron with the desired ending cash balance of $65 million, or will the company need additional financing? If so, how much?

Quiz

Test your understanding of internal control and cash by answering the following questions. Answer each question by selecting the best choice from among the options given.

Q4-34 All of the following are objectives of internal control except
  a. to safeguard assets.
  b. to ensure accurate and reliable accounting records.
  c. to maximize net income.
  d. to comply with legal requirements.

Q4-35 All of the following are internal control procedures except
  a. Sarbanes-Oxley reforms.
  b. assignment of responsibilities.
  c. internal and external audits.
  d. adequate records.

Q4-36 Requiring that an employee with no access to cash do the accounting is an example of which characteristic of internal control?
  a. Monitoring of controls
  b. Separation of duties
  c. Assignment of responsibility
  d. Competent and reliable personnel

Q4-37 All of the following are controls for cash received over the counter except
  a. the customer should be able to see the amounts entered into the cash register.
  b. the cash drawer should open only when the sales clerk enters an amount on the keys.
  c. a printed receipt must be given to the customer.
  d. the sales clerk must have access to the cash register tape.

Q4-38 In a bank reconciliation, an outstanding check is
  a. deducted from the book balance.
  b. deducted from the bank balance.
  c. added to the bank balance.
  d. added to the book balance.

Q4-39 In a bank reconciliation, an EFT cash payment is
  a. added to the bank balance.
  b. added to the book balance.
  c. deducted from the book balance.
  d. deducted from the bank balance.

Q4-40 If a bookkeeper mistakenly recorded a $72 deposit as $27, the error would be shown on the bank reconciliation as a

a. $45 deduction from the book balance.
b. $27 deduction from the book balance.
c. $45 addition to the book balance.
d. $27 addition to the book balance.

Q4-41 If a bank reconciliation included a deposit in transit of $790, the entry to record this reconciling item would include a

a. credit to Prepaid insurance for $790.
b. debit to Cash for $790.
c. credit to Cash for $790.
d. No entry is required.

Q4-42 In a bank reconciliation, interest revenue earned on your bank balance is

a. added to the book balance.
b. deducted from the book balance.
c. added to the bank balance.
d. deducted from the bank balance.

Q4-43 Before paying an invoice for goods received on account, the controller or treasurer should ensure that

a. the company is paying for the goods it ordered.
b. the company is paying for the goods it actually received.
c. the company has not already paid this invoice.
d. all of the above.

Q4-44 Lula's Bakery is budgeting cash for 2015. The cash balance at December 31, 2014, was $14,000. Lula's Bakery budgets 2015 cash receipts at $81,000. Estimated cash payments include $44,000 for inventory, $34,000 for operating expenses, and $25,000 to expand the store. Lula's Bakery needs a minimum cash balance of $13,000 at all times. Lula's Bakery expects to earn net income of $76,000 during 2015. What is the final result of the company's cash budget for 2015?

a. $21,000 available for additional investments.
b. Pay off $42,000 of debt.
c. Must arrange new financing for $21,000.
d. $42,000 available for additional investments.

Q4-45 Which of the following assets are *not* included in "cash equivalents" in a typical balance sheet?

a. Time deposits
b. U.S. government securities
c. Foreign government securities
d. Certain very low risk equity securities
e. All of the above might be included in "cash equivalents."

Problems

MyAccountingLab

All of the Group A and Group B problems can be found within MyAccountingLab, an online homework and practice environment. Your instructor may ask you to complete these problems using **MyAccountingLab**.

Group A

P4-46A *(Learning Objectives 1, 4: Describe fraud and its impact; evaluate internal controls)* English Imports is an importer of silver, brass, and antique furniture items from England. Patricia Kregg is the general manager of English Imports. Kregg employs two other people in the business. Polly O'Hara serves as the buyer for English Imports. In her work, O'Hara travels throughout England to find interesting new products. When O'Hara finds a new product, she arranges for English Imports to purchase and pay for the item. She helps the English artisans prepare their invoices and then faxes the invoices to Kregg in the company office.

Kregg operates out of an office in Boston, Massachusetts. The office is managed by Lesley Luck, who handles the mail, keeps the accounting records, makes bank deposits, and prepares the monthly bank reconciliation. Virtually all of English Imports' cash receipts arrive by mail—from sales made to Target, Pier 1 Imports, and specialty shops.

Luck also prepares checks for payment based on invoices that come in from the suppliers who have been contacted by O'Hara. To maintain control over cash payments, Kregg examines the paperwork and signs all checks.

Requirement

1. Identify all the major internal control weaknesses in English Imports' system and how the resulting action could hurt English Imports. Also state how to correct each weakness.

P4-47A *(Learning Objectives 2, 4: Explain the components of internal control; evaluate internal controls)* Each of the following situations reveals an internal control weakness:

    a. In evaluating the internal control over cash payments of J. Harley Manufacturing, an auditor learns that the purchasing agent is responsible for purchasing diamonds for use in the company's manufacturing process, approving the invoices for payment, and signing the checks. No supervisor reviews the purchasing agent's work.

    b. Raylene Lloyd owns an architectural firm. Lloyd's staff consists of 16 professional architects, and Lloyd manages the office. Often, Lloyd's work requires her to travel to meet with clients. During the past six months, Lloyd has observed that when she returns from a business trip, the architecture jobs in the office have not progressed satisfactorily. Lloyd learns that when she is away, two of her senior architects take over office management and neglect their normal duties. One employee could manage the office.

    c. Douglas Snell has been an employee of the city of Marion for many years. Because the city is small, Snell performs all accounting duties, in addition to opening the mail, preparing the bank deposit, and preparing the bank reconciliation.

Requirements

1. Identify the missing internal control characteristic in each situation.
2. Identify each firm's possible problem.
3. Propose a solution to the problem.

P4-48A *(Learning Objective 3: Design and use a bank reconciliation)* The cash data of Richmond Automotive for June 2014 follow:

Cash					Account No. 101
Date	**Item**	**Jrnl. Ref.**	**Debit**	**Credit**	**Balance**
June 1	Balance				7,300
30		CR6	10,167		17,467
30		CP11		10,169	7,298

	Cash Receipts (CR)		Cash Payments (CP)	
Date	**Cash Debit**	**Check No.**	**Cash Credit**	
June 2	$ 2,971	3113	$ 1,524	
8	507	3114	1,601	
10	1,661	3115	1,830	
16	827	3116	43	
22	415	3117	839	
29	982	3118	120	
30	2,804	3119	542	
Total	$10,167	3120	987	
		3121	277	
		3122	2,406	
		Total	$10,169	

Richmond Automotive received the following bank statement on June 30, 2014:

	A	B	C
	A1 ⬍		
1	**Bank Statement for June 2014**		
2	Beginning balance		$ 7,300
3	Deposits and other additions:		
4	June 1	$ 525 EFT	
5	4	2,971	
6	9	507	
7	12	1,661	
8	17	827	
9	22	415	
10	23	1,375 BC	8,281
11	Checks and other deductions:		
12	June 7	$ 1,524	
13	13	1,380	
14	14	455 US	
15	15	1,601	
16	18	43	
17	21	467 EFT	
18	26	839	
19	30	120	
20	30	10 SC	(6,439)
21	Ending balance		$ 9,142
22			

Explanation: BC—bank collection of note receivable from customer, EFT—electronic funds transfer, US—unauthorized signature, SC—service charge

Additional data for the bank reconciliation include the following:

   a. The EFT deposit was a receipt of monthly rent. The EFT debit was a monthly insurance payment.
   b. The unauthorized signature check was received from a customer and returned by the bank unpaid.
   c. The correct amount of check number 3115, a payment on account, is $1,380. (Richmond Automotive's accountant mistakenly recorded the check as $1,830.)

Requirements

   1. Prepare the Richmond Automotive bank reconciliation at June 30, 2014.
   2. Prepare the journal entries required at June 30, 2014.
   3. Describe how a bank account and the bank reconciliation help the general manager control Richmond Automotive's cash.

P4-49A *(Learning Objective 5: Construct and use a cash budget)* Herman Knorr, chief financial officer of Dallas Wireless, is responsible for the company's budgeting process. Knorr's staff is preparing the Dallas Wireless cash budget for 2015. A key input to the budgeting process is last year's statement of cash flows, which follows (amounts in thousands):

	A	B	C
	A1		
1	**Dallas Wireless** **Statement of Cash Flows** **For the Year Ended December 31, 2014**		
2	(In thousands)		
3	**Cash Flows from Operating Activities**		
4	Collections from customers		$ 61,000
5	Interest received		400
6	Cash payments for inventory		(46,000)
7	Cash payments for operating expenses		(13,200)
8	Net cash provided by operating activities		2,200
9	**Cash Flows from Investing Activities**		
10	Purchases of equipment		(4,500)
11	Purchases of investments		(800)
12	Sales of investments		900
13	Net cash used for investing activities		(4,400)
14	**Cash Flows from Financing Activities**		
15	Payment of long-term debt		(200)
16	Issuance of stock		1,400
17	Payment of cash dividends		(500)
18	Net cash provided by financing activities		700
19	**Cash**		
20	Increase (decrease) in Cash		(1,500)
21	Cash, beginning of year		3,100
22	Cash, end of year		$ 1,600
23			

Requirements

1. Prepare the Dallas Wireless cash budget for 2015. Date the budget simply "2015," and denote the beginning and ending cash balances as "beginning" and "ending." Assume the company expects 2015 to be the same as 2014, but with the following changes:
   a. In 2015, the company expects a 25% increase in collections from customers and a 26% increase in purchases of inventory.
   b. There will be no sales of investments in 2015.
   c. Dallas Wireless plans to issue no stock in 2015.
   d. Dallas Wireless plans to end the year with a cash balance of $4,675.

Group B

P4-50B *(Learning Objectives 1, 4: Describe fraud and its impact; evaluate internal controls)* Finnish Imports is an importer of silver, brass, and furniture items from Finland. Lois Ferguson is the general manager of Finnish Imports. Ferguson employs two other people in the business. Mandy Martin serves as the buyer for Finnish Imports. In her work, Martin travels throughout Finland to find interesting new products. When Martin finds a new product, she arranges for Finnish Imports to purchase and pay for the item. She helps the artisans prepare their invoices and then faxes the invoices to Ferguson in the company office.

Ferguson operates out of an office in Brooklyn, New York. The office is managed by Sandra Moore, who handles the mail, keeps the accounting records, makes bank deposits, and prepares the monthly bank reconciliation. Virtually all of Finnish Imports' cash receipts arrive by mail—from sales made to Target, Crate and Barrel, and Williams-Sonoma.

Moore also prepares checks for payment based on invoices that come in from the suppliers who have been contacted by Martin. To maintain control over cash payments, Ferguson examines the paperwork and signs all checks.

Requirement

1. Identify all the major internal control weaknesses in Finnish Imports' system and how the resulting action could hurt Finnish Imports. Also state how to correct each weakness.

P4-51B *(Learning Objectives 2, 4: Explain the components of internal control; evaluate internal controls)* Each of the following situations reveals an internal control weakness:

Situation a. In evaluating the internal control over cash payments of Burlington Manufacturing, an auditor learns that the purchasing agent is responsible for purchasing diamonds for use in the company's manufacturing process, approving the invoices for payment, and signing the checks. No supervisor reviews the purchasing agent's work.

Situation b. Wilma Klepper owns an architectural firm. Klepper's staff consists of 19 professional architects, and Klepper manages the office. Often, Klepper's work requires her to travel to meet with clients. During the past six months, Klepper has observed that when she returns from a business trip, the architecture jobs in the office have not progressed satisfactorily. Klepper learns that when she is away, two of her senior architects take over office management and neglect their normal duties. One employee could manage the office.

Situation c. Dale Potter has been an employee of the city of Southport for many years. Because the city is small, Potter performs all accounting duties, in addition to opening the mail, preparing the bank deposit, and preparing the bank reconciliation.

Requirements

1. Identify the missing internal control characteristic in each situation.
2. Identify each firm's possible problem.
3. Propose a solution to the problem.

P4-52B *(Learning Objective 3: Design and use a bank reconciliation)* The cash data of Big City Automotive for July 2014 follow:

Cash					Account No. 101
Date	Item	Jrnl. Ref.	Debit	Credit	Balance
July 1	Balance				7,750
31		CR 6	10,201		17,951
31		CP 11		10,993	6,958

Cash Receipts (CR)		Cash Payments (CP)	
Date	Cash Debit	Check No.	Cash Credit
July 2	$ 2,875	3113	$ 1,506
8	586	3114	1,838
10	1,695	3115	1,930
16	845	3116	95
22	413	3117	819
29	986	3118	174
30	2,801	3119	563
Total	$10,201	3120	972
		3121	265
		3122	2,831
		Total	$10,993

Big City Automotive received the following bank statement on July 31, 2014:

	A	B	C
	A1		
1	**Bank Statement for July 2014**		
2	Beginning balance		$ 7,750
3	Deposits and other additions:		
4	July 1	$ 850 EFT	
5	4	2,875	
6	9	586	
7	12	1,695	
8	17	845	
9	22	413	
10	23	1,350 BC	8,614
11	Checks and other deductions:		
12	July 7	$1,506	
13	13	1,390	
14	14	417 US	
15	15	1,838	
16	18	95	
17	21	407 EFT	
18	26	819	
19	30	174	
20	30	25 SC	(6,671)
21	Ending balance		$ 9,693
22			

Explanation: BC—bank collection of note receivable from customer, EFT—electronic funds transfer, US—unauthorized signature, SC—service charge

Additional data for the bank reconciliation include the following:
  a. The EFT deposit was a receipt of monthly rent. The EFT debit was a monthly insurance expense.
  b. The unauthorized signature check was received from a customer and returned by the bank unpaid.
  c. The correct amount of check number 3115, a payment on account, is $1,390. (Big City Automotive's accountant mistakenly recorded the check as $1,930.)
  d. The bank collected a note receivable for Big City Automotive.

Requirements

  1. Prepare the Big City Automotive bank reconciliation at July 31, 2014.
  2. Prepare the necessary journal entries at July 31, 2014.
  3. Describe how a bank account and the bank reconciliation help the general manager control Big City Automotives' cash.

P4-53B *(Learning Objective 5: Construct and use a cash budget)* Dan Beene, chief financial officer of Tampa Wireless, is responsible for the company's budgeting process. Beene's staff is preparing the Tampa cash budget for 2015. A key input to the budgeting process is last year's statement of cash flows, which follows (amount in thousands):

A1			
	A	**B**	**C**
1	**Tampa Wireless** **Statement of Cash Flows** **For the Year Ended December 31, 2014**		
2	(In thousands)		
3	**Cash Flows from Operating Activities**		
4	Collections from customers		$ 66,000
5	Interest received		100
6	Cash payments for inventory		(50,000)
7	Cash payments for operating expenses		(13,400)
8	Net cash provided by operating activities		2,700
9	**Cash Flows from Investing Activities**		
10	Purchases of equipment		(4,800)
11	Purchases of investments		(400)
12	Sales of investments		400
13	Net cash used for investing activities		(4,800)
14	**Cash Flows from Financing Activities**		
15	Payment of long-term debt		(600)
16	Issuance of stock		1,500
17	Payment of cash dividends		(200)
18	Net cash provided by financing activities		700
19	**Cash**		
20	Increase (decrease) in Cash		(1,400)
21	Cash, beginning of year		2,900
22	Cash, end of year		$ 1,500
23			

Requirements

1. Prepare the Tampa Wireless cash budget for 2015. Date the budget simply "2015," and denote the beginning and ending cash balances as "beginning" and "ending." Assume the company expects 2015 to be the same as 2014, but with the following changes:
   a. In 2015, the company expects a 25% increase in collections from customers and a 24% increase in purchases of inventory.
   b. There will be no sales of investments in 2015.
   c. Tampa Wireless plans to issue no stock in 2015.
   d. Tampa Wireless plans to end the year with a cash balance of $4,750.

Challenge Exercises and Problem

E4-54 *(Learning Objectives 1, 4: Describe fraud and its impact; evaluate internal control)* Julie Brown, the owner of Julie's Party Sandwiches, has delegated management of the business to Stacie Wood, a friend. Brown drops by to meet customers and check up on cash receipts, but Wood buys the merchandise and handles cash payments. Business has been very good lately, and cash receipts have kept pace with the apparent level of sales. However, for a year or so, the amount of cash on hand has been too low. When asked about this, Wood explains that suppliers are charging more for goods than in the past. During the past year, Wood has taken two expensive vacations, and Brown wonders how Wood can afford these trips on her $52,000 annual salary and commissions.

List at least three ways Wood could be defrauding Brown of cash. In each instance, also identify how Brown can determine whether Wood's actions are ethical. Limit your answers to the store's cash payments. The business pays all suppliers by check (no EFTs).

E4-55 *(Learning Objective 5: Construct and use a cash budget)* Tom Patterson, the chief financial officer, is responsible for Gateway Golf's cash budget for 2015. The budget will help Patterson determine the amount of long-term borrowing needed to end the year with a cash balance of $135,000. Patterson's assistants have assembled budget data for 2015, which the computer printed in alphabetical order. Not all the data items reproduced below are used in preparing the cash budget.

(Assumed Data)	(In thousands)
Actual cash balance, December 31, 2014	$ 145
Budgeted total assets, December 31, 2015	22,677
Budgeted total current assets, December 31, 2015	7,576
Budgeted total current liabilities, December 31, 2015	4,360
Budgeted total liabilities, December 31, 2015	11,588
Budgeted total stockholders' equity, December 31, 2015	11,089
Collections from customers	20,400
Dividend payments	307
Issuance of stock	632
Net income	1,213
Payment of long-term and short-term debt	990
Payment of operating expenses	2,849
Payments for inventory items	14,245
Purchase of property and equipment with cash	1,588

Requirements

1. Construct the cash budget of Gateway Golf, Inc.
2. Compute Gateway Golf's budgeted current ratio and debt ratio at December 31, 2015. Based on these ratio values, and on the cash budget, would you lend $95,000 to Gateway Golf? Give the reason for your decision.

P4-56 *(Learning Objective 3: Use a bank reconciliation to detect fraud)* The president of The Pembrook Company has recently become concerned that the bookkeeper has embezzled cash from the company. He asks you, confidentially, to look over the bank reconciliation that the bookkeeper has prepared to see if you discover any discrepancies between the books and the bank statement. He provides you with the Cash account from the general ledger, the bank statement, and the bank reconciliation as of December 31. You learn from the November bank reconciliation that the following checks were outstanding on November 30: No. 1560 for $185, No. 1880 for $565, No. 1882 for $122, and No. 1883 for $468. There was one deposit in transit on November 30 for $1,252. An examination of the actual deposit slips revealed no bank errors. Assume the cash deposit of $2,425 on December 24 is the correct amount. The January bank statement showed that a $650 deposit cleared the bank on January 2.

	A	B	C	D	E	F
	A1					
	A	B	C	D	E	F
1	**Pembrook Company Bank Reconciliation December 31**					
2	**Bank**			**Books**		
3	Balance, 12/31		$ 3,668	Balance, 12/31		$ 9,455
4	Add:			Add:		
5	Deposits in transit		3,150	EFT receipt from customer		52
6			6,818	Interest revenue		6
7	Less:					9,513
8	Outstanding checks			Less:		
9	No. 1560	$ 185		Book error	$ 3,000	
10	No. 1901	842		NSF check	135	
11	No. 1902	168	(1,195)	EFT payment of utilities	755	(3,890)
12	Adjusted bank balance		$ 5,623	Adjusted book balance		$ 5,623
13						

General Ledger
Cash

Bal 12/1	7,354		
Cash receipt 12/7	1,300	No. 1880	565
Cash receipt 12/15	4,193	No. 1882	122
Cash receipt 12/23	5,425	No. 1883	468
Cash receipt 12/30	650	No. 1884	1,284
		No. 1885	1,388
		No. 1886	700
		No. 1887	2,478
		No. 1888	1,030
		No. 1889	422
		No. 1901	842
		No. 1902	168
Bal 12/31	9,455		

	A	B	C
	A1 ⇕		
1	**Bank Statement for December 31**		
2	Bal 12/1		$ 3,787
3	Deposits		
4	Dec 1	$ 1,252	
5	8	1,300	
6	16	4,193	
7	24	2,425	
8	31	6	
9	31	52	
10	Total deposits		9,228
11	Checks and other debits:		
12	No. 1880	565	
13	No. 1882	122	
14	No. 1883	468	
15	No. 1884	1,284	
16	No. 1885	1,388	
17	No. 1886	700	
18	No. 1887	2,478	
19	No. 1888	1,030	
20	No. 1889	422	
21	NSF	135	
22	EFT	755	
23	Total checks and other debits		(9,347)
24	Bal 12/31		$ 3,668
25			

Explanation: BC—bank collection, EFT—electronic funds transfer, US—unauthorized signature, SC—service charge

Requirement

1. Prepare a corrected bank reconciliation. Show the unexplained difference as an adjustment to the book balance. Include in your analysis the amount of the theft and how the bookkeeper attempted to conceal the theft.

APPLY YOUR KNOWLEDGE

Decision Cases

Case 1. *(Learning Objectives 1, 3, 4: Describe fraud; use a bank reconciliation; evaluate internal controls)* Environmental Concerns, Inc., has poor internal control. Recently, Oscar Benz, the manager, has suspected the bookkeeper of stealing. Details of the business's cash position at September 30 follow.

  a. The Cash account shows a balance of $10,402. This amount includes a September 30 deposit of $3,794 that does not appear on the September 30 bank statement.

  b. The September 30 bank statement shows a balance of $8,224. The bank statement lists a $200 bank collection, an $8 service charge, and a $36 NSF check. The bookkeeper has not recorded any of these items.

  c. At September 30, the following checks are outstanding:

Check No.	Amount
154	$116
256	150
278	853
291	990
292	206
293	145

  d. The bookkeeper receives all incoming cash and makes the bank deposits. He also reconciles the monthly bank statement. Here is his September 30 reconciliation:

Balance per books, September 30		$10,402
Add: Outstanding checks		1,460
Bank collection.................................		200
Subtotal.......................................		12,062
Less: Deposits in transit...........................	$3,794	
Service charge	8	
NSF check.......................................	36	(3,838)
Balance per bank, September 30.................		$ 8,224

Requirement

  1. Benz has requested that you determine whether the bookkeeper has stolen cash from the business and, if so, how much. He also asks you to explain how the bookkeeper attempted to conceal the theft. To make this determination, you perform a proper bank reconciliation. There are no bank or book errors. Benz also asks you to evaluate the internal controls and to recommend any changes needed to improve them.

Case 2. *(Learning Objectives 1, 4: Describe fraud and its impact; evaluate internal control)* This case is based on an actual situation experienced by one of the authors. Gilead Construction, headquartered in Topeka, Kansas, built a motel in Kansas City. The construction foreman, Slim Pickins, hired the workers for the project. Pickins had his workers fill out the necessary tax forms and sent the employment documents to the home office.

Work on the motel began on May 1 and ended in December. Each Thursday evening, Pickins filled out a time card that listed the hours worked by each employee during the five-day work week ended at 5 P.M. on Thursday. Pickins faxed the time sheets to the home office, which prepared the payroll checks on Friday morning. Pickins drove to the home office after lunch on Friday, picked up the payroll checks, and returned to the construction site. At 5 P.M. on Friday, Pickins distributed the paychecks to the workers.

    a. Describe in detail the internal control weakness in this situation. Specify what negative result could occur because of the internal control weakness.

    b. Describe what you would do to correct the internal control weakness.

Ethical Issues

For each of the following situations, answer the following questions:

  1. What is the ethical issue in this situation?

  2. What are the alternatives?

  3. Who are the stakeholders? What are the possible consequences to each? Analyze from the following standpoints: (a) economic, (b) legal, and (c) ethical.

  4. Place yourself in the role of the decision maker. What would you do? How would you justify your decision?

Issue 1. Sunrise Bank recently appointed the accounting firm of Smith, Godfroy, and Hannaford as the bank's auditor. Sunrise quickly became one of Smith, Godfroy, and Hannaford's largest clients. Subject to banking regulations, Sunrise must provide for any expected losses on notes receivable that Sunrise may not collect in full.

During the course of the audit, Smith, Godfroy, and Hannaford determined that three large notes receivable of Sunrise seem questionable. The auditors discussed these loans with Susan Carter, controller of Sunrise. Carter assured the auditors that these notes were good and that the makers of the notes will be able to pay their notes after the economy improves.

Smith, Godfroy, and Hannaford stated that Sunrise must record a loss for a portion of these notes receivable to account for the likelihood that Sunrise may never collect their full amount. Carter objected and threatened to dismiss the auditors if they demanded that the bank record the loss. Smith, Godfroy, and Hannaford wants to keep Sunrise as a client. In fact, the firm was counting on the revenue from the Sunrise audit to finance an expansion.

Issue 2. Barry Galvin is executive vice president of Community Bank. Active in community affairs, Galvin serves on the board of directors of The Salvation Army. The Salvation Army is expanding rapidly and is considering relocating. At a recent meeting, The Salvation Army decided to buy 250 acres of land on the edge of town. The owner of the property is Olga Nadar, a major depositor in Community Bank. Nadar is completing a bitter divorce, and Galvin knows that Nadar is eager to sell her property. In view of Nadar's difficult situation, Galvin believes Nadar would accept a low offer for the land. Realtors have appraised the property at $3.6 million.

Issue 3. Community Bank has a loan receivable from IMS Chocolates. IMS is six months late in making payments to the bank, and Jan French, a Community Bank vice president, is assisting IMS to restructure its debt.

French learns that IMS is depending on landing a contract with Snicker Foods, another Community Bank client. French also serves as Snicker Foods' loan officer at the bank. In this capacity, French is aware that Snicker is considering bankruptcy. No one else outside Snicker Foods knows this. French has been a great help to IMS and IMS's owner is counting on French's expertise in loan workouts to advise the company through this difficult process. To help the bank collect on this large loan, French has a strong motivation to alert IMS of Snicker's financial difficulties.

Focus on Financials | Amazon.com, Inc.

(Learning Objective 6: Report cash on the balance sheet) Refer to the **Amazon.com, Inc.**, consolidated financial statements in Appendix A at the end of this book. The cash and cash equivalents section of the Consolidated Balance Sheet shows a balance of $8,084 as of December 31, 2012.

1. What are the general criteria for an asset to be classified as a "cash equivalent"?
2. Refer to Note 1—DESCRIPTION OF BUSINESS AND ACCOUNTING POLICIES. What types of assets does the company generally include in the category of "cash equivalents"?
3. Does the company include any more detailed description of "cash equivalents"? Where? Describe the categories.
4. Does Amazon.com, Inc. have any "restricted cash"? What is this? Why do you think these assets have to be separately disclosed? (Challenge)

Focus on Analysis | Yum! Brands, Inc.

(Learning Objectives 2, 5: Analyze internal controls and cash flows) Refer to the YUM! Brands, Inc., Financial Statements in Appendix B at the end of this book.

1. Focus on cash and cash equivalents. Why did cash change during 2012? The statement of cash flows holds the answer to this question. Analyze the seven largest *individual* items on the statement of cash flows (not the summary subtotals such as "net cash provided by operating activities"). For each of the seven individual items, state how YUM! Brand's Inc.'s actions affected cash. Show amounts in millions and round to the nearest $1 million. (Challenge)
2. YUM! Brands, Inc.'s Report of Management describes the company's internal controls. Show how the management report corresponds to the objectives of internal control included in this chapter. (Challenge)

Group Project

You are promoting a rock concert in your area. Assume you organize as a partnership, with each member of your group contributing $5,000 in exchange for an ownership interest and a share in the profits. Therefore, each of you is risking some hard-earned money on this venture. Assume it is April 1 and that the concert will be performed on June 30. Your promotional activities begin immediately, and ticket sales start on May 1. You expect to sell all of the firm's assets, pay all the liabilities, and distribute all remaining cash to the group members by July 31.

Requirements

Write an internal control manual that will help to safeguard the assets of the business. The manual should address the following aspects of internal control:

1. Assign responsibilities among the group members.
2. Authorize individuals, including group members and any outsiders that you need to hire to perform specific jobs.
3. Separate duties among the group and any employees.
4. Describe all documents needed to account for and safeguard the business's assets.

Quick Check Answers

1. *g, c, e, both d and f, a, b, h;*
   Unused: i

2. *a*

3. *b*

4. *b*

5. *a*

6. *d*

7. *d*

8. *e*

9. *c*

10. *d*

11. *c*

5 Short-Term Investments & Receivables

➤ **SPOTLIGHT:** Amazing Apple! Short-term investments and accounts receivable are 37 times as large as inventories!

How do you manage your busy life? You may use any of thousands of applications ("Apps") on a device made by Apple, Inc. Apple is a U.S.-based multinational corporation that designs, manufactures, and markets highly innovative and reliable consumer electronics and related peripheral equipment and software. The company sells its products worldwide through its retail stores, online stores, and direct sales force, as well as through third-party cellular network carriers, wholesalers, retailers, and value-added resellers. Sales of iPad, iPhone, iPod, and AppleTV products, along with the company's popular Macbook and iMac notebook computers, have generated hundreds of billions of dollars in profits for the company over the past decade, much of it in cold hard cash! You may be surprised to find that Apple, Inc., has not spent a great deal of this cash. In fact, according to the company's balance sheet at September 29, 2012 (see excerpt on the next page), much of that cash ($18.4 billion) went no further than the next category down the balance sheet—to short-term investments in marketable securities. In addition, company sales have also generated almost $11 billion in net accounts receivable. The company holds another $10.7 billion in cash and cash equivalents (another kind of short-term investment discussed in Chapter 4).

As Apple is a manufacturer, you might expect that inventories would comprise the largest single current asset account on its balance sheet, as is the case for many manufacturing companies. However, a closer look at the balance sheet shows that cash and cash equivalents, short-term marketable securities, and accounts receivable account for over $40 billion of its $57.7 billion in current assets. That's almost 70%. These liquid assets literally dwarf inventories. Short-term marketable securities and net accounts receivable together are 37 times as large as inventories! ●

Darrin Jenkins/Alamy

A1				
	A	**B**	**C**	**D**
1	Apple, Inc. Balance Sheet (Excerpt, Adapted)			
2	(In Millions of $)	Sep. 29, 2012	Sep. 24, 2011	
3	Current assets:			
4	Cash and cash equivalents	$ 10,746	$ 9,815	
5	Short-term marketable securities	18,383	16,137	
6	Accounts receivable, less allowances of $98 and $53,			
7	respectively	10,930	5,369	
8	Inventories	791	776	
9	Deferred tax assets	2,583	2,014	
10	Vendor non-trade receivables	7,762	6,348	
11	Other current assets	6,458	4,529	
12	Total current assets	57,653	44,988	
13	Long-term marketable securities	92,122	55,618	
14	Property, plant, and equipment, net	15,452	7,777	
15	Goodwill	1,135	896	
16	Acquired intangible assets, net	4,224	3,536	
17	Other assets	5,478	3,556	
18	Total assets	$ 176,064	$ 116,371	
19				

Try It in Excel

You can access the most current annual report of Apple, Inc., in Excel format at **www.sec.gov**. Using the "filings" link on the toolbar at the top of the home page, select "company filings search." This will take you to the "EDGAR Company Filings" page. Type "Apple" in the company name box, and select "search." This will produce the "EDGAR Search Results" page showing the company name. Click on the "CIK" link beside the company name. This will pull up all of the reports the company has filed with the SEC. Under the "filing type" box, type "10-K," and click on the search box. Form 10-K is the SEC form for the company's latest annual report. Find the year that you wish to view. Click on the "Interactive Data" box, which takes you to the "View Filing Data" page. Find and click on the "View Excel Document" link at the top of this page. You may choose to either open or download the Excel files containing the company's most recent financial statements. ■

This chapter shows how to account for short-term investments and receivables. We cover short-term investments along with receivables to emphasize their relative liquidity. Short-term investments are the next-most-liquid current assets after cash and cash equivalents. (Recall that *liquid* means "close to cash.")

Learning Objectives

1. **Account for** short-term investments

2. **Apply** GAAP for proper revenue recognition

3. **Account for and control** accounts receivable

4. **Evaluate** collectibility using the allowance for uncollectible accounts

5. **Account for** notes receivable

6. **Show** how to speed up cash flow from receivables

7. **Evaluate** liquidity using two new ratios

ACCOUNT FOR SHORT-TERM INVESTMENTS

Reasons to Invest in Other Companies

Companies invest in debt or equity securities of other companies for at least two reasons:

1 **Account for short-term investments**

1. They may have excess cash that they do not need immediately, and so they invest on a short-term basis in equity or debt securities in other companies, hoping to earn additional income to eventually use in operations; and/or

2. They may have long-term strategic reasons for investing, such as obtaining the ability to influence another company. For example, a company might acquire an investment in a supplier in order to obtain a steady stream of good quality, reasonably priced raw material to use in production.

Investments in debt or equity securities may be classified as either short-term or long-term. Short-term investments are reported as current assets on a company's balance sheet, and long-term investments are classified as long-term assets. To be classified as a current asset, an investment must meet *both* of the following criteria:

- The investment must be *liquid* (easily convertible to cash); and
- The investor must *intend* to either convert the investment to cash within one year or current operating cycle, whichever is longer, or use it to pay a current liability.

Otherwise, the investment is classified as a long-term asset.

Investments in securities are classified into three categories, as shown in Exhibit 5-1. These categories are (1) **trading securities**, (2) **held-to-maturity securities**, and (3) **available-for-sale securities**.

- *Trading securities* are debt (bonds, notes, etc.) or equity (stock) investments purchased and expected to be sold within the near term through active trading. These securities generate income or losses on a day-to-day basis through changes in their prices.
- *Available-for-sale securities* are debt or equity securities that are not classified as either trading or held-to-maturity. They are held with the intent of selling them some time in the future.

Exhibit 5-1 | Categories of Investments in Securities

Type of security	Trading (1)	Available-for-Sale (2)	(3)	Held-to-Maturity (4)	(5)
Asset classification	Current	Current	Long-term	Current	Long-term
Initial measurement	Cost	Cost	Cost	Cost	Cost
Subsequent measurement	Fair value	Fair value	Fair value	Amortized cost	Amortized cost
Unrealized gains/losses	Income statement (other income, gains and losses)	Other comprehensive income (OCI)	Other comprehensive income (OCI)	N/A	N/A
Chapter	5	5	8	8	8

■ *Held-to-maturity securities* are debt securities (bonds, notes, or other instruments with established maturity dates) that the investor has the intent and ability to hold until they mature.

Any of these categories of investments may be classified as a current asset, as long as it meets both of the stated criteria on page 247. However, of the three categories, only trading securities are always classified as current assets.

Let's examine how Apple, Inc., describes its investments (from Note 1, *Summary of Significant Accounting Policies*):

Cash Equivalents and Marketable Securities

All highly liquid investments with maturities of three months or less at the date of purchase are classified as cash equivalents. The Company's marketable debt and equity securities have been classified and accounted for as available-for-sale. Management determines the appropriate classification of its investments at the time of purchase and reevaluates the designations at each balance sheet date. The Company classifies its marketable debt securities as either short-term or long-term based on each instrument's underlying contractual maturity date. Marketable debt securities with maturities of 12 months or less are classified as short-term and marketable debt securities with maturities greater than 12 months are classified as long-term. The Company classifies its marketable equity securities, including mutual funds, as either short-term or long-term based on the nature of each security and its availability for use in current operations. The Company's marketable debt and equity securities are carried at fair value, with the unrealized gains and losses, net of taxes, reported as a component of shareholders' equity. The cost of securities sold is based upon the specific identification method.

Applying this explanation to the line items in the balance sheet, notice that it encompasses securities in three of the line items:

■ Line 4, "cash and cash equivalents," $10,746 million, includes a portfolio of debt securities with maturities of three months or less. These were discussed in Chapter 4.

■ Line 5, "short-term marketable securities," $18,383 million, includes a portfolio of both debt and equity securities that are classified as available-for-sale, as described in Note 1. These are current assets because they meet the criteria of being both highly liquid and the company intends to convert them to cash within the next operating cycle. However, the company has chosen not to treat them as trading securities because they do not trade them on a daily basis.

■ Line 13, "long-term marketable securities," $92,122 million, includes a portfolio of investment assets that does not meet at least one of the criteria for being classified as current. The company has made these investments for long-term strategic purposes. It does not plan to sell these investments within the next fiscal year.

Notice that cash and investment assets on these three line items together comprise $121.3 billion, or 68.9% of Apple, Inc.'s total assets as of September 29, 2012!

In this chapter, we discuss how companies measure and report investments in trading securities and available-for-sale securities that meet the criteria for inclusion in current assets. These are listed in columns (1) and (2) of Exhibit 5-1. We reserve the discussion of other types of available-for-sale securities, as well as long-term held-to-maturity securities, until Chapter 8.

Trading Securities

Suppose that, on June 18, 2014, Apple, Inc., purchases 5,000 shares of **Intel** stock as a trading security, intending to trade (sell) the stock on the active market within a few months. If the fair value of the Intel stock increases, Apple, Inc., will have a gain; if Intel's stock price drops, Apple, Inc., will have a loss. Along the way, Apple, Inc., will receive dividend revenue from Intel.

For simplicity, suppose first that the Intel stock is Apple, Inc.'s only short-term investment. Apple, Inc., buys the Intel stock during 2014 for $20 per share, paying $100,000 cash. Apple, Inc., records the purchase of the investment at cost:

	A1				
	A	**B**		**C**	**D**
1	2014				
2	June 18	Investment in Trading Securities		100,000	
3		Cash			100,000
4		Purchased investment.			
5					

Investment in Trading Securities

100,000 |

Assume that, on June 30, Apple, Inc., receives a cash dividend of $4,000 from Intel. Apple, Inc., records the dividend revenue as:

	A1				
	A	**B**		**C**	**D**
1	June 30	Cash		4,000	
2		Dividend Revenue			4,000
3		Received cash dividend.			
4					

Assets	=	Liabilities	+	Stockholders' Equity	+	Revenues
+ 4,000	=				+	4,000

Unrealized Gains and Losses. Apple, Inc.'s 2014 fiscal year ends on September 27, and Apple, Inc., prepares financial statements. On this date, the fair market value of Intel's stock is $22. The Intel stock has risen in value, and on September 27, Apple, Inc.'s investment has a current fair value of $110,000. Fair (market) value is the amount for which the owner can sell the securities. Apple, Inc., has an **unrealized gain** on the investment:

- *Gain* because the fair value ($110,000) of the portfolio of securities is greater than Apple, Inc.'s cost of the securities ($100,000). A gain has the same effect as a revenue.

- *Unrealized gain* because Apple, Inc., has not yet sold the securities.

Trading securities are reported on the balance sheet at current fair value, because fair (market) value is the amount the investor can receive by selling the securities. Prior to preparing financial statements on September 27, 2014, Apple, Inc., adjusts the investment in Intel securities to its current fair value with this year-end journal entry:

	A1				
	A	**B**		**C**	**D**
1	Sept 27	Investment in Trading Securities		10,000	
2		Unrealized Gain on Trading Securities			10,000
3		Adjusted investment to fair value.			
4					

Investment in Trading Securities

100,000 |
10,000 |
110,000 |

Unrealized Gain on Trading Securities (other income)

| 10,000

After the adjustment, Apple, Inc.'s Investment in Trading Securities account, reflecting its investment in Intel stock, is ready to be reported on the balance sheet at the current fair value of $110,000.

Suppose that Apple, Inc., decides to keep the Intel stock for another year, even though the company still regards the stock as a trading security. During 2015, the Intel stock declines in value. On September 26, 2015, the end of Apple, Inc.'s fiscal year, the fair value of Intel stock is $21 per share. In preparation for its 2015 balance sheet, Apple, Inc., makes the following adjusting entry:

	A1	⬦			
	A	**B**		**C**	**D**
1	2015				
2	Sept 26	Unrealized Loss on Trading Securities		5,000	
3		Investment in Trading Securities			5,000
4		*Adjusted investment to fair value.*			
5					

Investment in Trading Securities		Unrealized Loss on Trading Securities (other income)
100,000	5,000	5,000
10,000		
105,000		

Unrealized gains and losses on trading securities are reported as elements of "other income or losses" in the income statement, as shown in Exhibit 5-1.

At the end of each period, because they are reported on the income statement, unrealized gains and losses on trading securities are closed along with other revenue and expense accounts and eventually become a part of retained earnings on the balance sheet. In our case, an unrealized gain of $10,000 is reported on 2014's income statement and is closed to retained earnings at the end of that year. In 2015, an unrealized loss is reported on 2015's income statement and is closed to retained earnings at the end of that year. Thus, the company's retained earnings balance at the end of 2015 includes a net $5,000 unrealized gain from the Intel stock ($10,000 unrealized gain in 2014 − $5,000 unrealized loss in 2015).

Realized Gains and Losses. A *realized* gain or loss occurs only when the investor sells an investment. This gain or loss is different from the unrealized gain that we just reported for Apple, Inc. The result may be:

- Realized gain = Sale price is *greater than* the Investment carrying amount.
- Realized loss = Sale price is *less than* the Investment carrying amount.

Suppose Apple, Inc., sells its Intel stock on June 19, 2016. The sale price is $107,000, and Apple, Inc., makes this journal entry:

	A1	⬦			
	A	**B**		**C**	**D**
1	2016				
2	June 19	Cash		107,000	
3		Investment in Trading Securities			105,000
4		Gain on Sale of Trading Securities (other income)			2,000
5		*Sold investments at a gain.*			
6					

Accountants rarely use the word *realized* in the account title. A gain (or a loss) is understood to be a realized gain (or loss) arising from a sale transaction. Unrealized gains and losses are clearly labeled as *unrealized*.

Available-for-Sale Securities. Exhibit 5-2, Part A, contrasts the journal entries for Apple, Inc.'s hypothetical investment in Intel stock under two alternative sets of assumptions: (1) the securities are treated as trading securities; and (2) the securities are treated as available-for-sale securities.

We have already illustrated the journal entries under the assumption of the Intel stock being treated as a trading security. Now focus on the right-hand side of Exhibit 5-2. Entry 1 in 2014 for the initial purchase of available-for-sale securities is the same as it is for trading securities, except for the investment account title. In addition, accounting for periodic dividend revenue (entry 2) in 2014 for available-for-sale securities is identical to the entry for trading securities. However, the year-end adjustment in 2014 and 2015 to fair value (entries 3 and 4) for available-for-sale

Exhibit 5-2 | Accounting and Reporting for Short-Term Investments and Related Revenues, Gains, and Losses

Entry	Trading Securities (TS)			Available-for-Sale Securities (AFSS)		
	Part A. Journal Entries					
1	Purchase in 2014	Investment in TS..........................	100,000	Investment in AFSS..........................	100,000	
	($100,000 cash)	Cash......................................		100,000	Cash......................................		100,000
2	Receipt of dividends	Cash..	4,000	Cash..	4,000	
	$ 4,000	Dividend Revenue.................		4,000	Dividend Revenue....................		4,000
3	Year-end adjustment 2014 (unrealized gain $10,000)					
		Investment in TS*.......................	10,000	Investment in AFSS*.........................	10,000	
		Unrealized Gain on TS (other income)...............		10,000	Unrealized Gain on Investment in AFSS (OCI).........		10,000
4	Year-end adjustment 2015 (unrealized loss $5,000)					
		Unrealized Loss on TS (other loss)................................	5,000	Unrealized Gain on Investment in AFSS (OCI)................	5,000	
		Investment in TS.................		5,000	Investment in AFSS..................		5,000
5	Sale in 2016	Cash..	107,000	Cash..	107,000	
	($107,000 cash)	Investment in TS..................		105,000	Unrealized Gain on Investment in AFSS (OCI)................	5,000	
		Gain on Sale of TS (other income).....................		2,000	Investment in AFSS..................		105,000
					Gain on Sale of Investment in AFSS..................................		7,000

	Part B. Financial Reporting						
	Trading Securities (TS)				Available-for-Sale Securities (AFSS)		
Balance sheet	2014	2015	2016		2014	2015	2016
Assets				**Assets**			
Investment in TS......................................	110,000	105,000	0	Investment in AFSS......................	110,000	105,000	0
				Stockholders' equity			
				Accumulated OCI (other comprehensive income)......	10,000	5,000	0
Income statement	2014	2015	2016		2014	2015	2016
Dividend revenue......................	4,000	0	0		4,000	0	0
Unrealized gain (loss)................	10,000	(5,000)	0		0	0	0
Realized gain on sale................	0	0	2,000		0	0	7,000

*Many companies use an allowance account to record upward and downward movements in fair value of the investment, enabling them to maintain the original cost information for the security. The allowance account is added to (subtracted from) cost to reflect fair value on the balance sheet.

securities is different than it is for trading securities. Although the investment adjustment (a debit of $10,000 in 2014 and a credit of $5,000 in 2015) is the same, the offsetting unrealized gains and losses on available-for-sale securities are not reported as other income or other loss in the income statement for those years. Instead, they are reported as **other comprehensive income (loss)** for each period and are accumulated separately over time as **accumulated other comprehensive income (loss)**, which is a separate component of stockholders' equity. This is because an available-for-sale security, even if it is classified as short-term, is typically not sold as quickly or frequently as a trading security. So, prior to the actual sale, it is more likely that previously recorded unrealized gains and losses may be reversed for available-for-sale securities. These unrealized gains and losses are kept separate and are not reflected as part of net income of any period, as long as the securities remain unsold.

When the securities are sold in 2016 (entry 5), the unrealized gain or loss account remaining for the available-for-sale securities is eliminated from both the investment account and accumulated other comprehensive income. This entry returns the investment back to its original cost, which is then matched against the sales proceeds to calculate the realized gain or loss on the sale (in this case, a $7,000 gain). The terms "other comprehensive income" and "accumulated other comprehensive income" are discussed more thoroughly in Chapters 8, 10, and 11.

Reporting on the Balance Sheet and the Income Statement

Exhibit 5-2, Part B, illustrates the proper way to report investments in both trading and available-for-sale securities on the balance sheet and income statement.

The Balance Sheet. Short-term investments are current assets. They appear on the balance sheet immediately after cash because short-term investments are almost as liquid as cash. Report both short-term trading investments and short-term available-for-sale investments at their *current fair (market) values*.

For available-for-sale investments, report unrealized gains and losses as an element of other comprehensive income, which, over time, is accumulated in a separate section of stockholders' equity. In our simple case with only one stock, the balance in accumulated other comprehensive income at the end of 2015 is $5,000 and is the result of a $10,000 increase in 2014 offset by a $5,000 decrease in 2015. This balance is zeroed out when the securities are sold in 2016. The investment account ($105,000) is restored to original cost ($100,000) at this point so that it may be matched against the proceeds of the sale to reflect the realized gain or loss ($7,000).

Income Statement. Investments in debt and equity securities earn interest revenue and dividend revenue. Investments also create both unrealized and realized gains and losses. For trading investments, these items are reported on the income statement as other revenue, gains, and losses, reported in the periods in which they occur. For available-for-sale investments, dividends are reported in the same way as for trading securities, and realized gains and losses are recognized in other revenue, gains, and losses as the securities are sold. Notice that, regardless of whether the securities are treated as trading or available-for-sale, the impact on reported earnings over the three-year period is the same (+10,000 − $5,000 + $2,000 in 2014, 2015, and 2016, respectively, for trading versus $7,000 in 2016 for available-for-sale). The only difference between the two classification methods is in the timing (the period in which the net gains or losses are recognized on the income statement).

Ethics and the Current Ratio

Recall that the current ratio is computed as follows:

$$\text{Current ratio} = \frac{\text{Total current assets}}{\text{Total current liabilities}}$$

Lending agreements often require the borrower to maintain a current ratio at some specified level, say 1.50 or greater. What happens when the borrower's current ratio falls below 1.50? The consequences can be severe:

- The lender can call the loan for immediate payment.
- If the borrower cannot pay, then the lender may take over the company.

Suppose it's December 10 and it looks like Health Corporation of America's (HCA's) current ratio will end the year at a value of 1.48. That would put HCA in default on the lending agreement and create a bad situation. With three weeks remaining in the year, how can HCA improve its current ratio?

There are several strategies for increasing the current ratio, such as:

1. Launch a major sales effort. The increase in cash and receivables will more than offset the decrease in inventory, total current assets will increase, and the current ratio will improve.

2. Pay off some current liabilities before year-end. Both current assets in the numerator and current liabilities in the denominator will decrease by the same amount. The proportionate impact on current liabilities in the denominator will be greater than the impact on current assets in the numerator, and the current ratio will increase. This strategy increases the current ratio when the current ratio is already above 1.0, as it is for HCA.

3. A third strategy reveals one of the accounting games that companies with questionable ethics sometimes play. Suppose HCA owns some investments that it clearly plans to hold for strategic reasons for longer than a year. Suppose the company chooses to reclassify a sufficient amount of these as current assets for the sole purpose of increasing the current ratio to an acceptable level. This strategy would be acceptable if HCA does in fact plan to sell the investments within the next year. However, such a strategy would be unethical if HCA does it solely for the purpose of beefing up its current ratio.

From this example you can see that accounting is not all black-and-white. It takes good judgment—which includes a strong sense of ethics—to become a successful accountant.

⟩⟩ Mid-Chapter Summary Problem

The largest current asset on Waverly Corporation's balance sheet is Investment in Trading Securities. The investments consist of stock in other corporations and cost Waverly $8,660 (amounts in millions). At the balance sheet date, the fair value of these securities is $9,000.

Suppose Waverly holds the stock investments in the hope of trading them actively for a profit and converting them to cash within four to six months. How will Waverly classify the investments? What will Waverly report on the balance sheet at December 31, 2014? What will Waverly report on its 2014 income statement? Show a T-account for Investment in Trading Securities.

Answer

Investment in Trading Securities	
8,660	
340	
Balance 9,000	

These investments in trading securities are *current assets* as reported on the 2014 balance sheet, and Waverly's 2014 income statement will report as follows (amounts in millions):

Balance sheet		Income statement	
Current assets:		Other revenue and expense:	
Cash......................................	$ XX	Unrealized Gain on Trading Securities	
Investment in		($9,000 − $8,660)	$ 340
Trading Securities............	9,000		

Suppose Waverly sells the investment in securities for $8,700 in 2015. Journalize the sale and then show the Investment in Trading Securities T-account as it appears after the sale.

Answer

	(In millions)
Cash	8,700
Loss on Sale of Trading Securities...	300
Investment in Trading Securities	9,000
Sold investments at a loss.	

Investment in Trading Securities

8,660	
340	9,000

APPLY GAAP FOR PROPER REVENUE RECOGNITION

2 Apply GAAP for proper revenue recognition

A study of accounts and notes receivable would not be complete without a brief review of the principles of revenue recognition, which is the basis for accounts and notes receivable. Recall from the discussion of the revenue principle in Chapter 3 that revenue should be recognized when it is earned, and not before. Revenue recognition is proper when (or as) the entity satisfies the performance obligations in a contract. In other words, the entity has done everything required to earn the revenue by transferring the good or service to the customer, and when the customer has assumed ownership and control over goods or the service, the provider has substantially completed the service. In addition, the price of the goods or services is fixed or determinable, and collection is reasonably assured. The amount of the revenue to be recognized is the cash value of the goods or services transferred from the seller to the buyer.

For example, assume Apple, Inc., delivers a truckload of iPhones to an AT&T Wireless warehouse in Florida. On the truck are 30,000 iPhone 6s, each of which Apple, Inc., sells to AT&T Wireless for $100 on account. The amount of Apple, Inc.'s sale to AT&T Wireless is $3,000,000. At the point when Apple, Inc., delivers the phones to the warehouse, it fulfills its contract to supply the goods, and simultaneously, AT&T Wireless assumes ownership and acquires the obligation to pay for the iPhones. Apple, Inc., records the following transaction[1]:

	A1			C	D
	A	**B**		**C**	**D**
1		Accounts Receivable		3,000,000	
2		Sales Revenue			3,000,000
3		*To record sale of 30,000 iPhone 6s.*			
4					

---

[1]In this example, we ignore the cost of the product to Apple, Inc., which is accounted for both at the point of sale and the point of return. We will discuss this further when we cover inventories and cost of goods sold in Chapter 6.

The timing and amount of revenue recognized is determined by the shipping terms and payment incentives offered to the buyer by the seller.

Shipping Terms, Sales Discounts, and Sales Returns

Shipping Terms. The proper time to recognize sales revenue is often when ownership of goods changes hands between the seller and the buyer. This point is determined by the **shipping terms** in the sales contract. When goods are shipped **FOB (free on board)** *shipping point,* ownership changes hands and revenue is recognized at the point when the goods leave the seller's shipping dock. When goods are shipped FOB *destination*, ownership changes hands and revenue is recognized at the point of delivery to the customer.

Sales Discounts. Sometimes businesses offer customers **sales discounts** for early payment in order to speed up cash flow. A typical sales discount incentive might be stated as:

2/10, n/30

This expression means that the seller is willing to discount the order by 2% if the buyer pays the invoice within 10 days of the invoice date. After that time, the seller withdraws the discount offer. Regardless, the buyer *must* pay within 30 days. In the case of Apple, Inc.'s sale to AT&T Wireless, if AT&T Wireless pays the invoice within 10 days, it is entitled to a $60,000 discount, making the full amount due to settle Apple, Inc.'s invoice $2,940,000 rather than $3,000,000. The transaction to record the collection of this receivable would be as follows:

	A	B	C	D
		A1		
1		Cash	2,940,000	
2		Sales Discount	60,000	
3		Accounts Receivable		3,000,000
4		*To record collection of credit sale less 2% discount.*		
5				

Companies with plenty of cash often take advantage of early payment discounts on their purchases, thus adding to their reported profits and cash flows.

Sales Returns and Allowances. Consumers usually have a right to return unsatisfactory or damaged merchandise to the retailer for a refund or exchange. This is called a **sales return or allowance**. Retailers keep track of sales returns over time to make sure they are not excessive. Returned merchandise means lost profits. For example, suppose that of the 30,000 iPhones Apple, Inc., sells to AT&T Wireless, 100 are returned (or Apple, Inc., grants AT&T Wireless an allowance) because they are damaged in shipment. Apple, Inc., would record the following entry:

	A	B	C	D
		A1		
1		Sales Returns and Allowances	10,000	
2		Accounts Receivable		10,000
3		*To record return of 100 iPhones to vendor.*		
4				

Retailers, wholesalers, and manufacturers typically disclose sales revenue at the *net* amount, which means after sales discounts and sales returns and allowances have been subtracted. Using hypothetical data for discounts and returns, Apple, Inc.'s net sales (revenue) for 2012, compared with the last two years, is:

	A	B	C	D
	Apple, Inc. **(2012, Adapted)**			
1				
2	(in millions of $)			
3	Gross revenue	$ 159,390		
4	— Sales discounts	(2,390)		
5	— Sales returns and allowances	(492)		
6	= Net revenue	$ 156,508		
7				
8		2012	2011	2010
9	Net revenue (in millions)	$ 156,508	$ 108,249	$ 65,225
10				

ACCOUNT FOR AND CONTROL ACCOUNTS RECEIVABLE

3 **Account for and control** accounts receivable

Receivables are the third most liquid asset—after cash and short-term investments. Most of the remainder of this chapter shows how to account for receivables.

Types of Receivables

Receivables are monetary claims against others. Receivables are acquired mainly by selling goods and services (accounts receivable) and by lending money (notes receivable). The journal entries to record the receivables are

Performing a Service on Account		Lending Money on a Note Receivable	
Accounts Receivable....................	XXX	Notes Receivable.........................	XXX
Service Revenue......................	XXX	Cash..	XXX
Performed a service on account.		*Loaned money to another company.*	

The two major types of receivables are accounts receivable and notes receivable. A business's *accounts receivable* are the amounts collectible from customers from the sale of goods and services. Accounts receivable, which are *current assets*, are sometimes called *trade receivables* or merely *receivables*.

The Accounts Receivable account in the general ledger serves as a *control account* that summarizes the total amount receivable from all customers. Companies also keep a *subsidiary ledger* of accounts receivable with a separate account for each customer:

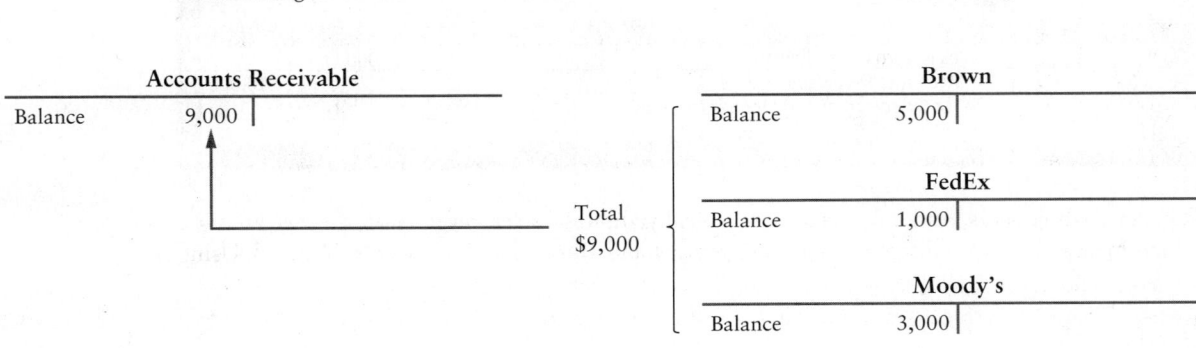

Notes receivable are more formal contracts than accounts receivable. For a note, the borrower signs a written promise to pay the lender a definite sum at the maturity date, plus interest. This is why notes are also called promissory notes. The note may require the borrower to pledge *security* for the loan. This means that the borrower gives the lender permission to claim certain assets, called *collateral*, if the borrower fails to pay the amount due. We cover the details of notes receivable later in this chapter.

Other receivables is a miscellaneous category for all receivables other than accounts receivable and notes receivable. Examples include interest receivable and advances to employees.

Internal Controls Over Cash Collections on Account

Businesses that sell on credit receive most of their cash receipts from collections of accounts receivable. Internal control over collections on account is important. Chapter 4 discusses control procedures for cash receipts, but another element of internal control deserves emphasis here—the separation of cash-handling and cash-accounting duties. Consider the following case:

> Central Paint Company is a small, family-owned business that takes pride in the loyalty of its workers. Most employees have been with Central for 10 or more years. The company makes 90% of its sales on account and receives most of its cash by mail.
>
> The office staff consists of a bookkeeper and an office supervisor. The bookkeeper maintains the general ledger and a subsidiary record of individual customer accounts receivable. The bookkeeper also makes the daily bank deposit.
>
> The supervisor prepares monthly financial statements and any special reports the company needs. The supervisor also takes sales orders from customers and serves as office manager.

Can you identify the internal control weakness here? The problem is that the bookkeeper makes the bank deposit. Remember the Mid-Atlantic Manufacturing case in Chapter 4? With this cash-handling duty, the bookkeeper could lap accounts receivable. Alternatively, he or she could steal an incoming customer check and write off the customer's account as uncollectible. The customer doesn't complain because the bookkeeper wrote off the customer's account, and Central therefore stops pursuing collection.

How can this weakness be corrected? The supervisor—not the bookkeeper—could open incoming mail and make the daily bank deposit. The bookkeeper should *not* be allowed to handle cash. Only the remittance advices should be forwarded to the bookkeeper to credit customer accounts receivable. Removing cash handling from the bookkeeper and keeping the accounts away from the supervisor separates duties and strengthens internal control.

Using a bank lockbox achieves the same separation of duties. Customers send their payments directly to a post office box owned by Central Paint Company's bank, which records cash as the cash goes into Central's bank account. The bank then forwards the remittance advice to Central's bookkeeper, who credits the customer account. No Central Paint employee even touches incoming cash.

How Do We Manage the Risk of Not Collecting?

In Chapters 1 to 4, we use many different companies to illustrate how to account for a business. Chapter 1 began with The Gap, Inc., a quality casual clothing chain, that sells clothes and accessories through a network of company-operated stores, as well as through its website. Consumer sales from company-owned stores are largely for cash, which includes credit card sales. Other exclusively retail businesses such as J. Crew and Whole Foods Market, Inc., make almost all their sales in cash. However, Apple, Inc., besides having its own retail outlet stores, also makes sales to independent distributors, such as AT&T Wireless. These sales are on credit, generating accounts receivable. Apple, Inc.'s balance sheet at September 29, 2012, reflects $10,930 million in accounts receivable, accounting for about 19% of the company's current assets. Chapter 3's opening vignette featured Starbucks Corporation. As of September 30, 2012, Starbucks Corporation held $486 million in receivables, which amounts to about 11.6% of its current assets (page 144).

By selling on credit, companies run the risk of not collecting some receivables. Unfortunately, some customers don't pay their debts. The prospect of failing to collect from a customer provides the biggest challenge in accounting for receivables. The Decision Guidelines address this challenge.

❯ Decision Guidelines

Managing and Accounting for Receivables

Here are the management and accounting issues a business faces when the company extends credit to customers. For each issue, the Decision Guidelines propose a plan of action. Let's look at a business situation: Suppose you open a health club near your college. Assume you will let customers use the club and bill them for their monthly dues. What challenges will you encounter by extending credit to customers?

The main issues in *managing* receivables, along with plans of action, are the following:

Issues	Plan of Action
1. What are the benefits and the costs of extending credit to customers?	1. Benefit—Increase in sales. Cost—Risk of not collecting.
2. Run a credit check on prospective customers.	2. Extend credit only to creditworthy customers.
3. Design the internal control system to separate duties.	3. Separate cash-handling and accounting duties to keep employees from stealing the cash collected from customers.
4. Keep a close eye on customer payment habits. Send second and third statements to slow-paying customers, if necessary.	4. Pursue collection from customers to maximize cash flow.

The main issues in accounting for receivables (amounts are assumed), and the related plans of action, are the following:

Issues	Plan of Action
1. Measure and report receivables on the balance sheet at net realizable value, the amount you expect to collect. This is the appropriate amount to report for receivables.	Report receivables at net realizable value: **Balance sheet** Receivables... $1,000 Less: Allowance for uncollectible accounts... (80) Receivables, net... $ 920
2. Measure and report the expense associated with failure to collect receivables. This expense is called *uncollectible-account expense* and is reported on the income statement.	Measure the expense of not collecting from customers: **Income statement** Sales (or service) revenue.............................. $8,000 Expenses: Uncollectible-account expense.................. 190

These guidelines lead to our next topic, accounting for uncollectible receivables.

EVALUATE COLLECTIBILITY USING THE ALLOWANCE FOR UNCOLLECTIBLE ACCOUNTS

4 **Evaluate** collectibility using the allowance for uncollectible accounts

A company acquires an account receivable only when it sells its product or service on credit (on account). You'll recall that the entry to record the earning of revenue on account is (amount assumed):

	A	B	C	D
1		Accounts Receivable	1,000	
2		Sales Revenue (or Service Revenue)		1,000
3		*Earned revenue on account.*		
4				

Ideally, the company would collect cash for all of its receivables. But unfortunately the entry to record cash collections on account is only for $950.

	A	B	C	D
1		Cash	950	
2		Accounts Receivable		950
3		*Collections on account.*		
4				

You can see that companies rarely collect all of their accounts receivable. So companies must account for their uncollectible accounts—$50 in this example. Selling on credit creates both a benefit and a cost:

- *Benefit:* Customers who cannot pay cash immediately can buy on credit, so sales and profits increase.

- *Cost:* The company cannot collect from some customers. Accountants label this cost **uncollectible-account expense, doubtful-account expense**, or **bad-debt expense**.

Apple, Inc., reports accounts receivable as follows on its 2012 balance sheet (in millions):

	Sep. 29, 2012	Sep. 24, 2011
Accounts receivable, less allowances of $98 and $53, respectively	$10,930	$5,369

The phrase "less allowances" means that a relatively small amount ($98 million, or less than 1% of the total) has been subtracted from total accounts receivable, representing the amount that Apple, Inc., does *not* expect to collect. Sometimes the amount of the allowance is not considered sufficiently material to separately disclose in the line item, so it is disclosed in an explanatory financial statement footnote and the line item in the balance sheet simply says "accounts receivable, net." Apple, Inc.'s net amount of the receivables ($10,930 million) is the amount that Apple, Inc., *does* expect to collect in cash receipts. Notice that the net amount of receivables more than doubled during the current year (from $5,369 million to $10,930 million) while the allowance amount almost doubled (from $53 million to $98 million).

Uncollectible-account expense is an operating expense in the selling, general, and administrative category along with salaries, rent, and utilities. To measure uncollectible-account expense, companies that follow GAAP use the allowance method.

Allowance Method

The best way to measure uncollectible accounts expense (bad debts) is by the **allowance method**. This method records losses from failure to collect receivables based on estimates developed from the company's collection experience. Apple, Inc., doesn't wait to see which customers will not pay. Instead, it records the estimated amount as Uncollectible-Account Expense and also sets up a contra-account to accounts receivable called **Allowance for Uncollectible Accounts**. In doing so, Apple follows the expense recognition principle discussed in Chapter 3, by matching the expense related to non-collection in the same period that the related sales revenue is recognized. On the balance sheet, the Allowance for Uncollectible Accounts reduces gross receivables to their net realizable value. Other titles for this account are **Allowance for Doubtful Accounts** and *Allowance for Bad Debts*. The allowance shows the amount of the receivables the business expects *not* to collect.

In Chapter 3 we used the Accumulated Depreciation account to show the amount of a plant asset's cost that has been expensed—the portion of the asset that's no longer a benefit to the company. Allowance for Uncollectible Accounts serves a similar purpose for Accounts Receivable.

The allowance shows how much of the receivable has been expensed. You'll find this diagram helpful (amounts are assumed):

Equipment.............................	$100,000	Accounts receivable.....................	$10,000
Less: Accumulated		Less: Allowance for	
depreciation	(40,000)	uncollectible accounts	(900)
Equipment, net...................	60,000	Accounts receivable, net.............	9,100

Focus on Accounts Receivable. Customers owe this company $10,000, but it expects to collect only $9,100. The *net realizable value* of the receivables is therefore $9,100. Another way to report these receivables is as follows:

Accounts receivable, less allowance of $900.................	$9,100

You can work backward to determine the full amount of the receivables, $10,000 (net realizable value of $9,100 plus the allowance of $900).

The income statement reports Uncollectible-Account Expense among the operating expenses, using assumed figures, as:

Income statement (partial):

Expenses:

Uncollectible-account expense:...............	$2,000

> Stop & Think...

Refer to the Apple, Inc., balance sheet at the beginning of the chapter. At September 29, 2012, how much in total did customers owe Apple, Inc.? How much did Apple, Inc., expect *not* to collect? How much did Apple, Inc., expect to collect? What was the net realizable value of Apple, Inc.'s receivables?

Answer:

	Millions
Customers owed Apple, Inc.	$11,028 ($10,930 + $98)
Apple, Inc. expected not to collect the allowance of....	(98)
Apple, Inc. expected to collect—net realizable value ...	$10,930

Notice that to determine the *total* (*gross*) amount customers owed, you have to add the amount of the allowance back to the "net realizable value" ($10,930 million + $98 million = $11,028 million). Of this amount, $98 million was expected not to be collected, leaving $10,930 million that the company expected to collect (i.e., its net realizable value). Although the gross amount is not shown in the financial statements, it is useful for analysis purposes, as shown on pages 265–266.

The best way to estimate uncollectibles uses the company's history of collections from customers. There are two basic ways to estimate uncollectibles:

- Percent-of-sales method
- Aging-of-receivables method

Percent-of-Sales. The **percent-of-sales method** computes uncollectible-account expense as a percent of revenue.[2] This method takes an *income-statement approach* because it focuses on the amount of expense to be reported on the income statement. Assume it is September 29, 2012, and Apple, Inc.'s accounts have these balances *before the year-end adjustments* (amounts in millions):

Accounts Receivable		Allowance for Uncollectible Accounts	
11,028			10

Customers owe Apple, Inc., $11,028 million, and the Allowance amount on the books is $10 million. But Apple, Inc.'s top managers know that the company will fail to collect more than $10 million. Suppose Apple, Inc.'s credit department estimates that uncollectible-account expense is 0.0005 (1/20 of 1%) of total revenues, which are $156,508 million. The entry that records uncollectible-account expense for the year also updates the allowance as follows (using Apple, Inc., figures):

	A	B	C	D
	A1			
1	Sep. 29	Uncollectible-Account Expense ($156,508 × .0005)	78	
2		Allowance for Uncollectible Accounts		78
3		*Recorded uncollectible account expense for the year.*		
4		*Calculations rounded to nearest million.*		
5				

The expense decreases Apple, Inc.'s assets, as shown by the accounting equation.

Assets	=	Liabilities	+	Stockholders' Equity	−	Expenses
− 78	=	0			−	78

The percent-of-sales method employs the expense recognition (matching) concept to estimate, probably on a monthly or quarterly basis, the cost that has been incurred in order to earn a certain amount of revenue, and to recognize both in the same time period.

Accounts Receivable		Allowance for Uncollectible Accounts		Uncollectible-Account Expense	
11,028			10	78	
		Adj	78		
		End Bal	88		

Net accounts receivable, $10,940

Using the percent-of-sales method, the net realizable value of accounts receivable, or the amount ultimately expected to be collected from customers, would be $10,940 ($11,028 − $88). This method will usually result in a different amount of estimated uncollectible-accounts expense and net realizable value of accounts receivable than would be produced by the aging method, discussed next.

Aging-of-Receivables. The other popular method for estimating uncollectibles is called **aging-of-receivables**. The aging method is a *balance-sheet approach* because it focuses on what should be the most relevant and faithful representation of accounts receivable as of the balance-sheet date. In the aging method, individual receivables from specific customers are analyzed based on how long they have been outstanding.

---

[2]In this text, we assume that all sales are on account, unless it is specifically stated that they are in cash.

Suppose it is September 29, 2012, and Apple, Inc.'s receivables accounts show the following before the year-end adjustment (amounts in millions):

Accounts Receivable		Allowance for Uncollectible Accounts	
$11,028			$10

These accounts are not yet ready for the financial statements because the allowance balance is not realistic.

Apple, Inc.'s computerized accounting package ages the company's accounts receivable. Exhibit 5-3 shows a representative aging schedule at September 29, 2012. Apple, Inc.'s gross receivables total $11,028. Of this amount, the aging schedule shows that the company will *not* collect $98 (lower right corner).

Exhibit 5-3 | Aging Accounts Receivable of Apple, Inc.

	Age of Account (Dollar amounts rounded to the nearest million)				
Customer	1–30 Days	31–60 Days	61–90 Days	Over 90 Days	Total Balance
Walmart					
Publix					
Totals	$10,164	$ 600	$ 200	$ 64	$11,028
Estimated percent uncollectible	× 0.75%	× 1%	× 5%	× 10%	
Allowance for Uncollectible Accounts balance should be	$ 76* +	$ 6 +	$ 10 +	$ 6* =	$ 98

*Computations are rounded

The aging method will bring the balance of the allowance account ($10) to the needed amount as determined by the aging schedule ($98). The lower right corner of the aging schedule gives the needed balance in the allowance account. To update the allowance, Apple, Inc., would make this adjusting entry at year-end:

	A	B	C	D
	A1			
1	2012			
2	Sep. 29	Uncollectible-Account Expense	88	
3		Allowance for Uncollectible Accounts ($98 – $10)		88
4		*Recorded uncollectible accounts expense for the year.*		
5				

The expense decreases Apple, Inc.'s assets and net income, as shown by the accounting equation.

Assets	=	Liabilities	+	Stockholders' Equity	−	Expenses
− 88	=	0			−	88

Now the balance sheet can report the amount that Apple, Inc., actually expects to collect from customers: $10,930 ($11,028 − $98). This is the net realizable value of Apple, Inc.'s accounts receivable.

Accounts Receivable		Allowance for Uncollectible Accounts		Uncollectible-Account Expense
11,028		Beg. bal.	10	88
		Adj.	88	
		End Bal	98	

Net accounts receivable, $10,930

Writing Off Uncollectible Accounts. Assume that at the beginning of fiscal 2013, Apple, Inc., had these accounts receivable (amounts in millions):

Accounts Receivable— RS		Accounts Receivable— TM		Allowance for Uncollectible Accounts	
9		3			98

Accounts Receivable— Other	
11,016	

Total Accounts Receivable = $11,028   Allowance = $98

Accounts Receivable, Net = $10,930

Suppose that, early in fiscal 2013, Apple, Inc.'s credit department determines that Apple, Inc., cannot collect from customers RS and TM. Apple, Inc., then writes off the receivables from these customers with the following entry:

	A	B	C	D
1	2013			
2	Jan 31	Allowance for Uncollectible Accounts	12	
3		Accounts Receivable—RS		9
4		Accounts Receivable—TM		3
5		*Wrote off uncollectible receivables.*		
6				

Assets	=	Liabilities	+	Stockholders' Equity
+ 12 − 12	=	0	+	0

After the write-off, Apple, Inc.'s accounts show these amounts:

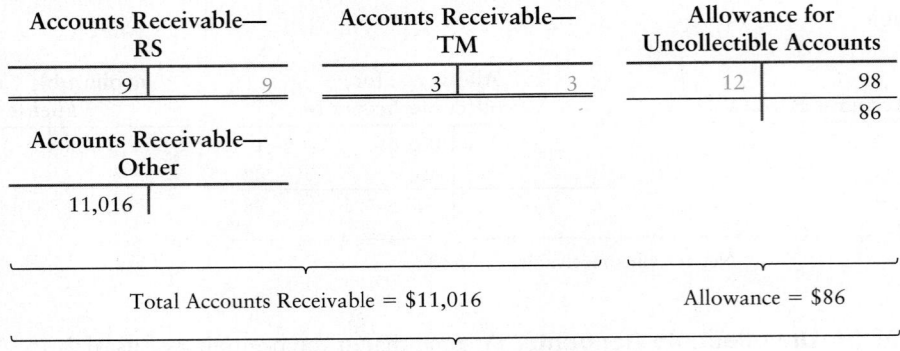

Accounts Receivable—RS		Accounts Receivable—TM		Allowance for Uncollectible Accounts	
9	9	3	3	12	98
					86

Accounts Receivable—Other

11,016

Total Accounts Receivable = $11,016   Allowance = $86

Accounts Receivable, Net = $10,930

The accounting equation shows that the write-off of uncollectibles has no effect on Apple, Inc.'s total assets, no effect on current assets, and no effect on net accounts receivable. Notice that Accounts Receivable, Net is still $10,930. There is no effect on net income either. Why is there no effect on net income? Net income is unaffected because the write-off of uncollectibles affects no expense account. If the company uses the allowance method, as discussed in the previous section, expenses would have been properly recognized in the period they were incurred, which is the same period in which the related sales took place.

Combining the Percent-of-Sales and the Aging Methods. Most companies use the percent-of-sales and aging-of-accounts methods together:

- For *interim statements* (monthly or quarterly), companies often use the percent-of-sales method because it is easier and quicker to apply. The percent-of-sales method focuses on the uncollectible-account *expense*, but that is not enough.

- At the end of the year, companies use the aging method to ensure that Accounts Receivable is reported at *net realizable value* on the balance sheet. The aging method focuses on the amount of the receivables that is uncollectible.

- Using the two methods together provides good measures of both the *expense* and the *asset*. Exhibit 5-4 compares the two methods.

Exhibit 5-4 | Comparing the Percent-of-Sales and Aging Methods for Estimating Uncollectible Accounts

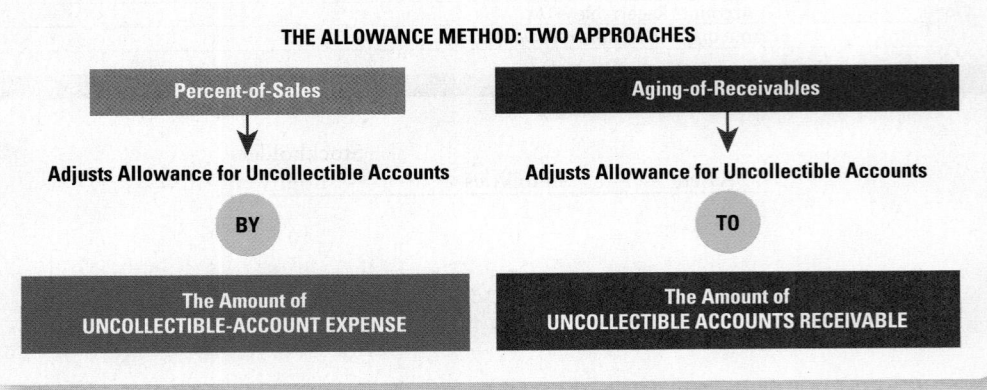

Direct Write-Off Method

There is another, less preferable way to account for uncollectible receivables. Under the **direct write-off method**, the company waits until a specific customer's receivable proves uncollectible. Then the accountant writes off the customer's account and records Uncollectible-Account Expense (using assumed data):

	A	B	C	D
1	2013			
2	Jan 31	Uncollectible-Account Expense	12	
3		Accounts Receivable—RS		9
4		Accounts Receivable—TM		3
5		*Wrote off uncollectible accounts by direct write-off method.*		
6				

The direct write-off method is not considered as being in keeping with generally accepted accounting principles (GAAP) for financial statement purposes, for two reasons:

1. It uses no allowance for uncollectibles. As a result, receivables are always reported at their full amount, which is more than the business expects to collect. *Assets on the balance sheet may be overstated.*

2. It fails to recognize the expense of uncollectible accounts in the same period in which the related sales revenue is earned. In this example, Apple, Inc., made the sales to RS and TM in 2012 and should have recorded the uncollectible-account expense during 2012, not in 2013 when it wrote off the accounts.

Because of these deficiencies, Apple, Inc., and virtually all other large companies use the allowance method for preparing their financial statements.

The direct write-off method is the *required* method of accounting for uncollectible accounts for federal income tax purposes. It is one of several sources of timing differences that may arise between net income for financial reporting purposes and net income for federal income tax purposes. We will discuss other differences between book and taxable income in later chapters.

Computing Cash Collections from Customers

A company earns revenue and then collects the cash from customers. For Apple, Inc., and most other companies, there is usually a time lag between earning the revenue and collecting the cash. Collections from customers are the single most important source of cash for any business. You can compute a company's collections from customers by analyzing its Accounts Receivable account. Receivables typically hold only five items, as reflected in the five elements of the following Accounts Receivable account balance (amounts assumed):

Accounts Receivable

Beg Bal (left over from last period)	200	Write-offs of uncollectibles	100**
Sales (or service) revenue on account	1,800*	Collections from customers	X = 1,500†
End Bal (carries over to next period)	400		

On the next page, we review the coded journal entries that affect Accounts Receivable.

*The journal entry that places revenue into the receivable account is:

	A	B	C
A1			
1	Accounts Receivable	1,800	
2	Sales (or Service) Revenue		1,800
3			

**The journal entry for write-offs of uncollectible accounts is:

	A	B	C
A1			
1	Allowance for Uncollectible Accounts	100	
2	Accounts Receivable		100
3			

†The journal entry that records cash collections of accounts receivable is:

	A	B	C
A1			
1	Cash	1,500	
2	Accounts Receivable		1,500
3			

Suppose you know all these amounts *except* collections from customers. You can compute collections by solving for X in the T-account.[3] Often write-offs are unknown and must be omitted. Then the computation of collections becomes an approximation.

ACCOUNT FOR NOTES RECEIVABLE

5 Account for notes receivable

As stated earlier, notes receivable are more formal than accounts receivable. Notes receivable due within one year or less are current assets. Notes due beyond one year are *long-term receivables* and are reported as long-term assets. Some notes receivable are collected in installments. The portion due within one year is a current asset and the remainder is long-term. Apple, Inc., may hold a $20,000 note receivable from a customer, but only the $6,000 that the customer must pay within one year is a current asset of Apple, Inc.

Before exploring accounting for notes receivable, let's define some key terms:

Creditor. The party to whom money is owed. The creditor is also called the *lender*.

Debtor. The party that borrowed and owes money on the note. The debtor is also called the *maker* of the note or the *borrower*.

Interest. Interest is the cost of borrowing money. The interest is stated in an annual percentage rate.

Maturity date. The date on which the debtor must pay the note.

Maturity value. The sum of principal and interest on the note.

Principal. The amount of money borrowed by the debtor and lent by the creditor.

Term. The length of time from when the note was signed by the debtor to when the debtor must pay the note.

---

[3]An equation may help you solve for X. The equation is $\$200 + \$1,800 - X - \$100 = \$400$. $X = \$1,500$.

There are two parties to a note:

- The *creditor* has a note receivable.
- The *debtor* has a note payable.

Exhibit 5-5 is a typical promissory note.

Exhibit 5-5 | Promissory Note

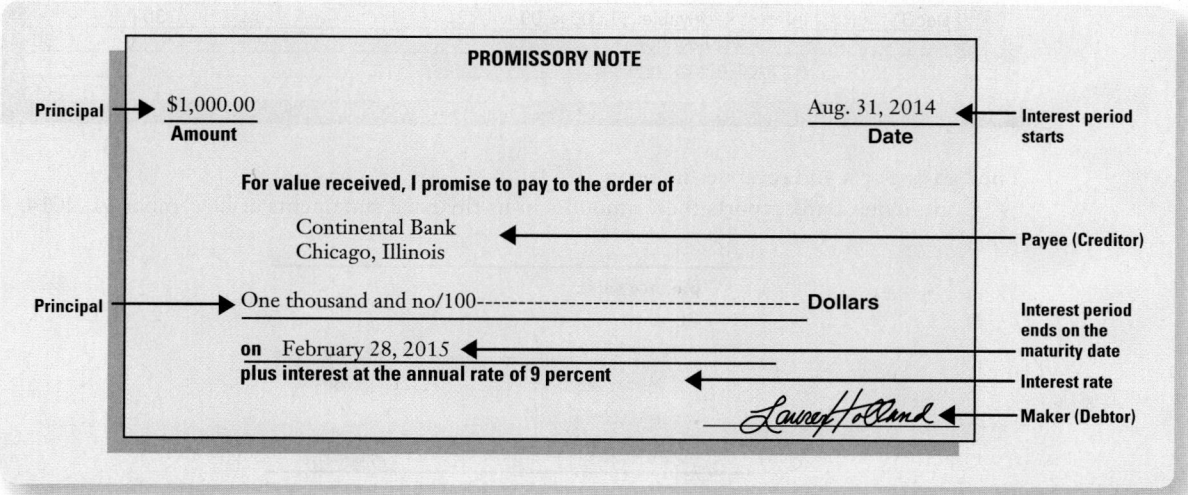

The **principal** amount of the note ($1,000) is the amount borrowed by the debtor and lent by the creditor. This six-month note receivable runs from August 31, 2014, to February 28, 2015, when Lauren Holland (the maker) promises to pay Continental Bank (the creditor) the principal of $1,000 plus 9% interest. Interest is revenue to the creditor (Continental Bank, in this case).

Accounting for Notes Receivable

Consider the promissory note in Exhibit 5-5. After Lauren Holland signs the note, Continental Bank gives her $1,000 cash. The bank's entries follow, assuming a December 31 year-end for Continental Bank:

	A	B	C	D
1	2014			
2	Aug 31	Note Receivable—L. Holland	1,000	
3		Cash		1,000
4		*Made a loan.*		
5				

Note Receivable—
L. Holland
_____
1,000 |

The bank gives one asset, cash, in exchange for another asset, a note receivable; so total assets do not change.

Continental Bank earns interest revenue during September, October, November, and December. At December 31, 2014, the bank accrues 9% interest revenue for four months:

	A1	⬍			
	A		**B**	**C**	**D**
1	Dec 31	Interest Receivable ($1,000 × .09 × 4/12)		30	
2		Interest Revenue			30
3		*Accrued interest revenue.*			
4					

The bank's assets and revenues increase.

Continental Bank reports these amounts in its financial statements at December 31, 2014:

Balance sheet

Current assets:

Note receivable $1,000

Interest receivable............... 30

Income statement

Interest revenue................... $ 30

The bank collects the note on February 28, 2015, and records the following:

	A1	⬍			
	A		**B**	**C**	**D**
1	2015				
2	Feb 28	Cash		1,045	
3		Note Receivable—L. Holland			1,000
4		Interest Receivable			30
5		Interest Revenue ($1,000 × .09 × 2/12)			15
6		*Collected note at maturity.*			
7					

This entry zeroes out Note Receivable and Interest Receivable and also records the interest revenue earned in 2015.

Note Receivable—
L. Holland

1,000	1,000

In its financial statements for the year ended December 31, 2015, the only item that Continental Bank will report is the interest revenue of $15 that was earned in 2015. There's no note receivable or interest receivable on the balance sheet because those items were zeroed out when the bank collected the note at maturity.

Three aspects of the interest computation deserve mention:

1. Interest rates are always for an annual period, unless stated otherwise. In this example, the annual interest rate is 9%. At December 31, 2014, Continental Bank accrues interest revenue for four months. The interest computation is:

Principal	×	Interest Rate	×	Time	=	Amount of Interest
$1,000	×	.09	×	4/12	=	$30

2. The time element (4/12) is the fraction of the year that the note has been in force during 2014.

3. Interest is often computed for a number of days. For example, suppose you loaned out $10,000 on April 10. The note receivable runs for 90 days and specifies interest at 8%.

    a. Interest starts accruing on April 11 and runs for 90 days, ending on the due date, July 9:

Month	Number of Days That Interest Accrues
April	20
May	31
June	30
July	9
Total	90

    b. The interest computation is
        $$\$10{,}000 \times 0.08 \times 90/365 = \$197$$

Some companies sell goods and services on notes receivable (versus selling on accounts receivable). This often occurs when the payment term extends beyond the customary accounts receivable period of 30 to 60 days.

Suppose that on March 20, 2015, Apple, Inc., sells a large number of iPads to Walmart. Apple, Inc., gets Walmart's three-month promissory note plus 10% annual interest. At the outset, Apple, Inc., would debit Notes Receivable and credit Sales Revenue.

A company may also accept a note receivable from a trade customer whose account receivable is past due. The company then debits Notes Receivable and credits Accounts Receivable. We would say the company "received a note receivable on account." Now let's examine some strategies to speed up cash flow from receivables.

SHOW HOW TO SPEED UP CASH FLOW FROM RECEIVABLES

All companies want speedy cash receipts. Rapid cash flow means companies have the ability to pay off current liabilities faster, as well as to finance new products, research, and development. Thus, companies such as Apple, Inc., develop strategies to shorten the credit cycle and collect cash more quickly. For example, they might offer sales discounts for early payment, as discussed earlier. They might also charge interest on customer accounts that exceed a certain age. They adopt more effective credit and collection procedures. In recent years, as electronic banking has become more popular, a common strategy has been to emphasize credit card or bankcard sales.

6 **Show** how to speed up cash flow from receivables

Credit Card or Bankcard Sales

The merchant sells merchandise and lets the customer pay with a credit card, such as Discover or American Express, or with a bankcard, such as VISA or MasterCard. This strategy may increase sales dramatically, but the added revenue comes at a cost, which is typically about 2% to 3% of the total amount of the sale. Let's see how credit cards and bankcards work from the seller's perspective.

Suppose Apple, Inc., sells a computer and peripheral devices for $5,000 at one of its stores, and the customer pays with a VISA card. Apple, Inc., records the sale:

	A	B	C
	A1		
1	Cash	4,900	
2	Credit Card Discount Expense	100	
3	Sales Revenue		5,000
4	*Recorded bankcard sales.*		
5			

Assets	=	Liabilities	+	Stockholders' Equity	+	Revenues	–	Expenses
+ 4,900	=	0	+			+ 5,000		– 100

Apple enters the transaction in its accounting system via a point-of-sale terminal. The terminal, linked to a VISA server, automatically credits Apple, Inc.'s bank account for a discounted portion, say $4,900, of the $5,000 sale amount. Two percent ($100) goes to VISA. To Apple, Inc., the credit card discount is an operating expense similar to interest expense.

Selling (Factoring) Receivables

Apple, Inc., makes some large sales to big-box electronics stores on account, debiting Accounts Receivable and crediting Sales Revenue. Apple, Inc., might then sell these accounts receivable to another business, called a *factor*. The factor earns revenue by paying a discounted price for the receivable and then hopefully collecting the full amount from the customer. The benefit to Apple, Inc., is the immediate receipt of cash. The biggest disadvantage of factoring is that it is often quite expensive when compared to the costs of retaining the receivable on the books and ultimately collecting the full amount. In addition, the company that factors its receivables loses control over the collection process. For these reasons, factoring is not often used by companies who have other, less costly means to raise cash, such as short-term borrowing from banks. Factoring may be used by start-up companies with insufficient credit history to obtain loans at a reasonable cost, by companies with weak credit history, or by companies that are already saddled with a significant amount of debt.

To illustrate selling, or *factoring*, accounts receivable, suppose a company wishes to speed up cash flow and therefore sells $100,000 of accounts receivable, receiving cash of $95,000. The company would record the sale of the receivables:

	A	B	C
1	Cash	95,000	
2	Financing Expense	5,000	
3	Accounts Receivable		100,000
4	*Sold accounts receivable.*		
5			

Again, Financing Expense is an operating expense, with the same effect as a loss. Some companies may debit a Loss account. Discounting a note receivable is similar to selling an account receivable. However, the credit is to Notes Receivable (instead of Accounts Receivable).

Notice the high price (5% of the face amount, or $5,000) the company has had to pay in order to collect the cash immediately, as opposed to waiting 30–60 days to collect the full amount. Therefore, if the company can afford to wait, it will probably not engage in factoring to collect the full amount of the receivables.

Reporting on the Statement of Cash Flows

Receivables and short-term investments appear on the balance sheet as current assets. We saw these in Apple, Inc.'s balance sheet at the beginning of the chapter. We've also seen how to report the related revenues, expenses, gains, and losses on the income statement. Because receivable and investment transactions affect cash, their effects must also be reported on the statement of cash flows.

Receivables bring in cash when the business collects from customers. These transactions are reported as *operating activities* on the statement of cash flows because they result from sales. Investment transactions show up as *investing activities* on the statement of cash flows. Chapter 12 shows how companies report their cash flows on the statement of cash flows. In that chapter, we will see exactly how to report cash flows related to receivables and investment transactions.

EVALUATE LIQUIDITY USING TWO NEW RATIOS

Investors and creditors use ratios to evaluate the financial health of a company. We introduced the current ratio in Chapter 3. Other ratios, including the **quick ratio** (or **acid-test ratio**) and the number of **days' sales in receivables**, help investors measure liquidity.

7 **Evaluate** liquidity using two new ratios

Quick (Acid-Test) Ratio

The balance sheet lists assets in the order of relative liquidity:

1. Cash and cash equivalents
2. Short-term investments
3. Accounts (or notes) receivable

Apple, Inc.'s balance sheet in the chapter-opening story lists these accounts in order.

Managers, stockholders, and creditors care about the liquidity of a company's assets. The current ratio measures ability to pay current liabilities with current assets. A more stringent measure of the ability to pay current liabilities is the quick (or *acid-test*) ratio:

Apple, Inc. 2012

(Dollars in millions, taken from Apple, Inc. balance sheet)

$$\text{Quick (acid-test) ratio} = \frac{\text{Cash and cash equivalents} + \text{Short-term investments} + \text{Net current receivables}}{\text{Total current liabilities}} = \frac{\$10,746 + \$18,383 + \$10,930}{\$38,542} = 1.04$$

The higher the quick ratio, the easier it is to pay current liabilities. Apple, Inc.'s quick ratio of 1.04 means that it has $1.04 of quick assets to pay each $1 of current liabilities. This ratio value is considered excellent. What is considered an acceptably high quick ratio? The answer depends on the industry. Auto dealers can operate smoothly with a quick ratio of 0.20, roughly one-fifth of Apple, Inc.'s ratio value. How can auto dealers survive with so low a quick ratio? The auto manufacturers help finance their dealers' inventory. Most dealers, therefore, have a financial safety net provided through the manufacturers. Retail stores often have relatively low quick ratios as well but compensate for it with high inventory turnover and virtually 100% cash sales, which keeps the cash flowing in fast enough to pay creditors.

Days' Sales in Receivables

After a business makes a credit sale, the *next* step is collecting the receivable. **Days' sales in receivables**, also called *days' sales outstanding* (*DSO*) or the *collection period*, tells a company how long it takes to collect its average level of receivables. Shorter is better because cash is coming in quickly. The longer the collection period, the less cash is available to pay bills and expand.

Days' sales in receivables can be computed in two logical steps. First, compute average daily sales (or average revenue for one day). Then divide average daily sales into average net receivables for the period. We show days' sales in receivables for Apple, Inc.

(Dollars in millions, taken from Apple, Inc.'s financial statements)		
Days' Sales in Receivables		(In millions)

1. $\dfrac{\text{Average}}{\text{daily sales}} = \dfrac{\text{Net sales}}{365 \text{ days}}$ $\qquad$ $\dfrac{\$156,508}{365 \text{ days}} = \$429 \text{ per day}$

2. $\dfrac{\text{Days' sales in receivables}}{} = \dfrac{\text{Average net receivables*}}{\text{Average daily sales}}$ $\qquad$ $\dfrac{\$8,150^*}{\$429 \text{ per day}} = 19 \text{ days}$

$^*\dfrac{\text{Average net receivables}}{} = \dfrac{\text{Beginning net receivables} + \text{Ending net receivables}}{2} = \dfrac{\$10,930 + \$5,369}{2} = \$8,150$

Net sales come from the income statement, and the net receivables amounts are taken from the balance sheet. Average net receivables is the simple average of the beginning and ending balances.

It takes Apple, Inc., 19 days to collect its average level of receivables. To evaluate Apple, Inc.'s collection period, we need to compare 19 days to the credit terms that Apple, Inc., offers customers when the company makes a sale, as well as the number of days on average that creditors typically allow Apple, Inc., to pay them without penalty. Suppose Apple, Inc., makes sales on "net 30" terms, which means that customers should pay Apple, Inc., within 30 days of the sale. That makes Apple, Inc.'s collection period very favorable in comparison to its credit terms. With regard to its credit terms for payables, if Apple, Inc.'s short-term creditors expect payment of their accounts payable within 30 days, Apple, Inc., enjoys use of its cash collections from receivables for 11 days before it must be paid out to creditors. The company can put that cash to work, investing it in "cash equivalents" or "trading securities" for additional short-term gains. No wonder that the company has so much invested in these types of assets, as we discussed in the chapter opening.

Companies watch their collection periods closely. Whenever collections slow down, the business must find other sources of financing, such as borrowing or selling receivables. During recessions, customers pay more slowly and a longer collection period may be unavoidable.[4]

---

[4]Another ratio, **accounts receivable turnover**, captures the same information as days' sales in receivables. Receivable turnover is computed as: Net sales/Average net accounts receivable. During 2012, Apple, Inc., had a receivable turnover ratio of 19.2 times. ($156,508/$8,150 = 19.2). Days sales' in receivables can then be computed by dividing 365 by the receivable turnover (365/19.2 = 19.01, rounded to 19). You can see that this method merely rearranges the equations in the body of the text, "going through the back door" to achieve the same result.

End-of-Chapter Summary Problem

Excelsior Technical Resources' (ETR's) balance sheet at December 31, 2014, reported the following:

	(In millions)
Accounts receivable	$382
Allowance for doubtful accounts	(52)

ETR uses both the percent-of-sales and the aging approaches to account for uncollectible receivables.

Requirements

1. How much of the December 31, 2014, balance of accounts receivable did ETR expect to collect? Stated differently, what was the net realizable value of ETR's receivables?
2. Journalize, without explanations, 2015 entries for ETR:
    a. Estimated doubtful-account expense of $40 million, based on the percent-of-sales method, all during the year.
    b. Write-offs of uncollectible accounts receivable totaling $58 million. Prepare a T-account for Allowance for Doubtful Accounts and post to this account. Show its unadjusted balance at December 31, 2015.
    c. December 31, 2015, aging of receivables, which indicates that $47 million of the total receivables of $409 million is uncollectible at year-end. Post to Allowance for Doubtful Accounts, and show its adjusted balance at December 31, 2015.
3. Show how ETR's receivables and the related allowance will appear on the December 31, 2015, balance sheet.
4. Show what ETR's income statement for the year ending December 31, 2015, will report for the transactions detailed.

Answers
Requirement 1

	(In millions)
Net realizable value of receivables ($382 − $52)	$330

Requirement 2

	A	B	C	D
1			(In millions)	
2	a.	Doubtful-Account Expense	40	
3		Allowance for Doubtful Accounts		40
4				
5	b.	Allowance for Doubtful Accounts	58	
6		Accounts Receivable		58
7				

Allowance for Doubtful Accounts

		Dec 31, 2014	52
2015 Write-offs	58	2015 Expense	40
		Unadjusted balance at Dec 31, 2015	34

A1	⇕				
	A	B		C	D
1				(In millions)	
2	c.	Doubtful-Account Expense ($47 – $34)		13	
3		Allowance for Doubtful Accounts			13
4					

Allowance for Doubtful Accounts

Dec 31, 2015 Unadj bal	34
2015 Expense	13
Dec 31, 2015 Adj bal	47

Requirement 3

	(In millions)
Accounts receivable......................................	$409
Allowance for doubtful accounts................	(47)
Accounts receivable, net.............................	$362

Requirement 4

	(In millions)
Expenses: Doubtful-account expense for 2015 ($40 + $13)	$53

REVIEW | Short-term Investments and Receivables

Quick Check (Answers are given on page 299.)

1. T-BAR-T Tennis Academy held investments in trading securities with a fair value of $90,000 at December 31, 2014. These investments cost T-BAR-T $76,000 on January 1, 2014. What is the appropriate amount for T-BAR-T to report for these investments on the December 31, 2014, balance sheet?

   a. $90,000
   b. $76,000
   c. $14,000 gain
   d. cannot be determined from the data given

2. Return to T-BAR-T Tennis Academy in question 1. What should appear on the T-BAR-T income statement for the year ended December 31, 2014, for the trading securities?

   a. $90,000
   b. $14,000 unrealized gain
   c. $76,000
   d. cannot be determined from the data given

Use the following information to answer questions 3–7.

R. Antonio Company had the following information in 2014:

Accounts receivable 12/31/14..	$ 26,000
Allowance for uncollectible accounts 12/31/14 (before adjustment).........	1,500
Credit sales during 2014	94,000
Cash sales during 2014	28,000
Collections from customers on account during 2014.............................	100,000

3. Uncollectible accounts are determined by the percent-of-sales method to be 3% of credit sales. How much is uncollectible-account expense for 2014?
   a. $4,320
   b. $3,240
   c. $1,500
   d. $2,820

4. Uncollectible-account expense for 2014 is $2,820. What is the adjusted balance in the Allowance account at year-end for 2014?
   a. $1,320
   b. $2,820
   c. $4,320
   d. $1,500

5. If uncollectible accounts are determined by the aging-of-receivables method to be $2,280, the uncollectible account expense for 2014 would be
   a. $2,280.
   b. $780.
   c. $2,280.
   d. $1,500.

6. Using the aging-of-receivables method, the balance of the Allowance account after the adjusting entry at year-end 2014 would be
   a. $2,280.
   b. $1,500.
   c. $780.
   d. $3,780.

7. Using the aging-of-receivables method, the net realizable value of accounts receivable on the December 31, 2014, balance sheet would be
   a. $22,220.
   b. $28,280.
   c. $23,720.
   d. $26,000.

8. Accounts Receivable has a debit balance of $3,600, and the Allowance for Uncollectible Accounts has a credit balance of $200. A $70 account receivable is written off. What is the amount of net receivables (net realizable value) after the write-off?
   a. $3,330
   b. $3,400
   c. $3,530
   d. $3,470

9. Angelina Corporation began 2014 with Accounts Receivable of $450,000. Sales for the year totaled $1,820,000. Angelina ended the year with accounts receivable of $525,000. Angelina's bad-debt losses are minimal. How much cash did Angelina collect from customers in 2014?
   a. $1,895,000
   b. $845,000
   c. $1,820,000
   d. $1,745,000

10. Stripes Ltd. received a four-month, 7%, $15,000 note receivable on March 1. The adjusting entry on March 31 will include
    a. a debit to Interest Receivable for $1,050.
    b. a debit to Interest Receivable for $350.
    c. a debit to Cash for $1,050.
    d. a credit Interest Revenue for $87.50.

11. What is the maturity value of a $40,000, 5%, six-month note?
    a. $42,000
    b. $39,000
    c. $41,000
    d. $40,000

12. If the adjusting entry to accrue interest on a note receivable is omitted, then
    a. assets, net income, and stockholders' equity are understated.
    b. liabilities are understated, net income is overstated, and stockholders' equity is overstated.
    c. assets, net income, and stockholders' equity are overstated.
    d. assets are overstated, net income is understated, and stockholders' equity is understated.

13. Net sales total $621,500. Beginning and ending accounts receivable are $36,000 and $46,000, respectively. Calculate days' sales in receivables.
    a. 30 days
    b. 27 days
    c. 21 days
    d. 24 days

14. From the following list of accounts, calculate the quick ratio.

Cash	$ 2,500	Accounts payable	$ 9,000
Accounts receivable	10,000	Salary payable	3,000
Inventory	14,000	Notes payable (due in two years)	11,000
Prepaid insurance	2,000	Short-term investments	6,400

    a. 1.5
    b. 1.7
    c. 1.6
    d. 2.7

Accounting Vocabulary

acid-test ratio (p. 271) Ratio of the sum of cash plus short-term investments plus net current receivables to total current liabilities. Tells whether the entity can pay all its current liabilities if they come due immediately. Also called the *quick ratio*.

accounts receivable turnover (p. 272) Net sales divided by average net accounts receivable.

accumulated other comprehensive income (p. 252) The cumulative amount of items reported as other comprehensive income; a separate category in the stockholders' equity section of the balance sheet.

aging-of-receivables (p. 261) A way to estimate bad debts by analyzing individual accounts receivable according to the length of time they have been receivable from the customer.

Allowance for Doubtful Accounts (p. 259) Another name for *Allowance for Uncollectible Accounts*.

Allowance for Uncollectible Accounts (p. 259) The estimated amount of collection losses. Another name for *Allowance for Doubtful Accounts*.

allowance method (p. 259) A method of recording collection losses based on estimates of how much money the business will not collect from its customers.

available-for-sale securities (p. 247) Securities that are not classified as held-to-maturity or trading securities.

bad-debt expense (p. 259) Another name for *uncollectible-account expense*.

creditor (p. 266) The party to whom money is owed.

days' sales in receivables (p. 271) Ratio of average net accounts receivable to one day's sales. Indicates how many days' sales remain in Accounts Receivable awaiting collection. Also called the *collection period*.

debtor (p. 266) The party who owes money.

direct write-off method (p. 265) A method of accounting for bad debts in which the company waits until a customer's account receivable proves uncollectible and then debits Uncollectible-Account Expense and credits the customer's Account Receivable.

doubtful-account expense (p. 259) Another name for *uncollectible-account expense*.

FOB (p. 255) Acronym for "free on board"; used in quoting shipping terms. See also *shipping terms*.

held-to-maturity securities (p. 248) Securities in which the investor has the intent and ability to hold until a maturity date stated on the face of the security.

interest (p. 266) The borrower's cost of renting money from a lender. Interest is revenue for the lender and expense for the borrower.

maturity date (p. 266) The date on which the debtor must pay the note.

maturity value (p. 266) The sum of principal and interest on the note.

other comprehensive income (p. 252) Certain types of revenue, expenses, gains, and losses that are allowed to bypass the income statement. These items are reported either in a separate statement or in a combined statement of net income and comprehensive income. At the end of a period, items of comprehensive income for that period are reported as accumulated other comprehensive income, a separate category of stockholders' equity.

percent-of-sales method (p. 261) Computes uncollectible-account expense as a percentage of net sales. Also called the *income-statement approach* because it focuses on the amount of expense to be reported on the income statement.

principal (p. 267) The amount borrowed by a debtor and lent by a creditor.

quick ratio (p. 271) Another name for *acid-test ratio*.

receivables (p. 256) Monetary claims against a business or an individual, acquired mainly by selling goods or services and by lending money.

sales discount (p. 255) Percentage reduction of sales price by the seller as an incentive for early payment before the due date. A typical way to express sales discount is "2/10, n/30." This means the seller will grant a 2% discount if the invoice is paid within 10 days, and the entire amount is due within 30 days.

sales return and allowance (p. 255) Merchandise returned for credit or refunds for services provided.

shipping terms (p. 255) Terms provided by the seller of merchandise that dictate the date on which title transfers to the buyer. A typical way to express shipping terms is through

FOB terms. For example, "FOB destination" means title to the goods passes to the buyer when the goods are delivered and the buyer assumes control over them. "FOB shipping point" means title passes on the date the goods are shipped from the seller's warehouse.

term (p. 266) The length of time from inception to maturity.

trading securities (p. 247) Debt or equity investments that are to be sold in the near future with the intent of generating profits on the sale.

uncollectible-account expense (p. 259) Cost to the seller of extending credit. Arises from the failure to collect from credit customers. Also called *doubtful-account expense* or *bad-debt expense*.

unrealized gain/loss (p. 249, 250) Gains and losses that occur on investments through fluctuations in market values, rather than through sales.

ASSESS YOUR PROGRESS

Short Exercises

S5-1. *(Learning Objective 1: Report trading investments)* Answer these questions about investments.
1. What is the amount to report on the balance sheet for a trading security?
2. Why is a trading security always a current asset? Explain.

S5-2. *(Learning Objective 1: Account for short-term investments)* Keystone Corp. holds a portfolio of trading securities. Suppose that on October 15, Keystone paid $160,000 for an investment in Shurock Co. shares to add to its portfolio. At December 31, the market value of Shurock Co. shares is $172,000. For this situation, show everything that Keystone would report on its December 31 balance sheet and on its income statement for the year ended December 31.

S5-3. *(Learning Objective 1: Account for short-term investments)* Inverness Investments purchased Dorr Corp. shares as a trading security on December 16 for $85,000.
1. Suppose the Dorr Corp. shares decreased in value to $78,000 at December 31. Make the Inverness journal entry to adjust the Investment in Trading Securities account to market value.
2. Show how Inverness would report the Investment in Trading Securities on its balance sheet and the unrealized gain or loss on its income statement.

S5-4. *(Learning Objective 2: Apply GAAP for proper revenue recognition)* On December 23, 2014, R Patrick Sports Manufacturing sells a truckload of sporting goods to the Sports R Us store in Amarillo, Texas. The terms of the sale are FOB destination. The truck runs into bad weather on the way to Amarillo and doesn't arrive until January 2, 2015. R Patrick Sports Manufacturing's invoice totals $308,000 including sales tax. The company's year-end is December 31. What should R Patrick Sports Manufacturing reflect in its 2014 income statement for this sale?

S5-5. *(Learning Objective 2: Apply GAAP for proper revenue recognition)* Refer to the facts in S5-4. The sales terms on the invoice are 2/10, net 30. What does this mean? What is Sports R Us' potential savings, if any? How much time does the company have to take advantage of these savings?

S5-6. *(Learning Objective 2: Apply GAAP for proper revenue recognition)* Refer to the facts in S5-4. Suppose that when store personnel uncrate the shipment of merchandise, they find that a shipment of clothing worth $6,100 is defective. They notify R Patrick of the problem and return the shipment to the company. What entry will R Patrick make?

S5-7. *(Learning Objective 3: Apply internal controls to accounts receivable)* As a recent college graduate, you land your first job in the customer collections department of NY Publishing. Spencer Crew, the manager, asked you to propose a system to ensure that cash received from customers by mail is handled properly. Draft a short memorandum to explain the essential element in your proposed plan; explain why this element is important.

S5-8. *(Learning Objective 4: Evaluate collectibility using the allowance for uncollectible accounts)* During its first year of operations, Nunley Chocolates, LTD., Inc., had sales of $483,000, all on account. Industry experience suggests that Nunley Chocolates, LTD.'s uncollectibles will amount to 2% of credit sales. At December 31, 2014, accounts receivable total $49,000. The company uses the allowance method to account for uncollectibles.
1. Make Nunley Chocolates, LTD.'s journal entry for uncollectible-account expense using the percent-of-sales method.
2. Show how Nunley Chocolates, LTD. should report accounts receivable on its balance sheet at December 31, 2014.

S5-9. *(Learning Objectives 3, 4: Account for accounts receivable and uncollectible accounts)* Perform the following accounting for the receivables of Hawkins & Harriss, a CPA firm, at December 31, 2014.

Requirements

1. Set up T-accounts and start with the beginning balances for these T-accounts:
   - Accounts Receivable, $303,000
   - Allowance for Uncollectible Accounts, $26,000

   Post the following 2014 transactions to the T-accounts:
   - **a.** Service revenue of $1,978,000, all on account
   - **b.** Collections on account, $2,010,000
   - **c.** Write-offs of uncollectible accounts, $29,000
   - **d.** Uncollectible-account expense (allowance method), $35,000
2. What are the ending balances of Accounts Receivable and Allowance for Uncollectible Accounts?
3. Show how Hawkins & Harriss will report accounts receivable on its balance sheet at December 31, 2014.

S5-10. *(Learning Objectives 2, 3, 4, 5, 6: Apply GAAP for revenue recognition; account for accounts receivable, uncollectible accounts, and notes receivable; show how to speed up cash flow from receivables)* Answer these questions about receivables and uncollectibles. For the true-false questions, explain any answers that turn out to be false.
1. True or false? Credit sales increase receivables. Collections and write-offs decrease receivables.
2. True or false? A proper way to express credit terms is "FOB shipping point."
3. Which receivables figure—the *total* amount that customers *owe* the company, or the *net* amount the company expects to collect—is more interesting to investors as they consider buying the company's stock? Give your reason.
4. Show how to determine net sales revenue.
5. Show how to determine net accounts receivable.

6. True or false? The direct write-off method of accounting for uncollectibles understates assets.

7. Texas Bank lent $150,000 to Kansas Company on a six-month, 6% note. Which party has interest receivable? Which party has interest payable? Interest expense? Interest revenue? How much interest will these organizations record one month after Kansas Company signs the note?

8. When Texas Bank accrues interest on the Kansas Company note, show the directional effects on the bank's assets, liabilities, and equity (increase, decrease, or no effect).

9. True or false? Credit card sales increase accounts receivable.

10. True or false? Companies with strong liquidity usually factor receivables.

S5-11. *(Learning Objective 5: Account for notes receivable)*

1. Compute the amount of interest during 2014, 2015, and 2016 for the following note receivable: On May 31, 2014, Main Street Bank lent $220,000 to Ron Rowlette on a two-year, 5% note.

2. Which party has a (an)
   a. note receivable?
   b. note payable?
   c. interest revenue?
   d. interest expense?

3. How much in total would Main Street Bank collect if Ron Rowlette paid off the note early—say, on November 30, 2014?

S5-12. *(Learning Objective 5: Account for notes receivable)* On August 31, 2014, Nina Herrera borrowed $5,000 from Second State Bank. Herrera signed a note payable, promising to pay the bank principal plus interest on August 31, 2015. The interest rate on the note is 6%. The accounting year of Second State Bank ends on June 30, 2015. Journalize Second State Bank's (a) lending money on the note receivable at August 31, 2014, (b) accrual of interest at June 30, 2015, and (c) collection of principal and interest at August 31, 2015, the maturity date of the note.

S5-13. *(Learning Objective 7: Evaluate liquidity using the quick (acid-test) ratio and days' sales in receivables)* Tovar Clothiers reported the following amounts in its 2015 financial statements. The 2014 amounts are given for comparison.

		2015		2014
Current assets:				
Cash...		$ 18,600		$ 18,000
Short-term investments................		27,500		20,500
Accounts receivable.....................	$161,000		$154,000	
Less: Allowance for				
uncollectibles........................	(14,200)	146,800	(12,200)	141,800
Inventory.....................................		393,000		404,000
Prepaid insurance.........................		4,100		4,100
Total current assets		590,000		588,400
Total current liabilities..................		203,000		220,000
Net sales.......................................		1,593,000		1,462,000

Requirements

1. Compute Tovar's quick (acid-test) ratio at the end of 2015. Round to two decimal places. How does the quick (acid-test) compare with the industry average of 0.92?

2. Compare days' sales in receivables for 2015 with the company's credit terms of net 30 days.

Exercises

Group A

E5-14A. *(Learning Objective 1: Apply GAAP for short-term investments)* Western Corporation, the investment banking company, often has extra cash to invest. Suppose Western buys 1,240 shares of Excelsior, Inc., stock at $57 per share. Assume Western expects to hold the Excelsior stock for one month and then sell it. The purchase occurs on December 15, 2014. At December 31, the market price of a share of Excelsior stock is $58 per share.

Requirements

1. What type of investment is this to Western? Give the reason for your answer.
2. Record Western's purchase of the Excelsior stock on December 15 and the adjustment to market value on December 31.
3. Show how Western would report this investment on its balance sheet at December 31 and any gain or loss on its income statement for the year ended December 31, 2014.
4. Suppose Western did *not* intend to treat the Excelsior stock as a trading security, but still intended to treat it as a short-term investment. How do your answers for parts 1–3 change? Follow Exhibit 5-2.

E5-15A. *(Learning Objectives 2, 3: Apply GAAP for sales, sales discount, and sales returns; account for accounts receivable)* Denver Interiors reported the following transactions in July:

Jul 2	Sold merchandise on account to Kara Elsworth, $450, terms 2/10, n/30.
10	Sold merchandise on account to Sedalia Bradley, $2,500, terms 2/10, n/30
11	Collected payment from Kara Elsworth for the Jul 2 sale.
15	Bradley returned $350 of the merchandise purchased on Jul 10.
19	Collected payment from Sedalia Bradley for the balance of the Jul 10 sale.

Requirements

1. Record the foregoing transactions in the journal of Denver Interiors.
2. Prepare a computation of net sales for the month of July.

E5-16A. *(Learning Objective 4: Apply GAAP for uncollectible receivables)* At December 31, 2014, State Line Window Sales has an Accounts Receivable balance of $96,000. Allowance for Doubtful Accounts has a credit balance of $1,340 before the year-end adjustment. Credit Sales Revenue for 2014 was $608,000. State Line Window Sales estimates that doubtful-account expense for the year is 1% of credit sales. Make the year-end entry to record Doubtful-Account Expense. Show how Accounts Receivable and Allowance for Doubtful Accounts are reported on the balance sheet at December 31, 2014.

E5-17A. *(Learning Objectives 2, 3, 4: Apply GAAP for revenue recognition, accounts receivable, and uncollectible receivables)* On November 30, Windsor Party Planners had a $43,000 balance in Accounts Receivable and a $3,700 credit balance in Allowance for Uncollectible Accounts. During December, Windsor Party Planners made credit sales of $195,000. December collections on account were $164,000, and write-offs of uncollectible receivables totaled $2,820. Uncollectible-accounts expense is estimated as 1% of credit sales.

Requirements

1. Journalize sales, collections, write-offs of uncollectibles, and uncollectible-account expense by the allowance method during December. Explanations are not required.
2. Show the ending balances in Accounts Receivable, Allowance for Uncollectible Accounts, and *Net* Accounts Receivable at December 31. How much does Windsor Party Planners expect to collect?
3. Show how Windsor Party Planners will report accounts receivable and net sales on its December 31 balance sheet and income statement for the month ended December 31.

E5-18A. *(Learning Objective 4: Apply GAAP to uncollectible receivables)* At December 31, 2014, before any year-end adjustments, the Accounts Receivable balance of Wynn Electronics is $360,000. The Allowance for Doubtful Accounts has a $22,500 credit balance. Wynn Electronics prepares the following aging schedule for Accounts Receivable:

		Age of Accounts		
Total Balance	1–30 Days	31–60 Days	61–90 Days	Over 90 Days
$360,000	$140,000	$100,000	$80,000	$40,000
Estimated uncollectible	0.5%	2.0%	8.0%	50.0%

Requirements

1. Based on the aging of Accounts Receivable, is the unadjusted balance of the allowance account adequate? Too high? Too low?
2. Make the entry required by the aging schedule. Prepare a T-account for the allowance.
3. Show how Wynn Electronics will report Accounts Receivable on its December 31 balance sheet.

E5-19A. *(Learning Objective 4: Applying GAAP for uncollectible accounts)* Assume All-Fresh Foods, Inc., experienced the following revenue, sales returns and allowances, and accounts receivable write-offs:

Month	Service Revenue	Sales Returns	Accounts Receivable Write-Offs in Month			
			March	April	May	Totals
March	$ 3,750		$50	$ 88		$138
April	3,950			64	$33	97
May	4,050	$106			53	53
	$11,750	$106	$50	$152	$86	$288

Suppose All-Fresh estimates that 2½% of (gross) revenues will become uncollectible. Assume all revenues are on credit.

Requirement

1. Journalize service revenue (all on account), bad-debt expense, sales returns and allowances, and write-offs during May. Include explanations.

E5-20A. *(Learning Objective 5: Apply GAAP for notes receivable)* Record the following note receivable transactions in the journal of Harland Services. How much interest revenue did Harland earn this year? *Use a 365-day year* for interest computations, and round interest amounts to the nearest dollar. Harland Services has an October 31 fiscal year-end.

Aug	1	Loaned $5,000 cash to Jill Waterman on a one-year, 7% note.
Oct	6	Performed service for King Properties, receiving a 90-day, 6% note for $12,000.
	16	Received a $2,000, six-month, 5% note on account from Vernon, Inc.
	31	Accrued interest revenue for the year.

E5-21A. *(Learning Objectives 6, 7: Show how to speed up cash flow from receivables; evaluate liquidity through ratios)* Sutterfield, Inc., reported the following items at December 31, 2014, and 2013:

	A	B	C	D	E	F
	A	**B**	**C**	**D**	**E**	**F**
1	**Balance Sheets (Summarized)**					
2						
3		**Year End**			**Year End**	
4		**2014**	**2013**		**2014**	**2013**
5	**Current assets:**			**Current liabilities:**		
6	Cash	$ 11,000	$ 7,000	Accounts payable	$ 20,000	$ 21,500
7	Marketable securities	27,000	16,000	Other current liabilities	112,000	114,000
8	Accounts receivable, net	61,000	75,000	Long-term liabilities	20,000	21,000
9	Inventory	198,000	194,000			
10	Other current assets	2,000	2,000	Stockholders' equity	147,000	147,500
11			10,000			
12	Total assets	$ 299,000	$ 304,000	Total liabilities and equity	$ 299,000	$ 304,000
13						
14	**Income statement (partial):**	**2014**				
15	Sales Revenue	$ 780,000				
17						

Requirements

1. Compute Sutterfield's (a) quick (acid-test) ratio and (b) days' sales in receivables for 2014. Evaluate each ratio value as strong or weak. Sutterfield sells on terms of net 30 days.
2. Recommend two ways for Sutterfield to speed up its cash flow from receivables.

E5-22A. *(Learning Objectives 6, 7: Show how to speed up cash flow from receivables; evaluate liquidity through ratios)* Jennings Co., Inc., an electronics and appliance chain, reported these figures in millions of dollars:

	2015	2014
Net sales..	$750,000	$689,000
Receivables at end of year	6,810	5,310

Requirements

1. Compute Jennings' days' sales in receivables or days' sales outstanding (DSO) during 2015.
2. Is Jennings' DSO long or short? Norton Networks takes 39 days to collect its average level of receivables. Fast Freight, the overnight shipper, takes 33 days. What causes Jennings' collection period to be so different?

Group B

E5-23B. *(Learning Objective 1: Apply GAAP for short-term investments)* Spring Corporation, the investment banking company, often has cash to invest. Suppose Spring buys 825 shares of TPG, Inc., stock at $59 per share. Assume Spring expects to hold the TPG stock for one month and then sell it. The purchase occurs on December 15, 2014. At December 31, the market price of a share of TPG stock is $62 per share.

Requirements

1. What type of investment is this to Spring? Give the reason for your answer.
2. Record Spring's purchase of the TPG stock on December 15 and the adjustment to market value on December 31.
3. Show how Spring would report this investment on its balance sheet at December 31 and any gain or loss on its income statement for the year ended December 31, 2014.
4. Suppose Spring did *not* intend to treat the TPG stock as a trading security, but still intended to treat it as a short-term investment. How do your answers for parts 1–3 change? Follow Exhibit 5-2.

E5-24B. *(Learning Objectives 2, 3: Apply GAAP for sales, sales discount, and sales returns; account for accounts receivable)* O'Kemo Designs reported the following transactions in November:

Nov	8	Sold merchandise on account to Tina Balise, $650, terms 2/10, n/30.
	15	Sold merchandise on account to Holyoke Glass, $1,800, terms 2/10, n/30.
	16	Holyoke Glass returned $500 of the merchandise purchased on Nov 15.
	17	Collected payment from Tina Balise for the Nov 8 sale.
	24	Collected payment from Holyoke Glass for the balance of the Nov 15 sale.

Requirements

1. Record the foregoing transactions in the journal of O'Kemo Designs.
2. Prepare a computation of net sales for the month of November.

E5-25B. *(Learning Objective 4: Apply GAAP for uncollectible receivables)* At December 31, 2014, Goldstone Travel has an Accounts Receivable balance of $82,000. Allowance for Doubtful Accounts has a credit balance of $730 before the year-end adjustment. Credit Service Revenue for 2014 was $795,000. Goldstone Travel estimates that Doubtful-Account Expense for the year is 2% of credit service revenue. Make the December 31 entry to record Doubtful-Account Expense. Show how the Accounts Receivable and the Allowance for Doubtful Accounts are reported on the balance sheet at December 31, 2014.

E5-26B. *(Learning Objectives 2, 3, 4: Apply GAAP for revenue recognition, accounts receivable, and uncollectible receivables)* On September 30, Pendley Party Shop had a $56,000 balance in Accounts Receivable and a $3,000 credit balance in Allowance for Uncollectible Accounts. During October, the store made credit sales of $323,000. October collections on account were $257,000, and write-offs of uncollectible receivables totaled $3,600. Uncollectible-account expense is estimated as 3% of credit sales.

Requirements

1. Journalize sales, collections, write-offs of uncollectibles, and uncollectible-account expense by the allowance method during October. Explanations are not required.
2. Show the ending balances in Accounts Receivable, Allowance for Uncollectible Accounts, and *Net* Accounts Receivable at October 31. How much does the store expect to collect?
3. Show how the store will report Accounts Receivable and net sales on its October 31 balance sheet and income statement for the month ended October 31.

E5-27B. *(Learning Objective 4: Apply GAAP for uncollectible receivables)* At December 31, 2014, before any year-end adjustments, the Accounts Receivable balance of RTS Manufacturing is $260,000. The Allowance for Doubtful Accounts has a $16,000 credit balance. RTS Manufacturing prepares the following aging schedule for Accounts Receivable:

	Age of Accounts			
Total Balance	1–30 Days	31–60 Days	61–90 Days	Over 90 Days
$260,000	$100,000	$80,000	$60,000	$20,000
Estimated uncollectible	0.5%	5.0%	6.0%	60.0%

Requirements

1. Based on the aging of Accounts Receivable, is the unadjusted balance of the Allowance account adequate? Too high? Too low?
2. Make the entry required by the aging schedule. Prepare a T-account for the allowance.
3. Show how RTS Manufacturing will report Accounts Receivable on its December 31 balance sheet.

E5-28B. *(Learning Objective 4: Apply GAAP for uncollectible receivables)* Assume Seaside Foods, Inc., experienced the following revenue, sales returns and allowances, and accounts receivable write-offs:

Month	Service Revenue	Sales Returns	Accounts Receivable Write-Offs in Month			
			March	April	May	Totals
March	$ 4,800		$43	$ 81		$124
April	5,000			100	$ 31	131
May	5,300	$104			219	219
	$15,100	$104	$43	$181	$250	$474

Suppose Seaside estimates that 4% of (gross) revenues will become uncollectible. Assume all sales are on credit.

Requirement

1. Journalize service revenue (all on account), bad-debt expense, sales returns and allowances, and write-offs during May. Include explanations.

E5-29B. *(Learning Objective 5: Applying GAAP for notes receivable)* Record the following note receivable transactions in the journal of Oak Tree Realty. How much interest revenue did Oak Tree earn this year? *Use a 365-day year* for interest computations, and round interest amounts to the nearest dollar. Assume that Oak Tree Realty has a July 31 fiscal year-end.

May 1	Loaned $19,000 cash to Rock Cason on a one-year, 6% note.
Jul 6	Performed service for Fairway Golf Course, receiving a 90-day, 5% note for $15,000.
16	Received a $5,000, six-month, 4% note on account from Hull, Inc.
31	Accrued interest revenue for the year.

E5-30B. *(Learning Objectives 6, 7: Show how to speed up cash flow from receivables; evaluate liquidity through ratios)* Cherokee, Inc., reported the following items at December 31, 2014, and 2013:

	A	B	C	D	E	F
1	Balance Sheets (Summarized)					
2						
3		Year End			Year End	
4		2014	2013		2014	2013
5	Current assets:			Current liabilities:		
6	Cash	$ 7,000	$ 13,000	Accounts payable	$ 23,000	$ 24,500
7	Marketable securities	29,000	18,000	Other current liabilities	109,000	110,000
8	Accounts receivable, net	62,000	76,000	Long-term liabilities	19,000	21,000
9	Inventory	201,000	197,000			
10	Other current assets	5,000	5,000	Stockholders' equity	153,000	153,500
11	Total assets	$ 304,000	$ 309,000	Total liabilities and equity	$ 304,000	$ 309,000
12						
13	Income statement (partial):	2014				
14	Sales Revenue	$ 812,500				
15						

Requirements

1. Compute Cherokee's (a) quick (acid-test) ratio and (b) days' sales in receivables for 2014. Evaluate each ratio value as strong or weak. Cherokee sells on terms of net 30 days.
2. Recommend two ways for Cherokee to improve its cash flow from receivables.

E5-31B. *(Learning Objectives 6, 7: Show how to speed up cash flow from receivables; evaluate liquidity through ratios)* City Electronics Co., Inc., an electronics and appliance chain, reported these figures in millions of dollars:

	2015	2014
Net sales...	$750,500	$683,000
Receivables at end of year...............	4,870	5,210

Requirements

1. Compute City Electronics' days' sales in receivables or days' sales outstanding (DSO) during 2015.
2. Is City Electronics' DSO long or short? Chang Networks takes 39 days to collect its average level of receivables. QuickShip, the overnight shipper, takes 33 days. What causes City Electronics' collection period to be so different?

Quiz

Test your understanding of receivables by answering the following questions. Select the best choice from among the possible answers given.

Q5-32. USA National Bank, the nationwide banking company, owns many types of investments. Assume that USA National Bank paid $650,000 for trading securities on December 5. Two weeks later, USA National Bank received a $45,000 cash dividend. At December 31, these trading securities were quoted at a market price of $655,000. USA National Bank's December income statement would include an

    a. unrealized loss of $5,000.   **c.** unrealized gain of $50,000.

    b. unrealized gain of $5,000.   **d.** unrealized loss of $3,000.

Q5-33. Refer to the USA National Bank data in Q5-32. At December 31, USA National Bank's balance sheet should report

    a. Investment in trading securities   **c.** Investment in trading securities

        of $650,000.   of $655,000.

    b. unrealized gain of $5,000.   **d.** dividend revenue of $45,000.

Q5-34. Under the allowance method for uncollectible receivables, the entry to record uncollectible-account expense has what effect on the financial statements?

    a. Decreases owners' equity and increases liabilities

    b. Decreases assets and has no effect on net income

    c. Increases expenses and increases owners' equity

    d. Decreases net income and decreases assets

Q5-35. Maverick Company uses the aging method to adjust the allowance for uncollectible accounts at the end of the period. At December 31, 2014, the balance of accounts receivable is $220,000 and the allowance for uncollectible accounts has a credit balance of $3,000 (before adjustment). An analysis of accounts receivable produced the following age groups:

Current	$170,000
60 days past due.........................	41,000
Over 60 days past due................	9,000
	$220,000

Based on past experience, Maverick estimates that the percentage of accounts that will prove to be uncollectible within the three age groups is 2%, 8%, and 20%, respectively. Based on these facts, the adjusting entry for uncollectible accounts should be made in the amount of

    a. $5,480.   **c.** $11,480.

    b. $12,480.   **d.** $8,480.

Q5-36. Refer to Q5-35. The net receivables on the balance sheet is _____.

Q5-37. Lemmon Company uses the percent-of-sales method to estimate uncollectibles. Net credit sales for the current year amount to $100,000, and management estimates 2% will be uncollectible. Allowance for Doubtful Accounts prior to adjustment has a credit balance of $3,000. The amount of expense to report on the income statement will be

    a. $5,000.   **c.** $2,000.

    b. $1,500.   **d.** $6,000.

Q5-38. Refer to Q5-37. The balance of Allowance for Doubtful Accounts, after adjustment, will be

    a. $2,000.   **c.** $1,000.

    b. $5,000.   **d.** $1,500.

Q5-39. Refer to questions 5-37 and 5-38. The following year, Lemmon Company wrote off $2,000 of old receivables as uncollectible. What is the balance in the Allowance account now?

Questions 5-40 through 5-44 use the following data:

On August 1, 2014, Deeva, Inc., sold equipment and accepted a six-month, 11%, $30,000 note receivable. Deeva's year-end is December 31.

Q5-40. How much interest revenue should Deeva accrue on December 31, 2014?
- **a.** $1,650
- **b.** $1,100
- **c.** $3,300
- **d.** $1,375

Q5-41. If Deeva, Inc., fails to make an adjusting entry for the accrued interest on December 31, 2014,
- **a.** net income will be understated and assets will be understated.
- **b.** net income will be understated and liabilities will be overstated.
- **c.** net income will be overstated and assets will be overstated.
- **d.** net income will be overstated and liabilities will be understated.

Q5-42. How much interest does Deeva, Inc., expect to collect on the maturity date (February 1, 2015)?
- **a.** $3,300
- **b.** $1,375
- **c.** $1,650
- **d.** $1,100

Q5-43. Which of the following accounts will Deeva credit in the journal entry at maturity on February 1, 2015, assuming collection in full?
- **a.** Interest Payable
- **b.** Interest Receivable
- **c.** Note Payable
- **d.** Cash

Q5-44. Write the journal entry on the maturity date (February 1, 2015).

Q5-45. Which of the following is included in the calculation of the quick (acid-test) ratio?
- **a.** Prepaid expenses and cash
- **b.** Inventory and short-term investments
- **c.** Cash and accounts receivable
- **d.** Inventory and prepaid expenses

Q5-46. A company with net credit sales of $1,095,000, beginning net receivables of $90,000, and ending net receivables of $114,000 has days' sales in accounts receivable of
- **a.** 40 days.
- **b.** 37 days.
- **c.** 34 days.
- **d.** 44 days.

Q5-47. A company sells on credit terms of "2/10, n/30" and has days' sales in accounts receivable of 31 days. Its days' sales in receivables is
- **a.** about right.
- **b.** too high.
- **c.** too low.
- **d.** not able to be evaluated from the data given.

Problems

All of the A and B problems can be found within MyAccountingLab, an online homework and practice environment. Your instructor may ask you to complete these problems using **MyAccountingLab**.

MyAccountingLab

Group A

P5-48A. *(Learning Objective 1: Apply GAAP to short-term investments)* During the fourth quarter of 2014, Flyer, Inc., generated excess cash, which the company invested in trading securities as follows:

2014	
Nov 16	Purchased 2,500 common shares as an investment in trading securities, paying $8 per share.
Dec 16	Received cash dividend of $0.23 per share on the trading securities.
Dec 31	Adjusted the trading securities to fair value of $7 per share.

Requirements

1. Open T-accounts for Cash (including its beginning balance of $38,000), Investment in Trading Securities, Dividend Revenue, and Unrealized Gain (Loss) on Trading Securities.
2. Journalize the foregoing transactions and post to the T-accounts.
3. Show how to report the short-term investment on Flyer's balance sheet at December 31, 2014.
4. Show how to report whatever should appear on Flyer's income statement for the year ended December 31, 2014.
5. Flyer sold the trading securities for $19,850 on January 14, 2015. Journalize the sale.
6. Assume that the securities were classified as available-for-sale. Further, assume that the fair value was $10 per share on December 31, 2015, and $10.50 per share on January 1, 2016 when they were sold. Re-perform steps 3–4 for 2014 and 2015, and journalize the sale of the securities on January 1, 2016. Follow the example in Exhibit 5-2.

P5-49A. *(Learning Objective 3: Apply controls to cash receipts from customers)* Brierra Products, Inc., makes all sales on account. Brittney Sims, accountant for the company, receives and opens incoming mail. Company procedure requires Sims to separate customer checks from the remittance slips, which list the amounts that Sims posts as credits to customer accounts receivable. Sims deposits the checks in the bank. At the end of each day, she computes the day's total amount posted to customer accounts and matches this total to the bank deposit slip. This procedure ensures that all receipts are deposited in the bank.

Requirement

1. As a consultant hired by Brierra Products, Inc., write a memo to management evaluating the company's internal controls over cash receipts from customers. If the system is effective, identify its strong features. If the system has flaws, propose a way to strengthen the controls.

P5-50A. *(Learning Objectives 2, 3, 4, 5: Apply GAAP for revenue, receivables, collections, and uncollectibles using the percent-of-sales method; account for notes receivable)* This problem takes you through the accounting for sales, receivables, uncollectibles, and notes receivable for Quick Mail Corp., the overnight shipper. By selling on credit, the company cannot expect to collect 100% of its accounts receivable. At July 31, 2014, and 2015, respectively, Quick Mail Corp. reported the following on its balance sheet (in millions of dollars):

	July 31, 2015	July 31, 2014
Accounts receivable	$6,990	$5,830
Less: Allowance for uncollectible accounts	(1,419)	(860)
Accounts receivable, net	$5,571	$4,970

During the year ended July 31, 2015, Quick Mail Corp. earned service revenue and collected cash from customers. Assume uncollectible-account expense for the year was 4% of service revenue on account and that Quick Mail wrote off uncollectible receivables and made other adjustments as necessary (see below). At year-end, Quick Mail ended with the foregoing July 31, 2015, balances.

Requirements

1. Prepare T-accounts for Accounts Receivable and Allowance for Uncollectible Accounts and insert the July 31, 2014, balances as given.
2. Journalize the following assumed transactions of Quick Mail Corp. for the year ended July 31, 2015 (explanations are not required):
   a. Service revenue was $98,480 million, of which 10% is cash and the remainder on account.
   b. Collections from customers on account were $84,341 million.
   c. Uncollectible-account expense was 4% of service revenue on account.
   d. Write-offs of uncollectible accounts receivable were $2,986 million.
   e. On July 1, Quick Mail received a 2-month, 6%, $203 million note receivable from a large corporate customer in exchange for the customer's past due account; Quick Mail made the proper year-end adjusting entry for the interest on this note.
   f. Quick Mail's July 31, 2015 year-end bank statement reported $58 million of NSF checks from customers.
3. Post your entries to the Accounts Receivable and the Allowance for Uncollectible Accounts T-accounts.
4. Compute the ending balances for Accounts Receivable and the Allowance for Uncollectible Accounts and compare your balances to the actual July 31, 2015, amounts. They should be the same. How much does Quick Mail expect to collect from its customers after July 31, 2015?
5. Show the net effect of these transactions on Quick Mail's net income for the year ended July 31, 2015.

P5-51A. *(Learning Objective 4: Apply GAAP for uncollectible receivables)* The September 30, 2015, records of Asher Communications include these accounts:

Accounts Receivable......................................	$473,000
Allowance for Doubtful Accounts...............	(15,100)

During the year, Asher Communications estimates doubtful-account expense at 1% of credit sales. At year-end (December 31), the company ages its receivables and adjusts the balance in Allowance for Doubtful Accounts to correspond to the aging schedule below.

	Age of Accounts			
Accounts Receivable	**1–30 Days**	**31–60 Days**	**61–90 Days**	**Over 90 Days**
$427,000	$259,000	$93,000	$39,000	$36,000
Estimated percent uncollectible	0.2%	2%	15%	35%

During the last quarter of 2015, the company completed the following selected transactions:

Nov 30	Wrote off as uncollectible the $3,100 account receivable from Proctor Carpets and the $800 account receivable from Antiques on Austin.
Dec 31	Adjusted the Allowance for Doubtful Accounts and recorded doubtful-account expense at year-end, based on the aging of receivables.

Requirements

1. Record the transactions for the last quarter of 2015 in the journal. Explanations are not required.
2. Prepare a T-account for Allowance for Doubtful Accounts with the appropriate beginning balance. Post the entries from Requirement 1 to that account.
3. Show how Asher Communications will report its accounts receivable in a comparative balance sheet for 2014 and 2015. Use the three-line reporting format. At December 31, 2014, the company's Accounts Receivable balance was $408,000, and the Allowance for Doubtful Accounts stood at $9,700.

P5-52A. *(Learning Objectives 1, 4, 7: Apply GAAP for short-term investments and uncollectible receivables; evaluate liquidity through ratios)* Assume Weithorn & Wesley, the accounting firm, advises Lakeside Seafood that its financial statements must be changed to conform to GAAP. At December 31, 2014, Lakeside's accounts include the following:

Cash	$21,000
Investment in trading securities, at cost	14,000
Accounts receivable	29,000
Inventory	28,000
Prepaid expenses	6,000
Total current assets	$98,000
Accounts payable	$30,000
Other current liabilities	27,000
Total current liabilities	$57,000

The accounting firm advised Lakeside of the following:

- Cash includes $9,000 that is deposited in a compensating balance account that is tied up until 2016.
- The market value of the trading securities is $12,000. Lakeside purchased the investments a couple of weeks ago.
- Lakeside has been using the direct write-off method to account for uncollectible receivables. During 2014, Lakeside wrote off bad receivables of $500. The aging of Lakeside's receivables at year-end indicated uncollectibles of $1,700.
- Lakeside reported net income of $46,000 in 2014.

Requirements

1. Restate Lakeside's current accounts to conform to GAAP. (Challenge)
2. Compute Lakeside's current ratio and quick (acid-test) ratio both before and after your corrections.
3. Determine Lakeside's correct net income for 2014. (Challenge)

P5-53A. *(Learning Objective 4: Apply GAAP for notes receivable)* Best Foods completed the following selected transactions.

2014		
	Oct 31	Sold goods to Stan's Foods, receiving a $24,000, three-month, 6% note.
	Dec 31	Made an adjusting entry to accrue interest on the Stan's Foods note.
2015		
	Jan 31	Collected the Stan's Foods note.
	Feb 18	Received a 90-day, 7.75%, $6,800 note from Dutton Market on account.
	19	Sold the Dutton Market note to United Bank, receiving cash of $6,600. (Debit the difference to financing expense.)
	Nov 11	Loaned $15,000 cash to Kosher Foods Co., receiving a 90-day, 4.75% note.
	Dec 31	Accrued the interest on the Kosher Foods Co. note.

Requirements

1. Record the transactions in Best Foods' journal. Round interest amounts to the nearest dollar. Explanations are not required.
2. Show what Best Foods will report on its comparative classified balance sheet at December 31, 2015, and December 31, 2014.

P5-54A. *(Learning Objectives 6, 7: Show how to speed up cash flow from receivables; evaluate liquidity using ratios)* The comparative financial statements of SunShine Pools, Inc., for 2015, 2014, and 2013 included the following select data:

	(In millions)		
	2015	2014	2013
Balance sheet			
Current assets:			
Cash...	$ 100	$ 80	$ 60
Investment in Trading Securities	145	165	120
Receivables, net of allowance			
for doubtful accounts of $7, $6,			
and $4, respectively	270	260	230
Inventories	365	330	300
Prepaid expenses	60	5	45
Total current assets	$ 940	$ 840	$ 755
Total current liabilities......................	$ 585	$ 650	$ 685
Income statement			
Net sales	$5,940	$5,200	$4,320

Requirements

1. Compute these ratios for 2015 and 2014:
   a. Current ratio
   b. Quick (acid-test) ratio
   c. Days' sales in receivables
2. Which ratios improved from 2014 to 2015 and which ratios deteriorated? Is this trend favorable or unfavorable?
3. Recommend two ways for SunShine Pools to improve cash flows from receivables.

Group B

P5-55B. *(Learning Objective 1: Apply GAAP for short-term investments)* During the fourth quarter of 2014, Beachwear Sales, Inc., generated excess cash, which the company invested in trading securities:

2014	
Nov 17	Purchased 2,100 common shares as an investment in trading securities, paying $11 per share.
Dec 19	Received cash dividend of $0.47 per share on the trading securities.
Dec 31	Adjusted the trading securities to fair value of $9 per share.

Requirements

1. Open T-accounts for Cash (including its beginning balance of $29,000), Investment in Trading Securities, Dividend Revenue, and Unrealized Gain (Loss) on Trading Securities.
2. Journalize the foregoing transactions and post to the T-accounts.

3. Show how to report the short-term investment on Beachwear Sales's balance sheet at December 31, 2014.

4. Show how to report whatever should appear on Beachwear Sales's income statement for the year ended December 31, 2014.

5. Beachwear Sales sold the trading securities for $21,928 on January 11, 2015. Journalize the sale.

6. Assume that the securities were classified as available-for-sale. Further, assume that the fair value was $10 per share on December 31, 2015, and $9 per share on January 1, 2016 when they were sold. Re-perform steps 3–4 for 2014 and 2015, and journalize the sale of the securities on January 1, 2016. Follow the example in Exhibit 5-2.

P5-56B. *(Learning Objective 3: Apply controls to cash receipts from customers)* Drury Computer Solutions makes all sales on account, so virtually all cash receipts arrive in the mail. Wes Cowley, the company president, has just returned from a trade association meeting with new ideas for the business. Among other things, Cowley plans to institute stronger internal controls over cash receipts from customers.

Requirement

1. Take the role of Wes Cowley, the company president. Write a memo to employees outlining procedures to ensure that all cash receipts are deposited in the bank and that the total amounts of each day's cash receipts are posted to customer accounts receivable.

P5-57B. *(Learning Objectives 2, 3, 4, 5: Apply GAAP for revenue, receivables, collections, and uncollectibles using the percent-of-sales method; account for notes receivable)* This problem takes you through the accounting for sales, receivables, uncollectibles, and notes receivable for Ship Fast Corp, the overnight shipper. By selling on credit, the company cannot expect to collect 100% of its accounts receivable. At July 31, 2014, and 2015, respectively, Ship Fast Corp. reported the following on its balance sheet (in millions of dollars):

	July 31,	
	2015	2014
Accounts receivable...	$6,095	$5,836
Less: Allowance for uncollectible accounts...............	(1,821)	(759)
Accounts receivable, net...	$4,274	$5,077

During the year ended July 31, 2015, Ship Fast Corp. earned sales revenue and collected cash from customers. Assume uncollectible-account expense for the year was 5% of service revenue on account, and Ship Fast wrote off uncollectible receivables and made other adjustments as necessary (see below). At year-end, Ship Fast ended with the foregoing July 31, 2015, balances.

Requirements

1. Prepare T-accounts for Accounts Receivable and Allowance for Uncollectible Accounts, and insert the July 31, 2014, balances as given.

2. Journalize the following transactions of Ship Fast for the year ended July 31, 2015. (Explanations are not required.)
   a. Service revenue was $99,484 million, of which 10% is for cash and the remainder on account.
   b. Collections from customers on account were $85,706 million.
   c. Uncollectible-account expense was 5% of service revenue on account.
   d. Write-offs of uncollectible accounts receivable were $3,415 million.
   e. On July 1, Ship Fast received a 2-month, 6%, $198 million note receivable from a large corporate customer in exchange for the customer's past due account; Ship Fast made the proper year-end adjusting entry for the interest on this note.
   f. Ship Fast's July 31, 2015 year-end bank statement reported $42 million of NSF checks from customers.

3. Post to the Accounts Receivable and Allowance for Uncollectible Accounts T-accounts.
4. Compute the ending balances for Accounts Receivable and Allowance for Uncollectible Accounts and compare your balances to the actual July 31, 2015, amounts. They should be the same. How much does Ship Fast expect to collect from its customers after July 31, 2015?
5. Show the net effect of these transactions on Ship Fast's net income for the year ended July 31, 2015.

P5-58B. *(Learning Objective 4: Apply GAAP for uncollectible receivables)* The September 30, 2015, records of Foglemann Communications include these accounts:

Accounts Receivable.....................................	$462,000
Allowance for Doubtful Accounts	(15,300)

During the year, Foglemann Communications estimates doubtful-account expense at 1% of credit sales. At year-end, the company ages its receivables and adjusts the balance in Allowance for Doubtful Accounts to correspond to the aging schedule.

	Age of Accounts			
Accounts Receivable	1–30 Days	31–60 Days	61–90 Days	Over 90 Days
$438,000	$255,000	$78,000	$26,000	$79,000
Estimated percent uncollectible	0.3%	3%	12%	25%

During the last quarter of 2015, the company completed the following selected transactions:

Nov 30	Wrote off as uncollectible the $2,500 account receivable from Frisco Carpets and the $900 account receivable from Antiques on the Avenue.
Dec 31	Adjusted the Allowance for Doubtful Accounts and recorded doubtful-account expense at year-end, based on the aging of receivables.

Requirements

1. Record the transactions for the last quarter of 2015 in the journal. Explanations are not required.
2. Prepare a T-account for Allowance for Doubtful Accounts with the appropriate beginning balance. Post the entries from requirement 1 to that account.
3. Show how Foglemann Communications will report its accounts receivable in a comparative balance sheet for 2015 and 2014. Use the three-line reporting format. At December 31, 2014, the company's Accounts Receivable balance was $432,000 and the Allowance for Doubtful Accounts stood at $7,300.

P5-59B. *(Learning Objectives 1, 4, 7: Apply GAAP for short-term investments and uncollectible receivables; evaluate liquidity through ratios)* Assume Killough & Kirkland, the accounting firm, advises Beachfront Seafood Sales that its financial statement must be changed to conform to GAAP. At December 31, 2014, Beachfront's accounts include the following:

Cash...	$15,000
Investment in Trading Securities, at cost	9,000
Accounts receivable..	31,000
Inventory..	28,000
Prepaid expenses	7,000
Total current assets	$90,000
Accounts payable	$30,000
Other current liabilities	19,000
Total current liabilities...............................	$49,000

The accounting firm advised Beachfront of the following:

- Cash includes $4,000 that is deposited in a compensating balance account that will be tied up until 2016.
- The market value of the trading securities is $8,700. Beachfront purchased the trading securities a couple of weeks ago.
- Beachfront has been using the direct write-off method to account for uncollectible receivables. During 2014, Beachfront wrote off bad receivables of $600. The aging of Beachfront's receivables at year-end indicated uncollectibles of $2,400.
- Beachfront reported net income of $54,000 for 2014.

Requirements

1. Restate Beachfront's current accounts to conform to GAAP. (Challenge)
2. Compute Beachfront's current ratio and quick (acid-test) ratio both before and after your corrections.
3. Determine Beachfront's correct net income for 2014. (Challenge)

P5-60B. *(Learning Objective 5: Apply GAAP for notes receivable)* Breckenridge Nutrition completed the following selected transactions:

2014	
Oct 31	Sold goods to Best-Yet Foods, receiving a $36,000, three-month 5.00% note.
Dec 31	Made an adjusting entry to accrue interest on the Best-Yet foods note.
2015	
Jan 31	Collected the Best-Yet Foods note.
Feb 18	Received a 90-day, 4.50%, $7,400 note from Daphne's Market on account.
19	Sold the Daphne's Market note to City Bank, receiving cash of $7,200. (Debit the difference to financing expense.)
Nov 11	Loaned $15,500 to Tiger Foods, receiving a 90-day, 6.00% note.
Dec 31	Accrued the interest on the Tiger Foods note.

Requirements

1. Record the transactions in Breckenridge Nutrition's journal. Round all amounts to the nearest dollar; explanations are not required.
2. Show what Breckenridge Nutrition will report on its comparative classified balance sheet at December 31, 2015, and December 31, 2014.

P5-61B. *(Learning Objectives 6, 7: Show how to speed up cash flow from receivables; evaluate liquidity through ratios)* The comparative financial statements of Southside Pools, Inc., for 2015, 2014, and 2013 included the following select data:

		(In millions)	
	2015	**2014**	**2013**
Balance sheet			
Current assets:			
Cash...	$ 110	$ 90	$ 60
Investment in Trading Securities	140	175	115
Receivables, net of allowance for doubtful accounts of $7, $6, and $4, respectively	290	260	250
Inventories	365	325	315
Prepaid expenses	45	20	30
Total current assets	$ 950	$ 870	$ 770
Total current liabilities......................	$ 545	$ 630	$ 645
Income statement			
Net sales	$5,960	$5,210	$4,340

Requirements

1. Compute these ratios for 2015 and 2014:
   a. Current ratio
   b. Quick (acid-test) ratio
   c. Days' sales in receivables
2. Which ratios improved from 2014 to 2015 and which ratios deteriorated? Is this trend favorable or unfavorable?
3. Recommend two ways for Southside Pools, Inc., to improve cash flow from receivables.

Challenge Exercises and Problem

E5-62. *(Learning Objective 6: Show how to speed up cash from receivables)* Retro Shirt Company sells on credit and manages its own receivables. Average experience for the past three years has been the following:

	Cash	Credit	Total
Sales	$250,000	$250,000	$500,000
Cost of goods sold	125,000	125,000	250,000
Uncollectible-account expense	—	12,000	12,000
Other expenses	82,500	82,500	165,000

Samuel Mormino, the owner, is considering whether to accept bankcards (VISA, MasterCard). Mormino expects total sales to increase by 10% but cash sales to remain unchanged. If Mormino switches to bankcards, the business can save $8,000 on other expenses, but VISA and MasterCard charge 3% on bankcard sales. Mormino figures that the increase in sales will be due to the increased volume of bankcard sales.

Requirement

1. Should Retro Shirt Company start selling on bankcards? Show the computations of net income under the present plan and under the bankcard plan.

E5-63. *(Learning Objectives 3, 4: Apply GAAP for receivables and uncollectible receivables)* Suppose Overpriced, Inc., reported net receivables of $2,582 million and $2,269 million at January 31, 2015, and 2014, respectively, after subtracting allowances of $71 million and $67 million at these respective dates. Overpriced earned total revenue of $26,667 million (all on account) and recorded doubtful-account expense of $8 million for the year ended January 31, 2015.

Requirement

1. Use this information to measure the following amounts for the year ended January 31, 2015:
   a. Write-offs of uncollectible receivables
   b. Collections from customers

P5-64. *(Learning Objectives 2, 3, 4: Analyze accounts receivable)* The balance sheet of InSpace, Inc., a world leader in the design and sale of telescopic equipment, reported the following information on its balance sheets for 2014 and 2013 (figures are in thousands):

(In thousands)	December 31, 2014	December 31, 2013
Accounts receivable (net of allowance of $1,000 and $930, respectively)	$8,300	$8,500

In 2014, InSpace recorded $16,500 in sales (all on account), of which $900 was returned for credit. InSpace offers its customers credit terms of 2/10, n/30. Seventy-five percent of collections on accounts receivable were made within the discount period. InSpace wrote off uncollectible accounts receivable in the amount of $130 during 2014.

Requirements

1. Compute the amount of uncollectible accounts expense recorded by InSpace in 2014.
2. Compute InSpace's cash collections from customers in 2014.
3. Open T-accounts for Accounts Receivable and Allowance for Uncollectible Accounts. Enter the beginning balances into each of these accounts. Prepare summary journal entries in the T-accounts to record the following for 2014:
   a. Sales
   b. Collections
   c. Sales returns
   d. Write-offs of uncollectible accounts
   e. Uncollectible-Accounts Expense

APPLY YOUR KNOWLEDGE

Decision Cases

Case 1. *(Learning Objectives 2, 3, 4: Apply GAAP for revenue, accounts receivable, and uncollectible receivables)* A fire during 2014 destroyed most of the accounting records of Clearview Cablevision, Inc. The only accounting data for 2014 that Clearview can come up with are the following balances at December 31, 2014. The general manager also knows that bad-debt expense should be 5% of service revenue on credit.

Accounts receivable, December 31, 2014	$180,000
Less: Allowance for bad debts	(22,000)
Total expenses, excluding bad-debt expense	670,000
Collections from customers	840,000
Write-offs of bad receivables	30,000
Accounts receivable, December 31, 2013	110,000

Prepare a summary income statement for Clearview Cablevision, Inc., for the year ended December 31, 2014. The stockholders want to know whether the company was profitable in 2014. Use a T-account for Accounts Receivable to compute service revenue. Assume that all revenues are on credit.

Case 2. *(Learning Objectives 4, 7: Apply GAAP for uncollectible receivables; evaluate liquidity through ratios)* Suppose you work in the loan department of Superior Bank. Dean Young, owner of Dean Young Beauty Aids, has come to you seeking a loan for $500,000 to expand operations. Young proposes to use accounts receivable as collateral for the loan and has provided you with the following information from the company's most recent financial statements:

	2015	2014	2013
	(In thousands)		
Sales	$1,475	$1,001	$902
Cost of goods sold	876	647	605
Gross profit	599	354	297
Other expenses	518	287	253
Net profit or (loss) before taxes	$ 81	$ 67	$ 44
Accounts receivable	$ 128	$ 107	$ 94
Allowance for doubtful accounts	13	11	9

Requirement

1. Analyze the trends of sales, days' sales in receivables, and cash collections from customers for 2015 and 2014. Would you make the loan to Young? Support your decision with facts and figures.

Ethical Issue

Sunnyvale Loan Company is in the consumer loan business. Sunnyvale borrows from banks and loans out the money at higher interest rates. Sunnyvale's bank requires Sunnyvale to submit quarterly financial statements to keep its line of credit. Sunnyvale's main asset is Notes Receivable. Therefore, Uncollectible-Account Expense and Allowance for Uncollectible Accounts are important accounts for the company.

Kimberly Burnham, the company's owner, prefers that net income reflect a steady increase in a smooth pattern, rather than an increase in some periods and a decrease in other periods. To report smoothly increasing net income, Burnham underestimates Uncollectible-Account Expense in some periods. In other periods, Burnham overestimates the expense. She reasons that the income overstatements roughly offset the income understatements over time.

Requirements

1. What is the ethical issue in this situation?
2. Who are the stakeholders? What are the possible consequences to each?
3. Analyze the alternatives from the following standpoints: (a) economic, (b) legal, (c) ethical.
4. What would you do? How would you justify your decision?

Focus on Financials | Amazon.com, Inc.

(Learning Objectives 1, 2: Account for short-term investments; apply GAAP for proper revenue recognition) Refer to **Amazon.com, Inc.'s** consolidated financial statements in Appendix A at the end of this book.

1. Examine the account "marketable securities" in the consolidated balance sheet, as well as Notes 1 and 2.
   a. What does this account consist of?
   b. Why do you think the company has made these investments?
   c. What percentage change has occurred in short-term investments from December 31, 2011, to December 31, 2012? What management business strategy might this reveal?
   d. Using the financial statement footnotes for reference, explain how Amazon.com, Inc., accounts for marketable securities. What footnote contains this information?
   e. Has the company profited from holding its portfolio of marketable securities during the year ended December 31, 2012? How do you know?
2. Using the "Description of Business" section of Note 1 as a reference, describe how Amazon.com, Inc., recognizes revenue.
3. The fourth account listed on Amazon.com's Consolidated Balance Sheet is called "accounts receivable, net and other." What does the "net" mean?
4. Refer to Note 1. What kinds of accounts receivable are included in Amazon.com, Inc.'s receivables?
5. How much is the allowance for doubtful accounts in 2012 and 2011?
6. Calculate the current ratio, quick (acid-test) ratio, and net working capital for Amazon.com, Inc. for 2012 and 2011. Evaluate Amazon.com, Inc.'s liquidity trend over the two years. What other information might be helpful in evaluating these statistics?

Focus on Analysis | Yum! Brands, Inc.

(Learning Objectives 2, 3: Apply GAAP for revenue recognition; account for and control accounts receivable) This case is based on **Yum! Brands, Inc.'s** consolidated balance sheets, consolidated statements of income, and Note 2 of its financial statements (Significant Accounting Policies) in Appendix B at the end of this book.

1. Describe Yum! Brands, Inc.'s revenue recognition policy. From what sources does it earn most of its revenue?
2. Since Yum! Brands, Inc., is a consumer retail business, most of its retail sales are cash sales. However, accounts receivable still comprise about 16% ($301/$1,909) of its current assets. What customers do business with Yum! Brands, Inc., on account? Why is this necessary? What is the average payment term for these receivables?
3. Compute the following for 2012:
   a. Average daily sales, using total revenues.
   b. Days' sales to collection for accounts receivable.
   c. Compare part b with the average payment term for accounts receivable. Did the company perform better or worse than its normal payment terms for its credit customers?
4. Calculate the current ratio, quick (acid-test) ratio, and net working capital for Yum! Brands, Inc. for 2012 and 2011. Evaluate the two year trend in Yum! Brands, Inc.'s liquidity. What other information might be helpful in evaluating these statistics?

Group Project

Jillian Michaels and Dee Childress worked for several years as sales representatives for Xerox Corporation. During this time, they became close friends as they acquired expertise with the company's full range of copier equipment. Now they see an opportunity to put their expertise to work and fulfill lifelong desires to establish their own business. Navarro Community College, located in their city, is expanding, and there is no copy center within five miles of the campus. Business in the area is booming, office buildings and apartments are springing up, and the population of the Navarro section of the city is growing.

Michaels and Childress want to open a copy center, similar to FedEx Kinko's, near the Navarro campus. A small shopping center across the street from the college has a vacancy that would fit their needs. Michaels and Childress each have $35,000 to invest in the business, but they forecast the need for $200,000 to renovate the store and purchase some equipment. Xerox Corporation will lease two large copiers to them at a total monthly rental of $6,000. With enough cash to see them through the first six months of operation, they are confident they can make the business succeed. The two women work very well together, and both have excellent credit ratings. Michaels and Childress must borrow $130,000 to start the business, advertise its opening, and keep it running for its first six months.

Requirements

Assume two roles: (1) Michaels and Childress, the partners who will own Navarro Copy Center; and (2) loan officers at Synergy Bank.

1. As a group, visit a copy center to familiarize yourselves with its operations. If possible, interview the manager or another employee. Then write a loan request that Michaels and Childress will submit to Synergy Bank with the intent of borrowing $130,000 to be paid back over three years. The loan will be a personal loan to the partnership of Michaels and Childress, not to Navarro Copy Center. The request should specify all the details of the plan that will motivate the bank to grant the loan. Include a budget for each of the first six months of operation of the proposed copy center.
2. As a group, interview a loan officer in a bank. Write Synergy Bank's reply to the loan request. Specify all the details that the bank should require as conditions for making the loan.
3. If necessary, modify the loan request or the bank's reply in order to reach agreement between the two parties.

Quick Check Answers

1. *a*
2. *b*
3. *d* ($94,000 × 0.03)
4. *c* ($1,500 + $2,820)
5. *b* ($2,280 − $1,500)
6. *a*
7. *c* ($26,000 − $2,280)
8. *b* ($3,600 − $70) − ($200 − $70)
9. *d* ($450,000 + $1,820,000 − $525,000)
10. *d* ($15,000 × 0.07 × 4/12 × 1/4)
11. *c* [$40,000 + ($40,000 × 0.05 × 6/12)]
12. *a*
13. *d* [($36,000 + $46,000)/2] ÷ ($621,500/365)
14. *c* ($2,500 + $10,000 + $6,400) ÷ ($9,000 + $3,000)

6 Inventory & Cost of Goods Sold

You've recently returned to college for the fall semester and taken a part-time campus job; you study in a small city in the Southeastern part of the United States. Your parents are doing everything they can to help you financially but, for the most part, you're on your own, using the income from the job, scholarships, and student loans to pay expenses. Money is tight, so you've moved into an unfurnished apartment on the edge of campus. The day you move in, you discover that you need a few basic household items: cleaning supplies, bath and kitchen towels, laundry detergent, paper products, a few small pieces of furniture, some frozen foods and bottled water for the fridge. Your car has broken down, and your work schedule makes it inconvenient for your friends to drive you to the giant discount store on the other side of town just to get a few basic items that might cost only pennies less. Then it hits you: How about trying the Family Dollar Store right down the block? You could walk to the store, pick these items up for a reasonable price, and be out in 10 minutes, saving both money and time.

Family Dollar Stores, Inc., operates more than 7,400 general merchandise retail discount stores in 45 states, providing value-conscious consumers with a selection of competitively-priced merchandise in a number of core categories: health and beauty aids, packaged food and refrigerated products, home cleaning supplies, housewares, stationery, seasonal goods, apparel, and home fashions. The majority of Family Dollar Stores, Inc.'s products are priced at $10 or less, with approximately 28% priced at $1 or less. Although the variety of products offered by Family Dollar Stores is not nearly as extensive as that of the giant discount retailers such as Walmart, its prices are competitive for the products it sells. It operates from 11 giant distribution centers that are centrally located in the states it serves. It buys in large quantities, allowing it to pass on lower prices from suppliers along to its customers.

Family Dollar Stores, Inc.'s consolidated balance sheets for fiscal 2012 and 2011 are summarized on the following page. You can see that, as of August 25, 2012, merchandise inventory is by far Family Dollar Stores' largest current asset ($1.4 billion, or 81% of the total). That's not surprising since Family Dollar Stores, like other retailers, relies on inventory as its lifeblood for everyday operations.

Ross Taylor/AP Images

If a customer walks into a Family Dollar Store looking for a certain type of laundry detergent, for example, and doesn't find it, they might not return; having the inventory on hand at a competitive price is a key element of the company's strategy. A closer look at the company's balance sheet shows that the company increased its merchandise inventory levels by about $271.5 million (23.5%) between fiscal 2011 and 2012. Why would it do that? The U.S. economy was struggling to recover from an economic recession in 2012, and cost-conscious consumers were looking for bargains at every turn, so the budget retail business was growing. Family Dollar Stores, Inc., increased inventory levels in anticipation of increased sales volume.

We also present Family Dollar Stores' Consolidated Statements of Income for the comparative fiscal years 2012 and 2011, on page 302. A few quick computations will show that, during fiscal 2012, net sales increased by $783 million (9.2%), compared with fiscal 2011. The corresponding increase in cost of goods sold (related to inventories, as we will see later) was $555.5 million (10.1%). The company also incurred an additional $177.6 million in selling, general, and administrative expenses (up only 7.4% over 2011). As a result, the company's operating profits increased by $50 million (about 7.8%), and pre-tax earnings increased by about $47 million (7.6%). In short, as revenues increased, cost of goods sold increased at a slightly greater pace, but the company made up the difference by cutting selling, general, and administrative expenses, resulting in an increased operating profit of about 7.8%. Net income for fiscal 2012 increased by about 8.7% over 2011.

A1				
	A	**B**	**C**	**D**
1	**Family Dollar Stores, Inc.** **Consolidated Balance Sheets** **(Adapted, In thousands of $)**	**Fiscal 2012**	**Fiscal 2011**	
2	**Assets**	**Aug. 25, 2012**	**Aug. 27, 2011**	**% change**
3	Current assets			
4	Cash and cash equivalents	$ 92,333	$ 141,405	
5	Short-term investment securities	6,271	96,006	
6	Restricted cash and investments	126,281	0	
7	Merchandise inventories	1,426,163	1,154,660	23.5%
8	Deferred income taxes	69,518	60,011	
9	Income tax refund receivable	0	10,326	
10	Prepayments and other	47,604	71,436	
11	Total current assets	1,768,170	1,533,844	
12	Property and equipment, net	1,496,360	1,280,589	
13	Investment securities	23,720	107,458	
14	Other Assets, Noncurrent	84,815	74,314	
15	Total assets	$ 3,373,065	$ 2,996,205	
16	**Liabilities and Stockholders' Equity**			
17	Current liabilities	$ 1,065,657	$ 1,017,055	
18	Long-term liabilities	1,009,781	892,076	
19	Total liabilities	2,075,438	1,909,131	
20	Stockholders' equity	1,297,627	1,087,074	
21	Total liabilities and stockholders' equity	$ 3,373,065	$ 2,996,205	
22				

A1			B	C	D	E
	Family Dollar Stores, Inc. Consolidated Statements of Income (Adapted, in thousands of $)		**Fiscal 2012**	**Fiscal 2011**		
1						
2			**12 Months Ended**			
3			**Aug. 25, 2012**	**Aug. 27, 2011**	**change**	**% change**
4	Net sales		$ 9,331,005	$ 8,547,835	$ 783,170	9.2%
5	Cost of goods sold		6,071,058	5,515,540	555,518	10.1%
6	Gross margin (gross profit)		3,259,947	3,032,295	227,652	7.5%
7	Selling, general and administrative		2,571,846	2,394,223	177,623	7.4%
8	Operating profit		688,101	638,072	50,029	7.8%
9	Other income (expense)		(24,163)	(20,914)	(3,249)	15.5%
10	Income before income taxes		663,938	617,158	46,780	7.6%
11	Income taxes		241,698	228,713	12,985	5.7%
12	Net income		$ 422,240	$ 388,445	$ 33,795	8.7%
13						

You can see that cost of goods sold is by far Family Dollar Stores' largest expense. The title Cost of Goods Sold[1] perfectly describes that expense. In short:

- Family Dollar Stores buys inventory, an asset carried on the books at the lower of its cost or market value (replacement cost).
- The goods that Family Dollar Stores sells are no longer Family Dollar Stores' assets. The cost of inventory that's sold gets shifted into the expense account Cost of Goods Sold. ●

Merchandise inventory is the heart of a merchandising business, and cost of goods sold is the most important expense for a company that sells goods rather than services. Gross profit (or gross margin) is the difference between net sales and cost of goods sold. **This chapter covers the accounting for inventory and cost of goods sold.** It also shows you how to analyze the impact of changes in this asset and expense on the financial statements. Here we focus on inventory, cost of goods sold, and gross margin (or gross profit).

Learning Objectives

1. **Show** how to account for inventory

2. **Apply and compare** various inventory cost methods

3. **Explain and apply** underlying GAAP for inventory

4. **Compute and evaluate** gross profit (margin) percentage and inventory turnover

5. **Use** the cost-of-goods-sold (COGS) model to make management decisions

6. **Analyze** effects of inventory errors

---

[1] In this chapter and throughout this text, you may assume that "cost of goods sold" and "cost of sales" are synonymous.

You can access the most current annual report of Family Dollar Stores, Inc., in Excel format at **www.sec.gov.** Using the "filings" link on the toolbar at the top of the page, select "company filings search." This will take you to the "EDGAR Company Filings" page." Type "Family Dollar Stores" in the company name box, and select "search." This will produce the "EDGAR search results" page showing the company name. Click on the "CIK" link beside the company name. This will pull up all of the reports that the company has filed with the SEC. Under the "filing type" box, type "10-K." Form 10-K is the SEC form for the company's latest annual report. Find the year that you wish to view. Click on the "Interactive Data" box, which takes you to the "View Filing Data" page. You may choose to either open or download the Excel files containing the company's most recent financial statements. ■

SHOW HOW TO ACCOUNT FOR INVENTORY

We begin by showing how the financial statements of a merchandiser such as Family Dollar Stores, Inc., or The Gap, Inc., differ from those of service entities such as FedEx and Century 21 Real Estate. The financial statements in Exhibit 6-1 highlight how service entities differ from merchandisers.

1 **Show** how to account for inventory

Exhibit 6-1 | Contrasting a Service Company with a Merchandising Company

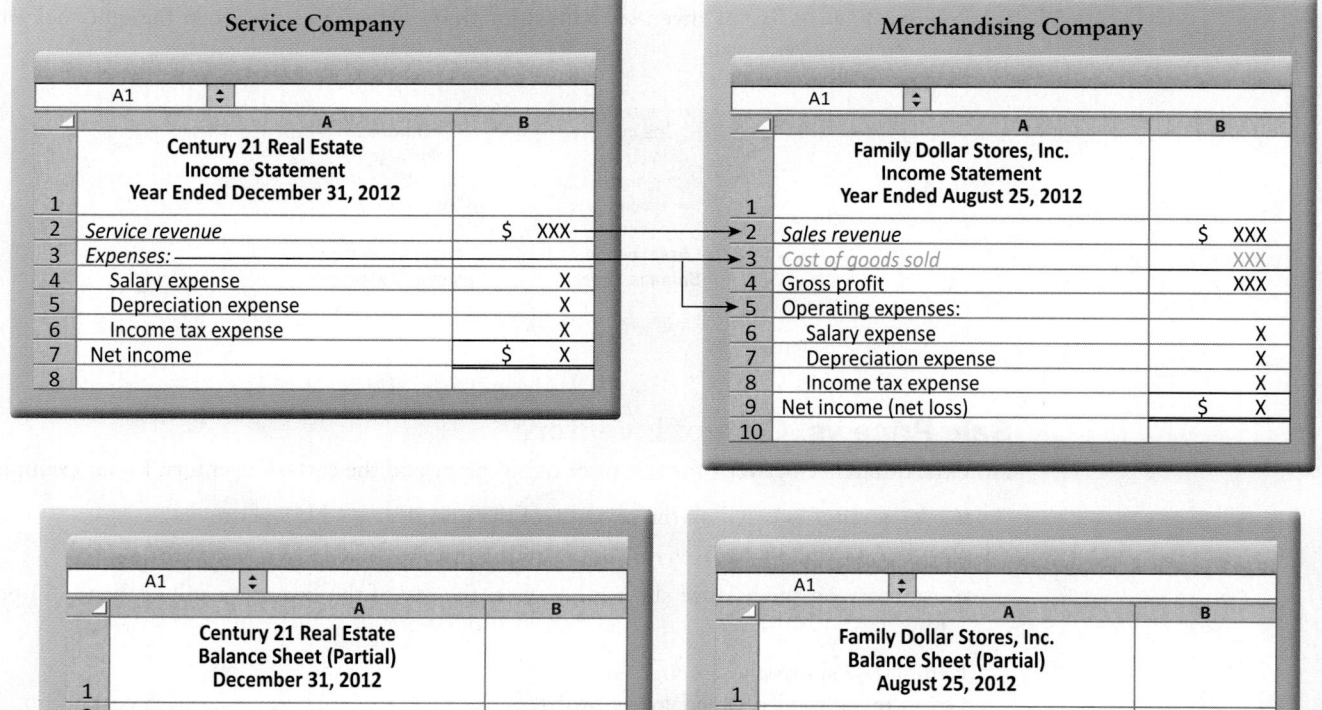

Merchandisers have two accounts that service entities don't need:
- Cost of goods sold on the income statement
- Inventory on the balance sheet

The basic concept of accounting for merchandise inventory can be illustrated with an example. Suppose that Family Dollar Stores, Inc., has in stock 300 towels that cost $3 each. Family Dollar Stores marks each towel up by $2 and sells 200 of the towels for $5 each.

- Family Dollar Stores, Inc.'s balance sheet reports the 100 towels that the company still holds in inventory.
- The income statement reports the cost of the 200 towels sold, as shown in Exhibit 6-2.

Exhibit 6-2 | Inventory and Cost of Goods Sold When Inventory Cost Is Constant

Balance Sheet (partial)		Income Statement (partial)	
Current assets		Sales revenue	
Cash	$XXX	(200 towels @ $5 each)	$1,000
Short-term investments	XXX	Cost of goods sold	
Accounts receivable	XXX	(200 towels @ $3 each)	600
Inventory (100 towels @ $3 each)	300	Gross profit	$ 400
Prepaid expenses	XXX		

Here is the basic concept of how we distinguish **inventory**, the asset, from **cost of goods sold**, the expense. The cost of the inventory sold shifts from asset to expense when the seller delivers the goods to the buyer.

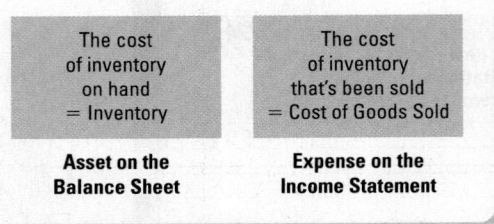

Sale Price vs. Cost of Inventory

Note the difference between the sale price of inventory and the cost of inventory. In our example,

- sales revenue is based on the *sale price* of the inventory sold ($5 per towel);
- cost of goods sold is based on the *cost* of the inventory sold ($3 per towel);
- inventory on the balance sheet is based on the *cost* of the inventory still on hand ($3 per towel).

Exhibit 6-2 shows these items.

Gross margin, also called **gross profit**, is the excess of sales revenue over cost of goods sold. It is called *gross* margin (profit) because operating expenses have not yet been subtracted. Exhibit 6-3 shows actual inventory and cost-of-goods-sold data adapted from the financial statements of Family Dollar Stores, Inc.

Exhibit 6-3 | Family Dollar Stores, Inc., Inventory and Cost of Sales

	A	B	C
	A1 ⬍		
	A	B	C
1	**Family Dollar Stores, Inc.** **Consolidated Balance Sheet (Partial, Adapted)** **August 25, 2012**		
2	**Assets**		
3	**(in millions)**		
4	Current assets		
5	Cash and cash equivalents		$ 92.3
6	Restricted cash and short-term investments		132.6
7	Merchandise inventories		1,426.2
8			

	A	B	C
	A1 ⬍		
	A	B	C
1	**Family Dollar Stores, Inc.** **Consolidated Statement of Income (Partial, Adapted)** **Year Ended August 25, 2012**		
2	**(In millions)**		
3	Net sales		$ 9,331.0
4	Cost of goods sold		6,071.1
5	Gross margin (gross profit)		$ 3,259.9
6			

Family Dollar Stores, Inc.'s inventory of $1,426.2 million represents

$$\begin{array}{c}\text{Inventory}\\\text{(balance sheet)}\end{array} = \begin{array}{c}\text{Number of units of}\\\text{inventory } on\ hand\end{array} \times \begin{array}{c}\text{Cost per unit}\\\text{of inventory}\end{array}$$

Family Dollar Stores, Inc.'s cost of goods sold ($6,071.1 million) represents

$$\begin{array}{c}\text{Cost of goods sold}\\\text{(income statement)}\end{array} = \begin{array}{c}\text{Number of units of}\\\text{inventory } sold\end{array} \times \begin{array}{c}\text{Cost per unit}\\\text{of inventory}\end{array}$$

Let's see what "units of inventory" and "cost per unit" mean.

Number of Units of Inventory. The number of inventory units on hand is determined from the accounting records, backed up by a physical count of the goods at year-end. Companies do not include in inventory any goods they hold on **consignment** because those goods belong to another company. But they do include their own inventory that is out on consignment and held for sale by another company. As discussed in Chapter 5, companies include inventory in transit from suppliers or in transit to customers that, according to shipping terms, legally belong to them as of the year-end. Shipping terms, otherwise known as *FOB (free on board) terms,* indicate who owns the goods at a particular time and, therefore, who must pay for the shipping costs. When the vendor invoice specifies *FOB shipping point* (the most common business practice), legal title to the goods passes from the seller to the purchaser when the inventory leaves the seller's place of business. The purchaser therefore owns the goods while they are in transit and must pay the transportation costs. In the case of goods purchased FOB shipping point, the company purchasing the goods must include goods in transit from suppliers as units in inventory as of the year-end. In the case of goods purchased *FOB destination,* title to the goods does not pass from the seller to the purchaser until the goods arrive at the purchaser's receiving dock. Therefore, these goods are not counted in year-end inventory of the purchasing company. Rather, the cost of these goods is included in inventory of the seller until the goods reach their destination.

Cost per Unit of Inventory. The cost per unit of inventory poses a challenge because companies purchase goods at different prices throughout the year. Which unit costs go into ending inventory? Which unit costs go to cost of goods sold?

Starting on page 308, we discuss how the selection between different accounting methods determines reported amounts on the balance sheet and the income statement. First, however, let's take a step back and cover how inventory accounting systems work.

Accounting for Inventory in the Perpetual System

There are two main types of inventory accounting systems: the periodic system and the perpetual system. The **periodic inventory system**, discussed in more detail in Appendix 6A, is used for inexpensive goods. A fabric store or a hardware store won't keep a running record of every bolt of fabric or every ten-penny nail. Instead, these stores count their inventory periodically—at least once a year—to determine the quantities on hand. Businesses such as restaurants and hometown nurseries also use the periodic system because the accounting cost of a periodic system is low.

A **perpetual inventory system** uses computer software to keep a running record of inventory on hand. This system achieves control over goods such as furniture, automobiles, jewelry, apparel, and most other types of inventory. Most businesses use the perpetual inventory system.

Even with a perpetual system, the business still counts the inventory on hand annually. The physical count establishes the correct amount of ending inventory for the financial statements and also serves as a check on the perpetual records. Here is a quick summary of the two main inventory accounting systems.

Perpetual Inventory System	Periodic Inventory System
• Used for all types of goods	• Used for inexpensive goods
• Keeps a running record of all goods bought, sold, and on hand	• Does *not* keep a running record of all goods bought, sold, and on hand
• Inventory counted at least once a year	• Inventory counted at least once a year

How the Perpetual System Works. Let's use an everyday situation to show how a perpetual inventory system works. When you check out at a Family Dollar, Walmart, or Whole Foods Market store, the clerk scans the bar codes on the labels of the items you buy. Exhibit 6-4 illustrates a typical bar code. Suppose you are buying a desk lamp from a Family Dollar Store. The bar code on the product label holds lots of information. The optical scanner reads the bar code, and the computer records the sale and updates the inventory records.

Exhibit 6-4 | Bar Code for Electronic Scanner

0 72512 06581 5

Recording Transactions in the Perpetual System. All accounting systems record each purchase of inventory. When Family Dollar makes a sale, two entries are needed in the perpetual system:

- The company records the sale—debits Cash or Accounts Receivable and credits Sales Revenue for the sale price of the goods.

- Family Dollar also debits Cost of Goods Sold and credits Inventory for the cost of the inventory sold.

Exhibit 6-5 shows the accounting for inventory in a perpetual system. Panel A gives the journal entries and the T-accounts, and Panel B shows the income statement and the balance sheet. All amounts are assumed. (Appendix 6A illustrates the accounting for these same transactions for a periodic inventory system.)

Exhibit 6-5 | Recording and Reporting Inventory—Perpetual System

PANEL A—Recording Transactions and the T-accounts (All amounts are assumed)

Journal Entry

	A	C	D	G
1	1. Inventory		560,000	
2	Accounts Payable			560,000
3	*Purchased inventory on account.*			
4	2. Accounts Receivable		900,000	
5	Sales Revenue			900,000
6	*Sold inventory on account.*			
7	Cost of Goods Sold		540,000	
8	Inventory			540,000
9	*Recorded cost of goods sold.*			
10				

Inventory

Beginning balance	100,000*		
Purchases	560,000	Cost of goods sold	540,000
Ending balance	120,000		

*Beginning inventory was $100,000

Cost of Goods Sold

Cost of goods sold	540,000

PANEL B—Reporting in the Financial Statements

Income Statement (partial)

Sales revenue	$900,000
Cost of goods sold	540,000
Gross profit	$360,000

Ending Balance Sheet (partial)

Current assets:		
Cash	$	XXX
Short-term investments		XXX
Accounts receivable		XXX
Inventory		120,000
Prepaid expenses		XXX

In Exhibit 6-5 (panel A), the first entry to Inventory summarizes in one entry what, in practice, may actually be several entries. The cost of the inventory, $560,000, is the *net* amount of the purchases, determined as follows (using assumed amounts):

Purchase price of the inventory	$600,000
+ **Freight in** (the cost to transport the goods from the seller to the buyer)	4,000
− **Purchase returns** for unsuitable goods returned to the seller	(25,000)
− **Purchase allowances** granted by the seller	(5,000)
− **Purchase discounts** for early payment by the buyer	(14,000)
= Net purchases of inventory—Cost to the buyer	$560,000

Freight in is the transportation cost, paid by the buyer, under terms FOB shipping point, to move goods from the seller to the buyer. Freight in is accounted for as part of the cost of inventory. Freight out is paid by the *seller,* under shipping terms FOB destination, and is not part of the cost of inventory. Instead, freight out is considered a delivery expense. It's the seller's expense of delivering merchandise to customers.

A **purchase return** represents a decrease in inventory and a corresponding decrease in accounts payable because the buyer returned the goods to the seller (vendor). With a **purchase allowance**, the buyer keeps the inventory but decreases its cost of inventory held because the buyer is granted an allowance (a deduction) from the amount owed. These terms are the "flip side" of the seller's *sales return* and *sales allowance* discussed in Chapter 5. To document approval of purchase returns, management issues a **debit memorandum**, meaning that accounts payable are reduced (debited) for the amount of the return. The offsetting credit is to inventory as the goods are shipped back to the seller (vendor). Purchase returns and allowances are usually documented on the final invoice received from the vendor. Throughout this book, we often refer to net purchases simply as Purchases.

A **purchase discount** (the "flip side" of a *sales discount* discussed in Chapter 5) is a decrease in the buyer's cost of inventory earned by paying quickly. Many companies offer payment terms of "2/10 n/30." This means the buyer can take, and the seller grants, a 2% discount for payment within 10 days, with the final amount due within 30 days. Another common credit term is "net 30," which tells the customer to pay the full amount within 30 days. In summary,

$$
\begin{aligned}
\text{Net purchases} = \ &\text{Purchases} \\
&- \text{Purchase returns and allowances} \\
&- \text{Purchase discounts} \\
&+ \text{Freight in}
\end{aligned}
$$

The journal entries for purchase returns and purchase discounts are as follows (assuming a purchase return of $500 in merchandise and a purchase of $1,000 in merchandise with terms of 2/10, n/30):

	A	B	C Debit	D Credit
1		Purchase returns:		
2		Accounts payable	500	
3		Inventory		500
4		*To record purchase return of merchandise that cost $500.*		
5				
6		Purchase discounts:		
7		Original purchase:		
8		Inventory (1,000 x 1)	1,000	
9		Accounts payable (1,000 x 1)		1,000
10		*To record a gross purchase of $1,000 in merchandise.*		
11				
12		Payment 10 days later (within discount period):		
13		Accounts payable	1,000	
14		Inventory		20
15		Cash		980
16		*To record payment for merchandise within 10 days at 2% discount.*		
17				

APPLY AND COMPARE VARIOUS INVENTORY COST METHODS

2 Apply and compare various inventory cost methods

Inventory is the first asset for which a manager can decide which accounting method to use. The accounting method selected affects the profits to be reported, the amount of income tax to be paid, and the values of the inventory turnover and gross margin percentage ratios derived from the financial statements.

What Goes into Inventory Cost?

The cost of inventory on Family Dollar Stores, Inc.'s balance sheet represents all the costs that the company incurred to bring its inventory to the point of sale. The following cost principle applies to all assets:

The cost of any asset, such as inventory, is the sum of all the costs incurred to bring the asset to its intended use, less any discounts.

The cost of inventory includes its basic purchase price, plus freight in, insurance while in transit, and any fees or taxes paid to get the inventory ready to sell, less returns, allowances, and discounts.

After a Family Dollar Store lamp is sitting on the shelf in the store, other costs, such as advertising and sales commissions, are *not* included as the cost of inventory. Advertising, sales commissions, and delivery costs are selling expenses that go in the income statement, rather than in the balance sheet.

Apply the Various Inventory Costing Methods

Determining the cost of inventory is easy when the unit cost remains constant, as in Exhibit 6-2. But the unit cost of merchandise usually fluctuates. For example, prices of products sometimes rise along with fuel prices that increase transportation costs of merchandise to retail stores. The lamp that cost Family Dollar $10 in January may cost $14 in June and $18 in October. Suppose Family Dollar sells 1,000 lamps in November. How many of those lamps cost $10, how many cost $14, and how many cost $18?

To compute cost of goods sold and the cost of ending inventory still on hand, we must assign a unit cost to the items. Accounting uses four generally accepted inventory methods:

1. **Specific unit cost**
2. **Average cost**
3. **First-in, first-out (FIFO) cost**
4. **Last-in, first-out (LIFO) cost**

A company can use any of these methods. The methods can have very different effects on reported profits, income taxes, and cash flow. Therefore, companies select their inventory method with great care.

Specific Unit Cost. Some businesses deal in unique inventory items, such as automobiles, antique furniture, jewels, and real estate. These businesses cost their inventories at the specific cost of the particular unit. For instance, a Toyota dealer may have two vehicles in the showroom—a "stripped-down" model that cost the dealer $19,000 and a "loaded" model that cost the dealer $30,000. If the dealer sells the loaded model, the cost of goods sold is $30,000. The stripped-down auto will be the only unit left in inventory, and so ending inventory is $19,000.

The **specific-unit-cost method** is also called the *specific identification method*. This method is too expensive to use for inventory items that have common characteristics, such as bushels of wheat, gallons of paint, or auto tires.

The other inventory accounting methods—average, FIFO, and LIFO—are fundamentally different. These other methods do not use the specific cost of a particular unit. Instead, they assume different flows of inventory costs. To illustrate average, FIFO, and LIFO costing, we use a common set of data, given in Exhibit 6-6.

Exhibit 6-6 | Inventory Data Used to Illustrate the Various Inventory Costing Methods

	Inventory			
Beg bal	(10 units @ $10)	100		
Purchases:			Cost of goods sold	
No. 1	(25 units @ $14)	350	(40 units @ ?)	?
No. 2	(25 units @ $18)	450		
End bal	(20 units @ ?)	?		

In Exhibit 6-6, Family Dollar began the period with 10 lamps that cost $10 each; the beginning inventory was therefore $100. During the period, Family Dollar bought 50 more lamps, sold 40 lamps, and ended the period with 20 lamps.

Goods Available		Number of Units	Total Cost
Goods available	=	10 + 25 + 25 = 60 units	$100 + $350 + $450 = $900
Cost of goods sold	=	40 units	?
Ending inventory	=	20 units	?

The big accounting questions are as follows:

1. What is the cost of goods sold for the income statement?
2. What is the cost of the ending inventory for the balance sheet?

The answers to these questions depend on which inventory method Family Dollar uses. Let's look at average costing first.

Average Cost. The **average-cost method**, sometimes called the **weighted-average method**, is based on the average cost of inventory during the period. Using data from Exhibit 6-6, the average cost per unit is determined as

$$\text{Average cost per unit} = \frac{\text{Cost of goods available}^2}{\text{Number of units available}} = \frac{\$900}{60} = \$15$$

$$
\begin{aligned}
\text{Cost of goods sold} &= \text{Number of units sold} \times \text{Average cost per unit} \\
&= 40 \text{ units} \times \$15 = \$600
\end{aligned}
$$

$$
\begin{aligned}
\text{Ending inventory} &= \text{Number of units on hand} \times \text{Average cost per unit} \\
&= 20 \text{ units} \times \$15 = \$300
\end{aligned}
$$

The following T-account shows the effects of average costing:

Inventory (at Average Cost)

Beg bal	(10 units @ $10)	100			
Purchases:					
No. 1	(25 units @ $14)	350			
No. 2	(25 units @ $18)	450	Cost of goods sold (40 units @ average cost of $15 per unit)		600
End bal	(20 units @ average cost of $15 per unit)	300			

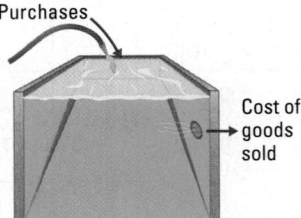

Average costing

Purchases

Cost of goods sold

FIFO Cost. Under the FIFO method, the first costs into inventory are the first costs assigned to cost of goods sold—hence the name **first-in, first-out**. The diagram on the next page shows the

---

[2]Cost of Goods Available (used synonymously with Cost of Goods Available for Sale throughout the chapter)
= Beginning inventory + Purchases

effect of FIFO costing. The following T-account shows how to compute FIFO cost of goods sold and ending inventory for the Family Dollar lamps (data from Exhibit 6-6):

Inventory (at FIFO cost)

Beg bal	(10 units @ $10)	100				
Purchases:			Cost of goods sold (40 units):			
No. 1	(25 units @ $14)	350	(10 units @ $10)	100	}	
No. 2	(25 units @ $18)	450	(25 units @ $14)	350		540
			(5 units @ $18)	90		
End bal	(20 units @ $18)	360				

First-in, first-out (FIFO) costing

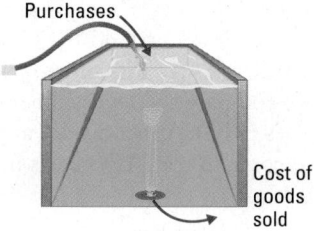

Under FIFO, the cost of ending inventory is always based on the latest costs incurred—in this case, $18 per unit.

LIFO Cost. LIFO (**last-in, first-out**) costing is the opposite of FIFO. Under LIFO, the last costs into inventory go immediately to cost of goods sold, as shown in the diagram below. Compare LIFO and FIFO, and you will see a vast difference.

The following T-account shows how to compute the LIFO inventory amounts for the Family Dollar lamps (data from Exhibit 6-6):

Inventory (at LIFO cost)

Beg bal	(10 units @ $10)	100				
Purchases:			Cost of goods sold (40 units):			
No. 1	(25 units @ $14)	350	(25 units @ $18)	450	}	660
No. 2	(25 units @ $18)	450	(15 units @ $14)	210		
End bal	(10 units @ $10)	} 240				
	(10 units @ $14)					

Last-in, first-out (LIFO) costing

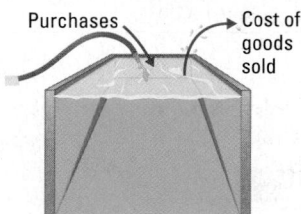

Under LIFO, the cost of ending inventory is always based on the oldest costs—from beginning inventory plus the early purchases of the period—$10 and $14 per unit.

Compare the Effects of FIFO, LIFO, and Average Cost on Cost of Goods Sold, Gross Profit, and Ending Inventory

When inventory unit costs change, the various inventory methods produce different cost-of-goods-sold figures. Exhibit 6-7 summarizes the income effects (Sales − Cost of goods sold = Gross profit) of the three inventory methods (remember that prices are rising). Study Exhibit 6-7 carefully, focusing on cost of goods sold and gross profit.

Exhibit 6-7 | Income Effects of the FIFO, LIFO, and Average Inventory Methods; Increasing Costs

	FIFO	LIFO	Average
Sales revenue (assumed)	$1,000	$1,000	$1,000
Cost of goods sold........................	540 (lowest)	660 (highest)	600
Gross profit.................................	$ 460 (highest)	$ 340 (lowest)	$ 400

Exhibit 6-8 shows the impact of both FIFO and LIFO costing methods on cost of goods sold and inventories during both increasing costs (Panel A) and decreasing costs (Panel B). Study this exhibit carefully; it will help you *really* understand FIFO and LIFO.

Financial analysts search the stock markets for companies with good prospects for income growth. Analysts sometimes need to compare the net income of a company that uses LIFO with the net income of a company that uses FIFO. Appendix 6B, at the end of this chapter, shows how to convert a LIFO company's net income to the FIFO basis in order to compare the companies.

Exhibit 6-8 | Cost of Goods Sold and Ending Inventory—FIFO and LIFO; Increasing Costs and Decreasing Costs

PANEL A—When Inventory Costs Are Increasing

	Cost of Goods Sold (COGS)	Ending Inventory (EI)
FIFO	FIFO COGS is lowest because it's based on the oldest costs, which are low. Gross profit is, therefore, the highest.	FIFO EI is highest because it's based on the most recent costs, which are high.
LIFO	LIFO COGS is highest because it's based on the most recent costs, which are high. Gross profit is, therefore, the lowest.	LIFO EI is lowest because it's based on the oldest costs, which are low.

PANEL B—When Inventory Costs Are Decreasing

	Cost of Goods Sold (COGS)	Ending Inventory (EI)
FIFO	FIFO COGS is highest because it's based on the oldest costs, which are high. Gross profit is, therefore, the lowest.	FIFO EI is lowest because it's based on the most recent costs, which are low.
LIFO	LIFO COGS is lowest because it's based on the most recent costs, which are low. Gross profit is, therefore, the highest.	LIFO EI is highest because it's based on the oldest costs, which are high.

Keeping Track of Perpetual Inventories under LIFO and Weighted-Average Cost Methods

The LIFO cost-flow assumption does not follow the logical flow of goods. Therefore, when costs are changing, it is physically impossible to apply LIFO unit costs to units purchased and sold as the transactions are happening using a perpetual inventory accounting system. Similarly, for large companies with millions of purchases and sales transactions, although it might be physically possible to do so, keeping track of perpetual inventories using weighted-average cost can be quite challenging, requiring sophisticated computer software to make constant updates to both changing quantities and changing unit prices on a daily basis. Therefore, many companies that use these methods keep track of perpetual inventories in quantities only during the period, making adjusting journal entries at the end of the period to apply either LIFO or weighted-average cost to both ending inventory and cost of goods sold. The details of this topic are reserved for more advanced accounting courses.

The Tax Advantage of LIFO

The Internal Revenue Service requires all U.S. companies to use the same method of costing inventories for tax purposes that they use for financial reporting purposes. Thus, the choice of inventory methods directly affects income taxes, which must be paid in cash. When prices are rising, LIFO results in the *lowest taxable income* and thus the *lowest income taxes*. Let's use the gross profit data of Exhibit 6-7 to illustrate.

	FIFO	LIFO
Gross profit (from Exhibit 6-7)	$460	$340
Operating expenses (assumed)................	260	260
Income before income tax	$200	$ 80
Income tax expense (40%).....................	$ 80	$ 32

Income tax expense is lowest under LIFO by $48 ($80 − $32). **This is the most attractive feature of LIFO—low income tax payments**, which is why about one-third of all U.S. companies use LIFO. During periods of inflation, companies that can justify it may switch to LIFO for its tax and cash-flow advantages.

Let's compare the FIFO and LIFO inventory methods from a couple of different standpoints.

1. *Measuring cost of goods sold.* How well does each method match inventory expense—cost of goods sold—against revenue? LIFO results in the most realistic net income figure because LIFO assigns the most recent inventory costs to expense. In contrast, FIFO matches old inventory costs against revenue—a poor measure of expense. FIFO income is therefore less realistic than LIFO income.

2. *Measuring ending inventory.* Which method reports the most up-to-date inventory cost on the balance sheet? FIFO. LIFO can value inventory at very old costs because LIFO leaves the oldest prices in ending inventory.

LIFO and Managing Reported Income. LIFO allows managers to manipulate net income by timing their purchases of inventory. When inventory prices are rising rapidly and a company wants to show less income (in order to pay less taxes), managers can buy a large amount of inventory near the end of the year. Under LIFO, these high inventory costs go straight to cost of goods sold. As a result, net income is decreased.

If the business is having a bad year, management may wish to report higher income. The company can delay the purchase of high-cost inventory until next year. This avoids decreasing current-year income. In the process, the company draws down inventory quantities, a practice known as *LIFO inventory liquidation*.

LIFO Liquidation. When LIFO is used and ending inventory quantities fall below the level of the previous period, the situation is called a *LIFO liquidation*. To compute cost of goods sold, the company must dip into older layers of inventory cost. Under LIFO, and when prices are rising, that action shifts older, lower costs into cost of goods sold. The result is higher net income. Managers try to avoid a LIFO liquidation because it increases income taxes.

International Perspective Many U.S. companies that currently use LIFO must use another method in foreign countries. Why? LIFO is not allowed in Australia, the United Kingdom, and some other British Commonwealth countries. Virtually all countries permit FIFO and the average-cost method.

These differences can create comparability problems for financial analysts when comparing a U.S. company against a foreign competitor. As discussed earlier, Appendix 6B illustrates how analysts convert reported income for a company that uses LIFO to income under FIFO.

International Financial Reporting Standards (IFRS) also do not permit the use of LIFO, although they do permit FIFO and other methods. If U.S. GAAP and IFRS become fully integrated in the future, U.S. companies that use LIFO might be forced to convert their inventory pricing to another method. As we discussed earlier in the chapter, in periods of rising prices, the use of LIFO inventories results in the lowest amount of reported income and, thus, the lowest amount of income taxes. If, as stated previously, about a third of U.S. companies continue to use LIFO through the next few years, conversion of inventories to methods other than LIFO may substantially increase income for them. This change has potentially far-reaching implications. For example, if the Internal Revenue Service were to continue to require companies to use the same inventory pricing methods for income tax purposes and financial statement purposes, conversion of LIFO inventories to another method would greatly increase the tax burden on many U.S. companies, including some small- and medium-sized businesses that can least afford it.

The disallowance of LIFO inventories under IFRS is only one of several rather thorny issues that must be resolved before the United States can adopt IFRS. Resolution of these differences will likely have political as well as financial implications. We will cover other key differences between U.S. GAAP and IFRS in later chapters. Appendix E summarizes all of these differences.

›› Mid-Chapter Summary Problem

Suppose a division of **Texas Instruments** that sells computer microchips has these inventory records for January 2015:

Date	Item	Quantity	Unit Cost	Total Cost
Jan 1	Beginning inventory	100 units	$ 8	$ 800
6	Purchase	60 units	9	540
21	Purchase	150 units	9	1,350
27	Purchase	90 units	10	900

Company accounting records show sales of 310 units for revenue of $6,770. Operating expense for January was $1,900.

Requirements

1. Prepare the January income statement, showing amounts for LIFO, average, and FIFO cost. Label the bottom line "Operating income." Round average cost per unit to three decimal places and all other figures to whole-dollar amounts. Show your computations.

2. Suppose you are the financial vice president of Texas Instruments. Which inventory method will you use if your motive is to

   a. minimize income taxes?

   b. report the highest operating income?

   c. report operating income between the extremes of FIFO and LIFO?

   d. report inventory on the balance sheet at the most current cost?

   e. attain the best measure of net income for the income statement?

State the reason for each of your answers.

Answers

Requirement 1

A1	⬍			
	A	**B**	**C**	**D**
1	**Texas Instruments Incorporated** **Income Statement for Microchip** **Month Ended January 31, 2015**			
2		**LIFO**	**Average**	**FIFO**
3	Sales revenue	$ 6,770	$ 6,770	$ 6,770
4	Cost of goods sold	2,870	2,782	2,690
5	Gross profit	3,900	3,988	4,080
6	Operating expenses	1,900	1,900	1,900
7	Operating income	$ 2,000	$ 2,088	$ 2,180
8				

Cost of goods sold computations:

LIFO: (90 @ \$10) + (150 @ \$9) + (60 @ \$9) + (10 @ \$8) = \$2,870

Average: 310 × \$8.975* = \$2,782

FIFO: (100 @ \$8) + (60 @ \$9) + (150 @ \$9) = \$2,690

$$*\frac{(\$800 + \$540 + \$1,350 + \$900)}{(100 + 60 + 150 + 90)} = \$8.975$$

Requirement 2

a. Use LIFO to minimize income taxes. Operating income under LIFO is lowest when inventory unit costs are increasing, as they are in this case (from \$8 to \$10). (If inventory costs were decreasing, income under FIFO would be lowest.)

b. Use FIFO to report the highest operating income. Income under FIFO is highest when inventory unit costs are increasing, as in this situation.

c. Use the average-cost method to report an operating income amount between the FIFO and LIFO extremes. This is true in this situation and in others when inventory unit costs are increasing or decreasing.

d. Use FIFO to report inventory on the balance sheet at the most current cost. The oldest inventory costs are expensed as cost of goods sold, leaving in ending inventory the most recent (most current) costs of the period.

e. Use LIFO to attain the best measure of net income. LIFO produces the best current expense recognition by matching the most current expense with current revenue. The most recent (most current) inventory costs are expensed as cost of goods sold.

3 **Explain and apply** underlying GAAP for inventory

EXPLAIN AND APPLY UNDERLYING GAAP FOR INVENTORY

Several accounting principles have special relevance to inventories:

- Consistency
- Disclosure
- Representational faithfulness

Disclosure Principle

The **disclosure principle** holds that a company's financial statements should report enough information for outsiders to make informed decisions about the company. The company should report *relevant* and *representationally faithful* information about itself. That means properly disclosing inventory accounting methods, as well as the substance of all material transactions impacting the existence and proper valuation of inventory. It also requires the use of *comparable* methods for *consistency* of presentation from period to period. The financial statements typically contain a footnote describing the inventory pricing method used, as well as the fact that inventory was valued at the lower of that method or market. The lower-of-cost-or-market rule is described next. Without knowledge of the accounting method and without clear, complete disclosures in the financial statements, a banker could make an unwise lending decision. Suppose the banker is comparing two companies—one using LIFO and the other, FIFO. The FIFO company reports higher net income but only because it uses FIFO. Without knowing this, the banker could loan money to the wrong business.

> **EXCERPT FROM NOTE 6 OF THE FINANCIAL STATEMENTS**
> . . . American-Saudi changed its method of accounting for the cost of crude oil . . . from the FIFO method to the LIFO method. The company believes that the LIFO method better matches current costs with current revenues. . . . The change decreased the Company's net income . . . by $3 million. . . .

Lower-of-Cost-or-Market Rule

The **lower-of-cost-or-market rule** (abbreviated as **LCM**) is based on the principles of relevance and representational faithfulness. LCM requires that inventory be reported in the financial statements at whichever is lower—the inventory's historical cost or its market value. Applied to inventories, *market value* generally means *current replacement cost* (that is, how much the business would have to pay now to replace its inventory). If the replacement cost of inventory falls below its historical cost, the business must write down the value of its goods to market value, which is the most relevant and representationally faithful measure of its true worth to the business. **The business reports ending inventory at its LCM value on the balance sheet.** All this can be done automatically by a computerized accounting system. How is the write-down accomplished?

Suppose Family Dollar, Inc., paid $3,000 for inventory on June 26. By August 25, its fiscal year-end, the inventory can be replaced for $2,000. Family Dollar's year-end balance sheet must report this inventory at the LCM value of $2,000. Exhibit 6-9 on the following page presents the effects of LCM on the balance sheet and the income statement. Before any LCM effect, cost of goods sold is $9,000. An LCM write-down decreases Inventory and increases Cost of Goods Sold:

	A	B	C	D
1		Cost of Goods Sold	1,000	
2		Inventory		1,000
3		*Wrote inventory down to market value.*		
4				

Exhibit 6-9 | Lower-of-Cost-or-Market (LCM) Effects on Inventory and Cost of Goods Sold

Balance Sheet

Current assets:

Cash	$ XXX
Short-term investments	XXX
Accounts receivable......................................	XXX
Inventories, at market	
(which is lower than $3,000 cost)	2,000
Prepaid expenses	XXX
Total current assets	$X,XXX

Income Statement

Sales revenue..	$21,000
Cost of goods sold ($9,000 + $1,000)	10,000
Gross profit..	$11,000

If the market value of Family Dollar's inventory had been above cost, it would have made no adjustment for LCM. In that case, simply report the inventory at cost, which is the lower of cost or market.

Companies disclose LCM in notes to their financial statements, as shown next for Family Dollar Stores, Inc.:

NOTE 1: ACCOUNTING POLICIES

- *Inventories.* Inventories are valued using the retail method, based on retail prices less mark-on percentages, which approximates the lower of first-in, first-out (FIFO) cost or market.

LCM is not optional. It is required by GAAP.

Global View

Another IFRS Difference IFRS defines "market" differently from U.S. GAAP. Under IFRS, "market" is always defined as "net realizable value," which, for inventories, is current market value. If IFRS is adopted in the United States, inventory write-downs may become less common than they are now, due to the fact that selling prices are usually greater than replacement cost.

Under U.S. GAAP, once the LCM rule is applied to write inventories down to current replacement cost, the write-downs may never be reversed. In contrast, under IFRS, some LCM write-downs may be reversed, and inventory may be subsequently written up again, not to exceed original cost. This may cause more fluctuation in the reported incomes of companies that sell inventories than we currently see.

Inventory and the Detailed Income Statement

Exhibit 6-10 provides an example of a detailed income statement, complete with all the discounts and expenses in their proper places. Study it carefully.

Exhibit 6-10 | Detailed Income Statement

A1 ⬍			
	A	**B**	**C**
1	New Jersey Technology, Inc. Income Statement Year Ended December 31, 2015		
2	Sales revenue	$ 100,000	
3	Less: Sales discounts	(2,000)	
4	Sales returns and allowances	(3,000)	
5	Net sales		$ 95,000*
6	Cost of goods sold		45,000
7	Gross profit		50,000
8	Operating expenses:		
9	Selling:		
10	Sales commission expense	$ 5,000	
11	Freight out (delivery expense)	1,000	
12	Other expenses (detailed)	6,000	12,000
13	Administrative:		
14	Salary expense	$ 2,000	
15	Depreciation expense	2,000	
16	Other expenses (detailed)	4,000	8,000
17	Income before income tax		30,000
18	Income tax expense (40%)		12,000
19	Net income		$ 18,000
20			

*Most companies report only the net sales figure, $95,000.

COMPUTE AND EVALUATE GROSS PROFIT (MARGIN) PERCENTAGE AND INVENTORY TURNOVER

4 Compute and evaluate gross profit (margin) percentage and inventory turnover

Owners, managers, and investors use ratios to evaluate a business. Two ratios relate directly to inventory: gross profit percentage and the rate of inventory turnover.

Gross Profit Percentage

Gross profit—sales minus cost of goods sold—is a key indicator of a company's ability to sell inventory at a profit. Merchandisers strive to increase **gross profit percentage**, also called the **gross margin percentage**. Gross profit percentage is markup stated as a percentage of sales. Gross profit percentage is computed as follows for Family Dollar Stores, Inc. Data (in millions) for the year ended August 25, 2012, are taken from Exhibit 6-3 earlier (figures rounded).

$$\text{Gross profit percentage} = \frac{\text{Gross profit}}{\text{Net sales revenue}} = \frac{\$3,260}{\$9,331} = 0.349 = 34.9\%$$

The gross profit percentage is watched carefully by managers and investors. A 34.9% gross margin means that each dollar of sales generates about $0.35 of gross profit. On average, cost of goods sold consumes $0.65 of each sales dollar for Family Dollar Stores, Inc. For most firms, the gross profit percentage changes little from year to year, so a small downturn may signal trouble, and an upturn by a small percentage can mean millions of dollars in additional profits. Family Dollar Stores, Inc.'s trend in gross profit for fiscal years 2010 through 2012 was 35.7%, 35.5%, and 34.9%, respectively. These figures reflect small but steady declines in gross profit over the three-year period. Only a fractional percentage decrease in gross profit (0.8% from 2010 to 2012), when applied to 2012 sales, computes to a decline in profits of $74.6 million (0.008 × $9,331,005,000). The big players in the discount store space are Walmart and Target Stores, each of which have tremendous leverage and power. Other staunch competitors for Family Dollar, Inc.'s customers are Dollar Tree and Dollar General Stores. All of these are competing for the business of the low- to medium-income family. It appears that Family Dollar Stores, Inc., is being challenged by large and small competitors to keep product cost increases in line with sales increases.

Family Dollar's gross profit percentage of 34.9% is greater than that of Walmart Stores, Inc. (24.5%) but smaller than the gross profit percentage of Nordstrom, Inc. (37.2%). Nordstrom's is a high-end retailer that caters to affluent customers, with high-priced designer merchandise, resulting in higher gross profits than those found in discount chains. Family Dollar Stores, Inc., and Walmart Stores, Inc., compete in the budget consumer space, handling lower-priced consumer products that are designed to move faster than those of a luxury retailer like Nordstrom. However, in terms of sales, Walmart is 52 times larger than Family Dollar Stores, Inc. ($466 billion vs. $9 billion in fiscal 2012). Thus, Walmart is capable of leveraging its buying power with vendors, purchasing the same products for much lower prices than Family Dollar and passing those savings along to customers in the form of lower sales prices, resulting in a lower gross margin percentage than Family Dollar Stores, Inc. We'll see in the next section how Walmart makes up for a lower gross profit percentage with volume by turning its inventory at a much faster rate than Family Dollar Stores and Nordstrom. Exhibit 6-11 graphs the gross profit percentages for these three companies.

Exhibit 6-11 | Gross Profit Percentages of Three Leading Retailers

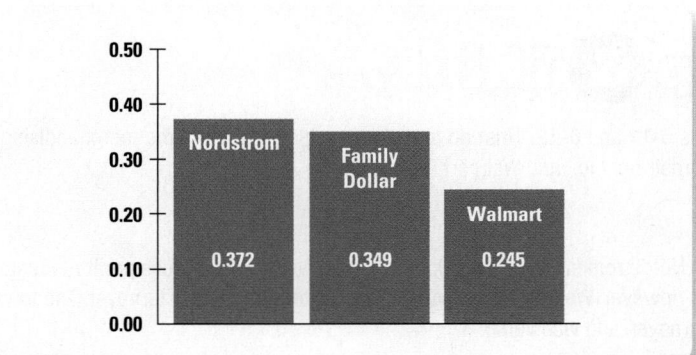

Inventory Turnover

Family Dollar Stores, Inc., strives to sell its inventory as quickly as possible because the goods generate no profit until they're sold. The faster the sales, the higher the income, and vice versa for slow-moving goods. Ideally, a business could operate with zero inventory, but most businesses, especially retailers, must keep some goods on hand. **Inventory turnover**, the ratio of cost of goods sold to average inventory, indicates how rapidly inventory is sold. The fiscal 2012 computation for Family Dollar Stores, Inc., follows (data in millions from the Consolidated Balance Sheets and Statements of Income):

$$\text{Inventory turnover} = \frac{\text{Cost of goods sold}}{\text{Average inventory}} = \frac{\text{Cost of goods sold}}{\left(\dfrac{\text{Beginning}}{\text{inventory}} + \dfrac{\text{Ending}}{\text{inventory}}\right) \div 2}$$

$$= \frac{\$6,071}{(\$1,155 + \$1,426)/2} = \begin{array}{l}\text{4.70 times per year} \\ \text{(every 78 days)}\end{array}$$

The inventory turnover statistic shows how many times the company sold (or turned over) its average level of inventory during the year. Inventory turnover varies from industry to industry.

Exhibit 6-12 graphs the rates of inventory turnover for the same three companies. Let's compare Family Dollar Stores, Inc.'s turnover with that of Nordstrom, Inc., and Walmart Stores, Inc.

You can see that both Nordstrom and Walmart turn inventory over faster than Family Dollar. Both Nordstrom and Walmart are large department stores. They sell a variety of products (Nordstrom sells clothing and Walmart sells virtually every kind of consumer item, including groceries) that sell faster than the more limited variety of household consumer goods sold by Family Dollar Stores, Inc. Thus, both Nordstrom, Inc., and Walmart Stores, Inc., report higher dollar amounts of gross profit and net income than Family Dollar Stores, Inc.

Exhibit 6-12 | Inventory Turnover Rates of Three Leading Retailers

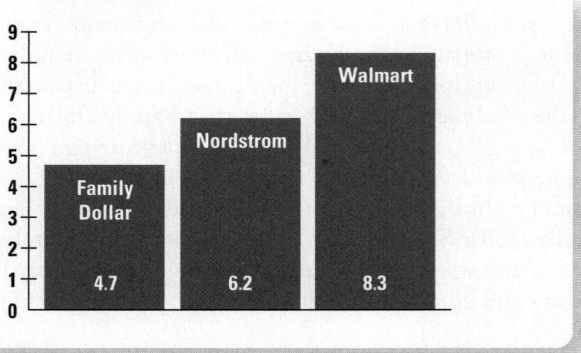

Examine Exhibits 6-11 and 6-12. What do those ratio values say about the merchandising (pricing) strategies of Nordstrom, Inc., and Walmart Stores, Inc.?

Answer:

It's obvious that Nordstrom sells high-end merchandise. Nordstrom's gross profit percentage is higher than Walmart's. However, Walmart has a much faster rate of inventory turnover. The lower the price, the faster the turnover, and vice versa.

USE THE COGS MODEL TO MAKE MANAGEMENT DECISIONS

5 **Use** the cost-of-goods-sold (COGS) model to make management decisions

Exhibit 6-13 presents the **cost-of-goods-sold (COGS) model**. Some may view this model as related to the periodic inventory system. But the COGS model is used by all companies, regardless of their accounting systems. The model is extremely powerful because it captures all the inventory information for an entire accounting period. Study this model carefully (all amounts are assumed).

Exhibit 6-13 | The Cost-of-Goods-Sold Model

	A	B
	A1	
1	Cost of goods sold:	
2	Beginning inventory	$1,200
3	+ Purchases	6,300
4	= Cost of goods available	7,500
5	− Ending inventory	(1,500)
6	= Cost of goods sold	$6,000
7		

Family Dollar Stores, Inc., uses a perpetual inventory accounting system. Let's see how the company can use the COGS model to manage the business effectively.

Computing Budgeted Purchases

1. What's the single most important question for Family Dollar Stores, Inc., to address?
   - What merchandise should Family Dollar Stores, Inc., offer to its customers? This is a *marketing* question that requires market research. If Family Dollar Stores continually stocks up on the wrong merchandise, sales will suffer and profits will drop.
2. What's the second most important question for Family Dollar Stores, Inc.?
   - How much inventory should Family Dollar Stores, Inc., buy? **This is an accounting question faced by all merchandisers**. If Family Dollar Stores, Inc., buys too much merchandise, it will have to lower prices, the gross profit percentage will suffer, and the company may lose money. Buying the right quantity of inventory is critical for success. This question can be answered with the COGS model. Let's see how it works.

We must rearrange the COGS formula. Then we can help a Family Dollar store manager know how much inventory to buy, as follows (using amounts from Exhibit 6-13):

1	Cost of goods sold (based on the plan for the next period)....................	$6,000
2	+ Ending inventory (based on the plan for the next period).......................	1,500
3	= Cost of goods available as planned...	7,500
4	− Beginning inventory (actual amount left over from the prior period)......	(1,200)
5	= Purchases (how much inventory the manager needs to buy)..................	$6,300

In this case, the manager should buy $6,300 of merchandise to work his plan for the upcoming period.

Estimating Inventory by the Gross Profit Method

Often a business must *estimate* the value of its goods. For example, suppose a fire destroys the warehouse, all inventory, and all records. The insurance company requires an estimate of the loss. In this case, the business must estimate the cost of ending inventory because the records have been destroyed.

The **gross profit method**, also known as the **gross margin method**, is widely used to estimate ending inventory. This method uses the familiar COGS model (amounts are assumed).

For the gross profit method, we rearrange *ending inventory* and *cost of goods sold* as follows:

Beginning inventory	$ 4,000
+ Purchases	16,000
= Cost of goods available	20,000
− Ending inventory....................................	(5,000)
= Cost of goods sold.................................	$15,000

Beginning inventory	$ 4,000
+ Purchases	16,000
= Cost of goods available	20,000
− Cost of goods sold..................................	(15,000)
= Ending inventory....................................	$ 5,000

Suppose a fire destroys some of Family Dollar Stores, Inc.'s inventory. To collect insurance, the company must estimate the cost of the ending inventory lost. Using its *actual gross profit rate* of 35%, you can estimate the cost of goods sold. Then subtract cost of goods sold from cost of goods available to estimate the amount of ending inventory. Exhibit 6-14 shows the calculations for the gross profit method, with new amounts assumed for the illustration.

You can also use the gross profit method to test the overall reasonableness of an ending inventory amount. This method also helps to detect large errors.

Exhibit 6-14 | Gross Profit Method of Estimating Inventory

	A	B	C
	A1		
1	Beginning inventory		$ 38,000
2	Purchases		72,000
3	Cost of goods available		110,000
4	Estimated cost of goods sold:		
5	Net sales revenue	$ 100,000	
6	Less estimated gross profit of 35%	35,000	
7	Estimated cost of goods sold		65,000
8	Estimated cost of ending inventory lost		$ 45,000
9			

Beginning inventory is $70,000, net purchases total $365,000, and net sales are $500,000. With a normal gross profit rate of 40% of sales (cost of goods sold = 60%), how much is ending inventory?

Answer:

$$\$135,000 = [\$70,000 + \$365,000 - (0.60 \times \$500,000)]$$

ANALYZE EFFECTS OF INVENTORY ERRORS

6 **Analyze** effects of inventory errors

Inventory errors sometimes occur. An error in ending inventory creates errors for two accounting periods. In Exhibit 6-15, start with period 1 in which ending inventory is *overstated* by $10,000 and cost of goods sold is therefore *understated* by $10,000. Then compare period 1 with period 3, which is correct. *Period 1 should look exactly like period 3.*

Inventory errors counterbalance in two consecutive periods. Why? Recall that period 1's ending inventory becomes period 2's beginning amount. Thus, the period 1 error carries over into period 2. Trace the ending inventory of $20,000 from period 1 to period 2. Then compare periods 2 and 3. *All three periods should look exactly like period 3.* The Exhibit 6-15 amounts in color are incorrect.

Exhibit 6-15 | Inventory Errors: An Example

	A	B	C	D	E	F	G
	A1						
1		Period 1 — Ending Inventory Overstated by $10,000		Period 2 — Beginning Inventory Overstated by $10,000		Period 3 — Correct	
2	Sales revenue		$ 100,000		$100,000		$ 100,000
3	Cost of goods sold:						
4	Beginning inventory	$ 10,000		$ 20,000		$ 10,000	
5	Purchases	50,000		50,000		50,000	
6	Cost of goods available	60,000		70,000		60,000	
7	Ending inventory	(20,000)		(10,000)		(10,000)	
8	Cost of goods sold		40,000		60,000		50,000
9	Gross profit		$ 60,000		$ 40,000		$ 50,000
10							
11				$ 100,000			
12							

Beginning inventory and ending inventory have opposite effects on cost of goods sold (beginning inventory is added; ending inventory is subtracted). Therefore, after two periods, an inventory error washes out (counterbalances). Notice that total gross profit is correct for periods 1 and 2 combined ($100,000) even though each year's gross profit is off by $10,000. The correct gross profit is $50,000 for each period, as shown in period 3.

We must have accurate information for all periods. Exhibit 6-16 summarizes the effects of inventory accounting errors.

Exhibit 6-16 | Effects of Inventory Errors

	A1		

	A	Period 1		Period 2	
		Cost of Goods Sold	Gross Profit and Net Income	Cost of Goods Sold	Gross Profit and Net Income
1					
2	Period 1				
3	Ending inventory overstated	Understated	Overstated	Overstated	Understated
4	Period 1				
5	Ending inventory understated	Overstated	Understated	Understated	Overstated
6					

Cooking the Books with Inventory

Crazy Eddie

It is one thing to make honest mistakes in accounting for inventory, but quite another to use inventory to commit fraud. The two most common ways to "cook the books" with inventory are

1. inserting fictitious inventory—thus overstating quantities—and

2. deliberately overstating unit prices used in the computation of ending inventory amounts.

Either one of these tricks has exactly the same effect on income as inventory errors, discussed in the previous section. The difference is that honest inventory errors are often corrected as soon as they are detected, thus minimizing their impact on income. In contrast, deliberate overstatement of inventories tends to be repeated over and over again throughout the course of months, or even years, thus causing the misstatement to grow ever higher until it is discovered. By that time, it can be too late for the company.

Crazy Eddie, Inc.,[3] was a retail consumer electronics store in 1987, operating 43 retail outlets in the New York City area, with $350 million in reported sales and reported profits of $10.5 million. Its stock was a Wall Street "darling," with a collective market value of $600 million. The only problem was that the company's reported profits had been grossly overstated since 1984, the year that the company went public.

Eddie Antar, the company's founder and major stockholder, became preoccupied with the price of his company's stock in 1984. Antar realized that the company, in an extremely competitive retail market in the largest city in the United States, had to keep posting impressive operating profits in order to maintain the upward trend in the company's stock price.

Within the first six months, Antar ordered a subordinate to double-count about $2 million of inventory in the company's stores and warehouses. Using Exhibits 6-15 and 6-16, you can see

---

[3]Michael C. Knapp, *Contemporary Auditing: Real Issues and Cases*, 6th edition, Mason, Ohio: Thomson Southwestern, 2009.

that the impact of this inventory overstatement went straight to the "bottom line," overstating profits by the same amount, ignoring income tax effects. Unfortunately, the company's auditors failed to detect the inventory overstatement. The following year, emboldened by the audit error, Antar ordered subordinates (now accomplices) to bump the overstatement to $9 million. In addition, he ordered employees to destroy incriminating documents to conceal the inventory shortage. When auditors asked for these documents, employees told them they had been lost. Antar also ordered that the company scrap its sophisticated computerized perpetual inventory system and return to an outdated manual system that was easier to manipulate. The auditors made the mistake of telling Antar which company stores and warehouses they were going to visit in order to observe the year-end physical count of inventory. Antar shifted sufficient inventory to those locations just before the counts to conceal the shortages. By 1988, when the fraud was discovered, the inventory shortage (overstatement) was larger than the total profits the company had reported since it went public in 1984.

In June 1989, Crazy Eddie, Inc., filed for Chapter 11 bankruptcy protection. Later that year, the company closed its stores and sold off its assets. Eddie Antar became a fugitive from justice, moved to Israel, and took an assumed name. He was arrested in 1992, extradited to the United States, and convicted on 17 counts of fraudulent financial reporting in 1993. He was ordered to pay $121 million in restitution to former stockholders and creditors.

A series of missteps by the courts led to a plea bargain agreement in 1996, a condition of which was Antar's admission, for the first time, that he had defrauded investors by manipulating the company's accounting records. One of the prosecuting attorneys was quoted as saying, "Crazy Eddie wasn't crazy, just crooked."

The following Decision Guidelines summarize the situations that call for (a) a particular inventory system and (b) the motivation for using each costing method.

❯ Decision Guidelines

ACCOUNTING FOR INVENTORY

Suppose a Williams-Sonoma store stocks two basic categories of merchandise:

- High-end cookware, small electric appliances, cutlery, and kitchen furnishings
- Small items of low value, near the checkout stations, such as cupholders and bottle openers

Jacob Stiles, the store manager, is considering how accounting will affect the business. Let's examine several decisions Stiles must make to properly account for the store's inventory.

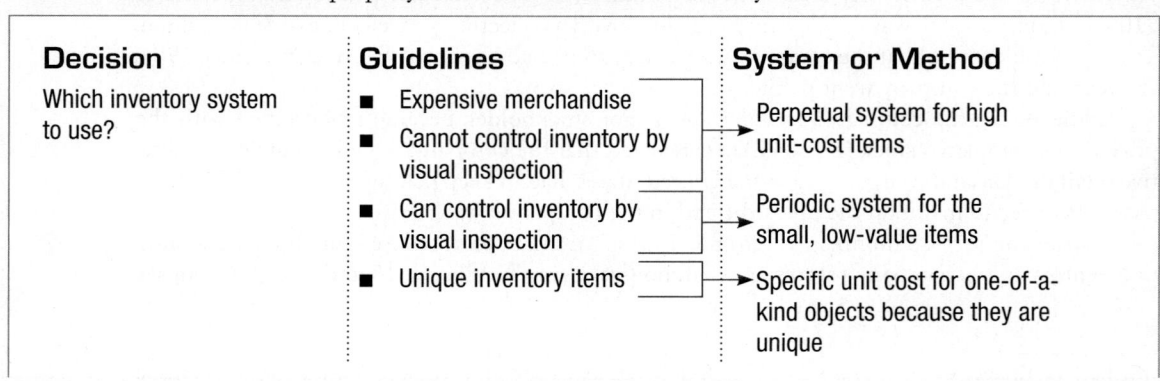

Decision	Guidelines	System or Method
Which inventory system to use?	■ Expensive merchandise ■ Cannot control inventory by visual inspection	Perpetual system for high unit-cost items
	■ Can control inventory by visual inspection	Periodic system for the small, low-value items
	■ Unique inventory items	Specific unit cost for one-of-a-kind objects because they are unique

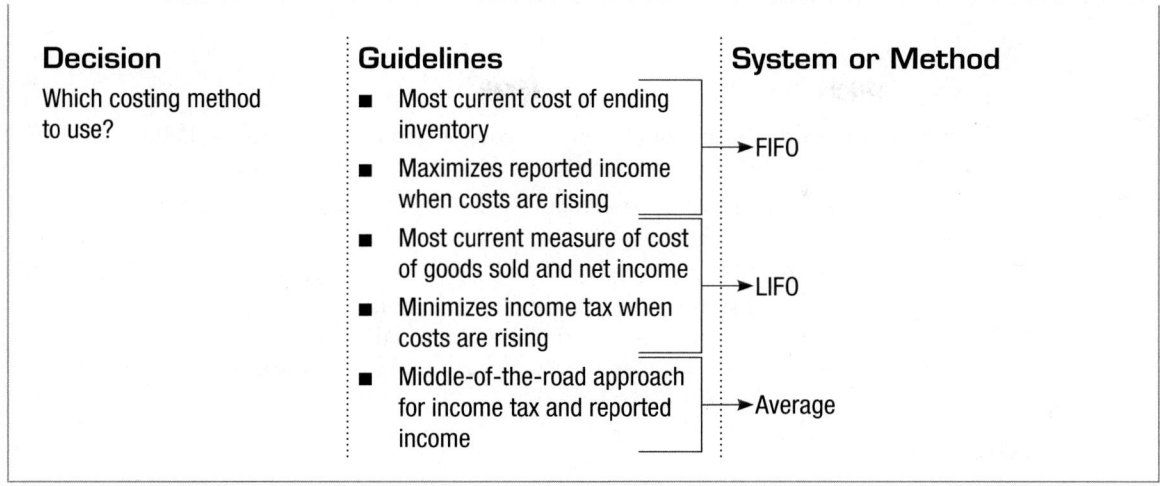

Decision	Guidelines	System or Method
Which costing method to use?	■ Most current cost of ending inventory ■ Maximizes reported income when costs are rising	→ FIFO
	■ Most current measure of cost of goods sold and net income ■ Minimizes income tax when costs are rising	→ LIFO
	■ Middle-of-the-road approach for income tax and reported income	→ Average

» End-of-Chapter Summary Problem

The Gift Horse began 2014 with 60,000 units of inventory that cost $36,000. During 2014, The Gift Horse purchased merchandise on account for $352,500:

Purchase 1	100,000 units costing	$ 65,000
Purchase 2	270,000 units costing	175,500
Purchase 3	160,000 units costing	112,000

Cash payments on account totaled $326,000 during the year (ignore purchase discounts).

The Gift Horse's sales during 2014 consisted of 520,000 units of inventory for $660,000, all on account. The company uses the FIFO inventory method.

Cash collections from customers were $630,000. Operating expenses totaled $240,500, of which The Gift Horse paid $211,000 in cash. The Gift Horse credited Accrued Liabilities for the remainder. At December 31, The Gift Horse accrued income tax expense at the rate of 35% of income before tax.

Requirements

1. Make summary journal entries to record The Gift Horse's transactions for the year, assuming the company uses a perpetual inventory system. Explanations are not required.

2. Determine the FIFO cost of The Gift Horse's ending inventory at December 31, 2014, two ways:

   a. Use a T-account.

   b. Multiply the number of units on hand by the unit cost.

3. Show how The Gift Horse would compute cost of goods sold for 2014. Follow the FIFO example on pages 310–311.

4. Prepare The Gift Horse's income statement for 2014. Show subtotals for the gross profit and income before tax.

5. Determine The Gift Horse's gross profit percentage, rate of inventory turnover, and net income as a percentage of sales for the year. In The Gift Horse's industry, a gross profit percentage of 40%, an inventory turnover of six times per year, and a net income percentage of 7% are considered excellent. How well does The Gift Horse compare to these industry averages?

Answers
Requirement 1

	A	B	C	D
1		Inventory ($65,000 + $175,500 + $112,000)	352,500	
2		Accounts Payable		352,500
3				
4		Accounts Payable	326,000	
5		Cash		326,000
6				
7		Accounts Receivable	660,000	
8		Sales Revenue		660,000
9				
10		Cost of Goods Sold (see Requirement 3)	339,500	
11		Inventory		339,500
12				
13		Cash	630,000	
14		Accounts Receivable		630,000
15				
16		Operating Expenses	240,500	
17		Cash		211,000
18		Accrued Liabilities		29,500
19				
20		Income Tax Expense (see Requirement 4)	28,000	
21		Income Tax Payable		28,000
22				

Requirement 2

Inventory

Beg bal	36,000		
Purchases	352,500	Cost of goods sold	339,500
End bal	49,000		

Number of units in ending inventory (60,000 + 100,000 + 270,000 + 160,000 − 520,000)		70,000
Unit cost of ending inventory at FIFO ($112,000 ÷ 160,000 from Purchase 3)....	×	$ 0.70
FIFO cost of ending inventory......................		$49,000

Requirement 3

Cost of goods sold (520,000 units):	
60,000 units costing...	$ 36,000
100,000 units costing...	65,000
270,000 units costing...	175,500
90,000 units costing $0.70 each*	63,000
Cost of goods sold..	$339,500

*From Purchase 3: $112,000/160,000 units = $0.70 per unit.

Requirement 4

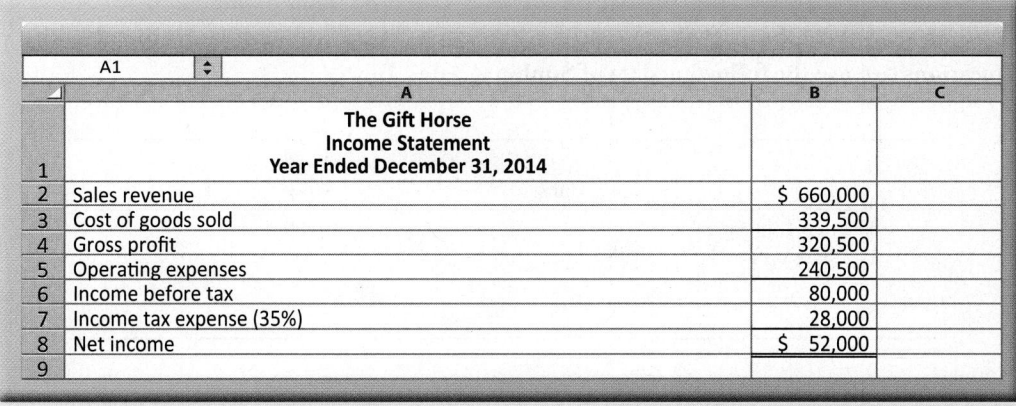

	A	B	C
1	**The Gift Horse** **Income Statement** **Year Ended December 31, 2014**		
2	Sales revenue	$ 660,000	
3	Cost of goods sold	339,500	
4	Gross profit	320,500	
5	Operating expenses	240,500	
6	Income before tax	80,000	
7	Income tax expense (35%)	28,000	
8	Net income	$ 52,000	
9			

Requirement 5

		Industry Average
Gross profit percentage:	$320,500 ÷ $660,000 = 48.6%	40%
Inventory turnover:	$\dfrac{\$339,500}{(\$36,000 + \$49,000)/2} = 8$ times	6 times
Net income as a percent of sales:	$52,000 ÷ $660,000 = 7.9%	7%

The Gift Horse's statistics are better than the industry averages.

REVIEW | Inventory & Cost of Goods Sold

Quick Check (Answers are given on page 356.)

1. Which statement is true?
   a. The Sales account is used to record only sales on account.
   b. Gross profit is the excess of sales revenue over cost of goods sold.
   c. A service company purchases products from suppliers and then sells them.
   d. Purchase returns and allowances increase the net amount of purchases.

2. Sales discounts should appear in the financial statements
   a. as an addition to sales.
   b. among the current liabilities.
   c. as a deduction from sales.
   d. as an operating expense.
   e. as an addition to inventory.

3. How is inventory classified in the financial statements?
   a. As a liability
   b. As a revenue
   c. As an expense
   d. As a contra account to Cost of Goods Sold
   e. As an asset

Questions 4–6 use the following data of Sunburst Sales, Inc.:

	Units	Unit Cost	Total Cost	Units Sold
Beginning inventory	25	$ 4	$100	
Purchase on Apr 25	41	5	205	
Purchase on Nov 16	17	10	170	
Sales	45	?	?	

4. Sunburst Sales uses a FIFO inventory system. Cost of goods sold for the period is
   a. $450.
   b. $257.
   c. $200.
   d. $310.

5. Sunburst Sales' LIFO cost of ending inventory would be
   a. $217.
   b. $165.
   c. $275.
   d. $450.

6. Sunburst Sales' average cost of ending inventory is
   a. $217.
   b. $275.
   c. $165.
   d. $450.

7. When applying the lower-of-cost-or-market rule to inventory, "market" generally means
   a. original cost, less physical deterioration.
   b. original cost.
   c. resale value.
   d. current replacement cost.

8. During a period of rising prices, the inventory method that will yield the highest net income and asset value is
   a. specific identification.
   b. average cost.
   c. LIFO.
   d. FIFO.

9. Which statement is true?

    a. An error overstating ending inventory in 2014 will understate 2014 net income.

    b. Application of the lower-of-cost-or-market rule often results in a lower inventory value.

    c. When prices are rising, the inventory method that results in the lowest ending inventory value is FIFO.

    d. The inventory method that best matches current expense with current revenue is FIFO.

10. The ending inventory of Carroll Co. is $46,000. If beginning inventory was $70,000 and goods available (cost of goods available for sale) totaled $115,000, the cost of goods sold is

    a. $69,000.   **c.** $45,000.

    b. $70,000.   **d.** $139,000.

11. Bell Company had cost of goods sold of $160,000. The beginning and ending inventories were $8,000 and $23,000, respectively. Purchases for the period must have been

    a. $183,000.   **d.** $191,000.

    b. $145,000.   **e.** $168,000.

    c. $175,000.

Use the following information for questions 12–14.

Palamino Company had an $18,000 beginning inventory and a $21,000 ending inventory. Net sales were $200,000; purchases, $95,000; purchase returns and allowances, $6,000; and freight in, $8,000.

12. Cost of goods sold for the period is

    a. $91,000.   **c.** $111,000.

    b. $100,000.   **d.** $94,000.

13. What is Palamino's gross profit percentage (rounded to the nearest percentage)?

    a. 53%   **c.** 9%

    b. 47%   **d.** 11%

14. What is Palamino's rate of inventory turnover?

    a. 4.5 times   **c.** 9.5 times

    b. 4.9 times   **d.** 4.8 times

15. Beginning inventory is $100,000, purchases are $240,000, and sales total $430,000. The normal gross profit is 45%. Using the gross profit method, how much is ending inventory?

    a. $96,500   **c.** $103,500

    b. $190,000   **d.** $193,500

16. An overstatement of ending inventory in one period results in

    a. no effect on net income of the next period.

    b. an understatement of the beginning inventory of the next period.

    c. an understatement of net income of the next period.

    d. an overstatement of net income of the next period.

Accounting Vocabulary

average-cost method (p. 310) Inventory costing method based on the average cost of inventory during the period. Average cost is determined by dividing the cost of goods available by the number of units available. Also called the *weighted-average method*.

consignment (p. 305) An inventory arrangement where the seller sells inventory that belongs to another party. The seller does not include consigned merchandise on hand in its balance sheet, because the seller does not own this inventory.

cost of goods sold (p. 304) Cost of the inventory the business has sold to customers.

cost-of-goods-sold model (p. 320) Formula that brings together all the inventory data for the entire accounting period: Beginning inventory + Purchases = Cost of goods available (i.e., cost of goods available for sale). Then, Cost of goods available − Ending inventory = Cost of goods sold.

debit memorandum (p. 308) A document issued to the seller (vendor) when an item of inventory that is unwanted or damaged is returned. This document authorizes a reduction (debit) to accounts payable for the amount of the goods returned.

disclosure principle (p. 316) A business's financial statements must report enough information for outsiders to make knowledgeable decisions about the business. The company should report relevant and representationally faithful information about its economic affairs.

first-in, first-out (p. 310) Inventory costing method by which the first costs into inventory are the first costs out to cost of goods sold. Ending inventory is based on the costs of the most recent purchases.

gross margin (p. 304) Another name for *gross profit*.

gross margin method (p. 321) Another name for the *gross profit method*.

gross margin percentage (p. 318) Another name for the *gross profit percentage*.

gross profit (p. 304) Sales revenue minus cost of goods sold. Also called *gross margin*.

gross profit method (p. 321) A way to estimate inventory based on a rearrangement of the cost-of-goods-sold model:

Beginning inventory + Net purchases = Cost of goods available − Cost of goods sold = Ending inventory. Also called the *gross margin method*.

gross profit percentage (p. 318) Gross profit divided by net sales revenue. Also called the *gross margin percentage*.

inventory (p. 304) The merchandise that a company sells to customers.

inventory turnover (p. 319) Ratio of cost of goods sold to average inventory. Indicates how rapidly inventory is sold.

last-in, first-out (p. 311) Inventory costing method by which the last costs into inventory are the first costs out to cost of goods sold. This method leaves the oldest costs—those of beginning inventory and the earliest purchases of the period—in ending inventory.

lower-of-cost-or-market (LCM) rule (p. 316) Requires that an asset be reported in the financial statements at whichever is lower—its historical cost or its market value (current replacement cost for inventory).

periodic inventory system (p. 306) An inventory system in which the business does not keep a continuous record of the inventory on hand. Instead, at the end of the period, the business makes a physical count of the inventory on hand and applies the appropriate unit costs to determine the cost of the ending inventory.

perpetual inventory system (p. 306) An inventory system in which the business keeps a continuous record for each inventory item to show the inventory on hand at all times.

purchase allowance (p. 307) A decrease in the cost of purchases because the seller has granted the buyer a subtraction (an allowance) from the amount owed.

purchase discount (p. 308) A decrease in the cost of purchases earned by making an early payment to the vendor.

purchase return (p. 307) A decrease in the cost of purchases because the buyer returned the goods to the seller.

specific-unit-cost method (p. 309) Inventory cost method based on the specific cost of particular units of inventory.

weighted-average method (p. 310) Another name for the *average-cost method*.

ASSESS YOUR PROGRESS

Short Exercises

S6-1. *(Learning Objective 1: Show how to account for inventory transactions)* Metricalla, Inc., purchased inventory costing $120,000 and sold 70% of the goods for $165,000. All purchases and sales were on account. Metricalla later collected 35% of the accounts receivable.
  1. Journalize these transactions for Metricalla, which uses the perpetual inventory system.
  2. For these transactions, show what Metricalla will report for inventory, revenues, and expenses on its financial statements at the end of the month. Report gross profit on the appropriate statement.

S6-2. *(Learning Objective 2: Apply the average, FIFO, and LIFO methods)* City Copy Center sells laser printers and supplies. Assume City Copy Center started the year with 100 containers of ink (average cost of $8.30 each, FIFO cost of $8.40 each, LIFO cost of $8.10 each). During the year, City Copy Center purchased 700 containers of ink at $9.90 and sold 600 units for $19.50 each. City Copy Center paid operating expenses throughout the year, a total of $3,750. Ignore income taxes for this exercise.

   Prepare City Copy Center's income statement for the current year ended December 31 under the average, FIFO, and LIFO inventory costing methods. Include a complete statement heading.

S6-3. *(Learning Objective 2: Compare income tax effects of the inventory costing methods)* This exercise should be used in conjunction with S6-2. City Copy Center is a corporation subject to a 40% income tax. Compute City Copy Center's income tax expense under the average, FIFO, and LIFO inventory costing methods. Which method would you select to (a) maximize income before tax and (b) minimize income tax expense?

S6-4. *(Learning Objective 2: Compare income and income tax effects of LIFO)* Univision.com uses the LIFO method to account for inventory. Univision is having an unusually good year, with net income well above expectations. The company's inventory costs are rising rapidly. What can Univision do immediately before the end of the year to decrease net income? Explain how this action decreases reported income, and tell why Univision might want to decrease its net income.

S6-5. *(Learning Objective 3: Apply the lower-of-cost-or-market rule to inventory)* It is December 31, the end of the year, and the controller of Raney Corporation is applying the lower-of-cost-or-market (LCM) rule to inventories. Before any year-end adjustments, Raney reports the following data:

Cost of goods sold...	$380,000
Historical cost of ending inventory,	
as determined by a physical count...............	56,000

Raney determines that the current replacement cost of ending inventory is $52,000. Show what Raney should report for ending inventory and for cost of goods sold. Identify the financial statement where each item appears.

S6-6. *(Learning Objective 2: Compare income, tax, and other effects of the inventory methods)* This exercise tests your understanding of the four inventory methods. List the name of the inventory method that best fits the description. Assume that the cost of inventory is rising.
  1. _____ Maximizes reported income
  2. _____ Used to account for automobiles, jewelry, and art objects
  3. _____ Results in a cost of ending inventory that is close to the current cost of replacing the inventory
  4. _____ Generally associated with saving income taxes
  5. _____ Enables a company to buy high-cost inventory at year-end and thereby decrease reported income and income tax

6. _____ Results in an old measure of the cost of ending inventory

7. _____ Provides a middle-ground measure of ending inventory and cost of goods sold

8. _____ Enables a company to keep reported income from dropping lower by liquidating older layers of inventory

9. _____ Writes inventory down when current replacement cost drops below historical cost

10. _____ Matches the most current cost of goods sold against sales revenue

S6-7. _(Learning Objective 4: Compute ratio data to evaluate operations)_ Pepper Company made sales of $53,376 million during 2014. Cost of goods sold for the year totaled $24,437 million. At the end of 2013, Pepper's inventory stood at $2,672 million, and Pepper ended 2014 with inventory of $2,908 million.

Compute Pepper's gross profit percentage and rate of inventory turnover for 2014.

S6-8. _(Learning Objective 5: Estimate ending inventory by the gross profit method)_ Prompt Technology began the year with inventory of $15,000 and purchased $420,000 of goods during the year. Sales for the year are $870,000, and Prompt Technology's gross profit percentage is 60% of sales. Compute Prompt Technology's estimated cost of ending inventory by using the gross profit method.

S6-9. _(Learning Objective 6: Analyze the effect of an inventory error on two years)_ Quick Office Supplies' $3.8 million cost of inventory at the end of last year was understated by $1.1 million.

1. Was last year's reported gross profit of $2.7 million overstated, understated, or correct? What was the correct amount of gross profit last year?
2. Is this year's gross profit of $3.6 million overstated, understated, or correct? What is the correct amount of gross profit for the current year?
3. Was last year's reported cost of goods sold of $5.1 million overstated, understated, or correct? What was the correct amount of cost of goods sold last year?
4. Is this year's cost of goods sold of $5.7 million overstated, understated, or correct? What is the correct amount of cost of goods sold for this year?

S6-10. _(Learning Objectives 3, 5: Explain underlying GAAP for inventory; evaluate management decisions)_ Determine whether each of the following actions in buying, selling, and accounting for inventories is ethical or unethical. Give your reason for each answer.

1. LLW Corporation deliberately overstated purchases to produce a high figure for cost of goods sold (low amount of net income). The real reason was to decrease the company's income tax payments to the government.
2. Lacey Pharmaceuticals purchased a large amount of inventory shortly before year-end to increase the LIFO cost of goods sold and decrease reported income for the year.
3. Johanson Sales, Inc., delayed the purchase of inventory until after December 31, 2014, to keep 2014's cost of goods sold from growing too large. The delay in purchasing inventory helped net income of 2014 to reach the level of profit demanded by the company's investors.
4. Davidson Sales Company deliberately overstated ending inventory in order to report higher profits (net income).
5. In applying the lower-of-cost-or-market rule to inventories, Coastal Coffee Company recorded an excessively low value for its ending inventory (below both cost and market). This allowed the company to pay less income tax for the year.

Exercises

Group A

E6-11A. *(Learning Objectives 1, 2: Show how to account for inventory transactions; apply the FIFO cost method)* Accounting records for Lyons Corporation yield the following data for the year ended June 30, 2014:

Inventory, June 30, 2013...	$15,000
Purchases of inventory (on account)...	68,000
Sales of inventory—83% on account; 17% for cash (cost $57,000).........	115,000
Inventory at FIFO, June 30, 2014	26,000

Requirements

1. Journalize Lyons' inventory transactions for the year under the perpetual system.
2. Report ending inventory, sales, cost of goods sold, and gross profit on the appropriate financial statement.

E6-12A. *(Learning Objectives 1, 2: Show how to account for inventory transactions; apply the FIFO cost method)* Bright Sales, Inc.'s inventory records for a particular development program show the following at January 31:

Jan	1	Beginning inventory	5 units @ $155	=	$ 775
	15	Purchase................................	8 units @ 156	=	$1,248
	26	Purchase................................	13 units @ 165	=	$2,145

At January 31, nine of these programs are on hand. Journalize the following for Bright Sales, Inc., under the perpetual system:
1. Total January purchases in one summary entry. All purchases were on credit.
2. Total January sales and cost of goods sold in two summary entries. The selling price was $600 per unit, and all sales were on credit. Assume that Bright Sales, Inc., uses the FIFO inventory method.
3. Under FIFO, how much gross profit would Bright Sales, Inc., earn on these transactions? What is the FIFO cost of Bright Sales, Inc.'s ending inventory?

E6-13A. *(Learning Objective 2: Compare ending inventory and cost of goods sold by four methods)* Use the data for Bright Sales, Inc., in E6-12A to answer the following:

Requirements

1. Compute cost of goods sold and ending inventory, using each of the following methods:
   a. Specific unit cost, with three $155 units and six $165 units still on hand at the end
   b. Average cost
   c. First-in, first-out
   d. Last-in, first-out
2. Which method produces the highest cost of goods sold? Which method produces the lowest cost of goods sold? What causes the difference in cost of goods sold?

E6-14A. *(Learning Objective 2: Compare the tax advantage of LIFO over FIFO)* Use the data for Bright Sales, Inc., in E6-12A to illustrate Bright Sales, Inc.'s income tax advantage from using LIFO over FIFO. Sales revenue is $10,200, operating expenses are $3,400, and the income tax rate is 28%. How much in taxes would Bright Sales, Inc., save by using the LIFO method versus FIFO?

E6-15A. *(Learning Objective 2: Compare ending inventory and cost of goods sold—FIFO vs. LIFO)* MusicWorld.net specializes in sound equipment. Because each inventory item is expensive, MusicWorld uses a perpetual inventory system. Company records indicate the following data for a line of speakers:

Date		Item	Quantity	Unit Cost	Sale Price
Jun	1	Balance..................	14	$45	
Jun	2	Purchase................	4	69	
Jun	7	Sale	6		$112
Jun	13	Sale	5		112

Requirements

1. Determine the amounts that MusicWorld should report for cost of goods sold and ending inventory two ways:
   a. FIFO
   b. LIFO
2. MusicWorld uses the FIFO method. Prepare MusicWorld's income statement for the month ended June 30, 2014, reporting gross profit. Operating expenses totaled $340, and the income tax rate was 40%.

E6-16A. *(Learning Objective 2: Compare gross profit—FIFO vs. LIFO—falling prices)* Suppose a Sams store in Kansas City, Missouri, ended May 2014 with 70,000 units of merchandise that cost an average of $7 each. Suppose the store then sold 65,000 units for $850,000 during June. Further, assume the store made two large purchases during June as follows:

Jun 10	10,000 units @ $5.10	=	$ 51,000
20	40,000 units @ $4.20	=	$168,000

Requirements

1. At June 30, the store manager needs to know the store's gross profit under both FIFO and LIFO. Supply this information.
2. What caused the FIFO and LIFO gross profit figures to differ?

E6-17A. *(Learning Objective 3: Apply the lower-of-cost-or-market rule to inventories)* Debbie's Garden Supplies uses a perpetual inventory system. Debbie's Garden Supplies has these account balances at October 31, 2014, prior to making the year-end adjustments:

Inventory		Cost of Goods Sold		Sales Revenue	
Beg bal 31,000					
End bal 33,000		Bal 120,000			Bal 246,000

A year ago, the replacement cost of ending inventory was $32,500, which exceeded the cost of $31,000. Debbie's Garden Supplies has determined that the replacement cost of the October 31, 2014, ending inventory is $31,500.

Requirement

1. Prepare Debbie's Garden Supplies' 2014 income statement through gross profit to show how the company would apply the lower-of-cost-or-market rule to its inventories.

E6-18A. *(Learning Objective 4: Compute cost of goods sold and gross profit)* Supply the missing income statement amounts for each of the following companies (amounts adapted, in millions):

Company	Net Sales	Beginning Inventory	Net Purchases	Ending Inventory	Cost of Goods Sold	Gross Profit
Cailley	$253,000	$41,000	$132,000	$37,000	(a)	(b)
Durango	137,000	26,000	(c)	21,000	(d)	44,000
Hartt	(e)	(f)	54,000	24,000	62,000	35,000
Rosen	82,000	9,000	29,000	(g)	33,000	(h)

Requirement

1. Prepare the income statement for Cailley Company for the year ended December 31, 2014. Use the cost-of-goods-sold model to compute cost of goods sold. Cailley's operating and other expenses, as adapted, for the year were $72,000. Ignore income tax.

Note: E6-19A builds on E6-18A with a profitability analysis of these companies.

E6-19A. *(Learning Objective 4: Evaluate profitability and inventory turnover)* Refer to the data in E6-18A. Compute all ratio values to answer the following questions:
- Which company has the highest, and which company has the lowest, gross profit percentage?
- Which company has the highest, and which has the lowest, rate of inventory turnover?

Based on your figures, which company appears to be the most profitable?

E6-20A. *(Learning Objective 4: Compute and evaluate gross profit percentage and inventory turnover)* Lasley & Linderman, a partnership, had the following inventory data:

	2013	2014
Ending inventory at:		
FIFO Cost..............	$18,000	$ 23,000
LIFO Cost..............	8,000	19,000
Cost of goods sold at:		
FIFO Cost..............		$ 80,900
LIFO Cost..............		84,900
Sales revenue..............		154,000

Lasley and Linderman need to know the company's gross profit percentage and rate of inventory turnover for 2014 under
1. FIFO.
2. LIFO.

Which method produces a higher gross profit percentage? Inventory turnover?

E6-21A. *(Learning Objective 5: Use the COGS model to make management decisions)* Dawson Drums prepares budgets to help manage the company. Dawson Drums is budgeting for the fiscal year ended January 31, 2014. During the preceding year ended January 31, 2013, sales totaled $9,400 million and cost of goods sold was $6,500 million. At January 31, 2013, inventory was $1,800 million. During the upcoming 2014 year, suppose Dawson Drums expects cost of goods sold to increase by 12%. The company budgets next year's ending inventory at $2,100 million.

Requirement

1. One of the most important decisions a manager makes is how much inventory to buy. How much inventory should Dawson Drums purchase during the upcoming year to reach its budget?

E6-22A. *(Learning Objective 5: Use the COGS model to make management decisions)* York Farm Supply, Inc., began September with inventory of $45,700. The business made net purchases of $62,300 and had net sales of $107,600 before a fire destroyed the company's inventory. For the past several years, York Farm Supply's gross profit percentage has been 45%. Estimate the cost of the inventory destroyed by the fire. Identify another reason that owners and managers use the gross profit method to estimate inventory.

E6-23A. *(Learning Objective 6: Analyze the effect of an inventory error)* Lake Anna Marine Supply reported the following comparative income statements for the years ended June 30, 2014, and 2013:

	A	B	C	D	E
1	**Lake Anna Marine Supply** **Income Statements** **For the Years Ended June 30, 2014 and 2013**				
2			**2014**		**2013**
3	Sales revenue		$ 216,000		$ 191,000
4	Cost of goods sold:				
5	Beginning inventory	$ 15,000		$ 11,500	
6	Net purchases	105,000		88,000	
7	Cost of goods available	120,000		99,500	
8	Ending inventory	(18,000)		(15,000)	
9	Cost of goods sold		102,000		84,500
10	Gross profit		114,000		106,500
11	Operating expenses		51,000		46,000
12	Net income		$ 63,000		$ 60,500
13					

Lake Anna's president and shareholders are thrilled by the company's boost in sales and net income during 2014. Then the accountants for the company discover that ending 2013 inventory was understated by $3,600. Prepare the corrected comparative income statements for the two-year period, complete with a heading for the statements. How well did Lake Anna really perform in 2014 as compared with 2013?

Group B

E6-24B. *(Learning Objectives 1, 2: Show how to account for inventory transactions; apply the FIFO cost method)* Accounting records for Yates Corporation yield the following data for the year ended March 31, 2014:

Inventory, March 31, 2013	$ 12,000
Purchases of inventory (on account)...	72,000
Sales of inventory—79% on account; 21% for cash (cost $56,000)	108,000
Inventory at FIFO, March 31, 2014..	28,000

Requirements

1. Journalize Yates's inventory transactions for the year under the perpetual system.
2. Report ending inventory, sales, cost of goods sold, and gross profit on the appropriate financial statement.

E6-25B. *(Learning Objectives 1, 2: Show how to account for inventory transactions; apply the FIFO cost method)* Nashville Sales, Inc.'s inventory records for a particular development program show the following at August 31:

Aug 1	Beginning inventory	6 units @ $170	=	$1,020
Aug 15	Purchase.................................	8 units @ 172	=	1,376
Aug 26	Purchase.................................	14 units @ 180	=	2,520

At August 31, eleven of these programs are on hand. Journalize the following for Nashville Sales, under the perpetual system:

1. Total August purchases in one summary entry. All purchases were on credit.
2. Total August sales and cost of goods sold in two summary entries. The selling price was $575 per unit, and all sales were on credit. Assume that Nashville Sales uses the FIFO inventory method.
3. Under FIFO, how much gross profit would Nashville Sales earn on these transactions? What is the FIFO cost of Nashville Sales, Inc.'s ending inventory?

E6-26B. *(Learning Objective 2: Compare ending inventory and cost of goods sold by four methods)* Use the data for Nashville Sales, Inc., in E6-25B to answer the following.

Requirements

1. Compute cost of goods sold and ending inventory using each of the following methods:
   a. Specific unit cost, with five $170 units and six $180 units still on hand at the end
   b. Average cost
   c. FIFO
   d. LIFO
2. Which method produces the highest cost of goods sold? Which method produces the lowest cost of goods sold? What causes the difference in cost of goods sold?

E6-27B. *(Learning Objective 2: Compare the tax advantage of LIFO over FIFO)* Use the data for Nashville Sales, Inc., in E6-25B to illustrate Nashville Sales' income tax advantage from using LIFO over FIFO. Sales revenue is $9,775, operating expenses are $3,800, and the income tax rate is 40%. How much in taxes would Nashville Sales save by using the LIFO method versus FIFO?

E6-28B. *(Learning Objective 2: Compare ending inventory and cost of goods sold—FIFO vs. LIFO)* MusicMagic.net specializes in sound equipment. Because each inventory item is expensive, MusicMagic uses a perpetual inventory system. Company records indicate the following data for a line of speakers:

Date	Item	Quantity	Unit Cost	Sale Price
Sep 1	Balance...................	17	$62	
Sep 3	Purchase................	3	71	
Sep 8	Sale	5		$114
Sep 12	Sale	7		114

Requirements

1. Determine the amounts that MusicMagic should report for cost of goods sold and ending inventory two ways:
   a. FIFO
   b. LIFO
2. MusicMagic uses the FIFO method. Prepare MusicMagic's income statement for the month ended September 30, 2014, reporting gross profit. Operating expenses totaled $320, and the income tax rate was 35%.

E6-29B. *(Learning Objective 2: Compare gross profit—FIFO vs. LIFO—falling prices)* Suppose a Costco store in Denver, Colorado, ended September 2014 with 100,000 units of merchandise that cost an average of $7.20 each. Suppose the store then sold 95,000 units for $1,235,000 during October. Further, assume the store made two large purchases during October as follows:

Oct 8	20,000 units @ $6.10	= $122,000
22	60,000 units @ $5.20	= $312,000

Requirements

1. At October 31, the store manager needs to know the store's gross profit under both FIFO and LIFO. Supply this information.
2. What caused the FIFO and LIFO gross profit figures to differ?

E6-30B. *(Learning Objective 3: Apply the lower-of-cost-or-market rule to inventories)* RoseTree Garden Supplies uses a perpetual inventory system. RoseTree Garden Supplies has these account balances at August 31, 2014, prior to making the year-end adjustments:

Inventory		Cost of Goods Sold		Sales Revenue	
Beg bal 30,000					
End bal 34,000		Bal 118,000			Bal 251,000

A year ago, the current replacement cost of ending inventory was $31,500, which exceeded the cost of $30,000. RoseTree Garden Supplies has determined that the replacement cost of the August 31, 2014, ending inventory is $32,000.

Requirement

1. Prepare RoseTree Garden Supplies' 2014 income statement through gross profit to show how the company would apply the lower-of-cost-or-market rule to its inventories.

E6-31B. *(Learning Objective 4: Compute cost of goods sold and gross profit)* Supply the missing amounts for each of the following companies:

Company	Net Sales	Beginning Inventory	Net Purchases	Ending Inventory	Cost of Goods Sold	Gross Profit
Epperson	$240,000	$41,000	$120,000	$39,000	(a)	(b)
Griffith	137,000	28,000	(c)	20,000	(d)	41,000
Norse	(e)	(f)	55,000	21,000	60,000	37,000
Victory	80,000	10,000	33,000	(g)	35,000	(h)

Requirement

1. Prepare the income statement for Epperson Company for the year ended December 31, 2014. Use the cost-of-goods-sold model to compute cost of goods sold. Epperson's operating and other expenses for the year were $72,000. Ignore income tax.

Note: E6-32B builds on E6-31B with a profitability analysis of these companies.

E6-32B. *(Learning Objective 4: Evaluate profitability and inventory turnover)* Refer to the data in E6-31B. Compute all ratio values to answer the following questions:

- Which company has the highest, and which company has the lowest, gross profit percentage?
- Which company has the highest, and which has the lowest, rate of inventory turnover?

Based on your figures, which company appears to be the most profitable?

E6-33B. *(Learning Objective 4: Compute and evaluate gross profit percentage and inventory turnover)* Pepper & Penson, a partnership, had these inventory data:

	2013	2014
Ending inventory at:		
FIFO Cost...............	$12,000	$ 24,000
LIFO Cost...............	7,000	14,000
Cost of goods sold at:		
FIFO Cost...............		$ 80,800
LIFO Cost...............		90,800
Sales revenue...............		158,000

Pepper and Penson need to know the company's gross profit percentage and rate of inventory turnover for 2014 under
1. FIFO.
2. LIFO.

Which method produces a higher gross profit percentage? Inventory turnover?

E6-34B. *(Learning Objective 5: Use the COGS model to make management decisions)* Teaching Toys prepares budgets to help manage the company. Teaching Toys is budgeting for the fiscal year ended January 31, 2014. During the preceding year ended January 31, 2013, sales totaled $9,600 million and cost of goods sold was $6,600 million. At January 31, 2013, inventory was $1,600 million. During the upcoming 2014 year, suppose Teaching Toys expects cost of goods sold to increase by 12%. The company budgets next year's inventory at $1,900 million.

Requirement

1. One of the most important decisions a manager makes is how much inventory to buy. How much inventory should Teaching Toys purchase during the upcoming year to reach its budget?

E6-35B. *(Learning Objective 5: Use the COGS model to make management decisions)* L5 Products Company began April with inventory of $46,500. The business made net purchases of $61,500 and had net sales of $104,600 before a fire destroyed the company's inventory. For the past several years, L5 Products' gross profit percentage has been 40%. Estimate the cost of the inventory destroyed by the fire. Identify another reason that owners and managers use the gross profit method to estimate inventory.

E6-36B. *(Learning Objective 6: Analyze the effect of an inventory error)* Lake Travis Marine Supply reported the following comparative income statements for the years ended June 30, 2014, and 2013:

A1					
	A	**B**	**C**	**D**	**E**
1	Lake Travis Marine Supply Income Statements For the Years Ended June 30, 2014 and 2013				
2			2014		2013
3	Sales revenue		$ 146,000		$ 124,600
4	Cost of goods sold:				
5	Beginning inventory	$ 12,000		$ 9,500	
6	Net purchases	82,000		79,000	
7	Cost of goods available	94,000		88,500	
8	Ending inventory	(16,500)		(12,000)	
9	Cost of goods sold		77,500		76,500
10	Gross profit		68,500		48,100
11	Operating expenses		29,000		21,000
12	Net income		$ 39,500		$ 27,100
13					

Lake Travis's president and shareholders are thrilled by the company's boost in sales and net income during 2014. Then the accountants for the company discover that ending 2013 inventory was understated by $7,000. Prepare the corrected comparative income statements for the two-year period, complete with a heading for the statements. How well did Lake Travis really perform in 2014 as compared with 2013?

Quiz

Test your understanding of accounting for inventory by answering the following questions. Select the best choice from among the possible answers given.

Q6-37. Raines Software began January with $3,400 of merchandise inventory. During January, Raines made the following entries for its inventory transactions:

	A1	⬍			
	A		**B**	**C**	**D**
1		Inventory		6,700	
2			Accounts Payable		6,700
3					
4		Accounts Receivable		7,700	
5			Sales Revenue		7,700
6					
7		Cost of Goods Sold		5,500	
8			Inventory		5,500
9					

How much was Raines' inventory at the end of January?
  a. $4,600   **c.** $10,100
  b. $6,700   **d.** $ – 0 –

Q6-38. What was Raines's gross profit for January?
  a. $5,500   **c.** $2,200
  b. $7,700   **d.** $ – 0 –

Q6-39. When does the cost of inventory become an expense?
  a. When payment is made to the supplier
  b. When inventory is purchased from the supplier
  c. When cash is collected from the customer
  d. When inventory is delivered to a customer

The next two questions use the following facts. Square Nails Frame Shop wants to know the effect of different inventory costing methods on its financial statements. Inventory and purchases data for June are:

			Units	Unit Cost	Total Cost
Jun 1		Beginning inventory	2,100	$11.00	$23,100
	4	Purchase	1,200	$11.50	13,800
	9	Sale	(1,400)		

Q6-40. If Square Nails Frame Shop uses the FIFO method, the *cost of the ending inventory* will be
  a. $21,500.   **c.** $13,800.
  b. $15,700.   **d.** $15,400.

Q6-41. If Square Nails Frame Shop uses the LIFO method, *cost of goods sold* will be
  a. $15,400.   **c.** $13,800.
  b. $16,000.   **d.** $15,700.

Q6-42. In a period of rising prices,
  a. net income under LIFO will be higher than under FIFO.
  b. LIFO inventory will be greater than FIFO inventory.
  c. cost of goods sold under LIFO will be less than under FIFO.
  d. gross profit under FIFO will be higher than under LIFO.

Q6-43. The income statement for Truly Fresh Foods shows gross profit of $153,000, operating expenses of $123,000, and cost of goods sold of $213,000. What is the amount of net sales revenue?
  a. $276,000
  b. $489,000
  c. $366,000
  d. $336,000

Q6-44. The word *market* as used in "the lower of cost or market" generally means
  a. current replacement cost.
  b. retail market price.
  c. original cost.
  d. liquidation price.

Q6-45. The sum of ending inventory and cost of goods sold is
  a. net purchases.
  b. cost of goods available (or cost of goods available for sale).
  c. beginning inventory.
  d. gross profit.

Q6-46. The following data come from the inventory records of Dean Company:

Net sales revenue	$627,000
Beginning inventory	61,000
Ending inventory	40,000
Net purchases	430,000

Based on these facts, the gross profit for Dean Company is
  a. $197,000.
  b. $190,000.
  c. $176,000.
  d. $166,000.

Q6-47. Flirt Cosmetics ended the month of March with inventory of $25,000. Flirt Cosmetics expects to end April with inventory of $17,000 after selling goods with a cost of $92,000. How much inventory must Flirt Cosmetics purchase during April in order to accomplish these results?
  a. $134,000
  b. $109,000
  c. $100,000
  d. $84,000

Q6-48. Two financial ratios that clearly distinguish a discount chain such as Walmart from a high-end retailer such as Gucci are the gross profit percentage and the rate of inventory turnover. Which set of relationships is most likely for Gucci?

Gross profit percentage	**Inventory turnover**
a. Low	High
b. High	Low
c. Low	Low
d. High	High

Q6-49. Sales are $580,000 and cost of goods sold is $310,000. Beginning and ending inventories are $23,000 and $38,000, respectively. How many times did the company turn its inventory over during this period?
  a. 10.2 times
  b. 11.7 times
  c. 19.0 times
  d. 8.9 times

Q6-50. Tusa, Inc., reported the following data:

Freight in....................	$ 21,000	Sales returns..............	$ 4,000
Purchases	202,000	Purchase returns........	6,000
Beginning inventory	55,000	Sales revenue.............	490,000
Purchase discounts	4,600	Ending inventory........	44,000

Tusa's gross profit percentage is
 a. 50.7.
 b. 54.0.
 c. 53.0.
 d. 46.0.

Q6-51. White Sales Company had the following beginning inventory, net purchases, net sales, and gross profit percentage for the first quarter of 2014:

Beginning inventory, $56,000	Net purchases, $79,000
Net sales revenue, $95,000	Gross profit rate, 40%

By the gross profit method, the ending inventory should be
 a. $57,000.
 b. $97,000.
 c. $78,000.
 d. $135,000.

Q6-52. An error understated RLR Corporation's December 31, 2014, ending inventory by $36,000. What effect will this error have on total assets and net income for 2014?

	Assets	**Net income**
a.	Understate	Understate
b.	No effect	No effect
c.	No effect	Overstate
d.	Understate	No effect

Q6-53. An error understated RLR Corporation's December 31, 2014, ending inventory by $36,000. What effect will this error have on net income for 2015?
 a. Understate
 b. Overstate
 c. No effect

Problems

MyAccountingLab

> All of the A and B problems can be found within MyAccountingLab, an online homework and practice environment. Your instructor may ask you to complete these problems using **MyAccountingLab**.

Group A

P6-54A. *(Learning Objectives 1, 2: Show how to account for inventory in a perpetual system using the average-costing method)* Big Buy purchases inventory in crates of merchandise; each crate of inventory is a unit. The fiscal year of Big Buy ends each January 31. Assume you are dealing with a single Big Buy store in Miami, Florida. The Miami store began 2014 with an inventory of 20,000 units that cost a total of $1,060,000. During the year, the store purchased merchandise on account as follows:

Jul (32,000 units at $58)	$1,856,000
Nov (52,000 units at $62)....................................	3,224,000
Dec (62,000 units at $68)....................................	4,216,000
Total purchases..	$9,296,000

Cash payments on account totaled $8,968,000. During fiscal year 2014, the store sold 154,000 units of merchandise for $15,785,000, of which $5,500,000 was for cash and the balance was on account. Big Buy uses the average-cost method for inventories. Operating expenses for the year were $3,750,000. Big Buy paid 70% in cash and accrued the rest as accrued liabilities. The store accrued income tax at the rate of 40%.

Requirements

1. Make summary journal entries to record the store's transactions for the year ended January 31, 2014. Big Buy uses a perpetual inventory system.
2. Prepare a T-account to show the activity in the Inventory account.
3. Prepare the store's income statement for the year ended January 31, 2014. Show totals for gross profit, income before tax, and net income.

P6-55A. *(Learning Objective 2: Apply various inventory costing methods)* Assume a Gold Starr Sports outlet store began August 2014 with 44 pairs of running shoes that cost the store $32 each. The sale price of these shoes was $67. During August, the store completed these inventory transactions:

		Units	Unit Cost	Unit Sale Price
Aug 2	Sale	15	$32	$67
9	Purchase......	79	34	
13	Sale	29	32	67
18	Sale	11	34	68
22	Sale	30	34	68
29	Purchase......	26	36	

Requirements

1. The preceding data are taken from the store's perpetual inventory records. Which cost method does the store use? Explain how you arrived at your answer.
2. Determine the store's cost of goods sold for August. Also compute gross profit for August.
3. What is the cost of the store's August 31 inventory of running shoes?

P6-56A. *(Learning Objective 2: Compare inventory by three methods)* Camp Surplus began May 2014 with 67 tents that cost $25 each. During the month, Camp Surplus made the following purchases at cost:

May 6	101 tents @ $27 =	$2,727
18	163 tents @ $29 =	4,727
26	41 tents @ $30 =	1,230

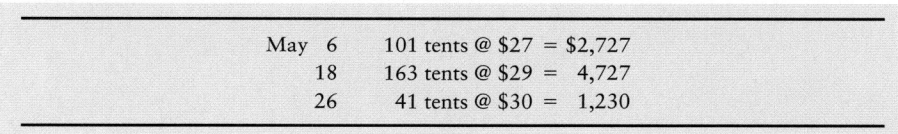

Camp Surplus sold 323 tents, and at May 31 the ending inventory consists of 49 tents. The sale price of each tent was $51.

Requirements

1. Determine the cost of goods sold and ending inventory amounts for May under the average cost, FIFO cost, and LIFO cost. Round average cost per unit to two decimal places, and round all other amounts to the nearest dollar.
2. Explain why cost of goods sold is highest under LIFO. Be specific.
3. Prepare the Camp Surplus income statement for May. Report gross profit. Operating expenses totaled $3,250. Camp Surplus uses average costing for inventory. The income tax rate is 30%.

P6-57A. *(Learning Objective 2: Compare various inventory costing methods)* The records of Fisher Aviation include the following accounts for inventory of aviation parts at July 31 of the current year:

Inventory			
Aug 1	Balance	720 units @ $7.15	$ 5,148
Nov 5	Purchase	400 units @ $7.20	2,880
Jan 24	Purchase	8,420 units @ $7.60	63,992
Apr 8	Purchase	480 units @ $8.30	3,984

Sales Revenue		
Jul 31	9,045 units	$128,560

Requirements

1. Prepare a partial income statement through gross profit under the average, FIFO, and LIFO methods. Round average cost per unit to two decimal places and all other amounts to the nearest dollar.
2. Which inventory method would you use to minimize income tax? Explain why this method causes income tax to be the lowest.

P6-58A. *(Learning Objective 3: Explain GAAP and apply the lower-of-cost-or-market rule to inventories)* Canton Trade Mart has recently had lackluster sales. The rate of inventory turnover has dropped, and the merchandise is gathering dust. At the same time, competition has forced Canton's suppliers to lower the prices that Canton will pay when it replaces its inventory. It is now December 31, 2014, and the current replacement cost of Canton's ending inventory is $7,000 below what Canton actually paid for the goods, which was $98,000. Before any adjustments at the end of the period, the Cost of Goods Sold account has a balance of $410,000.

    a. What accounting action should Canton take in this situation?
    b. Give any journal entry required.
    c. At what amount should Canton report Inventory on the balance sheet?
    d. At what amount should the company report Cost of Goods Sold on the income statement?
    e. Discuss the accounting principle or concept that is most relevant to this situation.

P6-59A. *(Learning Objective 4: Compute and evaluate gross margin and inventory turnover)*
Sweet Treats, Inc., and Coffee Time Corporation are both specialty food chains. The two
companies reported these figures, in millions:

	A1			B	C
		A		**B**	**C**
1	Sweet Treats, Inc. Income Statements (Adapted) Years Ended December 31				
2	(Amounts in millions)			**2014**	**2013**
3	Revenues:				
4	Net sales			$ 542	$ 704
5					
6	Costs and Expenses:				
7	Cost of goods sold			474	592
8	Selling, general, and administrative expenses			37	50
9					

	A1			B	C
		A		**B**	**C**
1	Sweet Treats, Inc. Balance Sheets (Adapted) December 31				
2	(Amounts in millions)			**2014**	**2013**
3	Assets				
4	Current assets:				
5	Cash and cash equivalents			$ 61	$ 26
6	Receivables			27	33
7	Inventories			20	36
8					

	A1			B	C
		A		**B**	**C**
1	Coffee Time Corporation Income Statements (Adapted) Years Ended December 31				
2	(Amounts in millions)			**2014**	**2013**
3	Net sales			$ 7,777	$ 6,369
4	Cost of goods sold			3,180	2,600
5	Selling, general, and administrative expenses			3,000	2,350
6					

	A1			B	C
		A		**B**	**C**
1	Coffee Time Corporation Balance Sheets (Adapted) December 31				
2	(Amounts in millions)			**2014**	**2013**
3	Assets				
4	Current assets:				
5	Cash and temporary investments			$ 318	$ 171
6	Receivables, net			227	194
7	Inventories			625	541
8					

Requirements

1. Compute the gross profit percentage and the rate of inventory turnover for Sweet Treats, Inc., and Coffee Time Corporation for 2014.
2. Based on these statistics, which company looks more profitable? Why? What other expense category should we consider in evaluating these two companies?

P6-60A. *(Learning Objectives 4, 5: Compute gross profit; Use the COGS model to make management decisions, and estimate inventory by the gross profit method)* Assume Whitfield Company, a camera store, lost some inventory in a fire on August 15. To file an insurance claim, Whitfield Company must estimate its August 15 inventory by the gross profit method. Assume that for the past two years Whitfield Company's gross profit has averaged 45% of net sales. Suppose that Whitfield Company's inventory records reveal the following data:

Inventory, August 1..................	$ 67,200
Transactions August 1–15:	
Purchases	410,800
Purchase discounts	15,000
Purchase returns........................	10,600
Sales...	695,000
Sales returns.............................	12,000

Requirements

1. Estimate the cost of the lost inventory using the gross profit method.
2. Prepare the income statement for August 1 to August 15 for this product through gross profit. Show the detailed computations of cost of goods sold in a separate schedule.

P6-61A. *(Learning Objective 5: Use the COGS model to make management decisions, and estimate amount of inventory to purchase)* Shorty's Convenience Stores' income statement for the year ended December 31, 2013, and its balance sheet as of December 31, 2013, reported the following:

A1	

	A	B
1	**Shorty's Convenience Stores** **Income Statement** **Year Ended December 31, 2013**	
2	Sales	$ 986,000
3	Cost of sales	721,000
4	Gross profit	265,000
5	Operating expenses	109,000
6	Net income	$ 156,000
7		

A1	

	A	B	C	D
1	**Shorty's Convenience Stores** **Balance Sheet** **December 31, 2013**			
2	**Assets**		**Liabilities and Capital**	
3	Cash	$ 43,000	Accounts payable	$ 32,000
4	Inventories	64,000	Note payable	185,000
5	Land and		Total liabilities	217,000
6	buildings, net	267,000	Owner, capital	157,000
7			Total liabilities	
8	Total assets	$ 374,000	and capital	$ 374,000
9				

The business is organized as a proprietorship, so it pays no corporate income tax. The owner is budgeting for 2014. He expects sales and cost of goods sold to increase by 5%. To meet customer demand, ending inventory will need to be $86,000 at December 31, 2014. The owner hopes to earn a net income of $178,000 next year.

Requirements

1. One of the most important decisions a manager makes is the amount of inventory to purchase. Show how to determine the amount of inventory to purchase in 2014.
2. Prepare the store's budgeted income statement for 2014 to reach the target net income of $178,000. To reach this goal, operating expenses must decrease by $8,750.

P6-62A. *(Learning Objective 6: Analyze the effects of inventory errors)* The accounting records of Downton Home Store show these data (in millions). The shareholders are very happy with Downton's steady increase in net income.

	2014		2013		2012
Net sales revenue..........................	$47		$44		$41
Cost of goods sold:					
Beginning inventory...................	$ 10		$ 9		$ 8
Net purchases	31		29		27
Cost of goods available..............	41		38		35
Less ending inventory................	(11)		(10)		(9)
Cost of goods sold		30		28		26
Gross profit.....................................		17		16		15
Operating expenses		8		8		8
Net income.....................................		$ 9		$ 8		$ 7

Auditors discovered that the ending inventory for 2012 was understated by $5 million and that the ending inventory for 2013 was understated by $3 million. The ending inventory at December 31, 2014, was correct.

Requirements

1. Show corrected income statements for each of the three years.
2. How much did these assumed corrections add to or take away from Downton's total net income over the three-year period? How did the corrections affect the trend of net income?
3. Will Downton's shareholders still be happy with the company's trend of net income? Give the reason for your answer.

Group B

P6-63B. *(Learning Objectives 1, 2: Show how to account for inventory in a perpetual system using the average-costing method)* Super Buy purchases inventory in crates of merchandise; each crate of inventory is a unit. The fiscal year of Super Buy ends each June 30. Assume you are dealing with a single Super Buy store in San Diego, California. The San Diego store began 2014 with an inventory of 23,000 units that cost a total of $1,196,000. During the year, the store purchased merchandise on account.

August (28,000 units at $54)................................	$1,512,000
March (48,000 units at $58)	2,784,000
May (58,000 units at $64)	3,712,000
Total purchases..	$8,008,000

Cash payments on account totaled $7,860,000. During fiscal 2014, the store sold 153,000 units of merchandise for $15,682,500, of which $5,400,000 was for cash and the balance was on account. Super Buy uses the average-cost method for inventories. Operating expenses for the year were $4,500,000. Super Buy paid 50% in cash and accrued the rest as accrued liabilities. The store accrued income tax at the rate of 35%.

Requirements

1. Make summary journal entries to record the store's transactions for the year ended June 30, 2014. Super Buy uses a perpetual inventory system.
2. Prepare a T-account to show the activity in the Inventory account.
3. Prepare the store's income statement for the year ended June 30, 2014. Show totals for gross profit, income before tax, and net income.

P6-64B. *(Learning Objective 2: Apply various inventory costing methods)* Assume a Bear Sports outlet store began January 2014 with 42 pairs of running shoes that cost the store $36 each. The sale price of these shoes was $68. During January, the store completed these inventory transactions:

		Units	Unit Cost	Unit Sale Price
Jan 3	Sale	15	$36	$68
8	Purchase......	82	38	
11	Sale	27	36	68
19	Sale	6	38	70
24	Sale	29	38	70
30	Purchase......	25	40	

Requirements

1. The preceding data are taken from the store's perpetual inventory records. Which cost method does the store use? Explain how you arrived at your answer.
2. Determine the store's cost of goods sold for January. Also compute gross profit for January.
3. What is the cost of the store's January 31 inventory of running shoes?

P6-65B. *(Learning Objective 2: Compare inventory by three methods)* Army-Navy Surplus began March 2014 with 75 camping stoves that cost $16 each. During the month, Army-Navy Surplus made the following purchases at cost:

Mar 3	95 stoves @ $18 = $1,710
17	165 stoves @ $20 = 3,300
23	36 stoves @ $21 = 756

Army-Navy Surplus sold 318 stoves, and at March 31, the ending inventory consists of 53 stoves. The sale price of each tent was $47.

Requirements

1. Determine the cost-of-goods-sold and ending inventory amounts for March under the average cost, FIFO cost, and LIFO cost. Round average cost per unit to two decimal places, and round all other amounts to the nearest dollar.
2. Explain why cost of goods sold is highest under LIFO. Be specific.
3. Prepare Army-Navy Surplus's income statement for March. Report gross profit. Operating expenses totaled $2,755. Army-Navy Surplus uses average costing for inventory. The income tax rate is 30%.

P6-66B. *(Learning Objective 2: Compare various inventory costing methods)* The records of Parker Aviation include the following accounts for inventory of aviation parts at October 31 of the current year:

Inventory			
Nov 1	Balance	700 units @ $7.35	$ 5,145
Jan 8	Purchase	350 units @ $7.50	2,625
May 21	Purchase	8,450 units @ $7.90	66,755
Jul 7	Purchase	480 units @ $8.60	4,128

Sales Revenue		
Oct 31	9,075 units	$129,369

Requirements

1. Prepare a partial income statement through gross profit under the average, FIFO, and LIFO methods. Round average cost per unit to two decimal places and all other amounts to the nearest whole dollar.
2. Which inventory method would you use to minimize income tax? Explain why this method causes income tax to be the lowest.

P6-67B. *(Learning Objective 3: Explain GAAP and apply the lower-of-cost-or-market rule to inventories)* Stillwater Trade Mart has recently had lackluster sales. The rate of inventory turnover has dropped, and the merchandise is gathering dust. At the same time, competition has forced Stillwater's suppliers to lower the prices that Stillwater will pay when it replaces its inventory. It is now December 31, 2014, and the current replacement cost of Stillwater's ending inventory is $8,000 below what Stillwater actually paid for the goods, which was $101,000. Before any adjustments at the end of the period, the Cost of Goods Sold account has a balance of $490,000.

   a. What accounting action should Stillwater take in this situation?
   b. Give any journal entry required.
   c. At what amount should Stillwater report Inventory on the balance sheet?
   d. At what amount should the company report Cost of Goods Sold on the income statement?
   e. Discuss the accounting principle or concept that is most relevant to this situation.

P6-68B. *(Learning Objective 4: Compute and evaluate gross margin and inventory turnover)* Magic Muffins, Inc., and Top Roast Coffee Corporation are both specialty food chains. The two companies reported these figures, in millions:

A1 ⬍			
	A	B	C
1	**Magic Muffins, Inc.** **Income Statements (Adapted)** **Years Ended December 31**		
2	**(Amounts in millions)**	**2014**	**2013**
3	Revenues:		
4	Net sales	$ 540	$ 705
5			
6	Costs and Expenses:		
7	Cost of goods sold	470	595
8	Selling, general, and administrative expenses	51	53
9			

A1 ⬍			
	A	B	C
1	**Magic Muffins, Inc.** **Balance Sheets (Adapted)** **December 31**		
2	**(Amounts in millions)**	**2014**	**2013**
3	Assets		
4	Current assets:		
5	Cash and temporary investments	$ 21	$ 24
6	Receivables	25	40
7	Inventories	18	30
8			

A1				B	C
	A				
1	**Top Roast Coffee Corporation** **Income Statements (Adapted)** **Years Ended December 31**				
2	**(Amounts in millions)**			**2014**	**2013**
3	Net sales			$ 7,710	$ 6,400
4	Cost of goods sold			3,170	2,600
5	Selling, general, and administrative expenses			2,975	2,360
6					

A1				B	C
	A				
1	**Top Roast Coffee Corporation** **Balance Sheets (Adapted)** **December 31**				
2	**(Amounts in millions)**			**2014**	**2013**
3	**Assets**				
4	Current assets:				
5	Cash and temporary investments			$ 320	$ 175
6	Receivables, net			220	195
7	Inventories			630	540
8					

Requirements

1. Compute the gross profit percentage and the rate of inventory turnover for Magic Muffins and Top Roast Coffee for 2014.
2. Based on these statistics, which company looks more profitable? Why? What other expense category should we consider in evaluating these two companies?

P6-69B. *(Learning Objectives 4, 5: Compute gross profit; Use the COGS model to make management decisions, and estimate inventory by the gross profit method)* Assume Sternberg Company, a music store, lost some inventory in a fire on March 15. To file an insurance claim, Sternberg Company must estimate its March 15 inventory by the gross profit method. Assume that for the past two years, Sternberg Company's gross profit has averaged 44% of net sales. Suppose Sternberg Company's inventory records reveal the following data:

Inventory, March 1	$ 67,300
Transactions March 1–15:	
Purchases	410,700
Purchase discounts	17,000
Purchase returns......................	10,500
Sales...	690,000
Sales returns............................	13,000

Requirements

1. Estimate the cost of the lost inventory using the gross profit method.
2. Prepare the income statement for March 1 through March 15 for this product through gross profit. Show the detailed computation of cost of goods sold in a separate schedule.

P6-70B. *(Learning Objective 5: Use the COGS model to make management decision of the amount of inventory to purchase)* Chuck's Convenience Stores' income statement for the year ended December 31, 2013, and its balance sheet as of December 31, 2013, reported the following. The business is organized as a proprietorship, so it pays no corporate income tax. The owner is budgeting for 2014. He expects sales and cost of goods sold to increase by 10%. To meet customer demand, ending inventory will need to be $84,000 at December 31, 2014. The owner hopes to earn a net income of $166,000 next year.

A1		
	A	**B**
1	**Chuck's Convenience Stores** **Income Statement** **Year Ended December 31, 2013**	
2	Sales	$ 975,000
3	Cost of sales	724,000
4	Gross profit	251,000
5	Operating expenses	113,000
6	Net income	$ 138,000
7		

A1				
	A	**B**	**C**	**D**
1	**Chuck's Convenience Stores** **Balance Sheet** **December 31, 2013**			
2	**Assets**		**Liabilities and Capital**	
3	Cash	$ 48,000	Accounts payable	$ 28,000
4	Inventories	69,000	Note payable	188,000
5	Land and		Total liabilities	216,000
6	buildings, net	262,000	Owner, capital	163,000
7			Total liabilities	
8	Total assets	$ 379,000	and capital	$ 379,000
9				

Requirements

1. One of the most important decisions a manager makes is the amount of inventory to purchase. Show how to determine the amount of inventory to purchase in 2014.
2. Prepare the store's budgeted income statement for 2014 to reach the target net income of $166,000. To reach this goal, operating expenses must decrease by $2,900.

P6-71B. *(Learning Objective 6: Analyze the effects of inventory errors)* The accounting records of Durango Furniture show these data (in millions). The shareholders are very happy with Durango's steady increase in net income.

	2014		2013		2012	
Net sales revenue............................		$41		$38		$35
Cost of goods sold:						
Beginning inventory....................	$ 13		$ 12		$ 11	
Net purchases	32		30		28	
Cost of goods available..............	45		42		39	
Less ending inventory.................	(14)		(13)		(12)	
Cost of goods sold		31		29		27
Gross profit....................................		10		9		8
Operating expenses		6		6		6
Net income.....................................		$ 4		$ 3		$ 2

Auditors discovered that the ending inventory for 2012 was understated by $3 million and that the ending inventory for 2013 was understated by $1 million. The ending inventory at December 31, 2014, was correct.

Requirements

1. Show corrected income statements for each of the three years.
2. How much did these assumed corrections add to or take away from Durango's total net income over the three-year period? How did the corrections affect the trend of net income?
3. Will Durango's shareholders still be happy with the company's trend of net income? Give the reason for your answer.

Challenge Exercises and Problem

E6-72. *(Learning Objective 2: Apply various inventory methods to make inventory policy decisions)*
For each of the following situations, identify the inventory method that you would use; or, given the use of a particular method, state the strategy that you would follow to accomplish your goal.

   a. Inventory costs are increasing. Your company uses LIFO and is having an unexpectedly good year. It is near year-end, and you need to keep net income from increasing too much in order to save on income tax.

   b. Suppliers of your inventory are threatening a labor strike, and it may be difficult for your company to obtain inventory. This situation could increase your income taxes.

   c. Company management, like that of Apple and Pottery Barn, prefers a middle-of-the-road inventory policy that avoids extremes.

   d. Inventory costs are *decreasing,* and your company's board of directors wants to minimize income taxes.

   e. Inventory costs are *increasing,* and the company prefers to report high income.

   f. Inventory costs have been stable for several years, and you expect costs to remain stable for the indefinite future. (Give the reason for your choice of method.)

E6-73. *(Learning Objective 2: Measure the effect of a LIFO liquidation)* Suppose In Style Fashions, a specialty retailer, had these records for ladies' evening gowns during 2014:

Beginning inventory (44 @ $975)	$ 42,900
Purchase in February (19 @ $1,050)	19,950
Purchase in June (55 @ $1,100)	60,500
Purchase in December (31 @ $1,200)	37,200
Cost of goods available for sale	$160,550

Assume that In Style sold 117 gowns during 2014 and uses the LIFO method to account for inventory. The income tax rate is 35%.

Requirements

1. Compute In Style's cost of goods sold for evening gowns in 2014.
2. Compute what cost of goods sold would have been if In Style had purchased enough inventory in December—at $1,200 per evening gown—to keep year-end inventory at the same level it was at the beginning of the year.

E6-74. *(Learning Objective 4: Evaluate profitability)* Z Mart, Inc., declared bankruptcy. Let's see why. Z Mart reported these figures:

	A	B	C	D	E
	A1 ⬍				
	Z Mart, Inc. **Statements of Income** **Years Ended December 31**				
1					
2	**Millions**	**2014**	**2013**	**2012**	**2011**
3	Sales	$ 36.6	$ 35.3	$ 34.3	
4	Cost of sales	29.4	27.6	26.8	
5	Selling expenses	7.5	6.3	6.0	
6	Other expenses	0.1	0.9	0.7	
7	Net income (net loss)	$ (0.4)	$ 0.5	$ 0.8	
8	Additional data:				
9	Ending inventory	$ 8.6	$ 7.2	$ 7.2	$ 6.4
10					

Requirement

1. Evaluate the trend of Z Mart's results of operations during 2012 through 2014. Consider the trends of sales, gross profit, and net income. Track the gross profit percentage and the rate of inventory turnover in each year. Also discuss the role that selling expenses must have played in Z Mart's difficulties.

P6-75. *(Learning Objectives 1, 4: Account for inventory; analyze two companies that use different inventory methods)* Arnold Financial Management believes that the biotechnology industry is a good investment and is considering investing in one of two companies. However, one company, HeartStart, Inc., uses the FIFO method of inventory, and another company, GeneTech, Inc., uses LIFO. The following information about the two companies is available from their annual reports:

HeartStart, Inc.	2013	2012
Inventory..	$ 101,000	$ 95,000
Cost of goods sold..	1,200,000	1,100,000
Sales..	2,000,000	1,850,000
Net income..	190,000	187,000
GeneTech, Inc.	**2013**	**2012**
Inventory (See Note)	$ 330,000	$ 300,000
Cost of goods sold..	3,900,000	3,800,000
Sales..	6,700,000	6,400,000
Net income..	870,000	770,000

Notes to the Financial Statement. If GeneTech had used the FIFO method, inventory would have been $20,000 higher at the end of 2012 and $22,000 higher at the end of 2013.

The income of the two companies is difficult to compare because GeneTech is a much larger company and uses a different inventory method. To better compare the two companies, Arnold wants you to prepare the following analysis.

Requirements

1. Show the computation of GeneTech's cost of goods sold in 2013 using the LIFO method. Refer to Appendix 6B for an illustration.
2. Prepare summary journal entries for 2013 for GeneTech's purchases of inventory (assume all purchases are on account), sales (assume all are on account), and cost of goods sold. Prepare a T-account for inventory and post these transactions into the T-account. The company uses the perpetual inventory method.
3. Show the computation of GeneTech's cost of goods sold for 2013 using the FIFO method.
4. Compute the gross profit percentage for 2013 for both HeartStart and GeneTech using FIFO figures for both.
5. Compute the inventory turnover for 2013 for both HeartStart and GeneTech using FIFO figures for both.
6. Which company appears stronger? Support your answer.

Apply Your Knowledge

Decision Cases

Case 1. *(Learning Objective 2: Apply and compare various inventory methods, and assess the impact of a year-end purchase of inventory)* Duracraft Corporation is nearing the end of its first year of operations. Duracraft made inventory purchases of $745,000 during the year, as follows:

January	1,000 units @	$100.00 =	$100,000
July	4,000	121.25	485,000
November	1,000	160.00	160,000
Totals	6,000		$745,000

Sales for the year are 5,000 units for $1,200,000 of revenue. Expenses other than cost of goods sold and income taxes total $200,000. The president of the company is undecided about whether to adopt the FIFO method or the LIFO method for inventories. The income tax rate is 40%.

Requirements

1. To aid company decision making, prepare income statements under FIFO and under LIFO.
2. Compare the net income under FIFO with net income under LIFO. Which method produces the higher net income? What causes this difference? Be specific.

Case 2. *(Learning Objectives 2, 3: Apply and compare various inventory methods; apply underlying GAAP for inventory)* The inventory costing method a company chooses can affect the financial statements and thus the decisions of the people who use those statements.

Requirements

1. Company A uses the LIFO inventory method and discloses its use of the LIFO method in notes to the financial statements. Company B uses the FIFO method to account for its inventory. Company B does *not* disclose which inventory method it uses. Company B reports a higher net income than Company A. In which company would you prefer to invest? Give your reason.
2. Representational faithfulness is an accepted accounting concept. Would you want management to be faithful in representing its accounting for inventory if you were a shareholder or a creditor of a company? Give your reason.

Ethical Issue

During 2014, Vanguard, Inc., changed to the LIFO method of accounting for inventory. Suppose that during 2013, Vanguard changes back to the FIFO method and the following year Vanguard switches back to LIFO again.

Requirements

1. What would you think of a company's ethics if it changed accounting methods every year?
2. What accounting principle would changing methods every year violate?
3. Who can be harmed when a company changes its accounting methods too often? How?

Focus on Financials | Amazon.com, Inc.

(Learning Objectives 1, 4: Show how to account for inventories; compute and evaluate gross profit and inventory turnover) The notes are part of the financial statements. They give details that would clutter the statements. This case will help you learn to use a company's inventory notes. Refer to **Amazon.com, Inc.**'s consolidated financial statements and related notes in Appendix A at the end of the book and answer the following questions:

1. How much was Amazon.com, Inc.'s merchandise inventory at December 31, 2012? At December 31, 2011? Does Amazon.com, Inc., include all inventory that it handles in the inventory account on its balance sheet?

2. How does Amazon.com, Inc., *value* its inventories? Which *cost* method does the company use?

3. Using the cost-of-goods-sold model, compute Amazon.com, Inc.'s purchases of inventory during the year ended December 31, 2012.

4. Did Amazon.com, Inc.'s gross profit percentage on company sales improve or deteriorate in the year ended December 31, 2012, compared to the previous year?

5. For this part, assume that beginning inventory on January 1, 2011 was $3,202 million. Compute inventory turnover for 2012 and 2011. Would you rate Amazon.com, Inc.'s rate of inventory turnover for the years ended December 31, 2012, and December 31, 2011, as fast or slow in comparison to most other companies in its industry? Explain your answer.

6. Go to the SEC's website (www.sec.gov). Find Amazon.com, Inc.'s most recent consolidated balance sheet and consolidated statement of operations. What has happened to the company's inventory turnover and gross profit percentages since December 31, 2012? Can you explain the reasons? Where would you find the company's explanations for these changes? (Challenge)

Focus on Analysis | Yum! Brands, Inc.

(Learning Objectives 1, 2, 4: Show how to account for inventory; explain GAAP for inventory; compute and evaluate gross profit and inventory turnover) Refer to the **Yum! Brands, Inc.,** consolidated financial statements in Appendix B at the end of this book. Show amounts in millions and round to the nearest $1 million.

1. Three important pieces of inventory information are (a) the cost of inventory on hand, (b) the cost of sales, and (c) the cost of inventory purchases. Identify or compute each of these items for Yum! Brands, Inc., at December 31, 2012. Assume "food and paper" are cost of goods sold.

2. Which item in requirement 1 is most directly related to cash flow? Why? (Challenge)

3. Assume that all inventory purchases were made on account and that only inventory purchases increased Accounts Payable and Other Current Liabilities. Compute Yum! Brands, Inc.'s cash payments for inventory during 2012.

4. How does Yum! Brands, Inc., *value* its inventories? Which *costing* method does Yum! Brands use?

5. Did Yum! Brands, Inc.'s gross profit percentage and rate of inventory turnover improve or deteriorate in 2012 (versus 2011)? Consider the overall effect of these two ratios. Did Yum! Brands, Inc., improve during 2012? How did these factors affect the net income for 2012? Yum! Brands, Inc.'s inventories totaled $189 million at the end of fiscal 2010. Round decimals to three places.

Group Project

(Learning Objective 4: Evaluate inventory turnover ratios) Obtain the annual reports of 10 companies, two from each of five different industries. Most companies' financial statements can be downloaded from their websites.

1. Compute each company's gross profit percentage and rate of inventory turnover for the most recent two years. If annual reports are unavailable or do not provide enough data for multiple-year computations, you can gather financial statement data from *Moody's Industrial Manual.*

2. For the industries of the companies you are analyzing, obtain the industry averages for gross profit percentage and inventory turnover from Robert Morris Associates, *Annual Statement Studies;* Dun and Bradstreet, *Industry Norms and Key Business Ratios;* or Leo Troy, *Almanac of Business and Industrial Financial Ratios.*

3. How well does each of your companies compare to the other company in its industry? How well do your companies compare to the average for their industry? What insight about your companies can you glean from these ratios?

4. Write a memo to summarize your findings, stating whether your group would invest in each of the companies it has analyzed.

For online homework, exercises, and problems that provide you with immediate feedback, please visit www.myaccountinglab.com.

Quick Check Answers

1. *b*
2. *c*
3. *e*
4. *c* [(25 × $4) + (20 × $5)]
5. *b* [(25 × $4) + ($13 × $5)]
6. *a* 38 × [($100 + $205 + $170) ÷ 83]
7. *d*
8. *d*
9. *b*
10. *a* ($115,000 − $46,000)
11. *c* ($160,000 + $23,000 − $8,000)
12. *d* ($18,000 + $95,000 + $8,000 − $6,000 − $21,000)
13. *a* ($200,000 − $94,000)/$200,000
14. *d* [$94,000 ÷ (($18,000 + $21,000)/2)]
15. *c* $100,000 + $240,000 − [$430,000 × (1 − 0.45)]
16. *c*

APPENDIX 6A

ACCOUNTING FOR INVENTORY IN THE PERIODIC SYSTEM

In the periodic inventory system, the business keeps no running record of the merchandise. Instead, at the end of the period, the business counts inventory on hand, and applies the unit costs to determine the cost of ending inventory. This inventory figure appears on the balance sheet and is used to compute cost of goods sold.

Recording Transactions in the Periodic System

In the periodic system, the Inventory account carries the beginning balance left over from the preceding period throughout the current period. The business records purchases of inventory in the Purchases account (an expense). Then, at the end of the period, the Inventory account must be updated for the financial statements. A journal entry removes the beginning balance by crediting Inventory and debiting Cost of Goods Sold. A second journal entry sets up (debits) the ending inventory balance, based on the physical count, and credits Cost of Goods Sold. The final entry in this sequence transfers the amount of Purchases to Cost of Goods Sold, crediting Purchases and debiting Cost of Goods Sold. These end-of-period entries can be made during the closing process.

Exhibit 6A-1 illustrates the accounting in the periodic system. After the process is complete, Inventory has its correct ending balance of $120,000, and Cost of Goods Sold shows $540,000.

Exhibit 6A-1 | Recording and Reporting Inventories—Periodic System (All amounts assumed)

PANEL A—Recording Transactions and the T-accounts (All amounts are assumed)

	A	B	C	D
	A1 ⬍			
1	1.	Purchases	560,000	
2		Accounts Payable		560,000
3		*Purchased inventory on account.*		
4				
5	2.	Accounts Receivable	900,000	
6		Sales Revenue		900,000
7		*Sold inventory on account.*		
8				
9	3.	End-of-period entries to update Inventory and record Cost of Goods Sold:		
10	a.	Cost of Goods Sold	100,000	
11		Inventory (beginning balance)		100,000
12		*Transferred beginning inventory to COGS.*		
13				
14	b.	Inventory (ending balance)	120,000	
15		Cost of Goods Sold		120,000
16		*Set up ending inventory based on physical count.*		
17				
18	c.	Cost of Goods Sold	560,000	
19		Purchases		560,000
20		*Transferred purchases to COGS.*		
21				

The T-accounts show the following:

Inventory				Cost of Goods Sold		
100,000*		100,000		100,000		120,000
120,000				560,000		
				540,000		

*Beginning inventory was $100,000

PANEL B—Reporting in the Financial Statements

Income Statement (Partial)			Ending Balance Sheet (Partial)	
Sales revenue...........................		$900,000	Current assets:	
Cost of goods sold:			Cash...	$ XXX
Beginning inventory	$ 100,000		Short-term investments	XXX
Purchases	560,000		Accounts receivable.....................	XXX
Cost of goods available	660,000		Inventory	120,000
Ending inventory................	(120,000)		Prepaid expenses	XXX
Cost of goods sold..................		540,000		
Gross profit........................		$360,000		

Appendix Assignments

Short Exercises

S6A-1. *(Record inventory transactions in the periodic system)* Flexon Technologies began the year with inventory of $580. During the year, Flexon purchased inventory costing $1,190 and sold goods for $2,900, with all transactions on account. Flexon ended the year with inventory of $650. Journalize all the necessary transactions under the periodic inventory system.

S6A-2. *(Compute cost of goods sold and prepare the income statement—periodic system)* Use the data in S6A-1 to do the following for Flexon Technologies.

Requirements

1. Post to the Inventory and Cost of Goods Sold accounts.
2. Compute cost of goods sold by the cost-of-goods-sold model.
3. Prepare the income statement of Flexon Technologies through gross profit.

Exercises

MyAccountingLab

> All of these exercises can be found within MyAccountingLab, an online homework and practice environment. Your instructor may ask you to complete these exercises using **MyAccountingLab**.

E6A-3A. *(Compute amounts for the GAAP inventory methods—periodic system)* Suppose Cambridge Corporation's inventory records for a particular computer chip indicate the following at October 31:

Oct	1	Beginning inventory	5 units @ $60 = $300
	8	Purchase.................................	4 units @ $60 = 240
	15	Purchase.................................	10 units @ $70 = 700
	26	Purchase.................................	1 units @ $80 = 80

The physical count of inventory at October 31 indicates that seven units of inventory are on hand.

Requirements

Compute ending inventory and cost of goods sold, using each of the following methods:
1. Specific unit cost, assuming three $60 units and four $70 units are on hand
2. Average cost (round average unit cost to the nearest cent)
3. First-in, first-out
4. Last-in, first-out

E6A-4A. *(Journal inventory transactions in the periodic system; compute cost of goods sold)* Use the data in E6A-3A.

Requirements

Journalize the following for the periodic system:
1. Total October purchases in one summary entry. All purchases were on credit.
2. Total October sales in a summary entry. Assume that the selling price was $300 per unit and that all sales were on credit.
3. October 31 entries for inventory. Cambridge uses LIFO. Post to the Cost of Goods Sold T-account to show how this amount is determined. Label each item in the account.
4. Show the computation of cost of goods sold by the cost-of-goods-sold model.

Problems

All of these problems can be found within MyAccountingLab, an online homework and practice environment. Your instructor may ask you to complete these problems using **MyAccountingLab**.

MyAccountingLab

P6A-5A. *(Compute cost of goods sold and gross profit on sales—periodic system)* Assume a Waverly outlet store began August 2014 with 52 units of inventory that cost $13 each. The sale price of these units was $67. During August, the store completed these inventory transactions:

		Units	Unit Cost	Unit Sale Price
Aug 3	Sale	14	$13	$67
8	Purchase......	78	14	69
11	Sale	38	13	67
19	Sale	7	14	69
24	Sale	32	14	69
30	Purchase......	20	15	70
31	Sale	9	14	69

Requirements

1. Determine the store's cost of goods sold for August under the periodic inventory system. Assume the FIFO method.
2. Compute gross profit for August.

P6A-6A. *(Record transactions in the periodic system; report inventory items in the financial statements)* Accounting records for Total Desserts, Inc., yield the following data for the year ended December 31, 2014 (amounts in thousands):

Inventory, Dec 31, 2013..	$ 490
Purchases of inventory (on account)...	2,000
Sales of inventory—75% on account, 25% for cash.......................	3,400
Inventory at the lower of FIFO cost or market, Dec 31, 2014	620

Requirements

1. Journalize Total Desserts' inventory transactions for the year under the periodic system. Show all amounts in thousands.
2. Report ending inventory, sales, cost of goods sold, and gross profit on the appropriate financial statement (amounts in thousands). Show the computation of cost of goods sold.

APPENDIX 6B

THE LIFO RESERVE—CONVERTING A LIFO COMPANY'S NET INCOME TO THE FIFO BASIS

Suppose you are a financial analyst and it is your job to recommend stocks for your clients to purchase as investments. You have narrowed your choice to **Walgreen Company** and **Kohl's Corporation.** Walgreen uses the LIFO method for inventories, and Kohl's uses FIFO. The two companies' net incomes are not comparable because they use different inventory methods. To compare the two companies, you need to place them on the same footing.

The Internal Revenue Service allows companies to use LIFO for income tax purposes only if they use LIFO for financial reporting, but companies may also report an alternative inventory amount in the financial statements. Doing so presents a rare opportunity to convert a company's net income from the LIFO basis to what the income would have been if the business had used FIFO. Fortunately, you can convert Walgreen's income from the LIFO basis, as reported in the company's financial statements, to the FIFO basis. Then you can compare Walgreen and Kohl's.

Like many other companies that use LIFO, Walgreen reports the FIFO cost, a LIFO Reserve, and the LIFO cost of ending inventory. The LIFO Reserve[3] is the difference between the LIFO cost of an inventory and what the cost of that inventory would be under FIFO. Assume that Walgreen reported the following amounts:

Walgreen Company Uses LIFO		
	(In millions)	
	2015	**2014**
From the Walgreen balance sheet:		
Inventories (approximate FIFO cost)...............	$ 25,056	$22,749
Less LIFO reserve...	(165)	(135)
LIFO cost...	24,891	22,614
From the Walgreen income statement:		
Cost of goods sold...	$191,838	
Net income...	8,039	
Income tax rate	35%	

Converting Walgreen's 2015 net income to the FIFO basis focuses on the LIFO Reserve because the reserve captures the difference between Walgreen's ending inventory costed at LIFO and at FIFO. Observe that during each year, the FIFO cost of ending inventory exceeded the LIFO cost. During 2015, the LIFO Reserve increased by $30 million ($165 million − $135 million). *The LIFO Reserve can increase only when inventory costs are rising.* Recall that during a period of rising costs, LIFO produces the highest cost of goods sold and the lowest net income. Therefore, for 2015, Walgreen's cost of goods sold would have been lower if the company had used the FIFO method for inventories. Walgreen's net income would have been higher, as the following computations show:

---

[3]The LIFO Reserve account is widely used in practice even though the word *reserve* is poor terminology.

If Walgreen Company Had Used FIFO in 2015	
	(In millions)
Cost of goods sold, as reported under LIFO..	$191,838
− Increase in LIFO Reserve ($165 − $135)	(30)
= Cost of goods sold, if Walgreen had used FIFO..	$191,808
Lower cost of goods sold → Higher pretax income by................................	$ 30
Minus income taxes (35%)	11
Higher net income under FIFO..	19
Net income as reported under LIFO...	8,039
Net income Walgreen would have reported for	
2015 if using FIFO	$ 8,058

Now you can compare Walgreen's net income with that of Kohl's Corporation. All the ratios used for the analysis—current ratio, inventory turnover, and so on—can be compared between the two companies as long as we use the FIFO figures for Cost of Goods Sold and Inventories for Walgreen.

The LIFO Reserve provides another opportunity for managers and investors to answer a key question about a company.

> **How much income tax has the company saved over its lifetime by using the LIFO method to account for inventory?**

Using Walgreen as an example, the computation at the end of 2015 is as follows (amounts in millions):

Income tax saved by using LIFO = LIFO Reserve × Income tax rate
$$\$58 \qquad = \qquad \$165 \quad \times \quad .35$$

With these price changes, by the end of 2015, Walgreen has saved a total of $58 million by using the LIFO method to account for its merchandise inventory. Had Walgreen used the FIFO method, Walgreen would have almost $58 million less cash to invest in the opening of new stores.

In recent years, many companies have experienced decreases in the cost of their inventories. When prices decline, cost of goods sold under FIFO is greater (LIFO cost of goods sold is less). This makes gross profit and net income less under FIFO than LIFO.

Plant Assets, Natural Resources, & Intangibles

> **SPOTLIGHT:** FedEx Corporation

If you need a document or package delivered across the country overnight or any of a number of other business services, FedEx can handle it. **FedEx Corporation** sets a high standard for quick delivery, as well as other transportation, e-commerce, and business services. For this reason, FedEx has, for the last decade, consistently made the list as one of the "World's Most Admired Companies" by *Fortune* magazine. As you can see from the company's Consolidated Balance Sheets on the following page, FedEx moves packages using property and equipment such as aircraft, package-handling equipment, computers, and vehicles. These are FedEx's most important resources (lines 11–15). The company owns over $36 billion of property and equipment as of May 31, 2012 (line 16), which is actually a little over $6 billion more than total assets (line 23)! How can this be? Notice that over the estimated useful lives of these assets, the company has built up accumulated depreciation of about $19 billion (line 17), indicating that the assets are more than half used up as of that date ($18,916/$36,164 = 52.3%). The net book value of FedEx's property and equipment is about $17 billion (line 18). The company also owns about $3.6 billion in goodwill and other tangible and intangible long-term assets (line 22). When you complete this chapter, you will understand better what these terms and concepts mean. ●

Marlene Ford/Alamy

	A	B	C
1	**FedEx Corporation** **Consolidated Balance Sheets (Partial, Adapted)**		
2	(In millions of $)	May 31, 2012	May 31, 2011
3	**CURRENT ASSETS**		
4	Cash and cash equivalents	$ 2,843	$ 2,328
5	Receivables, less allowances of $178 and $182	4,704	4,581
6	Spare parts, supplies and fuel, less allowances	440	437
7	Deferred income taxes	533	610
8	Prepaid expenses and other	536	329
9	Total current assets	9,056	8,285
10	**PROPERTY AND EQUIPMENT, AT COST**		
11	Aircraft and related equipment	14,360	13,146
12	Package handling and ground support equipment	5,912	5,591
13	Computer and electronic equipment	4,646	4,408
14	Vehicles	3,654	3,294
15	Facilities and other	7,592	7,247
16	Gross property and equipment	36,164	33,686
17	Less accumulated depreciation and amortization	(18,916)	(18,143)
18	Net property and equipment	17,248	15,543
19	**OTHER LONG-TERM ASSETS**		
20	Goodwill	2,387	2,326
21	Other assets	1,212	1,231
22	Total other long-term assets	3,599	3,557
23	TOTAL ASSETS	$ 29,903	$ 27,385
24			

This chapter covers the measurement and reporting principles for long-term tangible fixed assets (also known as *plant assets* or *property and equipment*) **as well as intangible assets.** Unlike inventories that are typically bought, manufactured, and sold, fixed tangible and intangible assets are used in the business to earn a profit. This chapter also briefly covers measurement and reporting principles for natural resources, which begin as long-term assets. Then, as they are extracted or depleted, their cost is transferred to the income statement as an expense.

Learning Objectives

1. **Measure and account for** the cost of plant assets

2. **Distinguish** a capital expenditure from an immediate expense

3. **Measure and record** depreciation on plant assets

4. **Analyze** the effect of a plant asset disposal

5. **Apply** GAAP for natural resources and intangible assets

6. **Explain** the effect of an asset impairment on the financial statements

7. **Analyze** rate of return on assets

8. **Analyze** the cash flow impact of long-lived asset transactions

> ## Try It in Excel
>
> You can access the most current annual report of FedEx Corporation in Excel format at **www.sec.gov**. Using the "filings" link on the toolbar at the top of the home page, select "company filings search." This will take you to the "EDGAR Company Filings" page. Type "FedEx" in the company name box, and select "search." This will produce the "EDGAR Search Results" page showing the company name. Click on the "CIK" link beside the company name. This will pull up all of the reports the company has filed with the SEC. Under the "filing type" box, type "10-K" and click the search box. Form 10-K is the SEC form for the company's latest annual report. Find the year that you wish to view. Click on the "Interactive Data" box, which takes you to the "View Filing Data" page. Find and click on the "View Excel Document" link at the top of this page. You may choose to either open or download the Excel files containing the company's most recent financial statements. ■

Businesses use several types of long-lived assets. We show these assets in Exhibit 7-1, along with the expense account that is typically associated with each one. For example, buildings, airplanes, and equipment depreciate. Natural resources deplete (often through cost of goods sold), and intangible assets are amortized.

Exhibit 7-1 | Long-Lived Assets and Related Expense Accounts

Asset Account (Balance Sheet)	Related Expense Account (Income Statement)
Plant Assets	
Land	None
Buildings, Machinery, and Equipment	Depreciation Expense
Furniture and Fixtures	Depreciation Expense
Land Improvements	Depreciation Expense
Natural Resources	Depletion Expense (through cost of goods sold)
Intangibles	Amortization Expense

- *Plant assets* (also known as *property, plant, and equipment* or *fixed assets)* are long-lived assets that are tangible—for instance, land, buildings, and equipment. The expense associated with plant assets is called *depreciation expense.* Of the plant assets, land is unique. Land is not expensed over time because its usefulness does not decrease. Most companies report plant assets as property, plant, and equipment on the balance sheet. **FedEx** uses the heading Property and Equipment in its balance sheet shown on page 363 (lines 10–18).

- *Natural resources* such as oil and gas reserves, coal mines, or stands of timber, are accounted for as long-term assets when they are purchased or developed. As the natural resource is extracted, its cost is transferred to inventory. Later, as the inventory is sold, its cost is transferred to cost of goods sold in a manner similar to that described in Chapter 6.

- *Intangible assets* are useful because of the special rights they carry. They have no physical form. Patents, copyrights, and trademarks are intangible assets, as is goodwill. Accounting for intangibles is similar to accounting for plant assets. FedEx reports Goodwill and Other Assets on its balance sheet (lines 20 and 21).

MEASURE AND ACCOUNT FOR THE COST OF PLANT ASSETS

Here is the basic working rule for measuring the cost of an asset:

The cost of any asset is the sum of all the costs incurred to bring the asset to its intended use.

The cost of a plant asset includes purchase price, plus any taxes, commissions, and other amounts paid to make the asset ready for use. Because the specific costs differ for the various types of plant assets, we discuss the major groups individually.

1 Measure and account for the cost of plant assets

Land

The cost of land includes its purchase price (cash plus any note payable given), brokerage commission, survey fees, legal fees, and any back property taxes that the purchaser pays. Land cost also includes expenditures for grading and clearing the land and for removing unwanted buildings.

The cost of land does *not* include the cost of fencing, paving, security systems, and lighting. These are separate plant assets—called *land improvements*—and they are subject to depreciation.

Suppose FedEx signs a $300,000 note payable to purchase 20 acres of land for a new shipping site. FedEx also pays $10,000 for real estate commission, $8,000 of back property tax, $5,000 for removal of an old building, a $1,000 survey fee, and $260,000 to pave the parking lot—all in cash. What is FedEx's cost of this land?

Purchase price of land......................		$300,000
Add related costs:		
Real estate commission	$10,000	
Back property tax........................	8,000	
Removal of building....................	5,000	
Survey fee...................................	1,000	
Total related costs.......................		24,000
Total cost of land...........................		$324,000

Note that the cost to pave the parking lot, $260,000, is *not* included in the land's cost, because the pavement is a land improvement. FedEx would record the purchase of this land as follows:

	A	B	C	D
1		Land	324,000	
2		Note Payable		300,000
3		Cash		24,000
4				

Assets	=	Liabilities	+	Stockholders' Equity
+ 324,000				
	=	+ 300,000	+	0
− 24,000				

This purchase of land increases both assets and liabilities. There is no effect on equity.

Buildings, Machinery, and Equipment

The cost of constructing a building includes architectural fees, building permits, contractors' charges, and payments for material, labor, and overhead. If the company constructs its own building, the cost will also include the cost of interest on money borrowed to finance the construction.

When an existing building (new or old) is purchased, its cost includes the purchase price, brokerage commission, sales and other taxes paid, and all expenditures to repair and renovate the building for its intended purpose.

The cost of FedEx's package-handling equipment includes its purchase price (less any discounts), plus transportation from the seller to FedEx, insurance while in transit, sales and other taxes, purchase commission, installation costs, and any expenditures to test the asset before it's placed in service. The equipment cost will also include the cost of any special platforms. Then after the asset is up and running, insurance, taxes, and maintenance costs are recorded as expenses, not as part of the asset's cost.

Land Improvements and Leasehold Improvements

For a FedEx shipping terminal, the cost to pave a parking lot ($260,000) would be recorded in a separate account entitled Land Improvements. This account includes costs for such other items as driveways, signs, fences, and sprinkler systems. Although these assets are located on the land, they are subject to decay, and their cost should therefore be depreciated.

FedEx may lease some of its airplanes and other assets. The company customizes these assets for its special needs. For example, FedEx paints its logo on delivery trucks. These improvements are assets of FedEx even though the company may not own the truck. The cost of leasehold improvements should be depreciated over the term of the lease. Most companies call the depreciation on leasehold improvements *amortization*, which is a similar concept to *depreciation*.

Lump-Sum (or Basket) Purchases of Assets

Businesses often purchase several assets as a group, or a "basket," for a single lump-sum amount. For example, FedEx may pay one price for land and a building. The company must identify the cost of each asset. The total cost is divided among the assets according to their relative sales (or market) values. This technique is called the *relative-sales-value method*.

Suppose FedEx purchases land and a building in Denver. The building sits on two acres of land, and the combined purchase price of land and building is $2,800,000. An appraisal indicates that the land's market value is $300,000 and that the building's market value is $2,700,000.

FedEx first figures the ratio of each asset's market value to the total market value. Total appraised value is $2,700,000 + $300,000 = $3,000,000. Thus, the land, valued at $300,000, is 10% of the total market value. The building's appraised value is 90% of the total. These percentages are then used to determine the cost of each asset:

Asset	Market (Sales) Value		Total Market Value		Percentage of Total Market Value		Total Cost	Cost of Each Asset
Land	$ 300,000	÷	$3,000,000	=	10%	× $2,800,000		$ 280,000
Building	2,700,000	÷	3,000,000	=	90%	× $2,800,000		2,520,000
Total	$3,000,000				100%			$2,800,000

If FedEx pays cash, the entry to record the purchase of the land and building is

	A1					
	A	**B**			**C**	**D**
1		Land			280,000	
2		Building			2,520,000	
3		Cash				2,800,000
4						

Assets	=	Liabilities	+	Stockholders' Equity
+ 280,000	=			
+ 2,520,000	=	0	+	0
− 2,800,000	=			

Total assets don't change—it is merely the makeup of FedEx's assets that changes.

> Stop & Think...

How would FedEx divide a $120,000 lump-sum purchase price for land, building, and equipment with estimated market values of $40,000, $95,000, and $15,000, respectively?

Answer:

	Estimated Market Value	Percentage of Total Market Value	×	Total Cost	=	Cost of Each Asset
Land..................	$ 40,000	26.7%*	×	$120,000	=	$ 32,040
Building..............	95,000	63.3%	×	$120,000	=	75,960
Equipment.........	15,000	10.0%	×	$120,000	=	12,000
Total	$150,000	100.0%				$120,000

*$40,000/$150,000 = 0.267, and so on

DISTINGUISH A CAPITAL EXPENDITURE FROM AN IMMEDIATE EXPENSE

2 **Distinguish** a capital expenditure from an immediate expense

When a company spends money on a plant asset, it must decide whether to record an asset or an expense. Examples of these expenditures range from FedEx's purchase of an airplane to replacing the tires on a FedEx truck.

Expenditures that increase the asset's capacity or extend its useful life are called **capital expenditures**. For example, the cost of a major overhaul that extends the useful life of a FedEx truck is a capital expenditure. Capital expenditures are said to be *capitalized, which means the cost is added to an asset account* and not expensed immediately. A major decision in accounting for plant assets is whether to capitalize or to expense a certain cost.

Costs that do not extend the asset's capacity or its useful life, but merely maintain the asset or restore it to working order, are recorded as expenses. For example, Repair Expense is reported on the income statement and matched against revenue. The costs of repainting a FedEx delivery truck, repairing a dented fender, and replacing tires are also expensed immediately. Exhibit 7-2 shows the distinction between capital expenditures and immediate expenses for ordinary repairs.

Exhibit 7-2 | Capital Expenditures vs. Immediate Expenses

Record an Asset for Capital Expenditures	Record Repair and Maintenance Expense (Not an Asset) for an Expense
Extraordinary repairs:	**Ordinary repairs:**
Major engine overhaul	Repair of transmission or other mechanism
Modification of body for new use of truck	Oil change, lubrication, and so on
Addition to storage capacity of truck	Replacement of tires and windshield, or a paint job

The distinction between a capital expenditure (a long-term asset) and an immediate expense requires judgment: Does the cost extend the asset's usefulness or its useful life? If so, record an asset. If the cost merely maintains the asset in its present condition or returns it to its prior condition, then record an expense.

Most companies expense all small (immaterial) costs (say, below $1,000) regardless of whether the costs are capital in nature. For larger (material) costs, they follow the capitalization rule stated in the previous paragraph. A conservative policy is one that avoids overstating assets and profits. A company that overstates its assets may eventually have to defend itself in court if investors or creditors lose money because of the company's improper accounting practices.

Accounting errors sometimes occur for plant asset costs. For example, a company may

- expense a cost that should have been capitalized. This error overstates expenses and understates net income in the year of the error.
- capitalize a cost that should have been expensed. This error understates expenses and overstates net income in the year of the error.

Cooking the Books

by Improper Capitalization

WorldCom

It is one thing to accidentally capitalize a plant asset instead of expensing it, but quite another to do it intentionally, thus deliberately overstating assets, understating expenses, and overstating net income. One well-known company committed one of the biggest financial statement frauds in U.S. history in this way.

In 2002, WorldCom, Inc., was one of the largest telecommunications service providers in the world. The company had grown rapidly from a small, regional telephone company in 1983 to a giant corporation in 2002 by acquiring an ever-increasing number of other such companies. But 2002 was a bad year for WorldCom, as well as for many others in the "telecom" industry. The United States was reeling from the effects of a deep economic recession spawned by the "bursting dot-com bubble" in 2000 and intensified by the terrorist attacks on U.S. soil in 2001. Wall Street was looking high and low for positive signs, pressuring public companies to keep profits trending upward in order to support share prices, without much success, at least for the honest companies.

Bernard J. ("Bernie") Ebbers, WorldCom's chief executive officer, was worried. He began to press his chief financial officer, Scott Sullivan, to find a way to make the company's income statement look healthier. After all legitimate attempts to improve earnings failed, Sullivan concocted a scheme to cook the books.

Like all telecommunications companies, WorldCom had signed contracts with other telephone companies, paying them fees so that WorldCom customers could use their lines for telephone calls and Internet activity. GAAP require such fees to be expensed as incurred, rather than capitalized. Overestimating the growth of its business, WorldCom had incurred billions of dollars in such costs, about 15% more than its customers would ever use.

In direct violation of GAAP, Sullivan rationalized that the excessive amounts WorldCom had spent on line costs would eventually lead to the company's recognizing revenue in future years (thus extending their usefulness and justifying, in his mind, their classification as assets). Sullivan directed the accountants working under him to reclassify line costs as property, plant, and equipment assets, rather than as expenses, and to amortize (spread) the costs over several years rather than to expense them in the periods in which they were incurred. Over several quarters, Mr. Sullivan and his assistants transferred a total of $3.1 billion in such charges from operating expense accounts to property, plant, and equipment, resulting in the transformation of what would have been a net loss for all of 2001 and the first quarter of 2002 into a sizeable profit. It was the largest single fraud in U.S. history to that point.

Sullivan's fraudulent scheme was discovered by the company's internal audit staff during a routine spot-check of the company's records for capital expenditures. The staff members reported Sullivan's (and his staff's) fraudulent activities to the head of the company's audit committee and its external auditor, setting in motion a chain of events that resulted in Ebbers' and Sullivan's firings and the company's eventual bankruptcy. Ebbers, Sullivan, and several of their assistants went to prison for their participation in this fraudulent scheme.

Shareholders of WorldCom lost billions of dollars in share value when the company went down, and more than 500,000 people lost their jobs.

The WorldCom scandal rocked the financial world, causing global stock markets to plummet from lack of confidence. This prompted action on the part of the U.S. Congress and President George W. Bush that eventually led to the passage of the Sarbanes-Oxley Act of 2002, the most significant piece of shareholder protection legislation since the Great Depression in the 1930s.

MEASURE AND RECORD DEPRECIATION ON PLANT ASSETS

As we've seen in previous chapters, plant assets are reported on the balance sheet at book value, which is calculated as follows:

3 **Measure and record** depreciation on plant assets

$$\text{Book Value of a Plant Asset} = \text{Cost} - \text{Accumulated Depreciation}$$

Plant assets wear out, grow obsolete, and lose value over time. To account for this process, we allocate a plant asset's cost to expense over its life—a process called *depreciation*. The depreciation process follows the expense recognition principle discussed in Chapter 3. Depreciation apportions the cost of using a fixed asset over time by allocating a portion of that cost against the revenue the asset helps earn each period. Exhibit 7-3 illustrates the accounting for a Boeing 737 jet by FedEx.

Exhibit 7-3 | Depreciation: Allocating Costs to Periods in Which Revenues Are Generated

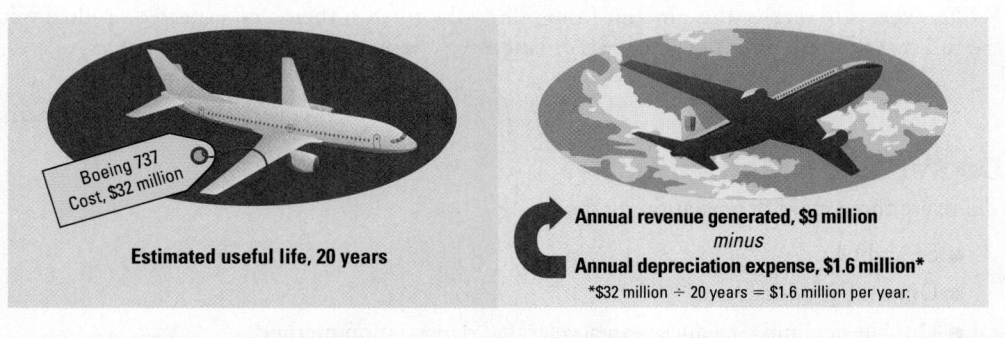

Boeing 737 Cost, $32 million

Estimated useful life, 20 years

Annual revenue generated, $9 million
minus
Annual depreciation expense, $1.6 million*
*$32 million ÷ 20 years = $1.6 million per year.

Recall that depreciation expense (not accumulated depreciation) is reported on the income statement.

Only land has an unlimited life and is not depreciated for accounting purposes. For most plant assets, depreciation is caused by one of the following:

- *Physical wear and tear.* For example, physical deterioration takes its toll on the usefulness of FedEx airplanes, equipment, delivery trucks, and buildings.
- *Obsolescence.* Computers and other electronic equipment may become *obsolete* before they deteriorate. An asset is obsolete when another asset can do the job more efficiently. An asset's useful life may be shorter than its physical life. FedEx and other companies depreciate their computers over a short period of time—perhaps four years—even though the computers will remain in working condition much longer.

Suppose FedEx buys a computer for use in tracking packages. FedEx believes it will get four years of service from the computer, which will then be worthless. Under straight-line depreciation, FedEx expenses one-quarter of the asset's cost in each of its four years of use.

You've just seen what depreciation is. Let's see what depreciation is *not*.

1. *Depreciation is not a process of valuation.* Businesses do *not* record depreciation based on changes in the market value of their plant assets. Instead, businesses allocate the asset's *cost* to the periods of its useful life.

2. *Depreciation does not mean setting aside cash to replace assets as they wear out.* Any cash fund is entirely separate from depreciation.

How to Measure Depreciation

To measure depreciation for a plant asset, we must know three things about it:

1. Cost
2. Estimated useful life
3. Estimated residual value

We have discussed cost, which is a known amount. The other two factors must be estimated.

Estimated useful life is the length of service expected from using the asset. Useful life may be expressed in years, units of output, miles, or some other measure. For example, the useful life of a building is stated in years. The useful life of a FedEx airplane or delivery truck may be expressed as the number of miles the vehicle is expected to travel. Companies base these estimates on their experience and trade publications.

Estimated residual value—also called *scrap value* or *salvage value*—is the expected cash value of an asset at the end of its useful life. For example, FedEx may believe that a package-handling machine will be useful for seven years. After that time, FedEx may expect to sell the machine as scrap metal. The amount FedEx believes it can get for the machine at disposal is the estimated residual value. In computing depreciation, the estimated residual value is *not* depreciated because FedEx expects to receive this amount from selling the asset. If there's no expected residual value, the full cost of the asset is depreciated. A plant asset's **depreciable cost** is measured as follows:

$$\text{Depreciable Cost} = \text{Asset's cost} - \text{Estimated residual value}$$

Depreciation Methods

There are three main depreciation methods:

- Straight-line
- Units-of-production
- Double-declining-balance—an accelerated depreciation method

These methods allocate different amounts of depreciation to each period. However, they all result in the same total amount of depreciation, which is the asset's depreciable cost. Exhibit 7-4 presents the data we use to illustrate depreciation computations for a FedEx truck.

Exhibit 7-4 | Depreciation Computation Data

Data Item	Amount
Cost of truck..	$41,000
Less: Estimated residual value..............	(1,000)
Depreciable cost.......................................	$40,000
Estimated useful life:	
Years	5 years
Units of production	100,000 units [miles]

Straight-Line Method. In the **straight-line (SL) method,** an equal amount of depreciation is assigned to each year (or period) of asset use. Depreciable cost is divided by useful life in years to determine the annual depreciation expense. Applied to the FedEx truck data from Exhibit 7-4, SL depreciation is

$$\text{Straight-line depreciation per year} = \frac{\text{Cost} - \text{Residual value}}{\text{Useful life, in years}}$$

$$= \frac{\$41,000 - \$1,000}{5}$$

$$= \$8,000$$

The entry to record depreciation is

	A	B	C	D
1		Depreciation Expense—Truck	8,000	
2		Accumulated Depreciation—Truck		8,000
3				

Assets	=	Liabilities	+	Stockholders' Equity	−	Expenses
− 8,000	=	0				− 8,000

Observe that depreciation decreases the asset (through Accumulated Depreciation) and also decreases equity (through Depreciation Expense). Let's assume that FedEx purchased this truck on January 1, 2011. Assume that FedEx's accounting year ends on December 31. Exhibit 7-5 gives a *straight-line depreciation schedule* for the truck. The final column of the exhibit shows the *asset's book value,* which is cost less accumulated depreciation.

Exhibit 7-5 | Straight-Line Depreciation Schedule for Truck

	A	B	C	D	E	F	G
1	Date	Cost	Rate*	Depreciable Cost	Yearly Expense	Accum. Deprec.	Book Value
2	1/1/2011	41,000		40,000			41,000
3	12/31/2011		0.2	40,000	8,000	8,000	33,000
4	12/31/2012		0.2	40,000	8,000	16,000	25,000
5	12/31/2013		0.2	40,000	8,000	24,000	17,000
6	12/31/2014		0.2	40,000	8,000	32,000	9,000
7	12/31/2015		0.2	40,000	8,000	40,000	1,000
8							

*1/years of useful life = 1/5 = 0.2

As an asset is used in operations,

■ accumulated depreciation increases.

■ the book value of the asset decreases.

You can estimate the age (or the "used up" amount) of a plant asset by calculating the ratio between accumulated depreciation on a straight-line basis and cost. For example, if accumulated depreciation is $500,000 and cost is $1,000,000, the plant asset is approximately half used up. An asset's final book value is its *residual value* ($1,000 in Exhibit 7-5). At the end of its useful life, the asset is said to be *fully depreciated.*

Building depreciation schedules such as the one in Exhibit 7-5 is easy with Excel. Use the information in Exhibit 7-4 and the formula on page 371 to help you program the cells. To construct Exhibit 7-5 in Excel:

1. Open a new workbook. In cells A1 through G1, insert column headings to correspond to those of Exhibit 7-5. You will have to adjust the column width of your spreadsheet to accommodate the headings.
2. In cells B2 and G2, (asset cost and book value) type in the original gross cost (41,000). The remainder of the cells in column B should be blank.
3. In cell A2, type in the original purchase date (1/1/2011). In cells A3 through A7, type in the year-end dates of 12/31/2011 through 12/31/2015, respectively. Change the formatting of these cells to "date."
4. In cells C3 through C7, enter the depreciation rate for each year, which is the reciprocal of the asset's useful life (1/5, or 20%). Enter .2 in cell C3 and copy this value down through cell C7.
5. In cell D2, calculate the depreciable cost of $40,000. Enter =B2−1000. Copy this value down through cell D7.
6. In cell E3, enter the formula =C3*D3. The value $8,000 should appear. Copy this formula to cells E4 through E7.
7. Column F keeps a running sum of accumulated depreciation. Start with cell F3. Enter the formula =F2+E3. $8,000 (accumulated depreciation at the end of year 1) should appear. Copy cell F3 down to cells F4 through F7. You should get the same values as you see in Exhibit 7-5.
8. Column G keeps a running calculation of the declining net book value of the asset. Start with cell G3. Freeze the value of the original cost of the asset ($41,000) in cell G2 by entering "$" before both the column and row. Then subtract the value of accumulated depreciation (cell F3). The formula in cell G3 becomes =$G$2−F3. The result should be $33,000 ($41,000 − $8,000). Copy cell G3 down through cell G7. ∎

> Stop & Think...

A FedEx sorting machine that cost $10,000 with a useful life of five years and a residual value of $2,000 was purchased on January 1. What is SL depreciation for each year?

Answer:

$$\$1,600 = (\$10,000 - \$2,000)/5$$

Units-of-Production Method. In the **units-of-production (UOP) method,** a fixed amount of depreciation is assigned to each *unit of output*, or service, produced by the asset. Depreciable cost is divided by useful life—in units of production—to determine this amount. This per-unit depreciation expense is then multiplied by the number of units produced each period to compute depreciation. The UOP depreciation per unit of output (mile) for the FedEx truck data in Exhibit 7-4 (p. 370) is

$$\text{Units-of-production depreciation per unit of output} = \frac{\text{Cost} - \text{Residual value}}{\text{Useful life, in units of production}}$$

$$= \frac{\$41,000 - \$1,000}{100,000 \text{ miles}} = \$0.40 \text{ per mile}$$

Assume that FedEx expects to drive the truck 20,000 miles during the first year, 30,000 during the second, 25,000 during the third, 15,000 during the fourth, and 10,000 during the fifth. Exhibit 7-6 shows the UOP depreciation schedule.

Exhibit 7-6 | Units-of-Production (UOP) Depreciation Schedule for Truck

	A	B	C	D	E	F	G
	Date	Cost	Rate per unit	Number Units	Yearly Expense	Accum. Deprec.	Book Value
1	Date	Cost	Rate per unit	Number Units	Yearly Expense	Accum. Deprec.	Book Value
2	1/1/2011	41,000					41,000
3	12/31/2011		0.4	20,000	8,000	8,000	33,000
4	12/31/2012		0.4	30,000	12,000	20,000	21,000
5	12/31/2013		0.4	25,000	10,000	30,000	11,000
6	12/31/2014		0.4	15,000	6,000	36,000	5,000
7	12/31/2015		0.4	10,000	4,000	40,000	1,000
8							

The amount of UOP depreciation varies with the number of units the asset produces. In our example, the total number of units (miles) produced is 100,000. UOP depreciation does not depend directly on time, as with the other methods.

Try It in Excel

If you built the straight-line depreciation schedule in Exhibit 7-5 with Excel, changing the spreadsheet for units-of-production depreciation is a snap. Steps 1–3 and 6–8 are identical. Only steps 4 and 5, dealing with columns C and D, change. You might want to start by opening the straight-line schedule you prepared and saving it under another name: "units-of-production depreciation." Next, change the column headings for column C and column D. Column C should be labeled "Rate per unit." Column D should be labeled "Number Units." Assuming you do this, here are the modified steps 4 and 5 of the process we used before:

4. In column C, calculate a per-unit (rather than per-year as we did with straight-line) depreciation rate by dividing the depreciable cost ($41,000 − $1,000 in Exhibit 7-4) by the number of units (100,000 miles) to get a fixed depreciation rate per mile ($0.40). Enter .4 in cell C3 and copy down through cell C7.

5. In cells D3 through D7, respectively, enter the number of miles driven in years 1 through 5 of the asset's useful life. These are 20,000, 30,000, 25,000, 15,000, and 10,000, respectively.

All of the other amounts in the table will automatically recalculate to reflect units-of-production depreciation, exactly as shown in Exhibit 7-6. ■

Double-Declining-Balance Method. An **accelerated depreciation method** writes off a larger amount of the asset's cost near the start of its useful life than the straight-line method does. **Double-declining-balance (DDB)** is the most frequently used accelerated depreciation method. It computes annual depreciation by multiplying the asset's declining book value at the beginning of the year by a constant percentage, which is two times the straight-line depreciation rate. DDB amounts are computed as follows:

$$\text{DDB depreciation rate per year} = \frac{1}{\text{Useful life, in years}} \times 2$$

$$= \frac{1}{5 \text{ years}} \times 2$$

$$= 20\% \times 2 = 40\%$$

- *First*, compute the straight-line depreciation rate per year. A truck with a 5-year useful life has a straight-line depreciation rate of 1/5, or 20%, each year. An asset with a 10-year useful life has a straight-line depreciation rate of 1/10, or 10%, and so on.
- *Second*, multiply the straight-line rate by 2 to compute the DDB rate. For a 5-year asset, the DDB rate is 40% (20% × 2). A 10-year asset has a DDB rate of 20% (10% × 2).
- *Third*, multiply the DDB rate by the period's *beginning* asset book value (cost less accumulated depreciation). Under the DDB method, ignore the residual value of the asset in computing depreciation, except during the last year. The DDB rate for the FedEx truck in in our example (p. 370) is 40%.
- *Fourth*, determine the final year's depreciation amount—that is, the amount needed to reduce the asset's book value to its residual value. In Exhibit 7-7, the fifth and final year's DDB depreciation is $4,314—book value, end of year 4 (2014) of $5,314 less the $1,000 residual value. *The residual value should not be depreciated* but should remain on the books until the asset is disposed of.

Exhibit 7-7 | Double-Declining-Balance (DDB) Depreciation Schedule for Truck

	A	B	C	D	E	F
1	Date	Cost	DDB Rate	Yearly Expense	Accum. Deprec.	Book Value
2	1/1/2011	41,000				41,000
3	12/31/2011		0.4	16,400	16,400	24,600
4	12/31/2012		0.4	9,840	26,240	14,760
5	12/31/2013		0.4	5,904	32,144	8,856
6	12/31/2014		0.4	3,542	35,686	5,314
7	12/31/2015		0.4	4,314	40,000	1,000*
8						

* Final-year depreciation is a plug amount needed to reduce asset book value to estimated salvage value

Try it in Excel

If you built the straight-line and UOP depreciation schedules in Exhibits 7-5 and 7-6 with Excel, changing the spreadsheet for DDB depreciation is easy. Steps 1–3 and 7–8 are identical. The other steps differ only slightly. You might want to start by opening the straight-line schedule you prepared and saving it under another name: "DDB depreciation." Next, change the column heading for column C to "DDB Rate." Right-click on column D (labeled "depreciable cost" in Exhibit 7-5) and delete the entire column. This moves the "yearly expense" over to column D. Here are modified steps 4 and 5 of the process we used for the straight-line rate:

4. In column C, calculate a new depreciation rate, which is double the straight-line rate. In our example, the straight-line rate is 20% per year. The DDB rate is 40% (2×20%). Enter .4 in cell C3 and copy down through cell C7.

5. Column D now contains a calculated amount for yearly depreciation expense. The yearly depreciation expense is the product of the previous book value of the asset (in column F) times the DDB rate (in column C). For 2011, depreciation expense is $16,400, which is calculated in Excel as =F2*C3. Enter this formula in cell D3. Your result should be $16,400. Copy this formula down through cell D6 (*not* cell D7, for reasons explained below).

All of the other amounts in the table through line 6 will automatically recalculate to reflect DDB depreciation, exactly as shown in Exhibit 7-7. ∎

The DDB method differs from the other methods in two ways:

1. Residual value is ignored initially; first-year depreciation is computed on the asset's full cost.

2. Depreciation expense in the final year is the "plug" amount needed to reduce the asset's book value to the residual amount. For this reason, depreciation expense in cell D7 of your Excel table should be 4,314, which is the amount needed to reduce the final book value to the residual amount of $1,000.

What is the DDB depreciation each year for the asset in the Stop & Think on page 372?

Answers:

Yr. 1: $4,000 ($10,000 × 40%)
Yr. 2: $2,400 ($6,000 × 40%)
Yr. 3: $1,440 ($3,600 × 40%)
Yr. 4: $160 ($10,000 − $4,000 − $2,400 − $1,440 − $2,000 = $160)*
Yr. 5: $0

*The asset is not depreciated below residual value of $2,000.

Comparing Depreciation Methods

Let's compare the three methods in terms of the yearly amount of depreciation. The yearly amount varies by method, but the total $40,000 depreciable cost is the same under all methods.

		Amount of Depreciation per Year	
Year	Straight-Line	Units-of-Production	Accelerated Method Double-Declining Balance
1	$ 8,000	$ 8,000	$16,400
2	8,000	12,000	9,840
3	8,000	10,000	5,904
4	8,000	6,000	3,542
5	8,000	4,000	4,314
Total	$40,000	$40,000	$40,000

GAAP requires expense recognition in such a way as to match an asset's depreciation against the revenue the asset produces. For a plant asset that generates revenue evenly over time, the straight-line method best meets the expense recognition principle. The units-of-production method best meets the principle for those assets that wear out because of physical use rather than obsolescence. The accelerated method (DDB) best meets the principle for those assets that generate more revenue earlier in their useful lives and less in later years.

Exhibit 7-8 graphs annual depreciation amounts for the straight-line, units-of-production, and accelerated depreciation (DDB) methods. The graph of straight-line depreciation is flat through time because annual depreciation is the same in all periods. Units-of-production depreciation follows no particular pattern because annual depreciation depends on the use of the asset. Accelerated depreciation is greatest in the first year and less in the later years.

Exhibit 7-8 | Depreciation Patterns Through Time

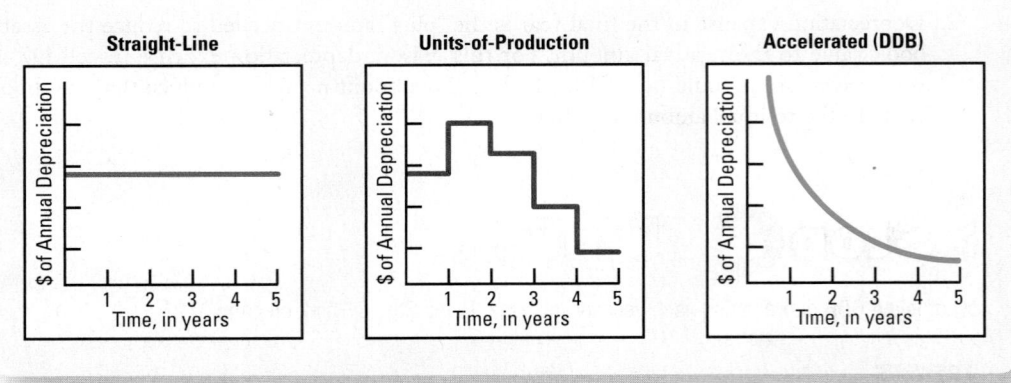

Exhibit 7-9 shows the percentage of companies that use each depreciation method from a recent survey of 600 companies conducted by the American Institute of Certified Public Accountants (AICPA).

Exhibit 7-9 | Depreciation Methods Used by 600 Companies

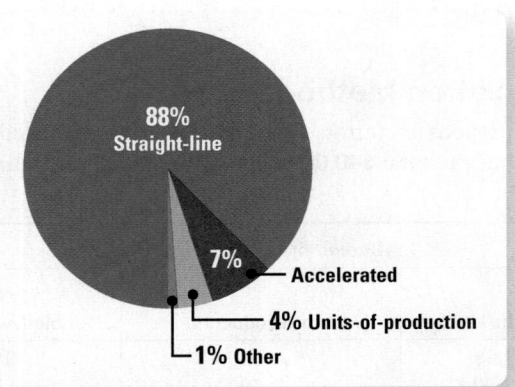

For reporting in the financial statements, straight-line depreciation is the most popular method. As we shall see, however, accelerated depreciation is most popular for income tax purposes.

Mid-Chapter Summary Problem

Suppose FedEx purchased equipment on January 1, 2014, for $44,000. The expected useful life of the equipment is 10 years or 100,000 units of production, and its residual value is $4,000. Under three depreciation methods, the annual depreciation expense and the balance of accumulated depreciation at the end of 2014 and 2015 are

	Method A		Method B		Method C	
Year	Annual Depreciation Expense	Accumulated Depreciation	Annual Depreciation Expense	Accumulated Depreciation	Annual Depreciation Expense	Accumulated Depreciation
2014	$4,000	$4,000	$8,800	$ 8,800	$1,200	$1,200
2015	4,000	8,000	7,040	15,840	5,600	6,800

Requirements

1. Identify the depreciation method used in each instance, and show the equation and computation for each; round to the nearest dollar.

2. Assume continued use of the same method through year 2016. Determine the annual depreciation expense, accumulated depreciation, and book value of the equipment for 2014 through 2016 under each method, assuming 12,000 units of production in 2016.

Answers

Requirement 1

Method A: Straight-Line

Depreciable cost = $40,000($44,000 − $4,000)

Each year: $40,000/10 years = $4,000

Method B: Double-Declining-Balance

$$\text{Rate} = \frac{1}{10 \text{ years}} \times 2 = 10\% \times 2 = 20\%$$

2014: 0.20 × $44,000 = $8,800

2015: 0.20 × ($44,000 − $8,800) = $7,040

Method C: Units-of-Production

$$\text{Depreciation per unit} = \frac{\$44,000 - \$4,000}{100,000 \text{ units}} = \$0.40$$

2014: $0.40 × 3,000 units = $1,200

2015: $0.40 × 14,000 units = $5,600

Requirement 2

Method A: Straight-Line

Year	Annual Depreciation Expense	Accumulated Depreciation	Book Value
Start			$44,000
2014	$4,000	$ 4,000	40,000
2015	4,000	8,000	36,000
2016	4,000	12,000	32,000

Method B: Double-Declining-Balance

Year	Annual Depreciation Expense	Accumulated Depreciation	Book Value
Start			$44,000
2014	$8,800	$ 8,800	35,200
2015	7,040	15,840	28,160
2016	5,632	21,472	22,528

Method C: Units-of-Production

Year	Annual Depreciation Expense	Accumulated Depreciation	Book Value
Start			$44,000
2014	$1,200	$ 1,200	42,800
2015	5,600	6,800	37,200
2016	4,800	11,600	32,400

Computations for 2016

Straight-line	$40,000/10 years = $4,000
Double-declining-balance	$28,160 × 0.20 = $5,632
Units-of-production	12,000 units × $0.40 = $4,800

Other Issues in Accounting for Plant Assets

Plant assets are complex because

- they have long lives.
- depreciation affects income taxes.
- companies may have gains or losses when they sell plant assets.
- international accounting changes in the future may affect the recognition as well as the carrying values of assets.

Depreciation for Tax Purposes

FedEx and most other companies use straight-line depreciation for reporting to stockholders and creditors on their financial statements. However, for income tax purposes they also keep a separate set of depreciation records, based on accelerated depreciation methods in the Internal Revenue Code (IRC) developed by the Internal Revenue Service (IRS). This is legal, ethical, and honest; U.S. tax law not only permits but expects it. The reason that different methods are typically used for financial statement and income tax purposes is that the objectives of GAAP are different from the tax reporting objectives of the IRC. The objective of GAAP is to provide useful information for making economic decisions. The objective of the IRC is to raise sufficient revenue to pay for federal government expenditures.

Suppose you are a business manager and the IRS allows an accelerated depreciation method. Why do FedEx managers prefer accelerated over straight-line depreciation for income tax purposes? Accelerated depreciation provides the fastest tax deductions, thus decreasing immediate tax payments. FedEx can reinvest the tax savings back into the business. FedEx has a choice—pay taxes or buy equipment. This choice is easy.

To understand the relationships between cash flow, depreciation, and income tax, recall our depreciation example of a FedEx truck:

- First-year depreciation is $8,000 under straight-line and $16,400 under double-declining-balance (DDB).
- DDB is permitted for income tax purposes.

Assume that this FedEx office has $400,000 in revenue and $300,000 in cash operating expenses during the truck's first year and an income tax rate of 30%. The cash flow analysis appears in Exhibit 7-10.

Exhibit 7-10 | The Cash Flow Advantage of Accelerated Depreciation for Tax Purposes

		SL	Accelerated
1	Cash revenue	$400,000	$400,000
2	Cash operating expenses	300,000	300,000
3	Cash provided by operations before income tax	100,000	100,000
4	Depreciation expense (a noncash expense)	8,000	16,400
5	Income before income tax	$ 92,000	$ 83,600
6	Income tax expense (30%)	$ 27,600	$ 25,080
	Cash-flow analysis:		
7	Cash provided by operations before tax	$100,000	$100,000
8	Income tax expense	27,600	25,080
9	Cash provided by operations	$ 72,400	$ 74,920
10	Extra cash available for investment if DDB is used ($74,920 – $72,400)		$ 2,520

You can see that, for income tax purposes, accelerated depreciation helps conserve cash for the business. That's why virtually all companies use accelerated depreciation to compute their income taxes.

There is a special depreciation method—used only for income tax purposes—called the **Modified Accelerated Cost Recovery System (MACRS)**. Under MACRS, each fixed asset is classified into one of eight classes identified by asset life (Exhibit 7-11 on the following page). Depreciation for the first four classes is computed by the double-declining-balance method. Depreciation for 15-year assets and 20-year assets is computed by the 150%-declining-balance method. Under 150% DB, annual depreciation is computed by multiplying the straight-line rate by 1.50 (instead of 2.00, as for DDB). For a 20-year asset, the straight-line rate is 0.05 per year (1/20 = 0.05), so the annual MACRS depreciation rate is 0.075 (0.05 × 1.50). The taxpayer computes annual depreciation by multiplying asset book value at the beginning of the year by 0.075 in a manner similar to the way that DDB works.

The IRC permits several other rapid depreciation methods that, in some cases, permit companies to take additional "bonus depreciation" on "tangible personal property" (fixed assets that are not real estate) for tax purposes in the year of initial purchase. In other cases, a certain amount of investment in these types of fixed assets may be deducted entirely from taxable income rather than capitalized and depreciated. All of these methods are intended to provide incentives for businesses to continually reinvest in new plant and equipment, saving them cash in tax outlays and providing stimulus for the U.S. economy.

Exhibit 7-11 | Modified Accelerated Cost Recovery System (MACRS)

Class Identified by Asset Life (years)	Representative Assets	Depreciation Method
3	Race horses	DDB
5	Automobiles, light trucks	DDB
7	Equipment	DDB
10	Equipment	DDB
15	Sewage-treatment plants	150% DB
20	Certain real estate	150% DB
27½	Residential rental property	SL
39	Nonresidential rental property	SL

Most real estate is depreciated by the straight-line method (see the last two categories in Exhibit 7-11).

Depreciation for Partial Years

Companies purchase plant assets whenever they need them, not just at the beginning of the year. Therefore, companies must compute *depreciation for partial years*. Suppose UPS purchases a warehouse building on April 1 for $500,000. The building's estimated life is 20 years, and its estimated residual value is $80,000. UPS's accounting year ends on December 31. Let's consider how UPS computes depreciation for April through December.

■ First, compute depreciation for a full year (unless you are using the units-of-production method, which automatically adjusts for partial periods by merely accounting for the number of units produced in the period).

■ Second, multiply full-year depreciation by the fraction of the year that you held the asset—in this case, 9/12. Assuming the straight-line method, the partial year's depreciation for this UPS building is $15,750, calculated as follows:

$$\text{Full-year depreciation} \qquad \frac{\$500,000 - \$80,000}{20} = \$21,000$$

$$\text{Partial year depreciation} \qquad \$21,000 \times 9/12 = \$15,750$$

What if UPS bought the asset on April 18? Many businesses record no monthly depreciation on assets purchased after the 15th of the month, and they record a full month's depreciation on an asset bought on or before the 15th.

Most companies use computerized systems to account for fixed assets. Each asset has a unique identification number, and the system will automatically calculate the asset's depreciation expense. Accumulated Depreciation is automatically updated.

Changing the Useful Life of a Depreciable Asset

After an asset is in use, managers may change its useful life on the basis of experience and new information. **Disney Enterprises, Inc.**, made such a change, called a *change in accounting estimate*. Disney recalculated depreciation on the basis of revised useful lives of several of its theme park assets. The following note in Disney Enterprises, Inc.'s financial statements reports this change in accounting estimate:

Note 5
...[T]he Company extended the estimated useful lives of certain theme park ride and attraction assets based upon historical data and engineering studies. The effect of this change was to decrease depreciation by approximately $8 million (an increase in net income of approximately $4.2 million...).

Assume that a Disney hot dog stand cost $50,000 and that the company originally believed the asset had a 10-year useful life with no residual value. Using the straight-line method, the company would record $5,000 depreciation each year ($50,000/10 years = $5,000). Suppose Disney used the asset for four years. Accumulated depreciation reached $20,000, leaving a remaining depreciable book value (cost less accumulated depreciation less residual value) of $30,000 ($50,000 − $20,000). From its experience, management believes the asset will remain useful for an *additional* 10 years. The company would spread the remaining depreciable book value over the asset's remaining life as follows:

$$\underset{\substack{\text{Asset's remaining} \\ \text{depreciable book value}}}{} \div \underset{\substack{\text{(New) Estimated} \\ \text{useful life remaining}}}{} = \underset{\substack{\text{(New) Annual} \\ \text{depreciation}}}{}$$

$$\$30,000 \quad \div \quad 10 \text{ years} \quad = \quad \$3,000$$

The yearly depreciation entry based on the new estimated useful life is as follows:

	A	C	D	G
A1				
1		Depreciation Expense—Hot Dog Stand	3,000	
2		Accumulated Depreciation—Hot Dog Stand		3,000
3				

Depreciation decreases both assets and equity.

Assets	=	Liabilities	+	Stockholders' Equity	−	Expenses
− 3,000	=	0				− 3,000

Cooking the Books

Through Depreciation

Waste Management

Since plant assets usually involve relatively large amounts and relatively large numbers of assets, sometimes a seemingly subtle change in the way they are accounted for can have a tremendous impact on the financial statements. When these changes are made in order to cook the books, the results can be devastating.

Waste Management, Inc., is North America's largest integrated waste service company, providing collection, transfer, recycling, disposal, and waste-to-energy services for commercial, industrial, municipal, and residential customers from coast to coast.

Starting in 1992, six top executives of the company, including its founder and chairman of the board, its chief financial officer, its corporate controller, its top lawyer, and its vice president of finance, decided that the company's profits were not growing fast enough to meet "earnings targets," which were tied to their executive bonuses. Among several fraudulent financial tactics these top executives employed to cook the books were (1) assigning unsupported and inflated salvage values to garbage trucks, (2) unjustifiably extending the estimated useful lives of their garbage trucks, and (3) assigning arbitrary salvage values to other fixed assets that previously had no salvage values. All of these tactics had the effect of decreasing the amount of depreciation expense in the income statements and increasing net income by a corresponding amount. While practices like this might seem relatively subtle and even insignificant when performed on an individual asset, remember that there were thousands of trash trucks and dumpsters involved, so the dollar amount grew huge in a short time. In addition, the company continued these practices for five years, overstating earnings by $1.7 billion.

The Waste Management fraud was the largest of its kind in history until the WorldCom scandal, discussed earlier in this chapter. In 1997, the company fired the officers involved and hired a new CEO who ordered a review of these practices, which uncovered the fraud. In the meantime, these dishonest executives had profited handsomely, receiving performance-based bonuses based on the company's inflated earnings, retaining their high-paying jobs, and receiving enhanced retirement benefits. One of the executives took the fraud to another level. Just 10 days before the fraud was disclosed, he enriched himself with a tax benefit by donating inflated company stock to his alma mater to fund a building in his name! Although the men involved were sued for monetary damages, none of them ever went to jail.

When the fraud was disclosed, Waste Management shareholders lost over $6 billion in the market value of their investments as the stock price plummeted by more than 33%. The company and these officers eventually settled civil lawsuits for approximately $700 million because of the fraud.

You might ask, "Where were the auditors while this was occurring?" The company's auditor was Arthur Andersen, LLP, whose partners involved on the audit engagement were eventually found to be complicit in the scheme. In fact, a few of the Waste Management officers who perpetrated the scheme had been ex-partners of the audit firm. As it turns out, the auditors actually identified many of the improper accounting practices of Waste Management. However, rather than insisting that the company fix the errors, or risk exposure, they merely "persuaded" management to agree not to repeat these practices in the future and entered into an agreement with them to write off the accumulated balance sheet overstatement over a period of 10 years. In June 2001, the SEC fined Arthur Andersen $7 million for "knowingly and recklessly issuing false and misleading audit reports" for Waste Management from 1993 through 1996.

In October 2001, immediately on the heels of these disclosures, the notorious Enron scandal broke. Enron, as well as WorldCom, were Arthur Andersen clients at the time. The Enron scandal finally put the firm out of business. Many people feel that, had it not been for Andersen's involvement in the Waste Management affair, the SEC might have been more lenient toward the company in the Enron scandal.

The Enron scandal is discussed in Chapter 10.

Fully Depreciated Assets

A *fully depreciated asset* is one that has reached the end of its estimated useful life. Suppose FedEx has fully depreciated equipment with zero residual value (cost was $60,000). FedEx accounts will appear as follows:

Equipment			Accumulated Depreciation		Book value
60,000		−		60,000	= $0

The equipment's book value is zero, but that doesn't mean the equipment is worthless. FedEx may use the equipment for a few more years, but FedEx will not record any more depreciation on a fully depreciated asset.

When FedEx disposes of the equipment, FedEx will remove both the asset's cost ($60,000) and its accumulated depreciation ($60,000) from the books. The next section shows how to account for plant asset disposals.

ANALYZE THE EFFECT OF A PLANT ASSET DISPOSAL

4 **Analyze** the effect of a plant asset disposal

Eventually, a plant asset ceases to serve a company's needs. The asset may wear out or become obsolete. Before accounting for the disposal of the asset, the business should bring depreciation up to date to

- measure the asset's final book value and
- record the expense up to the date of disposal.

Disposing of a Fully Depreciated Asset for No Proceeds

To account for disposal, remove the asset and its related accumulated depreciation from the books. Suppose the final year's depreciation expense has just been recorded for a machine that cost $60,000 and is estimated to have zero residual value. The machine's accumulated depreciation thus totals $60,000. Assuming that this asset is junked, the entry to record its disposal is as follows:

	A	C	D	G
1		Accumulated Depreciation—Machinery	60,000	
2		Machinery		60,000
3		To dispose of a fully depreciated machine.		
4				

A1

$$\frac{\text{Assets}}{\begin{array}{c} +\ 60{,}000 \\ -\ 60{,}000 \end{array}} = \frac{\text{Liabilities}}{0} + \frac{\text{Stockholders' Equity}}{0}$$

There is no gain or loss on this disposal, and there's no effect on total assets, liabilities, or equity.

If assets are disposed of for no proceeds before being fully depreciated, the company incurs a loss on the disposal in the amount of the asset's net book value. Suppose FedEx disposes of equipment that cost $60,000. This asset's accumulated depreciation is $50,000, and book value is, therefore, $10,000. Junking this equipment results in a loss equal to the book value of the asset:

	A	C	D	G
1		Accumulated Depreciation—Equipment	50,000	
2		Loss on Disposal of Equipment	10,000	
3		Equipment		60,000
4		To dispose of equipment.		
5				

A1

$$\frac{\text{Assets}}{\begin{array}{c} +\ 50{,}000 \\ -\ 60{,}000 \end{array}} = \frac{\text{Liabilities}}{0} + \frac{\text{Stockholders' Equity}}{} - \frac{\text{Losses}}{-\ 10{,}000}$$

FedEx disposed of an asset with $10,000 book value and received nothing. The result is a $10,000 loss, which decreases both total assets and equity.

The Loss on Disposal of Equipment is reported as Other income (expense) on the income statement. Losses decrease net income exactly as expenses do. Gains increase net income the same as revenues.

Selling a Plant Asset

Suppose FedEx sells equipment on September 30, 2014, for $7,300 cash. The equipment cost $10,000 when purchased on January 1, 2011, and has been depreciated straight-line. FedEx estimated a 10-year useful life and no residual value. Prior to recording the sale, FedEx accountants must update the asset's depreciation. Assume that FedEx uses the calendar year as its accounting period. Partial-year depreciation must be recorded for the asset's depreciation from January 1, 2014, to the sale date. The straight-line depreciation entry at September 30, 2014, is

	A	C	D	G
	A1			
1	Sep 30	Depreciation Expense ($10,000/10 years × 9/12)	750	
2		Accumulated Depreciation—Equipment		750
3		*To update depreciation.*		
4				

The Equipment account and the Accumulated Depreciation—Equipment account appear as follows. Observe that the equipment's book value is $6,250 ($10,000 − $3,750).

Equipment		Accumulated Depreciation—Equipment	
Jan 1, 2011 10,000		Dec 31, 2011 1,000	
		Dec 31, 2012 1,000	= Book value
	−	Dec 31, 2013 1,000	$6,250
		Sep 30, 2014 750	
		Balance 3,750	

The gain on the sale of the equipment for $7,300 is $1,050, computed as

Cash received from sale of the asset		$7,300
Book value of asset sold:		
Cost	$10,000	
Less: Accumulated depreciation	(3,750)	6,250
Gain on sale of the asset................................		$1,050

The entry to record sale of the equipment is

	A	C	D	G
	A1			
1	Sep 30	Cash	7,300	
2		Accumulated Depreciation—Equipment	3,750	
3		Equipment		10,000
4		Gain on Sale of Equipment		1,050
5		*To sell equipment.*		
6				

Total assets increase, and so does equity—by the amount of the gain.

Assets	=	Liabilities	−	Stockholders' Equity	+	Gains
+ 7,300						
+ 3,750	=	0			+	1,050
− 10,000						

Gains are recorded as credits on the income statement, just as revenues are. Gains and losses on asset disposals appear as Other income (expense), or Other gains (losses).

Exchanging a Plant Asset

Managers often trade in old assets for new ones. This is called a *nonmonetary exchange*. The accounting for nonmonetary exchanges is based on the *fair values of the assets involved*. Thus, the cost of an asset like plant and equipment received in a nonmonetary exchange is equal to the fair values of the assets given up (including the old asset and any cash paid). Any difference between the fair value of the old asset from its book value is recognized as gain (fair value of old asset exceeds book value) or loss (book value of old asset exceeds fair value) on the exchange. For example, assume Papa John's Pizza's

- old delivery car cost $9,000 and has accumulated depreciation of $8,000. Thus, the old car's book value is $1,000.

Assume Papa John's trades in the old automobile for a new one with a fair market value of $15,000 and pays cash of $10,000. Thus, the implied fair value of the old car is $5,000 ($15,000 − $10,000). This amount is treated as cash received by the business for the old vehicle.

- The cost of the new delivery car is $15,000 (fair value of the old asset, $5,000, plus cash paid, $10,000).

The pizzeria records the exchange transaction:

	A		C	D	G
1			Delivery Auto (new)	15,000	
2			Accumulated Depreciation (old)	8,000	
3			Delivery Auto (old)		9,000
4			Cash		10,000
5			Gain on Exchange of Delivery Auto		4,000
6			*Traded in old delivery car for new auto.*		
7					

Assets	=	Liabilities	+	Stockholders' Equity	+	Gains
+ 15,000						
+ 8,000	=	0			+	4,000
− 9,000						
− 10,000						

There was a net increase in total assets of $4,000 and a corresponding increase in stockholders' equity to reflect the gain on the exchange. Notice that this amount represents the excess of the fair value of the old asset ($5,000) over its book value ($1,000). Some special rules may apply here, but they are reserved for more advanced courses.

T-Accounts for Analyzing Plant Asset Transactions

You can perform quite a bit of analysis if you know how transactions affect the plant asset accounts. Here are the accounts with descriptions of the activity in each account.

Building (or Equipment)	
Beg bal	
Cost of assets purchased	Cost of assets disposed of
End bal	

Accumulated Depreciation	
Accumulated depreciation of assets disposed of	Beg bal
	Depreciation expense for the current period
	End bal

Cash	
Cash proceeds for assets disposed of	Cash paid for assets purchased

Long-Term Debt	
	New Debt incurred for assets purchased

Depreciation Expense		Gain on Sale of Building (or Equipment)	
Depreciation expense for the current period			Gain on sale

Loss on Sale of Building (or Equipment)	
Loss on sale	

You can analyze transactions as they flow through these accounts to answer very useful questions such as the amount of cash paid to purchase new plant assets, the amount of cash proceeds from disposal of plant assets, the cost of assets purchased, and the gross cost as well as net book value of assets disposed of.

Example: Suppose you started the year with buildings that cost $100,000. During the year, you bought another building for $150,000 and ended the year with buildings that cost $180,000. What was the cost of the building you sold?

Building

Beg bal	100,000			
Cost of assets purchased	150,000	Cost of assets sold	$X = 70,000^*$	
End bal	180,000			

$^*X = 100,000 + 150,000 - 180,000$

Global View

One of the most significant differences between U.S. GAAP and International Financial Reporting Standards (IFRS) is the permitted reported carrying values of property, plant, and equipment. Recall from Chapter 1 that U.S. GAAP has long advocated the historical cost principle as most appropriate for plant assets because it results in a more objective (nonbiased) and therefore more reliable (auditable) figure. It also supports the continuity assumption, which states that we expect the entity to remain in business long enough to recover the cost of its plant assets through depreciation.

In contrast, while historical cost is the primary basis of accounting under IFRS, it permits the periodic revaluation of plant assets to fair market value. The primary justification for this position is that the historical cost of plant assets purchased years ago does not properly reflect their current values. Thus, the amounts shown on the balance sheet for these assets do not reflect a relevant measure of what these assets are worth. For example, suppose a business bought a building in downtown Orlando, Florida, in 1960 for $1 million. Assume that this year the building has been appraised for $20 million. IFRS would permit the company periodically to revalue the building on its balance sheet.

The primary objection to the use of fair values on the balance sheet for plant assets is that these values are subjective and subject to change, sometimes quite rapidly. Consider, for example, residential and commercial real estate in California during the credit crisis of 2008 and 2009. The fair market values of these assets dropped by double-digit percentages in a period of less than one year. If these assets had been valued at fair market values on the books of the companies that held them, assets would have to have been adjusted accordingly, causing the balance sheet amounts to fluctuate wildly. Furthermore, if the assets had been depreciated, it is likely that both the depreciation expense and accumulated depreciation would also have had to be adjusted more frequently.

IFRS also differs substantially from U.S. GAAP with respect to accounting for depreciation. Whereas U.S. GAAP depreciates each asset as a composite whole (a building, manufactured equipment, an aircraft, etc.), IFRS uses a "components" approach. For example, suppose a company builds and owns a building that it is using for its operations. The total cost of the building, including all components (air-conditioning systems, roofing, duct work, plumbing, lighting systems, etc.) is $15 million. U.S. GAAP usually treats the building as a single composite asset within the class of buildings, with an estimated useful life of about 40 years that it depreciates using straight-line depreciation (about $375,000 per year). In contrast, IFRS does not view the building as a single composite asset, but recognizes the separate components of it—each with a different useful life and potentially accounted for with a different depreciation method. Thus, the frame of the building, the roof, air-conditioning systems, duct work, plumbing, light fixtures, and all other major components of the building each might have a different useful life (most being far less than 40 years) and be depreciated using a different method over shorter periods of time. Each has to be set up on the books as a separate plant asset with separate amounts of depreciation expense and accumulated depreciation. Converting a large enterprise's accounting system to a component approach for depreciation requires a massive one-time expenditure in information technology, as well as more extensive ongoing record-keeping requirements.

APPLY GAAP FOR NATURAL RESOURCES AND INTANGIBLE ASSETS

Accounting for Natural Resources

Natural resources are long-term assets of a special type, such as iron ore, petroleum (oil), and timber. These resources are often called *wasting assets* because, in contrast to property and equipment, they are actually physically used up over time. The process by which this occurs is called **depletion**. Depletion is distinctively different from depreciation, because it involves actually tracking the flow of a natural resource from its raw state, through inventory (to the extent not sold), to cost of goods sold or some other expense on the income statement. When a natural resource is acquired or developed, the entity follows the cost principle, similarly to that used in accounting for a plant asset. When the asset is extracted, the entity follows an approach much like the units-of-production depreciation method to account for the production. If all of the resource extracted is regarded as sold (as in the case of a drilling and exploration company), the amount depleted is transferred directly from long-term assets to the income statement in the form of an expense (such as depletion expense). However, as in the case of an integrated oil company (one with both production and refining operations), if a portion of the extracted resource is not immediately sold, it becomes saleable inventory (a current asset). Then, as the inventory is sold, its cost is transferred to an expense such as cost of goods sold, as discussed in Chapter 6.

For example, an oil reserve may cost **ExxonMobil** $100,000,000 and contain an estimated 10,000,000 barrels of oil. ExxonMobil is an integrated oil company, meaning it both drills for oil and refines it, so the company retains some inventory rather than selling all it produces. Upon purchase or development of the oil reserve (assuming the company paid cash), ExxonMobil makes the following entry:

	A1				
	A		**C**	**D**	**G**
1		Oil Reserve		100,000,000	
2		Cash			100,000,000
3					

The depletion rate is $10 per barrel ($100,000,000/10,000,000 barrels). If 3,000,000 barrels are extracted and 1,000,000 barrels are sold, the company's different divisions might make the following entries. First, the oil reserve (long-term asset) is depleted by $30,000,000 (3,000,000 barrels × $10 per barrel) and $30,000,000 is transferred to inventory. The depletion entry is:

	A1				
	A		**C**	**D**	**G**
1		Oil Inventory (3,000,000 barrels × $10)		30,000,000	
2		Oil Reserve			30,000,000
3					

5 Apply GAAP for natural resources and intangible assets

The following week, as the oil is sold, ExxonMobil makes the following entry:

	A		C	D	G
1			Cost of oil sold (1,000,000 barrels × $10)	10,000,000	
2			Oil Inventory		10,000,000
3					

This would assign $10 million to Cost of Sales (an expense), and leave $20 million in Oil Inventory (a current asset). The net book value of the oil reserve (the long-term asset) after these entries is $70 million ($100 million − $30 million).

Accounting for Intangible Assets

As we've seen, **intangible assets** are long-lived assets with no physical form. Intangibles are valuable because they carry special rights from patents, copyrights, trademarks, franchises, leaseholds, and goodwill. Like buildings and equipment, an intangible asset is recorded at its acquisition cost. Intangibles are the most valuable assets of high-tech companies and those that depend on research and development. The residual value of most intangibles is zero.

Intangible assets fall into two categories:

- Intangibles with *finite lives* that can be measured. We record amortization for these intangibles annually. **Amortization** expense is the title of the expense associated with intangibles. Amortization works like depreciation and is usually computed on a straight-line basis. Amortization can be credited directly to the asset account.

- Intangibles with *indefinite lives*. Record no amortization for these intangibles. Instead, check them annually for any loss in value (impairment), and record a loss when it occurs. Goodwill is the most prominent example of an intangible asset with an indefinite life.

In the following discussions, we illustrate the accounting for both categories of intangibles.

Accounting for Specific Intangibles

Each type of intangible asset is unique, and the accounting can vary from one asset to another.

Patents. **Patents** are federal government grants that give the holder the exclusive right for 20 years to produce and sell an invention. The invention may be a product or a process—for example, the Sony Blu-Ray disc players and the Dolby Laboratories surround-sound process. Like any other asset, a patent may be purchased. Suppose **Sony** pays $170,000 to acquire a patent on January 1, and the business believes the expected useful life of the patent is 5 years—not the entire 20-year period. Amortization expense is $34,000 per year ($170,000/5 years). Sony records the acquisition and amortization for this patent:

	A		C	D	G
1	Jan 1		Patents	170,000	
2			Cash		170,000
3			*To acquire a patent.*		
4					

	A		C	D	G
1	Dec 31		Amortization Expense—Patents ($170,000/5)	34,000	
2			Patents		34,000
3			*To amortize the cost of a patent.*		
4					

Assets	=	Liabilities	+	Stockholders' Equity	–	Expenses
– 34,000	=	0				– 34,000

You can see that we credited the Patents account directly (no Accumulated Amortization account). Amortization for an intangible decreases both assets and equity exactly as depreciation does for equipment or a building.

Copyrights. **Copyrights** are exclusive rights to reproduce and sell a book, musical composition, film, or other work of art. Copyrights also protect computer software programs, such as **Microsoft**'s Windows and Excel. Issued by the federal government, copyrights extend 70 years beyond the author's (composer's, artist's, or programmer's) life. The cost of obtaining a copyright from the government is low, but a company may pay a large sum to purchase an existing copyright from the owner. For example, a publisher may pay the author of a popular novel $1 million or more for the book copyright. Because the useful life of a copyright is usually no longer than two or three years, each period's amortization amount is a high proportion of the copyright cost.

Trademarks and Trade Names. **Trademarks** and **trade names** (or *brand names*) are distinctive identification of a product or service. The "eye" symbol that flashes across our television screens is the trademark that identifies the **CBS** television network. You are probably also familiar with **NBC**'s peacock. Advertising slogans that are legally protected include **American Airlines**' "AAdvantage" program and **Coca Cola Co.**'s "It's the real thing™" slogan. These are distinctive identifications of products or services, marked with the symbol™ or ®.

Some trademarks may have a definite useful life set by contract. We should amortize the cost of this type of trademark over its useful life. But a trademark or a trade name may have an indefinite life and not be amortized.

Franchises and Licenses. **Franchises** and **licenses** are privileges granted by a private business or a government to sell a product or service in accordance with specified conditions. The Chicago Cubs baseball organization is a franchise granted to its owner by the National League. **McDonald's** restaurants and **Holiday Inn**s are popular franchises. The useful lives of many franchises and licenses are indefinite and, therefore, not amortized.

Goodwill. In accounting, **goodwill** has a very specific meaning:

> **Goodwill is defined as the excess of the cost of purchasing another company over the sum of the market values of the acquired company's net assets (assets minus liabilities).**

A purchaser is willing to pay for goodwill when the purchaser buys another company that has abnormal earning power.

FedEx operates in several foreign countries. Suppose FedEx acquires Europa Company at a cost of $10 million. Europa's assets have a market value of $9 million, and the market value of its liabilities total $2 million, so Europa's net assets total $7 million at current market value. In this case, FedEx paid $3 million for goodwill:

Purchase price paid for Europa Company		$10 million
Sum of the market values of Europa Company's assets	$9 million	
Less: Market value of Europa Company's liabilities	(2 million)	
Market value of Europa Company's net assets		7 million
Excess is called *goodwill*		$ 3 million

FedEx's entry to record the acquisition of Europa Company, including its goodwill, would be

	A	C	D	G
1		Assets (Cash, Receivables, Inventories, Plant Assets,		
2		all at market value)	9,000,000	
3		Goodwill	3,000,000	
4		Liabilities		2,000,000
5		Cash		10,000,000
6				

Goodwill in accounting has special features:

1. Goodwill is recorded *only* when it is purchased in the acquisition of another company. A purchase transaction provides objective evidence of the value of goodwill. Companies never record goodwill that they create for their own business.

2. According to GAAP, goodwill is not amortized because the goodwill of many entities increases in value. Rather, each year, companies with goodwill on their financial statements are required to perform a special impairment test for goodwill, similar (but not identical) to the impairment test for other long-term assets described in the next section. If the test shows that goodwill is impaired, it must be written down to the impaired value. The details of this impairment test are beyond the scope of this text and are reserved for later courses.

Accounting for Research and Development Costs

Accounting for research and development (R&D) costs is one of the most difficult issues in accounting. R&D is the lifeblood of companies such as **Procter & Gamble, General Electric, Intel,** and **Boeing**. R&D is one of these companies' most valuable intangible assets. However, in general, U.S. companies do not report R&D assets on their balance sheets. Rather, they expense R&D costs as they are incurred.

EXPLAIN THE EFFECT OF AN ASSET IMPAIRMENT ON THE FINANCIAL STATEMENTS

6 Explain the effect of an asset impairment on the financial statements

Generally accepted accounting principles require that management of companies test both tangible and intangible long-term assets for impairment yearly. **Impairment** occurs when the expected future cash flows (which approximate the expected future benefits) from a long-term asset fall below the asset's net book (carrying) value (cost minus accumulated depreciation or amortization). If an asset is impaired, the company is required to adjust the carrying value downward from its book value to its **fair value**. In this case, fair value is based not on the expected future cash flows, but on the asset's estimated market value at the date of the impairment test. Exhibit 7-12 displays both the normal relationship and an impaired relationship between net book value, future cash flows, and fair value.

Exhibit 7-12 | Normal Relationship and Impaired Relationship among Values of an Asset

	Normal	Impaired
Largest:	Future cash flows	Net book value
Middle:	Fair value	Future cash flows
Smallest:	Net book value	Fair value

In a normal relationship, estimated future cash flows represents the largest of the three amounts, followed by fair value, and then net book value. An impaired relationship exists if net book value exceeds estimated future cash flows. The process of accounting for asset impairment requires two steps:

Step 1 **Test the asset for impairment.**
- **If net book value > Estimated future cash flows, then the asset is impaired.**

Step 2 **If the asset is impaired under step 1, compute the impairment loss.**
- **Impairment loss = Net book value − Fair value**

To illustrate, let's assume that FedEx has a long-term asset with the following information as of May 31, 2012:

- Net book value $100 million
- Estimated future cash flows   80 million
- Fair (market) value   70 million

The two-stage impairment process is

Step 1 **Impairment test: Is net book value > estimated future cash flows? (Answer: Yes, so the asset is impaired).**

Step 2 **Impairment loss = Net book value − Fair value ($100 − 70) = $30**

FedEx will make the following entry:

	A	C	D	G
1	2012			
2	May 31	Impairment Loss on Long-term Asset ($100 − $70)	30	
3		Long-term Asset		30
4				

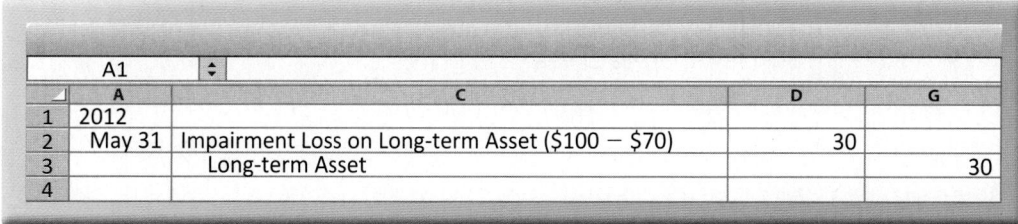

Assets	=	Liabilities	+	Stockholders' Equity	−	Losses
− 30	=	0				− 30

Both long-term assets and equity decrease (through the Loss account). Under U.S. GAAP, once a long-term asset has been written down because of impairment, it may never again be written back up, should it increase in value.

Global View

Like U.S. GAAP, IFRS also records impairments based on a two-step impairment process. The details of this process are covered in more advanced accounting courses. However, unlike U.S. GAAP, asset impairments under IFRS may be reversed in future periods for some types of long-term assets, in the event that the market price recovers. Thus, under IFRS, a company can record an impairment loss on certain long-term assets in one period and then write the asset back up with a corresponding gain in a later period.

Accounting for research and development costs represents another prominent difference between U.S. GAAP and IFRS. Whereas under U.S. GAAP, in general, both research and development costs are expensed as incurred, under IFRS, costs associated with the creation of intangible assets are classified into research-phase costs and development-phase costs. Costs in the research phase are always expensed. However, costs in the development phase are capitalized if the company can demonstrate meeting the following six criteria:

- The technical feasibility of completing the intangible asset
- The intention to complete the intangible asset
- The ability to use or sell the intangible asset

- The future economic benefits (e.g., the existence of a market or, if for internal use, the usefulness of the intangible asset)
- The availability of adequate resources to complete development of the asset
- The ability to reliably measure the expenditure attributable to the intangible asset during its development

Thus, IFRS are generally more permissive than U.S. GAAP toward capitalization of research and development costs. Adoption of IFRS should result in generally higher reported incomes for companies that incur research and development costs in periods in which these costs are incurred.

The Financial Accounting Standards Board (FASB) is currently working on a new accounting standard aimed at eliminating the differences between U.S. GAAP and IFRS in the area of research and development costs.

Still another difference between IFRS and U.S. GAAP lies in the capitalization of internally generated intangible assets such as brand names and patents. U.S. GAAP only permits capitalization of these when they are purchased from a source outside the company. The cost of internally generated brand names and patents must be expensed on the income statement. In contrast, IFRS allows the capitalization of internally generated intangible assets like these as long as it is probable (i.e., more likely than not) that the company will receive future benefits from them. Adoption of IFRS by U.S. companies is therefore expected to result in the recognition of more intangible assets on their balance sheets than presently exist. These assets may be either amortized over the assets' estimated useful lives or tested for impairment as they are held, depending on the asset.

ANALYZE RATE OF RETURN ON ASSETS

7 **Analyze** rate of return on assets

Evaluating company performance is a key goal of financial statement analysis. Shareholders entrust managers with the responsibility of developing a business strategy that utilizes company assets in a manner that both effectively and efficiently generates a profit. In this chapter, we begin to develop a framework by which company performance can be evaluated. The most basic framework for this purpose is **return on assets (ROA)**.

ROA, also known as *rate* of return on assets, measures how profitably management has used the assets that stockholders and creditors have provided the company. The basic formula for the ROA ratio is

$$\text{ROA} = \frac{\text{Net income}[1]}{\text{Average total assets}}$$

where Average total assets = (Beginning total assets + Ending total assets)/2

ROA measures how much the entity earned for each dollar of assets invested by both stockholders and creditors. Companies with high ROA have both selected assets and managed them more successfully than companies with low ROA. ROA is often computed on a divisional or product-line basis to help identify less profitable segments and improve their performance.

---

[1]For companies with significant debt, some analysts may add interest expense to net income. While it is theoretically correct to do so, in order to illustrate DuPont analysis, we do not. Adding back interest makes a material difference to ROA only when interest expense is relatively high compared to net income.

DuPont Analysis: A More Detailed View of ROA

To better understand why ROA increased or decreased over time, companies often perform a **DuPont Analysis**,[2] which breaks ROA down into two component ratios that drive it:

$$\text{Net profit margin ratio} = \frac{\text{Net income}}{\text{Net sales}}$$

$$\text{Total asset turnover} = \frac{\text{Net sales}}{\text{Average total assets}}$$

Net profit margin ratio measures how much every sales dollar generates in profit. Net profit margin can be increased in one of three ways: (1) increasing sales volume, or the amount of goods or services sold or performed; (2) increasing sales prices; or (3) decreasing cost of goods sold and operating expenses.

Total asset turnover measures how many sales dollars are generated for each dollar of assets invested. This is a measure of how effectively and efficiently the company manages its assets. Asset turnover can be increased by (1) increasing sales in the ways just described; (2) keeping less inventory on hand; or (3) closing unproductive facilities, selling idle assets, and consolidating operations to fewer places to reduce the amount of plant assets needed.

ROA is the product of net profit margin ratio and total asset turnover:

$$\text{ROA} = \text{Net profit margin ratio} \times \text{Total asset turnover}$$

$$\text{ROA} = \frac{\text{Net income}}{\text{Net sales}} \times \frac{\text{Net sales}}{\text{Average total assets}} = \frac{\text{Net income}}{\text{Average total assets}}$$

By influencing the drivers of net profit margin ratio and total asset turnover, management devises strategies to improve each one, thus increasing ROA. Successful companies often choose between a mixture of two different strategies: *product differentiation* or *low cost*. A company that follows a high product differentiation strategy usually spends a great deal on research and development and advertising to convince customers that the company's products (usually higher-priced) are worth the investment. **Apple, Inc.,** our spotlight company in Chapters 5 and 13, follows a product differentiation strategy, introducing innovative and attractive technology in the marketplace before any other competitor and always at a higher price. Alternatively, a low-cost strategy usually relies on efficient management of inventory and productive assets to produce a high asset turnover. **Dell, Inc.,** a competitor of Apple's, follows a low-cost strategy. Of course, all companies would like to have the best of both worlds by maximizing both net profit margin ratio and asset turnover, but some companies have to settle for one or the other.

To illustrate, let's consider **Masimo Corporation**, a company that produces electronic instruments used in the health-care industry. The following table contains approximate financial data adapted from Masimo's income statements and balance sheets for 2011 and 2012:

Masimo Corporation Selected (Adapted) Financial Data (Amounts in thousands)		
	2011	**2012**
Net sales	$350,000	$400,000
Net income	52,500	75,000
Average total assets	350,000	300,000

[2]The full DuPont Analysis model actually illustrates a way to compute Return on Common Stockholders' Equity (ROE), which is the product of three component ratios: net profit margin ratio, total asset turnover, and leverage. In this chapter, we discuss a partial version of the full DuPont model, ROA, which is the product of the first two component ratios. In Chapter 9 we introduce the third component ratio (leverage) and in Chapter 10 we illustrate how the leverage ratio is used to convert ROA to ROE.

	Masimo Corporation DuPont Analysis				
	Net profit margin ratio × (Net income/Net sales)	×	Total asset turnover (Net sales/Average total assets)	=	ROA (Net income/Average total assets)
2011	$\dfrac{\$52,500}{\$350,000}$	×	$\dfrac{\$350,000}{\$350,000}$	=	15%
2012	$\dfrac{\$75,000}{\$400,000}$	×	$\dfrac{\$400,000}{\$300,000}$	=	25%

In 2011, the company's net profit margin ratio was 15% ($52,500/$350,000). Its asset turnover was 1.0 ($350,000/$350,000), meaning that it earned $1 of sales revenue for every $1 of assets invested. In 2012, the company improved its net profit margin ratio to 18.75% ($75,000/$400,000) by reducing expenses, increasing sales, and introducing new and unique products to the market that no other competitor had. In addition, Masimo sold unproductive plant assets, reducing total average assets from $350,000 to $300,000 and increasing asset turnover from 1.0 to 1.33. Thus, the company used both product differentiation and low-cost strategies to its benefit, increasing return on assets from 15% to 25%.

Return on assets is the first of several ratios we will introduce over the next few chapters to show how analysts dissect financial statements to get behind the numbers, discover management's strategies, and evaluate their performance. In Chapters 9 and 10 we will add the component of financial leverage to the DuPont Analysis model and explain how it is combined with ROA to calculate return on common stockholders' equity (ROE).

ANALYZE THE CASH FLOW IMPACT OF LONG-LIVED ASSET TRANSACTIONS

8 **Analyze** the cash flow impact of long-lived asset transactions

Three main types of long-lived asset transactions appear on the statement of cash flows:

- acquisitions,
- sales, and
- depreciation (as well as amortization).

Acquisitions and sales of long-term assets are *investing* activities. Capital expenditures are examples of investing activities that appear on the statement of cash flows. The disposition of plant and other long-term assets results in a cash receipt, as illustrated in Exhibit 7-13, which excerpts data from the cash flow statement of FedEx Corporation. Depreciation, acquisitions, capital expenditures, and sales (dispositions) of long-term capital assets are denoted in color (lines 7, 11, and 12).

Exhibit 7-13 | Reporting Investing Activities on FedEx Corporation's Statement of Cash Flows

	A	B
A1		
	FedEx Corporation Statement of Cash Flows (Partial, Adapted) Year Ended May 31, 2012	
1		
2		(In millions)
3	**Cash Flows from Operating Activities:**	
4	Net income	$ 2,032
5	Adjustments to reconcile net income	
6	to net cash provided by operating activities:	
7	Depreciation and amortization	2,113
8	Other items (summarized)	690
9	Net cash provided by operating activities	4,835
10	**Cash Flows from Investing Activities:**	
11	Capital expenditures	(4,007)
12	Other asset acquisitions and dispositions, net	(42)
13	Net cash (used in) investing activities	(4,049)
14	**Cash Flows from Financing Activities:**	
15	Net cash (used in) financing activities	(244)
16	Effect of exchange rate changes on cash	(27)
17	**Net (increase) in cash and cash equivalents**	515
18	**Cash and cash equivalents, beginning of period**	2,328
19	**Cash and cash equivalents, end of period**	$ 2,843
20		

Let's examine FedEx's investing activities first. During 2012, FedEx invested $4,007 million in capital expenditures (line 11). FedEx also engaged in net acquisition and disposition of other long-term assets, spending another $42 million (line 12). FedEx's statement of cash flows reports Depreciation and amortization (line 7) of $2,113 million. Observe that "Depreciation and amortization" is listed as a positive item under "adjustments to reconcile net income to net cash provided by operating activities." Since depreciation and amortization do not affect cash, you may be wondering why these amounts appear on the statement of cash flows. In this format, the operating activities section of the statement of cash flows starts with net income (line 4) and reconciles to net cash provided by operating activities (line 9). Depreciation and amortization decrease net income but do not affect cash. Depreciation and amortization are therefore added back to net income to measure cash flow from operations. The add-back of depreciation and amortization to net income offsets the earlier subtraction of these expenses. The sum of net income plus depreciation and amortization, therefore, helps to reconcile net income (on the accrual basis) to cash flow from operations (a cash-basis amount). We revisit this topic in the full context of the statement of cash flows in Chapter 12.

FedEx's cash flows are strong. Net cash provided by operating activities exceeds net income by $2.8 billion. With this excess, the company has made sizeable capital expenditures, signaling that it has invested in new plant and equipment and other long-term assets needed to expand and run its business. The company has also had to borrow money in the past to help finance these purchases. The company used cash in financing activities ($244 million) to help pay off this debt. The company's cash and cash equivalents position at the end of 2012, in the amount of $2,843 million, is very strong.

● Decision Guidelines

PLANT ASSETS AND RELATED EXPENSES

FedEx Corporation, like all other companies, must make some decisions about how to account for its plant assets and intangibles. Let's review some of these decisions.

Decision	Guidelines
Capitalize or expense a cost?	General rule: Capitalize all costs that provide *future benefit for the business such as a new package-handling system. Expense all costs that provide no future benefit, such as a repair to an airplane.*
Capitalize or expense: • Cost associated with a new asset? • Cost associated with an existing asset?	Capitalize all costs that bring the asset to its intended use, including asset purchase price, transportation charges, and taxes paid to acquire the asset. Capitalize only those costs that add to the asset's capacity or to its useful life. Expense all other costs as maintenance or repairs.
Which depreciation method to use: • For financial reporting? • For income tax?	Use the method that best allocates the cost of an asset through depreciation expense against the revenues produced by the asset. Most companies use the straight-line method. Use the method that produces the fastest tax deductions (MACRS). A company can use different depreciation methods for financial reporting and for income tax purposes. In the United States, this practice is both legal and ethical.
How to account for natural resources?	Capitalize the asset's acquisition cost and all later costs that add to the natural resource's future benefit. Record depletion by the units-of-production method by transferring the amount extracted to inventory and eventually to cost of goods sold.
How to account for intangibles?	Capitalize acquisition cost and all later costs that add to the asset's future benefit. For intangibles with finite lives, record amortization expense. For intangibles with indefinite lives, do not record amortization. But if an intangible asset loses value, record a loss in the amount of the decrease in asset value.
How to record impairments in long-term assets?	Every year, conduct a two-step impairment process for long-term assets: STEP 1: Compare net book value with expected cash flows from the asset. If net book value > expected cash flows, the asset is impaired. Otherwise, the asset is not impaired. STEP 2: For all impaired assets under step 1, reduce the carrying value of the asset from net book value to fair value. Record a loss for the difference.
How profitable is the company?	Return on assets (ROA) = Net profit margin ratio × Total asset turnover = (Net income/Net sales) × (Net sales/Average total assets)

End-of-Chapter Summary Problem

The figures that follow appear in the *Answers to the Mid-Chapter Summary Problem*, Requirement 2, on page 378.

	Method A: Straight-Line			Method B: Double-Declining-Balance		
Year	Annual Depreciation Expense	Accumulated Depreciation	Book Value	Annual Depreciation Expense	Accumulated Depreciation	Book Value
Start			$44,000			$44,000
2014	$4,000	$ 4,000	40,000	$8,800	$ 8,800	35,200
2015	4,000	8,000	36,000	7,040	15,840	28,160
2016	4,000	12,000	32,000	5,632	21,472	22,528

Requirements

1. Suppose the income tax authorities permitted a choice between these two depreciation methods. Which method would FedEx select for income tax purposes? Why?

2. Suppose FedEx purchased the equipment described in the table on January 1, 2014. Management has depreciated the equipment by using the double-declining-balance method. On July 1, 2016, FedEx sold the equipment for $27,000 cash.

Record depreciation for 2016 and the sale of the equipment on July 1, 2016.

Answers

Requirement 1

For tax purposes, most companies select the accelerated method because it results in the most depreciation in the earliest years of the asset's life. Accelerated depreciation minimizes income tax payments in the early years of the asset's life. That maximizes the business's cash at the earliest possible time.

Requirement 2

Entries to record depreciation to date of sale, and then the sale of the equipment, follow:

	A	B	C	D
	A1			
1	2016			
2	Jul 1	Depreciation Expense—Equipment ($5,632 X 1/2 year)	2,816	
3		Accumulated Depreciation—Equipment		2,816
4		*To update depreciation.*		
5				
6	Jul 1	Cash	27,000	
7		Accumulated Depreciation—Equipment		
8		($15,840 + $2,816)	18,656	
9		Equipment		44,000
10		Gain on Sale of Equipment		1,656
11		*To record sale of equipment.*		
12				

REVIEW | Plant Assets and Intangibles

Quick Check (Answers are given on page 427.)

1. Bentley, Inc., purchased a tract of land, a small office building, and some equipment for $1,800,000. The appraised value of the land was $1,144,000, the building $660,000, and the equipment $396,000. What is the cost of the land?
   - **a.** $936,000
   - **b.** $600,000
   - **c.** $1,144,000
   - **d.** None of the above

2. Which statement is false?
   - **a.** Depreciation is based on the expense recognition principle because it apportions the cost of the asset against the revenue generated over the asset's useful life.
   - **b.** Depreciation is a process of allocating the cost of a plant asset over its useful life.
   - **c.** The cost of a plant asset minus accumulated depreciation equals the asset's book value.
   - **d.** Depreciation creates a fund to replace the asset at the end of its useful life.

   Use the following data for questions 3–6.

   On October 1, 2014, Freedom Communications purchased a new piece of equipment that cost $35,000. The estimated useful life is five years and estimated residual value is $8,000.

3. What is the depreciation expense for 2014 if Freedom uses the straight-line method?
   - **a.** $5,400
   - **b.** $1,350
   - **c.** $1,750
   - **d.** $7,000

4. Assume Freedom Communications purchased the equipment on January 1, 2014. If Freedom uses the straight-line method for depreciation, what is the asset's book value at the end of 2015?
   - **a.** $16,200
   - **b.** $21,000
   - **c.** $24,200
   - **d.** $32,200

5. Assume Freedom Communications purchased the equipment on January 1, 2014. If Freedom uses the double-declining-balance method, what is depreciation for 2015?
   - **a.** $14,000
   - **b.** $8,400
   - **c.** $22,400
   - **d.** $6,480

6. Return to Freedom's original purchase date of October 1, 2014. Assume that Freedom uses the straight-line method of depreciation and sells the equipment for $22,400 on October 1, 2018. The result of the sale of the equipment is a gain (loss) of
   - **a.** $9,000.
   - **b.** $1,000.
   - **c.** ($4,600).
   - **d.** $0.

7. A company bought a new machine for $23,000 on January 1. The machine is expected to last four years and to have a residual value of $3,000. If the company uses the double-declining-balance method, accumulated depreciation at the end of year 2 will be
   - **a.** $23,000.
   - **b.** $20,000.
   - **c.** $15,000.
   - **d.** $17,250.

8. Which of the following is *not* a capital expenditure?
   - **a.** A complete overhaul of an air-conditioning system
   - **b.** Replacement of an old motor with a new one in a piece of equipment
   - **c.** The cost of installing a piece of equipment
   - **d.** A tune-up of a company vehicle
   - **e.** The addition of a building wing

9. Which of the following assets is *not* subject to a decreasing book value through depreciation, depletion, or amortization?
   a. Natural resources
   b. Land improvements
   c. Goodwill
   d. Intangibles

10. Why would a business select an accelerated method of depreciation for tax purposes?
    a. Accelerated depreciation generates higher depreciation expense immediately and therefore lowers tax payments in the early years of the asset's life.
    b. MACRS depreciation follows a specific pattern of depreciation.
    c. Accelerated depreciation is easier to calculate because salvage value is ignored.
    d. Accelerated depreciation generates a greater amount of depreciation over the life of the asset than does straight-line depreciation.

11. A company purchased an oil well for $210,000. It estimates that the well contains 30,000 barrels, has an eight-year life, and no salvage value. If the company extracts and sells 2,000 barrels of oil in the first year, how much in cost of sales should be recorded?
    a. $26,250
    b. $105,000
    c. $21,000
    d. $14,000

12. Which item among the following is *not* an intangible asset?
    a. Goodwill
    b. A copyright
    c. A trademark
    d. A patent
    e. All of the above are intangible assets.

13. An important measure of profitability is
    a. inventory turnover.
    b. return on assets (ROA).
    c. quick (acid test) ratio.
    d. net sales.

14. In 2014, total asset turnover for JBC Company has increased. This means that the
    a. company has become more effective.
    b. company has become more efficient.
    c. company has become more effective and more efficient.
    d. company has neither become more effective nor more efficient.

Accounting Vocabulary

accelerated depreciation methods (p. 373) A depreciation method that writes off a relatively larger amount of the asset's cost nearer the start of its useful life than the straight-line method does.

amortization (p. 388) The systematic reduction of a lump-sum amount. Expense that applies to intangible assets in the same way depreciation applies to plant assets and depletion applies to natural resources.

capital expenditure (p. 367) Expenditure that increases an asset's capacity or extends its useful life. Capital expenditures are debited to an asset account.

copyright (p. 389) Exclusive right to reproduce and sell a book, musical composition, film, other work of art, or computer program. Issued by the federal government, copyrights extend 70 years beyond the author's life.

depletion (p. 387) That portion of a natural resource's cost that is used up in a particular period. Depletion expense is computed in the same way as units-of-production depreciation. A depleted asset usually flows into inventory and eventually to cost of goods sold as the resource is sold.

depreciable cost (p. 370) The cost of a plant asset minus its estimated residual value.

double-declining-balance (DDB) (p. 373) An accelerated depreciation method that computes annual depreciation by multiplying the asset's decreasing book value at the beginning of the year by a constant percentage, which is two times the straight-line rate.

DuPont Analysis (p. 393) A detailed approach to measuring rate of return on equity (see Chapter 10). In this chapter, we confine our discussion to return on assets, comprising the first two components of return on equity, calculated as follows: Net profit margin ratio (Net income/Net sales) × Total asset turnover (Net sales/Average total assets).

estimated residual value (p. 370) Expected cash value of an asset at the end of its useful life. Also called *residual value*, *scrap value*, or *salvage value*.

estimated useful life (p. 370) Length of service that a business expects to get from an asset. May be expressed in years, units of output, miles, or other measures.

fair value (p. 390) The asset's estimated market value at a particular date.

franchises and **licenses** (p. 389) Privileges granted by a private business or a government to sell a product or service in accordance with specified conditions.

goodwill (p. 389) Excess of the cost of an acquired company over the sum of the market values of its net assets (assets minus liabilities).

impairment (p. 390) The condition that exists when the carrying amount of a long-lived asset exceeds the amount of the future cash flows from the asset. Whenever long-term assets have been impaired, they have to be written down to fair market values using a two-step process. Under U.S. GAAP, once impaired, the carrying value of a long-lived asset may never again be increased. Under IFRS, if the fair value of impaired assets recovers in the future, the values may be increased.

intangible asset (p. 388) An asset with no physical form—a special right to current and expected future benefits.

Modified Accelerated Cost Recovery System (MACRS) (p. 379) A special depreciation method used only for income tax purposes. Assets are grouped into classes, and for a given class, depreciation is computed by the double-declining-balance method, the 150%-declining balance method, or, for most real estate, the straight-line method.

natural resources (p. 387) Assets such as oil and gas reserves, coal mines, or stands of timber—accounted for as long-term assets when purchased or developed; their cost is transferred to expense through a process called depletion.

net profit margin ratio (p. 393) Computed by the formula Net income/Net sales. This ratio measures the portion of each net sales dollar generated in net profit.

patent (p. 388) A federal government grant giving the holder the exclusive right for 20 years to produce and sell an invention.

plant assets (p. 364) Long-lived assets, such as land, buildings, and equipment, used in the operation of the business. Also called *fixed assets* or *property and equipment*.

return on assets (ROA) (p. 392) Also known as *rate of return on assets*. Measures how profitably management has used the assets that stockholders and creditors have provided the company.

straight-line (SL) method (p. 371) Depreciation method in which an equal amount of depreciation expense is assigned to each year of asset use.

total asset turnover (p. 393) A measure of efficiency in usage of total assets. The ratio calculates how many times per year average total assets are covered by net sales. Formula: Net sales/Average total assets. Also known as *asset turnover*.

trademark, trade name (p. 389) A distinctive identification of a product or service. Also called a *brand name*.

units-of-production (UOP) method (p. 372) Depreciation method by which a fixed amount of depreciation is assigned to each unit of output produced by the plant asset.

ASSESS YOUR PROGRESS

Short Exercises

S7-1. *(Learning Objective 1: Measure the cost and book value of a company's plant assets)* Examine the excerpt of a footnote from Whole Foods Market, Inc.'s September 30, 2012, annual report on the next page.

	A	B	C
1	Balances of Major Classes of Property and Equipment Are as Follows (in thousands)		
2		12 months ended	
3		Sep. 30 2012	Sep. 30 2011
4	Land	$ 76,592	$ 48,928
5	Buildings and leasehold improvements	2,219,763	1,958,612
6	Capitalized real estate leases	24,876	24,262
7	Fixtures and equipment	1,674,089	1,398,778
8	Construction in progress and equipment not yet in service	53,328	188,844
9		4,048,648	3,619,424
10	Less accumulated depreciation and amortization	(1,855,965)	(1,622,212)
11		$ 2,192,683	$ 1,997,212
12			

1. What are Whole Foods Market, Inc.'s largest two categories of property and equipment as of September 30, 2012? Describe in general terms the types of expenditures included in these categories.

2. What was Whole Foods Market, Inc.'s gross cost of property and equipment at September 30, 2012? What was the book value of property and equipment on this date? Why is book value less than cost?

S7-2. *(Learning Objective 1: Measure and record the cost of individual assets in a lump–sum purchase of assets)* Graves Automotive pays $320,000 for a group purchase of land, building, and equipment. At the time of acquisition, the land has a current market value of $112,000, the building's current market value is $227,500, and the equipment's current market value is $10,500. Journalize the lump-sum purchase of the three assets for a total cost of $320,000. The business signs a note payable for this amount.

S7-3. *(Learning Objective 2: Distinguish a capital expenditure from an immediate expense)* Identify each of the following items as either a capital expenditure (C), expense on the income statement (E), or neither (N):

Type of Expenditure C Capital expenditure E Expensed on income statement N Neither capital expenditure or expensed	Transaction
	1. Purchased a computer and peripheral equipment for $25,600 cash.
	2. Paved a parking lot on leased property for $100,000.
	3. Repaired plumbing in main plant, paying $150,000 cash.
	4. Purchased equipment for new manufacturing plant, $5,000,000; financed with long-term note.
	5. Paid $50,000 in cash for installation of equipment in (4).
	6. Paid $15,000 maintenance on equipment in (4) during its first year of use.
	7. Paid $150,000 to tear down old building on new plant site.
	8. Paid dividends of $50,000.
	9. Paid interest on construction note for new plant building, $550,000.
	10. Paid property taxes of $50,000 for the first year the new building is occupied.

S7-4. *(Learning Objective 3: Compute depreciation and book value by three methods—first year only)* Assume that at the beginning of 2013, DHL, a FedEx competitor, purchased a used Jumbo 747 aircraft at a cost of $52,400,000. DHL expects the plane to remain useful for five years (7.3 million miles) and to have a residual value of $6,400,000. DHL expects to fly the plane 835,000 miles the first year, 1,650,000 miles each year during the second, third, and fourth years, and 1,515,000 miles the last year.
1. Compute DHL's depreciation for the first two years on the plane using the following methods:
   a. Straight-line
   b. Units-of-production (round depreciation per mile to the closest cent)
   c. Double-declining-balance
2. Show the airplane's book value at the end of the first year under each depreciation method.

S7-5. *(Learning Objective 3: Select the best depreciation method for income tax purposes)* This exercise uses the assumed DHL's data from SE7-4. Assume DHL is trying to decide which depreciation method to use for income tax purposes. The company can choose from among the following methods: (a) straight-line, (b) units-of-production, or (c) double-declining-balance.
1. Which depreciation method offers the tax advantage for the first year? Describe the nature of the tax advantage.
2. How much income tax will DHL save for the first year of the airplane's use under the method you just selected as compared with using the straight-line depreciation method? The income tax rate is 36%. Ignore any earnings from investing the extra cash.

S7-6. *(Learning Objective 3: Compute partial year depreciation, and select the best depreciation method)* Assume that on September 30, 2013, Lufthansa, the national airline of Germany, purchased a Jumbo aircraft at a cost of €41,000,000 (€ is the symbol for the euro). Lufthansa expects the plane to remain useful for four years (5,200,000 miles) and to have a residual value of €5,200,000. Lufthansa will fly the plane 390,000 miles during the remainder of 2013. Compute Lufthansa's depreciation on the plane for the year ended December 31, 2013, using the following methods:
   a. Straight-line
   b. Units-of-production
   c. Double-declining-balance

Which method would produce the highest net income for 2013? Which method produces the lowest net income?

S7-7. *(Learning Objective 3: Compute and record depreciation after a change in useful life of the asset)* Seven Flags over Georgia paid $180,000 for a concession stand. Seven Flags started out depreciating the building straight-line over 10 years with zero residual value. After using the concession stand for 6 years, Seven Flags determines that the building will remain useful for only 2 more years. Record Seven Flags' depreciation on the concession stand for year 7 by the straight-line method.

S7-8. *(Learning Objectives 3, 4: Compute depreciation; record a gain or loss on disposal)* On January 1, 2013, Regal Manufacturing purchased a machine for $850,000. Regal Manufacturing expects the machine to remain useful for eight years and to have a residual value of $40,000. Regal Manufacturing uses the straight-line method to depreciate its machinery. Regal Manufacturing used the machine for five years and sold it on January 1, 2018, for $325,000.
1. Compute accumulated depreciation on the machine at January 1, 2018 (same as December 31, 2017).
2. Record the sale of the machine on January 1, 2018.

S7-9. *(Learning Objective 5: Account for the depletion of a company's natural resources)* TexAm Petroleum, the giant oil company, holds reserves of oil and gas assets. At the end of 2014, assume the cost of TexAM Petroleum's oil reserves totaled $204 billion, representing 12 billion barrels of oil in the ground.
1. Which depreciation method is similar to the depletion method that TexAM Petroleum and other oil companies use to compute their annual depletion expense for the oil removed from the ground?

2. Suppose the company removed 800 million barrels of oil during 2015. Record this event. Show amounts in billions.

3. Assume that, of the amount removed in (2), the company sold 300 million barrels. Make the cost of sales entry.

S7-10. *(Learning Objective 5: Measure and record goodwill)* Handy Snacks, Inc., dominates the snack-food industry with its Salty Chip brand. Assume that Handy Snacks, Inc., purchased Super Snacks, Inc., for $5.2 million cash. The market value of Super Snacks' assets is $9 million, and Super Snacks has liabilities with a market value of $7.1 million.

Requirements

1. Compute the cost of the goodwill purchased by Handy Snacks.
2. Explain how Handy Snacks will account for goodwill in future years.

S7-11. *(Learning Objective 7: Calculate return on assets)* In 2014, FPT, Inc., reported $200 million in sales, $15 million in net income, and average total assets of $83 million. What is FPT's return on assets in 2014?

S7-12. *(Learning Objective 7: Calculate return on assets)* Moore Optical, Inc., provides a full line of designer eyewear to optical dispensaries. Moore reported the following information for 2014 and 2013:

	2014	2013
Sales revenue	$500,000	$450,000
Net income	$ 37,500	$ 33,600
Average total assets	$250,000	$240,000

Compute return on assets (ROA) for 2014 and 2013. Using the DuPont model, identify the components and state whether each improved or worsened from 2013 to 2014.

S7-13. *(Learning Objective 8: Analyze the cash flow impact of investing activities on the statement of cash flows)* During 2014, Richardson Satellite Systems, Inc., purchased two other companies for $8 million in cash. Also during 2014, Richardson made capital expenditures of $4.2 million in cash to expand its market share. During the year, Richardson sold its North American operations, receiving cash of $6.4 million. Overall, Richardson reported a net income of $5.3 million during 2014.

Show what Richardson would report for cash flows from investing activities on its statement of cash flows for 2014. Report a total amount for net cash provided by (used in) investing activities.

S7-14. *(Learning Objective 6: Explain the effect of asset impairment on financial statements)* For each of the following scenarios, indicate whether a long-term asset has been impaired (Y for yes and N for no) and, if so, the amount of the loss that should be recorded.

Asset	Book Value	Estimated Future Cash Flows	Fair Value	Impaired? (Y or N)	Amount of Loss
a. Equipment	$160,000	$120,000	$ 100,000		
b. Trademark	$320,000	$420,000	$ 380,000		
c. Land	$56,000	$30,000	$ 28,000		
d. Factory building	$3 million	$3 million	$2 million		

Exercises

Group A

E7-15A. *(Learning Objective 1: Measure the cost of plant assets)* Lexington Self Storage pur-chased land, paying $125,000 cash as a down payment and signing a $140,000 note payable for the balance. Lexington also had to pay delinquent property tax of $2,500, title insurance costing $5,500, and $18,000 to level the land and remove an unwanted building. The company paid $54,000 to add soil for the foundation and then constructed an office building at a cost of $970,000. It also paid $36,000 for a fence around the property, $11,000 for the company sign near the property entrance, and $4,000 for lighting of the grounds. What is the capitalized cost of each of Lexington's land, land improvements, and building?

E7-16A. *(Learning Objectives 1, 4: Allocate costs to assets acquired in a lump-sum purchase; dispose of a plant asset)* DuBoise Manufacturing bought three used machines in a $164,000 lump-sum purchase. An independent appraiser valued the machines as shown in the table.

Machine No.	Appraised Value
1	$ 62,000
2	48,000
3	92,000

What is each machine's individual cost? Immediately after making this purchase, DuBoise sold machine 3 for its appraised value. What is the result of the sale? (Round decimals to three places when calculating proportions, and use your computed percentages throughout.)

E7-17A. *(Learning Objective 2: Distinguish capital expenditures from expenses)* Assume Safe Runner Products, Inc., purchased conveyor-belt machinery. Classify each of the following expenditures as a capital expenditure or an immediate expense related to machinery:
  a. Purchase price
  b. Transportation and insurance while machinery is in transit from seller to buyer
  c. Sales tax paid on the purchase price
  d. Installation
  e. Training of personnel for initial operation of the machinery
  f. Special reinforcement to the machinery platform
  g. Income tax paid on income earned from the sale of products manufactured by the machinery
  h. Major overhaul to extend the machinery's useful life by five years
  i. Ordinary repairs to keep the machinery in good working order
  j. Lubrication of the machinery before it is placed in service
  k. Periodic lubrication after the machinery is placed in service

E7-18A. *(Learning Objectives 1, 3: Measure, depreciate, and report plant assets)* During 2014, Lawson's Book Store paid $273,000 for land and built a store in Georgetown. Prior to construc-tion, the city of Georgetown charged Lawson's $1,300 for a building permit, which Lawson's paid. Lawson's also paid $15,300 for architect's fees. The construction cost of $745,000 was financed by a long-term note payable, with interest cost of $36,200 paid at completion of the project. The building was completed June 30, 2014. Lawson's depreciates the building by the straight-line method over 35 years, with estimated residual value of $332,300.

1. Journalize transactions for the following:
   a. Purchase of the land
   b. All the costs chargeable to the building in a single entry
   c. Depreciation on the building for 2014

Explanations are not required.
2. Report Lawson's Book Store's plant assets on the company's balance sheet at December 31, 2014.
3. What will Lawson's income statement for the year ended December 31, 2014, report for these facts?

E7-19A. *(Learning Objective 3: Determine depreciation amounts by three methods)* Dave's Pizza bought a used Toyota delivery van on January 2, 2014, for $28,600. The van was expected to remain in service for four years (154,000 miles). At the end of its useful life, Dave's officials estimated that the van's residual value would be $2,500. The van traveled 63,500 miles the first year, 51,000 miles the second year, 29,500 miles the third year, and 10,000 miles in the fourth year.

Requirements

1. Prepare a schedule of *depreciation expense* per year for the van under the three depreciation methods discussed in this chapter. (For units-of-production and double-declining-balance, round to the nearest two decimal places after each step of the calculation.)
2. Which method best tracks the wear and tear on the van?
3. Which method would Dave's prefer to use for income tax purposes? Explain in detail why Dave's prefers this method.

E7-20A. *(Learning Objectives 1, 3, 8: Report plant assets, depreciation, and investing cash flows)* Assume that on January 1, 2014, a Sunrise Bakery restaurant purchased a building, paying $53,000 cash and signing a $103,000 note payable. The restaurant paid another $66,000 to remodel the building. Furniture and fixtures cost $59,000, and dishes and supplies—a current asset—were obtained for $9,600. All expenditures were for cash. Assume that all of these expenditures occurred on January 1, 2014.

Sunrise Bakery is depreciating the building over 25 years by the straight-line method, with estimated residual value of $56,000. The furniture and fixtures will be replaced at the end of five years and are being depreciated by the double-declining-balance method, with zero residual value. At the end of the first year, the restaurant still has dishes and supplies worth $1,500.

Show what the restaurant will report for supplies, plant assets, and cash flows at the end of the first year on its

- income statement,
- balance sheet, and
- statement of cash flows (investing only).

Note: The purchase of dishes and supplies is an operating cash flow because supplies are a current asset.

E7-21A. *(Learning Objective 3: Change a plant asset's useful life)* Assume Harley Software Consultants purchased a building for $505,000 and depreciated it on a straight-line basis over 40 years. The estimated residual value was $80,000. After using the building for 20 years, Harley realized that the building will remain useful only 14 more years. Starting with the 21st year, Harley began depreciating the building over a revised total life of 34 years and decreased the residual value to $33,500. Record depreciation expense on the building for years 20 and 21.

E7-22A. *(Learning Objectives 3, 4: Measure DDB depreciation; analyze the effect of a sale of a plant asset)* Assume that on January 2, 2014, Design Guild of Vermont purchased fixtures for $9,700 cash, expecting the fixtures to remain in service for five years. Design Guild has depreciated the fixtures on a double-declining-balance basis, with $1,800 estimated residual value. On September 30, 2015, Design Guild sold the fixtures for $3,300 cash. Record both the depreciation expense on the fixtures for 2015 and the sale of the fixtures. Apart from your journal entry, also show how to compute the gain or loss on Design Guild's disposal of these fixtures.

E7-23A. *(Learning Objectives 1, 3, 4: Measure a plant asset's cost; calculate UOP depreciation; analyze the effect of a used asset trade-in)* TransAmerica Truck Company is a large trucking company that operates throughout the United States. TransAmerica Truck Company uses the units-of-production (UOP) method to depreciate its trucks. The company trades in trucks often to keep driver morale high and to maximize fuel economy. Consider these facts about one Mack truck in the company's fleet: When acquired in 2014, the tractor-trailer rig cost $360,000 and was expected to remain in service for 10 years or 1,000,000 miles. Estimated residual value was $50,000. During 2014, the truck was driven 75,000 miles; during 2015, 108,000 miles; and during 2016, 135,000 miles. After 99,000 miles in 2017, the company traded in the Mack truck for a less-expensive Freightliner with a sticker price (fair market value) of $240,000. TransAmerica Truck Company paid cash of $20,000. Determine TransAmerica's gain or loss on the transaction. Prepare the journal entry to record the trade-in of the old truck on the new one.

E7-24A. *(Learning Objective 5: Record natural resource assets and depletion)* Denver Mines paid $625,000 for the right to extract ore from a 250,000-ton mineral deposit. In addition to the purchase price, Denver Mines also paid a $810 filing fee, a $2,000 license fee to the state of Colorado, and $55,390 for a geologic survey of the property. Because the company purchased the rights to the minerals only, it expects the asset to have zero residual value when fully depleted. During the first year of production, Denver Mines removed 48,000 tons of ore, of which it sold 44,000 tons. Make journal entries to record (a) purchase of the mineral rights, (b) payment of fees and other costs, (c) depletion for first-year production, and (d) sales of ore. Round depletion per unit to the closest cent.

E7-25A. *(Learning Objectives 5, 6: Record intangibles, amortization, and impairment)*
1. Shermann Printers incurred external costs of $1,500,000 for a patent for a new laser printer. Although the patent gives legal protection for 20 years, it is expected to provide Shermann Printers with a competitive advantage for only 15 years. Assuming the straight-line method of amortization, make journal entries to record (a) the purchase of the patent and (b) amortization for year 1.
2. After using the patent for 10 years, Shermann Printers learns at an industry trade show that Fast Printers is designing a more efficient printer. On the basis of this new information, Shermann Printers determines that the expected future cash flows from the patent are only $400,000. Its fair value on the open market is zero. Is this asset impaired? If so, make the impairment adjusting entry.

E7-26A. *(Learning Objectives 5, 6: Compute and account for goodwill; explain the effect of asset impairment)* Assume Hughes Co. paid $30 million to purchase BaySide.com. Assume further that BaySide had the following summarized data at the time of the Hughes Co. acquisition (amounts in millions):

BaySide.com			
Assets		**Liabilities and Equity**	
Current assets	$18	Total liabilities	$35
Long-term assets	36	Stockholders' equity	19
	$54		$54

BaySide's long-term assets had a current market value of only $31 million, and the liabilities have a market value of $35 million.

Requirements

1. Compute the cost of goodwill purchased by Hughes Co.
2. Journalize Hughes Co.'s purchase of BaySide.
3. Explain how Hughes Co. will account for goodwill.

E7-27A. *(Learning Objective 7: Calculate return on assets)* Kroger, Inc., one of the nation's largest grocery retailers, reported the following information (adapted) in its comparative financial statements for the fiscal year ended January 31, 2013:

	January 31, 2013	January 31, 2012
Net sales....................................	$48,815	$47,220
Net earnings..............................	$ 2,010	$ 1,783
Average total assets..................	$33,699	$33,005

Requirements

1. Compute net profit margin ratio for the years ended January 31, 2013 and 2012. Did it improve or worsen in 2013?
2. Compute asset turnover for the years ended January 31, 2013 and 2012. Did it improve or worsen in 2013?
3. Compute return on assets for the years ended January 31, 2013 and 2012. Did it improve or worsen in 2013? Which component (net profit margin ratio or asset turnover) was mostly responsible?

E7-28A. *(Learning Objective 8: Report cash flows for plant assets)* Assume Gregg Manufacturing Corporation completed the following transactions:
 a. Sold a store building for $740,000. The building cost Gregg Manufacturing $1,600,000, and at the time of the sale, its accumulated depreciation totaled $920,000.
 b. Lost a store building in a fire. The building cost $460,000 and had accumulated depreciation of $310,000. The insurance proceeds received by Gregg Manufacturing totaled $185,000.
 c. Renovated a store at a cost of $203,000.
 d. Purchased store fixtures for $68,000. The fixtures are expected to remain in service for 10 years and then be sold for $29,000. Gregg Manufacturing uses the straight-line depreciation method.

For each transaction, show what Gregg Manufacturing would report for investing activities on its statement of cash flows. Show negative amounts in parentheses.

Group B

E7-29B. *(Learning Objective 1: Measure the cost of plant assets)* Atlanta Self Storage purchased land, paying $145,000 cash as a down payment and signing a $190,000 note payable for the balance. Atlanta also had to pay delinquent property tax of $5,000, title insurance costing $3,000, and $8,000 to level the land and remove an unwanted building. The company paid $58,000 to add soil for the foundation and then constructed an office building at a cost of $860,000. It also paid $39,000 for a fence around the property, $16,000 for the company sign near the property entrance, and $4,000 for lighting of the grounds. What is the capitalized cost of each of Atlanta's land, land improvements, and building?

E7-30B. *(Learning Objectives 1, 4: Allocate costs to assets acquired in a lump-sum purchase; dispose of a plant asset)* Greenview Manufacturing bought three used machines in a $175,000 lump-sum purchase. An independent appraiser valued the machines as shown:

Machine No.	Appraised Value
1	$68,000
2	$54,000
3	$88,000

What is each machine's individual cost? Immediately after making this purchase, Greenview sold machine 3 for its appraised value. What is the result of the sale? (Round decimals to three places when calculating proportions, and use your computed percentages throughout.)

E7-31B. *(Learning Objective 2: Distinguish capital expenditures from expenses)* Assume Blynn Athletic Products, Inc., purchased conveyor-belt machinery. Classify each of the following expenditures as a capital expenditure or an immediate expense related to machinery:

   a. Purchase price
   b. Transportation and insurance while machinery is in transit from seller to buyer
   c. Sales tax paid on the purchase price
   d. Installation
   e. Training of personnel for initial operation of the machinery
   f. Special reinforcement to the machinery platform
   g. Income tax paid on income earned from the sale of products manufactured by the machinery
   h. Major overhaul to extend the machinery's useful life by four years
   i. Ordinary repairs to keep the machinery in good working order
   j. Lubrication of the machinery before it is placed in service
   k. Periodic lubrication after the machinery is placed in service

E7-32B. *(Learning Objectives 1, 3: Measure, depreciate, and report plant assets)* During 2014, Garrett's Book Store paid $315,000 for land and built a store in Baltimore. Prior to construction, the city of Baltimore charged Garrett's $1,700 for a building permit, which Garrett's paid. Garrett's also paid $15,700 for architect's fees. The construction cost of $718,000 was financed by a long-term note payable, with interest cost of $35,900 paid at completion of the project. The building was completed August 31, 2014. Garrett's depreciates the building by the straight-line method over 35 years, with estimated residual value of $323,650.

   1. Journalize transactions for the following:
      a. Purchase of the land
      b. All the costs chargeable to the building in a single entry
      c. Depreciation on the building for 2014

Explanations are not required.

   2. Report Garrett's Book Store's plant assets on the company's balance sheet at December 31, 2014.
   3. What will Garrett's income statement for the year ended December 31, 2014, report for this situation?

E7-33B. *(Learning Objective 3: Determine depreciation amounts by three methods)* Royce's Pizza bought a used Honda delivery van on January 2, 2014, for $43,000. The van was expected to remain in service for four years (208,000 miles). At the end of its useful life, Royce's officials estimated that the van's residual value would be $3,500. The van traveled 65,000 miles the first year, 64,000 miles the second year, 42,000 miles the third year, and 37,000 miles in the fourth year.

Requirements

   1. Prepare a schedule of *depreciation expense* per year for the van under the three depreciation methods discussed in this chapter. (For units-of-production and double-declining-balance, round to the nearest two decimal places after each step of the calculation.)
   2. Which method best tracks the wear and tear on the van?
   3. Which method would Royce's prefer to use for income tax purposes? Explain in detail why Royce's prefers this method.

E7-34B. *(Learning Objectives 1, 3, 8: Report plant assets, depreciation, and investing cash flows)* Assume that on January 1, 2014, an Early Risers Café purchased a building, paying $54,000 cash and signing a $104,000 note payable. The restaurant paid another $65,000 to remodel the building. Furniture and fixtures cost $51,000, and dishes and supplies—a current asset—were obtained for $9,000. All expenditures were for cash. Assume that all of these expenditures occurred on January 1, 2014.

Early Risers Café is depreciating the building over 25 years by the straight-line method, with estimated residual value of $50,000. The furniture and fixtures will be replaced at the end of five years and are being depreciated by the double-declining-balance method, with zero residual value. At the end of the first year, the restaurant still has dishes and supplies worth $1,600.

Show what the restaurant will report for supplies, plant assets, and cash flows at the end of the first year on its

- income statement,
- balance sheet, and
- statement of cash flows (investing only).

Note: The purchase of dishes and supplies is an operating cash flow because supplies are a current asset.

E7-35B. *(Learning Objective 3: Change a plant asset's useful life)* Assume Simmons Security Consultants purchased a building for $540,000 and depreciated it on a straight-line basis over 40 years. The estimated residual value was $90,000. After using the building for 20 years, Simmons realized that the building will remain useful only 13 more years. Starting with the 21st year, Simmons began depreciating the building over the newly revised total life of 33 years and decreased the estimated residual value to $35,500. Record depreciation expense on the building for years 20 and 21.

E7-36B. *(Learning Objectives 3, 4: Measure DDB depreciation; analyze the effect of a sale of a plant asset)* Assume that on January 2, 2014, Design House of Nebraska purchased fixtures for $9,200 cash, expecting the fixtures to remain in service for five years. Design House has depreciated the fixtures on a double-declining-balance basis, with $1,100 estimated residual value. On October 31, 2015, Design House sold the fixtures for $2,700 cash. Record both the depreciation expense on the fixtures for 2015 and then the sale of the fixtures. Apart from your journal entry, also show how to compute the gain or loss on Design House's disposal of these fixtures.

E7-37B. *(Learning Objectives 1, 3, 4: Measure a plant asset's cost; calculate UOP depreciation; analyze the effect of a used asset trade-in)* USA Truck Company is a large trucking company that operates throughout the United States. USA Truck Company uses the units-of-production (UOP) method to depreciate its trucks.

USA Truck Company trades in trucks often to keep driver morale high and to maximize fuel economy. Consider these facts about one Mack truck in the company's fleet: When acquired in 2014, the tractor-trailer cost $430,000 and was expected to remain in service for 10 years or 1,000,000 miles. Estimated residual value was $20,000. During 2014, the truck was driven 81,000 miles; during 2015, 111,000 miles; and during 2016, 141,000 miles. After 75,000 miles in 2017, the company traded in the Mack truck for a less expensive Freightliner with a sticker price (fair market value) of $280,000. USA Truck Company paid cash of $25,000. Determine USA Trucks' gain or loss on the transaction. Prepare the journal entry to record the trade-in of the old truck on the new one.

E7-38B. *(Learning Objective 5: Record natural resource assets and depletion)* Charleston Mines paid $628,000 for the right to extract ore from a 325,000-ton mineral deposit. In addition to the purchase price, Charleston Mines also paid a $930 filing fee, a $2,300 license fee to the state of West Virginia, and $66,820 for a geologic survey of the property. Because the company purchased the rights to the minerals only, it expected the asset to have zero residual value when fully depleted. During the first year of production, Charleston Mines removed 58,000 tons of ore, of which it sold 53,000 tons. Make journal entries to record (a) purchase of the mineral rights, (b) payment of fees and other costs, (c) depletion for first-year production, and (d) sales of ore. Round depletion per unit to the closest cent.

E7-39B. *(Learning Objectives 5, 6: Record intangibles, amortization, and impairment)*
1. Morgan Printers incurred external costs of $1,200,000 for a patent for a new laser printer. Although the patent gives legal protection for 20 years, it is expected to provide Morgan Printers with a competitive advantage for only 12 years. Assuming the straight-line method of amortization, make journal entries to record (a) the purchase of the patent and (b) amortization for year 1.
2. After using the patent for 8 years, Morgan Printers learns at an industry trade show that Superb Printers is designing a more efficient printer. On the basis of this new information, Morgan Printers determines that the expected future cash flows from the patent are only $350,000 and that the patent is worthless on the open market. Is this asset impaired? If so, record the impairment adjusting entry.

E7-40B. *(Learning Objectives 5, 6: Compute and account for goodwill and impairment)* Assume Hurd Co. paid $28 million to purchase Southwest.com. Assume further that Southwest had the following summarized data at the time of the Hurd Co. acquisition (amounts in millions):

Southwest.com			
Assets		**Liabilities and Equity**	
Current assets	$14	Total liabilities	$29
Long-term assets	37	Stockholders' equity	22
	$51		$51

Southwest's long-term assets had a current market value of only $32 million, and liabilities have a market value of $29 million.

Requirements

1. Compute the cost of goodwill purchased by Hurd Co.
2. Journalize Hurd Co.'s purchase of Southwest.
3. Explain how Hurd Co. will account for goodwill.

E7-41B. *(Learning Objective 7: Calculate return on assets)* Lowe's Companies, Inc., the second-largest home improvement retailer, reported the following information (adapted) in its comparative financial statements for the fiscal year ended January 31, 2013:

	January 31, 2013	January 31, 2012
Net sales.....................................	$82,189	$76,733
Net earnings.............................	$ 1,116	$ 70
Average total assets..................	$23,505	$23,126

Requirements

1. Compute net profit margin ratio for the years ended January 31, 2013 and 2012. Did it improve or worsen in 2013?
2. Compute asset turnover for the years ended January 31, 2013 and 2012. Did it improve or worsen in 2013?
3. Compute return on assets for the years ended January 31, 2013 and 2012. Did it improve or worsen in 2013? Which component (net profit margin ratio or asset turnover) was mostly responsible?

E7-42B. *(Learning Objective 8: Report cash flows for plant assets)* Assume Gruen Manufacturing Corporation completed the following transactions:

   a. Sold a store building for $710,000. The building had cost Gruen Manufacturing $1,400,000, and at the time of the sale, its accumulated depreciation totaled $780,000.

   b. Lost a store building in a fire. The building cost $430,000 and had accumulated depreciation of $260,000. The insurance proceeds received by Gruen Manufacturing totaled $108,000.

   c. Renovated a store at a cost of $201,000.

   d. Purchased store fixtures for $73,000. The fixtures are expected to remain in service for 10 years and then be sold for $14,000. Gruen Manufacturing uses the straight-line depreciation method.

For each transaction, show what Gruen Manufacturing would report for investing activities on its statement of cash flows. Show negative amounts in parentheses.

Quiz

Test your understanding of accounting for plant assets, natural resources, and intangibles by answering the following questions. Select the best choice from among the possible answers given.

Q7-43. A capital expenditure
 a. adds to an asset.
 b. is a credit like capital (owners' equity).
 c. is expensed immediately.
 d. records additional capital.

Q7-44. Which of the following items should be accounted for as a capital expenditure?
 a. Maintenance fees paid with funds provided by the company's capital
 b. Taxes paid in conjunction with the purchase of office equipment
 c. Costs incurred to repair leaks in the building roof
 d. The monthly rental cost of an office building

Q7-45. Suppose you buy land for $3,000,000 and spend $1,000,000 to develop the property. You then divide the land into lots as follows:

Category	Sale Price per Lot
15 Hilltop lots.................	$480,000
15 Valley lots	$270,000

How much did each hilltop lot cost you?
 a. $133,333
 b. $480,000
 c. $170,667
 d. $96,000

Q7-46. Which statement about depreciation is false?
 a. Depreciation is a process of allocating the cost of an asset to expense over its useful life.
 b. Obsolescence as well as physical wear and tear should be considered when determining the period over which an asset should be depreciated.
 c. A major objective of depreciation accounting is to allocate the cost of using an asset against the revenues it helps to generate.
 d. Depreciation should not be recorded in years in which the market value of the asset has increased.

Q7-47. At the beginning of last year, Bremond Corporation purchased a piece of heavy equipment for $34,000. The equipment has a life of five years or 100,000 hours. The estimated residual value is $4,000. Bremond used the equipment for 22,000 hours last year and 25,000 hours this year. Depreciation expense for year 2 using double-declining-balance (DDB) and units-of-production would be as follows:

	DDB	**UOP**
a.	$7,200	$8,500
b.	$7,200	$7,500
c.	$8,160	$7,500
d.	$8,160	$8,500

Q7-48. Dykes Corporation acquired a machine for $26,000 and has recorded depreciation for 3 years using the straight-line method over a 6-year life and $2,000 residual value. At the start of the fourth year of use, Dykes revised the estimated useful life to a total of 10 years. Estimated residual value declined to $0.

How much depreciation should Dykes record in each of the asset's last 7 years (that is, year 4 through year 10), following the revision?
 a. $13,000
 b. $2,000
 c. $2,600
 d. Some other amount

Q7-49. Kline Company failed to record depreciation of equipment. How does this omission affect Kline's financial statements?
 a. Net income is overstated and assets are overstated.
 b. Net income is overstated and assets are understated.
 c. Net income is understated and assets are understated.
 d. Net income is understated and assets are overstated.

Q7-50. Suzy's Beauty, Inc., uses the double-declining-balance method for depreciation on its computers. Which item is *not* needed to compute depreciation for the first year?
 a. Expected useful life in years
 b. Original cost
 c. Estimated residual value
 d. All the above are needed.

Q7-51. Which of the following costs are reported on a company's income statement and balance sheet?

Income Statement	Balance Sheet
a. Accumulated depreciation	Land
b. Cost of goods sold	Accumulated deprecation
c. Gain on sale of land	Cost of goods sold
d. Goodwill	Accounts payable

Use the following information to answer questions 7-52 through 7-53.

Ringle Company purchased a machine for $10,200 on January 1, 2014. The machine has been depreciated using the straight-line method over an eight-year life and $800 residual value. Ringle sold the machine on January 1, 2016, for $8,900.

Q7-52. What is straight-line depreciation for the year ended December 31, 2014, and what is the book value on December 31, 2015?

Q7-53. What gain or loss should Ringle record on the sale?
 a. Loss, $1,050   c. Gain, $800
 b. Loss, $125   d. Gain, $1,050

Q7-54. A company purchased mineral assets costing $832,000 with estimated residual value of $68,800 and holding approximately 240,000 tons of ore. During the first year, 54,000 tons are extracted and sold. What is the amount of depletion for the first year?
 a. $187,200
 b. $171,720
 c. $156,620
 d. Cannot be determined from the data given

Q7-55. Suppose George's Delivery pays $66 million to buy Lone Star Overnight. The fair value of Lone Star's assets is $72 million, and the fair value of its liabilities is $23 million. How much goodwill did George's Delivery purchase in its acquisition of Lone Star Overnight?
 a. $43 million   c. $23 million
 b. $29 million   d. $17 million

Q7-56. Hydra, Inc., was reviewing its assets for impairment at the end of the current year. Information about one of its assets is as follows:

Net book value..........................	$1,000,000
Estimated future cash flows......	$ 850,000
Fair (market) value..................	$ 820,000

Hydra should report an impairment loss for the current year of
- **a.** $0.
- **b.** $150,000.
- **c.** $180,000.
- **d.** $30,000.

Q7-57. TextDat, Inc., reported sales revenue of $600,000, net income of $45,000, and average total assets of $500,000. TextDat's return on assets is
- **a.** 9.0%.
- **b.** 7.5%.
- **c.** 1.1%.
- **d.** 83.3%.

Problems

All of the A and B problems can be found within MyAccountingLab, an online home-work and practice environment. Your instructor may ask you to complete these problems using **MyAccountingLab**.

MyAccountingLab

Group A

P7-58A. *(Learning Objectives 1, 2, 3: Measure and account for plant assets; distinguish a capital expenditure from an expense; measure and record depreciation)* Assume Perez Sales, Inc., opened an office in Jacksonville, Florida. Further assume that Perez Sales incurred the following costs in acquiring land, making land improvements, and constructing and furnishing the new sales building:

a. Purchase price of land, including an old building that will be used for a garage (land market value is $320,000; building market value is $80,000)	$365,000
b. Landscaping (additional dirt and earth moving)	8,300
c. Fence around the land	35,400
d. Attorney fee for title search on the land	300
e. Delinquent real estate taxes on the land to be paid by Perez Sales	5,900
f. Company signs at entrance to the property	1,500
g. Building permit for the sales building	750
h. Architect fee for the design of the sales building	19,200
i. Masonry, carpentry, and roofing of the sales building	516,000
j. Renovation of the garage building	41,000
k. Interest cost on construction loan for sales building	9,600
l. Landscaping (trees and shrubs)	6,900
m. Parking lot and concrete walks on the property	52,500
n. Lights for the parking lot and walkways	7,800
o. Salary of construction supervisor (85% to sales building; 10% to land improvements; and 5% to garage building renovations)	45,000
p. Office furniture for the sales building	83,800
q. Transportation and installation of furniture	1,200

Assume Perez Sales depreciates buildings over 50 years, land improvements over 20 years, and furniture over 12 years, all on a straight-line basis with zero residual value.

Requirements

1. Show how to account for each of Perez Sales' costs by listing the cost under the correct account. Determine the total cost of each asset.
2. All construction was complete and the assets were placed in service on April 2. Record depreciation for the year ended December 31. Round to the nearest dollar.
3. How will what you learned in this problem help you manage a business?

P7-59A. *(Learning Objectives 1, 3: Measure and account for the cost of plant assets; measure and record depreciation under DDB)* Jersey Lake Resort reported the following on its balance sheet at December 31, 2014:

Property, plant, and equipment, at cost:	
Land...	$ 151,000
Buildings	739,000
Less: Accumulated depreciation	(348,000)
Equipment...	412,000
Less: Accumulated depreciation	(263,000)

In early July 2015, the resort expanded operations and purchased additional equipment for cash at a cost of $145,000. The company depreciates buildings by the straight-line method over 20 years with residual value of $87,000. Due to obsolescence, the equipment has a useful life of only 10 years and is being depreciated by the double-declining-balance method with zero residual value.

Requirements

1. Journalize Jersey Lake Resort's plant asset purchase and depreciation transactions for 2015.
2. Report plant assets on the December 31, 2015, balance sheet.

P7-60A. *(Learning Objectives 1, 3, 4: Measure and account for the cost of plant assets and depreciation; analyze and record a plant asset disposal)* Galaxy, Inc., has the following plant asset accounts: Land, Buildings, and Equipment, with a separate accumulated depreciation account for each of these except Land. Galaxy completed the following transactions:

Jan 3	Traded in equipment with accumulated depreciation of $68,000 (cost of $131,000) for similar new equipment with a cash cost of $175,000. Received a trade-in allowance of $71,000 on the old equipment and paid $104,000 in cash.
Jun 30	Sold a building that had a cost of $640,000 and had accumulated depreciation of $100,000 through December 31 of the preceding year. Depreciation is computed on a straight-line basis. The building has a 40-year useful life and a residual value of $240,000. Galaxy received $115,000 cash and a $420,000 note receivable.
Oct 31	Purchased land and a building for a single price of $320,000 cash. An independent appraisal valued the land at $70,200 and the building at $280,800.
Dec 31	Recorded depreciation as follows:
	Equipment has an expected useful life of 4 years and an estimated residual value of 12% of cost. Depreciation is computed on the double-declining-balance method.
	Depreciation on buildings is computed by the straight-line method. The new building carries a 40-year useful life and a residual value equal to 10% of its cost.

Requirement

1. Record the transactions in Galaxy, Inc.'s journal.

P7-61A. *(Learning Objectives 1, 3, 8: Measure and account for the cost of a plant asset; measure depreciation by three methods; identify the cash flow advantage of accelerated depreciation for tax purposes)* On January 4, 2014, Glennside Co. paid $235,000 for a computer system. In addition to the basic purchase price, the company paid a setup fee of $1,100, $6,200 sales tax, and $37,200 for a special platform on which to place the computer. Glennside management estimates that the computer will remain in service for five years and have a residual value of $24,500. The computer will process 35,000 documents the first year, with annual processing decreasing by 2,500 documents during each of the next four years (that is, 32,500 documents in

2015; 30,000 documents in 2016; and so on). In trying to decide which depreciation method to use, the company president has requested a depreciation schedule for each of the three depreciation methods (straight-line, units-of-production, and double-declining-balance).

Requirements

1. For each of the generally accepted depreciation methods, prepare a depreciation schedule showing asset cost, depreciation expense, accumulated depreciation, and asset book value.
2. Glennside reports to stockholders and creditors in the financial statements using the depreciation method that maximizes reported income in the early years of asset use. For income tax purposes, the company uses the depreciation method that minimizes income tax payments in those early years. Consider the first year Glennside Co. uses the computer. Identify the depreciation methods that meet Glennside's objectives, assuming the income tax authorities permit the use of any of the methods.
3. Cash provided by operations before income tax is $154,000 for the computer's first year. The income tax rate is 40%. For the two depreciation methods identified in requirement 2, compare the net income and cash provided by operations (cash flow). Show which method gives the net income advantage and which method gives the cash flow advantage.

P7-62A. *(Learning Objectives 1, 3, 4, 6, 8: Analyze plant asset transactions from a company's financial statements)* Khonner Stores, Inc., sells electronics and appliances. The excerpts that follow are adapted from Khonner Stores' financial statements for 2014 and 2013.

| | February 28, | |
Balance Sheet (dollars in millions)	2014	2013
Assets		
Total current assets	$7,987	$6,901
Property, plant, and equipment	5,631	4,997
Less: Accumulated depreciation	2,124	1,729
Goodwill	655	612

| | Year Ended February 28, | |
Statement of Cash Flows (dollars in millions)	2014	2013
Operating activities:		
Net income	$1,167	$1,586
Noncash items affecting net income:		
Depreciation	560	558
Gain on sale of property, plant and equipment	(11)	0
Investing activities:		
Additions to property, plant, and equipment	(913)	(819)
Sale of property, plant and equipment	125	0

Requirements

1. How much was Khonner Stores' cost of plant assets at February 28, 2014? How much was the book value of plant assets? Show computations.
2. The financial statements give three evidences that Khonner Stores purchased plant assets and goodwill during fiscal year 2014. What are they?

3. Prepare T-accounts for Property, Plant, and Equipment; Accumulated Depreciation; and Goodwill. Then fill in the T-accounts with information from the comparative balance sheets and cash flow statements. Label each increase or decrease and give its dollar amount.

4. Prepare the journal entry for the sale of property and equipment in 2014.

P7-63A. *(Learning Objective 5: Account for natural resources)* Mid Pacific Energy Company's balance sheet includes the asset Iron Ore. Mid Pacific Energy paid $2.55 million cash for the right to work a mine that contained an estimated 195,000 tons of ore. The company paid $63,000 to remove unwanted buildings from the land and $71,000 to prepare the surface for mining. Mid Pacific Energy also signed a $34,100 note payable to a landscaping company to return the land surface to its original condition after the lease ends. During the first year, Mid Pacific Energy removed 44,500 tons of ore, of which it sold 37,000 tons on account for $33 per ton. Operating expenses for the first year totaled $327,000, all paid in cash. In addition, the company accrued income tax at the tax rate of 28%.

Requirements

1. Record all of Mid Pacific Energy's transactions for the year. Round depletion per unit to the closest cent.
2. Prepare the company's single-step income statement for its iron ore operations for the first year. Evaluate the profitability of the company's operations.
3. What balances should appear from these transactions on Mid Pacific Energy's balance sheet at the end of its first year of operations?

P7-64A. *(Learning Objectives 1, 4, 8: Analyze the effect of a plant asset addition and disposal; report plant asset transactions on the financial statements)* At the end of 2013, Electric Power Associates (EPA) had total assets of $17.6 billion and total liabilities of $9 billion. Included among the assets were property, plant, and equipment with a cost of $4.1 billion and accumulated depreciation of $2.9 billion.

EPA completed the following selected transactions during 2014: The company earned total revenues of $26.6 billion and incurred total expenses of $21.7 billion, which included depreciation of $1.5 billion. During the year, EPA paid $1.7 billion for new property, plant, and equipment and sold old plant assets for $0.9 billion. The cost of the assets sold was $1.8 billion, and their accumulated depreciation was $1.2 billion.

Requirements

1. Explain how to determine whether EPA had a gain or loss on the sale of old plant assets during the year. What was the amount of the gain or loss, if any?
2. Show how EPA would report property, plant, and equipment on the balance sheet at December 31, 2014, after all the year's activity. What was the book value of property, plant, and equipment?
3. Show how EPA would report its operating activities and investing activities on its statement of cash flows for 2014. Ignore gains and losses.

P7-65A. *(Learning Objective 7: Calculate return on assets)* Target Corporation operates general merchandise and food discount stores in the United States. The company reported the following information for the three years ending February 2, 2013:

A1				
	A	B	C	D
1	**Target Corporation** **Consolidated Statements of Operations (Adapted)**			
2			For the year ended	
3	**In millions of USD**	**Feb. 2, 2013**	**Jan. 28, 2012**	**Jan. 29, 2011**
4	Total net revenue	$ 73,301	$ 69,865	$ 67,390
5	Cost of sales	50,568	47,860	45,725
6	Selling, general and administrative expenses	17,362	16,683	16,413
7	Net income from operations	5,371	5,322	5,252
8	Other revenue (expense)	(762)	(866)	(757)
9	Net income before income taxes	4,609	4,456	4,495
10	Income tax expense	(1,610)	(1,527)	(1,575)
11	Net income	$ 2,999	$ 2,929	$ 2,920
12				

A1				
	A	B	C	D
1	**Target Corporation** **Partial Balance Sheet (Condensed)**			
2	**In millions of USD**	**Feb. 2, 2013**	**Jan. 28, 2012**	**Jan. 29, 2011**
3	Total current assets	$ 16,388	$ 16,449	$ 17,213
4	Property, plant and equipment, net	30,653	29,149	25,493
5	Other assets	1,122	1,032	999
6	Total assets	$ 48,163	$ 46,630	$ 43,705
7				

Requirements

1. Compute net profit margin ratio for Target for the years ended February 2, 2013, and January 28, 2012.
2. Compute asset turnover for Target for the years ended February 2, 2013, and January 28, 2012.
3. Compute return on assets for Target for the years ended February 2, 2013, and January 28, 2012.
4. What factors contributed to the change in return on assets during the year?

P7-66A. *(Learning Objectives 4, 8: Analyze the effect of a plant asset disposal and the cash flow impact of long-lived asset transactions)* Wilson Corporation reported the following related to property and equipment (all in millions):

From the balance sheets:

	12/31/14	12/31/13
Property and equipment	$24,073	$22,011
Accumulated depreciation	(13,306)	(12,087)

From the investing activities section of the 2014 cash flow statement:

Cash used to purchase property and equipment	($2,510)
Proceeds from sale of property and equipment	48

From the 2014 income statement:

Depreciation expense	$1,546
Gain or loss on the sale of equipment	??

Requirements

1. Draw T-accounts for Property and Equipment and Accumulated Depreciation. Enter information as presented and solve for the unknown in each account. (*Hint*: Recall the types of transactions that make each of the two accounts increase and decrease. You are solving for the cost of property and equipment sold and the accumulated depreciation on those assets.)
2. Based on your calculations in requirement 1, calculate the book value of assets sold during 2014. What is the difference between the sales price and the book value?
3. Prepare the journal entry for the sale of property and equipment during 2014. Describe the effect of this transaction on the financial statements. Compare the sales price and the book value in the journal entry, and compare this to the difference you calculated in requirement 2; describe briefly.
4. Prepare a T-account for Property and Equipment, Net. Repeat requirement 1.

Group B

P7-67B. *(Learning Objectives 1, 2, 3: Measure and account for plant assets; distinguish a capital expenditure from an expense; measure and record depreciation)* Assume Pancake House, Inc., opened an office in Cocoa Beach, Florida. Further assume that Pancake House incurred the following costs in acquiring land, making land improvements, and constructing and furnishing the new sales building:

a.	Purchase price of land, including an old building that will be used for a garage (land market value is $330,000; building market value is $70,000)	$375,000
b.	Landscaping (additional dirt and earth moving)	8,000
c.	Fence around the land	35,300
d.	Attorney fee for title search on the land	600
e.	Delinquent real estate taxes on the land to be paid by Pancake House	5,200
f.	Company signs at entrance to the property	1,700
g.	Building permit for the sales building	670
h.	Architect fee for the design of the sales building	19,400
i.	Masonry, carpentry, and roofing of the sales building	512,000
j.	Renovation of the garage building	41,500
k.	Interest cost on construction loan for sales building	9,700
l.	Landscaping (trees and shrubs)	6,100
m.	Parking lot and concrete walks on the property	52,300
n.	Lights for the parking lot and walkways	7,200
o.	Salary of construction supervisor (83% to sales building; 10% to land improvements; and 7% to garage building renovations)	42,000
p.	Office furniture for the sales building	83,000
q.	Transportation and installation of furniture	1,400

Assume Pancake House depreciates buildings over 40 years, land improvements over 25 years, and furniture over 10 years, all on a straight-line basis with zero residual value.

Requirements

1. Show how to account for each of Pancake House's costs by listing the cost under the correct account. Determine the total cost of each asset.
2. All construction was complete and the assets were placed in service on July 2. Record depreciation for the year ended December 31. Round to the nearest dollar.
3. How will what you learned in this problem help you manage a business?

P7-68B. *(Learning Objectives 1, 3: Measure and account for the cost of plant assets; measure and record depreciation under DDB)* Maddison Lake Resort reported the following on its balance sheet at December 31, 2014:

Property, plant, and equipment, at cost:	
Land..	$ 156,000
Buildings	741,000
Less: Accumulated depreciation	(344,000)
Equipment..	410,000
Less: Accumulated depreciation	(264,000)

In early July 2015, the resort expanded operations and purchased additional equipment for cash at a cost of $135,000. The company depreciates buildings by the straight-line method over 20 years with residual value of $85,000. Due to obsolescence, the equipment has a useful life of only 10 years and is being depreciated by the double-declining-balance method with zero residual value.

Requirements

1. Journalize Maddison Lake Resort's plant asset purchase and depreciation transactions for 2015.
2. Report plant assets on the December 31, 2015, balance sheet.

P7-69B. *(Learning Objectives 1, 3, 4: Measure and account for the cost of plant assets and depreciation; analyze and record a plant asset disposal)* Morey, Inc., has the following plant asset accounts: Land, Buildings, and Equipment, with a separate accumulated depreciation account for each of these except Land. Morey completed the following transactions:

Jan 4	Traded in equipment with accumulated depreciation of $64,000 (cost of $134,000) for similar new equipment with a cash cost of $175,000. Received a trade-in allowance of $72,000 on the old equipment and paid $103,000 in cash.
Jun 29	Sold a building that had a cost of $650,000 and had accumulated depreciation of $140,000 through December 31 of the preceding year. Depreciation is computed on a straight-line basis. The building has a 40-year useful life and a residual value of $220,000. Morey received $125,000 cash and a $379,625 note receivable.
Oct 30	Purchased land and a building for a single price of $360,000 cash. An independent appraisal valued the land at $160,800 and the building at $241,200.

Dec 31	Recorded depreciation as follows:
	    Equipment has an expected useful life of 8 years and an estimated residual value of 3% of cost. Depreciation is computed on the double-declining-balance method.
	    Depreciation on buildings is computed by the straight-line method. The new building carries a 40-year useful life and a residual value equal to 30% of its cost.

Requirement

1. Record the transactions in Morey, Inc.'s journal.

P7-70B. *(Learning Objectives 1, 3, 8: Measure and account for the cost of a plant asset; measure depreciation by three methods; identify the cash flow advantage of accelerated depreciation for tax purposes)* On January 7, 2014, Plummer Co. paid $240,000 for a computer system. In addition to the basic purchase price, the company paid a setup fee of $1,400, $6,500 sales tax, and $29,100 for a special platform on which to place the computer. Plummer's management estimates that the computer will remain in service for five years and have a residual value of $25,000. The computer will process 50,000 documents the first year, with annual processing decreasing by 2,500 documents during each of the next four years (that is, 47,500 documents in year 2015; 45,000 documents in year 2016; and so on). In trying to decide which depreciation method to use, the company president has requested a depreciation schedule for each of the three depreciation methods (straight-line, units-of-production, and double-declining-balance).

Requirements

1. For each of the generally accepted depreciation methods, prepare a depreciation schedule showing asset cost, depreciation expense, accumulated depreciation, and asset book value.
2. Plummer reports to stockholders and creditors in the financial statements using the depreciation method that maximizes reported income in the early years of asset use. For income tax purposes, the company uses the depreciation method that minimizes income tax payments in those early years. Consider the first year Plummer Co. uses the computer. Identify the depreciation methods that meet Plummer's objectives, assuming the income tax authorities permit the use of any of the methods.
3. Cash provided by operations before income tax is $158,000 for the computer's first year. The income tax rate is 32%. For the two depreciation methods identified in requirement 2, compare the net income and cash provided by operations (cash flow). Show which method gives the net income advantage and which method gives the cash flow advantage.

P7-71B. *(Learning Objectives 1, 3, 4, 6, 8: Analyze plant asset transactions from a company's financial statements)* Jefferson Sales, Inc., sells electronics and appliances. The excerpts that follow are adapted from Jefferson Sales' financial statements for 2014 and 2013:

| | February 28, | |
Balance Sheet (dollars in millions)	2014	2013
Assets		
Total current assets	$7,988	$6,904
Property, plant, and equipment	5,638	4,992
Less: Accumulated depreciation	2,124	1,729
Goodwill..	657	610

| | Year Ended February 28, | |
Statement of Cash Flows (dollars in millions)	2014	2013
Operating activities:		
Net income	$1,650	$ 1,480
Noncash items affecting net income:		
Depreciation	561	559
Gain on sale of property, plant and equipment..........	(9)	0
Investing activities:		
Additions to property, plant, and equipment...............	(923)	(815)
Sale of property, plant and equipment.........................	120	0

Requirements

1. How much was Jefferson Sales' cost of plant assets at February 28, 2014? How much was the book value of plant assets? Show computations.
2. The financial statements give two evidences that Jefferson Sales purchased plant assets and goodwill during fiscal year 2014. What are they?
3. Prepare T-accounts for Property, Plant, and Equipment; Accumulated Depreciation; and Goodwill. Then fill in the T-accounts with information from the comparative balance sheets and cash flow statements. Label each increase or decrease and give its dollar amount.
4. Prepare the journal entry for the sale of property and equipment in 2014.

P7-72B. *(Learning Objective 5: Account for natural resources)* Central Atlantic Energy Company's balance sheet includes the asset Iron Ore. Central Atlantic Energy paid $2.75 million cash for the right to work a mine that contained an estimated 215,000 tons of ore. The company paid $67,000 to remove unwanted buildings from the land and $78,500 to prepare the surface for mining. Central Atlantic Energy also signed a $38,550 note payable to a landscaping company to return the land surface to its original condition after the lease ends. During the first year, Central Atlantic Energy removed 42,500 tons of ore, of which it sold 38,000 tons on account for $37 per ton. Operating expenses for the first year totaled $412,000, all paid in cash. In addition, the company accrued income tax at the tax rate of 35%.

Requirements

1. Record all of Central Atlantic Energy's transactions for the year. Round depletion per unit to the closest cent.
2. Prepare the company's single-step income statement for its iron ore operations for the first year. Evaluate the profitability of the company's operations.
3. What balances should appear from these transactions on Central Atlantic Energy's balance sheet at the end of its first year of operations?

P7-73B. *(Learning Objectives 1, 4, 8: Analyze the effect of a plant asset addition and disposal; report plant asset transactions on the financial statements)* At the end of 2013, Creative Legal Associates (CLA) had total assets of $17 billion and total liabilities of $9.2 billion. Included among the assets were property, plant, and equipment with a cost of $4.2 billion and accumulated depreciation of $2.7 billion.

CLA completed the following selected transactions during 2014: The company earned total revenues of $26.2 billion and incurred total expenses of $22 billion, which included depreciation of $1.6 billion. During the year, CLA paid $1.8 billion for new property, plant, and equipment and sold old plant assets for $0.7 billion. The cost of the assets sold was $1.1 billion, and their accumulated depreciation was $0.8 billion.

Requirements

1. Explain how to determine whether CLA had a gain or loss on the sale of old plant assets during the year. What was the amount of the gain or loss, if any?
2. Show how CLA would report property, plant, and equipment on the balance sheet at December 31, 2014, after all the year's activity. What was the book value of property, plant, and equipment?
3. Show how CLA would report its operating activities and investing activities on its statement of cash flows for 2014. Ignore gains and losses.

P7-74B. *(Learning Objective 7: Calculate return on assets)* Kohl's Corporation operates family-oriented department stores that sell moderately priced apparel and housewares. The company reported the following information (adapted) for the three years ending February 3, 2013:

	A	B	C	D
	Kohl's Corporation			
1	Consolidated Statements of Operations (Adapted)			
2	In millions of USD	For the year ended		
3		Feb. 2, 2013	Jan. 28, 2012	Jan. 29, 2011
4	Total net revenue	$ 19,279	$ 18,804	$ 18,391
5	Cost of sales	12,289	11,625	11,359
6	Selling, general and administrative expenses	5,100	5,021	5,118
7	Net income from operations	1,890	2,158	1,914
8	Other revenue (expense)	(329)	(299)	(132)
9	Net income before income taxes	1,561	1,859	1,782
10	Income tax expense	(575)	(692)	(668)
11	Net income	$ 986	$ 1,167	$ 1,114
12				

	A	B	C	D
	Kohl's Corporation			
1	Partial Balance Sheet (Condensed)			
2	In millions of USD	Feb. 2, 2013	Jan. 28, 2012	Jan. 29, 2011
3	Total current assets	$ 4,719	$ 4,829	$ 5,645
4	Property, plant and equipment, net	8,872	8,905	7,256
5	Other assets	314	414	663
6	Total assets	$ 13,905	$ 14,148	$ 13,564
7				

Requirements

1. Compute net profit margin ratio for Kohl's Corporation for the years ended February 2, 2013, and January 28, 2012.
2. Compute asset turnover for Kohl's Corporation for the years ended February 2, 2013, and January 28, 2012.
3. Compute return on assets for Kohl's Corporation for the years ended February 2, 2013, and January 28, 2012.
4. What factors contributed to the change in return on assets during the year?

P7-75B. *(Learning Objectives 4, 8: Analyze the effect of a plant asset disposal and the cash flow impact of long-lived asset transactions)* Sophie Corporation reported the following related to property and equipment (all in millions):

From the balance sheets:

	12/31/14	12/31/13
Property and equipment	$34,075	$32,009
Accumulated depreciation	(23,312)	(22,065)

From the investing activities section of the 2014 cash flow statement:

Cash used to purchase property and equipment	($3,518)
Proceeds from sale of property and equipment	71

From the 2014 income statement:

Depreciation expense	$2,149
Gain or loss on the sale of equipment	??

Requirements

1. Draw T-accounts for Property and Equipment and Accumulated Depreciation. Enter information as presented and solve for the unknown in each account. (*Hint*: Recall the types of transactions that make each of the two accounts increase and decrease. You are solving for the cost of Property and Equipment sold and the Accumulated Depreciation on those assets.)
2. Based on your calculations in requirement 1, calculate the book value of assets sold during 2014. What is the difference between the sales price and the book value?
3. Prepare the journal entry for the sale of property and equipment during 2014. Describe the effect of this transaction on the financial statements. Compare the sales price and the book value in the journal entry, and compare this to the difference you calculated in requirement 2; describe briefly.
4. Prepare a T-account for Property and Equipment, Net. Repeat requirement 1.

Challenge Exercises and Problem

E7-76. *(Learning Objective 3: Determine the effect on net income of a change in the depreciation method)* Kerusi, Inc., has a popular line of boogie boards. Kerusi reported net income of $64 million for 2014. Depreciation expense for the year totaled $30 million. Kerusi, Inc., depreciates plant assets over eight years using the straight-line method and no residual value.

Kerusi, Inc., paid $240 million for plant assets at the beginning of 2014. At the start of 2015, Kerusi changed its method of accounting for depreciation to double-declining-balance (DDB). The year 2015 is expected to be the same as 2014 except for the change in depreciation method. If Kerusi had been using DDB depreciation all along, how much net income can Kerusi, Inc., expect to earn during 2015? Ignore income tax.

E7-77. *(Learning Objective 2: Distinguish a capital expenditure from an expense, and measure the financial statement effects of an expensing error)* The European Press (TEP) is a major telecommunication conglomerate. Assume that early in year 1, TEP purchased equipment at a cost of 20 million euros (€20 million). Management expects the equipment to remain in service for four years and estimated residual value to be negligible. TEP uses the straight-line depreciation method. *Through an accounting error, TEP expensed the entire cost of the equipment at the time of purchase.* Because TEP is operated as a partnership, it pays no income tax.

Requirements

Prepare a schedule to show the overstatement or understatement in the following items at the end of each year over the four-year life of the equipment:
1. Total current assets
2. Equipment, net
3. Net income

P7-78. *(Learning Objective 4: Determine plant and equipment transactions for an actual company)* FedEx Corporation provides a broad portfolio of transportation, e-commerce, and business services. FedEx reported the following information in its 2012 annual report:

A1				
	A		B	C
1	**FedEx Corporation** **Partial Consolidated Balance Sheets**			
2			**May 31**	
3	(in millions)		2012	2011
4	**PROPERTY AND EQUIPMENT, AT COST**			
5	Aircraft and related equipment		$ 14,360	$ 13,146
6	Package handling and ground support equipment		5,912	5,591
7	Computer and electronic equipment		4,646	4,408
8	Vehicles		3,654	3,294
9	Facilities and other		7,592	7,247
10	Gross property and equipment		36,164	33,686
11	Less accumulated depreciation and amortization		(18,916)	(18,143)
12	Net property and equipment		$ 17,248	$ 15,543
13				

A1				
	A		B	C
1	**FedEx Corporation** **Partial Statements of Cash Flows**			
2	(In millions)		**May 31**	
3			2012	2011
4	**Investing Activities**			
5	Capital expenditures		$ (4,007)	$ (3,434)
6	Business acquisitions		(116)	(96)
7	Proceeds from asset dispositions and other		74	111
8	Cash used in investing activities		$ (4,049)	$ (3,419)
9				

NOTE 1: DESCRIPTION OF BUSINESS AND SUMMARY OF SIGNIFICANT ACCOUNTING POLICIES

Property and equipment (excerpted):

For financial reporting purposes, we record depreciation and amortization of property and equipment on a straight-line basis over the asset's service life or related lease term, if shorter. For income tax purposes, depreciation is computed using accelerated methods when applicable. Depreciation expense, excluding gains and losses on sales of property and equipment used in operations, was $2.1 billion in 2012 and $1.9 billion in 2011.

In May 2012, we made the decision to retire from service 18 Airbus A310-200 aircraft and 26 related engines, as well as six Boeing MD10-10 aircraft and 17 related engines. As a consequence of this decision, a noncash impairment charge of $134 million was recorded in the fourth quarter.

Requirements

1. Using the information provided from the balance sheet and statement of cash flows for FedEx, reconstruct the Property and Equipment and Accumulated Depreciation accounts. You will not have to account for individual asset categories, but only for the gross cost of property and equipment and accumulated depreciation. You will have to solve for the original gross cost and accumulated depreciation of the plant and equipment sold. Ignore business acquisitions for purposes of this part.

2. Prepare the journal entries to record total capital expenditures, total depreciation expense, asset impairments, and total sales of property, plant, and equipment. You will have to compute an implied gain or loss on equipment sold based on the information given.

APPLY YOUR KNOWLEDGE

Decision Cases

Case 1. *(Learning Objective 3: Measure profitability based on different inventory and depreciation methods)* Suppose you are considering investing in two businesses, La Petite France Bakery and Burgers Ahoy. The two companies are virtually identical, and both began operations at the beginning of the current year. During the year, each company purchased inventory:

Jan	4	10,000 units at $4 =	40,000
Apr	6	5,000 units at 5 =	25,000
Aug	9	7,000 units at 6 =	42,000
Nov	27	10,000 units at 7 =	70,000
Totals		32,000	$177,000

During the first year, both companies sold 25,000 units of inventory.

In early January, both companies purchased equipment costing $150,000 that had a 10-year estimated useful life and a $20,000 residual value. La Petite France uses the inventory and depreciation methods that maximize reported income. By contrast, Burgers Ahoy uses the inventory and depreciation methods that minimize income tax payments. Assume that both companies' trial balances at December 31 included the following:

Sales revenue	$350,000
Operating expenses	50,000

The income tax rate is 40%.

Requirements

1. Prepare both companies' multiple-step income statements.
2. Write an investment newsletter to address the following questions: Which company appears to be more profitable? Which company has more cash to invest in promising projects? If prices continue rising over the long term, which company would you prefer to invest in? Why? (Challenge)

Case 2. *(Learning Objectives 2, 5: Distinguish between capital expenditures and expense; account for plant assets and intangible assets)* The following questions are unrelated except that they all apply to plant assets and intangible assets:
1. The manager of Carpet World regularly debits the cost of repairs and maintenance of plant assets to Plant and Equipment. Why would she do that, since she knows she is violating GAAP?
2. The manager of Horizon Software regularly buys plant assets and debits the cost to Repairs and Maintenance Expense. Why would he do that, since he knows this action violates GAAP?
3. It has been suggested that because many intangible assets have no value except to the company that owns them, they should be valued at $1.00 or zero on the balance sheet. Many accountants disagree with this view. Which view do you support? Why?

Ethical Issue

United Jersey Bank of Princeton purchased land and a building for the lump sum of $6 million. To get the maximum tax deduction, the bank's managers allocated 80% of the purchase price to the building and only 20% to the land. A more realistic allocation would have been 60% to the building and 40% to the land.

Requirements

1. What is the ethical issue in this situation?
2. Who are the stakeholders? What are the possible consequences to each?
3. Analyze the alternatives from the following standpoints: (a) economic, (b) legal, and (c) ethical.
4. What would you do? How would you justify your decision?

Focus on Financials | Amazon.com, Inc.

(Learning Objectives 2, 3, 6: Analyze activity in plant assets) Refer to **Amazon.com, Inc.'s** Consolidated Financial Statements in Appendix A at the end of the book, and answer the following questions:

1. Refer to Note 1 and Note 3 of the Notes to Consolidated Financial Statements. What kinds of assets are included in fixed assets of Amazon.com, Inc?
2. Which depreciation method does Amazon.com, Inc., use for reporting to stockholders and creditors in the financial statements? What type of depreciation method does the company probably use for income tax purposes? Why is this method preferable for tax purposes?
3. Depreciation expense is embedded in operating expense accounts listed on the income statement, so you can't break out the actual figure for depreciation in that way. Refer to Note 3—Fixed Assets. How much was Amazon.com, Inc.'s depreciation expense on fixed assets during 2012? What did this figure include? How much was Amazon.com, Inc.'s accumulated depreciation on fixed assets at the end of 2012? Explain why accumulated depreciation exceeds depreciation expense for the current year.
4. How much did Amazon.com, Inc., spend on fixed assets, including internal-use software and website development, during 2012? In 2011? Evaluate the trend in these capital expenditures as to whether it conveys good news or bad news for Amazon.com, Inc. Explain.
5. Refer to Notes 1 and 4 of the Notes to Consolidated Financial Statements. What are Amazon.com, Inc.'s intangible assets? How does the company account for each of these intangibles over its lifetime?

Focus on Analysis | Yum! Brands, Inc.

(Learning Objectives 1, 5, 6, 7, 8: Measure the cost of plant assets,; explain plant asset activity; apply GAAP for intangible assets, explain an asset impairment, analyze rate of return on assets; analyze the cash flow impact of long-lived asset transactions) Refer to the **Yum! Brands, Inc.** Consolidated Financial Statements in Appendix B at the end of this book. This case leads you through an analysis of the activity for some of Yum! Brands, Inc.'s long-term assets, as well as the calculation of its rate of return on total assets.

1. On the statement of cash flows, how much did Yum! Brands, Inc., pay for capital expenditures during fiscal 2012? In what section of the cash flows statement do you find this amount?
2. Briefly describe Yum! Brands, Inc.'s policies for research and development costs, as well as for impairment or disposal of property, plant and equipment. You can find discussions of these matters in Note 2 (Summary of Significant Accounting Policies).
3. Which depreciation method does Yum! Brands, Inc., use? Over what range of useful lives does Yum! Brands, Inc., depreciate various types of fixed assets? You can find discussions of this in Note 2 (Summary of Significant Accounting Policies).
4. Review the information in Note 8 (Supplemental balance sheet disclosures). List the categories of Yum! Brands, Inc.'s property, plant and equipment as of December 29, 2012 and

December 31, 2011. How much depreciation expense is included in the calculation of net income for these two fiscal years? Does it appear that Yum! Brands, Inc.'s property, plant and equipment was proportionately newer or older at the end of fiscal 2012 (versus 2011)? Explain your answer. (Challenge)

5. Examine Notes 2 and 9. Briefly describe Yum! Brands, Inc.'s accounting for goodwill and other intangible assets. From what countries of the world does Yum! Brands derive its goodwill? Briefly analyze the activity in the goodwill account for the fiscal year ended December 29, 2012. What other types of intangible assets did Yum! Brands, Inc., own as of December 29, 2012?

6. Using DuPont Analysis, calculate Yum! Brands, Inc.'s rate of return on total assets for fiscal 2012 and fiscal 2011. Total assets at December 25, 2010 (the end of its 2010 fiscal year), were $8,316 million. Did the company perform better or worse in 2012 than in 2011?

Group Project

Visit a local business.

Requirements

1. List all its plant assets.
2. If possible, interview the manager. Gain as much information as you can about the business's plant assets. For example, try to determine the assets' costs, the depreciation method the company is using, and the estimated useful life of each asset category. If an interview is impossible, then develop your own estimates of the assets' costs, useful lives, and book values, assuming an appropriate depreciation method.
3. Determine whether the business has any intangible assets. If so, list them and gain as much information as possible about their nature, cost, and estimated useful lives.
4. Write a detailed report of your findings and be prepared to present your results to the class.

> **For online homework, exercises, and problems that provide you with immediate feedback, please visit www.myaccountinglab.com.**

MyAccountingLab

Quick Check Answers

1. a {[$1,144/($1,144 + $660 + $396)] × $1,800 = $936}

2. d

3. b ($35,000 − $8,000)/5 × 3/12 = $1,350

4. c [($35,000 − $8,000)/5 × 2 = $10,800; $35,000 − $10,800 = $24,200]

5. b [$35,000 × 0.4 = $14,000; ($35,000 − $14,000) × 0.4 = $8,400]

6. a [($35,000 − $8,000)/5 × 4 = $21,600; $35,000 − $21,600 = $13,400; $22,400 − $13,400 = gain of $9,000]

7. d [$23,000 × 2/4 = $11,500; ($23,000 − $11,500) × 2/4 = $5,750; $11,500 + $5,750 = $17,250]

8. d

9. c

10. a

11. d [$210,000 × (2,000/30,000) = $14,000]

12. e

13. b

14. c

8

Long-Term Investments & the Time Value of Money

> **SPOTLIGHT:** Intel Holds Several Different Types of Investments

Is it too early for you to start thinking about retirement? If you're smart, you'll start saving for retirement with your very first job out of college. You may use mutual funds, a savings plan at work, or make some investments on your own. The reasons people purchase long-term investments are for current income (interest and dividends) and appreciation of the investment's value (stocks, bonds, and real estate, for example). Some very wealthy individuals invest in a wide variety of traditional and nontraditional investments in order to obtain significant influence over, or even to control, corporate entities and to maximize their wealth.

Businesses such as **Intel, Apple, General Electric**, and **Coca-Cola** invest for the same reasons. In this chapter you'll learn how to account for long-term investments of several types. We use Intel Corporation as our example company because Intel has so many interesting in-

Robert Clare/Photographer's Choice/
Getty Images

vestments. You'll also learn about the time value of money, which is an essential factor in valuing some types of long-term investments as well as long-term liabilities (covered in Chapter 9).

What comes to mind when you think of Intel? Computer processors and microchips? Yes, but interestingly, 17.3% [($3,999 million + $5,685 million + $4,424 million + $493 million)/$84,351 million] of Intel's assets are tied up in investments in other companies. The assets section of Intel's 2012 balance sheet reports these investments on lines 5, 6, 12, and 13. Cash and cash equivalents ($8,478 million), which also includes some investments, comprises another 10% of total assets. ●

	A	B	C
	A1		
1	**Intel Corporation** **Consolidated Partial Balance Sheet (Partial, Adapted)**		
2	In Millions	Dec. 29, 2012	Dec. 31, 2011
3	Current assets:		
4	Cash and cash equivalents	$ 8,478	$ 5,065
5	Short-term investments	3,999	5,181
6	Trading assets	5,685	4,591
7	Accounts receivable, net	3,833	3,650
8	Inventories	4,734	4,096
9	Other current assets	4,629	3,289
10	Total current assets	31,358	25,872
11	Property, plant, and equipment, net	27,983	23,627
12	Marketable equity securities	4,424	562
13	Other long-term investments	493	889
14	Goodwill	9,710	9,254
15	Identified intangible assets, net	6,235	6,267
16	Other long-term assets	4,148	4,648
17	Total assets	$ 84,351	$ 71,119
18			

Throughout this course, you've become increasingly familiar with the financial statements of companies such as **Whole Foods Market, FedEx,** and **Starbucks**. You've seen most of the items that appear in a set of financial statements. One of your learning goals should be to develop the ability to analyze whatever you encounter in real-company statements. This chapter will help you advance toward that goal.

The first half of this chapter shows how to account for long-term investments, including a brief overview of consolidated financial statements and the translation of financial statements of U.S.-owned foreign companies into U.S. dollars. The second half of the chapter covers the impact of the time value of money on the valuation of investments.

Learning Objectives

1. Analyze and report investments in held-to-maturity debt securities

2. Analyze and report investments in available-for-sale securities

3. Analyze and report investments in affiliated companies using the equity method

4. Analyze and report controlling interests in other corporations using consolidated financial statements

5. Report investing activities on the statement of cash flows

6. Explain the impact of the time value of money on certain types of investments

>> **Try It** *in*
Excel

You can access the most current annual report of Intel Corporation in Excel format at **www.sec.gov**. Using the "filings" link on the toolbar at the top of the home page, select "company filings search." This will take you to the "Edgar Company Filings" page. Type "Intel" in the company name box, and select "search." This will produce the "EDGAR Search Results" page showing the company name. Click on the "CIK" link beside the company name. This will pull up all of the reports the company has filed with the SEC. Under the "filing type" box, type "10-K" and click the search box. Form 10-K is the SEC form for the company's latest annual report. Find the year that you wish to view. Click on the "Interactive Data" box, which takes you to the "View Filing Data" page. Find and click on the "View Excel Document" link at the top of this page. You may choose to either open or download the Excel files containing the company's most recent financial statements. ∎

Investments come in all sizes and shapes—ranging from a few shares of stock to a controlling interest in multiple corporations, or interests in other types of investments such as corporate or municipal bonds or real estate. In later chapters, we will discuss stocks and bonds from the perspective of the company that issues the securities. In this chapter, we examine *long-term investments* from the perspective of the purchaser, or investor.

To consider investments, we need to define two key terms. The entity that owns stock or bonds of a corporation or other entity is the *investor*. The corporation or other entity that issues the stock is the *investee*. A corporation or other entity, such as a municipality, that issues bonds is a *debtor*. If you own some shares of Intel common stock, you are an investor and Intel is the investee. If you own Intel bonds, you are an investor/creditor and Intel is the investee/debtor.

Stock and Bond Prices

You can log on to the Internet to learn Intel's current stock price or the current trading value of its publicly held debt. Exhibit 8-1 presents recent information from a popular financial website about Intel's stock on a particular day. During the previous 52 weeks, Intel common stock had a high price of $29.27 per share and a low of $19.23 per share. The annual cash dividend for the most recent full year was $0.90 per share. During the previous day, 17.34 million shares of Intel common stock were traded. At day's end, the price of the stock closed at $21.26, up $0.11 from the closing price of the preceding day.

Exhibit 8-1 │ Stock Information for Intel Corporation

52-Week						
Hi	Lo	Stock (sym)	Div	Volume	Close	Net Change
$29.27	$19.23	INTC	$0.90	17,340,000	$21.26	+0.11

Reporting Investments on the Balance Sheet

An investment is an asset to the investor. The investment may be short-term or long-term. **Short-term investments** in marketable equity or debt securities are current assets. They can be classified as either *trading*, *held-to-maturity*, or *available-for-sale*, depending on management's intent and ability to hold rather than liquidate (sell) them. To be listed as short-term on the balance sheet,

- the investment must be *liquid* (readily convertible to cash), and
- the investor must intend either to convert the investment to cash within one year or to use it to pay a current liability.

We saw how to account for short-term investments in Chapter 5.

Investments that aren't short-term are listed as **long-term investments**, a category of non-current assets. Long-term investments include stocks and bonds that the investor expects to hold for longer than one year. Exhibit 8-2 shows where short-term and long-term investments appear on the balance sheet.

Exhibit 8-2 | Reporting Investments on the Balance Sheet

	A	B	C
1	**Current Assets:**		
2	Cash	$ X	
3	Short-term investments	X	
4	Accounts receivable	X	
5	Inventories	X	
6	Prepaid expenses	X	
7	Total current assets		X
8	Property, plant, and equipment		X
9	Long-term investments [or simply Investments]		X
10	Intangible assets		X
11	Other assets		X
12			

Assets are generally listed on the balance sheet in the order of liquidity. Long-term investments are less liquid than short term investments because the company neither intends nor has the ability to liquidate them within the current year or operating cycle. Intel reports short-term investments as current assets, immediately after cash and cash equivalents (p. 429, lines 5 and 6). The company reports long-term investments in both debt securities (bonds) and equity securities (stock) in the non-current asset section of the balance sheet (p. 429, lines 12 and 13). We now discuss the financial reporting for each of these types of long-term investments.

ANALYZE AND REPORT INVESTMENTS IN HELD-TO-MATURITY DEBT SECURITIES

The major investors in debt securities such as bonds are financial institutions—pension funds, mutual funds, and insurance companies such as Intel Capital. The relationship between the issuing corporation and the investor (bondholder) may be diagrammed as follows:

1 Analyze and report investments in held-to-maturity debt securities

Chapter 8	Chapter 9
Investor (Bondholder)	**Issuing Corporation**
Investment in bonds ⟷	Bonds payable
Interest revenue ⟷	Interest expense

If the investor company intends to hold debt securities longer than a year, but not until maturity, they are categorized as available-for-sale securities and accounted for under the fair value method, described in the next section. If the investing company intends to hold a debt security until maturity, it accounts for the security at amortized cost, as a **held-to-maturity investment**, as described in this section.

Bonds of publicly traded companies are traded on the open market, just as stocks are. Like other forms of debt, bonds pay investors interest, usually semiannually (twice a year). The (face) interest rate of a particular bond is quoted on the face of the instrument and determines the cash amount of semiannual interest the debtor company pays. Bonds are usually issued in $1,000 face (par) denominations, but they typically do not sell at par value. The price of a bond at a particular time is quoted as a percentage of its par value. Market prices of bonds fluctuate inversely with market interest rates. If market rates on competing instruments are higher than the face rate of interest on a particular bond, the bond sells at a discount (below 100% of par, or face value). For example, a quoted bond price of 96.5 means that the $1,000 bond is selling for 96.5% of par, or $965 (discounted from par value). If market rates are lower than the face rate of interest on the bond being considered, the bond sells at a premium (above 100% of par). For example, a quoted bond price of 102.5 means that the bond is selling for 102.5% of par, or $1,025 (a premium over par value).

Held-to-maturity investments are reported by the *amortized cost method*, which determines the carrying amount. Bond investments are initially recorded at cost (market price as a percentage × par value of bonds issued). At each semiannual interest payment date, the investor records interest revenue (1/2 the annual face interest rate × the face amount of the bond). In addition, whenever there is an issue premium or discount, it is amortized by adjusting the carrying amount of the bond upward or downward toward its par or face value, with an offsetting entry being made to interest revenue. Years later, at maturity, the carrying amount will have been adjusted from the original issue amount to its par or face value, and the investor will receive the face amount upon redemption of the bond.

As an example, assume that Intel Capital purchases $10,000 of 6% CBS bonds at a price of 95.2 on April 1, 2014. Intel Capital intends to hold the bonds until their maturity date, April 1, 2018. Interest dates are semiannual, on April 1 and October 1. Because these bonds mature on April 1, 2018, they will be outstanding for four years (48 months). In this case, Intel Capital pays a discount price for the bonds (95.2% of face value), because the market rates of interest for other similar instruments are higher than 6%.[1] The initial purchase price and carrying value of the investment is $9,520 (95.2% × $10,000). Intel Capital must amortize the discount of $480, and thus adjust the bonds' carrying amount from cost of $9,520 up to $10,000 over their 48-month term to maturity. Assume Intel Capital amortizes discount on the bonds by the straight-line method. Following are the entries for this bond investment on April 1 and October 1, 2014, the issue date and the first interest payment date:

	A1				
	A	**B**	**C**	**D**	
1	2014				
2	Apr 1	Held-to-Maturity Investment in Bonds ($10,000 × 0.952)	9,520		
3		Cash		9,520	
4		*To purchase bond investment.*			
5					
6	Oct 1	Cash ($10,000 × 0.06 × 6/12)	300		
7		Interest Revenue		300	
8		*To receive semiannual interest.*			
9					
10	Oct 1	Held-to-Maturity Investment in Bonds [($10,000 − $9,520)/48] × 6	60		
11		Interest Revenue		60	
12		*To amortize discount on bond investment.*			
13					

At December 31, 2014, Intel Capital's year-end adjustments are

	A1				
	A	**B**	**C**	**D**	
1	2014				
2	Dec 31	Interest Receivable ($10,000 × 0.06 × 3/12)	150		
3		Interest Revenue		150	
4		*To accrue interest revenue.*			
5					
6	Dec 31	Held-to-Maturity Investment in Bonds [($10,000 − $9,520)/48] × 3	30		
7		Interest Revenue		30	
8		*To amortize discount on bond investment.*			
9					

---

[1]We will discuss how the time value of money impacts the price of an investment in the second half of this chapter.

This amortization entry has two effects:

- It increases the Held-to-Maturity Investment in Bonds account on its march toward maturity value, which will be $10,000 on April 1, 2018.

- It records the interest revenue earned from the increase in the carrying amount of the investment.

The financial statements of Intel Capital at December 31, 2014, would report the following for this investment in bonds:

Balance sheet at December 31, 2014:
   Current assets:
      Interest receivable... $ 150
      Held-to-maturity investments in bonds ($9,520 + $60 + $30)...   9,610
      Property, plant, and equipment......................................   X,XXX

Income statement for the year ended December 31, 2014:
   Other revenues:
      Interest revenue ($300 + $60 + $150 + $30)........................ $ 540

By April 1, 2018, the maturity date of the bonds, the carrying value will have been adjusted to equal the face value of $10,000, and Intel Capital will redeem the bonds for this amount.

ANALYZE AND REPORT INVESTMENTS IN AVAILABLE-FOR-SALE SECURITIES

Long-term **available-for-sale securities** may be debt securities not held to maturity or equity (stock) securities other than trading securities. *Cost* is used only as the initial amount for recording the purchase of these investments. At the end of each reporting period, these securities are adjusted to their current **fair values** because the company expects to sell the investments at these values at some point in the future, although not within the next year.

2 **Analyze and report** investments in available-for-sale securities

Accounting Methods for Long-Term Stock Investments

The accounting rules for long-term investments in equity securities (stock) depend on the percentage of ownership by the investor, as shown in Exhibit 8-3:

Exhibit 8-3 | Accounting Methods for Long-Term Stock Investments by Percentage of Ownership

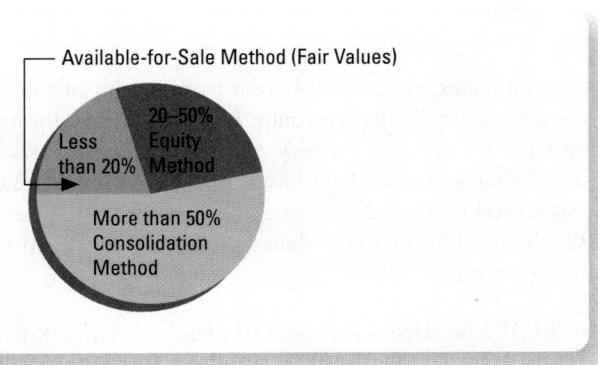

An investment less than, but up to, 20% is considered available-for-sale because the investor usually has little or no influence on the investee, in which case the strategy would be to hold the investment, making it available for sale in periods beyond the end of the fiscal year. Ownership

of 20% to 50%, provides the investor with the opportunity to significantly influence the investee's operating decisions and policies over the long run. An investment above 50% allows the investor a great deal of long-term influence—perhaps control—over the investee company. The methods of accounting for 20% or more equity interests are discussed in the two sections that follow. In this section, we discuss securities accounted for as available-for-sale investments. Let's begin with an example.

Suppose Intel purchases 1,000 shares of **Hewlett-Packard** common stock at the market price of $44 per share. Intel intends to hold this investment for longer than a year and therefore treats it as a long-term available-for-sale security (AFSS). Intel's entry to record the investment is

	A1			
	A	B	C	D
1	2014			
2	Oct 23	Investment in AFSS (1,000 × $44)	44,000	
3		Cash		44,000
4		*Purchased investment.*		
5				

$$\text{Assets} = \text{Liabilities} + \text{Stockholders' Equity}$$

$$\begin{array}{ccc} +\,44,000 \\ -\,44,000 \end{array} = \quad 0 \quad + \quad 0$$

Assume that Intel receives a $0.20 cash dividend per share on the Hewlett-Packard stock. Intel's entry to record receipt of the dividend is

	A1			
	A	B	C	D
1	2014			
2	Nov 14	Cash (1,000 × $0.20)	200	
3		Dividend Revenue		200
4		*Received cash dividend.*		
5				

$$\text{Assets} = \text{Liabilities} + \text{Stockholders' Equity} + \text{Revenues}$$

$$+200 \quad = \quad 0 \quad + \qquad\qquad\qquad\qquad +200$$

Receipt of a *stock* dividend is different from receipt of a cash dividend. For a stock dividend, the investor records no dividend revenue. Instead, the investor makes a memorandum entry in the accounting records to denote the new number of shares of stock held as an investment. Because the number of shares of stock held has increased, the investor's cost per share decreases. To illustrate, suppose Intel receives a 10% stock dividend from Hewlett-Packard Company. Intel would receive 100 shares (10% of 1,000 shares previously held) and make this memorandum entry in its accounting records:

> **MEMORANDUM—Receipt of stock dividend: Received 100 shares of Hewlett-Packard common stock in 10% stock dividend. New cost per share is $40.00 (cost of $44,000 ÷ 1,100 shares).**

In all future transactions affecting this investment, Intel's cost per share is now $40.

The Fair Value Adjustment

GAAP requires that companies adjust their portfolios of available-for-sale securities to *fair value* as of the balance sheet date. Fair value of an asset is the amount that would be received for the securities in an "orderly sale." GAAP recognizes three different approaches:

- Level 1: Quoted prices in active markets for identical assets
- Level 2: Estimates based on other observable inputs (e.g., prices for similar assets)
- Level 3: Estimates based on unobservable estimates (the company's own estimates based on certain assumptions)

Fair value should be determined using the most reliable method available. Level 1 is preferable, because it is considered easiest to verify. If no quoted prices in active markets are available, the investor moves to levels 2 and 3, in that order, to make the fair value adjustment. Companies must disclose the aggregate amounts of fair value for both trading and available-for-sale investments determined under each of these three levels in the financial statement footnotes. In our example of the investment in Hewlett-Packard stock, a level 1 fair value is available, because the stock has a quoted market price as of the end of the year. Returning to our original example before the stock dividend, assume that the quoted market price of the stock is $46.50, making fair value of the 1,000 shares of Hewlett-Packard common stock $46,500 on December 31, 2014. In this case, Intel makes the following entry to adjust the investment to fair value:

	A	B	C	D
	A1			
1	2014			
2	Dec 31	Allowance to Adjust Investment in AFSS to Market*		
3		($46,500 − $44,000)	2,500	
4		Unrealized Gain on Investment in AFSS		2,500
5		*Adjusted investment to fair value.*		
6				

*Alternatively, the entry may be made directly to the Investment in AFSS account.

The increase in the investment's fair value creates additional equity for the investor.

Assets	=	Liabilities	+	Stockholders' Equity
+ 2,500	=	0		+ 2,500

The Allowance to Adjust Investment in AFSS to Market is an optional companion account to the Investment in AFSS. Rather than use the allowance account, the company may make periodic adjustments directly to the Investment in AFSS account, as shown in Exhibit 5-2. In either case, the investment's cost ($44,000) plus the market adjustment ($2,500) equals the investment fair value carrying amount ($46,500), as follows:

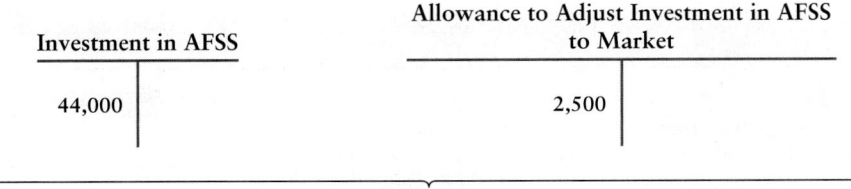

Investment in AFSS   44,000

Allowance to Adjust Investment in AFSS to Market   2,500

Investment carrying amount = Fair value of $46,500

Here the allowance has a debit balance because the fair value of the investment increased. If the investment's fair value declines, the allowance is credited. In that case, the carrying amount is its cost minus the allowance.

The other side of this adjustment entry is a credit to Unrealized Gain on Investment in AFSS. If the fair value of the investment declines, the company debits Unrealized Loss on Investment in AFSS. *Unrealized* gains and losses result from changes in fair value, not from sales of investments. For available-for-sale investments, the Unrealized Gain on Investment in AFSS account or the Unrealized Loss on Investment in AFSS account is reported as an element of *other comprehensive income*, which is a change in owners' equity that bypasses net income, reported in a separate statement of comprehensive income or in a separate section of the income statement below net income in a combined statement of income and comprehensive income.

The statement of comprehensive income is covered more thoroughly in Chapter 11. The following display shows one of the ways that Intel could report its regular net income plus comprehensive income from the unrealized gain in its combined Statement of Income and Other Comprehensive Income at the end of 2014 (all other figures are assumed for this illustration):

	A	B	C
	A1		
1	**Intel Corporation** **Consolidated Statement of Comprehensive Income** **For Year Ended December 29, 2014**		
2	(figures assumed, not actual)		
3	Revenues		$ 50,000
4	Expenses, including income tax		36,000
5	Net income		$ 14,000
6	Other comprehensive income:		
7	Unrealized gain on investment in AFSS	$ 2,500	
8	Less Income tax 40%	(1,000)	1,500
9	Comprehensive income		$ 15,500
10			

The preceding example assumes that the investor holds an investment in only one equity security: stock of another company. Usually, companies invest in a portfolio of securities (both equity and debt securities of more than one company). In this case, the periodic adjustment to fair value must be made for the portfolio as a whole. See the "Stop & Think" exercise at the end of this section (p. 437) for an example.

Selling an Available-for-Sale Investment

The sale of an available-for-sale investment usually results in a *realized* gain or loss. When an available-for-sale asset that has been revalued is subsequently sold, the amount of unrealized gain or loss existing on the asset at the date of sale is reversed, effectively returning the carrying value of the portion of the asset sold to its original cost. Realized gains and losses on the investment are then measured as the difference between the amount received from the sale and the cost of the investment.

Suppose Intel sells its entire investment in Hewlett-Packard stock for $43,000 during 2015. Intel would record the sale as follows:

	A	B	C	D
	A1			
1	2015	Unrealized Gain on Investment in AFSS	2,500	
2	May 19	Allowance to Adjust Investment in AFSS to Market		2,500
3		To eliminate unrealized gain on available-for-sale		
4		investments sold.		
5				
6	May 19	Cash	43,000	
7		Loss on Sale of Investment in AFSS	1,000	
8		Investment in AFSS (cost)		44,000
9		Sold investment.		
10				

Assets	=	Liabilities	+	Stockholders' Equity	−	Losses
− 2,500				− 2,500		
+ 43,000	=	0			−	1,000
− 44,000						

Intel would report Loss on Sale of Investment in AFSS as a realized loss in "Other income or loss" on the income statement.

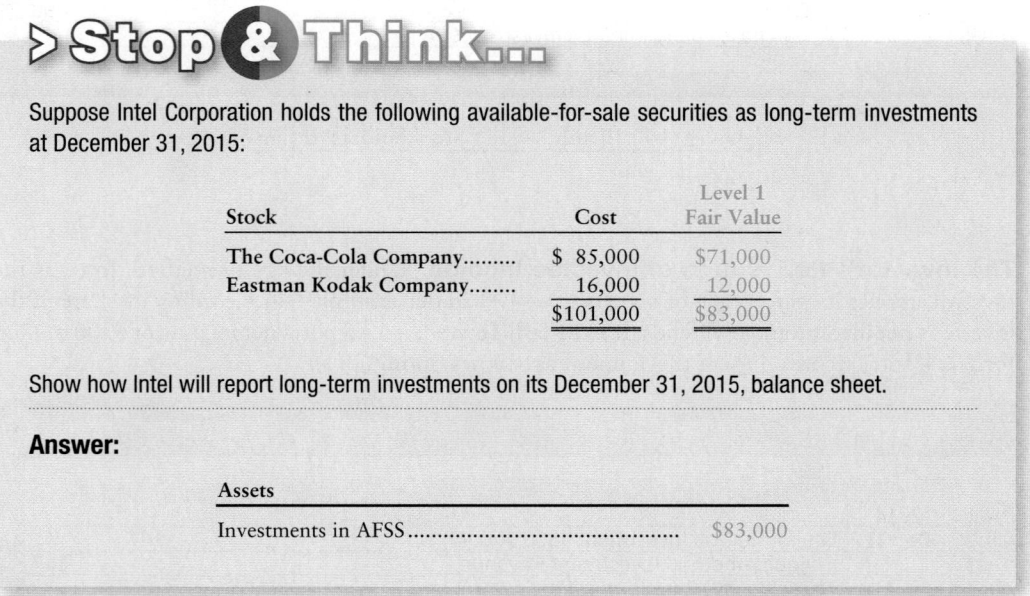

> Stop & Think...

Suppose Intel Corporation holds the following available-for-sale securities as long-term investments at December 31, 2015:

Stock	Cost	Level 1 Fair Value
The Coca-Cola Company.........	$ 85,000	$71,000
Eastman Kodak Company........	16,000	12,000
	$101,000	$83,000

Show how Intel will report long-term investments on its December 31, 2015, balance sheet.

Answer:

Assets	
Investments in AFSS...	$83,000

ANALYZE AND REPORT INVESTMENTS IN AFFILIATED COMPANIES USING THE EQUITY METHOD

Buying a Large Stake in Another Company

An investor owning between 20% and 50% of the investee's voting stock or other ownership interests may significantly influence the business activities of the investee. Such an investor can probably affect dividend policies, product lines, and other important matters. The investor company will more than likely hold one or more seats on the board of directors of the investee company. As shown in Exhibit 8-3, we use the **equity method** to account for these types of investments.

    Intel holds equity-method investments in IM Flash Technologies, LLC and Intel-GE Care Innovations, LLC. These investee companies are referred to as *affiliates* because the investor has a sufficient ownership percentage in them to significantly influence their operations. Because Intel has a voice in shaping the policy and operations of IM Flash Technologies, LLC, some measure of its profits and losses should be included in Intel's income.

3   **Analyze and report** investments in affiliated companies using the equity method

Accounting for Equity-Method Investments

Investments accounted for by the equity method are recorded initially at cost. Suppose that, on January 1, 2014, Intel pays $490 million for 49% of the ownership of IM Flash Technologies, LLC. Intel's entry to record the purchase of this investment follows (in millions):

	A	B	C	D
	A1			
1	2014			
2	Jan 1	Equity-method Investment	490	
3		Cash		490
4		*To purchase equity–method investment.*		
5				

Assets	=	Liabilities	+	Stockholders' Equity
+ 490	=	0	+	0
− 490				

The Investor's Percentage of Investee Income. Under the equity method, Intel, as the investor, applies its percentage of ownership—49% in our example—in recording its share of the investee's net income and dividends. If IM Flash Technologies reports net income of $300 million for 2014, Intel records 49% of this amount as follows (in millions):

	A	B	C	D
	A1			
1	2014			
2	Dec 31	Equity-method Investment (300 × 0.49)	147	
3		Equity-method Investment Revenue		147
4		*To record investment revenue.*		
5				

Assets	=	Liabilities	+	Stockholders' Equity (Revenue)
+ 147	=	0		+ 147

Because of the close relationship between Intel and IM Flash Technologies, Intel, the investor, increases the Equity-method Investment account and records Equity-method Investment Revenue when IM Flash Technologies, the investee, reports income. As IM Flash's stockholders' equity increases, so does the Equity-method Investment account on Intel's books.

Receiving Dividends Under the Equity Method. Intel records its proportionate part of cash dividends received from IM Flash. When IM Flash declares and pays a cash dividend of $200 million, Intel receives 49% of this dividend and records this entry (in millions):

	A	B	C	D
	A1			
1	2014			
2	Dec 31	Cash ($200 × 0.49)	98	
3		Equity-method Investment		98
4		*To receive cash dividend on equity-method investment.*		
5				

Assets	=	Liabilities	+	Stockholders' Equity
+ 98	=	0	+	0
− 98				

The Equity-method Investment account is *decreased* for the receipt of a dividend on an equity-method investment. Why? Because the dividend decreases the investee's owners' equity and thus the investor's investment.

After the preceding entries are posted, Intel's Equity-method Investment account at December 31, 2014, shows Intel's equity in the net assets of IM Flash Technologies (in millions):

Equity-method Investment

Jan 1	Purchase	490	Dec 31	Dividends	98
Dec 31	Net income	147			
Dec 31	Balance	539			

On December 31, 2014, Intel would report the Equity-method investment on the balance sheet and the Equity-method investment revenue on the income statement as follows:

	Millions
Balance sheet (partial):	
Assets	
Total current assets...	$XXX
Equity-method investment................................	539
Property, plant, and equipment, net...................	XXX
Income statement (partial):	
Income from operations......................................	$XXX
Other revenue:	
Equity-method investment revenue................	147
Net income..	$XXX

Gain or loss on the sale of an equity-method investment is measured as the difference between the sale proceeds and the carrying amount of the investment. For example, Intel's sale of 20% of the IM Flash Technologies common stock for $100 million on January 1, 2015 would be recorded as follows (in millions):

	A	B	C	D
	A1			
1	2015			
2	Jan 1	Cash	100.0	
3		Loss on Sale of Equity-method Investment	7.8	
4		Equity-method Investment ($539 × 0.20)		107.8
5		Sold 20% of investment.		
6				

Assets	=	Liabilities	+	Stockholders' Equity	−	Losses
+ 100	=	0			−	7.8
− 107.8						

Summary of the Equity Method. The following T-account illustrates the accounting for equity-method investments:

Equity-method Investment

Original cost	Share of losses
Share of income	Share of dividends
Balance	

ANALYZE AND REPORT CONTROLLING INTERESTS IN OTHER CORPORATIONS USING CONSOLIDATED FINANCIAL STATEMENTS

4 Analyze and report controlling interests in other corporations using consolidated financial statements

In this section, we cover the situation in which an investing corporation buys more than 50% of the voting stock of another company, permitting the investor to actually *control* the investee. Intel's ownership of Intel Capital is an example.

Why Buy Controlling Interest in Another Company?

Most large corporations own controlling interests in other companies. A **controlling** (or **majority**) **interest** is the ownership of more than 50% of the investee's voting stock. Such an investment enables the investor to elect a majority of the members of the investee's board of directors and thus control the investee's policies, such as its production, distribution (supply chain), financing, and investing decisions. The investor is called the **parent company**, and the investee company is called the **subsidiary**. For example, **McAfee, Inc.,** a computer data security company, is a subsidiary of Intel Corporation, the parent. Therefore, the stockholders of Intel control McAfee, Inc., as diagrammed in Exhibit 8-4.

Exhibit 8-4 | Ownership Structure of Intel Corporation and McAfee, Inc.

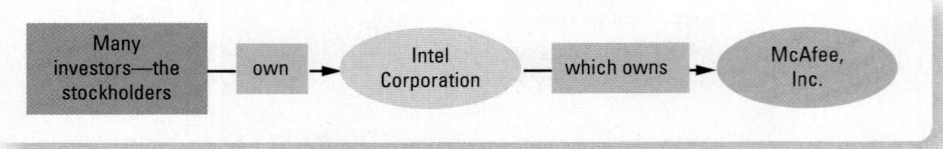

Intel Corporation owned controlling interests in 29 other subsidiary corporations as of the end of fiscal 2012. Exhibit 8-5 shows some of these other subsidiaries.

Exhibit 8-5 | Selected Subsidiaries of Intel Corporation

Intel Capital	Intel Americas, Inc.
Componentes Intel de Costa Rica, S.A.	Intel Europe, Inc.
Intel Asia Holding Limited	Wind River Systems, Inc.

Consolidation Accounting

Consolidation accounting is a method of combining the financial statements of all the companies controlled by the same stockholders. This method reports a single set of financial statements for the consolidated entity, which carries the name of the parent company.

Consolidated financial statements combine the balance sheets, income statements, statements of stockholders' equity, and cash flow statements of the parent company with those of its subsidiaries. The result is a single set of statements as if the parent and its subsidiaries were one company. Investors can gain a better perspective on total operations than they could by examining the reports of the parent and each individual subsidiary.

In consolidated financial statements, the assets, liabilities, revenues, and expenses of each subsidiary are added to the parent's accounts. For example, the balance in Intel Capital's Cash account is added to the balance in the Intel Corporation's Cash account and to the cash of all other subsidiaries. The sum of all of the cash amounts is presented as a single amount in the Intel consolidated balance sheet. Each account balance of a subsidiary, such as Intel Capital or Intel Europe, Inc., loses its identity in the consolidated statements, which bear the name of the parent, Intel Corporation. After a subsidiary's financial statements become consolidated into the parent company's statements, the subsidiary's statements are no longer available to the public.

Exhibit 8-6 diagrams a corporate structure for a parent corporation that owns controlling interests in five subsidiaries and an equity-method investment in another investee company.

Exhibit 8-6 | Parent Company with Consolidated Subsidiaries and an Equity-Method Investment

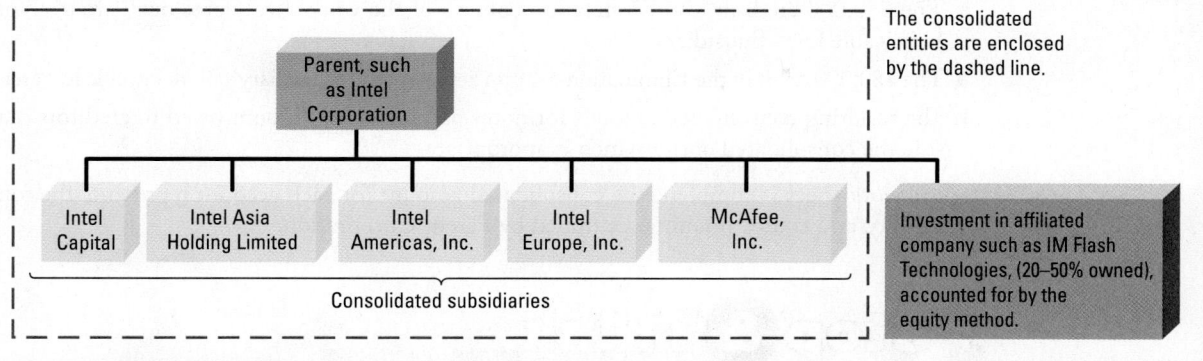

The Consolidated Balance Sheet and the Related Work Sheet

Intel Corporation owns all (100%) the outstanding voting common stock of McAfee, Inc. Both Intel and McAfee, Inc., keep separate sets of books. Intel, the parent company, uses a work sheet to prepare the consolidated statements of Intel and its consolidated subsidiaries. Then Intel's consolidated balance sheet shows the combined assets and liabilities of Intel and all its subsidiaries.

Exhibit 8-7 shows the work sheet for consolidating the balance sheets of Parent Corporation and Subsidiary Corporation. We use these hypothetical entities to illustrate the consolidation process. Consider elimination entry (a) for the parent-subsidiary ownership accounts. Entry (a) credits the parent's Investment account to eliminate its debit balance. Entry (a) also eliminates the subsidiary's stockholders' equity accounts by debiting the subsidiary's Common Stock and Retained Earnings for their full balances. Without this elimination, the consolidated financial statements would include both the parent company's investment in the subsidiary and the subsidiary company's equity. But these accounts represent the same thing—Subsidiary's equity—and so they must be eliminated from the consolidated totals. If they weren't, the same resources would be counted twice.

Exhibit 8-7 | Work Sheet for a Consolidated Balance Sheet

	A1					
	A	**B**	**C**	**D**	**E**	**F**
1		**Parent Corporation**	**Subsidiary Corporation**	**Eliminations** Debit	Credit	**Parent and Subsidiary Consolidated Amounts**
2						
3	**Assets**					
4	Cash	12,000	18,000			30,000
5	Note receivable from Subsidiary	80,000	—		(b) 80,000	—
6	Inventory	104,000	91,000			195,000
7	Investment in Subsidiary	150,000	—		(a) 150,000	—
8	Other assets	218,000	138,000			356,000
9	Total	564,000	247,000			581,000
10	**Liabilities and Stockholders' Equity**					
11	Accounts payable	43,000	17,000			60,000
12	Notes payable	190,000	80,000	(b) 80,000		190,000
13	Common stock	176,000	100,000	(a) 100,000		176,000
14	Retained earnings	155,000	50,000	(a) 50,000		155,000
15	Total	564,000	247,000	230,000	230,000	581,000
16						

The resulting Parent and Subsidiary consolidated balance sheet (far-right column) reports no Investment in Subsidiary account. Moreover, the consolidated totals for Common Stock and Retained Earnings are those of Parent Corporation only. Study the final column of the consolidation work sheet.

In this example, Parent Corporation has an $80,000 note receivable from Subsidiary, and Subsidiary has a note payable to Parent. The parent's receivable and the subsidiary's payable represent the same resources—all entirely within the consolidated entity. Both, therefore, must be eliminated, and entry (b) accomplishes this.

- The $80,000 credit in the Elimination column of the work sheet zeros out Parent's Note Receivable from Subsidiary.
- The $80,000 debit in the Elimination column zeros out the Subsidiary's Note Payable to Parent.
- The resulting consolidated amount for notes payable is the amount owed to creditors outside the consolidated entity, which is appropriate.

After the work sheet is complete, the consolidated amount for each account represents the total asset, liability, and equity amounts controlled by Parent Corporation.

> **Stop & Think...**

Examine Exhibit 8-7. Why does the consolidated stockholders' equity ($176,000 + $155,000) *exclude* the equity of Subsidiary Corporation?

Answer:

The stockholders' equity of the consolidated entity is that of the parent only. To include the stockholders' equity of the subsidiary as well as the investment in the subsidiary on the parent's books would be double counting.

Goodwill and Noncontrolling Interest

Goodwill and Noncontrolling (minority) Interest are two accounts that only a consolidated entity can have. As we saw in Chapter 7, goodwill is the intangible asset of the parent company that represents the parent company's excess payment over and above the fair market value of net assets of the acquired subsidiary.

Noncontrolling (minority) interest arises when a parent company owns less than 100% of the stock of a subsidiary. For example, General Electric (GE) owns less than 100% of some of the companies it controls. The remainder of the subsidiaries' stock is noncontrolling (minority) interest to GE. Noncontrolling Interest is reported as a separate account in the stockholders' equity section of the consolidated balance sheet of the parent company. The amount of noncontrolling interest in subsidiaries' stock must be clearly identified and labeled as such. GE reports noncontrolling interest in the stockholders' equity section on its balance sheet. By contrast, Intel reports no noncontrolling interest, which suggests that Intel owns 100% of all its subsidiaries.

Income of a Consolidated Entity

The income of a consolidated entity is the net income of the parent plus the parent's proportion of the subsidiaries' net income. Suppose Parent Company owns all the stock of Subsidiary S-1 and 60% of the stock of Subsidiary S-2. During the year just ended, Parent earned net income of $330,000, S-1 earned $150,000, and S-2 had a net loss of $100,000. Parent Company would report net income of $420,000, computed as

	Net Income (Net Loss) of Each Company		Parent's Ownership of Each Company		Parent's Consolidated Net Income (Net Loss)
Parent Company	$330,000	×	100%	=	$330,000
Subsidiary S-1	150,000	×	100%	=	150,000
Subsidiary S-2	(100,000)	×	60%	=	(60,000)
Consolidated net income					$420,000

Cooking the Books   with Investments and Debt

Enron Corporation

In 2000, Enron Corporation in Houston, Texas, employed approximately 22,000 people and was one of the world's leading electricity, natural gas, pulp and paper, and communications companies, with reported revenues of nearly $101 billion. *Fortune* had named Enron "America's Most Innovative Company" for six consecutive years. To many outside observers, Enron was the model corporation.

Enron's financial statements showed that the company was making a lot of money, but in reality, most of its profits were merely on paper. Rather than from operations, the great majority of the cash Enron needed to operate on a day-to-day basis came from bank loans. It was very important, therefore, that Enron keep its debt ratio (discussed in Chapter 3) as well as its return on assets (ROA, discussed in Chapter 7) at acceptable levels so the banks would continue to view the company as creditworthy. Enron's balance sheets contained large misstatements in the liabilities and stockholders' equity sections over a period of years. Many of the offsetting misstatements were in long-term assets. Specifically, Enron owned numerous long-term investments, including power plants; water rights; broadband cable; and sophisticated, complex, and somewhat dubious derivative financial instruments in such unusual things as the weather! Many of these investments actually had questionable value, but Enron had abused fair market value accounting to estimate them at grossly inflated values.

To create paper profits, Andrew Fastow, Enron's chief financial officer, created a veritable maze of "special purpose entities" (SPEs), financed with bank debt. He valued the investments mentioned above using "mark-to-market" (fair value accounting), using unrealistic assumptions that created inflated asset values on the financial statements. He then "sold" the dubious investments to the SPEs to get them off Enron's books. Enron recorded millions of dollars in "profits" from these transactions. Fastow then used Enron stock to collateralize the bank debt of the SPEs, making the transactions entirely circular. Unknown to Enron's board of directors, Fastow or members of his own family owned most of these entities, making them related parties to Enron. Enron was, in fact, the owner of the assets of the SPEs, and was, in fact, obligated for the debts of the SPEs since those debts were collateralized with Enron stock.

When Enron's fraud was discovered in late 2001, the company was forced to consolidate the assets of the SPEs, as well as all of their bank debt, into its own financial statements. The inflated assets had to be written down to impaired market values. The end result of the restatement impacted Enron's debt ratio and ROA so much that the banks refused to loan the company any more money to operate. Enron's energy trading business virtually dried up overnight, and it was bankrupt within 60 days. An estimated $60 billion in shareholder value, and 22,000 jobs, were lost. Enron's CEO, Jeffrey Skilling, its CFO, Andrew Fastow, and Board Chairman, Kenneth Lay, were all convicted of fraud. Skilling and Fastow both went to prison. Lay died suddenly of a heart attack before being sentenced.

Enron's audit firm, Arthur Andersen, was accused of trying to cover up its knowledge of Enron's practices by shredding documents. The firm was indicted by the U.S. Justice Department in March 2002. Because of the indictment, Andersen lost all of its public clients and was forced out of business. As a result, over 58,000 persons lost their jobs worldwide. A U.S. Supreme Court decision in 2005 eventually led to the withdrawal of the indictment, but it came much too late for the once "gold-plated" CPA firm. Allegations about the lack of quality of its work on Enron, as well as other well publicized cases such as Waste Management (p. 381) and WorldCom (p. 368), who were also clients, doomed Arthur Andersen.

◉ Decision Guidelines

ACCOUNTING METHODS FOR LONG-TERM INVESTMENTS

These guidelines show which accounting method to use for each type of long-term investment.

Intel has all types of investments—stocks, bonds, 25% interests, and controlling interests. How should Intel account for its various investments?

Type of Long-Term Investment	Accounting Method
Intel owns bonds that it intends to hold to maturity.	Amortized cost
Intel owns a portfolio of bond and other debt securities as well as equity securities in companies (less than 20%) that it intends to hold long-term.	Available-for-sale; fair value
Intel owns between 20% and 50% of investee/affiliate stock.	Equity
Intel owns more than 50% of investee stock.	Consolidation

≫ Mid-Chapter Summary Problem

1. Identify the appropriate accounting method for each of the following situations:
   a. Investment in 25% of investee's stock
   b. 10% investment in available-for-sale stock
   c. Investment in more than 50% of investee's stock
2. At what amount should the following long-term available-for-sale investment portfolio be reported on the December 31 balance sheet? All the investments are less than 5% of the investee's stock. Journalize any adjusting entry required by these data.

Stock	Investment Cost	Current Market Value
DuPont	$ 5,000	$ 5,500
ExxonMobil	61,200	53,000
Procter & Gamble	3,680	6,230

3. Investor paid $67,900 to acquire a 40% equity-method investment in the common stock of Investee. At the end of the first year, Investee's net income was $80,000, and Investee declared and paid cash dividends of $55,000. What is Investor's ending balance in its Equity-Method Investment account? Use a T-account to answer.

4. Parent company paid $85,000 for all the common stock of Subsidiary Company, and Parent owes Subsidiary $20,000 on a note payable. Complete the following consolidation work sheet:

A1						
	A	B	C	D	E	F
1		Parent Company	Subsidiary Company	Eliminations Debit	Credit	Consolidated Amounts
2	**Assets**					
3	Cash	7,000	4,000			
4	Note receivable from Parent	—	20,000			
5	Investment in Subsidiary	85,000	—			
6	Other assets	108,000	99,000			
7	Total	200,000	123,000			
8	**Liabilities and Stockholders' Equity**					
9	Accounts payable	15,000	8,000			
10	Notes payable	20,000	30,000			
11	Common stock	120,000	60,000			
12	Retained earnings	45,000	25,000			
13	Total	200,000	123,000			
14						

Answers

1. **a.** Equity method

   b. Available-for-sale, adjusted to fair value at end of each reporting period

   c. Consolidation

2. Report the investments in available-for-sale securities (AFSS) at fair value, $64,730, as follows:

Stock	Investment Cost	Current Market Value
DuPont	$ 5,000	$ 5,500
ExxonMobil	61,200	53,000
Procter & Gamble	3,680	6,230
Totals	$69,880	$64,730

Adjusting entry:

A1			
A	B	C	D
1	Unrealized Loss on Investment in AFSS ($69,880 – $64,730)	5,150	
2	Allowance to Adjust Investment in AFSS to Market		5,150
3	*To adjust investments to fair value.*		
4			

3.

Equity-method Investment

Cost	67,900	Dividends	22,000**
Income	32,000*		
Balance	77,900		

*$80,000 × .40 = $32,000
**$55,000 × .40 = $22,000

4. Consolidation work sheet:

	A	B	C	D	E	F
A1 ⇕						
	A	B	C	D	E	F
1		Parent Company	Subsidiary Company	Eliminations Debit	Eliminations Credit	Consolidated Amounts
2	**Assets**					
3	Cash	7,000	4,000			11,000
4	Note receivable from Parent	—	20,000		(a) 20,000	—
5	Investment in Subsidiary	85,000	—		(b) 85,000	—
6	Other assets	108,000	99,000			207,000
7	Total	200,000	123,000			218,000
8	**Liabilities and Stockholders' Equity**					
9	Accounts payable	15,000	8,000			23,000
10	Notes payable	20,000	30,000	(a) 20,000		30,000
11	Common stock	120,000	60,000	(b) 60,000		120,000
12	Retained earnings	45,000	25,000	(b) 25,000		45,000
13	Total	200,000	123,000	105,000	105,000	218,000
14						

Consolidation of Foreign Subsidiaries

Global View

Many U.S. companies conduct a large part of their business abroad. Intel, General Electric, and PepsiCo, among others, are more active in other countries than they are in the United States. In fact, Intel earns 84% of its revenue outside the United States. Exhibit 8-8 shows the approximate percentages of international revenues for these companies.

Exhibit 8-8 | Extent of International Business

Company	Percentage of International Revenues
Intel	84%
General Electric	54%
PepsiCo	40%

Foreign Currencies and Exchange Rates

Most countries use their own national currency. An exception is the European Union nations—France, Germany, Italy, Belgium, and others, use a common currency, the *euro*, whose symbol is €. If Intel, a U.S. company, sells computer processors to software developers in France, will Intel receive U.S. dollars or euros? If the transaction is in dollars, the company in France must buy dollars to pay Intel in U.S. currency. If the transaction is in euros, then Intel will collect euros and must sell euros for dollars.

The price of one nation's currency can be stated in terms of another country's monetary unit. This measure of one currency against another is called the **foreign-currency exchange rate**. In Exhibit 8-9, the dollar value of a euro is $1.35 as of September 30, 2013. This means that one euro can be bought for $1.35. Other currencies are also listed in Exhibit 8-9. These exchange rates vary daily.

Exhibit 8-9 | Foreign-Currency Exchange Rates

Country	Monetary Unit	U.S. Dollar Value	Country	Monetary Unit	U.S. Dollar Value
Brazil............	Real (R)........................	$0.44	United Kingdom........	Pound (£).........	$1.61
Canada.........	Canadian Dollar (C$)...	0.97	China	Yuan (元).........	0.163
France..........	Euro (€)........................	1.35	Japan........................	Yen (¥).............	0.010
Germany......	Euro (€)........................	1.35	Mexico....................	Peso (P)............	0.757

Source: *http://www.fms.treas.gov/intn.html#rates*

We can convert the cost of an item stated in one currency to its cost in a second currency on a given date. We call this conversion a *translation*. Suppose an item purchased on September 30, 2013, costs 200 euros. To compute its cost in dollars, we multiply the euro amount by the conversion rate: 200 euros × $1.35 = $270.

Two main factors affect the price (the exchange rate) of a particular currency:

1. The ratio of a country's imports to its exports
2. The rate of return available in the country's capital markets

The Import/Export Ratio. Japanese exports often exceed Japan's imports. Customers of Japanese companies must buy yen (the Japanese unit of currency) to pay for their purchases denominated in yen. This strong demand for yen drives up the price of the yen. In contrast, the United States imports more goods than it exports. Americans must sell dollars to buy the foreign currencies needed to pay for the foreign goods. As the supply of dollars increases, the price of the dollar falls relative to other currencies.

The Rate of Return. The rate of return available in a country's capital markets affects the amount of investment funds flowing into the country. When rates of return are high in a politically stable country such as the United States, international investors buy stocks, bonds, and real estate in that country. This activity increases the demand for the nation's currency and drives up its exchange rate.

Currencies are often described as "strong" or "weak." The exchange rate of a **strong currency** is rising relative to other nations' currencies. The exchange rate of a **weak currency** is falling relative to other currencies.

The exchange rate for the British pound was $1.61 on September 30, 2013. On October 17, that rate may rise to $1.62. We would say that the dollar has weakened against the pound. The pound has thus become more expensive, making travel and conducting business in England more expensive for Americans.

The Foreign-Currency Translation Adjustment

The process of translating a foreign subsidiary's financial statements into dollars usually creates a **foreign-currency translation adjustment**. This item appears in the consolidated financial statements of most multinational companies and is reported as part of other comprehensive income. The statement of other comprehensive income will be discussed in Chapter 11.

A translation adjustment arises due to changes in the foreign exchange rate over time. In general,

- *assets* and *liabilities* are translated into dollars at the current exchange rate on the date of the statements.
- *stockholders' equity* is translated into dollars at older, historical exchange rates. Paid-in capital accounts are translated at the historical exchange rate when the subsidiary was acquired. Retained earnings are translated at the average exchange rates applicable over the period in which interest in the subsidiary has been held.

This difference in exchange rates creates an out-of-balance condition on the balance sheet. The translation adjustment brings the balance sheet back into balance. Let's see how the translation adjustment works.

Suppose Intel has an Italian subsidiary whose financial statements are expressed in euros (the European currency). Intel must consolidate the Italian subsidiary's financials into its own statements. When Intel acquired the Italian company in 2009, a euro was worth $1.35 (assumed). When the Italian firm earned its retained income during 2009–2014, the average exchange rate was $1.30 (assumed). On the balance sheet date in 2014, a euro is worth only $1.20 (assumed). Exhibit 8-10 shows how to translate the Italian company's balance sheet into dollars.

Exhibit 8-10 | Translation of a Foreign-Currency Balance Sheet into Dollars

	A	B	C	D
	A1			
	A	**B**	**C**	**D**
1	**Italian Imports, Inc., Accounts**	**Euros**	**Exchange Rate**	**Dollars**
2				
3	Assets	€ 800,000	$ 1.20	$ 960,000
4				
5	Liabilities	€ 500,000	1.20	$ 600,000
6	Stockholders' equity			
7	Common stock	100,000	1.35	135,000
8	Retained earnings	200,000	1.30	260,000
9	Accumulated other comprehensive income:			
10	Foreign-currency translation adjustment			(35,000)
11		€ 800,000		$ 960,000
12				

The *foreign-currency translation adjustment* is the balancing amount that brings the dollar amount of total liabilities and equity of a foreign subsidiary into agreement with the dollar amount of total assets (in Exhibit 8-10, total assets equal $960,000). Only after the translation adjustment of $35,000 do total liabilities and equity equal total assets stated in dollars.

What caused the negative translation adjustment? The euro weakened after the acquisition of the Italian company.

- When Intel acquired the foreign subsidiary in 2009, a euro was worth $1.35.
- When the Italian company earned its income during 2009 through 2014, the average exchange rate was $1.30.
- On the balance sheet date in 2014, a euro is worth only $1.20.
- Thus, the Italian company's equity (assets minus liabilities) is translated into only $360,000 ($960,000 − $600,000).
- To bring stockholders' equity to $360,000 requires a $35,000 negative adjustment.

A negative translation adjustment is like a loss, reported as a negative item in the statement of other comprehensive income. Losses and gains from translation adjustments eventually are transferred to accumulated other comprehensive income in the stockholders' equity section of the balance sheet, as shown in Exhibit 8-10. The Italian firm's dollar figures in Exhibit 8-10 reflect what Intel would include in its consolidated balance sheet. The consolidation procedures would follow those illustrated in Exhibit 8-7.

REPORT INVESTING ACTIVITIES ON THE STATEMENT OF CASH FLOWS

5 Report investing activities on the statement of cash flows

Investing activities include many types of transactions. In Chapter 7, we covered the purchase and sale of long-term assets such as plant and equipment. In this chapter, we examine investments in stocks and bonds.

Exhibit 8-11 provides excerpts from Intel's 2012 consolidated statement of cash flows. During 2012, Intel sold available-for-sale investments and received $7.6 billion in cash. Intel purchased available-for-sale investments for $8.7 billion and sold equity-method investments for $100 million. These investing activities relate directly to the topics you studied in this chapter. They used $2.1 billion in cash to make other kinds of investments. Overall, investing activities consumed $14.1 billion of Intel Corporation's cash in 2012.

Exhibit 8-11 | Intel Corporation's Investing Activities on the Statement of Cash Flows

	A	B
	A1 ⬍	
1	**Intel Corporation** **Consolidated Statement of Cash Flows (Partial, Adapted)**	
2	**(In billions)**	**2012**
3	**Cash flows provided by (used for) investing activities:**	
4	Sales of available-for-sale investments	$ 7.6
5	Purchases of available-for-sale investments	(8.7)
6	Additions to property, plant, and equipment	(11.0)
7	Sales of equity-method investments	0.1
8	Other uses of cash	(2.1)
9	**Net cash (used for) investing activities**	$ (14.1)
10		

EXPLAIN THE IMPACT OF THE TIME VALUE OF MONEY ON CERTAIN TYPES OF INVESTMENTS

Which would you rather have: $1,000 received today, or $1,000 received a year from now? A logical person would answer: "I'd rather have the cash now, because if I get it now, I can invest it at some interest rate so that a year in the future I'll have more." The term **future value** means the sum of money that a given current investment will be "worth" at a specified time in the future, assuming a certain interest rate. The term *time value of money* refers to the fact that money earns interest over time. *Interest* is the cost of using money. To borrowers, interest is the fee paid to the lender for the period of the loan. To lenders, interest is the revenue earned from allowing someone else to use their money for a period of time.

> **6** **Explain** the impact of the time value of money on certain types of investments

Whether making investments or borrowing money long-term, we must always recognize the interest we receive or pay. Otherwise, we overlook an important part of the transaction. Suppose you invest $4,545 in corporate bonds that pay 10% interest (based on the original amount invested) each year. After one year, the value of your investment has grown to $5,000, as shown in Exhibit 8-12:

Exhibit 8-12 | Future Value of an Investment

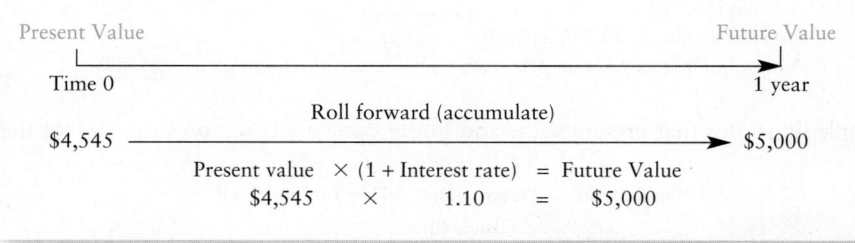

The difference between your original (present) investment ($4,545) and the future value of the investment ($5,000) is the amount of interest revenue you will earn during the year ($455). Interest becomes more important as the time period lengthens because the amount of interest depends on the span of time the money is invested. The time value of money plays a key role in measuring the value of certain long-term investments as well as long-term debt.

If the money were invested for five years, you would have to perform five calculations like the one described above. You would also have to consider the compound interest that your investment is earning. *Compound interest* is not only the interest you earn on your principal amount but also the interest you receive on the interest you have already earned. Most business applications include compound interest.

To calculate the future value of an investment, we need three inputs: (1) the *amount of initial payment* (*or receipt*), (2) the length of *time* between investment and future receipt (or *payment*), and (3) the *interest rate*. The following table shows the interest revenue earned on the original $4,545 investment each year for five years at 10%:

End of Year	Interest	Future Value
0	—	$4,545
1	$4,545 × 0.10 = $455	5,000
2	5,000 × 0.10 = 500	5,500
3	5,500 × 0.10 = 550	6,050
4	6,050 × 0.10 = 605	6,655
5	6,655 × 0.10 = 666	7,321

As shown in the table, earning 10% compounded annually, a $4,545 investment grows to $5,000 at the end of one year, to $5,500 at the end of two years, and to $7,321 at the end of five years.

Present Value

Often a person knows or is able to estimate a future amount and needs to determine the related present value (PV). The term **present value** means the value on a given date of a future payment or series of future payments, discounted to reflect the time value of money. In Exhibit 8-12, present value and future value are on opposite ends of the same time line. Suppose an investment promises to pay you $5,000 at the *end* of one year. How much would you pay *now* to acquire this investment? You would be willing to pay the present value of the $5,000 future amount, which, at 10% interest, is $4,545.

Like future value, present value depends on three factors: (1) the *amount of payment (or receipt)*, (2) the length of *time* between investment and future receipt (or *payment*), and (3) the *interest rate*. The process of computing a present value is called *discounting* because the present value is *less* than the future value.

In our investment example, the future receipt is $5,000. The investment period is one year. Assume that you demand an annual interest rate of 10% on your investment. With all three factors specified, you can compute the present value of $5,000 at 10% for one year:

$$\text{Present value} = \frac{\text{Future value}}{1 + \text{Interest rate}} = \frac{\$5,000}{1.10} = \$4,545$$

By turning the data around into a future-value problem, we can verify the present-value computation:

Amount invested (present value)	$4,545
Expected earnings ($4,545 × 0.10)	455
Amount to be received one year from now (future value)	$5,000

This example illustrates that present value and future value are based on variations of the same equation:

$$\text{Future value} = \text{Present value} \times (1 + \text{Interest rate})^n$$

$$\text{Present value} = \frac{\text{Future value}}{(1 + \text{Interest rate})^n}$$

Where n = number of periods

If the $5,000 is to be received two years from now, you will pay only $4,132 for the investment, as shown in Exhibit 8-13. By turning the data around, we verify that $4,132 accumulates to $5,000 at 10% for two years:

Amount invested (present value) $4,132
Expected earnings for first year ($4,132 × 0.10).......................... 413
Value of investment after one year 4,545
Expected earnings for second year ($4,545 × 0.10) 455
Amount to be received two years from now (future value) $5,000

$$\text{Formula: Present value} = \frac{\text{Future value}}{(1 + \text{Interest rate})^n}$$

$$4,132 = \frac{5,000}{(1 + 0.10)^2}$$

$$\text{Future value} = \text{Present value} \times (1 + \text{Interest rate})^n$$

$$5,000 = \$4,132 \times (1 + 0.10)^2$$

Exhibit 8-13 | Present Value: An Example

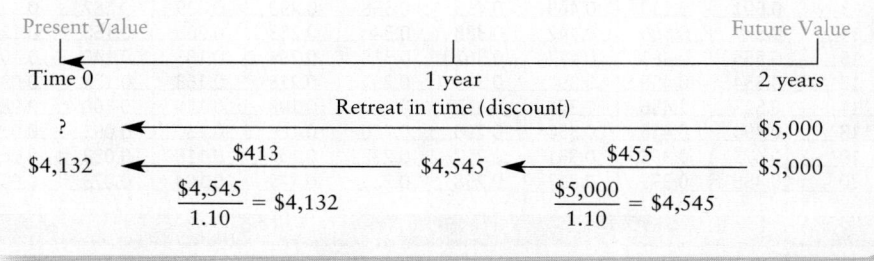

You would pay $4,132—the present value of $5,000—to receive the $5,000 future amount at the end of two years at 10% per year. The $868 difference between the amount invested ($4,132) and the amount to be received ($5,000) is the return on the investment, the sum of the two interest receipts: $413 + $455 = $868.

Present-Value Tables

We have shown the simple formula for computing present value. However, figuring present value "by hand" for investments spanning many years is time-consuming and presents too many opportunities for arithmetic errors. Present-value tables simplify our work. Let's review our examples of present value by using Exhibit 8-14, Present Value of $1.

Exhibit 8-14 | Present Value of $1

	A	B	C	D	E	F	G	H	I	J
	A1									
1					Present Value of $1					
2	Periods	4%	5%	6%	7%	8%	10%	12%	14%	16%
3										
4	1	0.962	0.952	0.943	0.935	0.926	0.909	0.893	0.877	0.862
5	2	0.925	0.907	0.890	0.873	0.857	0.826	0.797	0.769	0.743
6	3	0.889	0.864	0.840	0.816	0.794	0.751	0.712	0.675	0.641
7	4	0.855	0.823	0.792	0.763	0.735	0.683	0.636	0.592	0.552
8	5	0.822	0.784	0.747	0.713	0.681	0.621	0.567	0.519	0.476
9	6	0.790	0.746	0.705	0.666	0.630	0.564	0.507	0.456	0.410
10	7	0.760	0.711	0.665	0.623	0.583	0.513	0.452	0.400	0.354
11	8	0.731	0.677	0.627	0.582	0.540	0.467	0.404	0.351	0.305
12	9	0.703	0.645	0.592	0.544	0.500	0.424	0.361	0.308	0.263
13	10	0.676	0.614	0.558	0.508	0.463	0.386	0.322	0.270	0.227
14	11	0.650	0.585	0.527	0.475	0.429	0.350	0.287	0.237	0.195
15	12	0.625	0.557	0.497	0.444	0.397	0.319	0.257	0.208	0.168
16	13	0.601	0.530	0.469	0.415	0.368	0.290	0.229	0.182	0.145
17	14	0.577	0.505	0.442	0.388	0.340	0.263	0.205	0.160	0.125
18	15	0.555	0.481	0.417	0.362	0.315	0.239	0.183	0.140	0.108
19	16	0.534	0.458	0.394	0.339	0.292	0.218	0.163	0.123	0.093
20	17	0.513	0.436	0.371	0.317	0.270	0.198	0.146	0.108	0.080
21	18	0.494	0.416	0.350	0.296	0.250	0.180	0.130	0.095	0.069
22	19	0.475	0.396	0.331	0.277	0.232	0.164	0.116	0.083	0.060
23	20	0.456	0.377	0.312	0.258	0.215	0.149	0.104	0.073	0.051
24										

For the 10% investment for one year, we find the junction of the 10% column and row 4 (corresponding to period 1) in Exhibit 8-14. The figure 0.909 is computed as follows: 1/1.10 = 0.909. This work has been done for us, and only the present value factors are given in the table. To figure the present value for $5,000, we multiply 0.909 by $5,000. The result is $4,545, which matches the result we obtained by hand.

For the two-year investment, we read down the 10% column and across row 5 (corresponding to period 2). We multiply 0.826 (computed as 0.909/1.10 = 0.826) by $5,000 and get $4,130, which confirms our earlier computation of $4,132 (the difference is due to rounding in the present-value table). Using the table, we can compute the present value of any single future amount.

Present Value of an Ordinary Annuity

Return to the investment example at the top of page 451. That investment provided the investor with only a single future receipt ($5,000 at the end of two years). *Ordinary annuity investments* provide multiple receipts of an equal amount at fixed year-end intervals over the investment's duration.

Consider an investment that promises *annual* cash receipts of $10,000 to be received at the end of each year for three years. Assume that you demand a 12% return on your investment. What is the investment's present value? That is, what would you pay today to acquire the investment? The investment spans three periods, and you would pay the sum of three present values. The computation follows:

Year	Annual Cash Receipt	Present Value of $1 at 12% (Exhibit 8-14)	Present Value of Annual Cash Receipt
1	$10,000	0.893	$ 8,930
2	10,000	0.797	7,970
3	10,000	0.712	7,120
Total present value of investment..............			$24,020

The present value of this annuity is $24,020. By paying this amount today, you will receive $10,000 at the end of each of the three years while earning 12% on your investment.

This example illustrates repetitive computations of the three future amounts, a time-consuming process. One way to ease the computational burden is to add the three successive present value factors (0.893 + 0.797 + 0.712) and multiply their sum (2.402) by the annual cash receipt ($10,000) to obtain the present value of the annuity ($10,000 × 2.402 = $24,020).

An easier approach is to use a present-value-of-an-ordinary-annuity table. Exhibit 8-15 shows the present value of $1 to be received periodically for a given number of periods, at the end of each period. The present value of a three-period annuity at 12% is 2.402 (the junction of row 6 (corresponding to period 3) and the 12% column). Thus, $10,000 received annually at the end of each of three years, discounted at 12%, is $24,020 ($10,000 × 2.402), which is the present value.

Exhibit 8-15 | Present Value of Ordinary Annuity of $1

Periods	4%	5%	6%	7%	8%	10%	12%	14%	16%
1	0.962	0.952	0.943	0.935	0.926	0.909	0.893	0.877	0.862
2	1.886	1.859	1.833	1.808	1.783	1.736	1.690	1.647	1.605
3	2.775	2.723	2.673	2.624	2.577	2.487	2.402	2.322	2.246
4	3.630	3.546	3.465	3.387	3.312	3.170	3.037	2.914	2.798
5	4.452	4.329	4.212	4.100	3.993	3.791	3.605	3.433	3.274
6	5.242	5.076	4.917	4.767	4.623	4.355	4.111	3.889	3.685
7	6.002	5.786	5.582	5.389	5.206	4.868	4.564	4.288	4.039
8	6.733	6.463	6.210	5.971	5.747	5.335	4.968	4.639	4.344
9	7.435	7.108	6.802	6.515	6.247	5.759	5.328	4.946	4.608
10	8.111	7.722	7.360	7.024	6.710	6.145	5.650	5.216	4.833
11	8.760	8.306	7.887	7.499	7.139	6.495	5.938	5.453	5.029
12	9.385	8.863	8.384	7.943	7.536	6.814	6.194	5.660	5.197
13	9.986	9.394	8.853	8.358	7.904	7.103	6.424	5.842	5.342
14	10.563	9.899	9.295	8.745	8.244	7.367	6.628	6.002	5.468
15	11.118	10.380	9.712	9.108	8.559	7.606	6.811	6.142	5.575
16	11.652	10.838	10.106	9.447	8.851	7.824	6.974	6.265	5.669
17	12.166	11.274	10.477	9.763	9.122	8.022	7.120	6.373	5.749
18	12.659	11.690	10.828	10.059	9.372	8.201	7.250	6.467	5.818
19	13.134	12.085	11.158	10.336	9.604	8.365	7.366	6.550	5.877
20	13.590	12.462	11.470	10.594	9.818	8.514	7.469	6.623	5.929

Using Microsoft Excel to Calculate Present Value

While tables such as Exhibits 8-14 and 8-15 are helpful, they are limited to the interest rates in the columns or the periods of time in the rows. Using a computer program like Microsoft Excel provides an infinite range of interest rates and periods. For that reason, most businesspeople solve present-value problems quickly and easily using Excel rather than tables.

■ *To compute the present value of a single payment,* the following formula applies:

$$= \text{Payment}/(1 + i)^n$$

where i = interest rate
n = number of periods

■ In Excel, we use the $\wedge$ symbol to indicate the exponent. To illustrate, suppose you are expecting to receive a \$500,000 payment four years from now, and suppose that market interest rates are 8%. You would enter the following formula in Excel:

$$= 500000/(1.08)^{\wedge}4$$

You should calculate a present value of \$367,514.90 (rounded to \$367,515).

■ *To compute the present value of an annuity (stream of payments),* open an Excel spreadsheet to a blank cell. Click the insert function button (f_x). Then select the "Financial" category from the drop-down box. The following box will appear:

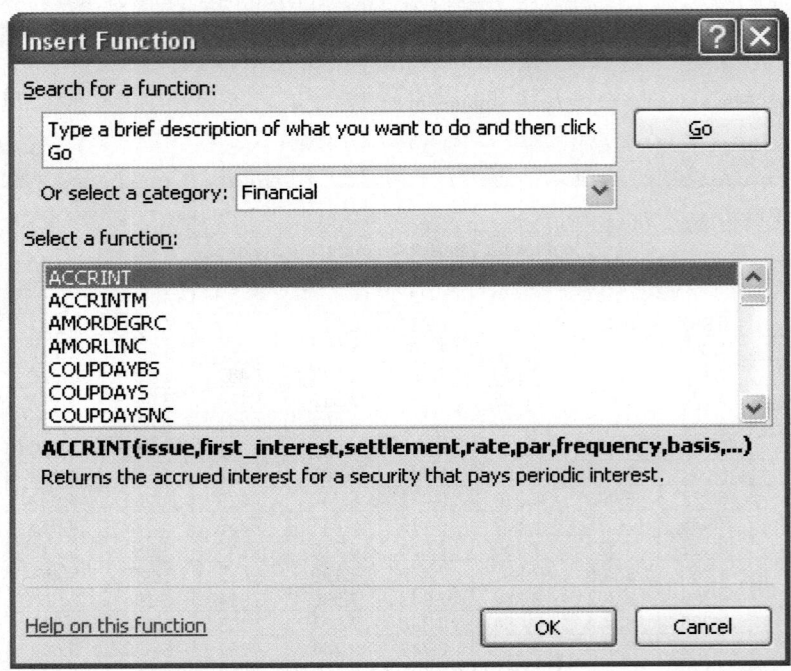

Scroll down the function list and select "PV." A description of the PV function will display beneath the function list, along with the following line: **PV (rate,nper,pmt,fv,type)**. Double-click PV, and the following box will appear:

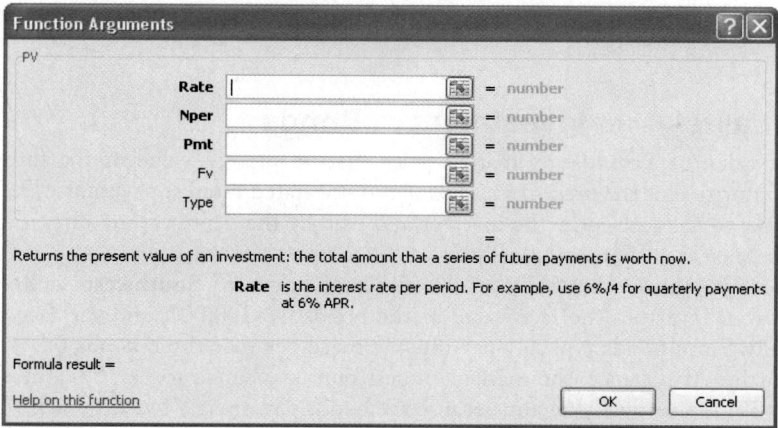

Enter the interest rate, the number of periods, and the payment (as a negative number). The present value of the annuity will appear at the bottom of the box after the "=" sign.

To illustrate, notice that we have assumed an investment that is expected to return $20,000 per year for 20 years and a market interest rate of 8%. The net present value of this annuity (rounded to the nearest cent) is $196,362.95, computed with Excel as follows:

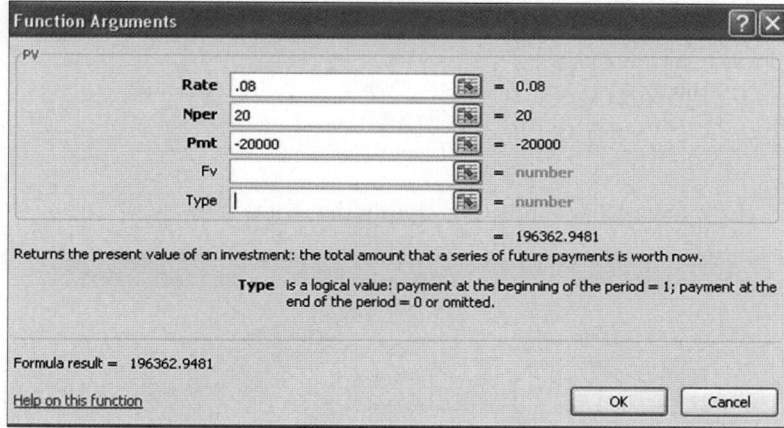

Using the PV Model to Compute Fair Value
of Available-for-Sale Investments

Earlier in the chapter, we discussed GAAP for available-for-sale investments. Recall that, at the end of each year, investors are required to adjust the portfolio of these types of investments to fair values, using one of three different approaches (in this order of preference):

■ Level 1: Quoted prices in active markets for identical assets

■ Level 2: Estimates based on other observable inputs (e.g., prices for similar assets)

■ Level 3: Estimates based on unobservable estimates (the company's own estimates based on certain assumptions)

Some types of investments (publicly traded stocks and bonds) have quoted prices in active markets. Determining fair value for these investments is easy: Merely obtain the quoted price from the financial media (usually the Internet or *Wall Street Journal* on the year-end). Other types of nontraditional investments (e.g., notes, bonds or stocks, contracts, annuities) may not have daily quoted market prices in active markets. Therefore, the company may use financial models that predict expected cash flows from these investments over a period of time and discount those cash flows back to the balance-sheet date. These are called level 2 or level 3 approaches to asset valuation. Use of these models may require a great deal of sophisticated judgment about the amount and timing of cash flows and sometimes a number of subjective estimates such as interest rates.

Models such as these are quite sensitive to changes in these judgments and estimates. Let's illustrate with a simple example.

Present Value of an Investment in Bonds

The present value of a bond—its market price—is the present value of the future principal amount at maturity plus the present value of the future stated interest payments. The principal is a *single amount* to be received by the investor and paid by the debtor at maturity. The interest is an *annuity* because it occurs periodically.

Let's compute the present value of 9% five-year bonds of **Southwest Airlines** from the standpoint of an investor. The face value of the bonds is $100,000, and the face interest rate is 9% annually. Since bonds typically pay interest twice per year, these bonds pay 4 1/2% interest semiannually. At issuance, the market interest rate is assumed to be 10% annually, but it is computed at 5% semiannually (again, because the bonds pay interest twice a year). Therefore, the effective (market) interest rate for each of the 10 semiannual periods is 5%. We thus use 5% in computing the present value of the sum of the principal and of the stream of interest payments. The market price of these bonds is $96,149:

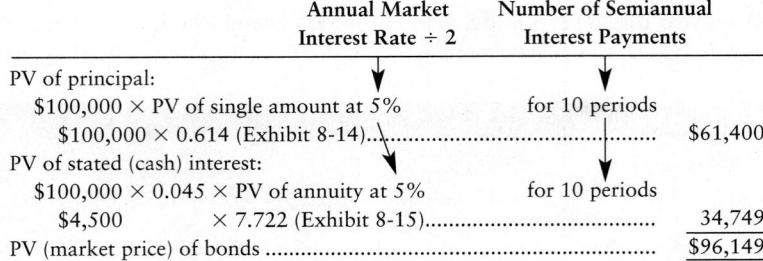

	Annual Market Interest Rate ÷ 2	Number of Semiannual Interest Payments	
PV of principal:			
$100,000 × PV of single amount at 5%		for 10 periods	
$100,000 × 0.614 (Exhibit 8-14)			$61,400
PV of stated (cash) interest:			
$100,000 × 0.045 × PV of annuity at 5%		for 10 periods	
$4,500 × 7.722 (Exhibit 8-15)			34,749
PV (market price) of bonds			$96,149

Using the Excel PV function as outlined previously, the inputs are[2]

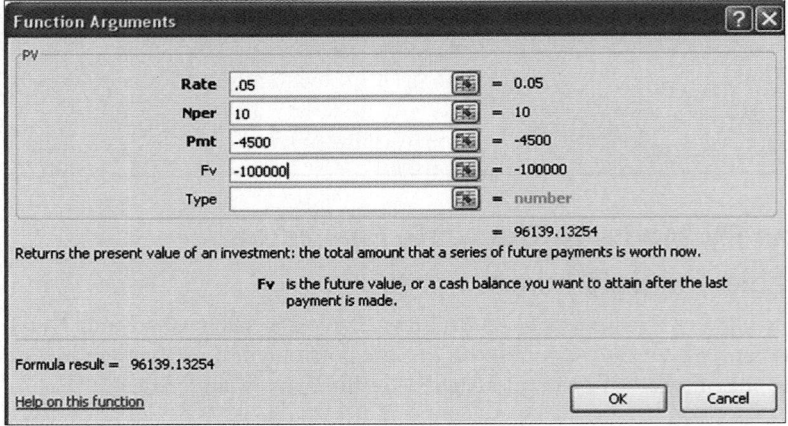

The fair value of the Southwest bonds on the investor's balance sheet would be $96,139 using Excel.[3] Amounts calculated from the PV tables ($96,149) and Excel ($96,139) differ merely by rounding. We discuss accounting for these bonds from the debtor's point of view in Chapter 9 on pages 497–507. It may be helpful for you to re-read this section before you study those pages.

---

[2]Assume that all payments of interest and principal occur at the end of the period, rather than the beginning. Therefore, it is appropriate to leave the Excel table field labeled "Type" blank.

[3]In the real world, bond investments in public companies are typically classified as level 1 investments because they are usually traded in active markets with quoted prices. We use an investment in bonds here to illustrate the valuation computation for level 3 investments because bonds are easier to understand than the more complex types of level 3 investments. The process of estimating fair value using discounted cash flow models is similar for all types of investments.

Intel reports the fair value of its long-term investments and other assets in a (partial) footnote to its 2012 financial statements as follows (in millions):

	Level 1	Level 2	Level 3	Total
Marketable equity securities	4,424	-		4,424
Other long-term assets	69	984	55	1,108

Some of the level 2 and level 3 fair value estimates use discounted cash flow projections such as the ones we have described in this section.

 # End-of-Chapter Summary Problems

1. Translate the balance sheet of the Brazilian subsidiary of **Wrangler Corporation**, a U.S. company, into dollars. When Wrangler acquired this subsidiary, the exchange rate of the Brazilian currency, the real, was $0.40. The average exchange rate applicable to retained earnings is $0.41. The real's current exchange rate is $0.43.

   Before performing the translation, predict whether the translation adjustment will be positive or negative. Does this situation generate a foreign-currency translation gain or loss? Give your reasons.

	Reals
Assets	900,000
Liabilities	600,000
Stockholders' equity:	
Common stock	30,000
Retained earnings	270,000
	900,000

Answers

Translation of foreign-currency balance sheet: This situation will generate a *positive* translation adjustment, which is like a gain. The gain occurs because the real's current exchange rate, which is used to translate net assets (assets minus liabilities), exceeds the historical exchange rates used for stockholders' equity.

The calculation follows:

	Reals	Exchange Rate	Dollars
Assets	900,000	0.43	$387,000
Liabilities	600,000	0.43	$258,000
Stockholders' equity:			
Common stock	30,000	0.40	12,000
Retained earnings	270,000	0.41	110,700
Accumulated other comprehensive income: Foreign-currency translation adjustment	—		6,300
	900,000		$387,000

2. You have invested in a commercial building that you are leasing to a national retail chain. The tenant has signed a 10-year lease agreement that cannot be canceled. You expect to collect $8,000 per month for the full term of the lease. What is the present value of this investment if prevailing interest rates are 12%, compounded monthly?

Answers

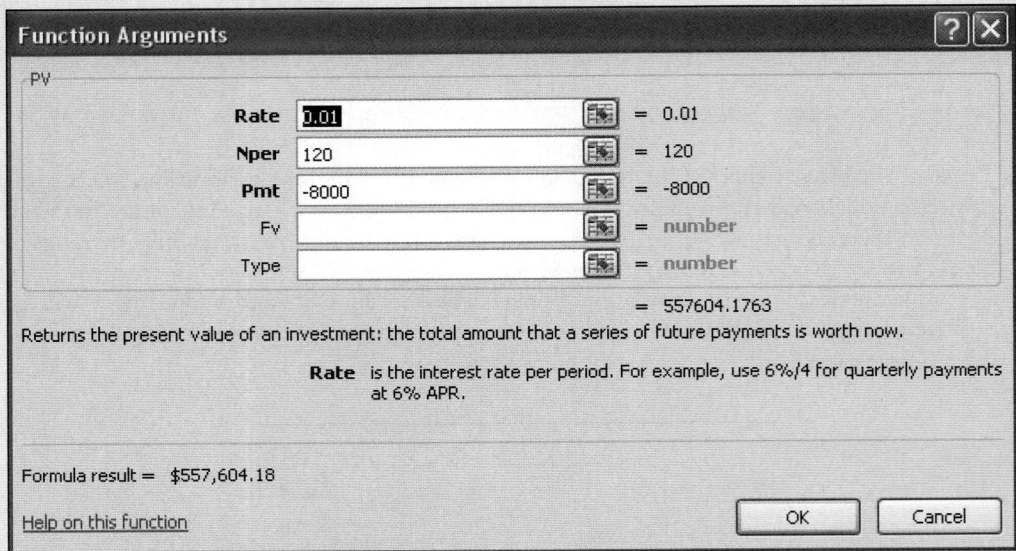

The interest compounds monthly, so it is appropriate to use 120 periods, the number of months in the lease, rather than 10 years. In addition, the yearly interest rate must be adjusted to a monthly rate of 1% (12% ÷ 12). The net present value of this lease is $557,604. Note that you cannot use Exhibit 8-15 since it does not include 1% and does not have 120 periods. The Excel PV function easily gives the result.

REVIEW | Long-Term Investments & the Time Value of Money

Quick Check (Answers are given on page 481.)

1. Mac's investment in less than 2% of Mobil's stock, which Mac expects to hold for three years and then sell, is what type of investment?

   a. Equity
   b. Available-for-sale

   c. Consolidation
   d. Trading

2. Langolis Corporation purchased an available-for-sale investment in 1,600 shares of Southwest Supplies stock for $26 per share. On the next balance-sheet date, Southwest Supplies stock is quoted at $29 per share. Langolis's *balance sheet* should report

   a. unrealized loss of $4,800.
   b. investments of $41,600.

   c. investments of $46,400.
   d. unrealized gain of $41,600.

3. Use the Langolis Corporation data in question 2. Langolis's *income statement* should report

   a. unrealized gain of $4,800.
   b. investments of $41,600.
   c. unrealized loss of $4,800.
   d. nothing, because Langolis hasn't sold the investment.

4. Langolis Corporation purchased an available-for-sale investment in 1,600 shares of Southwest Supplies for $26 per share. On the next balance-sheet date, Southwest Supplies stock is quoted at $29 per share. Langolis sold the Southwest Supplies stock for $55,000 two months later. Langolis's *income statement* for the period of the sale should report a(n)

   a. gain on sale of $13,400.
   b. unrealized gain of $4,800.

   c. loss on sale of $13,400.
   d. investments of $55,000.

5. Sheridan Moving & Storage Co. paid $80,000 for 25% of the common stock of Holland Co. Holland earned net income of $60,000 and declared and paid dividends of $40,000. The carrying value of Sheridan's investment in Holland is

   a. $80,000.
   b. $140,000.

   c. $85,000.
   d. $100,000.

6. Shore, Inc., owns 80% of Rockwall Corporation, and Rockwall owns 80% of Smith Company. During 2014, these companies' net incomes are as follows before any consolidations:

   - Shore, $160,000
   - Rockwall, $70,000
   - Smith, $40,000

   How much net income should Shore report for 2014?

   a. $270,000
   b. $241,600

   c. $248,000
   d. $160,000

7. Majestic, Inc., holds an investment in Cromwell bonds that pay interest each October 31. Majestic's *balance sheet* at December 31 should report

   a. interest receivable.
   b. interest revenue.

   c. interest expense.
   d. interest payable.

8. You are taking a vacation to Germany and you buy euros for $1.65. On your return, you cash in your unused euros for $1.40. During your vacation,
   a. the euro rose against the dollar.
   b. the euro gained value.
   c. the dollar rose against the euro.
   d. the dollar lost value.

9. Arnold Financing leases airplanes to airline companies. Arnold has just signed a 10-year lease agreement that requires annual year-end lease payments of $1,000,000. What is the present value of the lease using a 10% interest rate?
   a. $386,000
   b. $61,450,000
   c. $3,860,000
   d. $6,145,000

10. Sunnyside owns numerous foreign subsidiary companies. When Sunnyside consolidates its Swiss subsidiary, Sunnyside should translate the subsidiary's assets into dollars at the
    a. historical exchange rate when Sunnyside purchased the Swiss company.
    b. current exchange rate.
    c. average exchange rate during the period Sunnyside owned the Swiss subsidiary.
    d. none of the above; there's no need to translate the subsidiary's assets into dollars.

Accounting Vocabulary

available-for-sale securities (p. 433) All investments not classified as held-to-maturity or trading securities.

consolidated financial statements (p. 440) Financial statements of the parent company plus those of more-than-50%-owned subsidiaries as if the combination were a single legal entity.

controlling (majority) interest (p. 440) Ownership of more than 50% of an investee company's voting stock.

equity method (p. 437) The method used to account for investments in which the investor has 20%–50% of the investee's voting stock and can significantly influence the decisions of the investee.

fair value (p. 433) The amount that a seller would receive on the sale of an investment to a willing purchaser on a given date. Available-for-sale securities are valued at fair market values on the balance-sheet date.

foreign-currency exchange rate (p. 446) The measure of one country's currency against another country's currency.

foreign-currency translation adjustment (p. 447) The balancing figure that brings the dollar amount of the total liabilities and stockholders' equity of the foreign subsidiary into agreement with the dollar amount of its total assets.

future value (p. 449) Measures the future sum of money that a given current investment is "worth" at a specified time in the future assuming a certain interest rate.

held-to-maturity investments (p. 431) Bonds and notes that an investor intends to hold until maturity.

long-term investments (p. 431) Any investment that does not meet the criteria of a short-term investment; any investment that the investor expects to hold longer than a year or that is not readily marketable.

noncontrolling (minority) interest (p. 442) A subsidiary company's equity that is held by stockholders other than the parent company (i.e., less than 50%).

parent company (p. 440) An investor company that owns more than 50% of the voting stock of a subsidiary company.

present value (p. 450) The value on a given date of a future payment or series of future payments, discounted to reflect the time value of money.

short-term investments (p. 430) Investment that a company plans to hold for one year or less and the investment is liquid (readily convertible to cash). Also called *marketable securities*.

strong currency (p. 447) A currency whose exchange rate is rising relative to other nations' currencies.

subsidiary (p. 440) An investee company in which a parent company owns more than 50% of the voting stock.

weak currency (p. 447) A currency whose exchange rate is falling relative to that of other nations' currencies.

ASSESS YOUR PROGRESS

Short Exercises

S8-1. *(Learning Objective 2: Analyze and report an available-for-sale investment)* Tiffany Company completed these long-term available-for-sale investment transactions during 2014:

2014	
Apr 10	Purchased 600 shares of Byson stock, paying $17 per share. Tiffany Company intends to hold the investment for the indefinite future.
Jul 22	Received a cash dividend of $1.24 per share on the Byson stock.
Dec 31	Adjusted the Byson investment to its current market value of $5,500.

1. Journalize Tiffany Company's investment transactions. Explanations are not required.
2. Assume the Byson Co. stock is Tiffany Company's only investment. Explain how these transactions will be reflected on Tiffany Company's income statement and its statement of other comprehensive income.
3. Show how to report the investment and any unrealized gain or loss on Tiffany Company's balance sheet at December 31, 2014. Ignore income tax.

S8-2. *(Learning Objective 2: Account for the sale of an available-for-sale investment)* Use the data given in S8-1. On May 21, 2015, Tiffany Company sold its investment in Byson Co. stock for $23 per share.
1. Journalize the sale. No explanation is required.
2. How does the gain or loss that you recorded here differ from the gain or loss that was recorded at December 31, 2014?

S8-3. *(Learning Objective 3: Analyze and report an investment in an affiliate)* Suppose on January 1, 2014, Sperrey Motors paid $260 million for a 35% investment in Phase Motors. Assume Phase earned net income of $34 million and declared and paid cash dividends of $17 million during 2014.
1. What method should Sperrey Motors use to account for the investment in Phase? Give your reason.
2. Journalize these three transactions on the books of Sperrey Motors. Show all amounts in millions of dollars (rounded to the closest million), and include an explanation for each entry.
3. Post to the Equity-Method Investment T-account. What is its balance after all the transactions are posted?

S8-4. *(Learning Objective 3: Account for the sale of an equity-method investment)* Use the data given in S8-3. Assume that on January 1, 2015, Sperrey Motors sold half its investment in Phase Motors. The sale price was $115 million. Compute Sperrey Motors' gain or loss on the sale.

S8-5. *(Learning Objective 4: Define and explain controlling interests and consolidated financial statements)* Answer these questions about consolidation accounting:
1. Define "parent company." Define "subsidiary company."
2. How do consolidated financial statements differ from the financial statements of a single company?
3. Which company's name appears on the consolidated financial statements? How much of the subsidiary's shares must the parent own before reporting consolidated statements?

S8-6. *(Learning Objective 4: Explain goodwill and minority interest)* Two accounts that arise from consolidation accounting are goodwill and noncontrolling interest.

1. What is goodwill, and how does it arise? Which company reports goodwill, the parent or the subsidiary? Where is goodwill reported?
2. What is noncontrolling interest, and which company reports it, the parent or the subsidiary? Where is noncontrolling interest reported?

S8-7. *(Learning Objective 1: Analyze and report investments in held-to-maturity securities)* South Mark (SM) owns vast amounts of corporate bonds. Suppose that on June 30, 2014, SM buys $950,000 of CitiSide bonds at a price of 102. The CitiSide bonds pay cash interest at the annual rate of 7% and mature at the end of five years.

1. How much did SM pay to purchase the bond investment? How much will SM collect when the bond investment matures?
2. How much cash interest will SM receive each year from CitiSide?
3. Will SM's annual interest revenue on the bond investment be more or less than the amount of cash interest received each year? Give your reason.
4. Compute SM's annual interest revenue on this bond investment. Use the straight-line method to amortize the premium on the investment.

S8-8. *(Learning Objective 1: Record held-to-maturity investment transactions)* Return to S8-7, the South Mark (SM) investment in CitiSide bonds. Journalize the following on SM's books:

a. Purchase of the bond investment on June 30, 2014. SM expects to hold the investment to maturity.
b. Receipt of semiannual cash interest on December 31, 2014.
c. Amortization of the premium on the bonds on December 31, 2014. Use the straight-line method.
d. Collection of the investment's face value at the maturity date on June 30, 2019. (Assume the receipt of 2019 interest and the amortization of bonds for 2019 have already been recorded, so ignore these entries.)

S8-9. *(Learning Objective 6: Calculate present value)* Calculate the present value of the following amounts:

1. $10,000 at the end of five years at 8%
2. $10,000 a year at the end of the next five years at 8%

S8-10. *(Learning Objective 6: Calculate the present value of an investment)* Georgetown Leasing leased a car. Georgetown will receive $300 a month for 60 months.

1. What is the present value of the lease if the annual interest rate in the lease in 12%? Use the PV function in Excel to compute the present value.
2. What is the present value of the lease if the car can be sold for $5,000 at the end of five years?

S8-11. *(Learning Objective 5: Report investing transactions on the statement of cash flows)* Companies divide their cash flows into three categories for reporting on the cash flow statement.

1. List the three categories of cash flows in the order they appear on the cash flow statement. Which category of cash flows is most closely related to this chapter?
2. Identify two types of transactions that companies report as cash flows from investing activities.

S8-12. *(Learning Objective 5: Using a statement of cash flows)* Excerpts from The HLH Company statement of cash flows, as adapted, appear as follows:

A1		

	A	B	C
1	**The HLH Company and Subsidiaries** **Consolidated Statement of Cash Flows** **(Adapted)**		
2	(In millions)	**Years Ended December 31,** **2014**	**2013**
3	**Operating Activities**		
4	Net cash provided by operating activities	$ 5,404	$ 1,498
5	**Investing Activities**		
6	Purchases of property, plant, and equipment	(1,001)	(951)
7	Acquisitions and investments, principally		
8	trademarks and bottling companies	(851)	(521)
9	Purchases of investments	(590)	(668)
10	Proceeds from disposals of investments	608	384
11	Proceeds from disposals of property, plant,		
12	and equipment	128	72
13	Other investing activities	183	178
14	Net cash used in investing activities	(1,523)	(1,506)
15	**Financing Activities**		
16	Issuances of debt (borrowing)	3,867	4,704
17	Payments of debt	(5,142)	(5,477)
18	Issuances of stock	220	438
19	Purchases of stock for treasury	(358)	(186)
20	Dividends	(2,298)	(2,172)
21	Net cash used in financing activities	(3,711)	(2,693)
22			

As the chief executive officer of The HLH Company, your duty is to write the management letter to your stockholders explaining HLH's major investing activities during 2014. Compare the company's level of investment with previous years, and indicate how the company financed its investments during 2014. Net income for 2014 was $4,123 million.

Exercises

All of the A and B exercises can be found within MyAccountingLab, an online home-work and practice environment. Your instructor may ask you to complete these exercises using **MyAccountingLab**.

MyAccountingLab

Group A

E8-13A. *(Learning Objective 2: Record transactions for available-for-sale securities)* Journalize the following long-term available-for-sale security transactions of Rogers Brothers Department Stores:

    a. Purchased 520 shares of Florida Fine Foods common stock at $35 per share, with the intent of holding the stock for the indefinite future.
    b. Received a cash dividend of $1.80 per share on the Florida Fine Foods investment.
    c. At year-end, adjusted the investment account to fair value of $42 per share.
    d. Sold the Florida Fine Foods stock for the price of $27 per share.

E8-14A. *(Learning Objective 2: Analyze and report investments in available-for-sale securities)* Bellamonte Co. bought 3,000 shares of German common stock at $40; 620 shares of Chile stock at $47.75; and 1,800 shares of Sweden stock at $78—all as available-for-sale investments. At December 31, Hoover's Online reports German stock at $30.125, Chile at $50.00, and Sweden at $70.00.

Requirements

1. Determine the cost and the fair value of the long-term investment portfolio at December 31.
2. Record Bellamonte's adjusting entry at December 31.
3. What would Bellamonte Co. report on its statement of other comprehensive income and balance sheet for the information given? Make the necessary disclosures. Ignore income tax.

E8-15A. *(Learning Objective 3: Account for transactions using the equity method)* McCloud Corporation owns equity-method investments in several companies. Suppose McCloud paid $1,675,000 to acquire a 45% investment in Trumpp Software Company. Trumpp Software reported net income of $660,000 for the first year and declared and paid cash dividends of $460,000.

Requirements

1. Record the following in McCloud's journal: (a) purchase of the investment, (b) McCloud's proportion of Trumpp Software's net income, and (c) receipt of the cash dividends.
2. What is the ending balance in McCloud's investment account?

E8-16A. *(Learning Objective 3: Analyze gains or losses on equity-method investments)* Without making journal entries, record the transactions of E8-15A directly in the McCloud account, Equity-method Investment. Assume that after all the noted transactions took place, McCloud sold its entire investment in Trumpp Software for cash of $2,370,000. How much is McCloud's gain or loss on the sale of the investment?

E8-17A. *(Learning Objective 3: Apply the appropriate accounting method for a 35% investment)* Russell Financial paid $480,000 for a 35% investment in the common stock of Timberwood, Inc. For the first year, Timberwood reported net income of $185,000 and at year-end declared and paid cash dividends of $95,000. On the balance-sheet date, the fair value of Russell's investment in Timberwood stock was $390,000.

Requirements

1. Which method is appropriate for Russell Financial to use in accounting for its investment in Timberwood, Inc.? Why?
2. Show everything that Russell would report for the investment and any investment revenue in its year-end financial statements.

E8-18A. *(Learning Objective 4: Prepare a consolidated balance sheet)* Alpha, Inc., owns Beta Corp. The two companies' individual balance sheets follow:

	A	B	C	D	E
1	**Alpha, Inc.** **Consolidation Work Sheet**				
2		**Alpha, Inc.**	**Beta Corp.**	**Elimination** **Debit**	**Credit**
3	Cash	$ 46,000	$ 20,000		
4	Accounts receivable, net	75,000	52,000		
5	Note receivable from Alpha	—	29,000		
6	Inventory	56,000	80,000		
7	Investment in Beta	113,000	—		
8	Plant assets, net	283,000	97,000		
9	Other assets	29,000	13,000		
10	Total	$ 602,000	$ 291,000		
11					
12					
13	Accounts payable	$ 49,000	$ 22,000		
14	Notes payable	148,000	33,000		
15	Other liabilities	78,000	123,000		
16	Common stock	112,000	80,000		
17	Retained earnings	215,000	33,000		
18	Total	$ 602,000	$ 291,000		
19					

Requirements

1. Prepare a consolidated balance sheet of Alpha, Inc. It is sufficient to complete the consolidation work sheet. Use Exhibit 8-7 as a model.
2. What is the amount of stockholders' equity for the consolidated entity?

E8-19A. *(Learning Objective 1: Analyze and report held-to-maturity security transactions)* Assume that on September 30, 2014, Protex, Inc., paid 98 for 5.5% bonds of Booker Corporation as a long-term, held-to-maturity investment. The maturity value of the bonds will be $75,000 on September 30, 2019. The bonds pay interest on March 31 and September 30.

Requirements

1. What method should Protex use to account for its investment in the Booker Corp. bonds?
2. Using the straight-line method of amortizing the discount on bonds, journalize all of Protex's transactions on the bonds for 2014.
3. Show how Protex would report everything related to the bond investment on its balance sheet at December 31, 2014.

E8-20A. *(Learning Objective 6: Calculate the present value of a bond investment)* Donte Corp. purchased 10, $1,000, 5% bonds of General Electric Corporation when the market rate of interest was 4%. Interest is paid semiannually on the bonds, and the bonds will mature in six years. Using the PV function in Excel, compute the price Donte paid (the present value) on the bond investment.

E8-21A. *(Learning Objective 4: Translate a foreign-currency balance sheet into dollars)* Translate into dollars the balance sheet of Wyoming Leather Goods' German subsidiary. When Wyoming Leather Goods acquired the foreign subsidiary, a euro was worth $1.03. The current exchange rate is $1.36. During the period when retained earnings were earned, the average exchange rate was $1.15 per euro.

	Euros
Assets	450,000
Liabilities	150,000
Stockholders' equity:	
Common stock....................	90,000
Retained earnings...............	210,000
	450,000

During the period covered by this scenario, which currency was stronger, the dollar or the euro?

E8-22A. *(Learning Objective 5: Prepare and use the statement of cash flows)* During fiscal year 2014, Hearth & Home Bakery reported a net income of $122.9 million. Hearth & Home Bakery received $1.8 million from the sale of other businesses. Hearth & Home Bakery made capital expenditures of $8.1 million and sold property, plant, and equipment for $6.0 million. The company purchased long-term investments at a cost of $11.6 million and sold other long-term investments for $4.3 million.

Requirement

1. Prepare the investing activities section of Hearth & Home Bakery's statement of cash flows. Based solely on Hearth & Home Bakery's investing activities, does it appear that the company is growing or shrinking? How can you tell?

E8-23A. *(Learning Objective 5: Use the statement of cash flows)* At the end of the year, Campus Properties' statement of cash flows reported the following for investment activities:

	A	B
	A1	
	A	**B**
1	**Campus Properties** **Consolidated Statement of Cash Flows (Partial)**	
2	Cash flows from Investing Activities:	
3	Notes receivable collected	$ 2,515,000
4	Purchases of short-term investments	(3,030,000)
5	Proceeds from sales of equipment	630,000*
6	Proceeds from sales of investments (cost of $430,000)	438,000
7	Expenditures for property and equipment	(557,900)
8	Net cash used by investing activities	$ (4,900)
9		

*Cost $4,300,000; Accumulated depreciation, $3,670,000.

Requirement

1. For each item listed, make the journal entry that placed the item on Campus Properties' statement of cash flows.

Group B

E8-24B. *(Learning Objective 2: Record transactions for available-for-sale securities)* Journalize the following long-term, available-for-sale investment transactions of Kennedy Brothers Department Stores:

a. Purchased 650 shares of Cheng Fine Foods common stock at $33 per share, with the intent of holding the stock for the indefinite future.

b. Received a cash dividend of $1.75 per share on the Cheng Fine Foods investment.

c. At year-end, adjusted the investment account to fair value of $38 per share.

d. Sold the Cheng Fine Foods stock for the price of $26 per share.

E8-25B. *(Learning Objective 2: Analyze and report investments in available-for-sale securities)* California Co. bought 3,500 shares of New Brunswick common stock at $34; 740 shares of Paris stock at $46.25; and 1,380 shares of Ireland stock at $73—all as available-for-sale investments. At December 31, Hoover's Online reports New Brunswick stock at $28.125, Paris at $48.00, and Ireland at $68.00.

Requirements

1. Determine the cost and the fair value of the long-term investment portfolio at December 31.
2. Record California Co.'s adjusting entry at December 31.
3. What would California Co. report on its statement of other comprehensive income and balance sheet for the information given? Make the necessary disclosures. Ignore income tax.

E8-26B. *(Learning Objective 3: Account for transactions using the equity method)* Potter Corporation owns equity-method investments in several companies. Suppose Potter paid $1,420,000 to acquire a 35% investment in Needham Software Company. Needham Software reported net income of $660,000 for the first year and declared and paid cash dividends of $400,000.

Requirements

1. Record the following in Potter's journal: (a) purchase of the investment, (b) Potter's proportion of Needham Software's net income, and (c) receipt of the cash dividends.
2. What is the ending balance in Potter's investment account?

E8-27B. *(Learning Objective 3: Analyze gains or losses on equity-method investments)* Without making journal entries, record the transactions of E8-26B directly in the Potter account, Equity-method Investment. Assume that after all the noted transactions took place, Potter sold its entire investment in Needham Software for cash of $1,640,000. How much is Potter's gain or loss on the sale of the investment?

E8-28B. *(Learning Objective 3: Apply the appropriate accounting method for a 45% investment)* Humphrey Financial paid $495,000 for a 45% investment in the common stock of Holmes, Inc. For the first year, Holmes reported net income of $206,000 and at year-end declared and paid cash dividends of $97,000. On the balance-sheet date, the fair value of Humphrey's investment in Holmes stock was $402,000.

Requirements

1. Which method is appropriate for Humphrey Financial to use in its accounting for its investment in Holmes, Inc.? Why?
2. Show everything that Humphrey would report for the investment and any investment revenue in its year-end financial statements.

E8-29B. *(Learning Objective 4: Prepare a consolidated balance sheet)* Zeta, Inc., owns Theta Corp. These two companies' individual balance sheets follow:

	A	B	C	D	E
	A1				
1	**Zeta, Inc.** **Consolidation Work Sheet**				
2		Zeta, Inc.	Theta Corp.	Elimination Debit	Credit
3	Cash	$ 48,000	$ 18,000		
4	Accounts receivable, net	82,000	58,000		
5	Note receivable from Zeta	—	33,000		
6	Inventory	54,000	83,000		
7	Investment in Theta	119,000	—		
8	Plant assets, net	288,000	98,000		
9	Other assets	29,000	11,000		
10	Total	$ 620,000	$ 301,000		
11					
12					
13	Accounts payable	$ 49,000	$ 35,000		
14	Notes payable	152,000	23,000		
15	Other liabilities	78,000	124,000		
16	Common stock	107,000	82,000		
17	Retained earnings	234,000	37,000		
18	Total	$ 620,000	$ 301,000		
19					

Requirements

1. Prepare a consolidated balance sheet of Zeta, Inc. It is sufficient to complete the consolidation work sheet. Use Exhibit 8-7 as a model.
2. What is the amount of stockholders' equity for the consolidated entity?

E8-30B. *(Learning Objective 1: Analyze and report held-to-maturity security transactions)* Assume that on September 30, 2014, Rentex, Inc., paid 96 for 7% bonds of Oleander Corporation as a long-term held-to-maturity investment. The maturity value of the bonds will be $80,000 on September 30, 2019. The bonds pay interest on March 31 and September 30.

Requirements

1. What method should Rentex use to account for its investment in the Oleander Corp. bonds?
2. Using the straight-line method of amortizing the discount on bonds, journalize all of Rentex's transactions on the bonds for 2014.
3. Show how Rentex would report everything related to the bond investment on its balance sheet at December 31, 2014.

E8-31B. *(Learning Objective 6: Calculate the present value of a bond investment)* Itaska Corp. purchased 20 $1,000 4% bonds of Citigroup when the market rate of interest was 3%. Interest is paid semiannually, and the bonds will mature in five years. Using the PV function in Excel, compute the price Itaska paid (the present value) for the bond investment.

E8-32B. *(Learning Objective 4: Translate a foreign-currency balance sheet into dollars)* Translate into dollars the balance sheet of Colorado Leather Goods' Spanish subsidiary. When Colorado Leather Goods acquired the foreign subsidiary, a euro was worth $1.02. The current exchange rate is $1.34. During the period when retained earnings were earned, the average exchange rate was $1.17 per euro.

	Euros
Assets......................................	400,000
Liabilities	300,000
Stockholders' equity:	
Common stock....................	45,000
Retained earnings................	55,000
	400,000

During the period covered by this situation, which currency was stronger, the dollar or the euro?

E8-33B. *(Learning Objective 5: Prepare and use the statement of cash flows)* During fiscal year 2014, Creative Cupcakes reported a net income of $112.4 million. Creative Cupcakes received $1.9 million from the sale of other businesses. Creative Cupcakes made capital expenditures of $8.5 million and sold property, plant, and equipment for $5.8 million. The company purchased long-term investments at a cost of $12.1 million and sold other long-term investments for $4.3 million.

Requirement

1. Prepare the investing activities section of Creative Cupcakes' statement of cash flows. Based solely on Creative Cupcakes' investing activities, does it appear that the company is growing or shrinking? How can you tell?

E8-34B. *(Learning Objective 5: Use the statement of cash flows)* At the end of the year, Mosley Properties' statement of cash flows reported the following for investing activities:

	A	B
	A1	
	A	**B**
1	**Mosley Properties** **Consolidated Statement of Cash Flows (Partial)**	
2	Cash flows from Investing Activities:	
3	Notes receivable collected	$ 2,508,000
4	Purchases of short-term investments	(3,031,000)
5	Proceeds from sales of equipment	419,000*
6	Proceeds from sales of investments (cost of $410,000)	421,000
7	Expenditures for property and equipment	(326,800)
8	Net cash used by investing activities	$ (9,800)
9		

*Cost $4,100,000; Accumulated depreciation, $3,681,000.

Requirement

1. For each item listed, make the journal entry that placed the item on Mosley's statement of cash flows.

Quiz

Test your understanding of long-term investments and international operations by answering the following questions. Select the best choice from among the possible answers given.

Questions 35–37 use the following data:

Assume that Kensell Networks owns the following long-term available-for-sale investments:

Company	Number of Shares	Cost per Share	Year-end Fair Value per Share	Dividend per Share
Hoile Corp.	800	$56	$71	$1.90
Rosewood, Inc.	100	7	11	1.30
Sticks Ltd.	300	20	24	1.10

Q8-35. Kensell's balance sheet at year end should report

    a. investments of $51,500.   **c.** investments of $65,100.

    b. unrealized loss of $13,600.   **d.** dividend revenue of $1,980.

Q8-36. Kensell's income statement for the year should report

    a. unrealized loss of $13,600.   **c.** gain on sale of investment of $13,600.

    b. investments of $51,500.   **d.** dividend revenue of $1,980.

Q8-37. Suppose that, before year-end, Kensell sells the Hoile stock for $67 per share. Journalize the sale.

Q8-38. Dividends received on an equity-method investment

    a. increase owners' equity.   **c.** increase the investment account.

    b. decrease the investment account.   **d.** increase dividend revenue.

Q8-39. The starting point in accounting for all investments is

    a. cost.   **c.** equity value.

    b. cost minus dividends.   **d.** market value on the balance-sheet date.

Q8-40. Consolidation accounting

    a. reports the receivables and payables of the parent company only.

    b. combines the accounts of the parent company and those of the subsidiary companies.

    c. eliminates all liabilities.

    d. all of the above.

Q8-41. On January 1, 2014, Microsport, Inc., purchased $120,000 face value of the 9% bonds of Service Express, Inc., at 104. The bonds mature on January 1, 2019. For the year ended December 31, 2017, Microsport received cash interest of

    a. $10,800.   **c.** $9,800.

    b. $8,800.   **d.** $11,800.

Q8-42. Return to Microsport, Inc.'s bond investment in the preceding question. For the year ended December 31, 2017, Microsport received cash interest of $10,800. What was the interest revenue that Microsport earned in this period?

    a. $9,800   **c.** $9,840

    b. $11,800   **d.** $8,800

Q8-43. The present value of $5,000 at the end of eight years at 5% interest is

    a. $5,000.   **c.** $4,228.

    b. $32,315.   **d.** $3,385.

Q8-44. Which of the following is not needed to compute the present value of an investment?
   a. The interest rate
   b. The rate of inflation
   c. The amount of the receipt
   d. The length of time between the investment and future receipt

Q8-45. What is the present value of bonds with a face value of $5,000; a stated interest rate of 6%; a market rate of 8%; and a maturity date four years in the future? Interest is paid semiannually.
   a. $5,000   **c.** $4,663
   b. $5,393   **d.** $3,947

Q8-46. Consolidation of a foreign subsidiary usually results in a
   a. foreign-currency translation adjustment.
   b. foreign-currency transaction gain or loss.
   c. gain or loss on consolidation.
   d. LIFO/FIFO difference.

Problems

> All of the A and B problems can be found within MyAccountingLab, an online homework and practice environment. Your instructor may ask you to complete these problems using **MyAccountingLab**.

MyAccountingLab

Group A

P8-47A. *(Learning Objectives 2, 3: Analyze and report various long-term investment transactions on the balance sheet and income statement)* Illinois Exchange Company completed the following long-term investment transactions during 2014:

2014	
May 12	Purchased 28,000 shares, which make up 35% of the common stock of Brentwood Corporation at total cost of $420,000.
Jul 9	Received annual cash dividend of $1.25 per share on the Brentwood investment.
Sep 16	Purchased 800 shares of Detroit, Inc., common stock as an available-for-sale investment, paying $41.75 per share.
Oct 30	Received cash dividend of $0.39 per share on the Detroit investment.
Dec 31	Received annual report from Brentwood Corporation. Net income for the year was $475,000.

At year-end, the fair value of the Detroit stock is $31,600. The fair value of the Brentwood stock is $656,000.

Requirements

1. For which investment is fair value used in the accounting? Why is fair value used for one investment and not the other?
2. Show what Illinois Exchange would report on its year-end balance sheet, income statement, and statement of other comprehensive income for these investment transactions. It is helpful to use a T-account for the Equity-method Investment account. Ignore income tax.

P8-48A. *(Learning Objectives 2, 3: Analyze and report available-for-sale and equity-method investments)* The beginning balance sheet of Kendall Corporation included the following:

Equity-method Investment in Bailey Software	$581,000

Kendall Corporation completed the following investment transactions during the year:

Mar 16	Purchased 2,700 shares of Lawrence, Inc., common stock as a long-term available-for-sale investment, paying $12.00 per share.
May 21	Received cash dividend of $0.80 per share on the Lawrence investment.
Aug 17	Received cash dividend of $65,000 from Bailey Software.
Dec 31	Received annual reports from Bailey Software, net income for the year was $612,000. Of this amount Kendall's proportion is 30%.

At year-end, the fair values of Kendall Corporation's investments are as follows: Lawrence, $39,000; Bailey, $692,000.

Requirements

1. Record the transactions in the journal of Kendall Corporation.
2. Post entries to the T-account for Equity-method Investment in Bailey, and determine its balance at December 31.
3. Show how to report the Investment in Available-for-Sale Securities and the Equity-method Investment in Bailey accounts on Kendall Corporation's balance sheet at December 31.

P8-49A. *(Learning Objective 4: Analyze consolidated financial statements)* This problem demonstrates the dramatic effect that consolidation accounting can have on a company's ratios. Snider Motor Company (Snider) owns 100% of Snider Motor Credit Corporation (SMCC), its financing subsidiary. Snider's main operations consist of manufacturing automotive products. SMCC mainly helps people finance the purchase of automobiles from Snider and its dealers. The two companies' individual balance sheets are adapted and summarized as follows (amounts in billions):

	Snider (Parent)	SMCC (Subsidiary)
Total assets	$78.8	$163.1
Total liabilities	$63.8	$155.2
Total stockholders' equity	15.0	7.9
Total liabilities and equity................	$78.8	$163.1

Assume that SMCC's liabilities include $1.6 billion owed to Snider, the parent company.

Requirements

1. Compute the debt ratio of Snider Motor Company considered alone.
2. Determine the consolidated total assets, total liabilities, and stockholders' equity of Snider Motor Company after consolidating the financial statements of SMCC into the totals of Snider, the parent company.
3. Recompute the debt ratio of the consolidated entity. Why do companies prefer not to consolidate their financing subsidiaries into their own financial statements?

P8-50A. *(Learning Objective 4: Consolidate a wholly owned subsidiary)* Assume Jackson, Inc., paid $351,000 to acquire all the common stock of Marshall Corporation and Marshall owes Jackson $168,000 on a note payable. Immediately after the purchase on September 30, 2014, the two companies' balance sheets appear as follows:

	Jackson	Marshall
Assets		
Cash..	$ 48,000	$ 32,000
Accounts receivable, net.......................	179,000	88,000
Note receivable from Marshall..............	168,000	—
Inventory..	329,000	424,000
Investment in Marshall.........................	351,000	—
Plant assets, net....................................	407,000	477,000
Total	$1,482,000	$1,021,000
Liabilities and Stockholders' Equity		
Accounts payable	$ 134,000	$ 64,000
Notes payable	409,000	306,000
Other liabilities	215,000	300,000
Common stock......................................	587,000	260,000
Retained earnings.................................	137,000	91,000
Total	$1,482,000	$1,021,000

Requirement

1. Prepare the work sheet for the consolidated balance sheet of Jackson, Inc. Use Exhibit 8-7 as a model.

P8-51A. *(Learning Objective 1: Analyze and report held-to-maturity investments purchased at a premium)* Insurance companies and pension plans hold large quantities of bond investments. Neill Insurance Corp. purchased $2,500,000 of 6.0% bonds of Summerville, Inc., for 116 on January 1, 2014. These bonds pay interest on January 1 and July 1 each year. They mature on January 1, 2018. At October 31, 2014, the end of the company's fiscal year, the market price of the bonds is 109.

Requirements

1. Journalize Neill's purchase of the bonds as a long-term investment on January 1, 2014 (to be held to maturity), receipt of cash interest, and amortization of the bond premium at July 1, 2014. The straight-line method is appropriate for amortizing the bond investment.
2. Journalize the accrual of interest receivable and amortization of premium on October 31, 2014 (round the answer to the nearest whole number).
3. Show all financial statement effects of this long-term bond investment on Neill Insurance Corp.'s balance sheet at October 31, 2014, and income statement for the year ending October 31, 2014.

P8-52A. *(Learning Objective 6: Explain the impact of the time value of money on valuation of investments)* Annual cash inflows from two competing investment opportunities are given. Each investment opportunity will require the same initial investment.

	Investment	
Year	A	B
1	$14,000	$ 9,000
2	8,000	9,000
3	5,000	9,000
	$27,000	$27,000

Requirement

1. Assuming a 12% interest rate, which investment opportunity would you choose?

P8-53A. *(Learning Objective 4: Consolidate a foreign subsidiary)* Assume that Patel Corporation has a subsidiary company based in Japan.

Requirements

1. Translate into dollars the foreign-currency balance sheet of the Japanese subsidiary of Patel.

	Yen
Assets	¥515,000,000
Liabilities	¥145,000,000
Stockholders' equity:	
Common stock....................	18,000,000
Retained earnings...............	352,000,000
	¥515,000,000

When Patel acquired this subsidiary, the Japanese yen was worth $0.0092. The current exchange rate is $0.0107. During the period when the subsidiary earned its income, the average exchange rate was $0.0095 per yen. Before you perform the foreign-currency translation calculations, indicate whether Patel has experienced a positive or a negative translation adjustment. State whether the adjustment is a gain or a loss, and show where it is reported in the financial statements.

2. To which company does the foreign-currency translation adjustment "belong"? In which company's financial statements will the translation adjustment be reported?

Group B

P8-54B. *(Learning Objectives 2, 3: Analyze and report various long-term investment transactions on the balance sheet and income statement)* Indiana Exchange Company completed the following long-term investment transactions during 2014:

2014	
May 12	Purchased 21,000 shares, which make up 45% of the common stock of Portland Corporation at total cost of $370,000.
Jul 9	Received annual cash dividend of $1.28 per share on the Portland investment.
Sep 16	Purchased 1,100 shares of Sydney, Inc., common stock as an available-for-sale investment, paying $41.75 per share.
Oct 30	Received cash dividend of $0.36 per share on the Sydney investment.
Dec 31	Received annual report from Portland Corporation. Net income for the year was $465,000.

At year-end, the fair value of the Sydney stock is $31,600. The fair value of the Portland stock is $653,000.

Requirements

1. For which investment is fair value used in the accounting? Why is fair value used for one investment and not the other?
2. Show what Indiana Exchange would report on its year-end balance sheet, income statement, and statement of other comprehensive income for these investment transactions. It is helpful to use a T-account for the Equity-method Investment account. Ignore income tax.

P8-55B. *(Learning Objectives 2, 3: Analyze and report available-for-sale and equity-method investments)* The beginning balance sheet of Kyndra Corporation included the following:

Equity-method Investment in KTR Software..	$585,000

Kyndra Corporation completed the following investment transactions during the year:

Mar 16	Purchased 2,900 shares of Littleton, Inc., common stock as a long-term available-for-sale investment, paying $12.50 per share.
May 21	Received cash dividend of $1.20 per share on the Littleton investment.
Aug 17	Received cash dividend of $63,000 from KTR Software.
Dec 31	Received annual reports from KTR Software; net income for the year was $603,000. Of this amount, Kyndra's proportion is 30%.

At year-end, the fair values of Kyndra Corporation's investments are as follows: Littleton, $39,400; KTR, $695,000.

Requirements

1. Record the transactions in the journal of Kyndra Corporation.
2. Post entries to the T-account for Equity-method Investment in KTR Software, and determine its balance at December 31.
3. Show how to report the Investment in Available-for-Sale Securities and the Equity-method Investment in KTR Software accounts on Kyndra Corporation's balance sheet at December 31.

P8-56B. *(Learning Objective 4: Analyze consolidated financial statements)* This problem demonstrates the dramatic effect that consolidation accounting can have on a company's ratios. Race Motor Company (Race) owns 100% of Race Motor Credit Corporation (RMCC), its financing subsidiary. Race's main operations consist of manufacturing automotive products. RMCC mainly helps people finance the purchase of automobiles from Race and its dealers. The two companies' individual balance sheets are adapted and summarized as follows (amounts in billions):

	Race (Parent)	RMCC (Subsidiary)
Total assets	$78.1	$163.3
Total liabilities	$63.8	$155.3
Total stockholders' equity................	14.3	8.0
Total liabilities and equity................	$78.1	$163.3

Assume that RMCC's liabilities include $1.3 billion owed to Race, the parent company.

Requirements

1. Compute the debt ratio of Race Motor Company considered alone.
2. Determine the consolidated total assets, total liabilities, and stockholders' equity of Race Motor Company after consolidating the financial statements of RMCC into the totals of Race, the parent company.
3. Recompute the debt ratio of the consolidated entity. Why do companies prefer not to consolidate their financing subsidiaries into their own financial statements?

P8-57B. *(Learning Objective 4: Consolidate a wholly owned subsidiary)* Assume Abbey, Inc., paid $479,000 to acquire all the common stock of Maine Corporation and Maine owes Abbey $164,000 on a note payable. Immediately after the purchase on September 30, 2014, the two companies' balance sheets are as follows:

	Abbey	Maine
Assets		
Cash	$ 56,000	$ 28,000
Accounts receivable, net	169,000	86,000
Note receivable from Maine	164,000	—
Inventory	321,000	490,000
Investment in Maine	479,000	—
Plant assets, net	407,000	527,000
Total	$1,596,000	$1,131,000
Liabilities and Stockholders' Equity		
Accounts payable	$ 122,000	$ 61,000
Notes payable	409,000	289,000
Other liabilities	223,000	302,000
Common stock	561,000	253,000
Retained earnings	281,000	226,000
Total	$1,596,000	$1,131,000

Requirement

1. Prepare the work sheet for the consolidated balance sheet of Abbey, Inc. Use Exhibit 8-7 as a model.

P8-58B. *(Learning Objective 1: Analyze and report held-to-maturity investments purchased at a premium)* Insurance companies and pension plans hold large quantities of bond investments. Housemann Insurance Corp. purchased $2,600,000 of 10.0% bonds of Sardoan, Inc., for 114 on January 1, 2014. These bonds pay interest on January 1 and July 1 each year. They mature on January 1, 2018. At October 31, 2014, the end of the fiscal year, the market price of the bonds is 105.

Requirements

1. Journalize Housemann's purchase of the bonds as a long-term investment on January 1, 2014 (to be held to maturity), receipt of cash interest, and amortization of the bond premium at July 1, 2014. The straight-line method is appropriate for amortizing the bond investment.
2. Journalize the accrual of interest receivable and amortization of premium on October 31, 2014 (round answer to the nearest whole number).
3. Show all financial statement effects of this long-term bond investment on Housemann Insurance Corp.'s balance sheet at October 31, 2014, and income statement for the year ending October 31, 2014.

P8-59B. *(Learning Objective 6: Explain the impact of the time value of money on the valuation of investments)* Annual cash inflows from two competing investment opportunities are given. Each investment opportunity will require the same initial investment.

	Investment	
Year	X	Y
1	$17,000	$11,000
2	10,000	11,000
3	6,000	11,000
	$33,000	$33,000

Requirement

1. Assuming a 10% interest rate, which investment opportunity would you choose?

P8-60B. *(Learning Objective 4: Consolidate a foreign subsidiary)* Assume that Deepa Corporation has a subsidiary company based in Japan.

Requirements

1. Translate into dollars the foreign-currency balance sheet of the Japanese subsidiary of Deepa.

	Yen
Assets	¥390,000,000
Liabilities	¥145,000,000
Stockholders' equity:	
Common stock....................	21,000,000
Retained earnings................	224,000,000
	¥390,000,000

When Deepa acquired this subsidiary, the Japanese yen was worth $0.0088. The current exchange rate is $0.0103. During the period when the subsidiary earned its income, the average exchange rate was $0.0092 per yen. Before you perform the foreign-currency translation calculations, indicate whether Deepa has experienced a positive or a negative translation adjustment. State whether the adjustment is a gain or a loss, and show where it is reported in the financial statements.

2. To which company does the foreign-currency translation adjustment "belong"? In which company's financial statements will the translation adjustment be reported?

Challenge Exercises and Problem

E8-61. *(Learning Objectives 1, 2, 3, 5: Accounting for various types of investments)* Suppose MyPlace owns the following investments at December 31, 2014:

    a. 100% of the common stock of MyPlace United Kingdom, which holds assets of £600,000 and owes a total of £400,000. At December 31, 2014, the current exchange rate of the pound (£) is £1 = $1.97. The translation rate of the pound applicable to stockholders' equity is £1 = $1.63. During 2014, MyPlace United Kingdom earned net income of £75,000, and the average exchange rate for the year was £1 = $1.89. MyPlace United Kingdom declared and paid cash dividends of £40,000 during 2014.

    b. Investments that MyPlace is holding to sell beyond the current period. These investments comprise less than 20% of the voting stock in the investee. They cost $550,000 and declined in value by $250,000 during 2014, but they paid cash dividends of $25,000 to MyPlace. One year ago, at December 31, 2013, the fair value of these investments was $900,000.

    c. 35% of the common stock of MyPlace Financing Associates. During 2014, MyPlace Financing earned net income of $900,000 and declared and paid cash dividends of $80,000. The carrying amount of this investment was $700,000 at December 31, 2013.

Requirements

1. Which method is used to account for each investment?
2. By how much did each of these investments increase or decrease MyPlace's net income during 2014?
3. For investments b and c, show how MyPlace would report these investments on its balance sheet at December 31, 2014.

E8-62. *(Learning Objectives 2, 4: Explain and analyze accumulated other comprehensive income)*
Brown-Box Retail Corporation reported stockholders' equity on its balance sheet at December 31:

	A	B
	A1	
1	**Brown-Box Retail Corporation** **Balance Sheet (Partial)** **December 31, 2015**	
2	Stockholders' equity: (in millions)	
3	Common stock, $0.10 par value—	
4	1200 million shares authorized	
5	500 million shares issued	$ 50
6	Additional paid-in capital	1,098
7	Retained earnings	6,100
8	Accumulated other comprehensive (loss)	(?)
9	Less: Treasury stock, at cost	(80)
10		

Requirements

1. Identify the two components that typically make up accumulated other comprehensive income.
2. For each component of accumulated other comprehensive income, describe the event that can cause a *positive* balance. Also describe the events that can cause a *negative* balance for each component.
3. At December 31, 2014, Brown-Box Retail's accumulated other comprehensive loss was $57 million. Then during 2015, Brown-Box Retail had a positive foreign-currency translation adjustment of $25 million and an unrealized loss of $15 million on available-for-sale investments. What was Brown-Box Retail's balance of accumulated other comprehensive income (loss) at December 31, 2015?

E8-63. *(Learning Objective 6: Calculate present values of competing investments)* Which option is better: receive $100,000 now or $20,000, $25,000, $30,000, $25,000, and $20,000, respectively, over the next five years?

Requirements

1. Assuming a 5% interest rate, which investment opportunity would you choose?
2. If you could earn 10%, would your choice change?
3. Assuming a 10% interest rate, what would the cash flow in year 5 have to be in order for you to be indifferent to the two plans?

Apply Your Knowledge

Decision Cases

Case 1. *(Learning Objectives 2, 4: Make an investment decision)* Infografix Corporation's consolidated sales for 2014 were $26.6 billion, and expenses totaled $24.8 billion. Infografix operates worldwide and conducts 37% of its business outside the United States. During 2014, Infografix reported the following items in its financial statements (amounts in billions):

Foreign-currency translation adjustments..	$(202)
Unrealized holding _____ on available-for-sale investments.............	(328)

As you consider an investment in Infografix stock, some concerns arise. Answer each of the following questions:

1. What do the parentheses around the two dollar amounts signify?
2. Are these items reported as assets, liabilities, stockholders' equity, revenues, or expenses? Are they normal-balance accounts, or are they contra accounts?
3. Did Infografix include these items in net income? In retained earnings? In the final analysis, how much net income did Infografix report for 2014?
4. Should these items scare you away from investing in Infografix stock? Why or why not? (Challenge)

Case 2. *(Learning Objectives 1, 2, 5: Make an investment sale decision)* Cathy Talbert is the general manager of Barham Company, which provides data-management services for physicians in the Columbus, Ohio, area. Barham Company is having a rough year. Net income trails projections for the year by almost $75,000. This shortfall is especially important. Barham plans to issue stock early next year and needs to show investors that the company can meet its earnings targets.

Barham holds several investments purchased a few years ago. Even though investing in stocks is outside Barham's core business of data-management services, Talbert thinks these investments may hold the key to helping the company meet its net income goal for the year. She is considering what to do with the following investments:

1. Barham owns 50% of the common stock of Ohio Office Systems, which provides the business forms that Barham uses. Ohio Office Systems has lost money for the past two years but still has a retained earnings balance of $550,000. Talbert thinks she can get Ohio's treasurer to declare a $160,000 cash dividend, half of which would go to Barham.
2. Barham owns a bond investment purchased eight years ago for $250,000. The purchase price represents a discount from the bonds' maturity value of $400,000. These bonds mature two years from now, and Barham purchased them as a long-term investment intending to hold them until they matured. Their current market value is $380,000. Ms. Talbert has checked with a **Charles Schwab** investment representative, and she is considering selling the bonds. Schwab would charge a 1% commission on the sale transaction.
3. Barham owns 5,000 shares of **Microsoft** stock valued at $53 per share as a long-term investment. One year ago, Microsoft stock was worth only $28 per share. Barham purchased the Microsoft stock for $37 per share. Talbert wonders whether Barham should sell the Microsoft stock.

Requirement

1. Evaluate all three actions as a way for Barham Company to generate the needed amount of income. Recommend the best way for Barham to achieve its net income goal.

Ethical Issue

Media One owns 18% of the voting stock of Web Talk, Inc. The remainder of the Web Talk stock is held by numerous investors with small holdings. Austin Cohen, president of Media One and a member of Web Talk's board of directors, heavily influences Web Talk's policies.

Under the fair value method of accounting for investments, Media One's net income increases as it receives dividend revenue from Web Talk. Media One pays President Cohen a bonus computed as a percentage of Media One's net income. Therefore, Cohen can control his personal bonus to a certain extent by influencing Web Talk's dividends.

A recession occurs in 2014, and Media One's income is low. Cohen uses his power to have Web Talk pay a large cash dividend. The action requires Web Talk to borrow in order to pay the dividend.

Requirements

1. What are the ethical issues in the Media One case?
2. Who are the stakeholders? What are the possible consequences to each?
3. What are the alternatives for Austin Cohen to consider? Analyze each alternative from the following standpoints: (a) economic, (b) legal, (c) ethical.
4. If you were Cohen, what would you do?
5. Discuss how using the equity method of accounting for the investment would decrease Cohen's potential for manipulating his bonus.

Focus on Financials | Amazon.com, Inc.

(Learning Objectives 2, 3, 4: Analyze investments, consolidated subsidiaries, and international operations) The consolidated financial statements of **Amazon.com, Inc.**, are given in Appendix A at the end of this book.

1. Refer to Note 1—Description of Business and Accounting Policies, under *Investments*. Describe the method of accounting used for investments over which the company can exercise significant influence but not control. How does the company classify these investments on its balance sheet? How does the company account for these investments on its income statement?
2. Does Amazon.com have any other types of investments other than those described in (1)? How does the company account for them? Does it adjust for periodic changes in fair value of these investments? If so, where do these adjustments appear?
3. Does Amazon.com, Inc., make any fair value adjustments to its investment portfolio? Which levels of fair value does it use? Why do you think it uses these methods?
4. What are Amazon.com's principles of consolidation? Where do you find them?

Focus on Analysis | Yum! Brands, Inc.

(Learning Objectives 2, 3, 4: Analyze and report available-for-sale investments; analyze consolidated statements and international operations) This case is based on the consolidated financial statements of **Yum! Brands, Inc.** given in Appendix B at the end of this book.

1. Read Note 1—Description of Business. How many system units (company-owned as well as franchise) did the company operate as of December 31, 2012? What percentage of these units were outside the United States? In how many countries and/or territories do they operate?
2. Read Note 1—Description of Business—and Note 18—Reportable Operating Segments. The company lists six operating segments worldwide. List these segments. Which is the largest?
3. Read Note 2—Summary of Significant Accounting Policies—Principles of Consolidation and Basis of Preparation. Which entities does Yum! Brands, Inc., consolidate? How does it treat amounts that are owed to/from various subsidiaries?

Group Project

Pick a stock from *The Wall Street Journal* or another database or publication. Assume that your group purchases 1,000 shares of the stock as a long-term investment and that your 1,000 shares are less than 20% of the company's outstanding stock. Research the stock in *Value Line*, *Moody's Investor Record*, or another source to determine whether the company pays cash dividends and, if so, how much and at what intervals.

Requirements

1. Track the stock for a period assigned by your professor. Over the specified period, keep a daily record of the price of the stock to see how well your investment has performed. Each day, search the Corporate Dividend News in *The Wall Street Journal* to keep a record of any dividends you've received. End the period of your analysis with a month-end, such as September 30 or December 31.
2. Journalize all transactions that you have experienced, including the stock purchase, dividends received (both cash dividends and stock dividends), and any year-end adjustment required by the accounting method that is appropriate for your situation. Assume you will prepare financial statements on the ending date of your study.
3. Show what you will report on your company's balance sheet, income statement, and statement of cash flows as a result of your investment transactions.

> **For online homework, exercises, and problems that provide you with immediate feedback, please visit www.myaccountinglab.com.**

MyAccountingLab

Quick Check Answers

1. *b*
2. *c* (1,600 shares × $29 = $46,400)
3. *d*
4. *a* ($55,000 − $41,600 original cost)
5. *c* [$80,000 + 0.25($60,000 − $40,000) = $85,000]
6. *b* [$160,000 + 0.80($70,000) + 0.64($40,000) = $241,600]
7. *a*
8. *c*
9. *d*
10. *b*

Liabilities

9

Southwest Airlines has been charting its own course in the airline industry for over 40 years. The company began operating as a short-haul, no-frills carrier in 1971, with only three Boeing 737 aircraft, serving Dallas, Houston, and San Antonio, Texas, business commuters with peanuts and drinks rather than lunch or dinner between stops. The company has gained a reputation through the years of providing reliable, low-cost travel from close-in, smaller airports that are convenient for many business commuters or vacationers. Through the years, Southwest has determined to keep operating costs lower than other carriers, passing the savings on to customers in the form of low fares. As of December 31, 2012, Southwest was the largest domestic air carrier in the United States, serving 97 destinations in 41 states, the District of Columbia, Puerto Rico, and 6 "near-international countries," including Mexico, Jamaica, the Bahamas, Aruba, the Dominican Republic, and Bermuda, with a fleet of 694 aircraft. Despite turbulence in a very volatile industry, Southwest has managed to remain consistently profitable while other airlines have experienced consistent losses. In 2012, the company earned $421 million on operating revenue of $17 billion. The company has also remained much more healthy than other airline companies from a liquidity standpoint. In 2011, Southwest purchased AirTran Airways, a competitor, largely with cash and stock.

So why focus on its liabilities? Like other airlines, Southwest has reported some interesting liabilities on the face of its balance sheet, as seen on the next page. For example, Southwest's Rapid Rewards program awards points for paid miles flown that can be redeemed by customers for free flights in the future. Southwest accrues a frequent-flier liability for this program and reports "Accrued liabilities" on the company's consolidated balance sheets. Southwest also collects cash in advance for tickets sold that will be used at a later time. This creates unearned revenue that Southwest reports as "Air traffic liability," to be reversed later as customers redeem their tickets. Both of these types of liabilities are shown in the current liability section of the balance sheets. Southwest also reports "Long-term debt," which consists of notes and bonds payable. The company has incurred these liabilities to finance purchases of their largest class of assets, which is the fleet of purchased aircraft.

Ilene MacDonald/Alamy

One of the most interesting things about Southwest's obligations is not so much those that are reported as current or long-term liabilities on the face of the balance sheet, but those that are not. The footnotes to the financial statements disclose that the company leases many of its aircraft, for which it has future obligations to make lease payments. Most of these obligations are not recorded as liabilities, because the terms of the lease contracts are written in such a way that the company does not have ownership in the assets after the lease obligations are satisfied. In addition, the company has signed agreements with **Boeing Corporation** that obligate it to purchase a certain number of new aircraft per year for a number of years into the future. Although these obligations have not yet occurred, the company is required to disclose them in the footnotes. ●

	A1	⬍			
	A			**B**	**C**
1	**Southwest Airlines Company** **Consolidated Balance Sheets (Adapted)**				
2				**Dec. 31, 2012**	**Dec. 31, 2011**
3	**(In Millions of $)**				
4	**Current assets**				
5	Cash and cash equivalents			$ 1,113	$ 829
6	Short-term investments			1,857	2,315
7	Accounts and other receivables			332	299
8	Inventories of parts and supplies			469	401
9	Deferred income taxes			246	263
10	Prepaid expenses and other			210	238
11	Total current assets			4,227	4,345
12	Property and equipment, at cost				
13	Flight equipment			16,367	15,542
14	Ground property and equipment			2,714	2,423
15	Deposits on purchase contracts			416	456
16	Property and equipment, at cost			19,497	18,421
17	Accumulated depreciation			(6,731)	(6,294)
18	Property and equipment, net			12,766	12,127
19	Goodwill			970	970
20	Other assets			633	626
21	**Total assets**			$ 18,596	$ 18,068
22	**Current liabilities**				
23	Accounts payable			$ 1,107	$ 1,057
24	Accrued liabilities			1,102	996
25	Air traffic liability			2,170	1,836
26	Current maturities of long-term debt			271	644
27	Total current liabilities			4,650	4,533
28	Long-term debt less current maturities			2,883	3,107
29	Deferred income taxes			2,884	2,566
30	Other noncurrent liabilities			1,187	985
31	**Total liabilities**			11,604	11,191
32	**Stockholders' equity**				
33	Common stock			808	808
34	Capital in excess of par value			1,210	1,222
35	Retained earnings			5,768	5,395
36	Accumulated other comprehensive (loss)			(119)	(224)
37	Treasury stock, at cost			(675)	(324)
38	**Total stockholders' equity**			6,992	6,877
39	**Total liabilities and stockholders' equity**			$ 18,596	$ 18,068
40					

This chapter shows how to account for liabilities—both current and long-term— and those obligations that are merely footnote disclosures. We begin with current liabilities.

Learning Objectives

1. **Account for** current and contingent liabilities

2. **Account for** bonds payable, notes payable, and interest expense

3. **Analyze and differentiate** financing with debt vs. equity

4. **Understand** other long-term liabilities

5. **Report** liabilities

You can access the most current annual report of Southwest Airlines Company in Excel format at **www.sec.gov**. Using the "filings" link on the toolbar at the top of the home page, select "company filings search." This will take you to the "Edgar Company Filings" page. Type "Southwest Airlines" in the company name box, and select "search." This will produce the "EDGAR Search Results" page showing the company name. Click on the "CIK" link beside the company name. This will pull up all of the reports the company has filed with the SEC. Under the "filing type" box, type "10-K" and click the search box. Form 10-K is the SEC form for the company's latest annual report. Find the year that you wish to view. Click on the "Interactive Data" box, which takes you to the "View Filing Data" page. Find and click on the "View Excel Document" link at the top of this page. You may choose to either open or download the Excel files containing the company's most recent financial statements. ■

ACCOUNT FOR CURRENT AND CONTINGENT LIABILITIES

1 Account for current and contingent liabilities

Current liabilities are obligations due within one year or within the company's normal operating cycle if longer than a year. Obligations due beyond that period of time are classified as *long-term liabilities*.

Current liabilities are of two kinds:

- Known amounts
- Estimated amounts

We look first at current liabilities of a known amount.

Current Liabilities of Known Amount

Current liabilities of known amount include accounts payable, short-term notes payable, sales tax payable, accrued liabilities, payroll liabilities, unearned revenues, and the current portion of long-term debt.

Accounts Payable. Amounts owed for products or services purchased on account are *accounts payable*. Southwest Airlines Co. reported Accounts Payable of $1,107 million at December 31, 2012 (line 23 on page 483). For example, Southwest Airlines purchases soft drinks and napkins as well as spare parts for aircraft maintenance on accounts payable. We have seen many other accounts payable examples in preceding chapters. One of a merchandiser's most common transactions is the credit purchase of inventory. **Walmart Stores, Inc.,** and **Target Corp.** buy their inventory on account.

Accounts Payable Turnover. An important measure of liquidity for a retail business is **accounts payable turnover**, which measures the number of times a year a company is able to pay its accounts payable. The ratio is computed as follows:

Accounts payable turnover (T/O) = Purchases from suppliers (assumed all on credit)
÷ Average accounts payable
Turnover expressed in days = 365 ÷ T/O (computed above)

The difficulty of computing this ratio is that "purchases from suppliers" is not normally reflected in any number on the financial statements. Therefore, it must be computed. In a merchandising company, inventory purchases can be computed by analyzing the activity in the inventory account and solving for merchandise purchases, as follows:

Inventory

Beginning balance (from balance sheet)	Cost of goods sold (from income statement)
Purchases from suppliers*	
Ending balance (from balance sheet)	

*Purchases from suppliers (assumed all on credit) = Cost of goods sold (from income statement) + Ending inventory (from comparative balance sheet) – Beginning inventory (from comparative balance sheet)

Once the turnover is computed, it is usually expressed in number of days, or **days' payable outstanding (DPO)** by dividing the turnover into 365. Here are comparative ratios for accounts payable turnover for **Walmart Stores, Inc.,** and **Target Corp.** from their 2012 financial statements:

	Walmart Stores, Inc.	Target Corp.
Cost of goods sold	$ 352,488	$ 50,568
+ Ending inventory	+ 43,803	+ 7,903
− Beginning inventory	− 40,714	− 7,918
= Purchases	= 355,577	= 50,553
÷ Average accounts payable	÷ 37,344	÷ 6,957
= Accounts payable turnover	= 9.52	= 7.27
Days' payable outstanding (365/turnover)	38 days	50 days

If there is not a material difference between beginning and ending inventories (i.e., if they haven't increased or decreased very much during the year), it is not necessary to adjust for inventory amounts, as the difference has zero effect on the turnover ratio. This makes the computation easier; simply divide cost of goods sold by average accounts payable to compute accounts payable turnover, then divide the turnover ratio into 365 for DPO.

Walmart pays its accounts payable in about 38 days, whereas Target takes 50 days to pay its accounts payable. If you were a supplier of these two giant companies, which would you rather do business with, on the basis of this ratio? If cash collections are important to you in order to pay your own bills, the obvious answer is Walmart, based strictly on this ratio.

What makes an accounts payable turnover ratio strong or weak in the eyes of creditors and investors? Generally, a high turnover ratio (short period in days) is better than a low turnover ratio. Companies with shorter payment periods are generally better credit risks than those with longer payment periods. However, some companies with strong credit ratings strategically follow shrewd cash management policies, withholding payment to suppliers as long as possible, while speeding up collections, in order to conserve cash. For example, Walmart's accounts payable turnover of about 38 days and Target's 50 days are longer than a typical 30-day credit period. These huge companies strategically stretch payment periods in order to maximize returns on excess cash, which is tough on suppliers. However, because of their size, market share, and buying power, few suppliers can afford not to do business with Walmart and Target.

To be sure, credit and sales decisions are based on far more information than accounts payable turnover, so it's wise not to oversimplify. However, combined with inventory turnover (discussed in Chapter 6) and accounts receivable turnover (discussed in Chapter 5), all expressed in days, accounts payable turnover is an important ingredient in computing the *cash conversion cycle*, which is an overall measure of liquidity. Combined with the current ratio (discussed in Chapter 3) and the quick ratio (discussed in Chapter 5), studying the cash conversion cycle helps users of financial statements determine the overall liquidity of a company. We will discuss the cash conversion cycle in more depth in Chapter 13.

It is not possible to compute turnover ratios for inventory or accounts payable for a service business, because service businesses have neither cost of goods sold nor inventory. For example, Southwest Airlines, being a service company, has no cost of goods sold account on its financial statements. Although the company reports a small inventory of parts and supplies on its balance sheet, these are not comparable to inventories in a retail business. Therefore, neither inventory turnover nor accounts payable turnover for Southwest Airlines would be meaningful.

Short-Term Notes Payable. **Short-term notes payable**, a common form of financing, are notes payable due within one year. **Starbucks** lists its short-term notes payable as *short-term borrowings*. Starbucks may issue short-term notes payable to borrow cash or to purchase assets. On its notes payable, Starbucks must accrue interest expense and interest payable at the end of the period. The following sequence of entries covers the purchase of inventory, accrual of interest expense, and payment of a 10% short-term note payable that's due in one year:

	A1			
	A	**B**	**C**	**D**
1	2014			
2	Jan 1	Inventory	8,000	
3		Note Payable, Short-Term		8,000
4		*Purchase of inventory by issuing a note payable.*		
5				

This transaction increases both an asset and a liability.

Assets	=	Liabilities	+	Stockholders' Equity
+ 8,000	=	+ 8,000	+	0

The Starbucks fiscal year ends each September 30. At year-end, Starbucks must accrue interest expense at 10% for January through September:

	A1			
	A	**B**	**C**	**D**
1	Sep 30	Interest Expense ($8,000 × 0.10 × 9/12)	600	
2		Interest Payable		600
3		*Accrual of interest expense at year-end.*		
4				

Liabilities increase and equity decreases because of the expense.

Assets	=	Liabilities	+	Stockholders' Equity	−	Expenses
0	=	+ 600				− 600

The balance sheet at year-end will report the Note Payable of $8,000 and the related Interest Payable of $600 as current liabilities. The income statement will report interest expense of $600.

The following entry records the note's payment at maturity on January 1, 2015:

	A	B	C	D
		A1 ⬍		
1	2015			
2	Jan 1	Note Payable, Short-Term	8,000	
3		Interest Payable	600	
4		Interest Expense ($8,000 × 0.10 × 3/12)	200	
5		Cash [$8,000 + ($8,000 × 0.10)]		8,800
6		*Payment of a note payable and interest at maturity.*		
7				
8				

The debits zero out the payables and also record Starbucks' interest expense for October, November, and December.

Sales Tax Payable. Most states levy a sales tax on retail sales. Retailers collect the tax from customers and thus owe the state for sales tax collected. Suppose one Saturday's sales at a Home Depot store totaled $200,000 (assume this is all in cash). Home Depot collected an additional 5% ($10,000) of sales tax. The store would record that day's sales as follows:

	A	B	C
	A1 ⬍		
1	Cash ($200,000 × 1.05)	210,000	
2	Sales Revenue		200,000
3	Sales Tax Payable ($200,000 × 0.05)		10,000
4	*To record cash sales and the related sales tax.*		
5			

Assets, liabilities, and equity all increase—equity because of the revenues.

Assets	=	Liabilities	+	Stockholders' Equity	+	Revenues
+ 210,000	=	+ 10,000				+ 200,000

Accrued Liabilities (Accrued Expenses). An **accrued liability** usually results from an expense that the business has incurred but not yet paid. Therefore, an accrued expense creates a liability, which explains why it is also called an **accrued expense**. Southwest Airlines Co. reported Accrued liabilities of $1,102 million at December 31, 2012 (line 24 on page 483).

For example, Southwest Airlines' salary expense and salary payable occur as employees work for the company. Interest expense accrues with the passage of time. There are several categories of accrued expenses:

- Salaries and Wages Payable
- Interest Payable
- Income Taxes Payable

Salaries and Wages Payable is the liability for payroll expenses not yet paid at the end of the period. This category includes salaries, wages, and payroll taxes withheld from employee paychecks. *Interest Payable* is the company's interest payable on notes payable. *Income Taxes Payable* is the amount of income tax the company still owes at year-end.

Payroll Liabilities. **Payroll**, also called *employee compensation*, is a major expense. For service organizations—such as law firms, real estate companies, and airlines—compensation is *the* major expense, just as cost of goods sold is the largest expense for a merchandising company.

Employee compensation takes many different forms. A *salary* is employee pay stated at a monthly or yearly rate. A *wage* is employee pay stated at an hourly rate. Sales employees earn a *commission*, which is a percentage of the sales the employee has made. A *bonus* is an amount over and above regular compensation. Accounting for all forms of compensation follows the pattern illustrated in Exhibit 9-1 (using assumed figures):

Exhibit 9-1 | Accounting for Payroll Expenses and Liabilities

	A1 ‡				
		A		B	C
1	Salary Expense			10,000	
2	Employee Income Tax Payable				1,200
3	FICA Tax Payable				800
4	Salary Payable [take-home pay]				8,000
5	*To record salary expense.*				
6					

Every expense accrual has the same effect: Liabilities increase and equity decreases because of the expense. The accounting equation shows these effects.

Assets	=	Liabilities	+	Stockholders' Equity	−	Expenses
		+ 1,200				− 10,000
0	=	+ 800				
		+ 8,000				

Salary expense represents *gross pay* (that is, employee pay before subtractions for taxes and other deductions). Salary expense creates several payroll liabilities:

- *Employee Income Tax Payable* is the employees' income tax that has been withheld from paychecks.
- *FICA Tax Payable* includes the employees' Social Security tax and Medicare tax, which also are withheld from paychecks. (FICA stands for the Federal Insurance Contributions Act, which created the Social Security tax.)
- *Salary Payable* is their net (take-home) pay.

Companies must also pay some *employer* payroll taxes and expenses for employee benefits. Accounting for these expenses is similar to the illustration in Exhibit 9-1.

Unearned Revenues. *Unearned revenues* are also called *deferred revenues* and *revenues collected in advance.* For all unearned revenue, the business has received cash from customers before earning the revenue. The company has a liability—an obligation to provide goods or services to the customer. Let's consider an example.

Southwest Airlines sells tickets and collects cash in advance. Southwest therefore reports unearned ticket revenue (which it calls Air traffic liability) for airline tickets sold in advance. At December 31, 2012, Southwest owed customers $2,170 million of air travel (see line 25 on page 483). Let's see how Southwest accounts for its Air traffic liability.

To illustrate with a transaction during 2014, assume that, on December 15, that Southwest collects $300 for a round-trip ticket from Dallas to Los Angeles. Southwest records the cash collection and related liability as follows:

	A1 ‡				
	A		B	C	D
1	2014				
2	Dec 15	Cash		300	
3		Air traffic liability			300
4		*Received cash in advance for ticket sale.*			
5					

Air traffic liability

	300

Suppose the customer flies to Los Angeles late in December. Southwest records the revenue earned as follows:

	A	B	C	D
1	2014			
2	Dec 28	Air traffic liability	150	
3		Ticket Revenue ($300 × 1/2)		150
4		*Earned revenue that was collected in advance.*		
5				

Air traffic liability

150	300
	Bal 150

Ticket Revenue

	150

The liability decreases and the revenue increases.

At year-end, Southwest reports

- $150 of Air traffic liability on the balance sheet, and
- $150 of ticket revenue on the income statement.

The customer returns to Dallas in January 2015, and Southwest records the revenue earned with this journal entry:

	A	B	C	D
1	2015			
2	Jan 4	Air traffic liability	150	
3		Ticket Revenue ($300 × 1/2)		150
4		*Earned revenue that was collected in advance.*		
5				

Now the liability balance is zero because Southwest has earned all the revenue it collected in advance.

Air traffic liability

150	300
150	
	Bal 0

Current Portion of Long-Term Debt. Some long-term debt must be paid in installments. The **current portion of long-term debt** (also called *current maturity* or *current installment*) is the amount of the principal that is payable within one year. At the end of each year, a company reclassifies (from long-term debt to a current liability) the amount of its long-term debt that must be paid next year.

Southwest Airlines reports Current maturities of long-term debt in the amount of $271 million as of December 31, 2012 (line 26 on page 483). Southwest also reports a long-term liability (line 28) in the amount of $2,883 million for Long-term debt, which excludes the current maturities. *Long-term debt* refers to long-term notes payable and bonds payable, which we cover in the second half of this chapter.

Current Liabilities That Must Be Estimated

A business may know that a liability exists but not know its exact amount. The business must report the liability on the balance sheet. Estimated liabilities vary among companies. Let's look first at Estimated Warranty Payable, a liability account that most merchandisers have.

Estimated Warranty Payable. Many companies guarantee their products under *warranty* agreements. The warranty period may extend for 90 days to a year for consumer products. Automobile companies—like **General Motors, BMW**, and **Toyota**—accrue liabilities for vehicle warranties.

Whatever the warranty's life, the expense recognition (matching) principle demands that the company record the *warranty expense* in the same period that the business records sales revenue. After all, the warranty motivates customers to buy products, so the company must record warranty expense in the period of sale. At the time of the sale, however, the company doesn't know which products are defective. The exact amount of warranty expense cannot be known with certainty, so the business must estimate warranty expense and the related liability.

Assume that **Black & Decker**, which manufactures power tools, made sales of $100,000 subject to product warranties. Assume that in past years between 2% and 4% of products proved defective. Black & Decker could estimate that 3% of sales will require repair or replacement. In this case, Black & Decker would estimate warranty expense of $3,000 ($100,000 × 0.03) for the year and make the following entry:

	A	B	C	D
A1				
1		Warranty Expense	3,000	
2		Estimated Warranty Payable		3,000
3		*To accrue warranty expense.*		
4				

Estimated Warranty Payable

	3,000

Assume that defects add up to $2,800, and Black & Decker will replace the defective products. Black & Decker then records the following:

	A	B	C	D
A1				
1		Estimated Warranty Payable	2,800	
2		Inventory		2,800
3		*To replace defective products sold under warranty.*		
4				

Estimated Warranty Payable

2,800	3,000
	Bal 200

At the end of the year, Black & Decker will report Estimated Warranty Payable of $200 as a current liability. The income statement reports Warranty Expense of $3,000 for the year. Then, next year Black & Decker will repeat this process. The Estimated Warranty Payable account probably won't ever zero out. If Black & Decker paid cash to satisfy the warranty, then the credit would be to Cash rather than to Inventory.

Vacation pay is another expense that must be estimated. And income taxes must be estimated because the final amount isn't determined until early the next year.

Contingent Liabilities

A *contingent liability* is not an actual liability. Instead, it's a potential liability that depends on the future outcome of past events. Examples of contingent liabilities are future obligations that may arise because of lawsuits, tax disputes, or alleged violations of environmental protection laws. The principle of representational faithfulness, discussed in Chapter 1, requires that companies disclose the substance of their financial positions and results of operations in a way that is as transparent and complete as possible. With liabilities, that principle implies: "When in doubt, disclose. When necessary, accrue." The Financial Accounting Standards Board (FASB) provides these guidelines to account for contingent liabilities[1]:

1. *Accrue* (i.e., make an adjusting journal entry for) a contingent liability if, in management's opinion, it's *probable* that the loss (or expense) will occur *and* the *amount can be reasonably estimated*. Warranty expense, illustrated previously, is an example. Another example is a lawsuit that has been settled as of the balance-sheet date but has not yet been paid.

2. *Disclose* a contingency in a financial statement note if it's *reasonably possible* (less than probable but more than remote) that a loss (or expense) will occur. Lawsuits in progress are a prime example. Southwest Airlines includes a note in its 2012 financial statements to report contingent liabilities from examinations of its past income tax returns by the IRS.

> **Note 17, Contingencies**
>
> The Company is subject to various legal proceedings [...] including [...] examinations by the Internal Revenue Service (IRS). The IRS regularly examines the Company's federal income tax returns and, in the course thereof, proposes adjustments to the Company's federal income tax liability reported on such returns. The Company's management does not expect that [...] any of its currently ongoing legal proceedings or [...] any proposed adjustments [...] by the IRS [...] will have a material adverse effect on the Company's financial condition, results of operations, or cash flow.

3. There is no need to report a contingent loss that is unlikely to occur. Instead, wait until an actual transaction clears up the situation. For example, suppose **Del Monte Foods** grows vegetables in Nicaragua, and the Nicaraguan government threatens to confiscate the assets of all foreign companies. Del Monte will report nothing about the contingency if the probability of a loss is considered remote.

A contingent liability may arise from lawsuits that claim wrongdoing by the company. The plaintiff may seek damages through the courts. If the court rules in favor of Southwest, there is no liability. But if the ruling favors the plaintiff, then Southwest will have an actual liability. It would be unethical to omit these disclosures from the financial statements because investors need this information to properly evaluate a company.

Commitments. Disclosure of contractual commitments often fall in the same category as contingencies, although they are slightly different. Commitments represent contractual promises a company has made to enter into transactions in the future and thus obligate the company to

---

[1]The FASB is currently reconsidering its disclosure requirements for contingent liabilities. If the new requirements are adopted, entities will be required to expand and enhance disclosures of loss contingencies. Specifically, *regardless of likelihood*, entities would be required to *disclose* loss contingencies if, in the opinion of management, they could have a *severe impact* on the entity's financial position, cash flows, or results of operation. An example of such a situation is a lawsuit that could put the company out of business within the next *year*. Both quantitative (dollar amounts) and qualitative (descriptive) information would be included. In addition, for all amounts *accrued*, the entity would have to include a table and explanations that show how these accruals have changed from the previous period. These proposals are similar, but not identical to, proposed changes in IFRS requirements for loss contingencies.

commit resources toward a certain purpose. Note 4 of Southwest Airlines Company's financial statements (the same note that describes contingencies) also includes a chart that describes the company's contractual purchase commitments to take delivery of 563 new Boeing 737 aircraft during years 2013 through 2027. It would not be proper to accrue commitments because the transactions have not yet occurred as of the balance-sheet date. However, because of the substantial amount of money required to fulfill these commitments (one plane costs $50–$70 million), Southwest is obligated to disclose them to shareholders and creditors, because they will have a substantial impact on the company's financial statements in future years.

> ### Global View
>
> The international accounting standard for loss contingencies requires accrual (i.e., journal entries) for *both* probable and possible contingent liabilities. The threshold for *probable* under IFRS is lower than the threshold under U.S. GAAP, which means that IFRS requires accrual of loss contingencies more frequently than U.S. GAAP.
>
> The IASB is studying its existing standard with a view toward harmonizing it with the changes that are being contemplated by the FASB (discussed in the previous footnote). Regardless of the outcome of the changes that are being proposed by both the IASB and FASB, it is likely that future financial statements of all companies will include *more disclosures of both quantitative and qualitative information* for contingent liabilities than are presently required.
>
> Appendix E summarizes differences between U.S. GAAP and IFRS, cross-referenced by chapter.

Are All Liabilities Reported on the Balance Sheet?

The big danger with liabilities is that you may fail to report a large debt on your balance sheet. What is the consequence of missing a large liability? You will definitely understate your liabilities and your debt ratio. By failing to accrue interest on the liability, you'll probably overstate your net income as well. In short, your financial statements will make you look better than you really are. Any such error, if significant, hurts a company's credibility.

Contingent liabilities are very easy to overlook because they aren't actual debts. How would you feel if you owned stock in a company that failed to report a contingency that put the company out of business? If you had known of the contingency, you could have sold the stock and avoided the loss. In this case, you would hire a lawyer to file suit against the company for negligent financial reporting.

 **Cooking the Books** **with Liabilities**

Crazy Eddie, Inc.

Accidentally understating liabilities is one thing, but doing it intentionally is quite another. When unethical management decides to cook the books in the area of liabilities, its strategy is to *deliberately understate recorded liabilities*. This can be done by intentionally underrecording the amount of existing liabilities or by omitting certain liabilities altogether.

Crazy Eddie, Inc., first discussed in Chapter 6, used *multiple tactics* to overstate its financial position over a period of four consecutive years. In addition to overstating inventory (thus understating cost of goods sold and overstating income), the management of the company deliberately *understated accounts payable* by issuing fictitious (false) debit memoranda for suppliers (vendors). A debit memo is issued for goods returned to a vendor, such as Sony. When a debit memorandum is issued, accounts payable are debited (reduced), thus reducing current liabilities and increasing the current ratio. Eventually, expenses are also decreased, and profits are correspondingly increased through reduction of expenses. Crazy Eddie, Inc., issued $3 million of fictitious debit memoranda in one year, making the company's current ratio and debt ratio look better than they actually were, as well as overstating profits.

Summary of Current Liabilities

Let's summarize what we've covered thus far. A company can report its current liabilities on the balance sheet as follows:

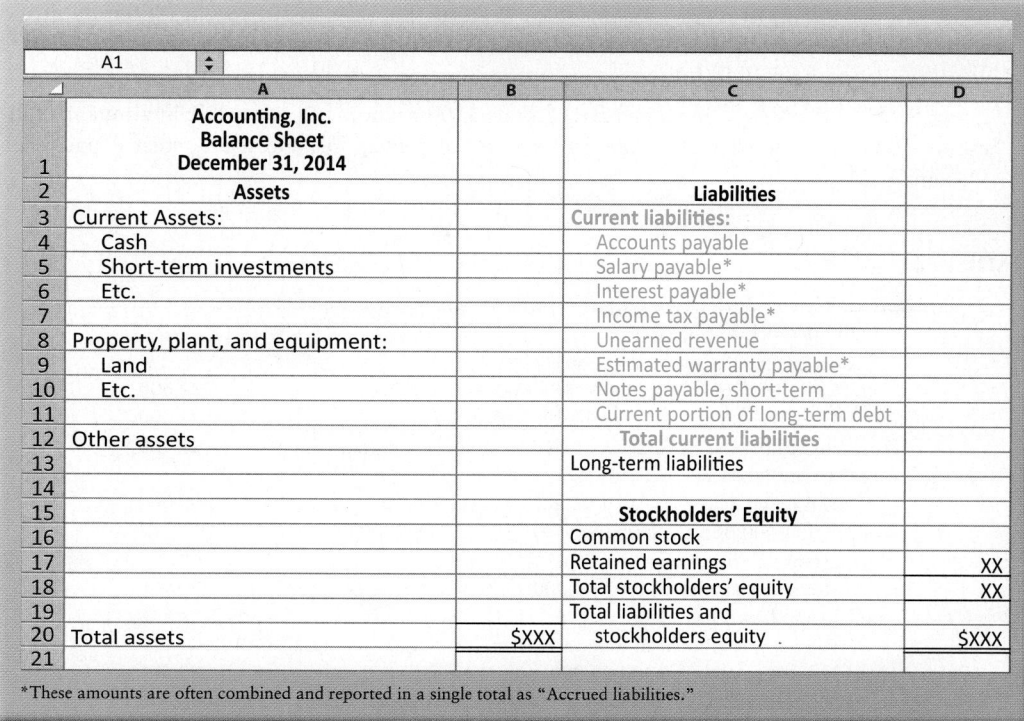

	A	B	C	D
	A1			
1	**Accounting, Inc.** **Balance Sheet** **December 31, 2014**			
2	**Assets**		**Liabilities**	
3	Current Assets:		Current liabilities:	
4	Cash		Accounts payable	
5	Short-term investments		Salary payable*	
6	Etc.		Interest payable*	
7			Income tax payable*	
8	Property, plant, and equipment:		Unearned revenue	
9	Land		Estimated warranty payable*	
10	Etc.		Notes payable, short-term	
11			Current portion of long-term debt	
12	Other assets		**Total current liabilities**	
13			Long-term liabilities	
14				
15			**Stockholders' Equity**	
16			Common stock	
17			Retained earnings	XX
18			Total stockholders' equity	XX
19			Total liabilities and	
20	Total assets	$XXX	stockholders equity	$XXX
21				

*These amounts are often combined and reported in a single total as "Accrued liabilities."

On its income statement this company would report the following:

- *Expenses* related to some of the current liabilities. Examples include Salary Expense, Interest Expense, Income Tax Expense, and Warranty Expense.

- *Revenue* related to the unearned revenue. Examples include Service Revenue and Sales Revenue that were collected in advance, but subsequently earned.

≫ Mid-Chapter Summary Problem

Assume that the **Estée Lauder Companies, Inc.**, faced the following liability situations at June 30, 2014, the end of the company's fiscal year. Show how Estée Lauder would report these liabilities on its balance sheet at June 30, 2014.

a. Salary expense for the last payroll period of the year was $900,000. Of this amount, employees' withheld income tax totaled $88,000 and FICA taxes were $61,000. These payroll amounts will be paid in early July.

b. On fiscal-year 2014 sales of $400 million, management estimates warranty expense of 2%. One year ago, at June 30, 2013, Estimated Warranty Payable stood at $3 million. Warranty payments were $9 million during the year ended June 30, 2014.

c. The company pays royalties on its purchased trademarks. Royalties for the trademarks are equal to a percentage of Estée Lauder's sales. Assume that sales in 2014 were $400 million and were subject to a royalty rate of 3%. At June 30, 2014, Estée Lauder owes two-thirds of the year's royalty, to be paid in July.

d. Long-term debt, outstanding since 2012, totals $100 million and is payable in annual installments of $10 million each. The interest rate on the debt is 7%, and the interest is paid each December 31.

Answer

Liabilities at June 30, 2014:	
a. Current liabilities:	
Salary payable ($900,000 − $88,000 − $61,000)	$ 751,000
Employee income tax payable	88,000
FICA tax payable	61,000
b. Current liabilities:	
Estimated warranty payable	2,000,000
[$3,000,000 + ($400,000,000 × 0.02) − $9,000,000]	
c. Current liabilities:	
Royalties payable ($400,000,000 × 0.03 × 2/3)	8,000,000
d. Current liabilities:	
Current installment of long-term debt	10,000,000
Interest payable ($100,000,000 × 0.07 × 6/12)	3,500,000
Long-term debt ($100,000,000 − $10,000,000)	90,000,000

ACCOUNT FOR BONDS PAYABLE, NOTES PAYABLE, AND INTEREST EXPENSE

2 Account for bonds payable, notes payable, and interest expense

In Chapter 8, we discussed bonds and notes from the standpoint of the investor, as held-to-maturity or available-for-sale investments (long-term assets). In this chapter, we examine bonds and notes from the flip-side, or the standpoint of the borrower, on whose balance sheets they appear as long-term liabilities. We treat bonds payable and notes payable together because the way they are accounted for is virtually the same.

Large companies such as Southwest Airlines, Home Depot, and **Toyota** cannot borrow billions from a single lender. So how do corporations borrow huge amounts? They issue (sell) bonds to the public. **Bonds payable** are groups of debt securities issued to multiple lenders, called *bondholders*. Southwest Airlines needs airplanes and can borrow large amounts by issuing bonds to thousands of individual investors, who each lend Southwest a modest amount. Southwest receives the cash it needs, and each investor limits his or her risk by diversifying investments—not putting all the investor's "eggs in one basket."

Bonds: An Introduction

Bonds payable are debts of the issuing company. Purchasers of bonds receive a bond certificate, which carries the issuing company's name. The certificate also states the *principal*, which is typically stated in units of $1,000; principal is also called the bond's *face value, maturity value*, or *par value*. The bond obligates the issuing company to pay the debt at a specific future time called the *maturity date*.

Interest is the rental fee on borrowed money. The bond certificate states the interest rate that the issuer will pay the holder and the dates that the interest payments are due (generally, twice a year). Exhibit 9-2 shows an actual bond certificate.

Exhibit 9-2 | Bond Certificate (Adapted)

Issuing bonds usually requires the services of a securities firm, such as Merrill Lynch, to act as the underwriter of the bond issue. The **underwriter** purchases the bonds from the issuing company and resells them to its clients, or it may sell the bonds to its clients and earn a commission on the sale.

Types of Bonds. All the bonds in a particular issue may mature at the same time (**term bonds**) or in installments over a period of time (**serial bonds**). Serial bonds are like installment notes payable. Some of Southwest Airlines' long-term debts are serial in nature because they are payable in installments.

Secured, or *mortgage*, *bonds* give the bondholder the right to take specified assets of the issuer if the company *defaults*—that is, fails to pay interest or principal. *Unsecured bonds*, called **debentures**, are backed only by the good faith of the borrower. Debentures carry a higher rate of interest than secured bonds because debentures are riskier investments.

Bond Prices. Investors may buy and sell bonds through bond markets. Bond prices are quoted at a percentage of their maturity value. For example,

- a $1,000 bond quoted at 100 is bought or sold for $1,000, which is 100% of its face value.
- the same bond quoted at 101.5 has a market price of $1,015 (101.5% of face value = $1,000 × 1.015).
- a $1,000 bond quoted at 88.375 is priced at $883.75 ($1,000 × 0.88375).

Bond Premium and Bond Discount. A bond issued at a price above its face (par) value is said to be issued at a **premium**, and a bond issued at a price below face (par) value has a **discount**. Premium on Bonds Payable has a *credit* balance and Discount on Bonds Payable carries a *debit* balance. Discount on Bonds Payable is therefore a contra liability account.

As a bond nears maturity, its market price moves toward par value. Therefore, the price of a bond issued at a

- premium decreases toward maturity value.
- discount increases toward maturity value.

On the maturity date, a bond's market value exactly equals its face value because the company that issued the bond pays that amount to retire the bond.

The Time Value of Money. We discussed the time value of money in Chapter 8. You should refresh your understanding of that material at this point because we will use it extensively in accounting for bonds payable and related interest expense. Let's examine how the *time value of money* affects the pricing of bonds, using the same example provided in Chapter 8—except this time, from the issuer (or debtor's) point of view.

Bond Interest Rates Determine Bond Prices. Bonds are always sold at their *market price*, which is the amount investors will pay for the bond. *Market price is the bond's present value*, which equals the present value of the principal payment plus the present value of the cash interest payments. Interest is usually paid semiannually (twice a year). Some companies pay interest annually or quarterly.

As discussed in Chapter 8, two interest rates work to set the price of a bond:

- The **stated interest rate**, also called the coupon rate, is the interest rate printed on the bond certificate. The stated interest rate determines the amount of cash interest the borrower pays—and the investor receives—each year. As shown in the example in Chapter 8, suppose Southwest Airlines bonds have a stated interest rate of 9%. Southwest would pay $9,000 of interest annually on $100,000 of bonds. Each semiannual payment would be $4,500 ($100,000 × 0.09 × 6/12).
- The **market interest rate**, or *effective interest rate*, is the rate that investors demand for loaning their money. The market interest rate varies by the minute.

A company may issue bonds with a stated interest rate that differs from the prevailing market interest rate. In fact, the two interest rates often differ.

Exhibit 9-3 shows how the stated interest rate and the market interest rate interact to determine the issue price of a bond payable for three separate cases.

Southwest Airlines may issue 9% bonds when the market rate has risen to 10%. Will the Southwest 9% bonds attract investors in this market? No, because investors can earn 10% on other bonds of similar risk. Therefore, investors will purchase Southwest bonds only at a price less than their face value. The difference between the lower price and face value is a *discount* (Exhibit 9-3). Conversely, if the market interest rate is 8%, Southwest's 9% bonds will be so attractive that investors will pay more than face value to purchase them. The difference between the higher price and face value is a *premium*.

Exhibit 9-3 | How Stated Interest Rates and Market Interest Rates Interact to Determine the Price of a Bond

Issue Price of Bonds Payable

Case A:

Stated interest rate on a bond payable	equals	Market interest rate	Therefore,	Price of face (par, or maturity) value
Example: 9%	=	9%	→	Par: $1,000 bond issued for $1,000

Case B:

Stated interest rate on a bond payable	less than	Market interest rate	Therefore,	Discount price (price below face value)
Example: 9%	<	10%	→	Discount: $1,000 bond issued for a price below $1,000

Case C:

Stated interest rate on a bond payable	greater than	Market interest rate	Therefore,	Premium price (price above face value)
Example: 9%	>	8%	→	Premium: $1,000 bond issued for a price above $1,000

Issuing Bonds Payable at Par (Face Value)

We start with the most straightforward situation—issuing bonds at their par value. There is no premium or discount on these bonds payable.

Suppose Southwest Airlines has $50,000 of 9% bonds payable that mature in five years. Assume that Southwest issued these bonds at par on January 1, 2014. The issuance entry is as follows:

	A	B	C	D
	A1			
1	2014			
2	Jan 1	Cash	50,000	
3		Bonds Payable		50,000
4		*To issue bonds at par.*		
5				

Bonds Payable

50,000

Assets and liabilities increase when a company issues bonds payable.

Assets	=	Liabilities	+	Stockholders' Equity
+ 50,000	=	+ 50,000	+	0

Southwest, the borrower, makes a one-time entry to record the receipt of cash and the issuance of bonds. Afterward, investors buy and sell the bonds through the bond markets. These later buy-and-sell transactions between outside investors do *not* involve Southwest at all.

Interest payments occur each January 1 and July 1. Southwest's entry to record the first semi-annual interest payment is as follows:

	A1	⬍			
	A	**B**		**C**	**D**
1	2014				
2	Jul 1	Interest Expense ($50,000 × 0.09 × 6/12)		2,250	
3		Cash			2,250
4		*To pay semiannual interest.*			
5					

The payment of interest expense decreases assets and equity. Bonds Payable is not affected.

Assets	=	Liabilities	+	Stockholders' Equity	−	Expenses
− 2,250	=	0	+			− 2,250

At year-end, Southwest accrues interest expense and interest payable for six months (July through December), as follows:

	A1	⬍			
	A	**B**		**C**	**D**
1	2014				
2	Dec 31	Interest Expense ($50,000 × 0.09 × 6/12)		2,250	
3		Interest Payable			2,250
4		*To accrue interest.*			
5					

Liabilities increase, and equity decreases.

Assets	=	Liabilities	+	Stockholders' Equity	−	Expenses
0	=	+ 2,250	+			− 2,250

On January 1, Southwest will pay the interest, debiting Interest Payable and crediting Cash. Then, at maturity, Southwest pays off the bonds as follows:

	A1	⬍			
	A	**B**		**C**	**D**
1	2019				
2	Jan 1	Bonds Payable		50,000	
3		Cash			50,000
4		*To pay bonds payable at maturity.*			
5					

Bonds Payable

50,000	50,000
	Bal 0

Assets	=	Liabilities	+	Stockholders' Equity
− 50,000	=	− 50,000		

Issuing Bonds Payable at a Discount

Market conditions may force a company to issue bonds at a discount. Suppose Southwest Airlines issued $100,000 of 9%, five-year bonds when the market interest rate is 10%. The market price of the bonds drops, and Southwest receives $96,149[2] at issuance. The transaction is recorded as follows:

	A1	◆			
	A	**B**		**C**	**D**
1	2014				
2	Jan 1	Cash		96,149	
3		Discount on Bonds Payable		3,851	
4		Bonds Payable			100,000
5		*To issue bonds at a discount.*			
6					

The accounting equation shows that Southwest has a net liability of $96,149—not $100,000.

$$\underline{\text{Assets}} \quad = \quad \underline{\text{Liabilities}} \quad + \quad \underline{\text{Stockholders' Equity}}$$

$$+\ 96,149 \quad = \quad -\ 3,851 \quad + \quad 0$$
$$+\ 100,000$$

The Bonds Payable accounts have a net balance of $96,149 as follows:

Bonds Payable		**Discount on Bonds Payable**		Net carrying amount
			=	of bonds payable
100,000	−	3,851		$96,149

Southwest's balance sheet immediately after issuance of the bonds would report the following:

Total current liabilities..................................		$ XXX
Long-term liabilities:		
Bonds payable, 9%, due 2019....................	$100,000	
Less: Discount on bonds payable...............	(3,851)	96,149

Discount on Bonds Payable is a contra account to Bonds Payable, a decrease in the company's liabilities. Subtracting the discount from Bonds Payable yields the *carrying amount* of the bonds. Thus, Southwest's liability is $96,149, which is the amount the company borrowed.

What Is the Interest Expense on These Bonds Payable?

Southwest pays interest on bonds semiannually, which is common practice. Each semiannual *interest payment* is set by the bond contract and therefore remains the same over the life of the bonds:

$$\text{Semiannual interest payment} = \$100,000 \times 0.09 \times 6/12$$
$$= \$4,500$$

But Southwest's *interest expense* increases as the bonds march toward maturity. Remember: These bonds were issued at a discount.

---

[2]The example in Chapter 8 on page 456 shows how to determine the price of this bond.

Panel A of Exhibit 9-4 repeats the Southwest Airlines bond data we've been using. Panel B provides an amortization table that does two things:

- Determines the periodic interest expense (column C)
- Shows the bond carrying amount (column F)

Study the exhibit carefully because the amounts we'll be using come directly from the amortization table. This exhibit shows the *effective-interest method of amortization*, which is the correct way to measure interest expense.

Exhibit 9-4 | Amortization of Bond Discount

Panel A—Bond Data

	A	B
	A1	
1	Issue date—January 1, 2014	Maturity date—January 1, 2019
2	Face (par or *maturity*) value—$100,000	Market interest rate at time of issue—10% annually, 5% semiannually
3	Stated interest rate—9%	Issue price—$96,149
4	Interest paid—4 1/2% semiannually, $4,500 = $100,000 × 0.09 × 6/12	
5		

Panel B—Amortization Table (Using Excel)

	A	B	C	D	E	F
	A1					
1	Semiannual Interest Date	Int Pmt (0.045* Maturity Value)	Interest Expense (0.05* Preceding Bond Carrying Value)	Discount Amortization (C – B)	Discount Account Balance (Preceding E – D)	Bond Carrying Amount ($100,000 – E)
2	1/1/2014				3,851	96,149
3	7/1/2014	4,500	4,807	307	3,544	96,456
4	1/1/2015	4,500	4,823	323	3,221	96,779
5	7/1/2015	4,500	4,839	339	2,882	97,118
6	1/1/2016	4,500	4,856	356	2,526	97,474
7	7/1/2016	4,500	4,874	374	2,152	97,848
8	1/1/2017	4,500	4,892	392	1,760	98,240
9	7/1/2017	4,500	4,912	412	1,348	98,652
10	1/1/2018	4,500	4,933	433	915	99,085
11	7/1/2018	4,500	4,954	454	461	99,539
12	1/1/2019	4,500	4,961*	461	(0)	100,000
13						

*Adjusted for effect of rounding

Notes
- Column B   The semiannual interest payments are constant—fixed by the bond contract.
- Column C   The interest expense each period = the preceding bond carrying amount × the market interest rate. Interest expense increases as the bond carrying amount (F) increases.
- Column D   The discount amortization (D) is the excess of interest expense (C) over interest payment (B).
- Column E   The discount balance (E) decreases when amortized.
- Column F   The bond carrying amount (F) increases from $96,149 at issuance to $100,000 at maturity.

Try It in **Excel**

Bond amortization tables are a snap when you prepare them in Excel. Open a blank Excel spreadsheet.

- In line 1, label the columns as shown in Panel B of Exhibit 9-4.

- Column A. Starting in line 2, enter the issue date (1/1/2014) followed by each of the semiannual interest payment dates. This will continue through line 12 with the last interest payment on January 1, 2019. Highlight all cell values in rows 2 through 12 of column A, and click on the drop down box in the "number" field on the ruler at the top of the spreadsheet. Choose the "date" category and click OK to change all cell values in Column A to the date format.

- Line 2, column E. Enter 3851 in cell E2. Enter the formula =100000−E2 in cell F2. The calculated value of 96149 should appear in cell F2, representing the initial carrying value of the bond.

- Line 3, column B. Enter formula =.045*100000 in cell B3. A calculated value of 4500 should appear, representing the amount of the first cash interest payment.

- Line 3, column C. In cell C3, enter formula =.05*F2. A calculated value of 4807 should appear, representing the calculated amount of interest expense, based on the carrying amount of the bond. If the cell shows a decimal fraction, use the "decrease decimal" command in the "number" field of the toolbar to reduce the decimals to none. This will round the value to the nearest dollar.

- Line 3, column D. In cell D3, enter formula =C3−B3. A value of 307 should appear, representing the amount of discount amortization included in interest expense on the first interest payment date.

- Line 3, column E. In cell E3, enter formula =E2−D3. A value of 3544 should appear, representing the unamortized discount remaining after the first interest payment.

- Line 3, column F. In cell F3, enter formula =100000−E3. A value of 96456 should appear, representing the adjusted carrying value of the bond after the first interest payment.

- For columns B through F, copy line 3 down through line 12. All of the numbers in the table should fill in. Line 12 will have to be adjusted for rounding by taking the remaining unamortized discount from cell E11 (461) and substituting that value in cell D12 (discount amortization). Also, substitute 4961 for interest expense in cell C12. This will adjust the final bond carrying amount to the maturity value of $100,000 and the unamortized discount to 0.

- Highlight cells B2 through F12, and insert commas to make table easier to read. When you insert the commas, Excel automatically inserts two decimals and zeros, so use the "decrease decimal" key to format the table to whole dollars. ■

Interest Expense on Bonds Issued at a Discount

In Exhibit 9-4, Southwest Airlines borrowed $96,149 cash but must pay $100,000 when the bonds mature. What happens to the $3,851 balance of the discount account over the life of the bond issue?

The $3,851 is additional interest expense to Southwest over and above the stated interest that Southwest pays each six months. Exhibit 9-5 graphs the interest expense (column C in Exhibit 9-4) and the interest payment (column B in Exhibit 9-4) on the Southwest bonds over their lifetime. Observe that the semiannual interest payment is fixed—by contract—at $4,500. But the amount of interest expense increases as the discount bond marches upward toward maturity.

Exhibit 9-5 | Interest Expense on Bonds Payable Issued at a Discount

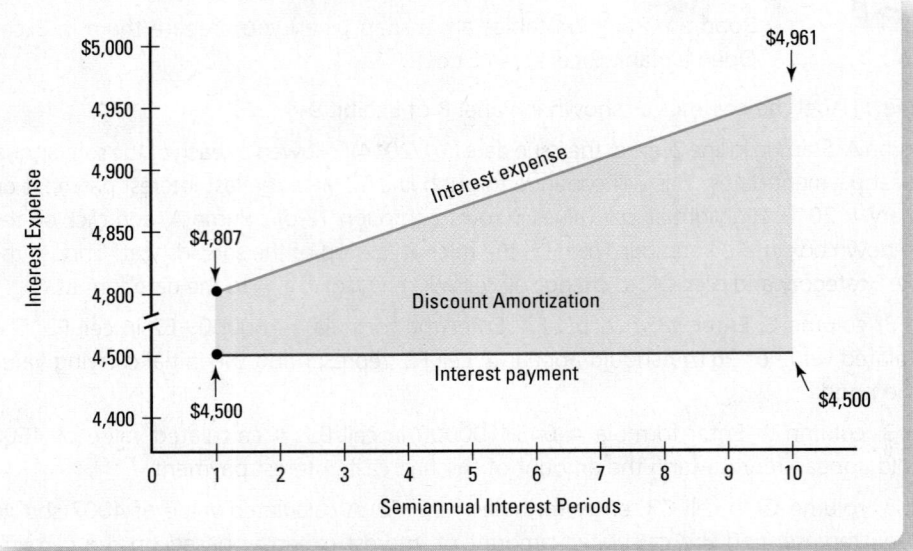

The discount is allocated to interest expense through amortization over the term of the bonds. Exhibit 9-6 illustrates the amortization of the bond discount so the carrying value of the bonds increases from $96,149 at the start to $100,000 at maturity. These amounts come from Exhibit 9-4, column F (p. 500).

Exhibit 9-6 | Amortizing Discount on Bonds Payable

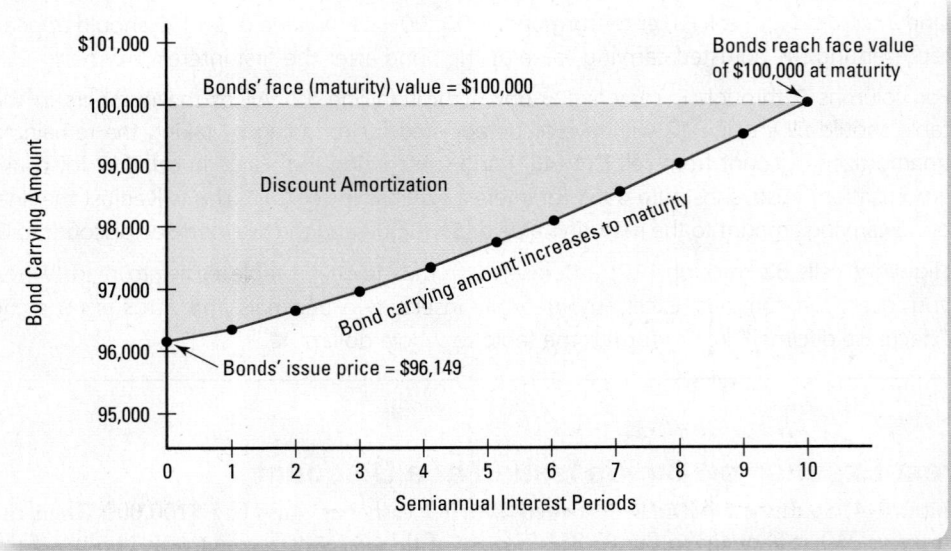

Now let's see how Southwest would account for these bonds issued at a discount. In our example, Southwest issued its bonds on January 1, 2014. On July 1, Southwest makes the first semiannual interest payment. But Southwest's interest expense is greater than its payment of

$4,500. Southwest's journal entry to record interest expense and the interest payment for the first six months follows (with all amounts taken from Exhibit 9-4):

	A		B	C	D
	A1	⇕			
	A		**B**	**C**	**D**
1	2014				
2	Jul 1		Interest Expense	4,807	
3			Discount on Bonds Payable		307
4			Cash		4,500
5			*To pay semiannual interest and amortize bond discount.*		
6					

The credit to Discount on Bonds Payable accomplishes two purposes:

- It adjusts the carrying value of the bonds as they march upward toward maturity value.
- It amortizes the discount to interest expense.

At December 31, 2014, Southwest accrues interest and amortizes the bond discount for July through December with this entry (amounts from Exhibit 9-4, page 500):

	A		B	C	D
	A1	⇕			
	A		**B**	**C**	**D**
1	2014				
2	Dec 31		Interest Expense	4,823	
3			Discount on Bonds Payable		323
4			Interest Payable		4,500
5			*To accrue semiannual interest and amortize bond discount.*		
6					

At December 31, 2014, Southwest's bond accounts appear as follows:

Bonds Payable		**Discount on Bonds Payable**	
	100,000	3,851	307
			323
		Bal 3,221	

Bond carrying amount, $96,779 = $100,000 − $3,221 from Exhibit 9-4, page 500.

Stop & Think...

What would Southwest Airlines' 2014 income statement and year-end balance sheet report for these bonds?

Answer:

Income Statement for 2014		
Interest expense ($4,807 + $4,823)		$ 9,630
Balance Sheet at December 31, 2014		
Current liabilities:		
Interest payable..		$ 4,500
Long-term liabilities:		
Bonds payable..	$100,000	
Less: Discount on bonds payable...............	(3,221)	96,779

At maturity on January 1, 2019, the discount will have been amortized to zero, and the bonds' carrying amount will be face value of $100,000. Southwest will retire the bonds by paying $100,000 to the bondholders.

Partial-Period Interest Amounts

Companies don't always issue bonds at the beginning or the end of their accounting year. They issue bonds when market conditions are most favorable, and that may be on May 16, August 1, or any other date. To illustrate partial-period interest, assume **Google, Inc.,** issues $100,000 of 8% bonds payable at 96 on August 31, 2014. The market rate of interest was 9%, and these bonds pay semiannual interest on February 28 and August 31 each year. The first few lines of Google's amortization table are as follows:

Semiannual Interest Date	4% Interest Payment	4 ½% Interest Expense	Discount Amortization	Discount Account Balance	Bond Carrying Amount
Aug 31, 2014				$4,000	$96,000
Feb 28, 2015	$4,000	$4,320	$320	3,680	96,320
Aug 31, 2015	4,000	4,334	334	3,346	96,654

Google's accounting year ends on December 31, so at year-end Google must accrue interest and amortize bond discount for four months (September through December). At December 31, 2014, Google will make this entry:

	A	B	C	D
1	2014			
2	Dec 31	Interest Expense ($4,320 × 4/6)	2,880	
3		Discount on Bonds Payable ($320 × 4/6)		213
4		Interest Payable ($4,000 × 4/6)		2,667
5		*To accrue interest and amortize discount at year-end.*		
6				

The year-end entry at December 31, 2014, uses 4/6 of the upcoming semiannual amounts at February 28, 2015. This example clearly illustrates the benefit of an amortization schedule.

Issuing Bonds Payable at a Premium

Let's modify the Southwest Airlines bond example to illustrate issuance of the bonds at a premium. Assume that, on January 1, 2014, Southwest issues $100,000 of five-year, 9% bonds that pay interest semiannually. If the 9% bonds are issued when the market interest rate is 8%, their issue price is $104,100.[3] The premium on these bonds is $4,100, and Exhibit 9-7 shows how to amortize the bonds by the effective-interest method. In practice, bond premiums are rare because few companies issue their bonds to pay cash interest above the market interest rate. We cover bond premiums for completeness.

Southwest's entry to record the issuance of the bonds on January 1, 2014, is as follows:

	A	B	C	D
1	2014			
2	Jan 1	Cash	104,100	
3		Bonds Payable		100,000
4		Premium on Bonds Payable		4,100
5		*To issue bonds at a premium.*		
6				

---

[3]You can use the same concepts in the example in Chapter 8 to determine the price of this bond.

At the beginning, Southwest's liability is $104,100—not $100,000. The accounting equation makes this clear.

Assets	=	Liabilities	+	Stockholders' Equity
+ 104,100	=	+ 100,000	+	0
		+ 4,100		

Exhibit 9-7 | Amortization of Bond Premium

Panel A—Bond Data

	A	B
	A1	
1	Issue date—January 1, 2014	Maturity date—January 1, 2019
2	Face (par or *maturity*) value—$100,000	Market interest rate at time of issue—8% annually, 4% semiannually
3	Stated interest rate—9%	Issue price—$104,100
4	Interest paid—4 1/2% semiannually, $4,500 = $100,000 × 0.09 × 6/12	
5		

Panel B—Amortization Table (Using Excel)

	A	B	C	D	E	F
	A1					
1	Semiannual Interest Date	Int Pmt (0.045* Maturity Value)	Interest Expense (0.04* Preceding Bond Carrying Value)	Premium Amortization (B − C)	Premium Account Balance (Preceding E − D)	Bond Carrying Amount ($100,000 + E)
2	1/1/2014				4,100	104,100
3	7/1/2014	4,500	4,164	336	3,764	103,764
4	1/1/2015	4,500	4,151	349	3,415	103,415
5	7/1/2015	4,500	4,137	363	3,051	103,051
6	1/1/2016	4,500	4,122	378	2,673	102,673
7	7/1/2016	4,500	4,107	393	2,280	102,280
8	1/1/2017	4,500	4,091	409	1,871	101,871
9	7/1/2017	4,500	4,075	425	1,446	101,446
10	1/1/2018	4,500	4,058	442	1,004	101,004
11	7/1/2018	4,500	4,040	460	544	100,544
12	1/1/2019	4,500	3,956*	544	0	100,000
13						

*Adjusted for effect of rounding

Notes
- Column B   The semiannual interest payments are constant—fixed by the bond contract.
- Column C   The interest expense each period = the preceding bond carrying amount × the market interest rate.
             Interest expense decreases as the bond carrying amount (F) decreases.
- Column D   The premium amortization (D) is the excess of interest payment (B) over interest expense (C).
- Column E   The premium balance (E) decreases when amortized.
- Column F   The bond carrying amount (F) decreases from $104,100 at issuance to $100,000 at maturity.

Try It in Excel

If you prepared a debt amortization table for bond discount with Excel (Exhibit 9-4), it's easy to prepare an amortization table for bond premium. Open a blank Excel spreadsheet.

- In line 1, label the columns as shown in Panel B of Exhibit 9-7.

- Column A. Starting in line 2, enter the issue date (1/1/2014) followed by each of the semiannual interest payment dates. This will continue through line 12 with the last interest payment on January 1, 2019. Highlight all cell values in rows 2 through 12 of column A, and click on the drop down box in the "number" field on the ruler at the top of the spreadsheet. Choose the "date" category and click OK to change all cell values in Column A to the date format.

- Line 2, column E. Enter 4100 in cell E2. Enter the formula =100000+E2 in cell F2. The calculated value of 104100 should appear in cell F2, representing the initial carrying value of the bond.

- Line 3, column B. In cell B3, enter formula =.045*100000. A calculated value of 4500 should appear, representing the first cash interest payment.

- Line 3, column C. In cell C3, enter formula =.04*F2. A calculated value of 4164 should appear, representing interest expense recognized on the first interest payment date. If the cell shows a decimal fraction, use the "decrease decimal" command in the "number" field of the toolbar to reduce the decimals to none. This will round the value to the nearest dollar.

- Line 3, column D. In cell D3, enter formula =B3−C3. A value of 336 should appear, representing the amount of premium amortization deducted from interest expense on the first interest payment date.

- Line 3, column E. In cell E3, enter formula =E2−D3. A value of 3764 should appear, representing the remaining unamortized premium after the first interest payment.

- Line 3, column F. In cell F3, enter formula =100000+E3. A value of 103764 should appear, representing the adjusted carrying value of the bond after the first interest payment.

- For columns B to F, copy line 3 down through line 12. All of the numbers in the table should fill in. Line 12 will have to be adjusted for rounding by taking the remaining unamortized premium from cell E11 (544) and substituting that value in cell D12 (premium amortization). Also, substitute 3956 for interest expense in cell C12. This will adjust the final bond carrying amount to the maturity value of $100,000 and the unamortized premium to 0. Your Excel table may be $1 off in some places because of rounding.

- Highlight cells B2 through F12 and format them for commas but no decimals, as you did for Exhibit 9-4. ■

Immediately after issuing the bonds at a premium on January 1, 2014, Southwest would report the bonds payable on the balance sheet as follows:

Total current liabilities		$ XXX
Long-term liabilities:		
Bonds payable	$100,000	
Premium on bonds payable	4,100	104,100

A premium is *added* to the balance of bonds payable to determine the carrying amount.

In Exhibit 9-7, Southwest borrowed $104,100 cash but must pay back only $100,000 at maturity. Amortization of the $4,100 premium will result in a reduction in Southwest's interest expense over the term of the bonds. The first interest payment on July 1, 2014, follows:

	A	B	C	D
	A1 ⬍			
1	2014			
2	Jul 1	Interest Expense (from Exhibit 9-7)	4,164	
3		Premium on Bonds Payable	336	
4		Cash		4,500
5		*To pay semiannual interest and amortize bond premium.*		
6				

This entry shows that amortization of premium over the first six months results in reducing interest expense to $4,164 ($4,500 – $336) while the cash interest paid remains at $4,500. Exhibit 9-8 graphs Southwest's interest payments (column B from Exhibit 9-7) and interest expense (column C).

Exhibit 9-8 | Interest Expense on Bonds Payable Issued at a Premium

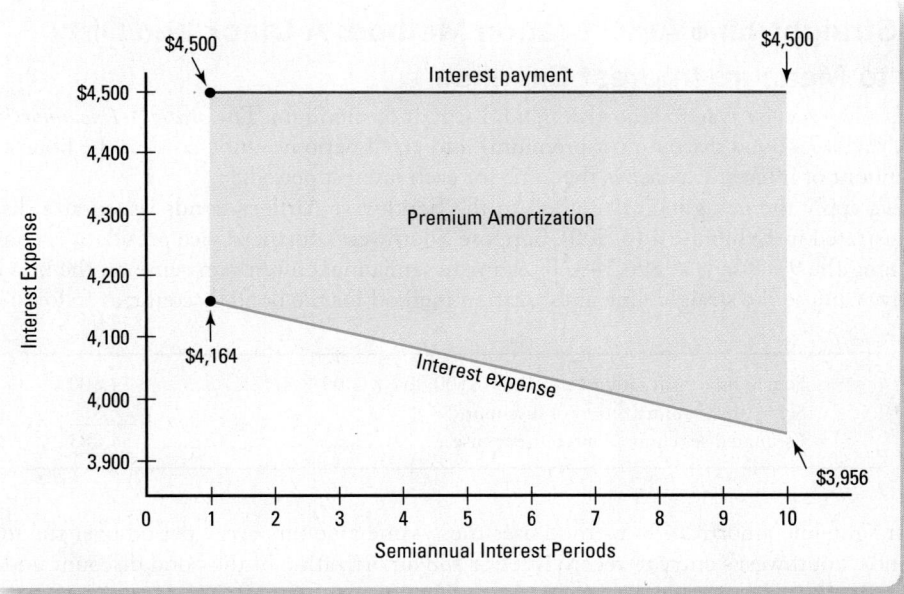

Through amortization, the premium decreases interest expense each period over the term of the bonds. Exhibit 9-9 on the following page diagrams the amortization of the bond premium so the carrying value of the bonds decreases from the issue price of $104,100 to maturity value of $100,000. All amounts are taken from Exhibit 9-7.

Exhibit 9-9 | Amortizing Premium on Bonds Payable

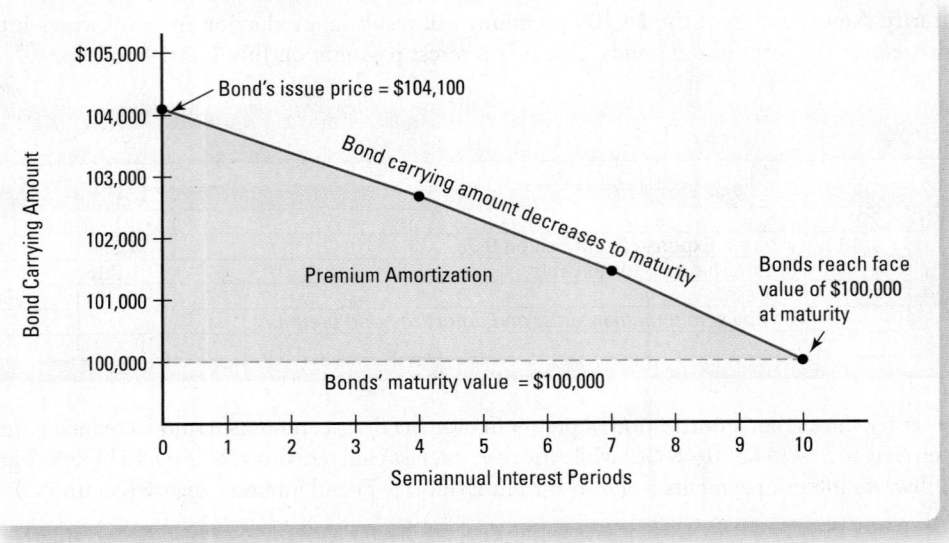

The Straight-Line Amortization Method: A Quick and Dirty Way to Measure Interest Expense

There's a less precise way to amortize bond discount or premium. The *straight-line amortization method* divides a bond discount (or premium) into equal periodic amounts over the bond's term. The amount of interest expense is the same for each interest period.

Let's apply the straight-line method to the Southwest Airlines bonds issued at a discount and illustrated in Exhibit 9-4 (p. 500). Suppose Southwest's financial vice president is considering issuing the 9% bonds at $96,149. To estimate semiannual interest expense on the bonds, the executive can use the straight-line amortization method for the bond discount, as follows:

Semiannual cash interest payment ($100,000 × 0.09 × 6/12).............	$4,500
+ Semiannual amortization of discount ($3,851 ÷ 10)...........................	385
= Estimated semiannual interest expense...	$4,885

The straight-line amortization method uses these same amounts every period over the term of the bonds. Southwest's entry to record interest and amortization of the bond discount under the straight-line amortization method would be as follows:

	A1	⬍		
	A	**B**	**C**	**D**
1	2014			
2	Jul 1	Interest Expense	4,885	
3		Discount on Bonds Payable		385
4		Cash		4,500
5		*To pay semiannual interest and amortize bond discount.*		
6				

Generally accepted accounting principles (GAAP) permit the straight-line amortization method only when its amounts differ insignificantly from the amounts determined by the effective-interest method.

Should We Retire Bonds Payable Before Their Maturity?

Normally, companies wait until maturity to pay off, or *retire*, their bonds payable. But companies sometimes retire bonds early. The main reason for retiring bonds early is to relieve the pressure of making high interest payments. Also, the company may be able to borrow at a lower interest rate.

Some bonds are **callable**, which means that the issuer may *call*, or pay off, those bonds at a prearranged price (this is the *call price*) whenever the issuer chooses. The call price is often a percentage point or two above the par value, perhaps 101 or 102. Callable bonds give the issuer the benefit of being able to pay off the bonds whenever it is most favorable to do so. The alternative to calling the bonds is to purchase them in the open market at their current market price.

Southwest Airlines has $300 million of debenture bonds outstanding. Assume the unamortized discount is $30 million. Lower interest rates may convince management to pay off these bonds now. Assume that the bonds are callable at 101. If the market price of the bonds is 99, will Southwest call the bonds at 101 or purchase them for 99 in the open market? Market price is the better choice because the market price is lower than the call price. Let's see how to account for an early retirement of bonds payable. Retiring the bonds at 99 results in a loss of $27 million, computed as follows:

	Millions
Par value of bonds being retired.............................	$300
Less: Unamortized discount......................................	(30)
Carrying amount of the bonds being retired............	270
Market price ($300 × 0.99).....................................	297
Loss on retirement of bonds payable.......................	$ 27

Gains and losses on early retirement of bonds payable are reported as Other income (loss) on the income statement.

Convertible Bonds and Notes

Some corporate bonds may be converted into the issuing company's common stock. These bonds are called **convertible bonds** (or **convertible notes**). For investors, these bonds combine the safety of (a) assured receipt of interest and principal on the bonds with (b) the opportunity for gains on the stock. The conversion feature is so attractive that investors usually accept a lower interest rate than they would on nonconvertible bonds. The lower cash interest payments benefit the issuer. If the market price of the issuing company's stock gets high enough, the bondholders will convert the bonds into stock.

Suppose Southwest Airlines has convertible notes payable of $100 million. If Southwest's stock price rises high enough, the note holders will convert the notes into the company's common stock. Conversion of the notes payable into stock will decrease Southwest's liabilities and increase its equity.

Assume the note holders convert the notes into four million shares of Southwest Airlines common stock ($1 par) on May 14. Southwest makes the following entry in its accounting records:

	A1	⬍			
	A	**B**		**C**	**D**
1	May 14	Convertible Notes Payable		100,000,000	
2		Common Stock (4,000,000 × $1 par)			4,000,000
3		Paid-in Capital in Excess of Par—Common			96,000,000
4		*To record conversion of notes payable.*			
5					

The accounting equation shows that liabilities decrease and stockholders' equity increases.

	Assets	=	Liabilities	+	Stockholders' Equity
	0	=	(100,000,000)		+ 4,000,000 + 96,000,000

The carrying amount of the notes ($100 million) ceases to be debt and becomes stockholders' equity. Common Stock is recorded at its *par value*, which is a dollar amount assigned to each share of stock. In this case, the credit to Common Stock is $4,000,000 (4,000,000 shares × $1 par value per share). The extra carrying amount of the notes payable ($96,000,000) is credited to another stockholders' equity account, Paid-in Capital in Excess of Par—Common. We'll be using this account in various ways in the next chapter.

ANALYZE AND DIFFERENTIATE FINANCING WITH DEBT VERSUS EQUITY

3 **Analyze and differentiate** financing with debt vs. equity

Managers must decide how to get the money they need to pay for assets. There are three main ways to finance operations:

- By retained earnings
- By issuing equity (stock)
- By issuing bonds (or notes) payable

Each strategy has its advantages and disadvantages.

1. *Financed by retained earnings* means that the company has enough cash from profitable operations to purchase the needed assets. There's no need to issue more stock or to borrow money. This strategy is low-risk to the company.

2. *Issuing equity (stock)* creates no liabilities or interest expense and is less risky to the issuing corporation. But issuing stock is more costly, as we shall see.

3. *Issuing bonds or notes payable* does not dilute control of the corporation. It often results in higher earnings per share because the earnings on borrowed money usually exceed interest expense. But creating more debt increases the risk of the company.

Earnings per share (EPS) is the amount of a company's net income for each share of its common stock. EPS is the single most important statistic for evaluating companies because EPS is a standard measure of operating performance that applies to companies of different sizes and from different industries.

Suppose Southwest Airlines needs $500,000 for expansion. Assume Southwest has net income of $300,000 and 100,000 shares of common stock outstanding. Management is considering two financing plans. Plan 1 is to issue $500,000 of 6% bonds payable, and plan 2 is to issue 50,000 shares of common stock for $500,000. Management believes the new cash can be invested in operations to earn income of $200,000 before interest and taxes.

Exhibit 9-10 shows the relative earnings-per-share advantage of borrowing. As you can see, Southwest's EPS amount is higher if the company borrows by issuing bonds (compare lines 12 and 13). Southwest earns more on the investment ($102,000) than the interest it pays on the bonds ($30,000). This is called **trading on the equity**, or using **leverage**. It is widely used to increase earnings per share of common stock.

Exhibit 9-10 | Relative Advantage of Borrowing

	A	B	C	D	E
	A1				
1			Plan 1		Plan 2
2			Borrow $500,000 at 6%		Issue 50,000 Shares of Common Stock for $500,000
3	1 Net income before expansion		$ 300,000		$ 300,000
4	2 Expected project income before interest and				
5	income tax	$ 200,000		$ 200,000	
6	3 Less interest expense ($500,000 × 0.06)	(30,000)		0	
7	4 Expected project income before income tax	170,000		200,000	
8	5 Less income tax expense (40%)	(68,000)		(80,000)	
9	6 Expected project net income		102,000		120,000
10	7 Total company net income		$ 402,000		$ 420,000
11	8 Earnings per share after expansion:				
12	9 Plan 1 Borrow ($402,000/100,000 shares)		$ 4.02		
13	10 Plan 2 Issue Stock ($420,000/150,000 shares)				$ 2.80
14					

In this case, borrowing results in higher earnings per share than issuing stock. Borrowing has its disadvantages, however. Interest expense may be high enough to eliminate net income and lead to losses. Also, borrowing creates liabilities that must be paid during bad years as well as good years. In contrast, a company that issues stock can omit its dividends during a bad year. The Decision Guidelines provide some help in deciding how to finance operations.

◉ Decision Guidelines

FINANCING WITH DEBT OR WITH STOCK

El Chico is one of the oldest chains of Tex-Mex restaurants in the United States, begun by the Cuellar family in the Dallas area in 1940. Suppose El Chico is expanding into neighboring states. Take the role of Miguel Cuellar and assume you must make some key decisions about how to finance the expansion.

Decision	Guidelines
How will you finance El Chico's expansion?	Your financing plan depends on El Chico's ability to generate cash flow, your willingness to give up some control of the business, the amount of financing risk you are willing to take, and El Chico's credit rating.
Do El Chico's operations generate enough cash to meet all its financing needs?	If yes, the business needs little outside financing. There is no need to borrow. If no, the business will need to issue additional stock or borrow the money.
Are you willing to give up some of your control of the business?	If yes, then issue stock to other stockholders, who can vote their shares to elect the company's directors. If no, then borrow from bondholders, who have no vote in the management of the company.
How much leverage (financing risk) are you willing or able to take?	If much, then borrow as much as you can, and you may increase El Chico's earnings per share. But this will increase the business's debt ratio and the risk of being unable to pay its debts. If little, then borrow sparingly. This will hold the debt ratio down and reduce the risk of default on borrowing agreements. But El Chico's earnings per share may be lower than if you were to borrow.
How good is the business's credit rating?	The better the credit rating, the easier it is to borrow on favorable terms. A good credit rating also makes it easier to issue stock. Neither stockholders nor creditors will entrust their money to a company with a bad credit rating.

The Leverage Ratio

As discussed and illustrated in the previous section, financing with debt can be advantageous, but management of a company must be careful not to incur too much debt. Chapter 3 discussed the debt ratio, which measures the proportion of total liabilities to total assets, two elements of the fundamental accounting equation:

$$\text{Debt ratio} = \frac{\text{Total debt (liabilities)}}{\text{Total assets}}$$

We can rearrange this relationship between total assets, total liabilities, and stockholders' equity in a different manner to illustrate the impact that leverage can have on profitability. The **leverage ratio** is calculated as follows:

$$\text{Leverage ratio} = \frac{\text{Total assets}}{\text{Total stockholders' equity}}$$

Also known as the **equity multiplier**, this ratio shows a company's total assets per dollar of stockholders' equity. A leverage ratio of exactly 1.0 would mean a company has no debt, because total assets would exactly equal total stockholders' equity. This condition is almost nonexistent, because virtually all companies have liabilities and, therefore, have leverage ratios in excess of 1.0. In fact, as we have shown previously, having a healthy amount of debt can actually enhance a company's profitability, in terms of the shareholders' investment. The leverage ratio is the third element of the *DuPont Analysis* model, introduced in part with the discussion of return on assets in Chapter 7.[4] The higher the leverage ratio, the more it magnifies return on stockholders' equity (Net income/Average stockholders' equity, or ROE). If net income is positive, return on assets (ROA) is positive. The leverage ratio magnifies this positive return to make return on equity (ROE) even more positive. This is because the company is using borrowed money to earn a profit (a concept known as *trading on the equity*).

However, if earnings are negative (losses), ROA is negative, and the leverage ratio makes ROE even more negative. We will discuss DuPont Analysis and ROE in more detail as we discuss stockholders' equity in Chapter 10. For now, let's just focus on understanding the meaning of the leverage ratio by looking at Southwest Airlines in comparison with one of its competitors, United Continental Holdings (parent company of United Airlines and Continental Airlines). Here are the leverage ratios and debt ratios for the two companies at the end of 2012:

(In millions) for 2012	Southwest	United Continental
1. Total assets	$18,596	$20,802
2. Stockholders' equity	$ 6,992	$ (3,184)
3. Leverage ratio (1 ÷ 2)	2.66	N/A
4. Total debt (1 − 2)	$11,604	$23,986
5. Debt ratio (4 ÷ 1)	62.4%	115.3%

These figures show that Southwest has $2.66 of total assets for each dollar of stockholders' equity. This translates to a debt ratio of 62.4%, which we learned in Chapter 3 is about normal for many companies. In comparison, United Continental has a deficit in stockholders' equity of about $3.2 billion, making the leverage ratio impossible to calculate. Rearranging the elements to show debt to total assets, United Continental has an astonishing ratio of 115.3%. This company is drowning in debt! A quick search of the SEC website for the balance sheets of AMR (the holding company of American Airlines) and Delta Airlines showed that both these companies were in similar straits. Southwest truly does stand alone in comparison with other major airlines from a leverage standpoint!

---

[4]The DuPont analysis model provides a detailed analysis of return on equity (ROE). It is the product of three elements: (Net income/Net sales) × (Net sales/Total assets) × (Total assets/Total stockholders' equity). When total assets and total stockholders' equity fluctuate materially from year to year, averages should be used for Total assets and Total stockholders' equity. Since these figures did not vary significantly for Southwest Airlines Co. from 2011 to 2012, we used year-end numbers to simplify. Notice that elements cross-cancel so that the model reduces to Net income/Stockholders' equity. See Chapter 10 for a more complete discussion of ROE. A modified version of the model considers only the first two elements to calculate return on assets (ROA), as discussed in Chapter 7.

The Times-Interest-Earned Ratio

Analysts use a second ratio—the **times-interest-earned ratio**—to relate income to interest expense. To compute this ratio, we divide *income from operations* (also called *operating income*) by interest expense. This ratio measures the number of times that operating income can *cover* interest expense. The times-interest-earned ratio is also called the **interest-coverage ratio**. A high times-interest-earned ratio indicates ease in paying interest expense; a low value suggests difficulty. Let's see how our competing airlines, Southwest and United Continental, compare on the times-interest-earned ratio (dollar amounts in millions taken from the companies' 2012 financial statements):

$$\text{Times–interest–earned ratio} = \frac{\text{Operating income}}{\text{Interest expense}}$$

$$\text{Southwest} \quad \frac{\$623}{\$147} = 4.24 \text{ times}$$

$$\text{United Continental} \quad \frac{\$39}{\$835} = 0.05 \text{ times}$$

Southwest's income from operations covers its interest expense 4.24 times. While not particularly strong, this ratio is much stronger for Southwest than other airlines. In contrast, United Continental's operating earnings of $39 million only measure a fraction (0.05) of its huge interest charges of $835 million. United Continental is clearly in trouble from an interest coverage perspective.

UNDERSTAND OTHER LONG-TERM LIABILITIES

Leases

A **lease** is a rental agreement in which the tenant (**lessee**) agrees to make rent payments to the property owner (**lessor**) in exchange for the use of the asset. Leasing allows the lessee to acquire the use of a needed asset without having to make the large up-front payment that purchase agreements require. Accountants distinguish between two types of leases: operating leases and capital leases.

4 **Understand** other long-term liabilities

Types of Leases

Operating leases are sometimes short-term or cancelable. However, often operating lease agreements are noncancelable and require the lessee to commit funds to pay the lessor for the use of property for years. They give the lessee the right to use the asset but provide no continuing rights to the asset. Instead, the lessor retains the usual risks and rewards of owning the leased asset. To account for an operating lease, the lessee debits Rent Expense (or Lease Expense) and credits Cash for the amount of the lease payment. Operating leases require the lessee to make rent payments, so an operating lease creates a liability even though that liability does not appear on the lessee's balance sheet. In recent years, Southwest Airlines has begun to lease most of its facilities (hangars; buildings; and equipment, including airplanes) under operating lease agreements. Following is an excerpt from Note 8 of Southwest's 2012 financial statements:

Note 8 Leases (partial)

Total rental expense for operating leases, both aircraft and other, charged to operations in 2012, 2011, and 2010 was $943 million, $847 million, and $631 million, respectively. The majority of the Company's terminal operations space, as well as 187 aircraft, were under operating leases at December 31, 2012. Future minimum lease payments under noncancelable operating leases with initial or remaining terms in excess of one year at December 31, 2012, were (in millions) as follows:

2013	$ 688
2014	614
2015	507
2016	392
2017	369
Thereafter	1,823
Total	$4,393

This essentially means that, although the company has merely signed rental agreements for these assets, it has an obligation over several years for almost $4.4 billion to the companies from which it is leasing these assets. Neither the obligation nor the associated assets are included in Southwest's balance sheet. This is an example of what is called "off-balance-sheet financing."

Capital leases are often used to finance the acquisition of long-term assets. A **capital lease** is a long-term, noncancelable debt. How do we distinguish a capital lease from an operating lease? The FASB provides the U.S. GAAP guidelines. To be classified as a capital lease, the lease must meet any *one* of the following criteria:

1. The lease transfers title of the leased asset to the lessee at the end of the lease term. Thus, the lessee becomes the legal owner of the leased asset.

2. The lease contains a *bargain purchase option*. The lessee can be expected to purchase the leased asset and become its legal owner.

3. The lease term is 75% or more of the estimated useful life of the leased asset. The lessee uses up most of the leased asset's service potential.

4. The present value of the lease payments is 90% or more of the market value of the leased asset. In effect, the lease payments are the same as installment payments for the leased asset.

If the lease does not meet one of these exact criteria, it is classified as an operating lease by default.

Accounting for a capital lease is much like accounting for the purchase of an asset. The lessee enters the asset into the lessee's long-term asset accounts at the present value of the future cash outflows from the lease contact and records a long-term lease liability at the beginning of the lease term. Thus, the lessee capitalizes the asset even though the lessee may never take legal title to it, because the lease agreement, in substance, makes the lessee assume the risks and rewards of ownership of the assets and the associated obligations. In lieu of rent expense, the lessee of the capital asset records depreciation expense on the asset (as required of an owner) and interest expense on the lease obligation each period. Both of these expenses are recorded over the term of the lease obligation.

At December 31, 2012, Southwest Airlines reported its capital leases in Note 8 of its financial statements, excerpted as follows:

The Company had two aircraft classified as capital leases at December 31, 2012, compared to seven aircraft classified as capital leases at December 31, 2011. Amounts applicable to these aircraft that are included in property and equipment were:

(in millions)	2012	2011
Flight equipment	$ 45	$177
Less: accumulated amortization	8	132
	$ 37	$ 45

The note shows that as of December 31, 2012, Southwest had only two aircraft classified as capital leased assets. This number was down from seven aircraft as of December 31, 2011, and from many more than that in previous years. In contrast, Southwest leases 187 aircraft on an operating lease basis.

Do Lessees Prefer Operating Leases or Capital Leases?

Suppose you were the chief financial officer (CFO) of Southwest Airlines. Southwest leases 187 of its 694 aircraft. Suppose the leases can be structured either as operating leases or as capital leases. Which type of lease would you prefer for Southwest? Why? Consider what would happen to Southwest's debt ratio if its operating leases in Note 8 were capitalized and the related liabilities recognized. Computing Southwest's debt ratio two ways (*operating* leases versus reclassifying them as *capital* leases) will make your decision clear (using Southwest's actual figures in millions):

		Operating Leases as Stated	Operating Leases Reclassified as Capital Leases	
Debt ratio	$= \dfrac{\text{Total liabilities}}{\text{Total assets}} =$	$\dfrac{\$11,604}{\$18,596}$	$\dfrac{\$11,604 + \$4,393}{\$18,596 + \$4,393} =$	$\dfrac{\$15,997}{\$22,989}$
		$= \quad 0.624$		$= \quad 0.696$

You can see that a capital lease increases the debt ratio—by over 7 percentage points for Southwest. By contrast, notice that operating leases don't affect the debt ratio that's reported on the balance sheet. For this reason, companies prefer operating leases. It is easy to see why Southwest's long-term commitment for operating leases, as disclosed in Note 8, far outweighs that of its capital lease agreements.

Ethical Challenge. Because of the relatively mechanical nature of the accounting criteria for capitalization of leases, it is possible under existing U.S. GAAP to purposely structure a company's lease agreements so that they barely miss meeting the third criterion (75% test) or the fourth criterion (90% test) for capitalization. Many U.S. companies have taken advantage of these mechanical rules, quite legally, to their economic advantage, thus obtaining almost all the same economic benefits associated with ownership of long-term assets, but avoiding the detrimental impact that recording those assets and obligations can have on their debt ratios.

Global View

In contrast to U.S. GAAP with its mechanical, or "bright line" tests for capitalization of leases, IFRS adopts a much broader approach. Rather than rules, IFRS employs "guidance" that focuses on the overall substance of the transaction, rather than on the mechanical form, and that leaves more to the judgment of the preparer of the financial statement. If, in the judgment of the company's accountants, the lease transfers "substantially all of the risks and rewards of ownership to the lessee," IFRS says the lease should be capitalized. Otherwise, the lease should be expensed as an operating lease.

As of the date of this text, the FASB and IASB have issued several joint exposure drafts proposing a new standard on long-term leases that will, for the great majority of such agreements, require capital lease treatment. This will essentially end the practice of operating leases and off-balance-sheet financing for leased equipment. A revised statement is expected sometime in 2013. When that happens, Southwest Airlines and many other companies with long-term operating leases for fixed assets could be forced to add billions of dollars to their long-term assets, as well as their long-term liabilities, with results as we just showed on their debt and other ratios.

Pensions and Postretirement Liabilities

Most companies have retirement plans for their employees. A **pension** is employee compensation that will be received during retirement. Companies also provide postretirement benefits, such as medical insurance for retired former employees. Because employees earn these benefits by their service, the company records pension and retirement-benefit expense while employees work for the company.

Pensions are one of the most complex areas of accounting. As employees earn their pensions and the company pays into the pension plan, the plan's assets grow. The obligation for future pension payments to employees also accumulates. At the end of each period, the company compares

- the fair market value of the assets in the retirement plans—cash and investments—with
- the plans' *projected benefit obligation*, which is the present value of promised future payments to retirees.

If the plan assets exceed the projected benefit obligation, the plan is said to be *overfunded*. In this case, the asset and obligation amounts are to be reported only in the notes to the financial statements. However, if the projected benefit obligation (the liability) exceeds plan assets, the plan is *underfunded*, and the company must report the excess liability on its balance sheet.

Southwest Airlines' retirement plans don't create large liabilities for Southwest. To illustrate pension liabilities, let's see the pension plan of AMR Corp., the parent company of American Airlines. At December 31, 2012, the retirement plans of AMR Corporation were underfunded. They had

- assets with a fair market value of $9,065 million.
- projected benefit obligations totaling $15,895 million.

AMR's balance sheet, therefore, included a Pension and Post-Retirement Liability of $6,830 million ($15,895 million – $9,065 million). This liability was split between current and long-term liabilities, in accordance with the due dates for the obligations.

REPORT LIABILITIES

Reporting on the Balance Sheet

5 Report liabilities

This chapter began with the liabilities reported on the consolidated balance sheets of Southwest Airlines. Exhibit 9-11 shows a standard way for Southwest to report its current liabilities and long-term debt.

Exhibit 9-11 includes Note 7 from Southwest's consolidated financial statements. The note gives additional details about the company's liabilities. Note 7 shows the interest rates and the maturity dates of Southwest's long-term debt. Investors need these data to evaluate the company. The note also reports

- current maturities of long-term debt ($271 million) as a current liability.
- long-term debt (less current maturities) of $2,883 million.

Trace these amounts from the note to the balance sheet. Working back and forth between the financial statements and the related notes is an important part of financial analysis. You now have the tools to understand the liabilities reported on an actual balance sheet.

Exhibit 9-11 | Reporting the Liabilities of Southwest Airlines Co.

	A	B	C	D	E
	A1				
1	**Southwest Airlines Co. Consolidated Balance Sheet (Partial, Adapted)**	**Dec. 31, 2012**		**Note 7 Long-term debt (In millions) (Adapted)**	**Dec. 31, 2012**
2	**Liabilities (in millions)**			Term loans due 2019–20	$ 787
3	Current Liabilities:			Fixed-rate notes on aircraft	93
4	Accounts payable	$ 1,107		Pass-through certificates due 2022	394
5	Accrued liabilities	1,102		Floating rate aircraft notes	527
6	Air traffic liability	2,170		7 3/8% debentures due 2027	138
7	Current maturities of			5 1/2% notes due 2014	366
8	long-term debt	271 ◄		5 3/4% notes due 2016	331
9	Total current liabilities	4,650		5 1/8% notes due 2017	329
10	Long-term debt, less current			5 1/4% convertible notes due 2016	117
11	maturities	2,883 ◄		Other long-term debt	93
12	Other long-term liabilities	4,071		Total long-term debt	3,175
13				Less current maturities	(271)
14	Total liabilities	$ 11,604		Less debt discounted and	
15				issuance costs	(21)
16				Long-term debt	$ 2,883
17					

Disclosing the Fair Value of Long-Term Debt

Generally accepted accounting principles require companies to report the fair value of their long-term debt. At December 31, 2012, Southwest Airlines' Note 11 included this excerpt (adapted, details omitted):

> **The estimated fair value of the Company's long-term debt was $3,250 million.**

Overall, the fair value of Southwest's long-term debt is about $367 million more than its carrying amount on the books ($2,883 million). Fair values of publicly traded debt are based on quoted market prices (level 1 measures, as discussed in Chapter 8), which fluctuate with interest rates and overall market conditions. Therefore, at any one time, fair values for various obligations can either exceed or be less than their carrying amounts.

Reporting Financing Activities on the Statement of Cash Flows

The Southwest Airlines consolidated balance sheet (p. 483) shows that the company finances about 62% of its operations with debt. Southwest's debt ratio is about 62%. Let's examine Southwest's financing activities as reported on its statement of cash flows. Exhibit 9-12 is an excerpt from Southwest's consolidated statement of cash flows.

Exhibit 9-12 | Consolidated Statement of Cash Flows (Partial, Adapted) for Southwest Airlines Co.

	A	B
1	**Southwest Airlines Co.** **Consolidated Statement of Cash Flows (Adapted)**	
2	(In millions)	**Year Ended December 31, 2012**
3	Cash Flow from Operating Activities:	
4	Net cash provided by operating activities	$ 2,064
5	Cash Flow from Investing Activities:	
6	Net cash used for investing activities	(833)
7	Cash Flow from Financing Activities:	
8	Payments of long-term debt and capital lease obligations	(578)
9	Repurchase of common stock	(400)
10	Other financing sources (net)	31
11	Net cash used for financing activities	(947)
12	Net increase in cash and cash equivalents	284
13		

Southwest has provided $2.06 billion more cash from operations than it used in 2012. The company has a long history of good financial management, and it is the most liquid and profitable airline company in the industry. With the excess cash generated from operations, Southwest has net investing activities of $833 million in property and equipment and investments of various types. In contrast, the company spent $578 million in payments on long-term debt and capital lease obligations and another $400 million repurchasing common stock, a topic we will cover in Chapter 10. Southwest has borrowed rather heavily in order to finance its growth and refurbish its fleet of aircraft. This is evident in the long-term debt footnote in Exhibit 9-11. Much of that debt has not yet come due as of the end of 2012, but current installments on the debt have been increasing in recent years. About $3.2 billion of the debt still remains, with current maturities of about $271 million and the remainder extending to 2027. Over the next several years, the company will have to pay the debt off, as it comes due in installments, with, it must hope, cash provided by operations.

The **Cessna Aircraft Company** has outstanding an issue of 4% convertible bonds that mature October 1, 2022. Suppose the bonds are dated October 1, 2014, and pay interest each April 1 and October 1.

Bond Data
Maturity (face) value—$100,000
Stated interest rate—4%
Interest paid—2% semiannually, $2,000 ($100,000 × 0.04 × 6/12)
Market interest rate at the time of issue—5% annually, 2½% semiannually

Requirements

1. Use Excel to build an amortization table through October 1, 2016. Use Excel to obtain the issue price.
2. Using the amortization table, record the following transactions:
   a. Issuance of the bonds on October 1, 2014.
   b. Accrual of interest and amortization of the bond discount on December 31, 2014.
   c. Payment of interest and amortization of the bond discount on April 1, 2015.
   d. Conversion of one-third of the bonds payable into no-par stock on October 2, 2016. For no-par stock, transfer the bond carrying amount into the Common Stock account. There is no Additional Paid-in Capital account.
   e. Retirement of two-thirds of the bonds payable on October 2, 2016. Purchase price of the bonds is based on their call price of 102.

Answers

Requirement 1

	A1					
	A	B	C	D	E	F
1			Amortization Table Cessna Aircraft Company			
2	Semiannual Interest Payment Date	Interest Payment (2% of Maturity Amount)	Interest Expense (2.5% of Preceding Bond Carrying Amount)*	Discount Amortization (C – B)*	Discount Account Balance (Preceding E – D)*	Bond Carrying Amount ($100,000 – E)*
3	10/1/2014				$ 6,528	$ 93,472
4	4/1/2015	$ 2,000	$ 2,337	$ 337	$ 6,191	$ 93,809
5	10/1/2015	$ 2,000	$ 2,345	$ 345	$ 5,845	$ 94,155
6	4/1/2016	$ 2,000	$ 2,354	$ 354	$ 5,492	$ 94,508
7	10/1/2016	$ 2,000	$ 2,363	$ 363	$ 5,129	$ 94,871
8						
9	Issue price	$ 93,472				
10						

*amounts may vary by $1 because of rounding

Requirement 2

	A	B	C	D	E
				Debit	Credit
1		2014			
2	a.	1-Oct	Cash	93,472	
3			Discount on Bonds Payable	6,528	
4			Bonds Payable		100,000
5			To issue bonds at a discount.		
6					
7	b.	31-Dec	Interest expense (2,337 × 3/6)	1,169	
8			Discount on Bonds Payable (337 × 3/6)		169
9			Interest Payable (2,000 × 3/6)		1,000
10			To accrue interest and amortize bond discount.		
11		2015			
12	c.	1-Apr	Interest expense (2,337 × 3/6)	1,168	
13			Interest payable	1,000	
14			Discount on Bonds Payable (337 × 3/6)		168
15			Cash		2,000
16			To pay semiannual interest, part of which		
17			was accrued, and amortize bond discount.		
18					
19	d.	2016			
20		2-Oct	Bonds Payable (100,000 × 1/3)	33,333	
21			Discount on Bonds Payable (5,129 × 1/3)		1,710
22			Common Stock (94,871 × 1/3)		31,623
23			To convert one-third of bonds to common stock.		
24					
25	e.	2-Oct	Bonds Payable (100,000 × 2/3)	66,667	
26			Loss on Retirement of Bonds	4,752	
27			Discount on Bonds Payable (5,129 × 2/3)		3,419
28			Cash (100,000 × 2/3 × 1.02)		68,000
29			To retire bonds payable before maturity at 102.		
30					

A1

REVIEW | Liabilities

Quick Check (Answers are given on page 549.)

1. Which of the following is *not* an estimated liability?
   - a. Product warranties
   - b. Allowance for bad debts
   - c. Income taxes
   - d. Vacation pay

2. Recording estimated warranty expense in the year the related products are sold *best* follows which accounting principle?
   - a. Full disclosure
   - b. Consistency
   - c. Historical cost
   - d. Materiality
   - e. Expense recognition (matching)

3. Accounts payable turnover for Big Blue, Inc., increased from 10 to 12 during 2014. Which of the following statements best describes what this means?
   - a. Inventory turned over faster in 2014, meaning sales increased.
   - b. The company paid its accounts payable more slowly in 2014, signaling a weaker liquidity position.
   - c. The company paid its accounts payable more quickly in 2014, signaling a stronger liquidity position.
   - d. Not enough information is provided to form a conclusion.

4. Packard Co. was organized to sell a single product that carries a 45-day warranty against defects. Engineering estimates indicate that 2% of the units sold will prove defective and require an average repair cost of $45 per unit. During Packard's first month of operations, total sales were 900 units; by the end of the month, 5 defective units had been repaired. The liability for product warranties at month-end should be

a. $225.

d. $585.

b. $1,035.

e. none of these.

c. $810.

5. A contingent liability should be recorded in the accounts

a. if the amount can be reasonably estimated.

b. if the amount is due in cash within one year.

c. if the related future event will probably occur.

d. both b and c.

e. both a and c.

6. An unsecured bond is a

a. debenture bond.

d. term bond.

b. registered bond.

e. serial bond.

c. mortgage bond.

7. The Discount on Bonds Payable account

a. is a miscellaneous revenue account.

d. is an expense account.

b. is a contra account to Bonds Payable.

e. has a normal credit balance.

c. is expensed at the bond's maturity.

8. The discount on a bond payable becomes

a. a liability in the year the bonds are sold.

b. a reduction in interest expense the year the bonds mature.

c. additional interest expense over the life of the bonds.

d. additional interest expense the year the bonds are sold.

e. a reduction in interest expense over the life of the bonds.

9. A bond that matures in installments is called a

a. callable bond.

d. serial bond.

b. zero coupon.

e. term bond.

c. secured bond.

10. The carrying value of Bonds Payable equals

a. Bonds Payable − Discount on Bonds Payable.

b. Bonds Payable + Accrued Interest.

c. Bonds Payable − Premium on Bonds Payable.

d. Bonds Payable + Discount on Bonds Payable.

11. Dart Corporation's leverage ratio increased from 2.5 in 2013 to 3.0 in 2014. Without looking at the financial statements, which statement best describes what may have occurred?

a. The company incurred new debt financing in 2014, but it may or may not have been more profitable.

b. The company incurred new equity financing in 2014, making it less profitable.

c. The company incurred new debt financing in 2014, making it more profitable.

d. The company incurred new equity financing in 2014, but it may or may not have been more profitable.

Use this information to answer questions 12–17.
McVay Corporation issued $100,000 of 4.5%, 10-year bonds. The bonds are dated and sold on January 1, 2015. Interest payment dates are January 1 and July 1. The bonds are issued to yield the market interest rate of 5%. Use the effective-interest method for questions 12–16.

12. Using the PV function in Excel, the price of the bonds (amount raised from issuance) is
   a. $100,000.
   b. $101,603.
   c. $94,303.
   d. $96,103.

13. What is the amount of interest expense that McVay Corporation will record on July 1, 2015, the first semiannual interest payment date? (All amounts rounded to the nearest dollar.)
   a. $2,250
   b. $2,403
   c. $3,745
   d. $153

14. What is the amount of discount amortization that McVay Corporation will record on July 1, 2015, the first semiannual interest payment date?
   a. $2,250
   b. $-0-
   c. $2,403
   d. $153

15. What is the total cash payment for interest for each 12-month period? (All amounts are rounded to the nearest dollar.)
   a. $4,809
   b. $5,000
   c. $4,500
   d. $3,588

16. What is the carrying amount of the bonds on the January 1, 2016, balance sheet?
   a. $96,255
   b. $96,412
   c. $100,000
   d. $96,103

17. Using straight-line amortization, the carrying amount of McVay Corporation's bonds at December 31, 2015, is
   a. $95,713.
   b. $95,908.
   c. $96,298.
   d. $96,493.

Accounting Vocabulary

accounts payable turnover (p. 485) The number of times per year a company pays off its accounts payable.

accrued expense (p. 487) An expense incurred but not yet paid in cash. Also called *accrued liability*.

accrued liability (p. 487) A liability for an expense that has not yet been paid. Also called *accrued expense*.

bonds payable (p. 494) Groups of debt securities issued to multiple lenders called *bondholders*.

callable bond (p. 509) Bonds that are paid off early at a specified price at the option of the issuer.

capital lease (p. 514) Lease agreement in which the lessee assumes, in substance, the risks and rewards of asset ownership. In the United States, a lease is assumed to be a capital lease if it meets any one of four criteria: (1) The lease transfers title of the leased asset to the lessee. (2) The lease contains a bargain purchase option. (3) The lease term is 75% or more of the estimated useful life of the leased asset. (4) The present value of the lease payments is 90% or more of the market value of the leased asset.

convertible bonds (or notes) (p. 509) Bonds or notes that may be converted into the issuing company's common stock at the investor's option.

current portion of long-term debt (p. 489) The amount of the principal that is payable within one year.

days' payable outstanding (DPO) (p. 485) Accounts payable turnover expressed in days (365/turnover).

debentures (p. 496) Unsecured bonds—bonds backed only by the good faith of the borrower.

discount (on a bond) (p. 496) Excess of a bond's face (par) value over its issue price.

earnings per share (EPS) (p. 510) Amount of a company's net income per share of its outstanding common stock.

equity multiplier (p. 512) Another name for *leverage ratio*.

interest-coverage ratio (p. 513) Another name for the *times-interest-earned ratio*.

lease (p. 513) Rental agreement in which the tenant (lessee) agrees to make rent payments to the property owner (lessor) in exchange for the use of the asset.

lessee (p. 513) Tenant in a lease agreement.

lessor (p. 513) Property owner in a lease agreement.

leverage (p. 510) Using borrowed funds to increase the return on equity. Successful use of leverage means earning more income on borrowed money than the related interest expense, thereby increasing the earnings for the owners of the business. Also called *trading on the equity.*

leverage ratio (p. 512) The ratio of total assets ÷ total stockholders' equity, showing the proportion of total assets to total stockholders' equity. This ratio, like the debt ratio introduced in Chapter 3, tells the mixture of a company's debt and equity financing and is useful in calculating rate of return on stockholders' equity (ROE) through the DuPont Model.

market interest rate (p. 496) Interest rate that investors demand for loaning their money. Also called *effective interest rate.*

operating lease (p. 513) A lease in which the lessee does not assume the risks or rewards of asset ownership.

payroll (p. 487) Employee compensation, a major expense of many businesses.

pension (p. 515) Employee compensation that will be received during retirement.

premium (on a bond) (p. 496) Excess of a bond's issue price over its face (par) value.

serial bonds (p. 495) Bonds that mature in installments over a period of time.

short-term notes payable (p. 486) Notes payable that are due within one year.

stated interest rate (p. 496) Interest rate that determines the amount of cash interest the borrower pays and the investor receives each year.

term bonds (p. 495) Bonds that all mature at the same time for a particular issue.

times-interest-earned ratio (p. 513) Ratio of income from operations to interest expense. Measures the number of times that operating income can cover interest expense. Also called the *interest-coverage ratio.*

trading on the equity (p. 510) Earning more income on borrowed money than the related interest expense, thereby increasing the earnings for the owners of the business. Also called *leverage*—the power of which is illustrated through the *leverage ratio.*

underwriter (p. 495) Organization that purchases the bonds from an issuing company and resells them to its clients or sells the bonds for a commission, agreeing to buy all unsold bonds.

ASSESS YOUR PROGRESS

Short Exercises

S9-1. *(Learning Objective 1: Account for a short-term note payable)* Jaska Sports Authority purchased inventory costing $22,500 by signing a 6% short-term note payable. The purchase occurred on July 31, 2014. Jaska pays annual interest each year on July 31. Journalize the company's (a) purchase of inventory; (b) accrual of interest expense on April 30, 2015, which is the year-end; and (c) payment of the note plus interest on July 31, 2015. (Round your answers to the nearest whole number.) (d) Show what the company would report for liabilities on its balance sheet at April 30, 2015, and on its income statement for the year ended on that date.

S9-2. *(Learning Objective 1: Analyze accounts payable turnover)* Jinna Sales, Inc.'s comparative income statements and balance sheets show the following selected information for 2013 and 2014:

	2014	2013
Cost of goods sold	$2,600,000	$2,400,000
Ending inventory	$1,000,000	$ 700,000
Beginning inventory	$ 700,000	$ 600,000
Average accounts payable	$ 317,600	$ 252,600

Requirements

1. Calculate the company's accounts payable turnover and days' payable outstanding (DPO) for 2013 and 2014.
2. On the basis of this computation alone, has the company's liquidity position improved or deteriorated during 2014?

S9-3. *(Learning Objective 1: Account for warranty expense and estimated warranty payable)*
Tires USA guarantees tires against defects for five years or 60,000 miles, whichever comes first.
Suppose Tires USA can expect warranty costs during the five-year period to add up to 5%
of sales. Assume that a Tires USA dealer in Atlanta, Georgia, made sales of $674,000 during
2014. Tires USA received cash for 35% of the sales and took notes receivable for the remainder.
Payments to satisfy customer warranty claims totaled $19,400 during 2014.
 1. Record the sales, warranty expense, and warranty payments for Tires USA.
 2. Post to the Estimated Warranty Payable T-account. The beginning balance was $14,000.
    At the end of 2014, how much in estimated warranty payable does Tires USA owe to its
    customers?

S9-4. *(Learning Objective 1: Report warranties in the financial statements)* Refer to the data
given in S9-3 . What amount of warranty expense will Tires USA report during 2014? Which
accounting principle addresses this situation? Does the warranty expense for the year equal the
year's cash payments for warranties? Explain the relevant accounting principle as it applies to
measuring warranty expense.

S9-5. *(Learning Objective 1: Interpret a company's contingent liabilities)* Wheels, Inc., the
motorcycle manufacturer, included the following note in its annual report:

NOTES TO CONSOLIDATED FINANCIAL STATEMENTS
7 (In Part): Commitments and Contingencies
   The Company self-insures its product liability losses in the United States up to $3.8 million
   (catastrophic coverage is maintained for individual claims in excess of $3.8 million up to $26.3 million).
   Outside the United States, the Company is insured for product liability up to $26.3 million per
   individual claim and in the aggregate.

---

 1. Why are these *contingent* (versus *real*) liabilities?
 2. In the United States, how can the contingent liability become a real liability for Wheels,
    Inc.? What are the limits to the company's product liabilities in the United States?
 3. How can a contingency outside the United States become a real liability for the company?
    How does Wheels, Inc.'s potential liability differ for claims outside the United States?

S9-6. *(Learning Objective 2: Review of bonds issued at a discount)* Read each statement below,
indicate if it is true or false, and give a brief explanation of your answer.
 1. When a bond is sold at a discount, the cash received is less than the present value of the
    future cash flows from the bond, based on the market rate of interest on the date of issue.
 2. When a bond is issued at a discount, the semiannual cash interest payments are calculated
    using the market rate on the date of issue.
 3. When a bond is issued at a discount, the semiannual amount of interest expense will be
    greater than the cash payment for interest.
 4. When a bond is sold at a discount, the maturity value is less than the present value of the
    principal and interest payments, based on the market rate of interest on the date of issue.
 5. The amortization of the discount on a bond payable results in additional interest expense
    recorded over the life of the bond.
 6. When the year-end accrual of interest and amortization of discount is recorded, the
    carrying value of Bonds Payable on the balance sheet will increase.

S9-7. *(Learning Objective 2: Determine bond prices at par, discount, or premium)* Determine
whether the following bonds payable will be issued at par value, at a premium, or at a discount:
   a. The market interest rate is 5%. Haylee Corp. issues bonds payable with a stated rate
       of 6½%.
   b. Samuel, Inc., issued 5% bonds payable when the market rate was 5¾%.
   c. Houston Corporation issued 3% bonds when the market interest rate was 3%.
   d. Ortloff Company issued bonds payable that pay stated interest of 7¼%. At issuance,
       the market interest rate was 7¾%.

S9-8. *(Learning Objective 2: Journalize basic bond payable transactions and bonds issued at par)* AJR Corp. issued 4% seven-year bonds payable with a face amount of $150,000 when the market interest rate was 4%. Assume that the accounting year of AJR ends on December 31 and that bonds pay interest on January 1 and July 1. Journalize the following transactions for AJR. Include an explanation for each entry.

    a. Issuance of the bonds payable at par on July 1, 2014
    b. Accrual of interest expense on December 31, 2014 (rounded to the nearest dollar)
    c. Payment of cash interest on January 1, 2015
    d. Payment of the bonds payable at maturity (give the date)

S9-9. *(Learning Objective 2: Issue bonds payable and amortize bonds by the effective-interest method)* Potter Investments, Inc., issued $560,000 of 2.5%, 10-year bonds payable on March 31, 2014. The market interest rate at the date of issuance was 3%, and the Potter Investments bonds pay interest semiannually. Potter's year-end is March 31.

    1. Using the PV function in Excel, calculate the issue price of the bonds.
    2. Prepare an effective-interest amortization table for the bonds through the first three interest payments. Round amounts to the nearest dollar.
    3. Record Potter Investments, Inc.'s issuance of the bonds on March 31, 2014, and payment of the first semiannual interest amount and amortization of the bond discount on September 30, 2014. Explanations are not required.

S9-10. *(Learning Objective 2: Account for bonds payable; analyze data on bonds)* Use the amortization table that you prepared for Potter Investment's bonds in S9-9 to answer the following questions:

    1. How much cash did Potter Investments borrow on March 31, 2014? How much cash will Potter Investments pay back at maturity on March 31, 2024?
    2. How much cash interest will Potter Investments pay each six months?
    3. How much interest expense will Potter Investments report on September 30, 2014, and on March 31, 2015? Why does the amount of interest expense increase each period?

S9-11. *(Learning Objective 2: Determine bonds payable amounts; amortize bonds by the straight-line method)* Moonlight Drive-Ins Ltd. borrowed money by issuing $2,000,000 of 4% bonds payable at 97.5 on July 1, 2014. The bonds are 10-year bonds and pay interest each January 1 and July 1.

    1. How much cash did Moonlight receive when it issued the bonds payable? Journalize this transaction.
    2. How much must Moonlight pay back at maturity? When is the maturity date?
    3. How much cash interest will Moonlight pay each six months?
    4. How much interest expense will Moonlight report each six months? Assume the straight-line amortization method. Journalize the entries for accrual of interest on December 31, 2014, and payment of interest on January 1, 2015.

S9-12. *(Learning Objective 3: Calculate the leverage ratio, debt ratio, and times-interest-earned ratio, and evaluate debt-paying ability)* Examine the following selected financial information for Best Buy Co., Inc., and Walmart Stores, Inc., as of the end of their 2012 fiscal years:

(In millions)	Best Buy Co., Inc.	Walnart Stores, Inc.
1. Total assets	$16,787	$203,105
2. Stockholders' equity	$ 3,061	$ 76,343
3. Operating income	$ 1,085	$ 27,801
4. Interest expense	$ 134	$ 2,064
5. Leverage ratio		
6. Total debt		
7. Debt ratio		
8. Times interest earned		

    1. Complete the table, calculating all the requested information for the two companies.
    2. Evaluate each company's long-term debt-paying ability (strong, medium, weak).

S9-13. *(Learning Objective 3: Compute earnings-per-share effects of financing with bonds versus stock)* Waterfront Marina needs to raise $1.5 million to expand the company. Waterfront Marina is considering the issuance of either

- $1,500,000 of 6% bonds payable to borrow the money, or
- 150,000 shares of common stock at $10 per share.

Before any new financing, Waterfront Marina expects to earn net income of $400,000, and the company already has 100,000 shares of common stock outstanding. Waterfront Marina believes the expansion will increase income before interest and income tax by $200,000. The income tax rate is 30%.

Prepare an analysis to determine which plan is likely to result in the higher earnings per share. Based solely on the earnings-per-share comparison, which financing plan would you recommend for Waterfront Marina?

S9-14. *(Learning Objective 3: Compute and evaluate three ratios)* Ferguson Plumbing Products Ltd. reported the following data in 2014 (in millions):

	2014
Net operating revenues................	$ 29.1
Operating expenses	25.0
Operating income.......................	4.1
Nonoperating items:	
Interest expense......................	(1.1)
Other	(0.2)
Net income..............................	$ 2.8
Total assets	$100.0
Total stockholders' equity	40.0

Compute Ferguson's leverage ratio, debt ratio, and times-interest-earned ratio, and write a sentence to explain what those ratio values mean. Would you be willing to lend Ferguson $1 million? State your reason.

S9-15. *(Learning Objectives 4, 5: Report liabilities, including capital lease obligations)* Royall, Inc., includes the following selected accounts in its general ledger at December 31, 2014:

Bonds payable (excluding current portion)..	$350,000
Equipment..	117,000
Current portion of bonds payable	56,000
Notes payable, long-term	125,000
Interest payable (due March 1, 2015)...	1,600
Accounts payable	28,500
Discount on bonds payable (all long-term)..	11,250
Accounts receivable..	31,000

Prepare the liabilities section of Royall, Inc.'s balance sheet at December 31, 2014, to show how the company would report these items. Report total current liabilities and total liabilities.

Exercises

MyAccountingLab

All of the A and B exercises can be found within MyAccountingLab, an online home-work and practice environment. Your instructor may ask you to complete these exercises using **MyAccountingLab**.

Group A

E9-16A. *(Learning Objective 1: Account for warranty expense and the related liability)* The accounting records of Dee's Appliances included the following balances at the end of the period:

Estimated Warranty Payable	Sales Revenue	Warranty Expense
Beg bal 4,500	108,000	

In the past, Dee's warranty expense has been 8% of sales. During the current period, the business paid $7,100 to satisfy the warranty claims.

Requirements

1. Journalize Dee's warranty expense for the period and the company's cash payments to satisfy warranty claims. Explanations are not required.
2. Show what Dee's Appliances will report on its income statement and balance sheet for this situation at the end of the period.
3. Which data item from requirement 2 will affect Dee's current ratio? Will Dee's current ratio increase or decrease as a result of this item?

E9-17A. *(Learning Objective 1: Record and report current liabilities)* Wortham Publishing completed the following transactions for one subscriber during 2014:

Oct 1	Sold a one-year subscription, collecting cash of $1,800, plus sales tax of 9%.
Nov 15	Remitted (paid) the sales tax to the state of Massachusetts.
Dec 31	Made the necessary adjustment at year-end.

Requirement

1. Journalize these transactions (explanations not required). Then report any liability on the company's balance sheet at December 31, 2014.

E9-18A. *(Learning Objective 1: Account for payroll expense and liabilities)* Southwest Talent Search has an annual payroll of $125,000. In addition, the company incurs payroll tax expense of 8%. At December 31, Southwest owes salaries of $9,500 and FICA and other payroll tax of $920. The company will pay these amounts early next year. Show what Southwest will report for the foregoing on its income statement for the year and on its year-end balance sheet.

E9-19A. *(Learning Objective 1: Record note-payable transactions)* Assume that Fallon Sales Company completed the following note-payable transactions:

2014		
Apr 1	Purchased delivery truck costing $58,000 by issuing a one-year, 4% note payable.	
Dec 31	Accrued interest on the note payable.	
2015		
Apr 1	Paid the note payable at maturity.	

Requirements

1. How much interest expense must be accrued at December 31, 2014? (Round your answer to the nearest whole dollar.)
2. Determine the amount of Fallon Sales' final payment on April 1, 2015.
3. How much interest expense will Fallon Sales report for 2014 and for 2015? (Round your answer to the nearest whole dollar.)

E9-20A. *(Learning Objective 1: Account for income tax)* At December 31, 2014, Bracken Real Estate reported a current liability for income tax payable of $75,000. During 2015, Bracken earned income of $680,000 before income tax. The company's income tax rate during 2015 was 29%. Also during 2015, Bracken paid income taxes of $177,600.

How much income tax payable did Bracken Real Estate report on its balance sheet at December 31, 2015? How much income tax expense did Bracken report on its 2015 income statement?

E9-21A. *(Learning Objectives 1, 3: Analyze current and long-term liabilities; evaluate debt-paying ability)* Greene Domes, Inc., builds environmentally sensitive structures. The company's 2014 revenues totaled $2,760 million. At December 31, 2014, and 2013, the company had, respectively, $658 million and $603 million in current assets. The December 31, 2014, and 2013, balance sheets and income statements reported the following amounts:

	A1	⬍		
	A		B	C
1	**At year-end (In millions)**		**2014**	**2013**
2	Liabilities and stockholders' equity			
3	Current liabilities			
4	Accounts payable		$ 107	$ 179
5	Accrued expenses		97	177
6	Employee compensation and benefits		45	15
7	Current portion of long-term debt		7	20
8	Total Current Liabilities		256	391
9	Long-term debt		1,384	1,300
10	Post-retirement benefits payable		102	154
11	Other liabilities		8	20
12	Stockholders' equity		1,951	1,492
13	Total liabilities and stockholders' equity		$ 3,701	$ 3,357
14	Year-end (in millions)			
15	Cost of goods sold		$ 1,546	$ 1,650
16				

Requirements

1. Describe each of Greene Domes, Inc.'s liabilities and state how the liability arose.
2. What were the company's total assets at December 31, 2014? Evaluate the company's leverage and debt ratios at the end of 2013 and 2014. Did the company improve, deteriorate, or remain about the same over the year?
3. Assume that beginning and ending inventories for both periods did not differ by a material amount. Accounts payable at the end of 2012 was $190 million. Calculate accounts payable turnover as a ratio and days' payable outstanding (DPO) for 2013 and 2014. Calculate current ratios for 2013 and 2014 as well. Evaluate whether the company improved or deteriorated from the standpoint of ability to cover accounts payable and current liabilities over the year.

E9-22A. *(Learning Objectives 1, 5: Report a contingent liability)* Strong Security Systems' revenues for 2014 totaled $25.8 million. As with most companies, Strong is a defendant in lawsuits related to its products. Note 14 of the Strong annual report for 2014 reported the following:

> **14. Contingencies**
> The company is involved in various legal proceedings.... It is the Company's policy to accrue for amounts related to these legal matters if it is probable that a liability has been incurred and an amount is reasonably estimable.

Requirements

1. Suppose Strong's lawyers believe that a significant legal judgment against the company is reasonably possible. How should Strong report this situation in its financial statements?
2. Suppose Strong's lawyers believe it is probable that a $2.1 million judgment will be rendered against the company. Report this situation in Strong's financial statements. Journalize any entry requirements by GAAP. Explanations are not required.

E9-23A. *(Learning Objectives 1, 5: Report current and long-term liabilities)* Assume that Best Electronics completed these selected transactions during March 2014:
   a. Sales of $1,800,000 are subject to estimated warranty cost of 4%. The estimated warranty payable at the beginning of the year was $41,000, and warranty payments for the year totaled $67,000.
   b. On March 1, Best Electronics signed a $75,000 note payable that requires annual payments of $15,000 plus 3% interest on the unpaid balance each March 2.
   c. Music For You, Inc., a chain of music stores, ordered $110,000 worth of CD players. With its order, Music For You, Inc., sent a check for $110,000 in advance, and Best shipped $80,000 of the goods. Best will ship the remainder of the goods on April 3, 2014.
   d. The March payroll of $260,000 is subject to employee withheld income tax of $27,900 and FICA tax of 7.65%. On March 31, Best pays employees their take-home pay and accrues all tax amounts.

Requirement

1. Report these items on Best Electronics' balance sheet at March 31, 2014.

E9-24A. *(Learning Objective 2: Issue bonds payable (discount), pay and accrue interest, and amortize bond discount by the straight-line method)* On January 31, 2014, Trapp Logistics, Inc., issued five-year, 3.5% bonds payable with a face value of $6,000,000. The bonds were issued at 96 and pay interest on January 31 and July 31. Trapp Logistics, Inc., amortizes bond discount by the straight-line method. Record (a) issuance of the bonds on January 31, (b) the semiannual interest payment and amortization of bond discount on July 31, and (c) the interest accrual and discount amortization on December 31.

E9-25A. *(Learning Objective 2: Measure cash amounts for a bond payable (premium); amortize bond premium by the straight-line method)* Berkley Bank has $200,000 of 4% debenture bonds outstanding. The bonds were issued at 106 in 2014 and mature in 2034.

Requirements

1. How much cash did Berkley Bank receive when it issued these bonds?
2. How much cash in *total* will Berkley Bank pay the bondholders through the maturity date of the bonds?
3. Take the difference between your answers to requirements 1 and 2. This difference represents Berkley Bank's total interest expense over the life of the bonds.
4. Compute Berkley Bank's annual interest expense by the straight-line amortization method. Multiply this amount by 20. Your 20-year total should be the same as your answer to requirement 3.

E9-26A. *(Learning Objective 2: Issue bonds payable (discount); record interest payments and the related bond amortization using the effective-interest method)* Hadley Ltd. is authorized to issue $5,000,000 of 4%, 10-year bonds payable. On December 31, 2014, when the market interest rate is 5%, the company issues $4,000,000 of the bonds. Hadley Ltd. amortizes bond discount by the effective-interest method. The semiannual interest dates are June 30 and December 31.

Requirements

1. Use the PV function in Excel to calculate the issue price of the bonds.
2. Using Exhibit 9-4 as a model, prepare a bond amortization table for the term of the bonds.
3. Record issuance of the bonds payable on December 31, 2014; the first semiannual interest payment on June 30, 2015; and the second payment on December 31, 2015.

E9-27A. *(Learning Objective 2: Issue bonds payable (premium); record interest payment and the related bond amortization using the effective-interest method)* On June 30, 2014, the market interest rate is 3.5%. First Base Sports Ltd. issues $4,000,000 of 4½%, 20-year bonds payable. The bonds pay interest on June 30 and December 31. First Base Sports Ltd. amortizes bond premium by the effective-interest method.

Requirements

1. Use the PV function in Excel to calculate the issue price of the bonds.
2. Using Exhibit 9-7 as a model, prepare a bond amortization table for the term of the bonds.
3. Record the issuance of bonds payable on June 30, 2014; the payment of interest on December 31, 2014; and the payment of interest on June 30, 2015.

E9-28A. *(Learning Objectives 3, 4: Interpret an operating lease footnote)* Footnote 10 of Abercrombie and Fitch Co.'s financial statements for fiscal year 2012 (January 29, 2013) contains the following information:

At January 29, 2013, the Company was committed to noncancelable leases with remaining terms of 1 to 17 years. A summary of operating lease commitments under noncancelable leases follows (thousands):

Fiscal 2013	$ 331,151
Fiscal 2014	$ 319,982
Fiscal 2015	$ 303,531
Fiscal 2016	$ 285,337
Fiscal 2017	$ 262,586
Thereafter	$1,110,598
Total	$2,613,185

Requirements

1. Interpret the information in the footnote. What rights does the company have? What obligations?
2. Are the rights and obligations discussed in requirement 1 reported in the liability section of the balance sheet? Why or why not? How does this impact the company's debt and leverage ratios?
3. How is this type of reporting likely to change in the future?

E9-29A. *(Learning Objective 3: Evaluate debt-paying ability)* Companies that operate in different industries may have very different financial ratio values. These differences may grow even wider when we compare companies located in different countries.

Compare three leading companies on their current ratio, debt ratio, leverage ratio, and times-interest-earned ratio. Compute the ratios for Company B, Company N, and Company V.

	A	C	D	E
	A1			
	A	**C**	**D**	**E**
1	**(Amounts in millions or billions)**	**Company B**	**Company N**	**Company V**
2	Income data			
3	Total revenues	$ 9,732	¥ 7,920	€ 136,146
4	Operating income	259	230	5,746
5	Interest expense	41	27	655
6	Net income	22	17	450
7	**Assets and liability data**			
8	**(Amounts in millions or billions)**			
9	Total current assets	429	5,321	144,720
10	Long-term assets	99	592	65,828
11	Total current liabilities	227	2,217	72,500
12	Long-term liabilities	86	2,277	111,177
13	Stockholders' equity	215	1,419	26,871
14				

Based on your computed ratio values, which company looks the least risky?

E9-30A. *(Learning Objective 3: Analyze alternative plans for raising money)* BBS Financial Services is considering two plans for raising $600,000 to expand operations. Plan A is to borrow at 4%, and plan B is to issue 200,000 shares of common stock at $3.00 per share. Before any new financing, BBS Financial Services has net income of $350,000 and 120,000 shares of common stock outstanding. Assume you own most of BBS Financial Services' existing stock. Management believes the company can use the new funds to earn additional income of $500,000 before interest and taxes. BBS Financial Services' income tax rate is 25%.

Requirements

1. Analyze BBS Financial Services' situation to determine which plan will result in higher earnings per share.
2. Which plan allows you to retain control of the company? Which plan creates more financial risk for the company? Which plan do you prefer? Why? Present your conclusion in a memo to BBS Financial Services' board of directors.

Group B

E9-31B. *(Learning Objective 1: Account for warranty expense and the related liability)* The accounting records of Tanner Appliances included the following balances at the end of the period:

Estimated Warranty Payable	Sales Revenue	Warranty Expense
Beg bal 2,800	147,000	

In the past, Tanner's warranty expense has been 9% of sales. During the current period the business paid $9,200 to satisfy the warranty claims.

Requirements

1. Journalize Tanner Appliance's warranty expense for the period and the company's cash payments to satisfy warranty claims. Explanations are not required.
2. Show what Tanner will report on its income statement and balance sheet for this situation at the end of the period.
3. Which data item from requirement 2 will affect Tanner Appliance's current ratio? Will Tanner's current ratio increase or decrease as a result of this item?

E9-32B. *(Learning Objective 1: Record and report current liabilities)* Stone Publishing completed the following transactions for one subscriber during 2014:

Oct 1	Sold a one-year subscription, collecting cash of $2,200, plus sales tax of 7%.
Nov 15	Remitted (paid) the sales tax to the state of Massachusetts.
Dec 31	Made the necessary adjustment at year-end.

Requirement

1. Journalize these transactions (explanations not required). Then report any liability on the company's balance sheet at December 31, 2014.

E9-33B. *(Learning Objective 1: Account for payroll expense and liabilities)* Northeast Talent Search has an annual payroll of $168,000. In addition, the company incurs payroll tax expense of 8%. At December 31, Northeast owes salaries of $7,900 and FICA and other payroll tax of $915. The company will pay these amounts early next year.

Show what Northeast will report for the foregoing on its income statement for the year and on its year-end balance sheet.

E9-34B. *(Learning Objective 1: Record note-payable transactions)* Assume that Fuller Sales Company completed the following note-payable transactions:

2014	
Oct 1	Purchased delivery truck costing $54,000 by issuing a one-year, 3% note payable.
Dec 31	Accrued interest on the note payable.
2015	
Oct 1	Paid the note payable at maturity.

Requirements

1. How much interest expense must be accrued at December 31, 2014? (Round your answer to the nearest whole dollar.)
2. Determine the amount of Fuller Sales' final payment on October 1, 2015.
3. How much interest expense will Fuller Sales report for 2014 and for 2015? (Round your answer to the nearest whole dollar.)

E9-35B. *(Learning Objective 1: Account for income tax)* At December 31, 2014, Branson Real Estate reported a current liability for income tax payable of $105,000. During 2015, Branson earned income of $1,040,000 before income tax. The company's income tax rate during 2015 was 36%. Also during 2015, Branson paid income taxes of $333,200.

How much income tax payable did Branson Real Estate report on its balance sheet at December 31, 2015? How much income tax expense did Branson report on its 2015 income statement?

E9-36B. *(Learning Objectives 1, 3: Analyze current and long-term liabilities; evaluate debt-paying ability)* Good Earth Homes, Inc., builds environmentally sensitive structures. The company's 2014 revenues totaled $2,785 million. At December 31, 2014 and 2013, the company had, respectively, $638 million and $604 million in current assets. The December 31, 2014 and 2013, balance sheets and income statements reported the following amounts:

	A	B	C
		2014	2013
1	**At year-end (In millions)**		
2	Liabilities and stockholders' equity		
3	Current liabilities		
4	Accounts payable	$ 134	$ 176
5	Accrued expenses	163	169
6	Employee compensation and benefits	51	16
7	Current portion of long-term debt	17	10
8	Total Current Liabilities	365	371
9	Long-term debt	1,487	1,346
10	Post-retirement benefits payable	138	112
11	Other liabilities	20	22
12	Stockholders' equity	2,027	1,492
13	Total liabilities and stockholders' equity	$ 4,037	$ 3,343
14	Year-end (in millions)		
15	Cost of goods sold	$ 1,765	$ 2,046
16			

Requirements

1. Describe each of Good Earth Homes, Inc.'s liabilities and state how the liability arose.
2. What were the company's total assets at December 31, 2014? Evaluate the company's leverage and debt ratios at the end of 2013 and 2014. Did the company improve, deteriorate, or remain about the same over the year?
3. Assume that beginning and ending inventories for both periods did not differ by a material amount. Accounts payable at the end of 2012 was $195. Calculate accounts payable turnover as a ratio and days' payable outstanding (DPO) for 2013 and 2014. Calculate current ratios for 2013 and 2014 as well. Evaluate whether the company improved or deteriorated from the standpoint of ability to cover accounts payable and current liabilities over the year.

E9-37B. *(Learning Objectives 1, 5: Report a contingent liability)* Nguyen Security Systems' revenues for 2014 totaled $21.9 million. As with most companies, Nguyen is a defendant in lawsuits related to its products. Note 14 of the Nguyen annual report for 2014 reported the following:

> **14. Contingencies**
> The company is involved in various legal proceedings.... It is the Company's policy to accrue for amounts related to these legal matters if it is probable that a liability has been incurred and an amount is reasonably estimable.

Requirements

1. Suppose Nguyen's lawyers believe that a significant legal judgment against the company is reasonably possible. How should Nguyen report this situation in its financial statements?
2. Suppose Nguyen's lawyers believe it is probable that a $1.7 million judgment will be rendered against the company. Report this situation in Nguyen's financial statements. Journalize any entry required by GAAP. Explanations are not required.

E9-38B. *(Learning Objectives 1, 5: Report current and long-term liabilities)* Assume Pippin Electronics completed these selected transactions during June 2014.

   a. Sales of $1,900,000 are subject to estimated warranty cost of 6%. The estimated warranty payable at the beginning of the year was $29,000, and warranty payments for the year totaled $46,000.
   b. On June 1, Pippin Electronics signed a $42,000 note payable that requires annual payments of $10,500 plus 4% interest on the unpaid balance each June 2.
   c. Music For You, Inc., a chain of music stores, ordered $125,000 worth of CD players. With its order, Music For You, Inc., sent a check for $125,000, and Pippin Electronics shipped $85,000 of the goods. Pippin Electronics will ship the remainder of the goods on July 3, 2014.

d. The June payroll of $270,000 is subject to employee withheld income tax of $28,300 and FICA tax of 7.65%. On June 30, Pippin Electronics pays employees their take-home pay and accrues all tax amounts.

Requirement

1. Report these items on Pippin Electronics' balance sheet at June 30, 2014.

E9-39B. *(Learning Objective 2: Issue bonds payable (discount); pay and accrue interest; amortize bond discount by the straight-line method)* On January 31, 2014, Kuhl Logistics, Inc., issued 10-year, 5% bonds payable with a face value of $8,000,000. The bonds were issued at 93 and pay interest on January 31 and July 31. Kuhl Logistics, Inc., amortizes bond discount by the straight-line method. Record (a) issuance of the bonds on January 31, (b) the semiannual interest payment and amortization of bond discount on July 31, and (c) the interest accrual and discount amortization on December 31.

E9-40B. *(Learning Objective 2: Measure cash amounts for a bond payable (premium); amortize bond premium by the straight-line method)* Clayton Bank has $400,000 of 3% debenture bonds outstanding. The bonds were issued at 102 in 2014 and mature in 2034.

Requirements

1. How much cash did Clayton Bank receive when it issued these bonds?
2. How much cash in *total* will Clayton Bank pay the bondholders through the maturity date of the bonds?
3. Take the difference between your answers to requirements 1 and 2. This difference represents Clayton Bank's total interest expense over the life of the bonds.
4. Compute Clayton Bank's annual interest expense by the straight-line amortization method. Multiply this amount by 20. Your 20-year total should be the same as your answer to requirement 3.

E9-41B. *(Learning Objective 2: Issue bonds payable (discount), and record interest payments and the related bond amortization using the effective-interest method)* Colorado Sports Ltd. is authorized to issue $5,000,000 of 4%, 10-year bonds payable. On December 31, 2014, when the market interest rate is 4.5%, the company issues $3,200,000 of the bonds. Colorado Sports amortizes bond discount by the effective-interest method. The semiannual interest dates are June 30 and December 31.

Requirements

1. Use the PV function in Excel to calculate the issue price of the bonds.
2. Using Exhibit 9-4 as a model, prepare a bond amortization table for the term of the bonds.
3. Record issuance of the bonds payable on December 31, 2014; the first semiannual interest payment on June 30, 2015; and the second payment on December 31, 2015.

E9-42B. *(Learning Objective 2: Issue bonds payable (premium); record interest payment and the related bond amortization using the effective-interest method)* On June 30, 2014, the market interest rate is 3%. Garden Groceries Ltd. issues $1,600,000 of 4%, 15-year bonds. The bonds pay interest on June 30 and December 31. Garden Groceries Ltd. amortizes bond premium by the effective-interest method.

Requirements

1. Use the PV function in Excel to calculate the issue price of the bonds.
2. Using Exhibit 9-7 as a model, prepare a bond amortization table for the term of the bonds.
3. Record the issuance of bonds payable on June 30, 2014; the payment of interest on December 31, 2014; and the payment of interest on June 30, 2015.

E9-43B. *(Learning Objectives 3, 4: Interpret an operating lease footnote)* Footnote 7 of Ann Taylor Stores Corp.'s financial statements for fiscal year 2012 contains the following information:

---

7. Commitments and Contingencies
Operating Leases

The Company occupies its retail stores and administrative facilities under operating leases, most of which are noncancelable. Some of the store leases grant the Company the right to extend the term for one or two additional five-year periods under substantially the same terms and conditions as the original leases. Some store leases also contain early termination options, which can be exercised by the Company under specific conditions. Most of the store leases require payment of a specified minimum rent, plus contingent rent based on a percentage of the store's net sales in excess of a specified threshold. The Company also leases certain office equipment for its corporate offices and store locations under noncancelable operating leases which generally have three-year terms.

Future minimum lease payments under noncancelable operating leases as of January 29, 2013, are as follows:

Fiscal Year	(in thousands)
2013	$ 177,337
2014	160,110
2015	149,471
2016	136,073
2017	118,096
Thereafter	306,139
Total	1,047,226
Sublease rentals	24,351
Net rentals	$1,022,875

Requirements

1. Interpret the information in the footnote. What rights does the company have? What obligations?
2. Are the rights and obligations discussed in requirement 1 reported in the liability section of the balance sheet? Why or why not? How does this impact the company's debt and leverage ratios?
3. How is this type of reporting likely to change in the future?

E9-44B. *(Learning Objective 3: Evaluate debt–paying ability)* Companies that operate in different industries may have very different financial ratio values. These differences may grow even wider when we compare companies located in different countries.

Compare three leading companies on their current ratio, debt ratio, leverage ratio, and times-interest-earned ratio. Compute the ratios for Company F, Company K, and Company R.

A1			
A	**B**	**C**	**D**
1 (Amounts in millions or billions)	Company F	Company K	Company R
2 Income data			
3 Total revenues	$ 9,724	¥ 7,907	€ 136,492
4 Operating income	239	224	5,692
5 Interest expense	46	33	736
6 Net income	23	15	448
7 **Assets and liability data**			
8 **(Amounts in millions or billions)**			
9 Total current assets	434	5,383	148,526
10 Long-term assets	114	405	49,525
11 Total current liabilities	207	2,197	72,600
12 Long-term liabilities	116	2,318	110,107
13 Stockholders' equity	225	1,273	15,344
14			

Based on your computed ratio values, which company looks the least risky?

E9-45B. *(Learning Objective 4: Analyze alternative plans for raising money)* RRS Financial Services is considering two plans for raising $900,000 to expand operations. Plan A is to borrow at 5%, and plan B is to issue 300,000 shares of common stock at $3.00 per share. Before any new financing, RRS Financial Services has net income of $650,000 and 225,000 shares of common stock outstanding. Assume you own most of RRS Financial Services' existing stock. Management believes the company can use the new funds to earn additional income of $800,000 before interest and taxes. RRS Financial Services' income tax rate is 40%.

Requirements

1. Analyze RRS Financial Services' situation to determine which plan will result in the higher earnings per share.
2. Which plan allows you to retain control of the company? Which plan creates more financial risk for the company? Which plan do you prefer? Why? Present your conclusion in a memo to RRS Financial Services' board of directors.

Quiz

Test your understanding of accounting for liabilities by answering the following questions. Select the best choice from among the possible answers given.

Q9-46. For the purpose of classifying liabilities as current or noncurrent, the term *operating cycle* refers to
  a. the average time period between business recessions.
  b. the time period between purchase of merchandise and the conversion of this merchandise back to cash.
  c. a period of one year.
  d. the time period between date of sale and the date the related revenue is collected.

Q9-47. Failure to accrue interest expense results in
  a. an overstatement of net income and an overstatement of liabilities.
  b. an understatement of net income and an overstatement of liabilities.
  c. an overstatement of net income and an understatement of liabilities.
  d. an understatement of net income and an understatement of liabilities.

Q9-48. Tennis Shoe Warehouse operates in a state with a 6.5% sales tax. For convenience, Tennis Shoe Warehouse credits Sales Revenue for the total amount (selling price plus sales tax) collected from each customer. If Tennis Shoe Warehouse fails to make an adjustment for sales taxes,
  a. net income will be overstated and liabilities will be understated.
  b. net income will be overstated and liabilities will be overstated.
  c. net income will be understated and liabilities will be overstated.
  d. net income will be understated and liabilities will be understated.

Q9-49. What kind of account is Unearned Revenue?
  a. Revenue account   **c.** Asset account
  b. Expense account   **d.** Liability account

Q9-50. An end-of-period adjusting entry that debits Unearned Revenue most likely will credit
  a. an expense.   **c.** a revenue.
  b. an asset.   **d.** a liability.

Q9-51. Dove, Inc., manufactures and sells computer monitors with a three-year warranty. Warranty costs are expected to average 7% of sales during the warranty period. The following table shows the sales and actual warranty payments during the first two years of operations:

Year	Sales	Warranty Payments
2014	$650,000	$ 5,200
2015	850,000	42,500

Based on these facts, what amount of warranty liability should Dove, Inc., report on its balance sheet at December 31, 2015?

    a. $47,700   **c.** $105,000

    b. $42,500   **d.** $57,300

Q9-52. Maridell's Fashions has a debt that has been properly reported as a long-term liability up to the present year (2014). Some of this debt comes due in 2014. If Maridell's Fashions continues to report the current position as a long-term liability, the effect will be to

    a. overstate the current ratio.   **c.** understate the debt ratio.

    b. understate total liabilities.   **d.** overstate net income.

Q9-53. A bond with a face amount of $10,000 has a current price quote of 102.875. What is the bond's price?

    a. $10,102.88   **c.** $102,875

    b. $10,287.50   **d.** $1,028.75

Q9-54. Bond carrying value equals Bonds Payable

    a. minus Premium on Bonds Payable.   **d.** minus Discount on Bonds Payable.

    b. plus Discount on Bonds Payable.   **e.** both a and b.

    c. plus Premium on Bonds Payable.   **f.** both c and d.

Q9-55. What type of account is Discount on Bonds Payable, and what is its normal balance?

    a. Contra liability; Debit   **c.** Adjusting account; Credit

    b. Contra liability; Credit   **d.** Reversing account; Debit

Questions 56–59 use the following data:

Day Company sells $400,000 of 5%, 10-year bonds for 97 on April 1, 2014. The market rate of interest on that day is 5.5%. Interest is paid each year on April 1.

Q9-56. The entry to record the sale of the bonds on April 1 would be as follows:

	A	B	C	D
	A1			
1	a.	Cash	388,000	
2		Bonds Payable		388,000
3				
4	b.	Cash	400,000	
5		Discount on Bonds Payable		12,000
6		Bonds Payable		388,000
7				
8	c.	Cash	388,000	
9		Discount on Bonds Payable	12,000	
10		Bonds Payable		400,000
11				
12	d.	Cash	400,000	
13		Bonds Payable		400,000
14				

Q9-57. Day Company uses the straight-line amortization method. The amount of interest expense for each year will be

    a. $10,600.   **d.** $23,200.

    b. $20,000.   **e.** none of these.

    c. $21,200.

Q9-58. Using straight-line amortization, write the adjusting entry required at December 31, 2014.

Q9-59. Using straight-line amortization, write the journal entry required at April 1, 2015.

Q9-60. Truitt Corporation issued $400,000 of 3%, 10-year bonds payable on January 1, 2014. The market interest rate when the bonds were issued was 4%. Interest is paid semiannually on January 1 and July 1. The first interest payment is July 1, 2014. Using the effective-interest amortization method, how much interest expense will Truitt record on July 1, 2014? Use Exhibit 9-4 as an example.

a. $6,000
b. $7,346
c. $8,000
d. $1,346
e. $5,509

Q9-61. Using the facts in the preceding question, Truitt's journal entry to record the interest expense on July 1, 2014, will include a

a. debit to Bonds Payable.
b. credit to Interest Expense.
c. debit to Premium on Bonds Payable.
d. credit to Discount on Bonds Payable.

Q9-62. Amortizing the discount on bonds payable
a. is necessary only if the bonds were issued at more than face value.
b. increases the recorded amount of interest expense.
c. reduces the carrying value of the bond liability.
d. reduces the semiannual cash payment for interest.

Q9-63. The journal entry on the maturity date to record the payment of $1,500,000 of bonds payable that were issued at a $70,000 discount includes
a. a debit to Bonds Payable for $1,500,000.
b. a credit to Cash for $1,570,000.
c. a debit to Discount on Bonds Payable for $70,000.
d. all of the above.

Q9-64. Is the payment of the face amount of a bond on its maturity date regarded as an operating activity, an investing activity, or a financing activity?
a. Investing activity
b. Operating activity
c. Financing activity

Problems

> All of the A and B problems can be found within MyAccountingLab, an online homework and practice environment. Your instructor may ask you to complete these problems using **MyAccountingLab**.

MyAccountingLab

Group A

P9-65A. *(Learning Objective 1: Measure and report current liabilities)* Gulfshore Marine experienced these events during the current year.

a. December revenue totaled $180,000; and, in addition, Gulfshore collected sales tax of 6%. The tax amount will be sent to the state of Alabama early in January.
b. On August 31, Gulfshore signed a six-month, 4% note payable to purchase a boat costing $78,000. The note requires payment of principal and interest at maturity.
c. On August 31, Gulfshore received cash of $5,000 in advance for service revenue. This revenue will be earned evenly over six months.
d. Revenues of $800,000 were covered by Gulfshore's service warranty. At January 1, estimated warranty payable was $9,600. During the year, Gulfshore recorded warranty expense of $32,000 and paid warranty claims of $29,900.
e. Gulfshore owes $100,000 on a long-term note payable. At December 31, 3.5% interest for the year plus $20,000 of this principal are payable within one year.

Requirement

1. For each item, indicate the account and the related amount to be reported as a current liability on the Gulfshore Marine balance sheet at December 31.

P9-66A. *(Learning Objective 1: Record liability-related transactions)* The following transactions of Big Bands Music Company occurred during 2014 and 2015:

2014	
Mar 3	Purchased a piano (inventory) for $52,000, signing a six-month, 4% note payable.
May 31	Borrowed $96,000 on a 3.5% note payable that calls for annual installment payments of $16,000 principal plus interest. Record the short-term note payable in a separate account from the long-term note payable.
Sep 3	Paid the six-month, 4% note at maturity.
Dec 31	Accrued warranty expense, which is estimated at 2.5% of sales of $216,000.
31	Accrued interest on the outstanding note payable.
2015	
May 31	Paid the first installment and interest for one year on the outstanding note payable.

Requirement

1. Record the transactions in Big Bands' journal. Explanations are not required.

P9-67A. *(Learning Objectives 1, 2: Record bond transactions (at par); report bonds payable on the balance sheet)* The board of directors of Media Plus authorizes the issue of $6,000,000 of 5%, 15-year bonds payable. The semiannual interest dates are May 31 and November 30. The bonds are issued on May 31, 2014, at par.

Requirements

1. Journalize the following transactions:
   a. Issuance of half of the bonds on May 31, 2014
   b. Payment of interest on November 30, 2014
   c. Accrual of interest on December 31, 2014
   d. Payment of interest on May 31, 2015
2. Report interest payable and bonds payable as they would appear on the Media Plus balance sheet at December 31, 2014.

P9-68A. *(Learning Objectives 1, 2, 5: Issue bonds at a discount; amortize by the straight-line method; report bonds payable and accrued interest on the balance sheet)* On February 28, 2014, Durmann Corp. issues 5%, 10-year bonds payable with a face value of $900,000. The bonds pay interest on February 28 and August 31. Durmann Corp. amortizes bond discount by the straight-line method.

Requirements

1. If the market interest rate is 4% when Durmann Corp. issues its bonds, will the bonds be priced at par, at a premium, or at a discount? Explain.
2. If the market interest rate is 6% when Durmann Corp. issues its bonds, will the bonds be priced at par, at a premium, or at a discount? Explain.
3. Assume that the issue price of the bonds is 95. Journalize the following bonds payable transactions.
   a. Issuance of the bonds on February 28, 2014
   b. Payment of interest and amortization of the bond discount on August 31, 2014
   c. Accrual of interest and amortization of the bond discount on December 31, 2014, the year-end
   d. Payment of interest and amortization of the bond discount on February 28, 2015
4. Report interest payable and bonds payable as they would appear on the Durmann Corp. balance sheet at December 31, 2014.

P9-69A. *(Learning Objective 2: Account for bonds payable at a discount; amortize by the straight-line method)*

Requirements

1. Journalize the following transactions of Trahan Communications, Inc.:

2014		
Jan	1	Issued $3,000,000 of 4%, 10-year bonds payable at 95. Interest payment dates are July 1 and January 1.
Jul	1	Paid semiannual interest and amortized bond discount by the straight-line method on the 4% bonds payable.
Dec	31	Accrued semiannual interest expense and amortized bond discount by the straight-line method on the 4% bonds payable.
2015		
Jan	1	Paid semiannual interest.
2024		
Jan	1	Paid the 4% bonds at maturity.

2. At December 31, 2014, after all year-end adjustments, determine the carrying amount of Trahan Communications bonds payable, net.

3. For the six months ended July 1, 2014, determine the following for Trahan Communications, Inc.:

    a. Interest expense

    b. Cash interest paid

What causes interest expense on the bonds to exceed cash interest paid?

P9-70A. *(Learning Objectives 2, 5: Analyze a company's long-term debt; report long-term debt on the balance sheet (effective-interest method))* The notes to the Wolfe Ltd. financial statements reported the following data on December 31, Year 1 (end of the fiscal year):

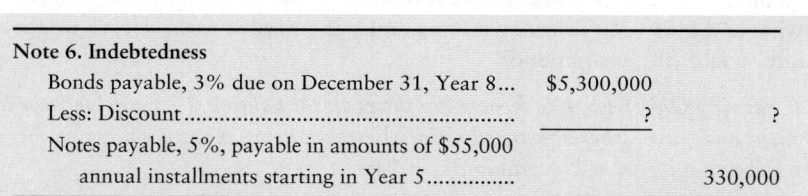

Note 6. Indebtedness		
Bonds payable, 3% due on December 31, Year 8...	$5,300,000	
Less: Discount..	?	?
Notes payable, 5%, payable in amounts of $55,000 annual installments starting in Year 5...............		330,000

Wolfe Ltd. amortizes bond discount by the effective-interest method and pays all interest amounts at December 31.

Requirements

1. Assume the market interest rate on January 1 of year 1, the date of issuance of the bonds, is 4%. Answer the following questions about Wolfe Ltd.'s long-term liabilities:

    a. Using the PV function in Excel, what is the issue price of the bonds?

    b. What is the maturity value of the 3% bonds?

    c. What is Wolfe Ltd.'s annual cash interest payment on the 3% bonds?

    d. What is the carrying amount of the 3% bonds at December 31, year 1?

2. Using Figure 9-4 as a model, prepare an amortization table through the maturity date for the 3% bonds. (Round all amounts to the nearest dollar.) How much is Wolfe Ltd.'s interest expense on the 3% bonds for the year ended December 31, Year 4?

3. Show how Wolfe Ltd. would report the 3% bonds payable and the 5% notes payable at December 31, Year 4.

P9-71A. *(Learning Objectives 2, 5: Issue convertible bonds at a discount, amortize by the effective-interest method, and convert bonds; report bonds payable on the balance sheet)* On December 31, 2014, Herndon Corp. issues 5½%, 10-year convertible bonds payable with a maturity value of $4,000,000. The semiannual interest dates are June 30 and December 31. The market interest rate is 6%. Herndon Corp. amortizes bond discount by the effective-interest method.

Requirements

1. Use the PV function in Excel to calculate the issue price of the bonds.
2. Using Exhibit 9-4 of the bond discount as a model, prepare an effective-interest method amortization table for the term of the bonds.
3. Journalize the following transactions:
   a. Issuance of the bonds on December 31, 2014. Credit Convertible Bonds Payable.
   b. Payment of interest and amortization of the bond discount on June 30, 2015.
   c. Payment of interest and amortization of the bond discount on December 31, 2015.
   d. Conversion by the bondholders on July 1, 2016, of bonds with face value of $1,600,000 into 120,000 shares of Herndon Corp.'s $1-par common stock.
4. Show how Herndon Corp. would report the remaining bonds payable on its balance sheet at December 31, 2016.

P9-72A. *(Learning Objective 3: Differentiate financing with debt vs. equity)* Hillside Medical Goods is embarking on a massive expansion. Assume plans call for opening 20 new stores during the next two years. Each store is scheduled to be 30% larger than the company's existing locations, offering more items of inventory and with more elaborate displays. Management estimates that company operations will provide $1 million of the cash needed for expansion. Hillside Medical must raise the remaining $6.75 million from outsiders.

The board of directors is considering obtaining the $6.75 million either through borrowing at 6% or by issuing an additional 100,000 shares of common stock. This year the company has earned $2 million before interest and taxes and has 100,000 shares of $1-par common stock outstanding. The market price of the company's stock is $67.50 per share. Assume that income before interest and taxes is expected to grow by 20% each year for the next two years. The company's marginal income tax rate is 35%.

Requirement

1. Use Excel to evaluate the effect of the above projected alternatives on net income and earnings per share two years from now.
2. Write a memo to Hillside's management discussing the advantages and disadvantages of borrowing and of issuing common stock to raise the needed cash. Which method of raising the funds would you recommend?

P9-73A. *(Learning Objectives 4, 5: Report liabilities on the balance sheet; calculate the leverage ratio, debt ratio, and times-interest-earned ratio)* The accounting records of Arroya Foods, Inc., include the following items at December 31, 2014:

Mortgage note payable, current portion	$ 86,000	Total assets	$4,574,000
Projected pension benefit obligation	461,000	Accumulated depreciation, equipment	167,000
Bonds payable, long-term	200,000	Discount on bonds payable (all long-term)	25,000
Mortgage note payable, long-term	386,000	Operating income	396,000
Bonds payable, current portion	515,000	Equipment	784,000
Interest expense	129,000	Pension plan assets (market value)	420,000
		Interest payable	43,000

Requirements

1. Show how each relevant item would be reported on the Arroya Foods, Inc., classified balance sheet, including headings and totals for current liabilities and long-term liabilities.
2. Answer the following questions about Arroya Food's financial position at December 31, 2014:
   a. What is the carrying amount of the bonds payable (combine the current and long-term amounts)?
   b. Why is the interest-payable amount so much less than the amount of interest expense?

3. How many times did Arroya Foods cover its interest expense during 2014?
4. Assume that all of the existing liabilities are included in the information provided. Calculate the leverage ratio and debt ratio of the company. Evaluate the health of the company from a leverage point of view. What other information would be helpful in making your evaluation?
5. Independent of your answer to (4), assume that Footnote 8 of the financial statements includes commitments for operating leases over the next 15 years in the amount of $3,000,000. If the company had to capitalize these leases in 2014, how would it change the leverage ratio and the debt ratio? How would this impact your assessment of the company's health from a leverage point of view?

Group B

P9-74B. *(Learning Objective 1: Measure and report current liabilities)* Merridian Marine experienced these events during the current year.
   a. December revenue totaled $145,000; and, in addition, Merridian collected sales tax of 7%. The tax amount will be sent to the state of Mississippi early in January.
   b. On August 31, Merridian signed a six-month, 6% note payable to purchase a boat costing $76,000. The note requires payment of principal and interest at maturity.
   c. On August 31, Merridian received cash of $3,600 in advance for service revenue. This revenue will be earned evenly over six months.
   d. Revenues of $850,000 were covered by Merridian's service warranty. At January 1, estimated warranty payable was $9,700. During the year, Merridian recorded warranty expense of $34,000 and paid warranty claims of $31,100.
   e. Merridian owes $90,000 on a long-term note payable. At December 31, 4% interest for the year plus $30,000 of this principal are payable within one year.

Requirement

1. For each item, indicate the account and the related amount to be reported as a current liability on the Merridian Marine balance sheet at December 31.

P9-75B. *(Learning Objective 1: Record liability-related transactions)* The following transactions of Concerto Music Company occurred during 2014 and 2015:

2014	
Mar 3	Purchased a piano (inventory) for $72,000, signing a six-month, 4% note payable.
May 31	Borrowed $85,000 on a 5% note payable that calls for annual installment payments of $17,000 principal plus interest. Record the short-term note payable in a separate account from the long-term note payable.
Sep 3	Paid the six-month, 4% note at maturity.
Dec 31	Accrued warranty expense, which is estimated at 2% of sales of $214,000.
31	Accrued interest on the outstanding note payable.
2015	
May 31	Paid the first installment and interest for one year on the outstanding note payable.

Requirement

1. Record the transactions in Concerto Music Company's journal. Explanations are not required.

P9-76B. *(Learning Objectives 1, 2: Record bond transactions (at par); report bonds payable on the balance sheet)* The board of directors of Cable Plus authorizes the issue of $7,000,000 of 6%, 20-year bonds payable. The semiannual interest dates are May 31 and November 30. The bonds are issued on May 31, 2014, at par.

Requirements

1. Journalize the following transactions:
   a. Issuance of half of the bonds on May 31, 2014
   b. Payment of interest on November 30, 2014
   c. Accrual of interest on December 31, 2014
   d. Payment of interest on May 31, 2015
2. Report interest payable and bonds payable as they would appear on the Cable Plus balance sheet at December 31, 2014.

P9-77B. *(Learning Objectives 1, 2, 5: Issue bonds at a discount; amortize by the straight-line method; report bonds payable and accrued interest payable on the balance sheet)* On February 28, 2014, Starr Corp. issues 4%, five-year bonds payable with a face value of $1,200,000. The bonds pay interest on February 28 and August 31. Starr Corp. amortizes bond discount by the straight-line method.

Requirements

1. If the market interest rate is 3% when Starr Corp. issues its bonds, will the bonds be priced at par, at a premium, or at a discount? Explain.
2. If the market interest rate is 5% when Starr Corp. issues its bonds, will the bonds be priced at par, at a premium, or at a discount? Explain.
3. Assume that the issue price of the bonds is 94. Journalize the following bond transactions.
   a. Issuance of the bonds on February 28, 2014
   b. Payment of interest and amortization of the bond discount on August 31, 2014
   c. Accrual of interest and amortization of the bond discount on December 31, 2014, the year-end
   d. Payment of interest and amortization of the bond discount on February 28, 2015
4. Report interest payable and bonds payable as they would appear on the Starr Corp. balance sheet at December 31, 2014.

P9-78B. *(Learning Objective 2: Account for bonds payable at a discount; amortize by the straight-line method)*

Requirements

1. Journalize the following transactions of Trahn Communications, Inc.:

2014		
Jan	1	Issued $4,000,000 of 5%, 10-year bonds payable at 94. Interest payment dates are July 1 and January 1.
Jul	1	Paid semiannual interest and amortized the bond discount by the straight-line method on the 5% bonds payable.
Dec 31		Accrued semiannual interest expense and amortized the bond discount by the straight-line method on the 5% bonds payable.
2015		
Jan	1	Paid semiannual interest.
2024		
Jan	1	Paid the 5% bonds at maturity.

2. At December 31, 2014, after all year-end adjustments, determine the carrying amount of Trahn Communications bonds payable, net.
3. For the six months ended July 1, 2014, determine the following for Trahn Communications Inc:
   a. Interest expense
   b. Cash interest paid

What causes interest expense on the bonds to exceed cash interest paid?

P9-79B. *(Learning Objectives 2, 5: Analyze a company's long-term debt; report the long-term debt on the balance sheet (effective-interest method)* The notes to the Bedford Ltd. financial statements reported the following data on December 31, Year 1 (end of the fiscal year):

Note 6. Indebtedness		
Bonds payable, 5% due December 31, Year 8........	$4,200,000	
Less: Discount..	?	?
Notes payable, 4%, payable in $40,000		
annual installments starting in Year 5...............		200,000

Bedford Ltd. amortizes bond discount by the effective-interest method and pays all interest amounts at December 31.

Requirements

1. Assume the market interest rate on January 1 of year 1, the date of issuance of the bonds, is 6%. Answer the following questions about Bedford Ltd. long-term liabilities:
   a. Using the PV function in Excel, what is the issue price of the bonds?
   b. What is the maturity value of the 5% bonds?
   c. What is Bedford Ltd.'s annual cash interest payment on the 5% bonds?
   d. What is the carrying amount of the 5% bonds at December 31, Year 1?
2. Using Exhibit 9-4 as a model, prepare an amortization table through the maturity date for the 5% bonds. Round all amounts to the nearest dollar. How much is Bedford Ltd.'s interest expense on the 5% bonds for the year ended December 31, Year 4?
3. Show how Bedford Ltd. would report the 5% bonds and the 4% notes payable at December 31, Year 4.

P9-80B. *(Learning Objectives 2, 5: Issue convertible bonds at a discount; amortize by the effective-interest method; convert bonds; report bonds payable on the balance sheet)* On December 31, 2014, Zunniga Corp. issues 4%, 10-year convertible bonds payable with a maturity value of $5,000,000. The semiannual interest dates are June 30 and December 31. The market interest rate is 5%. Zunniga Corp. amortizes bond discount by the effective-interest method.

Requirements

1. Use the PV function in Excel to calculate the issue price of the bonds.
2. Using Exhibit 9-4 as a model, prepare an effective-interest method amortization table for the term of the bonds.
3. Journalize the following transactions:
   a. Issuance of the bonds on December 31, 2014. Credit Convertible Bonds Payable.
   b. Payment of interest and amortization of the bond discount on June 30, 2015.
   c. Payment of interest and amortization of the bond discount on December 31, 2015.
   d. Conversion by the bondholders on July 1, 2016, of bonds with face value of $2,000,000 into 110,000 shares of Zunigga Corp. $1-par common stock.
4. Show how Zunigga Corp. would report the remaining bonds payable on its balance sheet at December 31, 2016.

P9-81B. *(Learning Objective 3: Differentiate financing with debt vs. equity)* Marcell Medical Goods is embarking on a massive expansion. Assume the plans call for opening 40 new stores during the next two years. Each store is scheduled to be 35% larger than the company's existing locations, offering more items of inventory and with more elaborate displays. Management estimates that company operations will provide $2.5 million of the cash needed for expansion. Marcell Medical must raise the remaining $7.75 million from outsiders.

The board of directors is considering obtaining the $7.75 million either through borrowing at 5% or by issuing an additional 100,000 shares of common stock. This year the company has earned $3 million before interest and taxes and has 100,000 shares of $1-par common stock outstanding. The market price of the company's stock is $77.50 per share. Assume that income before interest and taxes is expected to grow by 10% each year for the next two years. The company's marginal income tax rate is 35%.

Requirement

1. Use Excel to evaluate the effect of the above projected alternatives on net income and earnings per share two years from now.
2. Write a memo to Marcell's management discussing the advantages and disadvantages of borrowing and of issuing common stock to raise the needed cash. Which method of raising the funds would you recommend?

P9-82B. *(Learning Objectives 4, 5: Report liabilities on the balance sheet; calculate the leverage ratio, debt ratio, and times-interest-earned ratio)* The accounting records of Gilbert Foods, Inc., include the following items at December 31, 2014:

Mortgage note payable,		Total assets	$4,265,000
current portion.......................	$ 83,000	Accumulated depreciation,	
Projected pension		equipment	165,000
benefit obligation	467,000	Discount on bonds payable	
Bonds payable, long-term............	1,080,000	(all long-term)	322,000
Mortgage note payable,		Operating income...............	590,000
long-term	314,000	Equipment........................	731,000
Bonds payable, current portion ...	401,000	Pension plan assets	
Interest expense.........................	227,000	(market value)	425,000
		Interest payable.................	34,000

Requirements

1. Show how each relevant item would be reported on the Gilbert Foods, Inc., classified balance sheet, including headings and totals for current liabilities and long-term liabilities.
2. Answer the following questions about Gilbert Food's financial position at December 31, 2014:
   a. What is the carrying amount of the bonds payable (combine the current and long-term amounts)?
   b. Why is the interest-payable amount so much less than the amount of interest expense?
3. How many times did Gilbert Foods cover its interest expense during 2014?
4. Assume that all of the existing liabilities are included in the information provided. Calculate the leverage ratio and debt ratio of the company. Evaluate the health of the company from a leverage point of view. What other information would be helpful in making your evaluation?
5. Independent of your answer to (4), assume that Footnote 8 of the financial statements includes commitments for operating leases over the next 15 years in the amount of $3,000,000. If the company had to capitalize these leases in 2014, how would it change the leverage ratio and the debt ratio? How would this impact your assessment of the company's health from a leverage point of view?

Challenge Exercise and Problem

E9-83. *(Learning Objectives 1, 3, 5: Report current and long-term liabilities; evaluate leverage)* The top management of Murphee Marketing Services examines the following company accounting records at August 29, immediately before the end of the year, August 31:

Total current assets	$ 324,500
Noncurrent assets........................	1,098,500
	$1,423,000
Total current liabilities................	$ 173,800
Noncurrent liabilities	247,500
Stockholders' equity....................	1,001,700
	$1,423,000

1. Suppose Murphee's management wants to achieve a current ratio of 2. How much in current liabilities should Murphee pay off within the next two days in order to achieve its goal?
2. Calculate Murphee's leverage ratio and debt ratio. Evaluate the company's debt position. Is it low, high, or about average? What other information might help you to make a decision?

P9-84. *(Learning Objective 3: Understand how structuring debt transactions can affect a company)* The Fancy Cola Company reported the following comparative information at December 31, 2014, and December 31, 2013 (amounts in millions and adapted):

	2014	2013
Current assets	$21,579	$17,551
Total assets	72,921	48,671
Current liabilities	18,508	13,721
Total stockholders' equity	31,317	25,346
Net sales	35,119	30,990
Net income	11,809	6,824

Requirements

1. Calculate the following ratios for 2014 and 2013:
   a. Current ratio
   b. Debt ratio
2. During 2014, The Fancy Cola Company issued $1,590 million of long-term debt that was used to retire short-term debt. What would the current ratio and debt ratio have been if this transaction had not been made?
3. The Fancy Cola Company reports that its lease payments under operating leases will total $965 million in the future and $205 million will occur in the next year (2015). What would the current ratio and debt ratio have been in 2014 if these leases had been capitalized?

APPLY YOUR KNOWLEDGE

Decision Cases

Case 1. *(Learning Objective 3: Explore an actual bankruptcy; calculate leverage ratio, ROA, debt ratio, and times-interest-earned ratio)* In 2002, **Enron Corporation** filed for Chapter 11 bankruptcy protection, shocking the business community: How could a company this large and this successful go bankrupt? This case explores the causes and the effects of Enron's bankruptcy.

At December 31, 2000, and for the four years ended on that date, Enron reported the following (amounts in millions):

Balance Sheet (summarized)

Total assets	$65,503
Total liabilities	54,033
Total stockholders' equity	11,470

Income Statements (excerpts)

	2000	1999	1998	1997
Net income	$ 979*	$893	$703	$105
Revenues	100,789			

*Operating income = $1,953
Interest expense = $838

Unknown to investors and lenders, Enron also controlled hundreds of partnerships that owed vast amounts of money. These special-purpose entities (SPEs) did not appear on the

Enron financial statements. Assume that the SPEs' assets totaled $7,000 million and their liabilities stood at $6,900 million; assume a 10% interest rate on these liabilities.

During the four-year period up to December 31, 2000, Enron's stock price shot up from $17.50 to $90.56. Enron used its escalating stock price to finance the purchase of the SPEs by guaranteeing lenders that Enron would give them Enron stock if the SPEs could not pay their loans.

In 2001, the SEC launched an investigation into Enron's accounting practices. It was alleged that Enron should have been including the SPEs in its financial statements all along. Enron then restated net income for years up to 2000, wiping out nearly $600 million of total net income (and total assets) for this four-year period. Assume that $300 million of this loss applied to 2000. Enron's stock price tumbled, and the guarantees to the SPEs' lenders added millions to Enron's liabilities (assume the full amount of the SPEs' debt). To make matters worse, the assets of the SPEs lost much of their value; assume that their market value is only $500 million.

Requirements

1. Compute the debt ratio that Enron reported at the end of 2000. By using the DuPont Model, which we discussed in Chapter 7 (page 393), compute Enron's return on total assets (ROA) for 2000. For this purpose, use only total assets at the end of 2000, rather than the average of 1999 and 2000.
2. Compute Enron's leverage ratio for 2000. Now compute Enron's return on equity (ROE) by multiplying the ROA computed in part 1 by the leverage ratio. Can you see anything unusual in these ratios that might have caused you to question them? Why or why not?
3. Add the asset and liability information about the SPEs to the reported amounts provided in the table. Recompute all ratios after including the SPEs in Enron's financial statements. Also compute Enron's times-interest-earned ratio both ways for 2000. Assume that the changes to Enron's financial position occurred during 2000.
4. Why does it appear that Enron failed to include the SPEs in its financial statements? How do you view Enron after including the SPEs in the company's financial statements? (Challenge)

Case 2. *(Learning Objective 3: Analyze alternative ways of raising $5 million)* Business is going well for **Park 'N Fly**, the company that operates remote parking lots near major airports. The board of directors of this family-owned company believes that Park 'N Fly could earn an additional $1.5 million income before interest and taxes by expanding into new markets. However, the $5 million that the business needs for growth cannot be raised within the family. The directors, who strongly wish to retain family control of the company, must consider issuing securities to outsiders. The directors are considering three financing plans.

Plan A is to borrow at 6%. Plan B is to issue 100,000 shares of common stock. Plan C is to issue 100,000 shares of nonvoting, $3.75 preferred stock ($3.75 is the annual dividend paid on each share of preferred stock).[5] Park 'N Fly presently has net income of $3.5 million and 1 million shares of common stock outstanding. The company's income tax rate is 35%.

Requirements

1. Prepare an analysis to determine which plan will result in the highest earnings per share of common stock.
2. Recommend a plan to the board of directors. Give your reasons.

Ethical Issues

Issue 1. **Microsoft Corporation** is the defendant in numerous lawsuits claiming unfair trade practices. Microsoft has strong incentives not to disclose these contingent liabilities. However, GAAP requires that companies report their contingent liabilities.

Requirements

1. Why would a company prefer not to disclose its contingent liabilities?
2. Identify the parties involved in the decision and the potential consequences to each.

---

[5]For a discussion of preferred stock, see Chapter 10.

3. Analyze the issue of whether to report contingent liabilities from lawsuits from the following standpoints:
   a. Economic   **c.** Ethical
   b. Legal
4. What impact will future changes in accounting standards, both at the U.S. level and the international level, likely have on the issue of disclosure of loss contingencies?

Issue 2. When is a lease a capital idea? Laurie Gocker, Inc., entered into a lease arrangement with Nathan Morgan Leasing Corporation for an industrial machine. Morgan's primary business is leasing. The cash purchase price of the machine is $1,000,000. Its economic life is six years.

Gocker's balance sheet reflects total assets of $10 million and total liabilities of $7.5 million. Among the liabilities is a $2.5 million long-term note outstanding at Last National Bank. The note carries a restrictive covenant that requires the company's debt ratio to be no higher than 75%. The company's revenues have been falling of late and the shareholders are concerned about profitability.

Gocker and Morgan are engaging in negotiations for terms of the lease. Some other relevant facts are as follows:
1. Morgan wants to take possession of the machine at the end of the initial lease term.
2. The term may run from four to five years, at Gocker's discretion.
3. Morgan estimates the machine will have no residual value, and Gocker will not purchase it at the end of the lease term.
4. The present value of minimum lease payments on the machine is $890,000.

Requirements

1. What is (are) the ethical issue(s) in this case?
2. Who are the stakeholders? Analyze the consequences for each stakeholder from the following standpoints: (a) economic, (b) legal, and (c) ethical.
3. How should Gocker structure the lease agreement?
4. As of the date of this text, the FASB and IASB have issued a joint exposure draft of a new standard on long-term leases that will require companies to capitalize most leases like this one. How will the analysis of this case change when this standard is issued?

Focus on Financials | Amazon.com, Inc.

(Learning Objectives 1, 2, 3, 4, 5: Analyze current and long-term liabilities; evaluate debt-paying ability) Refer to **Amazon.com, Inc.**'s consolidated financial statements in Appendix A at the end of this book.

1. Did accounts payable for Amazon.com, Inc., increase or decrease in 2012? Calculate accounts payable turnover. How many days does it take Amazon.com, Inc. to pay an average account payable? Comment on the length of the period in days.
2. Examine Note 11—Income Taxes—in the Notes to Consolidated Financial Statements. Income tax provision is another title for income tax expense. What was Amazon.com, Inc.'s income tax provision in 2012? How much did the company pay in federal income taxes? In general, why were these amounts different? What was the company's marginal tax rate in 2012? Why? (Challenge)
3. Examine Note 6—Long-Term Debt. Did Amazon.com, Inc., borrow more or pay off more long-term debt during 2012? How can you tell? What was the company's effective interest rate on its long-term debt? Why do you think this rate was so low? (Challenge)
4. Examine Note 8—Commitments and Contingencies—in the Notes to Consolidated Financial Statements. Describe some of Amazon.com, Inc.'s commitments and contingent liabilities as of December 31, 2012. Are any of these amounts included in the numbers in the balance sheet line items?
5. How would you rate Amazon.com, Inc.'s overall debt position—risky, safe, or average? Compute three ratios at December 31, 2012 and 2011 that help answer this question.

Focus on Analysis | Yum! Brands, Inc.

(Learning Objectives 1, 2, 3, 4, 5: Analyze current liabilities and long-term debt) Refer to **Yum! Brands, Inc.'s** consolidated financial statements in Appendix B at the end of this book. These financial statements report a number of liabilities.

1. The current liability section of Yum! Brands, Inc.'s Consolidated Balance Sheet as of December 29, 2012, lists four different liabilities. List them and give a brief description of each.

2. Yum! Brands, Inc.'s largest single current liability at December 29, 2012 is "accounts payable and other current liabilities." Refer to "Supplemental Balance Sheet information." List the items that are included in this category, and give a brief description of each.

3. For 2012, calculate accounts payable turnover, both as a ratio and in number of days. Describe what this ratio means. Also compute the following other ratios for 2012 (if you have already computed them as part of your work in previous chapters, refer to them): (1) current ratio, (2) quick ratio, (3) days' sales to collection for accounts receivable, and (4) inventory turnover (express in days by dividing 365 by the turnover). How do you think you would combine the information in these ratios to assess Yum! Brands, Inc.'s current debt-paying ability? (Challenge)

4. Refer to the note entitled "Short-term Borrowings and Long-term Debt." What specific items are included? List them, including interest rates. Where is related interest information recorded? Are any of these amounts due currently? Which ones? How can you tell? When are the remainder due?

5. Refer to the note entitled "Contingencies." Describe the contents of this footnote. Are any of these items included in the liabilities recorded in either the current or long-term section of the balance sheet? Why or why not?

6. Refer to the note entitled "Leases." Compare the company's commitments under capital lease arrangements to its commitment under operating lease arrangements. Which dominates? Why do you think this is so? Calculate the impact on Yum! Brands, Inc.'s return on assets (ROA) and debt ratios if the company's operating lease commitments as of the end of 2012 were capitalized?

7. For 2012, compute the company's debt ratio, leverage ratio, and times-interest-earned ratio. Would you evaluate Yum! Brands, Inc. as risky, safe, or average in terms of these ratios?

8. Access Yum! Brands, Inc.'s most recent financial statements from www.sec.gov. Use the same method as described in the chapter opening for Southwest Airlines. What has happened to Yum! Brands, Inc.'s debt position since the end of 2012? (Challenge)

Group Projects

Project 1. Consider three different businesses:
1. A bank
2. A magazine publisher
3. A department store

For each business, list all of its liabilities—both current and long-term. Then compare the three lists to identify the liabilities that the three businesses have in common. Also identify the liabilities that are unique to each type of business.

Project 2. Alcenon Corporation leases the majority of the assets that it uses in operations. Alcenon prefers operating leases (versus capital leases) in order to keep the lease liability off its balance sheet and maintain a low debt ratio.

Alcenon is negotiating a 10-year lease on an asset with an expected useful life of 15 years. The lease requires Alcenon to make 10 annual lease payments of $20,000 each, with the first payment due at the beginning of the lease term. The leased asset has a market value of $135,180. The lease agreement specifies no transfer of title to the lessee and includes no bargain purchase option.

Write a report for Alcenon's management to explain what conditions must be present for Alcenon to be able to account for this lease as an operating lease.

Quick Check Answers

1. *b*

2. *e*

3. *c*

4. *d* [900 × 0.02 × $45 = warranty expense of $810; repaired $45 × 5 = $225; year-end liability = $585 ($810 − $225)]

5. *e*

6. *a*

7. *b*

8. *c*

9. *d*

10. *a*

11. *a*

12. *d*

13. *b*

14. *d*

15. *c*

16. *b* (See Amortization Schedule)

A	B Int Pmt (0.0225 × Maturity Value)	C Interest Expense (0.025 × Preceding Bond Carrying Value)	D Discount Amortization (C − B)	E Discount Account Balance (Preceding E − D)	F Bond Carrying Amount ($100,000 − E)
1/1/2015				3,897	96,103
7/1/2015	2,250	2,403	153	3,744	96,256
1/1/2016	2,250	2,406	156	3,588	96,412
7/1/2016	2,250	2,410	160	3,428	96,572

17. *d*

10 Stockholders' Equity

▶ **SPOTLIGHT:** The Home Depot: Building Toward Success

Founded in 1978, The Home Depot, Inc., is the world's largest home improvement specialty retailer. Home Depot has more than 2,200 retail stores in the United States, its territories, Canada, and Mexico. The Home Depot's common stock is traded on the New York Stock Exchange (NYSE) under the stock symbol HD. The company is included in the Dow Jones Industrial Average and Standard & Poor's 500 Index.

During its 2012 fiscal year, Home Depot reported sales of $74.8 billion, up 6.2% from fiscal year 2011; comparable store sales increased 4.6%. Basic Earnings per share on its common stock increased 21.7% to $3.03 per share. The company benefited not only from a recovery in the U.S. housing market but also from increased sales related to home repair due to Hurricane Sandy's damage to homes in the Northeast.

Based on these strong earnings and cash flows, Home Depot was able to increase its quarterly dividend at the end of 2012 to $0.39 per share, the fourth increase in as many years and the 104th consecutive quarter that the company has paid dividends. The company has a targeted dividend payout ratio (dividends ÷ earnings) of 50%. The company's board of directors also authorized a $17 billion treasury-stock repurchase program. From February 2002 until February 2013, the company has returned more than $37.5 billion in cash to shareholders through repurchases of its stock, which amounts to approximately 1 billion shares. The company also announced its "Return on Invested Capital Principle" to maintain a high return on stockholders' equity (ROE), with a goal of reaching 24% by 2015. On the next page, you'll find the company's Consolidated Balance Sheets as of February 3, 2013 and January 29, 2012. ●

Dwayne Newton/Photo Edit

	A	B	C	D
		A1		
		The Home Depot, Inc.		
1		**Consolidated Balance Sheets (Adapted)**		
2		(In Millions, unless otherwise specified)	**Feb. 03, 2013**	**Jan. 29, 2012**
3		Total Current Assets	$ 15,372	$ 14,520
4		Property and Equipment, at cost	38,491	38,975
5		Less Accumulated Depreciation and Amortization	(14,422)	(14,527)
6		Net Property and Equipment	24,069	24,448
7		Notes Receivable	140	135
8		Goodwill	1,170	1,120
9		Other Assets	333	295
10		Total Assets	$ 41,084	$ 40,518
11		Total Current Liabilities	$ 11,462	$ 9,376
12		Long-Term Debt, excluding current installments	9,475	10,758
13		Other Long-Term Liabilities	2,051	2,146
14		Deferred Income Taxes	319	340
15		Total Liabilities	23,307	22,620
16		**STOCKHOLDERS' EQUITY**		
17	1	Common Stock, par value $0.05; authorized: 10 billion shares;		
18		issued: 1.754 billion shares at February 3, 2013 and 1.733		
19		billion shares at January 29, 2012; outstanding: 1.484		
20		billion shares at February 3, 2013 and 1.537 billion shares		
21		at January 29, 2012	88	87
22	2	Paid-In Capital	7,948	6,966
23	3	Retained Earnings	20,038	17,246
24	4	Accumulated Other Comprehensive Income	397	293
25	5	Treasury Stock, at cost, 270 million shares at February 3, 2013		
26		and 196 million shares at January 29, 2012	(10,694)	(6,694)
27	6	**Total Stockholders' Equity**	17,777	17,898
28		Total Liabilities and Stockholders' Equity	$ 41,084	$ 40,518
29				

In this chapter, we focus on stockholders' equity. We'll show you how to account for the issuance of corporate capital stock to investors. We'll also cover the other elements of stockholders' equity—Additional Paid-in Capital, Retained Earnings, and Treasury Stock, plus dividends and stock splits. We'll conclude the chapter with a discussion of the Statement of Stockholders' Equity, in which we analyze the changes in all of the accounts in the stockholders' equity section of the balance sheet. By the time you finish this chapter, you may be ready to stop by a Home Depot store to get help in building something for yourself. Or you may find that you want to buy some stock in Home Depot or one of its competitors.

In this chapter, we discuss some of the decisions a company faces when

- issuing stock,
- buying back its stock, and
- paying dividends.

In addition, we discuss the factors that influence the evaluation of profitability in relation to stockholders' investment.

Let's begin with the organization of a corporation.

Learning Objectives

1. **Explain** the features of a corporation

2. **Account** for the issuance of stock

3. **Show** how treasury stock affects a company

4. **Account** for retained earnings, dividends, and splits

5. **Use** stock values in decision making

6. **Report** stockholders' equity transactions in the financial statements

You can access the most current annual report of The Home Depot, Inc. in Excel format at **www.sec.gov**. Using the "filings" link on the toolbar at the top of the home page, select "company filings search." This will take you to the "Edgar Company Filings" page. Type "Home Depot" in the company name box, and select "search." This will produce the "EDGAR Search Results" page showing the company name. Click on the "CIK" link beside the company name. This will pull up all of the reports the company has filed with the SEC. Under the "filing type" box, type "10-K" and click the search box. Form 10-K is the SEC form for the company's latest annual report. Find the year that you wish to view. Click on the "Interactive Data" box, which takes you to the "View Filing Data" page. Find and click on the "View Excel Document" link at the top of this page. You may choose to either open or download the Excel files containing the company's most recent financial statements. ■

EXPLAIN THE FEATURES OF A CORPORATION

1 **Explain** the features of a corporation

Anyone starting a business must decide how to organize the company. Corporations differ from proprietorships and partnerships in several ways.

Separate Legal Entity. A corporation is a business entity formed under state law. It is a distinct entity—an artificial person that exists apart from its owners, the **stockholders**, or **shareholders**. The corporation has many of the rights that a person has. For example, a corporation may buy, own, and sell property. Assets and liabilities in the business belong to the corporation and not to its owners. The corporation may enter into contracts, sue, and be sued.

Nearly all large companies, such as Home Depot, **Toyota**, and **Walmart**, are corporations. Their full names may include *Corporation* or *Incorporated* (abbreviated *Corp.* and *Inc.*) to indicate that they are corporations—like Intel Corporation and Home Depot, Inc., for example. Corporations can also use the word *Company*, such as Southwest Airlines Company.

Continuous Life and Transferability of Ownership. Corporations have *continuous lives* regardless of changes in their ownership. The stockholders of a corporation may buy more of the stock, sell the stock to another person, give it away, or bequeath it in a will. The transfer of the stock from one person to another does not affect the continuity of the corporation. In contrast, proprietorships and partnerships terminate when their ownership changes.

Limited Liability. Stockholders have **limited liability** for the corporation's debts. They have no personal obligation for corporate liabilities. The most that a stockholder can lose on an investment in a corporation's stock is the cost of the investment. Limited liability is one of the most attractive features of the corporate form of organization. It enables corporations to raise more capital from a wider group of investors than proprietorships and partnerships can. By contrast, proprietors and partners are personally liable for all the debts of their businesses.[1]

Separation of Ownership and Management. Stockholders own the corporation, but the *board of directors*—elected by the stockholders—appoints officers to manage the business. Thus, stockholders may invest $1,000 or $1 million in the corporation without having to manage it.

Management's goal is to maximize the firm's value for the stockholders. But the separation between owners and managers may create problems. Corporate officers may run the business for their own benefit and not for the stockholders. For example, in 2002, the CEO of **Tyco Corporation** was accused of defrauding Tyco of $600 million. In 2000, the CFO of **Enron Corporation** set up outside partnerships and paid himself millions to manage the partnerships—unbeknown to Enron stockholders. Both men went to prison.

Corporate Taxation. Corporations are separate taxable entities. They pay several taxes not borne by proprietorships or partnerships, including an annual franchise tax levied by the state. The franchise tax keeps the corporate charter in force. Corporations also pay federal and state income taxes.

Corporate earnings are subject to **double taxation** on their income to the extent they are distributed to shareholders in the form of dividends.

- First, corporations pay income taxes on their corporate income.
- Then stockholders pay income tax on the cash dividends received from corporations. Proprietorships and partnerships pay no business income tax. Instead, the business tax falls solely on the owners.

Government Regulation. Because stockholders have only limited liability for corporation debts, outsiders doing business with the corporation can look no further than the corporation if it fails to pay. To protect a corporation's creditors and stockholders, both federal and state governments monitor corporations. The regulations mainly ensure that corporations disclose the information that investors and creditors need to make informed decisions. Accounting provides much of this information.

Exhibit 10-1 summarizes the advantages and disadvantages of the corporate form of business organization.

Exhibit 10-1 | Advantages and Disadvantages of a Corporation

Advantages	Disadvantages
1. Can raise more capital than a proprietorship or partnership can	1. Separation of ownership and management
2. Continuous life	2. Double taxation of distributed profits
3. Ease of transferring ownership	3. Government regulation
4. Limited liability of stockholders	

Organizing a Corporation

The creation of a corporation begins when its organizers, called the *incorporators*, obtain a charter from the state. The charter includes the authorization for the corporation to issue a certain number of shares of stock. A share of stock is the basic unit of ownership for a corporation. The incorporators

- pay fees,
- sign the charter,
- file documents with the state, and
- agree to a set of **bylaws**, which act as the constitution for governing the company.

---

[1]Unless the business is organized as a limited-liability company (LLC) or a limited-liability partnership (LLP).

The corporation then comes into existence.

Ultimate control of the corporation rests with the stockholders, who elect a **board of directors** that sets company policy and appoints officers. The board elects a **chairperson**, who usually is the most powerful person in the organization. The chairperson of the board of directors often has the title chief executive officer (CEO). The board also designates the **president**, who is the chief operating officer (COO) in charge of day-to-day operations. Most corporations also have vice presidents in charge of sales, manufacturing, accounting and finance (the chief financial officer, or CFO), and other key areas. Exhibit 10-2 shows the authority structure in a corporation.

Exhibit 10-2 | Authority Structure of a Corporation

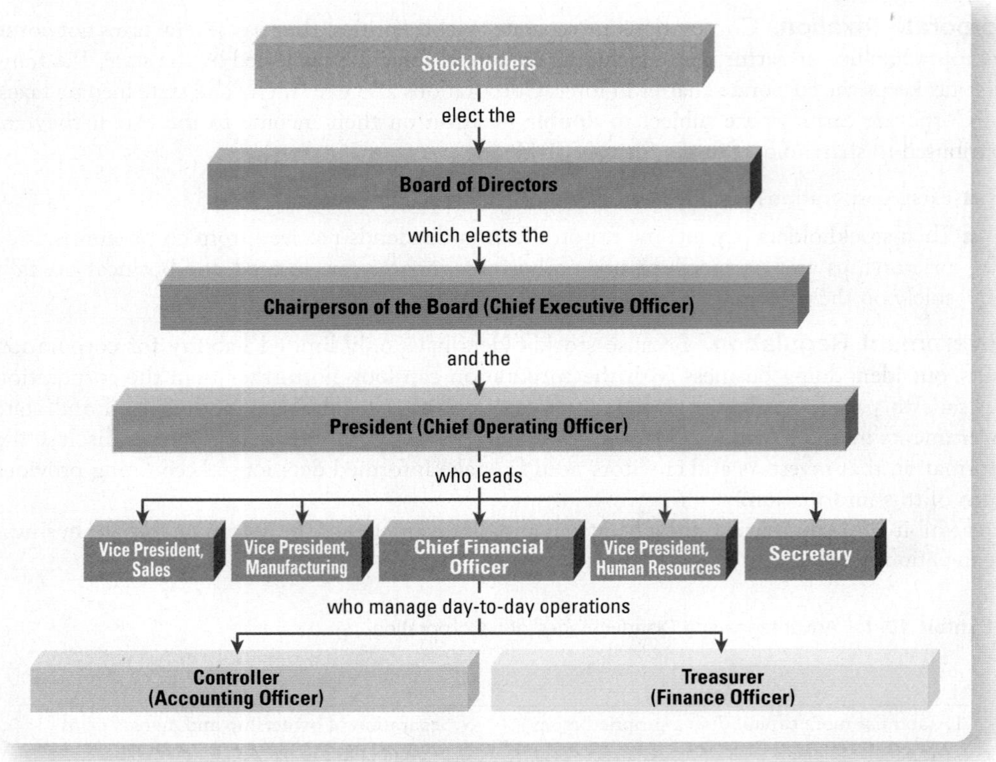

Stockholders' Rights

Ownership of stock entitles stockholders to four basic rights, unless a specific right is withheld by agreement with the stockholders:

1. *Vote.* The right to participate in management by voting on matters that come before the stockholders. This is the stockholder's sole voice in the management of the corporation. A stockholder gets one vote for each share of stock owned.

2. *Dividends.* The right to receive a proportionate part of any dividend. Each share of stock in a particular class receives an equal dividend.

3. *Liquidation.* The right to receive a proportionate share of any assets remaining after the corporation pays its liabilities in liquidation. Liquidation means to go out of business, sell the assets, pay all liabilities, and distribute any remaining cash to the owners.

4. *Preemption.* The right to maintain one's proportionate ownership in the corporation. Suppose you own 5% of a corporation's stock. If the corporation issues 100,000 new shares, it must offer you the opportunity to buy 5% (5,000) of the new shares. This right, called the *preemptive right*, is usually withheld from the stockholders.

Stockholders' Equity

As we saw in Chapter 1, **stockholders' equity** represents the stockholders' ownership interest in the assets of a corporation. Stockholders' equity is divided into two main parts:

1. **Paid-in capital**, also called **contributed capital**. This is the amount of stockholders' equity the stockholders have contributed to the corporation. Paid-in capital includes the stock accounts and any additional paid-in capital.

2. **Retained earnings**. This is the amount of stockholders' equity the corporation has earned through profitable operations and has not used for dividends.

Corporations report stockholders' equity by source. They report paid-in capital separately from retained earnings because most states prohibit the declaration of cash dividends from paid-in capital. Thus, cash dividends are declared from retained earnings.

The owners' equity of a corporation is divided into shares of **stock**. A corporation issues *stock certificates* to its owners when the company receives their investment in the business—usually cash. Because stock represents the corporation's capital, it is often called *capital stock*. The basic unit of capital stock is a *share*. A corporation may issue a stock certificate for any number of shares—1, 100, or any other number—but the total number of *authorized* shares is limited by charter. Exhibit 10-3 shows an actual stock certificate for Home Depot common stock.

Exhibit 10-3 | The Home Depot, Inc. Stock Certificate

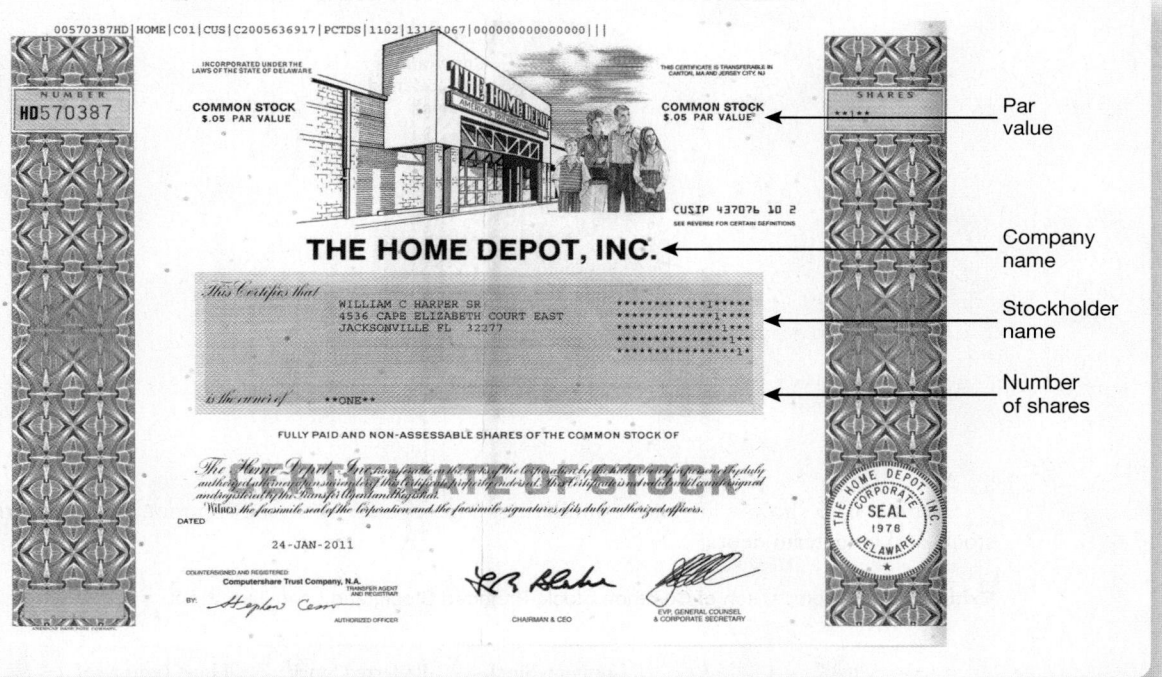

Stock in the hands of a stockholder is said to be *outstanding*. The total number of shares of stock outstanding at any time represents 100% ownership of the corporation.

Classes of Stock

Corporations issue different types of stock to appeal to a variety of investors. The stock of a corporation may be either

- common or preferred, and
- par or no-par.

Common and Preferred. Every corporation issues **common stock**, the basic form of capital stock. Unless designated otherwise, the word *stock* is understood to mean "common stock." Common stockholders have the four basic rights of stock ownership, unless a right is specifically withheld. The common stockholders are the owners of the corporation. They stand to benefit the most if the corporation succeeds because they take the most risk by investing in common stock.

Preferred stock gives its owners certain advantages over common stockholders. Preferred stockholders receive dividends before the common stockholders and they also receive assets before the common stockholders if the corporation liquidates. Owners of preferred stock also have the four basic stockholder rights, unless a right is specifically denied. Companies may issue different classes of preferred stock (Class A and Class B or Series A and Series B, for example). Each class of stock is recorded in a separate account. In most cases, the most preferred stockholders can expect to earn on their investments is a fixed dividend.

Preferred stock is a hybrid between common stock and long-term debt. Like interest on debt, preferred stock pays a fixed dividend. But, unlike interest on debt, the dividend is not required to be paid unless the board of directors declares the dividend. Also, companies have no obligation to pay back true preferred stock. Preferred stock that must be redeemed (paid back) by the corporation is a liability masquerading as a stock.

Preferred stock is rare. A recent survey of 600 corporations reveals that only 9% of them have issued preferred stock (Exhibit 10-4 below). In contrast, all corporations issue common stock. The balance sheet of Home Depot (p. 551) does not reflect any preferred stock issued.

Exhibit 10-4 | Percentage of Corporations Issuing Preferred Stock

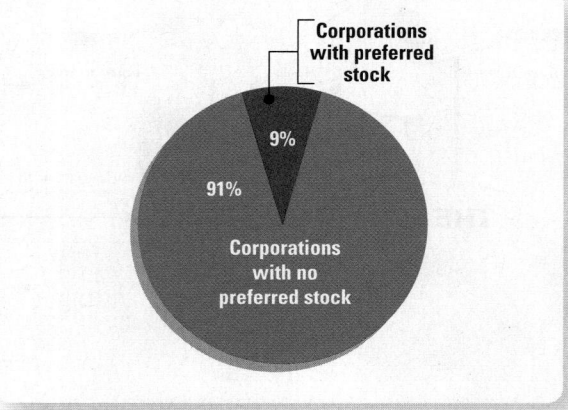

Exhibit 10-5 shows some of the similarities and differences among common stock, preferred stock, and long-term debt.

Exhibit 10-5 | Comparison of Common Stock, Preferred Stock, and Long-Term Debt

	Common Stock	Preferred Stock	Long-Term Debt
1. Obligation to repay principal	No	No	Yes
2. Dividends/interest	Dividends are not tax-deductible	Dividends are not tax-deductible	Interest expense is tax-deductible
3. Obligation to pay dividends/interest	Only after declaration	Only after declaration	At fixed rates and dates

Par Value and No-Par. Stock may be par-value stock or no-par stock. **Par value** is an arbitrary amount assigned by a company to a share of its stock upon original issuance. Most companies set the par value of their common stock low to avoid legal difficulties from issuing their stock below par. Most states require companies to maintain a minimum amount of stockholders' equity for the protection of creditors, and this minimum is often called the corporation's *legal capital*. For corporations with par-value stock, **legal capital** is the par value of the shares issued.

The par value of **PepsiCo** common stock is $0.0166 (1 2/3 cents) per share. **Best Buy**'s and **Southwest Airlines Company**'s common stock (p. 483) all carry a par value of $1 per share. Home Depot's common stock carries a par value of $0.05 per share.

No-par stock does not have a par value per share. Some no-par stock has a **stated value**, which makes it similar to par-value stock. The stated value is an arbitrary amount similar to par value. In a recent survey, only 9% of the companies had no-par stock outstanding. Apple, Inc., Krispy Kreme Doughnuts, and Sony all have no-par stock.

ACCOUNT FOR THE ISSUANCE OF STOCK

Large corporations such as **Home Depot, Google, Inc.,** and **Microsoft** sometimes need to raise huge amounts of money for specific purposes, such as operations or paying off long-term debt. The first time a private company issues stock to the public, it makes an **initial public offering (IPO)**. Corporations may sell stock directly to the stockholders or use the service of an *underwriter*, such as the investment banking firms **JP Morgan Chase & Co.** and **Goldman Sachs**. Companies often advertise the issuance of their stock to attract investors in the W*all Street Journal*, or the *Financial Times*. Let's see how a stock issuance works.

2 **Account** for the issuance of stock

Common Stock

Common Stock at Par. Assume that Home Depot needs to raise $100 million through issuance of stock. Suppose Home Depot's common stock had carried a par value equal to its issuance price of $10 per share. The entry for issuance of 10 million shares of stock at par would be

	A	B	C	D
	A1			
1	Jan 8	Cash (10,000,000 × $10)	100,000,000	
2		Common Stock		100,000,000
3		To issue common stock.		
4				

Home Depot's assets and stockholders' equity increase by the same amount.

Assets	=	Liabilities	+	Stockholders' Equity
+ 100,000,000	=	0		+ 100,000,000

Common Stock Above Par. Most corporations set par value low and issue common stock for a price above par. Rather than $10 as in the assumed example above, Home Depot's common stock has a par value of $0.05 per share. The $9.95 difference between issue price ($10) and par value ($0.05) is Paid-in Capital. Other names for this account are Additional Paid-in Capital or Paid-in Capital in Excess of Par. Both the par value of the stock and the additional amount are part of paid-in capital.

Because the entity is dealing with its own stockholders, a sale of stock is not gain, income, or profit to the corporation. This situation illustrates one of the fundamentals of accounting:

> **A company neither earns a profit nor incurs a loss when it sells its stock to, or buys its stock from, its own stockholders.**

With par value of $0.05 per share, Home Depot's actual entry to record the issuance of common stock looked something like this:

	A	B	C	D
	A1			
1	Jul 23	Cash (10,000,000 × $10)	100,000,000	
2		Common Stock (10,000,000 × $0.05)		500,000
3		Paid-in Capital		
4		(10,000,000 × $9.95)		99,500,000
5		To issue common stock.		
6				

Both assets and stockholders' equity increase by the same amount.

Assets	=	Liabilities	+	Stockholders' Equity
+ 100,000,000	=	0		+ 500,000
				+ 99,500,000

The Paid-in Capital Account is listed in the stockholders' equity section of the balance sheet immediately after the type of stock to which it relates (in the case of Home Depot, common stock). Hypothetically, then, after the last entry on page 557, the Stockholders' Equity section of The Home Depot, Inc.'s Balance Sheet might appear as follows (figures assumed):

	A	B
1	**Stockholders' Equity**	
2	Common stock, $.05 par, 10 billion shares	
3	authorized, 10 million shares issued and outstanding	$ 500,000
4	Paid-in Capital	99,500,000
5	Total paid-in capital	100,000,000
6	Retained earnings	500,000,000
7	Total stockholders' equity	$ 600,000,000
8		

All the transactions in this section include a receipt of cash by the corporation as it issues *new* stock. The transactions we illustrate are different from those reported in the daily news. In those transactions, one stockholder sold stock to another investor. The corporation doesn't record those transactions because they were between two outside parties.

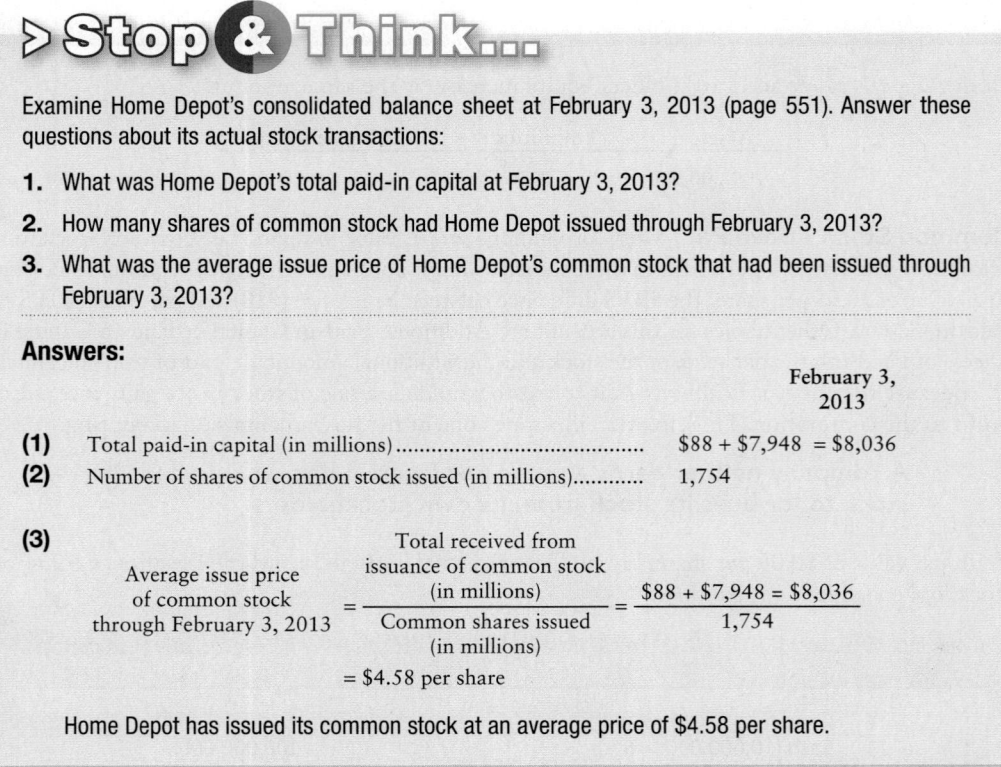

> **Stop & Think...**

Examine Home Depot's consolidated balance sheet at February 3, 2013 (page 551). Answer these questions about its actual stock transactions:

1. What was Home Depot's total paid-in capital at February 3, 2013?

2. How many shares of common stock had Home Depot issued through February 3, 2013?

3. What was the average issue price of Home Depot's common stock that had been issued through February 3, 2013?

Answers:

		February 3, 2013
(1)	Total paid-in capital (in millions)..	$88 + $7,948 = $8,036
(2)	Number of shares of common stock issued (in millions)............	1,754

(3)

$$\begin{array}{c}\text{Average issue price}\\\text{of common stock}\\\text{through February 3, 2013}\end{array} = \frac{\begin{array}{c}\text{Total received from}\\\text{issuance of common stock}\\\text{(in millions)}\end{array}}{\begin{array}{c}\text{Common shares issued}\\\text{(in millions)}\end{array}} = \frac{\$88 + \$7,948 = \$8,036}{1,754}$$

$$= \$4.58 \text{ per share}$$

Home Depot has issued its common stock at an average price of $4.58 per share.

No-Par Common Stock. To record the issuance of no-par stock, the company debits the asset received and credits the Common Stock account for the cash or fair market value of the asset received. Suppose Apple, Inc., issues 939 million shares of no-par common stock for $16,422 million. Apple's stock issuance entry is (in millions):

	A	B	C	D
	A1			
	A	**B**	**C**	**D**
1	Aug 14	Cash	16,422	
2		Common Stock		16,422
3		To issue no-par common stock.		
4				

$$\text{Assets} \quad = \quad \text{Liabilities} \quad + \quad \text{Stockholders' Equity}$$
$$+\ 16,422 \quad = \quad 0 \quad\quad\quad\quad\quad +\ 16,422$$

Apple's charter authorizes the company to issue 1,800 million shares of no-par stock, and the company has approximately $101,289 million in retained earnings and $499 of accumulated other comprehensive income. Apple, Inc., reports stockholders' equity on its balance sheet as follows (in millions):

	A	B
	A1	
	A	**B**
1	**Stockholders' Equity**	
2	(in millions)	
3	Common stock, no par, 1,800 shares	
4	authorized, 939 shares issued and outstanding	$ 16,422
5	Retained earnings	101,289
6	Accumulated other comprehensive income	499
7	Total stockholders' equity	$ 118,210
8		

You can see that a company with true no-par stock has no Additional Paid-in Capital account.

No-Par Common Stock with a Stated Value. Accounting for no-par stock with a stated value is identical to accounting for par-value stock. The excess over stated value is credited to Additional Paid-in Capital, or Paid-in Capital in Excess of Stated Value—Common.

Common Stock Issued for Assets Other Than Cash. When a corporation issues stock and receives assets other than cash, the company records the assets received at their current market value and credits the Common Stock and additional paid-in capital accounts accordingly. The assets' prior book values aren't relevant because the stockholder will demand stock equal to the market value of the asset given. On November 12, Kahn Corporation issued 15,000 shares of its $1 par common stock for equipment with a market value of $4,000 and a building with a market value of $120,000. Kahn's entry is

	A	B	C	D
	A1			
	A	**B**	**C**	**D**
1	Nov 12	Equipment	4,000	
2		Building	120,000	
3		Common Stock (15,000 × $1)		15,000
4		Paid-in Capital in Excess of Par—Common		
5		($124,000 − $15,000)		109,000
6		To issue $1-par common stock in exchange for		
7		equipment and a building.		
8				

Assets and equity both increase by $124,000.

Assets	=	Liabilities	+	Stockholders' Equity
+ 4,000	=	0		+ 15,000
+ 120,000				+ 109,000

Common Stock Issued for Services. Sometimes a corporation will issue shares of common stock in exchange for services rendered, either by employees or outsiders. In this case, no cash is exchanged. However, the transaction is recognized at fair market value. The corporation usually recognizes an expense for the fair market value of the services rendered. Common stock is increased for its par value (if any), and additional paid-in capital is increased for any difference. For example, assume that Kahn Corporation engages an attorney to represent the company on a legal matter. The attorney bills the corporation $25,000 for services and agrees to accept 2,500 shares of $1 par common stock, rather than cash, in settlement of the fee. The fair market value of the stock is $10 per share. The journal entry to record the transaction is

	A1	◆		
	A	**B**	**C**	**D**
1		Legal Expense	25,000	
2		Common Stock (2,500 × $1 par)		2,500
3		Paid-in Capital in Excess of Par—Common		
4		($25,000 – $2,500)		22,500
5				

In this case, retained earnings (stockholders' equity) is eventually decreased (through legal expense) by $25,000, and paid-in capital (stockholders' equity) is increased for the same amount.

A Stock Issuance for Other Than Cash Can Create an Ethical Challenge

Generally accepted accounting principles require a company to record the issuance of its stock at the fair market value of whatever the corporation receives in exchange for the stock. When the corporation receives cash, there is clear evidence of the value of the stock because cash is worth its face amount. But when the corporation receives an asset other than cash, the value of the asset can create an ethical challenge.

A computer whiz may start a new company by investing in computer software. The software may be market-tested or it may be new. The software may be worth millions, or it may be worthless. The corporation must record the asset received and the stock issued with a journal entry such as the following (assuming no-par stock is issued):

	A1	◆		
	A	**B**	**C**	**D**
1		Software	500,000	
2		Common Stock		500,000
3		*Issued stock in exchange for software.*		
4				

If the software is really worth $500,000, the accounting records are accurate. However, if the software is new and untested, both assets and stockholders' equity may be overstated.

Suppose your computer-whiz friend invites you to invest in the new business and shows you this balance sheet:

	A	B	C	D
1	**Gee-Whiz Computer Solutions, Inc.** **Balance Sheet** **December 31, 2014**			
2	**Assets**		**Liabilities and Stockholders' Equity**	
3	Computer software	$ 500,000	Total liabilities	$ -0-
4			**Stockholders' Equity**	
5			Common stock	500,000
6	Total assets	$ 500,000	Total liabilities and stockholders' equity	$ 500,000
7				

Companies like to report large asset and equity amounts on their balance sheets. That makes them look prosperous and creditworthy. Gee-Whiz looks debt-free and appears to have a valuable asset. Will you invest in this new business? Here are two takeaway lessons:

- Some accounting values are more solid than others.
- Not all financial statements mean exactly what they say—unless they are audited by independent CPAs.

Preferred Stock

Accounting for preferred stock follows the same pattern we illustrated for common stock. When a company issues preferred stock, it credits Preferred Stock at its par value, with any excess credited to Paid-in Capital in Excess of Par—Preferred.

There may be separate accounts for paid-in capital in excess of par for preferred and common stock, but not necessarily. Some companies combine paid-in capital in excess of par from both preferred and common stock transactions into one account. Accounting for no-par preferred follows the pattern for no-par common stock. When reporting stockholders' equity on the balance sheet, a corporation lists its accounts in this order:

- Preferred stock
- Common stock
- Additional paid-in capital
- Retained earnings

In Chapter 9, we saw how to account for convertible bonds payable (p. 509). Companies also issue convertible preferred stock. The preferred stock is usually convertible into the company's common stock at the discretion of the preferred stockholders, as the price of the common stock, as well as its dividend, rises to an attractive level in the future. Here are some representative journal entries for convertible preferred stock, using assumed amounts:

- Convertible preferred stock $1 par, 50,000 shares issued at par value

	A	B	C	D
1	2014	Cash	50,000	
2		Convertible Preferred Stock		50,000
3		*Issued convertible preferred stock.*		
4				

- Converted preferred stock to common stock at the rate of 6.25 to 1 (8,000 shares of $1 par-value common stock issued in exchange for 50,000 shares of preferred stock)

	A	B	C	D
A1				
1	2014	Convertible Preferred Stock	50,000	
2		Common Stock		8,000
3		Paid-in Capital in Excess of Par—Common		42,000
4		*Investors converted preferred into common.*		
5				

As you can see, we simply remove Convertible Preferred Stock from the books and assign the new Common Stock the prior book value of the preferred.

» Mid-Chapter Summary Problem

1. Test your understanding of the first half of this chapter by deciding whether each of the following statements is true or false.

   a. The policy-making body in a corporation is called the board of directors.

   b. The owner of 100 shares of preferred stock has greater voting rights than the owner of 100 shares of common stock.

   c. Par-value stock is worth more than no-par stock.

   d. Issuance of 1,000 shares of $5 par-value stock at $12 increases contributed capital by $12,000.

   e. The issuance of no-par stock with a stated value is fundamentally different from issuing par-value stock.

   f. A corporation issues its preferred stock in exchange for land and a building with a combined market value of $200,000. This transaction increases the corporation's owners' equity by $200,000 regardless of the assets' prior book values.

   g. Preferred stock is a riskier investment than common stock.

2. Adolfo Company has two classes of common stock. Only the Class A common stockholders are entitled to vote. The company's balance sheet included the following presentation:

	A	B
	A1	
1	**Stockholders' Equity**	
2	Capital stock:	
3	Class A common stock, voting, $1 par value,	
4	authorized, issued and outstanding 1,260,000 shares	$ 1,260,000
5	Class B common stock, nonvoting, no par value,	
6	authorized, issued, and outstanding 46,200,000 shares	11,000,000
7		12,260,000
8	Additional paid-in capital	2,011,000
9	Retained earnings	872,403,000
10	Total stockholders' equity	$ 886,674,000
11		

Requirements

a. Record the issuance of the Class A common stock for cash. Use the Adolfo account titles.

b. Record the issuance of the Class B common stock for cash. Use the Adolfo account titles.

c. How much of Adolfo's stockholders' equity was contributed by the stockholders? How much was provided by profitable operations? Does this division of equity suggest that the company has been successful? Why or why not?

d. Write a sentence to describe what Adolfo's stockholders' equity means.

Answers

1. a. True   b. False   c. False   d. True   e. False   f. True   g. False

2. a.

	A	B	C	D
	A1			
1		Cash	3,271,000	
2		Class A Common Stock		1,260,000
3		Additional Paid-in Capital		2,011,000
4		To record issuance of Class A common stock.		
5				

b.

	A	B	C	D
	A1			
1		Cash	11,000,000	
2		Class B Common Stock		11,000,000
3		To record issuance of Class B common stock.		
4				

c. Contributed by the stockholders: $14,271,000 ($12,260,000 + $2,011,000). Provided by profitable operations: $872,403,000. This division suggests that the company has been successful because most of its stockholders' equity has come from profitable operations.

d. Adolfo's stockholders' equity of $886,674,000 means that the company's stockholders own $886,674,000 of the business's assets.

Authorized, Issued, and Outstanding Stock

It is important to distinguish among three distinctly different numbers of a company's stock. The following examples use Home Depot's actual data from page 551.

- **Authorized stock** is the maximum number of shares the company can issue under its charter. As of February 3, 2013, Home Depot was authorized to issue 10 billion shares of common stock.

- **Issued stock** is the number of shares the company has issued to its stockholders. This is a cumulative total from the company's beginning up through the current date, less any shares permanently retired. As of February 3, 2013, Home Depot had issued 1,754 million common shares.

- **Outstanding stock** is the number of shares that the stockholders own (that is, the number of shares outstanding in the hands of the stockholders). Outstanding stock is issued stock minus treasury stock. At February 3, 2013, Home Depot had 1,484 million shares of common stock outstanding, computed as

Issued shares (line 1, in millions)	1,754
Less: Treasury shares (line 5, in millions)	(270)
Outstanding shares (in millions)	1,484

Now let's learn about treasury stock.

SHOW HOW TREASURY STOCK AFFECTS A COMPANY

3 **Show** how treasury stock affects a company

A company's own stock that it has issued and later reacquired is called **treasury stock**.[2] In effect, the corporation holds this stock in its treasury. Many public companies spend millions of dollars each year to buy back their own stock. Corporations purchase their own stock for several reasons:

1. The company has issued all its authorized stock and needs some stock for distributions to employees under stock purchase plans or compensation plans.

2. The business wants to increase net assets by buying its stock low and hoping to resell it for a higher price.

3. Management wants to avoid a takeover by an outside party.

4. Management wants to increase its reported earnings per share (EPS) of common stock (net income/number of common shares outstanding). Purchasing shares removes them from outstanding shares, thus decreasing the denominator of this fraction and increasing EPS. We cover the computation of EPS in more depth in Chapter 11.

5. Management uses a share repurchase program as a way to return excess cash to shareholders, in a manner similar to a dividend.

How Is Treasury Stock Recorded?

Treasury stock is recorded at cost (the market value of the stock on the date of the purchase) without regard to the stock's par value. Treasury stock is a *contra stockholders' equity* account. Therefore, the treasury-stock account carries a debit balance, the opposite of the other equity accounts. It is reported beneath the Retained Earnings account on the balance sheet as a negative amount.

To understand the way treasury-stock transactions work, it is helpful to analyze the changes that occur in the treasury-stock account during the year. Let's start with Home Depot's

---

[2]In this text, we illustrate the *cost* method of accounting for treasury stock because it is used most widely. Other methods are presented in intermediate accounting courses.

stockholders' equity at the end of the previous year, January 29, 2012 (we use rounded amounts in millions, except for shares):

	A	B
1	**The Home Depot, Inc.** **Stockholders' Equity** **January 29, 2012**	
2	**(in millions)**	
3	Common stock	87
4	Paid-in capital	6,966
5	Retained earnings	17,246
6	Accumulated other comprehensive income	293
7	Treasury stock (196,000,000 shares)	(6,694)
8	Total stockholders' equity	$ 17,898
9		

Notice that at January 29, 2012, Home Depot had spent $6,694 million to repurchase 196 million shares of its own stock. The average price it had paid for its shares through that date was about $34.15 per share ($6,694 million ÷ 196 million).

Repurchasing treasury stock provides a way for public companies to return cash to shareholders other than through dividends. The disadvantage to the shareholder of a share repurchase plan is that in order to receive cash, the shareholder has to surrender (dilute) ownership in the company.

Note 6 of Home Depot's financial statements gives more information about the company's accelerated share repurchase (ASR) program:

> In fiscal 2012, the Company entered into ASR agreements with third-party financial institutions to repurchase $3.05 billion of the Company's common stock. Under the agreements, the Company paid $3.05 billion to the financial institutions, using cash on hand, and received a total of 58 million shares in fiscal 2012. The final number of shares delivered upon settlement of each agreement was determined with reference to the average price of the Company's common stock over the term of the applicable ASR agreement. The $3.05 billion of shares repurchased are included in Treasury Stock in the accompanying Consolidated Balance Sheets.

The footnote reflects that, under its ASR program, the company paid $3.05 billion to purchase 58 million shares and included those shares in treasury stock. The Consolidated Statement of Stockholders' Equity (Exhibit 10-9) reflects that a total of 74 million shares were purchased for $4 billion, so an additional 16 million shares must have been purchased outside of the share repurchase program. This amounts to $54.05 per share ($4 billion ÷ 74 million). The entry to record the aggregate of these purchases is

	A	B	C	D
1	2012	Treasury Stock	4,000,000,000	
2	Various	Cash		4,000,000,000
3		*Purchased treasury stock.*		
4				

Assets	=	Liabilities	+	Stockholders' Equity
− 4,000,000,000	=	0		− 4,000,000,000

Notice that treasury stock is recorded at cost, which is the average market price of the stock on the various days that Home Depot purchased it. The financial statement impact of these transactions is decreased cash as well as stockholders' equity.

Retirement of Treasury Stock

A corporation may purchase its own stock and *retire* it by canceling the stock certificates. Retired stock cannot be reissued. Once the shares are repurchased, neither total assets nor total liabilities are affected, and a memorandum entry is made decreasing the number of shares issued in stockholders' equity.

Resale of Treasury Stock

Reselling treasury stock for cash grows assets and equity exactly as issuing new stock does. The sale increases assets and equity by the full amount of cash received. A company *never records gains or losses on transactions involving its own treasury stock*. Rather, amounts received in excess of amounts originally paid for treasury stock are recorded as Paid-in Capital from Treasury Stock Transactions, thus bypassing the income statement. If amounts received from resale of treasury stock were less than amounts originally paid, the difference would be debited to Paid-in Capital from Treasury Stock Transactions to the extent of that balance, and after that, to Retained Earnings. Home Depot did not resell any of its treasury stock in fiscal 2012, but suppose that on July 22, 2012, it had resold a million shares of treasury stock for $55 per share. Assuming that the average cost of treasury shares is $54.05 (calculated on page 565), the journal entry to record the resale of treasury shares would have been

	A	B	C	D
1	2012			
2	Jul 22	Cash	55,000,000	
3		Treasury Stock		54,050,000
4		Paid-in Capital from Treasury Stock Transactions		950,000
5		*Sold treasury stock.*		
6				

Assets	=	Liabilities	+	Stockholders' Equity
+ 55,000,000	=	0		+ 54,050,000
				+ 950,000

Issuing Stock for Employee Compensation

Sometimes companies supplement employee salaries by granting shares of stock rather than cash. Sometimes they use treasury shares for this purpose and sometimes they grant newly issued shares for various reasons. The Consolidated Statement of Stockholders Equity (Exhibit 10-9) shows that in fiscal 2012, Home Depot issued 21 million new (not treasury) shares in conjunction with an employee stock compensation plan. The entry the company made was

	A	B	C Debit	D Credit
1			**Debit**	**Credit**
2		Compensation Expense	679,000,000	
3		Common Stock		1,000,000
4		Paid-in Capital		678,000,000
5		*To record stock-based compensation plan.*		
6				

Now let's take a look at Home Depot's stockholders' equity as of February 3, 2013. For now, focus only on the treasury-stock account:

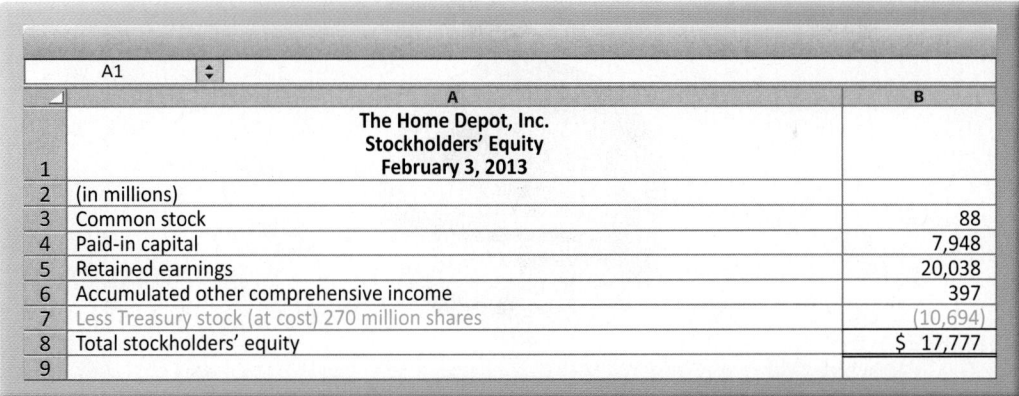

	A	B
1	The Home Depot, Inc. Stockholders' Equity February 3, 2013	
2	(in millions)	
3	Common stock	88
4	Paid-in capital	7,948
5	Retained earnings	20,038
6	Accumulated other comprehensive income	397
7	Less Treasury stock (at cost) 270 million shares	(10,694)
8	Total stockholders' equity	$ 17,777
9		

After treasury-stock transactions for 2012 have been recorded, the new number of treasury shares is 270 million. The balance in the treasury-stock account is $10,694 million. The new average purchase price of treasury shares is about $39.61 ($10,694 million ÷ 270 million).

Summary of Treasury-Stock Transactions

The types of treasury-stock transactions we have reviewed are

- *Buying treasury stock.* Assets and equity *decrease* by an amount equal to the cost of treasury stock purchased.

- *Reselling treasury stock.* Assets and equity *increase* by an amount equal to the sale price of the treasury stock sold.

- *Retiring treasury stock,* thus removing it from both common stock and from the treasury.

- *Reissuing treasury stock for employee compensation.* Expenses are increased, treasury stock is decreased, and additional paid-in capital is either increased or decreased for the difference.

ACCOUNT FOR RETAINED EARNINGS, DIVIDENDS, AND SPLITS

The Retained Earnings account carries the balance of the business's net income, less its net losses, and less any declared dividends that have been accumulated over the corporation's lifetime. *Retained* means "held onto." Successful companies grow by reinvesting in the business the assets they generate through profitable operations. Home Depot is an excellent example. Take another look at its stockholders' equity as of February 3, 2013 (p. 551). Notice that the Retained Earnings account ($20,038 million) is the largest account balance in stockholders' equity as of the end of fiscal 2012. In fact, because historically the company has spent so much money repurchasing treasury stock, retained earnings actually *exceeds* total stockholders' equity ($17,777 million).

4 **Account** for retained earnings, dividends, and splits

The Retained Earnings account is not a reservoir of cash for paying dividends to the stockholders. In fact, the corporation may have a large balance in Retained Earnings but not have enough cash to pay a dividend. Cash and Retained Earnings are two entirely separate accounts with no particular relationship. Retained Earnings says nothing about the company's cash balance.

A *credit* balance in Retained Earnings is normal, indicating that the corporation's lifetime earnings exceed lifetime losses and dividends. A *debit* balance in Retained Earnings arises when a corporation's lifetime losses and dividends exceed lifetime earnings. Called a **deficit**, this amount is subtracted to determine total stockholders' equity. In a recent survey, 15.5% of companies had a retained earnings deficit (Exhibit 10-6).

Exhibit 10-6 | Percentage of Companies with Positive Retained Earnings, Deficits

Should the Company Declare and Pay Cash Dividends?

A **dividend** is a distribution by a corporation to its stockholders, usually based on earnings. Dividends usually take one of three forms:

- Cash
- Stock
- Noncash assets

In this section we focus on cash dividends and stock dividends because noncash dividends are rare. For a noncash asset dividend, debit Retained Earnings and credit the asset (for example, Investment in Available-for-Sale Securities) for the current market value of the asset given.

Cash Dividends

Most dividends are cash dividends. Finance courses discuss how a company decides on its dividend policy. Accounting tells a company if it can pay a dividend. To do so, a company must have both

- enough retained earnings to *declare* the dividend, and
- enough cash to *pay* the dividend.

A corporation declares a dividend before paying it. Only the board of directors has the authority to declare a dividend. The corporation has no obligation to pay a dividend until the board declares one but, once declared, the dividend becomes a legal liability of the corporation. There are three relevant dates for dividends (using assumed amounts):

1. *Declaration date, June 19.* On the declaration date, the board of directors announces the dividend. Declaration of the dividend creates a liability for the corporation. Declaration is recorded by debiting Retained Earnings and crediting Dividends Payable. Assume a $50,000 dividend is declared.

	A1				
	A	**B**		**C**	**D**
1	Jun 19	Retained Earnings[3]		50,000	
2		Dividends Payable			50,000
3		*Declared a cash dividend.*			
4					

---

[3]In the early part of this book, we debited a Dividends account to clearly identify the purpose of the payment. From here on, we follow the more common practice of debiting the Retained Earnings account for dividend declarations.

Liabilities increase and stockholders' equity decreases.

Assets	=	Liabilities	+	Stockholders' Equity
0	=	+ 50,000		− 50,000

2. *Date of record, July 1.* As part of the declaration, the corporation announces the record date, which follows the declaration date by a few weeks. The stockholders on the record date will receive the dividend. There is no journal entry for the date of record.

3. *Payment date, July 10.* Payment of the dividend usually follows the record date by a week or two. Payment is recorded by debiting Dividends Payable and crediting Cash.

	A	B	C	D
1	Jul 10	Dividends Payable	50,000	
2		Cash		50,000
3		Paid cash dividend.		
4				

Both assets and liabilities decrease.

Assets	=	Liabilities	+	Stockholders' Equity
− 50,000	=	− 50,000		

The net effect of a dividend declaration and its payment, as shown in steps 1, 2, and 3, is a decrease in assets and a corresponding decrease in stockholders' equity.

Analyzing the Stockholders' Equity Accounts

By knowing accounting, you can look at a company's comparative year-to-year financial statements and tell a lot about what the company did during the current year. For example, Home Depot reported the following for Retained Earnings (in millions):

	Feb. 3, 2013	Jan. 29, 2012
Retained Earnings...............	$20,038	$17,246

What do these figures tell you about Home Depot's results of operations during fiscal 2012— did it earn net income or a net loss? How can you tell? Remember that

- net income is the only item that increases retained earnings;
- net losses decrease retained earnings;
- dividends declared decrease retained earnings; and
- other adjustments to retained earnings are usually relatively minor and relatively rare.

In most cases, if you know the amount of either net income or dividends, but not both, and if you know both beginning and ending balances of retained earnings, you can figure out the amount you don't know by analyzing the Retained Earnings account.

Let's analyze Home Depot's Retained Earnings account for the year ended February 3, 2013. As shown previously, the balance of Retained Earnings was $17,246 million on January 29, 2012. Net income for the year ended February 3, 2013, according to the company's consolidated statement of income, was $4,535 million. If there were no other changes in Retained Earnings besides dividends, how much in dividends did the company declare?

If you know accounting, you can compute Home Depot's dividend declarations during fiscal 2012 as (in millions)

		Retained earnings	
		Beg bal	17,246
Dividends	X	Net income	4,535
		End bal	20,038

Dividends (*X*) are $1,743 ($17,246 + $4,535 − *X*) = $20,038; *X* = $1,743. It really helps to be able to use accounting in this way!

Sometimes it doesn't work out this simply. From time to time, some corporations might record prior-period adjustments or other nonrecurring items to retained earnings. However, the two major elements that affect retained earnings are net income (loss) and dividends.

Dividends on Preferred Stock

When a company has issued both preferred and common stock, the preferred stockholders receive their dividends first. The common stockholders receive dividends only if the total dividend is large enough to pay the preferred stockholders first.

Avant Garde, Inc., has 100,000 shares of $1.50 preferred stock outstanding in addition to its common stock. The $1.50 designation means that the preferred stockholders receive an annual cash dividend of $1.50 per share. In 2014, Avant Garde declares an annual dividend of $500,000. The allocation to preferred and common stockholders is

Preferred dividend (100,000 shares × $1.50 per share)............	$150,000
Common dividend (remainder: $500,000 − $150,000)	350,000
Total dividend..	$500,000

If Avant Garde declares only a $200,000 dividend, preferred stockholders receive $150,000, and the common stockholders get the remainder, $50,000 ($200,000 − $150,000).

Two Ways to Express the Dividend Rate on Preferred Stock. Dividends on preferred stock are stated either as a

- percent of par value, or
- dollar amount per share.

For example, preferred stock may be "6% preferred," which means that owners of the preferred stock receive an annual dividend equal to 6% of the stock's par value. If par value is $100 per share, preferred stockholders receive an annual cash dividend of $6 per share (6% of $100). Alternatively, the preferred stock may be "$3 preferred," which means that the preferred stockholders receive an annual dividend of $3 per share regardless of the stock's par value. The dividend rate on no-par preferred stock is stated in a dollar amount per share.

Dividends on Cumulative and Noncumulative Preferred Stock. The balance-sheet classification of preferred stock, as well as the allocation of dividends, may be complex if the preferred stock is *cumulative*. Why? Corporations sometimes fail to pay a dividend to cumulative preferred stockholders. This is called *passing the dividend*, and the passed dividends are said to be *in arrears*. The owners of **cumulative preferred stock** must receive all dividends in arrears plus the current year's dividend before any dividends go to the common stockholders. In this sense, cumulative dividends almost take on the flavor of accrued interest on long-term debt, but not quite. Although cumulative dividends must be paid before other dividends, they must still be declared by the company's board of directors. *In most states, preferred stock is cumulative unless it is specifically labeled as noncumulative.*

Here's an example of how cumulative dividends work. Let's assume that the preferred stock of Avant Garde, Inc., is cumulative. Suppose Avant Garde passed the preferred dividend of $150,000 in 2013. Before paying dividends to common in 2014, Avant Garde must first pay preferred dividends of $150,000 for both 2013 and 2014—a total of $300,000. On September 6, 2014, Avant Garde declares a $500,000 dividend. The entry to record the declaration is as follows:

	A1			
	A	**B**	**C**	**D**
1	Sep 6	Retained Earnings	500,000	
2		Dividends Payable, Preferred ($150,000 × 2)		300,000
3		Dividends Payable, Common ($500,000 − $300,000)		200,000
4		*To declare a cash dividend.*		
5				

If the preferred stock is *noncumulative*, the corporation is not obligated to pay passed dividends.

Stock Dividends

A **stock dividend** is a proportional distribution by a corporation of its own stock to its stockholders. Stock dividends increase the Common Stock account, the Paid-in Capital in Excess of Par—Common and decrease Retained Earnings. Total equity is unchanged, and no asset or liability is affected.

The corporation distributes stock dividends to stockholders in proportion to the number of shares they already own. If you own 300 shares of Home Depot common stock and the corporation distributes a 10% common stock dividend, you get 30 (300 × 0.10) additional shares. You would then own 330 shares of the common stock. All other Home Depot stockholders would also receive 10% more shares, leaving all common stockholders' proportionate ownership unchanged.

In distributing a stock dividend, the corporation gives up no assets. Why, then, do companies issue stock dividends? A corporation may choose to distribute stock dividends for these reasons:

1. *To continue dividends but conserve cash.* A company may need to conserve cash and yet wish to continue dividends in some form. So the corporation may distribute a stock dividend. Stockholders pay no income tax on stock dividends.

2. *To reduce the per-share market price of its stock.* Distribution of a stock dividend usually causes the stock's market price to fall because of the increased number of outstanding shares that result from it. The objective is to make the stock less expensive and therefore attractive to more investors.

Generally accepted accounting principles (GAAP) label a stock dividend of 25% or less of outstanding common shares as *small* and suggest that the dividend be recorded at the market value of the shares distributed. Suppose Home Depot declared and distributed a 10% common stock dividend on February 3, 2013. At the time, Home Depot had approximately 1,484 million shares of common stock outstanding, and the corporation's stock was trading for $67 per share. Home Depot would have recorded this stock dividend as follows:

	A1			
	A	**B**	**C**	**D**
1	2013	Retained Earnings[4] (1,484,000,000 shares of		
2	Feb. 3	common outstanding × 0.10 stock dividend × $67		
3		market value per share of common)	9,942,800,000	
4		Common Stock (1,484,000,000 × 0.10 × $0.05		
5		par value per share)		7,420,000
6		Paid-in Capital		9,935,380,000
7		*Declared and distributed a 10% stock dividend.*		
8				

---

[4]Many companies debit Additional Paid-in Capital for their stock dividends.

The accounting equation clearly shows that a stock dividend has no effect on total assets, liabilities, or equity. The increases in equity offset the decreases, and the net effect is zero.

Assets	=	Liabilities	+	Stockholders' Equity
0	=	0		− 9,942,800,000
				+ 7,420,000
				+ 9,935,380,000

GAAP identifies stock dividends above 25% of outstanding common shares as *large* and permits large stock dividends to be recorded at par value. For a large stock dividend, therefore, The Home Depot, Inc. would debit Retained Earnings and credit Common Stock for the par value of the shares distributed in the dividend.

Stock Splits

A **stock split** is an increase in the number of shares of stock issued and outstanding, coupled with a proportionate reduction in the stock's par value. For example, if the company splits its stock 2 for 1, the number of outstanding shares is doubled and each share's par value is halved. A stock split, like a large stock dividend, decreases the market price of the stock—with the intention of making the stock more attractive in the market. Most leading companies in the United States— including **IBM**, **PepsiCo**, and Home Depot—have split their stock. The Home Depot, Inc.'s stock price has split 13 times since the company's initial IPO in 1978.

Assume the market price of a share of The Home Depot, Inc.'s common stock is approximately $100 per share. Assume that Home Depot wishes to decrease the market price to approximately $50 per share. Home Depot can split its common stock 2 for 1, and the stock price will fall to around $50. A 2-for-1 stock split means that

- the company will have twice as many shares of stock issued and outstanding after the split as it had before;
- each share's par value will be cut in half.

Assume that, before the split, The Home Depot, Inc. had approximately 500 million shares of $0.10 (10 cent) par common stock issued and outstanding. Compare The Home Depot, Inc.'s stockholders' equity before and after a 2-for-1 stock split (assumed, not actual numbers):

A1				
A	**B**	**C**	**D**
The Home Depot, Inc., Stockholders' Equity (Adapted, Assumed Numbers)			
Before **2-for-1 Stock Split**	(In millions)	After **2-for-1 Stock Split**	(In millions)
Common stock, $0.10 par, 1,000		Common stock, $0.05 par, 1,000	
shares authorized, 500 shares		shares authorized, 1,000 shares	
issued and outstanding	$ 50	issued and outstanding	$ 50
Additional paid-in capital	643	Additional paid-in capital	643
Retained earnings	4,304	Retained earnings	4,304
Other equity	260	Other equity	260
Total stockholders' equity	$ 5,257	Total stockholders' equity	$ 5,257

All account balances are the same after the stock split as before. Only three items are affected:

- Par value per share drops from $0.10 to $0.05.
- Shares *issued* double from 500 to 1,000 (both in millions).
- Shares *outstanding* double from 500 to 1,000 (both in millions).

Total equity doesn't change, nor do any assets or liabilities.

Summary of the Effects on Assets, Liabilities, and Stockholders' Equity

We've seen how to account for the basic stockholders' equity transactions:

- Issuance of stock—common and preferred (pp. 557–562)
- Purchase and sale of treasury stock (pp. 564–566)
- Cash dividends (pp. 568–571)
- Stock dividends and stock splits (pp. 571–573)

How do these transactions affect assets, liabilities, and equity? Exhibit 10-7 provides a helpful summary.

Exhibit 10-7 | Effects of Stock Transactions

Transaction	Assets	=	Liabilities	+	Stockholders' Equity
Issuance of stock—common and preferred	Increase		No effect		Increase
Purchase of treasury stock	Decrease		No effect		Decrease
Sale of treasury stock	Increase		No effect		Increase
Declaration of cash dividend	No effect		Increase		Decrease
Payment of cash dividend	Decrease		Decrease		No effect
Stock dividend—large and small	No effect		No effect		No effect*
Stock split	No effect		No effect		No effect

*The stock accounts increase and retained earnings decrease by offsetting amounts that net to zero.

USE STOCK VALUES IN DECISION MAKING

The business community measures *stock values* in various ways, depending on the purpose of the measurement. These values include market value, redemption value, liquidation value, and book value.

5 Use stock values in decision making

Market, Redemption, Liquidation, and Book Value

A stock's **market value**, or **market capitalization** *(market cap)*, is the market price of the common stock at a given date, multiplied by the number of shares of common stock outstanding. Market price varies with the corporation's net income, financial position, and future prospects, and with general economic conditions. *In almost all cases, stockholders are more concerned about the market value of a stock than any other value.* The overall market assessment of the worth of a share of common stock is reflected in the **price-earnings ratio**, expressed as

$$\text{Price-earnings ratio} = \frac{\text{Market price of one share of common stock}}{\text{Earnings per share of common stock}}$$

For example, on April 9, 2013, the market price of one share of The Home Depot, Inc.'s common stock was $71.20. The latest reported earnings per common share (basic) on its consolidated statement of earnings was $3.03. Therefore, its price-earnings ratio was 23.50 ($71.20 ÷ $3.03). The company reported 1,484 million shares of common stock outstanding (1,754 million shares issued − 270 million shares in treasury). Therefore, the market value (market capitalization) of The Home Depot, Inc. as of April 9, 2013, was approximately $105,661 million (1,484 million shares × $71.20.) We will discuss the concept of market capitalization further, in relation to investment decisions, in Chapter 11.

Preferred stock that requires the company to redeem the stock at a set price is called **redeemable preferred stock**. The company is *obligated* to redeem (pay to retire) the preferred stock. Therefore, redeemable preferred stock is really not stockholders' equity. Instead, it's a liability. The price the corporation agrees to pay for the stock, set when the stock is issued, is called the **redemption value**. **Liquidation value** is the amount that a company must pay a preferred stockholder in the event the company liquidates (sells out) and goes out of business.

The **book value per share** of common stock is the amount of common stockholders' equity on the company's books for each share of its stock. If the company has only common stock outstanding, its book value is computed by dividing total shareholders' equity by the number of shares of common stock *outstanding*. Recall that *outstanding* stock is *issued* stock minus *treasury* stock. For example, a company with only common stockholders' equity of $150,000 and 5,000 shares of common stock outstanding has a book value of $30 per share ($150,000 ÷ 5,000 shares).

If the company has both preferred and common outstanding, the preferred stockholders have the first claim to owners' equity, and thus preferred equity should be deducted from the numerator of the book value per share. Preferred stock often has a specified redemption value. In the book value per share ratio, the preferred equity is its redemption value plus any cumulative preferred dividends in arrears plus the current year dividend. Book value per share of common stock is then computed as follows:

$$\frac{\text{Book value per}}{\text{share of common stock}} = \frac{\text{Total stockholders' equity} - \text{Preferred equity}}{\text{Number of shares of common stock outstanding}}$$

Consider a hypothetical example. Crusader Corporation's balance sheet reports the following amounts:

	A	B
	A1	
1	**Stockholders' Equity**	
2	Preferred stock, 5%, $100 par, 400 shares issued, and outstanding,	
3	redemption value $130 per share	$ 40,000
4	Common stock, $10 par, 5,500 shares issued, 5,000 shares outstanding	55,000
5	Additional paid-in capital—common	72,000
6	Retained earnings	88,000
7	Treasury stock—common, 500 shares at cost	(15,000)
8	Total stockholders' equity	$ 240,000
9		

Cumulative preferred dividends are in arrears for four years (including the current year). Crusader's preferred stock has a redemption value of $130 per share. The book-value-per-share computations for Crusader Corporation are

Preferred Equity

Redemption value (400 shares × $130)	$52,000
Cumulative dividends ($40,000 × 0.05 × 4 years)	8,000
Preferred equity...	$60,000*

Common Equity

Total stockholders' equity..	$240,000
Less preferred equity	(60,000)
Common equity	$180,000
Book value per share [$180,000 ÷ 5,000 shares outstanding (5,500 shares issued minus 500 treasury shares)]	$ 36.00

*If the preferred stock had no redemption value, then preferred equity would be
$40,000 + preferred dividends in arrears.

Some investors search for stocks whose market price is below book value. They believe this indicates a good buy. Financial analysts often shy away from companies with a stock price at or below book value. To these analysts such a company is in trouble. As you can see, not all investors and analysts agree on a stock's value. In fact, wise investors base their decisions on more than a single ratio. In Chapter 13 you'll see the full range of financial ratios, plus more analytical techniques.

ROE: Relating Profitability to Stockholder Investment

Investors search for companies whose stocks are likely to increase in value. They're constantly comparing companies. But a comparison of The Home Depot, Inc. with a start-up company is not meaningful. Home Depot's profits run into the millions, far exceeding a new company's net income. In addition, management of the company has spent years investing in assets and managing both borrowed resources and stockholders' invested capital. Does this automatically make The Home Depot, Inc. a better investment? Not necessarily. To compare the profitability of companies of different sizes, investors use some standard profitability measures, including

- return on assets and
- return on equity.

DuPont Analysis, discussed earlier in Chapters 7 and 9, provides a convenient and meaningful way to analyze the various elements of profitability, as shown in the following diagram:

ROA		×	**Leverage Ratio**	=	**ROE**
Net Profit Margin Ratio ×	Asset Turnover Ratio	×	Leverage Ratio	=	Return on Equity
$\dfrac{\text{Net income*}}{\text{Net sales}}$	× $\dfrac{\text{Net sales}}{\text{Average total assets}}$	×	$\dfrac{\text{Average total assets}}{\text{Average common stockholders' equity}}$	=	$\dfrac{\text{Net income*}}{\text{Average common stockholders' equity}}$

* minus preferred dividends

The left-hand side of the diagram shows that **rate of return on total assets** or **return on assets (ROA)** is the product of two drivers: *net profit margin ratio* and *asset turnover*. Net profit margin ratio measures how effectively the company has earned revenue while controlling costs. Asset turnover measures how efficiently the company has managed its assets. We discussed these ratios as well as strategies that management uses to improve them in Chapter 7 (p. 392). In Chapter 9 (p. 512), we introduced the *leverage ratio*, or *equity multiplier*, that shows the impact of the use of debt, or leverage, to magnify ROA. Together, the three ratios combine to measure **rate of return on common stockholders' equity**, or **return on equity (ROE)**, in the last column on the right-hand side of the diagram.

ROE shows the relationship between net income and common stockholders' equity. Return on equity is computed only on common stock because the return to preferred stockholders is usually limited to a specified dividend (for example, 5%). The numerator of ROE is net income minus preferred dividends, if any. The denominator is *average common stockholders' equity*[5]—the average of total stockholders' equity minus preferred equity, if any. Since most companies do not have preferred stock, adjustments for preferred dividends and preferred equity are usually not necessary.

Let's use the DuPont Analysis model to analyze The Home Depot, Inc.'s ROE as of February 3, 2013. All balance sheet computations in this paragraph are based on figures taken from the company's comparative Consolidated Balance Sheets on page 551. You should re-compute the ratios and confirm the computations as you read. From its consolidated statements of earnings (www.sec.gov) (not reproduced in this chapter) we find that the company earned $4,535 million net income on $74,754 million in net sales for the year ended February 3, 2013, for a net profit margin ratio of 6.07%. This ratio is then combined with the balance-sheet information (in millions) to compute ROA and ROE as follows:

	ROA		×	**Leverage Ratio**	=	**ROE**
Net Profit Margin Ratio	×	Asset Turnover Ratio	×	Leverage Ratio	=	Return on Equity
$\dfrac{\text{Net income*}}{\text{Net sales}}$	×	$\dfrac{\text{Net sales}}{\text{Average total assets}}$	×	$\dfrac{\text{Average total assets}}{\text{Average common stockholders' equity}}$	=	$\dfrac{\text{Net income*}}{\text{Average common stockholders' equity}}$
$\dfrac{\$4,535}{\$74,754}$	×	$\dfrac{\$74,754}{\$40,801}$	×	$\dfrac{\$40,801}{\$17,838}$	=	$\dfrac{\$4,535}{\$17,838}$
$\{6.07\%\}$	×	$\{1.83\}$	×	$\{2.29\}$	=	$\{25.4\%\}$
	$\{\text{ROA} = 11.11\%\}$					

* minus preferred dividends

Each dollar of sales has resulted in about 6.1 cents of net profit. The company's asset turnover was 1.83, meaning that it earned $1.83 in sales for each average dollar invested in total assets. A leverage ratio of 2.29 to 1 means that the company owns $2.29 of assets for each dollar of stockholders' equity invested. Average total liabilities are $22,964 million, so the debt ratio for the company (based on average total liabilities to average total assets) is about 56% ($22,964/$40,801). The leverage ratio of 2.29, multiplied by ROA of 11.11%, magnifies profitability on shareholder investment to about 25.4%.

Are these returns strong, weak, or somewhere in between? To answer that question, it is necessary to have other information, such as

- comparative returns for The Home Depot, Inc. for prior years and
- comparative returns for other companies in the same industry.

For example, the following diagram compares The Home Depot, Inc.'s fiscal 2012 and 2011 ROE. It also compares The Home Depot, Inc.'s fiscal 2012 ROE with that of a competitor, **Lowes Companies, Inc.**

	Net Profit Margin Ratio	×	Asset Turnover Ratio	×	Leverage Ratio	=	Return on Equity
The Home Depot, Inc. 2012	6.07%	×	1.83	×	2.29	=	25.4%
The Home Depot, Inc. 2011	5.5%	×	1.75	×	2.19	=	21.1%
Lowes Companies, Inc. 2012	3.9%	×	1.53	×	2.18	=	13.0%

[5]In chapter 9, when we first introduced the leverage ratio, we used year end balance rather than the average for common stockholders' equity. Year end balances are acceptable as long as there are not material differences between beginning and ending balances. In this chapter, we assume that those differences exist. Therefore, we use averages for total assets and common stockholders' equity, which is technically more accurate.

In comparison with fiscal 2011, The Home Depot, Inc.'s fiscal 2012 ROE is substantially higher. Its net profit margin ratio in fiscal 2012 rose to 6.07% from 5.5% in fiscal 2011, meaning the company was more profitable on each dollar of sales. One-half of one percent improvement may not seem like much at first, but when multiplied by almost $75 billion in sales, it calculates to an extra $375 million in net profit! In addition, asset turnover increased from 1.75 to 1.83, which means the company earned more in sales per dollar invested and so was more efficient in fiscal 2012 than in fiscal 2011. The leverage ratio increased to 2.29 from 2.19 during fiscal 2012, indicating the company was using slightly more debt financing than in the previous year. With interest rates at all-time lows, 2012 was a good year to incur debt, as long as it could be repaid in a timely manner. All of this activity combined amounted to an increase of 4.3% in ROE—good news for investors, and good news for the company's share price.

In comparison with ROE data for Lowes Companies, Inc., The Home Depot, Inc.'s results in fiscal 2012 were higher in every dimension. Its net profit margin ratio (6.1%) bested Lowes by 2.2%, meaning Home Depot stores were significantly more profitable per dollar of sales. The likely explanation for this is that Home Depot's costs per dollar of sales were lower. The Home Depot, Inc. turned assets over more efficiently than Lowes in fiscal 2012 (1.83 vs. 1.53). Finally, The Home Depot, Inc. has slightly more leverage in its capital structure (2.29 vs. 2.18), thus magnifying its ROA from 11.1% to an ROE of 25.4%, compared to an ROE of only 13% for Lowes Companies, Inc.

What is a good rate of return on total assets? Ten percent is considered a strong benchmark in most industries. However, rates of return on assets vary by industry because the components of ROA are different across industries. Some high-technology companies earn much higher returns than do utility companies, grocery stores, and manufacturers of consumer goods such as toothpaste and paper towels. Companies that are efficient, generating a large amount of sales per dollar of assets invested, or companies that can differentiate their products and earn higher gross profit margins on them, have higher ROA than companies that do not have these attributes.

You can see by studying the DuPont model that whenever ROA is positive, ROE is always higher than ROA because of the leverage ratio (or equity multiplier). This also makes sense from an economic standpoint. Stockholders take a lot more investment risk than creditors, so the stockholders demand that ROE exceed ROA. They expect the return on their investment to exceed the cost of borrowed funds. Investors and creditors compare companies' ROE in much the same way they compare ROA. The higher the rate of return, the more successful the company. In many industries, 15% is considered a good ROE.

The Decision Guidelines at the end of the chapter (p. 580) offer suggestions for what to consider when investing in stock. You will also use all of these ratios more in Chapter 13.

REPORT STOCKHOLDERS' EQUITY TRANSACTIONS IN THE FINANCIAL STATEMENTS

The details of transactions impacting the various accounts in stockholders' equity are reported on the statement of cash flows as well as on the statement of stockholders' equity.

6 **Report** stockholders' equity transactions in the financial statements

Statement of Cash Flows

Many of the transactions we've covered are reported on the statement of cash flows. Equity transactions are *financing activities* because the company is dealing with its owners. Financing transactions that affect both cash and equity fall into three main categories:

- Issuance of stock
- Treasury stock
- Dividends

Financing activities from the Consolidated Statement of Cash Flows for The Home Depot, Inc., for the year ended February 3, 2013, are reported in Exhibit 10-8.

Issuances of Stock. The Home Depot, Inc. received cash of $784 million in conjunction with the issuance of new common stock during fiscal 2012.

Treasury Stock. During fiscal 2012, The Home Depot, Inc. spent $3,984 million in cash to repurchase shares of treasury stock and reported the payment as a financing activity.

Dividends. Most mature companies, including Home Depot, pay cash dividends to their stock-holders. Dividend payments are a type of financing transaction because the company is paying its stockholders for the use of their money. During fiscal 2012, Home Depot paid $1,743 million in cash dividends. Stock dividends are not reported on the statement of cash flows because the company pays no cash for them.

In Exhibit 10-8, cash payments for purchase of treasury stock and dividends appear as negative amounts, denoted by parentheses. Issuance of stock appears as a positive amount.

Exhibit 10-8 │ The Home Depot, Inc.'s Financing Activities Related to Stockholders' Equity

	A	B
	A1 ⬍	
1	**Cash Flows from Financing Activities**	**(In millions)**
2	Repurchases of common stock	(3,984)
3	Proceeds from sale of common stock	784
4	Cash Dividends Paid to Stockholders	(1,743)
5		

Statement of Stockholders' Equity

Businesses may report stockholders' equity in a way that differs from our examples. We use a detailed format in this book to help you learn all the components of stockholders' equity. Exhibit 10-9 contains the Consolidated Statements of Stockholders' Equity for The Home Depot, Inc. for the two fiscal years ended February 3, 2013.

Exhibit 10-9 │ The Home Depot, Inc.'s Consolidated Statements of Stockholders' Equity

	A	B	C	D	E	F	G	H	I
1	**The Home Depot, Inc. Consolidated Statements of Stockholders' Equity (Adapted)**								
2	**In Millions**	**Total**	**Common Stock**	**Shares**	**Paid-in Capital**	**Retained Earnings**	**Accumulated Other Comprehensive Income**	**Treasury Stock**	**Shares**
3	BALANCE at Jan. 30, 2011	$ 18,889	$ 86	1,722	$ 6,556	$ 14,995	$ 445	$ (3,193)	99
4	Net Earnings	3,883				3,883			
5	Shares Issued Under Employee Stock Plans, shares	197	1	11	196				
6	Tax Effect of Stock-Based Compensation	(2)			(2)				
7	Foreign-Currency Translation Adjustments	(143)					(143)		
8	Cash Flow Hedges, net of tax	5					5		
9	Stock Options, Awards and Amortization of Restricted Stock	215			215				
10	Repurchases of Common Stock	(3,501)						(3,501)	97
11	Cash Dividends	(1,632)				(1,632)			
12	Other	(13)			1		(14)		
13	BALANCE at Jan. 29, 2012	$ 17,898	$ 87	1,733	$ 6,966	$ 17,246	$ 293	$ (6,694)	196
14	Net Earnings	4,535				4,535			
15	Shares Issued Under Employee Stock Plans, shares	679	1	21	678				
16	Tax Effect of Stock-Based Compensation	82			82				
17	Foreign-Currency Translation Adjustments	100					100		
18	Cash Flow Hedges, net of tax	5					5		
19	Stock Options, Awards and Amortization of Restricted Stock	218			218				
20	Repurchases of Common Stock	(4,000)						(4,000)	74
21	Cash Dividends	(1,743)				(1,743)			
22	Other	3			4		(1)		
23	BALANCE at Feb. 03, 2013	$ 17,777	$ 88	1,754	$ 7,948	$ 20,038	$ 397	$ (10,694)	270
24									

Notice that, in contrast to the balance-sheet presentation (shown on p. 551), the Statement of Stockholders' Equity presents a detailed vertical analysis of the activity in each separate account in the Stockholders' Equity section over multiple years (usually three years although, for space purposes, our illustration covers only two). There are separate columns for each account in stockholders' equity: Common Stock (both dollar amounts and number of shares); Paid-in Capital; Retained Earnings; and Treasury Stock (both dollar amounts and number of shares). The statement also contains another column entitled Accumulated Other Comprehensive Income, which summarizes changes in the few elements of income that are permitted to bypass the income statement. These include foreign-currency translation adjustments resulting from consolidation of foreign subsidiaries and unrealized gains or losses on available-for-sale securities. Both of these were discussed in Chapter 8. Other comprehensive income will be covered again in Chapter 11.

A Detailed Stockholders' Equity Section of the Balance Sheet

One of the most important skills you will take from this course is the ability to understand the financial statements of real companies. Exhibit 10-10 presents a side-by-side comparison of the stockholders' equity section of the balance sheet using our general teaching format and the format you are likely to encounter in real-world balance sheets, such as that of The Home Depot, Inc. All amounts are assumed for this illustration.

Exhibit 10-10 | Formats for Reporting Stockholders' Equity

	A	B	C	D
	A1			
1	**General Teaching Format**		**Real-World Format**	
2	**Stockholders' Equity**		**Stockholders' Equity**	
3				
4	Paid-in capital:		┌─Preferred stock, 8%, $10 par, 30,000	
5	Preferred stock, 8%, $10 par, 30,000		shares authorized, issued, and outstanding	$ 330,000
6	shares authorized, issued, and outstanding	$ 300,000	Common stock, $1 par, 100,000 shares	
7	Paid-in capital in excess of		authorized, 60,000 shares issued,	60,000
8	par—preferred	30,000	58,600 shares outstanding	
9	Common stock, $1 par, 100,000 shares		┌─Additional paid-in capital	2,150,000
10	authorized, 60,000 shares issued,	60,000	Retained earnings	1,500,000
11	58,600 shares outstanding		Less treasury stock, common	
12	Paid-in capital in excess of		(1,400 shares at cost)	(40,000)
13	par—common	2,100,000	Accumulated other comprehensive income	200,000
14	Paid-in capital from treasury stock		Total stockholders' equity	$ 4,200,000
15	transactions, common	20,000		
17	Paid-in capital from retirement of			
18	preferred stock	30,000		
19	Total paid-in capital	2,540,000		
20	Retained earnings	1,500,000		
21	Subtotal	4,040,000		
22	Less treasury stock, common			
23	(1,400 shares at cost)	(40,000)		
24	Accumulated other comprehensive income	200,000		
25	Total stockholders' equity	$ 4,200,000		
26				

In general,

- Preferred stock (whenever its exists) comes first and is usually reported as a single amount.
- Common stock lists par value per share, the number of shares authorized, the number of shares issued, and the number of shares outstanding. The balance of the Common Stock account is determined as

$$\text{Common stock} = \text{Number of shares } \textit{issued} \times \text{Par value per share}$$

- Additional paid-in capital combines Paid-in capital in excess of par plus Paid-in capital from other sources. Additional paid-in capital belongs to the common stockholders.
- Outstanding stock equals issued stock minus treasury stock.
- Retained earnings comes after the paid-in capital accounts.
- Treasury stock is reported, usually at cost, as a deduction.
- Accumulated other comprehensive income is added (or accumulated other comprehensive loss is deducted). This account may be listed either before or after Treasury Stock.

● Decision Guidelines

INVESTING IN STOCK

Suppose you've saved $5,000 to invest. You visit a nearby **Edward Jones** office, where the broker probes for your risk tolerance. Are you investing mainly for dividends or for growth in the stock price? You must make some key decisions.

Investor Decision	Guidelines
Which category of stock to buy for:	
■ A safe investment?	Preferred stock is safer than common but, for even more safety, invest in high-grade corporate bonds or government securities.
■ Steady dividends?	Cumulative preferred stock. However, the company is not obligated to declare preferred dividends, and the dividends are unlikely to increase.
■ Increasing dividends?	Common stock, as long as the company's net income is increasing and the company has adequate cash flow to pay a dividend after meeting all obligations and other cash demands.
■ Increasing stock price?	Common stock, but again only if the company's net income and cash flow are increasing.
How to identify a good stock to buy?	There are many ways to pick stock investments. One strategy that works reasonably well is to invest in companies that consistently earn higher rates of return on assets and on equity than competing firms in the same industry. Also, select industries that are expected to grow.

End-of-Chapter Summary Problems

1. The balance sheet of Newline Corp. reported the following at December 31, 2014. The company has no transactions that produce other comprehensive income or loss.

	A	B
	A1	
1	**Stockholders' Equity**	
2	Preferred stock, 4%, $10 par, 10,000 shares authorized, issued,	
3	and outstanding, (redemption value, $110,000)	$ 100,000
4	Common stock, no-par, $5 stated value, 100,000 shares	
5	authorized, 50,000 shares issued, 49,000 shares outstanding	250,000
6	Paid-in capital in excess of stated value—Common	239,500
7	Retained earnings	395,000
8	Less: Treasury stock, common (1,000 shares)	(8,000)
9	Total stockholders' equity	$ 976,500
10		

Requirements

a. Is the preferred stock cumulative or noncumulative? How can you tell?

b. What is the total amount of the annual preferred dividend?

c. How many shares of common stock are outstanding?

d. Compute the book value per share of the common stock. No preferred dividends are in arrears, and Newline has not yet declared the 2014 dividend.

2. Use the following accounts and related balances to prepare the classified balance sheet of Whitewing, Inc., at September 30, 2014. Use the account format of the balance sheet.

Common stock, $1 par,		Long-term note payable	$ 80,000
50,000 shares authorized,		Inventory	85,000
20,000 shares issued	$ 20,000	Property, plant, and	
Dividends payable	4,000	equipment, net	226,000
Cash	9,000	Accounts receivable, net	23,000
Accounts payable	28,000	Preferred stock, $3.75, no-par,	
Paid-in capital in excess		10,000 shares authorized,	
of par—common	115,000	2,000 shares issued	24,000
Treasury stock, common,		Accrued liabilities	3,000
1,000 shares at cost	6,000	Retained earnings	75,000

Answers

1. a. The preferred stock is cumulative because it is not specifically labeled otherwise.

   b. Total annual preferred dividend: $4,000 ($100,000 × 0.04).

   c. Common shares outstanding: 49,000 (50,000 issued − 1,000 treasury).

   d. Book value per share of common stock:

Common:	
Total stockholders' equity...	$976,500
Less stockholders' equity allocated to preferred	(114,000)*
Stockholders' equity allocated to common	$862,500
Book value per share ($862,500 ÷ 49,000 shares)...............	$17.60

*Redemption value	$110,000
Cumulative dividend ($100,000 × 0.04)..	4,000
Stockholders' equity allocated to preferred..	$114,000

2.

	A	B	C	D	E
	Whitewing, Inc. **Balance Sheet** **September 30, 2014**				
1					
2	**Assets**		**Liabilities**		
3	Current Assets		Current Liabilities		
4	Cash	$ 9,000	Account payable		$ 28,000
5	Accounts receivable, net	23,000	Dividends payable		4,000
6	Inventory	85,000	Accrued liabilities		3,000
7	Total current assets	117,000	Total current liabilities		35,000
8	Property, plant, and		Long-term note payable		80,000
9	equipment, net	226,000	Total liabilities		115,000
10					
11			**Stockholders' Equity**		
12			Preferred stock, $3.75, no par,		
13			10,000 shares authorized,		
14			2,000 shares issued and		
15			outstanding	$ 24,000	
16			Common stock, $1 par,		
17			50,000 shares authorized,		
18			20,000 shares issued,		
19			19,000 shares outstanding	20,000	
20			Paid-in capital in excess of		
21			par—common	115,000	
22			Retained earnings	75,000	
23			Treasury stock, common,		
24			1,000 shares at cost	(6,000)	
25			Total stockholders' equity		228,000
26			Total liabilities and		
27	Total assets	$ 343,000	stockholders' equity		$ 343,000
28					

REVIEW | Stockholders' Equity

Quick Check (Answers are given on page 616.)

1. Dawson Company is authorized to issue 70,000 shares of $2 par common stock. On November 30, 2014, Dawson issued 10,000 shares at $22 per share. Dawson's journal entry to record these facts should include a
   a. credit to Paid-in Capital in Excess of Par for $220,000.
   b. debit to Common Stock for $220,000.
   c. credit to Common Stock for $20,000.
   d. Both a and c.

Questions 2–5 use the following account balances of McCorkle Co. at August 31, 2014:

Dividends Payable........................	$ 22,500	Cash..	$124,000
Preferred Stock, $100 par.............	150,000	Common Stock, $1 par	200,000
Paid-in Capital in Excess of Par—		Retained Earnings	400,000
Common..................................	100,000		

2. How many shares of common stock has McCorkle issued?
   a. 200,000   **c.** 300,000
   b. 124,000   **d.** Some other amount

3. McCorkle's total paid-in capital at August 31, 2014, is
   a. $427,500.   **c.** $827,500.
   b. $450,000.   **d.** $100,000.

4. McCorkle's total stockholders' equity as of August 31, 2014, is
   a. $951,500.   **c.** $827,500.
   b. $450,000.   **d.** $850,000.

5. What would McCorkle's total stockholders' equity be if McCorkle had $25,000 of treasury stock?
   a. $825,000   **c.** $827,500
   b. $951,500   **d.** $450,000

6. Trigg Corporation purchased treasury stock in 2014 at a price of $22 per share and resold the treasury stock in 2015 at a price of $42 per share. What amount should Trigg report on its income statement for 2015?
   a. $42 gain per share   **c.** $22 gain per share
   b. $20 gain per share   **d.** $0

7. The stockholders' equity section of a corporation's balance sheet reports

	Discount on Bonds Payable	*Treasury Stock*
a.	Yes	No
b.	No	No
c.	No	Yes
d.	Yes	Yes

8. The purchase of treasury stock

    a. decreases total assets and increases total stockholders' equity.

    b. decreases total assets and decreases total stockholders' equity.

    c. increases one asset and decreases another asset.

    d. has no effect on total assets, total liabilities, or total stockholders' equity.

9. When does a cash dividend become a legal liability?

    a. On date of payment   **c.** On date of record

    b. Never, because it is paid   **d.** On date of declaration

10. When do dividends increase stockholders' equity?

    a. On date of record   **c.** On date of declaration

    b. On date of payment   **d.** Never

11. Elm Tree Mall, Inc., has 3,000 shares of 5%, $40 par cumulative preferred stock and 140,000 shares of $1 par common stock outstanding. At the beginning of the current year, preferred dividends were four years in arrears. Elm Tree's board of directors wants to pay a $1.50 cash dividend on each share of outstanding common stock in the current year. To accomplish this, what total amount of dividends must Elm Tree declare?

    a. $240,000   **c.** $210,000

    b. $234,000   **d.** Some other amount

12. Stock dividends

    a. are distributions of cash to stockholders.

    b. have no effect on total stockholders' equity.

    c. reduce the total assets of the company.

    d. increase the corporation's total liabilities.

13. What is the effect of a stock dividend and a stock split on total assets?

	Stock Dividend	*Stock Split*
a.	Decrease	Decrease
b.	Decrease	No effect
c.	No effect	No effect
d.	No effect	Decrease

14. A 2-for-1 stock split has the same effect on the number of shares being issued as a

    a. 200% stock dividend.   **c.** 100% stock dividend.

    b. 50% stock dividend.   **d.** 20% stock dividend.

15. The numerator for computing the rate of return on total assets is

    a. net income.

    b. gross margin.

    c. net income minus preferred dividends.

    d. net income plus depreciation expense.

16. The denominator for computing the rate of return on equity is

    a. average total assets.

    b. average common stockholders' equity.

    c. net sales.

    d. net income.

Accounting Vocabulary

authorized stock (p. 564) Maximum number of shares a corporation can issue under its charter.

board of directors (p. 554) Group elected by the stockholders to set policy for a corporation and to appoint its officers.

book value per share (p. 574) Amount of common stockholders' equity on the company's books for each share of its stock.

bylaws (p. 553) Constitution for governing a corporation.

chairperson (p. 554) Elected by a corporation's board of directors, usually the most powerful person in the corporation.

common stock (p. 556) The most basic form of capital stock. The common stockholders own a corporation.

contributed capital (p. 555) The amount of stockholders' equity that stockholders have contributed to the corporation. Also called *paid-in capital*.

cumulative preferred stock (p. 570) Preferred stock whose owners must receive all dividends in arrears plus current year dividends before the corporation can pay dividends to the common stockholders.

deficit (p. 567) Debit balance in the Retained Earnings account.

dividend (p. 568) Distribution (usually cash) by a corporation to its stockholders.

double taxation (p. 553) Corporations pay income taxes on corporate income. Then the stockholders pay personal income tax on the cash dividends that they receive from corporations.

DuPont Analysis (p. 575) A detailed approach to measuring rate of return on equity (ROE), calculated as follows: Net profit margin ratio (net income minus preferred dividends/net sales) × Total asset turnover (net sales/average total assets) × Leverage ratio (average total assets/average common stockholders' equity). The first two components of the model comprise return on assets (ROA).

initial public offering (IPO) (p. 557) The first time a corporation issues stock to the public, which causes the number of issued and outstanding shares of stock to increase.

issued stock (p. 564) Number of shares a corporation has issued to its stockholders.

legal capital (p. 556) Minimum amount of stockholders' equity that a corporation must maintain for the protection of creditors. For corporations with par-value stock, legal capital is the par value of the stock issued.

limited liability (p. 552) No personal obligation of a stockholder for corporation debts. A stockholder can lose no more on an investment in a corporation's stock than the cost of the investment.

liquidation value (p. 574) The amount a corporation must pay a preferred stockholder in the event the company liquidates and goes out of business.

market capitalization (p. 573) The market price of one share of common stock × the total number of common shares outstanding at a particular date.

market value (of a stock) (p. 573) Price for which a person could buy or sell a share of stock.

outstanding stock (p. 564) Stock in the hands of stockholders.

paid-in capital (p. 555) The amount of stockholders' equity that stockholders have contributed to the corporation. Also called *contributed capital*.

par value (p. 556) Arbitrary amount assigned by a company to a share of its stock.

preferred stock (p. 556) Stock that gives its owners certain advantages, such as the priority to receive dividends before the common stockholders and the priority to receive assets before the common stockholders if the corporation liquidates.

president (p. 554) Chief operating officer in charge of managing the day-to-day operations of a corporation.

price-earnings (P/E) ratio (p. 573) The ratio of the market price of a share of common stock to its earnings per share.

rate of return on common stockholders' equity (p. 575) Net income minus preferred dividends, divided by average common stockholders' equity. A measure of profitability. Also called *return on equity*.

rate of return on total assets (p. 575) Net income minus preferred dividends divided by average total assets. This ratio measures a company's success in using its assets to earn income for the persons who finance the business. Also called *return on assets*.

redeemable preferred stock (p. 574) A corporation reserves the right to buy an issue of stock back from its shareholders, with the intent to retire the stock.

redemption value (p. 574) The price a corporation agrees to eventually pay for its redeemable preferred stock, set when the stock is issued.

retained earnings (p. 555) The amount of stockholders' equity that the corporation has earned through profitable operation of the business and has not given back to stockholders.

return on assets (ROA) (p. 575) Another name for *rate of return on total assets*.

return on equity (ROE) (p. 575) Another name for *rate of return on common stockholders' equity*.

shareholders (p. 552) Persons or other entities that own stock in a corporation. Also called *stockholders*.

stated value (p. 557) An arbitrary amount assigned to no-par stock; similar to par value.

stock (p. 555) Shares into which the owners' equity of a corporation is divided.

stock dividend (p. 571) A proportional distribution by a corporation of its own stock to its stockholders.

stockholder (p. 552) A person who owns stock in a corporation. Also called a *shareholder*.

stockholders' equity (p. 555) The stockholders' ownership interest in the assets of a corporation.

stock split (p. 572) An increase in the number of issued and outstanding shares of stock coupled with a proportionate reduction in the stock's par value.

treasury stock (p. 564) A corporation's own stock that it has issued and later reacquired.

ASSESS YOUR PROGRESS

Short Exercises

S10-1. *(Learning Objective 1: Explain advantages and disadvantages of a corporation)* What are two main advantages that a corporation has over a proprietorship and a partnership? What are two main disadvantages of a corporation? Describe the authority structure of a corporation. Who holds ultimate power?

S10-2. *(Learning Objective 1: Describe characteristics of preferred and common stock)* Answer the following questions about the characteristics of a corporation's stock:
1. Who are the real owners of a corporation?
2. What privileges do preferred stockholders have over common stockholders?
3. Which class of stockholders reaps greater benefits from a highly profitable corporation? Explain your answer.

S10-3. *(Learning Objective 2: Describe the effect of a stock issuance on paid-in capital)* LWL Corporation received $23,000,000 for the issuance of its stock on May 14. The par value of the LWL Corporation stock was only $23,000. Was the excess amount of $22,977,000 a profit to LWL Corporation? If not, what was it?

Suppose the par value of the LWL Corporation stock had been $4 per share, $8 per share, or $14 per share. Would a change in the par value of the company's stock affect LWL Corporation total paid-in capital? Give the reason for your answer.

S10-4. *(Learning Objective 2: Issue stock—par value stock and no-par stock)* At fiscal year-end 2014, Bragg Legal Services and Daylight Doughnuts reported these adapted amounts on their balance sheets (amounts in millions):

	A	B	C
1		Bragg Legal Services:	
2		Common stock, $0.01 par value, 3,100 shares issued	$ 31
3		Additional paid-in capital	19,800
4			

	A	B	C
1		Daylight Doughnuts:	
2		Common stock, no par value, 66 shares issued	$ 365
3			

Assume each company issued its stock in a single transaction. Journalize each company's issuance of its stock, using its actual account titles. Explanations are not required.

S10-5. *(Learning Objective 2: Issue stock to finance the purchase of assets)* This short exercise demonstrates the similarity and the difference between two ways to acquire plant assets.

Case A—Issue stock and buy the assets in separate transactions:

O'Dell, Inc., issued 17,000 shares of its $25 par common stock for cash of $756,000. In a separate transaction, O'Dell used the cash to purchase a building for $548,000 and equipment for $208,000. Journalize the two transactions.

Case B—Issue stock to acquire the assets in a single transaction:

O'Dell, Inc., issued 17,000 shares of its $25 par common stock to acquire a building with a market value of $548,000 and equipment with a market value of $208,000. Journalize this transaction.

Compare the balances in all the accounts after making both sets of entries. Are the account balances similar or different?

S10-6. *(Learning Objective 2: Prepare the stockholders' equity section of a balance sheet)* The financial statements of Cliffview Employment Services, Inc., reported the following accounts (adapted, with dollar amounts in thousands except for par value):

Paid-in capital in excess of par	$207	Total revenues	$1,450
Other stockholders' equity (negative)	(27)	Accounts payable	460
Common stock, $0.01 par		Retained earnings	643
900 shares issued	9	Other current liabilities	2,562
Long-term debt	23	Total expenses	836

Prepare the stockholders' equity section of Cliffview's balance sheet. Net income has already been closed to Retained Earnings.

S10-7. *(Learning Objectives 2, 5: Use stockholders' equity data)* Refer to the data in S10-6. Using only year-end figures rather than averages, compute the following for Cliffview Employment Services:
  a. Net income
  b. Total liabilities
  c. Total assets (use the accounting equation)
  d. Net profit margin ratio
  e. Asset turnover
  f. Leverage ratio
  g. Return on equity

What additional information do you need before you can use this data to make decisions?

S10-8. *(Learning Objective 3: Account for the purchase and sale of treasury stock)* Sanja Marketing Corporation reported the following stockholders' equity at December 31 (adapted and in millions):

Common stock	$ 365
Additional paid-in capital	286
Retained earnings	3,190
Treasury stock	(690)
Total stockholders' equity	$3,151

During the next year, Sanja Marketing purchased treasury stock at a cost of $34 million and resold treasury stock for $15 million (this treasury stock had cost Sanja Marketing $6 million). Record the purchase and resale of Sanja Marketing's treasury stock. Overall, how much did stockholders' equity increase or decrease as a result of the two treasury-stock transactions?

S10-9. *(Learning Objective 3: Explain purchase of treasury stock to fight off a takeover of the corporation)* Lucinda Lowery Exports, Inc., is located in Clancy, New Mexico. Lowery is the only company with reliable sources for its imported gifts. The company does a brisk business with specialty stores such as Neiman Marcus. Lowery's recent success has made the company a prime target for a takeover. An investment group named Alberton is attempting to buy 52% of Lowery's outstanding stock against the wishes of Lowery's board of directors. Board members are convinced that the Alberton investors would sell the most desirable pieces of the business and leave little of value.

At the most recent board meeting, several suggestions were advanced to fight off the hostile takeover bid. The suggestion with the most promise is to purchase a huge quantity of treasury stock. Lowery has the cash to carry out this plan.

Requirements

1. Suppose you are a significant stockholder of Lucinda Lowery Exports, Inc. Write a memorandum to explain to the board how the purchase of treasury stock would make it difficult for the Alberton group to take over Lowery. Include in your memo a discussion of the effect that purchasing treasury stock would have on stock outstanding and on the size of the corporation.
2. Suppose Lowery management is successful in fighting off the takeover bid and later sells the treasury stock at prices greater than the purchase price. Explain what effect these sales will have on assets, stockholders' equity, and net income.

S10-10. *(Learning Objective 4: Account for cash dividends)* Glenside Corporation earned net income of $97,000 during the year ended December 31, 2014. On December 15, Glenside declared the annual cash dividend on its 6% preferred stock (20,000 shares with total par value of $200,000) and a $0.14 per share cash dividend on its common stock (36,000 shares with total par value of $360,000). Glenside then paid the dividends on January 4, 2015.

Journalize the following for Glenside Corporation:
   a. Declaring the cash dividends on December 15, 2014
   b. Paying the cash dividends on January 4, 2015

Did Retained Earnings increase or decrease during 2014? By how much?

S10-11. *(Learning Objective 4: Divide cash dividends between preferred and common stock)* Bella, Inc., has 95,000 shares of $1.45 preferred stock outstanding in addition to its common stock. The $1.45 designation means that the preferred stockholders receive an annual cash dividend of $1.45 per share. In 2014, Bella declares an annual dividend of $503,000. The allocation to preferred and common stockholders is

Preferred dividend, (95,000 shares × $1.45 per share).............	$137,750
Common dividend (remainder: $503,000 − $137,750)	365,250
Total dividend...	$503,000

Answer these questions about Bella's cash dividends.
   1. How much in dividends must Bella declare each year before the common stockholders receive any cash dividends for the year?
   2. Suppose Bella, Inc., declares cash dividends of $550,000 for 2014. How much of the dividends goes to preferred? How much goes to common?
   3. Is Bella's preferred stock cumulative or noncumulative? How can you tell?
   4. Bella, Inc., passed the preferred dividend in 2013 and 2014. Then in 2015, Bella declares cash dividends of $1,400,000. How much of the dividends goes to preferred? How much goes to common?

S10-12. *(Learning Objective 4: Record a small stock dividend)* Tucson Bancshares has 34,000 shares of $3 par common stock outstanding. Suppose Tucson declares and distributes an 8% stock dividend when the market value of its stock is $20 per share.

1. Journalize Tucson's declaration and distribution of the stock dividend on May 11. An explanation is not required.
2. What was the overall effect of the stock dividend on Tucson's total assets? On total liabilities? On total stockholders' equity?

S10-13. *(Learning Objective 5: Compute book value per share)* Diamondback, Inc., has the following stockholders' equity:

Preferred stock, 1%, $12 par,	
40,000 shares authorized and issued.....................................	$ 480,000
Common stock, $8 par, 100,000 shares authorized,	
67,000 shares issued	536,000
Additional paid-in capital—Common	2,140,000
Retained earnings..	1,800,000
Less treasury stock, common (1,200 shares at cost)	(49,000)
Total stockholders' equity...	$4,907,000

The company has passed its preferred dividends for three years, including the current year. Compute the book value per share of the company's common stock. Refer to the "real-world format" for reporting stockholders' equity in Exhibit 10-10 (p. 579) as an example in making your computations.

S10-14. *(Learning Objective 5: Compute and explain return on assets and return on equity)* Give the DuPont model formula for computing (a) rate of return on total assets (ROA) and (b) rate of return on common stockholders' equity (ROE). Then answer these questions about the rate-of-return computations.

1. Explain the meaning of the component driver ratios in the computation of ROA.
2. What impact does the leverage ratio have on ROA?
3. Under what circumstances will ROE be higher than ROA? Under what circumstances would ROE be lower than ROA?

S10-15. *(Learning Objective 5: Compute return on assets and return on equity for a leading company)* KEH Corporation's 2014 financial statements reported the following items, with 2013 figures given for comparison (adapted, and in millions):

	A	B	C	D
			2014	**2013**
1				
2		**Balance Sheet**		
3		Total assets	¥ 10,632	¥ 9,523
4		Total liabilities	¥ 7,414	¥ 6,639
5		Total stockholders' equity (all common)	3,218	2,884
6		Total liabilities and stockholders' equity	¥ 10,632	¥ 9,523
7				
8		**Income Statement**		
9		Net sales revenue	¥ 7,632	
10		Operating expense	7,289	
11		Interest expense	31	
12		Other expense	194	
13		Net income	¥ 118	
14				

Use the DuPont model to compute KEH's return on assets and return on common equity for 2014. Evaluate the rates of return as strong or weak. What additional information would be helpful in making this decision? (¥ is the symbol for the Japanese yen.)

S10-16. *(Learning Objectives 1, 2, 5: Explain the features of a corporation's stock)* Wallace Corporation is conducting a special meeting of its board of directors to address some concerns raised by the stockholders. Stockholders have submitted the following questions. Answer each question.

1. Why are common stock and retained earnings shown separately in the shareholders' equity section of the balance sheet?
2. Larry Ramirez, a Wallace shareholder, proposes to transfer some land he owns to the company in exchange for shares of the company stock. How should Wallace Corporation determine the number of shares of our stock to issue for the land?
3. Preferred shares generally are preferred with respect to dividends and in the event of our liquidation. Why would investors buy our common stock when preferred stock is available?
4. What does the redemption value of our preferred stock require us to do?
5. One of our stockholders owns 200 shares of Wallace stock and someone has offered to buy her shares for the company's book value. Our stockholder asks us the formula for computing the book value of her stock.

S10-17. *(Learning Objective 6: Measure cash flows from financing activities)* During 2014, Oso Corporation earned net income of $6.3 billion and paid off $3.1 billion of long-term notes payable. Oso raised $2.4 billion by issuing common stock, paid $3.9 billion to purchase treasury stock, and paid cash dividends of $.7 billion. Report Oso's *cash flows from financing* activities on the statement of cash flows for 2014.

S10-18. *(Learning Objective 6: Analyze a statement of stockholders' equity)* Use the following statement of stockholders' equity to answer the following questions about Osborn Electronics Corporation:

	A	B	C	D	E	F	G
	A1						
1	Osborn Electronics Corporation Statement of Stockholders' Equity For the Year Ended December 31, 2014						
2		Common Stock $10 Par	Additional Paid-in Capital	Retained Earnings	Treasury Stock	Accumulated Other Comprehensive Income	Total Stockholders' Equity
3	Balance, December 31, 2013	$ 100,000	$ 83,000	$ 185,000	$ (18,000)	$ 4,000	$ 354,000
4	Issuance of stock	320,000	1,190,000				1,510,000
5	Net income			76,000			76,000
6	Cash dividends			(20,000)			(20,000)
7	Stock dividends—10%	42,000	62,000	(104,000)			0
8	Purchase of treasury stock				(13,000)		(13,000)
9	Sale of treasury stock		10,000		2,000		12,000
10	Other comprehensive income					19,000	19,000
11	Balance, December 31, 2014	$ 462,000	$ 1,345,000	$ 137,000	$ (29,000)	$ 23,000	$ 1,938,000
12							

1. How much cash did the issuance of common stock bring in during 2014?
2. What was the effect of the stock dividends on Osborn's retained earnings? On total paid-in capital? On total stockholders' equity? On total assets?
3. What was the cost of the treasury stock that Osborn purchased during 2014? What was the cost of the treasury stock that Osborn sold during the year? For how much did Osborn sell the treasury stock during 2014?
4. How much was Osborn's net income?
5. Osborn revalued available-for-sale investments during the year, resulting in an unrealized gain of $9,000. It also consolidated a foreign subsidiary, resulting in a currency translation gain of $10,000. How much was comprehensive income? How much should be added to Osborn's Accumulated Other Comprehensive Income?

Exercises

All of the A and B exercises can be found within MyAccountingLab, an online home-work and practice environment. Your instructor may ask you to complete these exercises using **MyAccountingLab**.

MyAccountingLab

Group A

E10-19A. *(Learning Objectives 2, 6: Account for issuance of stock; prepare the stockholders' equity section of a balance sheet)* Mulberry Sporting Goods is authorized to issue 18,000 shares of com-mon stock. During a two-month period, Mulberry completed these stock-issuance transactions:

Apr 23	Issued 4,000 shares of $1.00 par common stock for cash of $14.75 per share.	
May 12	Received inventory with a market value of $14,000 and equipment with market value of $51,000 for 3,400 shares of the $1.00 par common stock.	

Requirements

1. Journalize the transactions.
2. Prepare the stockholders' equity section of Mulberry Sporting Goods' balance sheet for the transactions given in this exercise. Retained Earnings has a balance of $53,900.

E10-20A. *(Learning Objective 2: Measure paid-in capital of a corporation)* City Publishing was recently organized. The company issued common stock to an attorney who provided legal services worth $17,000 to help organize the corporation. City Publishing also issued common stock to an inventor in exchange for his patent with a market value of $64,000. In addition, City received cash both for the issuance of 5,000 shares of its preferred stock at $70 per share and for the issuance of 16,000 of its common shares at $5 per share. During the first year of operations, City Publishing earned net income of $74,000 and declared a cash dividend of $26,000. With-out making journal entries, determine the total paid-in capital created by these transactions.

E10-21A. *(Learning Objectives 3, 6: Show how treasury stock affects a company; prepare the stockholders' equity section of a balance sheet)* Carey Software had the following selected account balances at December 31, 2014 (in thousands, except par value per share):

Inventory..	$ 1,120	Common stock, $0.25 par	
Property, plant, and		per share, 900 shares	
equipment, net	2,860	authorized, 500 shares	
Paid-in capital in excess of par	903	issued	$ 125
Treasury stock,		Retained earnings...............	2,316
90 shares at cost........................	1,485	Accounts receivable, net......	1,030
Accumulated other		Notes payable	1,274
comprehensive income (loss)	(732)*		

*Debit balance

Requirements

1. Prepare the stockholders' equity section of Carey's balance sheet (in thousands).
2. How can Carey have a larger balance of treasury stock than the sum of Common Stock and Paid-in Capital in Excess of Par?

E10-22A. *(Learning Objectives 2, 3, 4: Account for issuance of stock; show how treasury stock affects a company; account for dividends)* At December 31, 2014, Harelik Corporation reported the stockholders' equity accounts shown here (with dollar amounts in millions, except per-share amounts).

Common stock $1.50 par value per share,	
2,400 million shares issued...............	$ 3,600
Paid-in capital in excess of par value.....	7,200
Retained earnings...................................	1,490
Treasury stock, at cost	(85)
Total stockholders' equity.................	$12,205

Harelik's 2015 transactions included
  a. Net income, $380 million
  b. Issuance of 18 million shares of common stock for $12.00 per share
  c. Purchase of 8 million shares of treasury stock for $120 million
  d. Sold 5 million of the treasury shares purchased in part c for $80 million
  e. Declaration and payment of cash dividends of $24 million

Requirements

1. Journalize Harelik's transactions in parts b, c, d, and e. Explanations are not required.
2. What was the overall effect of these transactions (parts a through e) on Harelik's stockholders' equity?

E10-23A. *(Learning Objective 6: Report stockholders' equity after a sequence of transactions)* Use the Harelik Corporation data in E10-22A to prepare the stockholders' equity section of the company's balance sheet at December 31, 2015.

E10-24A. *(Learning Objectives 2, 3, 4, 6: Infer transactions from a company's comparative stockholders' equity)* Zion Products Company reported the following stockholders' equity on its balance sheet:

	A	B	C
		December 31,	
1	**Stockholders' Equity (Dollars and shares in millions)**	**2015**	**2014**
2	Convertible preferred stock—$1.00 par value; authorized 70 shares;		
3	issued and outstanding:		
4	2015 and 2014—8 and 16 shares, respectively	$ 8	$ 16
5	Common stock—$5 per share par value; authorized		
6	1,100 shares; issued: 2015 and 2014—500		
7	and 400 shares, respectively	2,500	2,000
8	Additional paid-in capital	2,800	1,950
9	Retained earnings	6,185	5,086
10	Treasury stock, common—at cost		
11	2015—23 shares; 2014—8 shares	(307)	(121)
12	Total stockholders' equity	11,186	8,931
13	Total liabilities and stockholders' equity	$ 51,323	$ 47,202
14			

Requirements

1. What caused Zion's preferred stock to decrease during 2015? Cite all possible causes.
2. What caused Zion's common stock to increase during 2015? Identify all possible causes.
3. How many shares of Zion's common stock were outstanding at December 31, 2015?
4. Zion's net income during 2015 was $1,350 million. How much were Zion's dividends during the year?
5. During 2015, Zion sold no treasury stock. What average price per share did Zion pay for the treasury stock that the company purchased during the year?

E10-25A. *(Learning Objective 4: Compute dividends on preferred and common stock)* Alabama Manufacturing, Inc., reported the following at December 31, 2014 and December 31, 2015:

	A1	⬍		
		A		B
1		**Stockholders' Equity**		
2	Preferred stock, cumulative, $1.00 par, 5%, 90,000 shares issued			$ 90,000
3	Common stock, $0.30 par, 9,450,000 shares issued			2,835,000
4				

Alabama Manufacturing has paid all preferred dividends through 2011.

Requirements

1. Compute the total amounts of dividends to both preferred and common for 2014 and 2015 if total dividends are $86,000 in 2014 and $264,000 in 2015.

E10-26A. *(Learning Objectives 4, 6: Record a stock dividend and report stockholders' equity)* The stockholders' equity for Dairy King Drive-Ins (DK) on April 16, 2015, follows:

	A1	⬍		
		A		B
1		**Stockholders' Equity**		
2	Common stock, $0.30 par, 2,600,000 shares			
3	authorized, 750,000 shares issued			$ 225,000
4	Paid-in capital in excess of par—common			1,614,400
5	Retained earnings			7,154,000
6	Accumulated other comprehensive income (loss)			(200,000)
7	Total stockholders' equity			$ 8,793,400
8				

On April 16, 2015, the market price of DK common stock was $20 per share. Assume DK declared and distributed a 15% stock dividend on this date.

Requirements

1. Journalize the declaration and distribution of the stock dividend.
2. Prepare the stockholders' equity section of the balance sheet after the stock dividend.
3. Why is total stockholders' equity unchanged by the stock dividend?
4. Suppose DK had a cash balance of $610,000 on April 17, 2015. What is the maximum amount of cash dividends DK can declare?

E10-27A. *(Learning Objectives 2, 3, 4: Measure the effects of stock issuance, dividends, splits, and treasury-stock transactions)* Identify the effects—both the direction and the dollar amount—of these assumed transactions on the total stockholders' equity of Silva Corporation. Each transaction is independent.

    a. Declaration of cash dividends of $58 million.
    b. Payment of the cash dividend in (a).
    c. A 20% stock dividend. Before the dividend, 72 million shares of $1.00 par common stock were outstanding; the market value was $12.87 at the time of the dividend.
    d. A 40% stock dividend. Before the dividend, 72 million shares of $1.00 par common stock were outstanding; the market value was $14.25 at the time of the dividend.
    e. Purchase of 1,700 shares of treasury stock (par value $1.00) at $13.25 per share.

f. Sale of 800 shares of the treasury stock for $16.00 per share. Cost of the treasury stock was $13.25 per share.

g. A 2-for-1 stock split. Prior to the split, 72 million shares of $1.00 par common stock were outstanding.

E10-28A. *(Learning Objective 5: Measure book value per share of common stock)* The balance sheet of Redd Rug Company reported the following:

Redeemable preferred stock, 5%, $70 par value, redemption value $40,000; outstanding 450 shares................	$ 31,500
Common stockholders' equity:	
6,000 shares issued and outstanding	80,000
Total stockholders' equity...	$111,500

Requirements

1. Compute the book value per share for the common stock, assuming all preferred dividends are fully paid up (none in arrears).
2. Compute the book value per share of the common stock, assuming that three years' cumulative preferred dividends, including the current year, are in arrears.
3. Redd Rug's common stock recently traded at a market price of $12.85 per share. Does this mean that Redd Rug's stock is a good buy at $12.85?

E10-29A. *(Learning Objective 5: Evaluate profitability)* NY Company included the following items in its financial statements for 2014, the current year (amounts in millions):

Payment of long-term debt..........	$8,145	Dividends paid	$ 324
Proceeds from issuance		Net sales:	
of common stock.....................	9,420	Current year.....................	60,000
Total liabilities:		Preceding year..................	55,000
Current year-end.....................	32,319	Net income:	
Preceding year-end..................	38,023	Current year.....................	1,884
Total stockholders' equity:		Preceding year..................	1,997
Current year-end.....................	23,479	Operating income:	
Preceding year-end..................	14,035	Current year.....................	9,980
Borrowings.................................	4,580	Preceding year..................	4,008

Requirements

1. Use DuPont Analysis to compute NY Company's return on assets and return on common equity during 2014 (the current year). NY Company has no preferred stock outstanding.
2. Do the company's rates of return look strong or weak? Give your reason.
3. What additional information do you need to make the decision in requirement 2?

E10-30A. *(Learning Objective 6: Report cash flows from financing activities)* Use the NY Company data in E10-29A to show how the company reported cash flows from financing activities during 2014 (the current year).

E10-31A. *(Learning Objective 6: Use a company's statement of stockholders' equity)* Robinson Water Company reported the following items on its statement of shareholders' equity for the year ended December 31, 2014 (amounts in thousands of $):

	$3.50 Par Common Stock	Additional Paid-in Capital	Retained Earnings	Accumulated Other Comprehensive Income	Total Shareholders' Equity
Balance, December 31, 2013.............	$395	$1,505	$4,700	$8	$6,608
Net earnings.......................................			1,050		
Other comprehensive income				1	
Issuance of stock	140	70			
Cash dividends..................................			(80)	—	
Balance, December 31, 2014.............					

1. Determine the December 31, 2014, balances in Robinson Water's shareholders' equity accounts and total shareholders' equity on this date.
2. Robinson Water's total liabilities on December 31, 2014, are $7,400. What is Robinson Water's debt ratio on this date?
3. Was there a profit or a loss for the year ended December 31, 2014? How can you tell?
4. At what price per share did Robinson Water issue common stock during 2014?

Group B

E10-32B. *(Learning Objectives 2, 6: Account for issuance of stock; prepare the stockholders' equity section of a balance sheet)* Bradley Sporting Goods is authorized to issue 13,000 shares of common stock. During a two-month period, Bradley completed these stock-issuance transactions:

Jul	23	Issued 4,200 shares of $1.00 par common stock for cash of $13.50 per share.
Aug	12	Received inventory with a market value of $13,000 and equipment with market value of $54,000 for 3,300 shares of the $1.00 par common stock.

Requirements

1. Journalize the transactions.
2. Prepare the stockholders' equity section of Bradley Sporting Goods' balance sheet for the transactions given in this exercise. Retained Earnings has a balance of $51,600.

E10-33B. *(Learning Objective 2: Measure paid-in capital of a corporation)* Campus Publishing was recently organized. The company issued common stock to an attorney who provided legal services worth $21,000 to help organize the corporation. Campus Publishing also issued common stock to an inventor in exchange for his patent with a market value of $67,000. In addition, Campus received cash both for the issuance of 2,000 shares of its preferred stock at $120 per share and for the issuance of 16,000 shares of its common shares at $6 per share. During the first year of operations, Campus Publishing earned net income of $68,000 and declared a cash dividend of $25,000. Without making journal entries, determine the total paid-in capital created by these transactions.

E10-34B. *(Learning Objectives 3, 6: Show how treasury stock affects a company; prepare the stockholders' equity section of a balance sheet)* Buffette Software had the following selected account balances at December 31, 2014 (in thousands, except par value per share):

Inventory..	$ 852	Common stock, $2.50 par	
Property, plant, and		per share, 1,000 shares	
equipment, net	2,859	authorized, 350 shares	
Paid-in capital in excess of par	900	issued	$ 875
Treasury stock,		Retained earnings...............	2,341
140 shares at cost.......................	1,820	Accounts receivable, net......	1,117
Accumulated other		Notes payable	1,188
comprehensive income (loss)	(727)*		

*Debit balance

Requirements

1. Prepare the stockholders' equity section of Buffette Software's balance sheet (in thousands).
2. How can Buffette have a larger balance of treasury stock than the sum of Common Stock and Paid-in Capital in Excess of Par?

E10-35B. *(Learning Objectives 2, 3, 4: Account for issuance of stock; show how treasury stock affects a company; account for dividends)* At December 31, 2014, Townlynn Corporation reported the stockholders' equity accounts shown here (with dollar amounts in millions, except per-share amounts).

Common stock $2.00 par value per share,	
2,300 million shares issued................	$ 4,600
Paid-in capital in excess of par value.....	4,100
Retained earnings...................................	1,565
Treasury stock, at cost	(48)
Total stockholders' equity.................	$10,217

Townlynn's 2015 transactions included

    a. Net income, $374 million
    b. Issuance of 9 million shares of common stock for $11 per share
    c. Purchase of 1 million shares of treasury stock for $12 million
    d. Sale of 500,000 of the treasury shares purchased for $7 million
    e. Declaration and payment of cash dividends of $23 million

Requirements

1. Journalize Townlynn's transactions in parts b, c, d, and e. Explanations are not required.
2. What was the overall effect of these transactions (parts a through e) on Townlynn Corporation's stockholders' equity?

E10-36B. *(Learning Objective 6: Report stockholders' equity after a sequence of transactions)* Use the Townlynn Corporation data in E10-35B to prepare the stockholders' equity section of the company's balance sheet at December 31, 2015.

E10-37B. *(Learning Objectives 2, 3, 4, 6: Infer transactions from a company's comparative stockholders' equity)* Delta Products Company reported the following stockholders' equity on its balance sheet:

A1		
A	**B**	**C**
Stockholders' Equity	**December 31,**	
(Dollars and shares in millions)	**2015**	**2014**
Convertible preferred stock—$1.00 par value; authorized 20 shares;		
issued and outstanding:		
2015 and 2014—4 and 8 shares, respectively	$ 4	$ 8
Common stock—$1 per share par value; authorized		
1,500 shares; issued: 2015 and 2014—300		
and 200 shares, respectively	300	200
Additional paid-in capital	1,400	650
Retained earnings	6,195	5,135
Treasury stock, common—at cost		
2015—24 shares; 2014—12 shares	(270)	(130)
Total stockholders' equity	7,629	5,863
Total liabilities and stockholders' equity	$ 48,484	$ 42,673

Requirements

1. What caused Delta's preferred stock to decrease during 2015? Cite all possible causes.
2. What caused Delta's common stock to increase during 2015? Identify all possible causes.
3. How many shares of Delta's common stock were outstanding at December 31, 2015?
4. Delta's net income during 2015 was $1,368 million. How much were Delta's dividends during the year?
5. During 2015, Delta sold no treasury stock. What average price per share did Delta pay for the treasury stock that the company purchased during the year?

E10-38B. *(Learning Objective 4: Compute dividends on preferred and common stock)* Mississippi Manufacturing, Inc., reported the following at December 31, 2014 and December 31, 2015:

A1	
A	**B**
Stockholders' Equity	
Preferred stock, cumulative, $2.00 par, 6%, 70,000 shares issued	$ 140,000
Common stock, $0.15 par, 9,428,000 shares issued	1,414,200

Mississippi Manufacturing has paid all preferred dividends through 2011.

Requirement

1. Compute the total amounts of dividends to both preferred and common for 2014 and 2015 if total dividends are $109,000 in 2014 and $364,000 in 2015.

E10-39B. *(Learning Objectives 4, 6: Record a stock dividend and report stockholders' equity)* The stockholders' equity for Dairy Land Drive-Ins (DL) on July 13, 2015, follows:

	A	B
	A1	
1	**Stockholders' Equity**	
2	Common stock, $0.75 par, 2,700,000 shares	
3	authorized, 650,000 shares issued	$ 487,500
4	Paid-in capital in excess of par—common	1,512,000
5	Retained earnings	7,123,000
6	Accumulated comprehensive income (loss)	(195,000)
7	Total stockholders' equity	$ 8,927,500
8		

On July 13, 2015, the market price of DL common stock was $17 per share. Assume DL declared and distributed a 20% stock dividend on this date.

Requirements

1. Journalize the declaration and distribution of the stock dividend.
2. Prepare the stockholders' equity section of the balance sheet after the stock dividend.
3. Why is total stockholders' equity unchanged by the stock dividend?
4. Suppose DL had a cash balance of $642,000 on July 14, 2015. What is the maximum amount of cash dividends DL can declare?

E10-40B. *(Learning Objectives 2, 3, 4: Measure the effects of stock issuance, dividends, splits, and treasury-stock transactions)* Identify the effects—both the direction and the dollar amount—of these assumed transactions on the total stockholders' equity of Toben Corporation. Each transaction is independent.

    a. Declaration of cash dividends of $58 million.
    b. Payment of the cash dividend in part a.
    c. A 25% stock dividend. Before the dividend, 69 million shares of $1.00 par common stock were outstanding; the market value was $19.88 at the time of the dividend.
    d. A 40% stock dividend. Before the dividend, 69 million shares of $1.00 par common stock were outstanding; the market value was $18.50 at the time of the dividend.
    e. Purchase of 1,800 shares of treasury stock (par value $1.00) at $14.00 per share.
    f. Sale of 800 shares of the treasury stock for $18.00 per share. Cost of the treasury stock was $14.00 per share.
    g. A 2-for-1 stock split. Prior to the split, 69 million shares of $1.00 par common stock were outstanding.

E10-41B. *(Learning Objective 5: Measure book value per share of common stock)* The balance sheet of Bleu Door Company reported the following:

Redeemable preferred stock, 6%, $90 par value,	
redemption value $30,000; outstanding 250 shares................	$22,500
Common stockholders' equity:	
5,000 shares issued and outstanding	60,000
Total stockholders' equity...	$82,500

Requirements

1. Compute the book value per share for the common stock, assuming all preferred dividends are fully paid up (none in arrears).
2. Compute the book value per share of the common stock, assuming that three years' cumulative preferred dividends, including the current year, are in arrears.
3. Bleu Door's common stock recently traded at a market price of $11.00 per share. Does this mean that Bleu Door's stock is a good buy at $11.00?

E10-42B. *(Learning Objective 5: Evaluate profitability)* Earlson Company included the following items in its financial statements for 2014, the current year (amounts in millions):

Payment of long-term debt..........	$ 9,041	Dividends paid.....................	$ 267
Proceeds from issuance		Net sales:	
of common stock.....................	9,405	Current year.....................	65,000
Total liabilities:		Preceding year.................	62,000
Current year-end....................	32,309	Net income:	
Preceding year-end.................	38,033	Current year.....................	2,200
Total stockholders' equity:		Preceding year.................	1,995
Current year-end....................	23,471	Operating income:	
Preceding year-end.................	14,037	Current year.....................	9,125
Borrowings................................	4,585	Preceding year.................	4,002

Requirements

1. Use DuPont Analysis to compute Earlson's return on assets and return on common equity during 2014 (the current year). Earlson has no preferred stock outstanding.
2. Do the company's rates of return look strong or weak? Give your reason.
3. What additional information do you need to make the decision in requirement 2?

E10-43B. *(Learning Objective 6: Report cash flows from financing activities)* Use the Earlson data in E10-42B to show how the company reported cash flows from financing activities during 2014 (the current year).

E10-44B. *(Learning Objective 6: Use a company's statement of stockholders' equity)* Whitney Water Company reported the following items on its statement of shareholders' equity for the year ended December 31, 2014 (amounts in thousands of $):

	$3 Par Common Stock	Additional Paid-in Capital	Retained Earnings	Accumulated Other Comprehensive Income	Total Shareholders' Equity
Balance, December 31, 2013..............	$375	$2,225	$4,200	$12	$6,812
Net earnings..			990		
Other comprehensive income				3	
Issuance of stock	120	240			
Cash dividends.....................................			(69)	—	
Balance, December 31, 2014..............					

Requirements

1. Determine the December 31, 2014, balances in Whitney Water's shareholders' equity accounts and total shareholders' equity on this date.
2. Whitney Water's total liabilities on December 31, 2014, are $7,800. What is Whitney Water's debt ratio on this date?
3. Was there a profit or a loss for the year ended December 31, 2014? How can you tell?
4. At what price per share did Whitney Water issue common stock during 2014?

Quiz

Test your understanding of stockholders' equity by answering the following questions. Select the best choice from among the possible answers given.

Q10-45. Which of the following is a characteristic of a corporation?

    a. Limited liability of stockholders   **c.** No income tax

    b. Mutual agency   **d.** Both b and c

Q10-46. Ramirez, Inc., issues 280,000 shares of no-par common stock for $15 per share. The journal entry is which of the following?

	A	B	C	D
1	a.	Cash	4,200,000	
2		Common Stock		280,000
3		Gain on the Sale of Stock		3,920,000
4				
5	b.	Cash	280,000	
6		Common Stock		280,000
7				
8	c.	Cash	4,200,000	
9		Common Stock		560,000
10		Paid-in Capital in Excess of Par		3,640,000
11				
12	d.	Cash	4,200,000	
13		Common Stock		4,200,000
14				

Q10-47. Par value

    a. is established for a share of stock after it is issued.

    b. represents the original selling price for a share of stock.

    c. represents what a share of stock is worth.

    d. may exist for common stock but not for preferred stock.

    e. is an arbitrary amount that establishes the legal capital for each share.

Q10-48. The paid-in capital portion of stockholders' equity does not include

    a. Paid-in Capital in Excess of Par Value.   **d.** Preferred Stock.

    b. Common Stock.   **e.** both c and d.

    c. Retained Earnings.

Q10-49. Preferred stock is least likely to have which of the following characteristics?

    a. Preference as to dividends

    b. Preference as to voting

    c. Preference as to assets on liquidation of the corporation

    d. The right of the holder to convert to common stock

Q10-50. Which of the following classifications represents the most shares of common stock?

    a. Issued shares   **d.** Treasury shares

    b. Outstanding shares   **e.** Authorized shares

    c. Unissued shares

Use the following information for questions Q10-51 to Q10-53:

These account balances at December 31 relate to Aqua Sport, Inc.:

Accounts Payable	$ 51,400	Paid-in Capital in Excess	
Accounts Receivable	81,950	of Par—Common	$260,000
Common Stock	313,000	Preferred Stock, 10%, $100 Par	81,000
Treasury Stock	5,700	Retained Earnings	71,600
Bonds Payable	3,900	Notes Receivable	12,300

Q10-51. What is total paid-in capital for Aqua Sport, Inc.?
- **a.** $654,000
- **b.** $648,300
- **c.** $725,600
- **d.** $659,700
- **e.** None of the above

Q10-52. What is total stockholders' equity for Aqua Sport, Inc.?
- **a.** $731,300
- **b.** $725,600
- **c.** $719,900
- **d.** $654,000
- **e.** None of the above

Q10-53. Aqua Sport's net income for the period is $119,300 and beginning common stockholders' equity is $681,200. Calculate Aqua Sport's return on common stockholders' equity.
- **a.** 18.1%
- **b.** 16.8%
- **c.** 17.0%
- **d.** 18.9%

Q10-54. A company paid $26 per share to purchase 500 shares of its common stock as treasury stock. The stock was originally issued at $10 per share. Which of the following is the journal entry to record the purchase of the treasury stock?

	A	B	C	D
1	a.	Treasury Stock	5,000	
2		Paid-in Capital in Excess of Par	8,000	
3		Cash		13,000
4				
5	b.	Common Stock	13,000	
6		Cash		13,000
7				
8	c.	Treasury Stock	13,000	
9		Cash		13,000
10				
11	d.	Treasury Stock	5,000	
12		Retained Earnings	8,000	
13		Cash		13,000
14				

Q10-55. When treasury stock is sold for less than its cost, the entry should include a debit to
- **a.** Gain on Sale of Treasury Stock.
- **b.** Loss on Sale of Treasury Stock.
- **c.** Paid-in Capital in Excess of Par.
- **d.** Retained Earnings.

Q10-56. A company purchased 100 shares of its common stock at $49 per share. It then sells 75 of the treasury shares at $58 per share. The entry to sell the treasury stock includes a
    a. credit to Paid-in Capital from Treasury Stock Transactions for $675.
    b. credit to Cash for $4,350.
    c. credit to Treasury Stock for $4,350.
    d. debit to Retained Earnings for $675.
    e. credit to Retained Earnings for $900.

Q10-57. Stockholders are eligible for a dividend if they own the stock on the date of
    a. issuance.   **c.** payment.
    b. declaration.   **d.** record.

Q10-58. Toni's Foods has outstanding 300 shares of 2% preferred stock, $100 par value; and 1,900 shares of common stock, $20 par value. Toni's declares dividends of $18,200. Which of the following is the correct entry?

	A	B	C	D
		A1		
1	a.	Dividends Payable, Preferred	600	
2		Dividends Payable, Common	17,600	
3		Cash		18,200
4				
5	b.	Retained Earnings	18,200	
6		Dividends Payable, Preferred		600
7		Dividends Payable, Common		17,600
8				
9	c.	Dividends Expense	18,200	
10		Cash		18,200
11				
12	d.	Retained Earnings	18,200	
13		Dividends Payable, Preferred		9,100
14		Dividends Payable, Common		9,100
15				

Q10-59. A corporation has 50,000 shares of 1% preferred stock outstanding. Also, there are 50,000 shares of common stock outstanding. Par value for each is $100. If a $450,000 dividend is paid, how much goes to the preferred stockholders?
    a. None   **d.** $450,000
    b. $50,000   **e.** $30,000
    c. $4,500

Q10-60. Assume the same facts as in Q10-59. What is the amount of dividends per share on common stock?
    a. $8.00   **d.** $9.00
    b. $11.00   **e.** None of these
    c. $4.50

Q10-61. Which of the following is *not* true about a 10% stock dividend?
    a. Total stockholders' equity remains the same.
    b. Paid-in Capital increases.
    c. Par value decreases.
    d. Retained Earnings decreases.
    e. The market value of the stock is needed to record the stock dividend.

Q10-62. A company declares a 5% stock dividend. The debit to Retained Earnings is an amount equal to
    a. the book value of the shares to be issued.
    b. the excess of the market price over the original issue price of the shares to be issued.
    c. the par value of the shares to be issued.
    d. the market value of the shares to be issued.

Q10-63. Which of the following statements is *not* true about a 3-for-1 stock split?
    a. A stockholder with 10 shares before the split owns 30 shares after the split.
    b. Par value is reduced to one-third of what it was before the split.
    c. Retained Earnings remains the same.
    d. The market price of each share of stock will decrease.
    e. Total stockholders' equity increases.

Q10-64. Gold Company's net income and net sales are $38,000 and $900,000, respectively, and average total assets are $250,000. What is Gold's return on assets?
    a. 27.8%   **c.** 17.2%
    b. 15.2%   **d.** 4.2%

Problems

> All of these A and B problems can be found within MyAccountingLab (MAL), an on-line homework and practice environment. Your instructor may ask you to complete these problems using **MyAccountingLab**.

MyAccountingLab

Group A

P10-65A. *(Learning Objectives 2, 6: Account for stock issuance; report stockholders' equity)* The partners who own Whitewater Rafts Co. wished to avoid the unlimited personal liability of the partnership form of business, so they incorporated as Whitewater Rafts, Inc. The charter from the state of Colorado authorizes the corporation to issue 150,000 shares of $8 par common stock. In its first month, Whitewater Rafts completed the following transactions:

Mar 6	Issued 800 shares of common stock to the promoter for assistance with issuance of the common stock. The promotional fee was $15,600. Debit Organization Expense.
9	Issued 10,000 shares of common stock to Blake Anderson and 25,000 shares to John Jefferson in return for cash equal to the stock's market value of $23 per share. The two men were partners in Whitewater Rafts Co.
26	Issued 1,400 shares of common stock for $24 cash per share.

Requirements

1. Record the transactions in the journal.
2. Prepare the stockholders' equity section of the Whitewater Rafts, Inc., balance sheet at March 31, 2015. The ending balance of Retained Earnings is $83,000.

P10-66A. *(Learning Objectives 6: Report stockholders' equity)* Dorton Corp. has the following stockholders' equity information:

    Dorton's charter authorizes the company to issue 7,500 shares of 10% preferred stock with par value of $150 and 700,000 shares of no-par common stock. The company issued 1,950 shares of the preferred stock at $150 per share. It issued 171,600 shares of the common stock for a total of $643,000. The company's retained earnings balance at the beginning of 2014 was $74,000, and net income for the year was $129,000. During 2014, Dorton declared the specified dividend on preferred and a $0.25 per-share dividend on common. Preferred dividends for 2013 were in arrears.

Requirement

1. Prepare the stockholders' equity section of Dorton Corp.'s balance sheet at December 31, 2014. Show the computation of all amounts. Journal entries are not required.

P10-67A. *(Learning Objectives 2, 4: Analyze stockholders' equity and dividends of a corporation)* Whitman Outdoor Furniture Company included the following stockholders' equity on its year-end balance sheet at February 28, 2015:

Stockholders' Equity	
Preferred stock, 6.5% cumulative—par value $15 per share;	
authorized 110,000 shares in each class	
Class A—issued 75,000 shares	$ 1,125,000
Class B—issued 96,000 shares	1,440,000
Common stock—$10 par value:	
authorized 2,000,000 shares,	
issued 245,000 shares	2,450,000
Additional paid-in capital—common	4,570,000
Retained earnings	8,890,000
	$18,475,000

Requirements

1. Identify the different issues of stock that Whitman Outdoor Furniture Company has outstanding.
2. Give the summary entries to record issuance of all the Whitman stock. Assume that all the stock was issued for cash. Explanations are not required.
3. Suppose Whitman passed its preferred dividends for three years. Would the company have to pay those dividends in arrears before paying dividends to the common stockholders? Give your reason.
4. What amount of preferred dividends must Whitman declare and pay each year to avoid having preferred dividends in arrears?
5. Assume that preferred dividends are in arrears for 2014. Journalize the declaration of an $825,000 dividend on February 28, 2015. An explanation is not required.

P10-68A. *(Learning Objectives 2, 3, 4: Account for stock issuance, dividends, and treasury stock)* CZ Jewelry Company reported the following summarized balance sheet at December 31, 2014:

Assets	
Current assets	$ 61,000
Property and equipment, net	108,700
Total assets	$169,700
Liabilities and Equity	
Liabilities	$ 34,000
Stockholders' equity:	
$0.50 cumulative preferred stock, $20 par, 900 shares issued	18,000
Common stock, $8 par, 7,100 shares issued	56,800
Paid-in capital in excess of par—common	17,900
Retained earnings	43,000
Total liabilities and equity	$169,700

During 2015, CZ Jewelry completed these transactions that affected stockholders' equity:

Feb	13	Issued 6,400 shares of common stock for $10 per share.
Jun	7	Declared the regular cash dividend on the preferred stock.
	24	Paid the cash dividend.
Aug	9	Declared and distributed a 10% stock dividend on the common stock. Market price of the common stock was $15 per share.
Oct	26	Reacquired 800 shares of common stock as treasury stock, paying $18 per share.
Nov	20	Sold 200 shares of the treasury stock for $20 per share.
Dec	31	Declared a cash dividend of $0.25 per share on the outstanding common stock; dividends will be paid in January, 2016.

Requirements

1. Journalize CZ Jewelry's transactions. Explanations are not required.
2. Report CZ Jewelry's stockholders' equity at December 31, 2015. Net income for 2015 was $36,000.

P10-69A. *(Learning Objectives 3, 4, 6: Measure the effects of stock-related transactions on a company)* Assume Fast Foods of Texas, Inc., completed the following transactions during 2014, the company's 10th year of operations:

Feb	3	Issued 11,000 shares of common stock ($3.00 par) for cash of $296,000.
Mar	19	Purchased 2,400 shares of the company's own common stock at $28 per share.
Apr	24	Sold 1,500 shares of treasury common stock for $34 per share.
Aug	15	Declared a cash dividend on the 8,000 shares of $0.90 no-par preferred stock.
Sep	1	Paid the cash dividends.
Nov	22	Declared and distributed a 10% stock dividend on the 98,000 shares of $3.00 par common stock outstanding. The market value of the common stock was $35 per share.

Requirements

1. Analyze each transaction in terms of its effect on the accounting equation of Fast Foods of Texas, Inc.
2. What impact did each transaction have on cash flows?

P10-70A. *(Learning Objectives 4, 5: Prepare a corporation's balance sheet; measure profitability)*
The following accounts and related balances of Cardinal Designers, Inc., as of December 31, 2014, are arranged in no particular order:

Cash..............................	$ 45,000	Interest expense........................	$ 16,300
Accounts receivable, net...............	25,000	Property, plant, and	
Paid-in capital in excess		equipment, net	359,000
of par—common.......................	53,800	Common stock, $2 par,	
Accrued liabilities........................	22,000	500,000 shares authorized,	
Long-term note payable	97,000	110,000 shares issued.............	220,000
Inventory.................................	89,000	Prepaid expenses	14,000
Dividends payable........................	9,000	Common stockholders'	
Retained earnings........................	?	equity, December 31, 2013	220,000
Accounts payable	135,000	Net income...............................	90,000
Trademarks, net..........................	9,000	Total assets,	
Goodwill....................................	18,000	December 31, 2013	500,000
		Treasury stock,	
		8,000 shares at cost...............	23,000
		Net sales....................................	750,000

Requirements

1. Prepare Cardinal's classified balance sheet in the account format at December 31, 2014.
2. Use DuPont Analysis to compute rate of return on total assets and rate of return on common stockholders' equity for the year ended December 31, 2014.
3. Do these rates of return suggest strength or weakness? Give your reason. What additional information might help you make your decision?

P10-71A. *(Learning Objective 6: Analyze a statement of stockholders' equity)* Marketing Specialties, Inc., reported the following statement of stockholders' equity for the year ended October 31, 2014:

A1						
	A	B	C	D	E	F
1	**Marketing Specialties, Inc.** **Statement of Stockholders' Equity** **For the Year Ended October 31, 2014**					
2	(In millions)	Common Stock	Additional Paid-in Capital	Retained Earnings	Treasury Stock	Total
3	Balance, October 31, 2013	$ 430	$ 1,640	$ 904	$ (115)	$ 2,859
4	Net income			480		480
5	Cash dividends			(190)		(190)
6	Issuance of stock (200 shares)	100	120			220
7	Stock dividend	106	127	(233)		—
8	Sale of treasury stock		11		7	18
9	Balance, October 31, 2014	$ 636	$ 1,898	$ 961	$ (108)	$ 3,387
10						

Requirements

Answer these questions about Marketing Specialties' stockholders' equity transactions.

1. What is the par value of the company's common stock?
2. At what price per share did Marketing Specialties issue its common stock during the year?
3. What was the cost of treasury stock sold during the year? What was the selling price of the treasury stock sold? What was the increase in total stockholders' equity?
4. Marketing Specialties' statement of stockholders' equity lists the stock transactions in the order in which they occurred. What was the percentage of the stock dividend? Round to the nearest percentage.

Group B

P10-72B. *(Learning Objectives 2, 6: Account for stock issuance; report stockholders' equity)* The partners who own Cadence Canoes Co. wished to avoid the unlimited personal liability of the partnership form of business, so they incorporated as Cadence Canoes, Inc. The charter from the state of Florida authorizes the corporation to issue 175,000 shares of $20 par common stock. In its first month, Cadence Canoes completed the following transactions:

Jan	6	Issued 200 shares of common stock to the promoter for assistance with issuance of common stock. The promotional fee was $5,000. Debit Organization Expense.
	9	Issued 10,000 shares of common stock to Bryce Kuhl and 24,000 shares to Arnold Ameen in return for cash equal to the stock's market value of $25 per share. The two men were partners in Cadence Canoes Co.
	26	Issued 1,200 shares of common stock for $30 cash per share.

Requirements

1. Record the transactions in the journal.
2. Prepare the stockholders' equity section of Cadence Canoes, Inc., balance sheet at January 31, 2015. The ending balance of Retained Earnings is $88,000.

P10-73B. *(Learning Objective 6: Report stockholders' equity)* Lehmann Corp. has the following stockholders' equity information:

Lehmann's charter authorizes the company to issue 15,000 shares of 6% preferred stock with par value of $95 and 725,000 shares of no-par common stock. The company issued 2,130 shares of the preferred stock at $95 per share. It issued 102,600 shares of the common stock for a total of $629,000. The company's retained earnings balance at the beginning of 2014 was $78,000, and net income for the year was $135,000. During 2014, Lehmann declared the specified dividend on preferred and a $0.90 per-share dividend on common. Preferred dividends for 2013 were in arrears.

Requirement

1. Prepare the stockholders' equity section of Lehmann Corp.'s balance sheet at December 31, 2014. Show the computation of all amounts. Journal entries are not required.

P10-74B. *(Learning Objectives 2, 4: Analyze stockholders' equity and dividends of a corporation)* Martin Outdoor Furniture Company included the following stockholders' equity on its year-end balance sheet at February 28, 2015:

Stockholders' Equity

Preferred stock, 5.0% cumulative—par value $25 per share authorized 140,000 shares in each class	
Class A—issued 75,000 shares	$ 1,875,000
Class B—issued 94,000 shares......................................	2,350,000
Common stock—$5 par value: authorized 1,400,000 shares,	
issued 268,000 shares..	1,340,000
Additional paid-in capital—common	4,560,000
Retained earnings..	8,470,000
	$18,595,000

Requirements

1. Identify the different issues of stock that Martin Outdoor Furniture Company has outstanding.
2. Give the summary entries to record issuance of all the Martin stock. Assume that all the stock was issued for cash. Explanations are not required.

3. Suppose Martin passed its preferred dividends for three years. Would the company have to pay these dividends in arrears before paying dividends to the common stockholders? Give your reasons.
4. What amount of preferred dividends must Martin declare and pay each year to avoid having preferred dividends in arrears?
5. Assume that preferred dividends are in arrears for 2014. Journalize the declaration of an $832,000 dividend on February 28, 2015. An explanation is not required.

P10-75B. *(Learning Objectives 2, 3, 4: Account for stock issuance, dividends, and treasury stock)*
London Jewelry Company reported the following summarized balance sheet at December 31, 2014:

Assets	
Current assets	$ 59,400
Property and equipment, net	101,300
Total assets	$160,700
Liabilities and Equity	
Liabilities	$ 34,500
Stockholders' equity:	
$0.40 cumulative preferred stock, $10 par, 800 shares issued	8,000
Common stock, $8 par, 6,700 shares issued	53,600
Paid-in capital in excess of par—common	18,600
Retained earnings	46,000
Total liabilities and equity	$160,700

During 2015, London Jewelry completed the following transactions that affected stockholders' equity:

Feb	13	Issued 6,200 shares of common stock for $11 per share.
Jun	7	Declared the regular cash dividend on the preferred stock.
	24	Paid the cash dividend.
Aug	9	Declared and distributed a 5% stock dividend on the common stock. Market price of the common stock was $15 per share.
Oct	26	Reacquired 200 shares of common stock as treasury stock, paying $17 per share.
Nov	20	Sold 50 shares of the treasury stock for $19 per share.
Dec	31	Declared a cash dividend of $0.25 per share on the outstanding common stock; dividends will be paid in January, 2016.

Requirements

1. Journalize London Jewelry's transactions. Explanations are not required.
2. Report London Jewelry's stockholders' equity at December 31, 2015. Net income for 2015 was $31,000.

P10-76B. *(Learning Objectives 3, 4, 6: Measure the effects of stock-related transactions on a company)* Assume Mable's of Montana, Inc., completed the following transactions during 2014, the company's 10th year of operations:

Feb	3	Issued 10,000 shares of common stock ($3.00 par) for cash of $297,000.
Mar	19	Purchased 2,700 shares of the company's own common stock at $31 per share.
Apr	24	Sold 1,400 shares of treasury stock for $32 per share.
Aug	15	Declared a cash dividend on the 16,000 shares of $0.50 no-par preferred stock.
Sep	1	Paid the cash dividends.
Nov	22	Declared and distributed a 20% stock dividend on the 94,000 shares of $3.00 par common stock outstanding. The market value of the common stock was $35 per share.

Requirements

1. Analyze each transaction in terms of its effect on the accounting equation of Mable's of Montana, Inc.
2. What impact did each transaction have on cash flows?

P10-77B. *(Learning Objectives 4, 5: Prepare a corporation's balance sheet; measure profitability)* The following accounts and related balances of Hunt Designers, Inc., as of December 31, 2014, are arranged in no particular order:

Cash	$53,000	Interest expense	$ 16,200
Accounts receivable, net	27,000	Property, plant, and	
Paid-in capital in excess		equipment, net	355,000
of par—common	75,600	Common stock, $2 par,	
Accrued liabilities	25,000	1,250,000 shares authorized,	
Long-term note payable	95,000	118,000 shares issued	236,000
Inventory	98,000	Prepaid expenses	14,000
Dividends payable	6,000	Common stockholders'	
Retained earnings	?	equity, December 31, 2013	233,000
Accounts payable	130,000	Net income	71,000
Trademarks, net	3,000	Total assets,	
Goodwill	18,000	December 31, 2013	495,000
		Treasury stock, common,	
		8,000 shares at cost	25,000
		Net sales	800,000

Requirements

1. Prepare Hunt's classified balance sheet in the account format at December 31, 2014.
2. Use DuPont Analysis to compute rate of return on total assets and rate of return on common stockholders' equity for the year ended December 31, 2014.
3. Do these rates of return suggest strength or weakness? Give your reason. What additional information might help you make your decision?

P10-78B. *(Learning Objective 5: Analyze a statement of stockholders' equity)* Medical Specialties, Inc., reported the following statement of stockholders' equity for the year ended October 31, 2014:

	A	B	C	D	E	F
		Common Stock	Additional Paid-in Capital	Retained Earnings	Treasury Stock	Total
1	**Medical Specialties, Inc.** **Statement of Stockholders' Equity** **For the Year Ended October 31, 2014**					
2	(In millions)					
3						
4	**Balance, October 31, 2013**	$ 470	$ 1,610	$ 911	$ (118)	$ 2,873
5	Net income			350		350
6	Cash dividends			(195)		(195)
7	Issuance of stock (40 shares)	80	100			180
8	Stock dividend	55	69	(124)		—
9	Sale of treasury stock		12		7	19
10	**Balance, October 31, 2014**	$ 605	$ 1,791	$ 942	$ (111)	$ 3,227
11						

Requirements

Answer these questions about Medical Specialties' stockholders' equity transactions.

1. What is the par value of the company's common stock?
2. At what price per share did Medical Specialties issue its common stock during the year?
3. What was the cost of treasury stock sold during the year? What was the selling price of the treasury stock sold? What was the increase in total stockholders' equity?
4. Medical Specialties' statement of stockholders' equity lists the stock transactions in the order in which they occurred. What was the percentage of the stock dividend? Round to the nearest percentage.

Challenge Exercises and Problem

E10-79. *(Learning Objectives 2, 3, 4: Reconstruct transactions from the financial statements)* I-9 Networking Solutions began operations on January 1, 2014, and immediately issued its stock, receiving cash. I-9's balance sheet at December 31, 2014, reported the following stockholders' equity:

Common stock, $1 par......................	$ 56,000
Additional paid-in capital..................	394,400
Retained earnings.............................	41,000
Treasury stock, 500 shares................	(2,000)
Total stockholders' equity............	$489,400

During 2014, I-9

    a. issued stock for $8 per share.
    b. purchased 800 shares of treasury stock, paying $4 per share.
    c. resold some of the treasury stock.
    d. declared and paid cash dividends.

Requirement

1. Journalize all of I-9's stockholders' equity transactions during the year. I-9's entry to close net income to Retained Earnings was

	A	B	C	D
1		Revenues	177,000	
2		Expenses		112,000
3		Retained Earnings		65,000
4				

E10-80. *(Learning Objective 6: Report financing activities on the statement of cash flows)* Use the I-9 Networking Solutions data in E10-79 to show how the company reported cash flows from financing activities during 2014.

E10-81. *(Learning Objectives 2, 3, 4: Account for issuance of stock and treasury stock; explain the changes in stockholders' equity)* Trufante Corporation reported the following stockholders' equity data (all dollars in millions except par value per share):

	A	B	C
		December 31,	
1		2014	2013
2	Preferred stock	$ 606	$ 738
3	Common stock, $1 par value	900	885
4	Additional paid-in capital—common	1,496	1,466
5	Retained earnings	20,661	19,104
6	Treasury stock, common	(2,800)	(2,640)
7			

Trufante earned net income of $2,920 during 2014. For each account except Retained Earnings, one transaction explains the change from the December 31, 2013, balance to the December 31, 2014, balance. Two transactions affected Retained Earnings. Give a full explanation, including the dollar amount, for the change in each account.

E10-82. *(Learning Objectives 2, 3, 4: Account for issuance of stock, treasury stock, and other changes in stockholders' equity)* Barkley Sales, Inc., ended 2014 with 10 million shares of $1 par common stock issued and outstanding. Beginning additional paid-in capital was $9 million, and retained earnings totaled $44 million.

- In April 2015, Barkley Sales issued 9 million shares of common stock at a price of $2 per share.
- In June, the company declared and distributed a 10% stock dividend at a time when Barkley's common stock had a market value of $12 per share.
- Then in September, Barkley's stock price dropped to $1 per share and the company purchased 9 million shares of treasury stock.
- For the year, Barkley Sales earned net income of $24 million and declared cash dividends of $13 million.

Requirement

1. Complete the following tabulation to show what Barkley Sales should report for stockholders' equity at December 31, 2015. Journal entries are not required.

(Amounts in millions)	Common Stock	+	Additional Paid-In Capital	+	Retained Earnings	−	Treasury Stock	=	Total Equity
Balance, Dec 31, 2014......................	$10		$9		$44		0		$63
Issuance of stock									
Stock dividend.................................									
Purchase of treasury stock................									
Net income.......................................									
Cash dividends.................................									
Balance, Dec 31, 2015......................									

P10-83. *(Learning Objective 5: Analyze information from stockholders' equity)* The stockholders' equity of All-Star Uniforms as of December 31, 2014 and 2013, follows:

	2014	2013
Common stock, 2,000,000 shares authorized, 1,000,000 and 950,000 shares issued, respectively	$ 100,000	$ 95,000
Paid-in capital in excess of par	39,980,000	37,905,000
Paid-in capital-treasury stock transactions	55,000	50,000
Retained earnings	67,000,000	60,000,000
Treasury stock, at cost, 20,000 and 25,000 shares, respectively	(792,000)	(990,000)
Total stockholders' equity	$106,343,000	$97,060,000

Requirements

1. What is the par value of the common stock?
2. How many shares of common stock were outstanding at the end of 2014?
3. As of December 31, 2014, what was the average price that stockholders paid for all common stock when issued?
4. Prepare a summary journal entry to record the change in common stock during the year.
5. What was the average price that stockholders paid for the common stock issued in 2014?
6. What was the average price paid by All-Star for the treasury stock at December 31, 2014?
7. Prepare a summary journal entry to record the change in treasury stock during the year.
8. Assuming net income for 2014 was $10,000,000, prepare a summary journal entry to record the dividends declared during 2014.

APPLY YOUR KNOWLEDGE

Decision Cases

Case 1. *(Learning Objectives 2, 6: Evaluate alternative ways of raising capital)* Nate Smith and Darla Jones have written a computer program for a video game that may rival PlayStation and Xbox. They need additional capital to market the product, and they plan to incorporate their business. Smith and Jones are considering alternative capital structures for the corporation. Their primary goal is to raise as much capital as possible without giving up control of the business. Smith and Jones plan to receive 50,000 shares of the corporation's common stock in return for the net assets of their old business. After the old company's books are closed and the assets are adjusted to current market value, Smith's and Jones's capital balances will each be $25,000.

The corporation's plans for a charter include an authorization to issue 10,000 shares of preferred stock and 500,000 shares of $1 par common stock. Smith and Jones are uncertain about the most desirable features for the preferred stock. Prior to incorporating, Smith and Jones are discussing their plans with two investment groups. The corporation can obtain capital from outside investors under either of the following plans:

■ *Plan 1.* Group 1 will invest $80,000 to acquire 800 shares of 6%, $100 par, nonvoting, preferred stock.

■ *Plan 2.* Group 2 will invest $55,000 to acquire 500 shares of $5, no-par preferred stock and $35,000 to acquire 35,000 shares of common stock. Each preferred share receives 50 votes on matters that come before the stockholders.

Requirements

Assume that the corporation is chartered.

1. Journalize the issuance of common stock to Smith and Jones. Debit each person's capital account for its balance.
2. Journalize the issuance of stock to the outsiders under both plans.
3. Assume that net income for the first year is $120,000 and total dividends are $30,000. Prepare the stockholders' equity section of the corporation's balance sheet under both plans.
4. Recommend one of the plans to Smith and Jones. Give your reasons. (Challenge)

Case 2. *(Learning Objective 4: Analyze cash dividends and stock dividends)* **United Parcel Service (UPS), Inc.,** had the following stockholders' equity amounts on December 31, 2014 (adapted, in millions):

Common stock and additional paid-in capital; 1,135 shares issued	$ 278
Retained earnings	9,457
Total stockholders' equity	$9,735

During 2014, UPS paid a cash dividend of $0.715 per share. Assume that, after paying the cash dividends, UPS distributed a 10% stock dividend. Assume also that during the following year, UPS declared and paid a cash dividend of $0.65 per share.

Suppose you own 10,000 shares of UPS common stock, acquired three years ago, prior to the 10% stock dividend. The market price of UPS stock was $61.02 per share before the stock dividend.

Requirements

1. How does the stock dividend affect your proportionate ownership in UPS? Explain.
2. What amount of cash dividends did you receive last year? What amount of cash dividends will you receive after the above dividend action?
3. Assume that immediately after the stock dividend was distributed, the market value of UPS's stock decreased from $61.02 per share to $55.473 per share. Does this decrease represent a loss to you? Explain.
4. Suppose UPS announces at the time of the stock dividend that the company will continue to pay the annual $0.715 *cash* dividend per share, even after distributing the *stock* dividend. Would you expect the market price of the stock to decrease to $55.473 per share as in requirement 3? Explain.

Ethical Issues

Ethical Issue 1. (*Note:* This case is based on a real situation.) George Campbell paid $50,000 for a franchise that entitled him to market Success Associates software programs in the countries of the European Union. Campbell intended to sell individual franchises for the major language groups of western Europe—German, French, English, Spanish, and Italian. Naturally, investors considering buying a franchise from Campbell asked to see the financial statements of his business.

Believing the value of the franchise to be greater than $50,000, Campbell sought to capitalize his own franchise at $500,000. The law firm of McDonald & LaDue helped Campbell form a corporation chartered to issue 500,000 shares of common stock with par value of $1 per share. Attorneys suggested the following chain of transactions:

   a. A third party borrows $500,000 and purchases the franchise from Campbell.
   b. Campbell pays the corporation $500,000 to acquire all its stock.
   c. The corporation buys the franchise from the third party, who repays the loan.

In the final analysis, the third party is debt-free and out of the picture. Campbell owns all of the corporation's stock, and the corporation owns the franchise. The corporation balance sheet lists a franchise acquired at a cost of $500,000. This balance sheet is Campbell's most valuable marketing tool.

Requirements

1. What is the ethical issue in this situation?
2. Who are the stakeholders in the suggested transaction?
3. Analyze this case from the following standpoints: (a) economic, (b) legal, and (c) ethical. What are the consequences to each stakeholder?
4. How should the transaction be reported?

Ethical Issue 2. St. Genevieve Petroleum Company is an independent oil producer in Baton Parish, Louisiana. In February, company geologists discovered a pool of oil that tripled the company's proven reserves. Prior to disclosing the new oil to the public, St. Genevieve quietly bought most of its stock as treasury stock. After the discovery was announced, the company's stock price increased from $6 to $27.

Requirements

1. What is the ethical issue in this situation? What accounting principle is involved?
2. Who are the stakeholders?
3. Analyze the facts from the following standpoints: (a) economic, (b) legal, and (c) ethical. What is the impact on each stakeholder?
4. What decision would you have made?

Focus on Financials | Amazon.com, Inc.

(Learning Objectives 2, 3, 5: Analyze common stock, retained earnings, return on equity, and return on assets) **Amazon.com's** consolidated financial statements appear in Appendix A at the end of this book.

1. Refer to Amazon's Consolidated Balance Sheets and Note 9 (Stockholders' Equity). Describe the classes of stock that Amazon.com, Inc., has authorized. How many shares of each class have been issued as of December 31, 2012? How many are outstanding as of December 31, 2012?
2. Refer to the Consolidated Balance Sheets and the Consolidated Statements of Stockholders' Equity. How many shares of treasury stock did the company purchase during the year ended December 31, 2012? What was the cost of the treasury stock? How much per share?
3. Examine Amazon.com's Consolidated Statement of Stockholders' Equity. Analyze the change that occurred in the company's Retained Earnings account during the year ended December 31, 2012. Can you trace the change to any of its other financial statements? Is this a good thing or a bad thing?
4. Use DuPont Analysis to compute Amazon.com's return on equity and return on assets for 2012. Pick a company that is a competitor of Amazon.com and compute these ratios for the competitor. Which ratios are similar? Which are different? Which company do you think is more profitable? Explain.

Focus on Analysis | Yum! Brands, Inc.

(Learning Objectives 2, 3, 4: Analyze treasury stock and retained earnings) This case is based on the consolidated financial statements of **Yum! Brands, Inc.** given in Appendix B at the end of this book. In particular, this case uses Yum! Brands, Inc.'s Consolidated Statement of Shareholders' Equity for the year 2012.

1. As of the end of December 31, 2012, how many shares of common stock does Yum! Brands, Inc., have authorized? Issued? Outstanding?
2. During 2012, Yum! Brands, Inc., purchased treasury stock. How many shares did it purchase? How much did it pay for the stock? What was the average price paid per share? Compare the price it paid for these shares with the market price of the company's stock today. Use any of the popular websites to look up the price of the stock. Does it look like the company got a "good deal" on the purchase of its stock? Why do you think the company purchased the shares? Do the financial statement footnotes give any clues? (Challenge)
3. Did Yum! Brands, Inc., issue any new shares of common stock during 2012? How can you tell? (Challenge)
4. Prepare a T-account to show the beginning and ending balances plus all the activity in Retained Earnings for 2012.

Group Project in Ethics

The global economic recession that started in 2007, and that persists in certain sectors, has impacted every business, but it was especially hard on banks, automobile manufacturing, and retail companies. Banks were largely responsible for the recession. Some of the biggest banks made excessively risky investments collateralized by real estate mortgages, and many of these investments soured when the real estate markets collapsed. When banks had to write these investments down to market values, the regulatory authorities notified them that they had inadequate capital ratios on their balance sheets to operate. Banks stopped loaning money. Because stock prices were depressed, companies could not raise capital by selling stock. With both debt and stock financing frozen, many businesses had to close their doors.

Fearing collapse of the whole economy, the central governments of the United States and several European nations loaned money to banks to prop up their capital ratios and keep them open. The government also loaned massive amounts to the largest insurance company in the United States (AIG) as well as to General Motors and Chrysler to help them stay in business. When asked why, many in government replied "these businesses were too important to fail." In several cases, the U.S. government has taken an "equity stake" in some banks and businesses by taking preferred stock in exchange for the cash infusion.

Because of the recession, corporate downsizing has occurred on a massive scale throughout the world. Although companies in the retail sector provide more jobs than the banking and automobile industry combined, the government has not chosen to "bail out" any retail businesses. Each company or industry mentioned in this book has pared down plant and equipment, laid off employees, or restructured operations. Some companies have been forced out of business altogether.

Requirements

1. Identify all the stakeholders of a corporation. A *stakeholder* is a person or a group who has an interest (that is, a stake) in the success of the organization.
2. Do you believe that some entities are "too important to fail"? Should the federal government help certain businesses to stay afloat during economic recessions and allow others to fail?
3. Identify several measures by which a company may be considered deficient and in need of downsizing. How can downsizing help to solve this problem?
4. Debate the bailout issue. One group of students takes the perspective of the company and its stockholders, and another group of students takes the perspective of the other stakeholders of the company (the community in which the company operates and society at large).
5. What is the problem with the government taking an equity position such as preferred stock in a private enterprise?

> **For online homework, exercises, and problems that provide you with immediate feedback, please visit www.myaccountinglab.com.**

Quick Check Answers

1. c (10,000 shares $\times$ \$2 = \$20,000)

2. a (\$200,000/\$1 par = 200,000 shares)

3. b (\$150,000 + \$100,000 + \$200,000)

4. d (\$150,000 + \$100,000 + \$200,000 + \$400,000)

5. a (\$850,000 − \$25,000)

6. d [No gain or loss (for the income statement) on treasury stock transactions]

7. c

8. b

9. d

10. d

11. a [First, annual preferred dividend = \$6,000 (3,000 $\times$ \$40 $\times$ 0.05)]. Five years of preferred dividends must be paid (four in arrears plus the current year). [(\$6,000 $\times$ 5) + (140,000 $\times$ \$1.50 per share common dividend) = \$240,000]

12. b

13. c

14. c

15. c

16. b

11

Evaluating Performance: Earnings Quality, the Income Statement, & the Statement of Comprehensive Income

> **SPOTLIGHT:** The Gap, Inc.: What a Difference a Year Makes!

Steve Vidler/Alamy

The Gap, Inc., is truly a case study in how a company has to adapt to changing market conditions in order to prosper in a highly competitive global economy. And what a difference a year can make! Turn back to Chapter 1's opening discussion. There we featured the financial statements of The Gap, Inc. for its fiscal 2011 year (ended January 28, 2012). The consolidated statements of income in that chapter showed flat sales combined with increased cost of goods sold and occupancy expenses, resulting in a 31% decline in net income compared to the 2010 fiscal year—not good news. The company responded with a renewed commitment to serve the needs of customers while delivering "quality earnings and long-term value to shareholders." Several years ago, The Gap, Inc., began adding stores in China, the world's largest developing economy with a huge and growing middle class, as well as in fashion-conscious Italy. The company also began adding to its online sales capability. What were the results of these efforts in fiscal 2012? Exhibit 11-1 on the next page presents the company's consolidated statements of earnings for the fiscal 2012 year (ended February 2, 2013). The change from fiscal 2011 is very impressive. Improved product performance and continued global expansion helped drive a 7.6% increase in net sales from the previous year while holding cost of goods sold and occupancy expenses to only a 2.2% increase. Glenn Murphy, chairman and CEO, stated, "Our results in 2012 were stellar in many ways, and I'm very pleased with how well our product resonated with customers. We enter 2013 focused on leveraging our global brands to gain more market share and continuing to increase shareholder value."[1] However, although sales revenues jumped significantly, the company's gross profit percentage of 39.4% ($6,171 million ÷ $15,651 million) in fiscal 2012 was still below the 40.2% gross profit margin ($5,889 million ÷ $14,664 million) achieved in fiscal 2010. Because operating results from The

---

[1]Gap, Inc. Reports Fourth Quarter Earnings Per Share Increase of 66 percent. The Street.com, 2/28/2013.

Exhibit 11-1 | The Gap, Inc., Consolidated Statements of Income

	A	B	C	D
	A1			
	The Gap, Inc.			
1	**Consolidated Statements of Income (Adapted)**	**Fiscal 2012**	**Fiscal 2011**	**Fiscal 2010**
2		**12 Months Ended**		
3	**($ and shares in millions, except per share amounts)**	**Feb. 02, 2013**	**Jan. 28, 2012**	**Jan. 29, 2011**
4	Net sales	$ 15,651	$ 14,549	$ 14,664
5	Cost of goods sold and occupancy expenses	9,480	9,275	8,775
6	Gross profit	6,171	5,274	5,889
7	Operating expenses	4,229	3,836	3,921
8	Operating income	1,942	1,438	1,968
9	Interest (expense)	(87)	(74)	8
10	Interest income	6	5	6
11	Income before income taxes	1,861	1,369	1,982
12	Income taxes	726	536	778
13	Net income	$ 1,135	$ 833	$ 1,204
14				
15	Weighted-average number of shares—basic	482	529	636
16	Weighted-average number of shares—diluted	488	533	641
17				
18	Earnings per share—basic (in dollars per share)	$ 2.35	$ 1.57	$ 1.89
19	Earnings per share—diluted (in dollars per share)	$ 2.33	$ 1.56	$ 1.88
20				
21	Cash dividends declared and paid per share	$ 0.50	$ 0.45	$ 0.40
22				

Gap, Inc., have followed a see-saw pattern, rather than a steady, even climb for several years, the market may not view The Gap, Inc., as favorably as some other companies for investment.

An interesting fact you may not know about The Gap, Inc., is the significant work the company is doing in the area of corporate social responsibility (CSR), a nonfinancial measure of performance that is becoming more important as a perceived measure of success. The company has set goals in four key areas to measure and improve its performance in being a good corporate citizen: its supply chain, the environment, its employees, and community investment. Each year, The Gap, Inc., along with many others like **The Home Depot, Inc.**, and **Starbucks Corporation** (focus companies in other chapters), issues a separate report on CSR. ●

When you finish this chapter, you will have a better understanding of earnings quality and how you can use a company's income statement (including footnotes) to estimate it. In addition, you'll learn about some other emerging ways to measure a company's performance that are not directly related to a company's earnings.

This chapter builds on your understanding of the corporate income statement. After studying this chapter, you will have seen all the types of items that typically appear on an income statement. You'll study the components of *income from operations,* which is the basis for many analysts' predictions about companies' future operations, as well as their current values. You'll learn to use information in the current financial statements, as well as the footnotes, to help decide whether to invest in a particular stock. You'll learn about how and why companies typically report income from discontinued operations separately from operating income. You'll also learn how conducting international business transactions in foreign currencies impacts net income. The chapter provides information about earnings per share, the most often-mentioned statistic in business, and about how to construct the statement of comprehensive income, which includes certain gains and losses that are allowed to bypass the income statement; they will eventually be reported as an element of stockholders' equity. Finally, you'll have a chance to see some reports issued by management and the company's auditors regarding both financial and nonfinancial measures of performance. The knowledge you get from this chapter will help you analyze financial statements and use the information in decision making.

We begin with a basic question: How do we evaluate the quality of a company's earnings? The term *quality of earnings* refers to the characteristics of an earnings number that make it most useful for decision making.

Learning Objectives

1. **Evaluate** quality of earnings

2. **Account** for foreign-currency gains and losses

3. **Account** for other items on the income statement

4. **Compute** earnings per share

5. **Analyze** the statement of comprehensive income, footnotes, and supplemental disclosures

6. **Differentiate** management's and auditors' reporting responsibilities

EVALUATE QUALITY OF EARNINGS

A corporation's net income, or net earnings (including earnings per share), receives more attention than any other single item in the financial statements. To stockholders, the larger the net income, the greater the likelihood of dividends. In addition, a steady and upward trend in *persistent* earnings generally translates sooner or later to a higher stock price.

1   **Evaluate** quality of earnings

Suppose you are considering investing in either the stock of **The Gap, Inc.**, or another major retailer. How do you make the decision? A knowledgeable investor will want to assess each company's **earnings quality**. The higher the quality of earnings in the current period as compared to its recent past, the more likely it is that the company is executing a successful business strategy to generate healthy earnings in the future, which is a key component in its stock price.

There are many components of earnings quality. Among the most prominent are (1) proper revenue and expense recognition; (2) high and persistently improving gross margin/sales ratio; (3) declining or stable operating expenses compared to sales; and (4) high and persistently improving operating earnings/sales ratio. To explore the makeup and the quality of earnings, let's examine its various sources. Exhibit 11-1 shows the Consolidated Statements of Income of The Gap, Inc., for fiscal years 2012, 2011, and 2010. We'll use these statements as a basis for our discussion of earnings quality.

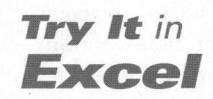

»   ***Try It** in* **Excel**

You can access the most current annual report of The Gap, Inc. in Excel format at **www.sec.gov**. Using the "filings" link on the toolbar at the top of the home page, select "company filings search." This will take you to the "Edgar Company Filings" page. Type "Gap" in the company name box, and select "search." This will produce the "EDGAR Search Results" page showing the company name. Click on the "CIK" link beside the company name. This will pull up all of the reports the company has filed with the SEC. Under the "filing type" box, type "10-K" and click the search box. Form 10-K is the SEC form for the company's latest annual report. Find the year that you wish to view. Click on the "Interactive Data" box, which takes you to the "View Filing Data" page. Find and click on the "View Excel Document" link at the top of this page. You may choose to either open or download the Excel files containing the company's most recent financial statements. ■

Revenue Recognition

The first component of earnings quality is proper recognition of net revenue, or *net sales*. You learned about revenue in Chapters 3 through 5. The *revenue principle*, discussed in Chapter 3 (p. 116), states that, under accrual accounting, revenue should be recognized when it is *earned*. For a retail business, revenue is generally considered earned when the selling business has fulfilled its obligation to either deliver the product or the service to the customer. In recognizing revenue, several important events usually have to occur: (1) The seller delivers the product or service to the customer; (2) the customer takes ownership of the product or service; and (3) the seller either collects cash or is reasonably assured of collecting the cash in the near future. In Chapter 4 (pp. 215–216), you learned about the importance of internal controls over the processes by which revenue is recognized and by which cash collections are entered into the accounting system. In Chapter 5 (pp. 254–256), you learned that net sales is the difference between gross sales and reductions made by sales returns and sales discounts. You also learned that credit sales, or sales on account, have to go through the process of collection, that some will ultimately not be collectible, and that a company must make an allowance for doubtful accounts. You studied the concept of *free on board* (FOB) terms, which governs the issue of who owns the goods during the shipment process, and therefore the timing of revenue. You must understand all of these concepts in order to grasp the meaning of proper revenue recognition.

Proper revenue recognition in a retail business like The Gap, Inc., is relatively straightforward. As explained in its Notes to Consolidated Financial Statements, The Gap, Inc., recognizes revenue as well as related cost of goods sold at the time customers receive the products. In the stores, revenue is recognized at the registers when the customers receive and pay for merchandise. For online sales (which in fiscal 2012 comprise about $1.9 billion, or 12% of total sales), the company has to estimate how long it takes the merchandise to reach customers by mail or courier. For both over-the-counter and online sales, the company estimates an allowance for returns and deducts it from gross sales to report *net sales*.

Let's examine Exhibit 11-1, and analyze the trend in The Gap's Net sales revenue (in millions, line 4). Notice that, over the past three years, Net sales for the company have followed a see-saw pattern. From fiscal year 2010 to 2011, Net sales declined from $14,664 million to $14,549 million (about 1%). Then, in fiscal 2012, Net sales jumped to $15,651 million (7.6% over 2011 and 6.7% over 2010). Same-store sales for all divisions, a key factor in growth for retail stores, increased for all four quarterly periods in 2012 compared with 2011. Sales to franchise stores (owned by other companies and not The Gap, Inc., but operated under its name) increased by 17%. The company opened 25 Althea stores, 33 Gap and outlet stores in China, and the first Old Navy store in Japan. All of these changes, obtained from reading the footnotes to the financial statements, as well as management's discussion and analysis, signal growth.

The real key to The Gap, Inc.'s future as an investment is whether it can continue growing its top line and break out of the see-saw pattern it has experienced for several years. Intense competition from other specialty retailers, as well as the frenetic pace of specialty fashion retailing, all present challenges to overcome. As a rule, markets tend to react negatively to volatile revenue patterns. The Gap, Inc.'s stock price, like that of other specialty retailers, has been no exception, fluctuating from a low of about $15.50 per share to a high of more than $38 per share over the three-year period.

Global View The FASB and IASB have reached agreement on a new standard, to be issued in 2013, that will bring the revenue recognition standards of the two bodies into much closer harmony and consistency than existed under previous standards. The new proposed standard, discussed in Chapter 3, has no impact on the material covered in this course, since the standards for revenue recognition in the retail industry were already closely aligned globally. You may cover the new standard in more detail in later accounting courses.

Cooking the Books **with Revenue**

Research has shown that roughly one-half of all financial statement fraud over the past two decades has involved improper revenue recognition.[2] Several of the more significant revenue recognition issues involving fraud, from the SEC's files follow:

■ *Recognizing revenue prematurely (before it is earned).* One of the common fraud techniques is **channel stuffing**, in which a company may ship inventory to regular customers in excess of amounts ordered. **Bristol-Myers Squibb**, a global pharmaceuticals company, was sued by the SEC in 2004 for channel stuffing during 2000 and 2001. The company allegedly stuffed its distribution channels with excess inventory near the end of every quarter in amounts sufficient to meet company sales targets (tied to executive bonuses), overstating revenue by about $1.5 billion. The company paid a civil fine of $100 million and established a $50 million fund to compensate shareholders for their losses.[3]

■ *Providing incentives for customers to purchase more inventory than is needed.* Incentives are given in exchange for future discounts and other benefits.

■ *Reporting revenue when significant services are still to be performed or goods are still to be delivered.*

■ *Reporting sales to fictitious or nonexistent customers.* This may include falsified shipping and inventory records.

Cost of Goods Sold and Gross Profit (Gross Margin)

After revenue, the next two important components in earnings quality are cost of goods sold and the resulting gross profit. Before we get to these components, however, it is important to emphasize that, just as avoiding premature or improper revenue recognition is important, it is equally important to make sure that *all expenses are accurately, completely, and transparently included* in the computation of net income. We saw with the example of the WorldCom fraud in Chapter 7 what can happen when a company manipulates reported earnings by deliberately understating expenses. Without the integrity that comes through full and complete disclosures of all existing expenses, and without recognizing those expenses in the proper periods, trends in earnings are at best meaningless and, at worst, downright misleading.

Cost of Goods Sold. As we learned in Chapter 6, cost of goods sold represents the direct cost of the goods sold to customers. In the case of The Gap, Inc., Cost of goods sold also includes

---

[2]*CPA Letter* (February 2003). American Institute of Certified Public Accountants. See www.aicpa.org/pubs/cpaltr/feb2003/financial.htm.

[3]Accounting and Auditing Enforcement Release No. 2075, August 4, 2004. *Securities and Exchange Commission v. Bristol-Myers Squibb Company*, 04-3680 DNJ (2004). See www.sec.gov/news/press/2004-105.htm.

the cost of occupying the space used to sell the product, or store rent. As shown on line 5 of Exhibit 11-1, Cost of goods sold and occupancy expenses represents the largest single operating expense for The Gap, Inc. Cost of goods sold and occupancy expenses as a percentage of sales rose from about 60% in fiscal 2010 to about 63.8% in fiscal 2011, then fell again to about 60.6% in fiscal 2012. In general, assuming cost of goods sold is accurately measured each period, steadily decreasing cost of goods sold as a percentage of net sales revenue is generally regarded as a sign of increasing earnings quality. This is usually accomplished through development of effective marketing strategies, establishment of a consistent supply chain for inventory purchases, and promoting long-term relationships with reliable vendors. Like other major retailers, The Gap, Inc.'s Cost of goods sold includes store occupancy expenses (rent). Controlling occupancy expense is usually a matter of effectively negotiating leases for new and established stores. Unfortunately, The Gap, Inc., has not always been able to perfectly control its store rents, which has contributed to an erratic cost pattern over the past several years.

Gross Profit (Gross Margin). Gross profit (Gross margin) represents the difference between Net sales and Cost of goods sold. Conversely, with steadily decreasing cost of goods sold, steadily increasing gross profit as a percentage of net sales revenue is considered a sign of increasing earnings quality. For The Gap, Inc., Gross profit decreased from 40.2% ($5,889/$14,664) in fiscal 2010 to 36.2% ($5,274/$14,549) in fiscal 2011 and increased to 39.4% ($6,171/$15,651) in fiscal 2012 (line 6 of Exhibit 11-1, all dollar amounts in millions). Fluctuating costs for The Gap, Inc.'s inventory purchases and store occupancy expenses are the culprit. The same general comments apply here as in our previous discussion of cost of goods sold.

Operating and Other Expenses

As implied in the title, operating expenses are the ongoing expenses incurred by the entity, other than direct expenses for merchandise and other costs directly related to sales. The largest operating expenses generally include salaries, wages, utilities, and supplies. Again, given that the entity takes care to accurately measure operating expenses, the lower these costs are relative to sales, we can assume management is operating the business more efficiently and, therefore, more profitably. As shown in line 7 of Exhibit 11-1, operating expenses of The Gap, Inc., have followed a rather stable pattern in relation to sales over the three-year period. From fiscal 2010 through fiscal 2012, operating expenses (in millions) were $3,921; $3,836; and $4,229 respectively. This kept operating expenses consistently in the range of 26.4% to 27% of net sales. When companies experience revenue difficulties, it is wise to try to trim fat from operations by cutting back on costs. The trick is knowing when and how much to cut, because indiscriminate cost cutting can erode perceived quality of the company's product or service, further damaging the bottom line. The Gap, Inc., apparently figured this out years ago, because its operating expenses as a percentage of net sales have been consistent for several years longer than is reflected in the fiscal 2010 through 2012 financial statements.

Operating Income (Earnings)

Given the integrity that comes with accuracy and transparency of reported revenues and expenses, a trend of high and persistently improving operating earnings in relation to net sales reflects increasing earnings quality. Operating income is a function of all of its individual ingredients: sales revenue, cost of goods sold, gross margin (gross profit), and operating expenses. For The Gap, Inc., because Net sales and Cost of goods sold and occupancy expenses have fluctuated, Operating income has also fluctuated. In fiscal 2010, it was $1,968 million (13.4% of net sales); in fiscal 2011, it fell to $1,438 million (9.9% of net sales); in fiscal 2012, it jumped to $1,942 million (12.4% of net sales). It is worth noting that fiscal 2012's rate of increase in operating income (2.5%) was the healthiest the company had seen in years. However, for reasons we have discussed throughout this section, there are doubts as to whether the company can continue to improve its operating earnings over the long term. As a matter of fact, if you analyzed the trend for the five years preceding fiscal 2012, you would see that the trend in the company's operating earnings has been erratic.

ACCOUNT FOR FOREIGN-CURRENCY GAINS AND LOSSES

International transactions are common in many businesses and can significantly influence reported earnings. Manufacturing of all kinds of products has migrated to places such as China, India, and Southeast Asia, where labor and materials are less costly. Transportation and communications systems, as well as manufacturing processes, have improved to the point at which it has become convenient and cost-effective for retailers to purchase virtually all items for resale from companies in these developing countries. According to The Gap, Inc.'s annual report, the company purchases nearly all of its inventories from sources outside the United States. Sometimes those purchases are made in currencies other than U.S. dollars, such as the Chinese yuan. The Gap, Inc., owns and operates stores in Canada, the United Kingdom, France, Ireland, Japan, China, and Italy. In addition, it has franchise agreements with unaffiliated companies to operate Gap and Banana Republic Stores in many other countries around the world.

2 Account for foreign-currency gains and losses

Dollars versus Foreign Currency

Assume The Gap, Inc., ships clothing and accessories to Republica, an unaffiliated franchise operation with stores in Mexico City, Monterrey, Guadalajara, and Cancun, Mexico. The sale can be made in dollars or in pesos. If Republica agrees to pay in dollars, The Gap, Inc., avoids the complication of dealing in a foreign currency, and the transaction is the same as selling to a Banana Republic store in San Francisco. But suppose Republica orders 1 million pesos (approximately $90,000) worth of inventory from The Gap, Inc., requests to pay in pesos, and The Gap, Inc., agrees to receive pesos in payment of its receivable instead of dollars.

The Gap, Inc., will need to convert the pesos to dollars; so the transaction poses a challenge. What if the peso weakens before The Gap, Inc., collects from the Mexican chain? In that case, The Gap, Inc., will not collect as many dollars as expected. The following example shows how to account for **foreign-currency exchange rate** gains and losses.

The Gap, Inc., sells goods to Republica on account for a price of 1 million pesos on July 28. On that date, a peso is worth $0.086. One month later, on August 28, the peso has weakened against the dollar so that a peso is worth only $0.083. The Gap, Inc., receives 1 million pesos from Republica on August 28, but the dollar value of The Gap, Inc.'s cash receipt is $3,000 less than expected. The Gap, Inc., ends up earning less than hoped for on the transaction. The following journal entries show how The Gap, Inc., would account for these transactions (ignore cost of goods sold):

	A1				
	A	**B**		**C**	**D**
1	Jul 28	Accounts Receivable—Republica (1,000,000 pesos × $0.086)		86,000	
2		Sales Revenue			86,000
3		*Sale on account.*			
4					

	A1				
	A	**B**		**C**	**D**
1	Aug 28	Cash (1,000,000 pesos × $0.083)		83,000	
2		Foreign-Currency Transaction Loss		3,000	
3		Accounts Receivable—Republica			86,000
4		*Collection on account.*			
5					

If The Gap, Inc., had required Republica to pay at the time of the sale, it would have received pesos worth $86,000. But by selling on account, The Gap, Inc., exposed itself to foreign-currency exchange risk. It therefore had a $3,000 *foreign-currency transaction loss* when it received $3,000 less cash than expected. If the peso had increased in value relative to the dollar, The Gap, Inc., would have had a *foreign-currency transaction gain*.

When a company holds a receivable denominated in a foreign currency, it wants the foreign currency to strengthen so that it can be converted into more dollars. Unfortunately, that did not occur for The Gap, Inc., on the sale in this example.

Purchasing in a foreign currency also exposes a company to foreign-currency exchange risk. To illustrate, assume The Gap, Inc., buys a shipment of watches on account from Excel, Ltd., a Swiss company. The price is 20,000 Swiss francs. On September 15, The Gap, Inc., receives the goods and the Swiss franc is quoted at $1.15. When The Gap, Inc., pays two weeks later, the Swiss franc has weakened against the dollar—to $1.10. The Gap, Inc., would record the purchase and payment as

	A	B	C	D
	A1			
1	Sep 15	Inventory (20,000 Swiss francs × $1.15)	23,000	
2		Accounts Payable—Excel, Ltd.		23,000
3		*Purchase on account.*		
4				

	A	B	C	D
	A1			
1	Sep 29	Accounts Payable—Excel, Ltd.	23,000	
2		Cash (20,000 Swiss francs × $1.10)		22,000
3		Foreign-Currency Transaction Gain		1,000
4		*Payment on account.*		
5				

The Swiss franc could have strengthened against the dollar, and The Gap, Inc., would have had a foreign-currency transaction loss. A company with a payable denominated in a foreign currency wants the dollar to get stronger: The payment then costs fewer dollars.

Reporting Foreign-Currency Gains and Losses on the Income Statement

The foreign-currency transaction gain account holds gains on transactions settled in a foreign currency. Likewise, the foreign-currency transaction loss account holds losses on transactions conducted in foreign currencies. Companies report the *net amount* of these two accounts on the income statement as Other Revenues and Gains, or Other Expenses and Losses, as the case may be. For example, assuming the two transactions we just described were the only two during the year, The Gap, Inc., would combine its $3,000 foreign-currency loss and the $1,000 gain and report the net loss of $2,000 on the income statement as

Other Expenses and Losses:
    Foreign-currency transaction loss, net $2,000

These gains and losses fall into the "Other" category because they arise from buying and selling foreign currencies, not from the company's main business. The Gap, Inc.'s foreign-currency losses amounted to $3 million in 2013, according to financial statement footnotes.

Reporting Foreign-Currency Exchange Gains and Losses on Cash and Cash Equivalents in the Statement of Cash Flows

Companies like The Gap, Inc., that maintain cash and cash equivalent balances denominated in foreign currencies are required to report the impact of foreign-currency exchange gains and losses on those balances as a separate line item on the statement of cash flows, directly after net cash provided by financing activities. We will cover this topic further in Chapter 12.

Should We Hedge Our Foreign-Currency-Transaction Risk?

One way for U.S. companies to avoid foreign-currency transaction losses is to insist that international transactions be settled in dollars. This requirement puts the burden of foreign currency translation on the foreign party. But this approach may alienate customers and decrease sales. Another way for a company to protect itself is by hedging. **Hedging** enables the entity to protect itself from losing money in one transaction by engaging in a counterbalancing transaction.

A U.S. company selling goods to be collected in Mexican pesos expects to receive a fixed number of pesos. If the peso is losing value, the U.S. company would expect the pesos to be worth fewer dollars than the amount of the receivable—an expected-loss situation, as we saw for The Gap, Inc.

The U.S. company may have accumulated payables in a foreign currency, such as The Gap, Inc.'s payable to the Swiss company. Losses on pesos may be offset by gains on Swiss francs. Most companies do not have equal amounts of receivables and payables in foreign currencies. To obtain a more precise hedge, companies can buy *futures contracts*. These are contracts for foreign currencies to be received in the future. Futures contracts can create a payable to exactly offset a receivable, and vice versa. Many companies that do business internationally, such as The Gap, Inc., use hedging techniques.

ACCOUNT FOR OTHER ITEMS ON THE INCOME STATEMENT

Interest Expense and Interest Income

Covered in Chapters 5, 8, and 9, respectively, interest income represents the return earned on invested money, and interest expense represents the cost of borrowed money. These items are not related to the company's operating activities, but to financing activities. Thus, they are segregated and reported in a separate section of the income statement. Note 5 to The Gap, Inc.'s consolidated financial statements indicates that the company issued notes payable of approximately $1.6 billion during the year ended January 28, 2012. The company repaid $400 million of these notes during the year ended February 2, 2013, leaving a balance of approximately $1.2 billion. Line 9 of the company's Consolidated Statements of Income reports $87 million and $74 million in interest expense for fiscal 2012 and 2011, respectively. Line 10 reports a very minor amount of interest income.

3 **Account** for other items on the income statement

Corporate Income Taxes

The next important ingredient of reported earnings on the statement of income is corporate income tax expense, which must be subtracted to arrive at net income. The current maximum federal income tax rate for corporations is 35%. In addition, state income taxes run about 5% in many states. The Gap, Inc.'s fiscal 2012 income tax provision (expense) of $726 million amounts to about 39% of earnings before income taxes. Thus, we use a rate of 40% to approximate income taxes in the illustrations that follow.

To account for income tax, the corporation measures

- *income tax expense*, an expense on the income statement. Income tax expense helps measure net income.

- *income tax payable*, a current liability on the balance sheet. Income tax payable is the amount of tax to be paid to the government based on the company's income tax return.

Accounting for income tax follows the principles of accrual accounting. Suppose, at the end of fiscal 2014, The Gap, Inc., reports income before tax (also called **pre-tax accounting income**) of $2 billion. As we saw previously, The Gap, Inc.'s combined income tax rate is close to 40%. To start this discussion, assume income tax expense and income tax payable are the same. Then on

January 31, 2015 (the end of its 2014 fiscal year) The Gap, Inc., would record income tax for the year as follows (amounts in millions):

	A	B	C	D
1	2015	(In millions)		
2	Jan 31	Income Tax Expense ($2,000 × 0.40)	800	
3		Income Tax Payable		800
4		*Recorded income tax for the year.*		
5				

The Gap, Inc.'s financial statements for fiscal 2014 would report these figures (partial, in millions):

Income statement (in millions)		**Balance sheet (in millions)**	
Income before income tax	$2,000	Current liabilities:	
Income tax expense	(800)	Income tax payable	$800
Net income.................................	$1,200		

In general, income tax expense and income tax payable can be computed as

$$\begin{array}{ccc} \text{Income} & \text{Income before} & \text{Income} \\ \text{tax} \quad = & \text{income tax} \quad \times & \text{tax} \\ \textit{expense} & \text{(from the} & \text{rate} \\ & \textit{income} & \\ & \textit{statement)} & \end{array} \qquad \begin{array}{ccc} \text{Income} & \text{Taxable} & \text{Income} \\ \text{tax} \quad = & \text{income tax (from} \quad \times & \text{tax} \\ \textit{payable} & \text{the } \textit{income tax} & \text{rate} \\ & \textit{return} \text{ filed with} & \\ & \text{the IRS)} & \end{array}$$

The income statement and the income tax return are entirely separate documents:

- The *income statement* reports the results of operations.
- The *income tax return* is filed with the Internal Revenue Service (IRS) to measure how much tax to pay the government.

For most companies, income tax expense and income tax payable differ. Some revenues and expenses affect income differently for accounting and for tax purposes. The most common difference between accounting income and **taxable income** occurs when a corporation uses straight-line depreciation in its financial statements and accelerated depreciation for the tax return.

Continuing with the The Gap, Inc., illustration, suppose for fiscal 2014 that it had

- pre-tax accounting income of $2 billion on its income statement, and
- taxable income of $1,600 million on its income tax return.

Taxable income is less than accounting income because The Gap, Inc., uses

- straight-line depreciation for accounting purposes (say, $200 million), and
- accelerated depreciation for tax purposes (say, $600 million).

The Gap, Inc., would record income tax for fiscal 2014 as follows (dollar amounts in millions and an income tax rate of 40%):

	A	B	C	D
1	2015	(In millions)		
2	Jan 31	Income Tax Expense ($2,000 × 0.40)	800	
3		Income Tax Payable ($1,600 × 0.40)		640
4		Deferred Tax Liability		160
5		*Recorded income tax for the year.*		
6				

Deferred Tax Liability is usually long-term.

The Gap, Inc.'s financial statements for fiscal 2014 will report

Income statement (in millions)		Balance sheet (in millions)	
Income before income tax	$2,000	Current liabilities:	
Income tax expense.....................	(800)	Income tax payable	$640
Net income.................................	$1,200	Long-term liabilities:	
		Deferred tax liability	160*

*Assuming the beginning balance of Deferred tax liability was zero.

In March 2015, The Gap, Inc., would pay income tax payable of $640 million because this is a current liability. The deferred tax liability can be paid later.

For a given year, Income Tax Payable can exceed Income Tax Expense. This occurs when, because of differences in revenue and expenses for book and tax purposes, taxable income exceeds book income. When that occurs, the company debits a Deferred Tax Asset. The remainder of this topic is reserved for a more advanced course.

Effective tax planning, both by in-house tax staff and externally through the counsel of the company's independent outside accountants and attorneys, can help lower the company's tax burden and can contribute substantially to improved operating profits.

Which Income Number Predicts Future Profits?

How is income from continuing operations used in investment analysis? Suppose Kimberly Kuhl, an analyst with **Morgan Stanley**, is estimating the value of The Gap, Inc.'s common stock. Kuhl believes that The Gap, Inc., can earn annual income each year equal to its income from ongoing (continuing) operations after tax—$1,135 million for fiscal 2012 for The Gap, Inc.

To estimate the value of The Gap, Inc.'s common stock, financial analysts use a method similar to that described in Chapter 8 to determine the present value of The Gap, Inc.'s stream of future income. Ms. Kuhl must use some interest rate to compute the present value. Assume that an appropriate interest rate (i) for the valuation of The Gap, Inc., is 6%. This rate is often based on the company's **weighted-average cost of capital** (WACC), which is a measure of the average returns that creditors and investors demand from the company. WACC is a major focus in corporate finance courses, so we do not discuss it, or how it is computed, in detail. However, you should know that WACC is influenced by the risk that a company might not be able to sustain a certain rate of return into the indefinite future. The higher the risk associated with an investment, the higher the rate of return demanded by investors and creditors, and vice versa. This rate is also called an **investment capitalization rate** because it is used to estimate the value of an investment. Assuming the capitalization rate is reasonable, and that the company can continue to earn this amount of income for an infinite period into the future, a simple way to estimate the value of the stock of The Gap, Inc., is

$$\begin{matrix} \text{Estimated value of} \\ \text{The Gap, Inc.,} \\ \text{common stock} \end{matrix} = \frac{\text{Estimated annual income in the future}}{\text{Investment capitalization rate}} = \frac{\$1,135 \text{ million}}{0.06} = \$18.92 \text{ billion}$$

Kuhl thus estimates that The Gap, Inc., as a company is worth $18.92 billion. She then computes the company's market capitalization based on its most recent stock price. The Gap, Inc.'s balance sheet at February 2, 2013, reports that the company has 463 million shares of common stock outstanding (1,106 million shares issued − 643 million shares in treasury). The market price of The Gap, Inc., common stock at the beginning of February 2013 is $32.59 per share. The current market value of The Gap, Inc., as a company (market capitalization) as of that date is

$$\begin{matrix} \text{Current market} \\ \text{value of the} \\ \text{company} \end{matrix} = \begin{matrix} \text{Number of shares} \\ \text{of common stock} \\ \text{outstanding} \end{matrix} \times \begin{matrix} \text{Current} \\ \text{market price} \\ \text{per share} \end{matrix}$$

$$\$15.09 \text{ billion} = 463 \text{ million} \times \$32.59$$

The investment decision rule is

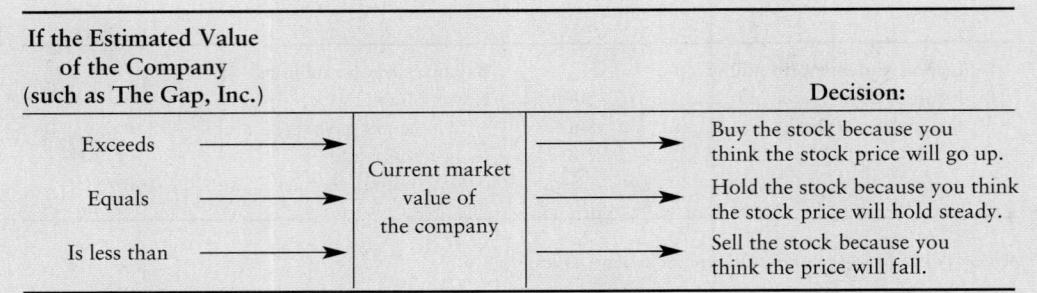

In this case,

			Decision:
Estimated Value of The Gap, Inc. $18.92 billion	Is greater than	Current market value of The Gap, Inc. $15.09 billion	→ Buy the stock
$40.86 per share*	Is greater than	$32.59 per share	→ Buy the stock

*$18.92 billion/463 million shares

Kuhl believes The Gap, Inc.'s stock price should rise above its current market value of $32.59 to somewhere in a range near $40. Based on this analysis, Morgan Stanley would recommend that investors buy The Gap, Inc., common stock. Tracking the stock over time will reveal whether Morgan Stanley's investment recommendation is correct. In early October, 2013, shares of The Gap, Inc., were selling for $40.31 per share. As of this date, it appears that Morgan Stanley made a good recommendation. You should use caution in making these types of estimates, because they do not include information about the company that might emerge at a later time or other market uncertainties. In reality, such estimates are only educated guesses. It is very difficult to predict stock price trends. Although some experts have better track records than others, even the experts can't predict stock prices perfectly!

Discontinued Operations

Most large companies engage in several lines of business. For example, The Gap, Inc., owns The Gap stores, its mid-line store, as well as **Old Navy** (its less-expensive lines), **Banana Republic** (its upscale lines) and **Piperlime**, a specialty line of women's shoes and handbags. **General Electric** makes household appliances and jet engines and owns **NBC**, the media network. We call each identifiable part of a company a *segment* of the business.

A company may sell or discontinue segments of its business from time to time. This did not happen to The Gap, Inc., during the fiscal years covered in Exhibit 11-1. However, as an example, during the second quarter of 2012, another well-known international company, **Nike, Inc.,** announced the sale of two of its major brands, Umbro and Cole Haan. Nike completed the sale of the assets of Umbro to Iconix Brand group for $225 million. The company reported a loss from discontinued operations of $107 million (net of the tax benefit it received from deducting the loss on its tax return) in the income statement of the second quarter of 2012. Also during the quarter, Nike reached an agreement to sell Cole Haan to Apax Partners for $570 million. The actual sale did not occur until 2013, but because it had agreed to sell this brand in 2012, Nike was entitled to report its loss from discontinued operations (net of tax benefit) in Loss from Discontinued Operations in 2012. Note that the caption "Discontinued Operations" includes *both* operating income or loss of the segment during the divestiture period *and* gains or losses on the transaction at the point of sale of the segment.

All gains and losses from discontinued operations are shown "net of tax"—that is, the income tax expense (or savings) from the gain (or loss) is subtracted from the item before reporting it in the income statement. *Financial analysts typically do not include discontinued operations in predictions of future corporate income because the discontinued segments will not continue to generate income for the company.* The end-of-chapter summary problem (pp. 637–638) contains an example and illustration of reporting for discontinued operations. The details of this topic are covered in more advanced accounting classes.

Extraordinary Items: An IFRS Difference **Extraordinary gains and losses**, also called **extraordinary items**, are both *unusual* in nature for the company and *infrequent* in occurrence. These gains and losses, like those from discontinued operations, are shown "net of tax" on the income statement. Losses from natural disasters (such as earthquakes, floods, and tornadoes) and the expropriation of company assets by a foreign government are extraordinary. The Gap, Inc., had no extraordinary items on its income statement for fiscal year 2012. Gains and losses due to lawsuits, restructuring, and the sale of plant assets are not extraordinary items. These gains and losses are considered normal business occurrences and are reported as Other Gains and Losses. The Gap, Inc., had none of these items on its income statement for fiscal 2012.

International Financial Reporting Standards (IFRS) do not give special treatment to extraordinary items. Instead, items that are "unusual" in nature or "infrequent" in occurrence are combined with operating income and expenses on the income statement. The result of U.S. companies' adoption of IFRS will be that extraordinary items will eventually disappear from the income statement. In fact, due to the narrow definition, extraordinary items are very rare, even under current U.S. GAAP.

Accounting Changes

Companies sometimes voluntarily change from one accounting method to another, such as from double-declining-balance (DDB) to straight-line depreciation, or from first-in, first-out (FIFO) to average cost for inventory. From time to time, companies might also be required to make accounting changes, whenever the FASB issues new accounting pronouncements. An accounting change makes it difficult to compare one period with preceding periods. Without detailed information, investors can be misled into thinking that the current year is better or worse than the preceding year, when in fact the only difference is a change in the accounting method.

Two types of accounting changes are most relevant to introductory accounting:

1. *Changes in accounting estimates* include changing the estimated life of a building or equipment and the estimated percent of uncollectible receivables. For these changes, companies report amounts for the *current and future* periods on the new basis. There is no looking back to the past. A change in depreciation method is treated as a change in estimate.

2. *Changes in accounting principles* include most changes in accounting methods, such as from FIFO to average cost for inventory and from one method to another for a revenue or an expense. For these changes, the company reports figures for all periods presented in the income statement—*past as well as current*—on the new basis. The company *retrospectively restates* (looks back and restates) all prior-period amounts that are presented for comparative purposes with the current year, as though the new accounting method had been in effect all along. This lets investors compare all periods that are presented on the same accounting basis. Other times, companies might discover errors they have made in applying accounting principles that must be corrected, requiring a change from the erroneous principle to one that is generally accepted.

    If an accounting change impacts periods prior to the earliest one presented in the current income statement, an adjustment, called a **prior-period adjustment**, must be made to the beginning balance of retained earnings in the current period's statement of stockholders' equity. The summary problem at the end of this chapter (pp. 637–638) contains an example of how this is done.

A detailed discussion of accounting changes is reserved for future accounting courses.

COMPUTE EARNINGS PER SHARE

4 **Compute** earnings per share

The final segment of the income statement reports **earnings per share (EPS)**, which is the amount of a company's net income per share of its *outstanding common stock*. EPS is a key measure of a business's success because it shows how much income the company earned for each share of stock. Stock prices are quoted at an amount per share, and investors buy a certain number of shares. EPS is used to help determine the value of a share of stock. EPS is computed as

$$\text{Earnings per share} = \frac{\text{Net income} - \text{Preferred dividends}}{\text{Weighted-average number of shares of common stock outstanding}}$$

The corporation lists its various sources of income separately: continuing operations, discontinued operations, and so on. It also lists the EPS figure for each of these elements of net income. Consider the EPS of The Gap, Inc. The final section of Exhibit 11-1 (lines 18 through 19) shows how companies report EPS. Notice that two EPS computations are made: one for "basic" (the currently outstanding shares) and one for "diluted" (which takes into account potential increases in outstanding shares). Companies must first compute a weighted-average number of shares outstanding. This computation, which is beyond the scope of this textbook, takes into account the changes that might occur in the number of shares outstanding during the year from such things as treasury stock purchases or reissuances. According to Exhibit 11-1, The Gap, Inc., has a "basic" weighted average of 482 million shares of common stock outstanding as of the end of fiscal 2012 (line 15) and "basic" earnings per share of $2.35 (line 18).

| 15 | Weighted-average number of shares—basic.................................. | 482 million |
| 18 | Earnings per share—basic ($1,135 million/482 million)................ | $2.35 |

Effect of Preferred Dividends on Earnings per Share. Recall that EPS is earnings per share of *common* stock. But the holders of preferred stock have first claim on dividends. Therefore, preferred dividends must be subtracted from net income and all income subtotals starting with income from continuing operations to compute EPS. Preferred dividends are not subtracted from discontinued operations or extraordinary items.

Like the vast majority of corporations, The Gap, Inc., has only one type of stock, which is common stock. However, for illustrative purposes only, suppose that The Gap, Inc., had 10,000,000 shares of preferred stock outstanding, each with a $1.00 dividend. The Gap, Inc.'s annual preferred dividends would be $10,000,000 (10,000,000 × $1.00). The $10,000,000 is subtracted from each net income, resulting in the following EPS amount (recall that The Gap, Inc., has a weighted average of 482 million shares of common stock outstanding):

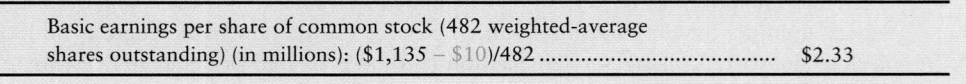

Basic earnings per share of common stock (482 weighted-average shares outstanding) (in millions): ($1,135 – $10)/482 .... $2.33

Earnings per Share Dilution. Some corporations have convertible preferred stock, which may be exchanged for common stock. For example, The Gap, Inc., is authorized to issue 30 million shares of preferred stock, which is convertible into shares of its current common stock. The company has not yet issued any of these shares, but could, at some date in the future. When preferred is converted to common, the EPS is *diluted*—reduced—because more common shares are divided into net income. Corporations with complex capital structures present two sets of EPS figures:

- EPS based on actual outstanding common shares (*basic* EPS)
- EPS based on outstanding common shares plus the additional shares that can arise from conversion of the preferred stock into common stock or other dilutive securities (*diluted* EPS)

The Gap, Inc.'s weighted-average diluted number of shares for the year ended February 2, 2013 is 488 million. Therefore, the EPS on a diluted basis is reduced by about $0.02 per share to account for the additional shares outstanding on a diluted basis (line 19 of Exhibit 11-1). The computations for diluted EPS are similar to those illustrated previously for basic EPS.

ANALYZE THE STATEMENT OF COMPREHENSIVE INCOME, FOOTNOTES, AND SUPPLEMENTAL DISCLOSURES

Reporting Comprehensive Income

All companies report net income or net loss on their income statements. As we saw in Chapter 8, companies with unrealized gains and losses on certain investments and foreign-currency translation adjustments also report another income figure. **Comprehensive income** is the company's change in total stockholders' equity from all sources other than from the owners of the business. Comprehensive income includes net income plus

5 **Analyze** the statement of comprehensive income, footnotes, and supplemental disclosures

- unrealized gains (losses) on available-for-sale investments, and
- foreign-currency translation gains/losses.

These types of other comprehensive income were discussed in Chapter 8. There are others, but discussion of them is reserved for later courses.

Items of comprehensive income, other than net income, do not enter into the determination of earnings per share.

Generally accepted accounting principles require that comprehensive income for a company be presented either alone in a separate **statement of comprehensive income** or combined with the "regular" income statement into a unified statement of comprehensive income. Exhibit 11-2 presents The Gap, Inc.'s separate Consolidated Statements of Comprehensive Income for the three fiscal years ended February 2, 2013. Notice that it starts on line 4 with net income of $1,135 million, $833 million, and $1,204 million for the three fiscal years from line 13 of the Consolidated Statements of Earnings in Exhibit 11-1. Lines 6 and 7 add foreign-currency translation gains (losses) (net of tax) for the three fiscal years. Lines 8 through 10 include adjustments for unrealized changes in fair value of derivative financial instruments (a type of available-for-sale investment) for the three fiscal years. Lines 11 through 13 make reclassifications from other comprehensive income to net income for realized gains and losses on derivative financial instruments sold during the three fiscal years.

Exhibit 11-2 | The Gap, Inc. Consolidated Statements of Comprehensive Income

	A	B	C	D
	A1			
1	**The Gap, Inc.** **Consolidated Statements of Comprehensive Income**			
2			**12 Months Ended**	
3	(in millions of USD)	Feb. 02, 2013	Jan. 28, 2012	Jan. 29, 2011
4	Net income	$ 1,135	$ 833	$ 1,204
5	Other comprehensive income (loss), net of tax:			
6	Foreign-currency translation, net of tax (tax benefit)			
7	of $–, $(2), and $6	(71)	24	37
8	Change in fair value of derivative			
9	financial instruments, net of tax (tax benefit)			
10	of $18, $(8), and $(19)	28	(11)	(31)
11	Reclassification adjustment for realized (gains) losses			
12	on derivative financial instruments, net of (tax)			
13	tax benefit of $(4), $20, and $14	(5)	31	24
14	Other comprehensive income (loss), net of tax	(48)	44	30
15	Comprehensive income	$ 1,087	$ 877	$ 1,234
16				

From this point, net income and other comprehensive income (lines 4 and 14, respectively) follow separate paths to the Stockholders' Equity section of the balance sheet. Net income from line 4 is added to Retained Earnings in the company's Consolidated Statements of Stockholders' Equity. Other Comprehensive Income (Loss) (net of tax) from line 14 is added to (subtracted from) Accumulated Other Comprehensive Income in the company's Consolidated Statements of Stockholders' Equity.

For Additional Details, Don't Forget the Footnotes

To fully understand the impact of information in the financial statements, and to form a more accurate opinion about the quality of a company's earnings, you need to become familiar with additional details found in the financial statement footnotes.

Footnote 1 of every public company's financial statements contains a summary of significant accounting policies used to prepare them. For example, in Note 1 of The Gap, Inc.'s consolidated financial statements, you can find the following information in narrative format that you may need to fully understand how The Gap, Inc., computes net income:

- Its principles of consolidation
- How it determines its fiscal year reporting period
- Its revenue recognition policy
- The types of costs it includes in cost of goods sold and operating expenses
- How it calculates rent, advertising, share-based compensation of employees, gift card revenue, earnings per share, foreign-currency gains and losses, comprehensive income, and income taxes
- The impact of recently issued accounting principles that might impact comparability of reported income and that might have required accounting changes

Other footnotes contain additional detail supporting reported information for balance sheet and income statement information. Here are some examples from The Gap, Inc.'s financial statement footnotes that impact the computation of net income and other comprehensive income:

- Note 2: Additional financial statement information, including details about property and equipment (including depreciation), accumulated other comprehensive income, and sales returns and allowances
- Note 4: Goodwill and intangible assets, including amortization expense
- Note 5: Long-term debt, including interest expense
- Note 10: Share-based compensation
- Note 11: Leases
- Note 12: Income taxes
- Note 13: Employee benefit plans
- Note 14: Earnings per share
- Note 16: Segment information

The last item in the list deserves special attention. Whenever it is relevant, companies have to break down key information (such as sales, operating income, and assets) by **segment**. For this purpose, a segment is defined as a division or subset of a business's operations. To be considered a segment, the division or operating unit must directly earn revenue for the company. Segments may be created by product line, type of business, geographic areas, or other logical divisions. Internally, each segment's revenues and expenses are accounted for separately.

The objective of requiring disclosures about operating information by segments is to provide the user with more detailed information about the different types of business activities in which a company engages and the different economic environments in which it operates. Seeing this detailed information helps users of financial statements to (a) better understand the company's performance; (b) better assess the company's prospects for future net cash flows; and (c) make more informed judgments about the company as a whole. For purposes of reporting segment information, companies are allowed to tailor the information toward their particular "management approach." That is, they may define segments in the same way they manage and evaluate their business activities (i.e., by geographic region, brand, type of revenue, etc.).

Exhibit 11-3 shows an excerpt from Note 16 of The Gap, Inc.'s consolidated financial statements showing the breakdown of net sales by its two management-defined segments: (1) stores and (2) direct (Internet sales, plus Piperlime and Althea).

Exhibit 11-3 | Excerpt of Note 16: Segment Information for Sales

We identify our operating segments according to how our business activities are managed and evaluated. All of our operating segments sell a group of similar products—apparel, accessories, and personal care products. As of February 2, 2013, we have two reportable segments:

- Stores—The Stores reportable segment includes the results of the retail stores for Gap, Old Navy, and Banana Republic. We have aggregated the results of all Stores operating segments into one reportable segment because the operating segments have similar economic characteristics.

- Direct—The Direct reportable segment includes the results of our online brands, as well as Piperlime and Athleta. Intermix is also a component of the Direct reportable segment; however, its results since the date of acquisition are immaterial.

The accounting policies for each of our operating segments are the same as those described in Note 1 of Notes to Consolidated Financial Statements.

Net sales by brand, region, and reportable segment are as follows:

	A1							
	A	**B**	**C**	**D**	**E**	**F**	**G**	**H**
1	($ in millions)							
2	Fiscal 2012	Gap	Old Navy	Banana Republic	Franchise	Other	Total	Percentage of Net Sales
3	U.S.	$ 3,323	$ 4,945	$ 2,171	$ —	$ —	$ 10,439	67%
4	Canada	352	410	216	—	—	978	6
5	Europe	691	—	66	63	—	820	5
6	Asia	1,062	9	148	86	—	1,305	9
7	Other regions	—	—	—	182	—	182	1
8	Total Stores reportable segment	5,428	5,364	2,601	331	—	13,724	88
9	Direct reportable segment	537	748	247	—	395	1,927	12
10	Total	$ 5,965	$ 6,112	$ 2,848	$ 331	$ 395	$ 15,651	100%
11	Sales growth	5%	8%	8%	17%	31%	8%	
12								

After reading this footnote, you should be much more informed of the geographic regions of the world where The Gap, Inc., earns its revenue, the brands (Gap, Old Navy, Banana Republic, and Franchise) that produce its revenue, the percentage of its sales that come from stores versus the Internet, and the amount of sales growth from each of its brands over its fiscal 2012 year. Totals of this detailed information tie back to total consolidated net sales reported in Exhibit 11-1 (p. 618). For example, you can readily see that 67% of total consolidated Net sales is earned in the United States, 21% is earned from stores in other countries, and 12% is earned from its Direct Reportable segment (which includes Internet sales as well as Piperlime and Althea). The segment with the highest reported sales growth over the latest fiscal year (31%) is the "other" category, which includes direct (Internet) sales, Piperlime and Althea. This footnote contains many more details than we can discuss here, including comparative information from prior years, enabling the analyst to compute trends over time. This detailed information should make a prospective investor better able to predict the direction the company may be headed in the future, as well as its prospects for growth and added share value.

Nonfinancial Reports

A growing number of companies now issue annual reports covering their performance in such nonfinancial areas as **corporate social responsibility (CSR).** For example, most of the focus companies in this textbook, such as **The Gap, Inc., Whole Foods Market, Inc., The Home Depot, Inc.,** and **Starbucks Corporation** issue annual **CSR reports.** These reports contain voluntary disclosures on how companies are conducting and governing their businesses in ways that benefit not only their shareholders but also the environment, their employees, and society as a whole. The Global Reporting Initiative (GRI) is an independent institution formed in 1997 to develop a common framework for sustainability reporting. Many of the world's largest businesses now issue CSR reports under GRI's strict guidelines. While reporting under this framework is voluntary rather than mandatory in the United States, the SEC has endorsed these types of reports. Other countries, such as France, South Africa, and The Netherlands, now mandate some form of CSR reporting in order to be listed on their stock exchanges.

You can find The Gap, Inc.'s CSR report at the following web address: http://www.gapinc .com/content/csr/html.html. Check it out! Reading this report may make you feel better about doing business at The Gap, Inc., or investing in its stock.

DIFFERENTIATE MANAGEMENT'S AND AUDITORS' RESPONSIBILITIES IN FINANCIAL REPORTING

Management's Responsibility

6 Differentiate management's and auditors' reporting responsibilities

Management issues a report on internal control over financial reporting along with the company's financial statements. Exhibit 11-4 is an excerpt from the report of management for The Gap, Inc.:

Exhibit 11-4 | Statement of Management's Responsibility

> Management is responsible for establishing and maintaining an adequate system of internal control over financial reporting. Management conducted an assessment of internal control over financial reporting based on the framework established by the Committee of Sponsoring Organizations of the Treadway Commission in *Internal Control—Integrated Framework*. Based on the assessment, management concluded that, as of February 2, 2013, our internal control over financial reporting is effective. The Company's internal control over financial reporting as of February 2, 2013, has been audited by an independent registered public accounting firm, as stated in its report, which is included herein.

Management declares its responsibility for the internal controls over financial reporting in accordance with the Sarbanes-Oxley Act of 2002. Management also states that it has conducted an assessment of internal controls over financial reporting based on the framework established by the Committee of Sponsoring Organizations (COSO) of the Treadway Commission and has concluded that, as of February 2, 2013, internal controls over financial reporting are effective. In addition, management states that the internal controls of the company have been audited by the company's outside auditors and refers to their report, which can be found in the company's annual report on the website of the U.S. Securities and Exchange Commission (www.sec.gov). See "Try It in Excel" on pages 619-620 for explicit instructions on how to access The Gap, Inc.'s most recent annual report. Exhibit 11-5 contains excerpts of the independent auditors' combined report on the financial statements as well as the internal controls of a hypothetical public company.

Auditor Report

The Securities Exchange Act of 1934 requires companies that issue their stock publicly to file audited financial statements with the SEC. Companies engage outside auditors who are certified

Exhibit 11-5 | Excerpts of Independent Auditors' Report for Hypothetical Public Company

To the Board of Directors and Stockholders of Superior Clothing, Inc.

We have audited the accompanying consolidated balance sheets of Superior Clothing, Inc., and subsidiaries (the "Company") as of February 2, 2013, and January 28, 2012, and the related consolidated statements of earnings, comprehensive income, stockholders' equity, and cash flows for each of the three fiscal years in the period ended February 2, 2013. We also have audited the Company's internal control over financial reporting as of February 2, 2013, based on criteria established by *Internal Control—Integrated Framework* issued by the Committee of Sponsoring Organizations of the Treadway Commission. The Company's management is responsible for these financial statements, for maintaining effective internal control over financial reporting, and for its assessment of the effectiveness of internal control over financial reporting, included in the accompanying Management's Report on Internal Control over Financial Reporting. Our responsibility is to express an opinion on these financial statements and opinion on the Company's internal control over financial reporting based on our audits.

We conducted our audits in accordance with the standards of the Public Company Accounting Oversight Board (United States). Those standards require that we plan and perform the audit to obtain reasonable assurance about whether the financial statements are free from material misstatements and whether effective internal control over financial reporting was maintained in all material respects…We believe that our audits provide a reasonable basis for our opinions.

A company's internal control over financial reporting is a process designed by, or under the supervision of, the company's…financial officers…and effected by the Company's board of directors…to provide reasonable assurance regarding the reliability of financial reporting and the preparation of financial statements…in accordance with generally accepted accounting principles.

Because of the inherent limitations of internal control over financial reporting, including the possibility of collusion or improper management override of controls, material misstatements due to error or fraud may not be prevented or detected on a timely basis. Also, projections of any evaluation of the effectiveness of internal control over financial reporting to future periods are subject to the risk that the controls may become inadequate because of changes in conditions, or that the degree of compliance with the policies or procedures may deteriorate.

In our opinion, the consolidated financial statement referred to above present fairly, in all material respects, the financial position of Superior Clothing, Inc., and subsidiaries as of February 2, 2013, and January 28, 2012, and the results of their operations and their cash flows for each of the three years in the period ended February 2, 2013, in conformity with accounting principles generally accepted in the United States of America. Also, in our opinion, the Company maintained, in all material respects, effective internal control over financial reporting as of February 2, 2013, based on the criteria established in *Internal Control—Integrated Framework* issued by the Committee of Sponsoring Organizations of the Treadway Commission.

/s/ Independent Auditing Firm

Anytown, U.S.A.

March 15, 2013

public accountants to examine their financial statements as well as their internal controls over financial reporting. The independent auditors decide whether the company's financial statements comply with GAAP. They must also decide whether the internal controls of the company meet certain standards. The firm then issues a combined audit report on both the financial statements and the company's system of internal controls over financial reporting.

The audit report is addressed to the board of directors and stockholders of the company. A partner of the auditing firm signs the firm's name to the report.

The combined audit report on financial statements and internal control over financial reporting typically contains five paragraphs:

- The first paragraph identifies the audited financial statements as well as the company being audited. It also states the responsibility of the company's management as well as the auditor's responsibilities.

- The second paragraph describes how the audit was performed in accordance with generally accepted auditing standards of the Public Company Accounting Oversight Board (an independent regulatory body with SEC oversight). These are the standards used by auditors as the benchmark for evaluating audit quality.

- The third paragraph describes in detail what a system of internal controls is, noting that it should be designed to provide reasonable assurance that transactions are recorded to permit preparation of financial statements that are fairly presented in conformity with GAAP.

- The fourth paragraph describes inherent limitations in the system of internal controls and notes that, at best, the system of internal controls can only provide reasonable assurance that financial statements are fairly presented.

- The fifth paragraph expresses the auditor's combined opinion on both the fairness of financial statements, in all material respects, in conformity with GAAP and the effectiveness of the company's internal controls over financial reporting. The auditing firm is expressing an **unqualified (clean) opinion** on both the fairness of the financial statements and the effectiveness of the company's internal controls. The unqualified opinion is the highest statement of assurance that an independent certified public accountant can express.

The independent audit adds credibility to the financial statements of a company as well as to its system of internal controls. It is no accident that financial reporting and auditing are more advanced in the United States than anywhere else in the world, and that U.S. capital markets are the envy of the world.

▶ Decision Guidelines

USING THE INCOME STATEMENT AND RELATED NOTES IN INVESTMENT ANALYSIS

Suppose you've completed your studies, taken a job, and have been fortunate to save $10,000. Now you are ready to start investing. These guidelines provide a framework for using accounting information for investment analysis.

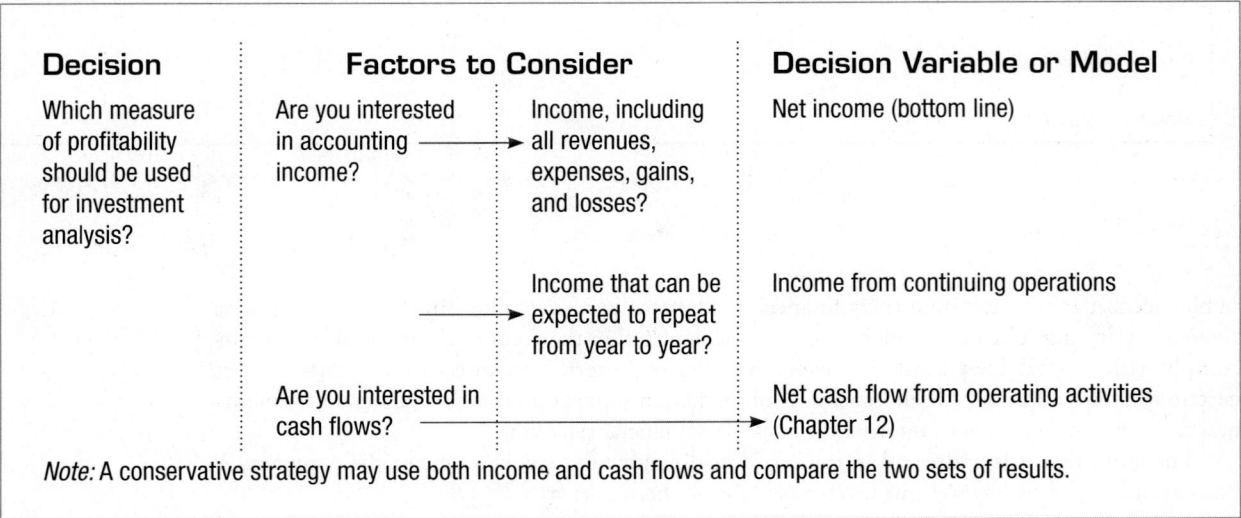

Decision	Factors to Consider		Decision Variable or Model
Which measure of profitability should be used for investment analysis?	Are you interested in accounting income?	Income, including all revenues, expenses, gains, and losses?	Net income (bottom line)
		Income that can be expected to repeat from year to year?	Income from continuing operations
	Are you interested in cash flows?		Net cash flow from operating activities (Chapter 12)

Note: A conservative strategy may use both income and cash flows and compare the two sets of results.

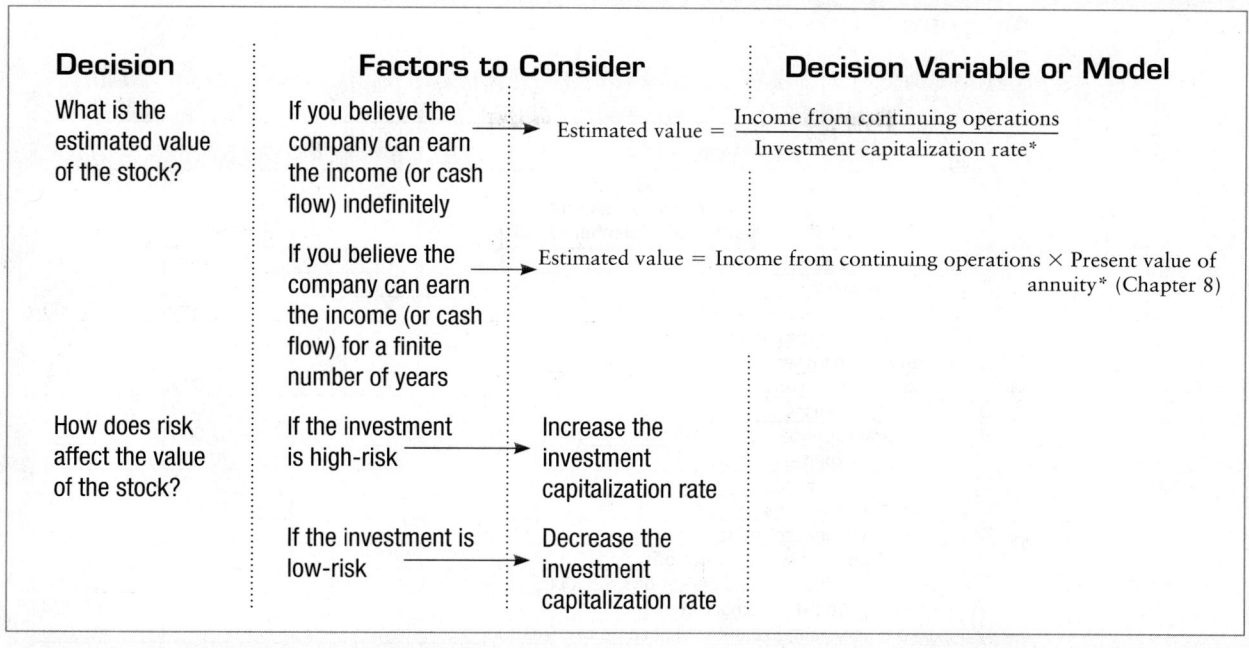

Decision	Factors to Consider	Decision Variable or Model
What is the estimated value of the stock?	If you believe the company can earn the income (or cash flow) indefinitely	Estimated value = $\dfrac{\text{Income from continuing operations}}{\text{Investment capitalization rate}^*}$
	If you believe the company can earn the income (or cash flow) for a finite number of years	Estimated value = Income from continuing operations × Present value of annuity* (Chapter 8)
How does risk affect the value of the stock?	If the investment is high-risk	Increase the investment capitalization rate
	If the investment is low-risk	Decrease the investment capitalization rate

*Use a rate that approximates the company's weighted-average cost of capital.

End-of-Chapter Summary Problems

The following information was taken from the ledger of Maxim, Inc.:

Prior-period adjustment—net of tax:		Treasury stock, common	
credit to Retained Earnings	$ 5,000	(5,000 shares at cost)	$ 25,000
Gain on sale of plant assets	21,000	Selling expenses................................	78,000
Cost of goods sold...........................	380,000	Common stock, no par,	
Income tax expense:		45,000 shares issued.....................	180,000
Continuing operations.................	32,000	Sales revenue	620,000
Discontinued operations.............	8,000	Interest expense................................	30,000
Extraordinary gain	10,000	Extraordinary gain	26,000
Preferred stock, 8%, $100 par,		Income from discontinued	
500 shares issued..........................	50,000	operations	20,000
Dividends...	16,000	Loss due to lawsuit...........................	11,000
Retained earnings, beginning,		General expenses..............................	62,000
as originally reported	103,000		

Requirement

1. Prepare a single-step income statement (with all revenues and gains grouped together) and a statement of retained earnings for Maxim, Inc., for the current year ended December 31, 2014. Include the earnings-per-share presentation and show computations. Assume no changes in the stock accounts during the year.

Answers

	A	B	C
	Maxim, Inc.		
	Income Statement		
1	**Year Ended December 31, 2014**		
2	**Revenue and gains:**		
3	Sales revenue		$ 620,000
4	Gain on sale of plant assets		21,000
5	Total revenues and gains		641,000
6	**Expenses and losses:**		
7	Cost of goods sold	$ 380,000	
8	Selling expenses	78,000	
9	General expenses	62,000	
10	Interest expense	30,000	
11	Loss due to lawsuit	11,000	
12	Income tax expense	32,000	
13	Total expenses and losses		593,000
14	Income from continuing operations		48,000
15	Income from discontinued operations, $20,000, less income tax, $8,000		12,000
16	Income before extraordinary item		60,000
17	Extraordinary gain, $26,000, less income tax, $10,000		16,000
18	Net income		$ 76,000
19	**Earnings per share:***		
20	Income from continuing operations		
21	[($48,000 − $4,000)/40,000 shares]		$ 1.10
22	Income from discontinued operations		
23	($12,000/40,000 shares)		0.30
24	Income before extraordinary item		
25	[($60,000 − $4,000)/40,000 shares]		1.40
26	Extraordinary gain ($16,000/40,000 shares)		0.40
27	Net income [($76,000 − $4,000)/40,000 shares]		$ 1.80
28			

*Computations:

$$EPS = \frac{Income - Preferred\ dividends}{Common\ shares\ outstanding}$$

Preferred dividends: $50,000 × 0.08 = $4,000
Common shares outstanding:
   45,000 shares issued − 5,000 treasury shares = 40,000 shares outstanding

	A	B
	Maxim, Inc.	
	Statement of Retained Earnings	
1	**Year Ended December 31, 2014**	
2	Retained earnings balance, beginning, as originally reported	$ 103,000
3	Prior-period adjustment—credit	5,000
4	Retained earnings balance, beginning, as adjusted	108,000
5	Net income for current year	76,000
6		184,000
7	Dividends for current year	(16,000)
8	Retained earnings balance, ending	$ 168,000
9		

Note: The Statement of Retained Earnings is usually incorporated into the Statement of Stockholders' Equity. See Chapter 10 for a more complete discussion.

REVIEW | The Income Statement

Quick Check (Answers are given on page 663.)

1. The quality of earnings suggests that
   a. continuing operations and one-time transactions are of equal importance.
   b. income from continuing operations is a more relevant predictor of future performance than income from one-time transactions.
   c. stockholders want the corporation to earn enough income to be able to pay its debts.
   d. net income is the best measure of the results of operations.

2. Which statement is true?
   a. Discontinued operations are a separate category on the income statement.
   b. Extraordinary items are combined with continuing operations on the income statement.
   c. Extraordinary items are part of discontinued operations.
   d. All of the above are true.

3. Kelley Corporation earned $6.39 per share of its common stock. Suppose you capitalize Kelley's income at 9%. How much are you willing to pay for a share of Kelley stock?
   a. $6.39
   b. $57.51
   c. $71.00
   d. $100.00

4. The following is a selected portion of Mod Style's income statement:

	Year Ended		
	2015	2014	2013
Income (loss) from continuing operations	$(20,000)	$61,000	$160,000
Income (loss) from discontinued operations	(17,000)	(1,500)	500
Net income (loss)	$(37,000)	$59,500	$160,500
Earnings (loss) per share from continuing operations:			
Basic	$ (0.40)	$ 1.20	$ 2.76
Earnings (loss) per share from discontinued operations:			
Basic	$ (0.34)	$ (0.03)	$ 0.01
Earnings (loss) per share:			
Basic	$ (0.74)	$ 1.17	$ 2.77

Mod Style has no preferred stock outstanding. How many shares of common stock did Mod Style have outstanding during fiscal year 2015?
   a. 27,027 shares
   b. 51,000 shares
   c. 92,500 shares
   d. 50,000 shares

5. You are taking a vacation to Italy, and you buy euros for $1.50. On your return, you cash in your unused euros for $1.20. During your vacation,
   a. the euro rose against the dollar.
   b. the euro gained value.
   c. the dollar rose against the euro.
   d. the dollar lost value.

6. Baylor County, Texas, purchased earth-moving equipment from a Canadian company. The cost was $1,400,000 Canadian, and the Canadian dollar was quoted at $0.97. A month later, Baylor County paid its debt, and the Canadian dollar was quoted at $0.98. What was Baylor County's cost of the equipment?
   a. $1,358,000
   b. $1,372,000
   c. $1,414,000
   d. $14,000

7. Why is it important for companies to report their accounting changes to the public?
    a. Accounting changes affect dividends, and investors want dividends.
    b. It is important for the results of operations to be compared between periods.
    c. Some accounting changes are more extraordinary than others.
    d. Most accounting changes increase net income, and investors need to know why the increase in net income occurred.

8. Other comprehensive income
    a. affects earnings per share.
    b. has no effect on income tax.
    c. includes extraordinary gains and losses.
    d. includes unrealized gains and losses on available-for-sale investments.

9. Go Home Systems earned income before tax of $180,000. Taxable income was $150,000, and the income tax rate was 32%. The journal entry to record Go Home's income tax expense and income tax liability was:

	A	B	C	D
		A1		
1	a.	Income Tax Payable	57,600	
2		Income Tax Expense		48,000
3		Deferred Tax Liability		9,600
4	b.	Income Tax Expense	48,000	
5		Income Tax Payable		48,000
6	c.	Income Tax Expense	57,600	
7		Income Tax Payable		57,600
8	d.	Income Tax Expense	57,600	
9		Income Tax Payable		48,000
10		Deferred Tax Liability		9,600
11				

10. Deferred Tax Liability is usually

Type of Account	Reported on the
a. Short-term	Income statement
b. Long-term	Balance sheet
c. Long-term	Income statement
d. Short-term	Statement of stockholders' equity

11. The main purpose of the statement of stockholders' equity is to report
    a. comprehensive income.
    b. results of operations.
    c. reasons for changes in the equity accounts.
    d. financial position.

12. An auditor report by independent accountants
    a. gives investors assurance that the company's financial statements conform to GAAP.
    b. ensures that the financial statements are error-free.
    c. gives investors assurance that the company's stock is a safe investment.
    d. is ultimately the responsibility of the management of the client company.

Accounting Vocabulary

channel stuffing (p. 621) A type of financial statement fraud that is accomplished by shipping more to customers (usually around the end of the year) than they ordered, with the expectation that they may return some or all of it. The objective is to record more revenue than the company has actually earned with legitimate sales and shipments.

clean opinion (p. 636) An *unqualified opinion*.

comprehensive income (p. 631) A company's change in total stockholders' equity from all sources other than from the owners of the business (including distributions to owners).

corporate social responsibility (CSR) (p. 634) A non-financial measure of a company's performance, including its investment in corporate governance, environmental conservation, and other socially responsible programs that benefit society as a whole.

earnings per share (EPS) (p. 630) Amount of a company's net income per share of its outstanding common stock.

earnings quality (p. 619) The characteristics of an earnings number that make it most useful for decision making; the degree to which earnings are an accurate reflection of underlying economic events for both revenues and expenses, and the extent to which earnings from a company's core operations are improving over time. Assuming that revenues and expenses are measured accurately, high-quality earnings are reflected in steadily improving sales and steadily declining costs over time, so that income from continuing operations follows a high and improving pattern over time.

extraordinary gains and losses (p. 629) Also called *extraordinary items*, these gains and losses are both unusual for the company and infrequent.

extraordinary items (p. 629) An *extraordinary gain or loss*.

foreign-currency exchange rate (p. 623) The measure of one country's currency against another country's currency.

hedging (p. 625) To protect oneself from losing money in one transaction by engaging in a counterbalancing transaction.

investment capitalization rate (p. 627) An assumed rate of return used to estimate the value of an investment in stock. This rate should approximate the weighted-average cost of capital (see below).

pre-tax accounting income (p. 625) Income before tax on the income statement.

prior-period adjustment (p. 629) A correction to the beginning balance of retained earnings for an error of an earlier period.

segment (p. 632) A division or subset of a business's operations, especially in large corporations. For a division to be considered a segment, it must directly earn revenue for the company. Segments may be created by product line, by type of business, by geographic areas, or other logical divisions for the corporation. Internally, each segment's revenues and expenses are accounted for separately.

statement of comprehensive income (p. 631) A statement showing all of the changes in stockholders' equity during a period other than transactions with owners. The statement of comprehensive income includes net income as well as other comprehensive income, such as unrealized gains/losses on available-for-sale securities and foreign-currency translation gains/losses.

taxable income (p. 626) The basis for computing the amount of tax to pay the government.

unqualified (clean) opinion (p. 636) An audit opinion stating that the financial statements are presented fairly in accordance with generally accepted accounting principles.

weighted-average cost of capital (p. 627) The combined rate of return expected for a company by its creditors and investors. In general, the higher the risk associated with the company, the greater the expected returns by creditors and investors.

ASSESS YOUR PROGRESS

Short Exercises

S11-1. *(Learning Objective 1: Evaluate quality of earnings)* Research has shown that over 50% of financial statement frauds are committed by companies that recognize revenue improperly. What does this mean? Describe the most common ways companies improperly recognize revenue.

S11-2. *(Learning Objective 1: Evaluate quality of earnings)* Study the 2014 income statement of Kristie's Imports, Inc., and answer these questions about the company:

	A	B	C
	A1 ⬍		
1	**Kristie's Imports, Inc.** **Consolidated Statement of Operations (Adapted)**		
2		**Year Ended**	
3	(In thousands except per share amounts)	**2014**	**2013**
4			
5	Net sales	$ 1,917,425	$ 1,806,475
6	Operating costs and expenses:		
7	Cost of sales (including buying and store occupancy costs)	1,013,490	1,045,580
8	Selling, general, and administrative expenses	549,850	526,150
9	Depreciation and amortization	55,275	48,450
10	Total operating costs and expenses	1,618,615	1,620,180
11	Operating income (loss)	298,810	186,295
12	Nonoperating (income) and expenses:		
13	Interest and investment income	(2,625)	(2,710)
14	Interest expense	1,725	1,630
15	Interest income, net	(900)	(1,080)
16	Income (loss) from continuing operations before income taxes	299,710	187,375
17	Provision (benefit) for income taxes	104,800	69,615
18	Income (loss) from continuing operations	194,910	117,760
19	Discontinued operations:		
20	Income (loss) from discontinued operations	(2,400)	280
21	Net income (loss)	$ 192,510	$ 118,040
22			
23	Earnings (loss) per share from continuing operations: Basic	$ 2.64	$ 1.62
24			
25	Earnings (loss) per share from discontinued operations: Basic	$ (0.03)	$ 0.00
26			
27	Earnings (loss) per share: Basic	$ 2.61	$ 1.62
28			

1. How much gross profit did Kristie's Imports earn on the sale of its products in 2014? How much was income from continuing operations? Net income?
2. At the end of 2014, what dollar amount of net income would most sophisticated investors use to predict Kristie's Imports' net income for 2015 and beyond? Name this item, give its amount, and state your reason.

S11-3. *(Learning Objective 1: Prepare a complex income statement)* Fisher Fine Coffees, Inc., reported the following items, listed in no particular order, at December 31, 2014 (in thousands):

Other gains (losses)	$(19,000)	Extraordinary gain	$ 3,000
Net sales revenue..................	197,000	Cost of goods sold.................	73,000
Loss on discontinued		Operating expenses	65,000
operations	13,000	Accounts receivable...............	21,000

Income tax of 35% applies to all items.

Prepare Fisher Fine Coffees' multi-step income statement for the year ended December 31, 2014. Omit earnings per share.

S11-4. *(Learning Objective 1: Value a company's stock)* For fiscal year 2014, Mango Computer, Inc., reported net sales of $19,323 million, net income of $1,997 million, and no significant discontinued operations, extraordinary items, or accounting changes. Earnings per share was $2.20. At a capitalization rate of 5%, how much should one share of Mango stock be worth? Compare your estimated stock price with the market price of $51.02 as quoted in the newspaper. Based on your estimated market value, should you buy, hold, or sell Mango stock?

S11-5. *(Learning Objective 2: Account for foreign-currency gains and losses)* Suppose Tex-Cola Corp. sells soft-drink syrup on account to a Russian company on September 12. Tex-Cola Corp. agrees to accept 400,000 Russian rubles. On the date of sale, the ruble is quoted at $0.34. Tex-Cola Corp. collects half the receivable on October 18 when the ruble is worth $0.31. Then on November 15, when the foreign-exchange rate of the ruble is $0.36, Tex-Cola Corp. collects the final amount.

Journalize these three transactions for Tex-Cola Corp. Ignore cost of goods sold.

S11-6. *(Learning Objective 2: Account for foreign-currency gains and losses)* Brandt Belting sells goods on account for 850,000 Mexican pesos. The foreign-exchange rate for a peso is $0.094 on the date of sale. Brandt Belting then collects cash on April 24 when the exchange rate for a peso is $0.099. Record Brandt's cash collection. Ignore cost of goods sold.

Brandt Belting buys inventory on account for 21,000 Swiss francs. A Swiss franc costs $1.12 on the purchase date. Record Brandt Belting's payment of cash on October 25, when the exchange rate for a Swiss franc is $1.14.

In these two scenarios, which currencies strengthened? Which currencies weakened?

S11-7. *(Learning Objectives 1, 3: Evaluate quality of earnings; use other information on an income statement)* Cool Cruise Lines, Inc., reported the following income statement for the year ended December 31, 2014:

	Millions
Operating revenues	$95,500
Operating expenses	84,100
Operating income	11,400
Other revenue (expense), net	1,000
Income from continuing operations	12,400
Discontinued operations, net of tax	1,100
Net income	$13,500

Requirements

1. Were Cool Cruise Line's discontinued operations more like an expense or revenue? How can you tell?
2. Should the discontinued operations of Cool Cruise Lines be included in or excluded from net income? State your reason.
3. Suppose you are working as a financial analyst and your job is to predict Cool Cruise Line's net income for 2015 and beyond. Which item from the income statement will you use for your prediction? Identify its amount. Why will you use this item?

S11-8. *(Learning Objective 3: Account for a corporation's income tax)* Elam Marine, Inc., had income before income tax of $171,000 and taxable income of $152,000 for 2014, the company's first year of operations. The income tax rate is 30%.
1. Make the entry to record Elam Marine's income taxes for 2014.
2. Show what Elam Marine will report on its 2014 income statement, starting with income before income tax. Also show what Elam Marine will report for current and long-term liabilities on its December 31, 2014, balance sheet.

S11-9. *(Learning Objective 4: Compute earnings per share)* Return to the Fisher Fine Coffees data in S11-3. Fisher Fine Coffees had 10,000 shares of common stock outstanding during 2014. Fisher Fine Coffees declared and paid preferred dividends of $5,000 during 2014.

Report Fisher Fine Coffees' earnings per share on the income statement. (Round all calculations to two decimal places.)

S11-10. *(Learning Objective 5: Report comprehensive income)* Use the Fisher Fine Coffees data in S11-3. In addition, Fisher Fine Coffees had unrealized gains of $2,300 on available-for-sale investments and a $2,900 foreign-currency translation adjustment (a gain) during 2014.

Both amounts are net of tax and in thousands. Start with Fisher Fine Coffees' net income from S11-3, and show how the company could report other comprehensive income on its 2014 financial statements.

Should Fisher Fine Coffees report earnings per share for other comprehensive income? State why or why not.

S11-11. *(Learning Objective 4: Interpret earnings-per-share data)* Bailey Motor Company has preferred stock outstanding and issued additional common stock during the year.
1. Give the basic equation to compute earnings per share of common stock for net income.
2. List the income items for which Bailey must report earnings-per-share data.
3. What makes earnings per share so useful as a business statistic?

S11-12. *(Learning Objective 5: Report a prior-period adjustment)* iLife, Inc., was set to report the following statement of retained earnings for the year ended December 31, 2014:

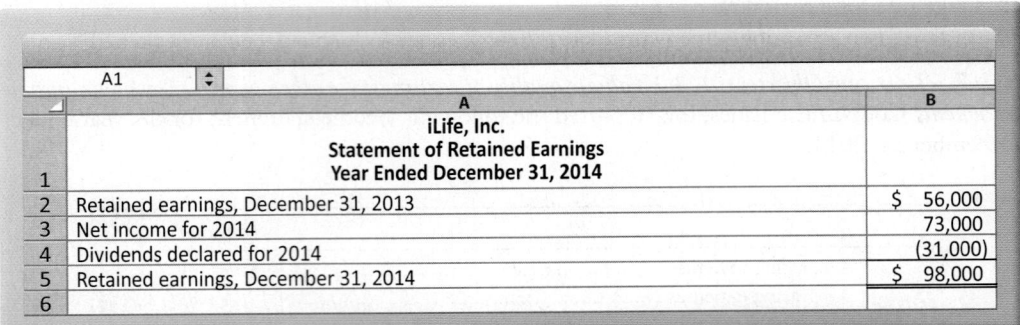

	A	B
	A1	
1	**iLife, Inc.** **Statement of Retained Earnings** **Year Ended December 31, 2014**	
2	Retained earnings, December 31, 2013	$ 56,000
3	Net income for 2014	73,000
4	Dividends declared for 2014	(31,000)
5	Retained earnings, December 31, 2014	$ 98,000
6		

Before issuing its 2014 financial statements, iLife learned that net income of 2013 was overstated by $12,500. Prepare iLife's 2014 statement of retained earnings to show the correction of the error—that is, the prior-period adjustment. (*Hint:* Use the end-of-chapter summary problem as an example.)

S11-13. *(Learning Objective 5: Analyze segment information)* Worldwide Electronics Corporation, based in New Jersey, sells electronics equipment through 150 retail and 25 outlet stores across the United States and in 18 different foreign countries. In addition, the company has a very well designed website through which it markets its products. The company manages and evaluates the retail, outlet, and Internet businesses through three separate divisions, each with its own management.
1. Define a "segment" of a business. What would be a logical way for Worldwide Electronics Corporation to segment its business for financial reporting purposes?
2. What is the purpose of segment reporting? In what ways might segment reporting benefit prospective investors in Worldwide Electronics?

S11-14. *(Learning Objective 6: Differentiate responsibility for financial statements)* The annual report of Meinike Computer, Inc., included the following:

Management's Annual Report on Internal Control over Financial Reporting

The Company's management is responsible for establishing and maintaining adequate control over financial reporting [....] Management conducted an evaluation of the effectiveness of the Company's internal control over financial reporting [....] Based on this evaluation, management has concluded that the Company's internal control over financial reporting was effective as of September 30, 2014....

> Report of Independent Registered Public Accounting Firm
> The Board of Directors and Shareholders
> Meinike Computer, Inc.:
>
> We have audited the accompanying consolidated balance sheets of Meinike Computer, Inc.,
> and subsidiaries (the Company) as of September 30, 2014, and September 30, 2013, and the
> related consolidated statements of operations, comprehensive income, shareholders' equity, and
> cash flows for each of the years in the three-year period ended September 30, 2014.
> We have also audited the company's internal control over financial reporting. These
> consolidated financial statements are the responsibility of the Company's management. Our
> responsibility is to express an opinion on these consolidated financial statements based on
> our audits and an opinion on the company's internal control over financial reporting
> based on our audits.
>
> We conducted our audits in accordance with the standards of the Public Company Accounting
> Oversight Board (United States)....
>
> In our opinion, the consolidated financial statements referred to above present fairly, in all
> material respects, the financial position of the Company as of September 30, 2014, and
> September 30, 2013, and the results of its operations and its cash flows for each of the
> years in the three-year period ended September 30, 2014, in conformity with accounting
> principles generally accepted in the United States of America. Also, in our opinion the company
> maintained effective internal control over financial reporting.
>
> SLMA LLP
>
> Aurora, Colorado
> December 28, 2014

1. Who is responsible for Meinike's financial statements?
2. By what accounting standards are the financial statements prepared?
3. Identify one concrete action that Meinike management takes to fulfill its responsibility for the reliability of the company's financial information.
4. Which entity gave an outside, independent opinion on the Meinike financial statements? Where was this entity located, and when did it release its opinion to the public?
5. Exactly what did the audit cover? Give names and dates.
6. By what standards did the auditor conduct the audit?
7. What was the auditor's opinion of Meinike's financial statements?

Exercises

> All of the A and B exercises can be found within MyAccountingLab, an online homework and practice environment. Your instructor might ask you to complete these exercises using **MyAccountingLab**.

MyAccountingLab

Group A

E11-15A. *(Learning Objective 1: Prepare and use a complex income statement; prepare a statement of comprehensive income)* Suppose Armstrong Cycles, Inc., reported a number of special items on its income statement. The following data, listed in no particular order, came from Armstrong's financial statements (amounts in thousands):

Income tax expense (savings):		Net sales..................................	$14,300
Continuing operations..................	$635	Foreign-currency translation	
Discontinued operations...............	94	gain, net of taxes...............................	310
Extraordinary loss........................	(4)	Extraordinary loss..................................	12
Unrealized gain on		Income from discontinued operations	320
available-for-sale investments,		Dividends declared and paid	650
net of taxes.................................	39	Total operating expenses........................	12,200
Short-term investments....................	45		

Requirements

1. Show how the Armstrong Cycles, Inc., multi-step income statement for the year ended September 30, 2014, should appear. Omit earnings per share. Use the end-of-chapter summary problem on pages 637–638 as an example.
2. Prepare the Statement of Comprehensive Income for Armstrong Cycles, Inc., for the year ended September 30, 2014. Use Exhibit 11-2 (p. 631) as an example.

E11-16A. *(Learning Objectives 1, 4: Prepare an income statement; compute earnings per share; evaluate quality of earnings; evaluate a company as an investment)* The Taavon Book Company accounting records include the following for 2014 (in thousands):

Other revenues	$ 1,700
Income tax expense	7,040
Sales revenue	124,000
Total operating expenses	101,600

Requirements

1. Prepare Taavon Book Company's single-step income statement for the year ended December 31, 2014, including EPS. Taavon had 1 million shares of common stock and no preferred stock outstanding during the year.
2. Assume Taavon Book Company's income from operations reflects that its core business has been steadily increasing by about 10% per year over the past three years and that none of its operations have been discontinued. What does this say about the quality of its earnings?
3. Assume investors capitalize Taavon Book's earnings from continuing operations at 9%. Estimate the price of one share of the company's stock.

E11-17A. *(Learning Objective 1: Use income data for investment analysis)* During 2014, Omega, Inc., had sales of $7.16 billion, operating profit of $2.70 billion, and net income of $3.70 billion. EPS was $6.50. On June 9, 2015, one share of Omega's common stock was priced at $75.60 on the New York Stock Exchange.

What investment capitalization rate did investors appear to be using to determine the value of one share of Omega stock? The formula for the value of one share of stock uses EPS in the calculation.

E11-18A. *(Learning Objective 2: Account for foreign-currency gains and losses)* Assume that Cooper Stores completed the following foreign-currency transactions:

Jun	9	Purchased DVD players as inventory on account from Moshu, a Japanese company. The price was 560,000 yen, and the exchange rate of the yen was $0.0078.
Jul	18	Paid Moshu when the exchange rate was $0.0072.
	22	Sold merchandise on account to Le Fleur, a French company, at a price of 45,000 euros. The exchange rate was $1.17. Ignore cost of goods sold.
	28	Collected from Le Fleur when the exchange rate was $1.14.

Requirements

1. Journalize these transactions for Cooper. Focus on the gains and losses caused by changes in foreign-currency rates. Round your answers to the nearest whole dollar.
2. On June 10, immediately after the purchase, and on July 23, immediately after the sale, which currencies did Cooper want to strengthen? Which currencies did in fact strengthen? Explain your reasoning.

E11-19A. *(Learning Objective 3: Account for income tax by a corporation)* During 2014, the Princeton Heights Corp. income statement reported income of $608,000 before tax. The company's income tax return filed with the IRS showed taxable income of $495,000. During 2014, Princeton Heights was subject to an income tax rate of 35%.

Requirements

1. Journalize Princeton Heights' income taxes for 2014.
2. How much income tax did Princeton Heights have to pay for the year 2014?
3. At the beginning of 2014, Princeton Heights' balance of Deferred Tax Liability was $25,600. How much Deferred Tax Liability did Princeton Heights report on its balance sheet at December 31, 2014?

E11-20A. *(Learning Objective 4: Compute earnings per common share)* Speedy Loan Company's balance sheet at December 31, 2014 reports the following:

Preferred stock, $20 par value, 3%, 11,000 shares issued	$ 220,000
Common stock, $2.50 par, 1,300,000 shares issued.....................	3,250,000
Treasury stock, common, 120,000 shares at cost	480,000

During 2014, Speedy earned net income of $5,700,000. Compute Speedy Loan's earnings per common share (EPS) for 2014; round EPS to two decimal places. Assume the number of shares issued and outstanding did not change during the year.

E11-21A. *(Learning Objective 4: Compute and use earnings per share)* Covey Holding Company operates numerous businesses, including motel, auto rental, and real estate companies. The year 2014 was interesting for Covey, which reported the following on its income statement (in millions):

Net revenues	$3,972
Total expenses and other..	3,227
Income from continuing operations.............................	745
Income from discontinued operations, net of tax	92
Income before extraordinary item	837
Extraordinary gain, net of tax.....................................	6
Net income..	$ 843

During 2014, Covey had the following (in millions, except for par value per share):

Common stock, $0.02 par value, 850 shares issued	$ 17
Treasury stock, 210 shares at cost..	(3,542)

Requirement

1. Using the end-of-chapter summary problem (pages 637–638) as an example, show how Covey should report earnings per share for 2014; round EPS to the nearest cent.

E11-22A. *(Learning Objective 5: Report a prior-period adjustment on the statement of retained earnings)* Sparkle, Inc., a household products chain, reported a prior-period adjustment in 2014. An accounting error caused net income of 2013 to be understated by $12 million. Retained earnings at December 31, 2013, as previously reported, was $463 million. Net income for 2014 was $81 million, and 2014 dividends declared were $42 million.

Requirement

1. Using the end-of-chapter summary problem (pages 637–638) as an example, prepare the company's statement of retained earnings for the year ended December 31, 2014. How does the prior-period adjustment affect Sparkle's net income for 2014?

E11-23A. *(Learning Objective 5: Prepare a statement of comprehensive income)* During the year ended December 31, 2014, Bowersox International Corporation earned $3,500,000 in net income after taxes. The company reported $100,000 of net unrealized gains on available-for-sale securities, net of taxes and $150,000 in foreign currency translation gains from consolidation of its Mexican subsidiary company, net of taxes.

Requirements

1. Prepare the Statement of Comprehensive Income for Bowersox International Corporation for the year ended December 31, 2014. Use Exhibit 11-2 on page 631 as an example.
2. Explain where the following items will appear in Bowersox International Corporation's Statement of Stockholder's Equity for the year ended December 31, 2014:
   a. Net income
   b. Net unrealized gains from available-for-sale securities, net of taxes
   c. Foreign currency translation gains from consolidation of Mexican subsidiary, net of taxes.

E11-24A. *(Learning Objective 5: Analyze segment information)* The following information appears in a footnote to the 2012 financial statements of Sears Holdings Corp.:

SUMMARY OF SEGMENT DATA

These reportable segment classifications are based on our business formats, as described in Note 1. Each of these segments derives its revenues from the sale of merchandise and related services to customers, primarily in the United States and Canada. The merchandise and service categories are as follows:

(i) Hardlines—consists of appliances, consumer electronics, lawn and garden, tools and hardware, automotive parts, household goods, toys, housewares and sporting goods;

(ii) Apparel and Soft Home—includes women's, men's, kids, footwear, jewelry, accessories and soft home;

(iii) Food and Drug—consists of grocery and household, pharmacy and drugstore; and

(iv) Service and Other—includes repair, installation and automotive service and extended contract revenue as well as revenues earned in connection with our agreements with SHO.

A1 ◆				
		B	C	D	E
1			2012		
2	*(In millions)*	Kmart	Sears Domestic	Sears Canada	Sears Holdings
3	Merchandise sales and services:				
4	Hardlines	$ 4,486	$ 11,870	$ 2,246	$ 18,602
5	Apparel and Soft Home	4,588	5,434	1,856	11,878
6	Food and Drug	5,398	38	—	5,436
7	Service and Other	95	3,635	208	3,938
8	Total merchandise sales and services	14,567	20,977	4,310	39,854
9	Operating income (loss)	$ 5	$ (656)	$ (187)	$ (838)
10					

A1 ◆				
		B	C	D	E
1			2011		
2	*(In millions)*	Kmart	Sears Domestic	Sears Canada	Sears Holdings
3	Merchandise sales and services:				
4	Hardlines	$ 4,765	$ 13,022	$ 2,377	$ 20,164
5	Apparel and Soft Home	4,723	5,471	2,011	12,205
6	Food and Drug	5,705	41	—	5,746
7	Service and Other	92	3,115	245	3,452
8	Total merchandise sales and services	15,285	21,649	4,633	41,567
9	Operating loss	$ (34)	$ (1,447)	$ (20)	$ (1,501)
10					

Requirements

1. What are Sears Holdings Corp.'s segments as of the end of its 2012 fiscal year?
2. Which segments appear to be performing better in 2012 than they did in 2011?
3. Which segments were the most profitable in 2012? Least profitable? Evaluate the overall profitability of Sears Holdings Corp. as of the close of 2012.
4. What can you learn from analyzing this segment information that helps make you a more prospective investor in Sears Holdings Corp.?

Group B

E11-25B. *(Learning Objective 1: Prepare and use a complex income statement; prepare a statement of comprehensive income)* Suppose Dion Cycles, Inc., reported a number of special items on its income statement. The following data, listed in no particular order, came from Dion's financial statements (amounts in thousands):

Income tax expense (savings):		Net sales.................................	$14,900
Continuing operations.................	$650	Foreign-currency translation	
Discontinued operations..............	83	gain, net of taxes	350
Extraordinary loss.......................	(4)	Extraordinary loss...............................	13
Unrealized gain on		Income from discontinued operations	280
available-for-sale investments,		Dividends declared and paid	640
net of taxes....................................	36	Total operating expenses.......................	12,700
Short-term investments....................	35		

Requirements

1. Show how the Dion Cycles, Inc., multi-step income statement for the year ended September 30, 2014, should appear. Omit earnings per share. Use the end-of-chapter summary problem (pages 637–638) as an example.
2. Prepare the Statement of Comprehensive Income for Dion Cycles, Inc., for the year ended September 30, 2014. Use Exhibit 11-2 (p. 631) as an example.

E11-26B. *(Learning Objectives 1, 4: Prepare an income statement; compute earnings per share; evaluate quality of earnings; evaluate a company as an investment)* The Berkstrom Book Company's accounting records include the following for 2014 (in thousands):

Other revenues..	$ 1,500
Income tax expense...	5,920
Sales revenue..	125,000
Total operating expenses...	106,200

Requirements

1. Prepare Berkstrom Book's single-step income statement for the year ended December 31, 2014, including EPS. Berkstrom Book had 800,000 shares of common stock and no preferred stock outstanding during the year.
2. Assume Berkstrom Book Company's income from operations reflects that its core business been steadily increasing by about 5% per year over the past three years and that none of its operations have been discontinued. What does this say about the quality of its earnings?
3. Assume investors capitalize Berkstrom Book earnings from continuing operations at 8%. Estimate the price of one share of the company's stock.

E11-27B. *(Learning Objective 1: Use income data for investment analysis)* During 2014, Alpha, Inc., had sales of $6.86 billion, operating profit of $2.20 billion, and net income of $3.40 billion. EPS was $6.75. On May 11, 2015, one share of Alpha's common stock was priced at $79.41 on the New York Stock Exchange.

What investment capitalization rate did investors appear to be using to determine the value of one share of Alpha stock? The formula for the value of one share of stock uses EPS in the calculation.

E11-28B. *(Learning Objective 2: Account for foreign-currency gains and losses)* Assume that Big Buy Stores completed the following foreign-currency transactions:

May 9	Purchased DVD players as inventory on account from Toyita, a Japanese company. The price was 350,000 yen, and the exchange rate of the yen was $0.0078.
Jun 18	Paid Toyita when the exchange rate was $0.0073.
22	Sold merchandise on account to Bon Appetit, a French company, at a price of 25,000 euros. The exchange rate was $1.17. Ignore cost of goods sold.
28	Collected from Bon Appetit when the exchange rate was $1.15.

Requirements

1. Journalize these transactions for Big Buy. Focus on the gains and losses caused by changes in foreign-currency rates; round your answers to the nearest whole dollar.
2. On May 10, immediately after the purchase, and on June 23, immediately after the sale, which currencies did Big Buy want to strengthen? Which currencies did in fact strengthen? Explain your reasoning.

E11-29B. *(Learning Objective 3: Account for income tax by a corporation)* During 2014, Yale Heights Corp.'s income statement reported income of $417,000 before tax. The company's income tax return filed with the IRS showed taxable income of $320,000. During 2014, Yale Heights was subject to an income tax rate of 30%.

Requirements

1. Journalize Yale Heights' income taxes for 2014.
2. How much income tax did Yale Heights have to pay for the year 2014?
3. At the beginning of 2014, Yale Heights' balance of Deferred Tax Liability was $23,700. How much Deferred Tax Liability did Yale Heights report on its balance sheet at December 31, 2014?

E11-30B. *(Learning Objective 4: Compute earnings per share)* Easy Loan Company's balance sheet at December 31, 2014 reports the following:

Preferred stock, $80 par value, 6%, 11,000 shares issued	$ 880,000
Common stock, $2.50 par, 1,400,000 shares issued.....................	3,500,000
Treasury stock, common, 130,000 shares at cost	900,000

During 2014, Easy Loan earned net income of $6,700,000. Compute Easy Loan's earnings per common share (EPS) for 2014. (Round EPS to two decimal places.) Assume the number of shares issued and outstanding did not change during the year.

E11-31B. *(Learning Objective 4: Compute and use earnings per share)* Werner Holding Company operates numerous businesses, including motel, auto rental, and real estate companies. The year 2014 was interesting for Werner, which reported the following on its income statement (in millions):

Net revenues	$3,950
Total expenses and other...	3,217
Income from continuing operations...............................	733
Loss from discontinued operations,	
net of tax savings	(57)
Income before extraordinary item	676
Extraordinary gain, net of tax..	4
Net income..	$ 680

During 2014, Werner had the following (in millions, except for par value per share):

Common stock, $0.25 par value, 840 shares issued	$ 210
Treasury stock, 170 shares at cost..	(3,600)

Requirement

1. Using the end-of-chapter summary problem (pages 637–638) as an example, show how Werner should report earnings per share for 2014; round EPS to the nearest cent.

E11-32B. *(Learning Objective 5: Report a prior-period adjustment on the statement of retained earnings)* Bright House, Inc., a household products chain, reported a prior-period adjustment in 2014. An accounting error caused net income of 2013 to be overstated by $13 million. Retained earnings at December 31, 2013, as previously reported, was $418 million. Net income for 2014 was $88 million, and 2014 dividends declared were $41 million.

Requirement

1. Using the end-of-chapter summary problem (pages 637–638) as an example, prepare the company's statement of retained earnings for the year ended December 31, 2014. How does the prior-period adjustment affect Bright House's net income for 2014?

E11-33B. *(Learning Objective 5: Prepare a statement of comprehensive income)* During the year ended December 31, 2014, Longman International Corporation earned $6,500,000 in net income after taxes. The company reported $100,000 of net unrealized losses on available-for-sale securities, net of taxes and $150,000 in foreign currency translation losses from consolidation of its Brazilian subsidiary company, net of taxes.

Requirements

1. Prepare the Statement of Comprehensive Income for Longman International Corporation for the year ended December 31, 2014. Use Exhibit 11-2 on page 631 as an example.
2. Explain where the following items will appear in Longman International Corporation's Statement of Stockholder's Equity for the year ended December 31, 2014:
   a. Net income
   b. Net unrealized losses from available-for-sale securities, net of taxes
   c. Foreign currency translation losses from consolidation of Mexican subsidiary, net of taxes.

E11-34B. *(Learning Objective 5: Analyze segment information)* The following information appears in a footnote to the 2012 financial statements of Nike, Inc.:

	A	B	C	D
			Year Ended May 31,	
1		2012	2011	2010
2	*(In millions)*			
3	**REVENUE**			
4	North America	$ 8,839	$ 7,579	$ 6,697
5	Western Europe	4,144	3,868	3,839
6	Central & Eastern Europe	1,200	1,040	999
7	Greater China	2,539	2,060	1,742
8	Japan	829	766	882
9	Emerging Markets	3,410	2,736	2,198
10	Global Brand Divisions	111	96	86
11	Total NIKE Brand	21,072	18,145	16,443
12	Other Businesses	3,095	2,786	2,564
13	Corporate	(39)	(69)	7
14	**TOTAL NIKE CONSOLIDATED REVENUES**	**$ 24,128**	**$ 20,862**	**$ 19,014**
15	**EARNINGS BEFORE INTEREST AND TAXES**			
16	North America	$ 2,007	$ 1,736	$ 1,538
17	Western Europe	597	730	807
18	Central & Eastern Europe	234	244	249
19	Greater China	911	777	637
20	Japan	136	114	180
21	Emerging Markets	853	688	521
22	Global Brand Divisions	(1,177)	(971)	(866)
23	Total NIKE Brand	3,561	3,318	3,066
24	Other Businesses	341	335	298
25	Corporate	(916)	(805)	(841)
26	Total NIKE Consolidated Earnings Before Interest and Taxes	2,986	2,848	2,523
27				

Requirements

1. Based on this information, what do you think are Nike, Inc.'s reportable segments as of the end of its 2012 fiscal year?
2. Which segments appear to be growing fastest in 2012? Slowest?
3. Which segments were the most profitable in 2012? Least profitable? Evaluate the overall profitability of Nike, Inc., as of the close of 2012.
4. What can you learn from analyzing this segment information that helps make you a more prospective investor in Nike, Inc.?

Quiz

Test your understanding of the corporate income statement and the statement of stockholders' equity by answering the following questions. Select the best choice from among the possible answers given.

Q11-35. What is the most relevant net income figure on a corporate multi-step income statement for predicting future profits and for use in investment valuation?

    a. Continuing operations   **c.** Discontinued operations

    b. Prior-period adjustments   **d.** Extraordinary items

Q11-36. Leslie's Lotion Company reports several earnings numbers on its current-year income statement (parentheses indicate a loss):

Gross profit.............................	$165,000	Income from continuing operations.......	$ 40,000
Net income...............................	41,000	Extraordinary gains.............................	11,000
Income before income tax	78,000	Discontinued operations......................	(10,000)

How much net income would most investment analysts predict for Leslie's to earn next year?

a. $41,000

b. $78,000

c. $40,000

d. $30,000

Q11-37. Return to the preceding question. Suppose you are evaluating Leslie's Lotion Company stock as an investment. You require an 8% rate of return on investments, so you capitalize Leslie's earnings at 8%. How much are you willing to pay for all of Leslie's stock?

a. $2,062,500

b. $500,000

c. $512,500

d. $975,000

Q11-38. Boston Systems purchased inventory on account from Megaplex. The price was ¥140,000, and a yen was quoted at $0.0091. Boston paid the debt in yen a month later when the price of a yen was $0.0092. Boston

a. recorded a foreign-currency transaction gain of $14.

b. debited Inventory for $1,288.

c. debited Inventory for $1,274.

d. None of the above.

Q11-39. One way to hedge a foreign-currency transaction loss is to

a. collect in your own currency.

b. pay in the foreign currency.

c. offset foreign-currency inventory and plant assets.

d. pay debts as late as possible.

Q11-40. Foreign-currency transaction gains and losses are reported on the

a. balance sheet.

b. consolidation work sheet.

c. statement of cash flows.

d. income statement.

Q11-41. Earnings per share is *not* reported for

a. discontinued operations.

b. comprehensive income.

c. extraordinary items.

d. continuing operations.

Q11-42. Copycat Corporation has income before income tax of $110,000 and taxable income of $100,000. The income tax rate is 30%. Copycat's income statement will report net income of

a. $30,000.

b. $33,000.

c. $107,000.

d. $77,000.

Q11-43. Copycat Corporation in the preceding question must immediately pay income tax of

a. $77,000.

b. $33,000.

c. $30,000.

d. $70,000.

Q11-44. Use the Copycat Corporation data in Q11-43. At the end of its first year of operations, Copycat's deferred tax liability is

a. $3,000.

b. $11,000.

c. $27,000.

d. $19,000.

Q11-45. Which of the following items is most closely related to prior-period adjustments?

a. Earnings per share

b. Retained earnings

c. Preferred stock dividends

d. Treasury stock

Q11-46. Segment information is reported in a company's

a. balance sheet.

b. income statement.

c. statement of stockholders' equity.

d. financial statement footnotes.

Q11-47. Which statement is true?

a. Auditors of public companies audit financial statements as well as internal controls.

b. GAAP requires companies to issue reports on corporate social responsibility (CSR).

c. Management audits the financial statements.

d. Independent auditors prepare the financial statements.

Problems

MyAccountingLab

All of the A and B problems can be found within MyAccountingLab, an online home-work and practice environment. Your instructor might ask you to complete these problems using **MyAccountingLab**.

Group A

P11-48A. *(Learning Objectives 1, 4: Prepare a complex income statement, including earnings per share; evaluate quality of earnings)* The following information was taken from the records of Ryder Cosmetics, Inc., at December 31, 2014:

Prior-period adjustment—net of taxes			Dividends on common stock	$ 38,000
debit to Retained Earnings	$ 8,400		Interest expense	23,000
Income tax expense (savings):			Gain on lawsuit settlement	8,100
Continuing operations	40,300		Dividend revenue	13,000
Income from discontinued			Treasury stock, common	
operations	4,600		(3,000 shares at cost)	15,000
Extraordinary loss	(8,570)		General expenses	71,900
Loss on sale of plant assets	11,000		Sales revenue	603,000
Income from discontinued			Retained earnings, beginning,	
operations	14,000		as originally reported	201,000
Preferred stock, 8%, $30 par,			Selling expenses	82,000
3,000 shares issued	90,000		Common stock, no par,	
Extraordinary loss	29,000		26,000 shares authorized	
Cost of goods sold	294,000		and issued	360,000

Requirements

1. Using the End-of-Chapter Summary Problem (pages 637–638) as an example, prepare Ryder Cosmetics' single-step income statement, which lists all revenues together and all expenses together, for the fiscal year ended December 31, 2014. Include earnings-per-share data. For purposes of earnings per share, assume dividends have been declared on preferred stock as of December 31.
2. Evaluate income for the year ended December 31, 2014. Ryder's top managers hoped to earn income from continuing operations equal to 15% of sales.

P11-49A. *(Learning Objective 5: Preparing a statement of retained earnings)* Use the data in P11-48A to prepare the Ryder Cosmetics statement of retained earnings for the year ended December 31, 2014. Use the Statement of Retained Earnings for Maxim, Inc., in the End-of-Chapter Summary Problem on pages 637–638 as a model.

P11-50A. *(Learning Objective 1: Use income data to make an investment decision)* Ryder Cosmetics in P11-48A holds significant promise for carving a niche in its industry. A group of Irish investors is considering purchasing the company's outstanding common stock. Ryder's stock is currently selling for $45 per share.

A *BetterLife Magazine* story predicted the company's income is bound to grow. It appears that Ryder can earn at least its current level of income for the indefinite future. Based on this information, the investors think that an appropriate investment capitalization rate for estimating the value of Ryder's common stock is 10%. How much will this belief lead the investors to offer for Ryder Cosmetics? Will Ryder's existing stockholders be likely to accept this offer? Explain your answers.

P11-51A. *(Learning Objective 2: Account for foreign-currency gains or losses)* Suppose Xavier Corporation completed the following international transactions:

May	1	Sold inventory on account to Giorgio, the Italian automaker, for €75,000. The exchange rate of the euro was $1.35, and Giorgio demands to pay in euros. Ignore cost of goods sold.
	10	Purchased supplies on account from a Canadian company at a price of Canadian $46,000. The exchange rate of the Canadian dollar was $0.76, and the payment will be in Canadian dollars.
	17	Sold inventory on account to an English firm for 139,000 British pounds. Payment will be in pounds, and the exchange rate of the pound was $1.91. Ignore cost of goods sold.
	22	Collected from Giorgio. The exchange rate is €1 = $1.38.
Jun	18	Paid the Canadian company. The exchange rate of the Canadian dollar is $0.75.
	24	Collected from the English firm. The exchange rate of the British pound was $1.88.

Requirements

1. Record these transactions in Xavier's journal and show how to report the foreign currency transaction gain or loss on the income statement.
2. How will what you learned in this problem help you structure international transactions?

P11-52A. *(Learning Objectives 1, 3, 4: Evaluate quality of earnings; compute earnings per share; estimate the price of a stock)* Capital Experts, Ltd. (CEL), specializes in taking underperforming companies to a higher level of performance. CEL's capital structure at December 31, 2013, included 28,000 shares of $2.25 preferred stock and 225,000 shares of common stock. During 2014, CEL issued common stock and ended the year with 243,000 shares of common stock outstanding. Average common shares outstanding during 2014 were 235,000. Income from continuing operations during 2014 was $485,000. The company discontinued a segment of the business at a loss of $89,000, and an extraordinary item generated a gain of $94,000. All amounts are after income tax. Assume the number of preferred shares outstanding did not change in 2014.

Requirements

1. Compute CEL's earnings per share. Start with income from continuing operations.
2. Analysts believe CEL can earn its current level of income for the indefinite future. Estimate the market price of a share of CEL common stock at investment capitalization rates of 9%, 11%, and 13%. Which estimate presumes an investment in CEL is the most risky? How can you tell?

P11-53A. *(Learning Objectives 3, 4, 5: Prepare an income statement; compute earnings per share; prepare a statement of comprehensive income)* Will Tompkins, accountant for Greene Harvest Foods, Inc., was injured in an auto accident. While he was recuperating, another, inexperienced employee prepared the following income statement for the fiscal year ended June 30, 2014:

	A	B	C
1	**Greene Harvest Foods, Inc.** **Income Statement** **June 30, 2014**		
2	**Revenue and gains:**		
3	Sales		$ 983,000
4	Paid-in capital in excess of par—common		11,000
5	Total revenues and gains		994,000
6	**Expenses and losses:**		
7	Cost of goods sold	$ 464,000	
8	Selling expenses	51,000	
9	General expenses	92,000	
10	Sales returns	20,000	
11	Unrealized loss on available-for-sale investments	10,000	
12	Dividends paid	16,000	
13	Sales discounts	14,000	
14	Income tax expense	102,600	
15	Total expenses and losses		769,600
16	Income from operations		224,400
17	**Other gains and losses:**		
18	Extraordinary gain	36,000	
19	Loss on discontinued operations	(25,000)	
20	Total other gains (losses)		11,000
21	Net income		$ 235,400
22	Earnings per share		$ 23.54
23			

The individual *amounts* listed on the income statement are correct. However, some *accounts* are reported incorrectly, and some accounts do not belong on the income statement at all. Also, income tax (30%) has not been applied to all appropriate figures. Greene Harvest Foods issued 27,000 shares of common stock back in 2004 and held 7,000 shares as treasury stock all during the fiscal year 2014.

Requirement

1. Using the End-of-Chapter Summary Problem (pages 637–638) as an example, prepare a corrected income statement for Greene Harvest Foods, Inc., for the fiscal year ended June 30, 2014. Use the single-step format, which lists all revenues together and all expenses together. Also prepare the earnings-per-share section of the statement.
2. Using Exhibit 11-2 (p. 631) as an example, prepare a Statement of Comprehensive Iincome for Greene Harvest Foods, Inc., for the fiscal year ended June 30, 2014. Start with net income, as computed in Requirement 1.

P11-54A. *(Learning Objective 3: Account for a corporation's income tax)* The accounting (not the income tax) records of Kaska Publications, Inc., provide the income statement for 2014.

	2014
Total revenue	$760,000
Expenses:	
Cost of goods sold	$355,000
Operating expenses	180,000
Total expenses before tax	535,000
Pretax accounting income	$225,000

Taxable income for 2014 includes these modifications from pre-tax accounting income:
  a. Additional taxable income of $16,000 earned in 2015 but taxed in 2014
  b. Additional depreciation expense of $38,000 for MACRS tax depreciation in 2014

The income tax rate is 33%.

Requirements

1. Compute Kaska's taxable income for 2014.
2. Journalize the corporation's income taxes for 2014.
3. Prepare the corporation's single-step income statement for 2014.

Group B

P11-55B. *(Learning Objectives 1, 4: Prepare a complex income statement, including earnings per share; evaluate quality of earnings)* The following information was taken from the records of Midler Cosmetics, Inc., at December 31, 2014:

Prior-period adjustment—net of taxes		Dividends on common stock	$37,000
debit to Retained Earnings.............	$ 9,300	Interest expense................................	25,000
Income tax expense (saving):		Gain on lawsuit settlement................	10,400
Continuing operations	35,950	Dividend revenue	16,000
Income from discontinued		Treasury stock, common	
operations......................................	6,100	(5,000 shares at cost)...............	15,000
Extraordinary loss	(4,300)	General expenses.............................	81,000
Loss on sale of plant assets.....................	15,000	Sales revenue	628,000
Income from discontinued		Retained earnings, beginning,	
operations......................................	20,000	as originally reported...............	202,000
Preferred stock, 6%, $30 par,		Selling expenses.................................	93,000
1,000 shares issued	30,000	Common stock, no par,	
Extraordinary loss.................................	14,000	36,000 shares authorized	
Cost of goods sold..................................	314,200	and issued..................................	390,000

Requirements

1. Using the End-of-Chapter Summary Problem (pages 637–638) as an example, prepare Midler Cosmetics' single-step income statement, which lists all revenues together and all expenses together, for the fiscal year ended December 31, 2014. Include earnings-per-share data. For purposes of earnings per share, assume dividends have been declared on preferred stock as of December.
2. Evaluate income for the year ended December 31, 2014. Midler's top managers hoped to earn income from continuing operations equal to 16% of sales.

P11-56B. *(Learning Objective 5: Prepare a statement of retained earnings)* Use the data in P11-55B to prepare the Midler Cosmetics statement of retained earnings for the year ended December 31, 2014. Use the Statement of Retained Earnings for Maxim, Inc., in the End-of-Chapter Summary Problem (pages 637–638) as a model.

P11-57B. *(Learning Objective 1: Use income data to make an investment decision)* Midler Cosmetics in Problem P11-55B holds significant promise for carving a niche in its industry. A group of Irish investors is considering purchasing the company's outstanding common stock. Midler's stock is currently selling for $38 per share.

A *Better Life Magazine* story predicted the company's income is bound to grow. It appears that Midler can earn at least its current level of income for the indefinite future. Based on this information, the investors think that an appropriate investment capitalization rate for estimating the value of Midler's common stock is 7%. How much will this belief lead the investors to offer for Midler Cosmetics? Will Midler's existing stockholders be likely to accept this offer? Explain your answers.

P11-58B. *(Learning Objective 2: Account for foreign-currency gains or losses)* Suppose Desmond Corporation completed the following international transactions:

May	1	Sold inventory on account to Aromando, the Italian automaker, for €65,000. The exchange rate of the euro was $1.33, and Aromando demands to pay in euros. Ignore cost of goods sold.
	10	Purchased supplies on account from a Canadian company at a price of Canadian $52,000. The exchange rate of the Canadian dollar was $0.72, and the payment will be in Canadian dollars.
	17	Sold inventory on account to an English firm for 125,000 British pounds. Payment will be in pounds, and the exchange rate of the pound was $1.93. Ignore cost of goods sold.
	22	Collected from Aromando. The exchange rate is €1 = $1.36.
Jun	18	Paid the Canadian company. The exchange rate of the Canadian dollar is $0.71.
	24	Collected from the English firm. The exchange rate of the British pound was $1.90.

Requirements

1. Record these transactions in Desmond's journal, and show how to report the foreign currency transaction gain or loss on the income statement.
2. How will what you learned in this problem help you structure international transactions?

P11-59B. *(Learning Objectives 1, 3, 4: Evaluate quality of earnings; compute earnings per share; estimate the price of a stock)* Better Experts, Ltd. (BEL), specializes in taking underperforming companies to a higher level of performance. BEL's capital structure at December 31, 2013, included 20,000 shares of $2.25 preferred stock and 240,000 shares of common stock. During 2014, BEL issued common stock and ended the year with 258,000 shares of common stock outstanding. Average common shares outstanding during 2014 were 245,000. Income from continuing operations during 2014 was $449,000. The company discontinued a segment of the business at a loss of $57,000, and an extraordinary item generated a gain of $94,000. All amounts are after income tax. Assume the number of preferred shares outstanding did not change in 2014.

Requirements

1. Compute BEL's earnings per share. Start with income from continuing operations.
2. Analysts believe BEL can earn its current level of income for the indefinite future. Estimate the market price of a share of BEL common stock at investment capitalization rates of 6%, 8%, and 10%. Which estimate presumes an investment in BEL is the most risky? How can you tell?

P11-60B. *(Learning Objectives 3, 4, 5: Prepare an income statement; compute earnings per share; prepare a statement of comprehensive income)* Carter Huntt, accountant for Southern Harvest Foods, Inc., was injured in an auto accident. While he was recuperating, another, inexperienced employee prepared the following income statement for the fiscal year ended June 30, 2014:

A1			
	A	**B**	**C**
1	**Southern Harvest Foods, Inc.** **Income Statement** **June 30, 2014**		
2	**Revenue and gains:**		
3	Sales		$ 897,000
4	Paid-in capital in excess of par—common		15,000
5	Total revenues and gains		912,000
6	**Expenses and losses:**		
7	Cost of goods sold	$ 363,000	
8	Selling expenses	49,000	
9	General expenses	75,000	
10	Sales returns	21,000	
11	Unrealized loss on available-for-sale investments	14,000	
12	Dividends paid	16,000	
13	Sales discounts	12,000	
14	Income tax expense	113,100	
15	Total expenses and losses		663,100
16	Income from operations		248,900
17	**Other gains and losses:**		
18	Extraordinary gain	44,000	
19	Loss on discontinued operations	(28,000)	
20	Total other gains (losses)		16,000
21	Net income		$ 264,900
22	Earnings per share		$ 13.25
23			

The individual *amounts* listed on the income statement are correct. However, some *accounts* are reported incorrectly, and some accounts do not belong on the income statement at all. Also, income tax (30%) has not been applied to all appropriate figures. Southern Harvest Foods issued 38,000 shares of common stock back in 2004 and held 8,000 shares as treasury stock all during the fiscal year 2014.

Requirement

1. Using the End-of-Chapter Summary Problem (pages 637–638) as an example, prepare a corrected Income Statement for Southern Harvest Foods, Inc., for the fiscal year ended June 30, 2014. Use the single-step format, which lists all revenues together and all expenses together. Also prepare the earnings-per-share section of the statement.
2. Using Exhibit 11-2 (p. 631) as an example, prepare a Statement of Comprehensive Income for Southern Harvest Foods, Inc., for the fiscal year ended June 30, 2014. Start with net income as computed in Requirement 1.

P11-61B. *(Learning Objective 3: Account for a corporation's income tax)* The accounting (not the income tax) records of Neighbors Publications, Inc., provide the income statement for 2014.

	2014
Total revenue	$790,000
Expenses:	
Cost of goods sold	$410,000
Operating expenses	175,000
Total expenses before tax	585,000
Pretax accounting income	$205,000

Taxable income for 2014 includes these modifications from pre-tax accounting income:

    a. Additional taxable income of $14,000 earned in 2015 but taxed in 2014

    b. Additional depreciation expense of $21,000 for MACRS tax depreciation in 2014

The income tax rate is 32%.

Requirements

1. Compute Neighbor's taxable income for 2014.
2. Journalize the corporation's income taxes for 2014.
3. Prepare the corporation's single-step income statement for 2014.

Challenge Problem

P11-62. *(Learning Objectives 1, 2, 4, 5: Analyze how various transactions affect the income statement and EPS)* Aerostar, Inc., operates as a retailer of casual apparel. A recent, condensed income statement for Aerostar follows:

	A1 ⬍			
	A		**B**	**C**
1	**Income Statement** **For the Year Ended January 31, 2012**			
2	Sales revenue			$ 2,400,000
3	Operating expenses:			
4	Cost of goods sold		$ 1,500,000	
5	Selling and administrative expenses		500,000	2,000,000
6	Operating income			400,000
7	Other revenue (expenses)			50,000
8	Income before tax			450,000
9	Income tax expense (40% tax rate)			180,000
10	Net income			$ 270,000
11	Earnings per share (50,000 shares)			$ 5.40
12				

Requirements

1. Assume that the following transactions were inadvertently omitted at the end of the year. Using the categories in the table, indicate the effect of each of the transactions on each category; use + for increase, − for decrease, and NE for no effect. Provide dollar amounts for each column except Earnings per Share.

Transaction	Operating Income	Income Before Tax	Net Income	Earnings per Share
Unadjusted balances	400,000	450,000	270,000	
a.				
b.				
c.				
d.				
e.				
f.				
g.				
h.				
i.				
Totals				

    a. Purchased inventory on account from a German company. The price was 100,000 euros. The exchange rate of the euro was $1.47.

    b. Sold inventory on account, $120,000 (cost of inventory, $75,000).

    c. Corrected a $50,000 overstatement of depreciation expense from a previous year.

    d. Paid the German company for the inventory purchased when the exchange rate was $1.50.

    e. Distributed 5,000 shares in a 10% stock dividend. The market value of the stock was $50.

    f. Recorded additional administrative expense, $5,000.

    g. Recorded interest earned, $20,000.

    h. Declared dividends on preferred stock, $50,000.

    i. Issued additional 5,000 shares of common stock, $260,000.

2. Determine the amount of Operating Income, Income Before Tax, Net Income, and Earnings Per Share after recording these transactions. Assume transactions (e) and (i) occurred on January 1.

APPLY YOUR KNOWLEDGE

Decision Cases

Case 1. *(Learning Objective 1: Evaluate quality of earnings)* Prudhoe Bay Oil Co. is having its initial public offering (IPO) of company stock. To create public interest in its stock, Prudhoe Bay's chief financial officer has blitzed the media with press releases. One in particular caught your eye. On November 19, Prudhoe Bay announced unaudited earnings per share (EPS) of $1.19—up 89% from last year's EPS of $0.63. An 89% increase in EPS is outstanding!

    Before deciding to buy Prudhoe Bay stock, you investigated further and found that the company omitted several items from the determination of unaudited EPS:

- Unrealized loss on available-for-sale investments, $0.06 per share
- Gain on sale of building, $0.05 per share
- Prior-period adjustment, increase in retained earnings, $1.10 per share
- Restructuring expenses, $0.29 per share
- Loss on settlement of lawsuit begun five years ago, $0.12 per share
- Lost income due to employee labor strike, $0.24 per share
- Income from discontinued operations, $0.09 per share

Wondering how to treat these "special items," you called your stockbroker at **Merrill Lynch**. She thinks that these items are nonrecurring and outside Prudhoe Bay's core operations. Furthermore, she suggests that you ignore the items and consider Prudhoe Bay's earnings of $1.19 per share to be a good estimate of long-term profitability.

Requirement

1. What EPS number will you use to predict Prudhoe Bay's future profits? Show your work, and explain your reasoning for each item.

Case 2. *(Learning Objective 1: Evaluate quality of earnings)* Mike Magid Toyota is an automobile dealership. Magid's annual report includes Note 1—Summary of Significant Accounting Policies as follows:

> **Income Recognition**
>
> **Sales are recognized when cash payment is received or, in the case of credit sales, which represent the majority of . . . sales, when a down payment is received and the customer enters into an installment sales contract. These installment sales contracts . . . are normally collectible over 36 to 60 months. . . .**
>
> **Revenue from auto insurance policies sold to customers are recognized as income over the life of the contracts.**

Bay Area Nissan, a competitor of Mike Magid Toyota, includes the following note in its Summary of Significant Accounting Policies:

> ### Accounting Policies for Revenues
>
> Sales are recognized when cash payment is received or, in the case of credit sales, which represent the majority of . . . sales, when the customer enters into an installment sales contract. Customer down payments are rare. Most of these installment sales contracts are normally collectible over 36 to 60 months. . . . Revenue from auto insurance policies sold to customers are recognized when the customer signs an insurance contract. Expenses are recognized over the life of the insurance contracts.

Suppose you have decided to invest in an auto dealership, and you've narrowed your choices to Magid and Bay Area. Which company's earnings are of higher quality? Why? Will their accounting policies affect your investment decision? If so, how? Mention specific accounts in the financial statements that will differ between the two companies. (Challenge)

Ethical Issue

The income statement of Royal Bank of Singapore reported the following results of operations:

Earnings before income taxes and extraordinary gain	$187,046
Income tax expense	72,947
Earnings before extraordinary gain	114,099
Extraordinary gain, net of income tax	419,557
Net earnings	$533,656

Suppose Royal Bank's management, in violation of International Financial Reporting Standards (IFRS), had reported the company's results of operations in this manner:

Earnings before income taxes	$706,603
Income tax expense	172,947
Net earnings	$533,656

Requirements

1. Identify the ethical issue in this situation.
2. Who are the stakeholders?
3. Evaluate the issue from the standpoint of (a) economic, (b) legal or regulatory, and (c) ethical dimensions. What are the possible effects on all stakeholders you identified?
4. Put yourself in the position of the controller of the bank. Your boss, the CEO, tries to pressure you to make the disclosure that violates IFRS. What would you do? What are the potential consequences?

Focus on Financials | Amazon.com, Inc.

(Learning Objective 1: Evaluate quality of earnings; evaluate an investment) Refer to the **Amazon.com, Inc.**, consolidated financial statements in Appendix A at the end of this book.

1. Amazon.com, Inc.'s consolidated statements of operations do not mention income from continuing operations. Why not? Focus your attention on the company's Consolidated Statements of Operations for the three years ended December 31, 2012, as well as the footnotes to financial statements and other materials. What clues do you find that help you evaluate the quality of Amazon.com, Inc.'s earnings?
2. Assume the role of an investor. Suppose you are determining the price to pay for a share of Amazon.com, Inc., stock. Assume you are considering three investment capitalization rates that depend on the risk of an investment in Amazon.com: 5%, 6%, and 7%. Compute your estimated value of a share of Amazon.com, Inc., stock, using each of the three capitalization rates. Which estimated value would you base your investment strategy on if you rate Amazon.com, Inc., risky? If you consider Amazon.com, Inc., a safe investment?

Note: Since earnings per share is negative, use (net cash provided by operations ÷ basic weighted average shares outstanding) as a basis for making your evaluation.

3. Go to Amazon.com's website and compare your computed estimates to its actual stock price. Which of your prices is most realistic? (Challenge)

Focus on Analysis | Yum! Brands, Inc.

(Learning Objectives 1, 5: Evaluate quality of earnings; evaluate an investment; analyze supplemental disclosures) This case is based on the **Yum! Brands, Inc.** consolidated financial statements in Appendix B at the end of this book.

1. Focus on the company's Consolidated Statements of Income for the three years ended December 31, 2012, as well as Note 2 summarizing the company's significant accounting policies. What is your evaluation of the quality of Yum! Brands, Inc.'s earnings? Explain how you formed your opinion.
2. Refer to Note 18 to the Consolidated Financial Statements. How does Yum! Brands, Inc.'s management define its operating segments? Which financial statement information does the company report by operating segment? Which segment appears to be the largest? What does this tell you about the international nature of Yum! Brands, Inc.'s business?
3. At the end of 2012, how much would you have been willing to pay for one share of Yum! Brands, Inc.'s stock if you had rated the investment as high risk? As low risk? Use even-numbered investment capitalization rates in the range of 4%–10% for your analysis, and use basic earnings per share for continuing operations.
4. Go to Yum! Brands, Inc.'s website and get the current price of a share of its common stock. Which value that you estimated in requirement 3 is closest to the company's actual stock price? (Challenge)
5. (Challenge) Does Yum! Brands, Inc., produce a corporate social responsibility report (CSR)? What are the company's CSR priorities?

Group Project

Select a company and research its business. Search the Internet for articles about this company. Obtain its latest available annual report from the company's website or from www.sec.gov. Click "Filings." Then, use the link entitled "Company Filings Search."

Requirements

1. Based on your group's analysis, come to class prepared to instruct the class on six interesting facts about the company that can be found in its financial statements and the related notes. Your group can mention only the obvious, such as net sales or total revenue, net income, total assets, total liabilities, total stockholders' equity, and dividends, in conjunction with other terms. Once you use an obvious item, you may not use that item again.
2. The group should write a paper discussing the facts that it has uncovered. Limit the paper to two double-spaced word-processed pages.

For online homework, exercises, and problems that provide you with immediate feedback, please visit www.myaccountinglab.com.

MyAccountingLab

Quick Check Answers

1. *b*	5. *c*	9. *d*
2. *a*	6. *a* ($1,400,000 × $0.97)	10. *b*
3. *c* ($6.39/0.09)	7. *b*	11. *c*
4. *d* (($37,000)/(0.74)) (rounding causes slight differences for computations of other lines)	8. *d*	12. *a*

12 The Statement of Cash Flows

> ➤ **SPOTLIGHT:** **Google: The Ultimate Answer (and Cash) Machine**

What Internet search engine do you use? When you're looking for an answer to a question, like most people, you may "just Google it." Google is the world's most popular search engine. Created by Larry Page and Sergey Brin when they were students at Stanford University, Google has grown from small beginnings to become a global technology leader that has helped transform the way people obtain all sorts of information. The company generates revenue primarily by delivering cost-effective online advertising. Google maintains an index of billions of web pages, which it makes freely available via its search engine to anyone with an Internet connection. Google stock has been a "hit" on Wall Street since its initial public offering (IPO). Recently, a share of Google, Inc., traded between $550 and $900 per share!

The beauty of Google is that it's so easy to use. Access the Internet at www.google.com, and you can simply enter what you want to find in the search box; you get a list of helpful websites. The world is literally at your fingertips. Google may be the ultimate answer machine and, in recent years, it has become a cash machine as well! In 2012, its Net cash provided by operating activities exceeded its Net income by almost $6 billion, and the company finished the year with almost $14.8 billion in Cash and cash equivalents on the books! ●

David Grossman/Photo Researchers, Inc.

A1		

	A	B	C
1	**Google, Inc.** **Consolidated Statements of Cash Flows (Adapted)**		
2		**12 Months Ended**	
3	(In millions of $)	Dec. 31, 2012	Dec. 31, 2011
4	**Operating activities**		
5	Net income	$ 10,737	$ 9,737
6	Adjustments:		
7	Depreciation and amortization, property and equipment	1,988	1,396
8	Amortization of intangible and other assets	974	455
9	Stock-based compensation, net of taxes	2,504	1,888
10	Deferred income taxes	(266)	343
11	Other gains and losses	(216)	116
12	Changes in current assets and liabilities		
13	Accounts receivable	(787)	(1,156)
14	Income taxes, net	1,492	731
15	Inventories	301	(30)
16	Prepaid revenue, expenses and other assets	(833)	(232)
17	Accounts payable	(499)	101
18	Accrued expenses and other liabilities	762	795
19	Accrued revenue share	299	259
20	Deferred revenue	163	162
21	Net cash provided by operating activities	16,619	14,565
22	**Investing activities**		
23	Purchases of property and equipment	(3,273)	(3,438)
24	Purchases of marketable securities	(33,410)	(61,672)
25	Maturities and sales of marketable securities	35,180	48,746
26	Other investments, net	(985)	(777)
27	Acquisitions of other companies	(10,568)	(1,900)
28	Net cash used in investing activities	(13,056)	(19,041)
29	**Financing activities**		
30	Stock-based compensation, net of taxes	(99)	81
31	Proceeds from issuance of debt, net of costs	16,109	10,905
32	Repayment of debt	(14,781)	(10,179)
33	Net cash provided by financing activities	1,229	807
34	Effect of exchange rate changes on cash and cash equivalents	3	22
35	Net increase (decrease) in cash and cash equivalents	4,795	(3,647)
36	Cash and cash equivalents at beginning of year	9,983	13,630
37	Cash and cash equivalents at end of year	$ 14,778	$ 9,983
38	Supplemental disclosures of cash flow information		
39	Cash paid for interest	$ 74	$ 40
40	Cash paid for taxes	2,034	1,471
41	Noncash financing activities	41	—
42			

In preceding chapters, we covered cash flows as they related to various topics: receivables, plant assets, and so on. **In this chapter, we show you how to prepare and use the statement of cash flows.** We begin with the statement format used by the vast majority of companies, the *indirect method*. We end with the alternate format of the statement of cash flows, the *direct method*, which is used by a minority of companies but is considered by many to be more informative. After working through this chapter, you will be able to analyze the cash flows of actual companies using both approaches.

This chapter has three sections:

- Introduction, consisting of Learning Objectives 1 and 2, beginning on this page.
- Preparing the Statement of Cash Flows: Indirect Method (Learning Objective 3), page 669
- Preparing the Statement of Cash Flows: Direct Method (Learning Objective 4), page 684

The introduction applies to all the cash flow topics. Professors who wish to cover only the indirect method can assign Learning Objectives 1, 2, and 3 of the chapter. Those interested only in the direct method can proceed from the introduction, which ends on page 669, to the direct method (Learning Objective 4), on page 684.

Learning Objectives

1. **Identify** the purposes of the statement of cash flows

2. **Distinguish** among operating, investing, and financing activities

3. **Prepare** a statement of cash flows by the indirect method

4. **Prepare** a statement of cash flows by the direct method

You can access the most current annual report of Google, Inc. in Excel format at **www.sec.gov**. Using the "filings" link on the toolbar at the top of the home page, select "company filings search." This will take you to the "Edgar Company Filings" page. Type "Google" in the company name box, and select "search." This will produce the "EDGAR Search Results" page showing the company name. Click on the "CIK" link beside the company name. This will pull up all of the reports the company has filed with the SEC. Under the "filing type" box, type "10-K" and click the search box. Form 10-K is the SEC form for the company's latest annual report. Find the year that you wish to view. Click on the "Interactive Data" box, which takes you to the "View Filing Data" page. Find and click on the "View Excel Document" link at the top of this page. You may choose to either open or download the Excel files containing the company's most recent financial statements. ■

IDENTIFY THE PURPOSES OF THE STATEMENT OF CASH FLOWS

1 | **Identify** the purposes of the statement of cash flows

The balance sheet reports a company's financial position, and balance sheets from two periods show whether cash increased or decreased. But that doesn't explain *why* the cash balance changed. The income statement reports net income and offers clues about cash, but the income statement doesn't tell *why* cash increased or decreased. We need a third financial statement.

The **statement of cash flows** reports **cash flows**—cash receipts and cash payments—in other words, where cash came from (receipts) and how it was spent (payments). The statement covers a span of time and therefore is dated "Year Ended December 31, 2014" or "Month Ended June 30, 2014." Exhibit 12-1 illustrates the relative timing of the four basic statements.

The statement of cash flows serves these purposes:

1. *Predicts future cash flows.* Past cash receipts and payments are reasonably good predictors of future cash flows.

2. *Evaluates management decisions.* Businesses that make wise decisions prosper, and those that make unwise decisions suffer losses. The statement of cash flows reports how managers got cash and how they used cash to run the business.

Exhibit 12-1 | Timing of the Financial Statements

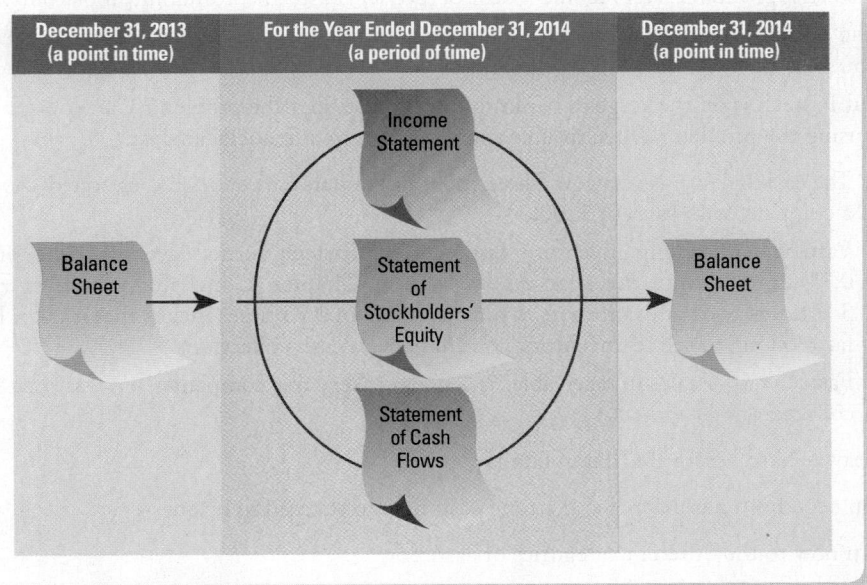

3. *Determines ability to pay dividends and interest.* Stockholders want dividends on their investments. Creditors demand interest and principal on their loans. The statement of cash flows reports on the ability to make these payments.

4. *Shows the relationship of net income to cash flows.* Usually, high net income eventually leads to an increase in cash, and vice versa. But cash flow can suffer even when net income is high.

On a statement of cash flows, *cash* means more than just cash in the bank. It includes **cash equivalents**, which are highly liquid short-term investments that can be converted into cash immediately. Examples include money-market accounts and investments in U.S. government securities. Throughout this chapter, the term *cash* refers to cash and cash equivalents.

How's Your Cash Flow? Telltale Signs of Financial Difficulty

Companies want to earn net income because profit measures success. Without net income, a business sinks. There will be no dividends, and the stock price suffers. High net income attracts investors, but you can't pay bills with net income. That requires cash.

A company needs both net income and strong cash flow. Income and cash flow usually move together because net income eventually generates cash. Sometimes, however, net income and cash flow take different paths. To illustrate, consider Fastech Company:

	A	B
	Fastech Company **Income Statement** **Year Ended December 31, 2014**	
1		
2	Sales revenue	$ 100,000
3	Cost of goods sold	30,000
4	Operating expenses	10,000
5	Net income	$ 60,000
6		

	A	B	C	D
1	**Fastech Company** **Balance Sheet** **December 31, 2014**			
2	Cash	$ 3,000	Total current liabilities	$ 50,000
3	Receivables	37,000	Long-term liabilities	20,000
4	Inventory	40,000		
5	Plant assets, net	60,000	Stockholders' equity	70,000
6	Total assets	$ 140,000	Total liabilities and equity	$ 140,000
7				

What can we glean from Fastech's income statement and balance sheet?

- Fastech is profitable. Net income is 60% of revenue. Fastech's profitability looks outstanding.
- The current ratio is 1.6, and the debt ratio is only 50%. These measures suggest little trouble in paying bills.
- But Fastech is on the verge of bankruptcy. Can you spot the problem? Can you see what is causing the problem? Three trouble spots leap out to a financial analyst.
  1. The cash balance is very low. Three thousand dollars isn't enough cash to pay the bills of a company with sales of $100,000.
  2. Fastech isn't selling inventory fast enough. Fastech turned over its inventory only 0.75 times during the year. As we saw in Chapter 6, inventory turnover rates of 3–8 times a year are common. A turnover ratio of 0.75 times means that it takes Fastech far too long to sell its inventory, and that delays cash collections.
  3. Fastech's days' sales in receivables is 135 days. Very few companies can wait that long to collect from customers.

The takeaway lesson from this discussion is

- you need both net income and strong cash flow to succeed in business.

Let's turn now to the different categories of cash flows.

DISTINGUISH AMONG OPERATING, INVESTING, AND FINANCING ACTIVITIES

2 Distinguish among operating, investing, and financing activities

A business engages in three types of business activities:

- Operating activities
- Investing activities
- Financing activities

Google's statement of cash flows reports cash flows under these three headings, as shown on page 665.

Operating activities create revenues, expenses, gains, and losses—*net income*, which is a product of accrual basis accounting. The statement of cash flows reports on operating activities. Operating activities are the most important of the three categories because they reflect the core of the organization. *A successful business must generate most of its cash from operating activities.*

Investing activities increase and decrease *long-term assets*, such as computers, land, buildings, equipment, and investments in other companies. Purchases and sales of these assets are investing activities. Investing activities are important, but they are less critical than operating activities.

Financing activities obtain cash from investors and creditors. Issuing stock, borrowing money, buying and selling treasury stock, and paying cash dividends are financing activities. Paying off a loan is another example. Financing cash flows relate to *long-term liabilities* and *stockholders' equity*. They are the least important of the three categories of cash flows, and that's why they come last. Exhibit 12-2 shows how operating, investing, and financing activities relate to the various parts of the balance sheet.

Exhibit 12-2 | How Operating, Investing, and Financing Activities Affect the Balance Sheet

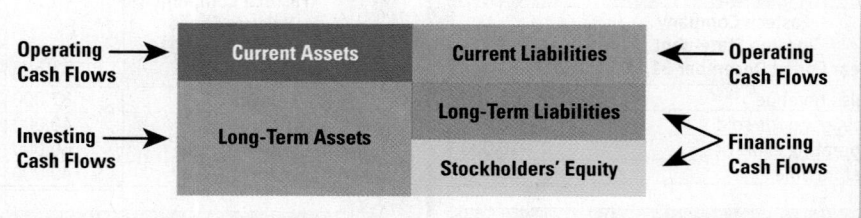

Examine Google's statement of cash flows on page 665. Focus on the final line of each section: Operating, Investing, and Financing. Google has very strong cash flows. During 2012, Google's operating activities provided about $16.6 billion of cash (line 21). Of that cash, $10.7 billion came from net income (line 5). We will explain the other adjustments later. Then, Google invested in the following: 3.3 billion in property and equipment (line 23); $10.6 billion in other companies (line 27); and $33.4 billion in marketable securities (line 24). The company sold another $35.2 billion in marketable securities or received maturity values (line 25). Finally, it received about $1.3 billion in net financing (it borrowed $16.1 billion and repaid $14.8 billion (lines 31 and 32, respectively)). These figures show that

- *operations* are Google's largest source of cash.
- the company is *investing* in the future.
- other companies, banks, and individuals are willing to *finance* Google by lending to and investing in the company.

Two Formats for Operating Activities

There are two ways to format operating activities on the statement of cash flows:

- **Indirect method**—reconciles from net income to net cash provided by operating activities. (pp. 669–684)
- **Direct method**—reports all cash receipts and cash payments from operating activities. (pp. 684–694)

The two methods use different computations, but they produce the same figure for Net cash provided by *operating activities*. The two methods do not affect *investing* or *financing activities*. The following table summarizes the differences between the indirect and direct methods:

Indirect Method		Direct Method	
Net income.................................	$600	Collections from customers..........	$2,000
Adjustments:		*Deductions:*	
Depreciation, etc.	300	Payments to suppliers, etc.	(1,100)
Net cash provided by operating activities..............	$900	Net cash provided by operating activities	$ 900

same

We begin with the indirect method because the vast majority of companies use it.

PREPARE A STATEMENT OF CASH FLOWS BY THE INDIRECT METHOD

To illustrate the statement of cash flows, we use **The Roadster Factory, Inc. (TRF)**, a dealer in auto parts for sports cars. Proceed as follows to prepare the statement of cash flows by using the indirect method:

3 Prepare a statement of cash flows by the indirect method

Step 1 Lay out the template as shown in Part 1 of Exhibit 12-3 (p. 670). The exhibit is comprehensive. The diagram in Part 2 (p. 671) gives a visual picture of the statement.

Step 2 Use the balance sheet to determine the increase or decrease in cash during the period. The change in cash is the "check figure" for the statement of cash flows. Exhibit 12-4 (p. 672) shows The Roadster Factory's (TRF's) comparative balance sheets, with Cash highlighted. TRF's cash decreased by $8,000 during 2014. *Why* did Cash decrease? The statement of cash flows will provide the answer.

Step 3 From the income statement, take Net income, Depreciation, depletion, and amortization expense, and any Gains or Losses on the sale of long-term assets. Insert these items on the statement of cash flows. Exhibit 12-5 (p. 672) gives TRF's income statement, with relevant items highlighted.

Step 4 Use the income statement and balance sheet data to prepare the statement of cash flows. The statement of cash flows is complete only after you have explained the year-to-year changes in all the balance-sheet accounts.

Exhibit 12-3 | Part 1: Template of the Statement of Cash Flows: Indirect Method

	A
	A1 ⬍
	A
1	**The Roadster Factory, Inc. (TRF)** **Statement of Cash Flows** **Year Ended December 31, 2014**
2	**Cash flows from operating activities:**
3	Net income
4	Adjustments to reconcile net income to net cash provided by operating activities:
5	+ Depreciation/depletion/amortization expense
6	+ Loss on sale of long-term assets
7	− Gain on sale of long-term assets
8	− Increases in current assets other than cash
9	+ Decreases in current assets other than cash
10	+ Increases in current liabilities
11	− Decreases in current liabilities
12	Net cash provided by (used for) operating activities
13	**Cash flows from investing activities:**
14	+ Sales of long-term assets (investments, land, building, equipment, and so on)
15	− Purchases of long-term assets
16	+ Collections of notes receivable
17	− Loans to others
18	Net cash provided by (used for) investing activities
19	**Cash flows from financing activities:**
20	+ Issuance of stock
21	+ Sale of treasury stock
22	− Purchase of treasury stock
23	+ Borrowing (issuance of notes or bonds payable)
24	− Payment of notes or bonds payable
25	− Payment of dividends
26	Net cash provided by (used for) financing activities
27	**Net increase (decrease) in cash during the year:**
28	+ Cash at December 31, 2013
29	= Cash at December 31, 2014
30	

Exhibit 12-3 | Part 2: Positive and Negative Items on the Statement of Cash Flows: Indirect Method

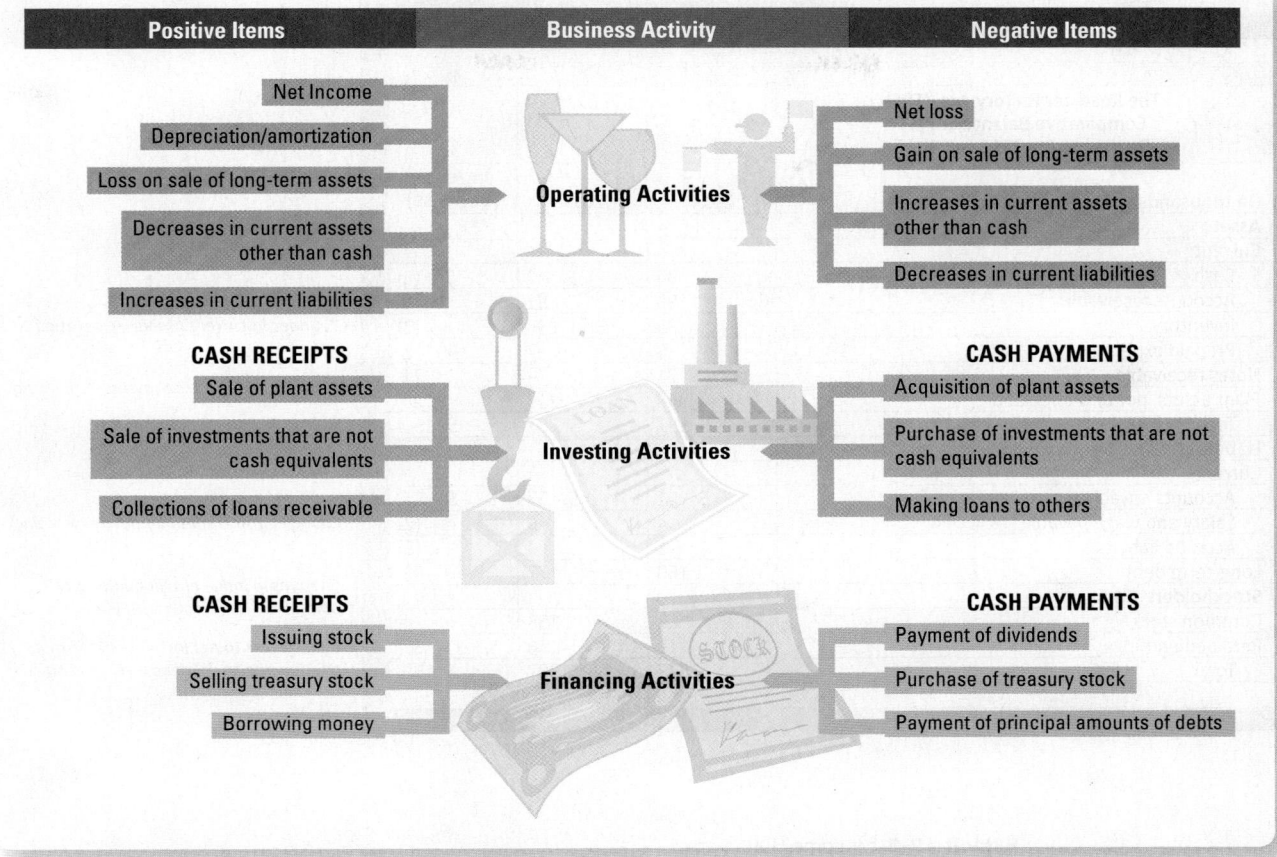

Cash Flows from Operating Activities

Operating activities are related to the transactions that make up net income.

Go to "Cash Flows from Operating Activities" in Exhibit 12-6 on page 673.

The operating section of the Statement of Cash Flows (Exhibit 12-6) begins with Net income, taken from the Income Statement (Exhibit 12-5) and is followed by "Adjustments to reconcile net income to net cash provided by operating activities." Let's discuss these adjustments.

Ⓐ **Depreciation, Depletion, and Amortization Expenses.** These expenses are added back to net income to convert net income to cash flow. Let's see why. Depreciation is recorded as

	A	B	C
	A1		
1	Depreciation Expense	18,000	
2	Accumulated Depreciation		18,000
3			

Depreciation Expense has no effect on cash. But depreciation, like all other expenses, decreases net income. Therefore, to convert net income to cash flows, we add depreciation back to net income. The add-back cancels the earlier deduction.

Exhibit 12-4 | Comparative Balance Sheets

	A	B	C	D
	A1			
1	**The Roadster Factory, Inc. (TRF)** **Comparative Balance Sheets** **December 31, 2014 and 2013**			
2	**(In thousands)**	**2014**	**2013**	**Increase (Decrease)**
3	**Assets**			
4	Current:			
5	Cash	$ 34	$ 42	$ (8)
6	Accounts receivable	96	81	15
7	Inventory	35	38	(3)
8	Prepaid expenses	8	7	1
9	Notes receivable	21	—	21
10	Plant assets, net of depreciation	343	219	124
11	Total	$ 537	$ 387	$ 150
12	**Liabilities**			
13	Current:			
14	Accounts payable	$ 91	$ 57	$ 34
15	Salary and wage payable	4	6	(2)
16	Accrued liabilities	1	3	(2)
17	Long-term debt	160	77	83
18	**Stockholders' Equity**			
19	Common stock	162	158	4
20	Retained earnings	119	86	33
21	Total	$ 537	$ 387	$ 150
22				

Changes in current assets—Operating (rows 6–8)

Changes in noncurrent assets—Investing (rows 9–10)

Changes in current liabilities—Operating (rows 14–16)

Changes in long-term liabilities and paid-in capital accounts—Financing

Change due to net income—Operating
Change due to dividends—Financing

Exhibit 12-5 | Income Statement

	A	B	C
	A1		
1	**The Roadster Factory, Inc. (TRF)** **Income Statement** **Year Ended December 31, 2014**		
2		**(In thousands)**	
3			
4	Revenues and gains:		
5	Sales revenue	$ 303	
6	Interest revenue	2	
7	Gain on sale of plant assets	8	
8	Total revenues and gains		$ 313
9	Expenses:		
10	Cost of goods sold	$ 150	
11	Salary and wage expense	56	
12	Depreciation expense	18	
13	Other operating expense	17	
14	Income tax expense	15	
15	Interest expense	7	
16	Total expenses		263
17	Net income		$ 50
18			

Exhibit 12-6 | Statement of Cash Flows—Operating Activities—Indirect Method

	A	B	C
		A1	
1	The Roadster Factory, Inc. (TRF) Partial Statement of Cash Flows (Indirect Method) For the Year Ended December 31, 2014		
2		(In thousands)	
3	Cash flows from operating activities:		
4	Net income		$ 50
5	Adjustments to reconcile net income to net cash		
6	provided by operating activities:		
7	Ⓐ Depreciation	$ 18	
8	Ⓑ Gain on sale of plant assets	(8)	
9	Increase in accounts receivable	(15)	
10	Decrease in inventory	3	
11	Increase in prepaid expenses	(1)	
12	Increase in accounts payable	34	
13	Decrease in salary and wage payable	(2)	
14	Decrease in accrued liabilities	(2)	27
15	Net cash provided by operating activities		$ 77
16			

Example: Suppose you had only two transactions, a $1,000 cash sale and depreciation expense of $300. Net cash flow from operations is $1,000, and Net income is $700 ($1,000 − $300). To go from net income ($700) to cash flow ($1,000), we add back the depreciation ($300). Depletion and amortization are treated like depreciation.

Ⓑ **Gains and Losses on the Sale of Long-Term Assets.** Sales of long-term assets are *investing* activities, and there's often a gain or loss on the sale. On the statement of cash flows, the gain or loss is an adjustment to net income. Exhibit 12-6 includes an adjustment for a gain. During 2014, The Roadster Factory sold equipment for $62,000. The book value was $54,000, so there was a gain of $8,000.

The $62,000 cash received from the sale is an investing activity (Exhibit 12-7, page 674), and the $62,000 includes the $8,000 gain. Net income also includes the gain, so we must subtract the gain from net cash provided by operations so that it may be added to the net book value of equipment sold in the investing section ($54,000 + $8,000 = $62,000). We explain investing activities in the next section.

A loss on the sale of plant assets also creates an adjustment in the operating section. Since the cash received from the sale of a long-term asset at a loss is less than the asset's book value, the amount of cash received reflects the loss. Losses are deducted from net income. Therefore, in order to show the amount of cash received from the sale of the asset in the investing section, losses are *added back* to net income in the operating section to compute Net cash flow from operations.

Ⓒ **Changes in the Current Asset and Current Liability Accounts, Excluding Cash.** Most current assets and current liabilities result from operating activities. For example, accounts receivable result from sales, inventory relates to cost of goods sold, and so on. Except for Cash, changes in the current accounts are adjustments to net income on the cash flow statement. The reasoning is as follows:

1. *An increase in a noncash current asset decreases cash.* It takes cash to acquire assets. Suppose you make a sale on account. Accounts receivable are increased, but cash isn't affected yet. Exhibit 12-4 (p. 672) reports that during 2014, The Roadster Factory's Accounts Receivable increased by $15,000. To compute cash flow from operations, we must subtract the $15,000 increase in Accounts Receivable, as shown in Exhibit 12-6. The reason is this: We have *not* collected this $15,000 in cash. Similar logic applies to all the other current assets. If they increase, cash decreases.

2. *A decrease in a noncash current asset increases cash.* Suppose TRF's Accounts Receivable balance decreased by $4,000. Cash receipts caused Accounts Receivable to decrease, so we add decreases in Accounts Receivable and the other current assets to net income.

3. *A decrease in a current liability decreases cash.* Payment of a current liability decreases both cash and the liability, so we subtract decreases in current liabilities from net income. In Exhibit 12-6, the $2,000 decrease in Accrued Liabilities is *subtracted* to compute Net cash provided by operations.

4. *An increase in a current liability increases cash.* The Roadster Factory's Accounts Payable increased. That can occur only if cash was not spent to pay this debt. Cash payments are therefore less than expenses, and TRF has more cash on hand. Thus, increases in current liabilities increase cash.

Evaluating Cash Flows from Operating Activities. Let's step back and evaluate The Roadster Factory's operating cash flows during 2014. TRF's operations provided net cash flow of $77,000. This amount exceeds net income, which is one sign of a healthy company. Now let's examine TRF's investing and financing activities, as reported in Exhibit 12-7.

Exhibit 12-7 | Statement of Cash Flows—Indirect Method

	A	B	C
	A1		
1	The Roadster Factory, Inc. (TRF) Statement of Cash Flows (Indirect Method) For the Year Ended December 31, 2014		
2			(In thousands)
3	Cash flows from operating activities:		
4	Net income		$ 50
5	Adjustments to reconcile net income to net cash		
6	provided by operating activities:		
7	ⒶDepreciation	$ 18	
8	ⒷGain on sale of plant assets	(8)	
9	Increase in accounts receivable	(15)	
10	Decrease in inventory	3	
11	Increase in prepaid expenses	(1)	
12	ⒸIncrease in accounts payable	34	
13	Decrease in salary and wage payable	(2)	
14	Decrease in accrued liabilities	(2)	27
15	Net cash provided by operating activities		77
16	Cash flows from investing activities:		
17	Acquisition of plant assets	$ (196)	
18	Loan to another company	(21)	
19	Proceeds from sale of plant assets	62	
20	Net cash used for investing activities		(155)
21	Cash flows from financing activities:		
22	Proceeds from issuance of long-term debt	$ 94	
23	Proceeds from issuance of common stock	4	
24	Payment of long-term debt	(11)	
25	Payment of dividends	(17)	
26	Net cash provided by financing activities		70
27	Net (decrease) in cash		$ (8)
28	Cash balance, December 31, 2013		42
29	Cash balance, December 31, 2014		$ 34
30			

Cash Flows from Investing Activities

Investing activities affect long-term assets, such as Plant Assets, Investments, and Notes Receivable. Increases in these accounts represent purchases of these assets and are offset by decreases to cash. Decreases to these accounts represent sales of these assets and are offset by increases to cash.

Most of the data come from the balance sheet.

Computing Purchases and Sales of Plant Assets. Companies keep a separate account for each plant asset. But for computing cash flows, it is helpful to combine all the plant assets into a single summary account. Also, we subtract accumulated depreciation and use the net figure. It's easier to work with a single plant asset account.

To illustrate, observe that The Roadster Factory's

- balance sheet reports beginning plant assets, net of accumulated depreciation, of $219,000. The ending balance is $343,000 (Exhibit 12-4).

- income statement shows depreciation expense of $18,000 and an $8,000 gain on sale of plant assets (Exhibit 12-5).

TRF's purchases of plant assets total $196,000 (take this amount as given; see Exhibit 12-7). How much, then, are the proceeds from the sale of plant assets? First, we must determine the book value of the plant assets sold:

Plant Assets, Net

Beginning balance	+	Acquisitions	−	Depreciation expense	−	Book value of assets sold	=	Ending balance
$219,000	+	$196,000	−	$18,000	−	−X	=	$343,000
						−X	=	$343,000 − $219,000 − $196,000 + $18,000
						X	=	$54,000

The sale proceeds are $62,000, determined as follows:

Sale proceeds	=	Book value of assets sold	+	Gain	−	Loss
X	=	$54,000	+	$8,000	−	$0
X	=	$62,000				

Trace the sale proceeds of $62,000 to the statement of cash flows in Exhibit 12-7. The Plant Assets T-account provides another look at the computation of the book value of the assets sold.

Plant Assets, Net

Beginning balance	219,000	Depreciation expense	18,000
Acquisitions	196,000	Book value of assets sold	54,000
Ending balance	343,000		

If the sale resulted in a loss of $3,000, the sale proceeds would be $51,000 ($54,000 − $3,000), and the statement of cash flows would report $51,000 as a cash receipt from this investing activity.

Computing Purchases and Sales of Investments, and Loans and Collections. The cash amounts of investment transactions can be computed in the manner illustrated for plant assets. Investments are easier because there is no depreciation, as shown in the following equation:

Investments (amounts assumed for illustration only)

Beginning balance	+	Purchases	−	Book value of investments sold	=	Ending balance
$100,000	+	$50,000		−X	=	$140,000
				−X	=	$140,000 − $100,000 − $50,000
				X	=	$10,000

The Investments T-account provides another look (amounts assumed).

Investments

Beginning balance	100,000	
Purchases	50,000	Book value of investments sold 10,000
Ending balance	140,000	

The Roadster Factory has a long-term receivable, and the cash flows from loan transactions on notes receivable can be determined as follows (data from Exhibit 12-4):

Notes Receivable

Beginning balance	+	New loans made	−	Collections	=	Ending balance
$0	+	X		−0	=	$21,000
		X			=	$21,000

Notes Receivable

Beginning balance	0	
New loans made	21,000	Collections 0
Ending balance	21,000	

Please refer to the investing section of the Statement of Cash Flows (Exhibit 12-7) to see all the investing activities listed together for TRF. Exhibit 12-8 summarizes the cash flows from investing activities, highlighted in color.

Cash Flows from Financing Activities

Financing activities affect liabilities and stockholders' equity, such as Notes Payable, Bonds Payable, Long-Term Debt, Common Stock, Paid-in Capital in Excess of Par, and Retained Earnings. Most of the data come from the balance sheet. Increases in these accounts are offset by increases in cash. Decreases in these accounts are offset by decreases in cash.

Computing Issuances and Payments of Long-Term Debt. The beginning and ending balances of Long-Term Debt, Notes Payable, or Bonds Payable come from the balance sheet. If either new issuances or payments are known, the other amount can be computed. Assume that proceeds from The Roadster Factory's new long-term debt issuances (represented as an increase

Exhibit 12-8 | Computing Cash Flows from Investing Activities

Receipts

From sale of plant assets	Beginning plant assets, net	+	Acquisition cost	−	Depreciation expense	−	Book value of assets sold	=	Ending plant assets, net
	Cash received	=	Book value of assets sold	+ or −	Gain on sale Loss on sale				
From sale of investments	Beginning investments	+	Purchase cost of investments	−	Book value of investments sold	=	Ending investments		
	Cash received	=	Book value of investments sold	+ or −	Gain on sale Loss on sale				
From collection of notes receivable	Beginning notes receivable	+	New loans made	−	Collections	=	Ending notes receivable		

Payments

For acquisition of plant assets	Beginning plant assets, net	+	Acquisition cost	−	Depreciation expense	−	Book value of assets sold	=	Ending plant assets, net
For purchase of investments	Beginning investments	+	Purchase cost of investments	−	Book value of investments sold	=	Ending investments		
For new loans made	Beginning notes receivable	+	New loans made	−	Collections	=	Ending notes receivable		

in cash) total $94,000 (take this amount as given in Exhibit 12-7). Debt payments (represented by a decrease in cash) are computed by performing an analysis of the Long-Term Debt account (see Exhibit 12-4).

Long-Term Debt (Notes Payable, Bonds Payable)

Beginning balance	+	Issuance of new debt	−	Payments of debt	=	Ending balance
$77,000	+	$94,000		−X	=	$160,000
				−X	=	$160,000 − $77,000 − $94,000
				X	=	$11,000

Long-Term Debt

		Beginning balance	77,000
Payments	11,000	Issuance of new debt	94,000
		Ending balance	160,000

Computing Issuances of Stock and Purchases of Treasury Stock.

These cash flows can be determined from the stock accounts. For example, cash received from issuing common stock is computed from Common Stock and Paid-in Capital in Excess of Par. We use a single summary Common Stock account as we do for plant assets. The Roadster Factory data are

Common Stock

Beginning balance	+	Issuance of new stock	=	Ending balance
$158,000	+	$4,000	=	$162,000

Common Stock

Beginning balance	158,000
Issuance of new stock	4,000
Ending balance	162,000

Increases in common stock and related additional paid-in capital are represented by offsetting increases in Cash.

The Roadster Factory has no treasury stock, but cash flows from purchasing treasury stock can be computed as follows (using assumed amounts):

Treasury Stock (amounts assumed for illustration only)

Beginning balance	+	Purchase of treasury stock	=	Ending balance
$16,000	+	$3,000	=	$19,000

Treasury Stock

Beginning balance	16,000	
Purchase of treasury stock	3,000	
Ending balance	19,000	

Increases (purchases) of treasury stock are represented by offsetting decreases in cash. If treasury stock is reissued for cash, the decrease in treasury stock is offset by an increase in cash.

Computing Dividend Declarations and Payments. If dividend declarations and payments are not given elsewhere, they can be computed. For The Roadster Factory, this computation is as follows:

Retained Earnings

Beginning balance	+	Net income	−	Dividend declarations and payments	=	Ending balance
$86,000	+	$50,000		−X	=	$119,000
				−X	=	$119,000 − $86,000 − $50,000
				X	=	$17,000

The T-account also shows the dividend computation. Dividends paid, represented by decreases in retained earnings, are offset by decreases in cash.

Retained Earnings

Dividend declarations and payments	17,000	Beginning balance	86,000
		Net income	50,000
		Ending balance	119,000

Please refer to the financing section of the Statement of Cash Flows (Exhibit 12-7) to see all the financing activities listed together for TRF.

Exhibit 12-9 summarizes the cash flows from financing activities, highlighted in color.

Exhibit 12-9 | Computing Cash Flows from Financing Activities

Receipts

From borrowing—issuance of long-term debt (notes payable)	Beginning long-term debt (notes payable) +	Cash received from issuance of long-term debt	− Payment of debt =	Ending long-term debt (notes payable)
From issuance of stock	Beginning stock +	Cash received from issuance of new stock	=	Ending stock

Payments

Of long-term debt	Beginning long-term debt (notes payable) +	Cash received from issuance of long-term debt	− Payment of debt =	Ending long-term debt (notes payable)
To purchase treasury stock	Beginning treasury stock + Purchase cost of treasury stock = Ending treasury stock			
Of dividends	Beginning retained earnings + Net income − Dividend declarations and payments = Ending retained earnings			

> Stop & Think...

Classify each of the following as an operating activity, an investing activity, or a financing activity as reported on the statement of cash flows prepared by the *indirect* method.

a. Issuance of stock	g. Paying bonds payable
b. Borrowing long-term	h. Interest expense
c. Sales revenue	i. Sale of equipment
d. Payment of dividends	j. Cost of goods sold
e. Purchase of land with cash	k. Purchase of another company with cash
f. Purchase of treasury stock	l. Making a loan

Answers:

a. Financing	g. Financing
b. Financing	h. Operating (included in net income)
c. Operating (included in net income)	i. Investing
d. Financing	j. Operating (included in net income)
e. Investing	k. Investing
f. Financing	l. Investing

Noncash Investing and Financing Activities

Companies make investments that do not require cash. They also obtain financing other than cash. Our examples have included none of these transactions. Now suppose The Roadster Factory issued common stock valued at $300,000 to acquire a warehouse. TRF would journalize this transaction as

	A	B	C
1	Warehouse Building	300,000	
2	Common Stock		300,000
3			

This transaction would not be reported as a cash payment because TRF paid no cash. But the investment in the warehouse and the issuance of stock are important. These noncash investing and financing activities should be reported in a separate schedule under the statement of cash flows. Exhibit 12-10 illustrates noncash investing and financing activities (all amounts are assumed).

Exhibit 12-10 | Noncash Investing and Financing Activities

	A	B
1		Thousands
2		
3	**Noncash investing and financing activities:**	
4	Acquisition of building by issuing common stock	$ 300
5	Acquisition of land by issuing note payable	70
6	Payment of long-term debt by issuing common stock	100
7	Total noncash investing and financing activities	$ 470
8		

Now let's apply what you've learned about the statement of cash flows prepared by the indirect method.

Mid-Chapter Summary Problem

Lucas Corporation reported the following income statement and comparative balance sheets, along with transaction data for 2014:

A1		
A	**B**	**C**
Lucas Corporation		
Income Statement		
Year Ended December 31, 2014		
Sales revenue		$ 662,000
Cost of goods sold		560,000
Gross profit		102,000
Operating expenses		
Salary expenses	$ 46,000	
Depreciation expense—equipment	7,000	
Amortization expense—patent	3,000	
Rent expense	2,000	
Total operating expenses		58,000
Income from operations		44,000
Other items:		
Loss on sale of equipment		(2,000)
Income before income tax		42,000
Income tax expense		16,000
Net income		$ 26,000

A1					
A	**B**	**C**	**D**	**E**	**F**
Lucas Corporation **Comparative Balance Sheets** **December 31, 2014 and 2013**					
Assets	**2014**	**2013**	**Liabilities**	**2014**	**2013**
Current:			Current:		
Cash and cash equivalents	$ 19,000	$ 3,000	Accounts payable	$ 35,000	$ 26,000
Accounts receivable	22,000	23,000	Accrued liabilities	7,000	9,000
Inventories	34,000	31,000	Income tax payable	10,000	10,000
Prepaid expenses	1,000	3,000	Total current liabilities	52,000	45,000
Total current assets	76,000	60,000	Long-term note payable	44,000	—
Long-term investments	18,000	10,000	Bonds payable	40,000	53,000
Equipment, net	67,000	52,000	**Stockholders' Equity**		
Patent, net	44,000	10,000	Common stock	52,000	20,000
			Retained earnings	27,000	19,000
			Less: Treasury stock	(10,000)	(5,000)
Total assets	$ 205,000	$ 132,000	Total liabilities and Stockholders' equity	$ 205,000	$ 132,000

681

Transaction Data for 2014:

Purchase of equipment with cash	$ 98,000	Issuance of long-term note payable	
Payment of cash dividends	18,000	to purchase patent......................................	$ 37,000
Issuance of common stock to		Issuance of long-term note payable to	
retire bonds payable..............................	13,000	borrow cash	7,000
Purchase of long-term investment		Issuance of common stock for cash	19,000
with cash..	8,000	Proceeds from sale of equipment	
Purchase of treasury stock.........................	5,000	(book value, $76,000)...............................	74,000

Requirement

1. Prepare Lucas Corporation's statement of cash flows (indirect method) for the year ended December 31, 2014. Follow the four steps outlined below. For Step 4, prepare a T-account to show the transaction activity in each long-term balance-sheet account. For each plant asset, use a single account, net of accumulated depreciation (for example: Equipment, Net).

   Step 1 Lay out the template of the statement of cash flows.

   Step 2 From the comparative balance sheets, determine the increase in cash and cash equivalents during the year, $16,000.

   Step 3 From the income statement, take net income, depreciation, amortization, and the loss on sale of equipment to the statement of cash flows.

   Step 4 Complete the statement of cash flows. Account for the year-to-year change in each balance-sheet account.

Answer

	A	B	C
1	**Lucas Corporation** **Statement of Cash Flows** **Year Ended December 31, 2014**		
2	**Cash flows from operating activities:**		
3	Net income		$ 26,000
4	Adjustments to reconcile net income to		
5	net cash provided by operating activities:		
6	Depreciation	$ 7,000	
7	Amortization	3,000	
8	Loss on sale of equipment	2,000	
9	Decrease in accounts receivable	1,000	
10	Increase in inventories	(3,000)	
11	Decrease in prepaid expenses	2,000	
12	Increase in accounts payable	9,000	
13	Decrease in accrued liabilities	(2,000)	19,000
14	Net cash provided by operating activities		45,000
15	**Cash flows from investing activities:**		
16	Purchase of equipment	$ (98,000)	
17	Sale of equipment	74,000	
18	Purchase of long-term investment	(8,000)	
19	Net cash used for investing activities		(32,000)
20	**Cash flows from financing activities:**		
21	Issuance of common stock	$ 19,000	
22	Payment of cash dividends	(18,000)	
23	Issuance of long-term note payable	7,000	
24	Purchase of treasury stock	(5,000)	
25	Net cash provided by financing activities		3,000
26	**Net increase in cash**		**16,000**
27	Cash balance, December 31, 2013		3,000
28	Cash balance, December 31, 2014		$ 19,000
29	**Noncash investing and financing activities:**		
30	Issuance of long-term note payable to purchase patent		$ 37,000
31	Issuance of common stock to retire bonds payable		13,000
32	Total noncash investing and financing activities		$ 50,000
33			

Long-Term Investments

Bal	10,000	
	8,000	
Bal	18,000	

Equipment, Net

Bal	52,000	
	98,000	76,000
		7,000
Bal	67,000	

Patent, Net

Bal	10,000	
	37,000	3,000
Bal	44,000	

Long-Term Note Payable

	Bal	0
		37,000
		7,000
	Bal	44,000

Bonds Payable

	Bal	53,000
13,000		
	Bal	40,000

Common Stock

	Bal	20,000
		13,000
		19,000
	Bal	52,000

Retained Earnings

	Bal	19,000
18,000		26,000
	Bal	27,000

Treasury Stock

Bal	5,000	
	5,000	
Bal	10,000	

PREPARE A STATEMENT OF CASH FLOWS BY THE DIRECT METHOD

4 Prepare a statement of cash flows by the direct method

The Financial Accounting Standards Board (FASB) and the International Accounting Standards Board (IASB) prefer the direct method of reporting operating cash flows because it provides clearer information about the sources and uses of cash. However, only a very small percentage of companies use this method because it requires more computations than the indirect method. Investing and financing cash flows are unaffected by the method used.

To illustrate the statement of cash flows, we use The Roadster Factory, Inc. (TRF), a dealer in auto parts for sports cars. To prepare the statement of cash flows by the direct method, proceed as follows:

Step 1 Lay out the template of the statement of cash flows by the direct method, as shown in Part 1 of Exhibit 12-11. Part 2 (p. 686) gives a visual presentation of the statement.

Step 2 Use the balance sheet to determine the increase or decrease in cash during the period. The change in cash is the "check figure" for the statement of cash flows. The Roadster Factory's comparative balance sheets show that cash decreased by $8,000 during 2014 (Exhibit 12-4, p. 672). *Why* did cash decrease during 2014? The statement of cash flows explains.

Step 3 Use the available data to prepare the statement of cash flows. The Roadster Factory's transaction data appear in Exhibit 12-12 on page 686. These transactions affected both the income statement (Exhibit 12-5, p. 672) and the statement of cash flows. Some transactions in Exhibit 12-12 affect one statement and some affect the other. For example, sales (item 1) are reported on the income statement. Cash collections (item 2) go on the statement of cash flows. Other transactions, such as interest expense and payments (item 12), affect both statements. *The statement of cash flows reports only those transactions with cash effects* (those with an asterisk in Exhibit 12-12). Exhibit 12-13 (on p. 687) gives The Roadster Factory's statement of cash flows for 2014.

Exhibit 12-11 | Part 1: Template of the Statement of Cash Flows—Direct Method

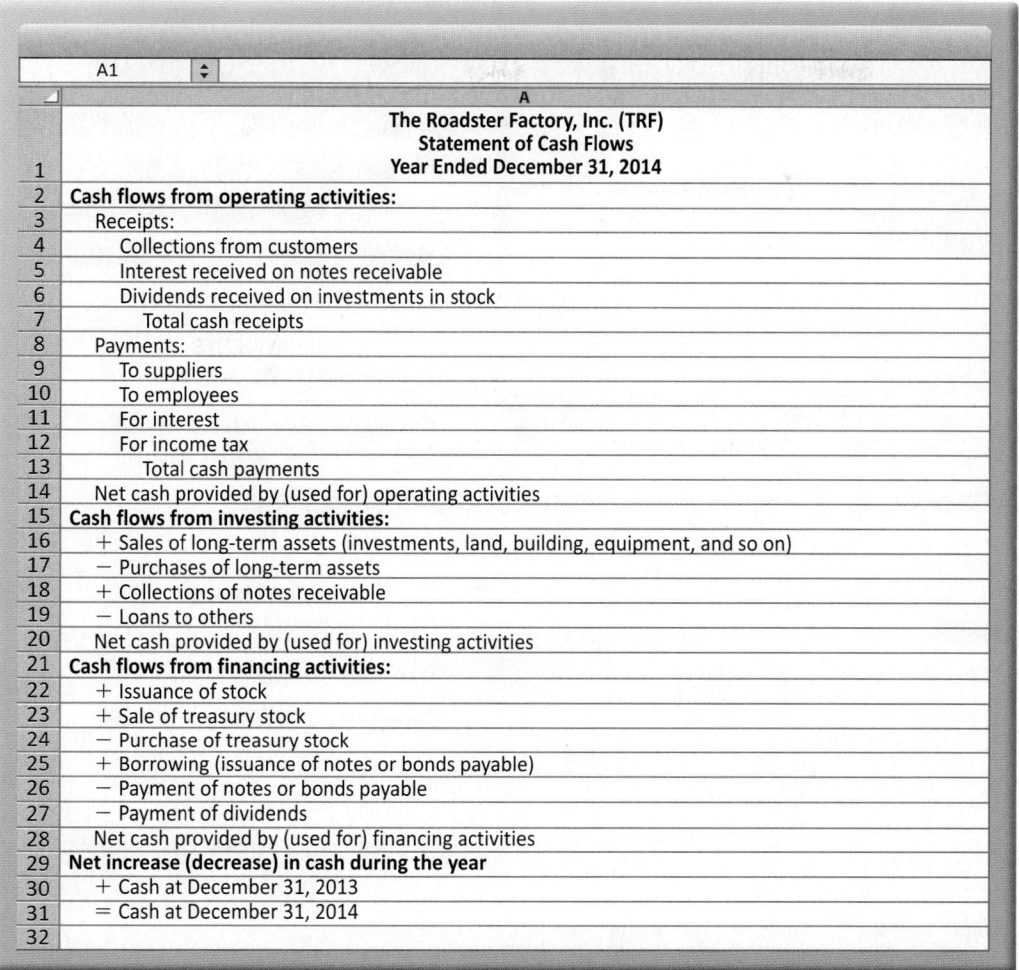

	A
	The Roadster Factory, Inc. (TRF)
	Statement of Cash Flows
1	**Year Ended December 31, 2014**
2	**Cash flows from operating activities:**
3	Receipts:
4	Collections from customers
5	Interest received on notes receivable
6	Dividends received on investments in stock
7	Total cash receipts
8	Payments:
9	To suppliers
10	To employees
11	For interest
12	For income tax
13	Total cash payments
14	Net cash provided by (used for) operating activities
15	**Cash flows from investing activities:**
16	+ Sales of long-term assets (investments, land, building, equipment, and so on)
17	− Purchases of long-term assets
18	+ Collections of notes receivable
19	− Loans to others
20	Net cash provided by (used for) investing activities
21	**Cash flows from financing activities:**
22	+ Issuance of stock
23	+ Sale of treasury stock
24	− Purchase of treasury stock
25	+ Borrowing (issuance of notes or bonds payable)
26	− Payment of notes or bonds payable
27	− Payment of dividends
28	Net cash provided by (used for) financing activities
29	**Net increase (decrease) in cash during the year**
30	+ Cash at December 31, 2013
31	= Cash at December 31, 2014
32	

Cash Flows from Operating Activities

Operating cash flows are listed first because they are the most important. Exhibit 12-13 shows that The Roadster Factory is sound; operating activities were the largest source of cash.

Cash Collections from Customers. Both cash sales and collections of accounts receivable are reported on the statement of cash flows as "Collections from customers . . . $288,000" in Exhibit 12-13.

Cash Receipts of Interest and Dividends. The income statement reports interest revenue and dividend revenue. Only the cash receipts of interest and dividends appear on the statement of cash flows—$2,000 of interest received in Exhibit 12-13. The Roadster Factory, Inc. received no revenue from dividends in 2014.

Payments to Suppliers. Payments to suppliers include all expenditures for inventory and operating expenses except employee pay, interest, and income taxes. *Suppliers* are those entities that provide inventory and essential services. For example, a clothing store's suppliers may include **Tommy Hilfiger, Adidas,** and **Ralph Lauren**. Other suppliers provide advertising, utilities, and office supplies. Exhibit 12-13 shows that The Roadster Factory paid suppliers $133,000.

Payments to Employees. This category includes salaries, wages, and other forms of employee pay. Accrued amounts are excluded because they have not yet been paid. The statement of cash flows reports only the cash payments of $58,000.

Exhibit 12-11 | Part 2: Cash Receipts and Cash Payments on the Statement of Cash Flows—Direct Method

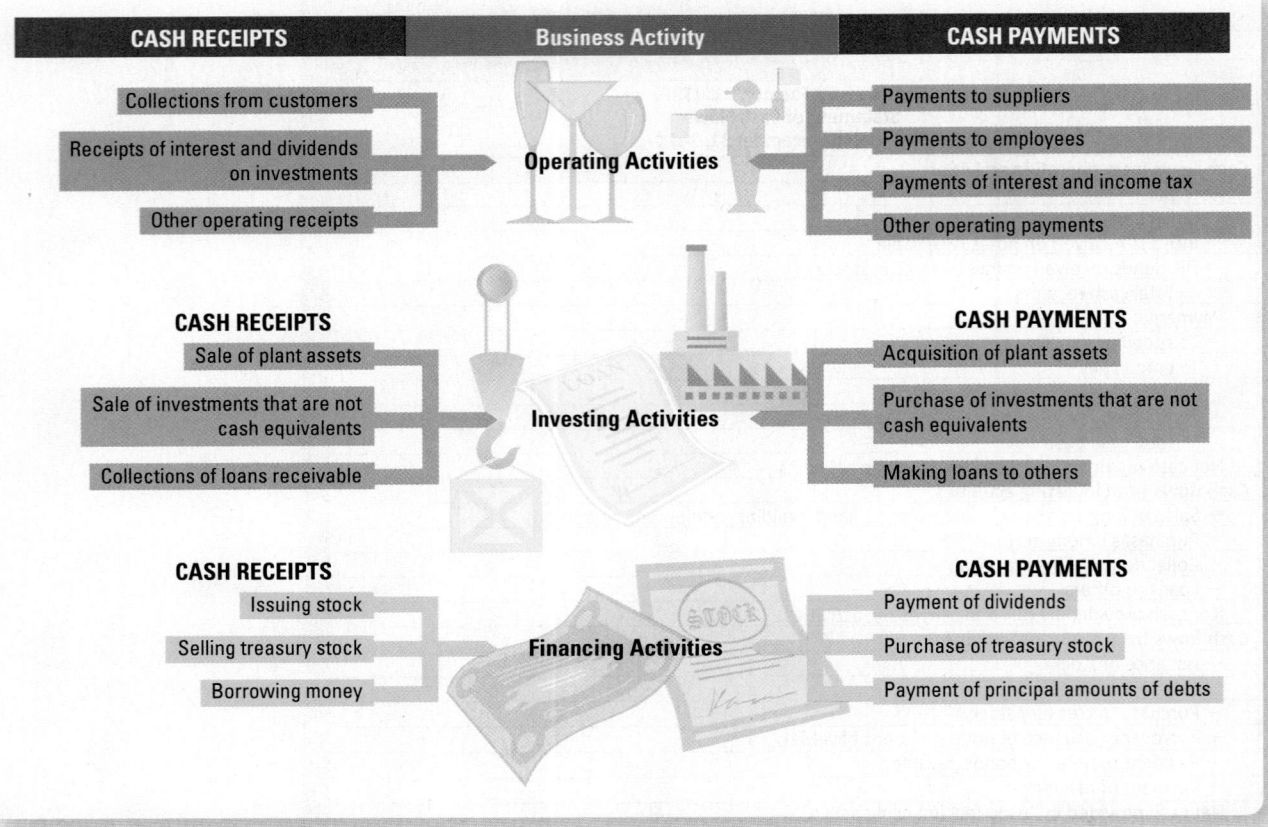

Exhibit 12-12 | Summary of the Roadster Factory's 2014 Transactions

Operating Activities
1. Sales on credit, $303,000
*2. Collections from customers, $288,000
*3. Interest revenue and receipts, $2,000
4. Cost of goods sold, $150,000
5. Purchases of inventory on credit, $147,000
*6. Payments to suppliers, $133,000
7. Salary and wage expense, $56,000
*8. Payments of salary and wages, $58,000
9. Depreciation expense, $18,000
10. Other operating expense, $17,000
*11. Income tax expense and payments, $15,000
*12. Interest expense and payments, $7,000

Investing Activities
*13. Cash payments to acquire plant assets, $196,000
*14. Loan to another company, $21,000
*15. Proceeds from sale of plant assets, $62,000, including $8,000 gain

Financing Activities
*16. Proceeds from issuance of long-term debt, $94,000
*17. Proceeds from issuance of common stock, $4,000
*18. Payment of long-term debt, $11,000
*19. Declaration and payment of cash dividends, $17,000

*Indicates a cash flow to be reported on the statement of cash flows.
Note: Income statement data are taken from Exhibit 12-16, page 690.

Exhibit 12-13 | Statement of Cash Flows—Direct Method

	A	B	C
	A1 ⬦		
1	The Roadster Factory, Inc. (TRF) Statement of Cash Flows (Direct Method) For Year Ended December 31, 2014		
2		(In thousands)	
3	Cash flows from operating activities:		
4	Receipts:		
5	Collections from customers	$ 288	
6	Interest received	2	
7	Total cash receipts		$ 290
8	Payments:		
9	To suppliers	$ (133)	
10	To employees	(58)	
11	For income tax	(15)	
12	For interest	(7)	
13	Total cash payments		(213)
14	Net cash provided by operating activities		77
15	Cash flows from investing activities:		
16	Acquisition of plant assets	$ (196)	
17	Loan to another company	(21)	
18	Proceeds from sale of plant assets	62	
19	Net cash used for investing activities		(155)
20	Cash flows from financing activities:		
21	Proceeds from issuance of long-term debt	$ 94	
22	Proceeds from issuance of common stock	4	
23	Payment of long-term debt	(11)	
24	Payment of dividends	(17)	
25	Net cash provided by financing activities		70
26	Net (decrease) in cash		(8)
27	Cash balance, December 31, 2013		42
28	Cash balance, December 31, 2014		$ 34
29			

Payments for Interest Expense and Income Tax Expense. Interest and income tax payments are reported separately. The Roadster Factory paid cash for all its interest and income taxes. Therefore, the same amount goes on the income statement and the statement of cash flows. These payments are operating cash flows because the interest and income tax are expenses.

Depreciation, Depletion, and Amortization Expense

These expenses are *not* listed on the direct-method statement of cash flows because they do not affect cash.

Cash Flows from Investing Activities

Investing is critical because a company's investments affect the future. Large purchases of plant assets signal expansion. Meager investing activity means the business is not growing.

Purchasing Plant Assets and Investments and Making Loans to Other Companies.

These cash payments acquire long-term assets. The Roadster Factory's first investing activity in Exhibit 12-13 is the purchase of plant assets ($196,000). TRF also made a $21,000 loan and thus got a note receivable.

Proceeds from Selling Plant Assets and Investments and from Collecting Notes Receivable.

These cash receipts are also investing activities. The sale of the plant assets needs explanation. The Roadster Factory received $62,000 cash from the sale of plant assets, and there was an $8,000 gain on this transaction. What is the appropriate amount to show on the cash flow statement? It is $62,000, the cash received from the sale, not the $8,000 gain.

Investors are often critical of a company that sells large amounts of its plant assets. That may signal an emergency. For example, problems in the airline industry have caused some companies to sell airplanes to generate cash.

Cash Flows from Financing Activities

Cash flows from financing activities include the following:

Proceeds from Issuance of Stock and Debt (Notes and Bonds Payable). Issuing stock and borrowing money are two ways to finance a company. In Exhibit 12-13, The Roadster Factory received $4,000 when it issued common stock. TRF also received $94,000 cash when it issued long-term debt (such as a note payable) to borrow money.

Payment of Debt and Purchasing the Company's Own Stock. Paying debt (notes payable) is the opposite of borrowing. TRF reports long-term debt payments of $11,000. The purchase of treasury stock is another example of a use of cash.

Payment of Cash Dividends. Paying cash dividends is a financing activity, as shown by The Roadster Factory's $17,000 payment in Exhibit 12-13. A *stock* dividend has no effect on Cash and is *not* reported on the cash flow statement.

Noncash Investing and Financing Activities

Companies make investments that do not require cash. They also obtain financing other than cash. Our examples thus far have included none of these transactions. Now suppose that The Roadster Factory issued common stock valued at $300,000 to acquire a warehouse. TRF would journalize this transaction as

	A	B	C
1	Warehouse Building	300,000	
2	Common Stock		300,000
3			

This transaction would not be reported as a cash payment because TRF paid no cash. But the investment in the warehouse and the issuance of stock are important. These noncash investing and financing activities can be reported in a separate schedule under the statement of cash flows. Exhibit 12-14 illustrates noncash investing and financing activities (all amounts are assumed).

Exhibit 12-14 | Noncash Investing and Financing Activities

	A	B
1		Thousands
2		
3	Noncash investing and financing activities:	
4	Acquisition of building by issuing common stock	$ 300
5	Acquisition of land by issuing note payable	70
6	Payment of long-term debt by issuing common stock	100
7	Total noncash investing and financing activities	$ 470
8		

> Stop & Think...

Using the direct method, classify each of the following as an operating activity, an investing activity, or a financing activity. Also identify those items that are not reported on the statement of cash flows prepared by the *direct* method.

a. Net income
b. Payment of dividends
c. Borrowing long-term
d. Payment of cash to suppliers
e. Making a loan
f. Sale of treasury stock
g. Depreciation expense
h. Purchase of equipment with cash

i. Issuance of stock
j. Purchase of another company with cash
k. Payment of a long-term note payable
l. Payment of income taxes
m. Collections from customers
n. Accrual of interest revenue
o. Expiration of prepaid expense
p. Receipt of cash dividends

Answers:

a. Not reported
b. Financing
c. Financing
d. Operating
e. Investing
f. Financing
g. Not reported
h. Investing

i. Financing
j. Investing
k. Financing
l. Operating
m. Operating
n. Not reported
o. Not reported
p. Operating

Now let's see how to compute the operating cash flows by the direct method.

Computing Operating Cash Flows by the Direct Method

To compute operating cash flows by the direct method, we use the income statement and the *changes* in the balance-sheet accounts. Exhibit 12-15 diagrams the process. Exhibit 12-16 is The Roadster Factory's income statement, and Exhibit 12-17 shows the comparative balance sheets.

Exhibit 12-15 | Direct Method of Computing Cash Flows from Operating Activities

RECEIPTS / PAYMENTS	Income Statement Account	Change in Related Balance Sheet Account	
RECEIPTS:			
From customers	Sales Revenue	+ Decrease in Accounts Receivable – Increase in Accounts Receivable	
Of interest	Interest Revenue	+ Decrease in Interest Receivable – Increase in Interest Receivable	
PAYMENTS:			
To suppliers	Cost of Goods Sold	+ Increase in Inventory – Decrease in Inventory	+ Decrease in Accounts Payable – Increase in Accounts Payable
	Operating Expense	+ Increase in Prepaids – Decrease in Prepaids	+ Decrease in Accrued Liabilities – Increase in Accrued Liabilities
To employees	Salary (Wage) Expense	+ Decrease in Salary (Wage) Payable – Increase in Salary (Wage) Payable	
For interest	Interest Expense	+ Decrease in Interest Payable – Increase in Interest Payable	
For income tax	Income Tax Expense	+ Decrease in Income Tax Payable – Increase in Income Tax Payable	

*We thank Professor Barbara Gerrity for suggesting this exhibit.

Exhibit 12-16 | Income Statement

	A	B	C
1	**The Roadster Factory, Inc. (TRF)** **Income Statement** **Year Ended December 31, 2014**		
2		**(In thousands)**	
3	Revenues and gains:		
4	Sales revenue	$ 303	
5	Interest revenue	2	
6	Gain on sale of plant assets	8	
7	Total revenues and gains		$ 313
8	Expenses:		
9	Cost of goods sold	$ 150	
10	Salary and wage expense	56	
11	Depreciation expense	18	
12	Other operating expense	17	
13	Income tax expense	15	
14	Interest expense	7	
15	Total expenses		263
16	Net income		$ 50
17			

Exhibit 12-17 | Comparative Balance Sheets

A1			
	A	**B**	**C**	**D**

	The Roadster Factory, Inc. (TRF) Comparative Balance Sheets December 31, 2014 and 2013			
1				
2	(In thousands)	**2014**	**2013**	**Increase (Decrease)**
3	**Assets**			
4	Current:			
5	Cash	$ 34	$ 42	$ (8)
6	Accounts receivable	96	81	15
7	Inventory	35	38	(3)
8	Prepaid expenses	8	7	1
9	Notes receivable	21	—	21
10	Plant assets, net of depreciation	343	219	124
11	Total	$ 537	$ 387	$ 150
12	**Liabilities**			
13	Current:			
14	Accounts payable	$ 91	$ 57	$ 34
15	Salary and wage payable	4	6	(2)
16	Accrued liabilities	1	3	(2)
17	Long-term debt	160	77	83
18	**Stockholders' Equity**			
19	Common stock	162	158	4
20	Retained earnings	119	86	33
21	Total	$ 537	$ 387	$ 150
22				

— Changes in noncash current assets—Operating

— Changes in noncurrent assets—Investing

— Changes in current liabilities—Operating

Changes in long-term liabilities and paid-in capital accounts—Financing

Change due to net income—Operating

Change due to dividends—Financing

Computing Cash Collections from Customers. Collections start with sales revenue (an accrual basis amount). The Roadster Factory's income statement (Exhibit 12-16) reports sales of $303,000. Accounts receivable increased from $81,000 at the beginning of the year to $96,000 at year-end, a $15,000 increase (Exhibit 12-17). Based on those amounts, Cash Collections equal $288,000, as follows. We must solve for cash collections (X):

Accounts Receivable

Beginning balance	+	Sales	−	Collections	=	Ending balance
$81,000	+	$303,000		−X	=	$96,000
				−X	=	$96,000 − $81,000 − $303,000
				X	=	$288,000

The T-account for Accounts Receivable provides another view of the same computation.

Accounts Receivable

Beginning balance	81,000		
Sales	303,000	Collections	288,000
Ending balance	96,000		

Accounts Receivable increased, so collections must be less than sales.

All collections of receivables are computed this way. Let's turn now to cash receipts of interest revenue. In our example, The Roadster Factory earned interest revenue and collected cash of $2,000. The amounts of interest revenue and cash receipts of interest often differ, and Exhibit 12-15 shows how to make this computation.

Computing Payments to Suppliers. This computation includes two parts:

- Payments for inventory
- Payments for operating expenses (other than interest and income tax)

Payments for inventory are computed by converting cost of goods sold to the cash basis. We use Cost of Goods Sold, Inventory, and Accounts Payable. First, we must solve for purchases. All the amounts come from Exhibits 12-16 and 12-17.

Cost of Goods Sold

Beginning inventory	+	Purchases	–	Ending inventory	=	Cost of goods sold
$38,000	+	X	–	$35,000	=	$150,000
		X			=	$150,000 – $38,000 + $35,000
		X			=	$147,000

Now we can compute cash payments for inventory (Y), as follows:

Accounts Payable

Beginning balance	+	Purchases	–	Payments for inventory	=	Ending balance
$57,000	+	$147,000		–Y	=	$91,000
				–Y	=	$91,000 – $57,000 – $147,000
				Y	=	$113,000

The T-accounts show where the data come from. Start with Cost of Goods Sold.

Cost of Goods Sold			
Beg inventory	38,000	End inventory	35,000
Purchases	147,000		
Cost of goods sold	150,000		

Accounts Payable			
Payments for inventory	113,000	Beg bal	57,000
		Purchases	147,000
		End bal	91,000

Accounts Payable increased, so payments for inventory are less than purchases.

Computing Payments for Other Operating Expenses. Payments for operating expenses other than interest and income tax are computed from three accounts: Prepaid Expenses, Accrued Liabilities, and Other Operating Expenses. All The Roadster Factory data come from Exhibits 12-16 and 12-17.

Prepaid Expenses

Beginning balance	+	Payments	–	Expiration of prepaid expense (assumed)	=	Ending balance
$7,000	+	X	–	$7,000	=	$8,000
		X			=	$8,000 – $7,000 + $7,000
		X			=	$8,000

Accrued Liabilities

Beginning balance	+	Accrual of expense at year-end (assumed)	–	Payments	=	Ending balance
$3,000	+	$1,000		–X	=	$1,000
				–X	=	$1,000 – $3,000 – $1,000
				X	=	$3,000

Other Operating Expenses

Accrual of expense at year-end	+	Expiration of prepaid expense	+	Payments	=	Ending balance
$1,000	+	$7,000		X	=	$17,000
				X	=	$17,000 − $1,000 − $7,000
				X	=	$9,000

Total payments for other operating expenses = $8,000 + $3,000 + $9,000

= $20,000

The T-accounts give another picture of the same data.

Prepaid Expenses						Accrued Liabilities				Other Operating Expenses		
Beg bal	7,000	Expiration of						Beg bal	3,000	Accrual of	1,000	
Payments	8,000	prepaid			Payment	3,000	Accrual of		expense at		
		expense	7,000				expense at		year-end		
End bal	8,000						year-end	1,000	Expiration of		
						End bal	1,000	prepaid		
									expense	7,000	
									Payments	9,000	
									End bal	17,000	

Total payments for other operating expenses = $20,000 ($8,000 + $3,000 + $9,000)

Now we can compute Payments to Suppliers:

Payments to suppliers	=	Payments for inventory	+	Payments for other operating expenses
$133,000	=	$113,000	+	$20,000

Computing Payments to Employees. It is convenient to combine all payments to employees into one account, Salary and Wage Expense. We then adjust the expense for the change in Salary and Wage Payable, as shown here:

Salary and Wage Payable

Beginning balance	+	Salary and wage expense	−	Payments	=	Ending balance
$6,000	+	$56,000		−X	=	$4,000
				−X	=	$4,000 − $6,000 − $56,000
				X	=	$58,000

Salary and Wage Payable

Payments to employees	58,000	Beginning balance	6,000
		Salary and wage expense	56,000
		Ending balance	4,000

Computing Payments of Interest and Income Taxes. The Roadster Factory's expense and payment amounts are the same for interest and income tax, so no analysis is required. If the expense and the payment differ, the payment can be computed as shown in Exhibit 12-15.

Computing Investing and Financing Cash Flows

Investing and financing activities are explained on pages 675–680. These computations are the same for both the direct and the indirect methods.

> Stop & Think...

Fidelity Company reported the following for 2014 and 2013 (in millions):

At December 31,	2014	2013
Receivables, net.........................	$3,500	$3,900
Inventory....................................	5,200	5,000
Accounts payable	900	1,200
Income taxes payable	600	700

Year Ended December 31,	2014
Revenues.......................................	$23,000
Cost of goods sold........................	14,100
Income tax expense......................	900

Based on these figures, how much cash did
- Fidelity collect from customers during 2014?
- Fidelity pay for inventory during 2014?
- Fidelity pay for income taxes during 2014?

Answers

		Beginning receivables	+	Revenues	−	Collections	=	Ending receivables
Collections from customers	= $23,400:	$3,900	+	$23,000	−	$23,400	=	$3,500

		Cost of goods sold	+	Increase in inventory	+	Decrease in accounts payable	=	Payments
Payments for inventory	= $14,600:	$14,100	+	($5,200 − $5,000)	+	($1,200 − $900)	=	$14,600

		Beginning income taxes payable	+	Income tax expense	−	Payment	=	Ending income taxes payable
Payment of income taxes	= $1,000:	$700	+	$900	−	$1,000	=	$600

Measuring Cash Adequacy: Free Cash Flow

Throughout this chapter, we have focused on cash flows from operating, investing, and financing activities. Some investors want to know how much cash a company can "free up" for new opportunities. **Free cash flow** is the amount of cash available from operations after paying for planned investments in plant assets. Free cash flow can be computed as follows:

$$\text{Free cash flow} = \frac{\text{Net cash provided}}{\text{by operating activities}} - \frac{\text{Cash payments earmarked for}}{\text{investments in plant assets}}$$

PepsiCo, Inc., uses free cash flow to manage its operations. Suppose PepsiCo expects net cash inflow of $2.3 billion from operations. Assume PepsiCo plans to spend $1.9 billion to modernize its bottling plants. In this case, PepsiCo's free cash flow would be $0.4 billion ($2.3 billion − $1.9 billion). If a good investment opportunity comes along, PepsiCo should have $0.4 billion to invest in the other company. **Shell Oil Company** also uses free-cash-flow analysis. A large amount of free cash flow is preferable because it means that a lot of cash is available for new investments. The Decision Guidelines that follow show some ways to use cash flow and income data for investment and credit analysis.

● Decision Guidelines

INVESTORS' AND CREDITORS' USE OF CASH FLOW AND RELATED INFORMATION

Jan Childres is a private investor. Through years of experience, she has devised some guidelines for evaluating both stock investments and bond investments. Childres uses a combination of accrual accounting data and cash flow information. Here are her decision guidelines for both investors and creditors.

▶ INVESTORS

Questions	Factors to Consider	Financial Statement Predictor/Decision Model*
1. How much in dividends can I expect to receive from an investment in stock?	Expected future net income	Income from continuing operations**
	Expected future cash balance	Net cash flows from (in order) ■ operating activities ■ investing activities ■ financing activities
	Future dividend policy	Current and past dividend policy
2. Is the stock price likely to increase or decrease?	Expected future net income	Income from continuing operations**
	Expected future cash flows from operating activities	Income from continuing operations** Net cash flow from operating activities
3. What is the future stock price likely to be?	Expected future income from	
	■ continuing operations, and	$$\text{Expected future price of a share of stock} = \frac{\text{Income from continuing operations per share**}}{\text{Investment capitalization rate**}}$$
	■ cash flow from operating activities	$$\text{Expected future price of a share of stock} = \frac{\text{Net cash flow from operations per share}}{\text{Investment capitalization rate**}}$$

▶ CREDITORS

Question	Factors to Consider	Financial Statement Predictor
Can the company pay the interest and principal at the maturity of a loan?	Expected future net cash flow from operating activities	Income from continuing operations** Net cash flow from operating activities

*There are many other factors to consider in making these decisions. These are some of the more common.
**See Chapter 11.

Adeva Health Foods, Inc., reported the following comparative balance sheets for 2014 and 2013 and the income statement for 2014:

A1		
	A	**B**	**C**

	A	**B**	**C**
1	**Adeva Health Foods, Inc.** **Comparative Balance Sheets** **December 31, 2014 and 2013**		
2		**2014**	**2013**
3	Cash	$ 19,000	$ 3,000
4	Accounts receivable	22,000	23,000
5	Inventories	34,000	31,000
6	Prepaid expenses	1,000	3,000
7	Equipment, net	90,000	79,000
8	Intangible assets	9,000	9,000
9		$ 175,000	$ 148,000
10			
11	Accounts payable	$ 14,000	$ 9,000
12	Accrued liabilities	16,000	19,000
13	Income tax payable	14,000	12,000
14	Notes payable	45,000	50,000
15	Common stock	31,000	20,000
16	Retained earnings	64,000	40,000
17	Treasury stock	(9,000)	(2,000)
18		$ 175,000	$ 148,000
19			

A1		
	A	**B**

	A	**B**
1	**Adeva Health Foods, Inc.** **Income Statement** **Year Ended December 31, 2014**	
2	Sales revenue	$ 190,000
3	Gain on sale of equipment	6,000
4	Total revenue and gains	196,000
5	Cost of goods sold	85,000
6	Depreciation expense	19,000
7	Other operating expenses	36,000
8	Total expenses	140,000
9	Income before income tax	56,000
10	Income tax expense	18,000
11	Net income	$ 38,000
12		

Assume that **Berkshire Hathaway** is considering buying Adeva. Berkshire Hathaway requests the following cash flow data for 2014. There were no noncash investing and financing activities.

a. Collections from customers.

b. Cash payments for inventory.

c. Cash payments for other operating expenses.

d. Cash payment for income tax.

e. Cash received from the sale of equipment. Adeva paid $40,000 for new equipment during the year.

f. Issuance of common stock.

g. Issuance of notes payable. Adeva paid off $20,000 during the year.

h. Cash dividends. There were no stock dividends.

Provide the requested data. Show your work.

Answers

a. Analyze Accounts Receivable: Let X = Collections from customers:

Beginning Accounts Receivable	+	Sales	−	Collections	=	Ending Accounts Receivable
$23,000	+	$190,000	−	X	=	$22,000
				X	=	$191,000

b. Analyze Inventory and Accounts Payable: Let X = Purchases, and let Y = Payments for inventory:

Beginning Inventory	+	Purchases	−	Cost of Goods Sold	=	Ending Inventory
$31,000	+	X	−	$85,000	=	$34,000
		X			=	$88,000

Beginning Accounts Payable	+	Purchases	−	Payments	=	Ending Accounts Payable
$9,000	+	$88,000	−	Y	=	$14,000
				Y	=	$83,000

c. Start with Other Operating Expenses, and adjust for the changes in Prepaid Expenses and Accrued Liabilities:

Other Operating Expenses	− Decrease in Prepaid Expenses	+ Decrease in Accrued Liabilities	=	Payments for Other Operating Expenses
$36,000	− $2,000	+ $3,000	=	$37,000

d. Analyze Income Tax Payable: Let X = Payment of income tax:

Beginning Income Tax Payable	+	Income Tax Expense	−	Payments	=	Ending Income Tax Payable
$12,000	+	$18,000	−	X	=	$14,000
				X	=	$16,000

e. Analyze Equipment, Net: Let X = Book value of equipment sold. Then combine with the gain or loss to compute cash received from the sale:

Beginning Equipment, net	+	Acquisitions	−	Depreciation Expense	−	Book Value Sold	=	Ending Equipment, net
$79,000	+	$40,000	−	$19,000	−	X	=	$90,000
						X	=	$10,000

Cash Received from Sale	=	Book Value Sold	+	Gain on Sale
$16,000	=	$10,000	+	$6,000

f. Analyze Common Stock: Let X = Issuance:

Beginning Common Stock	+	Issuance	=	Ending Common Stock
$20,000	+	X	=	$31,000
		X	=	$11,000

g. Analyze Notes Payable: Let X = Issuance:

Beginning Notes Payable	+	Issuance	−	Payment	=	Ending Notes Payable
$50,000	+	X	−	$20,000	=	$45,000
		X			=	$15,000

h. Analyze Retained Earnings: Let X = Dividends:

Beginning Retained Earnings	+	Net Income	−	Dividends	=	Ending Retained Earnings
$40,000	+	$38,000	−	X	=	$64,000
				X	=	$14,000

REVIEW | Statement of Cash Flows

Quick Check (Answers are given on page 738.)

1. All except which of the following activities are reported on the statement of cash flows?
   a. Marketing activities
   b. Operating activities
   c. Investing activities
   d. Financing activities

2. On the statement of cash flows, activities that create long-term liabilities are usually
   a. operating activities.
   b. investing activities.
   c. financing activities.
   d. noncash investing and financing activities.

3. On the statement of cash flows, activities affecting long-term assets are
   a. operating activities.
   b. investing activities.
   c. financing activities.
   d. marketing activities.

4. In 2014, MLL Corporation borrowed $90,000, paid dividends of $26,000, issued 12,000 shares of stock for $20 per share, purchased land for $25,000, and received dividends of $10,000. Net income was $120,000, and depreciation for the year totaled $11,000. Accounts receivable increased by $10,000. How much should be reported as net cash provided by operating activities by the indirect method?

a. $121,000
b. $115,000

c. $420,000
d. $131,000

5. On the statement of cash flows, activities that obtain the cash needed to launch and sustain a company are

a. marketing activities.
b. income activities.

c. financing activities.
d. investing activities.

6. On the statement of cash flows, the exchange of stock for land would be reported as which of the following?

a. Noncash investing and financing activities
b. Investing activities
c. Financing activities
d. Exchanges are not reported on the statement of cash flows

Use the following Georgia Company information for questions 7–10.

Net income	$40,000	Increase in accounts payable	$ 9,000
Depreciation expense	15,000	Acquisition of equipment	
Payment of dividends	1,000	with cash	25,000
Increase in accounts receivable	3,000	Sale of treasury stock	6,000
Collection of long-term notes receivable	11,000	Payment of long-term debt	13,000
Loss on sale of land	10,000	Proceeds from sale of land	42,000
		Decrease in inventories	6,000

7. Under the indirect method, net cash provided by operating activities would be

a. $94,000.
b. $97,000.

c. $71,000.
d. $77,000.

8. Net cash provided by (used for) investing activities would be

a. $94,000.
b. $28,000.

c. $71,000.
d. $(97,000).

9. Net cash provided by (used for) financing activities would be

a. $(8,000).
b. $1,000.

c. $5,000.
d. $94,000.

10. The net book value of land sold must have been

a. $42,000.
b. $5,000.
c. $52,000.
d. Cannot be determined from the data given.

11. Cold Cup Ice Cream began the year with $30,000 in accounts receivable and ended the year with $16,000 in accounts receivable. If credit sales for the year were $575,000, the cash collected from customers during the year amounted to

a. $561,000.
b. $605,000.

c. $591,000.
d. $589,000.

12. Berkshire Farms, Ltd., made sales of $680,000 and had cost of goods sold of $440,000. Inventory decreased by $25,000, and accounts payable decreased by $12,000. Operating expenses were $195,000. How much was Berkshire Farms' net income for the year?
    a. $20,000
    b. $45,000
    c. $240,000
    d. $33,000

13. Use the Berkshire Farms data from question 12. Accounts payable relates solely to the purchase of inventory. How much cash did Berkshire Farms pay for inventory during the year?
    a. $427,000
    b. $452,000
    c. $440,000
    d. $20,000

Accounting Vocabulary

cash equivalents (p. 667) Highly liquid short-term investments that can be converted into cash immediately.

cash flows (p. 666) Cash receipts and cash payments (disbursements).

direct method (p. 669) Format of the operating activities section of the statement of cash flows; lists the major categories of operating cash receipts (collections from customers and receipts of interest and dividends) and cash disbursements (payments to suppliers and employees, and for interest and income taxes).

financing activities (p. 668) Activities that obtain from investors and creditors the cash needed to launch and sustain the business; a section of the statement of cash flows.

free cash flow (p. 694) The amount of cash available from operations after paying for planned investments in plant assets.

indirect method (p. 669) Format of the operating activities section of the statement of cash flows; starts with net income and reconciles to net cash flow from operating activities.

investing activities (p. 668) Activities that increase or decrease the long-term assets available to the business; a section of the statement of cash flows.

operating activities (p. 668) Activities that create revenues, expenses, gains and losses; a section of the statement of cash flows. Operating activities affect the income statement.

statement of cash flows (p. 666) Reports cash receipts and cash payments classified according to the entity's major activities: operating, investing, and financing.

ASSESS YOUR PROGRESS

Short Exercises

S12-1. *(Learning Objective 1: Explain the purposes of the statement of cash flows)* State how the statement of cash flows helps investors and creditors perform each of the following functions:
   a. Predict future cash flows
   b. Evaluate management decisions

S12-2. *(Learning Objective 1: Explain the purposes of the statement of cash flows)* Kobe, Inc., has experienced an unbroken string of nine years of growth in net income. Nevertheless, the company is facing bankruptcy. Creditors are calling all of Kobe's loans for immediate payment, and the cash is simply not available. It is clear that the company's top managers overemphasized profits and gave too little attention to cash flows.

Write a brief memo, in your own words, to explain to the managers of Kobe, Inc., the purposes of the statement of cash flows.

S12-3. *(Learning Objective 2: Evaluate operating cash flows—indirect method)* Examine the statement of cash flows of Tubberfield, Inc.

	A	B	C
1	**Tubberfield, Inc.** **Consolidated Statement of Cash Flows (Adapted, In Millions)** **Year Ended December 31, 2014**		
2	**Cash flows from operating activities:**		
3	Net income	$ 875	
4	Adjustment to reconcile net income to net cash		
5	used in operating activities:		
6	Depreciation and amortization	222	
7	Change in assets and liabilities, net of acquired businesses:		
8	Accounts receivable	(470)	
9	Other current assets	(160)	
10	Accounts payable	(167)	
11	Accrued expenses and other liabilities	(238)	
12	Unearned revenue	25	
13	Income taxes payable	(266)	
14	Other, net	26	
15	Net cash used in operating activities		(153)
16	**Cash flows from investing activities:**		
17	Purchase of property and equipment	$ (1,593)	
18	Purchase of investments	(21,282)	
19	Sale of investments	19,286	
20	Acquisitions of other companies	(363)	
21	Net cash used in investing activities		(3,952)
22	**Cash flows from financing activities:**		
23	Proceeds from the issuance of common stock, net	$ 835	
24	Other financing activities, net	378	
25	Net cash provided by financing activities		1,213
26	Impact of foreign currency translation		18
27	Net increase (decrease) in cash and cash equivalents		(2,874)
28	Cash and cash equivalents at beginning of year		4,155
29	Cash and cash equivalents at end of year		$ 1,281
30			

Suppose Tubberfield's operating activities *provided*, rather than *used*, cash. Identify three things under the indirect method that could cause operating cash flows to be positive.

S12-4. *(Learning Objectives 1, 2: Use cash flow data to evaluate performance)* Top managers of Bayside Inns are reviewing company performance for 2014. The income statement reports a 20% increase in net income over 2013. However, most of the increase resulted from a gain on insurance proceeds from fire damage to a building. The balance sheet shows a large increase in receivables. The cash flows statement, in summarized form, reports the following:

Net cash used for operating activities	$(63,500)
Net cash provided by investing activities	42,000
Net cash provided by financing activities	29,100
Increase in cash during 2014	$ 7,600

Write a memo giving Bayside Inns' managers your assessment of 2014 operations and your outlook for the future. Focus on the information content of the cash flows data.

S12-5. *(Learning Objective 3: Report cash flows from operating activities—indirect method)* Incredibly Fast Transportation (IFT) began 2014 with accounts receivable, inventory, and prepaid expenses totaling $56,000. At the end of the year, IFT had a total of $59,000 for these current assets. At the beginning of 2014, IFT owed current liabilities of $41,000, and at year-end current liabilities totaled $45,000.

Net income for the year was $76,000. Included in net income were a $3,100 loss on the sale of land and depreciation expense of $12,000.

Show how IFT should report cash flows from operating activities for 2014. IFT uses the *indirect* method.

S12-6. *(Learning Objective 2: Distinguish among operating, financing, and investing activities—indirect method)* Smith Clinic, Inc., is preparing its statement of cash flows (*indirect* method) for the year ended March 31, 2014. Consider the following items in preparing the company's statement of cash flows. Identify each item as an operating activity—addition to net income (O+) or subtraction from net income (O−), an investing activity (I), a financing activity (F), or an activity that is not used to prepare the cash flows statement by the indirect method (N). Place the appropriate symbol in the blank space.

	a. Decrease in accrued liabilities
	b. Net income
	c. Decrease in prepaid expense
	d. Collection of cash from customers
	e. Purchase of equipment with cash
	f. Retained earnings
	g. Payment of dividends
	h. Increase in accounts payable
	i. Decrease in accounts receivable
	j. Gain on sale of building
	k. Loss on sale of land
	l. Depreciation expense
	m. Increase in inventory
	n. Issuance of common stock

S12-7. *(Learning Objective 3: Prepare operating cash flows—indirect method)* Adams Corporation accountants have assembled the following data for the year ended June 30, 2014:

Net income...............................	$?	Cost of goods sold....................	$198,000
Payment of dividends	6,400	Other operating expenses.........	64,000
Proceeds from the issuance		Purchase of equipment	
of common stock	24,000	with cash........................	37,000
Sales revenue...........................	376,000	Increase in current liabilities.....	20,100
Increase in current assets		Payment of note payable	37,000
other than cash	63,000	Proceeds from sale of land........	28,000
Purchase of treasury stock........	8,000	Depreciation expense	12,000

Prepare the *operating activities section* of Adams' statement of cash flows for the year ended June 30, 2014. Adams Corporation uses the *indirect* method for operating cash flows.

S12-8. *(Learning Objective 3: Prepare a statement of cash flows—indirect method)* Use the data in SE12-7 to prepare Adams Corporation's statement of cash flows for the year ended June 30, 2014. Adams uses the *indirect* method for operating activities.

S12-9. *(Learning Objective 3: Compute investing cash flows)* Dallas Computer Sales, Inc., reported the following financial statements for 2014:

	A	B
	Dallas Computer Sales, Inc.	
	Income Statement	
1	**Year Ended December 31, 2014**	
2	(In thousands)	
3	Service revenue	$ 819
4	Cost of goods sold	401
5	Salary expense	60
6	Depreciation expense	15
7	Other expenses	180
8	Total expenses	656
9	Net income	$ 163
10		

	A	B	C	D	E	F
	Dallas Computer Sales, Inc.					
	Comparative Balance Sheets					
1	**December 31, 2014 and 2013**					
2	(In thousands)					
3	**Assets**	**2014**	**2013**	**Liabilities**	**2014**	**2013**
4	Current:			Current:		
5	Cash	$ 53	$ 58	Accounts payable	$ 56	$ 54
6	Accounts receivable	62	53	Salary payable	26	22
7	Inventory	77	91	Accrued liabilities	13	16
8	Prepaid expenses	17	16	Long-term note payable	75	66
9	Long-term investments	65	88			
10	Plant assets, net	255	195	**Stockholders' Equity**		
11				Common stock	50	46
12				Retained earnings	309	297
13	Total	$ 529	$ 501	Total	$ 529	$ 501
14						

Compute the following investing cash flows; enter all amounts in thousands.
  a. Acquisitions of plant assets (all were for cash). Dallas Computer Sales sold no plant assets.
  b. Proceeds from the sale of investments. Dallas Computer Sales purchased no investments.

S12-10. *(Learning Objective 3: Compute financing cash flows)* Use the Dallas Computer Sales data in SE12-9 to compute the following; enter all amounts in thousands.
  a. New borrowing or payment of long-term notes payable. Dallas Computer Sales had only one long-term note payable transaction during the year.
  b. Issuance of common stock or retirement of common stock. Dallas Computer Sales had only one common stock transaction during the year.
  c. Payment of cash dividends (same as dividends declared).

S12-11. *(Learning Objective 4: Compute operating cash flows—direct method)* Use the Dallas Computer Sales data in SE12-9 to compute the following; enter all amounts in thousands.
  a. Collections from customers
  b. Payments for inventory

S12-12. *(Learning Objective 4: Compute operating cash flows—direct method)* Use the Dallas Computer Sales data in SE12-9 to compute the following; enter all amounts in thousands.
   a. Payments to employees
   b. Payments of other expenses

S12-13. *(Learning Objective 4: Prepare a statement of cash flows—direct method)* McCracken Horse Farms, Inc., began 2014 with cash of $58,000. During the year, McCracken earned service revenue of $694,000 and collected $640,000 from customers. Expenses for the year totaled $480,000, with $465,000 paid in cash to suppliers and employees. McCracken also paid $119,000 to purchase equipment and a cash dividend of $37,000 to stockholders. During 2014, McCracken borrowed $25,000 by issuing a note payable. Prepare the company's statement of cash flows for the year. Format operating activities by the *direct* method.

S12-14. *(Learning Objective 4: Computing operating cash flows—direct method)* Phoenix Golf Club, Inc., has assembled the following data for the year ended September 30, 2014:

Cost of goods sold...........................	$112,000	Payment of dividends.........................	$ 12,000
Payments to suppliers......................	124,000	Proceeds from issuance	
Purchase of equipment with cash	29,000	of common stock	30,000
Payments to employees....................	78,000	Sales revenue......................................	281,000
Payment of note payable	36,000	Collections from customers...............	263,000
Proceeds from sale of land...............	46,000	Payment of income tax......................	19,000
Depreciation expense	8,000	Purchase of treasury stock.................	5,400

Prepare the *operating activities section* of Phoenix Golf Club, Inc.'s statement of cash flows for the year ended September 30, 2014. Phoenix Golf Club uses the *direct* method for operating cash flows.

S12-15. *(Learning Objective 4: Preparing a statement of cash flows—direct method)* Use the data in SE12-14 to prepare Phoenix Golf Club, Inc.'s statement of cash flows for the year ended September 30, 2014. Phoenix uses the *direct* method for operating activities.

Exercises

Group A

E12-16A. *(Learning Objectives 2, 3: Distinguish among operating, investing, and financing activities for the statement of cash flows—indirect method)* Brothers Investments specializes in low-risk government bonds. Identify each of Brothers' transactions as operating (O), investing (I), financing (F), noncash investing and financing (NIF), or a transaction that is not reported on the statement of cash flows (N). Indicate whether each item increases (+) or decreases (−) cash. The *indirect* method is used for operating activities.

	a.	Purchase of long-term investment with cash
	b.	Issuance of long-term note payable to borrow cash
	c.	Increase in prepaid expenses
	d.	Decrease in accrued liabilities
	e.	Loss of sale of equipment
	f.	Decrease in accounts receivable
	g.	Depreciation of equipment
	h.	Increase in accounts payable
	i.	Amortization of intangible assets
	j.	Purchase of treasury stock
	k.	Payment of long-term debt
	l.	Increase in salary payable
	m.	Cash sale of land
	n.	Sale of long-term investment
	o.	Acquisition of building by cash payment
	p.	Net income
	q.	Issuance of common stock for cash
	r.	Payment of cash dividend
	s.	Acquisition of equipment by issuance of note payable

E12-17A. *(Learning Objectives 2, 3: Distinguish among operating, investing, and financing activities for the statement of cash flows—indirect method)* A company uses the indirect method to prepare the statement of cash flows. Indicate whether each of the following transactions affects an operating activity, an investing activity, a financing activity, or a noncash investing and financing activity:

	A	B	C	D	E	F	G	H
1	a.	Dividends Payable	25,000		h.	Equipment	28,000	
2		Cash		25,000		Cash		28,000
3	b.	Treasury Stock	12,000		i.	Bonds Payable	70,000	
4		Cash		12,000		Cash		70,000
5	c.	Land	123,000		j.	Cash	110,000	
6		Cash		123,000		Common Stock		17,000
7	d.	Cash	74,000			Capital in Excess of Par		93,000
8		Accounts Receivable	13,000		k.	Depreciation Expense	16,000	
9		Service Revenue		87,000		Accumulated Depreciation		16,000
10	e.	Salary Expense	36,000		l.	Loss on Disposal of Equipment	2,000	
11		Cash		36,000		Equipment, Net		2,000
12	f.	Furniture and Fixtures	36,000		m.	Building	235,000	
13		Cash		36,000		Note Payable, Long-Term		235,000
14	g.	Cash	10,000					
15		Long-Term Investment		10,000				
16								

E12-18A. *(Learning Objective 3: Compute cash flows from operating activities—indirect method)*
The accounting records of Capitol Distributors, Inc., reveal the following:

Net income...	$ 19,000	Depreciation expense	$ 7,000
Collection of dividend revenue..........	7,300	Increase in current liabilities...........	6,000
Payment of interest............................	17,000	Increase in current assets	
Sales revenue.....................................	206,000	other than cash	29,000
Gain on sale of land	8,000	Payment of dividends	7,300
Acquisition of land with cash............	38,000	Payment of income tax....................	4,000

Requirement

1. Compute cash flows from operating activities by the *indirect* method. Use the format of the operating activities section of Exhibit 12-6. Also evaluate the operating cash flow of Capitol Distributors. Give the reason for your evaluation.

E12-19A. *(Learning Objective 3: Compute cash flows from operating activities—indirect method)* The accounting records of Lane Fur Traders include these accounts:

Cash			
Dec 1	100,000		
Receipts	626,000	Payments	538,000
Dec 31	188,000		

Accounts Receivable			
Dec 1	5,000		
Credit sales	528,000	Collections	525,000
Dec 31	8,000		

Inventory			
Dec 1	7,500		
Purchases	451,000	Cost of Sales	449,500
Dec 31	9,000		

Equipment			
Dec 1	181,000		
Acquisition	10,000		
Dec 31	191,000		

Accumulated Deprec.—Equipment			
		Dec 1	60,000
		Depreciation	17,000
		Dec 31	77,000

Accounts Payable			
		Dec 1	14,500
Payments	389,000	Purchases	451,000
		Dec 31	76,500

Accrued Liabilities			
		Dec 1	19,000
Payments	29,000	Accruals	25,000
		Dec 31	15,000

Retained Earnings			
Quarterly		Dec 1	67,000
Dividend	19,000	Net Income	17,000
		Dec 31	65,000

Requirement

1. Compute Lane's net cash provided by (used for) operating activities during December. Use the *indirect* method. Do you see any potential problems in Lane's cash flows from operations? How can you tell?

E12-20A. *(Learning Objective 3: Preparing the statement of cash flows—indirect method)* The income statement and additional data of Tullis Travel Products, Inc., follow:

	A	B	C
1	**Tullis Travel Products, Inc.** **Income Statement** **Year Ended December 31, 2014**		
2	Revenues:		
3	Service revenue	$ 273,000	
4	Dividend revenue	8,700	$ 281,700
5	Expenses:		
6	Cost of goods sold	135,000	
7	Salary expense	59,000	
8	Depreciation expense	28,000	
9	Advertising expense	2,900	
10	Interest expense	2,100	
11	Income tax expense	16,400	243,400
12	Net income		$ 38,300
13			

Additional data:

a. Acquisition of plant assets was $95,000. Of this amount, $65,000 was paid in cash and $30,000 by signing a note payable.

b. Proceeds from sale of land totaled $17,000.

c. Proceeds from issuance of common stock totaled $46,000.

d. Payment of long-term note payable was $17,000.

e. Payment of dividends was $8,000.

The Statement of Cash Flows **707**

f. From the balance sheets:

A	B	C
A1		
	December 31,	
	2014	**2013**
Current assets:		
Cash	$ 118,300	$ 48,600
Accounts receivable	46,000	65,000
Inventory	87,000	77,000
Prepaid expenses	9,200	8,700
Current liabilities:		
Accounts payable	$ 33,900	$ 21,000
Accrued liabilities	66,000	57,000

Requirements

1. Prepare Tullis Travel Products's statement of cash flows for the year ended December 31, 2014, using the *indirect* method.
2. Evaluate Tullis' cash flows for the year. In your evaluation, mention all three categories of cash flows and give the reason for your evaluation.

E12-21A. *(Learning Objective 3: Evaluate a statement of cash flows—indirect method)* Consider three independent cases for the cash flows of Klein Merchandising Corp. For each case, identify from the statement of cash flows how Klein Merchandising Corp. generated the cash to acquire new plant assets. Rank the three cases from the most healthy financially to the least healthy.

A	B	C	D
A1			
	Case A	**Case B**	**Case C**
Cash flows from operating activities:			
Net income	$ 25,000	$ 25,000	$ 25,000
Depreciation and amortization	11,000	11,000	11,000
Increase in current assets	(2,000)	(14,000)	(27,000)
Decrease in current liabilities	(5,000)	(1,000)	(12,000)
	29,000	21,000	(3,000)
Cash flows from investing activities:			
Acquisition of plant assets	(102,000)	(102,000)	(102,000)
Sales of plant assets	46,000	111,000	11,000
	(56,000)	9,000	(91,000)
Cash flows from financing activities:			
Issuance of stock	76,000	18,000	119,000
Payment of debt	(47,000)	(28,000)	(27,000)
	29,000	(10,000)	92,000
Net increase (decrease) in cash	$ 2,000	$ 20,000	$ (2,000)

E12-22A. *(Learning Objectives 3, 4: Compute investing and financing amounts for the statement of cash flows)* Compute the following items for the statement of cash flows:

a. Beginning and ending Plant Assets, Net, are $129,000 and $122,000, respectively. Depreciation for the period was $16,000, and purchases of new plant assets were $47,000. Plant assets were sold at a $5,000 gain. What were the cash proceeds of the sale?

b. Beginning and ending Retained Earnings are $67,000 and $103,000, respectively. Net income for the period was $132,000, and stock dividends were $24,000. How much were cash dividends?

E12-23A. *(Learning Objective 4: Compute cash flows from operating activities—direct method)*
The accounting records of Demontre Pharmaceuticals, Inc., reveal the following:

Payment of salaries and wages	$47,000	Net income	$40,000
Depreciation expense	23,000	Payment of income tax	16,000
Decrease in current liabilities	18,000	Collection of dividend revenue	12,000
Increase in current assets other than cash	21,000	Payment of interest	8,000
		Cash sales	73,000
Payment of dividends	9,000	Gain on sale of land	7,000
Collection of accounts receivable	86,000	Acquisition of land with cash	25,000
		Payment of accounts payable	61,000

Requirement

1. Compute cash flows from operating activities by the *direct* method. Also evaluate Demontre's operating cash flow. Give the reason for your evaluation.

E12-24A. *(Learning Objective 4: Identify items for the statement of cash flows—direct method)*
Selected accounts of Callie Clara Antiques show the following:

Salary Payable

		Beginning bal	8,000
Payments	23,000	Salary expense	21,000
		Ending bal	6,000

Buildings

Beginning bal	60,000	Depreciation	15,000
Acquisitions with cash	90,000	Book value of building sold	89,000*
Ending bal	46,000		

*Sale price was $112,500.

Notes Payable

		Beginning bal	176,000
Payments	50,000	Issuance of note payable for cash	56,000
		Ending bal	182,000

Requirement

1. For each account, identify the item or items that should appear on a statement of cash flows prepared by the *direct* method. State where to report the item.

E12-25A. *(Learning Objective 4: Prepare the statement of cash flows—direct method)* The income statement and additional data of Office World, Inc., follow:

	A	B	C
	A1		
1	Office World, Inc. Income Statement Year Ended September 30, 2014		
2	Revenues:		
3	Sales revenue	$ 255,000	
4	Dividend revenue	9,500	$ 264,500
5	Expenses:		
6	Cost of goods sold	101,000	
7	Salary expense	43,000	
8	Depreciation expense	15,000	
9	Advertising expense	10,500	
10	Interest expense	2,200	
11	Income tax expense	22,500	194,200
12	Net income		$ 70,300
13			

Additional data:
  a. Collections from customers are $15,000 less than sales.
  b. Payments to suppliers are $1,600 more than the sum of cost of goods sold plus advertising expense.
  c. Payments to employees are $2,400 more than salary expense.
  d. Dividend revenue, interest expense, and income tax expense equal their cash amounts.
  e. Acquisition of plant assets is $195,000. Of this amount, $109,000 is paid in cash and $86,000 by signing a long-term note payable.
  f. Proceeds from sale of land total $27,000.
  g. Proceeds from issuance of common stock total $93,000.
  h. Payment of a long-term note payable is $17,000.
  i. Payment of dividends is $11,000.
  j. Cash balance, September 30, 2013, was $15,500.

Requirements

  1. Prepare Office World, Inc.'s statement of cash flows and accompanying schedule of noncash investing and financing activities. Report operating activities by the *direct* method.
  2. Evaluate Office World's cash flows for the year. In your evaluation, mention all three categories of cash flows, and give the reason for your evaluation.

E12-26A. *(Learning Objective 4: Compute amounts for the statement of cash flows—direct method)* Compute the following items for the statement of cash flows:
  a. Beginning and ending Accounts Receivable are $42,000 and $35,000, respectively. Credit sales for the period total $139,000. How much are cash collections from customers?
  b. Cost of Goods Sold is $67,000. Beginning Inventory was $56,000, and Ending Inventory balance is $59,000. Beginning and ending Accounts Payable are $24,000 and $26,000, respectively. How much are cash payments for inventory?

Group B

E12-27B. *(Learning Objectives 2, 3: Distinguish among operating, investing, and financing activities for the statement of cash flows—indirect method)* Donnahoo Investments specializes in low-risk government bonds. Identify each of Donnahoo's transactions as operating (O), investing (I), financing (F), noncash investing and financing (NIF), or a transaction that is not reported on the statement of cash flows (N). Indicate whether each item increases (+) or decreases (−) cash. The *indirect* method is used for operating activities.

	a.	Loss on sale of equipment
	b.	Decrease in accounts receivable
	c.	Acquisition of equipment by issuance of note payable
	d.	Increase in accounts payable
	e.	Payment of cash dividend
	f.	Purchase of long-term investment with cash
	g.	Cash sale of land
	h.	Increase in prepaid expenses
	i.	Increase in salary payable
	j.	Depreciation of equipment
	k.	Sale of long-term investment
	l.	Issuance of common stock for cash
	m.	Decrease in accrued liabilities
	n.	Amortization of intangible assets
	o.	Acquisition of building by cash payment
	p.	Payment of long-term debt
	q.	Issuance of long-term note payable to borrow cash
	r.	Purchase of treasury stock
	s.	Net income

E12-28B. *(Learning Objectives 2, 3: Distinguish among operating, investing, and financing activities for the statement of cash flows—indirect method)* A company uses the indirect method to prepare the statement of cash flows. Indicate whether each of the following transactions affects an operating activity, an investing activity, a financing activity, or a noncash investing and financing activity.

	A	B	C	D	E	F	G	H
			A1					
1	a.	Equipment	11,000		g.	Cash	61,000	
2		Cash		11,000		Common Stock		10,000
3	b.	Furniture and Fixtures	18,000			Capital in Excess of Par		51,000
4		Cash		18,000	h.	Dividends Payable	13,000	
5	c.	Cash	52,000			Cash		13,000
6		Accounts Receivable	11,000		i.	Cash	7,000	
7		Service Revenue		63,000		Long-Term Investment		7,000
8	d.	Salary Expense	14,000		j.	Building	105,000	
9		Cash		14,000		Note Payable—Long-Term		105,000
10	e.	Loss on Disposal of Equipment	1,000		k.	Treasury Stock	12,000	
11		Equipment, Net		1,000		Cash		12,000
12	f.	Bonds Payable	35,000		l.	Depreciation Expense	5,000	
13		Cash		35,000		Accumulated Depreciation		5,000
14					m.	Land	15,000	
15						Cash		15,000
16								

E12-29B. *(Learning Objective 3: Compute cash flows from operating activities—indirect method)* The accounting records of Chicago Distributors, Inc., reveal the following:

Net income..	$ 35,000	Depreciation expense	$ 7,000
Collection of dividend revenue..........	7,100	Decrease in current liabilities..........	19,000
Payment of interest............................	12,000	Increase in current assets	
Sales revenue.....................................	307,000	other than cash	25,000
Gain on sale of land	14,000	Payment of dividends.....................	7,700
Acquisition of land with cash............	35,000	Payment of income tax...................	14,000

Requirement

1. Compute cash flows from operating activities by the *indirect* method. Use the format of the operating activities section of Exhibit 12-6. Also evaluate the operating cash flow of Chicago Distributors. Give the reason for your evaluation.

E12-30B. *(Learning Objective 3: Compute cash flows from operating activities—indirect method)* The accounting records of Chaplaine Fur Traders include these accounts:

Cash			
Aug 1	80,000		
Receipts	618,000	Payments	650,000
Aug 31	48,000		

Accounts Receivable			
Aug 1	8,000		
Credit sales	522,000	Collections	441,000
Aug 31	89,000		

Inventory			
Aug 1	6,000		
Purchases	433,000	Cost of Sales	386,000
Aug 31	53,000		

Equipment		
Aug 1	181,000	
Acquisition	4,000	
Aug 31	185,000	

Accumulated Deprec.—Equipment		
	Aug 1	45,000
	Depreciation	6,000
	Aug 31	51,000

Accounts Payable			
		Aug 1	15,000
Payments	371,500	Purchases	433,000
		Aug 31	76,500

Accrued Liabilities			
		Aug 1	14,000
Payments	35,000	Accruals	30,000
		Aug 31	9,000

Retained Earnings			
Quarterly		Aug 1	63,000
Dividend	20,000	Net Income	21,000
		Aug 31	64,000

Requirement

1. Compute Chaplaine Fur Traders' net cash provided by (used for) operating activities during August. Use the *indirect* method. Do you see any potential problems in Chaplaine's cash flows from operations? How can you tell?

E12-31B. *(Learning Objective 3: Prepare the statement of cash flows—indirect method)* The income statement and additional data of Tyler Travel Products, Inc., follow:

	A	B	C
	A1		
1	**Tyler Travel Products, Inc.** **Income Statement** **Year Ended December 31, 2014**		
2	Revenues:		
3	Service revenue	$ 299,600	
4	Dividend revenue	8,700	$ 308,300
5	Expenses:		
6	Cost of goods sold	108,000	
7	Salary expense	44,000	
8	Depreciation expense	21,000	
9	Advertising expense	4,300	
10	Interest expense	2,100	
11	Income tax expense	19,500	198,900
12	Net income		$ 109,400
13			

Additional data:
  a. Acquisition of plant assets was $150,000. Of this amount, $95,000 was paid in cash and $55,000 by signing a note payable.
  b. Proceeds from sale of land totaled $14,000.
  c. Proceeds from issuance of common stock totaled $50,000.

d. Payment of a long-term note payable was $18,000.

e. Payment of dividends was $12,000.

f. From the balance sheets:

	A	B	C
	A1		
	A	B	C
1		December 31,	
2		2014	2013
3	**Current assets:**		
4	Cash	$ 85,200	$ 33,500
5	Accounts receivable	44,000	60,000
6	Inventory	84,000	62,000
7	Prepaid expenses	9,500	8,300
8			
9	**Current liabilities:**		
10	Accounts payable	$ 38,000	$ 36,500
11	Accrued liabilities	1,000	13,000
12			

Requirements

1. Prepare Tyler's statement of cash flows for the year ended December 31, 2014, using the *indirect* method.
2. Evaluate Tyler's cash flows for the year. In your evaluation, mention all three categories of cash flows, and give the reason for your evaluation.

E12-32B. *(Learning Objective 3: Evaluate a statement of cash flows—indirect method)* Consider three independent cases for the cash flows of Wynn Sporting Goods Corp. For each case, identify from the statement of cash flows how Wynn Sporting Goods Corp. generated the cash to acquire new plant assets. Rank the three cases from the most healthy financially to the least healthy.

	A	B	C	D
	A1			
	A	Case A	Case B	Case C
1		Case A	Case B	Case C
2	Cash flows from operating activities:			
3	Net income	$ 14,000	$ 14,000	$ 14,000
4	Depreciation and amortization	17,000	17,000	17,000
5	Increase in current assets	(3,000)	(1,000)	(7,000)
6	Decrease in current liabilities	(4,000)	(3,000)	(27,000)
7		24,000	27,000	(3,000)
8	Cash flows from investing activities:			
9	Acquisition of plant assets	(141,000)	(141,000)	(141,000)
10	Sales of plant assets	47,000	148,000	28,000
11		(94,000)	7,000	(113,000)
12	Cash flows from financing activities:			
13	Issuance of stock	104,000	26,000	149,000
14	Payment of debt	(45,000)	(38,000)	(28,000)
15		59,000	(12,000)	121,000
16	Net increase (decrease) in cash	$ (11,000)	$ 22,000	$ 5,000
17				

E12-33B. *(Learning Objectives 3, 4: Compute investing and financing amounts for the statement of cash flows)* Compute the following items for the statement of cash flows:

a. Beginning and ending Plant Assets, Net, are $152,000 and $147,000, respectively. Depreciation for the period was $28,000, and purchases of new plant assets were $91,000. Plant assets were sold at an $8,000 gain. What were the cash proceeds of the sale?

b. Beginning and ending Retained Earnings are $76,000 and $113,000, respectively. Net income for the period was $128,000, and stock dividends were $20,000. How much were cash dividends?

E12-34B. *(Learning Objective 4: Compute cash flows from operating activities—direct method)*
The accounting records of Greggory Pharmaceuticals, Inc., reveal the following:

Payment of salaries		Net income................................	$50,000
and wages..........................	$ 44,000	Payment of income tax...............	20,000
Depreciation expense	27,000	Collection of dividend	
Increase in current		revenue	14,000
liabilities	20,000	Payment of interest....................	9,000
Increase in current assets		Cash sales.....................................	51,000
other than cash	24,000	Gain on sale of land	3,000
Payment of dividends	12,000	Acquisition of land with cash	38,000
Collection of accounts		Payment of accounts	
receivable.........................	119,000	payable	63,000

Requirement

1. Compute cash flows from operating activities by the *direct* method. Also evaluate
   Greggory's operating cash flow. Give the reason for your evaluation.

E12-35B. *(Learning Objective 4: Identify items for the statement of cash flows—direct method)*
Selected accounts of Gracie Belle Antiques show the following:

Salary Payable

		Beginning bal	11,000
Payments	15,000	Salary expense	32,000
		Ending bal	28,000

Buildings

Beginning bal	75,000	Depreciation	17,000
Acquisitions with cash	116,000	Book value of building sold	88,000*
Ending bal	86,000		

*Sale price was $120,000.

Notes Payable

		Beginning bal	183,000
Payments	54,000	Issuance of note payable for cash	68,000
		Ending bal	197,000

Requirement

1. For each account, identify the item or items that should appear on a statement of cash
   flows prepared by the *direct* method. State where to report the item.

E12-36B. *(Learning Objective 4: Prepare the statement of cash flows—direct method)* The income statement and additional data of Quik Shop, Inc., follow:

	A	B	C
	A1 ⬍		
1	Quik Shop, Inc. Income Statement Year Ended June 30, 2014		
2	Revenues:		
3	Sales revenue	$ 275,000	
4	Dividend revenue	7,500	$ 282,500
5	Expenses:		
6	Cost of goods sold	106,000	
7	Salary expense	50,000	
8	Depreciation expense	14,000	
9	Advertising expense	12,500	
10	Interest expense	1,000	
11	Income tax expense	26,500	210,000
12	Net income		$ 72,500
13			

Additional data:
  a. Collections from customers are $30,000 more than sales.
  b. Payments to suppliers are $1,200 less than the sum of cost of goods sold plus advertising expense.
  c. Payments to employees are $1,800 less than salary expense.
  d. Dividend revenue, interest expense, and income tax expense equal their cash amounts.
  e. Acquisition of plant assets is $208,000. Of this amount, $133,000 is paid in cash and $75,000 by signing a long-term note payable.
  f. Proceeds from sale of land total $28,000.
  g. Proceeds from issuance of common stock total $33,000.
  h. Payment of a long-term note payable is $13,000.
  i. Payment of dividends is $8,000.
  j. Cash balance, June 30, 2013, was $12,400.

Requirements

  1. Prepare Quik Shop, Inc.'s statement of cash flows and accompanying schedule of noncash investing and financing activities. Report operating activities by the *direct* method.
  2. Evaluate Quik Shop's cash flows for the year. In your evaluation, mention all three categories of cash flows and give the reason for your evaluation.

E12-37B. *(Learning Objective 4: Compute amounts for the statement of cash flows—direct method)* Compute the following items for the statement of cash flows:
  a. Beginning and ending Accounts Receivable are $47,000 and $53,000, respectively. Credit sales for the period total $141,000. How much are cash collections from customers?
  b. Cost of Goods Sold is $76,000. Beginning Inventory balance is $39,000, and Ending Inventory balance is $35,000. Beginning and ending Accounts Payable are $29,000 and $32,000, respectively. How much are cash payments for inventory?

Quiz

Test your understanding of the statement of cash flows by answering the following questions. Select the best choice from among the possible answers given.

Q12-38. Paying off bonds payable is reported on the statement of cash flows under
  a. noncash investing and financing activities.
  b. financing activities.
  c. operating activities.
  d. investing activities.

Q12-39. The sale of inventory for cash is reported on the statement of cash flows under
  a. operating activities.
  b. noncash investing and financing activities.
  c. investing activities.
  d. financing activities.

Q12-40. Selling equipment for cash is reported on the statement of cash flows under
  a. financing activities.
  b. noncash investing and financing activities.
  c. investing activities.
  d. operating activities.

Q12-41. Which of the following terms appears on a statement of cash flows—indirect method?
  a. Collections from customers   **c.** Payments to suppliers
  b. Cash receipt of interest revenue   **d.** Depreciation expense

Q12-42. On an indirect method statement of cash flows, an increase in a prepaid insurance would be
  a. added to net income.
  b. added to increases in current assets.
  c. deducted from net income.
  d. included in payments to suppliers.

Q12-43. On an indirect method statement of cash flows, an increase in accounts payable would be
  a. reported in the financing activities section.
  b. added to net income in the operating activities section.
  c. deducted from net income in the operating activities section.
  d. reported in the investing activities section.

Q12-44. On an indirect method statement of cash flows, a gain on the sale of plant assets would be
  a. reported in the investing activities section.
  b. ignored, since the gain did not generate any cash.
  c. added to net income in the operating activities section.
  d. deducted from net income in the operating activities section.

Q12-45. A company uses the direct method to prepare the statement of cash flows. Select an activity for each of the following transactions:
  1. Receiving cash dividends is a/an _____ activity.
  2. Paying cash dividends is a/an _____ activity.

Q12-46. Photosmart Camera Co. sold equipment with a cost of $18,000 and accumulated depreciation of $6,000 for an amount that resulted in a gain of $4,000. What amount should Photosmart report on the statement of cash flows as "proceeds from sale of plant assets"?
  a. $12,000   **c.** $8,000
  b. $16,000   **d.** Some other amount

Questions 47–57 use the following data. Solomon Corporation formats operating cash flows by the *indirect* method in Questions 47–55. Solomon uses the direct method in Questions 56–57.

A1	◆			
	A		**B**	**C**
1	**Solomon's Income Statement for 2014**			
2	Sales revenue		$ 170,000	
3	Gain on sale of equipment		10,000*	$ 180,000
4	Cost of goods sold		112,000	
5	Depreciation		7,500	
6	Other operating expenses		24,000	143,500
7	Net income			$ 36,500
8				

*The book value of equipment sold during 2014 was $20,000.

A1	◆						
	A	**B**	**C**	**D**		**E**	**F**
1	**Solomon's Comparative Balance Sheets at the end of 2014**						
2		**2014**	**2013**			**2014**	**2013**
3	Cash	$ 3,000	$ 2,000	Accounts payable		$ 7,000	$ 8,000
4	Accounts receivable	6,000	11,000	Accrued liabilities		5,000	1,000
5	Inventory	8,000	7,000	Common stock		24,000	12,000
6	Plant and equipment, net	95,000	67,000	Retained earnings		76,000	66,000
7		$ 112,000	$ 87,000			$ 112,000	$ 87,000
8							

Q12-47. How many items enter the computation of Solomon's net cash provided by operating activities?

a. 7

b. 5

c. 3

d. 2

Q12-48. How do Solomon's accrued liabilities affect the company's statement of cash flows for 2014?

a. Increase in cash used by financing activities

b. They don't because the accrued liabilities are not yet paid

c. Increase in cash provided by operating activities

d. Increase in cash used by investing activities

Q12-49. How do accounts receivable affect Solomon's cash flows from operating activities for 2014?

a. Increase in cash provided by operating activities

b. Decrease in cash provided by operating activities

c. They don't because accounts receivable result from investing activities

d. Decrease in cash used by investing activities

Q12-50. Solomon's net cash provided by operating activities during 2014 was

a. $44,000.

b. $47,000.

c. $38,000.

d. $41,000.

Q12-51. How many items enter the computation of Solomon's net cash flow from investing activities for 2014?

a. 5

b. 2

c. 3

d. 7

Q12-52. The book value of equipment sold during 2014 was $20,000. Solomon's net cash flow from investing activities for 2014 was

   a. net cash used of $25,500.
   b. net cash used of $47,000.
   c. net cash used of $44,000.
   d. net cash used of $38,000.

Q12-53. How many items enter the computation of Solomon's net cash flow from financing activities for 2014?

   a. 3
   b. 7
   c. 5
   d. 2

Q12-54. Solomon's largest financing cash flow for 2014 resulted from (assume no stock dividends were distributed)

   a. payment of dividends.
   b. purchase of equipment.
   c. sale of equipment.
   d. issuance of common stock.

Q12-55. Solomon's net cash flow from financing activities for 2014 was (assume no stock dividends were distributed)

   a. net cash used of $25,500.
   b. net cash provided of $12,000.
   c. net cash used of $14,500.
   d. net cash used of $42,000.

Q12-56. Assume Solomon uses the direct method to prepare the statement of cash flows. Credit sales totaled $750,000, accounts receivable increased by $60,000, and accounts payable decreased by $40,000. How much cash did the company collect from customers?

   a. $810,000
   b. $690,000
   c. $730,000
   d. $750,000

Q12-57. Assume Solomon uses the direct method to prepare the statement of cash flows. Income tax payable was $5,000 at the end of the year and $2,600 at the beginning. Income tax expense for the year totaled $58,900. What amount of cash did the company pay for income tax during the year?

   a. $61,300
   b. $58,900
   c. $56,500
   d. $61,500

Problems

> All of the A and B problems can be found within MyAccountingLab, an online home-
> work and practice environment. Your instructor may ask you to complete these problems
> using **MyAccountingLab**.

MyAccountingLab

Group A

P12-58A. *(Learning Objectives 2, 3: Prepare an income statement, balance sheet, and statement of cash flows—indirect method)* Fairfax Fine Automobiles, Inc., was formed on January 1, 2014. The following transactions occurred during 2014:

On January 1, 2014, Fairfax issued its common stock for $300,000. Early in January, Fairfax made the following cash payments:

   a. $150,000 for equipment
   b. $136,000 for inventory (four cars at $34,000 each)
   c. $24,000 for 2014 rent on a store building

In February, Fairfax purchased nine cars for inventory on account. Cost of this inventory was $405,000 ($45,000 each). Before year-end, Fairfax paid $164,200 of this debt. Fairfax uses the FIFO method to account for inventory.

During 2014, Fairfax sold seven autos for a total of $497,000. Before year-end, Fairfax collected 90% of this amount.

The business employs three people. The combined annual payroll is $102,000, of which Fairfax owes $9,000 at year-end. At the end of the year, Fairfax paid income tax of $17,500.

Late in 2014, Fairfax declared and paid cash dividends of $20,000.

For equipment, Fairfax uses the straight-line depreciation method, over five years, with zero residual value.

Requirements

1. Prepare Fairfax Fine Automobiles, Inc.'s income statement for the year ended December 31, 2014. Use the single-step format, with all revenues listed together and all expenses together.
2. Prepare Fairfax's balance sheet at December 31, 2014.
3. Prepare Fairfax's statement of cash flows for the year ended December 31, 2014. Format cash flows from operating activities by using the *indirect* method.

P12-59A. *(Learning Objectives 2, 4: Prepare an income statement, balance sheet, and statement of cash flows—direct method)* Use the Fairfax Fine Automobiles Inc., data from P12-58A.

Requirements

1. Prepare Fairfax's income statement for the year ended December 31, 2014. Use the single-step format, with all revenues listed together and all expenses together.
2. Prepare Fairfax's balance sheet at December 31, 2014.
3. Prepare Fairfax's statement of cash flows for the year ended December 31, 2014. Format cash flows from operating activities by using the *direct* method.

P12-60A. *(Learning Objectives 2, 3: Prepare the statement of cash flows—indirect method)* DeWitt Software Corp. has assembled the following data for the years ending December 31, 2014 and 2013.

	A	B	C
		December 31,	
		2014	2013
3	Current Accounts:		
4	Current assets:		
5	Cash and cash equivalents	$ 96,400	$ 38,600
6	Accounts receivable	51,300	64,600
7	Inventories	34,600	67,000
8	Prepaid expenses	3,200	2,100
9	Current liabilities:		
10	Accounts payable	$ 27,100	$ 55,700
11	Income tax payable	18,600	16,300
12	Accrued liabilities	15,300	7,800
13			

Transaction Data for 2014:

Acquisition of land by issuing long-term note payable	$163,000	Purchase of treasury stock.....	$10,200
		Loss on sale of equipment	4,000
Stock dividends	31,600	Payment of cash dividends	18,100
Collection of loan..................	25,000	Issuance of long-term note	
Depreciation expense	13,000	payable to borrow cash.....	34,800
Purchase of building		Net income.........................	64,000
with cash..........................	95,000	Issuance of common stock	
Retirement of bonds payable		for cash	35,000
by issuing common stock	75,000	Proceeds from sale of	
Purchase of long-term		equipment	12,700
investment with cash.........	37,400	Amortization expense..........	4,200

Requirement

1. Prepare DeWitt Software Corp.'s statement of cash flows using the *indirect* method to report operating activities. Include an accompanying schedule of noncash investing and financing activities.

P12-61A. *(Learning Objectives 2, 3: Prepare the statement of cash flows—indirect method)* The comparative balance sheets of Orpheum Movie Theater Company at June 30, 2014, and 2013, reported the following:

A	B	C
	June 30,	
	2014	**2013**
Current assets:		
Cash and cash equivalents	$ 38,200	$ 21,700
Accounts receivable	14,800	20,200
Inventories	63,600	60,700
Prepaid expenses	3,700	1,600
Current liabilities:		
Accounts payable	$ 60,200	$ 55,200
Accrued liabilities	15,800	6,500
Income tax payable	9,500	10,500

Orpheum Movie Theater's transactions during the year ended June 30, 2014, included:

Acquisition of land		Proceeds from sale of long-	
by issuing note payable	$113,000	term investment	$13,600
Amortization expense............	3,000	Depreciation expense	14,700
Payment of cash dividend......	30,000	Cash purchase of building.....	50,000
Cash purchase of		Net income............................	65,200
equipment	58,700	Issuance of common	
Issuance of long-term note		stock for cash	5,000
payable to borrow cash	40,000	Stock dividend.......................	10,000

Requirements

1. Prepare Orpheum Movie Theater Company's statement of cash flows for the year ended June 30, 2014, using the *indirect* method to report cash flows from operating activities. Report noncash investing and financing activities in an accompanying schedule.
2. Evaluate Orpheum Movie Theater's cash flows for the year. Mention all three categories of cash flows, and give the reason for your evaluation.

P12-62A. *(Learning Objectives 2, 3: Prepare the statement of cash flows—indirect method)* The 2014 and 2013 comparative balance sheets and 2014 income statement of Sudan Medical Supply Corp. follow:

	A	B	C	D
	A1			
1	**Sudan Medical Supply Corp.** **Comparative Balance Sheets**			
2		December 31,		Increase
3		**2014**	**2013**	(Decrease)
4	Current assets:			
5	Cash and cash equivalents	$ 56,200	$ 21,900	$ 34,300
6	Accounts receivable	61,700	45,000	16,700
7	Inventories	54,400	52,200	2,200
8	Prepaid expenses	2,400	5,000	(2,600)
9	Plant assets:			
10	Land	67,200	39,800	27,400
11	Equipment, net	62,900	49,600	13,300
12	Total assets	$ 304,800	$ 213,500	$ 91,300
13	Current liabilities:			
14	Accounts payable	$ 35,500	$ 26,900	$ 8,600
15	Salary payable	18,000	13,100	4,900
16	Other accrued liabilities	16,100	23,700	(7,600)
17	Long-term liabilities:			
18	Notes payable	49,000	30,000	19,000
19	Stockholders' equity:			
20	Common stock, no-par	116,000	93,000	23,000
21	Retained earnings	70,200	26,800	43,400
22	Total liabilities and stockholders' equity	$ 304,800	$ 213,500	$ 91,300
23				

	A	B	C
	A1		
1	**Sudan Medical Supply Corp.** **Income Statement** **Year Ended December 31, 2014**		
2	Revenues:		
3	Sales revenue		$ 581,000
4	Expenses:		
5	Cost of goods sold	$ 249,500	
6	Salary expense	95,700	
7	Depreciation expense	16,100	
8	Other operating expense	59,000	
9	Interest expense	24,100	
10	Income tax expense	38,500	
11	Total expenses		482,900
12	Net income		$ 98,100
13			

Sudan Medical Supply had no noncash investing and financing transactions during 2014. During the year, there were no sales of land or equipment, no payment of notes payable, no retirements of stock, and no treasury stock transactions.

Requirements

1. Prepare the 2014 statement of cash flows, formatting operating activities by using the *indirect* method.
2. How will what you learned in this problem help you evaluate an investment?

P12-63A. *(Learning Objectives 2, 4: Prepare the statement of cash flows—direct method)* Use the Sudan Medical Supply Corp. data from P12-62A.

Requirements

1. Prepare the 2014 statement of cash flows by using the *direct* method.
2. How will what you learned in this problem help you evaluate an investment?

P12-64A. *(Learning Objectives 2, 4: Prepare the statement of cash flows—direct method)* Lane's Furniture Gallery, Inc., provided the following data from the company's records for the year ended March 31, 2015:

    a. Credit sales, $606,400
    b. Loan to another company, $11,300
    c. Cash payments to purchase plant assets, $92,100
    d. Cost of goods sold, $294,200
    e. Proceeds from issuance of common stock, $8,500
    f. Payment of cash dividends, $45,500
    g. Collection of interest, $4,900
    h. Acquisition of equipment by issuing short-term note payable, $24,200
    i. Payments of salaries, $97,000
    j. Proceeds from sale of plant assets, $21,800, including $6,400 loss
    k. Collections on accounts receivable, $416,000
    l. Interest revenue, $4,000
    m. Cash receipt of dividend revenue, $4,500
    n. Payments to suppliers, $386,400
    o. Cash sales, $170,200
    p. Depreciation expense, $48,000
    q. Proceeds from issuance of note payable, $25,000
    r. Payments of long-term notes payable, $60,400
    s. Interest expense and payments, $13,400
    t. Salary expense, $94,200
    u. Loan collections, $12,500
    v. Proceeds from sale of investments, $17,900, including $2,400 gain
    w. Payment of short-term note payable by issuing long-term note payable, $56,000
    x. Amortization expenses, $6,600
    y. Income tax expense and payments, $38,000
    z. Cash balance: March 31, 2014, $101,000; March 31, 2015, $38,200

Requirements

1. Prepare Lane Furniture Gallery, Inc.'s statement of cash flows for the year ended March 31, 2015. Use the *direct* method for cash flows from operating activities. Include an accompanying schedule of noncash investing and financing activities.
2. Evaluate 2015 from a cash flows standpoint. Give your reasons.

P12-65A. *(Learning Objectives 2, 3, 4: Prepare the statement of cash flows—direct and indirect methods)* To prepare the statement of cash flows, accountants for Tri-State Electric Company have summarized 2014 activity in two accounts:

Cash

Beginning bal	10,200	Payments on accounts payable	403,700
Sale of long-term investment	21,500	Payments of dividends	27,400
Collections from customers	664,200	Payments of salaries and wages	134,900
Issuance of common stock	61,600	Payments of interest	29,200
Receipts of dividends	17,500	Purchase of equipment	31,900
		Payments of operating expenses	34,000
		Payment of long-term note payable	35,400
		Purchase of treasury stock	19,000
		Payment of income tax	28,400
Ending Bal	31,100		

Common Stock

Beginning bal	56,200
Issuance for cash	61,600
Issuance to acquire land	84,300
Issuance to retire note payable	23,000
Ending bal	225,100

Tri-State Electric's 2014 income statement and balance sheet data follow:

	A	B	C
	A1		
1	**Tri-State Electric Company** **Income Statement** **Year Ended December 31, 2014**		
2	Revenues:		
3	Sales revenue		$ 681,900
4	Dividend revenue		17,500
5	Total revenue		699,400
6	Expenses and losses:		
7	Cost of goods sold	$ 347,200	
8	Salary and wage expense	142,800	
9	Depreciation expense	21,300	
10	Other operating expense	43,900	
11	Interest expense	28,300	
12	Income tax expense	26,000	
13	Loss on sale of investments	17,400	
14	Total expenses and losses		626,900
15	Net income		$ 72,500
16			

A1	⬍	
	A	**B**
1	**Tri-State Electric Company** **Selected Balance Sheet Data** **December 31, 2014**	
2		**Increase** **(Decrease)**
3	Current assets:	
4	Cash and cash equivalents	$ 20,900
5	Accounts receivable	27,900
6	Inventories	54,200
7	Prepaid expenses	600
8	Long-term investments	(38,900)
9	Equipment, net	10,600
10	Land	84,300
11	Current liabilities:	
12	Accounts payable	8,200
13	Interest payable	(900)
14	Salary payable	7,600
15	Other accrued liabilities	10,500
16	Income tax payable	(2,400)
17	Long-term note payable	(58,400)
18	Common stock	168,900
19	Retained earnings	45,100
20	Treasury stock	(19,000)
21		

Requirements

1. Prepare the statement of cash flows of Tri-State Electric Company for the year ended December 31, 2014, using the *direct* method to report operating activities. Also prepare the accompanying schedule of noncash investing and financing activities.
2. Use Tri-State Electric's 2014 income statement and balance sheet to prepare a supplementary schedule of cash flows from operating activities by using the *indirect* method.

P12-66A. *(Learning Objectives 2, 3, 4: Prepare the statement of cash flows—indirect and direct methods)* The comparative balance sheets of Victoria Vicente Design Studio, Inc., at June 30, 2014 and 2013, and transaction data for fiscal 2014, are as follows:

	A	B	C	D
	A1			
	Victoria Vicente Design Studio Comparative Balance Sheets			
1				
2			**June 30,**	**Increase**
3		**2014**	**2013**	**(Decrease)**
4	Current assets:			
5	Cash	$ 30,800	$ 12,200	$ 18,600
6	Accounts receivable	59,000	22,100	36,900
7	Inventories	78,400	40,400	38,000
8	Prepaid expenses	1,500	2,300	(800)
9	Long-term investment	20,400	2,700	17,700
10	Equipment, net	74,700	73,800	900
11	Land	49,700	92,800	(43,100)
12		$ 314,500	$ 246,300	$ 68,200
13	Current liabilities:			
14	Notes payable, short-term	$ 13,800	$ 18,700	$ (4,900)
15	Accounts payable	46,400	40,400	6,000
16	Income tax payable	13,400	15,100	(1,700)
17	Accrued liabilities	66,500	3,100	63,400
18	Interest payable	3,500	2,300	1,200
19	Salary payable	800	2,900	(2,100)
20	Long-term note payable	47,100	94,000	(46,900)
21	Common stock	69,300	51,200	18,100
22	Retained earnings	53,700	18,600	35,100
23		$ 314,500	$ 246,300	$ 68,200
24				

Transaction data for the year ended June 30, 2014, follows:

a. Net income, $72,800
b. Depreciation expense on equipment, $13,300
c. Purchased long-term investment with cash, $17,700
d. Sold land for $36,400, including $6,700 loss
e. Acquired equipment by issuing long-term note payable, $14,200
f. Paid long-term note payable, $61,100
g. Received cash for issuance of common stock, $13,200
h. Paid cash dividends, $37,700
i. Paid short-term note payable by issuing common stock, $4,900

Requirements

1. Prepare the statement of cash flows of Victoria Vicente Design Studio, Inc., for the year ended June 30, 2014, using the *indirect* method to report operating activities. Also prepare the accompanying schedule of noncash investing and financing activities. All current accounts except Notes Payable, short-term result from operating transactions.
2. Prepare a supplementary schedule showing cash flows from operations by the *direct* method. The accounting records provide the following: collections from customers, $230,800; interest received, $1,400; payments to suppliers, $98,400; payments to employees, $30,700; payments for income tax, $13,200; and payment of interest, $4,400.

Group B

P12-67B. *(Learning Objectives 2, 3: Prepare an income statement, balance sheet, and statement of cash flows—indirect method)* Lexington Luxury Automobiles, Inc., was formed on January 1, 2014. The following transactions occurred during 2014:

On January 1, 2014, Lexington issued its common stock for $450,000. Early in January, Lexington made the following cash payments:

a. $175,000 for equipment
b. $234,000 for inventory (six cars at $39,000 each)
c. $16,000 for 2014 rent on a store building

In February, Lexington purchased four cars for inventory on account. Cost of this inventory was $188,000 ($47,000 each). Before year-end, Lexington paid $75,300 of this debt. Lexington uses the FIFO method to account for inventory.

During 2014, Lexington sold seven vintage autos for a total of $490,000. Before year-end, Lexington collected 50% of this amount.

The business employs two people. The combined annual payroll is $78,000, of which Lexington owes $8,000 at year-end. At the end of the year, Lexington paid income tax of $19,500.

Late in 2014, Lexington declared and paid cash dividends of $22,000.

For equipment, Lexington uses the straight-line depreciation method, over five years, with zero residual value.

Requirements

1. Prepare Lexington Luxury Automobiles, Inc.'s income statement for the year ended December 31, 2014. Use the single-step format, with all revenues listed together and all expenses together.
2. Prepare Lexington's balance sheet at December 31, 2014.
3. Prepare Lexington's statement of cash flows for the year ended December 31, 2014. Format cash flows from operating activities by using the *indirect* method.

P12-68B. *(Learning Objectives 2, 4: Prepare an income statement, balance sheet, and statement of cash flows—direct method)* Use the Lexington Luxury Automobiles, Inc., data from P12-67B.

Requirements

1. Prepare Lexington's income statement for the year ended December 31, 2014. Use the single-step format, with all revenues listed together and all expenses together.
2. Prepare Lexington's balance sheet at December 31, 2014.
3. Prepare Lexington's statement of cash flows for the year ended December 31, 2014. Format cash flows from operating activities by using the *direct* method.

P12-69B. *(Learning Objectives 2, 3: Prepare the statement of cash flows—indirect method)* Watson Software Corp. has assembled the following data for the year ended December 31, 2014:

	A	B	C
		December 31,	
		2014	**2013**
3	**Current Accounts:**		
4	Current assets:		
5	Cash and cash equivalents	$ 100,700	$ 7,800
6	Accounts receivable	52,900	64,700
7	Inventories	39,000	68,000
8	Prepaid expenses	3,000	2,200
9	Current liabilities:		
10	Accounts payable	62,100	55,400
11	Income tax payable	18,400	16,300
12	Accrued liabilities	5,500	7,000
13			

Transaction Data for 2014:

Acquisition of land by issuing		Purchase of treasury stock	$10,900
long-term note payable	$163,000	Gain on sale of equipment.....	8,000
Stock dividends	40,100	Payment of cash dividends	19,000
Collection of loan..................	25,600	Issuance of long-term note	
Depreciation expense	19,000	payable to borrow cash.....	50,600
Purchase of building		Net income.........................	67,000
with cash...........................	116,000	Issuance of common stock	
Retirement of bonds payable		for cash	55,000
by issuing common stock	80,000	Proceeds from sale of	
Purchase of long-term		equipment	12,900
investment with cash.........	35,200	Amortization expense..........	4,600

Requirement

1. Prepare Watson Software Corp.'s statement of cash flows using the *indirect* method to report operating activities. Include an accompanying schedule of noncash investing and financing activities.

P12-70B. *(Learning Objectives 2, 3: Prepare the statement of cash flows—indirect method)* The comparative balance sheets of Majestic Movie Theater Company at September 30, 2014 and 2013, reported the following:

	A	B	C
		September 30,	
		2014	**2013**
3	**Current assets:**		
4	Cash and cash equivalents	$ 59,600	$ 26,700
5	Accounts receivable	14,300	23,800
6	Inventories	63,200	60,600
7	Prepaid expenses	11,700	6,000
8	**Current liabilities:**		
9	Accounts payable	$ 57,700	$ 35,800
10	Accrued liabilities	14,100	7,100
11	Income tax payable	15,300	10,300
12			

Majestic's transactions during the year ended September 30, 2014, included the following:

Acquisition of land by issuing note payable	$125,000	Proceeds from sale of long-term investment	$ 8,300
Amortization expense............	8,000	Depreciation expense	15,300
Payment of cash dividend......	25,000	Cash purchase of building	44,000
Cash purchase of equipment	82,200	Net income............................ Issuance of common	65,400
Issuance of long-term note payable to borrow cash	40,000	stock for cash .... Stock dividend........................	12,000 13,000

Requirements

1. Prepare Majestic Movie Theater Company's statement of cash flows for the year ended September 30, 2014, using the *indirect* method to report cash flows from operating activities. Report noncash investing and financing activities in an accompanying schedule.
2. Evaluate Majestic's cash flows for the year. Mention all three categories of cash flows, and give the reason for your evaluation.

P12-71B. *(Learning Objectives 2, 3: Prepare the statement of cash flows—indirect method)* The 2014 and 2013 comparative balance sheets and 2014 income statement of Sommar Medical Supply Corp. follow:

	A	B	C	D
	A1 ⬍			
	A	**B**	**C**	**D**
1	**Sommar Medical Supply Corp.** **Comparative Balance Sheets**			
2		December 31,		Increase
3		2014	2013	(Decrease)
4	Current assets:			
5	Cash and cash equivalents	$ 50,700	$ 15,200	$ 35,500
6	Accounts receivable	64,000	60,000	4,000
7	Inventories	65,200	53,200	12,000
8	Prepaid expenses	1,000	2,500	(1,500)
9	Plant assets:			
10	Land	48,400	32,600	15,800
11	Equipment, net	66,100	49,100	17,000
12	Total assets	$ 295,400	$ 212,600	$ 82,800
13	Current liabilities:			
14	Accounts payable	$ 35,400	$ 26,000	$ 9,400
15	Salary payable	32,000	36,500	(4,500)
16	Other accrued liabilities	22,800	24,100	(1,300)
17	Long-term liabilities:			
18	Notes payable	58,000	30,000	28,000
19	Stockholders' equity:			
20	Common stock, no-par	83,200	69,000	14,200
21	Retained earnings	64,000	27,000	37,000
22	Total liabilities and stockholders' equity	$ 295,400	$ 212,600	$ 82,800
23				

	A	B	C
	Sommar Medical Supply Corp. **Income Statement** **Year Ended December 31, 2014**		
1			
2	Revenues:		
3	Sales revenue		$ 571,000
4	Expenses:		
5	Cost of goods sold	$ 248,300	
6	Salary expense	94,900	
7	Depreciation expense	15,000	
8	Other operating expense	57,200	
9	Interest expense	24,800	
10	Income tax expense	39,100	
11	Total expenses		479,300
12	Net income		$ 91,700
13			

Sommar Medical Supply had no noncash investing and financing transactions during 2014. During the year, there were no sales of land or equipment, no payment of notes payable, no retirements of stock, and no treasury stock transactions.

Requirements

1. Prepare the 2014 statement of cash flows, formatting operating activities by using the *indirect* method.
2. How will what you learned in this problem help you evaluate an investment?

P12-72B. *(Learning Objectives 2, 4: Prepare the statement of cash flows—direct method)* Use the Sommar Medical Supply Corp. data from P12-71B.

Requirements

1. Prepare the 2014 statement of cash flows by using the *direct* method.
2. How will what you learned in this problem help you evaluate an investment?

P12-73B. *(Learning Objectives 2, 4: Prepare the statement of cash flows—direct method)* The Ritz Furniture Gallery, Inc., provided the following data from the company's records for the year ended December 31, 2014:

a. Credit sales, $560,100
b. Loan to another company, $7,900
c. Cash payments to purchase plant assets, $87,400
d. Cost of goods sold, $473,000
e. Proceeds from issuance of common stock, $10,800
f. Payment of cash dividends, $45,200
g. Collection of interest, $4,800
h. Acquisition of equipment by issuing short-term note payable, $56,300
i. Payments of salaries, $87,000
j. Proceeds from sale of plant assets, $23,000, including $6,600 loss
k. Collections on accounts receivable, $348,000
l. Interest revenue, $1,800
m. Cash receipt of dividend revenue, $4,000
n. Payments to suppliers, $325,400
o. Cash sales, $170,600
p. Depreciation expense, $49,800
q. Proceeds from issuance of note payable, $24,800
r. Payments of long-term notes payable, $48,000

s. Interest expense and payments, $13,800

t. Salary expense, $86,900

u. Loan collections, $18,500

v. Proceeds from sale of investments, $9,500, including $2,200 gain

w. Payment of short-term note payable by issuing long-term note payable, $74,000

x. Amortization expenses, $6,600

y. Income tax expense and payments, $36,000

z. Cash balance: December 31, 2013, $98,000; December 31, 2014, $61,300

Requirements

1. Prepare The Ritz Furniture Gallery, Inc.'s statement of cash flows for the year ended December 31, 2014. Use the *direct* method for cash flows from operating activities. Include an accompanying schedule of noncash investing and financing activities.

2. Evaluate 2014 from a cash flows standpoint. Give your reasons.

P12-74B. *(Learning Objectives 2, 3, 4: Prepare the statement of cash flows—direct and indirect methods)* To prepare the statement of cash flows, accountants for Four Star Electric Company have summarized 2014 activity in two accounts:

Cash

Beginning bal	45,400	Payments on accounts payable	401,000
Sale of long-term investment	32,400	Payments of dividends	27,800
Collections from customers	664,500	Payments of salaries and wages	143,900
Issuance of common stock	47,900	Payments of interest	27,000
Receipts of dividends	16,900	Purchase of equipment	31,900
		Payments of operating expenses	34,300
		Payment of long-term note payable	35,000
		Purchase of treasury stock	26,300
		Payment of income tax	28,600
Ending Bal	51,300		

Common Stock

	Beginning bal	56,300
	Issuance for cash	47,900
	Issuance to acquire land	56,000
	Issuance to retire note payable	25,000
	Ending bal	185,200

Four Star Electric's 2014 income statement and balance sheet data follow:

A1				
	A		**B**	**C**
1	**Four Star Electric Company** **Income Statement** **Year Ended December 31,2014**			
2	Revenues:			
3	Sales revenue			$ 635,900
4	Dividend revenue			16,900
5	Total revenue			652,800
6	Expenses and losses:			
7	Cost of goods sold		$ 346,500	
8	Salary and wage expense		151,500	
9	Depreciation expense		20,600	
10	Other operating expense		23,500	
11	Interest expense		28,700	
12	Income tax expense		25,200	
13	Loss on sale of investments		6,500	
14	Total expenses and losses			602,500
15	Net income			$ 50,300
16				

A1		
	A	**B**
1	**Four Star Electric Company** **Selected Balance Sheet Data** **December 31, 2014**	
2		**Increase** **(Decrease)**
3	Current assets:	
4	Cash and cash equivalents	$ 5,900
5	Accounts receivable	(27,500)
6	Inventories	61,600
7	Prepaid expenses	400
8	Long-term investments	(38,900)
9	Equipment, net	11,300
10	Land	56,000
11	Current liabilities:	
12	Accounts payable	8,200
13	Interest payable	1,700
14	Salary payable	7,600
15	Other accrued liabilities	(10,400)
16	Income tax payable	(3,400)
17	Long-term note payable	(60,000)
18	Common stock	128,900
19	Retained earnings	22,500
20	Treasury stock	(26,300)
21		

Requirements

1. Prepare the statement of cash flows of Four Star Electric Company for the year ended December 31, 2014, using the *direct* method to report operating activities. Also prepare the accompanying schedule of noncash investing and financing activities.
2. Use Four Star Electric's 2014 income statement and balance sheet to prepare a supplementary schedule of cash flows from operating activities by using the *indirect* method.

P12-75B. *(Learning Objectives 2, 3, 4: Prepare the statement of cash flows—indirect and direct methods)* The comparative balance sheets of Amanda Aguilar Design Studio, Inc., at June 30, 2014, and 2013, and transaction data for fiscal 2014, are as follows:

	A	B	C	D
			June 30,	Increase
1	Amanda Aguilar Design Studio Comparative Balance Sheets			
2			June 30,	Increase
3		2014	2013	(Decrease)
4	Current assets:			
5	Cash	$ 31,900	$ 18,500	$ 13,400
6	Accounts receivable	48,000	31,700	16,300
7	Inventories	68,700	50,200	18,500
8	Prepaid expenses	1,900	2,700	(800)
9	Long-term investment	10,000	5,200	4,800
10	Equipment, net	74,700	73,600	1,100
11	Land	33,100	89,900	(56,800)
12		$ 268,300	$ 271,800	$ (3,500)
13	Current liabilities:			
14	Notes payable, short-term	$ 13,800	$ 19,200	$ (5,400)
15	Accounts payable	39,500	40,900	(1,400)
16	Income tax payable	13,500	15,000	(1,500)
17	Accrued liabilities	20,700	9,600	11,100
18	Interest payable	3,300	2,800	500
19	Salary payable	4,500	4,900	(400)
20	Long-term note payable	38,400	84,100	(45,700)
21	Common stock	65,400	51,800	13,600
22	Retained earnings	69,200	43,500	25,700
23		$ 268,300	$ 271,800	$ (3,500)
24				

Transaction data for the year ended June 30, 2014, follows:
- **a.** Net income, $63,800
- **b.** Depreciation expense on equipment, $13,900
- **c.** Purchased long-term investment with cash, $4,800
- **d.** Sold land for $50,400, including $6,400 loss
- **e.** Acquired equipment by issuing long-term note payable, $15,000
- **f.** Paid long-term note payable, $60,700
- **g.** Received cash for issuance of common stock, $8,200
- **h.** Paid cash dividends, $38,100
- **i.** Paid short-term note payable by issuing common stock, $5,400

Requirements

1. Prepare the statement of cash flows of Amanda Aguilar Design Studio, Inc., for the year ended June 30, 2014, using the *indirect* method to report operating activities. Also prepare the accompanying schedule of noncash investing and financing activities. All current accounts except Notes Payable, short-term, result from operating transactions.
2. Prepare a supplementary schedule showing cash flows from operations by the *direct* method. The accounting records provide the following: collections from customers, $235,900; interest received, $1,600; payments to suppliers, $130,300; payments to employees, $29,500; payments for income tax, $13,500; and payment of interest, $5,800.

Challenge Exercises and Problem

E12-76. *(Learning Objectives 3, 4: Compute cash flow amounts)* Heartstrings, Inc., reported the following in its financial statements for the year ended May 31, 2014 (in thousands):

	A	B 2014	C 2013
1		**2014**	**2013**
2	Income Statement		
3	Net sales	$ 25,118	$ 21,543
4	Cost of sales	18,162	15,333
5	Depreciation	268	227
6	Other operating expenses	3,885	4,283
7	Income tax expense	537	488
8	Net income	$ 2,266	$ 1,212
9	Balance Sheet		
10	Cash and equivalents	$ 13	$ 10
11	Accounts receivable	597	612
12	Inventory	3,100	2,833
13	Property and equipment, net	4,345	3,431
14	Accounts payable	1,549	1,368
15	Accrued liabilities	939	636
16	Income tax payable	198	190
17	Long-term liabilities	477	466
18	Common stock	518	443
19	Retained earnings	4,374	3,783
20			

Requirement

1. Determine the following cash receipts and payments for Heartstrings, Inc., during 2014 (enter all amounts in thousands):
   a. Collections from customers
   b. Payments for inventory
   c. Payments for other operating expenses
   d. Payment of income tax
   e. Proceeds from issuance of common stock
   f. Payment of cash dividends

E12-77. *(Learning Objective 3: Use the balance sheet and the statement of cash flows together)* Hobby Specialties reported the following at December 31, 2014 (in thousands):

	A	B 2014	C 2013
1		**2014**	**2013**
2	From the comparative balance sheet:		
3	Property and equipment, net	$ 10,600	$ 9,640
4	Long-term notes payable	4,400	3,000
5	From the statement of cash flows:		
6	Depreciation	$ 1,910	
7	Capital expenditures	(4,175)	
8	Proceeds from sale of property and equipment	820	
9	Proceeds from issuance of long-term note payable	1,220	
10	Payment of long-term note payable	(140)	
11	Issuance of common stock	385	
12			

Requirement

1. Determine the following items for Hobby Specialties during 2014:
   a. Gain or loss on the sale of property and equipment
   b. Amount of long-term debt issued for something other than cash

P12-78. *(Learning Objectives 2, 3: Prepare a balance sheet from a statement of cash flows)* The December 31, 2013, balance sheet and the 2014 statement of cash flows for Mobley, Inc., follow:

	A	B
A1		
	Mobley, Inc. **Balance Sheet** **December 31, 2013**	
1		
2	**Assets:**	
3	Cash	$ 11,000
4	Accounts receivable (net)	92,000
5	Inventory	103,000
6	Prepaid expenses	6,000
7	Land	69,000
8	Machinery and equipment (net)	59,000
9	Total	$ 340,000
10	**Liabilities:**	
11	Accounts payable	$ 66,000
12	Unearned revenue	1,000
13	Income taxes payable	4,000
14	Long-term debt	75,000
15	**Total liabilities**	146,000
16	**Stockholders' equity:**	
17	Common stock, no par	26,000
18	Retained earnings	168,000
19	Total stockholders' equity	194,000
20	Total liabilities and stockholders' equity	$ 340,000
21		

	A	B	C
1	**Mobley, Inc.** **Statement of Cash Flows** **Year Ended December 31, 2014**		
2	**Cash flows from operating activities:**		
3	Net income		$ 18,000
4	Adjustments to reconcile net income to net cash		
5	provided by operating activities:		
6	Depreciation	$ 16,000	
7	Loss on sale of equipment	15,000	
8	Gain on sale of land	(6,000)	
9	Change in assets and liabilities:		
10	Accounts receivable	10,000	
11	Inventory	(7,000)	
12	Prepaid expenses	1,000	
13	Accounts payable	12,000	
14	Taxes payable	(2,500)	
15	Unearned revenue	1,500	40,000
16	Net cash provided by operating activities		$ 58,000
17	**Cash flows from investing activities:**		
18	Purchase of equipment	(25,000)	
19	Sale of equipment	9,000	
20	Sale of land	11,000	
21	Net cash used for investing activities		(5,000)
22	**Cash flows from financing activities:**		
23	Repayment of long-term debt	(16,000)	
24	Issuance of common stock	20,000	
25	Dividends paid (dividends declared, $7,000)	(5,000)	
26	Net cash used for financing activities		(1,000)
27	Increase (decrease) in cash		52,000
28	Cash balance, December 31, 2013		11,000
29	Cash balance, December 31, 2014		$ 63,000
30			

Requirement

1. Prepare the December 31, 2014, balance sheet for Mobley, Inc.

APPLY YOUR KNOWLEDGE

Decision Cases

Case 1. *(Learning Objective 3: Prepare and use the statement of cash flows to evaluate operations)*
The 2014 income statement and the 2014 comparative balance sheet of T-Bar-M Camp, Inc.,
have just been distributed at a meeting of the camp's board of directors. The directors raise a
fundamental question: Why is the cash balance so low? This question is especially trouble-
some since 2014 showed record profits. As the controller of the company, you must answer the
question.

	A	B
	A1	
1	**T–Bar–M Camp, Inc.** **Income Statement** **Year Ended December 31, 2014**	
2	(In thousands)	
3	Revenues:	
4	Sales revenue	$ 436
5	Expenses:	
6	Cost of goods sold	221
7	Salary expense	48
8	Depreciation expense	46
9	Interest expense	13
10	Amortization expense	11
11	Total expenses	339
12	Net income	$ 97
13		

	A	B	C
	A1		
1	**T–Bar–M Camp, Inc.** **Comparative Balance Sheets** **December 31, 2014 and 2013**		
2	(In thousands)	**2014**	**2013**
3	**Assets:**		
4	Cash	$ 17	$ 63
5	Accounts receivable, net	72	61
6	Inventories	194	181
7	Long-term investments	31	0
8	Property, plant, and equipment	369	259
9	Accumulated depreciation	(244)	(198)
10	Patents	177	188
11	Totals	$ 616	$ 554
12	**Liabilities and owners' equity:**		
13	Accounts payable	$ 63	$ 56
14	Accrued liabilities	12	17
15	Notes payable, long-term	179	264
16	Common stock, no par	149	61
17	Retained earnings	213	156
18	Totals	$ 616	$ 554
19			

Requirements

1. Prepare a statement of cash flows for 2014 in the format that best shows the relationship between net income and operating cash flow. The company sold no plant assets or long-term investments and issued no notes payable during 2014. There were *no* noncash investing and financing transactions during the year. Show all amounts in thousands.
2. Answer the board members' question: Why is the cash balance so low? Point out the two largest cash payments during 2014. (Challenge)
3. Considering net income and the company's cash flows during 2014, was it a good year or a bad year? Give your reasons.

Case 2. *(Learning Objectives 1, 2: Use cash flow data to evaluate an investment)* Applied Technology, Inc., and Four-Star Catering are asking you to recommend their stock to your clients. Because Applied and Four-Star earn about the same net income and have similar financial positions, your decision depends on their statements of cash flows, summarized as follows:

	Applied		Four–Star	
Net cash provided by operating activities:..................		$ 30,000		$ 70,000
Cash provided by (used for) investing activities:				
Purchase of plant assets	$(20,000)		$(100,000)	
Sale of plant assets...	40,000	20,000	10,000	(90,000)
Cash provided by (used for) financing activities:				
Issuance of common stock		—		30,000
Paying off long-term debt		(40,000)		—
Net increase in cash...		$ 10,000		$10,000

Based on their cash flows, which company looks better? Give your reasons. (Challenge)

Ethical Issue

Columbia Motors is having a bad year. Net income is only $37,000. Also, two important overseas customers are falling behind in their payments to Columbia, and Columbia's accounts receivable are ballooning. The company desperately needs a loan. The Columbia board of directors is considering ways to put the best face on the company's financial statements. Columbia's bank closely examines cash flow from operations. Daniel Peavey, Columbia's controller, suggests reclassifying as long-term the receivables from the slow-paying clients. He explains to the board that removing the $80,000 rise in accounts receivable from current assets will increase net cash provided by operations. This approach may help Columbia get the loan.

Requirements

1. Using only the amounts given, compute net cash provided by operations, both without and with the reclassification of the receivables. Which reporting makes Columbia look better?
2. Identify the ethical issue(s).
3. Who are the stakeholders?
4. Analyze the issue from the (a) economic, (b) legal, and (c) ethical standpoints. What is the potential impact on all stakeholders?
5. What should the board do?
6. Under what conditions would the reclassification of the receivables be considered ethical?

Focus on Financials | Amazon.com, Inc.

(Learning Objectives 1, 2, 3, 4: Use the statement of cash flows) Use **Amazon.com, Inc.'s** consolidated statement of cash flows along with the company's other consolidated financial statements, all in Appendix A at the end of the book, to answer the following questions.

Requirements

1. By which method does Amazon.com, Inc., report cash flows from operating activities? How can you tell?

2. Suppose Amazon.com, Inc., reported net cash flows from operating activities by using the direct method. Compute the following amounts for the year ended December 31, 2012 (ignore the statement of cash flows, and use only Amazon.com, Inc.'s income statement and balance sheet).

   a. Calculate collections from vendors, customers, and others. Use the information in Note 1—Description of Business and Accounting Policies. Prepare a T-account for Gross Accounts Receivable. Prepare another T-account for Allowance for Doubtful Accounts. Calculate the beginning and ending gross amounts of Gross Accounts Receivable by adding the beginning and ending balances of Allowance for Doubtful Accounts ($82 million and $116 million, respectively) to the net accounts receivable at both the beginning and end of the year. Assume that all sales are on account. Also assume that the company uses the percentage of net sales method for estimating doubtful accounts expense and that the company estimates this amount at 0.5%.

   b. Calculate payments to suppliers. Amazon.com, Inc., calls its Cost of Goods Sold "Cost of Sales." For this computation, use the format provided in Exhibit 12-15. Assume all inventory is purchased on account and that all cash payments to suppliers are made from accounts payable.

   c. Refer to Note 3—Property and Equipment. Prepare a T-account for Gross Fixed Assets and another T-account for Accumulated Depreciation. Fill in the beginning balances as supplied in Note 3. Analyze all activity in the fixed assets and accumulated depreciation accounts for 2012. In your analysis, make the following assumptions. Refer to the supplemental cash flow information at the bottom of the cash flow statement. Assume that both fixed asset acquisitions acquired under capital leases and fixed assets acquired under build-to-suit leases were noncash financing and investing activities. Assume that of the $2,159 million for depreciation and amortization (operating section of cash flow statement), $1,700 million is for depreciation expense. Prepare journal entries for (a) acquisition of leased equipment under capital leases, (b) acquisition of fixed assets for cash, (c) depreciation expense for fixed assets, and (d) for retirement of fixed assets. What is the gain or loss on retirement of fixed assets? Where would this gain or loss be reported? (Challenge)

   d. Evaluate 2012 for Amazon.com, Inc., in terms of net income, total assets, stockholders' equity, cash flows from operating activities, and overall results. Be specific. (Challenge)

Focus on Analysis | Yum! Brands, Inc.

(Learning Objectives 1, 2, 3, 4: Analyze cash flows) Refer to the **Yum! Brands, Inc.'s** consolidated financial statements in Appendix B at the end of this book. Focus on the year ended December 31, 2012.

1. What is Yum! Brands, Inc.'s main source of cash? Is this good news or bad news to its managers, stockholders, and creditors? What is Yum! Brands, Inc.'s main use of cash? Is this good news or bad news? Discuss your reasoning.

2. Explain briefly the three most significant differences between net cash provided by operations and net income.

3. Did Yum! Brands, Inc., buy or sell more fixed assets during 2012 than in previous years? How can you tell?

4. Identify the largest two items in the financing activities section of the Consolidated Statement of Cash Flows. Explain the company's probable reasoning behind these two expenditures.

5. Evaluate Yum! Brands, Inc.'s overall performance for 2012 in terms of cash flows. Be as specific as you can. What other information would be helpful to you in making your evaluation? (Challenge)

Group Projects

Project 1. Each member of the group should obtain the annual report of a different company. Select companies in different industries. Evaluate each company's trend of cash flows for the most recent two years. In your evaluation of the companies' cash flows, you may use any other information that is publicly available—for example, the other financial statements (income statement, balance sheet, statement of stockholders' equity, and the related notes) and news stories from magazines and newspapers. Rank the companies' cash flows from best to worst, and write a two-page report on your findings.

Project 2. Select a company and obtain its annual report, including all the financial statements. Focus on the statement of cash flows and, in particular, the cash flows from operating activities. Specify whether the company uses the direct method or the indirect method to report operating cash flows. As necessary, use the other financial statements (income statement, balance sheet, and statement of stockholders' equity) and the notes to prepare the company's cash flows from operating activities by using the *other* method.

MyAccountingLab | **For online homework, exercises, and problems that provide you with immediate feedback, please visit www.myaccountinglab.com.**

Quick Check Answers

1. *a*

2. *c*

3. *b*

4. *a* ($120,000 + $11,000 − 10,000)

5. *c*

6. *a*

7. *d* ($40,000 + $15,000 − $3,000 + $10,000 + $9,000 + $6,000)

8. *b* ($11,000 − $25,000 + $42,000)

9. *a* (− $1,000 + $6,000 − $13,000)

10. *c* ($42,000 + $10,000)

11. *d* ($30,000 + $575,000 − $16,000)

12. *b* ($680,000 − $440,000 − $195,000)

13. *a* ($440,000 − $25,000 + $12,000)

13

Financial Statement Analysis

Throughout this book we have shown how to account for the financial position, results of operations, and cash flows of companies such as **The Gap, Inc., Whole Foods Market, Inc.**, **Apple, Inc., Starbucks, Southwest Airlines Company**, and **Google, Inc.** Only one aspect of the course remains: financial statement analysis. In the first half of this chapter, armed with information about the company and its business strategy, we analyze the financial statements of Amazon.com, Inc. one of the book's focus companies, using horizontal and vertical analysis. In the second half of the chapter, we illustrate financial statement analysis of our focus company in Chapter 5, Apple, Inc., in comparison with those of a well-known competitor, **Dell, Inc.**, using the ratios covered in previous chapters of the text.

Amazon.com is the largest virtual supermarket on the globe. Since its inception as mostly a bookseller in 1995, the company has become synonymous with Internet retailing, expanding its lines of merchandise to cover almost every conceivable consumer item, and also acting as an intermediary marketer for the products of other companies. Amazon.com's most famous recent product is the Kindle, an integrated information retrieval system developed by an Amazon.com subsidiary, which has revolutionized the way people access books, newspapers, magazines, blogs, and other digital media. You may be reading this page on your Kindle reader! If you look a little more closely at the company's website (www.amazon.com), however, you will discover that it offers perhaps the world's biggest selection of merchandise: books; movies, music, and games; computer hardware and software; electronics; home and garden supplies; grocery, health, and beauty products; children's toys and apparel; adult apparel; sports and recreational gear; and auto and industrial tools. In fact, it is hard to think of any consumer item Amazon.com does not sell at competitive prices!

Internet marketing is the fastest-growing segment of the retail industry. When it comes to Internet retailing, nobody beats Amazon.com, Inc. One of

Ross D. Franklin/AP Images

the things that differentiates Amazon.com, Inc., from its competitors is that, in addition to handling its own products, Amazon.com offers its website to other retailers or manufacturers as an avenue to market their products as well. Click on the "Sell on Amazon.com" link and you will find instructions as to how other companies can upload information about inventory to the Amazon.com website, how customers can view and purchase these products, how Amazon.com can provide packing and shipping to customers through its "fulfillment" process, and how Amazon.com can even collect and transmit payments, all with just a few keystrokes or mouse clicks. Amazon.com is truly the ultimate electronic marketplace.

How well has Amazon.com been performing as the worldwide economy recovers from the most severe economic recession in 70 years? We can answer that question by financial statement analysis, and the answers may surprise you. We begin with the analysis of Amazon.com, Inc.'s comparative consolidated statements of operations for the years ended December 31, 2012, 2011, and 2010. In 2012, Amazon.com generated net sales of about $61 billion. Is that positive or negative news? To answer that question, we first need to learn more about the company's business strategy. Then we need not only to analyze the trend in net sales but to compare it with the trends in key expenses over the three years. We also need to compare Amazon.com's results with those of some of its competitors. ●

A1	

	A	B	C	D
1	**Amazon.com, Inc.** **Consolidated Statements of Operations (Adapted)** **12 Months Ended December 31, 2012, 2011, and 2010**			
2	**($ in millions)**	**Dec. 31, 2012**	**Dec. 31, 2011**	**Dec. 31, 2010**
3	Total net sales	$ 61,093	$ 48,077	$ 34,204
4	Cost of sales	45,971	37,288	26,561
5	Gross profit	15,122	10,789	7,643
6	Operating expenses			
7	Fulfillment	6,419	4,576	2,898
8	Marketing	2,408	1,630	1,029
9	Technology and content	4,564	2,909	1,734
10	General and administrative	896	658	470
11	Other operating expense (income), net	159	154	106
12	Total operating expenses	14,446	9,927	6,237
13	Income from operations	676	862	1,406
14	Interest income	40	61	51
15	Interest expense	(92)	(65)	(39)
16	Other income (expense), net	(80)	76	79
17	Total non-operating income (expense)	(132)	72	91
18	Income before income taxes	544	934	1,497
19	Provision for income taxes	(428)	(291)	(352)
20	Equity-method investment activity, net of tax	(155)	(12)	7
21	Net income (loss)	$ (39)	$ 631	$ 1,152
22	Basic earnings per share	$ (0.09)	$ 1.39	$ 2.58
23	Diluted earnings per share	$ (0.09)	$ 1.37	$ 2.53
24	Weighted average shares (millions)			
25	Basic	453	453	447
26	Diluted	453	461	456
27				

This chapter covers the basic tools of financial analysis. The first part of the chapter shows how to evaluate Amazon.com from year to year and how to compare Amazon.com to other companies that are in the same lines of business. For this comparison, we use a retail competitor, **Walmart Stores, Inc.**, a company that operates in both the Internet and store-front retail sectors. The second part of the chapter discusses the most widely used financial ratios. You have seen most of these ratios in earlier chapters. However, we have yet to use all of them in a comprehensive analysis of a company. By studying all these ratios together,

- you will learn the basic tools of financial analysis.
- you will enhance your business education.

Regardless of your chosen field—marketing, management, finance, entrepreneurship, or accounting—you will find these analytical tools useful as you move through your career.

Learning Objectives

1. Perform horizontal analysis

2. Perform vertical analysis

3. Prepare common-size financial statements

4. Analyze the statement of cash flows

5. Use ratios to make business decisions

6. Use other measures to make investment decisions

Try It in Excel

You can access the most current annual report of **Amazon.com**, Inc. in Excel format at **www.sec.gov**. Using the "filings" link on the toolbar at the top of the home page, select "company filings search." This will take you to the "Edgar Company Filings" page. Type "Amazon" in the company name box, and select "search." This will produce the "EDGAR Search Results" page showing the company name. Click on the "CIK" link beside the company name. This will pull up all of the reports the company has filed with the SEC. Under the "filing type" box, type "10-K" and click the search box. Form 10-K is the SEC form for the company's latest annual report. Find the year that you wish to view. Click on the "Interactive Data" box, which takes you to the "View Filing Data" page. Find and click on the "View Excel Document" link at the top of this page. You may choose to either open or download the Excel files containing the company's most recent financial statements. ■

It Starts with the Big Picture

It is impossible to evaluate a company effectively by examining only one year's numerical data. Financial analysis involves more than just doing the math. Thorough analysis of the financial position and results of operations of a company begins with understanding the business and industry of the company—the big picture. This usually entails quite a bit of reading and research, using all kinds of media—the business press, trade journals, and other publications.

You can often gain free access to this information on websites such as www.google.com/ finance. There are also some excellent "for pay" websites (such as the Motley fool—www.fool .com—and Hoovers, Inc.—www.hoovers.com) through which industry and company analyses may be purchased. Learning about what's happening in the industry, markets, general economic conditions, trends in product development, and specific company strategies puts the numbers in context and helps you understand why they turned out as they did. After all, accounting data should paint a picture of the results of implementing a particular business strategy.

For example, Amazon.com's Consolidated Statements of Operations on page 740 reveal that the company's income from operations has declined from $1,406 million in the year ended December 31, 2010 to $676 million in the year ended December 31, 2012. Income before income taxes has declined from $1,497 million to $544 million during the same period. A healthy net income after taxes of $1,152 million in 2010 deteriorated to a $39 million loss in 2012. Looking at these trends in isolation, without knowing some additional facts, seems alarming. The company could not remain in business if results of operations keep trending this negatively for many years. However, by reading industry and company analyses, we find that, over the past three years, the company has made a strategic decision to invest massive amounts of resources on growth-type projects to build the company's infrastructure, which are reflected in three major operating expense accounts: Fulfillment, Marketing, and Technology and content. So, the company has spent a huge portion of its profits on these projects, sacrificing immediate returns in order to prepare the way for long-term growth in the form of increased sales. Here are some examples of the projects in which Amazon.com, Inc. has invested:

■ The company has built a network of huge, strategically placed distribution (fulfillment) warehouses throughout the world to make it possible to get same-day shipping on Amazon .com products as well as those of the companies it represents. This is important in interpreting the huge increase in fulfillment costs (including both capacity and personnel) from $2,898 million in 2010 to $6,419 million in 2012 . The company believes that its capability to deliver products the same day they are purchased will greatly increase future sales.

■ The company is also investing heavily in digital content. It has filed for a patent that creates an exclusive marketplace for used digital goods. It is also developing another patent that creates an anonymous and exclusive system to facilitate customer mobile payments by cell phone or other mobile electronic device (such as a Kindle or iPad) without disclosing personal or private information of users to other parties. Knowing this helps explain the increase in Technology and content in operating expenses from $1,734 million in 2010 to $4,564 million in 2012. These expenses include adding capacity as well as personnel. Again, the company believes that this kind of sophisticated technology will draw sales from millions of new customers who now use portable digital devices more than they use their home computers.

Reading Management's Discussion and Analysis (MD&A) in a company's annual report gives management's perspectives on its own operations and lends insight into why they make certain strategic decisions. For example in the MD&A section of Amazon's annual report, you will find management's explanations for trends in sales and shipments, cost of sales and gross margins, operating expenses, general and administrative expense, compensation expense, and income taxes. The trend in every line item of the Consolidated Statements of Operations on page 740 is explained by management in MD&A.

Once we have an understanding of the big picture, we can start to dig deeper into the numbers, and they begin to make more sense. Public companies' financial statements are comparative, that is, they cover at least two periods. Amazon.com's Consolidated Statements of Operations on page 740 cover three fiscal years. In fact, most financial analysis covers trends in reported data over 3 to 10 years. Since one of the goals of financial analysis is to predict the future, it makes sense to start by mapping the trends of the past. This is particularly true of income statement data such as net sales and the various expenses that make up reported net income.

The graphs in Exhibit 13-1 show Amazon.com's three-year trend of net sales and income from operations. Reading from left to right, Amazon.com's net sales (panel A) increased at what looks like a healthy pace from 2010 through 2012. In fact, Amazon.com's net sales have been on the rise for the past eight years. This is generally a good sign, because increased sales often point the way to

Exhibit 13-1 | Comparative Net Sales and Income from Operations for Amazon.com (2010–2012)

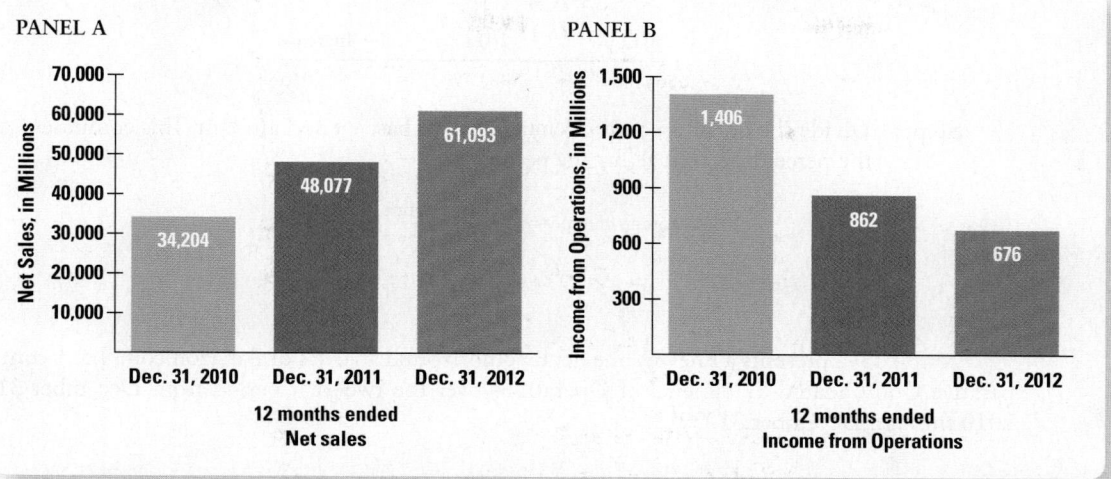

PANEL A

Net Sales, in Millions

| Dec. 31, 2010 | Dec. 31, 2011 | Dec. 31, 2012 |
| 34,204 | 48,077 | 61,093 |

12 months ended
Net sales

PANEL B

Income from Operations, in Millions

| Dec. 31, 2010 | Dec. 31, 2011 | Dec. 31, 2012 |
| 1,406 | 862 | 676 |

12 months ended
Income from Operations

expansion and growth in company value in future years. However, as we learned in Chapter 11, to experience high-quality earnings, typically profits must increase along with sales, and management must show that it is doing everything it can to control growth in expenses, or at least be able to explain reasons why it isn't. Let's look at Amazon.com's income from operations in Exhibit 13-1 (Panel B). We see that, in sharp contrast to net sales, operating income declined drastically over the same time period. When both sales and operating income are increasing proportionately year after year, it may seem easy to make a projection that they will continue to do so. The reality, however, is that they rarely follow such a simple pattern. How can we predict Amazon.com's net sales and income from operations for 2013 and beyond when the two numbers are headed in opposite directions? As we have seen, financial statement analysis is more than just finding a trend line. It also involves knowing key facts about the company's past actions, as well as its future plans. Let's do some horizontal analysis, and see if we can discover more about Amazon.com's story as we go.

PERFORM HORIZONTAL ANALYSIS

Many decisions hinge on the trend of revenues, expenses, income from operations, and so on. Have revenues increased this year? By how much? Suppose net sales have increased by $5 million this year. Is that a positive sign or not so positive? The response often is "compared to what?" The evaluation depends on net sales last period and the period before that. For example, if the $5 million increase in net sales this year represents a 20% increase from last year, and perhaps a 40% increase over a two-year period, this adds information that can improve the evaluation or decision.

1 **Perform** horizontal analysis

The study of percentage changes from year to year is called **horizontal analysis**. Computing a percentage change takes two steps:

1. Compute the dollar amount of the change from one period (the base period) to the next.
2. Divide the dollar amount of change by the base-period amount.

Illustration: Amazon.com, Inc.

Horizontal analysis is illustrated for Amazon.com, Inc., as follows (using the 2011 to 2012 figures, dollars in millions):

	2012	2011	Increase (Decrease)	
			Amount	Percentage
Net sales...............	$61,093	$48,077	$13,016	27.1%

Amazon.com's net sales (in millions) increased by 27.1% during 2012, computed as follows:

Step 1 Compute the dollar amount of change from 2011 to 2012:

2012		2011		Increase
$61,093	−	$48,077	=	$13,016

Step 2 Divide the dollar amount of change by the base-period amount. This computes the percentage change for the period:

$$\text{Percentage change} = \frac{\text{Dollar amount of change}}{\text{Base-year amount}}$$

$$= \frac{\$13,016}{\$48,077} = 27.1\%$$

Exhibit 13-2 presents a line-by-line detailed horizontal analysis of Amazon.com, Inc.'s comparative Consolidated Statements of Operations over the two-year period from December 31, 2010 through December 31, 2012.

Exhibit 13-2 | Comparative Consolidated Statements of Operations—Horizontal Analysis

A1						
	A	**B**	**C**	**D**	**E**	**F**
1	**Amazon.com, Inc.** **Comparative Horizontal Analysis of** **Consolidated Statements of Operations**					
2	**($ in millions)**	**2012**	**% change 2011–2012**	**2011**	**% change 2010–2011**	**2010**
3	Total net sales	$ 61,093	27%	$ 48,077	41%	$ 34,204
4	Cost of sales	45,971	23%	37,288	40%	26,561
5	Gross profit	15,122	40%	10,789	41%	7,643
6	Operating expenses					
7	Fulfillment	6,419	40%	4,576	58%	2,898
8	Marketing	2,408	48%	1,630	58%	1,029
9	Technology and content	4,564	57%	2,909	68%	1,734
10	General and administrative	896	36%	658	40%	470
11	Other operating expense (income), net	159	3%	154	45%	106
12	Total operating expenses	14,446	46%	9,927	59%	6,237
13	Income from operations	676	−22%	862	−39%	1,406
14	Interest income	40	−34%	61	20%	51
15	Interest expense	(92)	42%	(65)	67%	(39)
16	Other income (expense), net	(80)	−205%	76	−4%	79
17	Total nonoperating income (expense)	(132)	−283%	72	−21%	91
18	Income before income taxes	544	−42%	934	−38%	1,497
19	Provision for income taxes	(428)	47%	(291)	−17%	(352)
20	Equity-method investment activity, net	(155)	1,192%	(12)	−271%	7
21	Net income (loss)	$ (39)	−106%	$ 631	−45%	$ 1,152
22						

Try It in Excel

Formatting comparative financial statements for horizontal analysis when the financial statements are in Excel format is quite easy. Try reconstructing Exhibit 13-2 in Excel.

1. Start with the Consolidated Statements of Operations in the opening figure of the chapter.
2. Change the labels to correspond with Exhibit 13-2. Your spreadsheet might be slightly different from Exhibit 13-2, so the cells in which you start to enter formulas might have to be modified accordingly.

3. Insert one column between the 2012 and 2011 columns and another column between the 2011 and 2010 columns. Label these "% change."
4. Compute the percentage change as follows. We start in cell C3 (blank). Change the format of the data in the cell to % by clicking on the % box in the number field in the top toolbar. In cell C3, type the following: =(B3−D3)/D3. The result of 27% should appear in the cell. Copy this cell formula through line 21 of the sheet to perform this computation for all other income and expenses.
5. Repeat the process in (4) using blank cell E3, and using the formula: =(D3−F3)/F3. Copy this formula through line 21.
6. Pat yourself on the back. You've just performed horizontal analysis using Excel! ■

Now focus on the "% change" columns from 2010 to 2011 and from 2011 to 2012 in Exhibit 13-2; a much clearer picture of the company's results of operations than you have seen before will begin to appear. As discussed in the previous section, it was the company's strategy to invest massive amounts of resources in Fulfillment (line 7), Marketing (line 8), and Technology and content (line 9) in order to increase sales. Notice that the biggest year-over-year changes in these costs occurred in 2011 (58% increases in fulfillment and marketing and a 68% increase in technology and content). By 2012, the cost increases in these areas were beginning to taper off but were still substantial (40% increase from 2011 to 2012 in fulfillment, 48% in marketing, and 57% in technology and content). Remember, these percentage increases came *in addition to* already huge increases in 2011. Also remember why these costs were incurred: *to increase sales!* Now focus on line 3. Notice that sales increased 41% in 2011 compared with 2010, and again by 27 percent from 2011 to 2012. At first glance, these percentage changes look great. In comparison, cost of sales (line 4), increased by 40% from 2010 to 2011 year and 23% from 2011 to 2012, allowing the increase in gross profit (line 5) to equal or exceed the increase in sales over the two year period. But these increases in sales and gross margin pale in comparison with the percentage cost increases in Fulfillment, Marketing, and Technology and content expenses. Even more disappointing was the 2012 *decline in the rate of increase* in net sales (only 27% over 2011, compared with 41% in the prior year).

In summary, while sales were increasing over the course of 3 years, total operating expenses increased by far greater percentages. While gross profit increased by 41% and again by 40% in 2011 and 2012, respectively, income from operations plummeted by 39% and 22%, respectively, over the two-year period. These relationships are seen in Panel A and Panel B of Exhibit 13-1. It appears that the company's long-run strategy to increase sales by greatly increasing spending on fulfillment, marketing, and technology and content has yet to gain traction.

Now let's look at the year-to-year changes in lines 14–20 of Exhibit 13-2. As you learned in Chapter 11, these lines represent nonoperating income and expenses such as interest. Interest income (line 14) increased by 20% in 2011 but declined by 34% in 2012, signaling that the company owned fewer interest-bearing assets in 2012 than it did in 2011. Interest expense (line 15) increased by 67% from 2010 to 2011 and by another 42% from 2011 to 2012, indicating that the company increased its long-term borrowings significantly during the two-year period. Other income and expense (a net figure on line 16) flip-flopped from a net income to a net loss position over the two years. Remember from Chapter 11 that this account includes gains and losses from settling transactions in foreign currencies rather than U.S. dollars, which is becoming a larger part of Amazon .com, Inc.'s business. Whether a company incurs foreign exchange gains or losses depends on constantly fluctuating values of the U.S. dollar versus foreign currencies, which is often beyond a company's control. These changes produced a 38% drop in income before income taxes (line 18) from 2010 to 2011 and another 42% drop from 2011 to 2012. So far, the picture isn't very pretty.

Line 19 contains the company's provision for income taxes. While the details of the reasons for the changes in this expense account are often too complex to discuss in an elementary financial accounting text, these particular changes are not so complex that they cannot be understood. Normally, income tax expense fluctuates in the same direction with income before taxes, as it did with Amazon.com, Inc. in 2011. For example, income before income taxes (line 18) declined by 38% in 2011 versus 2010. The provision (expense) for income taxes also declined, but only by 17%.

The really puzzling change, however, came in 2012 when income before taxes went down by another 42%, and the provision for income taxes actually went *up* by 47%. As you will see in the next section on vertical analysis, the company's marginal income tax rate in 2012 (provision for income taxes/income before income taxes) was a staggering 78.7% ($428 million/$544 million)! How can this be? We find the explanation in the following excerpt from Note 11 to the Consolidated Financial Statements:

> Our effective tax rate in 2012, 2011, and 2010 was significantly affected by two factors: the favorable impact of earnings in lower-tax-rate jurisdictions and the adverse effect of losses incurred in certain foreign jurisdictions for which we may not realize a tax benefit. Income earned in lower-tax jurisdictions is primarily related to our European operations, which are headquartered in Luxembourg. Losses incurred in foreign jurisdictions for which we may not realize a tax benefit, primarily generated by subsidiaries located outside of Europe, reduce our pre-tax income without a corresponding reduction in our tax expense. . . .
>
> . . . Additionally, our effective tax rate in 2012 was more volatile as compared to prior years due to the lower level of pre-tax income generated during the year, relative to our tax expense. For example, the impact of non-deductible expenses on our effective tax rate was greater as a result of our lower pre-tax income. Our effective tax rate in 2012 was also adversely impacted by acquisitions (including integrations) and investments, audit developments, nondeductible expenses, and changes in tax law such as the expiration of the U.S. federal research and development credit at the end of 2011. These items collectively caused our annual effective tax rate to be higher than both the 35% U.S. federal statutory rate and our effective tax rates in 2011 and 2010.

A simplified explanation is that while the normal marginal income tax rates are about 35% of pre-tax income (the maximum rate in the United States), when companies such as Amazon.com, Inc., operate in multiple countries, they are subject to taxes in all of those countries as well. Amazon incurred some losses and expenses in foreign countries that were not deductible for U.S. tax purposes in both 2011 and 2012. Moreover, the relatively small amount of reported income before taxes in 2012 ($544 million) compared with the relatively large amount of income tax provision ($428 million) distorted the marginal tax rate in that year. In short, in addition to the fact that the company reported 42% less income before income taxes in 2012 versus 2011, its taxes went up by a significant amount, compounding its problems. So far, this looks like the perfect storm!

Finally, line 20 shows the net income or loss from equity-method investment activity, net of taxes. As we discussed in Chapter 8, equity-method investments are those that are from 20% to 50% owned. The equity method of accounting requires the investor to report its percentage share of the investee's after-tax net income or loss. From Note 5 of Amazon.com, Inc.'s financial statements, we find that the company owns a 29% interest in another company called LivingSocial, whose income statement in 2012 reported a net loss, in the amount of $650 million, of which Amazon.com's share was $155 million. In 2011, the equity-method investment loss was only $12 million. Therefore, over the 2012 year, the loss grew by 1,192%.

Studying year-to-year changes in balance-sheet accounts can enhance our total understanding of the current and long-term financial position of the entity. Let's look at a few balance-sheet changes in Exhibit 13-3.

First, cash and cash equivalents (line 6) increased by an astonishing 53.4% in 2012. Marketable equity securities decreased by 21.9%, but the company still owns about $3.4 billion of these highly liquid assets. These changes indicate that the company's liquid assets have increased significantly. Inventories (line 8) increased by 20.8%, indicating that the company is anticipating increased sales in the future. Accounts receivable, net and other (line 9) increased by 30.8%, faster than net sales (27% according to Exhibit 13-2). Accounts payable (line 19) increased by 19.5%, not quite as much as cost of goods sold (23%). This indicates that the company's rate of payments to its creditors is improving. Overall, total current assets (line 11) increased at the rate of 21.8% and total current liabilities (line 21) increased at a slightly higher rate (27.6%). Net working capital (current assets − current liabilities) declined from $2,594 million in 2011 to $2,294 million

Exhibit 13-3 | Horizontal Analysis: Consolidated Balance Sheets

	A	B	C	D	E
		A1 ⬍			
	A	**B**	**C**	**D**	**E**
1	**Amazon.com, Inc.** **Consolidated Balance Sheets** **December 31, 2012 and 2011**				
2	**In Millions, unless otherwise specified**			**Increase (decrease)**	
3		**2012**	**2011**	**Amount**	**Percentage**
4	**Assets**				
5	Current assets:				
6	Cash and cash equivalents	$ 8,084	$ 5,269	$ 2,815	53.4%
7	Marketable securities	3,364	4,307	(943)	−21.9%
8	Inventories	6,031	4,992	1,039	20.8%
9	Accounts receivable, net and other	3,364	2,571	793	30.8%
10	Deferred tax assets	453	351	102	29.1%
11	Total current assets	21,296	17,490	3,806	21.8%
12	Property and equipment, net	7,060	4,417	2,643	59.8%
13	Deferred tax assets	123	28	95	339.3%
14	Goodwill	2,552	1,955	597	30.5%
15	Other assets	1,524	1,388	136	9.8%
16	Total assets	$ 32,555	$ 25,278	$ 7,277	28.8%
17	**Liabilities and Stockholders' Equity**				
18	Current liabilities:				
19	Accounts payable	$ 13,318	$ 11,145	$ 2,173	19.5%
20	Accrued expenses and other	5,684	3,751	1,933	51.5%
21	Total current liabilities	19,002	14,896	4,106	27.6%
22	Long-term debt	3,084	255	2,829	1,109.4%
23	Other long-term liabilities	2,277	2,370	(93)	−3.9%
24	Commitments and contingencies			—	
25	Total liabilities	24,363	17,521	6,842	39.1%
26	Stockholders' equity:			—	
27	Preferred stock, $0.01 par value:			—	
28	Authorized shares—500			—	
29	Issued and outstanding shares—none			—	
30	Common stock, $0.01 par value:			—	
31	Authorized shares—5,000			—	
32	Issued shares—478 and 473			—	
33	Outstanding shares—454 and 455	5	5	—	0.0%
34	Treasury stock, at cost	(1,837)	(877)	960	109.5%
35	Additional paid-in capital	8,347	6,990	1,357	19.4%
36	Accumulated other comprehensive loss	(239)	(316)	(77)	−24.4%
37	Retained earnings	1,916	1,955	(39)	−2.0%
38	Total stockholders' equity	8,192	7,757	435	5.6%
39	Total liabilities and stockholders' equity	$ 32,555	$ 25,278	$ 7,277	28.8%
40					

in 2012. The aggregate impact of these changes in the current section of the balance sheet indicates that while the company produced a net loss for the year, it is still quite capable of paying its debts.

Property and equipment, net (line 12) increased by 59.8%, indicating that the company is investing huge amounts in long-term assets such as warehouses and technology. Long-term debt (line 22), which consists largely of amounts borrowed to finance international operations, as well as debt related to capital lease obligations, increased by $2.8 billion. According to Note 6 to the Consolidated Financial Statements, the company issued over $3 billion in very low cost (2.5% interest rate or less) notes for general corporate purposes. The company may redeem these notes (pay them off) at any time, and the company is not subject to any financial restrictions while the notes are outstanding. The company purchased $960 million in treasury stock (line 34) during 2012. The major reason for the increase in additional paid-in capital on line 35 ($1,357 million, or 19.4%) was stock-based compensation and issuance of employee benefit plan stock. Finally, the net loss of $39 million decreased retained earnings (line 37) by 2% during 2012. Overall, it appears that 2012, while not profitable overall, was a year when management decided to invest "big time" in the future. Now the company is waiting to see if its strategy pays off in terms of skyrocketing sales.

> **Stop & Think...**

Examine Exhibits 13-2 and 13-3. Which year-to-year fluctuations should cause the most concern for the investor? Explain your reasoning.

Answer:

On the Consolidated Statements of Operations, expenses for Fulfillment, Marketing, and Technology and content in 2011 and 2012 were made for the purpose of increasing sales but so far have greatly outpaced increases in sales. The company has hired additional employees and has taken steps to ensure that its products and those of its affiliated retailers and manufacturers are closer to the fingertips of Amazon.com's customers than ever before. At the same time, as reflected in the Consolidated Balance Sheets, the company is investing heavily in additional inventory and property and equipment (warehouses and information technology), betting that these investments are going to cause sales to grow at a faster pace. As of the end of 2012, sales had not responded as much as anticipated. The key question is "If you build it, will they come?" It will be interesting to see whether Amazon's big bet on the future will pay off—all the more reason to download the 2013 financial statements next year. Stay tuned.

Trend Percentages

Trend percentages are a form of horizontal analysis. Trends indicate the direction a business is taking. How have revenues changed over a five-year period? What trend does net income show? These questions can be answered by trend percentages over a representative period, such as the most recent five years.

Trend percentages are computed by selecting a base year whose amounts are set equal to 100%. The amount for each following year is stated as a percentage of the base amount. To compute a trend percentage, divide an item for a later year by the base-year amount, and multiply by 100.

$$\text{Trend \%} = \frac{\text{Any year \$}}{\text{Base year \$}} \times 100$$

Recall that, in Chapter 11, we established that income from operations is often viewed as the primary measure of a company's earnings quality. This is because it represents a company's best predictor of the future net inflows from its core business units. Income from continuing operations is often used in estimating the current value of the business.

Amazon.com, Inc., showed income from operations for 2008–2012 as follows:

(In millions)	2012	2011	2010	2009	2008 (Base)
Income from operations	$676	$862	$1,406	$1,129	$842

We want to calculate a trend for the period 2008 through 2012. The first year in the series (2008) is set as the base year. Trend percentages are computed by dividing each successive year's amount by the 2008 amount. The resulting trend percentages follow (2008 = 100%):

	2012	2011	2010	2009	2008 (Base)
Income from operations	80%	102%	167%	134%	100%

In 2009, Income from operations took a 34% jump, relative to the base year, and it took another 33% jump in 2010, before starting to decline. In 2011, it fell to 102% of its base level, and in 2012, it fell again to 80%, relative to the base year. The cause for these results is the tremendous growth occurring in online sales in the early years, followed by declining growth fueled by increased competition in more recent years. Amazon's most recent strategy has been investment in expansion, in the hopes that future sales will bounce back. You can perform a trend analysis on any item you consider important. Trend analysis using income-statement data is widely used for predicting the future.

Horizontal analysis highlights changes over time in financial statement line items. However, no single technique gives a complete picture of a business.

PERFORM VERTICAL ANALYSIS

Vertical analysis shows the relationship of a financial-statement item to its base, which is the 100% figure. All items on the particular financial statement are reported as a percentage of the base. For the income statement, total revenue (net sales) is usually the base. Suppose that investors have come to expect a company's net income to be greater than 8% of net sales. A drop to 4% over a period of two years while general economic conditions are improving may cause investors to become disappointed in the performance of company management. Thus, they might sell the company's stock in favor of companies with more attractive earnings potential.

2 Perform vertical analysis

Illustration: Amazon.com, Inc.

Exhibit 13-4 shows the vertical analysis of Amazon.com, Inc.'s Consolidated Statements of Operations. In this case,

$$\text{Vertical analysis \%} = \frac{\text{Each income statement item}}{\text{Net sales (revenue)}}$$

Exhibit 13-4 | Comparative Consolidated Statements of Operations—Vertical Analysis

	A1						
	A	**B**	**C**	**D**	**E**	**F**	**G**
1	**Amazon.com, Inc. Consolidated Statements of Operations—Vertical Analysis**						
2	**($ in millions)**	**2012**	**% of total**	**2011**	**% of total**	**2010**	**% of total**
3	Total net sales	$ 61,093	100.00%	$ 48,077	100.00%	$ 34,204	100.00%
4	Cost of sales	45,971	75.25%	37,288	77.56%	26,561	77.65%
5	Gross profit	15,122	24.75%	10,789	22.44%	7,643	22.35%
6	Operating expenses						
7	Fulfillment	6,419	10.51%	4,576	9.52%	2,898	8.47%
8	Marketing	2,408	3.94%	1,630	3.39%	1,029	3.01%
9	Technology and content	4,564	7.47%	2,909	6.05%	1,734	5.07%
10	General and administrative	896	1.47%	658	1.37%	470	1.37%
11	Other operating expense (income), net	159	0.26%	154	0.32%	106	0.31%
12	Total operating expenses	14,446	23.65%	9,927	20.65%	6,237	18.23%
13	Income from operations	676	1.11%	862	1.79%	1,406	4.11%
14	Interest income	40	0.07%	61	0.13%	51	0.15%
15	Interest expense	(92)	–0.15%	(65)	–0.14%	(39)	–0.11%
16	Other income (expense), net	(80)	–0.13%	76	0.16%	79	0.23%
17	Total nonoperating income (expense)	(132)	–0.22%	72	0.15%	91	0.27%
18	Income before income taxes	544	0.89%	934	1.94%	1,497	4.38%
19	Provision for income taxes	(428)	–0.70%	(291)	–0.61%	(352)	–1.03%
20	Equity-method investment activity, net	(155)	–0.25%	(12)	–0.02%	7	0.02%
21	Net income (loss)	$ (39)	–0.06%	$ 631	1.31%	$ 1,152	3.37%
22							

Formatting comparative financial statements for vertical analysis when the financial statements are in Excel format is just as easy as it was for horizontal analysis. Try reconstructing Exhibit 13-4 in Excel.

1. Start with the Consolidated Statements of Operations in the opening figure of the chapter. You will be ahead of the game if you have already prepared this in Excel.
2. Change the labels to correspond with Exhibit 13-4. Your spreadsheet might be slightly different than Exhibit 13-4, so the cells in which you start to enter formulas might have to be modified accordingly.
3. We are preparing three years of comparative data, so insert columns after each of the 2012, 2011, and 2010 financial columns. In our example, these become columns C, E, and G with blank cells; label these "% of total."
4. Common-sized income statements set net sales at 100% and express all other income and expenses as percentages of net sales. To set net sales at 100%, we start in cell C3 (blank). In the cell, type the following: =B3/$B$3. It is very important to insert the $ signs in the denominator both before and after the letter B. This "freezes" cell B3 to make it a constant denominator for the values in all other cells in the column. You may also use the F4 function key to freeze the cell value. The result of 100% should appear in the cell. To increase precision, use the "increase decimal" tab in the "number" field in the toolbar. We have adjusted to a precision of two decimal places. Copy this cell formula through line 21 of the sheet to perform this computation for all other income and expenses.
5. Repeat the process in (4) for the 2011 and 2010 figures columns by entering corresponding formulas in columns E and G. Copy these formulas through line 21. Use the "borders" tab (under "font" in the toolbar) to format the cells to extend the proper underscoring as shown in Exhibit 13-4.
6. Pat yourself on the back. You're learning to use Excel for the very valuable function of vertical analysis! Now let's dig into the numbers to interpret what they mean. ■

The vertical analysis format in Exhibit 13-4 permits us to study trends in key financial statistics such as gross profit, operating income, and net income over time. The absolute numbers are converted to percentages, permitting us to see fluctuations we might not see otherwise. Let's begin with gross profit and proceed through operating expenses.

Amazon's gross profit percentages over the three-year period have improved slightly (22.35% in 2010, 22.44% in 2011, and 24.75% in 2012). As we learned in Chapter 6, gross profit percentage measures the average percentage of profit generated per each dollar of sales. The company is steady to slightly improving in this area, meaning that it is controlling costs while slightly increasing its selling prices, perhaps to partially compensate for increased operating costs.

The real story behind the company's operating strategy over the period then starts to emerge, and it parallels what we learned in the horizontal analysis section, except that now we see it from a slightly different angle. The proportion of resources devoted, respectively, to Fulfillment, Marketing, and Technology and content steadily increased from a total of 16.55% of sales (8.47% + 3.01% + 5.07%) in 2010 to 21.92% of sales (10.51% + 3.94% + 7.47%) in 2012. These percentages reflect the company's operating strategy to increase these costs proportionately in order to attract more customers and increase sales. The company held general and administrative as well as other operating expenses relatively constant over the same period. Thus, total operating expenses increased from 18.23% of net sales in 2010 to 23.65% of net sales in 2012. Notice that the overall picture of how the company is implementing its strategy over time is complementary to the picture we saw with horizontal analysis, except from a slightly different angle.

Exhibit 13-5 shows the vertical analysis of Amazon.com's Consolidated Balance Sheets. The base amount (100%) is total assets for each year. The vertical analysis of Amazon.com's balance

Exhibit 13-5 | Comparative Consolidated Balance Sheets—Vertical Analysis

	A	B	C	D	E
1	**Amazon.com, Inc.** **Consolidated Balance Sheets**				
2	**(In millions, unless otherwise specified)**	**2012**	**% of total**	**2011**	**% of total**
3	**Assets**				
4	Current assets:				
5	Cash and cash equivalents	$ 8,084	24.8%	$ 5,269	20.8%
6	Marketable securities	3,364	10.3%	4,307	17.0%
7	Inventories	6,031	18.5%	4,992	19.7%
8	Accounts receivable, net and other	3,364	10.3%	2,571	10.2%
9	Deferred tax assets	453	1.4%	351	1.4%
10	Total current assets	21,296	65.4%	17,490	69.2%
11	Property and equipment, net	7,060	21.7%	4,417	17.5%
12	Deferred tax assets	123	0.4%	28	0.1%
13	Goodwill	2,552	7.8%	1,955	7.7%
14	Other assets	1,524	4.7%	1,388	5.5%
15	Total assets	$ 32,555	100.0%	$ 25,278	100.0%
16	**Liabilities and Stockholders' Equity**				
17	Current liabilities:				
18	Accounts payable	$ 13,318	40.9%	$ 11,145	44.1%
19	Accrued expenses and other	5,684	17.5%	3,751	14.8%
20	Total current liabilities	19,002	58.4%	14,896	58.9%
21	Long-term debt	3,084	9.5%	255	1.0%
22	Other long-term liabilities	2,277	7.0%	2,370	9.4%
23	Commitments and contingencies		0.0%		0.0%
24	Total liabilities	24,363	74.8%	17,521	69.3%
25	Stockholders' equity:				
26	Preferred stock, $0.01 par value:				
27	Authorized shares—500				
28	Issued and outstanding shares—none				
29	Common stock, $0.01 par value:				
30	Authorized shares—5,000				
31	Issued shares—478 and 473				
32	Outstanding shares—454 and 455	5	0.0%	5	0.0%
33	Treasury stock, at cost	(1,837)	−5.6%	(877)	−3.5%
34	Additional paid-in capital	8,347	25.6%	6,990	27.7%
35	Accumulated other comprehensive loss	(239)	−0.7%	(316)	−1.3%
36	Retained earnings	1,916	5.9%	1,955	7.7%
37	Total stockholders' equity	8,192	25.2%	7,757	30.7%
38	Total liabilities and stockholders' equity	$ 32,555	100.0%	$ 25,278	100.0%
39					

sheet reveals several things about Amazon.com's financial position at December 31, 2012, relative to 2011:

- Cash and cash equivalents increased in 2012 by 53.4% from 2011 (Exhibit 13-3, p. 747), and it also increased as a percentage of total assets from 20.8% to 24.8% (line 5 in Exhibit 13-5). This was accompanied by a decline in marketable securities (line 6) from 17.0% of total assets to 10.3% of total assets, indicating that marketable securities were likely sold to provide for the company's increasing cash needs for expansion of its fulfillment, technology and content facilities.

- Although inventories increased by 20.8% from 2011 to 2012 (Exhibit 13-3), they declined slightly as a percentage of total assets, from 19.7% in 2011 to 18.5% in 2012 (Exhibit 13-5, line 7). Still, inventory turnover (cost of goods sold ÷ average inventory) declined from about 9.1 times in 2011 to about 8.34 times in 2012.[1] This indicates that the company is building up inventories in anticipation of increased future sales.

---

[1] For computation of inventory turnover, see Chapter 6. Inventory as of December 31, 2010 was $3,202 million.

- The company made a huge investment in Property and equipment in 2012, consistent with its strategy to increase fulfillment capacity and information technology resources. This increased Property and equipment, net (line 11) from 17.5% of total assets in 2011 to 21.7% in 2012. Thus, the company invested a proportionately larger amount of resources in long-term assets than current assets in 2012 than it did in 2011.

- The company's debt ratio (total liabilities ÷ total assets), reflected clearly in line 24, rose from 69.3% of total assets in 2011 to 74.8% of total assets in 2012. This increase was caused by long-term borrowing (line 21) in 2012 in order to finance expansion. As we discussed in Chapter 3, a debt ratio of 74.8% is considered high. However, as mentioned earlier in the section on horizontal analysis, Note 6 to the Consolidated Financial Statements explained that the interest rates on this debt are quite low, which will allow the company to expand operations and service the debt as long as cash flow from operations remains healthy.

  Overall, Amazon.com, Inc., remained healthy from the standpoint of both liquidity and leverage in 2012, but both liquidity and leverage were trending negatively. Company management will need to monitor these two important metrics closely in future periods and be prepared to take corrective action if they do not improve.

PREPARE COMMON-SIZE FINANCIAL STATEMENTS

3 **Prepare** common-size financial statements

Exhibits 13-4 and 13-5 can be modified to report only percentages (no dollar amounts). Such financial statements are called **common-size statements**. A common-size financial statement assists in the comparison of different companies because all amounts are stated in percentages, thus expressing the financial results of each comparative company in terms of a common denominator.

> ## Stop & Think...

Calculate the common-size percentages for the following income statement:

Net sales...............................	$150,000
Cost of goods sold..................	60,000
Gross profit............................	90,000
Operating expense..................	40,000
Operating income....................	50,000
Income tax expense................	15,000
Net income.............................	$ 35,000

Answer:

Net sales...............................	100%	(= $150,000 ÷ $150,000)
Cost of goods sold..................	40	(= $ 60,000 ÷ $150,000)
Gross profit............................	60	(= $ 90,000 ÷ $150,000)
Operating expense..................	27	(= $ 40,000 ÷ $150,000)
Operating income....................	33	(= $ 50,000 ÷ $150,000)
Income tax expense................	10	(= $ 15,000 ÷ $150,000)
Net income.............................	23%	(= $ 35,000 ÷ $150,000)

Remember that you can use Excel, as pointed out earlier, to quickly and easily convert dollar-denominated data to percentages. You might want to practice doing this with the abbreviated data above, to assure yourself that you have mastered it.

Benchmarking

Benchmarking compares a company to some standard set by others. The goal of benchmarking is improvement. Suppose you are a financial analyst for **Goldman Sachs**, a large investment bank. You are considering investing in one of two different retailers, say Amazon.com, Inc., or Walmart Stores, Inc. A direct comparison of these companies' financial statements is not meaningful, in part because Walmart, Inc., is so much larger than Amazon.com. However, you can convert the companies' income statements to common size and compare the percentages. This comparison is meaningful, as we shall see.

Benchmarking Against a Key Competitor

Exhibit 13-6 presents the common-size income statement of Amazon.com, Inc., benchmarked against the common-size income statement of Walmart Stores, Inc. The companies are not exactly comparable because of differences in their business models. For example, Walmart has physical stores as well as online retail services. However, if you look at their websites, the two companies are very similar, organized in much the same way. They are close enough to illustrate the value of common-size vertical analysis.

Exhibit 13-6 | Common-Size Income Statements Benchmarked Against Competitor

A1		
A	**B**	**C**
Amazon.com, Inc. Common-Size Income Statement for Comparison with Key Competitor (Adapted) Year Ended During 2012		
	Amazon.com	**Walmart**
Net sales	100.0%	100.0%
Cost of sales	75.2%	75.1%
Gross profit	24.8%	24.9%
Operating expenses	23.7%	18.9%
Operating income	1.1%	6.0%

In this comparison, the results of the two companies are strikingly similar down through the gross margin percentages. As we have pointed out, Amazon.com's business strategy to increase operating expenses in the short run in order to attract long-run future sales is only a recent phenomenon. This is what caused Amazon.com's operating expenses to rise by 5.5% (from 18.2% in 2010 to 23.7% 2012), in comparison with Walmart's rather consistent level of operating expenses of 18.9% of net sales over the same period. Look back at Amazon.com, Inc.'s 2010 Consolidated Statement of Operations in Exhibit 13-4 and you will see that the company's operating expenses were 18.2% of net sales in that year, which is similar to that of Walmart's and much more typical for Amazon.com. The management of Amazon.com, Inc., is likely hoping that in the future operating expenses return to this range.

ANALYZE THE STATEMENT OF CASH FLOWS

This chapter has focused on the income statement and balance sheet. We may also perform horizontal analysis on the statement of cash flows. To continue our discussion of its role in decision making, let's use Exhibit 13-7, the comparative Consolidated Statements of Cash Flows of Amazon.com, Inc. on page 754. We have modified the statements somewhat to illustrate selected horizontal percentage changes.

For both 2012 and 2011, net cash provided by operating activities was the major source of cash for the company ($4,180 million in 2012 and $3,903 million in 2011). Net cash provided by operations increased by 7.1% in 2012 over 2011. Also, for both 2012 and 2011, net cash provided

4 Analyze the statement of cash flows

Exhibit 13-7 | Amazon.com, Inc., Comparative Consolidated Statements of Cash Flows

	A	B	C	D
	A1			
1	**Amazon.com, Inc.** **Comparative Consolidated Statements of Cash Flows (Adapted)**			
2		**Year Ended December 31**		
3	**(in millions of $)**	**2012**	**2011**	**% change**
4	CASH AND CASH EQUIVALENTS, BEGINNING OF PERIOD	$ 5,269	$ 3,777	39.5%
5	**OPERATING ACTIVITIES:**			
6	Net income (loss)	(39)	631	
7	Adjustments to reconcile net income (loss) to net cash			
8	provided by operating activities:			
9	Depreciation and amortization	2,159	1,083	
10	Stock-based compensation	833	557	
11	Other operating expense (income), net	154	154	
12	Losses (gains) on sales of marketable securities, net	(9)	(4)	
13	Other expense (income), net	253	(56)	
14	Deferred income taxes	(265)	136	
15	Excess tax benefits from stock-based compensation	(429)	(62)	
16	Changes in operating assets and liabilities:			
17	Inventories	(999)	(1,777)	
18	Accounts receivable, net and other	(861)	(866)	
19	Accounts payable	2,070	2,997	
20	Accrued expenses and other	1,038	1,067	
21	Additions to unearned revenue	1,796	1,064	
22	Amortization of previously unearned revenue	(1,521)	(1,021)	
23	Net cash provided by (used in) operating activities	4,180	3,903	7.1%
24	**INVESTING ACTIVITIES:**			
25	Purchases of property and equipment, including			
26	internal-use software and website development	(3,785)	(1,811)	109.0%
27	Acquisitions, net of cash acquired, and other	(745)	(705)	5.7%
28	Sales and maturities of marketable			
29	securities and other investments	4,237	6,843	−38.1%
30	Purchases of marketable securities and other investments	(3,302)	(6,257)	−47.2%
31	Net cash provided by (used in) investing activities	(3,595)	(1,930)	86.3%
32	**FINANCING ACTIVITIES:**			
33	Excess tax benefits from stock-based compensation	429	62	
34	Common stock repurchased	(960)	(277)	
35	Proceeds from long-term debt and other	3,378	177	1808.5%
36	Repayments of long-term debt, capital lease,			
37	and finance lease obligations	(588)	(444)	
38	Net cash provided by (used in) financing activities	2,259	(482)	
39	Foreign-currency effect on cash and cash equivalents	(29)	1	
40	Net increase (decrease) in cash and cash equivalents	2,815	1,492	88.7%
41	CASH AND CASH EQUIVALENTS, END OF PERIOD	$ 8,084	$ 5,269	53.4%
42				

by operating activities exceeded net income (net loss in 2012) by sizeable amounts. The ability to generate most of its cash from operations is one sign of a healthy company.

Now focus on the investing section. Notice that the company has increased spending for property and equipment by 109% from 2011 to 2012. Net spending from investing activities has increased by 86.3% from 2011 to 2012. This is a signal that the company is plowing cash back into the business and that excess cash generated from operations is being invested for future use. These are also signs of financial strength from a cash flow perspective. Finally, notice that the company is using long-term debt to finance the portion of its growth that it cannot provide through operations. Long-term debt proceeds increased by 1,808% in 2012 over 2011.

Analysts may find the statement of cash flows as helpful for spotting weakness as for gauging success. Why? Because a *shortage* of cash can throw a company into bankruptcy, but lots of cash doesn't ensure success. Let's look at the cash flow statement of Unix Corporation. See if you can find signals of cash flow distress.

A1				

	A	B	C
1	**Unix Corporation** **Statement of Cash Flows** **Year Ended June 30, 2014**		
2	**(In millions)**		
3	**Operating activities:**		
4	Net income		$ 35,000
5	Adjustments for noncash items:		
6	Depreciation	$ 14,000	
7	Net increase in current assets other than cash	(24,000)	
8	Net increase in current liabilities	8,000	(2,000)
9	Net cash provided by operating activities		33,000
10	**Investing activities:**		
11	Sale of property, plant, and equipment	$ 91,000	
12	Net cash provided by investing activities		91,000
13	**Financing activities:**		
14	Borrowing	$ 22,000	
15	Payment of long-term debt	(90,000)	
16	Purchase of treasury stock	(9,000)	
17	Payment of dividends	(23,000)	
18	Net cash used for financing activities		(100,000)
19	Increase (decrease) in cash		$ 24,000
20			

Unix Corporation's statement of cash flows reveals the following:

- Net cash provided by operating activities is less than net income. That's strange. Ordinarily, net cash provided by operating activities exceeds net income because of the add-back of depreciation and amortization. The increases in current assets and current liabilities should cancel out over time. For Unix Corporation, current assets increased far more than current liabilities during the year. This may be harmless. But it may signal difficulty in collecting receivables or selling inventory. Either event will cause trouble.

- The sale of plant assets is Unix's major source of cash. This is okay if this is a one-time situation. Unix may be shifting from one line of business to another, and it may be selling off old assets. But if the sale of plant assets is the major source of cash for several periods, Unix will face a cash shortage. A company can't sell off its plant assets forever. Soon it will go out of business.

- The only strength shown by the statement of cash flows is that Unix paid off more long-term debt than it borrowed. This will improve the debt ratio and Unix's credit standing.

In summary, here are some cash flow signs of a healthy company:

- Net cash flow provided by operating activities exceeds net income.
- Operations are the major *source* of cash (not a *use* of cash).
- Investing activities include more purchases than sales of long-term assets.
- Financing activities are not dominated by borrowing.

Perform a horizontal analysis and a vertical analysis of the comparative income statement of Hard Rock Products, Inc., which makes metal detectors. State whether 2014 was a good year or a bad year compared with 2013, and give your reasons. We encourage you to use Excel as a tool to perform your analysis.

	A1		
	A	**B**	**C**
1	**Hard Rock Products, Inc.** **Comparative Income Statements** **Years Ended December 31, 2014 and 2013**		
2		**2014**	**2013**
3	Total revenues	$ 275,000	$ 225,000
4	Expenses:		
5	Cost of goods sold	194,000	165,000
6	Engineering, selling, and administrative expenses	54,000	48,000
7	Interest expense	5,000	5,000
8	Income tax expense	9,000	3,000
9	Other expense (income)	1,000	(1,000)
10	Total expenses	263,000	220,000
11	Net income	$ 12,000	$ 5,000
12			

Answer

The horizontal analysis shows that total revenues increased 22.2%. This was greater than the 19.5% increase in total expenses, resulting in a 140% increase in net income.

	A1				
	A	**B**	**C**	**D**	**E**
1	**Hard Rock Products, Inc.** **Horizontal Analysis of Comparative Income Statements** **Years Ended December 31, 2014 and 2013**				
2		**2014**	**2013**	**Increase (Decrease)**	
				Amount	**Percent**
3	Total revenues	$ 275,000	$ 225,000	$ 50,000	22.2%
4	Expenses:				
5	Cost of goods sold	194,000	165,000	29,000	17.6
6	Engineering, selling, and				
7	administrative expenses	54,000	48,000	6,000	12.5
8	Interest expense	5,000	5,000	—	—
9	Income tax expense	9,000	3,000	6,000	200.0
10	Other expense (income)	1,000	(1,000)	2,000	—*
11	Total expenses	263,000	220,000	43,000	19.5
12	Net income	$ 12,000	$ 5,000	$ 7,000	140.0%
13					

*Percentage changes are typically not computed for shifts from a negative to a positive amount and vice versa.

The vertical analysis shows decreases in the percentages of net revenues consumed by the cost of goods sold (from 73.3% to 70.5%) and by the engineering, selling, and administrative expenses (from 21.3% to 19.6%). Because these two items are Hard Rock's largest dollar expenses, their percentage decreases are quite important. The relative reduction in expenses raised 2014 net income to 4.4% of revenues, compared with 2.2% the preceding year. The overall analysis indicates that 2014 was significantly better than 2013.

	A	B	C	D	E
		A1			
	A	B	C	D	E
1	**Hard Rock Products, Inc.** **Vertical Analysis of Comparative Income Statements** **Years Ended December 31, 2014 and 2013**				
2		**2014**		**2013**	
		Amount	**Percent**	**Amount**	**Percent**
3	Total revenues	$ 275,000	100.0 %	$ 225,000	100.0 %
4	Expenses:				
5	Cost of goods sold	194,000	70.5	165,000	73.3
6	Engineering, selling, and				
7	administrative expenses	54,000	19.6	48,000	21.3
8	Interest expense	5,000	1.8	5,000	2.2
9	Income tax expense	9,000	3.3	3,000	1.4**
10	Other expense (income)	1,000	0.4	(1,000)	(0.4)
11	Total expenses	263,000	95.6	220,000	97.8
12	Net income	$ 12,000	4.4 %	$ 5,000	2.2 %
13					

**Number rounded up.

USE RATIOS TO MAKE BUSINESS DECISIONS

Ratios are a major tool of financial analysis. We have discussed the use of many ratios in financial analysis in various chapters throughout the book. A ratio expresses the relationship between various types of financial information. In this section, we review how ratios are computed and used to make business decisions, using Apple, Inc., which was our spotlight company in Chapter 5.

Many companies include ratios in a special section of their annual reports. Exhibit 13-8 shows a summary of selected data from previous Apple, Inc., annual reports. Financial websites such as www.yahoofinance.com and www.googlefinance.com report many of these ratios. Exhibit 13-8 has been prepared in Excel format, with formulas for most of the ratios we have studied in this text. This template can be used as a template for any company's financial statements, but has been tailor-made in this chapter for Apple, Inc.

The ratios we discuss in this chapter are classified as follows:

1. Measuring ability to pay current liabilities
2. Measuring turnover and cash conversion cycle
3. Measuring leverage: overall ability to pay debts
4. Measuring profitability
5. Analyzing stock as an investment

You will find the skills you have acquired in earlier chapters in this book helpful when performing financial analysis using Microsoft Excel, as you work on the problems related to this section. Excel makes computation of financial ratios a breeze. However, interpretation of what the ratios mean and the use of the ratios to make decisions takes more time and effort! Now, let's analyze Apple, Inc.

5 Use ratios to make business decisions

Exhibit 13-8 | Financial Summary: Apple, Inc.

	A	B	C	D	E	F
		Apple, Inc.				
1	**Financial Summary and Key Ratios***					
2	(In millions of $)	**FY 2012**	**FY 2011**	**FY 2010**	**FY 2009**	**FY 2008**
3	**Results of operations**					
4	Net sales	$ 156,508	$ 108,249	$ 65,225	$ 42,905	$ 37,491
5	Cost of sales	87,846	64,431	39,541	25,683	24,294
6	Gross margin	68,662	43,818	25,684	17,222	13,197
7	Gross margin as percent of net sales	43.9%	40.5%	39.4%	40.1%	35.2%
8	Operating income	55,241	33,790	18,385	11,740	8,327
9	Operating income as percent of net sales	35.3%	31.2%	28.2%	27.4%	22.2%
10	Net income after taxes	41,733	25,922	14,013	8,235	6,119
11	Net income/sales (Return on Sales or ROS)	26.7%	23.9%	21.5%	19.2%	16.3%
12	ROA (line 11 × line 29)	28.6%	27.0%	22.9%	19.7%	
13	ROE (line 12 × line 40)	42.93%	41.58%	35.38%	30.55%	27.20%
14	Times interest earned	N/A	N/A	N/A	N/A	N/A
15	Average number of common shares outstanding (in thousands)	934,818	924,528	909,461	893,016	881,592
16	Earnings per common share, basic	$ 44.64	$ 28.05	$ 15.41	$ 9.22	$ 6.94
17	Price-earnings multiple	14.93	13.59	21.91	20.56	
18	Cash dividends	2,523	—	—	—	—
19	Dividends per common share	2.65	—	—	—	—
20	**Financial position**					
21	Accounts receivable	10,930	5,369	5,510	3,361	2,422
22	Average accounts receivable	8,150	5,440	4,436	2,892	
23	Inventories	791	776	1,051	455	509
24	Average inventories	783.5	913.5	753	482	
25	Current assets	57,653	44,988	41,678	31,555	30,006
26	Quick assets	40,059	31,321	31,130	26,825	
27	Total assets	176,064	116,371	75,183	47,501	36,171
28	Average total assets	146,218	95,777	61,342	41,836	
29	Asset turnover (line 4/line 28)	1.070	1.130	1.063	1.026	
30	Accounts payable	21,175	14,632	12,015	5,601	5,520
31	Average accounts payable	17,904	13,324	8,808	5,561	
32	Current liabilities	38,542	27,970	20,722	11,506	11,361
33	Total liabilities	57,854	39,756	27,392	15,861	13,874
34	Working capital (line 25 − line 32)	19,111	17,018	20,956	20,049	18,645
35	Current ratio (line 25/line 32)	1.50	1.61	2.01	2.74	2.64
36	Quick ratio (line 26/line 32)	1.04	1.12	1.50	2.33	
37	Debt ratio (line 33/line 27)	0.33	0.34	0.36	0.33	0.38
38	Total stockholders' equity	118,210	76,615	47,791	31,640	22,297
39	Average stockholders' equity	97,413	62,203	39,716	26,969	
40	Leverage ratio (line 28/line 39)	1.501	1.540	1.545	1.551	
41	Inventory turnover (line 5/line 24)	112.12	70.53	52.51	53.28	
42	Days' inventory outstanding (DIO)(365/line 41)	3.26	5.17	6.95	6.85	
43	Accounts receivable turnover (line 4/line 22)	19.20	19.90	14.70	14.84	
44	Days' sales outstanding (DSO)(365/line 43)	19.01	18.34	24.83	24.60	
45	Accounts payable turnover (line 5/line 31)	4.91	4.84	4.49	4.62	
46	Days' payable outstanding (DPO)(365/line 45)	74.34	75.41	81.29	79.00	
47	Cash conversion cycle (line 42 + line 44 − line 46)	(52.1)	(52.0)	(49.5)	(47.6)	
48						

*There may be some slight variation in the calculations of ratios due to rounding.

Remember to Start at the Beginning:
Company and Industry Information

As stated in the chapter opening, financial analysis is just manipulating numbers unless we give the numbers a context. That comes from understanding the company and the industry, and from knowing not only its history but where it appears to be headed in the future. Apple is known as perhaps the world's most innovative company. Founded as Apple Computer Company in Cupertino, California, in 1976 by two college dropouts, Steve Jobs and Michael Wozniak, the company first went public in 1977. For more than two decades, Apple was predominantly a manufacturer of personal computers. It faced intense competition from companies such as Dell, Inc., another upstart from Round Rock, Texas. Apple faced rocky sales and low market share during the 1990s. Jobs, who had been ousted from the company in 1985, returned to Apple in 1996 and shortly thereafter became the company's permanent CEO. Jobs subsequently instilled a new corporate philosophy of recognizable products and simple design, starting with the original iMac in 1998.

With the introduction of the successful iPod music player in 2001 and iTunes Music Store in 2003, Apple established itself as a leader in the consumer electronics and media sales industries, leading it to drop "Computer" from the company's name in 2007. The company is now also known for its iOS range of smart phone, media player, and tablet computer products that began with the iPhone, followed by the iPod Touch and then iPad. As of the end of its September 29, 2012 fiscal year, Apple was the largest publicly traded corporation in the world by market capitalization, with an estimated value of $626 billion, larger than that of Google and Microsoft combined. Jobs died prematurely in 2011, but under an able team of senior management, the company he founded continues to grow. As reflected in Exhibit 13-8, the company's net sales and profitability growth have been legendary. During the fiscal years 2008 through 2012, inclusive, worldwide net sales revenues (line 4) for Apple, Inc., grew from $37.5 billion to $156.5 billion. Net income after taxes (line 10) grew from $6.1 billion to $41.7 billion in this same period.

Meanwhile, the industry that Apple first joined (personal computers) is becoming a relic of the past. The first Internet-enabled mobile devices appeared in 1996. Now, the mobile Internet is set to dominate the computer world for the foreseeable future. By 2014, mobile devices are expected to replace the desktop computer as the most important way of accessing the Internet, eventually replacing search engines such as Google and Bing. Voice-activated devices and virtual assistants are expected to amplify this trend. "Cloud computing" is becoming the most common method of storing data online. Therefore, desktop computer and hard drive sales are expected to decline in the future. It has been predicted that by 2015, there will be 15 billion devices connected to the Internet. An "Internet of things" is expected to appear by 2017, allowing people to do such things as shop for groceries automatically online and have the goods delivered by driverless vehicles operated by global positioning systems (GPS). In homes, all electronic devices will be connected to the Internet via a central hub, with the high-definition television screen being the main home interface, operated almost entirely via gestures and voice. Apple, Inc., seems to be well positioned to prosper in this "brave new world" of technology because of its reputation as an innovator.

Now Let's Do the Numbers

Once you gain knowledge about a company and its industry, how do you determine whether the company's performance has been strong or weak, based on its current-period ratios? You can make that decision only if you have the following ratios to compare against the current period: (1) prior-year ratios, and (2) industry comparables, either in the form of an industry average or the ratios of a strong competitor. In the case of all the ratios in the following sections, we compare Apple's current-year ratios with (1) its prior-years' ratios (see Exhibit 13-8) and (2) ratios for the industry (if available), or ratios of one or more of Apple, Inc.'s competitors.

Measuring Ability to Pay Current Liabilities

Working capital is defined as

$$\text{Working capital} = \text{Current assets} - \text{Current liabilities}$$

Working capital measures the ability to pay current liabilities with current assets. In general, the larger the working capital, the better the ability to pay debts. Recall that capital is total assets minus total liabilities. Working capital is like a "current" version of total capital.

Consider two companies with equal working capital:

	Company	
	Jones	Smith
Current assets......................	$100,000	$200,000
Current liabilities	50,000	150,000
Working capital	$ 50,000	$ 50,000

Both companies have working capital of $50,000, but Jones's working capital is as large as its current liabilities. Smith's working capital is only one-third as large as current liabilities. Jones is in a better position because its working capital is a higher percentage of current liabilities. As shown in Exhibit 13-8 (line 34), Apple, Inc.'s working capital as of September 29, 2012 (the end of its 2012 fiscal year), was $19,111 million. This compares with $17,018 million and $20,956 million at the end of its 2011 and 2010 fiscal years, respectively. In comparison, the working capital of Dell, Inc., a competitor of Apple, Inc., as of the end of its 2012 fiscal year was $4,529 million. Apple, Inc., appears to be in a relatively very strong position from the standpoint of working capital. But the picture is incomplete. Let's look at two key ratios that help tell the rest of the story.

Current Ratio. The most common ratio evaluating current assets and current liabilities is the **current ratio**, which is current assets divided by current liabilities. As discussed in Chapter 3, the current ratio measures the ability to pay current liabilities with current assets. Exhibit 13-9 and Exhibit 13-10 show the Consolidated Statements of Operations and the Consolidated Balance Sheets of Apple, Inc., respectively.

Exhibit 13-9 | Comparative Consolidated Statements of Operations—Apple, Inc.

A1		

	A	B	C	D
1	Apple, Inc. Consolidated Statements of Operations			
2		12 Months Ended		
3	(In millions, except share data)	Sep. 29, 2012	Sep. 24, 2011	Sep. 25, 2010
4	Net sales	$ 156,508	$ 108,249	$ 65,225
5	Cost of sales	87,846	64,431	39,541
6	Gross margin	68,662	43,818	25,684
7	Operating expenses:			
8	Research and development	3,381	2,429	1,782
9	Selling, general and administrative	10,040	7,599	5,517
10	Total operating expenses	13,421	10,028	7,299
11	Operating income	55,241	33,790	18,385
12	Other income/(expense), net	522	415	155
13	Income before provision for income taxes	55,763	34,205	18,540
14	Provision for income taxes	14,030	8,283	4,527
15	Net income	$ 41,733	$ 25,922	$ 14,013
16	Earnings per share:			
17	Basic	$ 44.64	$ 28.05	$ 15.41
18	Diluted	$ 44.15	$ 27.68	$ 15.15
19	Shares (in thousands) used in computing earnings per share:			
20	Basic	934,818	924,258	909,461
21	Diluted	945,355	936,645	924,712
22	Cash dividends declared per common share	$ 2.65	$ –	$ –
23				

Exhibit 13-10 | Comparative Consolidated Balance Sheets—Apple, Inc.

	A	B	C
	A1		
1	**Apple, Inc.** **Consolidated Statements of Operations**		
2		Sep. 29, 2012	Sep. 24, 2011
3	(In millions, unless otherwise specified)		
4	**Current assets:**		
5	Cash and cash equivalents	$ 10,746	$ 9,815
6	Short-term marketable securities	18,383	16,137
7	Accounts receivable, less allowances of $98 and $53, respectively	10,930	5,369
8	Inventories	791	776
9	Deferred tax assets	2,583	2,014
10	Vendor nontrade receivables	7,762	6,348
11	Other current assets	6,458	4,529
12	**Total current assets**	57,653	44,988
13	Long-term marketable securities	92,122	55,618
14	Property, plant, and equipment, net	15,452	7,777
15	Goodwill	1,135	896
16	Acquired intangible assets, net	4,224	3,536
17	Other assets	5,478	3,556
18	**Total assets**	$ 176,064	$ 116,371
19	**Current liabilities:**		
20	Accounts payable	$ 21,175	$ 14,632
21	Accrued expenses	11,414	9,247
22	Deferred revenue	5,953	4,091
23	**Total current liabilities**	38,542	27,970
24	Deferred revenue — noncurrent	2,648	1,686
25	Other noncurrent liabilities	16,664	10,100
26	**Total liabilities**	57,854	39,756
27	Commitments and contingencies		
28	**Shareholders' equity:**		
29	Common stock, no par value; 1,800,000 shares authorized;	16,422	13,331
30	939,208 and 929,277 shares issued and outstanding, respectively		
31	Retained earnings	101,289	62,841
32	Accumulated other comprehensive income	499	443
33	**Total shareholders' equity**	118,210	76,615
34	**Total liabilities and shareholders' equity**	$ 176,064	$ 116,371

Using figures from Exhibit 13-10, the following are current ratios of Apple, Inc., at September 29, 2012, and September 24, 2011, along with the average for the computer manufacturing industry:

	Apple, Inc.'s Current Ratio		Industry
Formula (figures in millions)	2012	2011	Average
Current ratio = $\dfrac{\text{Current assets}}{\text{Current liabilities}}$	$\dfrac{\$57,653}{\$38,542} = 1.50$	$\dfrac{\$44,988}{\$27,970} = 1.61$	1.30

Although still strong, Apple, Inc.'s current ratio decreased during 2012, from 1.61 to 1.50. Line 35 of Exhibit 13-8 shows the current ratio declining significantly over the past five years from 2.64 in 2008 to 1.50 in 2012. Further examination of current assets and current liabilities in Exhibit 13-10 shows that current liabilities increased from $27,970 million to $38,542 million (about 38%) during 2012, while current assets increased from $44,988 million to $57,653 million (about 28%). Accounts payable increased from $14,632 million to $21,175 million (44.7%) in 2012 over 2011 and, according to Exhibit 13-8 (line 30), quadrupled in five years time. This is a natural consequence of the meteoric growth the company has experienced. It is hardly a sign of trouble, especially since the current ratio is well within the bounds of what is considered healthy from the standpoint of the ability to pay current liabilities. In general, a higher current ratio indicates a stronger financial position. Apple, Inc., certainly has more than sufficient current assets to maintain its operations. Apple's current ratio of 1.50 compares quite favorably with the current ratios of the industry as well as with two well-known competitors:

Company	Current Ratio
Dell, Inc...	1.49
Hewlett-Packard Company................	1.09

Quick (Acid-test) Ratio. As discussed in Chapter 5, the **quick (acid-test) ratio** tells us whether the entity could pass the acid test of paying all its current liabilities if they came due immediately (quickly). The quick ratio uses a narrower base to measure liquidity than the current ratio does.

To compute the quick ratio, we add cash, short-term investments, and accounts receivable (net of allowances), and divide by current liabilities. Inventory and prepaid expenses are excluded because they are less liquid. A business may be unable to convert inventory to cash immediately.

Using the information in Exhibits 13-8 (line 36) and 13-10, Apple, Inc.'s quick ratios for 2012 and 2011 are (in millions of $):

		Apple, Inc.'s Quick Ratio		Industry
	Formula	2012	2011	Average
Quick ratio =	$\dfrac{\text{Cash and cash equivalents} + \text{Short-term investments} + \text{Net current receivables}}{\text{Current liabilities}}$	$\dfrac{\$10,746 + \$18,383 + \$10,930}{\$38,542} = 1.04$	$\dfrac{\$9,815 + \$16,137 + \$5,369}{\$27,970} = 1.12$	0.80

Like the current ratio, the company's quick ratio declined somewhat from 2009 through 2012 but is still significantly better than the industry average. Compare Apple, Inc.'s quick ratio with the values of its leading competitors:

Company	Quick (Acid-Test) Ratio
Dell, Inc...	1.07
Hewlett-Packard Company................	0.65

A quick ratio of 0.90 to 1.00 is acceptable in most industries. How can many retail companies function with low quick ratios? Because their cash conversion cycles are so short. This points us to the next group of ratios, which measure turnover and the cash conversion cycle.

Measuring Turnover and the Cash Conversion Cycle

The ability to sell inventory and collect receivables, as well as pay accounts payable, is the lifeblood of any retail, wholesale, or manufacturing concern. In this section, we discuss three ratios that measure this ability—inventory turnover, accounts receivable turnover, and accounts payable turnover—as well as the relationship between them, called the *cash conversion cycle*.

Inventory Turnover. Companies generally strive to sell their inventory as quickly as possible. The faster inventory sells, the sooner cash comes in. **Inventory turnover**, discussed in Chapter 6, measures the number of times a company sells its average level of inventory during a year. A fast turnover indicates ease in selling inventory; a low turnover indicates difficulty. A value of 6 means that the company's average level of inventory has been sold six times during the year, and that's usually better than a turnover of three times. But too high a value can mean that the business is not keeping enough inventory on hand, which can lead to lost sales if the company can't fill orders. Therefore, a business strives for the most *profitable* rate of turnover, not necessarily the *highest* rate.

To compute inventory turnover, divide cost of goods sold by the average inventory for the period. We use the cost of goods sold—*not sales*—in the computation because both cost of goods sold and inventory are stated *at cost*. Apple, Inc.'s inventory turnover for 2012 is

Formula		Apple, Inc.'s Inventory Turnover	Competitor (Dell, Inc.)
Inventory turnover $= \dfrac{\text{Cost of goods sold}}{\text{Average inventory}}$		$\dfrac{\$87,846 \text{ million}}{\$783.5 \text{ million}} = 112.1$	26.33
Days' inventory outstanding (DIO) $= \dfrac{365}{\text{Turnover}}$		$\dfrac{365}{112.1} = 3.3 \text{ days}$	13.9 days

Cost of goods sold comes from the Consolidated Statements of Operations (Exhibit 13-9). Average inventory (from the balance sheets, Exhibit 13-10) is the average of beginning ($776 million) and ending inventory ($791 million). If inventory levels vary greatly from month to month, you should compute the average by adding the 12 monthly balances and dividing the sum by 12.

Inventory turnover varies widely with the nature of the business. For example, Apple's inventory turned over 112.1 times in 2012. On a daily basis (days' inventory outstanding), that means once every 3.3 days (365/112.1)! In 2011, Apple, Inc.'s inventory turned over 70.5 times. Lines 41 and 42 in Exhibit 13-8 show that inventory turnover has more than doubled since 2009, cutting the number of days it takes to sell inventory by more than half. In contrast, Dell, Inc.'s inventory turnover for 2012 was 26.3 times (once every 13.9 days). Hewlett-Packard Company's inventory turned over 8.61 times in 2012 (about once every 42 days). Computer manufacturers purposely keep very low inventory levels because of their ability to manufacture inventory quickly and because technology is subject to rapid obsolescence. Apple, Inc., is exceptional, even by these standards.

YUM! Brands, owner of fast-food restaurants Pizza Hut, Taco Bell, KFC, and Long John Silver's, has an inventory turnover ratio of 29 times per year because food spoils so quickly. By contrast, **Williams-Sonoma, Inc.**, the popular upscale housewares company, typically turns its inventory over only about 4 times per year (once with each season).

To evaluate inventory turnover, compare the ratio over time as well as with industry averages or competitors. Steadily increasing inventory turnover is a positive sign, particularly if gross profits are also increasing. A sharp decline in inventory turnover suggests the need to take action to increase sales, usually by lowering prices. Unfortunately, this will reduce gross margins until excess inventory can be disposed of.

Accounts Receivable Turnover. **Accounts receivable turnover** measures the ability to collect cash from credit customers. In general, the higher this ratio, the better. However, a receivable turnover that is too high may indicate that credit is too tight, and that may cause a company to lose sales to good customers.

To compute accounts receivable turnover, divide net sales (assumed all on credit) by average net accounts receivable. The ratio tells how many times during the year average receivables were turned into cash. Apple, Inc.'s accounts receivable turnover ratio for 2012 was

Formula		Apple, Inc.'s Accounts Receivable Turnover	Competitor (Dell, Inc.)
Accounts receivable turnover $= \dfrac{\text{Net sales}}{\text{Average net accounts receivable}}$		$\dfrac{\$156,508 \text{ million}}{\$8,150 \text{ million}} = 19.2$	8.7
Days' sales outstanding (DSO) (or days'-sales-in-receivables) $= \dfrac{365}{\text{Turnover}}$		$\dfrac{365}{19.2} = 19 \text{ days}$	42 days

Net sales comes from Exhibit 13-9 and from line 4 of Exhibit 13-8. Average net accounts receivable (line 22 of Exhibit 13-8) is figured by adding beginning ($5,369 million) and ending receivables ($10,930 million) from Exhibit 13-10, then dividing by 2. If accounts receivable vary widely during the year, compute the average by using the 12 monthly balances. Apple, Inc., collected its average accounts receivable 19.2 times during 2012. According to Exhibit 13-8 (line 43), accounts receivable turnover has been steadily increasing, from 14.8 times in fiscal 2009 to 19.2 times in 2012. In comparison, Dell, Inc.'s accounts receivable turnover for 2012 was 8.7 times.

Apple, Inc.'s accounts receivable turnover of 19.2 times per year is much faster than the industry average. Apple owns and operates a large number of retail stores, and much of its sales are for cash, which makes the receivables balance very low relative to the sales balance.

Days' Sales Outstanding. Businesses must convert accounts receivable to cash. All else being equal, the lower the receivable balance, the better the cash flow.

The *days' sales outstanding (DSO)* or **days'-sales-in-receivables**, discussed in Chapter 5, shows how many days' sales remain in accounts receivable. Days' sales in receivables can be calculated two different ways, each of which produces the identical result. First, if you have already calculated receivables turnover (see the previous section), simply divide the turnover into 365. For Apple, Inc., days' sales in receivables works out to about 19 days (365/19.2). Exhibit 13-8 (line 44) shows that DSO has declined by 5.6 days since 2009, meaning the company collected cash on receivables 5.6 days faster in 2012 than it did in 2009.

The second way to compute the ratio, described in Chapter 5, merely works from a different angle, by a two-step process:

1. Divide net sales by 365 days to figure average daily sales.
2. Divide average net receivables by average daily sales.

The data to compute this ratio for Apple, Inc., are taken from the 2012 income statement (Exhibit 13-9) and balance sheet (Exhibit 13-10):

Formula	Apple, Inc.'s Days' Sales in Accounts Receivable	Competitor (Dell, Inc.)
Days' sales outstanding (DSO) or days' sales in receivables:		
1. Average daily sales $= \dfrac{\text{Net sales}}{365 \text{ days}}$	$\dfrac{\$156,508 \text{ million}}{365 \text{ days}} = \$428.8$ million	
2. Convert average daily sales to DSO $= \dfrac{\text{Average net accounts receivable}}{\text{Average daily sales}}$	$\dfrac{\$8,150 \text{ million}}{\$428.8 \text{ million}} = 19$ days	42 days

By comparison, Dell, Inc.'s DSO in 2010 was 42 days (365/8.7). Dell owns far fewer retail outlets and sells fewer products than Apple.

Accounts Payable Turnover. Discussed in Chapter 9, **accounts payable turnover** measures the number of times per year that the entity pays off its accounts payable. To compute accounts payable turnover, divide cost of goods sold by average accounts payable.[2] For Apple, Inc., this ratio is

Formula	Apple, Inc.'s Accounts Payable Turnover	Competitor (Dell, Inc.)
Accounts payable turnover $= \dfrac{\text{Cost of goods sold}}{\text{Average accounts payable}}$	$\dfrac{\$87,846 \text{ million}}{\$17,904 \text{ million}} = 4.91$	3.85
Days' payable outstanding (DPO) $= \dfrac{365}{\text{Turnover}}$	$\dfrac{365}{4.91} = 74.3$ days	94.8 days

---

[2]For manufacturing or service-oriented companies, it is appropriate use purchases rather than cost of goods sold as the numerator of the fraction. This requires adjusting cost of goods sold for the difference between beginning and ending inventories. See Chapter 9 for details. When inventories are small in relation to cost of goods sold, and/or when there is virtually no change between beginning and ending inventories (as is the case for Apple, Inc.), this adjustment is insignificant. Therefore, to simplify, cost of goods sold may be used without adjustment.

Cost of goods sold comes from Exhibit 13-9 and line 5 of Exhibit 13-8, while average accounts payable comes from line 31 of Exhibit 13-8. On average, Apple, Inc., pays off its accounts payable 4.91 times per year, which is about every 74 days. To convert accounts payable turnover to days' payable outstanding (DPO), divide the turnover into 365 (365 ÷ 4.91 = 74 days). In comparison, Dell, Inc.'s accounts payable turnover is 3.85 times per year, or about every 95 days. The financial summary (Exhibit 13-8, line 46) shows that DPO has declined by about five days during the past four years, indicating that in 2012 Apple, Inc., is paying its suppliers about five days faster than it did in 2009.

Cash Conversion Cycle. By expressing the three turnover ratios in days, we can compute a company's **cash conversion cycle** as follows:

Formula			Apple, Inc.'s Cash Conversion Cycle	Competitor (Dell, Inc.)
Cash conversion cycle	=	DIO + DSO − DPO	3 + 19 − 74 = −52 days	−39 days
where DIO	=	Days' inventory outstanding		
DSO	=	Days' sales outstanding		
DPO	=	Days' payable outstanding		

At first glance, a negative amount for the cash conversion cycle looks odd. What does it mean? Apple, Inc., is in the enviable position of being able to sell inventory and collect from its customers 52 days before it has to pay its suppliers who provided the parts and materials to produce those inventories. This means that Apple can stock less inventory and hold onto cash longer than other companies. It also helps explain why the company could afford to keep over $18 billion in short-term marketable securities (Exhibit 13-10) to "sop up" its excess cash, using it to make still more money while waiting to pay off suppliers. According to Exhibit 13-8, line 47, Apple's negative cash conversion cycle has increased (become more favorable) by almost five days from 2009 through 2012. Apple's competitor, Dell, Inc., had a negative cash conversion cycle of −39 days in 2012.

Amazon.com, featured earlier in this chapter, also had a negative cash conversion cycle of about −33 days, whereas Barnes & Noble, a competitor of Amazon.com's, has a positive number because it has a much slower inventory turnover ratio than Amazon.com. Retail companies that have a more "normal" inventory turnover (about four times per year, or about every 90 days) have cash conversion cycles in the range of 30 to 60 days, depending on how long it takes to collect from customers. The cash conversion cycle for service-oriented businesses consists only of (DSO − DPO) because service businesses typically do not carry inventory.

Measuring Leverage: Overall Ability to Pay Debts

The ratios discussed so far relate to current assets and current liabilities. They measure the ability to sell inventory, collect receivables, and pay current bills. Two indicators of the ability to pay total liabilities are the debt ratio and the times-interest-earned ratio.

Debt Ratio. Suppose you are a bank loan officer and you have received loan applications for $500,000 from two similar companies. The first company already owes $600,000, and the second owes only $250,000. Which company gets the loan? Company 2 may look like the stronger candidate, because it owes less.

This relationship between total liabilities and total assets is called the **debt ratio**. Discussed in Chapters 3 and 9, the debt ratio tells us the proportion of assets financed with debt. A debt ratio of 1 reveals that debt has financed all the assets. A debt ratio of 0.50 means that debt finances half the assets. The higher the debt ratio, the greater the pressure to pay interest and principal. The lower the debt ratio, the lower the company's credit risk.

The debt ratios for Apple, Inc., in 2012 and 2011 follow ($ in millions):

Formula	Apple, Inc.'s Debt Ratio		Competitor (Dell, Inc.)
	2012	2011	
Debt ratio = $\dfrac{\text{Total liabilities}}{\text{Total assets}}$	$\dfrac{\$57,854}{\$176,064}$ = 0.33	$\dfrac{\$39,756}{\$116,371}$ = 0.34	0.78

This is an extremely low debt ratio, because of Apple, Inc.'s unusually healthy cash position described in the previous section. Exhibit 13-8 (line 37) shows that the debt ratio for Apple, Inc., has not exceeded 0.38 in the past five years. By contrast, notice that Dell, Inc., has a much higher debt ratio than Apple, Inc. The Risk Management Association reports that the average debt ratio for most companies ranges around 0.62, with relatively little variation from company to company. However, companies in certain industries such as airlines usually have higher debt ratios. The debt ratio is related to the leverage ratio discussed in the next section, which is used in DuPont Analysis to compute return on assets and return on equity.

Times-Interest-Earned Ratio. Analysts use a second ratio—the **times-interest-earned ratio** (introduced in Chapter 9)—to relate operating income to interest expense. To compute the times-interest-earned ratio, divide income from operations (operating income) by interest expense. This ratio measures the number of times operating income can *cover* interest expense and is also called the *interest-coverage ratio*. A high ratio indicates ease in paying interest; a low value suggests difficulty.

		Apple, Inc.'s Times-Interest-Earned Ratio		Competitor
	Formula	2012	2011	(Dell, Inc.)
Times-interest-earned ratio	$= \dfrac{\text{Income from operations}}{\text{Interest expense}}$	N/A	N/A	41.4

It is not possible to compute the times-interest-earned ratio for Apple, Inc., for one simple reason: The company has no interest-bearing debt. Why should it borrow money and pay interest, with so much cash on the balance sheet and the ability to generate cash from sales 52 days before having to pay creditors? From Exhibit 13-10, notice that $38 billion of the total $58 billion in liabilities is current, which is usually non-interest bearing. In addition, an examination of the financial statement footnotes reveals that of the $16.6 billion of "other non-current liabilities" none are interest bearing. Although Apple, Inc.'s competitor, Dell, Inc., has a relatively high debt ratio (0.78), its times-interest-earned ratio is quite high (41.4), meaning that Dell, Inc., is quite capable of servicing its interest payments. In contrast, in Chapter 9, we studied the financial statements of Southwest Airlines, with 4.2 times interest coverage, and United Continental with only 0.05 times interest coverage. In summary, the judgment about the adequacy of interest coverage, like so many other factors of financial statement analysis, is very much dependent on the industry, as well as the company being studied.

Measuring Profitability

The fundamental goal of business is to earn a profit, and so the ratios that measure profitability are reported widely.

Gross (Profit) Margin Percentage. In Chapter 6, we defined gross (profit) margin as net sales − cost of goods sold. That is, gross margin is the amount of profit that the entity makes from merely selling a product before other operating costs are subtracted. In Chapter 11, we emphasized that a persistently improving gross margin percentage is one important element of earnings quality. Let's look at Apple, Inc.'s gross margin percentages (see Exhibits 13-8 [line 7] and 13-9 for details):

		Apple, Inc.'s Gross Margin%		Competitor
	Formula	2012	2011	(Dell, Inc.)
Gross Margin %	$= \dfrac{\text{Gross margin}}{\text{Net sales}}$	43.9%	40.5%	21.4%

Apple is known as *the* innovator in the technology field. The company is constantly inventing new technology that people literally stand in line to purchase! Do you remember the last time you visited an Apple store (perhaps when a new version of the iPhone was introduced)? How much were you willing to pay for your new iPhone, iPad, or iMac? Do you remember how crowded the store was? As we discussed in Chapter 7, because of the creative talents of their people, some companies have been able to adopt a "product differentiation" business strategy, which allows them to sell their products for more than their competitors. When everyone wants the product, they are usually willing to pay more for it. As shown in Exhibit 13-8, line 7, Apple's gross margin percentage of 43.9% in 2012 is 3.4% greater in 2012 than it was in 2011, and 8.7% improved over fiscal 2008. This is quite an impressive number and is higher than that of any competitor. In contrast, Dell, Inc., with a 21.4% gross margin percentage, is known as a low-cost provider of computer equipment. Dell sells a lot of products, but it is usually not the first to introduce new products, so it has to sell products for lower prices, thus lowering its gross margin.

Operating Income (Profit) Percentage. Operating income (profit) percentage is net income from operations as a percentage of net sales. It is an important statistic, because it measures the percentage of profit earned from each sales dollar in a company's core business operations. In Chapter 11, we pointed out that a persistently high operating income compared to net sales is an important determinant of earnings quality. The first component of high operating earnings is a high gross margin percentage. After that, maximizing operating income depends on keeping operating costs as low as possible, given the level of desired product quality and customer service. Apple, Inc.'s operating income percentages, compared with Dell, Inc.'s, follow:

Formula	Apple, Inc.'s Operating Income %		Competitor (Dell, Inc.)
	2012	2011	
Operating Income % $=$ $\dfrac{\text{Operating Income}}{\text{Net sales}}$	35.3%	31.2%	5.3%

Apple is far ahead of the competition on earnings from its core operations and, according to Exhibit 13-8 (line 9), the company has improved the operating profit percentage from 22.2% to 35.3% over the past five years.

DuPont Analysis. In Chapters 7 (pp. 392–394) and 10 (pp. 575–577), we introduced **DuPont Analysis**, which is a detailed form of rate of return on total assets (ROA) and rate of return on common stockholders' equity (ROE). It might prove helpful to re-read those pages before you proceed with the following material. In Exhibit 13-11, we review the basic driver ratios for DuPont Analysis to provide a template for the analysis by component.

Exhibit 13-11 | DuPont Analysis Model

ROA			×	Leverage ratio (Equity multiplier)	=	ROE
Rate of return on sales (Net profit margin ratio)	× Asset turnover ratio	×		Leverage ratio (Equity multiplier)	=	Return on equity (ROE)
$\dfrac{\text{Net income*}}{\text{Net sales}}$	× $\dfrac{\text{Net sales}}{\text{Average total assets}}$		×	$\dfrac{\text{Average total assets}}{\text{Average common stockholders' equity}}$	=	$\dfrac{\text{Net income*}}{\text{Average common stockholders' equity}}$

*minus preferred dividends, if any

Notice that the ultimate goal of DuPont Analysis is to explain the rate of return on common stockholders' equity in a detailed fashion (far right-hand column) by breaking it down into its component elements: rate of return on sales, asset turnover, and leverage ratio. The first two components of the model combine to give rate of return on total assets (ROA). When the last component (leverage ratio) is incorporated into the model, it produces (by cross-cancellation) rate of return on common stockholders' equity (ROE). We now explain each component of the model, using figures for Apple, Inc., to illustrate.

Rate of Return (Net Profit Margin) on Sales. In business, *return* refers to profitability. Consider the **rate of return on net sales**, or simply *return on sales* (ROS). (The word *net* is usually omitted for convenience.) In Chapter 7, we referred to this ratio as *net profit margin ratio*. The initial element of DuPont Analysis, this ratio shows the percentage of each sales dollar earned as net income. The return-on-sales ratios for Apple, Inc., are as follows (using figures in millions from Exhibits 13-8 and 13-9):

		Apple, Inc.'s Rate of Return on Sales		Competitor (Dell, Inc.)
Formula		2012	2011	
Rate of return on sales (Net profit margin ratio)	$= \dfrac{\text{Net income} - \text{Preferred dividends}}{\text{Net sales}}$	$\dfrac{\$41,733}{\$156,508} = 26.7\%$	$\dfrac{\$25,922}{\$108,249} = 23.9\%$	4.2%

Companies strive for a high rate of return on sales. The higher the percentage, the more profit is being generated by sales dollars. Apple, Inc.'s return on sales is astoundingly high in 2012 (26.7%) and is over two percentage points higher than it was in 2011. According to Exhibit 13-8 (line 11), ROS for Apple has improved from 16.3% to 26.7% from 2008 through 2012. Compare Apple, Inc.'s rate of return on sales to the rates of some leading companies:

Company	Rate of Return on Sales
FedEx	5.6%
PepsiCo	11.9%
Intel	14.1%
Dell, Inc.	4.2%

Asset Turnover. As discussed in Chapter 7, **asset turnover** measures the amount of net sales generated for each dollar invested in assets. As such, it is a measure of how efficiently management is operating the company. Companies with high asset turnover tend to be more productive than companies with low asset turnover. Let's examine Apple, Inc.'s asset turnover for 2012 compared with 2011, and then compare it to competitor Dell, Inc.'s asset turnover (see Exhibit 13-8, line 28, for average total assets).

		Apple, Inc.'s Asset Turnover		Competitor (Dell, Inc.)
Formula		2012	2011	
Asset turnover ratio	$= \dfrac{\text{Net sales}}{\text{Average total Assets}}$	$\dfrac{\$156,508 \text{ million}}{\$146,218 \text{ million}} = 1.07$	$\dfrac{\$108,249 \text{ million}}{\$95,777 \text{ million}} = 1.13$	1.24

Compared to Dell, Apple has invested more in assets per dollar of sales. This is often the case with innovative companies, as opposed to companies that focus on low cost. To make major product innovations requires a significant investment in both tangible and intangible assets. So, while Apple, Inc., is significantly more profitable than Dell, Inc., it is less efficiently managed, at least by this measure.

Rate of Return on Total Assets (ROA). Having computed the "driver ratios" (rate of return on net sales and asset turnover), we are now prepared to combine them into the first two elements of DuPont Analysis to compute **rate of return on assets** (ROA):[3]

Rate of return on assets (ROA)	Apple, Inc.'s ROA		Competitor (Dell, Inc.)
	2012	2011	
Rate of return on sales	26.7%	23.9%	4.2%
×	×	×	×
Asset turnover ratio	1.07	1.13	1.24
=	=	=	=
ROA	28.6%	27.0%	5.2%

[3]Some analysts use net income before interest expense to compute ROA, since interest expense measures the return earned by creditors who provide the portion of total assets for which the company has used borrowed capital.

Again, the raw figures for our computations are based on income and asset figures from Exhibits 13-8 (line 12), 13-9, and 13-10, but the component ratios are based on the previous two illustrations. We see from these computations that for Apple, Inc., ROA is driven principally by its high profitability based on product differentiation, rather than efficiency. In contrast, Dell, Inc.'s ROA is based more on efficiency than profitability. Dell is a low-margin provider of basic computer technology, and as the low-cost provider, it is more efficient, generating more sales per dollar invested in total assets than Apple.

Leverage (Equity Multiplier) Ratio. The final element of DuPont Analysis is the **leverage ratio**, which measures the impact of debt financing on profitability. You learned in Chapters 9 and 10 that it can be advantageous to use borrowed capital to finance a business. Earlier, we expressed the debt ratio as the ratio of total liabilities to total assets. The leverage ratio, or equity multiplier, measures the proportion of each dollar of assets financed with stockholders' equity. Since Total assets − Stockholders' equity = Total liabilities, the leverage ratio is a way of inversely expressing the debt ratio—it merely looks at financing from the other side of the fundamental accounting equation. Let's examine Apple, Inc.'s leverage ratios for 2012 and 2011, compared with that of its competitor, Dell, Inc. (see Exhibit 13-8, line 28, for average total assets and line 39 for average stockholders' equity).

	Formula	Apple, Inc.'s Leverage Ratios		Competitor (Dell, Inc.)
		2012	2011	
Leverage ratio =	$\dfrac{\text{Average total assets}}{\text{Average common stockholders' equity}}$	$\dfrac{\$146{,}218 \text{ million}}{\$97{,}413 \text{ million}} = 1.50$	$\dfrac{\$95{,}777 \text{ million}}{\$62{,}203 \text{ million}} = 1.54$	4.693

As we pointed out earlier, Apple, Inc., has a comparatively low debt ratio (33% and 34% for 2012 and 2011, respectively). This translates to very low leverage ratios for Apple, Inc. (1.50 and 1.54 for 2012 and 2011, respectively). By comparison, Dell, Inc., has a comparatively high debt ratio (78% for 2012). Therefore, Dell uses much more borrowed capital than equity capital to finance its operations, and its leverage ratio is much higher (4.69).

Rate of Return on Common Stockholders' Equity (ROE). A popular measure of profitability is **rate of return on common stockholders' equity**, often shortened to *return on equity* (ROE). Also discussed in Chapter 10, this ratio shows the relationship between net income and common stockholders' investment in the company—how much income is earned for every $1 invested.

To compute this ratio by itself, first subtract preferred dividends, if any, from net income to measure income available to the common stockholders. Then divide income available to common stockholders by average common equity during the year. Common equity is total equity minus preferred equity. The vast majority of companies have no preferred equity, so common equity comprises the total. The 2012 return on common stockholders' equity, computed the traditional way, for Apple, Inc., is

	Formula	Apple, Inc.'s 2012 Rate of Return on Common Stockholders' Equity	Competitor (Dell, Inc.)
Rate of return on common stockholders' equity	$=\dfrac{\text{Net income} - \text{Preferred dividends}}{\text{Average common stockholders' equity}}$	$\dfrac{\$41{,}733 \text{ million} - \$0}{\$97{,}413 \text{ million}} = 42.8\%$	24.4%

DuPont Analysis ultimately reaches the same result (except for rounding error), but using it allows us to see much more information about the interaction between profitability (return on sales), asset utilization (turnover), and leverage:

Rate of Return on Stockholders' Equity (ROE)	*Apple, Inc.'s ROE* 2012	2011	Competitor (Dell, Inc.)
ROA	28.6%	27.0%	5.2%
×	×	×	×
Leverage ratio	1.50	1.54	4.69
=	=	=	=
ROE	42.9%	41.6%	24.4%

Apple, Inc., is by far a more profitable company than Dell, Inc. Dell is slightly more efficient in terms of asset turnover and more highly leveraged than Apple, having an asset turnover ratio of 1.2, a 78% debt ratio, and a leverage ratio of 4.69 ($4.69 of assets per dollar of stockholders' equity). To be sure, use of leverage is often a good thing, as long as it is kept within reasonable limits. The practice of using leverage is called **trading on the equity**, because it acts as a compounding factor for ROA. Companies like Dell that finance operations with debt are said to *leverage* their positions. However, Apple's superior profitability makes ROA, and also ROE, much higher. In fact, it is hard to find a company with higher ROE than Apple, Inc.

As we pointed out in Chapter 10, leverage can hurt ROE as well as help. If profits and cash flows decline, debts still must be paid. Therefore, leverage is a double-edged sword. It increases profits during good times but also magnifies losses during bad times.

Following are some recent ROE figures for a few other well-known companies:

Company	Rate of Return on Common Equity
General Electric..................	11.5%
Google..............................	19.2%
Starbucks	27.8%

Earnings per Share of Common Stock. As discussed in Chapters 9 and 11, *earnings per share of common stock*, or simply **earnings per share (EPS)**, is the amount of net income earned for each share of outstanding *common* stock. EPS is the most widely quoted of all financial statistics. It's the only ratio that appears on the income statement.

Earnings per share is computed by dividing net income available to common stockholders by the weighted average number of common shares outstanding during the year. Preferred dividends are subtracted from net income because the preferred stockholders have a prior claim to their dividends. Like most other companies, Apple, Inc., has no preferred stock and thus has no preferred dividends. The firm's EPS for 2012 and 2011 follow (based on Exhibits 13-8 (line 16) and 13-9):

	Formula	*Apple, Inc.'s Earnings per Share (Basic)* 2012	2011
Earnings per share of common stock	$= \dfrac{\text{Net income} - \text{Preferred dividends} \text{ (in thousands)}}{\text{Average number of shares of common stock outstanding (in thousands)}}$	$\dfrac{\$41,733,000 - \$0}{934,818} = \$44.64$	$\dfrac{\$25,922,000 - \$0}{924,258} = \$28.05$

Apple, Inc.'s EPS increased 59% ($44.64 vs. $28.05) during 2012, after an 82% increase ($28.05 vs. $15.41) during 2011. That's good news. In two years EPS for Apple, Inc. tripled! Such huge increases in earnings have certainly had an impact on the company's stock price. Apple, Inc., stockholders have been enjoying huge appreciation in their investment for several years. In mid-2013, the stock was selling for about $461 per share. That's tremendous appreciation if you had purchased the stock seven years ago, when it was selling for less than $100 per share. But the share price was over $700 in mid-2012. Shareholders who bought Apple, Inc.'s stock at that price were sorely disappointed by early 2013 after the stock lost 35% of its value. So with the stock fluctuating this wildly in price over a six-month period, would purchasing Apple, Inc., shares at $461 per share be a wise business decision? Where is the stock headed in 2014 and beyond? That's the relevant question to which a prospective stockholder wants an answer. The next section gives you some information on how analysts make this decision.

Analyzing Stock as an Investment

Investors buy stock to earn a return on their investment. This return consists of two parts: (1) gains (or losses) from selling the stock and (2) dividends.

Price-Earnings Ratio (Multiple). The **price-earnings ratio (multiple)** is the ratio of common stock price per share to earnings per share. This ratio, abbreviated P/E, appears in the *Wall Street Journal* stock listings and online. It shows the market price of $1 of earnings. Exhibit 13-8 (line 17) shows historical P/E multiples of Apple, Inc., stock at various times from 2009 through 2012.

Calculations for the P/E ratios of Apple, Inc., follow. The market price of Apple's common stock was $667.10 at September 29, 2012 (the end of its 2012 fiscal year), and $381.32 at September 24, 2011 (the end of its 2011 fiscal year). Stock prices can be obtained from a company's website or various other financial websites.

		Apple, Inc.'s Price/Earnings Ratio	
Formula		**2012**	**2011**
$\text{P/E ratio} = \dfrac{\text{Market price per share of common stock}}{\text{Earnings per share}}$		$\dfrac{\$667.10}{\$44.64} = 14.9$	$\dfrac{\$381.32}{\$28.05} = 13.6$

Given Apple, Inc.'s 2012 P/E ratio of 14.9, we would say that the company's stock is selling at 14.9 times earnings. Each $1 of Apple's earnings is worth $14.90 to the stock market.

Stocks trade in ranges, and public companies report updated EPS quarterly. These earnings are annualized and projected for the upcoming year (quarterly earnings multiplied by 4). Since Apple's yearly earnings were reported in 2012, its stock has traded in the range of $385 to $705 per share. Things change fast in the technology industry. New competitors, like Samsung, are threatening Apple with smart devices that perform comparably for a lower price. Apple's stock dropped drastically in price in late 2012, when first-quarter iPhone, iPad, and computer sales proved disappointing. Apple's gross margins plummeted, and its stock price with it, from $705 to $525 in a 60-day period.

Market prices of stocks are based on consensus estimations of what may happen in the future—business cycles, competition, government policies, new-product announcements, foreign trade deals, foreign currency fluctuations, and even the health of key company executives may significantly impact the estimates. Markets run on sentiment and are very difficult to predict. Some analysts study past trends in P/E multiples and try to estimate future trading ranges. If the P/E multiple of a particular stock drifts toward the low end of a range, and if its projected earnings are increasing, it means that the price of the stock is becoming more attractive, which is a signal to buy. As P/E multiples drift higher, given projected earnings, the stock becomes too expensive, and the analyst would recommend "hold" or "sell." Apple, Inc.'s historical P/E multiple on May 6, 2013, was 11.02 (stock price was $461.33 per share). The projected (forward) P/E multiple for Apple, Inc., from one popular website on that day was 10.47. Projected earnings per share for fiscal 2013 from the same website, based on the estimates of 57 stock analysts, were $39.76. Therefore, the projected price of Apple, Inc.'s stock as of September 2013 would be $416.29 (10.47 × $39.76). That would make Apple, Inc.'s shares appear overvalued at the price of $461.33 per share on May 6, 2013. Would you buy it?

Dividend Yield. **Dividend yield** is the ratio of dividends per share of stock to the stock's market price per share. This ratio measures the percentage of a stock's market value returned annually to the stockholders as dividends. Although dividends are never guaranteed, some well-established companies have continued to pay dividends even through turbulent economic times. *Preferred* stockholders pay special attention to this ratio because they invest primarily to receive dividends. However, certain companies, such as General Electric, **Merck Pharmaceuticals**, or IBM, also pay attractive dividends on their common stock. In periods of low interest rates on certificates of deposit or money-market funds, dividend-paying stocks become more attractive alternatives for conservative investors.

Because of its legendary profitability and phenomenal cash flows, Apple, Inc., paid the first quarterly dividend in its history ($2.65 per share) on August 16, 2012. In April 2013, the company announced it would increase the quarterly dividend to $3.05 per share ($12.20 per share per year). The company's board of directors also voted to return $100 billion to shareholders by 2015 in the form of dividend and stock repurchases (redemption of shares). On April 30, 2013, the company issued $17 billion in corporate bonds in order to finance these repurchases. This was the largest single bond issuance in history! Based on Apple, Inc.'s stock price of $442.78 on April 30, 2013, the dividend yield for shareholders on Apple, Inc.'s common stock on that date was

	Formula	*Dividend Yield on Apple, Inc. Common Stock*
		April 30, 2013
Dividend yield on common stock*	$= \dfrac{\text{Dividend per share of common stock}}{\text{Market price per share of common stock}}$	$\dfrac{\$12.20}{\$442.78} = 0.028$

*Dividend yields may also be calculated for preferred stock in a similar manner.

The company's dividend yield is about 2.8%. The company has pledged to issue quarterly dividends until its $100 billion promise has been fulfilled. If you think a dividend yield of 2.8% is low, you'd be correct but compared to current yields on certificates of deposit or bonds, it's pretty attractive. Dividend yields vary widely. They are generally higher for older, established firms (such as **Procter & Gamble** and General Electric) and lower to nonexistent for young, growth-oriented companies. Investors in Apple, Inc., have not historically purchased the stock for its dividend potential, because the stock is known for its capital appreciation. However, Apple, Inc.'s shareholders are now expecting both.

Book Value per Share of Common Stock. **Book value per share of common stock** is simply common stockholders' equity divided by the number of shares of common stock outstanding. Common equity equals total equity less preferred equity. Apple, Inc., has no preferred stock outstanding. Calculations of its book value per share of common follow. Numbers are based on Exhibit 13-10, using end-of-year number of shares outstanding.

	Formula (figures in thousands)	*Book Value per Share of Apple, Inc. Common Stock*	
		2012	2011
Book value per share of common stock	$= \dfrac{\text{Total stockholders' equity} - \text{Preferred equity}}{\text{Number of shares of common stock outstanding (basic)}}$	$\dfrac{\$118,210,000 - \$0}{939,208} = \$125.86$	$\dfrac{\$76,615,000 - \$0}{929,277} = \$82.45$

Book value per share indicates the recorded accounting amount for each share of common stock outstanding. Many experts believe book value is not useful for investment analysis because it bears no relationship to market value and provides little information beyond what's reported on the balance sheet. But some investors base their investment decisions on book value. For example, some investors rank stocks by the ratio of market price per share to book value per share. The lower the ratio, the more attractive the stock. These investors are called "value" investors, as contrasted with "growth" investors, who focus more on trends in net income.

What is the outlook for Apple, Inc.? Some have predicted that Apple has had its day and that the appeal of its stock may have peaked. But people have said that before about Apple, and they have been proven wrong because they failed to account for Apple's most valuable asset—its innovative and creative workforce. Apple's track record over the past five years is nothing short of astounding. Many people have made a lot of money from buying (and selling) its stock at the right time. Its earnings per share are solid, though perhaps on the decline in the short run, and its ROS, ROA, and ROE lead the industry. As of March 30, 2013, Apple had $40 billion in highly liquid assets on its books awaiting deployment in the creative process. In addition, the company has announced plans to distribute $100 billion to shareholders before 2015 in the form of dividends and share repurchases. From the standpoint of liquidity and leverage, the company is in stellar shape. It has a negative cash conversion cycle, meaning that it sells inventory and collects cash from customers weeks before accounts payable are due. As of the end of fiscal 2012, it had no interest-bearing debt and relatively little debt even after its issuance of corporate bonds in April of 2013. The company's recent P/E ratio of about 11 is relatively low.

Beyond that, Apple, Inc., is one of the largest, and perhaps the most innovative, companies in the world, continually producing new products that everyone wants. The future for the company in the "brave new world" of personal electronics depends on whether it can continue to provide the type of products that have so captured our fancy in the past. Stay tuned via your iPhone or iPad.

The Limitations of Ratio Analysis

Business decisions are made in a world of uncertainty. As useful as ratios are, they aren't a cure-all. Consider a physician's use of a thermometer. A reading of 102.0° Fahrenheit tells a doctor that something is wrong with the patient but doesn't indicate what the problem is or how to cure it.

In financial analysis, a sudden drop in the current ratio signals that *something* is wrong, but it doesn't identify the problem. A manager must analyze the figures to learn what caused the ratio to fall. A drop in current assets may mean a cash shortage or that sales are slow. The manager must evaluate all the ratios in the light of factors such as increased competition or a slowdown in the economy.

Legislation, international affairs, scandals, and other factors can turn profits into losses. To be useful, ratios should be analyzed over a period of years to consider all relevant factors. Any one year, or even any two years, may not represent the company's performance over the long term. The investment decision, whether in stocks, bonds, real estate, cash, or more exotic instruments, depends on one's tolerance for risk, and risk is the one factor that is always a certainty!

USE OTHER MEASURES TO MAKE INVESTMENT DECISIONS

Economic Value Added (EVA®)

The top managers of **Coca-Cola**, **Quaker Oats**, and other leading companies use **economic value added (EVA®)** to evaluate operating performance. EVA® combines accounting and finance to measure whether operations have increased stockholder wealth. EVA® can be computed as follows:

6 **Use** other measures to make investment decisions

$$EVA = \text{Net income before taxes} + \text{Interest expense} - \text{Capital charge}$$

$$\text{Capital charge} = \left(\begin{array}{c} \text{(Beginning balances)} \\ \text{Notes} + \begin{array}{c}\text{Current}\\\text{maturities}\\\text{of long-}\\\text{term debt}\end{array} + \begin{array}{c}\text{Long-term}\\\text{debt}\end{array} + \begin{array}{c}\text{Stockholders'}\\\text{equity}\end{array} \end{array} \right) \times \begin{array}{c}\text{Cost of}\\\text{capital}\end{array}$$

All amounts for the EVA® computation, except the cost of capital, come from the financial statements. The **weighted-average cost of capital**, discussed earlier in Chapter 11, is a weighted average of the returns demanded by the company's stockholders and lenders. Cost of capital varies with the company's level of risk. For example, stockholders would demand a higher return from a start-up company than from Amazon.com, Inc., because the new company is untested and therefore riskier. Lenders would also charge the new company a higher interest rate because of its greater risk. Thus, the new company has a higher cost of capital than Amazon.com, Inc.

The cost of capital is a major topic in finance classes. In the following discussions, we assume a value for the cost of capital (such as 10%, 12%, or 15%) to illustrate the computation of EVA®.

The idea behind EVA® is that the returns to the company's stockholders (net income) and to its creditors (interest expense) should exceed the company's capital charge. The **capital charge** is the amount that stockholders and lenders *charge* a company for the use of their money. A positive EVA® amount suggests an increase in stockholder wealth, and so the company's stock should remain attractive to investors. If EVA® is negative, stockholders will probably be unhappy with the company and sell its stock, resulting in a decrease in the stock's price. Different companies tailor the EVA® computation to meet their own needs.

Let's apply EVA® to Amazon.com, Inc. The company's EVA® for 2012 (see Exhibit 13-2 and Exhibit 13-3 for inputs) can be computed as follows, using net income before taxes (NIBT) and assuming an 8% weighted average cost of capital (dollars in millions):

				(Beginning balances)			
Amazon.com, Inc.'s EVA® =	NIBT	+ Interest expense	− [(Short-term borrowings	+ Long-term debt	+ Stockholders' equity	) ×	Cost of capital
=	\$544	+ \$92	− [(\$0	+ \$255	+ \$7,757	) ×	0.08]
=		\$636	−	\$8,012		×	0.08
=		\$636	−		\$641		
=			(\$5)				

By this measure, Amazon.com, Inc.'s operations subtracted \$5 million of value from its stockholders' wealth during 2012 after meeting the company's capital charge. This performance is considered relatively weak.

Red Flags in Financial Statement Analysis

Recent accounting scandals have highlighted the importance of *red flags* in financial analysis. The following conditions may mean a company is very risky:

- *Earnings problems.* Have income from continuing operations and net income decreased for several years in a row? Has income turned into a loss? This may be okay for a company in a cyclical industry, such as an airline or a home builder, but a company such as Amazon.com, Inc., may be unable to survive consecutive loss years.

- *Decreased cash flow.* Cash flow validates earnings. Is net cash provided by operations consistently lower than net income? Are the sales of plant assets a major source of cash? If so, the company may be facing a cash shortage.

- *Too much debt.* How does the company's debt ratio compare to that of major competitors and to the industry average? If the debt ratio is much higher than average, the company may be unable to pay debts during tough times. As we saw earlier, Apple, Inc.'s debt ratio of 33% in 2012 was much lower than Dell's 78% debt ratio.

- *Inability to collect receivables.* Are days' sales in receivables growing faster than for other companies in the industry? A cash shortage may be looming. Apple, Inc.'s cash collections from customers are very strong.

- *Buildup of inventories.* Is inventory turnover slowing down? If so, the company may be unable to move products, or it may be overstating inventory as reported on the balance sheet. Recall from the cost-of-goods-sold model that one of the easiest ways to overstate net income is to overstate ending inventory. Apple, Inc., has no problem here.

■ *Trends of sales, inventory, and receivables.* Sales, receivables, and inventory generally move together. Increased sales lead to higher receivables and require more inventory in order to meet demand. Strange movements among these items may spell trouble. Apple, Inc.'s relationships look normal.

Efficient Markets

An **efficient capital market** is one in which market prices fully reflect all information available to the public. Because stock prices reflect all publicly accessible data, it can be argued that the stock market is efficient. Market efficiency has implications for management action and for investor decisions. It means that managers cannot fool the market with accounting gimmicks. If the information is available, the market as a whole can set a "fair" price for the company's stock.

Suppose you are the president of Vitacomp Corporation. Reported earnings per share are $2, and the stock price is $40—so the P/E ratio is 20. You believe Vitacomp's stock is underpriced. To correct this situation, you are considering changing your depreciation method from accelerated to straight-line. The accounting change will increase earnings per share to $3. Will the stock price then rise to $60? Probably not; the company's stock price will probably remain at $40 because the market can understand the accounting change. After all, the company merely changed its method of computing depreciation. There is no effect on Vitacomp's cash flows, and the company's economic position is unchanged. An efficient market interprets data in light of their true underlying meaning.

In an efficient market, the search for "underpriced" stock is fruitless unless the investor has relevant *private* information. But it is unlawful as well as unethical to invest on the basis of *inside* information. An appropriate strategy seeks to manage risk, diversify investments, and minimize transaction costs. Financial analysis helps mainly to identify the risks of various stocks and then to manage the risk.

The Decision Guidelines feature summarizes the most widely used ratios.

▶ Decision Guidelines

USING RATIOS IN FINANCIAL STATEMENT ANALYSIS

Bobby and Kaye Simpson operate a financial services firm. They manage other people's money and do most of their own financial statement analysis. How do they measure companies' ability to pay bills, sell inventory, collect receivables, and so on? They use the standard ratios we have covered throughout this book.

Ratio	Computation	Information Provided
Measuring ability to pay current liabilities:		
1. Current ratio	$\dfrac{\text{Current assets}}{\text{Current liabilities}}$	Measures ability to pay current liabilities with current assets
2. Quick (acid-test) ratio	$\dfrac{\substack{\text{Cash and} \\ \text{cash equivalents}} + \substack{\text{Short-term} \\ \text{investments}} + \substack{\text{Net current} \\ \text{receivables}}}{\text{Current liabilities}}$	Shows ability to pay all current liabilities if they come due immediately

Ratio	Computation	Information Provided
Measuring turnover and cash conversion:		
3. Inventory turnover and days' inventory outstanding (DIO)	$$\text{Inventory turnover} = \frac{\text{Cost of goods sold}}{\text{Average inventory}}$$ $$\text{Days' inventory outstanding (DIO)} = \frac{365}{\text{Inventory turnover}}$$	Indicates salability of inventory—the number of times a company sells its average level of inventory during a year. DIO converts inventory turnover to number of days it takes to sell average inventory.
4. Accounts receivable turnover	$$\frac{\text{Net credit sales}}{\text{Average net accounts receivable}}$$	Measures ability to collect cash from credit customers
5. Days' sales in receivables or days' sales outstanding (DSO)	$$\frac{\text{Average net accounts receivable}}{\text{Average daily sales}}$$ or $$\frac{365}{\text{Accounts receivable turnover}}$$	Shows how many days' sales remain in Accounts Receivable—how many days it takes to collect the average level of receivables
6. Accounts payable turnover and days' payable outstanding (DPO)	$$\text{Accounts payable turnover} = \frac{\text{Cost of goods sold}}{\text{Average accounts payable}}$$ Days' payable outstanding (DPO) = 365/Accounts payable turnover	Shows how many times a year accounts payable turn over and how many days it takes the company to pay off accounts payable
7. Cash conversion cycle	Cash conversion cycle = DIO + DSO − DPO where DIO = Days' inventory outstanding DSO = Days' sales outstanding DPO = Days' payable outstanding	Shows overall liquidity by computing the total days it takes to convert inventory to receivables and back to cash, less the days to pay off its suppliers
Measuring ability to pay long-term debt:		
8. Debt ratio	$$\frac{\text{Total liabilities}}{\text{Total assets}}$$	Indicates percentage of assets financed with debt
9. Times-interest-earned ratio	$$\frac{\text{Income from operations}}{\text{Interest expense}}$$	Measures the number of times operating income can cover interest expense
Measuring profitability:		
10. Gross margin %	$$\frac{\text{Gross margin}}{\text{Net sales}}$$	Shows the percentage of profit that a company makes from merely selling the product, before any other operating costs are subtracted
11. Operating income %	$$\frac{\text{Income from operations}}{\text{Net sales}}$$	Shows the percentage of profit earned from each dollar of sales in the company's core business, after operating costs have been subtracted

Ratio	Computation	Information Provided
12. DuPont model	Exhibit 13-11	A detailed analysis of return on assets (ROA) and return on common stockholders' equity (ROE)
13. Rate of return on net sales	$$\frac{\text{Net income} - \text{Preferred dividends}}{\text{Net sales}}$$	Shows the percentage of each sales dollar earned as net income
14. Asset turnover ratio	$$\frac{\text{Net sales}}{\text{Average total assets}}$$	Measures the amount of net sales generated for each dollar invested in assets
15. Rate of return on total assets	DuPont method: Rate of return on net sales $\times$ Asset turnover $\quad$ or $\quad$ $\dfrac{\text{Net income} - \text{Preferred dividends}}{\text{Average total assets}}$	Measures how profitably a company uses its assets
16. Leverage ratio	$$\frac{\text{Average total assets}}{\text{Average common stockholders' equity}}$$	Otherwise known as the *equity multiplier*, measures the ratio of average total assets to average common stockholders' equity
17. Rate of return on common stockholders' equity	DuPont method: ROA $\times$ Leverage ratio $\quad$ or $\quad$ $\dfrac{\text{Net income} - \text{Preferred dividends}}{\text{Average common stockholders' equity}}$	Measures how much income is earned for every dollar invested by the company's common shareholders
18. Earnings per share of common stock	$$\frac{\text{Net income} - \text{Preferred dividends}}{\text{Average number of shares of common stock outstanding}}$$	Measures the amount of net income earned for each share of the company's common stock outstanding

Analyzing stock as an investment:

Ratio	Computation	Information Provided
19. Price-earnings ratio	$$\frac{\text{Market price per share of common stock}}{\text{Earnings per share}}$$	Indicates the market price of $1 of earnings
20. Dividend yield	$$\frac{\text{Dividend per share of common (or preferred) stock}}{\text{Market price per share of common (or preferred) stock}}$$	Shows the percentage of a stock's market value returned as dividends to stockholders each period
21. Book value per share of common stock	$$\frac{\text{Total stockholders' equity} - \text{Preferred equity}}{\text{Number of shares of common stock outstanding}}$$	Indicates the recorded accounting amount for each share of common stock outstanding

End-of-Chapter Summary Problems

The following financial data are adapted from the annual reports of Lear Corporation:

A1						
	A	**B**	**C**	**D**	**E**
1	**Lear Corporation** **Four-Year Selected Financial Data** **Years Ended January 31, 2014, 2013, 2012, and 2011**				
2	**Operating Results***	**2014**	**2013**	**2012**	**2011**
3	**Net Sales**	$ 13,848	$ 13,673	$ 11,635	$ 9,054
4	Cost of goods sold	8,715	8,599	6,775	5,318
5	Interest expense	109	75	45	46
6	Income from operations	1,675	1,445	1,817	1,333
7	Net earnings (net loss)	1,450	877	1,127	824
8	Cash dividends	76	75	76	77
9					
10	**Financial Position**				
11	Merchandise inventory	1,550	1,904	1,462	1,056
12	Total assets	7,591	7,012	5,189	3,963
13	Current ratio	1.48	0.95	1.25	1.20
14	Stockholders' equity	3,010	2,928	2,630	1,574
15	Average number of shares of				
16	common stock outstanding				
17	(in thousands)	850	879	895	576
18					

*Dollar amounts are in thousands.

Requirement

1. Compute the following ratios for 2012 through 2014, and evaluate Lear's operating results. Use the DuPont formula for ROA and ROE. Are operating results strong or weak? Did they improve or deteriorate during the three-year period?

   a. Inventory turnover

   b. Gross margin (profit) percentage

   c. Operating income (profit) percentage

   d. Rate of return on sales

   e. Asset turnover

   f. Rate of return on assets

   g. Leverage ratio

   h. Rate of return on stockholders' equity

   i. Times interest earned

   j. Earnings per share

Answer

	2014	2013	2012
a. Inventory turnover	$\dfrac{\$8,715}{(\$1,550 + \$1,904)/2} = 5.05$ times	$\dfrac{\$8,599}{(\$1,904 + \$1,462)/2} = 5.1$ times	$\dfrac{\$6,775}{(\$1,462 + \$1,056)/2} = 5.4$ times
b. Gross profit percentage	$\dfrac{\$13,848 - \$8,715}{\$13,848} = 37.1\%$	$\dfrac{\$13,673 - \$8,599}{\$13,673} = 37.1\%$	$\dfrac{\$11,635 - \$6,775}{\$11,635} = 41.8\%$
c. Operating income percentage	$\dfrac{\$1,675}{\$13,848} = 12.1\%$	$\dfrac{\$1,445}{\$13,673} = 10.6\%$	$\dfrac{\$1,817}{\$11,635} = 15.6\%$
d. Rate of return on sales	$\dfrac{\$1,450}{\$13,848} = 10.5\%$	$\dfrac{\$877}{\$13,673} = 6.4\%$	$\dfrac{\$1,127}{\$11,635} = 9.7\%$
e. Asset turnover	$\dfrac{\$13,848}{(\$7,591 + \$7,012)/2} = 1.897$	$\dfrac{\$13,673}{(\$7,012 + \$5,189)/2} = 2.241$	$\dfrac{\$11,635}{(\$5,189 + \$3,963)/2} = 2.543$
f. Rate of return on assets*	$10.5\% \times 1.897 = 19.9\%$	$6.4\% \times 2.241 = 14.3\%$	$9.7\% \times 2.543 = 24.7\%$
g. Leverage ratio	$\dfrac{\$7,301.50}{(\$3,010 + \$2,928)/2} = 2.459$	$\dfrac{\$6,100.50}{(\$2,928 + \$2,630)/2} = 2.195$	$\dfrac{\$4,576}{(\$2,630 + \$1,574)/2} = 2.177$
h. Rate of return on stockholders' equity*	$19.9\% \times 2.459 = 48.9\%$	$14.3\% \times 2.195 = 31.4\%$	$24.7\% \times 2.177 = 53.8\%$
i. Times-interest-earned ratio	$\dfrac{\$1,675}{\$109} = 15.4$ times	$\dfrac{\$1,445}{\$75} = 19.3$ times	$\dfrac{\$1,817}{\$45} = 40.4$ times
j. Earnings per share	$\dfrac{\$1,450}{850} = \$1.71$	$\dfrac{\$877}{879} = \$1.00$	$\dfrac{\$1,127}{895} = \$1.26$

* Used DuPont model in Exhibit 13-11.

Evaluation: After dipping a little in 2013, some of Lear's operating results started to recover in 2014. The gross profit percentage is consistent with 2013, and operating income percentage and all the return measures are improving in 2014. Asset turnover has fallen a little, but rate of return on assets is headed in the right direction because of the increases in profitability that the company has experienced over 2014. The final result in 2014 was a healthy net income and earnings per share for the year. This yielded a positive ROA and, because of leverage, an even more positive ROE.

REVIEW | Financial Statement Analysis

Quick Check (Answers are given at the end of the chapter.)

Analyze Clarke Company's financial statements by answering the questions that follow. Clarke owns a chain of restaurants.

	A1	B	C
	A	**B**	**C**
1	**Clarke Company** **Consolidated Statements of Income (Adapted)** **Years Ended December 31, 2014 and 2013**		
2	**(In millions, except per share data)**	**2014**	**2013**
3	Revenues		
4	Sales by Company-operated restaurants	$ 17,100	11,800
5	Revenues from franchised and affiliated restaurants	4,800	3,900
6	Total revenues	21,900	15,700
7	Food and paper (Cost of goods sold)	5,130	3,304
8	Payroll and employee benefits	3,800	3,500
9	Occupancy and other operating expenses	3,300	3,400
10	Franchised restaurants—occupancy expenses	947	845
11	Selling, general, and administrative expenses	1,825	1,720
12	Other operating expense, net	525	830
13	Total operating expenses	15,527	13,599
14	Operating income	6,373	2,101
15	Interest expense	340	350
16	Other nonoperating expense, net	92	63
17	Income before income taxes	5,941	1,688
18	Income tax expense	2,376	675
19	Net income	$ 3,565	$ 1,013
20	Per common share basic:		
21	Net income	$ 5.09	$ 1.69
22	Dividends per common share	$ 0.65	$ 0.40
23			

A1	⬥		
	A	**B**	**C**
1	**Clarke Company** **Consolidated Balance Sheets** **December 31, 2014 and 2013**		
2	**(In millions, except per share data)**	**2014**	**2013**
3	**Assets**		
4	Current assets:		
5	Cash and equivalents	$ 605	$ 420
6	Accounts and notes receivable	760	920
7	Inventories, at cost, not in excess of market	110	160
8	Prepaid expense and other current assets	570	390
9	Total current assets	2,045	1,890
10	**Property and equipment:**		
11	Property and equipment, at cost	28,710	26,400
12	Accumulated depreciation and amortization	(8,800)	(7,700)
13	Net property and equipment	19,910	18,700
14	**Other assets:**		
15	Investments in affiliates	1,160	1,019
16	Goodwill, net	1,790	1,520
17	Miscellaneous	970	1,090
18	Total other assets	3,920	3,629
19	Total assets	$ 25,875	$ 24,219
20	**Liabilities and Stockholders' Equity**		
21	Current liabilities:		
22	Accounts payable	$ 610	$ 615
23	Income taxes	75	17
24	Other taxes	230	190
25	Accrued interest	195	192
26	Accrued restructuring and restaurant closing costs	125	325
27	Accrued payroll and other liabilities	924	715
28	Current maturities of long-term debt	386	305
29	Total current liabilities	2,545	2,359
30	Long-term debt	8,700	9,700
31	Other long-term liabilities and minority interests	670	560
32	Deferred income taxes	995	995
33	**Total liabilities**	$ 12,910	$ 13,614
34	**Stockholders' equity:**		
35	Preferred stock, no par value; authorized—140.0 million shares;		
36	issued—none	—	—
37	Common stock, $0.01 par value; authorized—2.0 billion shares;		
38	issued—1,300 million shares	13	13
39	Additional paid-in capital	465	1,479
40	Unearned ESOP compensation	(88)	(97)
41	Retained earnings	22,910	19,800
42	Accumulated other comprehensive income (loss)	(845)	(1,600)
43	Common stock in treasury, at cost; 600 and 700 million shares	(9,490)	(8,990)
44	Total stockholders' equity	12,965	10,605
45	Total liabilities and stockholders' equity	$ 25,875	$ 24,219
46			

1. Horizontal analysis of Clarke's income statement for 2014 would show which of the following for Selling, General, and Administrative expenses?
   a. 0.94
   b. 0.08
   c. 6.1%
   d. None of the above

2. Vertical analysis of Clarke's income statement for 2014 would show which of the following for Selling, General, and Administrative expenses (use total revenues as the base)?

   a. 8.33%

   b. 11.80%

   c. 10.70%

   d. None of the above

3. Which item on Clarke's income statement has the most favorable trend during 2013–2014?

   a. Total revenues

   b. Payroll and employee benefits

   c. Food and paper costs

   d. Net income

4. On Clarke's common-size balance sheet for 2014, Goodwill would appear as

   a. up by 17.8%.

   b. 8.17% of total revenues.

   c. 6.9%.

   d. $1,790 million.

5. A good benchmark for Clarke Company would be

   a. Whataburger.

   b. Volvo.

   c. Microsoft.

   d. all of the above.

6. Clarke's inventory turnover for 2014 was

   a. 15 times.

   b. 38 times.

   c. 91 times.

   d. 61 times.

7. Clarke's quick (acid-test) ratio at the end of 2014 was

   a. 0.804.

   b. 0.54.

   c. 2.24.

   d. 0.05.

8. In 2014, using total revenues, Clarke's average collection period for accounts and notes receivable is

   a. 14 days.

   b. 2 days.

   c. 1 day.

   d. 32 days.

9. The average debt ratio for most companies is around 0.61. In 2014, Clarke's total debt position looks

   a. risky.

   b. middle-ground.

   c. safe.

   d. Cannot tell from the financial statements

10. Clarke's return on total revenues for 2014 is

    a. 13.78%.

    b. $5.09.

    c. $1.16.

    d. 16.3%.

11. Clarke's return on stockholders' equity for 2014 is

    a. 16.3%.

    b. 13.78%.

    c. $3,565 million.

    d. 30.3%.

12. On December 31, 2014, Clarke's common stock sold for $26 per share. At that price, how much did investors say $1 of the company's net income was worth?

    a. $0.14

    b. $26.00

    c. $5.11

    d. $1.00

13. On December 31, 2014, Clarke's common stock sold for $26 per share, and dividends per share were $0.65. Compute Clarke's dividend yield during 2014.

    a. 0.7%

    b. 2.5%

    c. 6.5%

    d. 5.7%

14. How much EVA® did Clarke generate for investors during 2014? Assume the cost of capital was 10%.

    a. $4,220 million

    b. $1,700 million

    c. $3,905 million

    d. $3,565 million

Accounting Vocabulary

accounts payable turnover (p. 764) Measures the number of times per year a company pays off its accounts payable. Assuming all purchases are on credit, to compute accounts payable turnover, divide purchases (cost of goods sold + ending inventory − beginning inventory) by average accounts payable. When inventories are immaterial, or when there is very little difference between beginning and ending inventories, substitute cost of goods sold for purchases.

accounts receivable turnover (p. 763) Measures a company's ability to collect cash from credit customers. To compute accounts receivable turnover, divide net credit sales by average net accounts receivable.

acid-test ratio (p. 762) Ratio of the sum of cash plus short-term investments plus net current receivables to total current liabilities. Tells whether the entity can pay all its current liabilities if they come due immediately. Also called the *quick ratio.*

asset turnover (p. 768) The dollars of sales generated per dollar of assets invested. Formula is Net sales ÷ Average total assets.

benchmarking (p. 753) The comparison of a company to a standard set by other companies, with a view toward improvement.

book value per share of common stock (p. 772) Common stockholders' equity divided by the number of shares of common stock outstanding. The recorded amount for each share of common stock outstanding.

capital charge (p. 774) The amount that stockholders and lenders charge a company for the use of their money. Calculated as (Notes payable + Loans payable + Long-term debt + Stockholders' equity) × Cost of capital.

cash conversion cycle (p. 765) The number of days it takes to convert inventory to receivables, and receivables into cash, after paying off payables. The formula is Days' inventory outstanding + Days' sales outstanding − Days' payables outstanding.

common-size statement (p. 752) A financial statement that reports only percentages (no dollar amounts).

current ratio (p. 760) Current assets divided by current liabilities. Measures a company's ability to pay current liabilities with current assets.

days' sales in receivables (p. 764) Ratio of average net accounts receivable to one day's sales. Indicates how many days' sales remain in Accounts Receivable awaiting collection. Also called the *collection period* and *days' sales outstanding.*

debt ratio (p. 765) Ratio of total liabilities to total assets. States the proportion of a company's assets that is financed with debt.

dividend yield (p. 771) Ratio of dividends per share of stock to the stock's market price per share. Tells the percentage of a stock's market value that the company returns to stockholders as dividends.

DuPont Analysis (p. 767) Detailed method of analyzing rate of return on common stockholders' equity. Rate of return on sales × Asset turnover × Leverage = Return on average common stockholders' equity.

earnings per share (EPS) (p. 770) Amount of a company's net income earned for each share of its outstanding common stock.

economic value added (EVA®) (p. 773) Used to evaluate a company's operating performance. EVA® combines the concepts of accounting income and corporate finance to measure whether the company's operations have increased stockholder wealth. EVA® = Net income + Interest expense − Capital charge.

efficient capital market (p. 775) A capital market in which market prices fully reflect all information available to the public.

horizontal analysis (p. 743) Study of percentage changes in line items on comparative financial statements.

inventory turnover (p. 762) Ratio of cost of goods sold to average inventory. Indicates how rapidly inventory is sold.

leverage ratio (p. 769) Ratio of average total assets to average common stockholders' equity. Measures the proportion of average total assets actually owned by the stockholders.

price-earnings ratio (p. 771) Ratio of the market price of a share of common stock to the company's earnings per share. Measures the value that the stock market places on $1 of a company's earnings.

quick (acid-test) ratio (p. 762) Another name for the *acid-test ratio.*

rate of return on common stockholders' equity (p. 769) Net income minus preferred dividends, divided by average common stockholders' equity. A measure of profitability. Also called *return on equity.* Also can be computed with DuPont Analysis.

rate of return on assets (p. 768) Net income − preferred dividends ÷ average total assets. This ratio measures a company's success in using its assets to earn income for the persons who finance the business. Also called *return on total assets.* Can also be computed using the first two elements of DuPont Analysis (Rate of return on net sales × Asset turnover).

rate of return on net sales (p. 767) Ratio of net income − preferred dividends to net sales. A measure of profitability. Also called *return on sales.*

times-interest-earned ratio (p. 766) Ratio of income from operations to interest expense. Measures the number of times that operating income can cover interest expense. Also called the *interest-coverage ratio.*

trading on the equity (p. 770) Another name for *leverage.*

trend percentages (p. 748) A form of horizontal analysis that indicates the direction a business is taking.

vertical analysis (p. 749) Analysis of a financial statement that reveals the relationship of each statement item to a specified base, which is the 100% figure.

weighted-average cost of capital (p. 773) A weighted average of the returns demanded by the company's stockholders and lenders. Often referred to as the *weighted-average cost of capital (WACC).*

working capital (p. 759) Current assets minus current liabilities; measures a business's ability to meet its short-term obligations with its current assets. Also called *net working capital.*

ASSESS YOUR PROGRESS

Short Exercises

S13-1. *(Learning Objective 1: Perform horizontal analysis of revenues and net income)* Celebrate! Corporation reported the following amounts on its 2014 comparative income statements:

(In thousands)	2014	2013	2012
Revenues	$20,289	$20,045	$18,449
Total expenses	10,915	10,338	10,100

Perform a horizontal analysis of revenues and net income—both in dollar amounts and in percentages—for 2014 and 2013.

S13-2. *(Learning Objective 1: Perform trend analysis of sales and net income)* Abbey, Inc., reported the following sales and net income amounts:

(In thousands)	2014	2013	2012	2011
Sales	$9,960	$9,260	$8,790	$8,410
Net income	670	500	480	432

Show Abbey's trend percentages for sales and net income. Use 2011 as the base year.

S13-3. *(Learning Objective 2: Perform vertical analysis to correct a cash shortage)* Robbles Software reported the following amounts on its balance sheets at December 31, 2014, 2013, and 2012:

	2014	2013	2012
Cash	$ 19,200	$ 13,600	$ 11,340
Receivables, net	34,700	20,800	23,900
Inventory	266,800	197,600	148,180
Prepaid expenses	34,900	41,600	33,460
Property, plant, and equipment, net	220,400	244,400	258,120
Total assets	$576,000	$518,000	$475,000

Sales and profits are high. Nevertheless, Robbles is experiencing a cash shortage. Perform a vertical analysis of Robbles Software's assets at the end of years 2014, 2013, and 2012. Use the analysis to explain the reason for the cash shortage.

S13-4. *(Learning Objective 3: Compare common-size income statements of two companies)* Kraft, Inc., and Claire Corporation are competitors. Compare the two companies by converting their condensed income statements to common size.

(In millions)	Kraft	Claire
Net sales..	$18,700	$7,869
Cost of goods sold...	10,573	4,965
Selling and administrative expenses................	4,895	1,521
Interest expense..	53	23
Other expenses...	89	38
Income tax expense	730	250
Net income..	$ 2,360	$1,072

Which company earned more net income? Which company's net income was a higher percentage of its net sales? Explain your answer.

S13-5. *(Learning Objective 5: Evaluate the trend in a company's current ratio)* Examine the financial data of Armistead Corporation.

Year Ended December 31	2014	2013	2012
Operating Results			
Net income..	$ 250	$ 340	$ 342
Earnings per common share	$1.37	$1.68	$1.99
Net income as a percent of sales..........................	19.9%	17.9%	19.3%
Return on average stockholders' equity................	21.0	18.0	19.0
Financial Position			
Current assets..	$ 610	$ 517	$ 465
Current liabilities	$ 382	$ 353	$ 359
Working capital	$ 228	$ 164	$ 106
Current ratio...	1.60	1.46	1.30

Show how to compute Armistead's current ratio for each year 2012 through 2014. Is the company's ability to pay its current liabilities improving or deteriorating?

S13-6. *(Learning Objective 5: Evaluate a company's quick (acid-test) ratio)* Use the AJ Cardenas, Inc., balance sheet data on the following page.
1. Compute AJ Cardenas, Inc.'s quick (acid-test) ratio at December 31, 2014, and 2013.
2. Use the comparative information from the table on the bottom of page 786 for Baker, Inc., Colvin Company, and Dunn Companies Limited. Is AJ Cardenas, Inc.'s quick (acid-test) ratio for 2014 and 2013 strong, average, or weak in comparison?

	A	B	C	D	E
	A1 ⬦				
1	AJ Cardenas, Inc. Balance Sheets (Adapted) December 31, 2014 and 2013				
2				Increase (Decrease)	
3	(Dollar amounts in millions)	2014	2013	Amount	Percentage
4	Assets				
5	Current assets:				
6	Cash and cash equivalents	$ 1,240	$ 900	$ 340	37.8%
7	Short-term investments	6	70	(64)	(91.4)
8	Receivables, net	230	250	(20)	(8.0)
9	Inventories	96	81	15	18.5
10	Prepaid expenses and other assets	243	363	(120)	(33.1)
11	Total current assets	1,815	1,664	151	9.1
12	Property, plant, and equipment, net	3,611	3,376	235	7.0
13	Intangible assets	1,011	878	133	15.1
14	Other assets	828	722	106	14.7
15	Total assets	$ 7,265	$ 6,640	$ 625	9.4%
16	Liabilities and Stockholders' Equity				
17	Current liabilities:				
18	Accounts payable	$ 1,000	$ 900	$ 100	11.1%
19	Income tax payable	39	61	(22)	(36.1)
20	Short-term debt	118	111	7	6.3
21	Other	70	73	(3)	(4.1)
22	Total current liabilities	1,227	1,145	82	7.2
23	Long-term debt	3,500	2,944	556	18.9
24	Other liabilities	1,117	1,036	81	7.8
25	Total liabilities	5,844	5,125	719	14.0
26	Stockholders' equity:				
27	Common stock	2	2	—	—
28	Retained earnings	1,573	1,689	(116)	(6.9)
29	Accumulated other comprehensive (loss)	(154)	(176)	22	(12.5)
30	Total stockholders' equity	1,421	1,515	(94)	(6.2)
31	Total liabilities and stockholders' equity	$ 7,265	$ 6,640	$ 625	9.4%
32					

Company	Quick (acid-test) Ratio
Baker, Inc. (Utility)...	0.74
Colvin Company (Department store)	1.06
Dunn Companies Limited (Grocery store)..............	1.09

S13-7. *(Learning Objective 5: Compute and evaluate turnover and the cash conversion cycle)* Use the AJ Cardenas 2014 income statement that follows and the balance sheet from S13-6 to compute the following:

A1		
	A	**B**	**C**

	A	B	C
1	**AJ Cardenas, Inc.** **Statements of Income (Adapted)** **Year Ended December 31, 2014 and 2013**		
2	(Dollar amounts in millions)	**2014**	**2013**
3	Revenues	$ 9,840	$ 9,309
4	Expenses:		
5	Food and paper (Cost of goods sold)	2,639	2,644
6	Payroll and employee benefits	2,138	2,211
7	Occupancy and other operating expenses	2,413	2,375
8	General and administrative expenses	1,217	1,148
9	Interest expense	184	117
10	Other expense (income), net	19	(34)
11	Income before income taxes	1,230	848
12	Income tax expense	385	267
13	Net income	$ 845	$ 581
14			

    a. AJ Cardenas Inc.'s rate of inventory turnover and days' inventory outstanding for 2014.

    b. Days' sales in average receivables (days' sales outstanding) during 2014 (round dollar amounts to one decimal place).

    c. Accounts payable turnover and days' payables outstanding for 2014. For this purpose, assume that the impact of inventories on cost of goods sold is immaterial, allowing you to use cost of goods sold rather than purchases in your computations.

    d. Length of cash conversion cycle in days for 2014.

Do these measures look strong or weak? Give the reason for your answer.

S13-8. *(Learning Objective 5: Measure ability to pay long-term debt)* Use the financial statements of AJ Cardenas, Inc., in S13-6 and S13-7.

    1. Compute the company's debt ratio at December 31, 2014.

    2. Compute the company's times-interest-earned ratio for 2014. For operating income, use income before both interest expense and income taxes. You can simply add interest expense back to income before taxes.

    3. Is AJ Cardenas's ability to pay liabilities and interest expense strong or weak? Comment on the value of each ratio computed for questions 1 and 2.

S13-9. *(Learning Objective 5: Measure profitability using DuPont Analysis)* Use the financial statements of AJ Cardenas, Inc., in S13-6 and S13-7 to compute these profitability measures for 2014. Show each computation.

    a. Rate of return on sales

    b. Asset turnover ratio

    c. Rate of return on total assets

    d. Leverage (equity multiplier) ratio

    e. Rate of return on common stockholders' equity

    f. Is AJ Cardenas, Inc.'s profitability strong, medium, or weak?

S13-10. *(Learning Objective 5: Compute EPS and the price-earnings ratio)* The annual report of Redd Cars, Inc., for the year ended December 31, 2014, included the following items (in millions):

Preferred stock outstanding, 3%	$700
Net income..	$620
Average number of shares of common stock outstanding...	700

1. Compute earnings per share (EPS) and the price-earnings ratio for Redd Cars' stock. Round to the nearest cent. The price of a share of Redd Car stock is $11.83.
2. How much does the stock market say $1 of Redd Cars' net income is worth?

S13-11. *(Learning Objective 5: Use ratio data to reconstruct an income statement)* A skeleton of Kathey's Florals' income statement appears as follows (amounts in thousands):

	A	B
1	**Income Statement**	
2	Net sales	$ 7,300
3	Cost of goods sold	(a)
4	Selling expenses	1,502
5	Administrative expenses	1,330
6	Interest expense	(b)
7	Other expenses	156
8	Income before taxes	1,038
9	Income tax expense	(c)
10	Net income	$ (d)
11		

Use the following ratio data to complete Kathey's Florals' income statement:
   a. Inventory turnover was 3 (beginning inventory was $800; ending inventory was $772).
   b. Rate of return on sales (after income taxes) is 0.08.

S13-12. *(Learning Objective 5: Use ratio data to reconstruct a balance sheet)* A skeleton of Kathey's Florals' balance sheet appears as follows (amounts in thousands):

	A	B	C	D
1	**Balance Sheet**			
2	Cash	$ 260	Total current liabilities	$ 2,100
3	Receivables	(a)	Long-term debt	(e)
4	Inventories	1,374	Other long-term liabilities	920
5	Prepaid expenses	(b)		
6	Total current assets	(c)		
7	Plant assets, net	(d)	Common stock	200
8	Other assets	2,375	Retained earnings	2,814
9	Total assets	$ 6,850	Total liabilities and equity	$ (f)
10				

Use the following ratio data to complete Kathey's Florals' balance sheet:
   a. Debt ratio is 0.56.
   b. Current ratio is 1.20.
   c. Quick (acid-test) ratio is 0.460.

S13-13. *(Learning Objective 5: Analyze a company based on its ratios)* Take the role of an investment analyst at Cole Binder. It is your job to recommend investments for your client. The only information you have is the following ratio values for two companies in the graphics software industry:

Ratio	Tower.org	Graphics Imaging
Days' sales in receivables............................	41	48
Inventory turnover......................................	7	11
Gross profit percentage	67%	58%
Net income as a percent of sales................	12%	13%
Times interest earned	19	13
Return on equity...	35%	30%
Return on assets...	14%	19%

Write a report to the Cole Binder investment committee. Recommend one company's stock over the other. State the reasons for your recommendation.

S13-14. *(Learning Objective 6: Measure economic value added)* Compute economic value added (EVA®) for Schaeffer Software. The company's cost of capital is 4%. Net income was $761 thousand, interest expense $401 thousand, beginning long-term debt $620 thousand, and beginning stockholders' equity was $3,010 thousand. Round all amounts to the nearest thousand dollars. Should the company's stockholders be happy with the EVA®?

Exercises

All of the A and B exercises can be found within MyAccountingLab, an online home-work and practice environment. Your instructor may ask you to complete these exercises using **MyAccountingLab**.

MyAccountingLab

Group A

E13-15A. *(Learning Objective 1: Compute year-to-year changes in working capital)* What were the dollar amount of change and the percentage of each change in Winding Lane Lodge's working capital during 2014 and 2013? Is this trend favorable or unfavorable?

	2014	2013	2012
Total current assets	$330,000	$291,000	$260,000
Total current liabilities	156,000	148,000	130,000

E13-16A. *(Learning Objective 1: Perform horizontal analysis of an income statement)* Prepare a horizontal analysis of the comparative income statements of Garza Music Co. Round percentage changes to the nearest one-tenth percent (three decimal places).

	A	B	C
A1			
1	**Garza Music Co.** **Comparative Income Statements** **Years Ended December 31, 2014 and 2013**		
2		**2014**	**2013**
3	Total revenue	$ 971,000	$ 868,000
4	Expenses:		
5	Cost of goods sold	$ 437,000	$ 408,750
6	Selling and general expenses	287,000	265,000
7	Interest expense	23,500	13,500
8	Income tax expense	105,500	84,650
9	Total expenses	853,000	771,900
10	Net income	$ 118,000	$ 96,100
11			

E13-17A. *(Learning Objective 1: Compute trend percentages)* Compute trend percentages for Overland Valley Sales & Service's total revenue and net income for the following five-year period, using year 0 as the base year. Round to the nearest full percent.

(In thousands)	Year 4	Year 3	Year 2	Year 1	Year 0
Total revenue	$1,365	$1,242	$1,102	$1,001	$1,024
Net income	128	109	105	97	86

Which grew faster during the period, total revenue or net income?

E13-18A. *(Learning Objective 2: Perform vertical analysis of a balance sheet)* Patterson Golf Company has requested that you perform a vertical analysis of its balance sheet to determine the component percentages of its assets, liabilities, and stockholders' equity.

	A	B
A1		
	Patterson Golf Company **Balance Sheet** **December 31, 2014**	
1		
2	**Assets**	
3	Total current assets	$ 63,000
4	Property, plant, and equipment, net	206,000
5	Other assets	40,000
6	Total assets	$ 309,000
7		
8	**Liabilities**	
9	Total current liabilities	$ 49,000
10	Long-term debt	107,000
11	Total liabilities	156,000
12		
13	**Stockholders' Equity**	
14	Total stockholders' equity	153,000
15	Total liabilities and stockholders' equity	$ 309,000
16		

E13-19A. *(Learning Objective 3: Prepare a common-size income statement)* Prepare a comparative common-size income statement for Garza Music Co., using the 2014 and 2013 data of E13-16A and rounding to four decimal places.

E13-20A. *(Learning Objective 4: Analyze the statement of cash flows)* Identify any weaknesses revealed by the statement of cash flows of Michigan Apple Farms, Inc.

	A	B	C
A1			
1	**Michigan Apple Farms, Inc.** **Statement of Cash Flows** **For the Current Year**		
2	**Operating activities:**		
3	Net income		$ 72,100
4	Add (subtract) noncash items:		
5	Depreciation	$ 11,250	
6	Net increase in current assets other than cash	(53,500)	
7	Net decrease in current liabilities		
8	exclusive of short-term debt	(19,750)	(62,000)
9	Net cash provided by operating activities		10,100
10			
11	**Investing activities:**		
12	Sale of property, plant, and equipment		124,200
13			
14	**Financing activities:**		
15	Issuance of bonds payable	$ 117,050	
16	Payment of short-term debt	(180,525)	
17	Payment of long-term debt	(89,025)	
18	Payment of dividends	(39,500)	
19	Net cash used for financing activities		(192,000)
20	Increase (decrease) in cash		$ (57,700)
21			

E13-21A. *(Learning Objective 5: Compute ratios; evaluate turnover, liquidity, and current debt–paying ability)* The financial statements of Big City News, Inc., include the following items:

	2014	2013	2012
Balance sheet:			
Cash	$ 48,000	$ 84,000	
Short-term investments	17,000	21,000	
Net receivables	72,000	75,000	55,000
Inventory......................................	85,000	72,000	60,000
Prepaid expenses..........................	8,000	6,000	
Total current assets	230,000	258,000	
Accounts payable..........................	75,000	65,000	50,000
Total current liabilities.................	131,000	94,000	
Income statement:			
Net credit sales	$484,000	$507,000	
Cost of goods sold	266,000	254,000	

Requirements

1. Using Exhibit 13-8 as a model, compute the following ratios for 2014 and 2013:
   a. Current ratio
   b. Quick (acid-test) ratio
   c. Inventory turnover and days' inventory outstanding (DIO)
   d. Accounts receivable turnover
   e. Days' sales in average receivables or days' sales outstanding (DSO)
   f. Accounts payable turnover and days' payable outstanding (DPO). Use cost of goods sold in the formula for accounts payable turnover
   g. Cash conversion cycle (in days)

(When computing days, round your answer to the nearest whole number.)

2. Evaluate the company's liquidity and current debt-paying ability for 2014. Has it improved or deteriorated from 2013?

3. As a manager of this company, what would you try to improve next year?

E13-22A. *(Learning Objective 6: Analyze the ability to pay liabilities)* LA Furniture Company has requested that you determine whether the company's ability to pay its current liabilities and long-term debts improved or deteriorated during 2014. To answer this question, compute the following ratios for 2014 and 2013:

  a. Working capital
  b. Current ratio
  c. Quick (acid-test) ratio
  d. Debt ratio
  e. Times-interest-earned ratio

Use Exhibit 13-8 as a model. Round your answers to two decimal places. Summarize the results of your analysis in a short paragraph.

	2014	2013
Cash	$ 51,000	$ 47,000
Short-term investments	28,000	27,000
Net receivables	114,000	126,000
Inventory	236,000	265,000
Prepaid expenses	22,000	8,000
Total assets	518,000	535,000
Total current liabilities	224,000	262,000
Long-term debt	97,000	174,000
Income from operations	261,000	150,000
Interest expense	41,000	42,000

E13-23A. *(Learning Objective 5: Analyze profitability)* For 2014 and 2013, compute return on sales (ROS), asset turnover (AT), return on assets (ROA), leverage (L), return on common stockholders' equity (ROE), gross profit percentage (GP), operating income percentage (OI), and earnings per share (EPS) to measure the ability to earn profits for Hearth & Home Decor, Inc., whose comparative income statements follow. Use DuPont Analysis for ROA and ROE, and round each component ratio to three decimals; for other ratio computations, round to two decimals.

	A	B	C
	A1		
1	Hearth and Home Decor, Inc. Comparative Income Statements Years Ended December 31, 2014 and 2013		
2		2014	2013
3	Net sales	$ 263,000	$ 199,000
4	Cost of goods sold	131,000	97,000
5	Gross profit	132,000	102,000
6	Selling and general expenses	55,000	48,000
7	Income from operations	77,000	54,000
8	Interest expense	14,000	18,000
9	Income before income tax	63,000	36,000
10	Income tax expense	21,000	13,000
11	Net income	$ 42,000	$ 23,000
12			

Additional data:

	2014	2013	2012
Total assets..	$390,000	$365,000	$350,000
Common stockholders' equity................	$196,000	$194,000	$192,000
Preferred dividends................................	$ 2,000	$ 1,000	$ 0
Average common shares outstanding			
during the year	15,000	14,000	13,000

Did the company's operating performance improve or deteriorate during 2014?

E13-24A. *(Learning Objectives 5, 6: Evaluate a stock as an investment)* Evaluate the common stock of Nate Distributing Company as an investment. Specifically, use the three common stock ratios to determine whether the common stock increased or decreased in attractiveness during the past year. Round calculations and your final answer to three decimal places.

	2014	2013
Net income...	$ 84,000	$ 93,000
Dividends to common	28,000	16,000
Total stockholders' equity at year-end................	580,000	500,000
(includes 92,000 shares of common stock)		
Preferred stock, 10%...	115,000	115,000
Market price per share of common		
stock at year-end	$ 19.50	$ 11.50

E13-25A. *(Learning Objective 6: Use economic value added to measure corporate performance)* Two companies with different economic-value-added (EVA®) profiles are Dakota Oil Pipeline, Inc., and Arkansas Bank Limited. Adapted versions of the two companies' financial statements are presented here (in millions):

	Dakota Oil Pipeline, Inc.	Arkansas Bank Limited
Balance sheet data (beginning of year):		
Total assets	$ 4,331	$13,403
Interest-bearing debt	$ 1,244	$ 7
All other liabilities...........................	2,550	2,575
Stockholders' equity.........................	537	10,821
Total liabilities and equity...............	$ 4,331	$13,403
Income statement data:		
Total revenue	$10,772	$ 4,000
Interest expense...............................	83	1
Net income.......................................	$ 200	$ 1,706

Requirements

1. Before performing any calculations, which company do you think represents the better investment? Give your reason.
2. Compute the EVA® for each company, and then decide which company's stock you would rather hold as an investment. Assume that both companies' cost of capital is 9.0%.

Group B

E13-26B. *(Learning Objective 1: Compute year-to-year changes in working capital)* What were the dollar amount of change and the percentage of each change in Oak Hill Lodge's working capital during 2014 and 2013? Is this trend favorable or unfavorable?

	2014	2013	2012
Total current assets	$60,000	$215,000	$250,000
Total current liabilities	25,000	108,000	125,000

E13-27B. *(Learning Objective 1: Perform horizontal analysis of an income statement)* Prepare a horizontal analysis of the comparative income statements of Murillo Music Co. Round percentage changes to the nearest one-tenth percent (three decimal places).

A1	◆		
	A	B	C
1	Murillo Music Co. Comparative Income Statements Years Ended December 31, 2014 and 2013		
2		2014	2013
3	Total revenue	$ 839,000	$ 897,000
4	Expenses:		
5	Cost of goods sold	$ 401,000	$ 400,000
6	Selling and general expenses	234,000	263,000
7	Interest expense	9,300	12,000
8	Income tax expense	84,000	86,000
9	Total expenses	728,300	761,000
10	Net income	$ 110,700	$ 136,000
11			

E13-28B. *(Learning Objective 1: Compute trend percentages)* Compute trend percentages for Pecan Valley Sales & Service's total revenue and net income for the following five-year period, using year 0 as the base year. Round to the nearest full percent.

(In thousands)	Year 4	Year 3	Year 2	Year 1	Year 0
Total revenue	$1,328	$1,206	$1,043	$1,001	$1,022
Net income	120	113	99	95	90

Which grew faster during the period, total revenue or net income?

E13-29B. *(Learning Objective 2: Perform vertical analysis of a balance sheet)* VanKlief Golf Company has requested that you perform a vertical analysis of its balance sheet to determine the component percentages of its assets, liabilities, and stockholders' equity.

	A	B
1	**VanKlief Golf Company** **Balance Sheet** **December 31, 2014**	
2	**Assets**	
3	Total current assets	$ 65,000
4	Property, plant, and equipment, net	199,000
5	Other assets	37,000
6	Total assets	$ 301,000
7		
8	**Liabilities**	
9	Total current liabilities	$ 51,000
10	Long-term debt	102,000
11	Total liabilities	153,000
12		
13	**Stockholders' Equity**	
14	Total stockholders' equity	148,000
15	Total liabilities and stockholders' equity	$ 301,000
16		

E13-30B. *(Learning Objective 3: Prepare a common-size income statement)* Prepare a comparative common-size income statement for Murillo Music Co. using the 2014 and 2013 data of E13-27B and rounding to four decimal places.

E13-31B. *(Learning Objective 4: Analyze the statement of cash flows)* Identify any weaknesses revealed by the statement of cash flows of California Oranges, Inc.

	A	B	C
1	**California Oranges, Inc.** **Statement of Cash Flows** **For the Current Year**		
2	**Operating activities:**		
3	Net income		$ 104,000
4	Add (subtract) noncash items:		
5	Depreciation	$ 32,000	
6	Net increase in current assets other than cash	(65,000)	
7	Net decrease in current liabilities		
8	exclusive of short-term debt	(44,000)	(77,000)
9	Net cash provided by operating activities		27,000
10			
11	**Investing activities:**		
12	Sale of property, plant, and equipment		151,000
13			
14	**Financing activities:**		
15	Issuance of bonds payable	$ 110,000	
16	Payment of short-term debt	(186,000)	
17	Payment of long-term debt	(101,000)	
18	Payment of dividends	(56,000)	
19	Net cash used for financing activities		(233,000)
20	Increase (decrease) in cash		$ (55,000)
21			

E13-32B. *(Learning Objective 5: Compute ratios; evaluate turnover, liquidity, and current debt-paying ability)* The financial statements of Omni News, Inc., include the following items:

	2014	2013	2012
Balance sheet:			
Cash	$ 34,000	$ 40,000	
Short-term investments	12,000	23,000	
Net receivables	68,000	71,000	60,000
Inventory......................................	86,000	77,000	62,000
Prepaid expenses..........................	11,000	5,000	
Total current assets	211,000	216,000	
Accounts payable..........................	80,000	65,000	50,000
Total current liabilities.................	133,000	96,000	
Income statement:			
Net credit sales	$481,000	$509,000	
Cost of goods sold	267,000	254,000	

Requirements

1. Using Exhibit 13-8 as a model, compute the following ratios for 2014 and 2013:
   a. Current ratio
   b. Quick (acid-test) ratio
   c. Inventory turnover and days' inventory outstanding (DIO)
   d. Accounts receivable turnover
   e. Days' sales in average receivables or days' sales outstanding (DSO)
   f. Accounts payable turnover and days' payable outstanding (DPO). Use cost of goods sold in the formula for accounts payable turnover
   g. Cash conversion cycle (in days)

When computing days, round your answer to the nearest whole number.

2. Evaluate the company's liquidity and current debt-paying ability for 2014. Has it improved or deteriorated from 2013?
3. As a manager of this company, what would you try to improve next year?

E13-33B. *(Learning Objective 5: Analyze the ability to pay liabilities)* NY Furniture Company has requested that you determine whether the company's ability to pay its current liabilities and long-term debts improved or deteriorated during 2014. To answer this question, compute the following ratios for 2014 and 2013. Use Exhibit 13-8 as a model. Round your answers to two decimal places.
   a. Working capital
   b. Current ratio
   c. Quick (acid-test) ratio
   d. Debt ratio
   e. Times-interest-earned ratio

Summarize the results of your analysis in a short paragraph.

	2014	2013
Cash	$ 42,000	$ 48,000
Short-term investments.................	31,000	6,000
Net receivables............................	118,000	125,000
Inventory.....................................	235,000	261,000
Prepaid expenses	15,000	5,000
Total assets.................................	572,000	534,000
Total current liabilities	249,000	151,000
Long-term debt	87,000	255,000
Income from operations	210,000	199,000
Interest expense..........................	38,000	40,000

E13-34B. *(Learning Objective 5: Analyze profitability)* For 2014 and 2013, compute return on sales (ROS), asset turnover (AT), return on assets (ROA), leverage (L), return on common stockholders' equity (ROE), gross profit percentage (GP), operating income percentage (OI), and earnings per share (EPS) to measure the ability to earn profits of Yard & Garden Decor, Inc., whose comparative income statements follow (use DuPont Analysis for ROA and ROE, and round each component ratio to three decimals; for other ratio computations, round to two decimals):

A1			
	A	**B**	**C**
1	**Yard and Garden Decor, Inc.** **Comparative Income Statements** **Years Ended December 31, 2014 and 2013**		
2		**2014**	**2013**
3	Net sales	$ 363,000	$ 290,000
4	Cost of goods sold	175,000	139,000
5	Gross profit	188,000	151,000
6	Selling and general expenses	100,000	94,000
7	Income from operations	88,000	57,000
8	Interest expense	13,000	10,000
9	Income before income tax	75,000	47,000
10	Income tax expense	26,000	11,000
11	Net income	$ 49,000	$ 36,000
12			

Additional data:

	2014	2013	2012
Total assets	$408,000	$402,000	$398,000
Common stockholders' equity	$149,000	$140,000	$131,000
Preferred dividends	$ 11,000	$ 9,000	$ 7,000
Average common shares outstanding during the year	20,000	15,000	5,000

Did the company's operating performance improve or deteriorate during 2014?

E13-35B. *(Learning Objectives 5, 6: Evaluate a stock as an investment)* Evaluate the common stock of Mark Distributing Company as an investment. Specifically, use the three common stock ratios to determine whether the common stock increased or decreased in attractiveness during the past year. Round calculations and your final answer to three decimal places.

	2014	2013
Net income..	$ 143,000	$ 97,000
Dividends to common	23,000	19,000
Total stockholders' equity at year-end...............	550,000	500,000
(includes 92,000 shares of common stock)		
Preferred stock, 6%..	170,000	110,000
Market price per share of common		
stock at year-end	$ 17.50	$ 12.25

E13-36B. *(Learning Objective 6: Use economic value added to measure corporate performance)*
Two companies with different economic-value-added (EVA®) profiles are Carolina Oil Pipeline, Inc., and Indiana Bank Limited. Adapted versions of the two companies' financial statements are presented here (in millions):

(In millions)	Carolina Oil Pipeline, Inc.	Indiana Bank Limited
Balance sheet data (beginning of year):		
Total assets	$ 4,353	$14,200
Interest-bearing debt	$ 1,246	$ 17
All other liabilities............................	2,800	2,605
Stockholders' equity.........................	307	11,578
Total liabilities and equity................	$ 4,353	$14,200
Income statement data:		
Total revenue	$10,807	$ 3,697
Interest expense................................	77	8
Net income.......................................	$ 195	$ 1,496

Requirements

1. Before performing any calculations, which company do you think represents the better investment? Give your reason.
2. Compute the EVA® for each company, and then decide which company's stock you would
   rather hold as an investment. Assume that both companies' cost of capital is 9.5%. (Round
   your EVA® calculation to the nearest whole number.)

Quiz

Use the Gateway Medical Corporation financial statements that follow to answer questions 13-37 through 13-48.

A1	⬍		
	A	**B**	**C**
1	**Gateway Medical Corporation** **Consolidated Statements of Financial Position**		
2		December 31,	
3	(In Millions)	**2014**	**2013**
4	**Assets:**		
5	Current Assets		
6	Cash and cash equivalents	$ 4,333	$ 4,226
7	Accounts and notes receivable	3,400	2,403
8	Short-term investments	845	520
9	Inventories, at cost	433	411
10	Prepaid expense and other current assets	1,638	1,226
11	Total current assets	10,649	8,786
12	Property and equipment, net	1,555	907
13	Investments	6,804	5,199
14	Other non-current assets	303	155
15	Total assets	$ 19,311	$ 15,047
16	**Liabilities and stockholders' equity:**		
17	Current liabilities		
18	Accounts payable	$ 7,708	$ 6,009
19	Accrued and other liabilities	3,676	3,033
20	Total current liabilities	11,384	9,042
21	Long-term debt	304	305
22	Other non-current liabilities	1,701	1,179
23	Total liabilities	13,389	10,526
24	Stockholders' equity		
25	Preferred stock and capital in excess of $0.02 par value;		
26	shares issued and outstanding: none	—	—
27	Common stock and capital in excess of $0.05 par value;		
28	shares authorized: 6,000; shares issued: 2,163 and		
29	1,903, respectively	7,803	7,001
30	Treasury stock, at cost: 183 and 123 shares, respectively	(6,444)	(4,401)
31	Retained earnings	4,676	1,990
32	Other comprehensive loss	(79)	(25)
33	Other	(34)	(44)
34	Total stockholders' equity	5,922	4,521
35	Total liabilities and stockholders' equity	$ 19,311	$ 15,047
36			

	A	B	C	D
1	**Gateway Medical Corporation** **Consolidated Statements of Income**			
2		**Year ended December 31,**		
3	**(In Millions, Except per Share Amounts)**	**2014**	**2013**	**2012**
4	Net Revenue	$ 42,666	$ 35,220	$ 31,111
5	Cost of goods sold	35,147	29,255	25,492
6	Gross profit	7,519	5,965	5,619
7	Operating expenses:			
8	Selling, general, and administrative	3,341	3,250	2,985
9	Research, development, and engineering	544	553	536
10	Special charges	—	—	512
11	Total operating expenses	3,885	3,803	4,033
12	Operating income	3,634	2,162	1,586
13	Investment and other income (loss), net	153	196	(30)
14	Income before income taxes	3,787	2,358	1,556
15	Income tax expense	1,136	940	472
16	Net income	$ 2,651	$ 1,418	$ 1,084
17	Earnings per common share:			
18	Basic	$ 1.41	$ 0.95	$ 0.37
19				

Q13-37. During 2014, Gateway Medical's total assets
   a. increased by $1,863 million.
   b. increased by 28.3%.
   c. Both a and b.
   d. increased by 22.1%.

Q13-38. Gateway Medical's current ratio at year-end 2014 is closest to
   a. $735.
   b. 22.1.
   c. 0.94.
   d. 1.2.

Q13-39. Gateway Medical's quick (acid-test) ratio at year-end 2014 is closest to
   a. 0.68.
   b. $8,578 million.
   c. 0.45.
   d. 0.75.

Q13-40. What is the largest single item included in Gateway Medical's debt ratio at December 31, 2014?
   a. Accounts payable
   b. Common stock
   c. Cash and cash equivalents
   d. Investments

Q13-41. Using the earliest year available as the base year, the trend percentage for Gateway Medical's net revenue during 2014 was
   a. 121%.
   b. up by 21.1%.
   c. up by $11,555 million.
   d. 137%.

Q13-42. Gateway Medical's common-size income statement for 2014 would report cost of goods sold as
   a. 82.4%.
   b. $35,147 million.
   c. up by 20.1%.
   d. 137.9%.

Q13-43. Gateway Medical's days' sales in receivables during 2014 was
   a. 137.9 days.
   b. 25 days.
   c. 35 days.
   d. 20.1 days.

Q13-44. Gateway Medical's inventory turnover during fiscal year 2014 was
   a. $35,147.
   b. very slow.
   c. 83 times.
   d. 137.9 times.

Q13-45. Gateway Medical's long-term debt bears interest at 11%. During the year ended December 31, 2014, Gateway's times-interest-earned ratio was

a. 137.9 times.
b. $35,147.

c. 20.1 times.
d. 108 times.

Q13-46. Gateway Medical's trend of return on sales is

a. improving.
b. declining.

c. stuck at 22.1%.
d. worrisome.

Q13-47. How many shares of common stock did Gateway Medical have outstanding, on average, during 2014? (*Hint*: Compute earnings per share.)

a. 137.9 million
b. 1,880 million

c. 20.1 million
d. 35,147 million

Q13-48. Book value per share of Gateway Medical's common stock outstanding at December 31, 2014, was

a. 137.9.
b. $35,147.

c. $2.99.
d. 20.1.

Problems

All of the A and B exercises can be found within MyAccountingLab, an online home-work and practice environment. Your instructor may ask you to complete these exercises using **MyAccountingLab**.

MyAccountingLab

Group A

P13-49A. *(Learning Objectives 1, 5: Compute trend percentages, return on sales, asset turnover, and ROA, and compare with industry)* Net sales, net income, and total assets for Westover Shipping, Inc., for a five-year period follow:

(In thousands)	2014	2013	2012	2011	2010
Net sales...	$510	$400	$362	$314	$296
Net income.......................................	53	47	50	37	24
Total assets......................................	297	269	246	231	209

Requirements

1. Compute trend percentages for each item for 2011 through 2014. Use 2010 as the base year, and round to the nearest percent.
2. Compute the rate of return on net sales for 2012 through 2014, rounding to three decimal places. Explain what this means.
3. Compute asset turnover for 2012 through 2014. Explain what this means.
4. Use DuPont Analysis to compute rate of return on average total assets (ROA) for 2012 through 2014.
5. How does Westover Shipping's return on net sales for 2014 compare with previous years? How does it compare with that of the industry? In the shipping industry, rates above 9% are considered good, and rates above 11% are outstanding.
6. Evaluate Westover Shipping, Inc.'s ROA for 2014, compared with previous years, and against an 18% benchmark for the industry.

P13-50A. *(Learning Objectives 3, 5: Prepare common-size statements; analyze profitability; make comparisons with the industry)* Top managers of CC Oliver Products, Inc., have asked for your help in comparing the company's profit performance and financial position with the average for the industry. The accountant has given you the company's income statement and balance sheet and also the following data for the industry:

	A1			B	C
	A			**B**	**C**
1	**CC Oliver Products, Inc.** **Income Statement Compared with Industry Average** **Year Ended December 31, 2014**				
2				**C.C. Oliver**	**Industry Average**
3	Net sales			$ 960,000	100.0%
4	Cost of goods sold			662,400	57.3
5	Gross profit			297,600	42.7
6	Operating expenses			220,800	29.4
7	Operating income			76,800	13.3
8	Other expenses			9,600	2.5
9	Net income			$ 67,200	10.8%
10					

	A1			B	C
	A			**B**	**C**
1	**CC Oliver Products, Inc.** **Balance Sheet Compared with Industry Average** **December 31, 2014**				
2				**C.C. Oliver**	**Industry Average**
3	Current assets			$ 292,000	72.1%
4	Fixed assets, net			72,800	19.0
5	Intangible assets, net			14,000	4.8
6	Other assets			21,200	4.1
7	Total			$ 400,000	100.0%
8					
9	Current liabilities			$ 188,000	47.2%
10	Long-term liabilities			84,000	21.0
11	Stockholders' equity			128,000	31.8
12	Total			$ 400,000	100.0%
13					

Requirements

1. Prepare a common-size income statement and balance sheet for CC Oliver Products. The first column of each statement should present CC Oliver Products' common-size statement, and the second column should show the industry averages.

2. For the profitability analysis, compare CC Oliver Products' (a) ratio of gross profit to net sales, (b) ratio of operating income to net sales, and (c) ratio of net income to net sales with the industry averages. Is CC Oliver Products' profit performance better or worse than the average for the industry?

3. For the analysis of financial position, compute CC Oliver Products' (a) ratios of current assets and current liabilities to total assets and (b) ratio of stockholders' equity to total assets. Compare these ratios with the industry averages. Is CC Oliver Products' financial position better or worse than the average for the industry?

P13-51A. *(Learning Objective 4: Use the statement of cash flows for decision making)* You are evaluating two companies as possible investments. The two companies, which are similar in size, are commuter airlines that fly passengers up and down the West Coast. All other available information has been analyzed, and your investment decision depends on the statements of cash flows.

A1				
	A	**B**	**C**	**D**	**E**

West Coast Airlines
Statements of Cash Flows
Years Ended November 30, 2015 and 2014

	A	B	C	D	E
1					
2			2015		2014
3	Operating activities:				
4	Net income (net loss)		$ (63,000)		$ 160,000
5	Adjustments for noncash items:				
6	Total		79,000		(13,000)
7	Net cash provided by operating activities		16,000		147,000
8					
9	Investing activities:				
10	Purchase of property, plant,				
11	and equipment	$ (67,000)		$ (140,000)	
12	Sale of long-term investments	58,000		9,000	
13	Net cash provided by (used for)				
14	investing activities		(9,000)		(131,000)
15					
16	Financing activities:				
17	Issuance of short-term notes payable	$ 198,000		$ 218,000	
18	Payment of short-term notes payable	(246,000)		(183,000)	
19	Payment of cash dividends	(51,000)		(92,000)	
20	Net cash provided (used) by financing activities		(99,000)		(57,000)
21	Increase (decrease) in cash		$ (92,000)		$ (41,000)
22	Cash balance at beginning of year		106,000		147,000
23	Cash balance at end of year		$ 14,000		$ 106,000
24					

Holiday Flights, Inc.
Statements of Cash Flows
Years Ended September 30, 2015 and 2014

	A	B	C	D	E
1					
2			2015		2014
3	Operating activities:				
4	Net income		$ 264,000		$ 193,000
5	Adjustments for noncash items:				
6	Total		67,000		79,000
7	Net cash provided by operating activities		331,000		272,000
8					
9	Investing activities:				
10	Purchase of property, plant,				
11	and equipment	$ (395,000)		$ (610,000)	
12	Sale of property, plant, and equipment	69,000		119,000	
13	Net cash used for investing activities		(326,000)		(491,000)
14					
15	Financing activities:				
16	Issuance of long-term notes payable	$ 198,000		$ 131,000	
17	Payment of short-term notes payable	(95,000)		(26,000)	
18	Net cash provided by financing activities		103,000		105,000
19	Increase (decrease) in cash		$ 108,000		$ (114,000)
20	Cash balance at beginning of year		176,000		290,000
21	Cash balance at end of year		$ 284,000		$ 176,000
22					
23					
24					

Requirement

1. Discuss the relative strengths and weaknesses of West Coast Airlines and Holiday Flights, Inc. Conclude your discussion by recommending one of the companies' stocks as an investment.

P13-52A. *(Learning Objective 5: Compute effects of business transactions on selected ratios)* Financial statement data of Whitworth Engineering include the following items:

Cash	$ 23,000	Accounts payable	$107,000
Short-term investments	36,000	Accrued liabilities	35,000
Accounts receivable, net	87,000	Long-term notes payable	163,000
Inventories	141,000	Other long-term liabilities	33,000
Prepaid expenses	4,000	Net income	95,000
Total assets	675,000	Number of common	
Short-term notes payable	42,000	shares outstanding	51,000

Requirements

1. Compute Whitworth's current ratio, debt ratio, and earnings per share. Round all ratios to two decimal places.
2. Compute the three ratios after evaluating the effect of each transaction that follows. Consider each transaction *separately*.
   a. Borrowed $150,000 on a long-term note payable
   b. On January 1, issued 14,000 shares of common stock, receiving cash of $304,000
   c. Paid short-term notes payable, $24,000
   d. Purchased merchandise of $64,000 on account, debiting Inventory
   e. Received cash on account, $15,000

P13-53A. *(Learning Objective 5: Use ratios to evaluate a stock investment)* Comparative financial statement data of Robinson Optical Mart follow:

	A	B	C
	A1		
1	**Robinson Optical Mart** **Comparative Income Statements** **Years Ended December 31, 2014 and 2013**		
2		**2014**	**2013**
3	Net sales	$ 957,000	$ 875,000
4	Cost of goods sold	675,000	576,000
5	Gross profit	282,000	299,000
6	Operating expenses	129,000	142,000
7	Income from operations	153,000	157,000
8	Interest expense	37,000	45,000
9	Income before income tax	116,000	112,000
10	Income tax expense	40,000	39,000
11	Net income	$ 76,000	$ 73,000
12			

		B	C	D
	A			
1	**Robinson Optical Mart** **Comparative Balance Sheets** **December 31, 2014 and 2013**			
2		**2014**	**2013**	**2012***
3	Current assets:			
4	Cash	$ 45,000	$ 49,000	
5	Current receivables, net	217,000	158,000	$ 200,000
6	Inventories	302,000	286,000	181,000
7	Prepaid expenses	4,000	29,000	
8	Total current assets	568,000	522,000	
9	Property, plant, and equipment, net	285,000	277,000	
10	Total assets	$ 853,000	$ 799,000	700,000
11				
12	Accounts payable	$ 160,000	$ 110,000	112,000
13	Other current liabilities	135,000	188,000	
14	Total current liabilities	295,000	298,000	
15	Long-term liabilities	243,000	231,000	
16	Total liabilities	538,000	529,000	
17	Common stockholders' equity, no par	315,000	270,000	199,000
18	Total liabilities and stockholders' equity	$ 853,000	$ 799,000	
19				

*Selected 2012 amounts.

Other information:
1. Market price of Robinson common stock: $88.17 at December 31, 2014, and $77.01 at December 31, 2013
2. Common shares outstanding: 18,000 during 2014 and 17,800 during 2013
3. All sales on credit

Requirements

1. Compute the following ratios for 2014 and 2013:
   a. Current ratio
   b. Quick (acid-test) ratio
   c. Receivables turnover and days' sales outstanding (DSO) (round to the nearest whole day)
   d. Inventory turnover and days' inventory outstanding (DIO) (round to the nearest whole day)
   e. Accounts payable turnover and days' payable outstanding (DPO) (use cost of goods sold in the numerator of the turnover ratio and round DPO to the nearest whole day).
   f. Cash conversion cycle (in days)
   g. Times-interest-earned ratio
   h. Return on assets (use DuPont Analysis)
   i. Return on common stockholders' equity (use DuPont Analysis)
   j. Earnings per share of common stock
   k. Price-earnings ratio
2. Decide whether (a) Robinson's financial position improved or deteriorated during 2014 and (b) the investment attractiveness of Robinson's common stock appears to have increased or decreased.
3. How will what you learned in this problem help you evaluate an investment?

P13-54A. *(Learning Objectives 5, 6: Use ratios to decide between two stock investments; measure economic value added)* Assume that you are considering purchasing stock as an investment. You have narrowed the choice to EShop.com and TopSales Stores and have assembled the following data.

Selected income statement data for the current year:

	EShop.com	TopSales Stores
Net sales (all on credit)..................	$598,000	$518,000
Cost of goods sold..........................	452,000	382,000
Income from operations	95,000	69,000
Interest expense.............................	—	11,000
Net income....................................	63,000	37,000

Selected balance-sheet and market price data at *end* of current year:

	EShop.com	TopSales Stores
Current assets:		
Cash	$ 28,000	$ 36,000
Short-term investments	9,000	11,000
Current receivables, net	187,000	166,000
Inventories..	219,000	186,000
Prepaid expenses...	15,000	13,000
Total current assets	458,000	412,000
Total assets...	984,000	935,000
Total current liabilities	371,000	340,000
Total liabilities	663,000	700,000
Preferred stock, 8%, $150 par................................		30,000
Common stock, $1 par (100,000 shares)................	100,000	
$5 par (10,000 shares)...................		50,000
Total stockholders' equity	321,000	235,000
Market price per share of common stock	$ 6.93	$ 58.82

Selected balance-sheet data at *beginning* of current year:

	EShop.com	TopSales Stores
Balance sheet:		
Current receivables, net...	$143,000	$194,000
Inventories	212,000	199,000
Total assets...	853,000	913,000
Long-term debt	—	310,000
Preferred stock, 8%, $150 par................................		30,000
Common stock, $1 par (100,000 shares)................	100,000	
$5 par (10,000 shares).................		50,000
Total stockholders' equity	259,000	219,000

Your strategy is to invest in companies that have low price-earnings ratios but appear to be in good shape financially. Assume that you have analyzed all other factors and that your decision depends on the results of ratio analysis.

Requirements

1. Compute the following ratios for both companies for the current year, and decide which company's stock better fits your investment strategy.
   a. Quick (acid-test) ratio
   b. Inventory turnover
   c. Days' sales in average receivables
   d. Debt ratio
   e. Times-interest-earned ratio

f. Return on common stockholders' equity

g. Earnings per share of common stock

h. Price-earnings ratio

2. Compute each company's economic-value-added (EVA®) measure and determine whether the companies' EVA®s confirm or alter your investment decision. Each company's cost of capital is 7%.

Group B

P13-55B. *(Learning Objectives 1, 5: Compute trend percentages, return on sales, asset turnover, and ROA, and compare with industry)* Net sales, net income, and total assets for Lloyd Shipping, Inc., for a five-year period follow:

(In thousands)	2014	2013	2012	2011	2010
Net sales....................	$500	$418	$365	$309	$299
Net income.................	51	39	43	34	27
Total assets	298	262	249	223	201

Requirements

1. Compute trend percentages for each item for 2011 through 2014. Use 2010 as the base year and round to the nearest percent.
2. Compute the rate of return on net sales for 2012 through 2014, rounding to three decimal places. Explain what this means.
3. Compute asset turnover for 2012 through 2014. Explain what this means.
4. Use DuPont Analysis to compute rate of return on average total assets (ROA) for 2012 through 2014.
5. How does Lloyd Shipping's return on net sales compare with previous years? How does it compare with that of the industry? In the shipping industry, rates above 9% are considered good, and rates above 11% are outstanding.
6. Evaluate Lloyd Shipping, Inc.'s ROA for 2014, compared with previous years, and against an 18% benchmark for the industry.

P13-56B. *(Learning Objectives 3, 5: Prepare common-size statements; analyze profitability; make comparisons with the industry)* Top managers of Sharp Products, Inc., have asked for your help in comparing the company's profit performance and financial position with the average for the industry. The accountant has given you the company's income statement and balance sheet and also the following data for the industry:

	A1	

	A	B	C
1	**Sharp Products, Inc.** **Income Statement Compared with Industry Average** **Year Ended December 31, 2014**		
2		**Sharp**	**Industry Average**
3	Net sales	$ 800,000	100.0%
4	Cost of goods sold	552,000	57.3
5	Gross profit	248,000	42.7
6	Operating expenses	184,000	29.4
7	Operating income	64,000	13.3
8	Other expenses	4,000	2.5
9	Net income	$ 60,000	10.8%
10			

	A	B	C
1	**Sharp Products, Inc.** **Balance Sheet Compared with Industry Average** **December 31, 2014**		
2		**Sharp**	**Industry Average**
3	Current assets	$ 377,600	72.1%
4	Fixed assets, net	113,920	19.0
5	Intangible assets, net	19,200	4.8
6	Other assets	129,280	4.1
7	Total	$ 640,000	100.0%
8			
9	Current liabilities	$ 300,800	47.2%
10	Long-term liabilities	134,400	21.0
11	Stockholders' equity	204,800	31.8
12	Total	$ 640,000	100.0%
13			

Requirements

1. Prepare a common-size income statement and balance sheet for Sharp Products. The first column of each statement should present Sharp Products' common-size statement, and the second column should show the industry averages.
2. For the profitability analysis, compare Sharp Products' (a) ratio of gross profit to net sales, (b) ratio of operating income to net sales, and (c) ratio of net income to net sales with the industry averages. Is Sharp Products' profit performance better or worse than the average for the industry?
3. For the analysis of financial position, compare Sharp Products' (a) ratios of current assets and current liabilities to total assets and (b) ratio of stockholders' equity to total assets with the industry averages. Is Sharp Products' financial position better or worse than the average for the industry?

P13-57B. *(Learning Objective 4: Use the statement of cash flows for decision making)* You are evaluating two companies as possible investments. The two companies, which are similar in size, are commuter airlines that fly passengers up and down the West Coast. All other available information has been analyzed, and your investment decision depends on the statements of cash flows.

A1

	A	B	C	D	E
1	**High Flight Airlines** **Statements of Cash Flows** **Years Ended May 31, 2015 and 2014**				
2			2015		2014
3	**Operating activities:**				
4	Net income (net loss)		$ (105,000)		$ 214,000
5	Adjustments for noncash items:				
6	Total		118,000		(44,000)
7	Net cash provided by operating activities		13,000		170,000
8					
9	**Investing activities:**				
10	Purchase of property, plant, and				
11	equipment	$ (94,000)		$ (147,000)	
12	Sale of long-term investments	98,000		29,000	
13	Net cash provided by (used for)				
14	investing activities		4,000		(118,000)
15					
16	**Financing activities:**				
17	Issuance of short-term notes payable	$ 149,000		$ 185,000	
18	Payment of short-term notes payable	(256,000)		(134,000)	
19	Payment of cash dividends	(67,000)		(106,000)	
20	Net cash used for financing activities		(174,000)		(55,000)
21	Increase (decrease) in cash		$ (157,000)		$ (3,000)
22	Cash balance at beginning of year		168,000		171,000
23	Cash balance at end of year		$ 11,000		$ 168,000
24					

A1

	A	B	C	D	E
1	**Mountain Air, Inc.** **Statements of Cash Flows** **Years Ended May 31, 2015 and 2014**				
2			2015		2014
3	**Operating activities:**				
4	Net income		$ 201,000		$ 147,000
5	Adjustments for noncash items				
6	Total		92,000		66,000
7	Net cash provided by operating activities		293,000		213,000
8					
9	**Investing activities:**				
10	Purchase of property, plant, and equipment	$ (448,000)		$(630,000)	
11	Sales of property, plant, and equipment	87,000		113,000	
12	Net cash used for investing activities		(361,000)		(517,000)
13					
14	**Financing activities:**				
15	Issuance of long-term notes payable	$ 244,000		$ 168,000	
16	Payment of short-term notes payable	(107,000)		(16,000)	
17	Net cash provided by financing activities		137,000		152,000
18	Increase (decrease) in cash		$ 69,000		$ (152,000)
19	Cash balance at beginning of year		135,000		287,000
20	Cash balance at end of year		$ 204,000		$ 135,000
21					

Requirement

1. Discuss the relative strengths and weaknesses of High Flight and Mountain Air. Conclude your discussion by recommending one of the companies' stocks as an investment.

P13-58B. *(Learning Objective 5: Compute effects of business transactions on selected ratios)* Financial statement data of Harper Engineering include the following items:

Cash	$ 30,000	Accounts payable	$107,000
Short-term investments	32,000	Accrued liabilities	31,000
Accounts receivable, net	86,000	Long-term notes payable	163,000
Inventories	147,000	Other long-term liabilities	31,000
Prepaid expenses	5,000	Net income	91,000
Total assets	673,000	Number of common	
Short-term notes payable	48,000	shares outstanding	50,000

Requirements

1. Compute Harper's current ratio, debt ratio, and earnings per share. Round all ratios to two decimal places.
2. Compute the three ratios after evaluating the effect of each transaction that follows. Consider each transaction *separately*.
   a. Borrowed $160,000 on a long-term note payable
   b. On January 1, issued 18,000 shares of common stock, receiving cash of $308,000
   c. Paid short-term notes payable, $30,000
   d. Purchased merchandise of $84,000 on account, debiting Inventory
   e. Received cash on account, $24,000

P13-59B. *(Learning Objective 5: Use ratios to evaluate a stock investment)* Comparative financial statement data of McClaine Optical Mart follow:

	A1	⬍		
	A		**B**	**C**
1	**McClaine Optical Mart** **Comparative Income Statements** **Years Ended December 31, 2014 and 2013**			
2			**2014**	**2013**
3	Net sales		$986,000	$892,000
4	Cost of goods sold		680,000	581,000
5	Gross profit		306,000	311,000
6	Operating expenses		127,000	148,000
7	Income from operations		179,000	163,000
8	Interest expense		30,000	50,000
9	Income before income tax		149,000	113,000
10	Income tax expense		41,000	41,000
11	Net income		$108,000	$ 72,000
12				

	A	B	C	D
1	**McClaine Optical Mart** **Comparative Balance Sheets** **December 31, 2014 and 2013**			
2		**2014**	**2013**	**2012***
3	Current assets:			
4	Cash	$ 32,000	$ 82,000	
5	Current receivables, net	227,000	157,000	$200,000
6	Inventories	297,000	294,000	258,000
7	Prepaid expenses	7,000	29,000	
8	Total current assets	563,000	562,000	
9	Property, plant, and equipment, net	273,000	261,000	
10	Total assets	$836,000	$823,000	701,000
11				
12	Accounts payable	$150,000	$105,000	112,000
13	Other current liabilities	135,000	187,000	
14	Total current liabilities	285,000	292,000	
15	Long-term liabilities	240,000	233,000	
16	Total liabilities	525,000	525,000	
17	Common stockholders' equity, no par	311,000	298,000	199,000
18	Total liabilities and stockholders' equity	$836,000	$823,000	
19				

*Selected 2012 amounts.

Other information:
1. Market price of McClaine common stock: $89.38 at December 31, 2014, and $85.67 at December 31, 2013
2. Common shares outstanding: 15,000 during 2014 and 10,000 during 2013
3. All sales on credit

Requirements

1. Compute the following ratios for 2014 and 2013:
    a. Current ratio
    b. Quick (acid-test) ratio
    c. Receivables turnover and days' sales outstanding (DSO); round to nearest whole day
    d. Inventory turnover and days' inventory outstanding (DIO); round to nearest whole day
    e. Accounts payable turnover and days' payable outstanding (DPO); (use cost of goods sold in the turnover ratio and round DPO to nearest whole day
    f. Cash conversion cycle (in days)
    g. Times-interest-earned ratio
    h. Return on assets; use DuPont Analysis
    i. Return on common stockholders' equity; use DuPont Analysis
    j. Earnings per share of common stock
    k. Price-earnings ratio
2. Decide whether (a) McClaine's financial position improved or deteriorated during 2014 and (b) the investment attractiveness of McClaine's common stock appears to have increased or decreased.
3. How will what you learned in this problem help you evaluate an investment?

P13-60B. *(Learning Objectives 5, 6: Use ratios to decide between two stock investments; measure economic value added)* Assume that you are considering purchasing stock as an investment. You have narrowed the choice to BuyHere.com and EasySales Stores and have assembled the following data.

Selected income statement data for current year:

	BuyHere.com	EasySales Stores
Net sales (all on credit).................	$601,000	$523,000
Cost of goods sold.........................	455,000	382,000
Income from operations	95,000	76,000
Interest expense............................	—	11,000
Net income	68,000	39,000

Selected balance-sheet and market price data at the *end* of the current year:

	BuyHere.com	EasySales Stores
Current assets:		
Cash	$ 31,000	$ 36,000
Short-term investments	7,000	11,000
Current receivables, net	182,000	165,000
Inventories..	208,000	184,000
Prepaid expenses...	15,000	14,000
Total current assets	443,000	410,000
Total assets	984,000	927,000
Total current liabilities	368,000	332,000
Total liabilities	665,000	710,000
Preferred stock: 6%, $100 par		20,000
Common stock, $1 par (150,000 shares)..............	150,000	
$5 par (10,000 shares)................		50,000
Total stockholders' equity	319,000	217,000
Market price per share of common stock	$ 4.95	$ 64.26

Selected balance-sheet data at the *beginning* of the current year:

	BuyHere.com	EasySales Stores
Balance sheet:		
Current receivables, net...	$144,000	$192,000
Inventories	204,000	198,000
Total assets..	841,000	912,000
Long-term debt	—	307,000
Preferred stock, 6%, $100 par		20,000
Common stock, $1 par (150,000 shares)................	150,000	
$5 par (10,000 shares)..................		50,000
Total stockholders' equity	263,000	217,000

Your strategy is to invest in companies that have low price-earnings ratios but appear to be in good shape financially. Assume that you have analyzed all other factors and that your decision depends on the results of ratio analysis.

Requirements

1. Compute the following ratios for both companies for the current year, and decide which company's stock better fits your investment strategy.
   a. Quick (acid-test) ratio
   b. Inventory turnover
   c. Days' sales in average receivables
   d. Debt ratio

   e. Times-interest-earned ratio

   f. Return on common stockholders' equity

   g. Earnings per share of common stock

   h. Price-earnings ratio

2. Compute each company's economic-value-added (EVA®) measure and determine whether the companies' EVA®s confirm or alter your investment decision. Each company's cost of capital is 9%.

Challenge Exercises and Problem

E13-61. *(Learning Objectives 2, 3, 5: Use ratio data to reconstruct a company's balance sheet)*
The following data (dollar amounts in millions) are taken from the financial statements of Number 1 Industries, Inc.:

Total liabilities	$12,500
Total current assets	$13,500
Accumulated depreciation	$ 1,600
Debt ratio	50%
Current ratio	1.50

Requirement

1. Complete the following condensed balance sheet. Report amounts to the nearest million dollars.

	(In millions)
Current assets	☐
Property, plant, and equipment ☐	
Less: Accumulated depreciation ☐	☐
Total assets	☐
Current liabilities	☐
Long-term liabilities	☐
Stockholders' equity	☐
Total liabilities and stockholders' equity	☐

E13-62. *(Learning Objectives 2, 3, 5: Use ratio data to reconstruct a company's income statement)*
The following data (dollar amounts in millions) are from the financial statements of Valley Corporation:

Average stockholders' equity	$5,400
Interest expense	$ 800
Operating income as a percent of sales	25%
Rate of return on stockholders' equity	10%
Income tax rate	40%

Requirement

1. Complete the following condensed income statement. Report amounts to the nearest million dollars.

Sales..	
Operating expense...................	
Operating income....................	
Interest expense.......................	
Pretax income	
Income tax expense	
Net income.............................	

P13-63. *(Learning Objectives 1, 2, 3, 4: Use trend percentages, common-size percentages, and ratios to reconstruct financial statements)* An incomplete comparative income statement and balance sheet for Amherst Corporation follow:

	A1	⬍			
		A		**B**	**C**
1	**Amherst Corporation** **Comparative income Statements** **Years Ended December 31, 2014 and 2013**				
2				**2014**	**2013**
3	Sales revenue			$2,100,000	$2,000,000
4	Cost of goods sold			?	1,400,000
5	Gross profit			?	600,000
6	Operating expense			?	400,000
7	Operating income			?	200,000
8	Interest expense			40,000	40,000
9	Income before income tax			?	160,000
10	Income tax expense (30%)			?	48,000
11	Net income			?	$ 112,000
12					

	A1	⬍			
		A		**B**	**C**
1	**Amherst Corporation** **Balance Sheet** **December 31, 2014 and 2013**				
2				**2014**	**2013**
3	ASSETS				
4	Current:				
5	Cash			$?	$ 30,000
6	Accounts receivable, net			?	135,000
7	Inventory			?	180,000
8	Total current assets			?	345,000
9	Plant and equipment, net			?	555,000
10	Total assets			$?	$900,000
11	LIABILITIES				
12	Current liabilities			$160,000	$140,000
13	10% Bonds payable			?	400,000
14	Total liabilities			?	540,000
15	STOCKHOLDERS' EQUITY				
16	Common stock, $5 par			?	220,000
17	Retained earnings			?	140,000
18	Total stockholders' equity			?	360,000
19	Total liabilities and stockholders' equity			$?	$900,000
20					

Requirement

1. Using the ratios, common-size percentages, and trend percentages given, complete the income statement and balance sheet for Amherst for 2014. Additional information:

	A	B	C
	A1		
	A	B	C
1	**Additional information:**	**2014**	**2013**
2	Common size cost of goods sold %:	65%	70%
3	Common size common stock %:	30%	24.4%
4	Trend percentage, Operating income	135%	100%
5	Asset turnover	2	
6	Accounts receivable turnover	14	
7	Quick (acid-test) ratio	1.25	
8	Current ratio	2.75	
9	Return on equity (DuPont model)	32.2%	
10			

Apply Your Knowledge

Decision Cases

Case 1. *(Learning Objectives 5, 6: Assess the effects of transactions on a company)* Suppose **Time Warner, Inc.,** is having a bad year in 2014, as the company has incurred a $4.9 billion net loss. The loss has pushed most of the return measures into the negative column, and the current ratio dropped below 1.0. The company's debt ratio is still only 0.27. Assume top management of Time Warner is pondering ways to improve the company's ratios. In particular, management is considering the following transactions:

1. Selling off the cable television segment of the business for $30 million (receiving half in cash and half in the form of a long-term note receivable). Book value of the cable television business is $27 million.
2. Borrowing $100 million on long-term debt.
3. Purchasing treasury stock for $500 million cash.
4. Writing off one-fourth of goodwill carried on the books at $128 million.
5. Selling advertising at the normal gross profit of 60%. The advertisements run immediately.
6. Purchasing trademarks from **NBC**, paying $20 million cash and signing a one-year note payable for $80 million.

Requirements

1. Top management wants to know the effects of these transactions (increase, decrease, or no effect) on the following ratios of Time Warner:
   a. Current ratio
   b. Debt ratio
   c. Times-interest-earned ratio (measured as [Net income + Interest expense]/Interest expense)
   d. Return on equity
   e. Book value per share of common stock
2. Some of these transactions have an immediately positive effect on the company's financial condition. Some are definitely negative. Others have an effect that cannot be judged as clearly positive or negative. Evaluate each transaction's effect as positive, negative, or unclear. (Challenge)

Case 2. *(Learning Objectives 5, 6: Analyze the effects of an accounting difference on the ratios)* Assume that you are a financial analyst. You are trying to compare the financial statements of **Caterpillar, Inc.,** with those of **CNH Global**, an international company that uses international financial reporting standards (IFRS). Caterpillar, Inc., uses the last-in, first-out (LIFO) method to account for its inventories. IFRS does not permit CNH Global to use LIFO, so they use FIFO. Analyze the effect of this difference in accounting method on the two companies' ratio values. For each ratio discussed in this chapter, indicate which company will have the higher (and the lower) ratio value. Also identify those ratios that are unaffected by the FIFO/LIFO difference. Ignore the effects of income taxes, and assume inventory costs are increasing. Then, based on your analysis of the ratios, summarize your conclusions as to which company looks better overall.

Case 3. *(Learning Objectives 2, 5: Identify action to cut losses and establish profitability)* Suppose you manage Outward Bound, Inc., a Vermont sporting goods store that lost money during the past year. To turn the business around, you must analyze the company and industry data for the current year to learn what is wrong. The company's data follow:

	A	B	C
	A1		
1	Outward Bound, Inc. Common-Size Balance Sheet Data		
2		Outward Bound	Industry Average
3	Cash and short-term investments	3.0%	6.8%
4	Trade receivables, net	15.2	11.0
5	Inventory	64.2	60.5
6	Prepaid expenses	1.0	0.0
7	Total current assets	83.4%	78.3%
8	Fixed assets, net	12.6	15.2
9	Other assets	4.0	6.5
10	Total assets	100.0%	100.0%
11			
12	Notes payable, short-term, 12%	17.1%	14.0%
13	Accounts payable	21.1	25.1
14	Accrued liabilities	7.8	7.9
15	Total current liabilities	46.0	47.0
16	Long-term debt, 11%	19.7	16.4
17	Total liabilities	65.7	63.4
18	Common stockholders' equity	34.3	36.6
19	Total liabilities and stockholders' equity	100.0%	100.0%
20			

	Outward Bound	Industry Average
Outward Bound, Inc. Common-Size Income Statement Data		
	Outward Bound	Industry Average
Net sales	100.0%	100.0%
Cost of sales	(68.2)	(64.8)
Gross profit	31.8	35.2
Operating expense	(37.1)	(32.3)
Operating income (loss)	(5.3)	2.9
Interest expense	(5.8)	(1.3)
Other revenue	1.1	0.3
Income (loss) before income tax	(10.0)	1.9
Income tax (expense) saving	4.4	(0.8)
Net income (loss)	(5.6)%	1.1%

Requirement

1. On the basis of your analysis of these figures, suggest four courses of action Outward Bound might take to reduce its losses and establish profitable operations. Give your reason for each suggestion. (Challenge)

Ethical Issue

Turnberry Golf Corporation's long-term debt agreements make certain demands on the business. For example, Turnberry may not purchase treasury stock in excess of the balance of retained earnings. Also, long-term debt may not exceed stockholders' equity, and the current ratio may not fall below 1.50. If Turnberry fails to meet any of these requirements, the company's lenders have the authority to take over management of the company.

Changes in consumer demand have made it hard for Turnberry to attract customers. Current liabilities have mounted faster than current assets, causing the current ratio to fall to 1.47. Before releasing financial statements, Turnberry management is scrambling to improve the current ratio. The controller points out that the company owns an investment that is currently classified as long-term. The investment can be classified as either long-term or short-term, depending on management's intention. By deciding to convert an investment to cash within one year, Turnberry can classify the investment as short-term—a current asset. On the controller's recommendation, Turnberry's board of directors votes to reclassify long-term investments as short-term.

Requirements

1. What is the accounting issue in this case? What ethical decision needs to be made?
2. Who are the stakeholders?
3. Analyze the potential impact on the stakeholders from the following standpoints: (a) economic, (b) legal, and (c) ethical.
4. Shortly after the financial statements are released, sales improve; so, too, does the current ratio. As a result, Turnberry management decides not to sell the investments it had reclassified as short-term. Accordingly, the company reclassifies the investments as long-term. Has management acted unethically? Give the reasoning underlying your answer.

Focus on Financials | Amazon.com, Inc.

(Learning Objectives 4, 5, 6: Compute standard financial ratios; use the statement of cash flows; measure liquidity and profitability; analyze stock as an investment) Use the consolidated financial statements and the data in **Amazon.com, Inc.'s** annual report (Appendix A at the end of the book) to evaluate the company's comparative performance for 2012 versus 2011. Use all

the ratio analysis tools described in this chapter. Does the company appear to be improving or declining in the following dimensions?

Requirements

1. The ability to pay its current liabilities.
2. The ability to sell inventory and collect receivables. Accounts receivable balance as of December 31, 2010, was $1,587 million; inventory balance as of December 31, 2010, was $3,202 million.
3. The ability to pay long-term debts.
4. Profitability (use DuPont Analysis). Total assets as of December 31, 2010, were $18,797 million. Total stockholders' equity as of December 31, 2010, was $6,864 million.
5. Cash flows from operations.
6. The potential of the company's stock as a long-term investment. Use year-end stock prices, when applicable, as found on investment websites such as www.googlefinance.com. (Challenge)

Focus on Analysis | Yum! Brands, Inc.

(Learning Objectives 1, 5: Analyze trend data; compute the standard financial ratios and use them to make decisions) Use the Yum! Brands, Inc. consolidated financial statements in Appendix B at the end of this book to address the following questions.

1. Perform a trend analysis of Yum! Brands, Inc.'s net sales, gross profit, operating income, and net income. Use 2010 as the base year, and compute trend figures for 2010 through 2012.
2. Find Yum! Brands, Inc.'s annual report for 2013 at www.sec.gov. Also perform research at a popular investment website such as www.msnmoney.com or www.finance.yahoo.com to update the information from part 1. (Challenge)
3. What in your opinion is the company's outlook for the future? Would you buy the company's stock as an investment? Why or why not? (Challenge)

Group Projects

Project 1. Select an industry in which you are interested, and use the leading company in that industry as the benchmark. Then select two other companies in the same industry. For each category of ratios in the Decision Guidelines feature on pages 775–777, compute at least two ratios for all three companies. Write a two-page report that compares the two companies with the benchmark company.

Project 2. Select a company and obtain its financial statements. Convert the income statement and the balance sheet to common size and compare the company you selected to the industry average. **Risk Management Association's** *Annual Statement Studies*, **Dun & Bradstreet's** *Industry Norms & Key Business Ratios*, and **Prentice Hall's** *Almanac of Business and Industrial Financial Ratios* by Leo Troy publish common-size statements for most industries. You will find these and other resources in your campus library and on the Internet.

MyAccountingLab | **For online homework, exercises, and problems that provide you with immediate feedback, please visit www.myaccountinglab.com.**

Quick Check Answers

1. c ($1,825 - $1,720)/$1,720

2. a ($1,825/$21,900)

3. d

4. c ($1,790/$25,875)

5. a

6. $b\left[\dfrac{\$5,130}{(\$160 + \$110)/2}\right] = 38$ *times*

7. $b[(\$605 + \$760)/\$2,545 = 0.54]$

8. $a \left[\dfrac{\$760 + \$920/2}{(\$21,900/365)} \right] = 14 \, days$

9. c

10. $d \, (\$3,565/\$21,900 = .163)$

11. $d \left[\dfrac{\$3,565}{(\$12,965 + \$10,605/2)} \right] = .303$

12. $c \, (\$26/\$5.09)$

13. $b \, (\$0.65/\$26)$

14. $a \, [\$5,941 + \$340 - (\$305 + \$9,700 + \$10,605) \times 0.10] = \$4,220$

Comprehensive Financial Statement Analysis Project

The objective of this exercise is to develop your ability to perform a comprehensive analysis on a set of financial statements. Obtain a copy of the 2012 annual report (10-K) of Kohl's Corporation (year end February 2, 2013) from www.sec.gov. (Note: The proper term to use in the company search box is "Kohls").

Requirement 1

Basic information (provide sources):
   a. Using a site such as www.hoovers.com or www.finance.yahoo.com, research the discount variety store industry. List two competitors of Kohl's Corporation.
   b. Describe Kohl's business and risk factors.
   c. List three Kohl's brands.
   d. What is Kohl's largest asset? Largest liability?
   e. How many shares of common stock are authorized? Issued? Outstanding?
   f. Did Kohl's repurchase any shares of common stock during the year? If so, how many?
   g. When does Kohl's record revenue?
   h. What inventory method does Kohl's use?
   i. What was Kohl's bad debt expense for the year?
   j. Does Kohl's have any business interests in foreign countries? Explain your answer.

Requirement 2

Evaluate profitability. Using information you have learned in the text and elsewhere, evaluate Kohl's profitability for 2012 compared with 2011. In your analysis, you should compute the following ratios and then comment on what those ratios indicate. NOTE: You will have to look up the 10-K for 2011 to obtain total assets and stockholders' equity for 2010. See www.sec.gov.
   a. Rate of return on sales
   b. Asset turnover
   c. Return on assets (DuPont model)
   d. Leverage ratio
   e. Return on equity (DuPont model)
   f. Gross margin percentage
   g. Earnings per share (show computation)
   h. Book value per share

Requirement 3

Evaluate the company's ability to sell inventory and pay debts during 2012 and 2011. You should note that the company does not hold traditional accounts receivable, because it sells all of its receivables to Capital One which is a credit card company. Therefore, it is impossible to compute accounts receivable turnover and days sales to collection. However, in your analysis, you should compute the following ratios, and then comment on what those ratios indicate.

Since the 2012 annual report only includes the balance sheets for 2012 and 2011, you will need to look up the 10-K for 2011 for information about 2010 inventory and accounts payable.

    a. Inventory turnover and days' inventory outstanding (DIO)

    b. Accounts payable turnover and days' payable outstanding (DPO)

    c. Cash conversion cycle (DIO-DPO)

    d. Current ratio

    e. Quick (acid-test) ratio

    f. Debt ratio

    g. Times interest earned

Requirement 4

Evaluate Kohl's cash flow.

    a. For 2012, what are Kohl's two main sources of cash?

    b. For 2012, is Kohl's net cash flow from operations greater than or less than net income? What is the primary cause of the difference?

    c. For 2012, what is the primary source of cash from investing activities? Is this the same as in 2011 and 2010? If not, state the primary source(s) of cash from investing activities in 2011 and 2010.

    d. For 2012, what is the primary source of cash from financing activities? Is this the same as in 2011 and 2010? If not, state the primary source(s) of cash from financing activities in 2011 and 2010.

    e. What trend(s) do you detect from this analysis?

Requirement 5

Other financial analysis.

    a. Compute common-size percentages for sales, gross profit, operating income, and net income for 2009–2012. Comment on your results.

    b. Find the selected financial data in the 10-K where Kohl's reports selected information since 2009. Compute trend percentages, using 2009 as the base year, for total revenues and net earnings. Comment on your results.

Requirement 6

Evaluate Kohl's Corporation stock as an investment.

    a. What was the closing market price of Kohl's Corporation stock on February 4, 2013, the next trading day after the balance-sheet date of February 2, 2013?

    b. Compute the price-earnings ratio using your EPS calculation and the market price you just determined.

    c. Assume that Kohl's Corporation's weighted-average cost of capital, and therefore, the relevant capitalization rate for projected earnings from operations, is 8%. Using the methods you learned in Chapter 11, calculate a projected value of Kohl's Corporation as of February 4, 2013. Compare that calculated value with the company's market capitalization (market cap) as of that date. Based on comparison of these two computations, would you evaluate the company's stock as a "buy," "hold," or "sell"? State your reasons. Now compare the price of the stock as of the date you are making this evaluation (it will be later than February 4, 2013) with the price as of that date. In retrospect, would your decision using the data as of February 4, 2013 have been a wise one? State your reasons.

2 0 1 2

ANNUAL REPORT

UNITED STATES
SECURITIES AND EXCHANGE COMMISSION
Washington, D.C. 20549

FORM 10-K

(Mark One)

☒   **ANNUAL REPORT PURSUANT TO SECTION 13 OR 15(d) OF THE SECURITIES EXCHANGE ACT OF 1934**
For the fiscal year ended December 31, 2012

or

☐   **TRANSITION REPORT PURSUANT TO SECTION 13 OR 15(d) OF THE SECURITIES EXCHANGE ACT OF 1934**
For the transition period from   to   .

Commission File No. 000-22513

AMAZON.COM, INC.
(Exact name of registrant as specified in its charter)

Delaware	**91-1646860**
(State or other jurisdiction of incorporation or organization)	(I.R.S. Employer Identification No.)

410 Terry Avenue North
Seattle, Washington 98109-5210
(206) 266-1000
(Address and telephone number, including area code, of registrant's principal executive offices)

Securities registered pursuant to Section 12(b) of the Act:

Title of Each Class	Name of Each Exchange on Which Registered
Common Stock, par value $.01 per share	Nasdaq Global Select Market

Securities registered pursuant to Section 12(g) of the Act:
None

Indicate by check mark if the registrant is a well-known seasoned issuer, as defined in Rule 405 of the Securities Act.   Yes ☒   No ☐

Indicate by check mark if the registrant is not required to file reports pursuant to Section 13 or Section 15(d) of the Exchange Act.   Yes ☐   No ☒

Indicate by check mark whether the registrant (1) has filed all reports required to be filed by Section 13 or 15(d) of the Securities Exchange Act of 1934 during the preceding 12 months (or for such shorter period that the registrant was required to file such reports), and (2) has been subject to such filing requirements for the past 90 days.   Yes ☒   No ☐

Indicate by check mark whether the registrant has submitted electronically and posted on its corporate Web site, if any, every Interactive Data File required to be submitted and posted pursuant to Rule 405 of Regulation S-T during the preceding 12 months (or for such shorter period that the registrant was required to submit and post such files).   Yes ☒   No ☐

Indicate by check mark if disclosure of delinquent filers pursuant to Item 405 of Regulation S-K is not contained herein, and will not be contained, to the best of registrant's knowledge, in definitive proxy or information statements incorporated by reference in Part III of this Form 10-K or any amendment to this Form 10-K.   ☐

Indicate by check mark whether the registrant is a large accelerated filer, an accelerated filer, or a non-accelerated filer. See definition of "accelerated filer and large accelerated filer" in Rule 12b-2 of the Exchange Act.

Large accelerated filer ☒	Accelerated filer	☐
Non-accelerated filer ☐ (Do not check if a smaller reporting company)	Smaller reporting company	☐

Indicate by check mark whether the registrant is a shell company (as defined in Rule 12b-2 of the Exchange Act).   Yes ☐   No ☒

Aggregate market value of voting stock held by non-affiliates of the registrant as of June 30, 2012	$ 83,001,105,646
Number of shares of common stock outstanding as of January 18, 2013	454,551,069

DOCUMENTS INCORPORATED BY REFERENCE

AMAZON.COM, INC.

PART I

Item 1. *Business*

This Annual Report on Form 10-K and the documents incorporated herein by reference contain forward-looking statements based on expectations, estimates, and projections as of the date of this filing. Actual results may differ materially from those expressed in forward-looking statements. See Item 1A of Part I—"Risk Factors."

Amazon.com, Inc. was incorporated in 1994 in the state of Washington and reincorporated in 1996 in the state of Delaware. Our principal corporate offices are located in Seattle, Washington. We completed our initial public offering in May 1997 and our common stock is listed on the Nasdaq Global Select Market under the symbol "AMZN."

As used herein, "Amazon.com," "we," "our," and similar terms include Amazon.com, Inc. and its subsidiaries, unless the context indicates otherwise.

General

Amazon.com opened its virtual doors on the World Wide Web in July 1995 and offers Earth's Biggest Selection. We seek to be Earth's most customer-centric company for four primary customer sets: consumers, sellers, enterprises, and content creators. In addition, we provide services, such as advertising services and co-branded credit card agreements.

We have organized our operations into two principal segments: North America and International. See Item 8 of Part II, "Financial Statements and Supplementary Data—Note 12—Segment Information." See Item 7 of Part II, "Management's Discussion and Analysis of Financial Condition and Results of Operations—Results of Operations—Supplemental Information" for supplemental information about our net sales.

Consumers

We serve consumers through our retail websites, and focus on selection, price, and convenience. We design our websites to enable millions of unique products to be sold by us and by third parties across dozens of product categories. Customers access our websites directly and through our mobile websites and apps. We also manufacture and sell Kindle devices. We strive to offer our customers the lowest prices possible through low everyday product pricing and shipping offers, including through membership in Amazon Prime, and to improve our operating efficiencies so that we can continue to lower prices for our customers. We also provide easy-to-use functionality, fast and reliable fulfillment, and timely customer service.

We fulfill customer orders in a number of ways, including through the U.S. and international fulfillment centers and warehouses that we operate, through co-sourced and outsourced arrangements in certain countries, and through digital delivery. We operate customer service centers globally, which are supplemented by co-sourced arrangements. See Item 2 of Part I, "Properties."

Sellers

We offer programs that enable sellers to sell their products on our websites and their own branded websites and to fulfill orders through us. We are not the seller of record in these transactions, but instead earn fixed fees, revenue share fees, per-unit activity fees, or some combination thereof.

Enterprises

We serve developers and enterprises of all sizes through Amazon Web Services ("AWS"), which provides access to technology infrastructure that enables virtually any type of business.

Content Creators

We serve authors and independent publishers with Kindle Direct Publishing, an online platform that lets independent authors and publishers choose a 70% royalty option and make their books available in the Kindle Store, along with Amazon's own publishing arm, Amazon Publishing. We also offer programs that allow authors, musicians, filmmakers, app developers, and others to publish and sell content.

Competition

Our businesses are rapidly evolving and intensely competitive. Our current and potential competitors include: (1) physical-world retailers, publishers, vendors, distributors, manufacturers, and producers of our products; (2) other online e-commerce and mobile e-commerce sites, including sites that sell or distribute digital content; (3) media companies, web portals, comparison shopping websites, and web search engines, either directly or in collaboration with other retailers; (4) companies that provide e-commerce services, including website development, fulfillment, customer service, and payment processing; (5) companies that provide information storage or computing services or products, including infrastructure and other web services; and (6) companies that design, manufacture, market, or sell consumer electronics, telecommunication, and media devices. We believe that the principal competitive factors in our retail businesses include selection, price, and convenience, including fast and reliable fulfillment. Additional competitive factors for our seller and enterprise services include the quality, speed, and reliability of our services and tools. Many of our current and potential competitors have greater resources, longer histories, more customers, and greater brand recognition. They may secure better terms from suppliers, adopt more aggressive pricing, and devote more resources to technology, infrastructure, fulfillment, and marketing. Other companies also may enter into business combinations or alliances that strengthen their competitive positions.

Intellectual Property

We regard our trademarks, service marks, copyrights, patents, domain names, trade dress, trade secrets, proprietary technologies, and similar intellectual property as critical to our success, and we rely on trademark, copyright, and patent law, trade-secret protection, and confidentiality and/or license agreements with our employees, customers, partners, and others to protect our proprietary rights. We have registered, or applied for the registration of, a number of U.S. and international domain names, trademarks, service marks, and copyrights. Additionally, we have filed U.S. and international patent applications covering certain of our proprietary technology. We have licensed in the past, and expect that we may license in the future, certain of our proprietary rights to third parties.

Seasonality

Our business is affected by seasonality, which historically has resulted in higher sales volume during our fourth quarter, which ends December 31. We recognized 35%, 36%, and 38% of our annual revenue during the fourth quarter of 2012, 2011, and 2010.

Employees

We employed approximately 88,400 full-time and part-time employees at December 31, 2012. However, employment levels fluctuate due to seasonal factors affecting our business. Additionally, we utilize independent contractors and temporary personnel to supplement our workforce, particularly on a seasonal basis. Although we have works councils and statutory employee representation obligations in certain countries, our employees are not represented by a labor union except where required by law and we consider our employee relations to be good. Competition for qualified personnel in our industry has historically been intense, particularly for software engineers, computer scientists, and other technical staff.

Available Information

Our investor relations website is www.amazon.com/ir and we encourage investors to use it as a way of easily finding information about us. We promptly make available on this website, free of charge, the reports that we file or furnish with the Securities and Exchange Commission ("SEC"), corporate governance information (including our Code of Business Conduct and Ethics), and select press releases and social media postings.

AMAZON.COM, INC.

CONSOLIDATED STATEMENTS OF CASH FLOWS
(in millions)

	Year Ended December 31,		
	2012	2011	2010
CASH AND CASH EQUIVALENTS, BEGINNING OF PERIOD	$ 5,269	$ 3,777	$ 3,444
OPERATING ACTIVITIES:			
Net income (loss)	(39)	631	1,152
Adjustments to reconcile net income (loss) to net cash from operating activities:			
Depreciation of property and equipment, including internal-use software and website development, and other amortization	2,159	1,083	568
Stock-based compensation	833	557	424
Other operating expense (income), net	154	154	106
Losses (gains) on sales of marketable securities, net	(9)	(4)	(2)
Other expense (income), net	253	(56)	(79)
Deferred income taxes	(265)	136	4
Excess tax benefits from stock-based compensation	(429)	(62)	(259)
Changes in operating assets and liabilities:			
Inventories	(999)	(1,777)	(1,019)
Accounts receivable, net and other	(861)	(866)	(295)
Accounts payable	2,070	2,997	2,373
Accrued expenses and other	1,038	1,067	740
Additions to unearned revenue	1,796	1,064	687
Amortization of previously unearned revenue	(1,521)	(1,021)	(905)
Net cash provided by (used in) operating activities	4,180	3,903	3,495
INVESTING ACTIVITIES:			
Purchases of property and equipment, including internal-use software and website development	(3,785)	(1,811)	(979)
Acquisitions, net of cash acquired, and other	(745)	(705)	(352)
Sales and maturities of marketable securities and other investments	4,237	6,843	4,250
Purchases of marketable securities and other investments	(3,302)	(6,257)	(6,279)
Net cash provided by (used in) investing activities	(3,595)	(1,930)	(3,360)
FINANCING ACTIVITIES:			
Excess tax benefits from stock-based compensation	429	62	259
Common stock repurchased	(960)	(277)	—
Proceeds from long-term debt and other	3,378	177	143
Repayments of long-term debt, capital lease, and finance lease obligations	(588)	(444)	(221)
Net cash provided by (used in) financing activities	2,259	(482)	181
Foreign-currency effect on cash and cash equivalents	(29)	1	17
Net increase (decrease) in cash and cash equivalents	2,815	1,492	333
CASH AND CASH EQUIVALENTS, END OF PERIOD	$ 8,084	$ 5,269	$ 3,777
SUPPLEMENTAL CASH FLOW INFORMATION:			
Cash paid for interest on long-term debt	$ 31	$ 14	$ 11
Cash paid for income taxes (net of refunds)	112	33	75
Property and equipment acquired under capital leases	802	753	405
Property and equipment acquired under build-to-suit leases	29	259	172

See accompanying notes to consolidated financial statements.

AMAZON.COM, INC.

CONSOLIDATED STATEMENTS OF OPERATIONS
(in millions, except per share data)

	Year Ended December 31,		
	2012	**2011**	**2010**
Net product sales	$51,733	$42,000	$30,792
Net services sales	9,360	6,077	3,412
Total net sales	61,093	48,077	34,204
Operating expenses (1):			
Cost of sales	45,971	37,288	26,561
Fulfillment	6,419	4,576	2,898
Marketing	2,408	1,630	1,029
Technology and content	4,564	2,909	1,734
General and administrative	896	658	470
Other operating expense (income), net	159	154	106
Total operating expenses	60,417	47,215	32,798
Income from operations	676	862	1,406
Interest income	40	61	51
Interest expense	(92)	(65)	(39)
Other income (expense), net	(80)	76	79
Total non-operating income (expense)	(132)	72	91
Income before income taxes	544	934	1,497
Provision for income taxes	(428)	(291)	(352)
Equity-method investment activity, net of tax	(155)	(12)	7
Net income (loss)	$ (39)	$ 631	$ 1,152
Basic earnings per share	$ (0.09)	$ 1.39	$ 2.58
Diluted earnings per share	$ (0.09)	$ 1.37	$ 2.53
Weighted average shares used in computation of earnings per share:			
Basic	453	453	447
Diluted	453	461	456

AMAZON.COM, INC.

CONSOLIDATED STATEMENTS OF COMPREHENSIVE INCOME
(in millions)

	Year Ended December 31,		
	2012	**2011**	**2010**
Net income (loss)	$(39)	$ 631	$1,152
Other comprehensive income (loss):			
Foreign currency translation adjustments, net of tax of $(30), $20, and $29	76	(123)	(137)
Net change in unrealized gains on available-for-sale securities:			
Unrealized gains (losses), net of tax of $(3), $1, and $(2)	8	(1)	5
Reclassification adjustment for losses (gains) included in net income, net of tax effect of $3, $1, and $0	(7)	(2)	(2)
Net unrealized gains (losses) on available-for-sale securities	1	(3)	3
Total other comprehensive income (loss)	77	(126)	(134)
Comprehensive income	$ 38	$ 505	$1,018

See accompanying notes to consolidated financial statements.

AMAZON.COM, INC.

CONSOLIDATED BALANCE SHEETS
(in millions, except per share data)

	December 31, 2012	December 31, 2011
ASSETS		
Current assets:		
Cash and cash equivalents	$ 8,084	$ 5,269
Marketable securities	3,364	4,307
Inventories	6,031	4,992
Accounts receivable, net and other	3,364	2,571
Deferred tax assets	453	351
Total current assets	21,296	17,490
Property and equipment, net	7,060	4,417
Deferred tax assets	123	28
Goodwill	2,552	1,955
Other assets	1,524	1,388
Total assets	$32,555	$25,278
LIABILITIES AND STOCKHOLDERS' EQUITY		
Current liabilities:		
Accounts payable	$13,318	$11,145
Accrued expenses and other	5,684	3,751
Total current liabilities	19,002	14,896
Long-term debt	3,084	255
Other long-term liabilities	2,277	2,370
Commitments and contingencies		
Stockholders' equity:		
Preferred stock, $0.01 par value:		
Authorized shares — 500		
Issued and outstanding shares — none	—	—
Common stock, $0.01 par value:		
Authorized shares — 5,000		
Issued shares — 478 and 473		
Outstanding shares — 454 and 455	5	5
Treasury stock, at cost	(1,837)	(877)
Additional paid-in capital	8,347	6,990
Accumulated other comprehensive loss	(239)	(316)
Retained earnings	1,916	1,955
Total stockholders' equity	8,192	7,757
Total liabilities and stockholders' equity	$32,555	$25,278

See accompanying notes to consolidated financial statements.

AMAZON.COM, INC.

CONSOLIDATED STATEMENTS OF STOCKHOLDERS' EQUITY
(in millions)

	Common Stock		Treasury Stock	Additional Paid-In Capital	Accumulated Other Comprehensive Income (Loss)	Retained Earnings	Total Stockholders' Equity
	Shares	Amount					
Balance at January 1, 2010	444	$ 5	$ (600)	$5,736	$ (56)	$ 172	$5,257
Net income	—	—	—	—	—	1,152	1,152
Other comprehensive income (loss)	—	—	—	—	(134)	—	(134)
Exercise of common stock options	7	—	—	16	—	—	16
Excess tax benefits from stock-based compensation	—	—	—	145	—	—	145
Stock-based compensation and issuance of employee benefit plan stock	—	—	—	428	—	—	428
Balance at December 31, 2010	451	5	(600)	6,325	(190)	1,324	6,864
Net income	—	—	—	—	—	631	631
Other comprehensive income (loss)	—	—	—	—	(126)	—	(126)
Exercise of common stock options	5	—	—	7	—	—	7
Repurchase of common stock	(1)	—	(277)	—	—	—	(277)
Excess tax benefits from stock-based compensation	—	—	—	62	—	—	62
Stock-based compensation and issuance of employee benefit plan stock	—	—	—	569	—	—	569
Issuance of common stock for acquisition activity	—	—	—	27	—	—	27
Balance at December 31, 2011	455	5	(877)	6,990	(316)	1,955	7,757
Net income (loss)	—	—	—	—	—	(39)	(39)
Other comprehensive income	—	—	—	—	77	—	77
Exercise of common stock options	4	—	—	8	—	—	8
Repurchase of common stock	(5)	—	(960)	—	—	—	(960)
Excess tax benefits from stock-based compensation	—	—	—	429	—	—	429
Stock-based compensation and issuance of employee benefit plan stock	—	—	—	854	—	—	854
Issuance of common stock for acquisition activity	—	—	—	66	—	—	66
Balance at December 31, 2012	454	$ 5	$(1,837)	$8,347	$(239)	$1,916	$8,192

See accompanying notes to consolidated financial statements.

AMAZON.COM, INC.

NOTES TO CONSOLIDATED FINANCIAL STATEMENTS

Note 1—DESCRIPTION OF BUSINESS AND ACCOUNTING POLICIES

Description of Business

Amazon.com opened its virtual doors on the World Wide Web in July 1995 and offers Earth's Biggest Selection. We seek to be Earth's most customer-centric company for four primary customer sets: consumers, sellers, enterprises, and content creators. We serve consumers through our retail websites and focus on selection, price, and convenience. We also manufacture and sell Kindle devices. We offer programs that enable sellers to sell their products on our websites and their own branded websites and to fulfill orders through us, and programs that allow authors, musicians, filmmakers, app developers, and others to publish and sell content. We serve developers and enterprises of all sizes through AWS, which provides access to technology infrastructure that enables virtually any type of business. In addition, we generate revenue through services, such as advertising services and co-branded credit card agreements.

We have organized our operations into two principal segments: North America and International. See "Note 12—Segment Information."

Prior Period Reclassifications

Certain prior period amounts have been reclassified to conform to the current period presentation. Long-term debt is now presented separately on our consolidated balance sheets.

Principles of Consolidation

The consolidated financial statements include the accounts of Amazon.com, Inc., its wholly-owned subsidiaries, and those entities in which we have a variable interest and are the primary beneficiary. Intercompany balances and transactions between consolidated entities are eliminated.

Use of Estimates

The preparation of financial statements in conformity with GAAP requires estimates and assumptions that affect the reported amounts of assets and liabilities, revenues and expenses, and related disclosures of contingent liabilities in the consolidated financial statements and accompanying notes. Estimates are used for, but not limited to, determining the selling price of products and services in multiple element revenue arrangements and determining the lives of these elements, incentive discount offers, sales returns, vendor funding, stock-based compensation, income taxes, valuation and impairment of investments, inventory valuation and inventory purchase commitments, collectability of receivables, valuation of acquired intangibles and goodwill, depreciable lives of property and equipment, internally-developed software, acquisition purchase price allocations, investments in equity interests, and contingencies. Actual results could differ materially from those estimates.

Earnings per Share

Basic earnings per share is calculated using our weighted-average outstanding common shares. Diluted earnings per share is calculated using our weighted-average outstanding common shares including the dilutive effect of stock awards as determined under the treasury stock method.

The following table shows the calculation of diluted shares (in millions):

	Year Ended December 31,		
	2012	2011	2010
Shares used in computation of basic earnings per share	453	453	447
Total dilutive effect of outstanding stock awards (1)	—	8	9
Shares used in computation of diluted earnings per share	453	461	456

(1) Calculated using the treasury stock method, which assumes proceeds are used to reduce the dilutive effect of outstanding stock awards. Assumed proceeds include the unrecognized deferred compensation of stock awards, and assumed tax proceeds from excess stock-based compensation deductions.

Cash and Cash Equivalents

We classify all highly liquid instruments with an original maturity of three months or less at the time of purchase as cash equivalents.

Inventories

Inventories, consisting of products available for sale, are primarily accounted for using the FIFO method, and are valued at the lower of cost or market value. This valuation requires us to make judgments, based on currently-available information, about the likely method of disposition, such as through sales to individual customers, returns to product vendors, or liquidations, and expected recoverable values of each disposition category.

We provide Fulfillment by Amazon services in connection with certain of our sellers' programs. Third-party sellers maintain ownership of their inventory, regardless of whether fulfillment is provided by us or the third-party sellers, and therefore these products are not included in our inventories.

Accounts Receivable, Net, and Other

Included in "Accounts receivable, net and other" on our consolidated balance sheets are amounts primarily related to vendor and customer receivables. At December 31, 2012 and 2011, vendor receivables, net, were $1.1 billion and $934 million, and customer receivables, net, were $1.5 billion and $1.2 billion.

Allowance for Doubtful Accounts

We estimate losses on receivables based on known troubled accounts and historical experience of losses incurred. Receivables are considered impaired and written-off when it is probable that all contractual payments due will not be collected in accordance with the terms of the agreement. The allowance for doubtful accounts was $116 million and $82 million at December 31, 2012 and 2011.

Internal-use Software and Website Development

Costs incurred to develop software for internal use and our websites are capitalized and amortized over the estimated useful life of the software. Costs related to design or maintenance of internal-use software and website development are expensed as incurred. For the years ended 2012, 2011, and 2010, we capitalized $454 million (including $74 million of stock-based compensation), $307 million (including $51 million of stock-based compensation), and $213 million (including $38 million of stock-based compensation) of costs associated with internal-use software and website development. Amortization of previously capitalized amounts was $327 million, $236 million, and $184 million for 2012, 2011, and 2010.

Property and Equipment, Net

Property and equipment are stated at cost. Property includes buildings and land that we own, along with property we have acquired under build-to-suit, financing, and capital lease arrangements. Equipment includes assets such as furniture and fixtures, heavy equipment, servers and networking equipment, and internal-use software and website development. Depreciation is recorded on a straight-line basis over the estimated useful lives of the assets (generally the lesser of 40 years or the remaining life of the underlying building, two years for assets such as internal-use software, three years for our servers, five years for networking equipment, five years for furniture and fixtures, and ten years for heavy equipment). Depreciation expense is classified within the corresponding operating expense categories on our consolidated statements of operations.

Leases and Asset Retirement Obligations

We categorize leases at their inception as either operating or capital leases. On certain of our lease agreements, we may receive rent holidays and other incentives. We recognize lease costs on a straight-line basis without regard to deferred payment terms, such as rent holidays that defer the commencement date of required payments. Additionally, incentives we receive are treated as a reduction of our costs over the term of the agreement. Leasehold improvements are capitalized at cost and amortized over the lesser of their expected useful life or the non-cancellable term of the lease.

We establish assets and liabilities for the estimated construction costs incurred under build-to-suit lease arrangements to the extent we are involved in the construction of structural improvements or take construction risk prior to commencement of a lease. Upon occupancy of facilities under build-to-suit leases, we assess whether these arrangements qualify for sales recognition under the sale-leaseback accounting guidance. If we continue to be the deemed owner, the facilities are accounted for as financing leases.

We establish assets and liabilities for the present value of estimated future costs to retire long-lived assets at the termination or expiration of a lease. Such assets are depreciated over the lease period into operating expense, and the recorded liabilities are accreted to the future value of the estimated retirement costs.

Goodwill

We evaluate goodwill for impairment annually or more frequently when an event occurs or circumstances change that indicate that the carrying value may not be recoverable. We test goodwill for impairment by first comparing the book value of net assets to the fair value of the reporting units. If the fair value is determined to be less than the book value or qualitative factors indicate that it is more likely than not that goodwill is impaired, a second step is performed to compute the amount of impairment as the difference between the estimated fair value of goodwill and the carrying value. We estimate the fair value of the reporting units using discounted cash flows. Forecasts of future cash flows are based on our best estimate of future net sales and operating expenses, based primarily on expected category expansion, pricing, market segment share, and general economic conditions.

We conduct our annual impairment test as of October 1 of each year, and have determined there to be no impairment for any of the periods presented. There were no triggering events identified from the date of our assessment through December 31, 2012 that would require an update to our annual impairment test. See "Note 4—Acquisitions, Goodwill, and Acquired Intangible Assets."

Other Assets

Included in "Other assets" on our consolidated balance sheets are amounts primarily related to acquired intangible assets, net of amortization; digital video content, net of amortization; certain equity investments; marketable securities restricted for longer than one year, the majority of which are attributable to collateralization of bank guarantees and debt related to our international operations; and intellectual property rights, net of amortization.

Investments

We generally invest our excess cash in investment grade short-to intermediate-term fixed income securities and AAA-rated money market funds. Such investments are included in "Cash and cash equivalents," or "Marketable securities" on the accompanying consolidated balance sheets, classified as available for sale, and reported at fair value with unrealized gains and losses included in "Accumulated other comprehensive loss."

Equity investments, including our 29% investment in LivingSocial, are accounted for using the equity method of accounting if the investment gives us the ability to exercise significant influence, but not control, over an investee. The total of our investments in equity-method investees, including identifiable intangible assets, deferred tax liabilities, and goodwill, is included within "Other assets" on our consolidated balance sheets. Our share of the earnings or losses as reported by equity method investees, amortization of the related intangible assets, and related gains or losses, if any, are classified as "Equity-method investment activity, net of tax" on our consolidated statements of operations. Our share of the net income or loss of our equity method investees includes operating and non-operating gains and charges, which can have a significant impact on our reported equity-method investment activity and the carrying value of those investments. We regularly evaluate these investments, which are not carried at fair value, for other-than-temporary impairment. We also consider whether our equity method investments generate sufficient cash flows from their operating or financing activities to meet their obligations and repay their liabilities when they come due.

We record purchases, including incremental purchases, of shares in equity-method investees at cost. Reductions in our ownership percentage of an investee, including through dilution, are generally valued at fair value, with the difference between fair value and our recorded cost reflected as a gain or loss in our equity-method investment activity. In the event we no longer have the ability to exercise significant influence over an equity-method investee, we would discontinue accounting for the investment under the equity method.

Equity investments without readily determinable fair values for which we do not have the ability to exercise significant influence are accounted for using the cost method of accounting and classified as "Other assets" on our consolidated balance sheets. Under the cost method, investments are carried at cost and are adjusted only for other-than-temporary declines in fair value, certain distributions, and additional investments.

Equity investments that have readily determinable fair values are classified as available for sale and are included in "Marketable securities" in our consolidated balance sheet and are recorded at fair value with unrealized gains and losses, net of tax, included in "Accumulated other comprehensive loss."

We periodically evaluate whether declines in fair values of our investments below their book value are other-than-temporary. This evaluation consists of several qualitative and quantitative factors regarding the severity and duration of the unrealized loss as well as our ability and intent to hold the investment until a forecasted recovery occurs. Additionally, we assess whether we have plans to sell the security or it is more likely than not we will be required to sell any investment before recovery of its amortized cost basis. Factors considered include quoted market prices; recent financial results and operating trends; implied values from any recent transactions or offers of investee securities; credit quality of debt instrument issuers; other publicly available information that may affect the value of our investments; duration and severity of the decline in value; and our strategy and intentions for holding the investment.

Long-Lived Assets

Long-lived assets, other than goodwill, are reviewed for impairment whenever events or changes in circumstances indicate that the carrying amount of the assets might not be recoverable. Conditions that would necessitate an impairment assessment include a significant decline in the observable market value of an asset, a significant change in the extent or manner in which an asset is used, or any other significant adverse change that would indicate that the carrying amount of an asset or group of assets may not be recoverable.

For long-lived assets used in operations, impairment losses are only recorded if the asset's carrying amount is not recoverable through its undiscounted, probability-weighted future cash flows. We measure the impairment loss based on the difference between the carrying amount and estimated fair value. Long-lived assets are considered held for sale when certain criteria are met, including when management has committed to a plan to sell the asset, the asset is available for sale in its immediate condition, and the sale is probable within one year of the reporting date. Assets held for sale are reported at the lower of cost or fair value less costs to sell. Assets held for sale were not significant at December 31, 2012 or 2011.

Accrued Expenses and Other

Included in "Accrued expenses and other" at December 31, 2012 and 2011 were liabilities of $1.1 billion and $788 million for unredeemed gift certificates. We reduce the liability for a gift certificate when redeemed by a customer. If a gift certificate is not redeemed, we recognize revenue when it expires or, for a certificate without an expiration date, when the likelihood of its redemption becomes remote, generally two years from the date of issuance.

Unearned Revenue

Unearned revenue is recorded when payments are received in advance of performing our service obligations and is recognized over the service period. Unearned revenue primarily relates to Amazon Prime memberships and AWS services. Current unearned revenue is included in "Accrued expenses and other" and non-current unearned revenue is included in "Other long-term liabilities" on our consolidated balance sheets. Current unearned revenue was $792 million and $462 million at December 31, 2012 and 2011. Non-current unearned revenue was $108 million and $87 million at December 31, 2012 and 2011.

Income Taxes

Income tax expense includes U.S. and international income taxes. Except as required under U.S. tax law, we do not provide for U.S. taxes on our undistributed earnings of foreign subsidiaries that have not been previously taxed since we intend to invest such undistributed earnings indefinitely outside of the U.S. If our intent changes or if these funds are needed for our U.S. operations, we would be required to accrue or pay U.S. taxes on some or all of these undistributed earnings. Undistributed earnings of foreign subsidiaries that are indefinitely invested outside of the U.S were $2.1 billion at December 31, 2012. Determination of the unrecognized deferred tax liability that would be incurred if such amounts were repatriated is not practicable.

Deferred income tax balances reflect the effects of temporary differences between the carrying amounts of assets and liabilities and their tax bases and are stated at enacted tax rates expected to be in effect when taxes are actually paid or recovered.

Deferred tax assets are evaluated for future realization and reduced by a valuation allowance to the extent we believe a portion will not be realized. We consider many factors when assessing the likelihood of future realization of our deferred tax assets, including our recent cumulative earnings experience and expectations of future taxable income and capital gains by taxing jurisdiction, the carry-forward periods available to us for tax reporting purposes, and other relevant factors. We allocate our valuation allowance to current and long-term deferred tax assets on a pro-rata basis.

We utilize a two-step approach to recognizing and measuring uncertain income tax positions (tax contingencies). The first step is to evaluate the tax position for recognition by determining if the weight of available evidence indicates it is more likely than not that the position will be sustained on audit, including resolution of related appeals or litigation processes. The second step is to measure the tax benefit as the largest amount which is more than 50% likely of being realized upon ultimate settlement. We consider many factors when evaluating and estimating our tax positions and tax benefits, which may require periodic adjustments and which may not accurately forecast actual outcomes. We include interest and penalties related to our tax contingencies in income tax expense.

Fair Value of Financial Instruments

Fair value is defined as the price that would be received to sell an asset or paid to transfer a liability in an orderly transaction between market participants at the measurement date. To increase the comparability of fair value measures, the following hierarchy prioritizes the inputs to valuation methodologies used to measure fair value:

Level 1—Valuations based on quoted prices for identical assets and liabilities in active markets.

Level 2—Valuations based on observable inputs other than quoted prices included in Level 1, such as quoted prices for similar assets and liabilities in active markets, quoted prices for identical or similar assets and liabilities in markets that are not active, or other inputs that are observable or can be corroborated by observable market data.

Level 3—Valuations based on unobservable inputs reflecting our own assumptions, consistent with reasonably available assumptions made by other market participants. These valuations require significant judgment.

We measure the fair value of money market funds and equity securities based on quoted prices in active markets for identical assets or liabilities. All other financial instruments were valued either based on recent trades of securities in inactive markets or based on quoted market prices of similar instruments and other significant inputs derived from or corroborated by observable market data. We did not hold any cash, cash equivalents, or marketable securities categorized as Level 3 as of December 31, 2012, or December 31, 2011.

Revenue

We recognize revenue from product sales or services rendered when the following four criteria are met: persuasive evidence of an arrangement exists, delivery has occurred or services have been rendered, the selling price is fixed or determinable, and collectability is reasonably assured. Revenue arrangements with multiple deliverables are divided into separate units and revenue is allocated using estimated selling prices if we do not have vendor-specific objective evidence or third-party evidence of the selling prices of the deliverables. We allocate the arrangement price to each of the elements based on the estimated selling prices of each element. Estimated selling prices are management's best estimates of the prices that we would charge our customers if we were to sell the standalone elements separately and include considerations of customer demand, prices charged by us and others for similar deliverables, and the price if largely based on costs. Sales of our Kindle device are considered arrangements with multiple deliverables, consisting of the device, 3G wireless access and delivery for some models, and software upgrades. The revenue related to the device, which is the substantial portion of the total sale price, and related costs are recognized upon delivery. Revenue related to 3G wireless access and delivery and software upgrades is amortized over the average life of the device, which is estimated to be three years.

We evaluate whether it is appropriate to record the gross amount of product sales and related costs or the net amount earned as commissions. Generally, when we are primarily obligated in a transaction, are subject to inventory risk, have latitude in establishing prices and selecting suppliers, or have several but not all of these indicators, revenue is recorded at the gross sales price. We generally record the net amounts as commissions earned if we are not primarily obligated and do not have latitude in establishing prices. Such amounts earned are determined using a fixed percentage, a fixed-payment schedule, or a combination of the two.

Product sales represent revenue from the sale of products and related shipping fees and digital content where we are the seller of record. Product sales and shipping revenues, net of promotional discounts, rebates, and return allowances, are recorded when the products are shipped and title passes to customers. Kindle devices sold through retailers are recognized at the point of sale to consumers. Retail sales to customers are made pursuant to a sales contract that provides for transfer of both title and risk of loss upon our delivery to the carrier.

Services sales represent third-party seller fees earned (including commissions) and related shipping fees, and non-retail activities such as AWS, advertising services, and our co-branded credit card agreements. Services sales, net of promotional discounts and return allowances, are recognized when services have been rendered. Amounts received in advance for services, including amounts received for Amazon Prime and web services, are deferred and recognized as revenue over the term.

Return allowances, which reduce revenue, are estimated using historical experience. Revenue from product sales and services rendered is recorded net of sales and consumption taxes. Additionally, we periodically provide incentive offers to our customers to encourage purchases. Such offers include current discount offers, such as percentage discounts off current purchases, inducement offers, such as offers for future discounts subject to a minimum current purchase, and other similar offers. Current discount offers, when accepted by our customers, are treated as a reduction to the purchase price of the related transaction, while inducement offers, when accepted by our customers, are treated as a reduction to purchase price based on estimated future redemption rates. Redemption rates are estimated using our historical experience for similar inducement offers. Current discount offers and inducement offers are presented as a net amount in "Total net sales."

Cost of Sales

Cost of sales consists of the purchase price of consumer products and digital content where we are the seller of record, inbound and outbound shipping charges, and packaging supplies. Shipping charges to receive products from our suppliers are included in our inventory, and recognized as cost of sales upon sale of products to our customers. Payment processing and related transaction costs, including those associated with seller transactions, are classified in "Fulfillment" on our consolidated statements of operations.

Content Costs

We obtain digital video content through licensing agreements that have a wide range of licensing provisions and are generally from one to five years with fixed payment schedules. When the license fee for a specific movie or television title is determinable or reasonably estimable and available for streaming, we recognize an asset representing the fee per title and a corresponding liability for the amounts owed. We amortize the asset on a straight-line basis over each title's contractual window of availability, which typically ranges from six months to five years. If we are unable to reasonably estimate the cost per title, no asset or liability is recorded and licensing costs are expensed as incurred.

Vendor Agreements

We have agreements to receive cash consideration from certain of our vendors, including rebates and cooperative marketing reimbursements. We generally consider amounts received from our vendors as a reduction of the prices we pay for their products and, therefore, record such amounts as a reduction of the cost of inventory we buy from them. Vendor rebates are typically dependent upon reaching minimum purchase thresholds. We evaluate the likelihood of reaching purchase thresholds using past experience and current year forecasts. When volume rebates can be reasonably estimated, we record a portion of the rebate as we make progress towards the purchase threshold.

When we receive direct reimbursements for costs incurred by us in advertising the vendor's product or service, the amount we receive is recorded as an offset to "Marketing" on our consolidated statements of operations.

Fulfillment

Fulfillment costs represent those costs incurred in operating and staffing our fulfillment and customer service centers, including costs attributable to buying, receiving, inspecting, and warehousing inventories;

picking, packaging, and preparing customer orders for shipment; payment processing and related transaction costs, including costs associated with our guarantee for certain seller transactions; responding to inquiries from customers, and supply chain management for our manufactured Kindle devices. Fulfillment costs also include amounts paid to third parties that assist us in fulfillment and customer service operations.

Marketing

Marketing costs consist primarily of targeted online advertising, television advertising, public relations expenditures; and payroll and related expenses for personnel engaged in marketing, business development, and selling activities. We pay commissions to participants in our Associates program when their customer referrals result in product sales and classify such costs as "Marketing" on our consolidated statements of operations. We also participate in cooperative advertising arrangements with certain of our vendors, and other third parties.

Advertising and other promotional costs are expensed as incurred and were $2.0 billion, $1.4 billion, and $890 million in 2012, 2011, and 2010. Prepaid advertising costs were not significant at December 31, 2012 and 2011.

Technology and Content

Technology and content expenses consist principally of technology infrastructure expenses and payroll and related expenses for employees involved in application, product, and platform development, category expansion, editorial content, buying, merchandising selection, systems support, and digital initiatives, as well as costs associated with the compute, storage, and telecommunications infrastructure used internally and supporting AWS.

Technology and content costs are expensed as incurred, except for certain costs relating to the development of internal-use software and website development, including software used to upgrade and enhance our websites and applications supporting our business, which are capitalized and amortized over two years.

General and Administrative

General and administrative expenses consist of payroll and related expenses for employees involved in general corporate functions, including accounting, finance, tax, legal, and human relations, among others; costs associated with use by these functions of facilities and equipment, such as depreciation expense and rent; professional fees and litigation costs; and other general corporate costs.

Stock-Based Compensation

Compensation cost for all stock-based awards expected to vest is measured at fair value on the date of grant and recognized over the service period. The fair value of restricted stock units is determined based on the number of shares granted and the quoted price of our common stock. Such value is recognized as expense over the service period, net of estimated forfeitures, using the accelerated method. The estimation of stock awards that will ultimately vest requires judgment, and to the extent actual results or updated estimates differ from our current estimates, such amounts will be recorded as a cumulative adjustment in the period estimates are revised. We consider many factors when estimating expected forfeitures, including employee class, economic environment, and historical experience.

Other Operating Expense (Income), Net

Other operating expense (income), net, consists primarily of intangible asset amortization expense and expenses related to legal settlements.

Other Income (Expense), Net

Other income (expense), net, consists primarily of foreign currency gains and losses of $(95) million, $64 million, and $75 million in 2012, 2011, and 2010, and realized gains and losses on marketable securities sales of $10 million, $4 million, and $1 million in 2012, 2011, and 2010.

Foreign Currency

We have internationally-focused websites for the United Kingdom, Germany, France, Japan, Canada, China, Italy, Spain, and Brazil. Net sales generated from these websites, as well as most of the related expenses directly incurred from those operations, are denominated in the functional currencies of the resident countries. The functional currency of our subsidiaries that either operate or support these websites is the same as the local currency. Assets and liabilities of these subsidiaries are translated into U.S. Dollars at period-end exchange rates, and revenues and expenses are translated at average rates prevailing throughout the period. Translation adjustments are included in "Accumulated other comprehensive income (loss)," a separate component of stockholders' equity, and in the "Foreign-currency effect on cash and cash equivalents," on our consolidated statements of cash flows. Transaction gains and losses including intercompany transactions denominated in a currency other than the functional currency of the entity involved are included in "Other income (expense), net" on our consolidated statements of operations. In connection with the settlement and remeasurement of intercompany balances, we recorded gains (losses) of $(95) million in 2012 and $70 million in both 2011 and 2010.

Recent Accounting Pronouncements

In 2011, the Financial Accounting Standards Board ("FASB") issued two Accounting Standard Updates ("ASU"), which amend guidance for the presentation of comprehensive income. The amended guidance requires an entity to present components of net income and other comprehensive income in one continuous statement, referred to as the statement of comprehensive income, or in two separate, but consecutive statements. The option to report other comprehensive income and its components in the statement of stockholders' equity has been eliminated. Although the new guidance changes the presentation of comprehensive income, there are no changes to the components that are recognized in net income or other comprehensive income under existing guidance. We adopted these ASUs using two consecutive statements for all periods presented.

Note 2—CASH, CASH EQUIVALENTS, AND MARKETABLE SECURITIES

As of December 31, 2012 and 2011, our cash, cash equivalents, and marketable securities primarily consisted of cash, U.S. and foreign government and agency securities, AAA-rated money market funds, and other investment grade securities. Our marketable fixed-income securities have effective maturities of less than 5 years. Cash equivalents and marketable securities are recorded at fair value. The following table summarizes, by major security type, our cash, cash equivalents, and marketable securities that are measured at fair value on a recurring basis and are categorized using the fair value hierarchy (in millions):

	December 31, 2012			
	Cost or Amortized Cost	Gross Unrealized Gains	Gross Unrealized Losses	Total Estimated Fair Value
Cash	$ 2,595	—	—	$ 2,595
Level 1 securities:				
Money market funds	5,561	—	—	5,561
Equity securities	2	—	—	2
Level 2 securities:				
Foreign government and agency securities	763	9	—	772
U.S. government and agency securities	1,809	3	(2)	1,810
Corporate debt securities	719	6	—	725
Asset-backed securities	49	—	—	49
Other fixed income securities	33	—	—	33
	$11,531	$ 18	$ (2)	$11,547
Less: Restricted cash, cash equivalents, and marketable securities (1)				(99)
Total cash, cash equivalents, and marketable securities				$11,448

---

(1) We are required to pledge or otherwise restrict a portion of our cash, cash equivalents, and marketable securities as collateral for standby and trade letters of credit, guarantees, debt, and real estate lease agreements. We classify cash and marketable securities with use restrictions of less than twelve months as "Accounts receivable, net and other" and of twelve months or longer as non-current "Other assets" on our consolidated balance sheets. See "Note 8—Commitments and Contingencies."

The following table summarizes gross gains and gross losses realized on sales of available-for-sale marketable securities (in millions):

	Year Ended December 31,		
	2012	2011	2010
Realized gains	$20	$15	$5
Realized losses	10	11	4

The following table summarizes the maturities of our cash equivalent and marketable fixed-income securities as of December 31, 2012 (in millions):

	Amortized Cost	Estimated Fair Value
Due within one year	$6,689	$6,691
Due after one year through five years	1,968	1,981
Due after five years	277	278
	$8,934	$8,950

Actual maturities may differ from the contractual maturities because borrowers may have certain prepayment conditions.

Note 3—PROPERTY AND EQUIPMENT

Property and equipment, at cost, consisted of the following (in millions):

	December 31,	
	2012	2011
Gross Property and Equipment (1):		
Land and buildings	$2,966	$1,437
Equipment and internal-use software (2)	6,228	4,106
Other corporate assets	174	137
Construction in progress	214	106
Gross property and equipment	$9,582	$5,786
Total accumulated depreciation (1)	2,522	1,369
Total property and equipment, net	$7,060	$4,417

(1) Excludes the original cost and accumulated depreciation of fully-depreciated assets.
(2) Includes internal-use software of $866 million and $623 million at December 31, 2012 and 2011.

In December 2012, we acquired our corporate headquarters for $1.2 billion consisting of land and 11 buildings that were previously accounted for as financing leases. The acquired building assets will be depreciated over their estimated useful lives of 40 years. We also acquired three city blocks of land for the expansion of our corporate headquarters for approximately $210 million.

Depreciation expense on property and equipment was $1.7 billion, $1.0 billion, and $552 million, which includes amortization of property and equipment acquired under capital lease obligations of $510 million, $335 million, and $164 million for 2012, 2011, and 2010. Gross assets remaining under capital leases were $2.3 billion and $1.6 billion at December 31, 2012 and 2011. Accumulated depreciation associated with capital leases was $1.1 billion and $603 million at December 31, 2012 and 2011. Cash paid for interest on capital leases was $51 million, $44 million, and $26 million for 2012, 2011, and 2010.

Note 6—LONG-TERM DEBT

In November 2012, we issued $3.0 billion of unsecured senior notes in three tranches as described in the table below (collectively, the "Notes"). The net carrying amount of the Notes was $3.0 billion and the unamortized discount was $27 million at December 31, 2012. We also have other long-term debt with a carrying amount, including the current portion, of $691 million and $384 million at December 31, 2012 and 2011. The face value of our total long-term debt obligations is as follows (in millions):

	December 31, 2012	2011
0.65% Notes due on November 27, 2015	$ 750	$ —
1.20% Notes due on November 29, 2017	1,000	—
2.50% Notes due on November 29, 2022	1,250	—
Other long-term debt	691	384
Total debt	3,691	384
Less current portion of long-term debt	(579)	(129)
Face value of long-term debt	$3,112	$ 255

The effective interest rates of the 2015, 2017, and 2022 Notes were 0.84%, 1.38%, and 2.66%. Interest on the Notes is payable semi-annually in arrears in May and November. We may redeem the Notes at any time in whole, or from time to time, in part at specified redemption prices. We are not subject to any financial covenants under the Notes. We used the net proceeds from the issuance of the Notes for general corporate purposes. The estimated fair value of the Notes was approximately $3.0 billion at December 31, 2012, which is based on quoted prices for our publicly-traded debt as of that date.

The other debt, including the current portion, had a weighted average interest rate of 6.4% and 5.9% in 2012 and 2011. We used the net proceeds from the issuance of the debt to fund certain international operations. The estimated fair value of the other long-term debt, which is based on Level 2 inputs, approximated its carrying value at December 31, 2012 and December 31, 2011.

At December 31, 2012, future principal payments for debt were as follows (in millions):

Year Ended December 31,	
2013	$ 579
2014	46
2015	816
2016	—
2017	1,000
Thereafter	1,250
	$3,691

Note 8—COMMITMENTS AND CONTINGENCIES

Commitments

We have entered into non-cancellable operating, capital, and financing leases for equipment and office, fulfillment center, and data center facilities. Rental expense under operating lease agreements was $541 million, $362 million, and $225 million for 2012, 2011, and 2010.

The following summarizes our principal contractual commitments, excluding open orders for purchases that support normal operations, as of December 31, 2012 (in millions):

	Year Ended December 31,					Thereafter	Total
	2013	2014	2015	2016	2017		
Operating and capital commitments:							
Debt principal and interest	$ 656	$ 105	$ 866	$ 43	$1,069	$1,380	$ 4,119
Capital leases, including interest	562	403	214	51	17	95	1,342
Financing lease obligations, including interest	1	1	1	1	1	9	14
Operating leases	595	634	570	514	453	2,688	5,454
Unconditional purchase obligations (1)	302	239	143	38	1	—	723
Other commitments (2) (3)	380	276	253	110	78	436	1,533
Total commitments	$2,496	$1,658	$2,047	$757	$1,619	$4,608	$13,185

(1) Includes unconditional purchase obligations related to agreements to acquire and license digital video content that represent long-term liabilities or that are not reflected on the consolidated balance sheets.
(2) Includes the estimated timing and amounts of payments for rent and tenant improvements associated with build-to-suit lease arrangements that have not been placed in service.
(3) Excludes $294 million of tax contingencies for which we cannot make a reasonably reliable estimate of the amount and period of payment, if any.

Pledged Securities

We have pledged or otherwise restricted $99 million and $156 million in 2012 and 2011 of our cash and marketable securities as collateral for standby and trade letters of credit, guarantees, debt related to our international operations, as well as real estate leases.

Inventory Suppliers

During 2012, no vendor accounted for 10% or more of our inventory purchases. We generally do not have long-term contracts or arrangements with our vendors to guarantee the availability of merchandise, particular payment terms, or the extension of credit limits.

Legal Proceedings (Selected)

The Company is involved from time to time in claims, proceedings, and litigation, including the following:

Beginning in March 2003, we were served with complaints filed in several different states, including Illinois, by a private litigant, Beeler, Schad & Diamond, P.C., purportedly on behalf of the state governments under various state False Claims Acts. The complaints allege that we (along with other companies with which we have commercial agreements) wrongfully failed to collect and remit sales and use taxes for sales of personal property to customers in those states and knowingly created records and statements falsely stating we were not required to collect or remit such taxes. In December 2006, we learned that one additional complaint was filed in the state of Illinois by a different private litigant, Matthew T. Hurst, alleging similar violations of the Illinois state law. The Hurst case was dismissed with prejudice in June 2012. All of the complaints seek injunctive relief, unpaid taxes, interest, attorneys' fees, civil penalties of up to $10,000 per violation, and treble or punitive damages under the various state False Claims Acts. It is possible that we have been or will be named in similar cases in other states as well. We dispute the allegations of wrongdoing in these complaints and intend to vigorously defend ourselves in these matters.

Note 9—STOCKHOLDERS' EQUITY

Preferred Stock

We have authorized 500 million shares of $0.01 par value Preferred Stock. No preferred stock was outstanding for any period presented.

Common Stock

Common shares outstanding plus shares underlying outstanding stock awards totaled 470 million, 468 million, and 465 million, at December 31, 2012, 2011, and 2010. These totals include all vested and unvested stock-based awards outstanding, including those awards we estimate will be forfeited.

Stock Repurchase Activity

In January 2010, our Board of Directors authorized the Company to repurchase up to $2.0 billion of our common stock with no fixed expiration. We have $763 million remaining under the $2.0 billion repurchase program.

Stock Award Plans

Employees vest in restricted stock unit awards over the corresponding service term, generally between two and five years.

Note 11—INCOME TAXES

In 2012, 2011, and 2010, we recorded net tax provisions of $428 million, $291 million, and $352 million. A majority of this provision is non-cash. We have tax benefits relating to excess stock-based compensation that are being utilized to reduce our U.S. taxable income. As such, cash taxes paid, net of refunds, were $112 million, $33 million, and $75 million for 2012, 2011, and 2010.

The components of the provision for income taxes, net are as follows (in millions):

| | Year Ended December 31, | | |
	2012	2011	2010
Current taxes:			
U.S. and state	$ 562	$103	$311
International	131	52	37
Current taxes	693	155	348
Deferred taxes:			
U.S. and state	(156)	157	1
International	(109)	(21)	3
Deferred taxes	(265)	136	4
Provision for income taxes, net	$ 428	$291	$352

U.S. and international components of income before income taxes are as follows (in millions):

| | Year Ended December 31, | | |
	2012	2011	2010
U.S.	$ 882	$658	$ 886
International	(338)	276	611
Income before income taxes	$ 544	$934	$1,497

The items accounting for differences between income taxes computed at the federal statutory rate and the provision recorded for income taxes are as follows:

	Year Ended December 31,		
	2012	2011	2010
Federal statutory rate	35.0%	35.0%	35.0%
Effect of:			
Impact of foreign tax differential	31.5	(8.4)	(12.7)
State taxes, net of federal benefits	0.2	1.5	1.5
Tax credits	(4.4)	(3.2)	(1.1)
Nondeductible stock-based compensation	11.1	4.1	1.6
Other, net	5.2	2.2	(0.8)
Total	78.6%	31.2%	23.5%

Our effective tax rate in 2012, 2011, and 2010 was significantly affected by two factors: the favorable impact of earnings in lower tax rate jurisdictions and the adverse effect of losses incurred in certain foreign jurisdictions for which we may not realize a tax benefit. Income earned in lower tax jurisdictions is primarily related to our European operations, which are headquartered in Luxembourg. Losses incurred in foreign jurisdictions for which we may not realize a tax benefit, primarily generated by subsidiaries located outside of Europe, reduce our pre-tax income without a corresponding reduction in our tax expense, and therefore increase our effective tax rate. We have recorded a valuation allowance against the related deferred tax assets.

In 2012, the adverse impact of such foreign jurisdiction losses was partially offset by the favorable impact of earnings in lower tax rate jurisdictions. Additionally, our effective tax rate in 2012 was more volatile as compared to prior years due to the lower level of pre-tax income generated during the year, relative to our tax expense. For example, the impact of non-deductible expenses on our effective tax rate was greater as a result of our lower pre-tax income. Our effective tax rate in 2012 was also adversely impacted by acquisitions (including integrations) and investments, audit developments, nondeductible expenses, and changes in tax law such as the expiration of the U.S. federal research and development credit at the end of 2011. These items collectively caused our annual effective tax rate to be higher than both the 35% U.S. federal statutory rate and our effective tax rates in 2011 and 2010.

APPENDIX B

YUM! BRANDS, INC.
ANNUAL REPORT
2012

UNITED STATES
SECURITIES AND EXCHANGE COMMISSION
Washington, D. C. 20549

FORM 10-K

YUM! BRANDS, INC.

(Exact name of registrant as specified in its charter)

North Carolina   13-3951308
(State or other jurisdiction of   (I.R.S. Employer
incorporation or organization)   Identification No.)

1441 Gardiner Lane, Louisville, Kentucky   40213
(Address of principal executive offices)   (Zip Code)

Registrant's telephone number, including area code: (502) 874-8300
Securities registered pursuant to Section 12(b) of the Act

Title of Each Class	**Name of Each Exchange on Which Registered**
Common Stock, no par value	New York Stock Exchange

The aggregate market value of the voting stock (which consists solely of shares of Common Stock) held by non-affiliates of the registrant as of June 16, 2012 computed by reference to the closing price of the registrant's Common Stock on the New York Stock Exchange Composite Tape on such date was approximately $29,700,000,000. All executive officers and directors of the registrant have been deemed, solely for the purpose of the foregoing calculation, to be "affiliates" of the registrant. The number of shares outstanding of the registrant's Common Stock as of February 12, 2013 was 450,729,244 shares.

Consolidated Statements of Income

YUM! Brands, Inc. and Subsidiaries

Fiscal years ended December 29, 2012, December 31, 2011 and December 25, 2010

(in millions, except per share data)

	2012	2011	2010
Revenues			
Company sales	$ 11,833	$ 10,893	$ 9,783
Franchise and license fees and income	1,800	1,733	1,560
Total revenues	13,633	12,626	11,343
Costs and Expenses, Net			
Company restaurants			
Food and paper	3,874	3,633	3,091
Payroll and employee benefits	2,620	2,418	2,172
Occupancy and other operating expenses	3,358	3,089	2,857
Company restaurant expenses	9,852	9,140	8,120
General and administrative expenses	1,510	1,372	1,277
Franchise and license expenses	133	145	110
Closures and impairment (income) expenses	37	135	47
Refranchising (gain) loss	(78)	72	63
Other (income) expense	(115)	(53)	(43)
Total costs and expenses, net	11,339	10,811	9,574
Operating Profit	2,294	1,815	1,769
Interest expense, net	149	156	175
Income Before Income Taxes	2,145	1,659	1,594
Income tax provision	537	324	416
Net Income – including noncontrolling interest	1,608	1,335	1,178
Net Income – noncontrolling interest	11	16	20
Net Income – YUM! Brands, Inc.	$ 1,597	$ 1,319	$ 1,158
Basic Earnings Per Common Share	$ 3.46	$ 2.81	$ 2.44
Diluted Earnings Per Common Share	$ 3.38	$ 2.74	$ 2.38
Dividends Declared Per Common Share	$ 1.24	$ 1.07	$ 0.92

See accompanying Notes to Consolidated Financial Statements.

Consolidated Statements of Comprehensive Income

YUM! Brands, Inc. and Subsidiaries

Fiscal years ended December 29, 2012, December 31, 2011 and December 25, 2010

(in millions)

	Year Ended		
	2012	2011	2010
Net income - including noncontrolling interests	$1,608	$1,335	$1,178
Other comprehensive income, net of tax:			
Translation adjustments and gains (losses) from intra-entity transactions of a long-term investment nature	27	88	7
Tax (expense) benefit	(3)	3	5
Reclassifications of currency translation adjustments into Net income	3	—	—
Tax (expense) benefit	—	—	—
Net unrealized losses arising during the year on pension and post-retirement plans	(19)	(205)	(48)
Tax (expense) benefit	9	77	18
Reclassification of pension and post-retirement losses to net income	156	34	28
Tax (expense) benefit	(57)	(12)	(8)
Net unrealized gain (loss) on derivative instruments	—	1	(2)
Tax (expense) benefit	—	—	1
Other comprehensive income, net of tax	116	(14)	1
Comprehensive income - including noncontrolling interests	1,724	1,321	1,179
Comprehensive income - noncontrolling interests	12	22	24
Comprehensive Income - Yum! Brands, Inc.	$1,712	1,299	$1,155

See accompanying Notes to Consolidated Financial Statements.

Consolidated Statements of Cash Flows

YUM! Brands, Inc. and Subsidiaries

Fiscal years ended December 29, 2012, December 31, 2011 and December 25, 2010

(in millions)

	2012	2011	2010
Cash Flows – Operating Activities			
Net Income – including noncontrolling interest	$ 1,608	$ 1,335	$ 1,178
Depreciation and amortization	645	628	589
Closures and impairment (income) expenses	37	135	47
Refranchising (gain) loss	(78)	72	63
Contributions to defined benefit pension plans	(119)	(63)	(52)
YUM Retirement Plan settlement charge	84	—	—
Gain upon consolidation of a former unconsolidated affiliate in China	(74)	—	—
Deferred income taxes	28	(137)	(110)
Equity income from investments in unconsolidated affiliates	(47)	(47)	(42)
Distributions of income received from unconsolidated affiliates	41	39	34
Excess tax benefit from share-based compensation	(98)	(66)	(69)
Share-based compensation expense	50	59	47
Changes in accounts and notes receivable	(18)	(39)	(12)
Changes in inventories	9	(75)	(68)
Changes in prepaid expenses and other current assets	(14)	(25)	61
Changes in accounts payable and other current liabilities	9	144	61
Changes in income taxes payable	126	109	104
Other, net	105	101	137
Net Cash Provided by Operating Activities	2,294	2,170	1,968
Cash Flows – Investing Activities			
Capital spending	(1,099)	(940)	(796)
Proceeds from refranchising of restaurants	364	246	265
Acquisitions	(543)	(81)	(62)
Changes in restricted cash	300	(300)	—
Other, net	(27)	69	14
Net Cash Used in Investing Activities	(1,005)	(1,006)	(579)
Cash Flows – Financing Activities			
Proceeds from long-term debt	—	404	350
Repayments of long-term debt	(282)	(666)	(29)
Revolving credit facilities, three months or less, net	—	—	(5)
Short-term borrowings by original maturity			
More than three months – proceeds	—	—	—
More than three months – payments	—	—	—
Three months or less, net	—	—	(3)
Repurchase shares of Common Stock	(965)	(752)	(371)
Excess tax benefit from share-based compensation	98	66	69
Employee stock option proceeds	62	59	102
Dividends paid on Common Stock	(544)	(481)	(412)
Other, net	(85)	(43)	(38)
Net Cash Used in Financing Activities	(1,716)	(1,413)	(337)
Effect of Exchange Rates on Cash and Cash Equivalents	5	21	21
Net Increase (Decrease) in Cash and Cash Equivalents	(422)	(228)	1,073
Cash and Cash Equivalents – Beginning of Year	1,198	1,426	353
Cash and Cash Equivalents – End of Year	$ 776	$ 1,198	$ 1,426

See accompanying Notes to Consolidated Financial Statements.

Consolidated Balance Sheets

YUM! Brands, Inc. and Subsidiaries

December 29, 2012 and December 31, 2011

(in millions)

	2012	2011
ASSETS		
Current Assets		
Cash and cash equivalents	$ 776	$ 1,198
Accounts and notes receivable, net	301	286
Inventories	313	273
Prepaid expenses and other current assets	272	338
Deferred income taxes	111	112
Advertising cooperative assets, restricted	136	114
Total Current Assets	1,909	2,321
Property, plant and equipment, net	4,250	4,042
Goodwill	1,034	681
Intangible assets, net	690	299
Investments in unconsolidated affiliates	72	167
Restricted cash	—	300
Other assets	575	475
Deferred income taxes	481	549
Total Assets	$ 9,011	$ 8,834
LIABILITIES AND SHAREHOLDERS' EQUITY		
Current Liabilities		
Accounts payable and other current liabilities	$ 1,945	$ 1,874
Income taxes payable	97	142
Short-term borrowings	10	320
Advertising cooperative liabilities	136	114
Total Current Liabilities	2,188	2,450
Long-term debt	2,932	2,997
Other liabilities and deferred credits	1,579	1,471
Total Liabilities	6,699	6,918
Redeemable noncontrolling interest	59	—
Shareholders' Equity		
Common Stock, no par value, 750 shares authorized; 451 shares and 460 shares issued in 2012 and 2011, respectively	—	18
Retained earnings	2,286	2,052
Accumulated other comprehensive income (loss)	(132)	(247)
Total Shareholders' Equity – YUM! Brands, Inc.	2,154	1,823
Noncontrolling interests	99	93
Total Shareholders' Equity	2,253	1,916
Total Liabilities, Redeemable Noncontrolling Interest and Shareholders' Equity	$ 9,011	$ 8,834

See accompanying Notes to Consolidated Financial Statements.

Consolidated Statements of Shareholders' Equity (Deficit)

YUM! Brands, Inc. and Subsidiaries

Fiscal years ended December 29, 2012 and December 31, 2011

| | Yum! Brands, Inc. | | | | | |
| (in millions) | Issued Common Stock | | Retained Earnings | Accumulated Other Comprehensive Income(Loss) | Noncontrolling Interests | Total |
	Shares	Amount				
Balance at December 25, 2010	469	$ 86	$ 1,717	$ (227)	$ 93	$1,669
Net Income			1,319		16	1,335
Translation adjustments and gains (losses) from intra-entity transactions of a long-term investment nature (net of tax impact of $3 million)				85	6	91
Pension and post-retirement benefit plans (net of tax impact of $65 million)				(106)		(106)
Net unrealized gain on derivative instruments (net of tax impact of less than $1 million)				1		1
Comprehensive Income						1,321
Dividends declared			(501)		(22)	(523)
Repurchase of shares of Common Stock	(14)	(250)	(483)			(733)
Employee stock option and SARs exercises (includes tax impact of $71 million)	5	119				119
Compensation-related events (includes tax impact of $5 million)	—	63				63
Balance at December 31, 2011	460	$ 18	$ 2,052	$ (247)	$ 93	$1,916
Net Income			1,597		11	1,608
Translation adjustments and gains (losses) from intra-entity transactions of a long-term investment nature (net of tax impact of $3 million)				23	1	24
Reclassification of translation adjustments into income				3		3
Pension and post-retirement benefit plans (net of tax impact of $48 million)				89		89
Comprehensive Income						1,724
Noncontrolling Interest - Little Sheep acquisition					16	16
Dividends declared			(569)		(22)	(591)
Repurchase of shares of Common Stock	(15)	(191)	(794)			(985)
Employee stock option and SARs exercises (includes tax impact of $89 million)	6	111				111
Compensation-related events (includes tax impact of $11 million)		62				62
Balance at December 29, 2012	451	$ —	$ 2,286	$ (132)	$ 99	$2,253

See accompanying Notes to Consolidated Financial Statements.

Notes to Consolidated Financial Statements
(Tabular amounts in millions, except share data)

Note 1 – Description of Business

YUM! Brands, Inc. and Subsidiaries (collectively referred to herein as "YUM" or the "Company") comprises primarily the worldwide operations of KFC, Pizza Hut and Taco Bell (collectively the "Concepts"). YUM is the world's largest quick service restaurant company based on the number of system units, with over 39,000 units of which approximately 54% are located outside the U.S. in more than 125 countries and territories. YUM was created as an independent, publicly-owned company on October 6, 1997 via a tax-free distribution by our former parent, PepsiCo, Inc., of our Common Stock to its shareholders. References to YUM throughout these Consolidated Financial Statements are made using the first person notations of "we," "us" or "our."

Through our widely-recognized Concepts, we develop, operate, franchise and license a system of both traditional and non-traditional quick service restaurants. Each Concept has proprietary menu items and emphasizes the preparation of food with high quality ingredients as well as unique recipes and special seasonings to provide appealing, tasty and attractive food at competitive prices. Our traditional restaurants feature dine-in, carryout and, in some instances, drive-thru or delivery service. Non-traditional units, which are principally licensed outlets, include express units and kiosks which have a more limited menu and operate in non-traditional locations like malls, airports, gasoline service stations, train stations, subways, convenience stores, stadiums, amusement parks and colleges, where a full-scale traditional outlet would not be practical or efficient. We also operate multibrand units, where two or more of our Concepts are operated in a single unit.

YUM consists of six operating segments: YUM Restaurants China ("China" or "China Division"), YUM Restaurants International ("YRI" or "International Division"), KFC U.S., Pizza Hut U.S., Taco Bell U.S., and YUM Restaurants India ("India" or "India Division"). The China Division includes mainland China, and the India Division includes India, Bangladesh, Mauritius, Nepal and Sri Lanka. YRI includes the remainder of our international operations. For financial reporting purposes, management considers the three U.S. operating segments to be similar and, therefore, has aggregated them into a single reportable operating segment ("U.S."). As a result of changes to our management reporting structure, in 2012 we began reporting information for our India business as a standalone reporting segment separated from YRI. While our consolidated results are not impacted, our historical segment information has been restated to be consistent with the current period presentation. In December 2011 we sold our Long John Silver's ("LJS") and A&W All American Food Restaurants ("A&W") brands to key franchise leaders and strategic investors in separate transactions. The results for these businesses through the sale date are included in the Company's results for 2011 and 2010.

Note 2 – Summary of Significant Accounting Policies (selected data)

Our preparation of the accompanying Consolidated Financial Statements in conformity with Generally Accepted Accounting Principles in the United States of America ("GAAP") requires us to make estimates and assumptions that affect reported amounts of assets and liabilities, disclosure of contingent assets and liabilities at the date of the financial statements, and the reported amounts of revenues and expenses during the reporting period. Actual results could differ from these estimates.

Principles of Consolidation and Basis of Preparation. Intercompany accounts and transactions have been eliminated in consolidation. We consolidate entities in which we have a controlling financial interest, the usual condition of which is ownership of a majority voting interest. We also consider for consolidation an entity, in which we have certain interests, where the controlling financial interest may be achieved through arrangements that do not involve voting interests. Such an entity, known as a variable interest entity ("VIE"), is required to be consolidated by its primary beneficiary. The primary beneficiary is the entity that possesses the power to direct the activities of the VIE that most significantly impact its economic performance and has the obligation to absorb losses or the right to receive benefits from the VIE that are significant to it.

Certain investments in entities that operate KFCs in China are accounted for by the equity method. These entities are not VIEs and our lack of majority voting rights precludes us from controlling these affiliates. Thus, we do not consolidate these affiliates, instead accounting for them under the equity method. Our share of the net income or loss of those unconsolidated affiliates is included in Other (income) expense. On February 1, 2012, we acquired an additional 66% interest in Little Sheep Group Limited ("Little Sheep"). As a result, we began consolidating this business, which was previously accounted for using the equity method. See Note 4 for a further description of the accounting upon acquisition of additional interest in Little Sheep.

We report Net income attributable to non-controlling interests, which include the minority shareholders of the entities that operate the KFCs in Beijing and Shanghai, China and the minority shareholders of Little Sheep, separately on the face of our Consolidated Statements of Income. The portion of equity not attributable to the Company is reported within equity, separately from the Company's equity on the Consolidated Balance Sheets. The shareholder that owns the remaining 7% ownership interest in Little Sheep holds an option that, if exercised, requires us to redeem their non-controlling interest. Redemption may occur any time after the third anniversary of the acquisition. This Redeemable non-controlling interest is classified outside permanent equity and recorded in the Consolidated Balance Sheet as the greater of the initial carrying amount adjusted for the non-controlling interest's share of net income (loss) or its redemption value.

Fiscal Year. Our fiscal year ends on the last Saturday in December and, as a result, a 53rd week is added every five or six years. The first three quarters of each fiscal year consist of 12 weeks and the fourth quarter consists of 16 weeks in fiscal years with 52 weeks and 17 weeks in fiscal years with 53 weeks. Our subsidiaries operate on similar fiscal calendars except that China, India and certain other international subsidiaries operate on a monthly calendar, and thus never have a 53rd week, with two months in the first quarter, three months in the second and third quarters and four months in the fourth quarter. YRI closes one period earlier to facilitate consolidated reporting.

Fiscal year 2011 included 53 weeks for our U.S. businesses and a portion of our YRI business. The 53rd week in 2011 added $91 million to total revenues, $15 million to Restaurant profit and $25 million to Operating Profit in our 2011 Consolidated Statement of Income. The $25 million benefit was offset throughout 2011 by investments, including franchise development incentives, as well as higher-than-normal spending, such as restaurant closures in the U.S. and YRI.

Foreign Currency. The functional currency of our foreign entities is the currency of the primary economic environment in which the entity operates. Functional currency determinations are made based upon a number of economic factors, including but not limited to cash flows and financing transactions. The operations, assets and liabilities of our entities outside the United States are initially measured using the functional currency of that entity. Income and expense accounts for our operations of these foreign entities are then translated into U.S. dollars at the average exchange rates prevailing during the period. Assets and liabilities of these foreign entities are then translated into U.S. dollars at exchange rates in effect at the balance sheet date. As of December 29, 2012, net cumulative translation adjustment gains of $166 million are recorded in Accumulated other comprehensive income (loss) in the Consolidated Balance Sheet.

As we manage and share resources at either the country level for all of our brands in a country or, for some countries in which we have more significant operations, at the individual brand level within the country, cumulative translation adjustments are recorded and tracked at the foreign-entity level that represents either our entire operations within a country or the operations of our individual brands within that country. Translation adjustments recorded in Accumulated other comprehensive income (loss) are subsequently recognized as income or expense generally only upon sale or upon complete or substantially complete liquidation of the related investment in a foreign entity. For purposes of determining whether a sale or complete or substantially complete liquidation of an investment in a foreign entity has occurred, we consider those same foreign entities for which we record and track cumulative translation adjustments. Restaurant closures and refranchising transactions during the periods presented constituted disposals or sales of assets within our foreign entities and thus did not result in any translation adjustments being recognized as income or expense.

Gains and losses arising from the impact of foreign currency exchange rate fluctuations on transactions in foreign currency are included in Other (income) expense in our Consolidated Statement of Income.

Reclassifications. We have reclassified certain items in the Consolidated Financial Statements for prior periods to be comparable with the classification for the fiscal year ended December 29, 2012. These reclassifications had no effect on previously reported Net Income - YUM! Brands, Inc.

Franchise and License Operations. We execute franchise or license agreements for each unit operated by third parties which set out the terms of our arrangement with the franchisee or licensee. Our franchise and license agreements typically require the franchisee or licensee to pay an initial, non-refundable fee and continuing fees based upon a percentage of sales. Subject to our approval and their payment of a renewal fee, a franchisee may generally renew the franchise agreement upon its expiration.

Revenue Recognition. Revenues from Company-owned restaurants are recognized when payment is tendered at the time of sale. The Company presents sales net of sales-related taxes. Income from our franchisees and licensees includes initial fees, continuing fees, renewal fees and rental income from restaurants we lease or sublease to them. We recognize initial fees received from a franchisee or licensee as revenue when we have performed substantially all initial services required by the franchise or license agreement, which is generally upon the opening of a store. We recognize continuing fees based upon a percentage of franchisee and licensee sales and rental income as earned. We recognize renewal fees when a renewal agreement with a franchisee or licensee becomes effective. We present initial fees collected upon the sale of a restaurant to a franchisee in Refranchising (gain) loss.

Direct Marketing Costs. We charge direct marketing costs to expense ratably in relation to revenues over the year in which incurred and, in the case of advertising production costs, in the year the advertisement is first shown. Deferred direct marketing costs, which are classified as prepaid expenses, consist of media and related advertising production costs which will generally be used for the first time in the next fiscal year and have historically not been significant. To the extent we participate in advertising cooperatives, we expense our contributions as incurred which are generally based on a percentage of sales. Our advertising expenses were $608 million, $593 million and $557 million in 2012, 2011 and 2010, respectively. We report substantially all of our direct marketing costs in Occupancy and other operating expenses.

Research and Development Expenses. Research and development expenses, which we expense as incurred, are reported in G&A expenses. Research and development expenses were $30 million, $34 million and $33 million in 2012, 2011 and 2010, respectively.

Share-Based Employee Compensation. We recognize all share-based payments to employees, including grants of employee stock options and stock appreciation rights ("SARs"), in the Consolidated Financial Statements as compensation cost over the service period based on their fair value on the date of grant. This compensation cost is recognized over the service period on a straight-line basis for the fair value of awards that actually vest. We present this compensation cost consistent with the other compensation costs for the employee recipient in either Payroll and employee benefits or G&A expenses.

Legal Costs. Settlement costs are accrued when they are deemed probable and estimable. Anticipated legal fees related to self-insured workers' compensation, employment practices liability, general liability, automobile liability, product liability and property losses (collectively, "property and casualty losses") are accrued when deemed probable and estimable. Legal fees not related to self-insured property and casualty losses are recognized as incurred.

Impairment or Disposal of Property, Plant and Equipment. Property, plant and equipment ("PP&E") is tested for impairment whenever events or changes in circumstances indicate that the carrying value of the assets may not be recoverable. The assets are not recoverable if their carrying value is less than the undiscounted cash flows we expect to generate from such assets. If the assets are not deemed to be recoverable, impairment is measured based on the excess of their carrying value over their fair value.

When we decide to close a restaurant, it is reviewed for impairment and depreciable lives are adjusted based on the expected disposal date. Other costs incurred when closing a restaurant such as costs of disposing of the assets as well as other facility-related expenses from previously closed stores are generally expensed as incurred. Additionally, at the date we cease using a property under an operating lease, we record a liability for the net present value of any remaining lease obligations, net of estimated sublease income, if any. Any costs recorded upon store closure as well as any subsequent adjustments to liabilities for remaining lease obligations as a result of lease termination or changes in estimates of sublease income are recorded in Closures and impairment (income) expenses. To the extent we sell assets, primarily land, associated with a closed store, any gain or loss upon that sale is also recorded in Closures and impairment (income) expenses.

Considerable management judgment is necessary to estimate future cash flows, including cash flows from continuing use, terminal value, sublease income and refranchising proceeds. Accordingly, actual results could vary significantly from our estimates.

Impairment of Investments in Unconsolidated Affiliates. We record impairment charges related to an investment in an unconsolidated affiliate whenever events or circumstances indicate that a decrease in the fair value of an investment has occurred which is other than temporary. In addition, we evaluate our investments in unconsolidated affiliates for impairment when they have experienced two consecutive years of operating losses. We recorded no impairment associated with our investments in unconsolidated affiliates during 2012, 2011 and 2010.

Guarantees. We recognize, at inception of a guarantee, a liability for the fair value of certain obligations undertaken. The majority of our guarantees are issued as a result of assigning our interest in obligations under operating leases as a condition to the refranchising of certain Company restaurants. We recognize a liability for the fair value of such lease guarantees upon refranchising and upon subsequent renewals of such leases when we remain contingently liable. The related expense and any subsequent changes in the guarantees are included in Refranchising (gain) loss. The related expense and subsequent changes in the guarantees for other franchise support guarantees not associated with a refranchising transaction are included in Franchise and license expense.

Income Taxes. We record deferred tax assets and liabilities for the future tax consequences attributable to temporary differences between the financial statement carrying amounts of existing assets and liabilities and their respective tax bases as well as operating loss, capital loss and tax credit carryforwards. Deferred tax assets and liabilities are measured using enacted tax rates expected to apply to taxable income in the years in which those differences are expected to be recovered or settled. The effect on deferred tax assets and liabilities of a change in tax rates is recognized in income in the period that includes the enactment date. Additionally, in determining the need for recording a valuation allowance against the carrying amount of deferred tax assets, we consider the amount of taxable income and periods over which it must be earned, actual levels of past taxable income and known trends and events or transactions that are expected to affect future levels of taxable income. Where we determine that it is more likely than not that all or a portion of an asset will not be realized, we record a valuation allowance.

The Company recognizes accrued interest and penalties related to unrecognized tax benefits as components of its Income tax provision.

See Note 17 for a further discussion of our income taxes.

Fair Value Measurements. Fair value is the price we would receive to sell an asset or pay to transfer a liability (exit price) in an orderly transaction between market participants. For those assets and liabilities we record or disclose at fair value, we determine fair value based upon the quoted market price, if available. If a quoted market price is not available for identical assets, we determine fair value based upon the quoted market price of similar assets or the present value of expected future cash flows considering the risks involved, including counterparty performance risk if appropriate, and using discount rates appropriate for the duration. The fair values are assigned a level within the fair value hierarchy, depending on the source of the inputs into the calculation.

Level 1   Inputs based upon quoted prices in active markets for identical assets.

Level 2   Inputs other than quoted prices included within Level 1 that are observable for the asset, either directly or indirectly.

Level 3   Inputs that are unobservable for the asset.

Cash and Cash Equivalents. Cash equivalents represent funds we have temporarily invested (with original maturities not exceeding three months), including short-term, highly liquid debt securities.

Receivables. The Company's receivables are primarily generated as a result of ongoing business relationships with our franchisees and licensees as a result of franchise, license and lease agreements. Trade receivables consisting of royalties from franchisees and licensees are generally due within 30 days of the period in which the corresponding sales occur and are classified as Accounts and notes receivable on our Consolidated Balance Sheets. Our provision for uncollectible franchise and licensee receivable balances is based upon pre-defined aging criteria or upon the occurrence of other events that indicate that we may not collect the balance due. Additionally, we monitor the financial condition of our franchisees and licensees and record provisions for estimated losses on receivables when we believe it probable that our franchisees or licensees will be unable to make their required payments. While we use the best information available in making our determination, the ultimate recovery of recorded receivables is also dependent upon future economic events and other conditions that may be beyond our control. Uncollectible franchise and license trade receivables consisted of $1 million in net recoveries and $7 million and $3 million in net provisions which were included in Franchise and license expenses in 2012, 2011 and 2010, respectively. Trade receivables that are ultimately deemed to be uncollectible, and for which collection efforts have been exhausted, are written off against the allowance for doubtful accounts.

	2012	2011
Accounts and notes receivable	$ 313	$ 308
Allowance for doubtful accounts	(12)	(22)
Accounts and notes receivable, net	$ 301	$ 286

Inventories. We value our inventories at the lower of cost (computed on the first-in, first-out method) or market.

Property, Plant and Equipment. We state property, plant and equipment at cost less accumulated depreciation and amortization. We calculate depreciation and amortization on a straight-line basis over the estimated useful lives of the assets as follows: 5 to 25 years for buildings and improvements, 3 to 20 years for machinery and equipment and 3 to 7 years for capitalized software costs. As discussed above, we suspend depreciation and amortization on assets related to restaurants that are held for sale.

Leases and Leasehold Improvements. The Company leases land, buildings or both for nearly 6,700 of its restaurants worldwide. Lease terms, which vary by country and often include renewal options, are an important factor in determining the appropriate accounting for leases including the initial classification of the lease as capital or operating and the timing of recognition of rent expense over the duration of the lease. We include renewal option periods in determining the term of our leases when failure to renew the lease would impose a penalty on the Company in such an amount that a renewal appears to be reasonably assured at the inception of the lease. The primary penalty to which we are subject is the economic detriment associated with the existence of leasehold improvements which might be impaired if we choose not to continue the use of the leased property. Leasehold improvements, which are a component of buildings and improvements described above, are amortized over the shorter of their estimated useful lives or the lease term. We generally do not receive leasehold improvement incentives upon opening a store that is subject to a lease.

Goodwill and Intangible Assets. From time to time, the Company acquires restaurants from one of our Concept's franchisees or acquires another business. Goodwill from these acquisitions represents the excess of the cost of a business acquired over the net of the amounts assigned to assets acquired, including identifiable intangible assets and liabilities assumed. Goodwill is not amortized and has been assigned to reporting units for purposes of impairment testing. Our reporting units are our operating segments in the U.S. (see Note 18), our YRI business units (which are aligned based on geography), our India Division, and our China Division brands. Goodwill is assigned to reporting units that are expected to benefit from the synergies of the combination even though other assets or liabilities acquired may not be assigned to that reporting unit. The amount of goodwill assigned to a reporting unit that has not been assigned any of the other assets acquired or liabilities assumed is determined by comparing the fair value of the reporting unit before the acquisition to the fair value of the reporting unit after the acquisition.

We evaluate goodwill for impairment on an annual basis or more often if an event occurs or circumstances change that indicate impairments might exist.

Common Stock Share Repurchases. From time to time, we repurchase shares of our Common Stock under share repurchase programs authorized by our Board of Directors. Shares repurchased constitute authorized, but unissued shares under the North Carolina laws under which we are incorporated. Additionally, our Common Stock has no par or stated value. Accordingly, we record the full value of share repurchases, upon the trade date, against Common

Stock on our Consolidated Balance Sheet except when to do so would result in a negative balance in such Common Stock account. In such instances, on a period basis, we record the cost of any further share repurchases as a reduction in retained earnings. Due to the large number of share repurchases and the increase in the market value of our stock over the past several years, our Common Stock balance is frequently zero at the end of any period. Accordingly, $794 million and $483 million in share repurchases were recorded as a reduction in Retained Earnings in 2012 and 2011, respectively. Our Common Stock balance was such that no share repurchases impacted Retained Earnings in 2010. See Note 16 for additional information.

Pension and Post-retirement Medical Benefits. We measure and recognize the overfunded or underfunded status of our pension and post-retirement plans as an asset or liability in our Consolidated Balance Sheet as of our fiscal year end. The funded status represents the difference between the projected benefit obligations and the fair value of plan assets. The projected benefit obligation is the present value of benefits earned to date by plan participants, including the effect of future salary increases, as applicable. The difference between the projected benefit obligations and the fair value of plan assets that has not previously been recognized in our Consolidated Statement of Income is recorded as a component of Accumulated other comprehensive income (loss).

Note 8 – Supplemental Balance Sheet Information

Prepaid Expenses and Other Current Assets	2012	2011
Income tax receivable	$ 55	$ 150
Assets held for sale[a]	56	24
Other prepaid expenses and current assets	161	164
	$ 272	$ 338

Property, Plant and Equipment	2012	2011
Land	$ 469	$ 527
Buildings and improvements	4,093	3,856
Capital leases, primarily buildings	200	316
Machinery and equipment	2,627	2,568
Property, Plant and equipment, gross	7,389	7,267
Accumulated depreciation and amortization	(3,139)	(3,225)
Property, Plant and equipment, net	$ 4,250	$ 4,042

Depreciation and amortization expense related to property, plant and equipment was $629 million, $599 million and $565 million in 2012, 2011 and 2010, respectively.

Accounts Payable and Other Current Liabilities	2012	2011
Accounts payable	$ 684	$ 712
Accrued capital expenditures	264	229
Accrued compensation and benefits	487	440
Dividends payable	151	131
Accrued taxes, other than income taxes	103	112
Other current liabilities	256	250
	$ 1,945	$ 1,874

Note 9 – Goodwill and Intangible Assets (selected data)

The changes in the carrying amount of goodwill are as follows:

	China	YRI	U.S.	India	Worldwide
Balance as of December 31, 2011(c)					
Goodwill, gross	88	299	311	—	698
Accumulated impairment losses	—	(17)	—	—	(17)
Goodwill, net	88	282	311	—	681
Acquisitions(d)	376	—	—	—	376
Disposals and other, net(b)	2	(11)	(14)	—	(23)
Balance as of December 29, 2012					
Goodwill, gross	466	288	297	—	1,051
Accumulated impairment losses	—	(17)	—	—	(17)
Goodwill, net	$ 466	$ 271	$ 297	$ —	$ 1,034

(d) We recorded goodwill of $376 million related to our acquisition of Little Sheep. See Note 4.

Note 11 – Leases

At December 29, 2012 we operated nearly 7,600 restaurants, leasing the underlying land and/or building in nearly 6,700 of those restaurants with the vast majority of our commitments expiring within 20 years from the inception of the lease. Our longest lease expires in 2151. We also lease office space for headquarters and support functions, as well as certain office and restaurant equipment. We do not consider any of these individual leases material to our operations. Most leases require us to pay related executory costs, which include property taxes, maintenance and insurance.

Future minimum commitments and amounts to be received as lessor or sublessor under non-cancelable leases are set forth below:

	Commitments		Lease Receivables	
	Capital	Operating	Direct Financing	Operating
2013	$ 18	$ 678	$ 2	$ 57
2014	18	634	2	52
2015	19	592	2	49
2016	19	556	2	45
2017	17	500	2	41
Thereafter	189	2,714	12	185
	$ 280	$ 5,674	$ 22	$ 429

At December 29, 2012 and December 31, 2011, the present value of minimum payments under capital leases was $170 million and $279 million, respectively. At December 29, 2012, unearned income associated with direct financing lease receivables was $12 million.

Note 18 – Reportable Operating Segments (selected data)

We are principally engaged in developing, operating, franchising and licensing the worldwide KFC, Pizza Hut and Taco Bell concepts. KFC, Pizza Hut and Taco Bell operate in 120, 97, and 27 countries and territories, respectively. Our five largest international markets based on operating profit in 2012 are China, Asia Franchise, United Kingdom, Australia and Latin America Franchise.
(Note then gives segment breakdowns for revenues, operating profits, interest expense, income before income taxes, depreciation and amortization, capital spending, identifiable assets, long-lived assets)

Note 19 – Contingencies (selected data)

Legal Proceedings

We are subject to various claims and contingencies related to lawsuits, real estate, environmental and other matters arising in the normal course of business. An accrual is recorded with respect to claims or contingencies for which a loss is determined to be probable and reasonably estimable.

Beginning on January 24, 2013 four purported class actions were filed in the United States District Court for the Central District of California against the Company and certain of its executive officers. The complaints allege claims under sections 10(b) and 20(a) of the Securities Exchange Act of 1934 against defendants on behalf of a purported class of all persons who purchased or otherwise acquired the Company's publicly traded securities between October 9, 2012 and January 7, 2013, inclusive (the "class period"). Plaintiffs allege that during the class period, defendants purportedly made materially false and misleading statements concerning the Company's current and future business and financial condition, thereby inflating the prices at which the Company's securities traded. The complaints seek damages in an undefined amount. The Company denies liability and intends to vigorously defend against all claims in these complaints. However, in view of the inherent uncertainties of litigation, the outcome of this case cannot be predicted at this time. Likewise, the amount of any potential loss cannot be reasonably estimated.

Item 9A.   **Controls and Procedures.**

<u>Evaluation of Disclosure Controls and Procedures</u>

The Company has evaluated the effectiveness of the design and operation of its disclosure controls and procedures pursuant to Rules 13a-15(e) and 15d-15(e) under the Securities Exchange Act of 1934 as of the end of the period covered by this report. Based on the evaluation, performed under the supervision and with the participation of the Company's management, including the Chairman and Chief Executive Officer (the "CEO") and the Chief Financial Officer (the "CFO"), the Company's management, including the CEO and CFO, concluded that the Company's disclosure controls and procedures were effective as of the end of the period covered by this report.

<u>Management's Report on Internal Control Over Financial Reporting</u>

Our management is responsible for establishing and maintaining adequate internal control over financial reporting, as such term is defined in Rules 13a-15(f) under the Securities Exchange Act of 1934. Under the supervision and with the participation of our management, including our principal executive officer and principal financial officer, we conducted an evaluation of the effectiveness of our internal control over financial reporting based on the framework in *Internal Control – Integrated Framework* issued by the Committee of Sponsoring Organizations of the Treadway Commission. Based on our evaluation under the framework in *Internal Control – Integrated Framework*, our management concluded that our internal control over financial reporting was effective as of December 29, 2012.

KPMG LLP, an independent registered public accounting firm, has audited the Consolidated Financial Statements included in this Annual Report on Form 10-K and the effectiveness of our internal control over financial reporting and has issued their report, included herein.

<u>Changes in Internal Control</u>

There were no changes with respect to the Company's internal control over financial reporting or in other factors that materially affected, or are reasonably likely to materially affect, internal control over financial reporting during the quarter ended December 29, 2012.

TYPICAL CHARTS OF ACCOUNTS FOR DIFFERENT TYPES OF BUSINESSES

A Simple Service Corporation

Assets	Liabilities	Stockholders' Equity
Cash	Accounts Payable	Common Stock
Accounts Receivable	Notes Payable, Short-Term	Retained Earnings
Allowance for Uncollectible Accounts	Salary Payable	Dividends
Notes Receivable, Short-Term	Wages Payable	**Revenues and Gains**
Interest Receivable	Payroll Taxes Payable	
Supplies	Employee Benefits Payable	Service Revenue
Prepaid Rent	Interest Payable	Interest Revenue
Prepaid Insurance	Unearned Service Revenue	Gain on Sale of Land (Furniture,
Notes Receivable, Long-Term	Notes Payable, Long-Term	Equipment, or Building)
Land		**Expenses and Losses**
Building		
Accumulated Depreciation—Building		Salary Expense
Equipment		Payroll Tax Expense
Accumulated Depreciation—Equipment		Employee Benefits Expense
Furniture		Rent Expense
Accumulated Depreciation—Furniture		Insurance Expense
		Supplies Expense
		Uncollectible Accounts Expense
		Depreciation Expense—Furniture
		Depreciation Expense—Equipment
		Depreciation Expense—Building
		Income Tax Expense
		Interest Expense
		Miscellaneous Expense
		Loss on Sale (or Exchange) of Land
		(Furniture, Equipment, or Building)

A Service Partnership

Same as service corporation, except for owners' equity

Owners' Equity

Partner 1, Capital
Partner 2, Capital
.
.
.
Partner N, Capital

Partner 1, Drawing
Partner 2, Drawing
.
.
.
Partner N, Drawing

(*continued*)

TYPICAL CHARTS OF ACCOUNTS FOR DIFFERENT TYPES OF BUSINESSES *(continued)*

A Complex Merchandising Corporation

Assets

Cash
Investments in Trading Securities
 or Investments in Available-
 for-Sale Securities
Accounts Receivable
Allowance for Uncollectible
 Accounts
Notes Receivable, Short-Term
Interest Receivable
Inventory
Supplies
Prepaid Rent
Prepaid Insurance
Notes Receivable, Long-Term
Equity-Method Investment
Investments in Available-
 for-Sale Securities
Investment in Bonds Held-to-
 Maturity
Other Receivables, Long-Term
Land
Land Improvements
Buildings
Accumulated Depreciation—
 Buildings
Equipment
Accumulated Depreciation—
 Equipment
Furniture and Fixtures
Accumulated Depreciation—
 Furniture and Fixtures
Franchises
Patents
Leasehold Improvements
Goodwill

Liabilities

Accounts Payable
Notes Payable, Short-Term
Current Portion of Bonds
 Payable
Salary Payable
Wages Payable
Payroll Taxes Payable
Employee Benefits Payable
Interest Payable
Income Tax Payable
Unearned Sales Revenue
Notes Payable, Long-Term
Bonds Payable
Lease Liability

Stockholders' Equity

Preferred Stock
Paid-in Capital in Excess of
 Par—Preferred
Common Stock
Paid-in Capital in Excess of
 Par—Common
Paid-in Capital from Treasury
 Stock Transactions
Paid-in Capital from
 Retirement of Stock
Retained Earnings
Accumulated Other
 Comprehensive Income
 (or Loss)
Unrealized Gain (or Loss)
 on Investments
 in Available-for-Sale
 Securities
Foreign Currency Translation
 Adjustment
Treasury Stock
Noncontrolling Interest

Revenues and Gains

Sales Revenue
Interest Revenue
Dividend Revenue
Equity-Method Investment
 Revenue
Unrealized Gain on
 Trading Securities
Gain on Sale of Investments
Gain on Sale of Land
 (Furniture and Fixtures,
 Equipment, or Buildings)
Discontinued Operations—
 Gain
Extraordinary Gains

Expenses and Losses

Cost of Goods Sold
Salary Expense
Wage Expense
Commission Expense
Payroll Tax Expense
Employee Benefits Expense
Rent Expense
Insurance Expense
Supplies Expense
Uncollectible Accounts Expense
Depreciation Expense—Land
 Improvements
Depreciation Expense—
 Furniture and Fixtures
Depreciation Expense—
 Equipment
Depreciation Expense—
 Buildings
Organization Expense
Amortization Expense—
 Franchises
Amortization Expense—
 Leasehold Improvements
Amortization Expense—
 Patent
Income Tax Expense
Unrealized Loss on
 Trading Securities
Loss on Sale of Investments
Loss on Sale (or Exchange) of
 Land (Furniture and
 Fixtures, Equipment, or
 Buildings)
Discontinued Operations—
 Loss
Extraordinary Losses

A Manufacturing Corporation

Same as merchandising corporation, except for assets

Assets

Inventories:
 Materials Inventories
 Work-in-Process Inventories
 Finished Goods Inventories
Factory Wages
Factory Overhead

SUMMARY OF GENERALLY ACCEPTED ACCOUNTING PRINCIPLES (GAAP)

Every technical area has professional associations and regulatory bodies that govern the practice of the profession. Accounting is no exception. In the United States, generally accepted accounting principles (GAAP) are written by the Financial Accounting Standards Board (FASB). The FASB has seven full-time members and a large staff. An independent organization with no government or professional affiliation, the FASB is subject to oversight by the Financial Accounting Foundation (FAF), which selects its members and funds its work. In order to ensure impartiality, FASB members are required to sever all ties to previous firms and institutions that they may have served prior to joining the FASB. Each member is appointed for a five-year term and is eligible for one additional five-year term.

FASB pronouncements are called *Statements of Financial Accounting Standards.* Once issued, these pronouncements are added to the *Accounting Standards Codification™*, which is the single source of authoritative nongovernmental U.S. GAAP. The codification organizes the many pronouncements that constitute U.S. GAAP–each of which specifies how to measure and report a particular type of business event or transaction–into a consistent, searchable format. GAAP is the "accounting law of the land." In the same way that our laws draw authority from their acceptance by the people, GAAP depends on general acceptance by the business community. Throughout this book, we refer to GAAP as the proper way to measure and report business activity.

In 2002, the FASB and the International Accounting Standards Board (IASB) announced a convergence project, whereby both bodies agreed to combine international financial reporting standards (IFRS) and U.S. GAAP into one set of global, compatible, high-quality standards. All new FASB and IASB standards written since that time have been written to measure and report various types of business activities in compatible (if not identical) ways. However, some differences between the two sets of standards still exist. Those differences are discussed in Appendix E.

The U.S. Congress has given the Securities and Exchange Commission (SEC), a government organization that regulates the trading of investments, ultimate responsibility for establishing accounting rules for companies that are owned by the general investing public. However, the SEC has delegated much of its rule-making power to the FASB. Exhibit D-1 outlines the flow of authority for developing GAAP.

EXHIBIT D-1 | Flow of Authority for Developing GAAP

United States Congress   Securities and Exchange Commission   Financial Accounting Standards Board   Pronouncements that make up generally accepted accounting principles (GAAP)

The Objective of Financial Reporting

The basic objective of financial reporting is to provide information that is useful in making investment and lending decisions. The FASB believes that accounting information can be useful in decision making only if it is *relevant* and if it *faithfully represents* economic reality.

Relevant information is useful in making predictions and for evaluating past performance–that is, the information has feedback value. For example, PepsiCo's disclosure of the profitability of each of its lines of business is relevant for investor evaluations of the company. To be relevant, information must be timely. To faithfully represent, the information must be complete, neutral (free from bias), and without material error (accurate). Accounting information must focus on the *economic substance* of a transaction, event, or circumstance, which may or may not always be the same as its legal form. Faithful representation makes the information *reliable* to users. Exhibit 1-3 on page 7 of Chapter 1 presents the objective of accounting, its fundamental and enhancing qualitative characteristics, and its constraint. These characteristics and constraint combine to shape the concepts and principles that make up GAAP. Exhibit D-2 summarizes the assumptions, concepts, and principles that accounting has developed to provide useful information for decision making.

EXHIBIT D-2 | Summary of Important Accounting Concepts, Principles, and Financial Statements

Assumptions, Concepts, Principles, and Financial Statements	Quick Summary	Text Reference
Assumptions and Concepts		
Entity assumption	Accounting draws a boundary around each organization to be accounted for.	Chapter 1, page 8
Continuity (going-concern) assumption	Accountants assume the business will continue operating for the foreseeable future.	Chapter 1, page 8
Stable-monetary-unit assumption	Accounting information is expressed primarily in monetary terms that ignore the effects of inflation.	Chapter 1, page 9
Time-period concept	Ensures that accounting information is reported at regular intervals.	Chapter 3, page 116
Materiality	Accounting information must be important enough to the user so that if it were omitted or incorrect, it would make a difference in the user's decision.	Chapter 1, page 6
Cost	A constraint of accounting, meaning that the cost of producing information should not exceed the expected benefits to users.	Chapter 1, page 7
Principles		
Historical cost principle	Assets are recorded at their actual historical cost.	Chapter 1, page 8
Revenue principle	Tells accountants when to record revenue (only after it has been earned) and the amount of revenue to record (the cash value of what has been received).	Chapter 3, page 116, and Chapter 11, page 620
Expense recognition (matching) principle	Directs accountants to (1) identify and measure all expenses incurred during the period and (2) match the expenses against the revenues earned during the period. The goal is to measure net income.	Chapter 3, page 118
Consistency principle	Businesses should use the same accounting methods from period to period.	Chapter 6, page 316
Disclosure principle	A company's financial statements should report enough information for outsiders to make informed decisions about the company.	Chapter 6, page 316
Financial Statements		
Balance sheet	Assets = Liabilities + Owners' Equity at a point in time.	Chapter 1
Income statement	Revenues and gains − Expenses and losses = Net income or net loss for the period	Chapters 1 and 11
Statement of cash flows	Cash receipts − Cash payments = Increase or decrease in cash during the period, grouped under operating, investing, and financing activities	Chapters 1 and 12
Statement of Comprehensive Income	Net income (from income statement) + Other comprehensive income − Other comprehensive loss = Comprehensive income	Chapter 11
Statement of retained earnings	Beginning retained earnings + Net income (or − Net loss) − Dividends Declared = Ending retained earnings	Chapters 1 and 10
Statement of stockholders' equity	Shows the reason for the change in each stockholders' equity account, including retained earnings.	Chapter 10, page 578
Financial statement notes	Provide information that cannot be reported conveniently on the face of the financial statements. The notes are an integral part of the statements.	Chapter 11, page 632

SUMMARY OF DIFFERENCES BETWEEN U.S. GAAP AND IFRS CROSS REFERENCED TO CHAPTER

The following table describes some of the current differences between U.S. generally accepted accounting principles (GAAP) and International Financial Reporting Standards (IFRS) that relate to topics (by chapter) covered in this textbook. The U.S. Securities and Exchange Commission (SEC) has adopted a timetable whereby U.S. public companies may adopt IFRS by 2016. Because of a global economic recession and a crisis in the financial markets, a significant number of informed persons believe that this time table may be delayed. Nevertheless, most people believe that the integration of GAAP and IFRS will eventually become a reality. The last column of the table explains what could happen if the U.S. GAAP of today were to switch to IFRS as they currently exist. This will help you assess the impact of these changes on U.S. financial statements.

Accounts	Topic	U.S. GAAP Position	IFRS Position	Implications of Switch to IFRS
Inventory and Cost of Goods Sold Chapter 6	Inventory costing	Companies can choose to use LIFO inventory costing, if desired. A large portion of U.S. companies currently use LIFO for its tax benefits.	LIFO is not allowed under any circumstances.	LIFO could be eliminated. Companies could still choose to use FIFO, average, or specific identification methods.
	Lower-of-cost-or market (LCM)	Market is usually determined to be replacement cost. LCM write-downs cannot be reversed.	Market is always net realizable value (fair market value). LCM write-downs can be reversed under certain conditions.	LCM write-downs may become less common, as selling prices are usually greater than replacement costs. Some write-downs might be reversed over time.
Property, Plant, and Equipment Chapter 7	Asset impairment and revaluation	If long-term assets are impaired, they are written down. Write-downs may not be reversed.	Long-term assets may be written up or down, based on fair market value (appraisals). Adjustments may be potentially reversed.	The cost principle might not apply to long-term assets as strongly. Assets could be evaluated by independent appraisers and adjusted either up or down.
	Depreciation	Assets are depreciated by classes (i.e., buildings, equipment, etc.).	Assets are depreciated by component (much more detailed than by classes).	Much more detailed records would have to be kept over depreciation.
Research and Development Chapter 7	Development costs	All research and development costs are expensed. Only exception is for computer software development costs, which can be capitalized and amortized over future sales revenues.	All research is expensed, but development costs are capitalized if six criteria are met, and amortized over future sales revenues.	Standards already developed by U.S. GAAP might be extended to apply to all development costs, not just computer software development.
Intangible Assets Chapter 7	Capitalization and recognition of intangible assets on balance sheet	Only recognized when purchased. Internally developed not recognized.	Recognized if future benefit is probable and reliably measurable (same criteria as recognition of contingencies). May be purchased or internally developed.	More intangible assets could be recognized on balance sheet. Adjusted for amortization or impairment over time.
Contingent Liabilities Chapter 9	Recording of contingent liabilities	Accrued (recorded in journal entry) if probable and reliably measurable. Contingent liabilities that are reasonably possible are disclosed in notes to financial statements.	Both probable and possible contingent liabilities are recorded in journal entries.	More liabilities will likely be recorded, regardless of the outcome of proposals being studied by FASB and IASB.

Accounts	Topic	U.S. GAAP Position	IFRS Position	Implications of Switch to IFRS
Contingent Liabilities Chapter 9	Disclosure of contingencies	The FASB has proposed that the standard for disclosure of loss contingencies be increased to include all such matters that are expected to be resolved in the near term (i.e., within the next year) and that could have a severe impact (higher than material, disruptive to the business). In addition, the proposal requires a quantitative tabular reconciliation of accrued loss contingencies that includes increases or decreases in such amounts during the most recent year.	IASB is studying its present requirements with a view to increase required disclosures in the next few years.	More liabilities will likely be recorded, regardless of the outcome of proposals being studied by the FASB and IASB.
Lease Liabilities Chapter 9	Classification of leases	FASB and IASB have issued a joint exposure draft that would eliminate virtually all operating leases. The present value of all future payments on leased assets would be capitalized under the category of "right to use" assets. The related obligations would be reported as "future lease payment" long-term liabilities. As of this publication, the exposure draft is still being debated.	Same as U.S. GAAP Position.	More leases could be classified as capital leases, resulting in more frequent recognition of long-term assets as well as long-term liabilities.
Revenue Chapter 11	Revenue recognition	Until recently, U.S. GAAP allowed many different ways to recognize revenues, depending on the industry and type of contract. However, the FASB and IASB have recently issued a joint exposure draft of a standard that greatly eliminates differences, requiring an entity to recognize revenue when it transfers goods or services to a customer in the amount of consideration it expects to receive from the customer. For the retail industry (largely featured in this book), U.S. GAAP and IFRS for revenue recognition were already essentially identical.	Revenue recognition based mainly on a single standard that contains general principles applied to different types of transactions.	The new standard will standardize the way in which revenues are recognized, resulting in changes in the timing of revenue recognition.
Extraordinary Items Chapter 11	Recording of extraordinary items	Allows separate disclosure of extraordinary items (unusual in nature and infrequent in occurrence) after income from continuing operations. The use of extraordinary items, although allowed, is extremely rare under U.S. GAAP.	Extraordinary items do not have special treatment. Even "unusual and infrequent" items are reported in income from continuing operations.	Extraordinary items may disappear from the income statement, to be reclassified as "ordinary" revenues and expenses.
Interest Revenue and Interest Expense Chapter 12	Indirect method cash flows statement presentation Direct method cash flows statement presentation	Interest revenue and interest expense are part of net income, and as such are included in operating activities (as part of net income) on an indirect method cash flows statement. Interest income is not reported under investing activities.	Interest revenue and interest expense are removed from net income (as an adjustment, similar to the adjustment for depreciation expense) in the operating activities section of the indirect method cash flows statement. Interest income is reported under investing activities, and interest expense is reported under financing activities for both direct and indirect methods.	Interest revenue and interest expense reclassified to different sections of the cash flows statement.

Company Index

Glindex A Combined Glossary and Subject Index

A

Above par common stock, 557–558

Accelerated depreciation. A depreciation method that writes off a relatively larger amount of the asset's cost nearer the start of its useful life than the straight-line method does, 373–374

Account. The record of the changes that have occurred in a particular asset, liability, or stockholders' equity during a period. The basic summary device of accounting, 55–57. *See also* Adjustments to entries
  adjusting, 119–133
  analyzing, 79
  asset accounts, 55
  chart of, 80–81
  formats for, 81–82
  impact of transactions on, 68–70
  liabilities accounts, 55
  normal balance of, 81
  permanent, 141–143
  posted to ledger, 77–78
  stockholders' equity accounts, 56–57
  temporary, 141
  types of, 55
  uncollectible, 259–264, 263–264

Account format. A balance-sheet format that lists assets on the left and liabilities and stockholders' equity on the right, 143

Account numbers, list of, 80–81

Accounting. The information system that measures business activities, processes that information into reports and financial statements, and communicates the results to decision makers, 3. *See also* Accounting decisions; Accounting equation; Accounting information; Assumptions

Accounting decisions, 23–24

Accounting equation. The most basic tool of accounting: Assets = Liabilities + Owners' equity, 11

Accounting errors, correcting, 80

Accounting estimates, changes in, 629

Accounting information
  accuracy of, 7
  comparability of, 7
  completeness of, 7
  disclosure of, 6
  on economic substance, 6
  enhancing qualitative characteristics, 7
  flow of, 73–77
  freedom from bias, 6
  global, 9–11
  and internal control, 201
  material, 6
  relevance, 6, 8
  understandability of, 7
  users of, 4
  verifiability of, 7

Accounting principles, 6
  vs. bookkeeping, 3
  changing methods of, 629
  fair value, 9–10
  faithful representation, 6
  financial, 4
  generally accepted accounting principles (GAAP), 6–7, 9–11
  historical cost principle, 8–9
  management, 4–5

Accounts payable, 56, 484

Accounts payable turnover. Measures the number of times per year a company pays off its accounts payable. Assuming all purchases are on credit, to compute accounts payable turnover, divide purchases (cost of goods sold + ending inventory – beginning inventory) by average accounts payable. When inventories are immaterial, or when there is very little difference between beginning and ending inventories, substitute cost of goods sold for purchases, 485–486, 764–765

Accounts receivable, 55

Accounts receivable turnover. Measures a company's ability to collect cash from credit customers. To compute accounts receivable turnover, divide net credit sales by average net accounts receivable, 272, 763–764

Accrual. An expense or a revenue that occurs before the business pays or receives cash. An accrual is the opposite of a deferral, 120

Accrual accounting. Accounting that records the impact of a business event as it occurs, regardless of whether the transaction affected cash
  and cash flows, 116
  cash-basis accounting vs., 115
  defined, 115
  ethical issues in, 119

Accrued expense. An expense incurred but not yet paid in cash. Also called *accrual liability*, 19, 56, 125–127, 487

Accrued liability. A liability for an expense that has not yet been paid by the company. Also called accrued expense, 56, 125–127, 487

Accrued revenue. A revenue that has been earned but not yet received in cash, 127

Accumulated depreciation. The cumulative sum of all depreciation expense from the date of acquiring a plant asset, 18, 124

Accumulated depreciation account, 124

Accumulated other comprehensive income. The cumulative amount of items reported as other comprehensive income; a separate category in the stockholders' equity section of the balance sheet, 252, 631

Acid-test ratio. Ratio of the sum of cash plus short-term investments plus net current receivables to total current liabilities. Tells whether the entity can pay all its current liabilities if they come due immediately. Also called the *quick ratio*, 271, 762

Adjusted trial balance. A list of all the ledger accounts with their adjusted balances, 132

Adjustments to entries
  accruals, 120
  accrued expenses, 125–127
  accrued revenues, 127
  deferrals, 120
  depreciation, 120
  prepaid expenses, 120–123
  summary of, 129–131
  trial balance, 132
  unearned revenue, 128–129

Aging-of-receivables. A way to estimate bad debts by analyzing individual accounts receivable according to the length of time they have been receivable from the customer, 261–263, 264

Allowance for Bad Debts, 259

Allowance for Doubtful Accounts. Another name for *Allowance for Uncollectible Accounts*, 259–264

Allowance for Uncollectible Accounts. The estimated amount of collection losses. Another name for *Allowance for Doubtful Accounts*, 259–264

Allowance method. A method of recording collection losses based on estimates of how much money the business will not collect from its customers, 259–264

Amortization. The systematic reduction of a lump-sum amount. Expense that applies to intangible assets in the same way depreciation applies to plant assets and depletion applies to natural resources, 388
  for bond premium, 504–508
  depreciation on leasehold improvements, 364
  on statement of cash flows, 671, 673, 687
  straight-line method, 508

Amortized cost method, 432

Approvals, proper, for internal control, 201–202

Asset. An economic resource that is expected to be of benefit in the future. *See also* Intangible asset; Plant assets
  accounts receivable, 18, 55
  asset accounts, 55–56
  asset transactions, 394–395
  assumptions about, 8–9
  basket purchases of, 366
  buildings, 55
  cash/cash equivalents, 18, 55
  classifying by liquidity, 142–143
  current, 18, 143, 673–674
  current, liquidity of, 143
  defined, 11, 55
  depreciable, useful life of, 380–381
  equipment, furniture, fixtures, 56
  fixed, 12
  fully depreciated, 382, 383
  impairment of, 390–392
  improper access to, 197
  intangible, 18
  inventory, 12, 18, 55
  kinds of, 12
  land, 55
  long-term, 18
  long-term, liquidity of, 143
  notes receivable, 18, 55
  prepaid expenses, 18, 55
  property and equipment, 12, 18
  reporting, 143
  return on, 392–394
  safeguarding, 197
  sale of, 673
  short-term investments, 18
  wasting, 387

Asset turnover. The dollars of sales generated per dollar of assets invested. Formula is Net sales ÷ Average total assets, 393, 575, 768

Assumptions
  continuity (going-concern), 8
  entity, 8
  historical cost, 8–9
  stable monetary unit, 9

Audit. A periodic examination of a company's financial statements and the accounting systems, controls, and records that produce them. Audits may be either external or internal. External audits are usually performed by certified public accountants (CPAs), 201

Periodic inventory system. An inventory system in which the business does not keep a continuous record of the inventory on hand. Instead, at the end of the period, the business makes a physical count of the inventory on hand and applies the appropriate unit costs to determine the cost of the ending inventory, 306, 324, 356–357

Permanent accounts. Asset, liability, and stockholders' equity accounts that are not closed at the end of the period, 141

Perpetual inventory system. An inventory system in which the business keeps a continuous record for each inventory item to show the inventory on hand at all times, 306–308, 324

Petty cash. Fund containing a small amount of cash that is used to pay minor amounts, 218

Phish. Creating bogus websites for the purpose of stealing unauthorized data, such as names, addresses, Social Security numbers, bank account, and credit card numbers, 203

Physical wear and tear, 369

Plant assets. Long-lived assets, such as land, buildings, and equipment, used in the operation of the business. Also called *fixed assets* or *property and equipment*, 364
  accounting for, 378
  analyzing transactions, 385–386
  buildings, machinery, and equipment, 365–366
  cash flow impact, 394–395
  depreciable cost of, 370
  depreciation for tax purposes, 378–380
  depreciation of, 369–376
  disposing of for no proceeds, 383
  effects of disposal of, 382–387
  exchanging, 384–385
  land, 364, 365
  land improvements and leasehold improvements, 366
  lump-sum purchases of assets, 366
  purchases and sales of, 675, 687–688
  selling, 383–384

Plant assets. Long-lived assets, such as land, buildings, and equipment, used in the operation of the business. Also called fixed assets
  book value of, 124
  buildings, machinery, and equipment, 18, 56
  defined, 123
  depreciation of, 123–125
  land, 55

Posting. Copying amounts from the journal to the ledger, 72

Postretirement liabilities, 515–516

Preemption, 554

Preferred dividends, effect on earnings per share, 630

Preferred stock. Stock that gives its owners certain advantages, such as the priority to receive dividends before the common stockholders and the priority to receive assets before the common stockholders if the corporation liquidates, 556, 561–562
  dividends on, 570–571, 630
  redeemable, 574

Premium (on a bond). Excess of bond's issue price over its face (par) value, 496

Prepaid expense. A category of miscellaneous assets that typically expire or get used up in the near future. Examples include prepaid rent, prepaid insurance, and supplies
  adjusting entries, 120–123

on the balance sheet, 18
prepaid rent, 121–122
supplies, 122

Present value. The value on a given date of a future payment or series of future payments, discounted to reflect the time value of money, 450
  of an annuity, 452–453
  of available-for-sale investments, 455–456
  calculating with Microsoft Excel, 454–455
  of investments in bonds, 456–457
  of money, 450–451

Present-value tables, 451–452

President. Chief operating officer in charge of managing the day-to-day operations of a corporation, 554

Pre-tax accounting income. Income before tax on the income statement, 625

Price-earnings (P/E) ratio. The ratio of the market price of a share of common stock to the company's earnings per share, 573–574

Price-earnings ratio. Ratio of the market price of a share of common stock to the company's earnings per share. Measures the value that the stock market places on $1 of a company's earnings, 771

Principal. The amount borrowed by a debtor and lent by a creditor, 266, 267, 494

Prior-period adjustment. A correction to the beginning balance of retained earnings for an error of an earlier period, 629

Profit margin. *See* Gross margin

Profitability, and stockholder investment, 575–577

Projected benefit obligation, 515

Promissory note, 257

Proper approvals, and internal control, 201–202

Property and equipment. *See* Plant assets

Proprietorship. A business with a single owner, 5, 13

Public Company Accounting Oversight Board, 198

Purchase, budgeted, 321

Purchase allowance. A decrease in the cost of purchases because the seller has granted the buyer a subtraction (an allowance) from the amount owed, 307

Purchase discount. A decrease in the cost of purchases earned by making an early payment to the vendor, 308

Purchase return. A decrease in the cost of purchases because the buyer returned the goods to the seller, 307

Purchasing department, 202

Q

Quality of earnings. *See* Earnings quality

Quick ratio. Another name for the *acid-test ratio*, 271, 762

Quitting concern, 8

R

Rate of return, foreign currencies and exchange rates, 447

Rate of return on assets (ROA). Net income – preferred dividends divided by average total assets. This ratio measures a company's success in using its assets to earn income for the persons who finance the business. Also called *return on total assets*. Can also be computed using the first two elements of DuPont Analysis (Rate of return on net sales X Asset turnover), 768–769

Rate of return on common stockholders' equity. Net income minus preferred dividends, divided by average common stockholders' equity. A measure of profitability. Also called *return on equity*, 575, 769–770

Rate of return on net sales. Ratio of net income – preferred dividends to net sales. A measure of profitability. Also called *return on sales*, 767–768

Rate of return on total assets. Net income minus preferred dividends divided by average total assets. This ratio measures a company's success in using its assets to earn income for the persons who finance the business. Also called *return on assets*, 392–394, 575, 768–769

Ratio analysis, limitations of, 773

Rationalization for fraud, 197

Ratios. *See also* Current ratio
  analysis, limitations of, 773
  for business decisions, 757–773
  days' sales in receivables, 271–272, 764
  debt ratio, 145–150, 545–546, 765–766
  decision guidelines, 545–546, 775–777
  dividend yield, 771–772
  gross margin/sales, 619, 622
  Import/Export, 447
  inventory turnover, 319–320, 762–763
  leverage ratio, 512, 769
  net profit margin, 393, 575
  price-earnings ratio, 573–574, 771
  quick (acid-test), 271, 762
  rate of return on assets, 768–769
  rate of return on net sales, 767–768
  rate of return on total assets, 392–394, 575, 768–769
  times-interest-earned ratio, 513, 766
  total asset turnover, 393, 575, 768

Realized gain or loss, 250, 436

Receivables. Monetary claims against a business or an individual, acquired mainly by selling goods or services and by lending money, 256
  accounting for, 258
  cash flow from, 269–270
  factoring, 270
  inability to collect, 774
  managing, 258
  other receivables, 257
  selling, 270
  trends in, 775
  types of, 256–257

Records, adequate, and internal control, 201

Redeemable preferred stock. A corporation reserves the right to buy an issue of stock back from its shareholders, with the intent to retire the stock, 574

Redemption value. The price a corporation agrees to eventually pay for its redeemable preferred stock, set when the stock is issued, 574

Regulatory bodies, 4

Remittance advice. An optional attachment to a check (sometimes a perforated tear-off document and sometimes capable of being electronically scanned) that indicates the payer, date, and purpose of the cash payment. The remittance advice is often used as the source document for posting cash receipts or payments, 205

Rent, prepaid, 121–122

Report format. A balance-sheet format that lists assets at the top, followed by liabilities and stockholders' equity below, 143

Research and development, costs of, 390